Craigievar Castle

AA ILLUSTRATED ROAD BOOK OF SCOTLAND

WITH GAZETTEER, ITINERARIES, MAPS AND TOWN PLANS

Published in 1974 by The Automobile Association, Fanum House, Basing View, Basingstoke, Hants.

1953 First impression
1954 Second Impression
1957 Third Impression, with minor corrections
1960 Second Post-War Edition, completely revised and reset
1960 Second Post-War Edition
Illustrated
1961 Second Impression
Illustrated
1963 Reprinted with minor corrections
Illustrated
1964 Third Post-War Edition, revised
1965 Fourth Edition
Illustrated
1969 Reprinted with minor corrections
Illustrated
1971 Reprinted with minor corrections
Illustrated
1972 Fifth Edition
Illustrated
1974 Sixth Edition
Illustrated

85097 065 2
 BM165 Printed and Bound in England by Hazell Watson & Viney Ltd Aylesbury, Bucks

Come forth, the sky is wide and it is a far cry to the world's end . . . There is a road which leads to the moon and the Great Waters . . . and it has no end; but it is a fine road, a braw road—who will follow it? . . .

JOHN BUCHAN *The Rime of True Thomas*

Contents

Preface

In this new edition of the Road Book of Scotland the information that it contains has been brought up to date. Most of the town plans have been redrawn to incorporate recent alterations, in the gazetteer the latest available population figures have been included, and current opening and closing times of places of interest are given.

As in previous editions, the illustrations in the gazetteer have been so arranged as to fall opposite the places described. The illustrations, of which there are over a thousand, are in most cases things that can be seen by the traveller without intruding on private property.

The Place Index on pages 278–282 lists some 1100 places which appear in the gazetteer as part of longer articles. Port Erroll, for example, does not appear as an entry in the gazetteer, but the entry under that name in the Place Index refers the reader to Cruden Bay, under which Port Erroll is described in the gazetteer.

We are indebted to HM Ministry of Works, the National Trust for Scotland, the Scottish Tourist Board, and the British Travel and Holidays Association, for permission to make use of photographs from their collections for illustrating places and objects of special interest in the Hebrides, the islands of Orkney and Shetland, and elsewhere; also to the West Highland Museum, Fort William, for permission to make use of an official photograph to illustrate the interesting Secret Portrait of Prince Charles Edward on Plate 68. In addition, we acknowledge the many sources from which information has been obtained. *Scottish Country Life*, *Country Life*, *The Field*, *The Autocar*, *The Motor*, *The Times*, *The Guardian*, and *The Scotsman*, have all provided information and suggested subjects for illustration.

How to use this book

This book is in four main parts—the counties of Scotland, with short descriptive articles; itineraries; a gazetteer; and an atlas.

TO CHOOSE A ROUTE

Consult the key map to the itineraries (following page 40) or the maps of selected through routes which follow the key map. The numbers shown on all these maps are itinerary numbers—they are not road numbers. For a general tour, see the map and article on pages 28-29.

On the key map, through routes are shown by a heavy black line and local and touring routes by a thin black line.

Instructions for reading the itineraries are given on page 50.

Routes can be traced in more detail on the atlas on which are shown the road numbers referred to in the itineraries.

TO LOCATE A PLACE

Refer to the gazetteer in which places are listed alphabetically; all but the smallest places in the itineraries are included. For each place, the appropriate page number in the atlas is given, followed by the National Grid reference (fully explained in pages ii and iii of the atlas). The county is also given, and a county map appears on page i of the atlas.

The gazetteer and itineraries are cross-referenced; itinerary numbers are given in the gazetteer, and in the itineraries there is an asterisk against places listed in the gazetteer.

THE COUNTIES OF SCOTLAND

The following articles are designed to present a general picture of the topography and outstanding characteristics of the counties. Each is followed by classified lists showing the best of the various ecclesiastical buildings, ancient and historic castles, the most notable houses, attractive villages, and places with the greatest scenic interest. All places mentioned are listed separately in the Gazetteer, except certain Abbeys, Castles and Houses, which are described under the place-names given after them in brackets.

A striking feature of Scotland is its wealth of picturesque islands, large and small, said to number in all some 787, and situated mostly off the north and west coasts, the most important being Arran, Bute, the Inner and Outer Hebrides, and the Orkney and Shetland groups. Arran and Bute together constitute the county of Bute, while the Hebrides are divided between Argyll, Inverness and Ross and Cromarty, All these islands, together with Orkney and Shetland, both of which are counties in their own right. are fully described under their own headings in the Gazetteer, so that only a bare mention of them has been made in the county articles.

The mainland of Scotland is traditionally divided into the Highlands and the Lowlands, the two districts being described in detail in the Gazetteer. The Lowlands belie their name, in that they are largely hilly, though only in the Galloway area and the Peebles-Selkirk border are heights of near 3,000 ft. approached. Included in the Lowlands are the Border Country, the Burns Country and the Scott Country, all of which are popular touring grounds, and for which there are a number of convenient centres.

The Highlands cover a much larger area, and in view of the mountainous nature of the country, narrower, and in general less well-surfaced roads are to be expected, but the magnificent scenery will more than compensate for this. Among the most notable examples of Highland grandeur are the wild peaks of historic Glencoe; the Lochaber district, with Ben Nevis, Britain's highest peak, facing the Mamores; the great Cairngorm range, incorporating a 64,118-acre National Nature Reserve; and, above all, the superb stretch of undeveloped hill country, ideal for one of the proposed Scottish National Parks, occupying almost the whole of the land to the north-west of the Great Glen, or Glen More, which virtually divides Scotland into two portions. These North-West Highlands contain the wildest mountain and loch scenery on the mainland, the greater part of it being concentrated near the deeply-indented coastline of Inverness, Wester Ross and Sutherland, with their many superb sea lochs. An outstanding exception is the grand inland scenery of Glen Affric and Glen Cannich, in northern Inverness-shire, where a great hydro-electric scheme, providing power for the Highlands, has opened up new vistas for the tourist by means of reconstructed roads.

Mountain scenery of an equally grand nature will be found also in the Hebridean islands of Mull, Rum, and in particular Skye, where the sensational knife-edge ridges of the Coolins are unique in Britain.

Extensive Forest Parks have been established in certain districts and are mentioned under their respective counties, in addition to being marked on the atlas.

A county map will be found on the first page of the atlas at the end of the book.

ABERDEENSHIRE

(County Town: Aberdeen)

Scotland's most easterly county, and one of the largest in area, is divided into the five districts of Mar, Garioch, Formartine, Strathbogie and Buchan. Aberdeenshire is noted particularly for the breeding of prize pedigree cattle.

The Mar district includes the impressive granite-built Cathedral and University city of Aberdeen, the third largest in the country, and stretches westwards along the richly wooded valley of the Dee to take in Royal Deeside, beloved of Queen Victoria and all the Royal Family. Also within the confines of Mar rise the heights of the eastern Grampians, on the Angus and Banff borders. Garioch and Formartine are smaller districts, situated to the north of the fertile and winding Don valley, the former including the prominent hill of Bennachie, with the Mither Tap, to the west of Inverurie, and the latter taking in the flat coastal area around Newburgh and the Ythan river estuary. Strathbogie, near the Banff border, is mainly hilly, and watered by the Deveron, its chief centre being Huntly, with the ruined Palace, or Castle of the Gordons. Finally, Buchan is the name given to the rather bleak north-east corner of the county, which includes a lonely and undeveloped stretch of the North Sea coast between the herring fishing ports of Peterhead and Fraserburgh. A more attractive and rocky seaboard lies to the west of the last-named, in the direction of Troup Head, in Banffshire. The interior of Buchan is almost entirely flat, the monotony being relieved by the isolated Mormond Hill, near Strichen, with its carvings of a white horse and a stag.

Deeside is by far the best known and most beautiful part of the county, the scenery becoming gradually more mountainous towards the west, where the lofty Cairngorm plateau and ridges, the source of the River Dee, and now partly a large National Nature Reserve, are situated. Here, Ben Macdhui, the second highest of Scotland's peaks, rises on the Banff border; Braeriach, overlooking the famous Lairig Ghru pass, is shared with the county of Inverness; while Cairn Toul is wholly within Aberdeenshire. Away to the north-east of the Cairngorms is Cock Bridge, on the upper Don, from where the desolate and lonely Lecht road climbs steeply to 2,090 ft., near the Banff border, on its way to Tomintoul.

The county is also famous for its splendid series of baronial castles, many being still inhabited, and foremost among which must be placed the modern Royal Castle of Balmoral. This stands in a beautiful forest setting on the Dee, to the east of the well-known Highland resort of Braemar, and has for its southern background the outline of the famous peak of Lochnagar. Among the more ancient castles, those of Fyvie, Craigievar, Midmar and Castle Fraser are the finest, and together form a group that is without equal of its kind in Scotland. Of numerous still earlier, but ruined structures, the picturesque castles of Kildrummy, Huntly, and Tolquhon, near Tarves, are outstanding.

Places of Scenic Interest. Aboyne, Ballater, Braemar, Cock Bridge, Collieston, Cruden Bay, Inverey, Lochnagar, Old Deer, Oyne, Pennan, Rosehearty.

Places of Architectural or Historic Interest. Aberdeen, Balmoral Castle, Braemar, Castle Fraser (Kemnay), Craig Castle (Lumsden), Craigievar Castle, Crathie, Delgatie Castle (Turriff), Drum Castle (Drumoak), Fyvie, Huntly, Inveramsay, Kildrummy, Kintore, Midmar Castle, Old Meldrum, Pitsligo, Tolquhon Castle (Tarves).

ANGUS

(County Town: Forfar)

The name of this county, which extends from the North Sea to the heights of the Grampians, was formerly Forfarshire. The title Forfar is, however, now confined to the county town.

The most picturesque part of Angus is known as the " Braes of Angus ", and lies to the north-west and north, where the lofty outliers of the eastern Grampian, or Benchinnan mountains penetrate into the county, which is here broken up into a series of deep and lonely glens of great beauty. The best known are Glen Isla, Glen Prosen, Glen Clova, and the delightful valley of the North Esk river, terminating with Loch Lee, backed by the lonely peak of Mount Keen, on the Aberdeen border. These glens, although traversed by roads, are comparatively little visited, due perhaps to the fact that none of them, except Lower Glen Isla, provides a through route to the west for motorists. For long-distance walkers, however, a wide field of exploration is opened up by means of the various lofty tracks leading towards the Dee valley and the White Mounth and Lochnagar mountains from a number of points at the remote heads of the glens.

In the highly cultivated south-west corner of Angus, which is famous also for its prize cattle, the Sidlaw Hills extend towards Forfar. In the vicinity of this town are two of the most interesting places in the county: Kirriemuir, with its memories of Sir James Barrie; and Glamis, famous for the great Castle, so intimately associated with the present Royal family, and overlooking the Howe of Angus in the fertile Vale of Strathmore.

The finest part of the coast lies between Arbroath and the port and resort of Montrose, where much wild rock scenery and sandstone cliffs will be found around Red Head, and also near the quaint fishing village of Auchmithie, lying to the south. Dundee is by far the largest centre in Angus, and ranks fourth in population among Scottish cities, being famous for jute, and noted also for the fine Old Steeple of the City Churches. Linking it to the Fife coast across the Firth of Tay is the celebrated two-mile-long Tay Bridge, carrying the main railway line to the south. A new road bridge was opened in 1966.

Among ecclesiastical buildings, Brechin Cathedral, where one of Scotland's three round towers, reminiscent of those found in Ireland, can be seen, is of interest, while the ruined Abbey at Arbroath is also notable. The Parish Church at Fowlis Easter contains an elaborately carved Sacrament House, one of the finest to have survived. Claypotts Castle, near Broughty Ferry, is a curious old stronghold, and at Edzell is a ruined castle preserving an early 17th cent. walled garden, which is unique in the country.

Places of Scenic Interest. Auchmithie, Braedownie, Clova, Dykehead, Edzell, Gannochy Bridge, Kirkton of Glenisla, Kirriemuir, Lochlee, Tarfside, Usan.

Places of Architectural or Historic Interest. Affleck Castle (Monikie), Arbroath, Brechin, Claypotts Castle (Broughty Ferry), Cortachy Castle, Dundee, Edzell, Fowlis Easter, Glamis, Guthrie, Hospitalfield (Arbroath), Inverquharity Castle (Kirriemuir), Kirriemuir, Pitcur, Restenneth Priory (Forfar), St. Vigean's.

ARGYLL

(County Town: Inveraray)

Second in size among the Scottish counties, and at one time known as the kingdom of Dalriada, Argyll incorporates in addition many of the Inner Hebridean islands. One of the largest of these is the rugged and picturesque Isle of Mull, in which Ben More rises to more than 3,000 ft. Jura and Islay are also of considerable size, but more famous are the small islands of Iona and Staffa, off the coast of Mull, the former celebrated for its Cathedral and associations with St. Columba, and the latter renowned for some remarkable basaltic rock scenery and the well-known Fingal's Cave.

The mainland of Argyll is cut up into peninsulas, and deeply indented by magnificent sea lochs. Outstanding among these are Loch Sunart, dividing the districts of Ardnamurchan and Morven; Outer Loch Linnhe, which separates Morven and Ardgour from Appin; the narrow trough of Loch Etive, situated in the land of Benderloch and

Lorne; and the long and narrow Loch Fyne, which divides Knapdale from the hilly land of Cowal, the shores of which are washed by the well-known Kyles of Bute. South and east of Cowal, in which the large resort of Dunoon faces Cloch Point on the Renfrew coast, are the waters of the Firth of Clyde, beloved of yachtsmen, and of which the Holy Loch and Loch Long are picturesque inlets. The head of the latter is dominated by Ben Arthur, popularly known as The Cobbler, overlooking the extensive Argyll Forest Park in the vicinity of Glen Croe, with its well-known hill of Rest and be Thankful. Farther south, the long and narrow Kintyre peninsula stretches away from Knapdale to terminate in the wild headland of the Mull of Kintyre, with its lighthouse.

Inland, far to the north, on the Inverness border, the beautiful southern, but roadless shores of Loch Shiel, with its memories of Prince Charles Edward, belong to Argyll, and here mountain and loch combine to portray an exceptionally rich and varied picture. Eastwards of Ballachulish and its well-known car ferry, finely situated on Loch Leven, lies the entrance to the grim and forbidding Pass of Glencoe, scenically and historically probably the most famous in Scotland, and hemmed in by 3,000-ft. high rock peaks culminating in Bidean nam Bian, the monarch of Argyll. Near the eastern entrance to the glen, where the finely-engineered new road is at a lower level than the disused old road, stands the "Kingshouse" Inn. Above it rises the spectacular rock bastion of Buchaille Etive Mor, the "Shepherd of Etive," famous among climbers, and towering above the lonely wastes of Rannoch Moor, one of the country's principal watersheds, dominated to the east by the lofty Drum Alban ridge of the Grampian range. Much of all this grand mountain district is the property of the National Trust for Scotland, notably the Dalness Forest area, which borders Glen Etive, leading towards the lonely shores of Loch Etive, at the head of which rises Ben Starav.

Beyond Loch Linnhe stretch the remote, but picturesque districts of Ardgour and Morven, threaded by Loch Sunart, to the north of which rise the fine peaks of Garbh Bheinn and Ben Resipol, the former being a prominent feature in the view across Loch Linnhe from the ferry at Ballachulish. Farther west still is Ardnamurchan, providing glorious views of the Hebridean islands of Rum and Eigg from many points, notably Kentra Bay, near Acharacle. The lonely Ardnamurchan Point marks the most westerly point on the Scottish mainland. The few roads in these districts are narrow and at times poorly surfaced, but there are frequent passing-places on certain stretches.

Loch Awe, dominated at its head by the twin-peaked Ben Cruachan, is the largest inland loch, with roads traversing the whole length of both its southern and northern shores. To the west lies Oban, perhaps the best known resort in the county, and an excellent centre for visiting the various Inner Hebridean islands by steamer. Near Ardrishaig, on Loch Fyne, is the eastern end of the Crinan Canal, built originally to provide an easier passage for ships making for the Sound of Jura and the Atlantic, thus avoiding the often stormy voyage round the Mull of Kintyre.

The Royal Burgh of Inveraray, on Loch Fyne, where the 18th cent. Castle is the ancestral home of the Duke of Argyll, the head of Clan Campbell, forms one of the pleasantest of small Scottish towns. The county also possesses a number of romantically situated old castles, now mostly in ruins, notably Kilchurn Castle on Loch Awe, Castle Stalker near Portnacroish in Appin, Castle Tioram near Acharacle, and Dunstaffnage Castle to the north of Oban.

In addition, a number of prehistoric antiquities, notably Chambered Cairns and Cup and Ring marked rocks from the Bronze Age, as well as several finely sculptured churchyard Crosses, are a feature of the county, particularly in the neighbourhood of Kilmartin.

Places of Scenic Interest. Acharacle, Ardgour, Ballachulish, Benmore Estate, Bridge of Orchy, Clachan Bridge, Falls of Cruachan, Glencoe, Inversanda, Kilchoan, Kilmelford, Kingshouse, Loch Awe, Loch Fyne, Lochgoilhead, Loch Shiel, Mull of Kintyre, Oban, Rest-and-be-Thankful, Southend, Strontian, Tarbert.

Places of Architectural or Historic Interest. Ardtornish Castle (Lochaline), Barcaldine Castle, Carnasserie Castle (Kilmartin), Carrick Castle (Lochgoilhead), Castle Stalker (Portnacroish), Castle Sween (Kilmory Knap), Castle Tioram (Acharacle), Dundarave Castle (Inveraray), Dunstaffnage Castle, Glencoe, Gylen Castle (Oban), Inveraray, Kilchurn Castle, Kilmartin, Kilmichael, Mingary Castle (Kilchoan), Saddell.

Places of interest in the Inner Hebridean islands of Colonsay, Iona, Jura and Staffa will be found by referring to the gazetteer articles for those islands. Islay and Mull have separate entries for all individual places of interest, these being cross-indexed in the parent articles.

AYRSHIRE

(County Town: Ayr)

The name of Robert Burns is inseparably bound up with Ayrshire, and of the various places with which his name is associated, Ayr itself and its neighbour Alloway, with the famous Auld Brig spanning the River Doon, are perhaps the most visited. Nevertheless, Catrine, Kilmarnock, Kirkoswald, Mauchline and Tarbolton all have their own special claims.

The county is divided from north to south into the three districts of Cunningham, Kyle and Carrick, the last-named having once formed part of Galloway. A long coastline on the shores of the Firth of Clyde gives splendid views from many places towards the island of Bute, the twin

Cumbraes, and the lofty mountains of Arran. Facing the resort of Girvan, and situated some ten miles out to sea, is the prominent, lonely isle of Ailsa Craig, with its lighthouse and ruined castle. Between the Renfrew border in the north and the town of Ayr on its bay are situated a number of well-known coastal resorts, including historic Largs, and Ardrossan, a port for Arran. Among numerous golfing centres, Troon, Turnberry and Prestwick are perhaps most renowned, the last-named now doubly famous due to the proximity of the great airport. Away to the south, between Girvan and the mouth of Loch Ryan, which bites deep into Wigtownshire, lies perhaps the finest coastal stretch in southern Scotland. This is traversed by the picturesque road through Kennedy's Pass and round Bennane Head to Ballantrae and the finely wooded Glen App, this glen lying a little inland.

Parts of the Cunningham district have been industrialised, the most important town being Kilmarnock, but the remainder of the county is devoted mainly to agriculture and dairy farming, the Ayrshire breed of cattle being world famous. There are lonely hills and moors bordering Dumfries and Kirkcudbright, to the south-east, rising in places to more than 2,500 ft. in height, and to the south of Dalmellington, in the foothills of Galloway, lies Loch Doon, which forms the Kirkcudbright boundary for most of its length. In the heart of the Carrick country are the pleasant villages of Straiton and Barr, the latter situated in the delightful Stinchar valley, while in the neighbourhood are the Carrick and Changue Forests, forming part of the Glen Trool Forest Park. To the east of Barr, a narrow hill road leads southwards over the Nick o' the Balloch pass, with views of the Galloway hills, and giving access to Glen Trool, in Kirkcudbrightshire.

Ayr itself, apart from its links with Burns, is a town and resort of varied interest, having associations with William Wallace, and being also the birthplace of John Macadam, of road-making fame. To the south of Ayr stands the small town of Maybole, once the capital of Carrick, preserving in the High Street the former town house of the Earls of Cassillis. In the vicinity stands the ruined Crossraguel Abbey, neighboured by the old tower of Baltersan.

Among numerous ancient castles, the finest are Culzean, where the former Kennedy stronghold is incorporated in Robert Adam's fine mansion of 1777, now the property of the Scottish National Trust; Killochan, near Girvan; and Rowallan, to the north-east of Kilmaurs. The remaining fragment at Turnberry is of interest as having perhaps been the birthplace of Robert Bruce. A feature of the county which is possibly unique is the so-called "Electric Brae" at Croy, near Dunure, where, as the result of a curious optical illusion, a car will roll backwards along what would appear to be a descending gradient, this being nevertheless an ascent.

Places of Scenic Interest. Ballantrae, Barr, Colmonell, Dunure, Kirkoswald, Lendalfoot, Pinwherry, Sorn, Straiton.

Places of Architectural or Historic Interest. Alloway, Ardstinchar Castle (Ballantrae), Auchinleck, Ayr, Crossraguel Abbey, Culzean Castle, Dumfries House (Cumnock), Kelburne Castle (Fairlie), Kilbirnie, Killochan Castle (Girvan), Largs, Loch Doon Castle, Loudoun Castle (Galston), Mauchline, Maybole, Penkill Castle (Dailly), Rowallan Castle (Kilmaurs), Tarbolton, Turnberry.

BANFFSHIRE

(County Town: Banff)

A long and narrow county of considerable physical contrasts, Banffshire extends from the lofty fastnesses of the Cairngorms and eastern Grampians in the south-western extremity, through a predominantly agricultural countryside around Keith to the characteristic fishing villages and towns along the rocky, cliffbound coast.

Ben Macdhui, Scotland's second highest mountain, and Cairn Gorm, almost as lofty, two famous Cairngorm peaks, are situated on the Aberdeen and Inverness borders respectively, while the remote Loch Avon, with its well-known Shelter Stone, lies under Beinn Mheadoin between the two first-mentioned mountains. An extensive National Nature Reserve is now included within the Cairngorms. The boundary with Aberdeen traverses the summits of Beinn a'Bhuird and Ben Avon, and away to the north-east, the remarkable Lecht road, reaching an altitude of 2,090 ft., crosses from the Aberdeenshire village of Cock Bridge to enter Banffshire on its way towards Tomintoul. This is the loftiest village in the Highlands, though not in the whole of Scotland.

The River Avon flows northwards through the county from its source in the Cairngorms, and beyond Tomintoul is overlooked by the Cromdale Hills on the Inverness and Moray borders. Later it unites with the rapid-flowing Spey beyond Delnashaugh Inn and the Bridge of Avon in a picturesque wooded setting. Northwards from here, the Spey forms the Moray boundary for some distance, with a particularly lovely stretch around Craigellachie, where it is joined by the Fiddich. To the south stands Dufftown, at the head of the long and pleasant Glen Rinnes, with Ben Rinnes rising in the background. Farther away to the south-west is Glen Livet, where the famous distillery is perhaps the best known of the many which are to be found in the county. Through the flatter north-east sector of Banffshire flows the Deveron, on the Aberdeen border, reaching the sea between the twin ports of Banff and Macduff, with their important fisheries.

The coastline is flat in the west, but often rocky

and cliffbound in the east, with a number of prominent headlands between Logie Head, near Cullen, and Troup Head, far to the east on the Aberdeen border. Among various picturesque, though often lonely fishing villages are Findochty and Portknockie, to the west of Cullen, and also Crovie and Gardenstown, lying under the cliffs to the east of Macduff. In the pleasant village of Fordyce, between Cullen and Portsoy, stands a delightful little 16th cent. castle, while Balvenie Castle, outside Dufftown, is a picturesque ruin. At Deskford, the Church preserves what is perhaps the finest of the interesting Sacrament Houses which are almost confined to this area of Scotland. Another example can be seen in the church at Cullen, which stands almost adjacent to Cullen House, where the old town was formerly situated.

Places of Scenic Interest. Craigellachie, Crovie, Delnashaugh, Findochty, Gardenstown, Glenlivet, Portknockie, Tomintoul.

Places of Architectural or Historic Interest. Auchindoun, Balvenie Castle (Dufftown), Boyne Castle (Portsoy), Cullen, Deskford, Duff House (Banff), Findlater Castle (Cullen), Fordyce, Kinnairdy Castle (Aberchirder).

BERWICKSHIRE

(County Town: Duns)

The name of the county is taken from the town of Berwick-upon-Tweed, though this latter is now regarded as belonging to Northumberland. At one time Berwickshire was known as The Merse, and this title is still applied to the wide plain which lies to the north of the River Tweed, and contains some of the richest agricultural land in Scotland.

The Tweed, a famous salmon stream, forms the southern border with England for some miles. Farther to the south-west, parts of Roxburgh extend northwards across the river, and at the seaward end the Tweed flows through a small portion of Northumberland and is joined by the Whiteadder Water. In the northern half of Berwickshire, the long range of the Lammermuirs, is tenanted largely by sheep. Its rather bleak moorlands slope gradually towards the Merse, extending from the viewpoint of Soutra Hill, on the borders of East Lothian and Midlothian, to the coast in the neighbourhood of Cockburnspath, and traversed by several narrow and hilly roads. To the south-west of the main Lammermuir ridge is the district of Lauderdale, watered by the Leader Water, and containing the small, but historic town of Lauder, the sole Royal Burgh in the county. In the vicinity of the town stand the old and new castles of Thirlestane.

The coast is largely rocky, with lofty, red cliffs in many places, the most notable headland being that of St. Abb's Head, to the west and south of which the maritime scenery is at its most impressive. Both Eyemouth and picturesque Burnmouth are noted for their fisheries, and to the north-west of the former is Coldingham, where the interesting Priory has been restored, and is now in use as the Parish Church.

The most famous building in the county is Dryburgh Abbey, which, apart from its beautiful situation near the Tweed, and also its architectural interest, is visited yearly by thousands who come to pay homage to Sir Walter Scott and to Field-Marshal Earl Haig, both of whom lie buried within its walls. Bemersyde House, the old home of the Haigs, is situated a little to the north of the Abbey, and the view from Bemersyde Hill, ranging over the windings of the Tweed backed by the Eildon Hills, was particularly loved by Scott.

At Coldstream, with its fine bridge spanning the Tweed, the famous Coldstream Guards were first raised in 1650 by General Monk, and away to the north-east, facing the river, is the beautiful old church of Ladykirk, built originally by James IV.

Places of Scenic Interest. Burnmouth, Cockburnspath, Cranshaws, Duns, Earlston, Eyemouth, St. Abb's, Soutra Hill.

Places of Architectural or Historic Interest. Abbey St. Bathans, Bemersyde, Chirnside, Coldingham, Cranshaws, Dryburgh Abbey, Greenknowe Castle (Gordon), Hume Castle (Greenlaw), Ladykirk, Mellerstain, Nisbet House (Duns), Thirlestane Castle (Lauder).

BUTE

(County Town: Rothesay)

This county consists of the large islands of Arran and Bute, together with the smaller Cumbraes, all of which are situated in the Firth of Clyde. The two first-named are fully described under their own headings in the gazetteer, while individual places of interest on both islands have their own separate entries, which are cross-indexed in the parent articles. A description of the twin Cumbraes will be found under the heading of Millport, their chief centre.

CAITHNESS

(County Town: Wick)

Situated in the distant and somewhat bleak far north-eastern corner of Scotland, and largely unknown to the majority of tourists, Caithness is in some respects more akin to a Lowland county. It contains nevertheless an irresistible magnet for the curious traveller in the magic name of John o' Groats, the fame of which rests largely on its very remoteness. This is the terminal point of the great trunk road from Edinburgh through the central Highlands to the lonely outpost facing the little island of Stroma. Although John o' Groats is scenically of minor interest, only a few miles to the east is the magnificent headland of Duncansby Head, with its lighthouse, and a trio of prominent detached sandstone stacks to the south, which should certainly be seen by all visitors to this " Ultima Thule."

The northern shores of Caithness are washed by the turbulent waters of the Pentland Firth, beyond which lie the Orkneys, of which the great cliffs and isolated Old Man of Hoy are often visible from a number of points on the mainland. The fishing port of Thurso is noted also for its quarries, from which emanate the characteristic Caithness flagstones lining so many of the local roads and fields. Across Thurso Bay, to the west, is the little harbour of Scrabster, the port for the Orkney mail steamer, and beyond it are the riven cliffs of Holborn Head, looking across the expanse of the bay towards Dunnet Head, the most northerly point on the mainland. Farther west along the coast is Dounreay, where Scotland's first experimental nuclear power station has been built.

Wick, on the east coast, is an important fishing port and Royal Burgh, with splendid cliff scenery, both to the south and north of the town, while the hilly coast road leading south-westwards gives an excellent picture of the southern Caithness landscape. Beyond Dunbeath this is composed mainly of an elevated tableland, broken up in various places by streams, the scenery being particularly impressive and picturesque around Berriedale, and near the Ord of Caithness on the Sutherland border.

Inland from Berriedale rise the lonely hills of Scaraben and Morven, the latter being the best known height in the county, and forming a landmark for many miles. Much of the interior of Caithness is boggy and undeveloped, and the early Norse invaders are recalled by many of the place-name terminations, while numerous prehistoric antiquities, such as hut circles and Pictish remains, have survived, notably in the Latheron valley between Dunbeath and Lybster.

Place of Scenic Interest. Berriedale, Bridge of Forss, John o' Groats, Latheron, Wick.

Places of Architectural or Historic Interest. Ackergill Tower (Reiss), Brawl Castle (Halkirk), Canisbay Church, Castle Girnigo (Wick), Castle of Mey (East Mey), Dunbeath, Dunnet, Keiss, Mid Clyth.

CLACKMANNANSHIRE

(County Town: Alloa)

Scotland's smallest county is situated between the widening Forth estuary and the highest parts of the Ochil Hills, with the fertile, low-lying country below the range traversed by the serpentine windings of the River Devon, which flows into the estuary near Tullibody.

The grass-covered Ochils extend along the whole northern border of the county, facing Perthshire, the highest point in the range, Ben Cleuch, attaining well over 2,000 ft. It rises above the little weaving towns of Alva and Tillicoultry, both of which stand at the foot of delightful glens, the meeting-point of tiny burns flowing down from the hills. In the foothills of the Ochils, below King's Seat Hill, and looking down towards the town of Dollar, noted for its Academy, stands the ancient, ruined Castle Campbell, in one of the most picturesque settings in Scotland, giving a view across the Fife levels to the Forth estuary and the distant Pentland Hills.

Both Alloa and Clackmannan have preserved ancient towers, the former, which has associations with Mary, Queen of Scots, standing in close proximity to a modern mansion.

Places of Scenic Interest. Alva, Dollar, Tillicoultry.

Places of Architectural or Historic Interest. Alloa, Castle Campbell (Dollar), Clackmannan.

DUMFRIESSHIRE

(County Town: Dumfries)

Extending from the low, sandy shores of the Solway Firth into the heart of the Lowlands, this county displays a wealth of hills and dales, outstanding among which are the three parallel dales of Nithsdale, Annandale and Eskdale. In the first-named is some of the loveliest scenery in Dumfries, notably between Thornhill and Sanquhar, where the Nith flows between ranges of shapely, green hills. A trio of picturesque passes, those of Dalveen, Mennock and Enterkin, link the Nith valley with Clydesdale, in Lanarkshire, the two first-named being traversed by good motoring roads. The last-named is a mere track, and joins the Mennock near the mining village of Wanlockhead, the highest situated in Scotland, overlooked by the bulky hill of Green Lowther.

Annandale stretches northwards from the Solway Firth, the river flowing between Lockerbie and Lochmaben, and the dale becoming lonelier and at its wildest to the north of the little spa of Moffat. Here, it is noted for the winding pass overlooking the Devil's Beef Tub, a hollow lying below steep green hills near the borders of Dumfries, Lanark and Peebles, close to the important watershed where the Rivers Clyde, Tweed and Annan rise. Beyond Moffat, the Selkirk road to the north-east follows the Moffat Water under the slopes of Hart Fell and White Coomb, and passes near the well-known waterfall of the Grey Mare's Tail, at the summit of the Birkhill Pass, looking into Selkirkshire. The burn at this point comes down from the high-lying Loch Skene, in the vicinity of which Dumfries, Peebles and Selkirk meet.

Eskdale, the most easterly of the three dales, commences near the English border, here guarded by the Scots Dyke, on the borders of the former "Debatable Land." It continues through Canonbie and Langholm, amid characteristic Border scenery, to lose itself away to the north in the wild and lonely Ettrick hills beyond Eskdalemuir.

The town of Dumfries, situated on the Nith near its estuary, has important Burns associations, and near Auldgirth, also on the river, is the well-known farmhouse of Ellisland, where the poet composed " Tam o' Shanter " among other works. Another famous literary association is claimed by Ecclefechan, where Thomas Carlyle was born, and near Dunscore is the farm of Craigenputtock, where his great work " Sartor Resartus " was written.

Among other places of interest in the county are Lochmaben, said to have been the birthplace of Robert Bruce, and Gretna, which was long notorious for its runaway marriage ceremonies. Sanquhar, in Nithsdale, together with the Lowther Hills to the east, has many associations with the persecuted Covenanters. In the little Church at Ruthwell is preserved the celebrated 8th cent. Ruthwell Cross, the most notable of the county's ecclesiastical remains, and at Durisdeer the Church contains a remarkable range of monuments. Drumlanrig Castle is a magnificent Renaissance house in a lovely setting, and Maxwelton House, near Moniaive, is famous as the one-time home of Annie Laurie. Among numerous castles and towers, Caerlaverock Castle, with its remarkable facade; Comlongon Castle near Clarencefield; and the exceptionally well-preserved Amisfield Tower, are perhaps the most notable.

Places of Scenic Interest. Auldgirth, Birkhill, Canonbie, Carronbridge, Enterkinfoot, Eskdalemuir, Langholm, Mennock, Moffat, Wanlockhead.

Places of Architectural or Historic Interest. Amisfield, Caerlaverock, Closeburn, Comlongon Castle (Clarencefield), Craigenputtock (Dunscore), Drumlanrig Castle, Dumfries, Durisdeer, Ecclefechan, Ellisland (Auldgirth), Gretna, Hollows Tower (Canonbie), Isle Tower (Auldgirth), Lochmaben, Maxwelton House (Moniaive), Moniaive, Rammerscales (Hightae), Ruthwell, Spedlins Tower (Lockerbie).

DUNBARTONSHIRE

(County Town: Dumbarton)

This county was at one time known as Lennox, and formed part of an ancient district comprising also portions of Stirling, Perth and Renfrew. This name is now preserved in the general title of the Lennox Hills, which is applied to the Kilpatricks, the Campsie Fells and the neighbouring hill ranges. Dunbarton is unique among Scottish counties in that it possesses also a small detached portion on the mainland, lying to the east, bordered by Lanark and Stirling. This includes the town of Kirkintilloch, where a fort on the Antonine, or Roman Wall, was formerly situated.

The bulk of the county stretches north-westwards from the environs of Glasgow, its boundaries being the Clyde estuary, Loch Long and Loch Lomond, while at the northern extremity it meets Perthshire beyond Ardlui at the head of the last-named loch. The great mass of Ben Vorlich dominates the scene at this point, and to the south-west of the mountain lies Loch Sloy, whose waters have been harnessed to one of Scotland's large hydro-electric schemes. Some of the loveliest scenery in the country is to be found on the road which traverses the whole length of Loch Lomond's western shores, passing the attractive village of Luss. Another scenic road is that which follows the Gare Loch to its head, and then continues along the eastern shores of the lengthy and narrow Loch Long to Arrochar, situated on the narrow neck of land separating Loch Long from Loch Lomond. Several of the well-known Clyde coast resorts lie on the shore of the Gare Loch, and also in the narrow Rosneath peninsula separating its waters from those of Loch Long, the best known being perhaps Helensburgh.

The Royal Burgh of Dumbarton, an important shipbuilding town, is noted for its castle, which dominates the Clyde estuary from the heights of Dumbarton Rock. To the north of the town, along the shores of the River Leven, which issues from Loch Lomond at the railhead of Balloch, is a district specialising in bleaching, and in which the town of Alexandria has associations with Tobias Smollett. Nearer to Glasgow the Clyde becomes highly industrialised, and Clydebank, which was severely damaged during the second World War, is famous for its shipbuilding yards, where, among many historic ships, the great liners *Queen Mary* and the two *Queen Elizabeths* were built. At Bowling, below the Kilpatrick Hills, between Dumbarton and Clydebank, the Forth and Clyde canal enters the estuary, and here was the western terminus of the Roman Wall, which stretched across the narrow waist of the country to the Forth estuary. Some portions are still to be seen in Dunbartonshire near the town of Bearsden.

Places of Scenic Interest. Ardlui, Arrochar, Garelochhead, Loch Lomond, Luss, Rosneath, Tarbet.

Places of Architectural or Historic Interest. Bearsden, Bowling, Dumbarton, Knockderry Castle (Kilcreggan), Ross Priory (Gartocharn).

EAST LOTHIAN

(County Town: Haddington)

One of the most fertile of the Scottish counties, notably near Dunbar, where, in the red soil, are grown the celebrated " Red Dunbar " potatoes. The long and lonely range of the Lammermuirs, given over largely to sheep, forms the southern background to East Lothian, while the land to the north of the hills slopes gradually towards the coastal plain overlooking the Firth of Forth. Lammer Law, rising to the south of Gifford, is the highest point in the Lammermuirs, and to the west, near the Midlothian and Berwick borders, is Soutra Hill, a well-known viewpoint on the main Edinburgh to Jedburgh road.

East Lothian has a coastline which is mainly flat, and the neighbourhood of the famous resorts of Gullane and North Berwick is largely devoted to golf. Out to sea beyond North Berwick, and a prominent object in the view from the picturesque, ruined castle of Tantallon, is the notable landmark of the Bass Rock, now a haunt of sea birds.

Both Dunbar and Prestonpans are renowned in Scottish history for the battles with which they are associated and near the latter is the little fishing village of Cockenzie. The Royal Burgh of Haddington, which formerly gave its name to the county, is supposed to be the birthplace of John Knox, and its fine, though mutilated Church has been called the " Lamp of Lothian." Dirleton, East Linton and Gifford are attractive villages, the first-named having an old castle, while near the last-named is the Adam mansion of Yester House, beyond which lies the curious underground " Goblin Ha' " from the former castle. At Whitekirk and Seton there are interesting churches, the latter, which is unfinished, being collegiate, and noted for its vaulted chancel and apse. A number of other fine old houses grace the county, among which may be mentioned Gosford House, Pilmuir near Bolton, and both Winton House and Penkaet in the vicinity of Pencaitland.

Places of Scenic Interest. Dirleton, East Linton, Garvald, Gifford, Pencaitland, Soutra Hill.

Places of Architectural or Historic Interest. Biel (Stenton), Dirleton, Dunbar, Dunglass, Elphinstone Tower (Tranent), Falside Castle (Tranent), Gosford House, Haddington, Hailes Castle (East Linton), Lennoxlove (Bolton), Northfield (Prestonpans), Pencaitland, Penkaet (Pencaitland), Pilmuir (Bolton), Prestonpans, Saltcoats Castle (Gullane), Seton, Spott, Tantallon Castle (North Berwick), Tynninghame, Whitekirk, Whittinghame, Winton House (Pencaitland), Yester (Gifford).

FIFE

(County Town: Cupar)

Situated between the Firths of Forth and Tay, and sometimes still known as the " Kingdom of Fife," this pleasant county included, until 1426, also Kinross within its boundaries. Although lacking the more spectacular physical features associated with some other Scottish counties, Fife has nevertheless achieved a niche of its own by virtue of the world-wide fame of St. Andrews, and the delightful old-world maritime burghs gracing the shores of the Firth of Forth, the most picturesque surviving of their kind. On the extreme north-west border rise the Ochil Hills, separated by the fertile Howe of Fife from the Lomonds, which lie farther south, and are shared with Kinross. Away to the south-west, Benarty Hill and the Cleish Hills, with their high point of Dumglow, are also situated on the Kinross border.

The remainder of Fife is mostly fertile and undulating, with flat country along the eastern shores from Tents Moor, beyond Leuchars, to Fife Ness, the most easterly point, facing the North Sea from the promontory known as the East Neuk of Fife. The two most famous railway bridges in Scotland link the county with West Lothian and Angus respectively, the Forth Bridge, spanning the Firth of Forth from Queensferry North, and the less impressive, but longer Tay Bridge crossing the Firth of Tay from Wormit, to the south-west of Newport-on-Tay. The new Forth road bridge was, in 1966, supplemented by one spanning the Tay. An important coalfield lies in the south-western sector of the county around Cowdenbeath.

St. Andrews is by far the most renowned Royal Burgh in Fife, and is today best known as the Mecca of golf, its Royal and Ancient Club ranking as the ruling authority on the game. The Cathedral, now reduced to ruin, and neighboured by the tall tower of St. Rule's Church, was once the largest in Scotland, while the University, with its fine chapel of St. Salvator, is the oldest in the country. The picturesque remains of the castle are impregnated with memories of Cardinal Beaton and John Knox. To the north of the town, beyond the Eden estuary, is Leuchars, with its famous Norman church and the fine old mansion of Earlshall. Westwards lies the very attractive little village of Ceres.

Among the small coastal towns, Crail, Pittenweem and St. Monance are all delightful, with their fishing harbours and numerous old houses, while near Pittenweem is the fine 16th cent. Kellie Castle. Farther west are situated Largo, associated with " Robinson Crusoe," and Dysart, another attractive old burgh, now linked to the larger town of Kirkcaldy. Dunfermline, a Royal Burgh with a long history, retains a striking Norman nave in its restored Abbey Church, in which Robert Bruce lies buried, and the town was the birthplace of the great philanthropist, Andrew Carnegie. Falkland, another pleasant little Royal Burgh, situated below the Lomonds, is famous for the delightful 16th century Palace, with its memories of Scottish kings.

Lastly, and the loveliest of its kind in Scotland, is Culross, now largely cared for by the Scottish National Trust, and situated on the Forth estuary west of Dunfermline, being easily reached by means of the fine new Forth road bridge. At Culross, the numerous old houses of the tiny Royal Burgh, with their crow-stepped gables and red pantiled roofs, the picturesque Tolbooth, and the beautiful little Palace, with its painted rooms and quaint walled gardens, are overlooked by the Abbey Church on the hillside above. They combine to produce a picture that is without a peer, and are deserving of even greater fame than they have already achieved.

Places of Scenic Interest. Auchtermuchty, Ceres, Crail, Culross, Dairsie, Falkland, Kilconquhar, Pitscottie, Pittenweem, St. Monance, Tayport.

Places of Architectural or Historic Interest. Balmerino Abbey, Crail, Culross, Dunfermline, Dysart, Earlshall (Leuchars), Falkland Palace, Inchcolm Island, Kellie Castle (Pittenweem),

Kincardine-on-Forth, Leslie, Leuchars, Lindores Abbey, Melville House (Monimail), St. Andrews, St. Monance, Scotstarvit (Cupar).

INVERNESS-SHIRE

(County Town: Inverness)

The largest county in Scotland, extending from the Atlantic to the North Sea, and scenically perhaps the finest, including within its boundaries examples of almost every type of Highland scenery. Its deeply indented western shores are notable for the magnificent sea lochs of Hourn and Nevis, the first-named of which exhibits scenery comparable with the fjords of Norway. These lochs are, however, difficult of access by road, though the inner and outer reaches of Loch Hourn can be visited by means of rough and narrow roads from Tomdoun and Glenelg respectively. The road leading to Glenelg from the shores of Loch Duich, in Ross and Cromarty, climbs over the lofty Mam Rattachan pass, one of the finest viewpoints in the Highlands. Several other sea lochs farther to the south are only little less remarkable for their wild beauty, and have, in addition, romantic associations with Prince Charles Edward and the '45. These Jacobite memories extend to the whole of the Moidart district, bordered by the highly picturesque, but roadless Loch Shiel, on the Argyll border, at the head of which stands Glenfinnan, with the well-known monument to the Prince in its superb mountain setting.

To Inverness-shire belongs also a large part of the Inner and Outer Hebrides, including the beautiful island of Skye, in which the spectacular, jagged rock peaks of the Coolins overlook the wild and desolate Loch Coruisk. In the extreme north of the island, near Staffin, is situated the strange, rocky amphitheatre known as the Quiraing. Both Eigg and mountainous Rum, whose outlines figure so prominently in views from the mainland, in addition to the whole chain of the Outer Hebrides, with the exception of Lewis, but including the lonely and distant islands of St. Kilda, are all also Inverness territory.

On the mainland, the Great Glen of Alban, or Glen More, with its chain of lochs, linked by the Caledonian Canal, is overlooked in the Lochaber district by Ben Nevis (4,406 ft.), the highest mountain in the British Isles. This glen virtually divides Scotland into two portions, and is one of its most remarkable physical features. The largest of the lochs in the Great Glen is Loch Ness, which has achieved fame as the domicile of the fabulous Loch Ness Monster, first seen in 1932. North-west of the Great Glen lies a wild and lonely area of mountain and loch, including the remote Knoydart and " Rough Bounds " district beyond picturesque Loch Quoich, where a hydro-electric scheme now operates. This district is as yet comparatively poorly developed for touring, but displays a rugged landscape ranking among the finest in the country. Much of the varied beauty of this part of Scotland can be appreciated from two roads; first, the far-famed Road to the Isles, " By Ailort and by Morar to the sea," linking Fort William with Morar, famous for its white sands and deep inland loch, and terminating at Mallaig, on Outer Loch Nevis; and secondly the roads through Glen Garry and Glen Moriston, which meet near Loch Cluanie, in Ross and Cromarty, to form an alternative Road to the Isles and lead by way of Glen Shiel to Kyle of Lochalsh, the well-known " Gateway to Skye." The views from the improved Mallaig road, in particular, will come as a revelation to those without previous experience of West Highland scenery, and the exceptionally lovely colourings are at times more akin to Mediterranean surroundings, while the picturesque, island-studded Loch Eilt, near Lochailort, is one of the gems of the Scottish mainland. A fine new road now links Kinlochmoidart with Lochailort, thus opening up the beautiful coastline of the Sound of Arisaig, backed by the hills of Moidart.

Some of the roads in the wilder parts of the county, and also in the Island of Skye and the Outer Hebrides are narrow and at times poorly surfaced, but frequent passing-places have been constructed on a number of stretches.

In the north of the county, the delightful valley of Strath Glass gives access from Cannich to the superbly-wooded mountain scenery of Glen Affric and Glen Cannich, with their lochs, which are, however, not through routes to the west. Their erstwhile peace has been somewhat shattered by the introduction of a large hydro-electric scheme, though the re-aligned and well-surfaced roads which have now been provided along these two glens are of considerable benefit to motorists.

To the east of Loch Ness and the Great Glen are the Monadhliath mountains, and below them lies Badenoch, and also Speyside, or Strath Spey, richly wooded in parts, and overlooked by the great range of the Cairngorms, now including an extensive National Nature Reserve. Their remote, flat-topped 4,000-ft. high summits, partly shared by the counties of Aberdeen and Banff, at whose meeting-point rises Ben Macdhui (4,275 ft.), the loftiest of the peaks, are surpassed only by Ben Nevis.

On Speyside are situated a number of pleasant summer and winter resorts, the best known being the newly-developed Aviemore. This is convenient for the Glenmore Forest Park, with Loch Morlich and the new ski road to Coire Cas, below the peak of Cairn Gorm, and also for Rothiemurchus Forest, at the entrance to the famous Lairig Ghru pass in the Cairngorms. Inverness and Fort William, the most important touring centres in the county, guard the eastern and western extremities of the Great Glen respectively, and are linked by a splendid modern highway, which traverses the entire length of the glen. Easy of access from Fort William, and reached by way of Spean Bridge and Roy Bridge, are the remarkable "Parallel Roads" of Glen Roy. Inverness has memories of Prince Charles

Edward, while the battlefield of Culloden, where the tragic finale of the '45 was played out, lies a little to the east.

Places of Scenic Interest. Arnisdale, Aviemore, Ben Nevis, Cannich, Fort William, Foyers, Glenelg, Glenfinnan, Kingussie, Kinloch Hourn, Kinlochmoidart, Lairig Ghru, Lochailort, Loch Arkaig, Loch Hourn, Loch Lochy, Loch nan Uamh, Loch Ness, Loch Nevis, Loch Quoich, Loch Shiel, Mallaig, Morar, Rothiemurchus, Roy Bridge, Spean Bridge, Struy Bridge, Tomdoun.

Places of Architectural or Historic Interest. Beaufort Castle (Kilmorack), Beauly, Castle Stewart (Inverness), Culloden, Dalcross Castle (Croy), Fort Augustus, Glenelg, Invergarry, Inverlochy Castle (Fort William), Inverness, Kilravock Castle (Croy), Urquhart Castle (Drumnadrochit).

A description of the Inner Hebridean island of Skye will be found by referring to its gazetteer article, while separate entries are made for all individual places of interest, most of which are also cross-indexed in the parent article. For the Outer Hebrides, see under Hebrides, Outer.

KINCARDINESHIRE

(County Town: Stonehaven)

Known also by the alternative name of The Mearns, this county has a long North Sea coastline, with rock scenery at various points, notably in the stretch between Bervie, or Inverbervie and Johnshaven, and also in the neighbourhood of Muchalls. Inland, between the River North Esk and the Bervie Water, is a fertile, level tract of country called the " Howe of the Mearns," an extension of the Howe of Angus and Strathmore valley lying away to the south-west.

Beyond the flat country, the level of the land rises gradually to the foothills of the eastern Grampians, much of them given over to grouse and deer, with Mount Battock rising to more than 2,500 ft. near the meeting point of Kincardine, Angus and Aberdeen. The only road to traverse this mountain district is the famous Cairn o' Mounth pass, attaining nearly 1,500 ft., and linking the attractive village of Fettercairn, known for its Macbeth associations, with Banchory, situated on wooded Deeside. This small Kincardineshire stretch of the Dee valley, overlooked to the north by the Hill of Fare, on the Aberdeen border, includes the notable 16th century Crathes Castle, a valuable acquisition of the Scottish National Trust and perhaps the finest building in the county.

Another hill road, known in part as the Slug Road, goes south-eastwards from Banchory to link Deeside with the coast. The river divides the county from Aberdeenshire from a point east of Banchory to Girdle Ness, on the coast, overlooking Aberdeen Bay. Away to the south of the Ness, beyond Muchalls, is the fishing port and resort of Stonehaven, near which, in a picturesque setting of cliffs, are considerable remains of the historic Dunnottar Castle.

Places of Scenic Interest. Banchory, Cairn o' Mounth, Cove, Fettercairn, Inverbervie, Johnshaven, Muchalls, St. Cyrus.

Places of Architectural or Historic Interest. Allardyce Castle (Inverbervie), Arbuthnott, Crathes Castle, Dunnottar Castle, Fiddes Castle (Drumlithie), Kincardine Castle (Fettercairn), Muchalls.

KINROSS-SHIRE

(County Town: Kinross)

One of the smallest in area among the Scottish counties, at one time forming part of Fife, from which it was separated in 1426.

Kinross is bordered to the north by the Ochil Hills, and to the east by the lesser range of the Lomonds, the county boundary in each case traversing some of the highest of the ridges. Between the hills lies Loch Leven, well known to fishermen, and perhaps the most notable physical feature of the county, being also historically famous for the celebrated escape of Mary, Queen of Scots, from its romantically-situated island castle. Part of Benarty Hill, and much of the Cleish Hills are included within the southern half of Kinross. In the extreme south-west, the picturesque gorges and waterfalls of the winding River Devon provide the county's finest scenery, notably in the vicinity of Rumbling Bridge and Crook of Devon, where the river forms the boundary with Perthshire.

The manufacture of woollens and linens is of some importance, and one of the chief centres of the industry is the small town of Milnathort, situated to the north-west of Loch Leven. Kinross House, in its splendid setting, is one of the finest houses of its period in Scotland, and the mansion of Blairadam is associated with William Adam, the architect, one of whose sons was the even more famous architect, Robert Adam.

Places of Scenic Interest. Crook of Devon, Kinnesswood, Loch Leven, Rumbling Bridge.

Places of Architectural or Historic Interest. Aldie Castle (Cleish), Blairadam, Burleigh Castle (Milnathort), Kinross, Loch Leven Castle, Portmoak, Tullibole Castle (Crook of Devon).

KIRKCUDBRIGHTSHIRE

(County Town: Kirkcudbright)

Sometimes also referred to as The Stewartry, recalling its former jurisdiction by a Royal Steward, this county, together with its western neighbour, Wigtown, constitutes the Galloway district, and includes within its borders the wild and beautiful scenery of the " Galloway Highlands." This mountain landscape, which has been graphically described in the novels of S. R. Crockett, is concentrated in the north-western corner, on the

Ayrshire border, where the lonely Merrick rises above the surrounding heights to take its place as the highest mainland hill south of the Highlands proper. Below the Merrick, to the west and south, lie, among others, the remote lochs of Enoch and Neldricken, and beyond the former rise Corserine and Carlins Cairn, the monarchs of the Rhinns of Kells range. These are only a little inferior in height to the Merrick itself, and look northwards across the valley of the Gala Lane to the shores of Loch Doon, which forms the boundary with Ayrshire.

To the south-west of the hills lies Glen Trool, the loveliest in Galloway, with the Bruce Memorial overlooking Loch Trool in a delightful and picturesque setting. The extensive Glen Trool Forest Park includes much of this fine country, while two of its outlying sub-divisions, Cairn Edward Forest, west of New Galloway, and Kirroughtree Forest, north-east of the little Wigtownshire town of Newton Stewart, and overlooked by the lofty Cairnsmore of Fleet, also lie within the county boundaries.

The remaining parts of Kirkcudbright are largely undulating, and given over to cattle and sheep rearing, the dark Galloway cattle and the local breed of horses both being well known. The county extends eastwards as far as the Nith estuary, over which towers the bulky hill of Criffell, while Maxwelltown, which is divided from the town of Dumfries by the river, was united to the latter in 1929. Much of the long coastline overlooks the Solway Firth and the distant Cumbrian mountains, and, while mainly flat in the east, becomes increasingly bolder and more scenic to the west, with a number of " Smugglers " caves, and also associations with Scott's " Guy Mannering." There are several large inlets, notably Rough Firth and Auchencairn Bay south of Dalbeattie; Kirkcudbright Bay, below the county town; and Fleet Bay, to the south-west of Gatehouse of Fleet. The coast road from the last-mentioned town along the shores of Wigtown Bay to Creetown, on the Cree estuary, is one of the loveliest in Scotland, passing several ruined castles, and also Dirk Hatteraick's Cave, west of Ravenshall Point.

The extensive Galloway Power Scheme utilises much of the local water power, notably in the Ken basin around New Galloway in the Glenkens district, and a number of reservoirs and power stations have been brought into operation, of which the Clatteringshaws reservoir and dam are outstanding.

The chief architectural interest lies in the Abbeys of Dundrennan, Lincluden, and New, or Sweetheart Abbey. Among the ruined castles, Cardoness and Rusco near Gatehouse of Fleet, Threave, to the west of Castle Douglas, and Maclellan's Castle at Kirkcudbright are all of note.

Places of Scenic Interest. Auchencairn, Bargrennan, Carsphairn, Clatteringshaws, Creetown, Douglas Hall, Gatehouse of Fleet, Irongray, Kippford, Loch Trool, Southerness.

Places of Architectural or Historic Interest. Anwoth Church, Cardoness Castle (Gatehouse of Fleet), Dundrennan Abbey, Hills Castle (Lochfoot), Lincluden Abbey, Maclellan's Castle (Kirkcudbright), New (or Sweetheart) Abbey, Orchardton Tower (Palnackie), Rusco Castle (Gatehouse of Fleet), Shawhead, Threave Castle (Castle Douglas).

LANARKSHIRE

(County Town: Hamilton)

The county of Lanark is sub-divided into three districts, known as the Upper, Middle and Lower Wards. The first-named is pastoral, and includes the range of the Lowther Hills; the second is largely composed of the orchard country of Lower Clydesdale, between Lanark and Hamilton, to the north-west of which stands the imposing ruin of Bothwell Castle; and the last-named contains the industrial area in the neighbourhood of Glasgow, where, in the city, stands one of Scotland's finest Cathedrals. The Upper Ward is the home of the well-known Clydesdale draught-horse, and the mining of lead and other minerals has long been associated with the district around Leadhills.

Due to the inclusion within its boundaries of the great city and seaport of Glasgow, and also the extensive coal and iron basin to the south-east, Lanarkshire has the largest population of all the Scottish counties. Although often thought of primarily as given over to industry, there is nevertheless much attractive scenery, commencing with the long valley of the River Clyde. Above its junction with the Avon near Motherwell, the Clyde traverses a landscape becoming increasingly pastoral, notably around Crossford, in a rich setting of orchards, near which stands Craignethan Castle, supposed to be the Tillietudlem of Scott's " Old Mortality." In the vicinity of the town of Lanark are the picturesque Falls of the Clyde, of which Cora Linn is perhaps the finest.

Away to the south-east, near Symington, is the isolated Tinto Hill, a prominent landmark and viewpoint, from which the even higher Culter Fell, on the Peebles border, can be seen. In the extreme south of the county, overlooking the heart of Upper Clydesdale, are the green hills of Lowther, rising to more than 2,000 ft. in places, and famous as the haunt of persecuted Covenanters in the latter half of the 17th century. Facing the hills is the bleak and loftily situated village of Leadhills, exceeded in altitude only by its Dumfriesshire neighbour Wanlockhead. From Elvanfoot, two roads link Clydesdale with the Nith valley across the Dumfries border, the former going through Leadhills and the Mennock Pass, and the latter keeping farther south and traversing the Dalveen Pass.

Places of Scenic Interest. Crawford, Douglas, Elvanfoot, Kirkfieldbank, Leadhills.

Places of Architectural or Historic Interest. Barncluith (Hamilton), Biggar, Bothwell, Cadzow Castle (Hamilton), Craignethan Castle (Crossford), Crookston Castle (Paisley), Dalzell House (Motherwell), Douglas, Glasgow, Hallbar Tower (Crossford), Pollok House (Pollokshaws).

MIDLOTHIAN

(County Town: Edinburgh)

The fame of the city of Edinburgh has very largely overshadowed the county in which it is situated. Nevertheless, Midlothian, or Edinburghshire, contains architectural features of considerable interest, some of the best farming land in the whole of Scotland, and scenery of a pleasantly diversified nature, from the Pentland Hills in the west to the Moorfoots in the east.

The Pentlands, which are some 16 miles in length, and attain nearly 2,000 ft. at Scald Law near Penicuik, were much beloved of Robert Louis Stevenson, and form an admirable outlet for the energies of Edinburgh's citizens. A number of reservoirs are situated on their slopes, and the range is crossed by numerous footpaths, and also various old drove roads, of which the Cauld Stane Slap, between the East and West Cairn Hills, is one of the best known. The Moorfoots are lonelier hills, exceeding the 2,000-ft. level at Blackhope Scar, while a narrow, but picturesque road threads their southern slopes, commencing at Heriot, and reaching a height of more than 1,000 ft. before descending into Tweeddale.

Soutra Hill, a well-known viewpoint on the main Edinburgh to Jedburgh road, and situated at the junction of Midlothian, East Lothian and Berwickshire, links the Moorfoot outliers with the Lammermuir Hills farther to the east. Away to the south lies the delightful winding valley of the Gala Water, in which lies the pleasant village of Stow in its setting of hills.

Among the notable buildings of Midlothian are the churches of Crichton, Duddingston, Temple, and above all Roslin; the castles of Borthwick, Craigmillar, Crichton and Roslin; and the fine old houses of Dalkeith, Pinkie, Hawthornden, to the south-west of Lasswade, and Auchendinny near Penicuik. Edinburgh, with its wealth of historic and architectural interest in the city, and also a number of interesting old mansions in the outer suburbs of Colinton, Corstorphine, Duddingston and Liberton, is, of course, a chapter in itself, and is very fully described in the gazetteer section of the book.

Places of Scenic Interest. Cramond Bridge, Duddingston, Glencorse, Lasswade, Roslin, Soutra Hill, Stow, Swanston, Temple.

Places of Architectural or Historic Interest. Arniston (Gorebridge), Auchendinny (Penicuik), Borthwick, Cakemuir Castle (Blackshiels), Carrington, Colinton, Corstorphine, Craigmillar Castle, Crichton, Dalhousie (Cockpen), Dalkeith, Drum (Gilmerton), Duddingston, Edinburgh, Glencorse, Hawthornden (Lasswade), Holyroodhouse (Edinburgh), Lauriston Castle (Barnton), Liberton, Mid Calder, Newbattle, Pinkie House, Preston (Pathhead), Prestonfield (Duddingston), Roslin, Temple.

MORAY

(County Town: Elgin)

This maritime county, once part of a province extending over a much larger area, has low, sandy shores facing the Moray Firth. Farther inland lies the broad and fertile Laigh of Moray, in the centre of which stands Elgin, famous for the ruins of its once-magnificent Cathedral, desecrated in 1390 by the notorious Wolf of Badenoch.

The fast-flowing River Findhorn traverses part of north-west Moray, exhibiting picturesque, wooded scenery at Randolph's Leap by its junction with the Divie, near Logie, to the north-east of Ferness, which lies just inside the county of Nairn. Later, the Findhorn flows between Darnaway Forest and Altyre Woods in the vicinity of Forres, before entering Findhorn Bay, an inlet of the Moray Firth. This is bordered to the west by the former Culbin Sands, now completely afforested. In the great sandstorm of 1694, they had engulfed a formerly fertile and prosperous district.

The southern half of the county is hilly, an altitude of more than 2,300 ft. being reached in the Cromdale Hills, on the Inverness and Banff border. To the north-west of the hills flows the turbulent River Spey, the second longest in Scotland, and famous for its salmon, forming the county boundary with Banff for some miles, and reaching the end of its long journey from Badenoch at Spey Bay beyond Fochabers. There are beautiful stretches near the point where it is joined by the Avon below the Hill of Delnapot, near Delnashaugh Inn, in Banffshire, and again in the neighbourhood of Craigellachie, also just over the Banff border. Here, the Fiddich enters the main stream, before the latter turns northwards towards Rothes, beyond which lies the pleasant Glen of Rothes.

Two well-known resorts in the county are Lossiemouth, on the coast, and the delightful Highland resort and touring centre of Grantown-on-Spey, with the massed summits of the Cairngorms rising away to the south. Among the old buildings of Moray, Elgin Cathedral, Pluscarden Priory and Spynie Palace, together with the sinister island castle of Lochindorb, and Coxton Tower near Lhanbryde, are perhaps of the greatest interest. Darnaway Castle, in its forest setting near Forres, although considerably later in date, preserves portions of an earlier structure.

Places of Scenic Interest. Findhorn, Forres, Grantown-on-Spey, Lochindorb, Logie, Mosstodloch, Rothes.

Places of Architectural or Historic Interest. Birnie, Castle Grant (Grantown-on-Spey), Coxton Tower (Lhanbryde), Darnaway Castle (Forres), Duffus, Elgin, Forres, Innes House (Elgin), Lochindorb, Pluscarden Priory, Spynie Palace.

NAIRNSHIRE

(County Town: Nairn)

One of the smaller Scottish counties, with an expanse of flat coastline on the shores of the Moray Firth, which is overlooked by the well-known resort and golfing centre of Nairn, noted for its dry and sunny climate. A little to the east is the pleasant village of Auldearn, where Montrose, in 1645, won a battle against the Covenanters. To the south-west of the town, beyond the River Nairn, stands the fine old castle of Cawdor, one of the most interesting and picturesque in the whole country, and associated with Shakespeare's "Macbeth." In the vicinity is Kilravock Castle, which has links with Prince Charles Edward, and to the south of Nairn stands the ruined Rait Castle.

The southern half of Nairn is hilly and sparsely populated, an altitude of more than 2,000 ft. being reached on the Inverness border in Strath Dearn. Here, the lonely Streens district is traversed by the River Findhorn, a rapid-flowing stream, on the banks of which the finest scenery in the county is to be found. At Dulsie Bridge, the river flows through a narrow, rocky gorge, overlooked by woodlands, and the view from the single-span 18th century bridge is exceptionally picturesque. Beyond the bridge, to the north-east, in the grounds of Glenferness House, is the romantic Princess Stone, and from this point the Findhorn flows in a series of curves to reach Ferness. Still farther north-east is Daltulich Bridge, where the river again threads its way through delightful wooded scenery to enter Morayshire, near the beauty spot of Randolph's Leap, where the Divie joins the main stream.

Places of Scenic Interest. Auldearn, Dulsie Bridge, Ferness.

Places of Architectural or Historic Interest. Ardclach Church, Brodie, Cawdor Castle, Inshoch Tower (Auldearn), Kilravock Castle (Croy), Rait Castle (Nairn).

ORKNEY

(County Town: Kirkwall)

The islands forming this group are fully described, both generally and individually, including all places of interest, under their own heading in the gazetteer.

PEEBLESSHIRE

(County Town: Peebles)

This pleasant Border county exhibits the characteristic valleys and rounded green hills of the Lowlands, and much of its scenery and past history has been used for local colour in the works of Sir Walter Scott and John Buchan. Peeblesshire is devoted mainly to agriculture and sheep farming, but the wool industry is of importance in several of the towns in the Tweed valley, notably Peebles and Innerleithen.

The River Tweed, famous for its salmon, flows through the centre of the county, which is known sometimes by the alternative name of Tweeddale. Some of the loveliest scenery associated with the river will be found around Peebles itself, and in particular farther to the west, where the hills become higher and lonelier. Here, the infant river has its source at Tweed's Well, near the watershed on the borders of Dumfries and Lanark in the shadow of Hart Fell, one of the loftiest of the Lowland hills. To the north of Hart Fell rises the flat-topped Broad Law, inferior in height among Lowland hills only to the Merrick, in Kirkcudbrightshire. Below, to the south-west lies the Talla reservoir, which is reached from Tweedsmuir, on the fine road linking Peebles with Moffat. Among the numerous tributaries of the Tweed, one of the best known is the Leithen Water. This joins the parent stream at Innerleithen, after flowing through picturesque Glentress, surrounded by hills, of which Windlestraw Law, rising near the meeting-point of Peebles, Midlothian and Selkirk, is the highest.

In the vicinity of the Royal Burgh and inland resort of Peebles are several delightful valleys, notably that of the Manor Water, which extends southwards into the hills from Manor Church. The attractive, but much less known and roadless Glensax lies to the south-east of the town. The Pentland Hills rise in the extreme north of the county, the boundary line with Midlothian traversing the lofty East and West Cairn Hills, between which goes the old drove road known as the Cauld Stane Slap, commencing beyond the village of West Linton. Outliers of the slightly higher Moorfoot Hills extend into the north-eastern corner of Peebleshire beyond the valleys of the Eddleston and Leithen Waters, and on the slopes of the hills lies the little Portmore Loch, near Eddleston.

There are interesting small churches at Stobo and Lyne, the former of which is backed by the celebrated Dawyck Woods. Facing the Tweed, outside Peebles, stands the very picturesque, ruined tower of Neidpath, once battered by Cromwell's guns, and associated later with the Dukes of Queensberry. The finest old house in the county is the mansion of Traquair, with its romantic associations and delightful setting in the valley of the Quair Water. Beyond Traquair village rises the hill road known as the "Paddy Slacks," forming the boundary with Selkirk, and crossing into Ettrick Forest and the Vale of Yarrow.

Places of Scenic Interest. Carlops, Crook Inn, Manor, Peebles, Skirling, Stobo, Traquair, Tweedsmuir, West Linton.

Places of Architectural or Historic Interest. Barns Tower (Lyne), Drochil Castle (Romanno Bridge), Lyne, Neidpath Castle (Peebles), Stobo, Traquair House, Whim (Leadburn).

PERTHSHIRE

(County Town: Perth)

Situated almost in the centre of the country, with the grassy, or heather-clad Grampian mountains and their subsidiary spurs occupying the greater part of the northern half, Perthshire is one of the loveliest of Scottish counties, and exhibits Highland scenery in its most characteristic vein, while its historical associations are no less outstanding.

In the south-eastern corner rise the Ochil and Sidlaw Hills, the latter separated from the Firth of Tay by the low-lying and fertile Carse of Gowrie. Away to the west, beyond the windings of the Forth, on the Stirling border, lies the romantic and beautifully wooded Trossachs district, overlooked by Ben Venue, with Lochs Katrine and Vennachar, made famous by the genius of Sir Walter Scott, and visited annually by thousands of tourists. Some of Perthshire's best known mountains lie to the north of this area, notably Ben Ledi near Callander; Ben More and its neighbour Stobinian dominating Crianlarich; Ben Vorlich, forming the background to Loch Earn; and Ben Lui, on the Argyll border, south-west of Tyndrum.

The fracture known as the Highland Line, or "fault," which divides the Highlands from the Lowlands, as shown by the changes in the rock structure of the hills, passes across Perthshire in a line going from Aberfoyle to the River Tay south-east of Dunkeld, and in the vicinity of Comrie slight earth tremors are occasionally felt.

Loch Tay and Loch Rannoch are the largest of the lochs, both being traversed by roads on either bank, this applying also to the smaller, but very delightful Loch Earn. Above the northern shores of Loch Tay towers Ben Lawers (3,984 ft.), a botanist's paradise (N.T. Scotland), and the highest mountain in the county. Beyond the Ben, and parallel to the loch, stretches Glen Lyon, one of the longest in Scotland, being particularly lovely immediately to the west of Fortingall. The lonely head of the glen is closed in by the lofty Drum Alban ridge of the Grampians, and hydro-electric developments have taken place in the vicinity. Much of General Wade's great military road from Dunkeld to Inverness, now part of the splendid modern highway, passes through the county, crossing the Grampians by means of the bleak Drumochter Pass. On his link road, commencing at Crieff, and joining the main highway at Dalnacardoch, lies Aberfeldy, where what is perhaps Wade's finest bridge still spans the Tay. To the north of Aberfeldy is the delightful Tummel valley, with the famous Queen's View, looking towards the prominent cone of Schiehallion and the Rannoch country. Extensive hydro-electric developments which have taken place between Loch Tummel and Piltochry are creating new interests for the tourist.

The picturesque, wooded gorge of Killiecrankie, near the meeting-place of Tummel and Garry, was the scene, in 1689, of a memorable battle; at Sheriffmuir, near Dunblane, in 1715, the Old Pretender's forces fought an indecisive action; and the legendary battle of Mons Graupius, c. A.D. 84, was responsible for the erroneous naming of the Grampian mountains. South of the fertile vale of Strathmore, and situated on the Tay, which has the largest volume of water in Scotland, stands the "Fair City" of Perth, boasting a long and interesting history. It is today an important touring centre, being within easy reach of the very lovely Sma' Glen, leading to Glen Almond; the gorges and waterfalls of the Devon near Rumbling Bridge, on the Kinross border; and the pleasant valley of Strath Earn, linking Crieff with St. Fillan's.

Aberfoyle, on the threshold of the Queen Elizabeth Forest Park; Callander, in a district beloved by Scott; the famous golfing centre at Gleneagles Hotel; and both Killin and Pitlochry, are all well-known Perthshire resorts. Far to the north-east of the last-named, beyond Glen Shee, is the Cairnwell Pass, in the Grampians, near the Aberdeen border, where the summit, at 2,199 ft., is the highest main road altitude reached in Great Britain. Among the notable buildings of the county are the Cathedrals of Dunblane and Dunkeld; the round tower of the church at Abernethy; the interesting group of domestic buildings at Stobhall; and the fine castles of Blair, at Blair Atholl, Castle Huntly near Longforgan, Doune and Huntingtower.

Places of Scenic Interest. Bridge of Balgie, Callander, Crianlarich, Fortingall, Glenshee, Killiecrankie, Killin, Kinloch Rannoch, Lochearnhead, Loch Tay, Meikleour, Moulin, Pitcairngreen, Pitlochry, Queen's View, Rumbling Bridge, St. Fillan's, Sma' Glen, Struan, Trossachs, Tummel Bridge, Tyndrum.

Places of Architectural or Historic Interest. Aberfoyle, Abernethy, Ardoch (Braco), Blair Castle (Blair Atholl), Bridge of Earn, Castle Huntly (Longforgan), Doune, Drummond Castle (Crieff), Dunblane, Dunkeld, Elcho Castle (Perth), Finlarig Castle (Killin), Fowlis Wester, Grandtully, Huntingtower, Inchmahome Priory (Port of Menteith), Innerpeffray (Crieff), Killiecrankie, Kinnaird, Meggernie Castle (Bridge of Balgie), Menzies Castle (Weem), Perth, Scone, Sheriffmuir (Dunblane), Stobhall, Tullibardine.

RENFREWSHIRE

(County Town: Renfrew)

A small county, bounded to the north by the widening estuary of the Clyde, which is backed by the distant hills of Cowal. In population Renfrewshire ranks high, including within its boundaries the important industrial towns of Paisley, Greenock and Renfrew, in addition to a part of Glasgow itself. Paisley is the world's largest thread-producing centre, and both Renfrew and Greenock are noted for shipbuilding. The roadstead in the

Clyde off the shores of the latter is famous as the "Tail of the Bank."

To the north-west of Paisley, the well-known Erskine Ferry across the Clyde gives access to the Highlands, and is much used by travellers from the south wishing to by-pass Glasgow. It is planned to replace it by a bridge. On the fringe of the industrial area are large stretches of moorland, notably to the south, where the high-lying Eaglesham Moor lies beyond the 18th century village of that name. Again near the Ayrshire border, west of Lochwinnoch, there are lonely moors attaining a height of over 1,700 ft.

Along the shores of the Clyde coast are situated the well-known resorts of Wemyss Bay and Gourock, linked by a road which passes the white Cloch lighthouse, and giving fine views over the estuary towards Dunoon. To the south-east of Greenock lies the fertile valley of Strath Gryfe, with its reservoirs, and in the centre of which is situated the pleasant inland resort of Kilmacolm.

The fine, restored Abbey Church at Paisley is the most important building in the county. The ruined castle of Newark, outside Port Glasgow, on the Clyde, and the old mansion of Dargavel, near Bishopton, are also of some interest.

Places of Scenic Interest. Eaglesham, Gourock, Inverkip, Kilmacolm.

Places of Architectural or Historic Interest. Cathcart Castle (Clarkston), Dargavel (Bishopton), Eaglesham, Houston, Kilbarchan, Newark Castle (Port Glasgow), Paisley, Renfrew.

ROSS AND CROMARTY

(County Town: Dingwall)

A large and mountainous northern county, only a small proportion of which is arable, stretching across Scotland from coast to coast and exhibiting some notable physical contrasts, from the North-West Highland grandeur of Wester Ross to the comparatively level country of Easter Ross.

The finest scenery is concentrated in the hill country, mainly deer forest, adjacent to its western shores. Here, the beautiful seaboard is deeply indented by picturesque lochs along the entire distance from the Coigach district near Ullapool, on Loch Broom, in the north, to Loch Alsh and lovely Loch Duich, with its perfect background of shapely hills, in the south. The grand defile of Glen Shiel, which gives access to the last-named loch, is thought by many competent judges to be even more impressive than the better-known Glencoe. It owes much of its fame to the finely-grouped quintet of peaks known as the Five Sisters of Kintail, which face the knife-edge ridges of The Saddle across the glen, to form the centrepiece of the superb view from the lofty Mam Rattachan Pass leading over to Glenelg, in Inverness-shire. The Five Sisters are part of the magnificent National Trust estate of Kintail, contiguous to which is another estate, also Trust property, with the spectacular but remote Falls of Glomach, some of the highest in Britain, and accessible, partly on foot, from Ardelve on Loch Alsh. A picturesque road from Kyle of Lochalsh, the terminal point of one of the Roads to the Isles, and the "Gateway to Skye," traverses the shores of Loch Alsh and beautiful Loch Duich, on which stands the romantic Eilean Donan Castle near Dornie bridge. The road then climbs through Glen Shiel to Cluanie, with its loch, and crosses some low hills to reach Loch Garry, now harnessed to a hydro-electric scheme, to the east of Tomdoun, before descending to Invergarry, in Inverness-shire. The scenery along the whole of this partly reconstructed route is comparable with the grandest in Britain.

Gairloch, on its beautiful sandy bay, is one of the most delightful of small Wester Ross resorts, and away to the south, beyond Outer Loch Torridon, lies the almost isolated Applecross peninsula, accessible only by sea, or by the road over the notorious Bealach nam Bo, or Pass of the Cattle. This climbs very steeply through wild hills, reaching a height of 2,054 ft., with a series of acute hairpin bends, affording magnificent views from the summit, and provides the nearest approach in these islands to the conditions of an Alpine pass.

Inner Loch Torridon and Glen Torridon are dominated by the great peaks of Ben Eighe, Liathach (the highest), and Ben Alligin, where the contrast between the red Torridon sandstone and the white quartzite is of great geological interest. These mountains are well seen by taking the new road from Shieldaig along the south side of the Inner Loch and continuing through the glen to Kinlochewe. Here, in Kinlochewe deer forest, is situated Britain's first National Nature Reserve, on the slopes of Ben Eighe above the picturesque, wooded shores of Loch Maree. Beyond its eastern shores, dominated by the fine peak of Slioch, lies a wilderness of trackless, rocky hills, notably A'Mhaighdean and Beinn Dearg Mhor, and culminating in An Teallach, near Dundonnell, perhaps the wildest peak on the mainland. Westwards are the inlets of Little Loch Broom and Gruinard Bay, the latter one of the loveliest in the Highlands, in a setting of low, rocky hills, well seen from the steep Gruinard Hill.

To the north of Ullapool, in the extreme north-western corner of Ross and Cromarty, is the fascinating, but lesser known Loch Lurgain. Its shores are traversed by a narrow, winding road, overlooked by the fantastic, rock-crowned hill known as Stack Polly, with the isolated peaks of Cul Mor and Cul Beag rising in the background. The coast beyond Loch Lurgain, on the northern fringe of the wild Coigach district, is traversed by an exceptionally lovely, but winding and hilly road overlooking Enard Bay which leads towards the Sutherland border at Inverkirkaig.

Many of the roads in the hilly western half of the

county are narrow and at times poorly-surfaced, but frequent passing-places have been constructed on certain stretches.

In the eastern half of the county, the bulky mass of Ben Wyvis towers over a comparatively low-lying district, and to the south lies the well-known inland resort of Strathpeffer. Easter Ross is composed mainly of the former county of Cromarty, which was annexed to Ross in 1889. The inlets of the Dornoch and Moray Firths, with their low, sandy shores, form the boundaries of this area, which is almost cut in half by the narrow Cromarty Firth lying to the north of the fertile Black Isle. In addition to its territory on the mainland, the Outer Hebridean island of Lewis, with the exception of the Harris peninsula, and famous for the Standing Stones of Callanish, belongs to Ross and Cromarty, as do also several of the outlying islands, among them the Flannan group.

Places of Scenic Interest. Achiltibuie, Applecross, Ardelve, Baddagyle, Braemore Lodge, Cluanie, Dornie, Dundonnell, Falls of Glomach, Gairloch, Glen Shiel, Gruinard Bay, Kinlochewe, Loch Broom, Loch Duich, Loch Lurgain, Loch Maree, Mam Rattachan, Plockton, Shiel Bridge, Strathpeffer, Tornapress, Torridon, Ullapool.

Places of Architectural or Historic Interest. Balnagown Castle (Logie Easter), Castle Leod (Strathpeffer), Dingwall, Edderton, Eilean Donan Castle (Dornie), Fortrose, Foulis Castle (Evanton), Kilcoy Castle (Muir of Ord), Tain.

Places of interest in the Outer Hebridean island of Lewis will be found by referring to its gazetteer entry under Hebrides, Outer.

ROXBURGHSHIRE

(County Town: Jedburgh)

In this Lowland county will be found the quintessence of Border scenery in its most characteristic vein, a land of rounded green hills, rushing streams and delightful valleys, of which Liddesdale and Teviotdale, both traversed by picturesque roads, are the best known. Part of the Border Forest Park, which extends also into England, lies in Liddesdale.

Many places in Roxburghshire are impregnated with memories of Border legends and warfare, and the presence of Abbotsford House makes the county of the very greatest interest to lovers of Sir Walter Scott. Other places having links with the great writer are Branxholm Tower near Hawick, Darnick Tower near Melrose, and the lonely Smailholm Tower, in its wild setting, neighboured by Sandyknowe farm, where part of Scott's youth was spent. Abbotsford, beautifully situated on the Tweed, and accessible to the public, was the writer's last and favourite home, remaining today almost untouched since the Waverley novels were written.

The three great ruined Abbeys of Melrose, Kelso and Jedburgh are among the finest in Scotland, the very notable architectural features and beautiful setting of the first-named, situated between the Tweed and the triple-peaked Eildon Hills, being quite outstanding. Of Kelso Abbey, perhaps once the greatest of the trio, the existing remains are less extensive, but the town, with its wide square, and Rennie's five-arched bridge spanning the Tweed looking towards the splendid pile of Floors Castle, is most attractive. The red sandstone Abbey at Jedburgh is still most impressive in its roofless state, while in the town stands the fine old Queen Mary's House, associated with that ill-fated monarch.

Liddesdale stretches northwards from the English border, where the Cheviot foothills near Newcastleton have been thickly afforested by the State, and in a branch valley which forks north-westwards is situated the ruined, but immensely strong Hermitage Castle, where Mary, Queen of Scots, nearly died from fever in 1566. The longer valley of Teviotdale is threaded by the Teviot Water, which flows across the northern half of the county from the lonely hills on the Dumfries border, and unites finally with the Tweed outside Kelso. In the heart of the dale lies the important woollen manufacturing town of Hawick, and to the north-west, near Denholm, is the lofty height of " dark " Ruberslaw, an ancient haunt of the persecuted Covenanters.

To the south of Jedburgh stands the picturesque old Ferniehirst Castle, now a Youth Hostel, beyond which a fine road follows the Jed Water towards England. This ascends gradually on to the Cheviot ridge, the 1,371-ft. high summit being reached at the splendid viewpoint of Carter Bar, from which the panorama across the Lowlands extends from the Cheviot itself to the Eildons far away to the north-west. Another road descends back into Scotland from this ridge towards Bonchester Bridge, on the Rule Water, where it is joined by the road from Liddesdale, which has climbed previously to well over 1,000 ft. at Note o' the Gate. Eastwards of Carter Bar, the line of the Roman " Dere Street " of Agricola crosses the Cheviots near the remarkable Chew Green earthworks, just inside the Northumbrian border. It then descends towards Oxnam, beyond which stands the ruined Cessford Castle, preserving walls 14 ft. in thickness. In the vicinity is Morebattle, at the foot of the lonely Kale Water valley, once a Covenanters' refuge, and away to the north-east, at the foot of the Cheviots, are the adjacent villages of Kirk and Town Yetholm. These lie on either side of the Bowmont Water, and were formerly the headquarters of the Scottish gipsies.

Places of Scenic Interest. Ancrum Bridge, Bonchester Bridge, Carter Bar, Denholm, Melrose, Morebattle, Newcastleton, Oxnam, Riccarton, Teviothead, Yetholm.

Places of Architectural or Historic Interest. Abbotsford House, Bowden, Branxholm Tower (Hawick), Cessford Castle (Morebattle), Darnick Tower, Fatlips Castle (Denholm), Ferniehirst Castle, Floors Castle, Hermitage Castle, Jedburgh Abbey, Kelso Abbey, Melrose Abbey, Newstead, Sandyknowe, Smailholm, Southdean.

SELKIRKSHIRE

(County Town: Selkirk)

At one time known as Ettrick Forest, which consisted largely of a vast Royal hunting ground, Selkirkshire is a Border county of much scenic beauty, showing characteristic Lowland hills, particularly in the west, near the boundaries of Peebles and Dumfries. Here, Broad Law, the second-highest of the Lowland hills, and the lonely Ettrick Pen are two of the most prominent heights, and Lochcraig Head rises at the meeting-point of all the three counties. To the east of the higher hills, in what is still described as Ettrick Forest, lie St. Mary's Loch and its neighbour the tiny Loch of the Lowes, beyond which stretches the celebrated Yarrow Vale, threaded by the Yarrow Water, and in parts richly wooded. The praises of this delectable region have been sung by many well-known writers, among them being Sir Walter Scott and William Wordsworth. St. Mary's Loch is the most picturesque sheet of water in the Borders, and its romantic associations with James Hogg, the "Ettrick Shepherd," give it an added interest. The well-known "Tibbie Shiel's" Inn, at its southern extremity, has been visited by many famous personages. The Megget Water flows into the loch from the west, and near the northern shore, beyond the churchyard of St. Mary's Kirk, stands the ruined Dryhope Tower, which has associations with Scott's ancestors.

To the south of Yarrow Vale is the valley of the Ettrick Water, where, at Tushielaw, in 1528, James V hanged a notorious Border raider in his own stronghold. Two picturesque roads diverge from here into the hills, the easterly branch leading towards Hawick, and the more southerly climbing to nearly 1,100 ft., on its way into Upper Eskdale.

Galashiels and Selkirk are both noted for their tweed mills, and the first-named is situated on the pleasant Gala Water, which joins the Tweed beyond the town. On the south bank of the Tweed, near Clovenfords, stands the mansion of Ashiestiel, where Scott lived for 8 years as sheriff of the county, and where several of the best known of his earlier works were written. To the north-west of Galashiels, a small portion of Selkirkshire projects into a district of lonely hills in which the Caddon Water rises, and near the meeting-point with Peebles and Midlothian is the high point of Windlestraw Law.

Selkirk itself, a Royal Burgh, noted for a picturesque annual Border Riding ceremony, stands in a delightful setting, and to the west of the town the Yarrow and the Ettrick Water unite, the combined streams flowing north-eastwards to join the Tweed within a short distance. The little church at Ettrick was the burial-place of both Hogg and Tibbie Shiel. Among the numerous ruined castles, or towers in the county, those of Newark near Broadmeadows, Oakwood near Ettrick Bridge End, and Elibank, facing the Tweed east of Walkerburn, are perhaps of most interest.

Places of Scenic Interest. Broadmeadows, Ettrick Bridge End, Fairnilee, Gordon Arms, St. Mary's Loch, Selkirk, Tushielaw, Yarrow.

Places of Architectural or Historic Interest. Ashiestiel, Bowhill (Selkirk), Elibank Tower (Walkerburn), Ettrick, Newark Castle (Broadmeadows), Oakwood Tower (Ettrick Bridge End), "Tibbie Shiel's" Inn.

SHETLAND

(County Town: Lerwick)

The islands forming this group are fully described, both generally and individually, including all places of interest, under their own heading in the gazetteer.

STIRLINGSHIRE

(County Town: Stirling)

Occupying a strategic position across the narrow waist of Scotland, at the meeting of the Lowlands and the Highlands, Stirlingshire has played a leading part in the history of the country. No place was of greater importance in the Middle Ages than the old bridge over the River Forth at Stirling, which is still in use for foot passengers, and stands near a newer bridge. Farther down the estuary, beyond Airth, the more recent Kincardine Bridge spans the widening course of the river, giving access to the Fife coast.

The county can be divided into three sectors. The first lies to the east, and includes the industrial area around Falkirk, with its coal and iron industry, and also the oil refineries and docks of Grangemouth on the Forth estuary. The second sector takes in the winding and fertile valley of the Forth to the east and west of Stirling, mainly on the Perthshire border. Lastly, and occupying the central area of the county, are the hills, comprising the Fintry, Gargunnock and Kilsyth ranges and also the Campsie Fells, in what is known as the land of Lennox. The heart of the hills is threaded by a road leading westwards from Denny, which follows the course of the River Carron and the Endrick Water towards the village of Fintry before debouching into the flat country to the east of Loch Lomond. Another road leads southwards over the Campsies to reach the well-known Campsie Glen.

A narrow tongue of Stirlingshire extends north-westwards along the picturesque shores of Loch

Lomond towards its head, with Loch Arklet and Loch Katrine farther to the east, and Glen Gyle, preserving memories of Rob Roy, forming the boundary with Perthshire beyond Stronachlachar. Above Rowardennan, on Loch Lomond, where the road along the eastern shore terminates, rises Ben Lomond, a noted viewpoint and the monarch of the surrounding district.

Stretching from east to west across the county, and often in close proximity, are the Forth and Clyde canal and the line of the Antonine, or Roman Wall, the remains of which, though slight compared with the more famous Hadrian's Wall in Northumberland, are nevertheless of interest. Some of the best preserved portions are situated in the vicinity of Falkirk, notably in the grounds of Callendar House.

The historic town of Stirling, known as the "Gateway to the Highlands," is the most important in the county, and is renowned for its great Castle and Palace, which has been associated with several Scottish Kings, and also with Mary, Queen of Scots. The fine old houses of Argyll's Lodging and Mar's Wark give an added interest to the town, while the Church of the Holy Rude is one of the finest in Scotland. In the immediate neighbourhood of Stirling are the loftily situated Wallace Monument at Causewayhead; the remains of Cambuskenneth Abbey, situated in the fertile Links of the Forth; and the famous battlefield of Bannockburn, which lies beyond St. Ninian's.

Places of Scenic Interest. Bridge of Allan, Campsie Glen, Fintry, Inversnaid, Killearn, Kippen, Loch Lomond, Rowardennan, St. Ninian's, Stockiemuir, Strathblane.

Places of Architectural or Historic Interest. Airth, Bannockburn, Callendar House (Falkirk), Cambuskenneth Abbey (Stirling), Culcreuch Tower (Fintry, Gargunnock, Kilsyth, Kippen, Stirling, Touch House (Gargunnock), Wallace Monument (Stirling).

SUTHERLAND

(County Town: Dornoch)

This maritime and sparsely populated county has a rugged Atlantic seaboard occupying the far north-west corner of Scotland. Its less spectacular eastern shores are washed by the waters of the North Sea. The western coast, stretching from lonely Cape Wrath to the borders of Ross and Cromarty at Enard Bay, is wild and beautiful, and indented by the sea lochs of Inchard, Laxford, and Cairnbawn, the last-named being an inlet of the lovely island-studded Eddrachillis Bay. This lies to the south of Scourie, a small fishing resort, well known for the nearby island of Handa, now a sanctuary for sea-fowl.

The scenery in the south-western part of the county is bare and mountainous, and of exceptional geological interest in the Assynt district. Here, the strangely-shaped peaks of Suilven, Canisp and Quinag, in particular the first-named, described sometimes as the "Matterhorn" of Scotland, are built up of red Torridon sandstone and rise individually in isolated majesty from a bed of Archæan pinky-grey gneiss, some of the oldest rocks in the world. The highest mountain in the county, Ben More Assynt (3,273 ft.), near Inchnadamph, is composed almost entirely of this gneiss, while other peaks farther to the north in the remote Reay Forest, notably Foinaven and Arcuil, which dominate the neighbourhood of Rhiconich, are composed mainly of quartzite. Almost the whole of this wild Northern Highland district is given over to deer forest. From the small Assynt resorts of Lochinver and Inchnadamph, and, in particular from the steep and narrow coastal road linking the first-named with the ferry at Kylesku, in its exceptionally wild and beautiful setting at the meeting-point of three lochs, a good idea can be obtained of the memorable, though bare and austere scenery of this fascinating landscape. Due to the innumerable small lochans, this is a fisherman's paradise, and, when viewed from the summit of any of the mountain tops in the district, the impression is given that there is almost more water than land. The roads in this part of the county are narrow and at times rough, but frequent passing places have been constructed on a number of stretches.

On the bleak northern coast is Loch Eriboll, a good anchorage, and a long and beautiful inlet, with roads on both the eastern and western shores. Westwards, beyond the celebrated Smoo Cave, is Durness, overlooking the Kyle of Durness and the lonely moors leading to Cape Wrath and its lighthouse. The mountains in this area include Ben Hope, the most northerly 3,000-ft. peak in Scotland. Farther to the east rises the many-peaked Ben Loyal, well seen from the Kyle of Tongue and forming a notable landmark. Much of this part of the country suffered severely as a result of the penal enactments of 1747, and also from the "Sutherland Clearances" in the early 19th century, when some 15,000 of the inhabitants were forced to move elsewhere. In more recent years efforts have, however, been made to improve conditions for the crofting population.

Near the Caithness border, on the east coast, the landscape resembles a lofty plateau, which has been carved out by its rivers, the shores being rocky, with some cliff scenery. Farther south, near the Dornoch Firth, the seaboard is for the most part low and sandy, and to the north-east of Golspie, overlooking the sea, stands the great pile of Dunrobin Castle in its park.

Places of Scenic Interest. Altnaharra, Cape Wrath, Drumbeg, Durness, Eriboll, Inchnadamph, Inverkirkaig, Kinlochbervie, Kylesku, Laxford Bridge, Loch Assynt, Lochinver, Rhiconich, Rispond, Scourie, Smoo Cave, Stoer, Tongue.

Places of Architectural or Historic Interest. Altnaharra, Ardvreck Castle (Inchnadamph), Dornoch, Dunrobin Castle, Golspie, Helmsdale, Skibo Castle.

WEST LOTHIAN

(County Town: Linlithgow)

This small county has for its northern boundary the flat shores of the Forth estuary, and is composed mainly of good farming land, though visible signs of the oil-shale industry in the vicinity of Winchburgh somewhat mar the landscape. West Lothian is less remarkable for its scenic beauty than for its architectural interest, which is dominated by the famous Palace and Church at Linlithgow, the name of which was formerly applied to the county as a whole.

The short coastline, from the mouth of the River Avon in the west to that of the Almond in the east, is mainly flat, with a harbour at Bo'ness. This town marks the terminal point of the Antonine, or Roman Wall, which extends across the waist of Scotland to the Clyde estuary. From Queensferry South, the spectacular Forth Bridge, an outstanding achievement of the late 19th cent., spans the widening estuary and carries the main railway line from Edinburgh to the Fife coast and the north. This has now been supplemented by the splendid new Forth road bridge, opened in 1964.

Linlithgow Palace, though largely in ruins, is of considerable interest, and here was born the ill-fated Mary, Queen of Scots, who played such a vital part in Scottish history, and is associated also with another West Lothian stronghold, that of Niddry near Kirkliston. The splendid church at Linlithgow is one of the finest in the country, and exhibits unusual French characteristics. To the south are the low Bathgate Hills, and on their western fringe lies Torphichen, where the church is also of much interest. Dalmeny church is perhaps the finest of Scottish Norman churches, and the little church at Abercorn is remarkable for its furnishings. Among the old mansions of West Lothian, that of Hopetoun House, the work of Sir William Bruce and William and Robert Adam, is outstanding. The Binns, now Scottish National Trust property, near Abercorn, and also Houston, near Uphall, are other fine old buildings.

Places of Scenic Interest. Cramond Bridge, Linlithgow, Torphichen.

Places of Architectural or Historic Interest. Abercorn, The Binns (Abercorn), Blackness, Bridge Castle (Torphichen), Dalmeny, Hopetoun House, Houston (Uphall), Kinneil (Bo'ness), Kirkliston, Linlithgow, Niddry Castle (Kirkliston), Queensferry South, Torphichen.

WIGTOWNSHIRE

(County Town: Wigtown)

The extreme south-western county of Scotland, forming, together with its eastern neighbour Kirkcudbright, the attractive district known as Galloway. Wigtown is divided into three distinct regions: the double peninsula of the Rhinns of Galloway, washed by the waters of Loch Ryan and Luce Bay; the Machers peninsula, separating Luce Bay from Wigtown Bay; and the inland country around New Luce, known as The Moors.

The whole county, with the exception of some low hills and moorlands on the Ayrshire border, is flat, or undulating, and devoted mainly to agriculture and grazing. There is a long coastline, often characterised by rock scenery, with "Smugglers" caves in places, while three prominent headlands stand out, those of Corsewall Point on Loch Ryan; the Mull of Galloway, Scotland's most southerly point; and Burrow Head, at the bleak extremity of the Machers district. A coastal road makes the almost complete circuit of Luce Bay, from the Mull of Galloway in the west to Whithorn in the east, providing some notable seascapes. Stranraer, at the head of Loch Ryan, is of importance as a port for Northern Ireland, and has superseded Portpatrick, where the harbour was too exposed to gales.

Newton Stewart, on the River Cree, one of the most delightful of small Scottish towns, stands on the threshold of much lovely country, including part of the Forest Park of Glen Trool, and the river forms the boundary with Kirkcudbright for some miles to the north. Monreith House in the Machers peninsula, and Logan House near Port Logan, in the southern horn of the Rhinns of Galloway, are both famous for their very beautiful woodland gardens, and at Port Logan is a remarkable tidal fish-pond, where the fish are tame and fed by hand. The ruins of the ancient Castle Kennedy are neighboured by the modern Lochinch Castle, also well known for its splendid grounds, the two buildings being situated on a narrow neck of land separating the Black and White Lochs. Other interesting old buildings in the county are Craigcaffie Tower at Innermessan, the Old Place of Mochrum near Kirkcowan, and Carscreuch Castle, in the vicinity of Glenluce.

Both Whithorn and the nearby Isle of Whithorn, on the coast, claim to be the site of the early Chapel of St. Ninian, who first introduced Christianity into Scotland, and his shrine at the former place became later an important place of pilgrimage, being visited regularly by James IV.

Places of Scenic Interest. Bargrennan, Cairn Ryan, Glenluce, Lochnaw Castle, Mull of Galloway, Newton Stewart, Port Logan, Portpatrick, Port William.

Places of Architectural or Historic Interest. Castle Kennedy, Castle of Park (Glenluce), Craigcaffie Castle (Innermessan), Cruggleton, Isle of Whithorn, Lochinch Castle (Castle Kennedy), Lochnaw Castle, Logan House (Port Logan), Luce Abbey (Glenluce), Monreith, Old Place of Mochrum (Kirkcowan), Whithorn.

LITERARY ASSOCIATIONS OF PLACES NAMED IN GAZETTEER

Many places in Scotland have interesting associations with famous or lesser-known men and women of letters. In the case of certain authors, entire districts have come to be associated with their works, such as the Scott Country, covering much of the Border Country in the Lowlands, and the Burns Country, which covers a different part of the Lowlands, centred on Ayrshire. Certain parts of Argyllshire have many links with the works of Robert Louis Stevenson.

Of the individual towns and villages, some are of interest for one or more literary works, others as the birthplace or place of rest of a particular writer. The following list, though not exhaustive, does give a comprehensive picture of the literary haunts of Scotland and all the places mentioned will be found in the gazetteer section of the book.

Joanna Baillie (1762–1851)	Bothwell.
Sir James Barrie (1860–1937)	Outer Hebrides (Harris), Kirriemuir.
James Boswell (1740–95)	Auchinleck, Broadford, Glenelg, Mam Rattachan Pass, Skye.
George Douglas Brown (1869–1902)	Ochiltree.
Dr. John Brown (1810–82)	Biggar.
Michael Bruce (1746–67)	Kinnesswood, Portmoak.
John Buchan (1875–1940)	Broughton, Clatteringshaws Dam, Creetown, Galloway, Loch Coruisk, Peebles, Tweedsmuir.
Robert Burns (1759–96)	Alloway, Auldgirth, Ayr, Dumfries, Gatehouse of Fleet, Kilmarnock, Kirkoswald, Lincluden Abbey, Mauchline, Moffat, Tarbolton.
Lord Byron (1788–1824)	Banff, Bridge of Ess, Cambus o'May.
Thomas Campbell (1777–1844)	Calgary, Salen (Isle of Mull), Ulva.
Thomas Carlyle (1795–1881)	Annan, Ecclefechan, Kirkcaldy.
S. R. Crockett (1860–1914)	Auchencairn, Castle Douglas, Galloway, Laurieston, Lendalfoot, Loch Trool, Peebles.
R. B. Cunninghame-Graham (1852–1936)	Cardross, Dumbarton, Port of Menteith.
John Davidson (1857–1909)	Barrhead.
Daniel Defoe (c. 1660–1731)	Largo.
Sir Arthur Conan Doyle (1859–1930)	Edinburgh.
William Drummond (1585–1649)	Hawthornden, Lasswade.
John Galt (1779–1839)	Irvine.
James Hogg (1770–1835)	Ettrick, St. Mary's Loch, Selkirk, "Tibbie Shiel's" Inn, Yarrow.
Dr. Johnson (1709–84)	Banff, Broadford, Dundonald, Glenelg, Glen Shiel, Renton, Skye.
Ben Jonson (1572–1637)	Lasswade.
Margaret Kennedy-Fraser (1857–1930)	Iona.
John Knox (1505–72)	Edinburgh, Perth, St. Andrews.
Andrew Lang (1844–1922)	Selkirk.
J. G. Lockhart (1794–1854)	Darnick, Dryburgh Abbey, Wishaw.
H. F. Lyte (1793–1847)	Ednam.
Hugh McDairmid (C. M. Grieve)	Langholm.
Alexander Macdonald (1700–70)	Arisaig, Dalilea.
Duncan Ban MacIntyre (1724–1812)	Dalmally.
Dr. Kenneth MacLeod (1871–1955)	Gigha.
James Macpherson (1736–96)	Kingussie, Moffat.
Thomas Macaulay (1800–59)	Killiecrankie.
Hugh Miller (1802–56)	Cromarty.
Neil Munro (1864–1930)	Corrieyairack Pass, Inveraray, Kingshouse.
Alexander Peden (c. 1626–86)	Denholm, Sorn.
Thomas de Quincey (1785–1859)	Lasswade.
Allan Ramsay (1686–1758)	Carlops, Leadhills, Penicuik.
Dante Gabriel Rossetti (1828–82)	Dailly.
John Ruskin (1819–1900)	Perth.
Sir Walter Scott (1771–1832)	Abbotsford, Aberfoyle, Ashiestiel, Blairgowrie, Caddonfoot, Callander, Clovenfords, Crossford, Darnick, Dryburgh, Dunfermline, Edinburgh, Gordon Arms, Innerleithen, Irongray, Lasswade, Loch Leven, Melrose, Orkney, Peebles, St. Mary's Loch, Selkirk, Smailholm, Trossachs.
William Shakespeare (1564–1616)	Birnam, Cawdor, Inverness.
Adam Smith (1723–90)	Edinburgh, Kirkcaldy.
Alexander Smith (1829–67)	Isle Ornsay.
Tobias Smollett (1721–71)	Alexandria, Renton.
Robert Southey (1774–1843)	Banff.
Robert Louis Stevenson (1850–94)	Appin, Ballachulish, Ballantrae, Borgue, Bridge of Allan, Bunessan, Cramond Bridge, Dalwhinnie, Dirleton, Edinburgh, Fairmilehead, Glencoe, Glencorse, Kingshouse, Lanark, Moulin, Peebles, Swanston, Torryburn.
Robert Tannahill (1774–1810)	Paisley.
James Thomson (1700–48)	Ednam, Southdean.
Dorothy Wordsworth (1771–1855)	Inversnaid.
William Wordsworth (1770–1850)	Broadmeadows, Lanark, St. Mary's Loch, Sma' Glen, Yarrow.

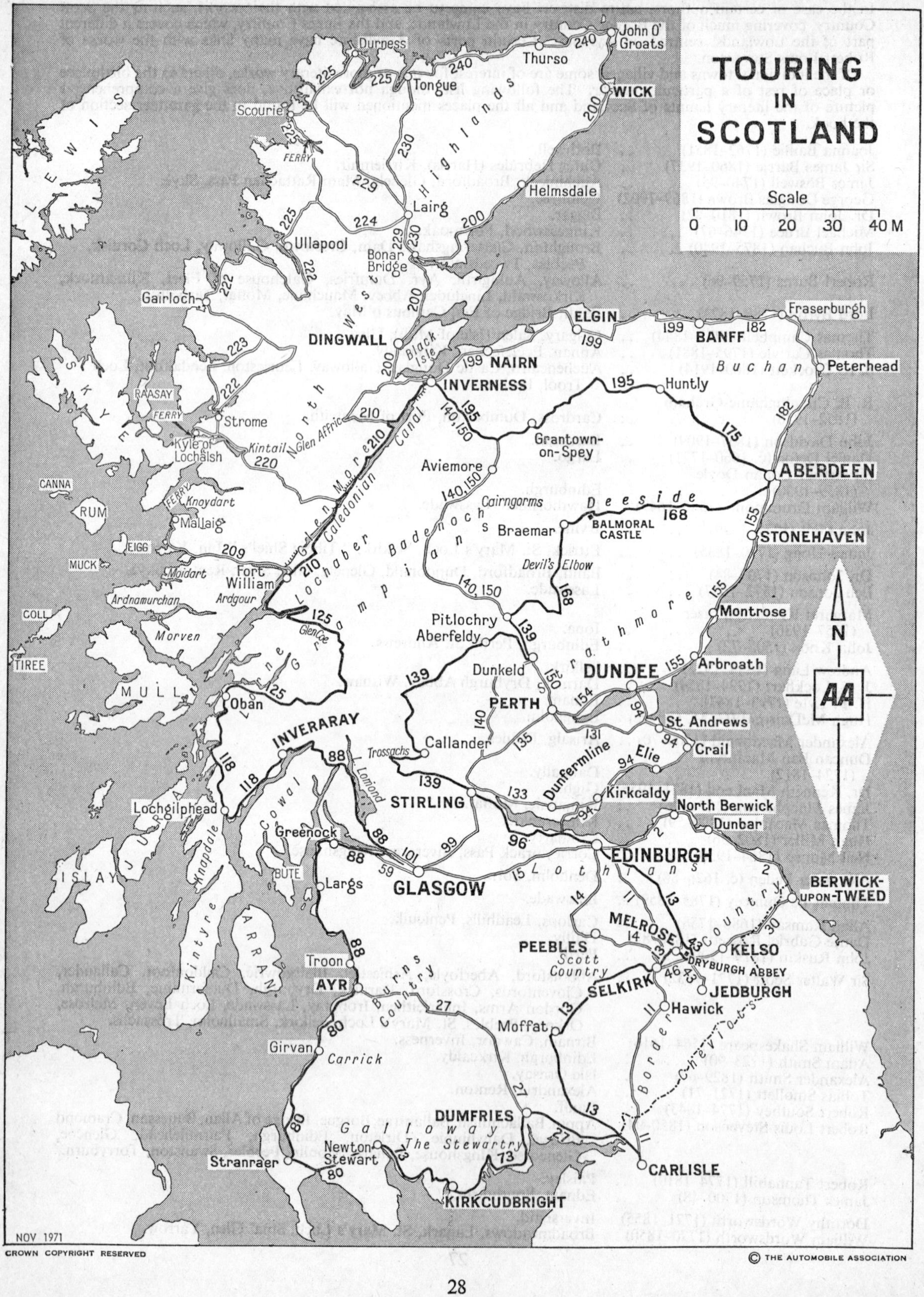
TOURING IN SCOTLAND
Scale
0 10 20 30 40 M
N
AA
John O' Groats
Thurso
Durness
Tongue
WICK
Scourie
FERRY
Highlands
Helmsdale
Lairg
Ullapool
Bonar Bridge
Gairloch
North West Highlands
DINGWALL
Black Isle
ELGIN
NAIRN
INVERNESS
BANFF
Fraserburgh
Buchan
Peterhead
Huntly
RAASAY
SKYE
LEWIS
Strome
Kyle of Lochalsh
Kintail
Glen Affric
Glen More
Caledonian Canal
Grantown-on-Spey
Aviemore
ABERDEEN
CANNA
RUM
Knoydart
Mallaig
EIGG
MUCK
Moidart
Fort William
Ardnamurchan
Ardgour
Lochaber
Badenoch
Cairngorms
Deeside
Braemar
BALMORAL CASTLE
Grampians
Devil's Elbow
STONEHAVEN
COLL
TIREE
Morven
MULL
GlenCoe
Lorne
Pitlochry
Aberfeldy
Strathmore
Montrose
Arbroath
Dunkeld
DUNDEE
PERTH
Oban
St. Andrews
INVERARAY
Trossachs
Callander
Crail
Elie
Dunfermline
Kirkcaldy
Lomond
Cowal
STIRLING
North Berwick
Dunbar
Lochgilphead
JURA
Greenock
Knapdale
ISLAY
BUTE
Largs
GLASGOW
EDINBURGH
Lothians
BERWICK-UPON-TWEED
Kintyre
ARRAN
MELROSE
Border Country
PEEBLES
Scott Country
DRYBURGH ABBEY
KELSO
Troon
AYR
Burns Country
SELKIRK
JEDBURGH
Hawick
Cheviots
Moffat
Girvan
Carrick
Border
DUMFRIES
Galloway
The Stewartry
Newton Stewart
Stranraer
KIRKCUDBRIGHT
CARLISLE
NOV 1971

TOURING IN SCOTLAND

Scotland has a twofold appeal for the motor tourist. He can enjoy both the wild mountain and loch scenery of the Highlands, and the less spectacular but none the less beautiful Lowland country, with its strong romantic and literary flavour. Except for the industrial area concentrated in the narrow waist of Scotland between the Clyde and the Forth, the land is sparsely populated, and nowhere else in Great Britain can one find such solitude as off the beaten track in the remote Highlands.

The map opposite shows the itinerary numbers for a suggested tour through the more popular touring districts. A few of the many alternatives possible are also indicated, including an extended tour to the North-West Highlands. The main tour totals approximately one thousand miles, and tourists with time at their disposal will find it convenient to choose suitable centres from which to explore the surrounding countryside. With the aid of the itinerary key map and the road atlas, tours covering most of the less-frequented districts can be planned. These should appeal to those already familiar with the better-known touring areas. Any comprehensive tour of Scotland should include a visit to some of the many islands situated off the west coast. Details of tours in these islands are given in the itinerary section of the book, beginning with number 241. More detailed descriptions will be found under individual headings in the gazetteer. A map showing the line of the various car-carrying services will be found on pages 34 and 35 of the atlas, though in some cases it is not worth the cost to take a car.

Although much fine scenery can be enjoyed without leaving main roads, the motorist will miss a great deal if he is not prepared to venture occasionally onto the lesser-used roads. Do not be deterred by fear of rough or dangerous stretches; main roads to the south and east of a line Fort William–Inverness are generally good, and severe gradients are few. Owing to the indented nature of the coastline there are a number of ferry crossings, full details of which are given later in the book. Delays may sometimes be experienced due to tide and weather conditions and also to the traffic demands during the touring season. Certain ferries do not operate on Sunday. Most of the ferry crossings can be avoided, but the necessary detours are mostly lengthy. In the wilder parts of the north and west the roads generally are of a lower standard, some being very narrow and occasionally rough. See 'Driving on Highland Roads' overleaf.

As hotel accommodation in the north-west is limited, it is important to make allowances when estimating the daily average mileage. If advance bookings have not been made when touring, hotels at intended stopping places should be telephoned as early as possible; during the touring season it is always advisable to arrange hotel accommodation in advance. It should also be remembered that in the north-west there are often long distances without garages or filling stations.

The early visitor to Scotland has the advantage of long hours of daylight, but the grandeur of the Highlands is probably seen at its best in September when the hillsides are covered with heather. July and August are best for seeing traditional events such as Highland Gatherings, festivals, and other summer events. Access to some hills is restricted during the August shooting season.

ROAD NUMBERS AND CLASSIFICATIONS

Originally introduced for administrative reasons, road numbers, as well as place names, appear on all official signs erected on classified roads. These road numbers are shown throughout the itineraries and on the maps in the Atlas contained in this book.

Numbered roads, besides helping a traveller to find his way, give him an assurance that—except perhaps in the more remote Highlands—he will find a reasonable surface and that the road will eventually lead somewhere.

The classification of roads in Class I, II and III for the purpose of grants from central funds towards highway expenditure, is now replaced by a single category of roads called "principal" roads. The method of designating roads as 'A' and 'B', formerly used in connection with the Class I and II roads respectively, is, however, retained and these prefixes to the road numbers are still being used on directional signs. Route numbers in brackets indicate that the routes are turnings off the road indicated, and can be reached by taking the direction indicated.

The plan for numbering is a simple one, though some anomalies have arisen during the years. Scotland is split up into three main zones centred on Edinburgh, with key highways forming the boundaries. Zones are numbered 7, 8, and 9 according to the number of the boundary highway;

zones 1 to 6 are centred on London. The three key highways for the road numbering system of Scotland are:

The Edinburgh–Carlisle Road	A7
The Edinburgh–Glasgow Road	A8
The Edinburgh–Inverness–John O'Groats Road	A9

Each zone comprises the area from one of these highways to the next in numerical sequence. For example, Zone 7 is from the Edinburgh–Carlisle road (A7), to the Edinburgh–Glasgow road (A8), and Zone 8 is from the Edinburgh–Glasgow road (A8) to the Edinburgh–Inverness–John O'Groats road (A9). Zone 9 lies east of A9 in roughly the area covered by the triangle Edinburgh, Nairn, Peterhead. The area Edinburgh, Berwick-upon-Tweed, Carlisle, includes the Scottish portion of Zone 6 with small portions of Zone 1 east of the Great North Road (A1) between Edinburgh and Berwick-upon-Tweed.

In general, the roads in any zone begin with the zone number, no matter how many figures the number may have. For example, A70 Edinburgh–Ayr and A76 Dumfries–Kilmarnock are in Zone 7, and all the Class B roads originating in this zone begin with 7, followed by 3 or 4 more numerals; similarly in Zones 8 and 9. Occasionally a road number is carried beyond the zone boundary by an important highway, an example being A73 which crosses A8 from Zone 7 into Zone 8 at Newhouse and continues through Airdrie to Cumbernauld on the Glasgow–Stirling road (A80).

Road numbers have yet another important use. With the aid of a map showing them—such as the atlas at the end of this book—a motorist can pinpoint his exact position at any signpost showing two or more numbers. For example B8074 joins A85 between Dalmally and Tyndrum at the south end of Glen Orchy, and farther north A832 joins A835 between Ullapool and Garve at the Braemore AA Box. Following the introduction of the new signposting system, a network of Primary Routes has been designated which comprises, apart from motorways, the most important traffic routes in both rural and urban areas. These primary routes are distinguished from other routes by the green background of their directional signs.

DRIVING ON HIGHLAND ROADS

In general, Scottish roads are of a good standard, but in the extreme north-west the fact that a road is labelled and numbered as Class A or Class B does not necessarily mean that its surface, width, or condition is going to be anything like similarly classified roads farther south. This is also true of many of the roads in other wild and mountainous parts of the country.

In the Highlands many garages are closed on Sundays and petrol pumps are scarce, so it is a good plan to keep the tank full.

In the north-west corner, substantial improvements have been made to road surfaces in recent years, but there are still rough stretches, especially on the western seaboard and on unclassified roads. There is, however, nothing that cannot be negotiated by reducing speed and by judicious use of the gearbox. Estimates of journey times should allow for these slower speeds and also for probable delays at ferries. Most roads are narrow—some little more than single-car width—but passing bays are provided, and with care no difficulty should be experienced. In view of the narrow roads motorists with trailer caravans may find it more convenient to select a centre and tour the surrounding area by car only.

There are a few simple rules to remember when using these narrow Highland roads.

1. Please be courteous and considerate in the use of passing bays on single-track roads. The bays are usually well marked by white, diamond-shaped signs, thus: If due care is exercised, it should not be necessary for vehicles to be reversed. It should be remembered that it is more difficult for buses, transport vehicles, or cars towing caravans to reverse on a single-lane road than it is for a car to do so.

2. Always adjust the speed of the vehicle to the prevailing conditions, and keep in mind the lack of visibility on bends.

3. The driver nearest to a passing bay should give way to an approaching vehicle.

4. It is not necessary for a driver to draw across the road into a passing bay on his right, or off-side, if another vehicle is approaching. He should stop opposite the bay, allowing the other vehicle enough carriageway to turn into it.

5. Passing bays are provided for vehicles to pass in safety, and, except in an emergency, should not be used as lay-bys for parking purposes.

6. Drivers of vehicles such as caravans, whose speed is restricted, should draw into or stop opposite a passing bay to allow a faster-moving vehicle to overtake.

HISTORIC BUILDINGS, THE FOREST PARKS, NATURE RESERVES AND SCOTLAND'S GARDENS

A very comprehensive booklet, entitled "Seeing Scotland", which contains also information on historic buildings, castles, houses, gardens and other places open to the public, is published by the National Trust for Scotland, 5, Charlotte Square, Edinburgh, 2, at a price of 5s. Copies are available from the Trust.

HISTORIC BUILDINGS. The monuments of Scotland can be divided into two classes. Firstly there are the prehistoric remains from those dim times before Scotland was a kingdom proper, when wolves were nearly as common as foxes today, when the land was covered by the great "Caledonian Forest" and when that mysterious race, the Picts, occupied most of the land. Secondly there are those Castles, Abbeys, Churches, palaces and historical houses which are a product of the last thousand years of Scotland's life and are a part of her recorded history.

Some 280 of the best of these monuments are under the guardianship of the Ministry of Public Building and Works. They vary from the prehistoric village of Jarlshof and the celebrated broch at Mousa, both in Shetland, to the exquisite beauty of the partially destroyed Melrose Abbey in the Border Country. Apart from these there are many relics of early Christian times, and secular buildings such as the Palace of Holyroodhouse and Edinburgh Castle, two very famous examples.

All guardianship monuments are accessible to the public. Admission is sometimes free, but is usually 1s. or 2s. according to the importance and size of the monument or building. Except in places of military importance, visitors are allowed to take photographs. Nearly all the important places of historical interest are easily accessible by road. An illustrated guide, *Ancient Monuments of Scotland*, is published by H.M. Stationery Office, Castle Street, Edinburgh, at 10s. (paper cover 6s.) Individual guides to many monuments are also published.

FOREST PARKS. The large amount of public forestry work which began after World War I, and which has increased since World War II, has resulted in the establishment of Forest Parks for public recreation. State afforestation has thrown open to all who love the countryside of Scotland and who like to roam and camp in it at leisure, several large tracts of the wilder parts of Scotland: The Argyll Forest Park embraces 60,000 acres and extends from Arrochar near Loch Long to Loch Goil and the Holy Loch near Dunoon. There are camping and caravan sites near Arrochar.

On the east side of Loch Lomond there is the Queen Elizabeth Forest Park which stretches for about twelve miles to the north and east of Rowardennan, and includes Ben Lomond (3,192 ft.). The approach is from Drymen in Stirlingshire. A camping ground and caravan park are situated close together in Rowardennan Forest (42,000 acres). Another caravan park (Cobleland site) is available at Gartmore station, near Aberfoyle.

Glenmore Forest Park is conveniently reached from Aviemore, in Inverness-shire. It extends for 12,500 acres and includes several of the highest peaks in Britain, including Cairn Gorm (4,084 ft.) In addition to mountain climbing, the area is now an important centre for winter sports, and there is a public camping ground near Glen More Lodge. Beyond here the new ski road rises to 2,100 feet, and a ski lift gives access to the higher slopes of Cairn Gorm.

In the south-west of Scotland lies the Glen Trool Forest Park, reached from Bargrennan. Though perhaps less rugged than the others, this area contains 130,000 acres of beautiful Galloway hill country and includes a chain of lovely lochs. There is a site for caravans and camping close to Loch Trool. Also in the south is the Border Forest Park which contains the largest planted forest in Great Britain, and again bears witness, as in other cases, to the very important work of the Forestry Commission. The main area lies over the Border in England, but two of the chief parts, namely Wauchope and Newcastleton, are in Scotland. Road access is not too easy. The approach points from the Scottish side are Hawick for Wauchope, and Langholm or Newcastleton for the Newcastleton Forest. The approach from the south is via Bellingham. A camping and caravan park is provided.

NATURE RESERVES. Scotland led the way with the first nationally owned Nature Reserve in Great Britain. This is near Kinlochewe in Ross and Cromarty, and is known as the Beinn Eighe National Nature Reserve, which was opened in 1951 and contains some 10,507 acres. Since then the work of the Nature Conservancy has expanded in area and in interest, and there are now 37 reserves in Scotland, the largest being the 64,118 acres in the Cairngorms.

The majority of the Nature Reserves are still privately owned, having been set up under special agreements with the Nature Conservancy. Most of the reserves are open to the public and details of any can be obtained on application to The Nature Conservancy, 12 Hope Terrace, Edinburgh 9.

SCOTLAND'S GARDENS SCHEME. Throughout the country during the spring, summer and autumn, many private gardens attached to houses and castles are open to the public by courtesy of their owners. In some cases the houses and castles themselves are open. Those interested in gardens will find these garden openings very well worth while. Admission charges vary, but are about 1s. to 2s. per person, and parking is 2s. to 2s. 6d.

Of the money raised, 60% is allocated to the Scottish Queen's Nurses benevolent and educational funds which receive two-thirds, and the gardens fund of the National Trust for Scotland which receives one-third. The garden owner may then give the remaining 40% to any charity he chooses. Full information about these garden openings may be obtained from the Secretary of Scotland's Garden Scheme, 26 Castle Terrace, Edinburgh 1. Additional details are given in the booklet "Seeing Scotland", which is described in the first paragraph of the preceding page.

THE NATIONAL TRUST FOR SCOTLAND

The National Trust for Scotland is an independent body and is recognised by Act of Parliament as a charity. Relying entirely on donations, legacies and the subscriptions of its members, the Trust exists to preserve for public enjoyment, places and buildings of historical and architectural interest and also areas of natural beauty in the Scottish countryside. More than sixty castles and country houses, cottages and gardens are now included in Trust properties.

The Trust owns and guards large stretches of Scotland's superb mountain scenery which are now made accessible to all. Among these are the wild beauty of Glencoe, the Pass of Killiecrankie, Ben Lawers, renowned for its alpine flowers, Goat Fell, the highest peak on Arran, and, perhaps finest of all, Kintail in Wester Ross.

A number of the great houses and castles of Scotland are now in the Trust's care, such as Crathes Castle on Deeside, Craigievar Castle in Aberdeenshire, the Royal Palace of Falkland in Fife, Culzean Castle in Ayrshire (associated with the late General Eisenhower), and Brodick Castle on the Isle of Arran. These properties, with the gardens which surround many of them, are part of the nation's heritage. Among other outstanding gardens which the Trust maintains are the famous Highland garden of Inverewe in Wester Ross, the unique 17th-century garden of Pitmedden in Aberdeenshire, and the remarkable Branklyn Gardens at Perth.

Not only the great houses attract the attention of the Trust, but many of the " little houses," built in the vernacular style of the past have now been restored and preserved. At Culross in Fife and Dunkeld in Perthshire, imaginative group restoration schemes have been undertaken. Often of equal delight to the eye are the cottages and humble houses which were associated with famous Scots. Hugh Miller, J. M. Barrie, Thomas Carlyle and Robert Burns are honoured by the Trust in this way, whilst what is often called Prince Charles's Monument at lonely Glenfinnan is now preserved as a memorial to the Highlanders who followed the Prince in the '45 Rising. It is fitting, therefore, that Culloden, the scene of the last battle on British soil, is also now a property of the Trust.

At properties where a charge is made, N.T.S. members have free admission, and members of the National Trust too have this privilege. Minimum annual subscription is 20s. for N.T.S. membership. Guide-books and leaflets giving information about its work, its properties and details of membership are readily available from the Trust Offices at 5 Charlotte Square, Edinburgh 2, or any property.

LIST OF COUNTIES WITH 1961 CENSUS POPULATION FIGURES

Aberdeen	298,503	East Lothian	52,653	Peebles	14,117
Angus	278,370	Fife	320,541	Perth	127,018
Argyll	59,345	Inverness	83,425	Renfrew	338,815
Ayr	342,855	Kincardine	48,810	Ross and Cromarty	57,607
Banff	46,400	Kinross	6,704	Roxburgh	43,171
Berwick	22,441	Kirkcudbright	28,877	Selkirk	21,055
Bute	15,129	Lanark	1,626,317	Shetland	17,809
Caithness	27,345	Midlothian	580,332	Stirling	194,858
Clackmannan	41,391	Moray	49,156	Sutherland	13,442
Dumfries	88,423	Nairn	8,421	West Lothian	92,764
Dunbarton	184,546	Orkney	18,743	Wigtown	29,107

SPORT IN SCOTLAND

GOLF. In this particular volume mention of golf is of course a " must "; Scotland and the royal and ancient game have always been and remain inseparables and the motorist, visitor or resident, will, except perhaps in the North-West Highlands, almost always find a course within easy distance.

Amid the many changes the years have brought in many things, Scotland's place in golf remains unique as the very fount and home of the game, its traditional and still operative seat of government whose writ runs to the end of the earth and whose repute for courses of characteristic quality is world-wide.

Whatever your starting point, or whichever way you head your car in this country of so many spots obviously intended by Providence for golf, you will find your journey rewarding. You may play in the northern isolation of Sutherland's Brora, or after your rounds at glorious Argyllshire's Machrihanish, be lulled to slumber by the Atlantic, and between these distant points experience the pleasures and variety, seaside and inland alike, of the game at many places.

You can still play, for instance, on links of apparent popularity in 1457, when King James II's Parliament, concerned at the neglect of archery, " decreed and ordained that wapinschawingis (weapon show) be halden be the Lordis and Barinis spirituale and temporale foure times in the zeir (year), and that the Fute-ball and Golf be utterly cryit doune and nocht usit."

At St. Andrews, for example, the centuries meet, for its classic green is at once an honoured shrine and a supreme test for modern champions; while guests of members may still view in the treasure case of the Royal and Ancient Club priceless relics of the past, including the first Silver Club and the original Championship Belt.

For the rich attractions, however, awaiting the golfing motorist north of the Border, and which are too numerous for mention or description here, the appended list will supply some finger-posts.

You will find them in Fife, where beside storied St. Andrews are other delights; East Lothian, the fabled " Holy Land of Golf " including much-picturised North Berwick; the shores of the Firth of Clyde where, with your score good, bad or indifferent, you will have scenery and sunsets that will linger in your memory for long; and finally the famous Gleneagles Hotel courses carved out of the moorland in and adjacent to Strath Earn.

But see for yourself, and you will agree that Robert Louis Stevenson needs in this case some amendment, for while you will travel hopefully you will not necessarily find that better than to arrive.

The following list of golf-courses has been arranged in County order. The name of the club or course is followed, in brackets, by the number of holes. The letter S denotes Sunday play, but information should be obtained locally as to the hours of play. The list includes courses owned by local authorities and many clubs where visitors are admitted without introduction. A few clubs at which it is necessary for an intending player to be introduced by a member have been omitted from the list, although the Gazetteer entry may include the word GOLF.

ABERDEENSHIRE

Aberdeen
- Balnagask (18. S.)
- King's Links (18 and 9. S.)
- Hazelhead (18 and 9 (2). S.)
- Murcar G.C. (18 and 9. S.)
- Royal Aberdeen, Balgownie (18. S.)

Aboyne G.C. (18)
Ballater G.C. (18. S.)
Braemar G.C. (18. S.)
Cruden Bay G.C. (18. S.)
Deeside (18. S.)
Ellon G.C. (9. S.)
Fraserburgh G.C. (18. S.)
Huntly G.C. (9)
Inverurie G.C. (9. S.)
Kemnay G.C. (9. S.)
Kintore G.C. (9. S.)
Peterhead G.C. (18. S.)
Tarland G.C. (9. S.)
Torphins (9. S.)
Turriff G.C. (9. S.)

ANGUS

Arbroath G.C. (18. S.)

Barry
- Panmure G.C. (18. S.)

Brechin G.C. (18. S.)

Carnoustie
- Medal Course (18. S.)
- Burnside Course (18. S.)

Dundee
- Caird Park Public G.C. (18 and 9. S.)
- Downfield G.C. (18. S.)
- Camperdown G.C. (18. S.)

Edzell G.C. (18. S.)

Forfar G.C. (18. S.)

Kirriemuir G.C. (18. S.)

Monifieth G.C. (18. S.) 2 courses

Montrose
- Medal Course (18. S.)
- Broomfield Course (18. S.)

ARGYLL

Blairmore and Strone G.C. (9. S.)

Dunoon. Cowal G.C. (18. S.)

Innellan G.C. (9. S.)

Islay, Isle of, G.C., Port Ellen (18. S.)

Machrihanish G.C. (18. S.) (Ladies Course (9))

Mull, Isle of
- Western Isles G.C. Tobermory (9)

Oban
- Glen Cruitten (18. S.)

Southend
- Dunaverty G.C. (18)

AYRSHIRE

Ayr. Belleisle G.C. (18. S.)
Seafield (18)
Dalmilling-Whitletto (18. S.)
Barassie G.C. (18. S.)
Beith G.C. (9. S.)
Gailes Western G.C. (18. S.)
Girvan Burgh G.C. (18. S.)
Irvine Municipal Course (18. S.)
Bogside (18. S.)
Kilbirnie
Place G.C. (9. S.)
Kilmarnock Caprington Course (18. S.)
Annanhill (18. S.)
Largs G.C. (18. S.)
Routenburn G.C. (18. S.)
Mauchline. Ballochmyle G.C. (18. S.)
Maybole G.C. (9. S.)
Newmilns Loudoun G.C. (18. S.)
Prestwick
St. Nicholas G.C. (18. S.)
Prestwick G.C. (18. S.) Introduction
Skelmorlie G.C. (13. S.)
Stevenston
Ardeer G.C. (18. S.)
Troon Municipal G.C. (18) 3 courses
Old Course (18. S.)
Portland Course (18. S.)
Turnberry G.C. (18. S.) 2 courses
West Kilbride G.C. (18)

BANFFSHIRE

Banff
Duff House Royal G.C. (18. S.)
Buckie
Strathlene G.C. (18. S.)
Cullen Municipal G.C. (18)
Macduff
Royal Tarlair G.C. (18. S.)

BERWICKSHIRE

Eyemouth G.C. (9)

BUTE

Arran, Isle of
Lamlash G.C. (18. S.)
Lochranza G.C. (9)
Machrie Bay G.C. (9)
Shiskine G.C., Nr. Blackwaterfoot (12)
Whiting Bay G.C. (18. S.)
Bute, Isle of
Rothesay G.C. (18. S.)
Cumbrae, Isle of
Millport G.C. (18. S.)

CAITHNESS-SHIRE

Castletown, Reay (9. S.)
Thurso G.C. (9)
Wick G.C. (18)

CLACKMANNANSHIRE

Alloa G.C. (18. S.)
Braehead G.C. (9. S.)
Dollar G.C. (18)
Tillicoultry G.C. (9. S.)

DUMFRIESSHIRE

Annan
Powfoot G.C. (18. S.)
Dumfries
Dumfries and Galloway G.C. (18. S.)
Dumfries and County G.C. (18. S.)
Lockerbie G.C. (9. S.)
Moffat G.C. (18. S.)
Sanquhar G.C. (9. S.)
Thornhill G.C. (9. S.)

DUNBARTONSHIRE

Alexandria
Vale of Leven G.C. (18. S.)
Bearsden
Douglas Park G.C. (18. S.)
Bearsden G.C. (9. S.)
Cardross G.C. (18)
Clydebank and District G.C. (18. S.)
Dalmuir Municipal G.C. (18. S.)
Dumbarton G.C. (18. S.)
Helensburgh G.C. (18)
Kirkintilloch G.C. (18)
Milngavie G.C. (18. S.)
Hilton Park G.C. (18)
Allander G.C. (18)

EAST LOTHIAN

Aberlady
Kilspindie G.C. (18)
Dunbar G.C. (18. S.)
Winterfield G.C. (18. S.)
Gifford G.C. (9. S.)
Gullane Nos. 1, 2 and 3 courses (18. S.)
Haddington G.C. (18. S.)
Longniddry G.C. (18. S.)
North Berwick G.C. (18. S.)
West Links G.C. (18 and 9)

FIFE

Aberdour G.C. (18. S.)
Anstruther G.C. (9)
Burntisland G.C. (18. S.)
Cardenden-Auchterderran G.C. (9. S.)
Crail. Balcomie (18. S.)
Cupar G.C. (9. S.)
Dunfermline G.C., Nr. Newmills (18. S.)
Canmore G.C. (18. S.)
Pitreavie G.C. (18. S.)
Elie (18. S.)
Earlsferry and Elie G.C. (18)
Elie Sports Club (9. S.)
Kincardine-on-Forth
Tulliallan G.C. (18. S.)
Kirkcaldy G.C. (18. S.)
Dunnikier Municipal Course (18. S.)
Ladybank G.C. (18. S.)
Leuchars
St. Michael's G.C. (9. S.)
Leven G.C. (18) 2 courses
Lundin Links G.C. (18. S.)
Ladies G.C. (18. S.)
St. Andrews G.C. (18. S.) 4 courses
Saline G.C. (9. S.)
Tayport
Scotscraig G.C. (18. S.)

INVERNESS-SHIRE

Boat of Garten G.C. (18. S.)
Carrbridge G.C. (9. S.)
Fort Augustus (9. S.)
Inverness G.C. (18. S.)
Kingussie G.C. (18. S.)
Newtonmore G.C. (18. S.)
Skye, Isle of
Portree (9)
Spean Bridge (9. S.)

KINCARDINESHIRE

Banchory G.C. (18. S.)
Stonehaven G.C. (18. S.)

KINROSS-SHIRE

Kinross G.C. (9. S.)
Milnathort G.C. (9. S.)

KIRKCUDBRIGHTSHIRE

Castle Douglas (9. S.)
Colvend G.C. (9. S.)
Gatehouse of Fleet G.C. (9. S.)
Kirkcudbright G.C. (9. S.)
New Galloway G.C. (9)
Southerness-on-Solway G.C. (18. S.)

LANARKSHIRE

Airdrie G.C. (18)
Easter Moffat G.C. (18. S.)
Bellshill G.C. (18. S.)
Biggar G.C. (18)
Cambuslang
Kirkhill G.C. (18. S.)
Carluke G.C. (18. S.)
Carnwath G.C. (18. S.)
Coatbridge. Drumpelier G.C. (18. S.)
East Kilbride G.C. (18. S.)
Glasgow
Public courses 8 (18 and 9. S.)
Glasgow G.C. (18. S.)
Balmore G.C. (18. S.)
Bishopbriggs G.C. (18)
Cathkin Braes G.C. (18. S.)
Cowglen G.C. (18. S.)
Crow Wood G.C. (18. S.)
East Renfrewshire G.C. (18)

Gartcosh
Mount Ellen G.C. (18)
Haggs Castle (18)
Sandyhills G.C. (18. S.)
Windy Hill G.C. (18. S.)
Hamilton Municipal G.C. (9. S.)
Lanark G.C. (18)
Leadhills G.C. (9. S.)
Lenzie G.C., Nr. Kirkintilloch (18)
Lesmahagow Muirsland G.C. (9. S.)
Motherwell
Colville Park G.C. (18)
Shotts G.C. (18. S.)
Strathaven G.C. (9. S.)
Wishaw G.C. (18. S.)
Cawder G.C. (18) 2 courses
Cathcart Castle G.C. (18. S.)

MIDLOTHIAN

Dalkeith
Newbattle G.C. (18. S.)
Edinburgh
Public courses 6 (18 and 9)
Royal Burgess Golfing Society (18. S.)
Baberton G.C. (18. S.)
Bruntsfield, Davidsons Mains (18. S.)
Craigmillar Park G.C. (18. S.)
Dalmahoy G.C. (18. S.) 2 courses
Duddingston G.C. (18. S.)
Kingsknowe G.C. (18. S.)
Liberton G.C. (18. S.)
Lothianburn G.C. (18. S.)
Merchants of Edinburgh (18. S.)
Mortonhall G.C. (18. S.)
Murrayfield G.C. (18. S.)
Prestonfield G.C. (18. S.)
Ratho Park G.C. (18. S.)
Swanston G.C. (18. S.)
Torphin Hill G.C. (18. S.)
Turnhouse G.C. (18)
Harburn G.C., Nr. West Calder (18. S.)
Lasswade
Broomieknowe G.C. (18. S.)
Milton Bridge
Glencorse G.C. (18. S.)
Musselburgh G.C. (18. S.)
Royal Musselburgh G.C. (18. S.)

MORAY

Elgin G.C. (18. S.)
Forres G.C. (18. S.)
Grantown-on-Spey G.C. (18. S.)
Hopeman G.C. (9. S.)
Lossiemouth
Moray G.C. (18 and 9. S.)
Spey Bay G.C. (18. S.)

NAIRNSHIRE

Nairn G.C. (18 and 9)
Dunbar G.C. (18. S.)

ORKNEY

Kirkwall
Orkney G.C. (18. S.)
Stromness G.C. (18)

PEEBLESSHIRE

Peebles Municipal G.C. (18. S.)
West Linton G.C. (9. S.)

PERTHSHIRE

Aberfeldy G.C. (9. S.)
Aberfoyle G.C. (9)
Alyth G.C. (18. S.)
Auchterarder G.C. (9. S.)
Blair Atholl G.C. (9. S.)
Blairgowrie G.C. (18 and 9. S.)
Callander G.C. (18. S.)
Comrie G.C. (9. S.)
Crieff G.C. (18. S.)
Dunblane New G.C. (18. S.)
Dunkeld and Birnam G.C. (9. S.)
Gleneagles Hotel G.C. (18. S. and 9. S.) 3 courses
Glenshee (6. S.)
Kenmore
Taymouth Castle (18. S.)
Killin G.C. (9. S.)
Muckhart G.C. Nr. Yetts of Muckhart (9. S.)
Muthill G.C. (9. S.)
Perth Municipal G.C. (18)
King James VI G.C. (18. S.)
Craigie Hill G.C. (18. S.)
Pitlochry G.C. (18 and 9. S.)
St. Fillan's G.C. (9. S.)

RENFREWSHIRE

Barrhead
Fereneze G.C. (18)
Bishopton
Erskine G.C. (18. S.)
Bridge of Weir
Ranfurly Castle G.C. Ltd. (18)
Ranfurly Old Course G.C. (18. S.)
Caldwell G.C. (18. S.)
Eaglesham G.C. (18)
Gourock G.C. (18. S.)
Greenock G.C. (18. S. and 9)
Whinhill G.C. (18. S.)
Johnstone
Cochrane Castle G.C. (18)
Kilmacolm G.C. (18. S.)
Lochwinnoch G.C. (9. S.)
Paisley G.C. (9. S.)
Ralston G.C. (18. S.)
Port Glasgow G.C. (18. S.)
Renfrew G.C. (18. S.)

ROSS AND CROMARTY

Alness G.C. (9)
Fortrose and Rosemarkie G.C. (18. S.)
Gairloch G.C. (9)
Invergordon G.C. (9. S.)
Muir of Ord G.C. (18. S.)
Portmahomack
Tarbat G.C. (9)

Stornoway G.C. (18)
Strathpeffer G.C. (18. S.)
Tain G.C. (18. S.)

ROXBURGHSHIRE

Hawick G.C. (18. S. and 9)
Minto G.C. (9. S.)
Jedburgh G.C. (9. S.)
Kelso G.C. (9. S.)
Melrose G.C. (9. S.)
St. Boswells G.C. (9. S.)

SELKIRKSHIRE

Galashiels G.C. (18. S.)
Torwoodlee G.C. (9. S.)
Selkirk G.C. (9. S.)

SHETLAND

Lerwick
Shetland G.C. Nr. Bressay (9. S.)

STIRLINGSHIRE

Bonnybridge G.C. (9. S.)
Drymen
Buchanan Castle G.C. (18)
Strathendrick G.C. (9. S.)
Falkirk
Falkirk G.C. (18)
Kilsyth
Burgh of Kilsyth G.C. (9. S.)
Larbert
Falkirk Tryst G.C. (18. S.)
Glenbervie G.C. (18)
Polmont G.C. (9. S.)
Stirling G.C. (18. S.)

SUTHERLAND

Brora G.C. (18. S.)
Dornoch
Royal Dornoch G.C. (18 and 9. S.)
Golspie G.C. (18)
Helmsdale G.C. (9. S.)

WEST LOTHIAN

Bathgate G.C. (18. S.)
Fauldhouse G.C. (18. S.)
Linlithgow G.C. (9. S.)
Uphall G.C. (18. S.)

WIGTOWNSHIRE

Glenluce
Wigtownshire County G.C. (9. S.)
Newton Stewart G.C. (9. S.)
Portpatrick
Dunskey G.C. (18. S.)
Port William
St. Medan G.C. (9. S.)
Stranraer G.C. (18. S.)

ANGLING in Scotland is, in the best sense of that much misused word, a " democratic " sport. That is to say it is enjoyed by all members of society and by those from all income groups. Moreover, the fish that these anglers pursue are for the most part game fish—salmon, sea trout, trout, and occasionally char. This may surprise visitors who have looked upon angling for game fish as the recreation of the rich or the comparatively well-off. This is not so in Scotland, where to be seen carrying a trout or salmon rod is the surest way of getting into conversation in a railway carriage, bus, or village street, or in more luxurious surroundings.

While it is true that there are in Scotland waters where game fish are highly preserved, and waters which are expensive to fish, it is also true that the majority of trouting water in this country can be fished for the cost of reasonably priced and often cheap tickets, or is attached free of charge to hotels. In many instances trouting water is altogether open and free. To a lesser extent this also applies to salmon and sea trout. You may fish for salmon on a ticket for five shillings or even less. For the motorist, then, Scotland offers a larger variety of angling for game fish suited to any purse than does anywhere else in Britain.

Roughly speaking, the mainland of Scotland is for the angler divided into two halves. These two halves are not the north and south of the country, but are marked by a diagonal line from the North-East to the South-West, again very roughly speaking, coinciding with the line that separates the Highlands from the Lowlands. (The Highland line is fully described in the article on the Highlands in the Gazetteer section of the book.) North and west of this line loch fishing predominates; south and east of it the rivers and streams hold pride of place.

For the motoring angler who wishes to " get about " as well as enjoy his sport this generalisation is capable of further sub-divisions:—

(1) In the extreme south-west, in Galloway (that little Highlands beyond the Lowlands) there is both loch and river fishing. The lochs provide fair sport in brown trout. Some are attached to hotels in Gatehouse of Fleet, Castle Douglas and Newton Stewart. Others are free, or are fishable on cheap tickets. There is good salmon and sea-trout to be had in the rivers of the Nith, the Fleet, the Border Esk, the Cree, and the Annan.

(2) In the south-east (the Borders proper) that noble river the Tweed is king of the waters; therein are born, and to it return each year, some of the finest salmon in Western Europe. Parts are carefully preserved, others can be fished on a very reasonably priced ticket. (3s. day; 10s. week; £2.2s. season.) There are also free stretches. The Tweed contains sea trout and some excellent brown trout, though naturally in so popular a water they tend to be highly educated. This also applies to the trout in the upper stretches of the Clyde and other smaller rivers amongst the Border hills. There is not much loch fishing in south-east Scotland; but if one stretches one's definition to include Fife and Kinross, there is, of course, the celebrated Loch Leven, with its own special trout, of recent years averaging over a pound. There are some who find fishing on Loch Leven " too commercial." But it is worthy of note that there are few who would refuse a day on that world-famous water.

(3) In central Scotland, which is largely occupied by Perthshire and parts of Inverness-shire, the Highland line is crossed and loch fishing predominates. It is easy to get permits through hotels or associations to fish most lochs, though some (notably Loch Lubnaig, south of Strathyre, which contains salmon as well as trout) are free. Loch Lomond, though so near to Glasgow, may be included in this area. It is famous for its salmon and sea trout and the price of tickets on it is reasonable (10s. day; 30s. week).

(4) The Western Central Highlands, so noted for their beauty, give the angler a continuation of the loch fishing of the more central parts. Though most of the rivers running into the Atlantic on this coast are preserved, there is salmon and sea-trout fishing to be had here on enquiry.

(5) In Aberdeenshire and the Buchan bulge to the north-east, there is practically no loch fishing, but there is some of the best river fishing in Scotland. The Dee, the Don (by some held to be " the best trouting river in Scotland "), the Ythan, the Deveron and other streams flow easily and at length through country that is not nearly so precipitous as in the west. The waters are therefore not subject to sudden rises and falls. Fish can linger in and return to them sure of comfort and feeding. From these facts the river angler profits in the " near North-East." Naturally such waters, particularly the Dee, are preserved. But by means of hotels and with tickets it is possible for the visiting angler to have a large variety of excellent river fishing—salmon, sea trout and trout.

(6) Away and across the Moray Firth in the far north-east the river fishing is largely preserved. In Caithness, however, the most northerly county on the mainland of Britain, there are a number of lochs which yield a good average of brown trout nearly up to the present Loch Leven size, and more numerous. The rights of fishing these lochs are nearly all held by hotels, and

most lochs are easily accessible by road and from the hotels. The charges are not high.

(7) The extreme North-West of Scotland, which is occupied by the counties of Sutherland and Ross, is the goal of angling motorists who love remote scenery, loch fishing, and large numbers of brown trout, without being consistently ambitious about size. This is not to say that there are not lochs in these parts containing large trout. At Durness, for instance, near to Cape Wrath, there are four lochs in which some of the record brown trout of Scotland have been taken. The average weight too is remarkably high; but for the most part of Sutherland the myriad little hill lochs do not yield trout of much over half a pound in weight, sometimes three to the pound or even less. But if you like plenty of fish with plenty of fight in their small bodies this is the place to find them. The hill lochs are so numerous that some of them are free, but most are attached to the hotels in this district.

Apart from these seven divisions of the mainland of Scotland there are, of course, the islands (the Hebrides, and Orkney and Shetland), in which in certain places some of the best angling in Scotland is to be found.

The average visiting motorist may find them difficult and expensive of access, but this article would not be complete without mention of fishing in the islands.

To fish for game fish in Scotland in any comfort one is confined to the months of mid-April to the end of September. There is of course a spring run of salmon beginning earlier, and an autumn run in places going on till November, but the average motorist who wishes to fish will probably be mostly concerned with brown trout, the fishing grounds for which are so easy of access and which can, even in the most unpromising weather, be guaranteed to provide *some* sport.

As brown trout are so plentiful in Scotland, especially in the lochs of the West and North-West the visiting angler must not expect in these places anything very large. He will, especially if he fishes the rivers on the east side, get trout of between one and two pounds, sometimes over, but in the majority of open or easily accessible lochs and streams and burns he must recognise that a trout of three-quarters of a pound is a reasonable size and that the average is more like half a pound.

Moderate tackle then is all that is needed for the motorist who wishes to try for trout in various districts of Scotland. A rod of nine and a half or ten feet will do excellently for all brown-trout fishing. A smooth-running reel, to give plenty of play and light gut or nylon of 3X or 3X equivalent, gives the best fun on nearly all trout waters of the country. Flies naturally vary according to district and season, but as far as wet fly fishing is concerned, the ordinary well-tried favourites, Peter Ross, Greenwell's Glory, Woodcock and Yellow, March brown, the butcher, grouse and claret, teal and green, soldier palmer and Zulu (the last named being more effective the farther north you go) as well as others of stock pattern will provide the basis of, if not all, the collection of flies you need. Others can be bought locally.

Wet fly fishing is most extensively used upon the lochs, though it also has its uses in fast-flowing rivers and streams. On the whole, however, dry fly fishing is becoming more extensively used upon Scottish rivers, and there are days when only the dry fly will do upon lochs. There is nothing like the regular pattern amongst dry flies as there is among wet. Visiting anglers should not only study the local conditions for the right dry flies but take the advice of local tackle-dealers.

Salmon and sea trout naturally require heavier tackle. But in these days of high prices it is quite possible to use a ten-and-a-half or eleven-foot rod which will give you pleasure when into sea trout, but which is quite capable of dealing with the ordinary salmon.

Fishing with fly (wet or dry) is the traditional method of angling for all game fish in Scotland; and, despite a certain amount of perennial discussion on the subject, most Scottish anglers get the greatest pleasure from catching their fish on the fly. Nevertheless, whether he be a fly purist or not, the visitor to Scotland must reconcile himself to the prospect (and the pleasure of variety) of using bait and other lures than fly. This is particularly true of the months of July and August, which are not the best fly months, and yet are the usual holiday months for motoring visitors.

It may surprise trout anglers accustomed to the waters of Southern England to learn that the humble worm is by no means despised by all in Scotland. Indeed there are days when the worm is almost the only lure for trout. A heavy spate (or flood) makes the use of fly impracticable. Worm fishing in such conditions is the only resource the angler has. Nor should he despise its use. While it is true that nothing like the same delicacy that goes with fly fishing is needed, there is a certain amount of skill in using your worm in swollen waters and studying the bed of the river to make its passage in the water natural. Moreover this is the kind of time when the large trout who have resisted the fly over many summers can be tempted from their lairs.

At the opposite extreme, and when the summer streams are very low, clear water worm angling with small red worms on the finest gut imaginable not only offers good sport, but calls for a high degree of skill. That is to say skill in negotiating the shallow clear pools, working one's worm in them in a lifelike way and, above all, keeping out of sight.

It may be added (though with a distinct reserve) that even the lordly salmon has been known to take a large lob worm or a bunch of worms on a hook. Anyone who intends to try this last extremity of salmon angling should make careful enquiries as to whether such methods are permissible on the water he intends to fish.

Finally, as an alternative to fly, both for trout and salmon, there is that method which has sprung into such prominence of recent years—spinning with a thread-line from a fixed spool reel. This art or craft in angling has made great strides owing to the scientific advances which the makers of rods, and particularly the new reels, have achieved. As with the worm on clear water days, spinning can prove deadly. Most keen resident anglers in Scotland carry at least one fly rod and a bait-casting rod with a bait-casting reel as well. It is, however, possible to buy a rod which will cope with the fly and with bait-casting, but in the long run this is an economy that is not recommended. The two styles of fishing are different, and a compromise is inclined to reduce the pleasure of each.

At the risk of repetition it must be stressed that the visitor will be surprised at the amount of angling for game fish that is available in Scotland. Indeed it is so obvious that many an angling motorist, especially in the wilder, remoter, more loch and burn filled districts, will be tempted to stop his car by the roadside and " have a go " at a lochan or running water that clearly " smells of trout." While it is true that in these remote districts such waters are sometimes free, or so nearly free that no one will object, the conscientious angler should make enquiries (usually in advance of his day's journey) as to whether there is any objection to him fishing the roadside waters. If he is lucky enough in Sutherland or the more remote west to strike such a patch of free, or near-free waters, he will find great pleasure in wandering on in his car from lochan to lochan, from burn to burn, trying his luck as he goes. But he *should make sure in advance* that he is entitled to do so. There is no licence for game fishing in Scotland, and if a water is free it is completely free to any legitimate method of angling; at the same time it should be stressed that even the remotest hill lochs are often preserved by hotels and angling associations, as well as by private individuals.

Salmon fishing, occurring as it does in spring and late autumn, is largely outside the scope of this article, which is primarily addressed to touring motorists. It is possible, however, to secure permission on the East Coast rivers and in some of the Highland lochs for late spring or early summer salmon. But luck plays a large part in such fishing. No one should count on salmon during the holiday months.

Luck, but to a lesser degree, arises in the angling for that lively and sporting fish, the sea trout. In most parts of the mainland of Scotland sea trout start coming up the rivers and streams and into the lochs in July. Dry weather, however, may hold them back, or, if they have got into fresh water the same dry weather may drive them down to the depths to sulk. Therefore, while sea trout during the holiday months are not nearly so chancy as salmon, they are not nearly so reliable as those delightful and usually smaller fish (whom some would call their humbler cousins) the brown trout. But, if a visiting angler is fortunate enough to strike a time when the sea trout are running, he will have an unforgettable experience. Pound for pound there is no game fish that in sport can surpass the sea trout. He fights like a demon to the last, and has an exciting trick of spending almost as much time in the air as in the water after he is hooked. He is the world's high jump expert amongst fish.

Sea trout waters are not *usually* free. They are generally attached to hotels (when not privately owned) and these hotels are mostly on the West Coast. The usual sea trout flies are all that the angler needs, but when fishing in estuary waters such as the Ythan, a famous sea trout spot, those long feathered contraptions known as demons, or sand eels, or even strips from a mackerel belly, are used with great effect. In certain parts of Scotland, notably in Shetland, anglers go after sea trout outside the actual estuaries and in the purely salt-water sea lochs, known in Shetland as " voes."

The preponderance of game fish in Scotland does not mean that there is not some excellent coarse fishing to be had. There is not the variety of coarse fish that there is in England, and as the season for most of them is in the winter they will not usually interest the tourist. There are grayling, particularly in the Perthshire streams, which can be fished for in the summer months. There are perch in many lochs; and the pike of the south-west lochs in Galloway and in the Lake of Menteith (the only lake as distinct from loch in Scotland) are not to be despised.

Finally there is sea fishing. In Scotland, where some really large pollock as well as cod are to be had in the north-west waters, the sport has been not so much neglected as not mapped out. The angler who finds himself near the coast during a dry holiday spell when the game fish are sulking at the bottom or off the take can have something of the pleasures of an explorer as well as of a sportsman if he can persuade a fisherman to take him out in his boat off the rock-bound and fish-teeming coast.

The angler coming to Scotland is indeed a fortunate man—or should be with such a wide variety of fishing at his disposal and at very moderate outlay. All over the country angling clubs, hotels and other proprietors of fishing rights expend a great deal of care and money in restocking or improving their waters. In recent years too the Hydro Electric Board has spent many thousands of pounds in re-stocking their reservoirs.

To sum up: the motoring angler on a holiday, even if he carries only one trout rod and a moderate

KEY MAP TO THE ITINERARIES

SCALE: TWELFTH-INCH TO MILE

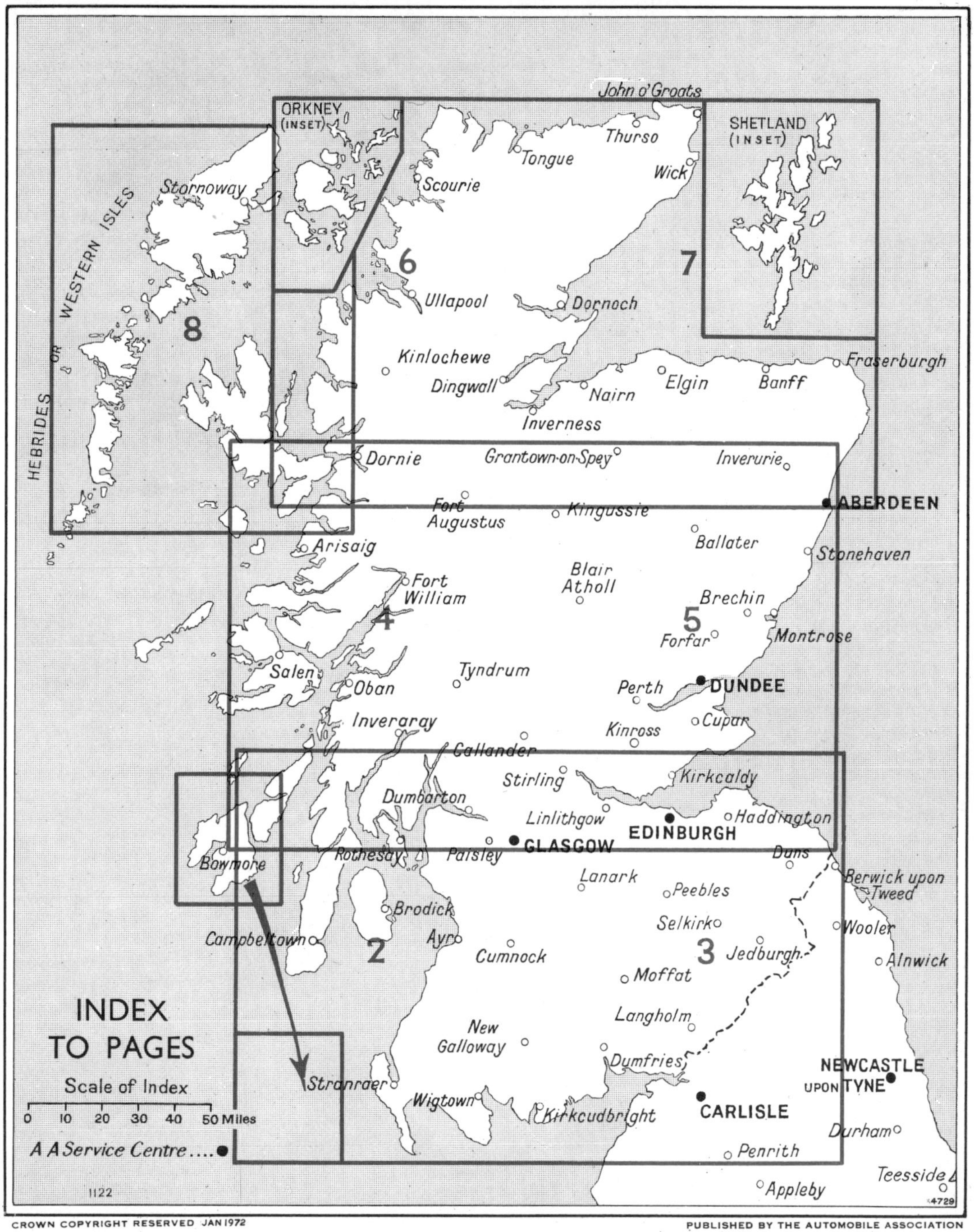

PUBLISHED BY THE AUTOMOBILE ASSOCIATION

REFERENCE TO MAP PAGES

Through-route Itineraries 100 Other Itineraries 74 Alternative Routes (80)

Car Ferries F Car-carrying Services (*see also pages 34 & 35 of atlas*)

Motorways and access points Motorways under construction

SCALE OF MAP PAGES

0 5 10 15 20 25 30 35 Statute Miles

0 5 10 15 20 25 30 35 40 45 50 55 Kilometres

4

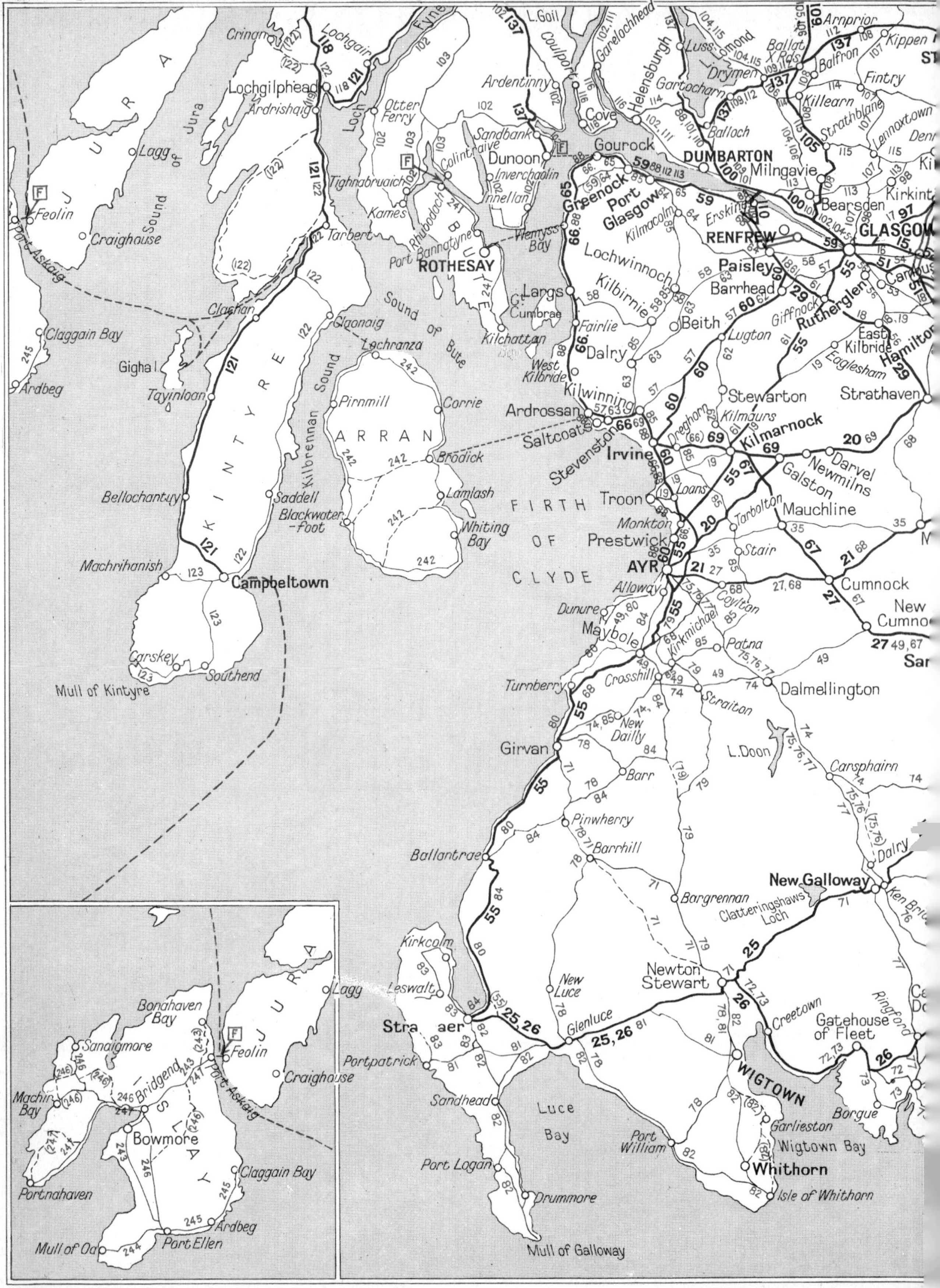

See special Through Ro

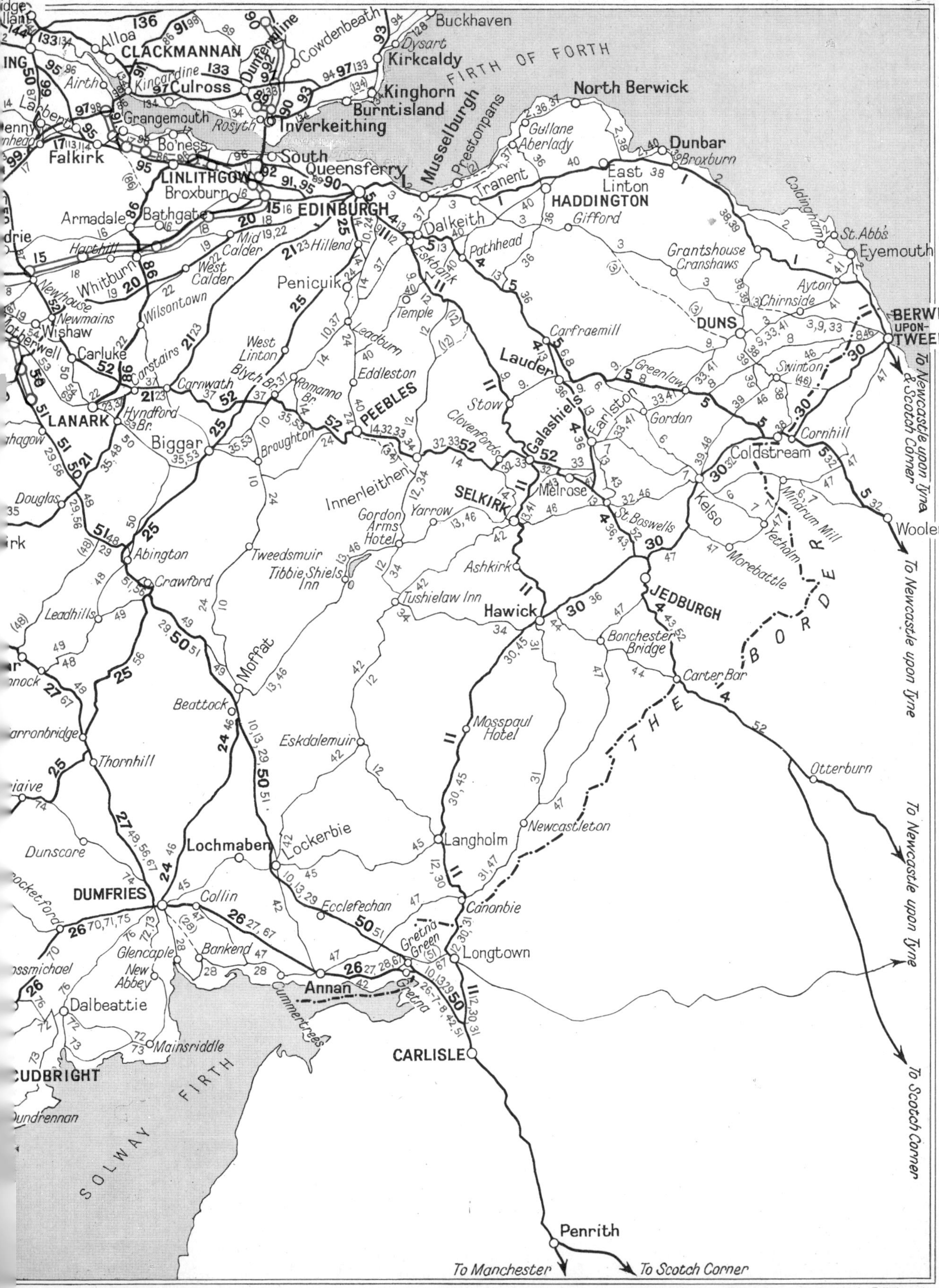

Printed by John Bartholomew & Son Ltd., Edinburgh

…s following Key Map

6

8

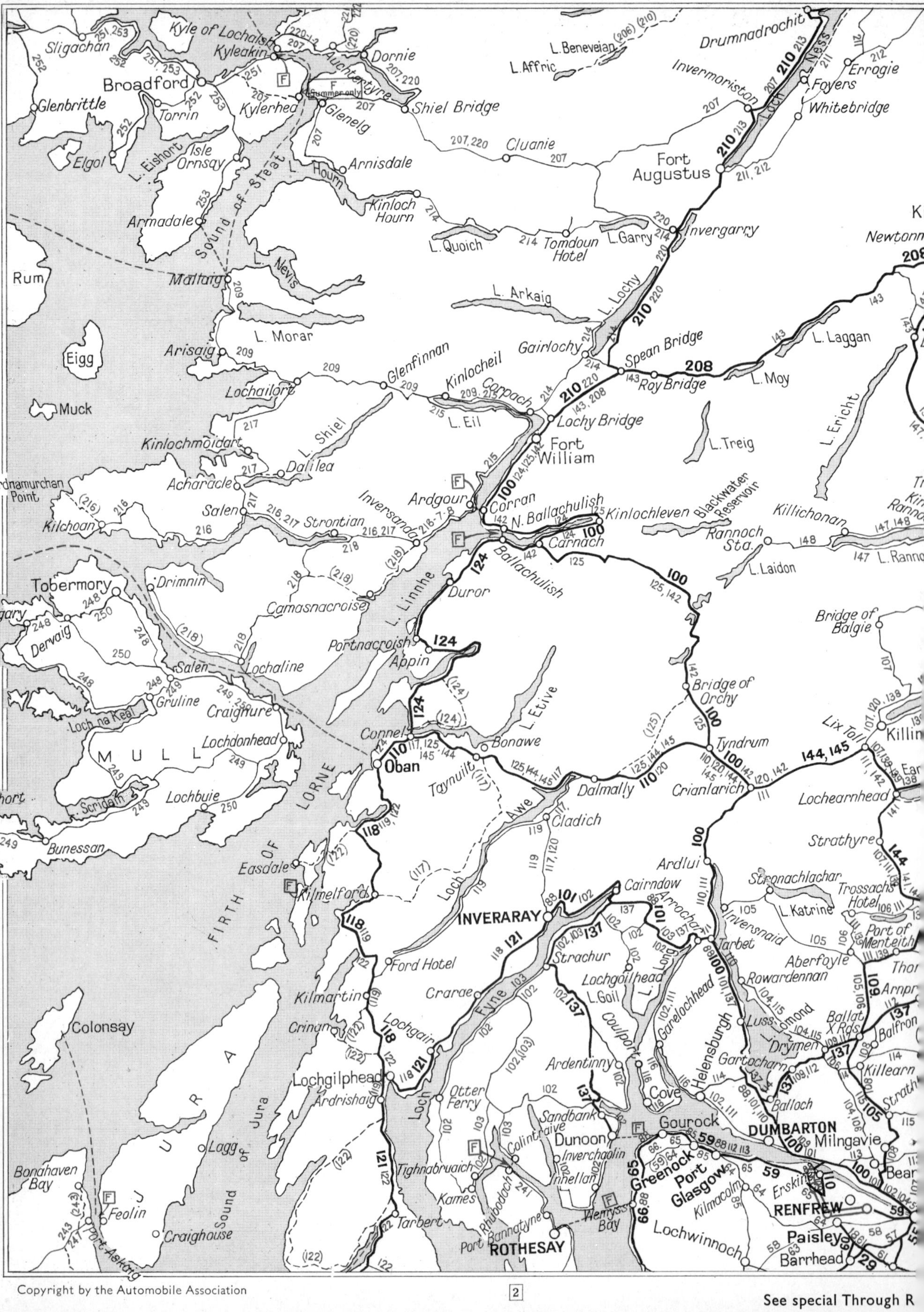

2

See special Through R

7

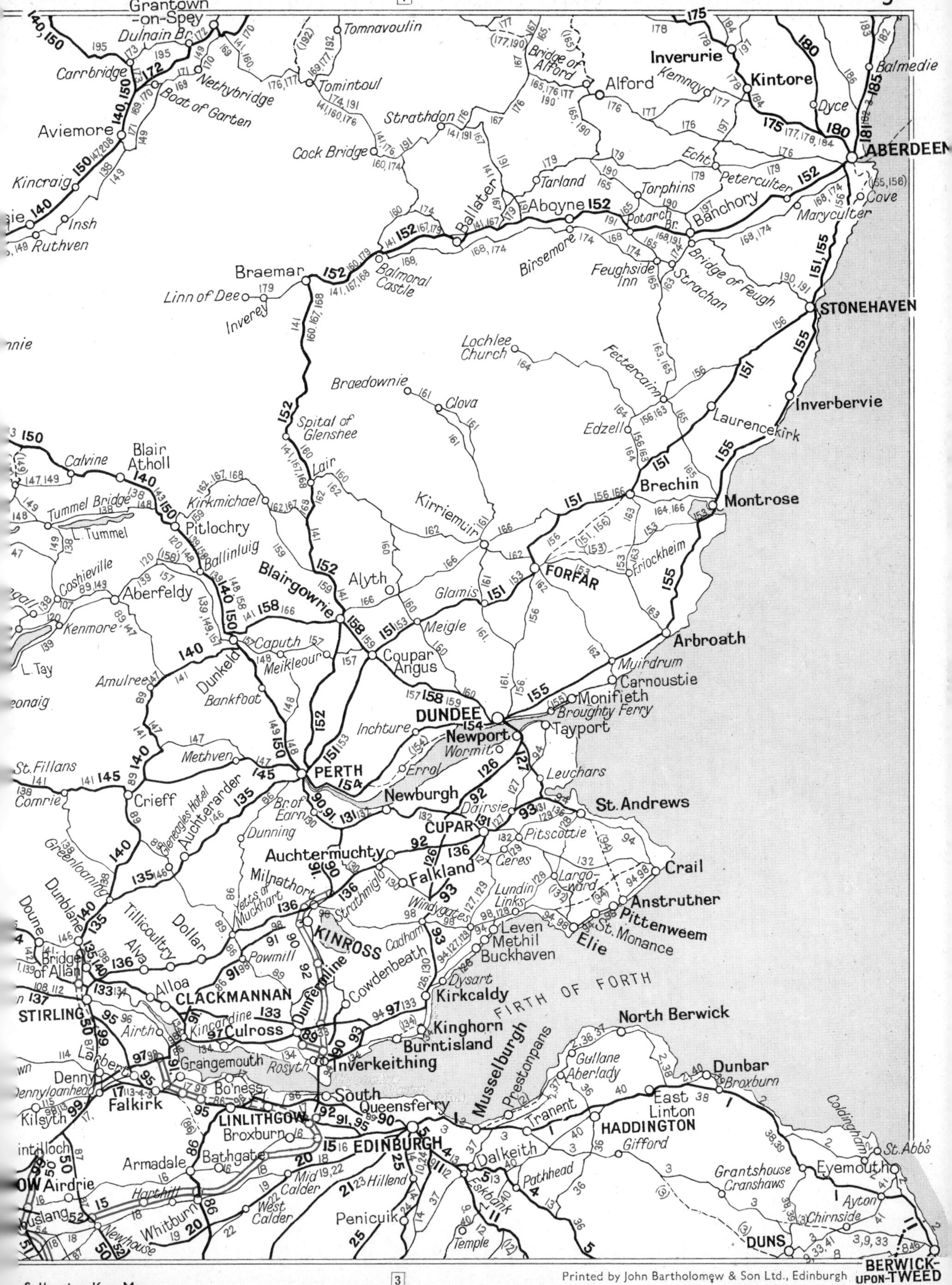

3

Printed by John Bartholomew & Son Ltd., Edinburgh

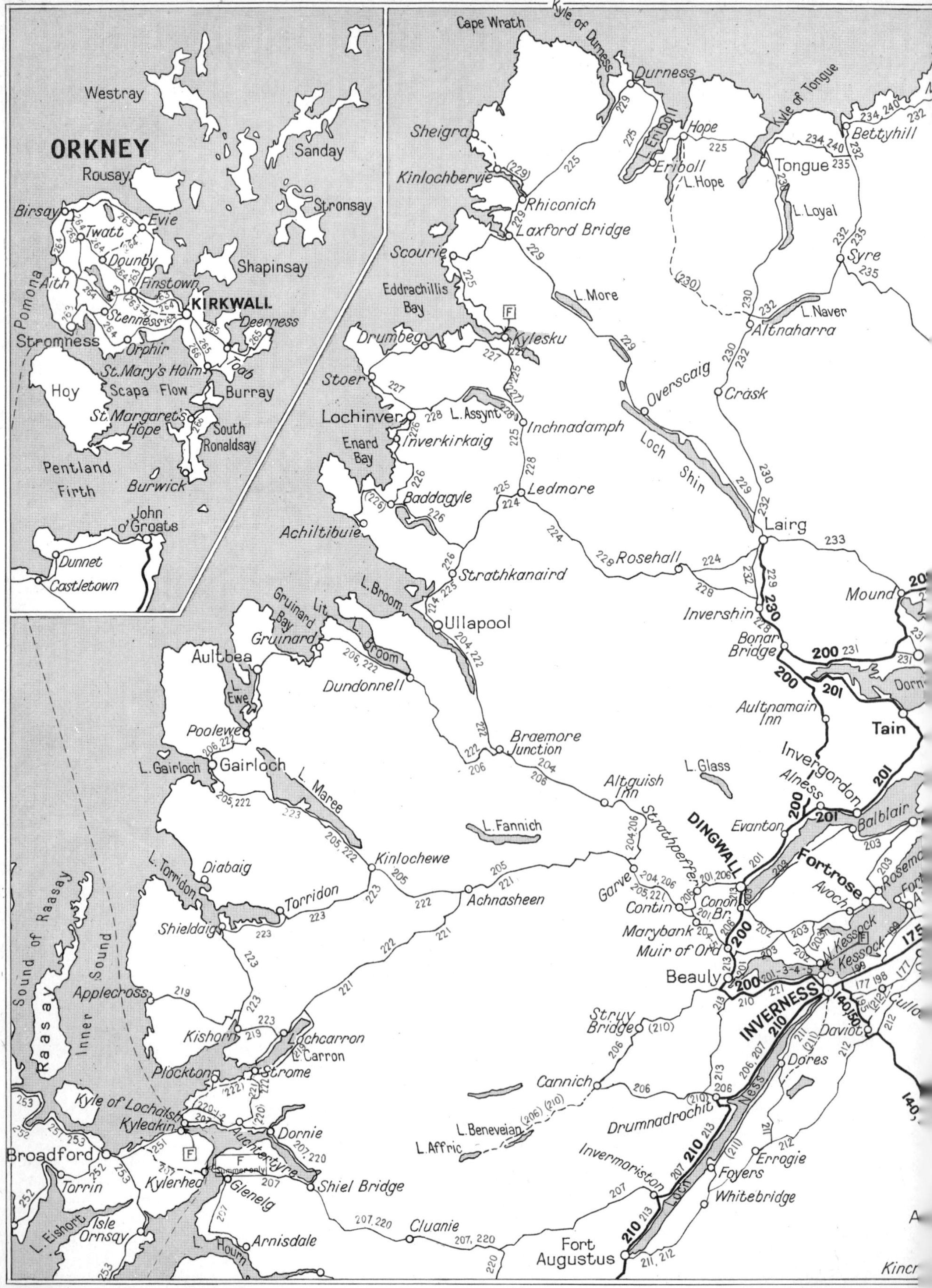

4

See special Through R

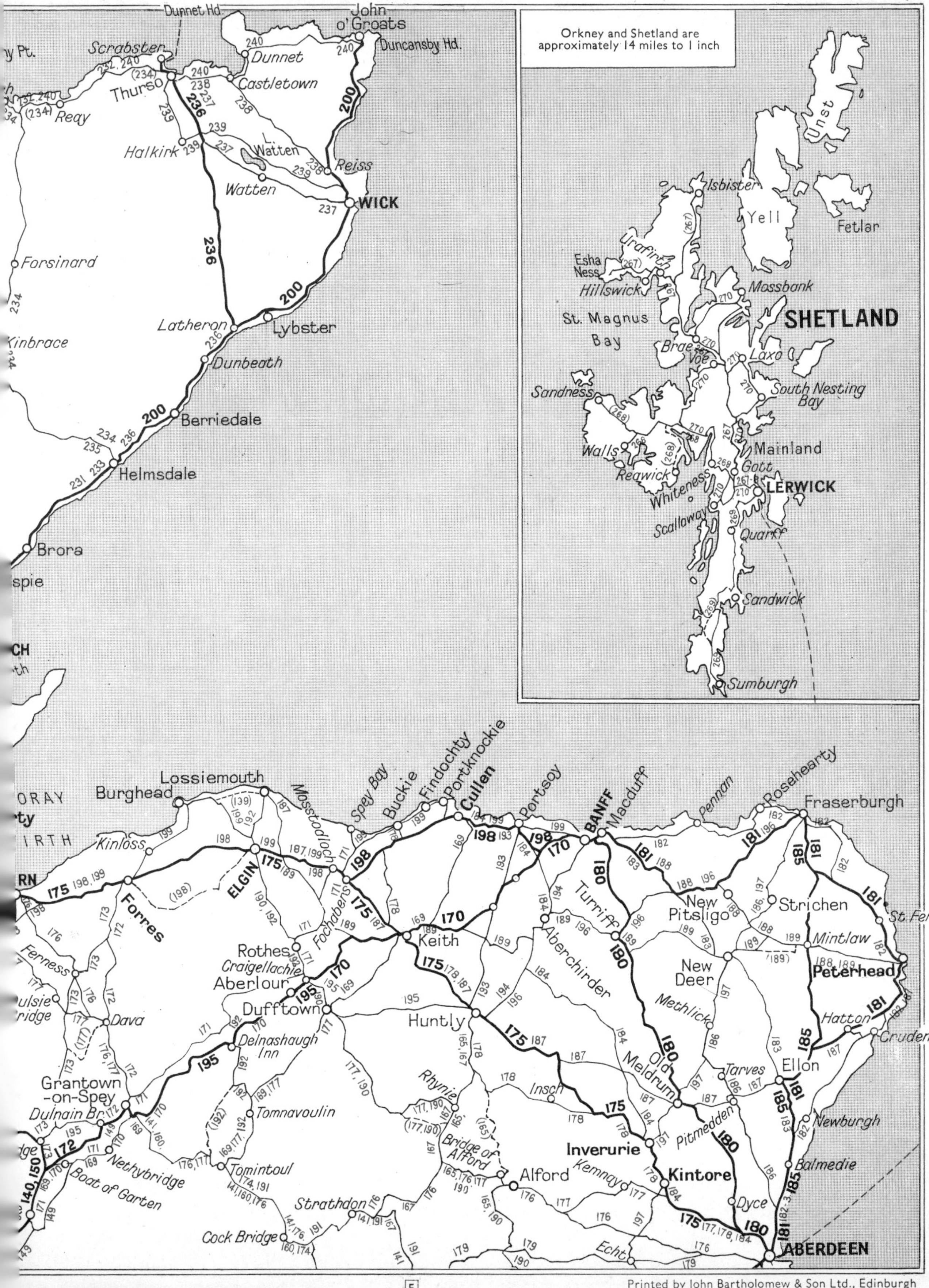

Printed by John Bartholomew & Son Ltd., Edinburgh

following Key Map

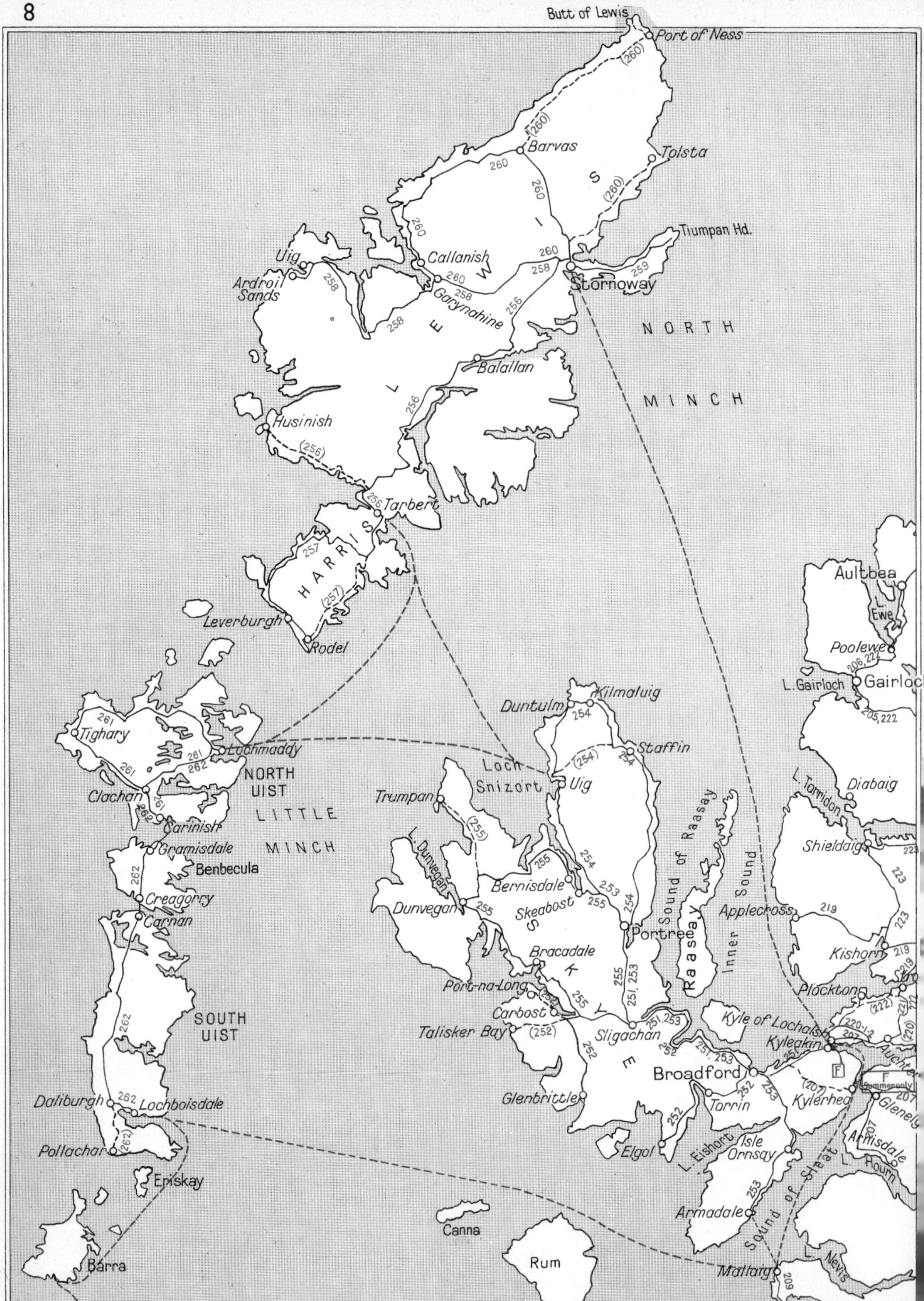

Printed by John Bartholomew & Son Ltd., Edinburgh

Weather Readings

Through-Route Maps

ITINERARIES

AVERAGE WEATHER READINGS FOR SCOTLAND

This table shows **Temperature:** *Maximum and minimum daily temperatures in degrees Centigrade.* **Rainfall:** *the average monthly rainfall in inches.* **Sunshine:** *the average monthly totals of bright sunshine, in hours.*

Town	Jan	Feb	Mar	Apr	May	June	July	Aug	Sept	Oct	Nov	Dec
Aberdeen												
Temperature...	6–2	6–2	8–2	9–4	12–6	16–9	17–11	17–11	15–9	12–6	8–4	7–2
Rainfall ...	3·0	2·2	2·0	2·2	2·7	2·1	3·3	2·8	2·7	3·5	3·4	3·1
Sunshine ...	47	68	106	136	170	183	150	144	123	96	57	37
Achnashellach (Wester Ross)												
Temperature...	6–1	7–1	8–2	11–3	14–5	16–8	17–10	17–9	15–8	12–5	8–2	7–1
Rainfall ...	8·9	6·8	5·6	5·6	3·8	5·0	5·7	6·6	7·1	9·1	8·0	8·7
Sunshine ...	31	58	93	135	171	165	124	124	105	77	45	15
Banff												
Temperature...	6–1	6–2	8–2	10–4	13–6	16–9	17–11	17–11	15–9	12–6	8–3	7–2
Rainfall ...	2·4	1·9	1·6	1·8	2·0	2·1	2·9	3·0	3·0	2·9	3·1	2·5
Sunshine ...	44	70	112	139	174	176	147	147	119	91	53	30
Dumfries												
Temperature...	6–1	7–1	9–2	11–3	15–6	18–9	19–11	18–11	16–8	13–6	9–3	7–2
Rainfall ...	4·7	2·9	2·7	2·4	2·7	2·7	3·9	4·0	3·7	4·6	4·1	4·3
Sunshine ...	40	62	103	137	184	192	151	142	112	88	56	35
Dundee												
Temperature...	6–1	6–1	8–2	11–3	14–6	18–8	19–11	19–10	16–8	13–5	8–2	7–1
Rainfall ...	2·8	2·2	2·0	1·7	2·6	2·0	3·2	3·3	2·7	3·3	2·9	2·4
Sunshine ...	50	76	105	140	166	182	154	141	122	95	63	41
Duntulm(Skye)												
Temperature...	7–3	7–2	8–3	9–4	12–6	14–9	16–11	16–11	14–9	12–7	9–5	7–3
Rainfall ...	5·8	3·9	3·2	3·4	2·9	3·3	3·8	4·4	5·1	6·0	5·6	5·6
Sunshine ...	34	57	101	129	203	161	130	127	97	72	42	25
Edinburgh												
Temperature...	6–2	6–2	8–2	10–4	13–6	17–9	18–11	18–11	16–9	12–7	8–4	7–2
Rainfall ...	2·5	1·6	1·6	1·6	2·2	1·9	3·1	3·1	2·6	2·9	2·4	2·1
Sunshine ...	52	76	114	139	172	196	161	143	127	100	62	43
Fort William												
Temperature...	7–1	7–1	9–3	11–4	15–6	17–9	18–11	18–11	16–9	12–6	9–3	7–2
Rainfall ...	8·9	7·1	5·0	5·2	3·2	4·5	5·3	5·8	7·7	9·1	7·8	9·4
Sunshine ...	13	46	82	108	173	154	116	118	82	56	26	7
Glasgow												
Temperature...	6–1	7–2	9–2	12–3	15–6	18–8	19–11	18–11	16–8	12–6	8–3	6–2
Rainfall ...	4·7	3·2	2·5	2·3	2·6	2·4	3·1	3·3	3·6	4·7	4·1	4·2
Sunshine ...	31	53	93	134	172	182	150	134	111	74	43	28
Helensburgh												
Temperature...	6–1	7–1	8–2	11–3	14–6	17–9	18–11	18–11	16–8	12–6	9–3	7–2
Rainfall ...	6·6	4·6	3·7	3·3	3·6	3·4	4·2	4·9	4·8	6·6	5·9	6·1
Sunshine ...	32	56	96	133	176	178	143	131	104	72	49	28

Town	Jan	Feb	Mar	Apr	May	June	July	Aug	Sept	Oct	Nov	Dec
Inverness												
Temperature...	6–1	6–1	8–2	10–3	13–6	16–8	17–11	17–11	15–8	12–6	8–3	7–2
Rainfall ...	2·7	1·9	1·5	1·8	2·2	1·9	3·1	3·1	2·7	3·0	2·4	2·4
Sunshine ...	45	67	108	132	164	169	141	138	109	86	50	30
Kelso												
Temperature...	6–0	7–0	9–1	12–3	14–5	18–8	19–11	19–9	16–8	13–5	8–2	7–1
Rainfall ...	2·3	1·7	1·6	1·6	1·9	1·9	2·8	3·0	2·3	2·7	2·3	1·9
Sunshine ...	40	58	109	135	171	180	171	139	120	93	60	31
North Berwick												
Temperature...	6–1	7–1	9–2	11–4	14–6	17–8	19–11	18–11	16–9	13–6	9–3	7–2
Rainfall ...	2·1	1·5	1·6	1·5	2·1	1·9	2·7	3·1	2·4	2·7	2·3	1·8
Sunshine ...	39	68	109	145	178	200	170	147	123	87	51	28
Oban												
Temperature...	7–2	7–2	9–3	11–4	14–7	16–9	17–11	17–11	15–9	12–7	9–4	7–3
Rainfall ...	6·2	4·3	3·2	3·3	3·2	3·5	4·3	4·7	5·3	6·7	6·0	6·0
Sunshine ...	29	57	98	140	191	176	135	131	102	70	44	27
Perth												
Temperature...	6–0	7–1	9–2	12–3	15–6	18–8	20–11	19–11	17–8	13–5	8–2	7–1
Rainfall ...	3·1	2·2	1·9	1·7	2·3	2·0	3·1	2·9	2·8	3·3	2·7	2·7
Sunshine ...	38	69	104	142	173	196	161	141	123	88	54	34
Prestwick												
Temperature...	7–2	7–2	9–3	11–4	14–7	16–9	18–12	18–12	16–9	13–7	9–4	7–3
Rainfall ...	3·7	2·4	2·1	1·9	2·2	2·3	3·0	3·1	3·3	4·0	3·4	3·5
Sunshine ...	35	66	102	146	189	176	145	141	111	78	47	24
Rothesay												
Temperature...	7–2	7–2	8–3	11–4	14–6	17–9	18–11	17–11	15–9	12–7	9–4	7–3
Rainfall ...	6·0	4·1	3·3	3·3	3·5	3·5	4·3	4·8	5·0	6·7	5·8	5·9
Sunshine ...	35	57	100	143	186	187	149	140	112	75	50	30
St Andrews												
Temperature...	6–1	7–1	8–2	11–3	13–6	17–8	19–11	18–11	16–8	12–6	9–3	7–2
Rainfall ...	2·7	1·8	1·8	1·6	2·3	1·8	2·8	2·8	2·4	2·9	2·8	2·4
Sunshine ...	50	78	114	153	181	204	170	149	133	99	66	40
Stornoway												
Temperature...	7–3	7–3	8–3	9–4	12–6	14–8	16–11	16–11	14–9	12–7	9–4	7–3
Rainfall ...	6·4	3·2	3·2	3·1	2·5	2·4	3·0	4·3	4·7	6·2	4·6	5·5
Sunshine ...	32	57	104	146	190	165	135	132	107	77	47	24
Wick												
Temperature...	6–2	6–2	7–2	9–3	11–6	13–8	15–10	15–10	14–8	11–6	8–4	7–3
Rainfall ...	2·9	2·1	1·8	2·1	1·8	2·0	2·6	2·6	2·9	3·2	3·1	2·9
Sunshine ...	43	74	111	143	174	175	147	144	117	85	53	33

Temperature equivalents to the nearest degree Fahrenheit

°C	0	1	2	3	4	5	6	7	8	9	10	11	12	13	14	15	16	17	18	19	20
°F	32	34	36	38	40	41	43	45	47	49	50	52	54	56	58	59	61	63	65	67	68

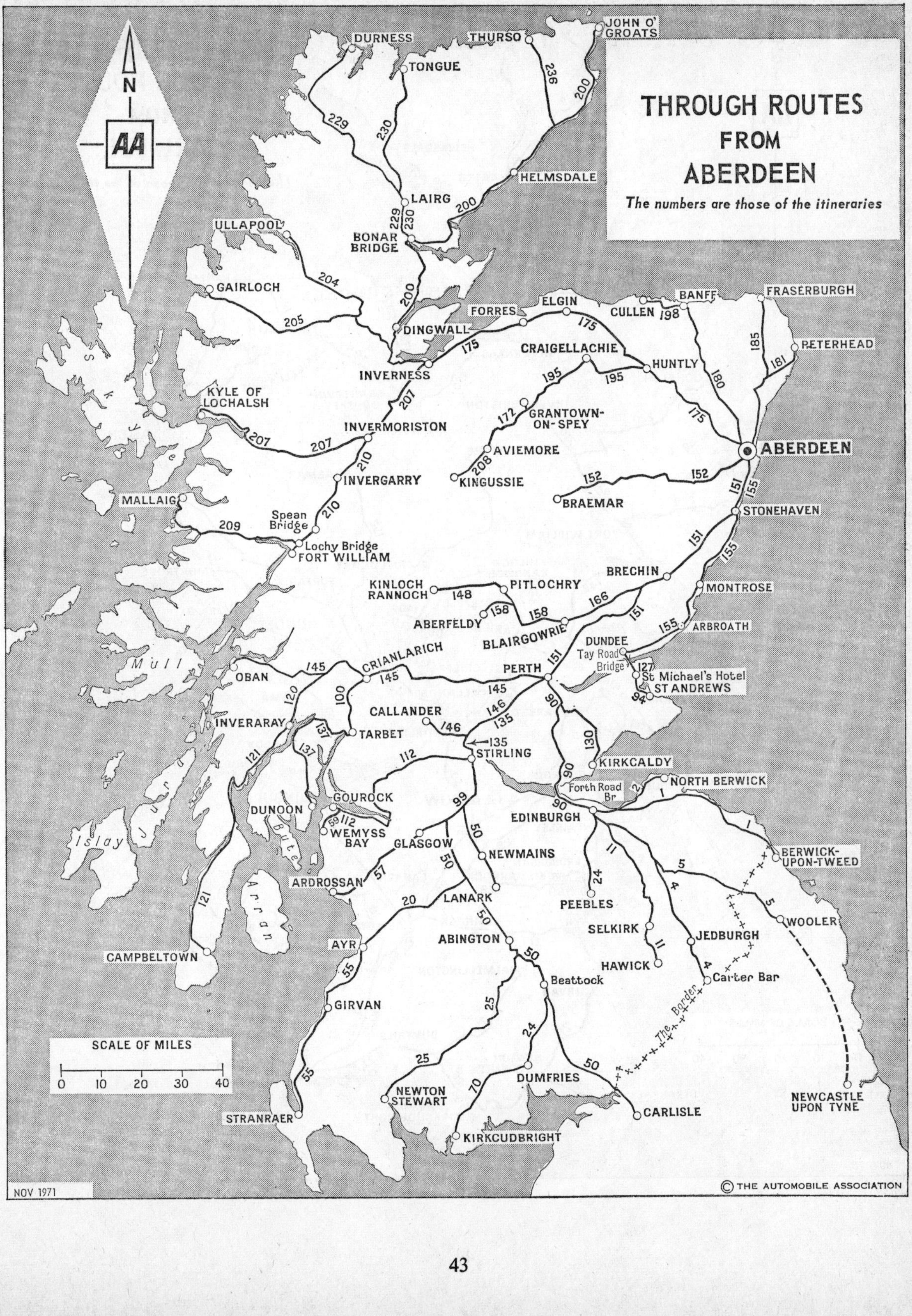
THROUGH ROUTES
FROM
ABERDEEN
The numbers are those of the itineraries
N
AA
SCALE OF MILES
0 10 20 30 40
NOV 1971
© THE AUTOMOBILE ASSOCIATION
JOHN O' GROATS
THURSO
DURNESS
TONGUE
HELMSDALE
LAIRG
BONAR BRIDGE
ULLAPOOL
GAIRLOCH
DINGWALL
FORRES
ELGIN
CULLEN
BANFF
FRASERBURGH
PETERHEAD
CRAIGELLACHIE
HUNTLY
INVERNESS
KYLE OF LOCHALSH
GRANTOWN-ON-SPEY
INVERMORISTON
AVIEMORE
ABERDEEN
KINGUSSIE
INVERGARRY
BRAEMAR
MALLAIG
Spean Bridge
STONEHAVEN
Lochy Bridge
FORT WILLIAM
BRECHIN
KINLOCH RANNOCH
PITLOCHRY
MONTROSE
ABERFELDY
BLAIRGOWRIE
ARBROATH
DUNDEE
Tay Road Bridge
St Michael's Hotel
ST ANDREWS
CRIANLARICH
OBAN
PERTH
CALLANDER
INVERARAY
TARBET
STIRLING
KIRKCALDY
NORTH BERWICK
Forth Road Br
GOUROCK
DUNOON
EDINBURGH
WEMYSS BAY
GLASGOW
NEWMAINS
BERWICK-UPON-TWEED
ARDROSSAN
LANARK
PEEBLES
WOOLER
SELKIRK
JEDBURGH
ABINGTON
CAMPBELTOWN
AYR
HAWICK
Carter Bar
Beattock
GIRVAN
The Border
DUMFRIES
NEWTON STEWART
NEWCASTLE UPON TYNE
CARLISLE
STRANRAER
KIRKCUDBRIGHT
Skye
Mull
Jura
Islay
Bute
Arran

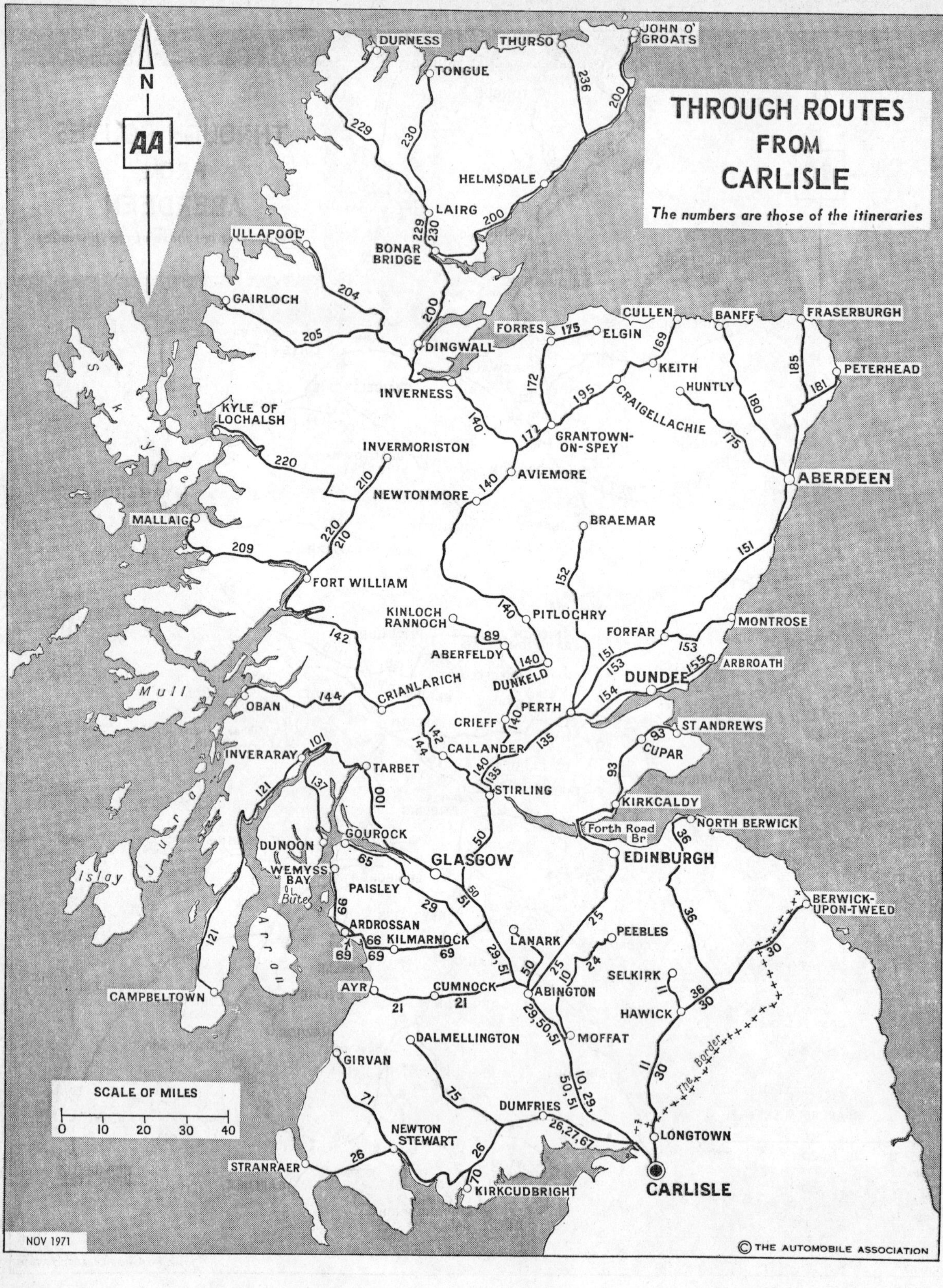
THROUGH ROUTES
FROM
CARLISLE
The numbers are those of the itineraries
N
AA
DURNESS
THURSO
JOHN O' GROATS
TONGUE
HELMSDALE
LAIRG
ULLAPOOL
BONAR BRIDGE
GAIRLOCH
DINGWALL
FORRES
ELGIN
CULLEN
BANFF
FRASERBURGH
PETERHEAD
KEITH
HUNTLY
INVERNESS
CRAIGELLACHIE
KYLE OF LOCHALSH
INVERMORISTON
GRANTOWN-ON-SPEY
AVIEMORE
ABERDEEN
NEWTONMORE
MALLAIG
BRAEMAR
FORT WILLIAM
KINLOCH RANNOCH
PITLOCHRY
MONTROSE
FORFAR
ABERFELDY
ARBROATH
DUNDEE
DUNKELD
CRIANLARICH
OBAN
PERTH
CRIEFF
ST ANDREWS
CUPAR
CALLANDER
INVERARAY
TARBET
STIRLING
KIRKCALDY
NORTH BERWICK
Forth Road Br
DUNOON
GOUROCK
EDINBURGH
GLASGOW
WEMYSS BAY
PAISLEY
BERWICK-UPON-TWEED
ARDROSSAN
KILMARNOCK
LANARK
PEEBLES
SELKIRK
AYR
CUMNOCK
ABINGTON
CAMPBELTOWN
HAWICK
MOFFAT
DALMELLINGTON
GIRVAN
DUMFRIES
NEWTON STEWART
LONGTOWN
STRANRAER
KIRKCUDBRIGHT
CARLISLE
Skye
Mull
Jura
Islay
Arran
Bute
The Border
SCALE OF MILES
0 10 20 30 40
NOV 1971
© THE AUTOMOBILE ASSOCIATION

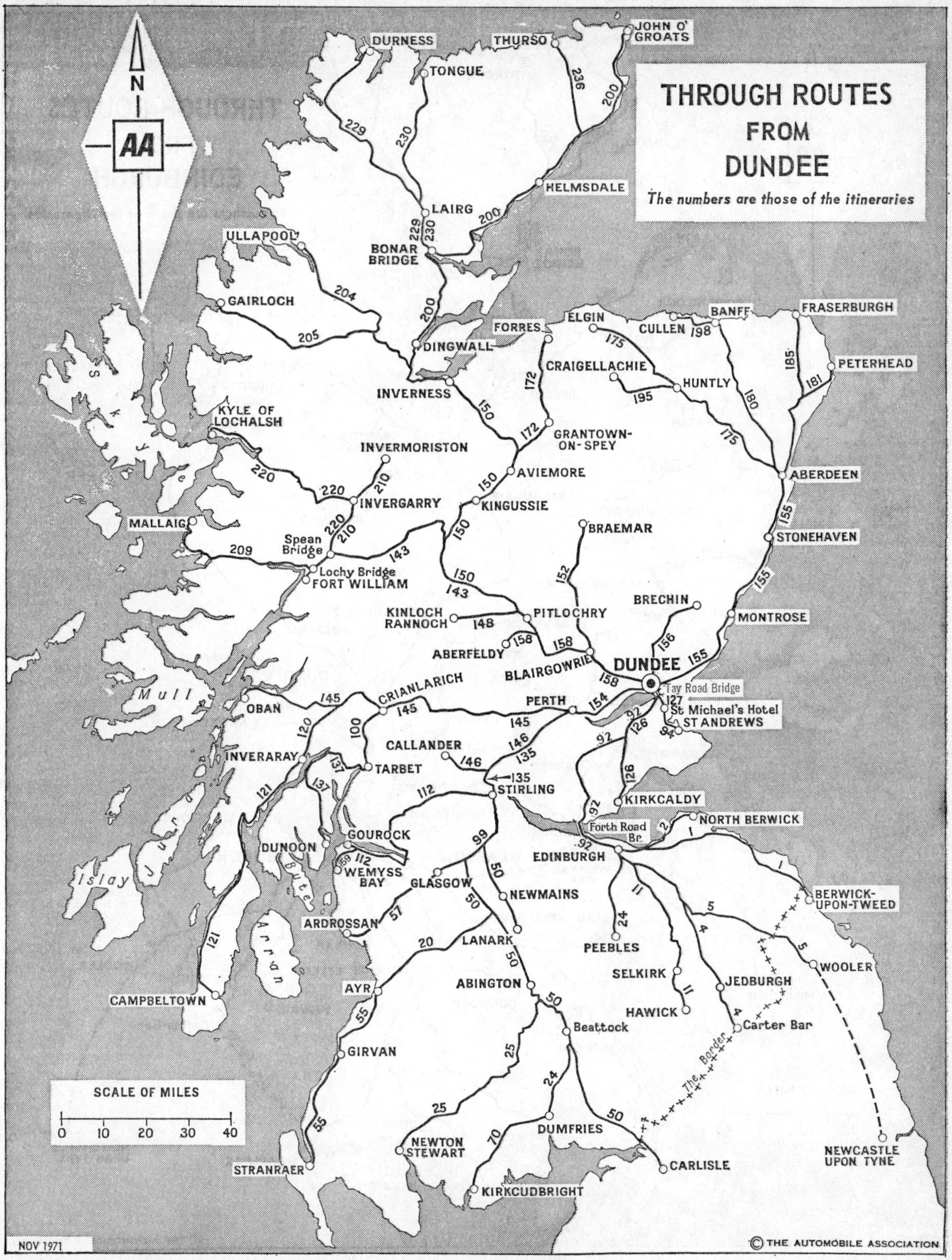
THROUGH ROUTES
FROM
DUNDEE
The numbers are those of the itineraries
N
AA
DURNESS
THURSO
JOHN O' GROATS
TONGUE
HELMSDALE
LAIRG
BONAR BRIDGE
ULLAPOOL
GAIRLOCH
DINGWALL
FORRES
ELGIN
CULLEN
BANFF
FRASERBURGH
PETERHEAD
CRAIGELLACHIE
HUNTLY
INVERNESS
KYLE OF LOCHALSH
GRANTOWN-ON-SPEY
INVERMORISTON
AVIEMORE
KINGUSSIE
ABERDEEN
INVERGARRY
MALLAIG
Spean Bridge
BRAEMAR
STONEHAVEN
Lochy Bridge
FORT WILLIAM
BRECHIN
KINLOCH RANNOCH
PITLOCHRY
MONTROSE
ABERFELDY
BLAIRGOWRIE
DUNDEE
Tay Road Bridge
St Michael's Hotel
ST ANDREWS
Mull
OBAN
CRIANLARICH
PERTH
CALLANDER
INVERARAY
TARBET
STIRLING
KIRKCALDY
NORTH BERWICK
Forth Road Br.
GOUROCK
DUNOON
WEMYSS BAY
EDINBURGH
Islay
Jura
Bute
GLASGOW
NEWMAINS
BERWICK-UPON-TWEED
ARDROSSAN
Arran
LANARK
PEEBLES
SELKIRK
WOOLER
JEDBURGH
ABINGTON
AYR
CAMPBELTOWN
HAWICK
Beattock
Carter Bar
The Border
GIRVAN
SCALE OF MILES
0 10 20 30 40
DUMFRIES
NEWTON STEWART
STRANRAER
CARLISLE
NEWCASTLE UPON TYNE
KIRKCUDBRIGHT
NOV 1971
© THE AUTOMOBILE ASSOCIATION

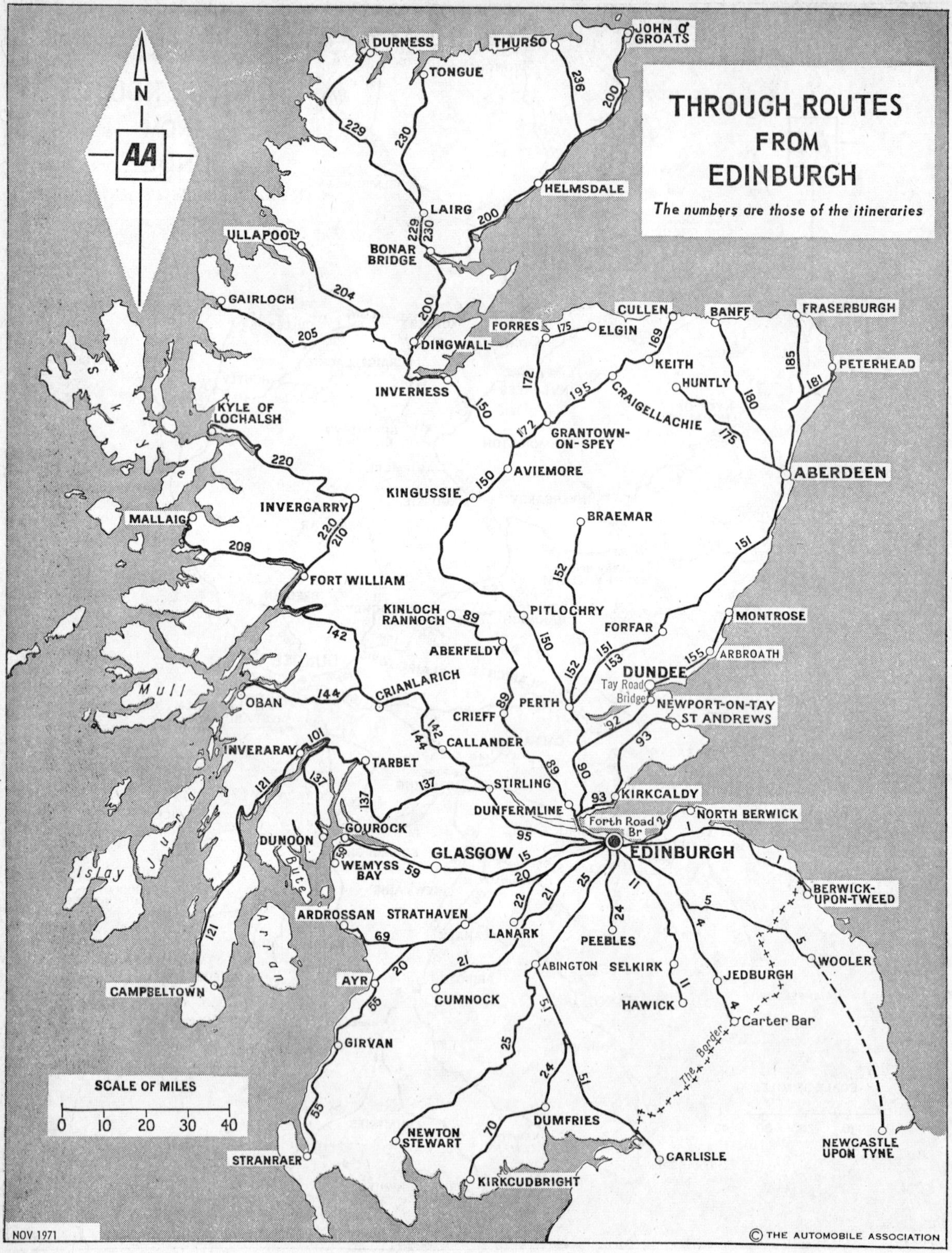
THROUGH ROUTES
FROM
EDINBURGH
The numbers are those of the itineraries
N
AA
DURNESS
THURSO
JOHN O' GROATS
TONGUE
HELMSDALE
LAIRG
ULLAPOOL
BONAR BRIDGE
GAIRLOCH
DINGWALL
FORRES
ELGIN
CULLEN
BANFF
FRASERBURGH
PETERHEAD
KEITH
HUNTLY
INVERNESS
CRAIGELLACHIE
GRANTOWN-ON-SPEY
KYLE OF LOCHALSH
AVIEMORE
ABERDEEN
KINGUSSIE
INVERGARRY
MALLAIG
BRAEMAR
FORT WILLIAM
KINLOCH RANNOCH
PITLOCHRY
MONTROSE
FORFAR
ABERFELDY
ARBROATH
DUNDEE
Tay Road Bridge
CRIANLARICH
PERTH
NEWPORT-ON-TAY
ST ANDREWS
OBAN
CRIEFF
Mull
CALLANDER
INVERARAY
TARBET
STIRLING
KIRKCALDY
DUNFERMLINE
Forth Road Br
NORTH BERWICK
GOUROCK
DUNOON
GLASGOW
EDINBURGH
WEMYSS BAY
Islay
Jura
Bute
Arran
BERWICK-UPON-TWEED
ARDROSSAN
STRATHAVEN
LANARK
PEEBLES
WOOLER
ABINGTON
SELKIRK
JEDBURGH
AYR
CAMPBELTOWN
CUMNOCK
HAWICK
Carter Bar
GIRVAN
The Border
SCALE OF MILES
0 10 20 30 40
DUMFRIES
NEWTON STEWART
CARLISLE
NEWCASTLE UPON TYNE
STRANRAER
KIRKCUDBRIGHT
NOV 1971
© THE AUTOMOBILE ASSOCIATION

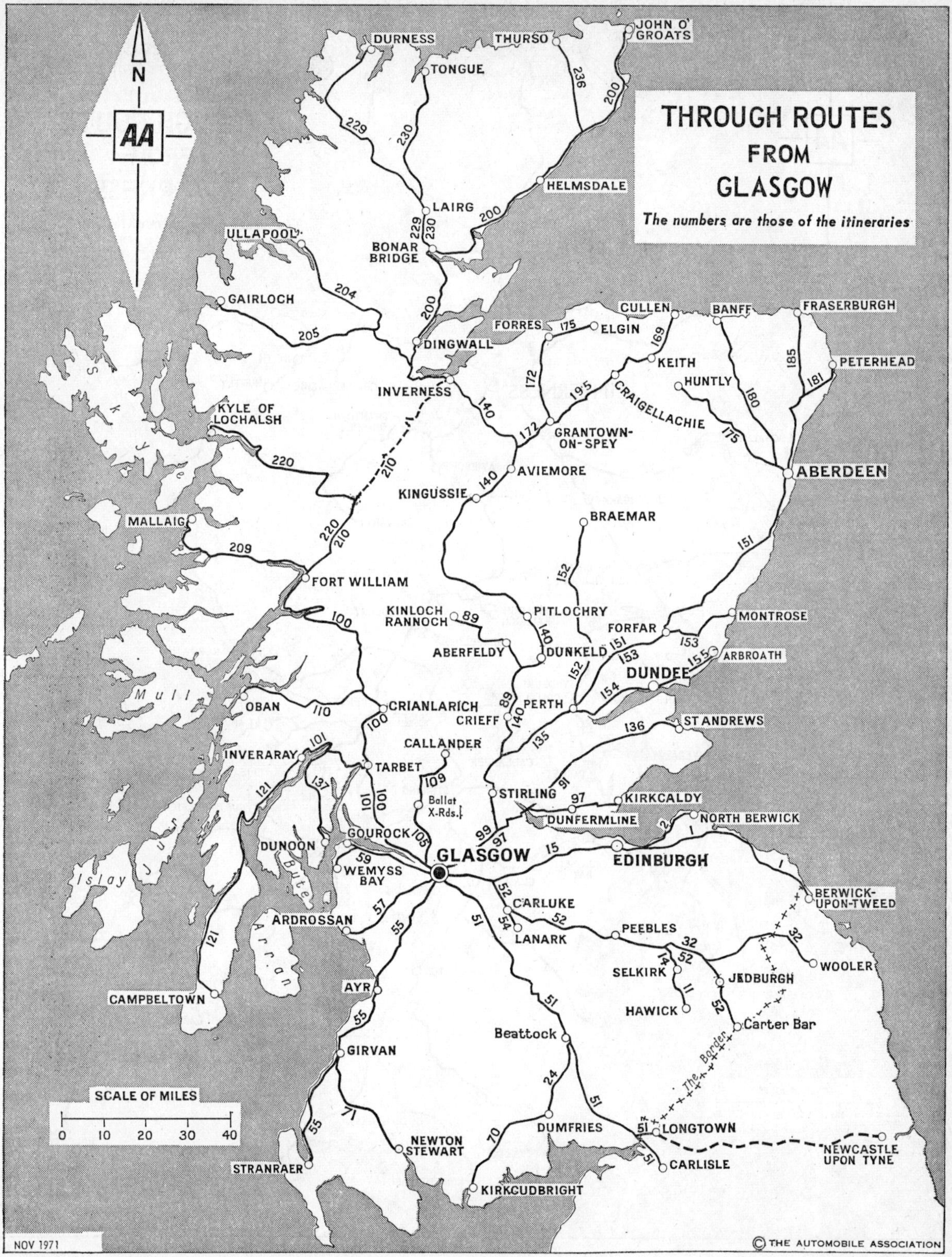
THROUGH ROUTES
FROM
GLASGOW
The numbers are those of the itineraries
N
AA
SCALE OF MILES
0 10 20 30 40
DURNESS
THURSO
JOHN O' GROATS
TONGUE
HELMSDALE
LAIRG
BONAR BRIDGE
ULLAPOOL
GAIRLOCH
DINGWALL
INVERNESS
KYLE OF LOCHALSH
MALLAIG
FORT WILLIAM
KINGUSSIE
AVIEMORE
GRANTOWN-ON-SPEY
FORRES
ELGIN
CULLEN
BANFF
FRASERBURGH
PETERHEAD
KEITH
HUNTLY
CRAIGELLACHIE
ABERDEEN
BRAEMAR
PITLOCHRY
KINLOCH RANNOCH
ABERFELDY
DUNKELD
FORFAR
MONTROSE
ARBROATH
DUNDEE
PERTH
CRIEFF
ST ANDREWS
OBAN
CRIANLARICH
CALLANDER
INVERARAY
TARBET
Ballat X-Rds.
STIRLING
KIRKCALDY
DUNFERMLINE
NORTH BERWICK
GOUROCK
DUNOON
WEMYSS BAY
GLASGOW
EDINBURGH
BERWICK-UPON-TWEED
CARLUKE
LANARK
PEEBLES
ARDROSSAN
SELKIRK
JEDBURGH
WOOLER
HAWICK
Carter Bar
AYR
CAMPBELTOWN
GIRVAN
Beattock
The Border
DUMFRIES
LONGTOWN
CARLISLE
NEWCASTLE UPON TYNE
NEWTON STEWART
STRANRAER
KIRKCUDBRIGHT
Skye
Mull
Islay
Jura
Bute
Arran
NOV 1971
© THE AUTOMOBILE ASSOCIATION

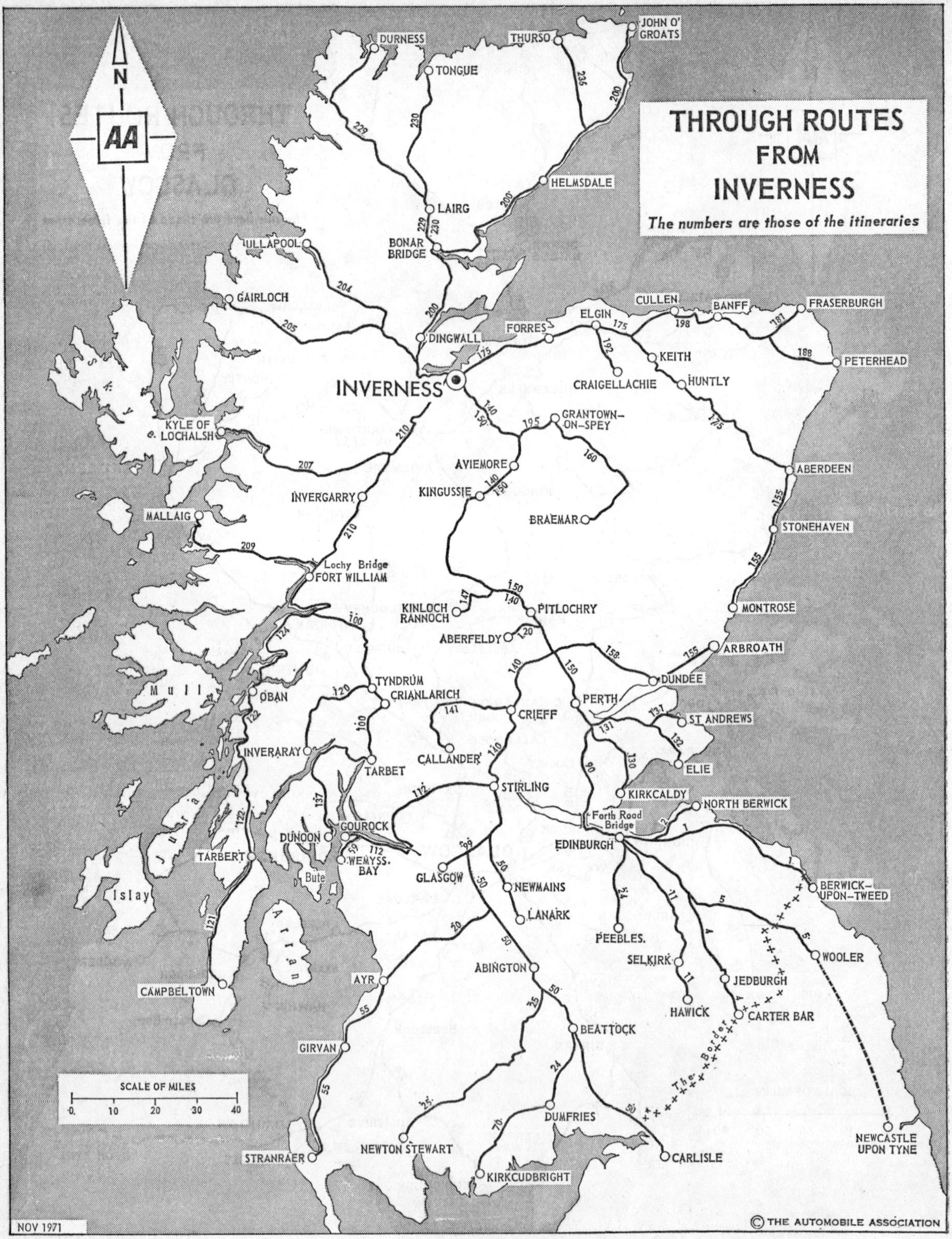
THROUGH ROUTES FROM INVERNESS
The numbers are those of the itineraries
N
AA
DURNESS
TONGUE
THURSO
JOHN O' GROATS
HELMSDALE
LAIRG
BONAR BRIDGE
ULLAPOOL
GAIRLOCH
DINGWALL
INVERNESS
FORRES
ELGIN
CULLEN
BANFF
FRASERBURGH
PETERHEAD
KEITH
CRAIGELLACHIE
HUNTLY
GRANTOWN-ON-SPEY
KYLE OF LOCHALSH
AVIEMORE
KINGUSSIE
BRAEMAR
ABERDEEN
STONEHAVEN
INVERGARRY
MALLAIG
Lochy Bridge
FORT WILLIAM
KINLOCH RANNOCH
PITLOCHRY
ABERFELDY
MONTROSE
ARBROATH
DUNDEE
TYNDRUM
CRIANLARICH
OBAN
Mull
PERTH
ST ANDREWS
CRIEFF
CALLANDER
INVERARAY
TARBET
ELIE
STIRLING
KIRKCALDY
NORTH BERWICK
Forth Road Bridge
EDINBURGH
GOUROCK
DUNOON
WEMYSS BAY
Bute
TARBERT
Jura
Islay
GLASGOW
NEWMAINS
LANARK
PEEBLES
BERWICK-UPON-TWEED
Arran
SELKIRK
WOOLER
JEDBURGH
ABINGTON
AYR
CAMPBELTOWN
HAWICK
CARTER BAR
BEATTOCK
GIRVAN
The Border
SCALE OF MILES
0 10 20 30 40
DUMFRIES
NEWCASTLE UPON TYNE
CARLISLE
NEWTON STEWART
STRANRAER
KIRKCUDBRIGHT
NOV 1971
© THE AUTOMOBILE ASSOCIATION

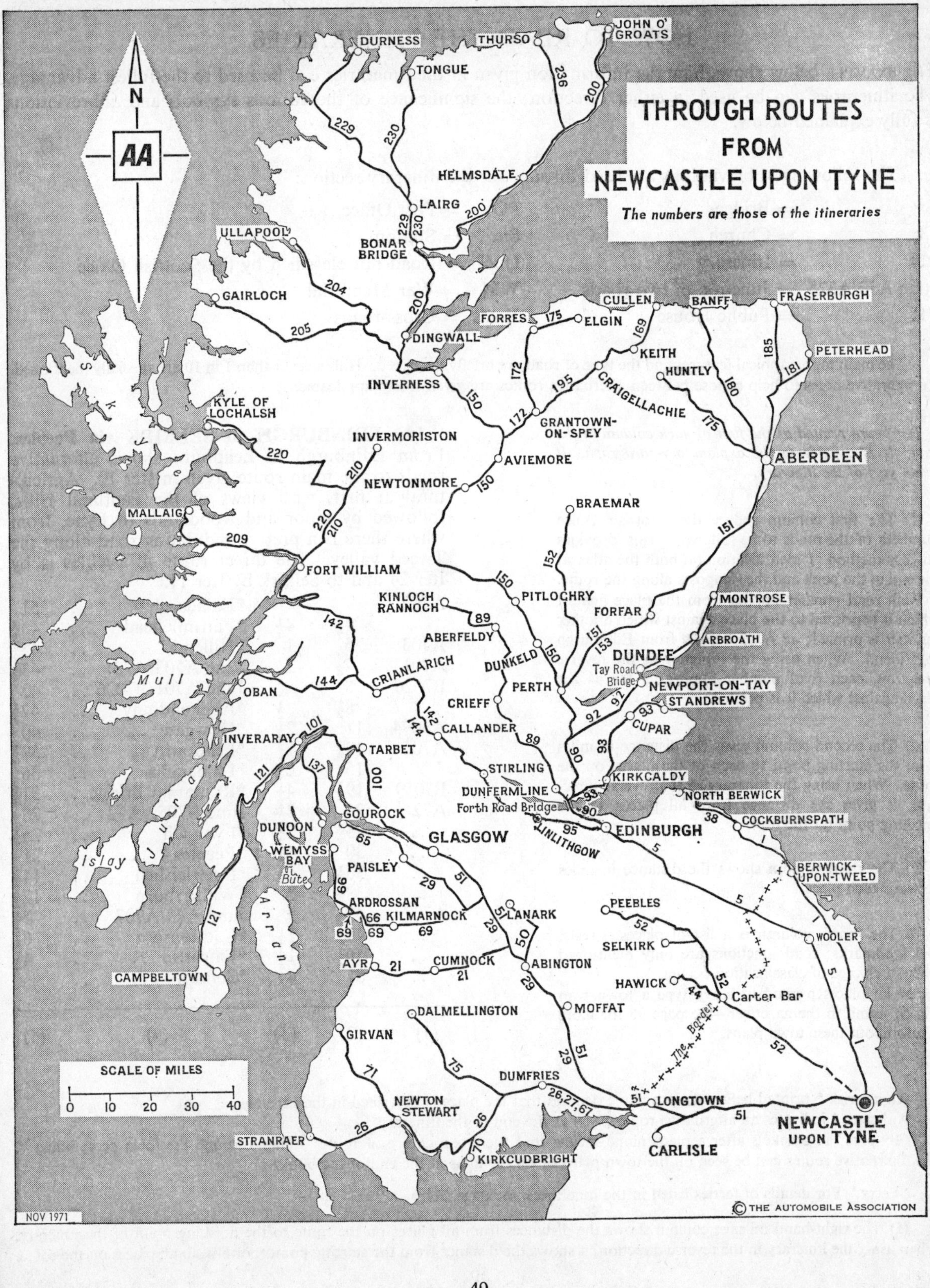
THROUGH ROUTES
FROM
NEWCASTLE UPON TYNE
The numbers are those of the itineraries
N
AA
SCALE OF MILES
0 10 20 30 40
JOHN O' GROATS
DURNESS
THURSO
TONGUE
HELMSDALE
LAIRG
ULLAPOOL
BONAR BRIDGE
GAIRLOCH
DINGWALL
INVERNESS
KYLE OF LOCHALSH
INVERMORISTON
NEWTONMORE
AVIEMORE
GRANTOWN-ON-SPEY
FORRES
ELGIN
CULLEN
BANFF
FRASERBURGH
PETERHEAD
KEITH
HUNTLY
CRAIGELLACHIE
ABERDEEN
BRAEMAR
MALLAIG
FORT WILLIAM
KINLOCH RANNOCH
PITLOCHRY
MONTROSE
FORFAR
ARBROATH
ABERFELDY
DUNKELD
DUNDEE
Tay Road Bridge
NEWPORT-ON-TAY
ST ANDREWS
CUPAR
PERTH
CRIEFF
CRIANLARICH
OBAN
Mull
INVERARAY
TARBET
CALLANDER
STIRLING
KIRKCALDY
DUNFERMLINE
Forth Road Bridge
NORTH BERWICK
COCKBURNSPATH
LINLITHGOW
EDINBURGH
GOUROCK
DUNOON
GLASGOW
WEMYSS BAY
Bute
PAISLEY
Islay
Jura
Arran
ARDROSSAN
KILMARNOCK
LANARK
BERWICK-UPON-TWEED
PEEBLES
SELKIRK
WOOLER
HAWICK
Carter Bar
The Border
AYR
CUMNOCK
ABINGTON
CAMPBELTOWN
MOFFAT
DALMELLINGTON
GIRVAN
DUMFRIES
NEWTON STEWART
LONGTOWN
NEWCASTLE UPON TYNE
CARLISLE
STRANRAER
KIRKCUDBRIGHT
NOV 1971
© THE AUTOMOBILE ASSOCIATION

HOW TO READ THE ITINERARIES

THE EXAMPLE below shows how the information given in the itineraries can be used to the fullest advantage. The itineraries can be used in either direction; the significance of the various symbols and abbreviations is fully explained below.

The following abbreviations are used throughout the itinerary section:

Br	= Bridge	PO	= Post Office
Ch	= Church	Sta	= Station
Iter	= Itinerary	Uncl	= Road not classified by the Scottish Office
Junc A30/A325	= Junction of two roads	WM	= War Memorial
PH	= Public House	X-rds	= Cross-roads

The main topographical features and the type of road are briefly described. Hills steeper than 1 in 10 are specially mentioned. Comparative notes to help choose between alternative routes are given where applicable.

The figure printed at the foot of each column in the example is a guide to the explanatory-paragraph. It is not part of the itinerary.

(1) The first column shows the Scottish Office numbers of the roads to be followed. This provides an easy method of identification on both the atlas at the end of the book and the signposts along the route.

Each road number applies from the place against which it is printed to the place against which another number is printed; *eg* A702 applies from Edinburgh to Hillend. When using the itinerary in the reverse direction, each road number applies as far as the place against which it is printed.

(2) The second column gives the distance in miles from the starting point to each of the places on the route. When using the itinerary in the reverse direction, it gives the distance from all places to the finishing point (at the top).

(3) The third column shows the distance in miles between each place.

(4) The fourth column is a list of places, streets, and landmarks; road junctions are only mentioned where a change of classification occurs.

For all places printed in **heavy** type a town plan will be found in the gazetteer—see page 98 for more details about these town plans.

14. EDINBURGH to SELKIRK via Peebles. From Edinburgh to Leadburn shows alternative roads to the main route given in Iter 10. Agricultural at first, with views of the Pentland Hills, followed by moor and woodlands to Lyne, from where there is a pretty, undulating road along the Tweed valley. The direct route to Peebles is by Iter 24 and to Selkirk by Iter 11.

A702			***Edinburgh**	51
..	4¼	4¼	*Fairmilehead ..	46¾
A703	5¼	1	*Hillend	45¾
A701	7¼	2	Junc A703/A701 ..	43¾
B7026	8	¾	Junc A701/B7026 ..	43
..	8½	½	*Auchendinny ..	42½
A6094	11	2½	*Howgate	40
A701	12¾	1¾	*Leadburn	38¼
..	15	2¼	*Lamancha ..	36
B7059	19½	4½	*Romanno Bridge ..	31½
A72	23	3½	Junc B7059/A72 ..	28
..	25¾	2¾	*Lyne Ch ..	25¼
..	30	4¼	***Peebles**	21
..	36½	6½	*Innerleithen ..	14½
..	38½	2	*Walkerburn ..	12½
A707	43½	5	Junc A72/A707 ..	7½
..	44¾	1¼	*Caddonfoot ..	6¼
..	46½	1¾	*Fairnilee	4½
..	51	4½	***Selkirk**	
(1)	(2)	(3)	(4)	(5)

An asterisk * printed before a place name denotes that the place is described in the gazetteer.

A dagger † indicates an alternative route given at the end of the itinerary.

'By-pass' in brackets after a place name means that there is a choice of routes, either through the town or avoiding it. The alternative routes can be seen on the town plans or on the atlas at the end of the book.

'Ferry.' For details of ferries listed in the itineraries, see page 284.

(5) The right-hand mileage column shows the distances from all places on the route to the finishing point of the itinerary. When using the itinerary in the reverse direction, it shows the distance from the starting point (bottom) to all places on the route.

ITINERARIES

An example showing how to read an itinerary is given on the opposite page

To Select a Route

Consult the Key Maps between pages 40 and 41, or—for longer journeys—refer to the Through Route Maps on pages 43-49. The numbers on these maps are those of the itineraries—they are *not* book pages or road numbers. The topographical descriptions given at the beginning of each itinerary include notes on the selection of alternative routes. See also ' Touring in Scotland ' and map (pages 28-29).

Mileages

The distances on the mileage chart are all assessed over the shortest practicable route, including ferries, to the centres of the towns concerned. The shortest distance is a matter of fact, but the best route is a matter of opinion, therefore the AA recommended route is not necessarily the shortest route.

1. EDINBURGH to BERWICK-UPON-TWEED for NEWCASTLE UPON TYNE. A pleasant, easy route following the Great North Road, with coast scenery between Broxburn and Cockburnspath and again between Ayton and Berwick. A stone near Broxburn commemorates the battle of Dunbar. A quicker route to Newcastle is given in Iter 5. If proceeding beyond Newcastle the City may be avoided by using A108 and Tyne Tunnel.

A1			***Edinburgh**	56¾
..	5¾	5¾	*Musselburgh	51
..	10	4¼	*Tranent	46¾
..	11¾	1¾	Macmerry	45
..	13¼	1½	Gladsmuir	43½
..	16½	3¼	*Haddington (By-pass)	40¼
..	22	5½	*East Linton (By-pass)	34¾
..	28½	6½	*Broxburn	28¼
..	35½	7	*Cockburnspath	21¼
..	40¼	4¾	*Grantshouse	16½
..	48¾	8½	*Ayton	8
..	53¾	5	*Lamberton Toll (The Border)	3
..	56¾	3	***Berwick-upon-Tweed**	
			Thence by A1:	
..	119½	62¾	Newcastle upon Tyne	

2. EDINBURGH to BERWICK-UPON-TWEED via the Coast. A coastal route for the greater part, and passes through the golfing district and seaside resorts of East Lothian. *Cockenzie and *Port Seton can be visited by following B1348 between Musselburgh and Aberlady, whilst *Portobello may be included by leaving Edinburgh by A1140, thence by A199 to Musselburgh. On leaving the Great North Road this route skirts the battlefield of Prestonpans, and passes *Seton Castle to reach the coast by *Gosford Bay. After North Berwick there is a fine view of the *Bass Rock from Canty Bay, while just beyond are the ruins of *Tantallon Castle. After Dunbar, a stone is passed near Broxburn commemorating the battle of Dunbar, and beyond Cockburnspath, a detour is made to visit the fine cliff scenery in the vicinity of St Abb's.

A1			***Edinburgh**	69¾
..	5¾	5¾	*Musselburgh	64
A198	7¾	2	Junc A1/A198	62
..	9¼	1½	*Prestonpans	60½
..	12¾	3½	*Longniddry	57
..	16	3¼	*Aberlady	53¾
..	18¾	2¾	*Gullane	51
..	19¼	½	*Muirfield	50½
..	21	1¾	*Dirleton	48¾
..	23½	2½	***North Berwick**	46¼
..	29	5½	*Whitekirk	40¾
..	30¾	1¾	*Tynninghame	39
A1	31¾	1	Junc A198/A1	38
A1087	33½	1¾	Junc A1/A1087	36¼
..	34¼	¾	West Barns	35½
..	35	¾	Belhaven	34¾
..	36	1	***Dunbar**	33¾
A1	37½	1½	*Broxburn	32¼
..	44½	7	*Cockburnspath	25¼
A1107	45¾	1¼	Junc A1/A1107	24
B6438	54½	8¾	*Coldingham	15¼
..	56¼	1¾	*St Abb's	13½
			Return to:	
A1107	58	1¾	*Coldingham	11¾
..	61	3	*Eyemouth	8¾
..	63½	2½	*Burnmouth	6¼
A1	63¾	¼	Junc A1107/A1	6
..	66¾	3	*Lamberton Toll (The Border)	3
..	69¾	3	***Berwick-upon-Tweed**	

3. EDINBURGH to BERWICK-UPON-TWEED via the Lammermuir Hills. An attractive by-road crossing the Lammermuir Hills beyond Gifford. Between Gifford and Cranshaws the road is hilly and narrow in parts, with gradients up to 1 in 6, and includes the crossing of two easy fords between which the road is known as the Hungry Snout. The direct road via Preston (B6355) avoids Duns. 5 miles from Gifford another narrow and hilly road, with a good surface, branches off by way of *Longformacus to Duns. The easiest route between Edinburgh and Duns is by Greenlaw, Iter 5 and 33, and the quickest to Berwick is by Iter 1.

A1			***Edinburgh**	57
..	5¾	5¾	*Musselburgh	51¼
B6371	10	4¼	*Tranent	47
B6355	10½	½	Junc B6371/B6355	46½
..	11¾	1¼	*Winton	45¼
..	13¾	2	*Pencaitland	43¼
..	16	2¼	*East Saltoun	41
..	19¾	3¾	*Gifford	37¼
..	32	12¼	*Cranshaws	25
..	37¼	5¼	*Burnhouses	19¾
B6365	38	¾	Junc B6355/B6365	19
A6112	40¼	2¼	Junc B6365/A6112	16¾
A6105	41½	1¼	***Duns**	15½
..	52	10½	*Foulden	5
A699	56	4	Junc A6105/A699	1
..	57	1	***Berwick-upon-Tweed**	

4. EDINBURGH to CARTER BAR for NEWCASTLE UPON TYNE. A pleasant, easy run through agricultural and moorland country, with fine open views to the north from the summit of Soutra Hill (1,131 feet), followed by a gradual descent through Lauderdale to cross the River Tweed at Leaderfoot Bridge, with the Eildon Hills to the west. After Jedburgh, *Ferniehirst Castle is passed, and there are extensive views to the north on the ascent approaching the summit at Carter Bar (1,371 feet) on the Cheviot ridge, where the Border is crossed into England. Owing to the high altitudes and undulating open roads it is advisable to use the route via Newcastle to Scotch Corner during the winter months (see Iters 1 and 5).

A7			***Edinburgh**	58½
	4¼	4¼	*Gilmerton	54¼
A6106	6	1¾	Junc A7/A6106	52½
A68	6¼	¼	Junc A6106/A68	52¼
..	7	¾	***Dalkeith**	51½
..	12¼	5¼	*Pathhead	46¼
..	15½	3¼	*Blackshields	43
..	18½	3	*Soutra Hill	40
..	22¾	4¼	*Carfraemill	35¾
..	26¾	4	*Lauder	31¾
..	33¾	7	*Earlston	24¾
..	38½	4¾	*Newtown St Boswells	20
..	39½	1	*St Boswells Green	19
..	44	5½	*Ancrum Bridge	13¾
..	48	3½	***Jedburgh**	10½
..	58½	10½	*Carter Bar (The Border)	
			Thence by A68 and A696 to:	
..	105¾	47¼	Newcastle upon Tyne	
			OR	
			A68 and A1(M):	
..	142	83½	Scotch Corner A1	
..	378	236	London	

5. EDINBURGH to WOOLER for NEWCASTLE UPON TYNE. Pleasant moorland scenery, with open view to the north from the summit of Soutra Hill (1,131 feet), afterwards descending along the east side of Lauderdale to Greenlaw. The River Tweed is reached at Coldstream, where the Border is crossed into England. A stone to the south of the road between Cornhill and Milfield commemorates the battle of Flodden, and there are views of the Cheviots hereabouts. If proceeding beyond Newcastle the City may be avoided by using A108 and Tyne Tunnel.

A7			***Edinburgh**	62¾
..	4¼	4¼	*Gilmerton	58½
A6106	6	1¾	Junc A7/A6106	56¾
A68	6¼	¼	Junc A6106/A68	56½
..	7	¾	***Dalkeith**	55¾
..	12¼	5¼	*Pathhead	50½
..	15½	3¼	*Blackshiels	47¼
..	18½	3	*Soutra Hill	44¼
A697	22¾	4¼	*Carfraemill	40
..	38	15¼	*Greenlaw	24¾
A698	46¾	8¾	Junc A697/A698	16
..	48¼	1½	*Coldstream	14½
A697	49½	1¼	Cornhill	13¼
..	56¾	7¼	Milfield	6
..	59¾	3	Akeld	3
..	62¾	3	Wooler	
			Thence by A697 and A1 to:	
..	108½	45¾	Newcastle upon Tyne	

6. EDINBURGH to WOOLER via Kelso. After Carfraemill, the road gradually descends along the east side of Lauderdale, with moorland and agricultural scenery, and passes close to *Mellerstain House before reaching the Tweed valley at Kelso. A pleasant, hilly by-road is then followed skirting the *Cheviot Hills, and the Border is crossed into England before reaching Mindrum Mill. The main road via Greenlaw is given in Iter. 5, whilst a better route between Kelso and Wooler is via Coldstream, see Iter 32.

			***Edinburgh**	64½
			By Iter 4 to:	
A697	22¾	22¾	*Carfraemill	41½
A6089	40¼	7½	Junc A697/A6089	34
..	35	4¾	*Gordon	29½
..	39½	4½	*Nenthorn	24¾
A698	43¼	3¾	***Kelso**	21
B6352	44	¾	Junc A698/B6352	20¼
..	44¼	¼	Maxwellheugh	20
B6396	45½	1¼	Junc B6352/B6396	18¾
B6352	53	7½	Mindrum Mill	11¼
B6351	55½	2½	Junc B6352/B6351	8¾
..	58½	3	Kirknewton	5¾
A697	61¼	2¾	Akeld	3
..	64¼	3	Wooler	

7. EDINBURGH to WOOLER via Smailholm and Yetholm. This forms a pleasant winding, but less hilly alternative to Iter 6 between Carfraemill and Kelso, passing near *Mellerstain House before Smailholm. After Kelso, a detour through Yetholm passes along the foothills of the *Cheviots, the Border being crossed into England between Yetholm and Mindrum Mill. The quickest way from Kelso to Wooler is by Coldstream (Iter 32), whilst the best road from Edinburgh to Wooler is by Iter 5.

			***Edinburgh**	69¼
			By Iter 4 to:	
A6105	33¾	33¾	*Earlston	35½
B6397	35	1¼	Junc A6015/B6397	34¼
..	39¾	4¾	*Smailholm	29½
A6089	44¼	4½	Junc B6397/A6089	25
A698	46	1¾	***Kelso**	23¼
B6352	46¾	¾	Junc A698/B6352	22½
..	47	¼	Maxwellheugh	22¼
..	53¾	6¾	*Yetholm	15½
..	58	4¼	Mindrum Mill	11¼
B6351	60½	2½	Junc B6352/B6351	8¾
..	63½	3	Kirknewton	5¾
A697	66¼	2¾	Akeld	3
	69¼	3	Wooler	

8. EDINBURGH to BERWICK-UPON-TWEED via Greenlaw. An alternative to the main road given in Iter 1. Beyond Carfraemill traverses the east side of Lauderdale through pleasant moorland country to Greenlaw, thence undulating agricultural districts.

			***Edinburgh**	58¼
			By Iter 4 to:	
A697	22¾	22¾	*Carfraemill	35½
..	38	15¼	*Greenlaw	20¼
B6460	39½	1½	Junc A697/B6460	18¾
..	42¾	4¼	Fogorig ..	15½
..	44¾	2	Mount Pleasant X-rds ..	13½
..	53½	8¾	*Paxton	4¾
A699	53¾	¼	Junc B6460/A699	4½
..	58¼	4½	***Berwick-upon-Tweed**	

9. EDINBURGH to BERWICK-UPON-TWEED via Stow. A pleasant touring route utilising by-roads on the middle part. At Eskbank, a short detour can be made past *Newbattle Abbey, afterwards rejoining the winding road across the moors to Stow, where there is an ascent of 1 in 8 from the main road. Hilly, cross country moorland roads are then followed to Duns, after which the country is flat and rural. The quickest way from A697 to Duns is by Greenlaw (Iters 8 and 33).

A7			***Edinburgh**	64½
..	4¼	4¼	*Gilmerton	60¼
..	6½	2¼	*Eskbank	58
..	11¼	4¾	*Fushiebridge	53¼
..	12¼	1	*Middleton	52¼
..	17	4¾	*Heriot ..	47½
B6362	25¼	8¼	*Stow ..	39¼
A68	30½	5¼	Junc B6362/A68	34
..	30¾	¼	*Lauder ..	33¾
A697	31¼	½	Junc A68/A697	33¼
B6456	36	4¾	Junc A697/B6456	28½
..	38½	2½	*Westruther	26
A6105	46	7½	Junc B6456/A6105	18½
..	49	3	***Duns** ..	15½
..	59½	10½	*Foulden	5
A699	63½	4	Junc A6105/A699	1
..	64½	1	***Berwick-upon-Tweed**	

10. EDINBURGH to CARLISLE. via Moffat. At first through agricultural districts, with views of the Pentland Hills, until beyond Broughton, where lonely moorland country is traversed. Near the summit, between Tweedsmuir and Moffat, is the source of the River Tweed, and shortly afterwards the famous *Devil's Beef Tub is passed on the descent into Annandale. A pleasant, undulating road through picturesque scenery then leads to the Border, which is crossed into England at Sark Bridge. The best route to Carlisle is via Abington (Iters 25 and 51).

A7			***Edinburgh**	93
A701	2¼	2¼	Junc A7/A701 ..	90¾
..	3	¾	*Liberton ..	90
..	6½	3½	*Bilston ..	86½
..	8	1½	*Milton Bridge ..	85
..	8½	½	*Glencorse ..	84½
..	10	1½	*Penicuik ..	83
..	13¼	3¼	*Leadburn ..	79¾
..	15½	2¼	*Lamancha ..	77½
..	20	4½	*Romanno Bridge	73
A72	22½	2½	*Blyth Bridge ..	70½
A701	25¾	3¼	Junc A72/A701 ..	67¼
..	28¾	3	*Broughton ..	64¼
..	35¾	7	*Crook Inn ..	57¼
..	37	1¼	*Tweedsmuir ..	56
..	52¼	15¼	***Moffat**	40¾
A74	53¾	1½	Junc A701/A74 ..	39¼
..	54¼	½	*Beattock Bypass ..	38¾
..	61	6¾	*Johnstone Bridge	32
..	68¼	7¼	*Lockerbie Bypass ..	24¾
..	74	5¾	*Ecclefechan Bypass ..	19
..	77½	3½	*Kirtlebridge Bypass ..	15¾
..	80¼	3	*Kirkpatrick Fleming ..	12¾
..	83½	3¼	*Gretna Green ..	9½
..	84	½	*Gretna ..	9
..	84¼	¼	*Sark Bridge (The Border) ..	8¾
A7	90½	6¼	†Junc A74/M6/A7	2½
	93	2½	Carlisle	
			†Thence by: M6 Motorway M61 Motorway	
	212	119	Manchester	
			† OR M6 Motorway M1 Motorway	
	404	311	London	

11. EDINBURGH to CARLISLE via Selkirk. At Eskbank, a short detour can be made past *Newbattle Abbey, afterwards rejoining the winding main road across the moorlands to Galashiels. Becoming rather hilly between Selkirk and Hawick, followed by a fine scenic run through Teviotdale to Langholm in Eskdale. This is a pleasant, but slower alternative to the recommended route given in Iter 10. A detour to include the many places of interest adjacent to the road is shown in Iter 13.

A7			***Edinburgh** ..	94
..	4¼	4¼	*Gilmerton ..	89¾
..	6½	2¼	*Eskbank ..	87½
..	11¼	4¾	*Fushiebridge ..	82¾
..	12¼	1	*Middleton ..	81¾
..	17	4¾	*Heriot ..	77
..	25¼	8¼	*Stow	86¾
..	29	3¾	*Bowland ..	65
..	33¼	4¼	***Galashiels** ..	60¾
..	39	5¾	***Selkirk**	55
..	44½	5½	Ashkirk	49½
..	50¾	6¼	***Hawick**	43¼
..	55¼	4½	Newmill	38¾
..	59½	4¼	*Teviothead ..	34½
..	63¼	3¾	Mosspaul Hotel	30¾
..	69¼	6	*Ewes PO ..	24¾
..	73½	4¼	*Langholm ..	20½
..	79¾	6¼	*Canonbie ..	14¼
..	82	2¼	The Border ..	12
..	85½	3½	Longtown ..	8¾
..	91½	6¼	Junc A7/M6 ..	2½
..	94	2½	Carlisle	

12. EDINBURGH to CARLISLE via the Moorfoot Hills and Ettrick Forest. An attractive by-road to Langholm through moorland country, narrow in places, but with a good surface. At Eskbank, a short detour can be made past *Newbattle Abbey, afterwards rejoining the main road. Beyond Middleton, a secondary road is followed over the Moorfoot Hills to Innerleithen. There is an alternative valley road (B709) leaving A7 farther south at Heriot Station. Between Traquair and Gordon Arms this is known as the Paddy Slacks road. The descent through Ettrick Forest to Yarrow Water is followed by another climb to reach the Ettrick valley, and the road then descends the Tima valley to cross the ridge into Eskdale, where the Thomas Telford memorial is passed before reaching Bentpath. A pleasant run through wooded country then follows until the Border is crossed into England between Canonbie and Longtown. In general this is a hilly route without any serious gradients.

A7			***Edinburgh** ..	93¼
..	4¼	4¼	*Gilmerton ..	89
..	6½	2¼	*Eskbank ..	86¾
..	11¼	4¾	*Fushiebridge ..	82
..	12¼	1	*Middleton ..	81
B7007	13¼	1	Junc A7/B7007 ..	80
B709	19¼	6	Junc B7007/B709	74
..	29	9¾	*Innerleithen ..	64¼
..	30½	1½	*Traquair ..	62¾
..	37½	7	*Gordon Arms Hotel	55¾
..	44	6½	*Tushielaw Inn	49¼
..	46¾	2¾	*Ettrick ..	46½
..	59¼	12½	*Eskdalemuir Ch	34
..	67	7¾	Bentpath ..	26¼
A7	72¾	5¾	*Langholm ..	20½
..	79	6¼	*Canonbie ..	14¼
..	81¼	2¼	The Border ..	12
..	84½	3¼	Longtown ..	8¾
..	93¼	6¼	Junc A7/M6 ..	2½
..	93¼	2½	Carlisle	

13. EDINBURGH to CARLISLE via the Scott Country and Yarrow Vale. A touring route in the Lowlands through mainly agricultural and moorland districts and including places of interest in the *Scott Country. From the summit of Soutra Hill (1,131 feet) there are fine open views to the north, and after a gradual descent through Lauderdale to Earlston, the main road is left to visit Bemersyde and Dryburgh Abbey. On returning to the main road at St Boswells, the Eildon Hills are encircled by way of Melrose and Abbotsford House. A short detour can be made to include the old-world village of *Newstead between St Boswells and Melrose, and on leaving the town another detour would include *Darnick Tower. Beyond Selkirk, the road ascends the picturesque Yarrow Vale, which is well wooded on the earlier part. Crosses the moorlands of Ettrick Forest and then passes the delightful *St Mary's Loch, to reach the summit at Birkhill (1,105 feet). Descends past the Grey Mare's Tail waterfall (on rt) to Moffat, then by a pleasant, undulating road in Annandale to cross the Border into England at Sark Bridge.

A7			***Edinburgh** ..	129¼
..	4¼	4¼	*Gilmerton ..	125
A6106	6	1¾	Junc A7/A6106 ..	123¼
A68	6¼	¼	Junc A6106/A68	123
..	7	¾	***Dalkeith** ..	122¼
..	12¼	5¼	*Pathhead ..	117
..	15½	3¼	*Blackshiels ..	113¾
..	18½	3	*Soutra Hill ..	110¾
..	22¾	4¼	*Carfraemill ..	106½
..	26¾	4	*Lauder ..	102½
A6105	33¾	7	*Earlston ..	95½
B6356	34	¼	Junc A6105/B6356 ..	95¼
..	37¼	3¼	*Bemersyde Hill	92
..	38	¾	*Bemersyde House ..	91¼
..	39½	1½	*Dryburgh Abbey	89¾
B6404	41½	2	Junc B6356/B6404 ..	87¾
..	43	1½	*St Boswells ..	86¼
A68	43¼	¼	Junc B6404/A68	86
..	44¼	1	*Newtown St Boswells ..	85
A6091	4¾	½	Junc A68/A6091	84½
..	47	2¼	***Melrose**	82¼
B6360	48½	1½	Junc A6091/B6360 ..	80¾
..	50	1½	*Abbotsford House	79¼
A7	52¼	2¼	Junc B6360/A7	77
A707	54½	2¼	***Selkirk** ..	74¾
A708	55	½	Junc A707/A708	74¼
..	59	4	*Broadmeadows	70¼
..	63	4	*Yarrow Ch ..	66¼
..	67	4	*Gordon Arms Hotel	62¼
..	72¼	5¼	*Rodono Hotel	57
..	73¼	1	*Tibbie Shiel's Inn	56
..	77¼	4	*Birkhill ..	52
..	78½	1¼	*Grey Mare's Tail	50¾
A701	88½	10	***Moffat**	40¾
A74	90	1½	Junc A701/A74 ..	39¼
..	90½	½	*Beattock Bypass ..	38¾
..	97¼	6¾	*Johnstone Bridge	32
..	104½	7¼	*Lockerbie Bypass ..	24¾
..	110¼	5¾	*Ecclefechan Bypass.. ..	19
..	113½	3¼	*Kirtlebridge Bypass.. ..	15¾
..	116½	3	*Kirkpatrick Fleming By pass	12¾
..	119¾	3¼	*Gretna Green ..	9½

..	120½	½	*Gretna	9
..	120½	¼	*Sark Bridge (The Border)	8¾
A7	126¾	6¼	Junc A74/M6/A7	2½
..	129¼	2½	Carlisle	

14. EDINBURGH to SELKIRK via Peebles. From Edinburgh to Leadburn shows alternative roads to the main route given in Iter 10. Agricultural at first, with views of the Pentland Hills, followed by moor and woodlands to Lyne, from where there is a pretty, undulating road along the Tweed valley. The direct route to Peebles is by Iter 24 and to Selkirk by Iter 11.

A702			***Edinburgh**	51
..	4¼	4¼	*Fairmilehead	46¾
A703	5¼	1	*Hillend	45¾
A701	7¼	2	Junc A703/A701	43¾
B7026	8	¾	Junc A701/B7026	43
..	8½	½	*Auchendinny	42½
A6094	11	2½	*Howgate	40
A701	12¾	1¾	*Leadburn	38¼
..	15	2¼	*Lamancha	36
B7059	19½	4½	*Romanno Bridge	31½
A72	23	3½	Junc B7059/A72	28
..	25¾	2¾	*Lyne Ch	25¼
..	30	4¼	***Peebles**	21
..	36½	6½	*Innerleithen	14½
..	38½	2	*Walkerburn	12½
A707	43½	5	Junc A72/A707	7½
..	44¾	1¼	*Caddonfoot	6¼
..	46½	1¾	*Fairnilee	4½
..	51	4½	***Selkirk**	

15. EDINBURGH to GLASGOW. A fast, industrial road linking the two cities, with no scenic interest. The mast of the BBC Kirk O'Shotts television transmitter is beside the road near Harthill Service Area.

A8			***Edinburgh**	45
..	4¼	4¼	*Corstorphine	40¾
..	6	1¾	*Gogar	39
M8	8½	2½	Junc A8/M8	36½
..	14¼	5¾	Junc for *Livingston	30¾
..	24¾	10½	*Harthill Service Area	20¼
A8	32	7¼	Junc M8/A8	13
..	45	13	***Glasgow**	

16. EDINBURGH to GLASGOW via Airdrie. An industrial road with no special features of interest. See Iter 15 for the main road avoiding the towns.

A8			***Edinburgh**	45
..	4¼	4¼	*Corstorphine	40¾
..	6	1¾	*Gogar	39
A89	8½	2½	Junc A8/A89	36½
..	9	½	*Newbridge	36
..	11¾	2¾	*Broxburn	33¼
..	13	1¼	*Uphall	32
..	14¾	1¾	Dechmont	30¼
..	19½	4¾	*Bathgate	25½
..	21¾	2¼	*Armadale	23¼
..	29½	7¾	*Caldercruix	15½
..	33½	4	***Airdrie**	11½
..	35½	2	***Coatbridge**	9½
..	38¾	3¼	*Baillieston	6¼
..	41¼	2½	*Shettleston	3¾
..	45	3¾	***Glasgow**	

17. EDINBURGH to GLASGOW via Bo'ness and Falkirk. At first a pleasant, easy road with views across the Forth estuary to Fife. Becomes industrial beyond Grangemouth, the latter part being mainly a commercial route through agricultural and mining districts. For the direct road to Falkirk see Iter 95 and for Glasgow Iter 15. Some places of interest near the south bank of the River Forth are visited in Iter 96.

A90			***Edinburgh**	49
..	2½	2½	Blackhall	46½
..	4½	2	*Barnton	44½
..	5	½	*Cramond Bridge	44
A904	8¾	3¾	Junc A90/A904	40¼
..	10¾	2	Newton	38¼
..	18	7¼	*Bo'ness	31
..	23	5	*Grangemouth	26
A9	26¼	3¼	***Falkirk**	22¾
A803	27¼	1	*Camelon	21¾
..	30¼	3	*Bonnybridge	18¾
..	31¾	1½	*Dennyloanhead	17¼
A80	32½	¾	Junc A803/A80	16½
..	33¼	¾	*Castlecary	15¾
..	35	1¾	*Cumbernauld Bypass	14
..	38	3	Condorrat	11
..	39½	1½	Mollinburn	9½
..	42	2½	*Muirhead	7
..	43¾	1¾	*Stepps	5¼
..	44½	¾	Millerston	4½
..	49	4½	***Glasgow**	

18. EDINBURGH to PAISLEY via Mid Calder. Mainly industrial, until joining the main Edinburgh-Glasgow road near Whitburn. The mast of the BBC Kirk O'Shotts television transmitter is beside the road between Harthill and Salsburgh. Avoids Glasgow, but there are built-up areas beyond Newhouse and the route is complicated.

A71			***Edinburgh**	55¼
..	5½	5½	*Hermiston	49¾
..	11¾	6¼	*East Calder	43½
A705	12½	¾	*Mid Calder	42¾
..	15	2½	*Livingston	40¼
..	18¼	3¼	Blackburn	36¾
A706,	21	2¾	*Whitburn	34¼
A8	21½	½	Junc A705/A8	33¾
..	23½	2	*Harthill	31¾
..	29	5½	Salsburgh	26¼
A775	31¾	2¾	Newhouse	23½
..	33¾	2	*Holytown	21½
..	35	1¼	Mossend	20¼
A725	35¾	¾	*Bellshill	19½
B7012	37¾	2	*Bothwell Bridge	17½
A776	39½	1¾	Junc B7012/A776	15¾
..	39¾	¼	*High Blantyre	15½
A749	42½	2¾	Junc A776/A749	12¾
A726	43¼	¾	*East Kilbride	12
..	47	3¾	Busby	8¼
	47¾	¾	*Clarkston	7½
..	49	1¼	*Giffnock	6¼
..	51¾	2¾	Nitshill	3½
..	55¼	3½	***Paisley**	

19. EDINBURGH to TROON via Motherwell. Agricultural on the earlier part, with mining districts on the moors to Newmains, and becoming industrial approaching the Clyde valley. After East Kilbride, Eaglesham Moor is crossed, and beyond Kilmarnock passes through flat agricultural country. Through traffic can avoid the centre of Motherwell by following road B754. The fastest road from Edinburgh to Motherwell is via M8 and A723, and Hamilton and East Kilbride via M8, A8 and A725. The recommended route between Edinburgh and Kilmarnock is by Strathaven, see Iters 20 and 69.

A71			***Edinburgh**	72¼
..	5½	5½	*Hermiston	66¾
..	11¾	6¼	*East Calder	60½
..	12½	¾	*Mid Calder	59¾
..	15	2½	Bellsquarry	57¼
..	17¼	2¼	*West Calder	55
A722	30¾	13½	***Newmains**	41½
A721	32¾	2	*Wishaw	39½
A723	36¼	3½	***Motherwell**	36
A724	38½	2¼	***Hamilton**	33¾
A776	40	1½	Burnbank	32¼
..	40¾	¾	*High Blantyre	31½
A749	43½	2¾	Junc A776/A749	28¾
A726	44¼	¾	*East Kilbride	28
B764	45¼	1	Junc A726/B764	27
..	48¾	3½	*Eaglesham	23½
A77	54¾	6	Junc B764/A77	17½
..	57¾	3	*Fenwick Bypass	14½
A759	62	4¼	***Kilmarnock**	10¼
A78	68¾	6¾	Junc A759/A78	3½
A759	70¼	1½	*Loans	2
..	72¼	2	***Troon**	

20. EDINBURGH to AYR. Agricultural then mining districts to Strathaven, afterwards becoming mainly agricultural. See Iter 21 for an alternative summer route with greater scenic interest.

A71			***Edinburgh**	73¼
..	5½	5½	*Hermiston	67¾
..	11¾	6¼	*East Calder	61½
..	12½	¾	*Mid Calder	60¾
..	15	2½	Bellsquarry	58¼
..	17¼	2¼	*West Calder	56
A73	30¾	13½	***Newmains**	42½

A71	31¼	½	Junc A73/A71	42
..	33¼	2	Overtown	40
..	39	1¾	Stonehouse	34¼
		4	Junc with M74	36
..	43	4	***Strathaven**	30¼
..	48¾	5¾	*Drumclog	24½
..	52	3¼	*Loudounhill	21¼
..	54	2	*Darvel	19¼
..	55¾	1¾	*Newmilns	17½
A719	58¼	2½	*Galston	15
..	71¼	13	Whitletts	2
..	73¼	2	***Ayr**	

21. EDINBURGH to AYR via Cumnock. A fine, open moorland road to Carnwath, skirting the Pentland Hills on the line of the old drove road known as the Lang Whang. Traverses rural country to Cumnock, where there is some mining. Mainly agricultural on the latter part. With fewer restricted areas than in the previous route, this makes a pleasant summer run, but during winter months the Strathaven route (Iter 20) is to be preferred.

A70			***Edinburgh**	77¼
..	6½	6½	*Currie	70¾
..	14	7½	*Causewayend	63¼
..	26	12	*Carnwath	51¼
..	28¾	2¾	*Carstairs	48½
..	32¼	3½	*Hyndford Bridge	45
..	37½	5¼	Rigside	39¾
..	39½	2	Junc with A74	37¾
..	41½	2	*Douglas	35¾
..	51¾	10¼	*Muirkirk	25½
..	59½	7¾	*Lugar	17¾
..	61½	2	***Cumnock**	15¾
..	65¾	4¼	*Ochiltree	11½
..	71¾	6	*Coylton	5½
..	77¼	5½	***Ayr**	

22. EDINBURGH to LANARK. Mainly agricultural to West Calder, thence a fine moorland road. During the summer months the more scenic route via Carnwath (Iter 23) may be preferred, but otherwise there is little to choose.

A71			***Edinburgh**	33½
..	5½	5½	*Hermiston	28
..	11¾	6¼	*East Calder	21¾
..	12½	¾	*Mid Calder	21
..	15	2½	Bellsquarry	18½
..	17¼	2¼	*West Calder	16¼
A704	18¼	1	Junc A71/A704	15¼
A706	22¼	4	Junc A704/A706	11¼
..	24½	2¼	*Wilsontown	9
..	25¼	¾	Forth	8¼
..	33½	8¼	***Lanark**	

23. EDINBURGH to LANARK via Carnwath. A fine, open moorland run to Carnwath, skirting the Pentland Hills along the line of the old drove road known as the Lang Whang. The alternative given in Iter 22 is a slightly easier road.

A70			***Edinburgh**	32¾
..	6½	6½	*Currie	26¼
..	14	7½	*Causewayend	18¾
..	26	12	*Carnwath	6¾
..	28¾	2¾	*Carstairs	4
A743	29¾	1	Junc A70/A743	3
..	32¾	3	***Lanark**	

24. EDINBURGH to DUMFRIES via Peebles. Pleasant agricultural country, with views of the Pentland Hills to Leadburn, followed by moorland scenery and becoming wooded in the Tweed valley after Peebles. Near the summit between Tweedsmuir and Moffat is the source of the Tweed, and shortly afterwards the famous *Devil's Beef Tub is passed on the descent to Annandale, where the country becomes wooded and agricultural. See Iter 10 for the direct road to Moffat.

A7			***Edinburgh**	77
A701	2¼	2¼	Junc A7/A701	74¾
..	3	¾	*Liberton	74
..	6½	3½	*Bilston	70½
..	8	1½	*Milton Bridge	69
..	8½	½	*Glencorse	68½
..	10	1½	*Penicuik	67
A703	13¼	3¼	*Leadburn	63¾
..	18½	5¼	*Eddleston	58½
A72	23	4½	***Peebles**	54
Uncl	26	3	Junc A72/Uncl	51
B712	27	1	Junc Uncl/B712	50
..	29¾	2¾	*Stobo	47¼
..	32½	2¾	*Drumelzier	44½
A701	34	1½	Junc B712/A701	43
..	39½	5½	*Crook Inn	37½
..	40¾	1¼	*Tweedsmuir	36¼
..	56	15¼	***Moffat**	21
A74	57½	1½	Junc A701/A74	19½
..	58	½	*Beattock Bypass	19
A701	59	1	Junc A74/A701	18
..	63¾	4¾	*St Ann's	13¼
..	69½	5¾	*Ae Bridge	7½
..	72½	3	*Amisfield	4½
..	73¾	1¼	Locharbriggs	3¼
..	77	3¼	***Dumfries**	

25. EDINBURGH to NEWTON STEWART and STRANRAER. An easy, undulating road to Dolphinton, with views of the Pentland Hills, thence through fine, open country. Follows the Clyde valley from Biggar to Elvanfoot, after which there are extensive views of the Lowther Hills, and reaching an altitude of 1,140 feet before descending through the winding Dalveen Pass. *Durisdeer Church lies to the east of the road before reaching Carronbridge in Nithsdale. Moor and hill scenery in the Galloway district, becoming agricultural beyond Newton Stewart. A quicker route to Stranraer is via Ayr (Iters 20 and 55).

A702			***Edinburgh**	129¼
..	4¼	4¼	*Fairmilehead	125
..	5¼	1	*Hillend	124
..	10½	5¼	*Silverburn	118¾
..	12¾	2¼	Nine Mile Burn	116½
..	14¼	1½	*Carlops	115
..	17	2¾	*West Linton	112¼
..	20¾	3¾	*Dolphinton	108½
A72	27½	6¾	Junc A702/A72	101¾
..	28½	1	*Biggar	100¾
A702	29½	1	Junc A72/A702	99¾
..	31¼	1¾	*Culter	98
..	34½	3¼	*Lamington	94¾
A73	39	4½	Junc A702/A73	90¼
A74	40¾	1¾	***Abington** Bypass	88½
..	44	3¼	*Crawford Bypass	85¼
A702	45½	1½	Junc A74/A702	83¾
..	46½	1	*Elvanfoot	82¾
A76	61¾	15¼	*Carronbridge	67½
B732	62¾	1	Junc A76/B732	66½
A702	63½	¾	Junc B732/A702	65¾
..	64¼	¾	Burnhead	65
..	65½	1¼	*Penpont	63¾
..	69¾	4¼	*Kirkland	59½
..	71¾	2	*Moniaive	57½
A769	82¾	11	Bogue Toll	46½
A712	84½	1¾	Junc A769/A712	44¾
..	85	½	Ken Br	44¼
..	85¾	¾	*New Galloway	43½
..	92¼	6½	*Clatteringshaws Dam	37
A75	103	10¾	Junc A712/A715	26¼
..	104¼	1¼	***Newton Stewart**	25
..	119½	15¼	*Glenluce	9¾
..	123	3½	Dunragit	6¼
..	126	3	*Castle Kennedy	3¼
..	129¼	3¼	***Stranraer**	

26. CARLISLE to STRANRAER. The main road to Galloway, crossing the Border at Sark Bridge. Pleasant agricultural and moorland country is traversed, with coastal scenery between Gatehouse of Fleet and Creetown.

A7			Carlisle	108¾
A74	2¼	2¼	Junc A7/M6/A74	106¼
..	8¾	6¼	*Sark Bridge (The Border)	100
A75	9	¼	*Gretna	99¾
..	11	2	Rigg	97¾
..	14	3	Eastriggs	94¾
..	14¾	¾	*Dornock	94
..	17¼	2½	*Annan	91½
..	29¼	12	Collin	79½
..	32¾	3½	***Dumfries**	76
..	42¼	9½	*Crocketford	66½
..	44½	2¼	Springholm	64¼
..	50¾	6¼	*Castle Douglas	58
..	56¼	5½	*Ringford	52½
..	59½	2¾	*Twynholm	49½
..	65¼	6	*Gatehouse of Fleet	43½
..	77¼	12	*Creetown	31½
..	80½	3¼	*Palnure	28¼
..	83¾	3¼	*Newton Stewart	25
..	99	15¼	*Glenluce	9¾

..	102½	3½	Dunragit	6¼
..	105½	3	***Castle Kennedy**	3¼
..	108¾	3¼	***Stranraer**	

27. CARLISLE to AYR. After crossing the Border at Sark Bridge, passes through pleasant agricultural country to Dumfries, where a short detour can be made to visit *Lincluden Abbey. Traverses the pretty Nith valley to Sanquhar, with mining in places towards Cumnock, but becoming mainly agricultural again on the latter part. Dumfries, Auldgirth and **Ayr** have associations with the poet **Burns.** A better route is via A74 and A70 (Iters 50 and 21).

A7			Carlisle	92
A74	2½	2½	Junc A7/M6/A74	89½
..	8¾	6¼	*Sark Bridge (The Border)	83¼
A75	9	¼	*Gretna	83
..	11	2	Rigg	81
..	14	3	Eastriggs	78
..	14¾	¾	*Dornock	77¼
..	17¼	2½	*Annan	74¾
..	29¼	12	Collin	62¾
A76	32¾	3½	***Dumfries**	59¼
..	35½	2¾	*New Bridge	56½
..	40½	5	*Auldgirth	51½
..	45	4½	*Closeburn	47
..	47¼	2¼	*Thornhill	44¾
..	49	1¾	*Carronbridge	43
..	53	4	*Enterkinfoot	39
..	57¼	4¼	*Mennock	34¾
..	59½	2¼	*Sanquhar	32½
..	63	3½	*Kirkconnel	29
..	70¾	7¾	*New Cumnock	21¼
A70	76¼	5½	***Cumnock**	15¾
..	80½	4¼	*Ochiltree	11½
..	86½	6	*Coylton	5½
..	92	5½	***Ayr**	

28. CARLISLE to DUMFRIES via the Coast. After crossing the Border at Sark Bridge, this forms an interesting alternative to the main road (Iter 26) and is mainly through flat country close to the Solway Firth. Between Cummertrees and Bankend, a short detour can be made to visit *Ruthwell Church, which lies north-east of the junction of roads B724 and B725, from which point the direct road to Dumfries is given in Iter 47. There is also a direct unclassified road from Bankend to Dumfries.

A7			Carlisle	39¼
A74	2½	2½	Junc A7/M6/A74	36¾
..	8¾	6¼	*Sark Br (Border)	30½
A75	9	¼	*Gretna	30¼
..	11	2	Rigg	28¼
..	14	3	Eastriggs	25¼
..	14¾	¾	*Dornock	24½
..	17¼	2½	*Annan	22
B724	17¾	½	Junc A75/B724	21½
..	20¾	3	*Cummertrees	18½
B725	24	3¼	Junc B724/B725	15¼
..	28¾	4¾	*Bankend (for *Caerlaverock Church)	10½
..	30½	1¾	*Caerlaverock (Castle)	8¾
..	34	3½	*Glencaple	5¼
..	39¼	5¼	***Dumfries**	

29. CARLISLE to PAISLEY. Continuous dual-carriageway between Gretna Green and Lesmahagow. After crossing the Border into Scotland at Sark Bridge, there is a fine open run through agricultural country in Annandale, changing to moorland on the gradual ascent over Beattock summit (1,029 feet). Beyond Lesmahagow a mining and industrial district is entered.

A7			Carlisle	103¼
A74	2½	2½	Junc A7/M6/A74	100¾
..	8¾	6¼	*Sark Bridge (The Border)	94½
..	9	¼	*Gretna	94¼
..	9½	½	*Gretna Green	93¾
..	12¾	3¼	*Kirkpatrick Fleming Bypass	90½
..	15¾	3	*Kirtlebridge Bypass	87½
..	19	3¼	*Ecclefechan Bypass	84¼
..	24¾	5¾	*Lockerbie Bypass	78½
..	32	7¼	*Johnstone Bridge	71¼
..	38¾	6¾	*Beattock Bypass	64½
..	49¼	10½	*Beattock Summit	54
..	54¼	5	*Crawford Bypass	49
..	57½	3¼	***Abington** Bypass	45¾
..	72	14½	*Lesmahagow	31¼
A71	77½	5½	Junc A74/A71	25¾
..	79	1½	Stonehouse	24¼
A726	83	4	***Strathaven**	20¼
..	85¾	2¾	Chapelton	17½
..	91¼	5½	*East Kilbride	12
..	95	3¾	Busby	8¼
..	95¾	¾	*Clarkston	7½
..	97	1¼	*Giffnock	6¼
..	99¾	2¾	Nitshill	3½
..	103¼	3½	***Paisley**	

30. CARLISLE to BERWICK-UPON-TWEED. A fine scenic run by the main road through the *Border Country. This route crosses the Border twice, entering Scotland between Longtown and Canonbie, and re-entering England at Cornhill. Open country at first in the Esk valley, then crosses the moors into Teviotdale for Hawick, where the country becomes agricultural. Flat in the Tweed valley beyond Kelso, with views of the *Cheviot Hills.

A7			Carlisle	88
..	2½	2½	Junc A7/M6	85½
..	8¾	6¼	Longtown	79¼
..	12	3¼	The Border	76
..	14¼	2¼	*Canonbie	73¾
..	20½	6¼	*Langholm	67½
..	24¾	4¼	*Ewes PO	63¼
..	30¾	6	Mosspaul Hotel	57¼
..	34½	3¾	*Teviothead	53½
..	38¾	4¼	Newmill	49¼
A698	43¼	4½	***Hawick**	44¾
..	48¼	5	*Denholm	39¾
..	57¼	9	Crailing	30¾
..	59¼	2	*Eckford Church	28¾
..	64¼	5	***Kelso**	23¾
..	69½	5¼	*Birgham	18½
..	73½	4	*Coldstream	14½
..	74¾	1¼	Cornhill	13¼
..	88	13¼	***Berwick-upon-Tweed**	

31. CARLISLE to HAWICK via Newcastleton. Crosses the Border into Scotland between Longtown and Canonbie, with pleasant scenery in *Liddesdale on the earlier part. Traverses moorlands after Newcastleton, 5 miles beyond which *Hermitage Castle lies to the west of the road. This is an alternative to the main road given in Iter 30.

A7			Carlisle	45
..	2½	2½	Junc A7/M6	42½
..	8¾	6¼	Longtown	36¼
..	12	3¼	The Border	33
..	14¼	2¼	*Canonbie	30¾
B6357	14½	¼	Junc A7/B6357	30½
..	15½	1	Rowanburn	29½
..	24½	9	*Newcastleton	20½
B6399	26	1½	Junc B6357/B6399	19
..	37¾	11¾	*Shankend	7¼
..	40¾	3	Stobs Camp (entrance)	4¼
..	45	4¼	***Hawick**	

32. PEEBLES to WOOLER. A scenic road mainly following the Tweed valley. After passing near the Eildon Hills at Melrose, the country is agricultural and becomes less hilly. Approaching Kelso the scanty remains of *Roxburgh Castle are passed, and there is a fine view of *Floors Castle on the north bank of the River Tweed, while at Cornhill the Border is crossed into England. A stone to the south of the road between Cornhill and Milfield commemorates the battle of Flodden. Views of the *Cheviot Hills to the south, on the latter part.

A72			***Peebles**	60¼
..	6½	6½	*Innerleithen	53¾
..	8½	2	*Walkerburn	51¾
..	15	6½	*Clovenfords	45¼
A6091	18½	3½	***Galashiels**	41¾
..	22½	4	***Melrose**	37¾
A68	24¾	2¼	Junc A6091/A68	35½
..	25¼	½	*Newtown St Boswells	35
A699	26¼	1	*St Boswells Green	34
..	28	1¾	*Maxton	32¼
A698	36½	8½	***Kelso**	23¾
..	41¾	5¼	*Birgham	18½
..	45¾	4	*Coldstream	14½
A697	47	1¼	Cornhill	13¼
..	54¼	7¼	Milfield	6
..	57¼	3	Akeld	3
..	60¼	3	Wooler	

33. PEEBLES to BERWICK-UPON-TWEED via Duns. A cross-country route at first along the pleasant Tweed valley to Galashiels, then avoiding Melrose, using narrow, undulating roads in places, to reach Greenlaw. Flat rural country between Duns and Berwick. The recommended route to Berwick is by Coldstream Iter 32 and 30, and the shortest way from Greenlaw to Berwick is by Iter 8.

A72			***Peebles**	59¾
..	6½	6½	*Innerleithen	53¼
..	8½	2	*Walkerburn	51¼
..	15	6½	*Clovenfords	44¾
A6091	18½	3½	***Galashiels**	41¼
B6360	21¼	2¾	Junc A6091/B6360	38½
..	22	¾	Gattonside	37¾
A68	24	2	Junc B6360/A68	35¾
A6105	26½	2½	*Earlston	33¼
..	32¾	6¼	*Gordon	27
..	37¼	4½	*Greenlaw	22½
..	40½	3¼	*Polwarth	19¼
..	44¼	3¾	***Duns**	15½
..	54¾	10½	*Foulden	5
A699	58¾	4	Junc A6105/A699	1
..	59¾	1	***Berwick-upon-Tweed**	

34. PEEBLES to HAWICK via Ettrick Forest. A cross-country moorland route utilizing narrow and hilly roads in places, but with no serious gradients. If preferred, an alternative road (B7062) along the south bank of the wooded River Tweed can be used to Traquair instead of the main road via Innerleithen. Between Traquair and Gordon Arms the route crosses from the Tweed valley to Yarrow Vale in Ettrick Forest and is known as the Paddy Slacks road. The climb over the next ridge to reach the Ettrick valley is followed by a winding moorland road leading to Hawick, in Teviotdale. The main road route is by Selkirk, Iters 14 and 11.

A72			***Peebles**	37¼
B709	6½	6½	*Innerleithen	30¾
..	8	1½	*Traquair	29¼
..	15	7	*Gordon Arms Hotel	22¼
B711	21½	6½	*Tushielaw Inn	15¾
..	24¼	2¾	*Buccleuch	13
..	32¼	8	*Roberton	5
A7	35½	3¼	Junc B711/A7	1¾
..	37¼	1¾	***Hawick**	

35. PEEBLES to AYR via Mauchline. Pleasant moorlands beyond the Lyne valley, and later through agricultural country, with mining developments in places. A better way between Muirkirk and Ayr is by Cumnock, see Iter 21.

A72			***Peebles**	72
..	4¼	4¼	*Lyne Ch	67¾
..	9¾	5½	*Blyth Bridge	62¼
..	15¼	5½	*Skirling	56¾
..	17¾	2½	*Biggar	54¼
..	21¼	3½	*Symington	50¾
A73	22	¾	Junc A72/A73	50
A70	27¾	5¾	*Hyndford Bridge	44¼
..	33	5¼	Rigside	39
..	37	4	*Douglas	35
..	47¼	10¼	*Muirkirk	24¾
B743	49¼	2	Junc A70/B743	22¾
..	56¾	7½	*Sorn	15¼
A758	60¾	4	*Mauchline	11¼
..	63¼	2½	*Failford	8¾
..	68¾	5½	*Auchincruive	3¼
A719	70	1	Whitletts	2
..	72	2	***Ayr**	

36. NORTH BERWICK to HAWICK. A cross-country route to Humbie through the golfing district of East Lothian, with coastal scenery at first. Fine, open views to the north from the summit of Soutra Hill (1,131 feet), then through moorland and agricultural country in Lauderdale. The Eildon Hills are seen to the west after crossing the Tweed at Leaderfoot Bridge, after which an easy road beyond Ancrum Bridge leads through Teviotdale.

A198			***North Berwick**	63½
..	2½	2½	*Dirleton	61
..	4¼	1¾	*Muirfield	59¼
..	4¾	½	*Gullane	58¾
A6137	7½	2¾	*Aberlady	56
..	13	5½	*Haddington	50½
..	16	3	*Bolton	47½
..	22	6	*Humbie (PO)	41½
A68	24½	2½	Junc A6137/A68	39
..	30½	6	*Carfraemill	33
..	34½	4	*Lauder	29
..	41½	7	*Earlston	22
..	46¼	4¾	*Newtown St Boswells	17¼
..	47¼	1	*St Boswells Green	16¼
..	52½	5¼	*Ancrum Bridge	11
A698	52¾	¼	Junc A68/A698	10¾
..	58¼	5¾	*Denholm	5
..	63½	5	***Hawick**	

37. NORTH BERWICK to LANARK via Dalkeith. A cross-country link, at first through the golfing district of East Lothian. Coastal scenery at *Gosford Bay, near Aberlady, then passing *Seton Castle beyond Longniddry and skirting the battlefield of Prestonpans. After Leadburn, mainly agricultural to Lanark. The quickest way is by Edinburgh, Iters 2 and 22.

A198			***North Berwick**	57¼
..	2½	2½	*Dirleton	54¾
..	4¼	1¾	*Muirfield	53
..	4¾	½	*Gullane	52½
..	7½	2¾	*Aberlady	49¾
..	10¾	3¼	*Longniddry	46½
..	14¼	3½	*Prestonpans	43
A6094	15¾	1½	Junc A198/A6094	41½
..	16¼	½	Wallyford	41
..	20¼	4	***Dalkeith**	37
..	20¾	½	*Eskbank	36½
..	22	1¼	*Bonnyrigg	35¼
..	24¼	2¼	Rosewell	33
..	28½	4¼	*Howgate	28¾
A701	30¼	1¾	*Leadburn	27
..	32½	2¼	*Lamancha	24¾
..	37	4½	*Romanno Bridge	20¼
..	39½	2½	*Blyth Bridge	17¾
A721	40¼	¾	Junc A701/A721	17
..	44¼	4	Elsrickle	13
..	48¼	4	*Newbigging	9
A70	50½	2¼	*Carnwath	6¾
..	53¼	2¾	*Carstairs	4
A743	54¼	1	Junc A70/A743	3
..	57¼	3	***Lanark**	

38. NORTH BERWICK to COLDSTREAM. A pleasant road, touching the coast in places, to Cockburnspath, after which the road is rather winding through mainly agricultural country. Two miles from North Berwick there is a fine view of the *Bass Rock from Canty Bay and the ruins of *Tantallon Castle lie just beyond. At Broxburn a stone commemorates the Battle of Dunbar (1650).

A198			***North Berwick**	46½
..	5½	5½	*Whitekirk	41
..	7¼	1¾	*Tynninghame	39¼
A1	8¼	1	Junc A198/A1	38¼
..	13¼	5	*Broxburn	33¼
..	20¼	7	*Cockburnspath	26¼
A6112	25	4¾	*Grantshouse	21½
..	31¼	6¼	*Preston	15¼
..	34	2¾	***Duns**	12½
..	37	3	Mount Pleasant X-rds	9½
..	40	3	*Swinton	6½
..	45½	5½	Lennel	1
..	46½	1	*Coldstream	

39. DUNBAR to KELSO. Pleasant coast scenery to Cockburnspath, then a rather winding road through a mainly agricultural district. At Broxburn a stone commemorates the Battle of Dunbar.

A1087			***Dunbar**	38
A1	1½	1½	*Broxburn	36½
..	8½	7	*Cockburnspath	29½
A6112	13¼	4¾	*Grantshouse	24¾
..	19½	6¼	*Preston	18½
..	22¼	2¾	***Duns**	15¾
B6460	25¼	3	Mount Pleasant X-rds	12¾
Uncl	25½	¼	Junc B6460/Uncl	12½
A699	28¼	2¾	Swinton Mill X-rds	9¾
..	30	1¾	Leitholm	8
..	32¼	2¼	*Eccles	5¼
..	35¾	3½	*Ednam	2¼
..	38	2¼	***Kelso**	

40. DUNBAR to PEEBLES via TEMPLE. A fast and easy road to

Haddington, then a cross-country route, with rural scenery changing to moorland approaching the Moorfoot Hills, beyond Temple.

A1087			***Dunbar**	42¾
..	1	1	Belhaven	41¾
..	1¾	¾	West Barns	41
A1	2½	¾	Junc A1087/A1	40¼
..	5¾	3¼	*East Linton Bypass	37
A6093	10½	4¾	Junc A1/A6093	32¼
..	11¼	¾	*Haddington	31½
..	16¾	5½	*Pencaitland	26
A68	21¼	4½	Junc A6093/A68	21½
B6372	21¾	½	Junc A68/B6372	21
..	25¼	3½	*Gorebridge	17½
..	28¼	3	*Temple	14½
Uncl	31	2¾	Junc B6372/Uncl	11¾
A703	35¾	4¾	Junc Uncl/A703	7
..	38¼	2½	*Eddleston	4½
..	42¾	4½	***Peebles**	

41. SELKIRK to EYEMOUTH. A cross-country link, with pleasant scenery in the *Scott Country and Tweed valley at first. Narrow, undulating roads between Earlston and Greenlaw, moorland in places, becoming mainly agricultural on the latter part. The fastest way to Duns is by Kelso, see Iters 46 and 39.

A7			***Selkirk**	44
B6360	2¼	2¼	Junc A7/B6360	41¾
..	4½	2¼	*Abbotsford House	39½
A6091	6	1½	Junc B6360/A6091	38
B6361	7½	1½	***Melrose**	36½
..	8¾	1¼	*Newstead	35¼
A68	9¾	1	Junc B6361/A68	34¼
A6105	12¼	2½	*Earlston	31¾
..	18½	6¼	*Gordon	25½
..	23	4½	*Greenlaw	21
..	26¼	3¼	*Polwarth	17¾
..	30	3¾	***Duns**	14
B6355	36	6	Junc A6105/B6355	8
..	36½	½	*Chirnside	7½
A1	41¼	4¾	Junc B6355/A1	2¾
B6355	41½	¼	*Ayton	2½
..	44	2½	*Eyemouth	

42. SELKIRK to CARLISLE via Ettrick Forest and Annan. A touring route, through fine open moorlands following the Ettrick and Tima valleys over the ridge into Eskdale. Narrow between Eskdalemuir and Lockerbie. Flat agricultural scenery in Annandale.

B7009			***Selkirk**	72¼
..	7¼	7¼	*Ettrick Bridge End	65
B709	14½	7¼	Junc B7009/B709	57¾
..	15	½	*Tushielaw Inn	57¼
..	17¾	2¾	*Ettrick	54½
B723	30¼	12½	*Eskdalemuir Ch	42
..	37½	7¼	Boreland	34¾
..	44½	7	*Lockerbie	27¾
..	50½	6	*Hoddom Bridge	21¾
A75	54¼	3¾	Junc B723/A75	18
..	55	¾	*Annan	17¼
..	57½	2½	*Dornock	14¾
..	58¼	¾	Eastriggs	14
..	61¼	3	Rigg	11
A74	63¼	2	*Gretna	9
..	63½	¼	*Sark Bridge (The Border)	8¾
A7	69¾	6¼	Junc A74/M6/A7	2½
..	72¼	2½	Carlisle	

43. SELKIRK to CARTER BAR via the Scott Country. A touring route visiting places of interest in the *Scott Country. Between Abbotsford House and Melrose the Eildon Hills are seen to the south-east, and a detour can be made to *Darnick Tower. The tour then proceeds via Earlston to reach Bemersyde and Dryburgh Abbey, returning to the main road at St Boswells. *Ferniehirst Castle is passed just beyond Jedburgh, and there are extensive views northwards on the ascent approaching the summit at Carter Bar (1,371 feet) on the Cheviot ridge, where the Border is crossed into England.

A7			***Selkirk**	41
B6360	2¼	2¼	Junc A7/B6360	38¾
..	4½	2¼	*Abbotsford House	36½
A6091	6	1½	Junc B6360/A6091	35
B6361	7½	1½	***Melrose**	33½
..	8¾	1¼	*Newstead	32¼
A68	9¾	1	Junc B6361/A68	31¼
A6105	12¼	2½	*Earlston	28¾
B6356	12½	¼	Junc A6105/B6356	28½
..	15¾	3¼	*Bemersyde Hill	25¼
..	16½	¾	*Bemersyde House	24½
..	18	1½	*Dryburgh Abbey	23
B6404	20	2	Junc B6356/B6404	21
..	21½	1½	*St Boswells	19½
A68	21¾	¼	Junc B6404/A68	19¼
..	22	¼	*St Boswells Green	19
..	27¼	5¼	*Ancrum Bridge	13¾
..	30½	3¼	***Jedburgh**	10½
..	41	10½	*Carter Bar	

44. HAWICK to CARTER BAR. An undulating road, with fine moorland scenery, gradually ascending to Carter Bar (1,371 feet) on the Cheviot ridge.

A698			***Hawick**	16
A6088	1¾	1¾	Junc A698/A6088	14¼
..	3¾	2	Kirkton	12¼
..	7½	3¾	*Bonchester Bridge	8½
..	10½	3	*Southdean	5½
A68	15¾	5¼	Junc A6088/A68	¼
..	16	¼	*Carter Bar	

45. DUMFRIES to HAWICK. Agricultural to Lockerbie, then a scenic cross-country moorland road to Langholm. An easy climb to Mosspaul is followed by a pleasant run through Teviotdale.

A709			***Dumfries**	53¼
..	4¼	4¼	*Torthorwald	49
..	8½	4¼	*Lochmaben	44¾
B7068	12½	4	*Lockerbie	40¾
..	15½	3	Tundergarth	37¾
..	16¾	1¼	Bankshill	36½
A7	30½	13¾	*Langholm	22¾
..	34¾	4¼	*Ewes PO	18½
..	40¾	6	Mosspaul Hotel	12½
..	44½	3¾	*Teviothead	8¾
..	48¾	4¼	Newmill	4½
..	53¼	4½	***Hawick**	

46. DUMFRIES to BERWICK-UPON-TWEED via Selkirk. Pleasant, wooded agricultural country to Moffat. After passing the Grey Mare's Tail waterfall (on left), the road climbs to the moorlands of Ettrick Forest. Picturesque scenery on the descent past *St Mary's Loch to Yarrow Vale, and well wooded in places approaching Selkirk. Hilly to St Boswells, passing close to the village of *Bowden at the foot of the Eildon Hills, then an easy road in the Tweed valley, passing the scanty remains of *Roxburgh Castle. *Floors Castle is well seen entering Kelso. The quickest way from Dumfries to Kelso is by Hawick, Iter 45 and 30, while places of interest in the *Scott Country can be visited by following Iter 43 from Selkirk to St Boswells. Between Kelso and Berwick agricultural districts are traversed, but the main road (Iter 30) continues with the Tweed valley via Coldstream, although there is little to choose between these two roads. At Swinton a diversion can be made to include *Ladykirk and Norham Castle, by following B6470 across the Tweed (The Border) and thence by A698 to Berwick.

A701			***Dumfries**	97¼
..	3¼	3¼	Locharbriggs	94
..	4½	1¼	*Amisfield	92¾
..	7½	3	*Ae Bridge	89¾
..	13¼	5¾	*St Ann's	84
A74	18	4¾	Junc A701/A74	79¼
..	19	1	*Beattock Bypass	78¼
A701	19½	½	Junc A74/A701	77¾
A708	21	1½	***Moffat**	76¼
..	31	10	*Grey Mare's Tail	66¼
..	32¼	1¼	*Birkhill	65
..	36¼	4	*Tibbie Shiel's Inn	61
..	37¼	1	*Rodono Hotel	60
..	42½	5¼	*Gordon Arms Hotel	54¾
..	46½	4	*Yarrow Ch	50¾
..	50½	4	*Broadmeadows	46¾
A707	54½	4	Junc A708/A707	42¾
A7	55	½	***Selkirk**	42¼

A699	55¾	¾	Junc A7/A699 ..	41½
..	63¾	8	*St Boswells Green	33½
..	65½	1¾	*Maxton	31¾
..	74	8½	***Kelso**	23¼
..	76¼	2¼	*Ednam	21
..	79½	3¼	*Eccles	17¾
..	82	2½	Leitholm	15¼
..	83¾	1¾	Swinton Mill X-rds	13½
..	85½	1¾	*Swinton	11¾
..	97¼	11¾	***Berwick-upon-Tweed**	

47. DUMFRIES to BERWICK-UPON-TWEED via the Border Country. A touring route, utilizing by-roads in the *Border Country for the greater part. A pleasant alternative to the main road as far as Annan, passing near *Ruthwell Church, which lies to the north of the road just beyond Clarencefield, then an undulating by-road to Canonbie. The quickest way to Canonbie is by Iter 67 to Gretna Green thence by roads A6071 and A7 (32½ miles). Pretty scenery in Liddesdale to Riccarton, after which the road ascends across lonely moorlands to the summit (1,250 feet) near Note o' the Gate, 5 miles beyond Riccarton. There are extensive views hereabouts before descending to Bonchester Bridge. A hilly by-road is then followed to Jedburgh, and after a short stretch of main road a detour is made past the foothills of the *Cheviots to Yetholm. The Border is then crossed into England, close to the scene of the battle of Flodden, which lies to the north of the road. Traverses pleasant undulating agricultural country on the latter part.

A75			***Dumfries** ..	107¼
B724	3½	3½	Collin	103¾
..	9¾	6¼	*Clarencefield ..	97½
..	13¼	3½	*Cummertrees ..	94
A75	16¼	3	Junc B724/A75 ..	91
..	16¾	½	*Annan	90½
B6357	17¼	½	Junc A75/B6357	90
..	23	5¾	*Kirkpatrick Fleming ..	84¼
..	26	3	Chapelknowe ..	81¼
A7	32	6	*Canonbie ..	75¼
B6357	32¼	¼	Junc A7/B6357 ..	75
..	33¼	1	Rowanburn ..	74
..	42¼	9	*Newcastleton ..	65
..	49	6¾	*Riccarton ..	58¼
A6088	60	11	Junc B6357/A6088 ..	47¼
B6357	61	1	*Bonchester Bridge	46¼
A68	67	6	Junc B6357/A68	40¼
..	68¾	1¾	***Jedburgh** ..	38½
..	70¾	2	Junc A68/A698	36½
..	73	2¼	Crailing	34¼
..	75	2	*Eckford Ch	32¼
B6401	75¼	¼	Junc A698/B6401	32
..	79¾	4½	*Morebattle	27½
B6352	84	4¼	*Yetholm ..	23¼
..	88¼	4¼	Mindrum Mill ..	19
A697	94	5¾	Junc B6352/A697 ..	13¼
B6354	94½	½	Junc A697/B6354 ..	12¾
..	97	2½	Etal ..	10¼
..	107¼	10¼	***Berwick-upon-Tweed**	

48. DUMFRIES to LANARK via Mennock Pass or via Sanquhar. On leaving Dumfries, a short detour can be made to visit *Lincluden Abbey before joining the main road along the pretty Nith valley, afterwards ascending the winding Mennock Pass to Wanlockhead, the highest village in Scotland (1,380 feet). The summit is reached between Wanlockhead and Leadhills where the road attains a height of 1,531 feet, with extensive views of the Lowther Hills. A long descent leads to Abington through moorland country, afterwards becoming agricultural. The alternative by Sanquhar follows the narrow, winding valleys of the Crawick and Duneaton Waters to A74. The recommended route to Abington is by Beattock (Iters 46 and 50) and between Abington and Lanark by Iter 50. A further alternative is via the Dalveen Pass, see Iter 56.

A76			***Dumfries** ..	57
..	2¾	2¾	*New Bridge ..	54¼
..	7¾	5	*Auldgirth ..	49¼
..	12¼	4½	*Closeburn ..	44¾
..	14½	2¼	*Thornhill ..	42½
..	16¼	1¾	*Carronbridge ..	40¾
..	20¼	4	†*Enterkinfoot ..	36¾
B797	24¼	4	Junc A76/B797 ..	32¾
..	30½	6¼	*Wanlockhead ..	26½
..	32¼	1¾	*Leadhills ..	24¾
A74	38¾	6½	***Abington** (By-pass) ..	18¼
A70	47½	8¾	Junc A74/A70 ..	9½
..	49¼	1¾	Rigside	7¾
A73	54½	5¼	*Hyndford Bridge	2½
..	57	2½	***Lanark**	
			† OR via Sanquhar	
A76	20¼		*Enterkinfoot	
..	24½	4¼	*Mennock	
..	26¾	2¼	*Sanquhar	
B740	27½	¾	Junc A76/B740	
..	39¾	12¼	*Crawfordjohn	
A74	41½	1¾	Junc B740/A74	
A70	46¾	5¼	Junc A74/A70	
..	48½	1¾	Rigside	
A73	53¾	5¼	*Hyndford Bridge	
..	56¼	2½	***Lanark**	

49. MOFFAT to AYR via the Mennock Pass. A touring route through the Lowlands, reaching an altitude of 1,029 feet at Beattock summit, and again ascending from Elvanfoot, with views of the Lowther Hills, to another summit (1,531 feet) between Leadhills and Wanlockhead, the latter being the highest village in Scotland (1,380 feet). Descends by the Mennock Pass, over 1,400 feet high, to the main road in upper Nithsdale, until, beyond Kirkconnel, a hilly cross-country moorland road is followed to Straiton. Afterwards continues through undulating country, and, nearing the coast between Maybole and Dunure, the *Croy (electric) Brae is traversed. A short diversion is made to visit Dunure, whence there is a fine coastal run into Ayr.

A701			***Moffat**	77½
B719	2½	2½	Junc A701/B719	75
A74	5½	3	Junc B719/A74 ..	72
..	9¼	3¾	*Beattock Summit	68¼
A702	12¾	3½	Junc A74/A702 ..	64¾
B7040	13¾	1	*Elvanfoot ..	63¾
B797	18½	4¾	*Leadhills ..	59
..	20¼	1¾	*Wanlockhead ..	57¼
A76	26½	6¼	Junc B797/A76 ..	51
..	26¾	¼	*Mennock ..	50¾
..	29	2¼	*Sanquhar ..	48½
..	32½	3½	*Kirkconnel ..	45
B741	39¾	7¼	Junc A76/B741 ..	37¾
A713	50	10¼	*Dalmellington ..	27½
B741	50½	½	Junc A713/B741	27
..	57	6½	*Straiton.. ..	20½
Uncl	60	3	Junc B741/Uncl	17½
B7023	60¾	¾	Crosshill ..	16¾
..	63½	2¾	*Maybole ..	14
A719	65¾	2¼	Junc B7023/A719 ..	11¾
Uncl	69¼	3½	*Dunure Mains ..	8¼
..	70¼	1	*Dunure ..	7¼
A719	71	¾	Junc Uncl/A719	6½
..	77½	6½	***Ayr**	

50. CARLISLE to STIRLING. After crossing the Border at Sark Bridge there is a long stretch of continuous dual-carriageway extending from Kirkpatrick to Denny Bypass. Picturesque open country in Annandale followed by moorland scenery reaching an altitude of 1,029 feet after Beattock. Mining and industrial districts between Newmains and Stirling.

A7			Carlisle ..	112¼
A74	2½	2½	Junc A7/M6/A74	109¾
..	8¾	6¼	*Sark Bridge (The Border) ..	103½
..	9	¼	*Gretna ..	103¼
..	9½	½	*Gretna Green	102¾
..	12¾	3¼	*Kirkpatrick Fleming Bypass	99½
..	15¾	3	*Kirtlebridge Bypass.. ..	96½
..	19	3¼	*Ecclefechan Bypass.. ..	93¼
..	24¾	5¾	*Lockerbie Bypass	87½
..	32	7¼	*Johnstone Bridge ..	80¼
..	38¾	6¾	*Beattock Bypass	73½
..	49¼	10½	*Beattock Summit	63
..	54¼	5	*Crawford Bypass	58
..	57½	3¼	†***Abington** Bypass ..	54¾
..	65½	8	Junc with A70 ..	46¾
..	71½	6	*Lesmahagow ..	40¾
M74	74½	3	Junc A74/M74 ..	37¾
..	77	2½	Junc with A71 ..	35¼
..	82¾	5¾	Junc for *Hamilton	29½
M73	87¾	5	Junc M74/M73 ..	24½
A80	94¾	7	Junc M73/A80 ..	17½
..	99½	4¾	*Cumbernauld Bypass ..	12¾
..	101¼	1¾	*Castlecary ..	11
..	105¼	4	*Denny Bypass ..	7
..	111	5¾	*St Ninian's ..	1¼
..	112¼	1¼	***Stirling**	

† OR via Lanark

A73	57½		*Abington Bypass	
..	72½	15	*Hyndford Bridge	
..	75	2½	***Lanark**	
..	79¼	4¼	*Braidwood	
..	80¾	1½	*Carluke	
..	84½	3¾	***Newmains**	
..	91¾	7¼	***Airdrie**	
A80	98	6¼	Junc A73/A80	
..	100¼	2¼	*Cumbernauld Bypass	

51. GLASGOW to CARLISLE or LONGTOWN (for Newcastle upon Tyne). Continuous dual-carriageway between M74 and Gretna. An easy road through industrial and mining districts on the earlier part, later crossing open moorlands. Beyond Crawford, the road reaches an altitude of 1,029 feet at Beattock summit, and then descends through picturesque open country in Annandale. Crosses the Border into England at Sark Bridge. Near Gretna Green, an alternative road branches across the Border to Longtown.

A74			***Glasgow**	94¾
..	4¾	4¾	*Mount Vernon	90
M74	6¼	1½	Junc A74/M74	88½
..	11¼	5	Junc for ***Hamilton**	83½
..	17	5¾	Junc with A71	77¾
A74	19¾	2¾	Junc M74/A74	75
..	22¾	3	*Lesmahagow	72
..	37¼	14½	***Abington** Bypass	57½
..	40½	3¼	*Crawford Bypass	54¼
..	45½	5	*Beattock Summit	49¼
..	56	10½	*Beattock Bypass	38¾
..	62¾	6¾	*Johnstone Bridge	32
..	70	7¼	*Lockerbie Bypass	24¾
..	75¾	5¾	*Ecclefechan Bypass	19
..	79	3¼	*Kirtlebridge Bypass	15¾
..	82	3	†*Kirkpatrick Fleming Bypass	12¾
..	85¼	3¼	*Gretna Green	9½
..	85¾	½	*Gretna	9
..	86	¼	*Sark Br (Border)	8¾
A7	92½	6¼	†Junc A74/M6/A74	
	94¾	2¼	Carlisle	
			†Thence by:	
			M6 Motoreay	
			M61 Motorway	
—	214	119	Manchester	
			OR	
..			M6 Motorway	
..			M1 Motorway	
..	406	311	London Bypass	
			† OR	
			*Kirkpatrick Fleming	
A6071	84½	2½	Junc A74/A6071	
..	85	½	*Springfield	
	85½	½	The Border	
A7	88¼	2¾	Junc A6071/A7	
..	88¾	½	Longtown	
			Thence A6071 and A69 to:	
..	149¾	61	Newcastle upon Tyne	

52. GLASGOW to CARTER BAR (for Newcastle upon Tyne). A fast road, at first through industrial and mining districts, with several level crossings between Newhouse and Carluke. Afterwards, a moorland road is succeeded by a fine scenic run, mainly along the Tweed valley to Melrose, where the Eildon Hills are seen to the south. After Jedburgh, *Ferniehirst Castle is passed, and there are extensive views to the north on the ascent approaching the summit at Carter Bar (1,371 feet) on the Cheviot ridge, where the Border is crossed into England. A detour to include the places of interest in the *Scott Country can be made via Selkirk, see Iters 14 and 43. For the recommended route to Newcastle upon Tyne see Iter 51.

A8			***Glasgow**	96
A73	13¼	13¼	Newhouse	82¾
..	17¼	4	***Newmains**	78¾
A721	21	3¾	*Carluke	75
A70	27½	6½	Junc A721/A70	68½
A721	30	2½	*Carnwath	66
..	32¼	2¼	*Newbigging	63¾
..	36¼	4	Elsrickle	59¾
A72	40¼	4	Junc A721/A72	55¾
..	41	¾	*Blyth Bridge	55
..	46½	5½	*Lyne Church	49½
..	50¾	4¼	***Peebles**	45¼
..	57¼	6½	*Innerleithen	38¾
..	59¼	2	*Walkerburn	36¾
..	65¾	6½	*Clovenfords	30¼
A6091	69¼	3½	***Galashiels**	26¾
..	73¼	4	***Melrose**	22¾
A68	75½	2¼	Junc A6091/A68	20½
..	76	½	*Newtown St Boswells	20
..	77	1	*St Boswells Green	19
..	82¼	5¼	*Ancrum Bridge	13¾
..	85½	3¼	***Jedburgh**	10½
..	96	10½	*Carter Bar (The Border)	
			Thence A68 and A696 to:	
..	143¼	47¼	Newcastle upon Tyne	

53. GLASGOW to PEEBLES via the Clyde Valley. Heavy traffic through an industrial district to Hamilton, then pleasant orchard scenery in the Clyde valley to Lanark. Crosses moorland country before joining the Tweed valley near Lyne. The fastest route to Peebles is by Newhouse and Carluke (Iter 52), while a better way to Hamilton is by A74 and Uddingston.

A724			***Glasgow**	55¾
..	4¾	4¾	*Cambuslang	51
..	9¾	5	Burnbank	46
A74	11¼	1½	***Hamilton**	44½
A72	14	2¾	Junc A74/A72	41¾
..	18¼	4¼	Rosebank	37½
..	20¾	2½	*Crossford	35
..	22	1¼	Hazelbank	33¾
..	24½	2½	*Kirkfieldbank	31¼
A73	25½	1	***Lanark**	30¼
..	28	2½	*Hyndford Bridge	27¾
A72	33¾	5¾	Junc A73/A72	22
..	34½	¾	*Symington	21¼
..	38	3½	*Biggar	17¾
..	40½	2½	*Skirling	15¼
..	46	5½	*Blyth Bridge	9¾
..	51½	5½	*Lyne Ch	4¼
..	55¾	4¼	***Peebles**	

54. GLASGOW to LANARK via Motherwell. Mainly industrial in character with heavy traffic to Wishaw. For fast travel the route via Newhouse is recommended, see Iter 52.

A74			***Glasgow**	26
..	4¾	4¾	*Mount Vernon	21¼
A721	6¾	2	Junc A74/A721	19¼
..	9½	2¾	*Bellshill	16½
..	12	2½	***Motherwell**	14
..	15½	3½	*Wishaw	10½
A73	18	2½	Junc A721/A73	8
..	20¼	2¼	*Carluke	5¾
..	21¾	1½	*Braidwood	4¼
..	26	4¼	***Lanark**	

55. GLASGOW to STRANRAER. Heavy traffic to Giffnock, then a fast arterial road, with open moorland in places, to Kilmarnock and then becoming agricultural and skirting *Prestwick Airport. After Ayr, the road is undulating with pleasant valley scenery, returning to the coast at Girvan, afterwards following the shore through Kennedy's Pass to Ballantrae, beyond which there is a climb inland before descending through Glen App to the shores of Loch Ryan. If proceeding to Glenluce, Stranraer may be avoided by following A751 from Innermessan to join A75 east of Stranraer.

A77			***Glasgow**	86½
..	5	5	*Giffnock	81½
..	7¼	2¼	*Newton Mearns	79¼
..	16¾	9½	*Fenwick Bypass	69¾
..	21	4¼	***Kilmarnock**	65½
..	22¼	1¼	Riccarton	64¼
..	34¾	12½	***Ayr** Bypass	51¾
..	40¼	5½	Minishant	46¼
..	44	3¾	*Maybole	42½
..	46¼	2¼	*Crossraguel Abbey	40¼
..	48½	2¼	*Kirkoswald	38
..	56¼	7¾	***Girvan**	30¼
..	62¾	6½	*Lendalfoot	23¾
..	69	6¼	*Ballantrae	17½
..	80½	11½	*Cairn Ryan	6
..	84	3½	*Innermessan	2½
..	86½	2½	***Stranraer**	

56. GLASGOW to DUMFRIES via Strathaven and the Dalveen Pass. A good alternative exit from Glasgow, with heavy traffic at first, then climbing to the moorlands, with pleasant views in places. Follows the Clyde valley for several miles beyond Abington, after which there are extensive views towards the Lowther Hills, and reaches an altitude of 1,140 feet at the head of the Dalveen Pass, before descending towards the Nith. *Durisdeer Church lies to the east of the road before Carronbridge in Nithsdale, and after New Bridge a short detour can be made to visit *Lincluden Abbey. The main road is by Beattock, Iters 51 and 24.

A749			***Glasgow**	77¾
..	3¼	3¼	*Rutherglen	74½
A726	8½	5¼	*East Kilbride	69¼
..	14	5½	Chapelton	63¾
..	16¾	2¾	***Strathaven**	61
A74	23½	6¾	Junc A726/A74	54¼
..	26	2½	*Lesmahagow	51¾
..	40½	14½	***Abington** Bypass	37¼
..	43¾	3¼	*Crawford Bypass	34
A702	45¼	1½	Junc A74/A702	32½
..	46¼	1	*Elvanfoot	31½
A76	61½	15¼	*Carronbridge	16¼
..	63¼	1¾	*Thornhill	14½
..	65½	2¼	*Closeburn	12¼
..	70	4½	*Auldgirth	7¾
..	74	4	Holywood	3¾
..	75	1	*New Bridge	2¾
..	77¾	2¾	***Dumfries**	

57. GLASGOW to ARDROSSAN. An easy road through agricultural country beyond the suburbs of Glasgow. Becomes industrial near Kilwinning.

A736			***Glasgow**	29¼
..	3½	3½	*Pollokshaws	25¾
..	8	4½	***Barrhead**	21¼
..	14¾	6¾	Lugton	14½
..	17¼	2½	Burnhouse	12
B778	19½	2¼	Junc A736/B778	9¾
A738	24¼	4¾	*Kilwinning	5
A78	25¾	1½	Junc A738/A78	3½
..	26¾	1	*Stevenston Bypass	2½
A738	28¾	2	Junc A78/A738	½
..	29¼	½	***Ardrossan**	

58. GLASGOW to LARGS. Industrial to Paisley, then through agricultural country. Ascends to the moors beyond Kilbirnie; care required on the descent of Hailey Brae (1 in 10) with two hairpin bends half a mile before joining the main coast road.

A737			***Glasgow**	30
..	7	7	***Paisley**	23
..	9½	2½	*Elderslie	20½
..	13¼	3¾	*Howwood	16¾
A760	16	2¾	Junc A737/A760	14
..	16¾	¾	*Lochwinnoch	13¼
..	20¾	4	*Kilbirnie	9¼
A78	29	8¼	Junc A760/A78	1
..	30	1	***Largs**	

59. GLASGOW to GOUROCK or WEMYSS BAY. Busy industrial route at first then using the *Renfrew Bypass Motorway. The alternative shows the direct road from Greenock to Inverkip and Wemyss Bay.

A8			***Glasgow**	26¾
..	4	4	*Govan Bypass	22¾
M8	5	1	Junc A8/A8	21¾
..	8	3	*Abbotsinch Airport	18¾
A8	11½	3½	Junc M8/A8	15¼
..	13¼	1¾	*Bishopton	13½
..	16¾	3½	Langbank	10
..	20½	3¾	*Port Glasgow	6¼
..	23¾	3¼	†***Greenock**	3
..	26¾	3	***Gourock**	
		†	OR	
A742	23¾		***Greenock**	
A78	28¼	4½	Junc A742/A78	
..	29	¾	*Inverkip	
..	31¾	2¾	***Wemyss Bay**	

60. PAISLEY to AYR. An easy road through agricultural districts, becoming flat beyond Irvine. Passes Prestwick Airport between Monkton and Prestwick. The latter two places may be avoided by using the Prestwick By-pass (A77).

A726			***Paisley**	33½
B771	1¾	1¾	Junc A726/B771	31¾
A736	4	2¼	***Barrhead**	29½
..	10¾	6¾	Lugton	22¾
..	13¼	2½	Burnhouse	20¼
A78	22	8¾	***Irvine**	11½
..	27	5	*Loans	6½
A778	29	2	Junc A78/A778	4½
A79	29½	½	*Monkton	4
..	30¾	1¼	*Prestwick	2¾
..	33½	2¾	***Ayr**	

61. PAISLEY to KILMARNOCK. Industrial at first, then mainly agricultural districts, but crossing moorlands between Newton Mearns and Fenwick.

A726			***Paisley**	22¼
..	3½	3½	Nitshill	18¾
A77	6¼	2¾	*Giffnock	16
..	8½	2¼	*Newton Mearns	13¾
..	18	9½	*Fenwick Bypass	4¼
..	22¼	4¼	***Kilmarnock**	

62. PAISLEY to KILMARNOCK via Kilmaurs. Mainly agricultural, with industrial development in places.

A726			***Paisley**	21½
B771	1¾	1¾	Junc A726/B771	19¾
A736	4	2¼	***Barrhead**	17½
A735	10¾	6¾	Lugton	10¾
..	13¼	2½	*Dunlop	8¼
..	15¾	2½	*Stewarton	5¾
..	19	3¼	*Kilmaurs	2½
..	21½	2½	***Kilmarnock**	

63. PAISLEY to ARDROSSAN. Agricultural scenery for the greater part, with industrial districts at each end.

A737			***Paisley**	25½
..	2½	2½	*Elderslie	23
..	6¼	3¾	*Howwood	19¼
..	11¾	5½	*Beith Bypass	13¾
..	16½	4¾	*Dalry	9
A738	20½	4	*Kilwinning	5
A78	22	1½	Junc A738/A78	3½
..	23	1	*Stevenston Bypass	2½
A738	25	2	Junc A78/A738	½
..	25½	½	***Ardrossan**	

64. PAISLEY to WEMYSS BAY via Kilmacolm. Industrial at first, but avoids *Johnstone, afterwards traversing pleasant, open countryside through Strath Gryfe to Port Glasgow. Industrial along the Clyde estuary to Greenock. Views across the Firth of Clyde beyond Inverkip.

A737			***Paisley**	26
A761	1½	1½	Junc A737/A761	24½
..	2¾	1¼	*Linwood	23¼
..	7	4¼	*Bridge of Weir	19
..	10½	3½	*Kilmacolm	15½
A8	14½	4	Junc A761/A8	11½
..	14¾	¼	*Port Glasgow	11¼
A742	18	3¼	***Greenock**	8
A78	22½	4½	Junc A742/A78	3½
..	23¼	¾	*Inverkip	2¾
..	26	2¾	***Wemyss Bay**	

65. PAISLEY to GOUROCK or WEMYSS BAY. Mainly industrial districts at first. Uses part of the *Renfrew Bypass Motorway and passes *Abbotsinch Airport. Views across the Firth of Clyde beyond Langbank.

A726			***Paisley**	27½
M8	1¼	1¼	Junc A726/M8	26¼
A8	4	2¾	Junc M8/A8	23½
..	5¾	1¾	*Bishopton	21¾
..	9¼	3½	Langbank	18¼
..	13	3¾	*Port Glasgow	14½
..	16¼	3¼	†***Greenock**	11¼
A78	19¼	3	***Gourock**	8¼
		†	OR	
A742			***Greenock**	
A78	20¾	4½	Junc A742/A78	3½
..	21½	¾	*Inverkip	2¾
..	24¼	2¾	***Wemyss Bay**	

66. GOUROCK to AYR or KILMARNOCK. A fine coastal route, close to the shore for several miles with views of the islands of Bute, the *Cumbraes and Arran in the Firth of Clyde and across to the hills of Cowal. *West Kilbride lies to the east of the main road beyond Fairlie, and the other coastal resorts including Ardrossan and Troon can also be included by reference to Iter 88. Partly industrial near Stevenston and flat beyond Irvine. Passes Prestwick Airport between Monkton and Prestwick, and these two places may be avoided by using the Prestwick By-pass (A77).

A78			***Gourock**	44¼
..	2¾	2¾	*Cloch Lighthouse	41½
..	5½	2¾	*Inverkip	38¾
..	8¼	2¾	***Wemyss Bay**	36
..	8¾	½	*Skelmorlie	35½
..	14¼	5½	***Largs**	30
..	17	2¾	*Fairlie	27¼

..	22	5	*Sea Mill ..	22¼
..	27¾	5¾	*Stevenston Bypass ..	16½
			*Kilwinning Bypass	
..	31¾	4	Rd to Bogside Race-course ..	12½
..	32¾	1	†***Irvine**	11½
..	37¾	5	*Loans	6½
A778	39¾	2	Junc A78/A778 ..	4½
A79	40¼	½	*Monkton ..	4
..	41½	1¼	*Prestwick ..	2¾
..	44¼	2¾	***Ayr**	
		†	OR	
A71	33½		*Irvine	
..	35¾	2¼	*Dreghorn	
..	38½	2¾	Crosshouse	
..	41	2½	***Kilmarnock**	

67. KILMARNOCK to LONGTOWN. Through agricultural country, with mining developments and moorland in a few places to Sanquhar. Pretty in Nithsdale to New Bridge, after which a short detour can be made to visit *Lincluden Abbey. Beyond Dumfries, flat agricultural districts are traversed to Gretna Green, later crossing the Border into England. A quicker route is via A71 M74 and A74. (Iters 69 in reverse and 51).

A71			***Kilmarnock** ..	86¾
A76	1¾	1¾	*Hurlford ..	85
..	8¾	7	*Mauchline ..	78
..	13½	4¾	*Auchinleck ..	73¼
..	15¼	1¾	***Cumnock** ..	71½
..	20¾	5½	*New Cumnock ..	66
..	28½	7¾	*Kirkconnel ..	58¼
..	32	3½	*Sanquhar ..	54¾
..	34¼	2¼	*Mennock ..	52½
..	38½	4¼	*Enterkinfoot ..	48¼
..	42½	4	*Carronbridge ..	44¼
..	44¼	1¾	*Thornhill ..	42½
..	46½	2¼	*Closeburn ..	40¼
..	51	4½	*Auldgirth ..	35¾
..	56	5	*New Bridge ..	30¾
A75	58¾	2¾	***Dumfries** ..	28
..	62¼	3½	Collin	24¼
..	74½	12	*Annan	12½
..	76¾	2½	*Dornock ..	10
..	77½	¾	Eastriggs	9¼
..	80½	3	Rigg	6¼
B721	81½	1	Junc A75/B721 ..	5¼
..	82½	1	*Gretna Green ..	4¼
A6071	82¾	¼	Junc B721/A6071	4
..	83	¼	*Springfield ..	3¾
..	83½	½	The Border ..	3¼
A7	86¼	2¾	Junc A6071/A7 ..	½
	86¾	½	Longtown	

68. STRATHAVEN to GIRVAN via Cumnock. An undulating cross-country road with open moorland scenery to Cumnock, then through rural countryside to reach the coast 5 miles before Girvan. A faster route is via Ayr, see Iter 20 and 55.

A723			***Strathaven** ..	55¾
A70	13¼	13¼	*Muirkirk ..	42½
..	21	7¾	*Lugar	34¾
..	23	2	***Cumnock** ..	32¾
..	27¼	4¼	*Ochiltree ..	28½
B742	33¼	6	*Coylton	22½
..	38½	5¼	Dalrymple ..	17¼
A77	42	3½	Junc B742/A77 ..	13¾
..	43½	1½	*Maybole ..	12¼
..	45¾	2¼	*Crossraguel Abbey	10
..	48	2¼	*Kirkoswald ..	7¾
..	55¾	7¾	***Girvan**	

69. LANARK to ARDROSSAN. Pleasant in the Clyde valley at first, then undulating across moorlands. Later passes through an agricultural district, with mining developments in places, and industrial towards the end.

A72			***Lanark**	51¾
..	1	1	*Kirkfieldbank ..	50¾
..	4¾	3¾	*Crossford ..	47
..	7¼	2½	Rosebank ..	44½
A71	8½	1¼	Junc with A72/A71	43¼
..	10½	2	Junc with M74 ..	41¼
..	12¾	2¼	Stonehouse ..	39
..	16¾	4	***Strathaven** ..	35
..	22½	5¾	*Drumclog ..	29¼
..	25¾	3¼	*Loudounhill ..	26
..	27¾	2	*Darvel	24
..	29½	1¾	*Newmilns ..	22¼
..	32	2½	*Galston ..	19¾
..	35	3	*Hurlford ..	16¾
..	36¾	1¾	***Kilmarnock** ..	15
..	39¼	2½	Crosshouse ..	12½
..	42	2¾	*Dreghorn ..	9¾
A78	44¼	2¼	***Irvine**	7½
..	45¼	1	Rd to Bogside Race-course ..	6½
			*Kilwinning By-pass	
..	49¼	4	*Stevenston (By-pass) ..	2½
A738	51¼	2	Junc A78/A738 ..	½
..	51¾	½	***Ardrossan**	

70. DUMFRIES to KIRKCUDBRIGHT. Pleasant agricultural scenery.

A75			***Dumfries** ..	27½
..	9½	9½	*Crocketford ..	18
..	11¾	2¼	Springholm ..	15¾
..	18	6¼	*Castle Douglas ..	9½
A711	22	4	Junc A75/A711 ..	5½
..	25½	3½	*Tongland ..	2
..	27½	2	***Kirkcudbright**	

71. DUMFRIES to GIRVAN via New Galloway. At first a lonely road through the hills of Galloway with fine moorland scenery, followed by attractive wooded country in the Cree valley as far as Bargrennan. Thence a fine moorland run, after which a pleasant valley road leads to the coast at Girvan. A short but interesting detour can be made from Bargrennan to visit the picturesque *Loch Trool, for the Glen Trool National Forest Park. Between Challoch and Barrhill there is a less-frequented route (B7027). The normal route to Newton Stewart is via Castle Douglas (Iter 26).

A75			***Dumfries** ..	73¾
A712	9½	9½	*Crocketford ..	64¼
..	15½	6	Corsock ..	58¼
..	23	7½	*Balmaclellan ..	50¾
..	24¼	1¼	Ken Bridge ..	49½
..	25	¾	*New Galloway ..	48¾
..	31½	6½	*Clatteringshaws Dam	42¼
A75	42¼	10¾	Junc A712/A75 ..	31½
A714	43½	1¼	***Newton Stewart**	30¼
..	45¾	2¼	Challoch ..	28
..	52¼	6½	*Bargrennan ..	21½
..	61¼	9	*Barrhill	12½
..	65½	4¼	*Pinwherry ..	8¼
..	69	3½	Pinmore ..	4¾
A77	72¾	3¾	Junc A714/A77 ..	1
..	73¾	1	***Girvan**	

72. DUMFRIES to NEWTON STEWART via Dalbeattie and Kirkcudbright. A touring route traversing pleasant agricultural districts, passing New (or Sweetheart) Abbey before circling Criffell Hill to Dalbeattie and touching the coast at several places. Rather narrow between Dalbeattie and Kirkcudbright. The shores of Wigtown Bay are followed between Gatehouse of Fleet and Creetown, with views of the Galloway Hills.

A710			***Dumfries** ..	64
..	7¼	7¼	*New Abbey ..	56¾
..	12	4¾	*Kirkbean ..	52
..	14½	2½	*Mainsriddle ..	49½
A745	16¼	1¾	*Southwick ..	47¾
A711	23¾	7½	*Dalbeattie ..	40¼
A745	24½	¾	Junc A711/A745	39½
B727	26¼	1¾	Junc A745/B727 ..	37¾
..	29	2¾	Gelston	35
A755	37¼	8¼	***Kirkcudbright** ..	26¾
A75	42	4¾	Junc A755/A75 ..	22
..	45½	3½	*Gatehouse of Fleet	18½
..	57½	12	*Creetown ..	6½
..	60¾	3¼	*Palnure ..	3¼
..	64	3¼	***Newton Stewart**	

73. DUMFRIES to NEWTON STEWART via the Coast. An interesting touring route following the coast as far as possible and passing New (or Sweetheart) Abbey and Dundrennan Abbey. At Mainsriddle a side road leads to *Southerness lighthouse, and between Colvend and Dalbeattie short detours can be made to visit the small resorts of *Rockcliffe and *Kippford. Views of the Galloway hills on the latter part.

A710			***Dumfries** ..	74¾
..	7¼	7¼	*New Abbey ..	67½
..	12	4¾	*Kirkbean ..	62¾
..	14½	2½	*Mainsriddle ..	60¼
..	16¼	1¾	*Southwick ..	58½
..	19	2¾	*Douglas Hall ..	55¾

..	20¾	1¾	*Colvend ..	54
..	22¾	2	Barnbarroch ..	52
A711	25¾	3	*Dalbeattie ..	49
..	29¼	3½	*Palnackie ..	45½
..	33¼	4	*Auchencairn ..	41½
..	38	4¾	*Dundrennan ..	36¾
A755	44¼	6¼	***Kirkcudbright** ..	30½
B727	45¼	1	Junc A755/B727..	29½
..	50	4¾	*Borgue	24¾
A75	53½	3½	Junc B727/A75 ..	21¼
..	56¼	2¾	*Gatehouse of Fleet	18½
..	68¼	12	*Creetown ..	6½
..	71½	3¼	*Palnure	3¼
..	74¾	3¼	***Newton Stewart**	

74. DUMFRIES to GIRVAN via Moniaive. On leaving Dumfries, short detours can be made to visit *Lincluden Abbey and *Irongray. A quiet cross-country route, hilly and winding to Moniaive, then across moorland, passing Kendoon Loch nearing Carsphairn. The northern extremity of *Loch Doon is passed on the way to Dalmellington, where there are some mining developments. Pleasant valley scenery beyond Straiton. The quickest way to Carsphairn is by Dalry, see Iter 75.

A76			***Dumfries** ..	64¾
B729	2¾	2¾	*New Bridge ..	62
..	9¼	6½	*Dunscore ..	55½
A702	14¾	5½	*Kirkland ..	50
B729	16¾	2	*Moniaive ..	48
A713	31¾	15	Junc B729/A713..	33
..	32¼	½	*Carsphairn ..	32½
..	42½	10¼	*Dalmellington ..	22¼
B741	43	½	Junc A713/B741..	21¾
..	49½	6½	*Straiton.. ..	15¼
..	57¾	8¼	*New Dailly ..	7
A77	64	6¼	Junc B741/A77 ..	¾
..	64¾	¾	***Girvan**	

75. DUMFRIES to AYR via Dalmellington. Pleasant moorland scenery in the Galloway Hills for the greater part. Mining in the vicinity of Dalmellington, which stands near the northern extremity of *Loch Doon. Agricultural on the latter part. The quickest way is by Cumnock (Iter 27). Another road (B7000) from Dalry to Carsphairn follows the eastern side of Glen Ken and passes the shores of Kendoon Loch.

A75			***Dumfries** ..	61¼
A712	9½	9½	*Crocketford ..	51¾
..	15½	6	Corsock	45¾
..	23	7½	*Balmaclellan ..	38¼
A713	24¼	1¼	Ken Bridge ..	37
..	26¾	2½	*Dalry	34½
..	36	9¼	*Carsphairn ..	25¼
..	46¼	10¼	*Dalmellington ..	15
..	51¼	5	*Patna	10
..	61¼	10	***Ayr**	

76. DUMFRIES to AYR via Dalbeattie. Pleasant agricultural district at first, and then follows the shores of Loch Ken between Castle Douglas and Ken Bridge. Crosses moorland and passes near the northern extremity of *Loch Doon, before Dalmellington, where there are some mining developments. Agricultural on the latter part. Another road (B7000) from Dalry to Carsphairn follows the eastern side of Glen Ken and passes the shores of Kendoon Loch. For the recommended routes from Dumfries to Ayr, see Iter 27; to Ken Bridge, see Iter 75; and to Castle Douglas, see Iter 70.

A711			***Dumfries** ..	70½
..	6½	6½	Beeswing.. ..	64
..	9	2½	*Kirkgunzeon ..	61½
..	13½	4½	*Dalbeattie ..	57
A745	14¼	¾	Junc A711/A745	56¼
A75	19½	5¼	Junc A745/A75 ..	51
A713	20	½	*Castle Douglas	50½
..	23¾	3¾	*Crossmichael ..	46¾
..	27	3¼	Parton	43½
..	33½	6½	Ken Br	37
..	36	2½	*Dalry	34½
..	45¼	9¼	*Carsphairn ..	25¼
..	55½	10¼	*Dalmellington ..	15
..	60½	5	*Patna	10
..	70½	10	***Ayr**	

77. KIRKCUDBRIGHT to AYR. Pretty scenic road, agricultural at first, then past lochs, hills, moors and close to the northern extremity of *Loch Doon, near Dalmellington, where there is some mining. Developments in connection with hydro-electric power schemes north of New Galloway. Agricultural on the latter part.

A711			***Kirkcudbright**	56
A762	1½	1½	Junc A711/A762	54½
A75	3½	2	Junc A762/A75 ..	52½
A762	4¾	1¼	*Ringford ..	51¼
..	9¾	5	*Laurieston ..	46¼
..	18¾	9	*New Galloway..	37¼
A713	22¼	3½	Junc A762/A713	33¾
..	30¾	8½	*Carsphairn ..	25¼
..	41	10¼	*Dalmellington ..	15
..	46	5	*Patna	10
..	56	10	***Ayr**	

78. NEWTON STEWART to GIRVAN via Luce Bay and New Luce. Pleasant rural scenery to the coast at Port William, then follows the sandy shores of Luce Bay to Auchenmalg, later passing Luce Abbey between Glenluce and New Luce. Beyond this point, narrow and hilly moorland by-roads are traversed between New Luce and Barrhill. After Pinwherry, a detour is made to include part of the Stinchar valley to Barr, whence the road over the hills is narrow and winding. The quickest way from Glenluce to Girvan is by A75 and A751 to Innermessan, thence by the coast road, A77. The direct road from Newton Stewart to Pinwherry and Girvan is shown in Iter 80.

A714			***Newton Stewart**	68½
B7005	6	6	Junc A714/B7005	62½
A714	7¾	1¾	*Bladnoch ..	60¾
..	11	3¼	Whaup Hill ..	57½
A747	17¼	6¼	*Port William ..	51¼
..	26½	9¼	Auchenmalg ..	42
A75	30½	4	Junc A747/A75 ..	38
..	31¼	¾	*Glenluce ..	37¼
Uncl	31¾	½	Junc A75/Uncl ..	36¾
..	36½	4¾	*New Luce ..	32
..	41½	5	*Glenwhilly ..	27
..	42¾	1¼	Miltonish ..	25¾
..	45¼	2½	Chirmorie ..	23¼
A714	49¼	4	*Barrhill	19¼
..	53½	4¼	*Pinwherry ..	15
B734	55¼	1¾	Junc A714/B734..	13¼
..	60¾	5½	*Barr	7¾
..	65¾	5	*Old Dailly ..	2¾
A77	68	2¼	Junc B734/A77 ..	½
..	68½	½	***Girvan**	

79. NEWTON STEWART to AYR via the Galloway and Carrick Hills. A touring route across the Galloway Hills, following the wooded Cree valley to Bargrennan, where a short detour can be made to visit the picturesque *Loch Trool for the Glen Trool National Forest Park. Care required on the section from Bargrennan to Straiton, which is a narrow, hilly and winding moorland road, rising to 1,421 feet, with a descent of 1 in 10, 3 miles before Straiton. A winding, valley road is then followed until joining the main road near Minishant. From Rowantree, an alternative road leads over the hills by the Nick o' the Balloch Pass (1,280 feet) to the Stinchar valley at North Balloch, thence by Iter 84 to Ayr (42 miles).

A714			***Newton Stewart**	44½
..	2¼	2¼	Challoch ..	42¼
Uncl	8¾	6½	*Bargrennan ..	35¾
..	18¼	9½	*Rowantree ..	26¼
B741	30	11¾	*Straiton.. ..	14½
B7045	30¼	¼	Junc B741/B7045	14¼
..	34¼	4	Kirkmichael ..	10¼
A77	38¼	4	Junc B7045/A77..	6¼
..	39	¾	Minishant ..	5½
..	44½	5½	***Ayr**	

80. NEWTON STEWART to AYR, touring route. At first the road passes through pleasant agricultural and moorland country, thence along the east side of Loch Ryan. It then turns inland along Glen App and later descends to the coast at Ballantrae. Thereafter it is a fine coast road, and passes Turnberry golf course. There are views of Culzean Castle and Dunure Castle (ruins), between which the famous *Croy (Electric) Brae is traversed.

A75			***Newton Stewart**	74¾
..	15¼	15¼	*Glenluce ..	59½
..	18¾	3½	Dunragit	56
..	21¾	3	*Castle Kennedy	53
A751	23	1¼	Junc A75/A751 ..	51¾
A77	24¾	1¾	*Innermessan ..	50
..	28¼	3½	*Cairn Ryan ..	46½
..	39¾	11½	*Ballantrae ..	35
..	46	6¼	*Lendalfoot ..	28¾
..	52½	6½	***Girvan**	22¼
A719	57½	5	Junc A77/A719 ..	17¼
..	57¾	¼	*Turnberry ..	17
..	59¼	1½	*Maidens ..	15½
..	61½	2¼	*Culzean Castle ..	13¼
..	67	5½	*Dunure Mains ..	7¾
..	73	6	Doonfoot ..	1¾
..	74¾	1¾	***Ayr**	

81. NEWTON STEWART to PORTPATRICK via Wigtown. Agricultural and moorland country. The direct road to Glenluce is given in Iter 25.

A714			***Newton Stewart**	38½
B733	7	7	*Wigtown ..	31½
..	15¼	8¼	*Kirkcowan ..	23¼
A75	16¾	1½	Junc B733/A75 ..	21¾
..	24¼	7½	*Glenluce ..	14¼
A715	26¾	2½	Junc A75/A715	11¾
A757	29	2¼	Junc A715/A757	9½
A716	32½	3½	Kildrochet ..	6
A757	33	½	Junc A716/A757	5½
A77	33½	½	*Lochans ..	5
..	38½	5	***Portpatrick**	

82. NEWTON STEWART to STRANRAER via Luce Bay and the Mull of Galloway. Pleasant rural scenery along the coast of Wigtownshire to the Mull of Galloway, touching the shores of Luce Bay between Monreith and Auchenmalg, and again between Sandhead and Drummore. A short detour can be made from Kirkinner via B7004 to *Garliestown and on to Whithorn, or by B7004 and B7063 passing *Cruggleton Church and direct to Isle of Whithorn. From Drummore to the Mull of Galloway, the most southerly point in Scotland, can be omitted by proceeding direct from Damnaglaur to Kirkmaiden. The direct road to Port William is given in Iter 78.

A714			***Newton Stewart**	92¾
..	7	7	*Wigtown ..	85¾
..	8¼	1¼	*Bladnoch ..	84½
A746	9½	1¼	Junc A714/A746	83¼
..	10¼	¾	*Kirkinner ..	82½
..	13½	3¼	*Sorbie	79¼
A750	18	4½	*Whithorn ..	74¾
..	21½	3½	*Isle of Whithorn	71¼
			Return to:	
A747	23¼	1¾	Junc A750/A747	69½
..	25¾	2½	*Glasserton ..	67
..	30	4¼	*Monreith ..	62¾
..	32½	2½	*Port William ..	60¼
..	41¾	9¼	Auchenmalg ..	51
A75	45¾	4	Junc A747/A75 ..	47
..	46½	¾	*Glenluce ..	46¼
A715	49	2½	Junc A75/A715 ..	43¾
A716	54¾	5¾	Junc A715/A716	38
..	55¾	1	*Sandhead ..	37
..	58¾	3	*Ardwell (PO) ..	34
B7041	65¼	6½	*Drummore ..	27½
..	66¼	1	Damnaglaur ..	26½
Uncl	67½	1¼	Junc B7041/Uncl	25¼
..	70¼	2¾	*Mull of Galloway	22½
			Return to:	
B7065	74¼	4	Damnaglaur ..	18½
..	75¼	1	*Kirkmaiden ..	17½
..	78¾	3½	*Port Logan ..	14
A716	80¾	2	Junc B7065/A716	12
..	82¼	1½	*Ardwell (PO) ..	10½
..	85¼	3	*Sandhead ..	7½
..	87¼	2	Stoneykirk ..	5½
..	89¼	2	Kildrochet ..	3½
A77	90¼	1	Junc A716/A77 ..	2½
..	92¾	2½	***Stranraer**	

83. A Tour from STRANRAER via Aldouran Glen and Loch Ryan. A picturesque tour in the quiet by-ways of the northern half of the Rhinns of Galloway, with distant glimpses of Ireland after Portpatrick. After passing Lochnaw Castle, the road follows the wooded Aldouran Glen, and a short detour is then made before approaching the shores of Loch Ryan.

A77			***Stranraer** ..	30¼
..	2¾	2¾	*Lochans ..	27½
..	7¾	5	***Portpatrick** ..	22½
			Return to:	
A764	8½	¾	Junc A77/A764 ..	21¾
B738	11¾	3¼	Junc A764/B738 ..	18½
..	13	1¼	Larbrax School ..	17¼
B7043	14½	1½	Junc B738/B7043 ..	15¾
..	15	½	*Lochnaw Castle	15¼
B798	17	2	Leswalt	13¼
..	19½	2½	Ervie (PO) ..	10¾
B738	19¾	¼	Junc B798/B738 ..	10½
A718	22¾	3	Junc B738/A718 ..	7½
..	24	1¼	*Kirkcolm ..	6¼
..	30¼	6¼	***Stranraer**	

84. STRANRAER to AYR via the Stinchar Valley. A touring route following the main road by the shores of Loch Ryan for some miles before ascending Glen App, then descending to the coast at Ballantrae. Thence by a pretty, undulating road along the wooded valley of the River Stinchar to North Balloch, followed by a narrow, moorland run over the hills to Crosshill. Care required when passing on this section. An easy run through agricultural districts on the latter part.

A77			***Stranraer** ..	57
..	2½	2½	*Innermessan ..	54½
..	6	3½	*Cairn Ryan ..	51
B7044	17½	11½	*Ballantrae ..	39½
A765	20¾	3¼	Junc B7044/A765	36¼
..	22¼	1¾	*Colmonell ..	34¾
A714	25¾	3¼	*Pinwherry ..	31¼
B734	27½	1¾	Junc A714/B734	29½
Uncl	33	5½	*Barr	24
..	37¼	4¼	*North Balloch ..	19¾
B7023	45¾	8½	Crosshill ..	11¼
A77	48½	2¾	*Maybole ..	8½
B7024	48¾	¼	Junc A77/B7024	8¼
..	54¼	5½	*Brig o' Doon ..	2¾
..	54¾	½	*Alloway ..	2¼
..	57	2¼	***Ayr**	

85. A tour from GIRVAN to GOUROCK. A by-road route through Ayrshire, following the Girvan valley to Kirkmichael, then a cross-country road to Irvine through mainly agricultural districts and visiting Tarbolton, in the Burns country. Beyond Lochwinnoch, crosses moorland to Kilmacolm and becomes industrial on the estuary of the Clyde.

A77			***Girvan**	78
B741	¾	¾	Junc A77/B741	77¼
..	7	6¼	*New Dailly ..	71
B7023	10¾	3¾	Junc B741/B7023	67¼
Uncl	12¾	2	Crosshill ..	65¼
B7045	14½	1¾	Junc Uncl/B7045	63½
Uncl	15	½	Kirkmichael ..	63
A713	20¼	5¼	*Patna	57¾
B730	21¼	1	Junc A713/B730	56¾
..	26¾	5½	*Drongan ..	51¼
A70	27½	¾	Junc B730/A70	50½
B730	27¾	¼	Junc A70/B730	50¼
..	29	1¼	Trabboch	49
..	30	1	*Stair	48
..	32½	2½	*Tarbolton ..	45½
A719	33¾	1¼	Junc B730/A719	44¼
B730	34¼	½	Junc A719/B730	43¾
..	39½	5¼	*Dundonald ..	38½
A71	42	2½	*Dreghorn ..	36
A78	44¼	2¼	***Irvine**	33¾
..	45¼	1	Rd to Bogside Race-course ..	32¾
A737	46¼	1	Junc A78/A737 ..	31¾
..	47½	1¼	*Kilwinning ..	30½
B780	51½	4	*Dalry	26½
A760	55¼	3¾	*Kilbirnie ..	22¾
B786	59¼	4	*Lochwinnoch ..	18¾
A761	67½	8¼	*Kilmacolm ..	10½
A8	71½	4	Junc A761/A8 ..	6½
..	71¾	¼	*Port Glasgow ..	6¼
..	75	3¼	***Greenock** ..	3
..	78	3	***Gourock**	

86. LANARK to PERTH via Kincardine Bridge and the Ochil Hills. Open moorland to Longridge, then agricultural and mining districts, whilst the interesting village of *Torphichen lies to the east of the road between Armadale and Linlithgow. Crosses the River Forth at Kincardine Bridge, and beyond Rumbling Bridge traverses the Ochil Hills by a pleasant scenic route with fine views. This forms an alternative to the main road across the Ochils by Glenfarg (Iter 91). Attractive at Forteviot in Strath Earn. The direct road (A801) avoiding Linlithgow via Maddiston is narrow and difficult to follow.

A706			***Lanark** ..	69¾
..	8¼	8¼	Forth	61½
..	9	¾	*Wilsontown ..	60¾
..	13¾	4¾	Longridge ..	56
..	15½	1¾	*Whitburn ..	54¼
..	18	2½	*Armadale ..	51¾

			***Linlithgow**	44¼
M9	29¼	3¾	Junc A9/M9	40½
A876	34½	5¼	Junc M9/A876	35¼
..	37½	3	*Kincardine Bridge	32¼
A977	38	½	*Kincardine-on-Forth	31¾
..	42¾	4¾	Forest Mill	27
..	46	3¼	Blairingone	23¾
..	48½	2½	Powmill	21¼
A823	49½	1	*Rumbling Bridge	20¼
..	51	1½	*Yetts of Muckhart	18¾
B934	51¼	¼	Junc A823/B934	18½
..	60¼	9	*Dunning	9½
..	63	2¾	*Forteviot	6¾
B9112	63½	½	Junc B934/B9112	6¼
..	66	2½	Aberdalgie	3¾
A9	68¼	2¼	Cherrybank	1½
..	69¾	1½	***Perth**	

87. STRATHAVEN to STIRLING via Motherwell. Traverses mining and agricultural districts.

A723			***Strathaven**	39¼
..	7½	7½	***Hamilton**	31¾
..	9¾	2¼	***Motherwell**	29½
..	11¾	2	*Carfin	27½
..	12½	¾	*Newarthill	26¾
A73	14¼	1¾	Newhouse	25
..	15½	1¼	Chapelhall	23¾
..	17½	2	*Airdrie	21¾
A80	24¼	6¾	Junc A73/A80	15
..	26½	2¼	*Cumbernauld Bypass	12¾
..	28¼	1¾	*Castlecary	11
..	32¼	4	*Denny Bypass	7
A9	38	5¾	*St Ninian's	1¼
..	39¼	1¼	***Stirling**	

88. AYR to INVERARAY, touring route. Fine scenery along the Ayrshire coast, the Firth of Clyde, Loch Lomond, and in the hills and by the sea lochs of Argyll. Prestwick Airport is passed before leaving the main road to visit the golfing centre of Troon. After a brief stretch of industrial development near Stevenston, a short detour leads to Saltcoats and Ardrossan, while after rejoining the main road another can be made from Sea Mill to *West Kilbride. The road then keeps close to the shore for several miles through the Clyde resorts, with views of the islands of Arran, the Cumbraes and Bute, in the Firth of Clyde, and across to the hills of Cowal. It is mainly industrial along both sides of the river for some miles and Glasgow is avoided by utilising the Erskine Bridge. Attractive scenery along the shores of *Loch Lomond from Arden to Tarbet, with views of Ben Lomond. Turning westward through the hills of Argyll, there are views of Ben Arthur (The Cobbler) approaching Arrochar, at the head of Loch Long. A gradual ascent is made by the reconstructed road in Glen Croe to the summit at Rest and be Thankful, with an undulating descent to the shores of *Loch Fyne.

A79			***Ayr**	112¾
..	2¾	2¾	*Prestwick	110
A778	4	1¼	*Monkton	108¾
B749	4½	½	*Junc A778/B749	108¼
A759	7¾	3¼	***Troon**	105
B746	8	¼	Junc A759/B746	104¾
..	9	1	*Barassie	103¾
A78	10	1	Junc B746/A78	102¾
..	14	4	***Irvine**	98¾
..	15	1	Rd to Bogside Race-course	97¾
			*Kilwinning By-pass	
A738	18½	3½	Junc A78/A738	94¼
..	19	½	*Stevenston	93¾
..	20½	1½	*Saltcoats	92¼
..	22	1½	***Ardrossan**	90¾
A78	22½	½	Junc A738/A78	90¼
..	26¼	3¾	*Sea Mill	86½
..	31¼	5	*Fairlie	81½
..	34	2¾	***Largs**	78¾
..	39½	5½	*Skelmorlie	73¼
..	40	½	***Wemyss Bay**	72¾
..	42¾	2¾	*Inverkip	70
..	45½	2¾	*Cloch Lighthouse	67¼
A8	48¼	2¾	***Gourock**	64½
..	51¼	3	***Greenock**	61½
..	54½	3¼	*Port Glasgow	58¼
..	58¼	3¾	Langbank	54½
B815	61	2¾	Junc A8/B815	51¾
A898	62½	1½	Junc B815/A898	50¼
..	63	½	*Erskine Bridge (Toll)	49¾
A82	63¾	¾	Junc A898/A82	49
..	71¾	8	*Alexandria	41
..	75¼	3½	Arden	37½
..	80¾	5½	*Luss	32
A83	89¼	8½	***Tarbet**	23½
..	91	1¾	*Arrochar	21¾
..	97¾	6¾	*Rest and be Thankful	15
..	103	5¼	*Cairndow	9¾
..	112¾	9¾	***Inveraray**	

89. EDINBURGH to KINLOCH RANNOCH. A scenic, but hilly road throughout, winding in places. An easy pleasant run at first with excellent views of the Forth estuary. Fine mountain views near Rumbling Bridge, approaching the Ochil Hills, which are crossed by a winding road in Glen Devon followed by the long descent to Gleneagles. Pleasant in Strath Earn to Crieff, after which there is fine Highland scenery as the road traverses the *Sma' Glen to Amulree. At Milton, a long climb over the hills by Glen Cochill is followed by a lengthy descent to Aberfeldy. Fine views of the Perthshire Hills hereabouts. Beyond Coshieville, ascends across moorland country skirting the peak of Schiehallion. Care on the winding descent three miles before Kinloch Rannoch.

A90			***Edinburgh**	88½
..	2½	2½	Blackhall	86
..	4½	2	*Barnton	84
A90	5	½	*Cramond Bridge	83½
..	10	5	Forth Road Bridge (Toll)	78½
A823	13	3	Junc A90/A823	75½
..	16	3	***Dunfermline**	72½
..	25¾	9¾	Powmill	62¾
..	26¾	1	*Rumbling Bridge	61¾
..	28¼	1½	*Yetts of Muckhart	60¼
..	30½	2¼	*Glendevon	58
..	36¾	6¼	Loaninghead X-rds	51¾
..	37½	¾	*Gleneagles Hotel	51
A822	42	4½	Junc A823/A822	46½
..	44	2	*Muthill	44½
A85	47½	3½	***Crieff**	41
A822	49½	2	*Gilmerton	39
..	56	6½	*Newton Bridge	32½
..	59¾	3¾	*Amulree	28¾
A826	61½	1¾	*Milton	27
B846	70¾	9¼	***Aberfeldy**	17¾
..	71¾	1	*Weem	16¾
..	76	4¼	*Coshieville	12½
..	79¼	3¼	*White Bridge	9¼
Uncl	79¾	½	Junc B846/Uncl	8¾
..	88½	8¾	***Kinloch Rannoch**	

90. EDINBURGH to PERTH. A 26 mile stretch of dual carriageway and motorway between Cramond Bridge and Glenfarg. Views of the Forth estuary and *Loch Leven. Picturesque in Glen Farg.

A90			***Edinburgh**	43¾
..	2½	2½	Blackhall	41¼
..	4½	2	*Barnton	39¼
..	5	½	*Cramond Bridge	38¾
..	10	5	†Forth Road Bridge (Toll)	33¾
M90	13¼	3¼	Junc A90/M90	30½
..	14	¾	Junc for ***Dunfermline**	29¾
..	17	3	Junc for ***Cowdenbeath**	26¾
..	26½	9½	Junc for *Kinross	17¼
A90	30¾	4¼	Junc M90/A90	13
..	33	2¼	*Glenfarg	10¾
..	39¾	6¾	*Bridge of Earn	4
..	43¾	4	***Perth**	
			†OR Avoiding Motorway Forth Road Bridge	34¾
B981	12¼	2¼	Junc A90/B981	32½
..	13¼	1	*Inverkeithing	31½
A910	17¼	4	*Crossgates	27½
A909	19½	2¼	*Cowdenbeath	25¼
B996	21½	2	road to *Kelty	23¼
..	25¼	3¾	*Gairneybridge	19½
A922	27½	2¼	*Kinross	17¼
B996	29¼	1¾	*Milnathort	15½
A90	31¾	2½	Junc B996/A90	13
..	34	2¼	*Glenfarg	10¾
..	40¾	6¾	*Bridge of Earn	4
..	44¾	4	***Perth**	

91. EDINBURGH to PERTH via Kincardine Bridge. A pleasant, easy road to Kincardine Bridge, then mainly rural scenery. Picturesque in Glen Farg. Milnathort and Kinross may be avoided by using the M90 Motorway.

A8			***Edinburgh**	65½
..	4¼	4¼	*Corstorphine	61¼
B9080	5¼	1	Junc A8/B9080	60¼
..	7¼	2	*Turnhouse Airport	58¼
..	9	1¾	*Kirkliston	56½
A9	10½	1½	Junc B9080/A9	
..	11¼	¾	*Winchburgh	54¼

			***Linlithgow** ..	48¼
M9	21	3¾	Junc A9/M9 ..	44½
A876	26¼	5¼	Junc M9/A876 ..	39¼
..	29¼	3	*Kincardine Bridge	36¼
A977	29¾	½	*Kincardine-on-Forth	35¾
..	34½	4¾	Forest Mill ..	31
..	37¾	3¼	Blairingone ..	27¾
..	40¼	2½	Powmill	25¼
..	42¼	2	*Crook of Devon	23¼
B918	47½	5¼	Junc with M90 ..	18
A922	48¾	¾	*Kinross	17¼
B996	50	1¾	*Milnathort ..	15½
A90	52½	2½	Junc B996/A90 ..	13
..	54¾	2¼	*Glenfarg ..	10¾
..	61½	6¾	*Bridge of Earn ..	4
..	65½	4	***Perth**	

92. EDINBURGH to DUNDEE. An easy pleasant run at first with excellent views of the Forth estuary. Pretty scenery. Views of *Loch Leven. Later through open agricultural country. The ruined *Balmerino Abbey can be reached by turning left before Kilmany. Crosses the Tay Road Bridge between Newport-on-Tay and Dundee.

A90			***Edinburgh**	56¾
..	2½	2½	Blackhall ..	54¼
..	4½	2	*Barnton ..	52¼
..	5	½	*Cramond Bridge	51¾
..	10	5	Forth Road Bridge (Toll)	46¾
M90	13¼	3¼	Junc A90/M90 ..	43½
..	14	¾	Junc for ***Dunfermline** ..	42¾
..	17	3	Junc for ***Cowdenbeath**	39¾
..	26½	9½	Junc for *Kinross	30¼
A91	30	3½	Junc M90/A91 ..	26¾
..	33	3	Gateside	23¾
..	35	2	*Strathmiglo ..	21¾
..	37	2	*Auchtermuchty	19¾
A914	41¼	4¼	Junc A91/A914 ..	15½
..	49¾	8½	*Kilmany ..	7
A92	53¾	4	Junc A914/A92 ..	3
..	54½	¾	*Newport-on-Tay Bypass ..	2¼
			Tay Road Bridge (Toll)	
..	56¾	2¼	***Dundee**	

93. EDINBURGH to ST ANDREWS. A pleasant, easy road through rural scenery, except for a small industrial area near Kirkcaldy. A quicker route is via Auchtermuchty Iters 92, 136.

A90			***Edinburgh** ..	52
..	2½	2½	Blackhall ..	49½
..	4½	2	*Barnton ..	47½
..	5	½	*Cramond Bridge	47
..	10	5	Forth Road Bridge (Toll)	42
A92	12½	2½	Junc A90/A92 ..	39½
..	13	½	*Inverkeithing Bypass ..	39
..	14	1	Hillend	38
..	15¼	1¼	Rd to *Dalgety Bay	36¾
B924	16	¾	Junc A92/B924 ..	36
A907	18½	2½	Junc B924/A907 ..	33½
A92	24¾	6¼	***Kirkcaldy** ..	27¼
..	26¼	1½	Sinclairtown ..	25¾
..	26¾	½	Gallatown ..	25¼
..	29¼	2½	*Thornton ..	22¾
..	31	1¾	*Glenrothes ..	21
..	32	1	Cadham	20
..	36	4	Kettlebridge ..	16
..	38¼	2¼	*Pitlessie	13¾
..	42½	4¼	***Cupar**	9½
..	45½	3	*Dairsie	6½
..	48	2½	*Guardbridge ..	2½
..	52	4	***St Andrews**	

94. EDINBURGH to DUNDEE via the Fife Coast. A pleasant, easy run at first with excellent views of the Forth estuary, before reaching the small industrial area near Kirkcaldy. This route avoids the industrial district on the coast road through Leven (see Iter 128), and later follows a winding, scenic road through some of the Fife coast Royal Burghs to St Andrews. Beyond Guardbridge, a short detour is made to Tayport, where there are views across the Firth of Tay. Pretty scenery throughout, although the road only occasionally approaches the seashore. A direct road (A921) from Upper Largo to Crail through *Colinsburgh passes *Kellie Castle; there is also a direct road (A959) from Anstruther to St Andrews (9½ miles).

A90			***Edinburgh** ..	77¾
..	2½	2½	Blackhall ..	75¼
..	4½	2	*Barnton ..	73¼
..	5	½	*Cramond Bridge	72¾
..	10	5	Forth Road Bridge (Toll)	67¾
A92	12½	2½	Junc A90/A92 ..	65¼
..	13	½	*Inverkeithing Bypass ..	64¾
..	14	1	Hillend	63¾
..	15¼	1¼	Rd to *Dalgety Bay	62½
B924	16	¾	Junc A92/B924 ..	61¾
A907	18½	2½	Junc B924/A907 ..	59¼
A92	24¾	6¼	***Kirkcaldy** ..	53
..	26¼	1½	Sinclairtown ..	51½
..	26¾	½	Gallatown ..	51
A915	27¼	½	Junc A92/A915 ..	50½
..	32½	5¼	*Windygates ..	45¼
..	35	2½	*Scoonie ..	42¾
..	37	2	*Lundin Links ..	40¾
A921	38	1	*Upper Largo ..	39¾
A917	40½	2½	Junc A921/A917	37¼
..	43¼	2¾	*Elie	34½
..	45¾	2½	*St Monance ..	32
..	47¾	2	*Pittenweem ..	30
..	48¾	1	*Anstruther ..	29
..	49¾	1	*Kilrenny ..	28
A918	53	3¼	*Crail	24¾
..	56	3	*Kingsbarns ..	21¾
A91	62¾	6¾	***St Andrews** ..	15
A919	66¾	4	*Guardbridge ..	11
..	68½	1¾	*Leuchars ..	9¼
B945	69¾	1¼	St Michael's Hotel	8
B946	74	4¼	*Tayport	3¾
A92	76	2	Junc B946/A92	1¾
			Tay Road Bridge (Toll)	
..	77¾	1¾	***Dundee**	

95. EDINBURGH to STIRLING. A pleasant, easy road for the greater part, with narrow streets in Falkirk and Camelon. Later passes near to the battlefield at Bannockburn. A quicker route is via the M9 Motorway avoiding Falkirk.

A8			***Edinburgh** ..	36
..	4¼	4¼	*Corstorphine ..	31¾
B9080	8¼	1¼	Junc A8/B9080 ..	30¾
..	7¼	2	*Turnhouse Airport	28¾
..	9	1¾	*Kirkliston ..	27
A9	10½	1½	Junc B9080/A9	
..	11¼	2¼	*Winchburgh ..	24¾
..	17¼	6	***Linlithgow** ..	18¾
..	21¼	4	Junc with M9 ..	14¾
..	21¾	½	*Polmont ..	14¼
..	23½	1¾	Laurieston ..	12½
..	25	1½	***Falkirk**	11
..	26	1	*Camelon ..	10
..	27½	1½	*Larbert	8½
..	31¼	3¾	Plean	4¾
..	33½	2¼	*Bannockburn ..	2½
..	34¾	1¼	*St Ninian's ..	1¼
..	36	1¼	***Stirling**	

96. EDINBURGH to STIRLING, touring route. A pleasant, easy touring route, visiting places of interest near the south bank of the River Forth. 3 miles from Barnton, a short detour can be made to visit the famous Norman church at *Dalmeny before passing beneath the impressive Forth Bridges, where there are views across the river. Very shortly, between Queensferry and Abercorn, *Hopetoun House is passed, after which another detour is made past the mansion of The *Binns to include Blackness Castle. After Linlithgow follows the M9 Motorway.

A90			***Edinburgh** ..	42½
..	2½	2½	Blackhall ..	40
..	4½	2	*Barnton ..	38
..	5	½	*Cramond Bridge	37½
B924	6¼	1¼	Junc A90/B924 ..	36¼
..	8¾	2½	*South Queensferry	33¾
A904	9¾	1	Junc B924/A904	32¾
Uncl	10¾	1	Junc A904/Uncl ..	31¾
..	12½	1¾	*Abercorn ..	30
A904	13¾	1¼	Junc Uncl/A904 ..	28¾
B9109	15½	1¾	Junc A904/B9109 ..	27
B903	17½	2	Junc B9109/B903 ..	25
..	19	1½	*Blackness ..	23½
A9	22¾	3¾	***Linlithgow** ..	19¾
M9	26½	3¾	Junc A9/M9 ..	16
A876	31¾	5¼	Junc M9/A876 ..	10¾
A905	33¼	1½	Junc A876/A905	9¼
..	34½	1¼	*Airth	8
..	39¾	5¼	Fallin	2¾
..	42½	2¾	***Stirling**	

97. GLASGOW to KIRKCALDY via Kincardine Bridge. A commercial route at first, through industrial, mining and agricultural districts. Later utilizes the Kincardine Bridge to cross the River Forth, after which pleasant rural countryside is traversed. See Iter 134 for an alternative road from Kincardine passing through the very interesting little Royal Burgh of *Culross (NT Scot).

A80			***Glasgow** ..	52½
..	4½	4½	Millerston ..	48
..	5¼	¾	*Stepps	47¼
..	7	1¾	*Muirhead ..	45½
..	9½	2½	Mollinburn ..	43
..	11	1½	Condorrat ..	41½
..	14	3	*Cumbernauld Bypass.. ..	38½
..	15¾	1¾	*Castlecary ..	36¾
A876	17¾	2	Junc A80/A876 ..	34¾
..	27¾	10	*Kincardine Bridge	24¾
A985	28¼	½	*Kincardine-on-Forth	24¼
..	34½	6¼	*Torryburn Bypass.. ..	18
A994	35¼	¾	Junc A985/A994 ..	17¼
..	36	¾	Cairneyhill ..	16½
..	37¼	1¼	Crossford ..	15¼
A907	39	1¾	***Dunfermline** ..	13½
..	41¼	2¼	Halbeath.. ..	11¼
..	42½	1¼	*Crossgates ..	10
..	44	1½	*Donibristle ..	8½
..	52½	8½	***Kirkcaldy**	

98. GLASGOW to CRAIL via Kincardine Bridge. Commercial at first, then through an agricultural district, with mining developments. Pleasant rural scenery after crossing the River Forth by Kincardine Bridge, with views of the Ochil Hills nearing Kinross. Pleasant by *Loch Leven, shortly after Milnathort, and later reaches the coast near Lundin Links, afterwards traversing a winding road, with pretty scenery, through the Fife coast Royal Burghs. There is a direct road (A921) from Upper Largo to Crail, through *Colinsburgh, which passes *Kellie Castle.

A803			***Glasgow** ..	86½
..	2¾	2¾	Springburn ..	83¾
..	4¼	1½	*Bishopbriggs ..	82¼
..	8¼	4	*Kirkintilloch Bypass ..	78¼
..	13¼	5	*Kilsyth	73¼
A80	18	4¾	Junc A803/A80 ..	68½
A876	19¼	1¼	June A80/A876 ..	67¼
..	29¼	10	*Kincardine Bridge ..	57¼
			*Kincardine Bridge	
A977	29¾	6¼	*Kincardine-on-Forth	56¾
..	34½	4¾	Forest Mill ..	52
..	37¾	3¼	Blairingone ..	48¾
..	40¼	2½	Powmill	46¼
..	42¼	2	*Crook of Devon	44¼
A90	48¼	6	*Kinross ..	38¼
A911	50	1¾	*Milnathort ..	36½
..	54	4	*Kinnesswood ..	32½
..	54¾	¾	*Portmoak ..	31¾
..	55	¼	*Scotlandwell ..	31½
..	59¼	4¼	*Leslie	27¼
..	61¼	2	Cadham	25¼
..	62½	1¼	*Markinch ..	24
..	64¼	1¾	*Milton of Balgonie ..	22¼
A915	66	1¾	*Windygates ..	20½
..	68½	2½	*Scoonie ..	18
..	70½	2	*Lundin Links ..	16
A921	71½	1	*Upper Largo ..	15
A917	74	2½	Junc A921/A917	12½
..	76¾	2¾	*Elie	9¾
..	79¼	2½	*St Monance ..	7¼
..	81¼	2	*Pittenweem ..	5¼
..	82¼	1	*Anstruther ..	4¼
..	83¼	1	*Kilrenny ..	3¼
..	86½	3¼	*Crail	

99. GLASGOW to STIRLING. A commercial route through industrial, mining and agricultural districts.

A80			***Glasgow** ..	26¾
..	4½	4½	Millerston ..	22¼
..	5¼	¾	*Stepps	21½
..	7	1¾	*Muirhead ..	19¾
..	9½	2½	Mollinburn ..	17¼
..	11	1½	Condorrat ..	15¾
..	14	3	*Cumbernauld Bypass.. ..	12¾
..	15¾	1¾	*Castlecary ..	11
..	19¾	4	*Denny Bypass ..	7
A9	25½	5¾	*St Ninian's ..	1¼
	26¾	1¼	***Stirling**	

100. GLASGOW to FORT WILLIAM. This main road to the Western Highlands is one of the finest highways in Scotland. There is a variety of loch, woodland and mountain scenery on the journey from the industrial banks of the Clyde, by *Loch Lomond and historic *Glencoe to Fort William, which lies at the foot of *Ben Nevis, the highest mountain in Great Britain. After Alexandria, the road, winding in places, follows the west shore of Loch Lomond for more than twenty miles into the Highlands through woodland scenery, with views of Ben Lomond, which rises from the far side of the Loch. Beyond Inveruglas, where the Loch Sloy hydro-electric power station is passed, the road ascends through Glen Falloch to Crianlarich. For 30 miles commencing at Tyndrum, the re-constructed Glencoe road is carefully graded and has an excellent surface. Beyond Bridge of Orchy, Loch Tulla is attractive and contrasts with the bleaker aspect as the Black Mount is skirted to reach a height of 1,143 feet on the open Moor of Rannoch, where part of the old road is seen leading past the *Kingshouse Hotel, on the right. There are magnificent views of the Three Sisters of Glencoe as the road enters the rugged and historic pass of Glencoe and descends past Loch Triochatan to sea level at Carnach (see Iter 142 for an alternative route from this point, avoiding Kinlochleven and the circuit of the Loch by means of the Ballachulish Ferry, saving 12¼ miles). The main road then circles Loch Leven, passing some industrial developments at Kinlochleven, afterwards continuing along the shore of *Loch Linnhe, with extensive views towards the *Ardgour Hills.

A82			***Glasgow** ..	115
..	3	3	Anniesland ..	112
..	7¾	4¾	*Duntocher ..	107¼
..	11¾	4	Milton	103¼
..	16	4¼	*Bonhill	99
..	16¾	¾	*Alexandria ..	98¼
..	20¼	3½	Arden	94¾
..	25¾	5½	*Luss	89¼
..	34¼	8½	***Tarbet**	80¾
..	37¾	3½	*Inveruglas ..	77¼
..	42½	4¾	*Ardlui	72½
..	51	8½	*Crianlarich ..	64
..	56½	5½	*Tyndrum ..	58½
..	63	6½	*Bridge of Orchy	52
..	86¾	23¾	*Carnach ..	28¼
..	93¼	6½	*Kinlochleven ..	21¾
..	102¾	9½	*N Ballachulish..	12¼
..	104¾	2	*Onich	10¼
..	106¼	1½	Rd to *Corran Ferry	8¾
..	115	8¾	***Fort William**	

101. GLASGOW to INVERARAY. Industrial along Clydeside, but beyond Alexandria a scenic road, at first along the shores of *Loch Lomond to Tarbet, with views of Ben Lomond. Beyond Arrochar, at the head of Loch Long, is the Argyll Forest Park with a fine view of Ben Arthur (The Cobbler). Then the gradual ascent of the reconstructed road in Glen Croe to the summit at Rest and be Thankful is made, followed by an undulating descent to the shores of *Loch Fyne.

A82			***Glasgow** ..	57¾
..	3	3	Anniesland ..	54¾
..	7¾	4¾	*Duntocher ..	50
..	11¾	4	Milton	46
..	16	4¼	*Bonhill	41¾
..	16¾	¾	*Alexandria ..	41
..	20¼	3½	Arden	37½
..	25¾	5½	*Luss	32
A83	34¼	8½	***Tarbet**	23½
..	36	1¾	*Arrochar ..	21¾
..	42¾	6¾	*Rest and be Thankful ..	15
..	48	5¼	*Cairndow ..	9¾
..	57¾	9¾	***Inveraray**	

102. A tour from GLASGOW to INVERARAY through Cowal. Industrial along Clydeside to Dumbarton, then fine mountain and loch scenery by the shores of the Gare Loch and Loch Long, with an ascent of 1 in 7 between Garelochhead and Whistlefield, followed by a similar descent. Views of Ben Arthur (The Cobbler) approaching Arrochar. See Iter 101 for an alternative route by Loch Lomond to Arrochar. Passes through the *Cowal district with the lochs and mountains of the Argyll Forest Park, partly by narrow roads with steep gradients, portions of which can be omitted as desired. Leaving Loch Long, there is a gradual ascent by the reconstructed road in Glen Croe to the summit at Rest and be Thankful, where a detour is made to picturesque Lochgoilhead. This narrow road has passing places and a gradient of 1 in 7. The tour then traverses Hell's Glen (1 in 5) to *Loch Fyne, and after a short stretch along the shore goes inland through the hills overlooking Loch Eck, to turn off by a narrow, hilly road (1 in 4) to Glen Finart and the shores of Loch Long at Ardentinny. Thereafter a level coast road gives views of the Rosneath peninsula, before circling the Holy Loch by Hunter's Quay to Dunoon. See Iter 137 for the direct route. On the detour along the coast past Toward Point to the road end at Inverchaolin, there are views of the islands of Bute and the *Cumbraes in the Firth of Clyde. Leaving Dunoon, the tour turns inland again by a scenic, narrow and winding road through hills, near the head of pretty Loch Striven. After an ascent of 1 in 5 the tour follows a new road with views of Loch Riddon to reach Tighnabruaich on the well-known *Kyles of Bute, then from Kames the road becomes narrow and hilly and beyond Otter Ferry follows the shore of Loch Fyne and rounds the head of the loch.

A82			*Glasgow	191
..	3	3	Anniesland	188
..	7¾	4¾	*Duntocher	183¼
..	11¾	4	Milton	179¼
A814	12	¼	Junc A82/A814	179
..	14	2	**Dumbarton**	177
..	17½	3½	*Cardross	173½
..	21¼	3¾	Rd to *Craigendoran Pier	169¾
..	22	¾	*Helensburgh	169
..	24¼	2¼	*Rhu	166¾
..	28½	4¼	*Faslane	162½
..	29½	1	*Garelochhead	161½
..	31	1½	*Whistlefield	160
..	32½	1½	*Finnart	158½
..	39½	7	*Arrochar	151½
B828	46½	6¾	*Rest and be Thankful	144¾
B839	49½	3¼	Junc B828/B839	141½
..	52¼	2¾	*Lochgoilhead	138¾
			Return	
A815	58½	6¼	Junc B839/A815	132½
..	61¼	2¾	*St Catherine's	129¾
..	65¼	4	Creggans Inn	125¾
..	66¼	1	*Strachur Bypass	124¾
Uncl	72½	6¼	Junc A815/Uncl	118½
A880	77¾	5¼	*Ardentinny	113¼
..	81½	3¾	*Blairmore	109½
..	82¼	¾	*Strone	108¾
..	83¾	1½	*Kilmun	107¼
A815	85¼	1½	Cothouse Bridge	105¾
..	87½	2¼	*Sandbank	103½
..	88	½	*Ardnadam	103
..	89½	1½	*Hunter's Quay	101½
..	90¼	¾	*Kirn	100¾
..	91½	1¼	***Dunoon**	99½
..	95¾	4¼	*Innellan	95¼
Uncl	102	6¼	Junc A815/Uncl	89
..	105½	3½	*Inverchaolin Ch	85½
			Return to:	
A885	119½	14	***Dunoon**	71½
A815	122¼	2¾	*Sandbank	68¾
B836	123½	1¼	Junc A815/B836	67½
..		2	Clachaig	65½
A886		8½	Rd to *Colintraive	57
A8003	135½	1½	Junc A886/A8003	55½
B8000	143½	8	*Tighnabruaich	47½
..	144	½	*Auchenlochan	47
..	144½	½	*Kames	46½
..	145¾	1¼	Millhouse	45¼
..	151½	5¾	*Kilfinan	39½
..	155½	4	*Otter Ferry	35½
..	166¼	10¾	*Strathlachan	24¾
A886		1½	Junc B8000/A886	
A815		3¼	*Strachur	
..	175½	4½	*St Catherines	15½
..	180½	5	Junc A815/A83	10½
..	181¼	¾	*Cairndow	9¾
..	191	9¾	***Inveraray**	

103. GLASGOW to TIGHNABRUAICH or COLINTRAIVE (for the Kyles of Bute). Fine mountain and loch scenery in the *Cowal district of Argyll, with views of Ben Arthur (The Cobbler) across Loch Long approaching Arrochar. See Iter 102 for an alternative route to Arrochar, by Loch Long. A gradual ascent from Loch Long by the reconstructed road in Glen Croe to the summit at Rest and be Thankful is followed by an undulating descent to *Loch Fyne, the shores of which are followed for over 25 miles. Pretty scenery in Glendaruel thence a scenic shore road along Loch Riddon to the *Kyles of Bute.

			*Glasgow	80½
			By Iter 100 to:	
A83	34¼	34¼	***Tarbet**	46¼
..	36	1¾	*Arrochar	44½
..	42¾	6¾	*Rest and be Thankful	37¾
A815	47¼	4½	Junc A83/A815	33¼
..	52¼	5	*St Catherine's	28¼
..	56¼	4	†Creggans Inn	24¼
A886	56½	¼	Junc A815/A886	23¾
..	71¼	14¾	*Glendaruel	9
A8003	72¼	1	†Junc A886/A8003	8
..	80½	8	*Tighnabruaich	
			† OR	
A886			Junc A886/A8003	
..	79½	7	*Colintraive	

104. GLASGOW to ROWARDENNAN. After leaving the suburbs of Glasgow, there is a pleasant run across *Stockiemuir, passing the AA viewpoint at *Auchineden. Between Balmaha and Rowardennan, at the foot of Ben Lomond, a narrow, wooded road (with several short hills up to 1 in 6), follows the shores of *Loch Lomond, with views of the prettily wooded islands on the loch.

A82			*Glasgow	28¼
A806	3	3	Anniesland	25¼
A809	4½	1½	Junc A806/A809	23¾
..	5½	1	*Bearsden	22¾
A811	17	11½	Junc A809/A811	11¼
B837	17¾	¾	*Drymen	10½
Uncl	21¾	4	*Balmaha	6½
..	28¼	6½	*Rowardennan	

105. GLASGOW to INVERSNAID. Pleasant in Strathblane, after leaving the suburbs of Glasgow, with views of the Campsie Fells. Open country to Aberfoyle, after which the narrow road passes between the hills and by several lochs, including Loch Arklet. There is a steep descent (1 in 10) to Inversnaid on *Loch Lomond. The steamer pier on Loch Katrine, at *Stronachlachar, lies ¾ mile to the east from the end of B829.

A82			*Glasgow	42¼
A806	3	3	Anniesland	39¼
A81	4½	1½	Junc A806/A81	37¾
..	5¼	¾	Hillfoot (Sta)	37
..	6¾	1½	*Milngavie	35½
..	11	4¼	*Strathblane	31¼
..	11¾	¾	Blanefield	30½
..	19¾	8	Ballat X-rds	22½
A821	26¼	6½	Junc A81/A821	16
B829	27¼	1	*Aberfoyle	15
Uncl	38¼	11	Junc B829/Uncl	4
..	42¼	4	*Inversnaid	

106. GLASGOW to CALLANDER via the Trossachs. A touring route, with splendid loch and woodland scenery on the latter part. After leaving the suburbs of Glasgow, there is a pleasant run across *Stockiemuir, passing the AA viewpoint at *Auchineden, to Drymen, followed by open country to Aberfoyle. A picturesque, winding road then climbs over the hills, with magnificent views towards Loch Vennachar and the Trossachs. Returning from Loch Katrine, the prettily wooded shores of Loch Achray are followed at first, then on by the larger Loch Vennachar to Callander.

A82			*Glasgow	45¼
A806	3	3	Anniesland	42¼
A809	4½	1½	Junc A806/A809	40¾
..	5½	1	*Bearsden	39¾
A811	17	11½	Junc A809/A811	28¼
..	17¾	¾	*Drymen	27½
A81	21½	3¾	Ballat X-rds	23¾
A821	28	6½	Junc A81/A821	17¼
..	29	1	*Aberfoyle	16¼
..	35½	6½	*Loch Katrine Pier	9¾
..	36¾	1¼	*Trossachs Hotel	8½

..	38½	1¾	*Brig o' Turk	6¾
A84	44	5½	Kilmahog	1¼
..	45¼	1¼	***Callander**	

107. GLASGOW to ABERFELDY via the Campsie Fells and Glen Lyon. A touring route throughout, using narrow and hilly by-roads in places, although these can easily be omitted as desired. Leaves the main road before Torrance, crosses flat country to Lennoxtown, then a long climb by *Campsie Glen to the summit (1,154 feet) on the Campsie Fells, from which there are extensive views. A long descent leads through Fintry and skirts the Fintry Hills to Kippen, followed by a flat stretch to Thornhill, whence it is rather hilly to Callander. Alternatively the touring route via The Trossachs (Iter 106) can be used. Onwards to Killin is by the main road, with an attractive stretch between Callander and Strathyre, by the Falls of Leny, where road and river wind through the pass to the shores of Loch Lubnaig. Views of Loch Earn approaching Lochearnhead, after which there is a gradual ascent through Glen Ogle over the ridge to descend into Glen Dochart and Killin. After a short run along *Loch Tay, the route turns off by the slopes of Ben Lawers along a narrow track, towards a gap in the hills. This is a rough and rutted mountain road, giving magnificent views on the gradual 4 miles ascent (max gradient 1 in 6). The lonely Lochan na Lairige is passed before reaching the summit at 1,805 feet, after which there is a similar 4 miles descent to Bridge of Balgie in Glen Lyon. This road is easier to traverse from north to south, but can be omitted if desired, by proceeding direct along the north shore of Loch Tay to Fortingall (Iter 138) or to Lawers and Aberfeldy (Iter 120). Glen Lyon is one of the longest in the country, and for those not venturing by the direct road over to Bridge of Balgie, a delightful and easy return journey can be made from Fortingall through the pretty Pass of Lyon. From Bridge of Balgie, a motoring road continues, past Meggernie Castle, with a gradually deteriorating surface, towards the wild head of the glen. Between Fortingall and Aberfeldy it is an easy valley road.

A803			***Glasgow**	90
..	2¾	2¾	Springburn	87¼
..	4¼	1½	*Bishopbriggs	85¾
A807	6¼	2	Junc A803/A807	83¾
B822	7	¾	Junc A807/B822	83
..	7¼	¼	Torrance	82¾
A891	10	2¾	Junc B822/A891	80
B822	10¾	¾	*Lennoxtown	79¼
B818	18	7¼	Junc B822/B818	72
..	18½	½	*Fintry	71½
B822	19¼	¾	Junc B818/B822	70¾
..	25¾	6½	*Kippen	64¼
..	30	4¼	Thornhill	60
A81	33¾	3¾	Junc B822/A81	56¼
A84	35¾	2	***Callander**	54¼
..	37	1¼	Kilmahog	53
..	44½	7½	*Strathyre	45½
..	46½	2	(road to) *Balquhidder	43½
A85	49¼	2¾	*Lochearnhead	40¾
A827	54¼	5	Lix Toll	35¾
..	56¾	2½	*Killin	33¼
Uncl	61¼	4½	Junc A827/Uncl	28¾
..	70¼	9	*Bridge of Balgie	19¾
..	71¼	1	*Innerwick Ch	18¾
..	73¼	2	Camusvrachan	16¾
..	76¼	3	Invervar	13¾
..	81¾	5½	*Fortingall	8¼
B846	84¾	3	*Coshieville	5¼
..	89	4¼	*Weem	1
..	90	1	***Aberfeldy**	

108. GLASGOW to STIRLING via Killearn. Pleasant in Strathblane, after leaving the suburbs of Glasgow, with views of the Campsie Fells, later through open country and following a level road for the last ten miles. Passes close to the villages of *Kippen and *Gargunnock.

A82			***Glasgow**	38½
A806	3	3	Anniesland	35½
A81	4½	1½	Junc A806/A81	34
..	5¼	¾	Hillfoot	33¼
..	6¾	1½	*Milngavie	31¾
..	11	4¼	*Strathblane	27½
..	11¾	¾	Blanefield	26¾
A875	14½	2¾	Junc A81/A875	24
..	16¾	2¼	*Killearn	21¾
..	19½	2¾	*Balfron	19
A811	21½	2	Junc A875/A811	17
..	23¾	2¼	*Buchlyvie	14¾
..	26¼	2½	Arnprior	12¼
..	38½	12¼	***Stirling**	

109. PAISLEY to CALLANDER via Erskine Ferry. A useful link route avoiding Glasgow by means of the Erskine Bridge. Featureless country to Bonhill, then fine open scenery, later passing the Lake of Menteith before reaching Port of Menteith. About half-way between this point and Callander the road is hilly, with an ascent and descent of 1 in 9.

A726			***Paisley**	44¾
M8	1½	1½	Junc A726/M8	43¼
M898	4¾	3¼	Junc M8/M898	40
A898	6	1¼	Junc M898/A898	38¾
..	6½	½	*Erskine Bridge (Toll)	38¼
A82	7¼	¾	Junc A898/A82	37½
A811	12¾	5½	Junc A83/A811	32
..	15	2¼	*Bonhill	29¾
..	16	1	Jamestown	28¾
..	20	4	*Gartocharn	24¾
..	24½	4½	*Drymen	20¼
A81	28	3½	Ballat X-rds	16¾
..	38	10	*Port of Menteith	6¾
..	44¾	6¾	***Callander**	

110. PAISLEY to OBAN via Erskine Bridge. This is an excellent road through beautiful loch and mountain scenery. After Alexandria, the road winds along the shores of *Loch Lomond into the Highlands, with views of Ben Lomond. At Inveruglas is the Loch Sloy hydro-electric power station, and the road then goes by way of Glen Falloch to Crianlarich and Tyndrum, near which Ben Lui is well seen. There is a fine view of Ben Cruachan approaching Dalmally, before crossing Loch Awe by the new bridge near *Kilchurn Castle, and there are more extensive views as the road follows the lochside towards the narrowing Pass of Brander. Pleasant along the shore road of Loch Etive before passing beneath Connel Bridge, after which *Dunstaffnage Castle lies just north of the road.

A726			***Paisley**	92¼
M8	1½	1½	Junc A726/M8	90¾
M898	4¾	3¼	Junc M8/M898	87½
A898	6	1¼	Junc M898/A898	86¼
..	6½	½	*Erskine Bridge (Toll)	85¾
A82	7¼	¾	Junc A898/A82	85
..	15¾	8½	*Alexandria	76½
..	19¼	3½	Arden	73
..	24¾	5½	*Luss	67½
..	33¼	8½	***Tarbet**	59
..	36¾	3½	*Inveruglas	55½
..	41½	4¾	*Ardlui	50¾
..	50	8½	*Crianlarich	42¼
A85	55½	5½	*Tyndrum	36¾
..	67½	12	*Dalmally	24¾
..	70½	3	*Loch Awe (Hotel)	21¾
..	74	3½	*Falls of Cruachan	18¼
..	77½	3½	Bridge of Awe	14¾
..	80	2½	*Taynuilt	12¼
..	87	7	*Connel	5¼
..	92¼	5¼	***Oban**	

111. A tour from PAISLEY to STIRLING via Loch Long and the Trossachs. A tour embracing the sea lochs of Dunbartonshire, together with some of the lochs and mountains of the Perthshire Highlands, and including the Trossachs district. Avoiding Glasgow by the Erskine Bridge, the tour traverses flat country on the industrial north bank of the Clyde to Dumbarton. Beyond Helensburgh, there is fine mountain and loch scenery on the shores of the Gare Loch and Loch Long. Between Garelochhead and Whistlefield there is an ascent of 1 in 7 followed by a similar descent. Views of Ben Arthur (The Cobbler) approaching Arrochar, before crossing to the shore of *Loch Lomond, where there is a fine view of Ben Lomond. If preferred, the direct road along Loch Lomondside can be followed from the Bridge, see Iter 110. Continuing into the Highlands, by the shores of Loch Lomond, the Loch Sloy hydro-electric power station is passed by Inveruglas, the tour then ascending through Glen Falloch to Crianlarich, and traversing in turn Glen Dochart and Glen Ogle, with Ben More overlooking the former. Lochearnhead is situated above Loch Earn, and an attractive stretch beyond Strathyre leads by the winding shores of pretty Loch Lubnaig, and afterwards by way of the Pass and Falls of Leny to Kilmahog, where a short detour can be made to visit Callander, before taking the road to the Trossachs along the edge of Loch Vennachar and the wooded Loch Achray. Returning from Loch Katrine, a picturesque, winding road crosses over the hills, giving extensive views, before descending to Aberfoyle and past the Lake of Menteith to the open country.

A726			***Paisley** ..	120¼
M8	1½	1½	Junc A726/M8 ..	118¾
M898	4¾	3¼	Junc M8/M898 ..	115½
A898	6	1¼	Junc M898/A898	114¼
..	6½	½	*Erskine Bridge (Toll)	113¾
A82	7¼	¾	Junc A898/A82 ..	113
A814	11¼	4	Junc A82/A814 ..	109
..	13¼	2	***Dumbarton** ..	107
..	16¾	3½	*Cardross ..	103½
..	20½	3¾	Rd to *Craigendoran Pier ..	99¾
..	21¼	¾	*Helensburgh ..	99
..	22½	2¼	*Rhu	96¾
..	27¾	4¼	*Faslane ..	92½
..	28¾	1	*Garelochhead ..	91½
..	30¼	1½	*Whistlefield ..	90
..	31¾	1½	*Finnart ..	88½
A83	38¾	7	*Arrochar ..	81½
A82	40½	1¾	***Tarbet**	79¾
..	43	3½	*Inveruglas ..	76¼
..	48¾	4¾	*Ardlui	71½
A85	57¼	8½	*Crianlarich ..	63
..	68½	11¼	Lix Toll ..	51¾
A84	73½	5	*Lochearnhead ..	46¾
..	76¼	2¾	(road to) *Balquhidder	44
..	78¼	2	*Strathyre ..	42
A821	85¾	7½	Kilmahog ..	34½
..	91¼	5½	*Brig o' Turk ..	29
..	93	1¾	*Trossachs Hotel	27¼
..	94¼	1¼	*Loch Katrine Pier	26
..	100¾	6½	*Aberfoyle ..	19½
A81	101¾	1	Junc A821/A81 ..	18½
..	105¼	3½	*Port of Menteith	15
A873	106½	1¼	Junc A81/A873 ..	13¾
..	110½	4	Thornhill ..	9¾
A84	114¼	3¾	Junc A873/A84 ..	6
..	120¼	6	***Stirling**	

112. GOUROCK to STIRLING via Erskine Bridge. Industrial on the south bank of the River Clyde, then utilizes the Erskine Bridge to avoid Glasgow. Traverses pleasant, open agricultural country beyond Bonhill, with views of the Campsie Fells, to the south-east, and following a level road for the last ten miles, passing close to the villages of *Kippen and *Gargunnock.

A8			***Gourock** ..	54¼
..	3	3	***Greenock** ..	51¼
..	6¼	3¼	*Port Glasgow ..	48
..	10	3¾	Langbank ..	44¼
B815	12¾	2¾	Junc A8/B815 ..	41½
A898	14¼	1½	Junc B815/A898 ..	40
..	14¾	½	*Erskine Bridge (Toll)	39½
A82	15½	¾	Junc A898/A82 ..	38¾
A811	20¾	5¼	Junc A82/A811 ..	33½
..	22¾	2	*Bonhill	31½
..	23¾	1	Jamestown ..	30½
..	27¾	4	*Gartocharn ..	26½
..	32¼	4½	*Drymen ..	22
..	36	3¾	Ballat X-rds ..	18¼
..	39½	3½	*Buchlyvie ..	14¾
..	42	2½	Arnprior ..	12¼
..	54¼	12¼	***Stirling**	

113. FALKIRK to GOUROCK via Erskine Bridge. At first through agricultural districts, with mining developments in places. From Kirkintilloch an intricate cross-country route is followed, avoiding Glasgow to the north and crossing the River Clyde by the Erskine Bridge. Industrial on the banks of the Clyde.

A9			***Falkirk**	46¼
A803	1	1	*Camelon ..	45¼
..	4	3	*Bonnybridge ..	42¼
..	5½	1½	*Dennyloanhead	40¾
..	11	5½	*Kilsyth	35¼
..	16	5	*Kirkintilloch (Bypass) ..	30¼
A807	18¼	2¼	Junc A803/A807	28
..	19	¾	Torrance ..	27¼
..	20¼	1¼	Balmore	26
A81	23½	3¼	Junc A807/A81 ..	22¾
A808	24¾	1¼	Hillfoot (Sta) ..	21½
A809	25¼	½	*Bearsden ..	21
A810	25¾	½	Junc A809/A810	20½
..	28¼	2½	Hardgate ..	18
	29	¾	*Duntocher ..	17¼
A82	29¾	¾	Junc A810/A82 ..	16½
A898	30¾	1	Junc A82/A898 ..	15½
..	31½	¾	*Erskine Bridge (Toll)	14¾
B815	32	½	Junc A898/B815 ..	14¼
A8	33½	1½	Junc B815/A8 ..	12¾
..	36¼	2¾	Langbank ..	10
..	40	3¾	*Port Glasgow ..	6¼
..	43¼	3¼	***Greenock** ..	3
..	46¼	3	***Gourock**	

114. FALKIRK to HELENSBURGH via Fintry. Industrial to Denny, then a tourist route by a narrow and hilly moorland road to Fintry, which lies between the Fintry Hills and Campsie Fells. Undulating on the latter part, and touches the shore of Loch Lomond for a short distance. The quickest way to Gartocharn is by Stirling (Iters 95 and 137).

A9			***Falkirk**	45¼
A803	1	1	*Camelon ..	44¼
A883	2¼	1¼	Junc A803/A883	43
B818	5½	3¼	*Denny	39¾
..	18½	13	*Fintry	26¾
A875	24¾	6¼	Junc B818/A875	20½
B834	25¾	1	*Killearn ..	19½
A809	28	2¼	Junc B834/A809	17¼
A811	30¼	2¼	Junc A809/A811	15
..	33¾	3½	*Gartocharn ..	11½
A813	37	3¼	Junc A811/A813	8¼
..	37½	½	*Balloch ..	7¾
A82	37¾	¼	Junc A813/A82 ..	7½
B831	40¼	2½	Arden	5
B832	41¾	1½	Junc B831/A832	3½
..	45¼	3½	*Helensburgh	

115. FALKIRK to ROWARDENNAN via Kilsyth. A cross-country link, with mining developments in places to Kilsyth, then pleasant agricultural scenery with views of the Campsie Fells to the north. Between Balmaha and Rowardennan, at the foot of Ben Lomond, a narrow, wooded road (with several short hills up to 1 in 6) follows the shores of *Loch Lomond, with views of the prettily wooded islands on the loch. Iter 114 shows an alternative route through Fintry, but the quickest route is via Stirling (Iters 95 and 137) to Drymen.

A9			***Falkirk**	42
A803	1	1	*Camelon ..	41
..	4	3	*Bonnybridge ..	38
..	5½	1½	*Dennyloanhead	36½
..	11	5½	*Kilsyth	31
A891	14	3	Junc A803/A891	28
..	15¾	1¾	Milton	26¼
..	17½	1¾	*Lennoxtown ..	24½
..	18¾	1¼	*Campsie Glen ..	23¼
A81	22¼	3½	*Strathblane ..	19¾
..	23	¾	Blanefield ..	19
B834	27½	4½	Junc A81/B834	14½
A809	28½	1	Junc B834/A809	13½
A811	30¾	2¼	Junc A809/A811	11¼
B837	31½	¾	*Drymen ..	10½
Uncl	35½	4	*Balmaha ..	6½
..	42	6½	*Rowardennan	

116. HELENSBURGH to COULPORT (Rosneath peninsula). Except between Rosneath and Kilcreggan, where there is a short ascent and descent, this is a practically level road circling the shores of the Gare Loch to the Rosneath peninsula, and finally along the shores of Loch Long.

A814			*Helensburgh ..	21¾
..	2¼	2¼	*Rhu	19½
..	6½	4¼	*Faslane ..	15¼
..	7½	1	*Garelochhead ..	14¼
B833	7¾	¼	Junc A814/B833	14
..	12½	4¾	Clynder	9¼
..	13¼	¾	*Rosneath ..	8½
..	15¾	2½	*Kilcreggan ..	6
..	17¾	2	*Cove	4
..	21¾	4	*Coulport	

117. INVERARAY to OBAN. Splendid views of Loch Awe and Ben Cruachan from the crest of the hill between Inveraray and Cladich, where there is a short 1 in 8 gradient. Crosses the new bridge near *Kilchurn Castle and follows the banks of Loch Awe towards the narrowing Pass of Brander. Pleasant along the shore road by Loch Etive before passing under Connel Bridge, after which *Dunstaffnage Castle lies just to the north of the road. For alternative routes see Iter 118 and 119.

A819			***Inveraray** ..	38¾
..	9¼	9¼	*Cladich ..	29½
A85	15	5¾	Junc A819/A85 ..	23¾
..	17	2	*Loch Awe Hotel	21¾
..	20½	3½	*Falls of Cruachan	18½
..	24	3½	Bridge of Awe ..	14¾
..	26½	2½	*Taynuilt ..	12¼
..	33½	7	*Connel ..	5¼
..	38¾	5¼	***Oban**	

118. INVERARAY to OBAN via Lochgilphead. A very fine scenic route, with a variety of loch and mountain scenery, becoming hilly on the latter part. Follows the shore of *Loch Fyne to Lochgilphead, and is level to Kilmartin. Approaching Kintraw the road becomes hilly (max gradient 1 in 8). Later follows the edge of Loch Melfort, through the wooded Pass of Melfort to Kilninver, after which there is a pleasant stretch along Loch Feochan.

A83			***Inveraray** ..	61¾
..	6	6	*Auchindrain ..	55¾
..	8	2	*Furnace ..	53¾
..	10	2	*Crarae	51¾
..	11½	1½	*Minard ..	50¼
..	17	5½	*Lochgair ..	44¾
A816	24½	7½	*Lochgilphead ..	37¼
..	28¼	3¾	*Kilmichael Glassary ..	33½
..	32¾	4½	*Kilmartin ..	29
..	38¼	5½	*Kintraw ..	23½
..	46½	8¼	*Kilmelford ..	15¼
..	53½	7	*Kilninver ..	8¼
..	61¾	8¼	***Oban**	

119. INVERARAY to OBAN or ARDRISHAIG via Loch Awe. Splendid views of Ben Cruachan and *Loch Awe from the crest of the hill between Inveraray and Cladich, afterwards following a secondary road with fair surface alongside Loch Awe for many miles. Hilly after joining the main road beyond Ford Hotel, with a maximum gradient of 1 in 8. Later follows the edge of Loch Melfort and through the wooded Pass of Melfort to Kilninver, after which there is a pleasant stretch along Loch Feochan. The alternative follows a level road back to Loch Fyne at Ardrishaig.

A819			***Inveraray** ..	60¾
B840	9¼	9¼	*Cladich ..	51¾
..	13¾	3½	*Portsonachan ..	48
..	21¼	8½	*Portinnisherrich	39½
..	30½	9¼	†*Ford (Hotel) ..	30¼
A816	33¼	2¾	Junc B840/A816	27½
..	37¼	4	*Kintraw ..	23½
..	45½	8¼	*Kilmelford ..	15¼
..	52½	7	*Kilninver ..	8¼
..	60¾	8¼	***Oban**	
			† OR	
B840	30½		*Ford Hotel	
A816	33¼	2¾	Junc B840/A816	
	34¾	1½	*Kilmartin	
..	39¼	4½	*Kilmichael Glassary	
A817	42¼	3	Junc A816/A817	
A83	42¾	½	Junc A817/A83	
..	44¼	1½	***Ardrishaig**	

120. INVERARAY to PITLOCHRY. Splendid views of Ben Cruachan and Loch Awe from the crest of the hill between Inveraray and Cladich, then an easy, undulating road through the hills to Killin, where there is a grand view of Ben Lawers. The whole length of *Loch Tay is then traversed to Kenmore, after which it is pleasant in the Tay and Tummel valleys.

A819			***Inveraray** ..	84¼
..	9¼	9¼	*Cladich ..	75
A85	15	5¾	Junc A819/A85 ..	69¼
..	16	1	*Dalmally ..	68¼
A82	28	12	*Tyndrum ..	56¼
..	33½	5½	*Crianlarich ..	50¾
A827	44¾	11¼	Lix Toll	39½
..	47¼	2½	*Killin	37
..	55¾	8½	*Lawers	28½
..	60	4¼	*Fearnan ..	24¼
..	63½	3½	*Kenmore ..	20¾
..	69¾	6¼	***Aberfeldy** ..	14½
..	74¾	5	*Grandtully ..	9½
..	79	4¼	*Logierait ..	5¼
A9	79¾	¾	Ballinluig ..	4½
..	84¼	4½	***Pitlochry**	

121. INVERARAY to CAMPBELTOWN. A fine scenic run at first along the shores of *Loch Fyne to Tarbert, then crossing a narrow isthmus to the shores of West Loch Tarbert, and following the Atlantic coast road on the west side of the *Kintyre peninsula. Hilly between Whitehouse and Clachan, with a maximum gradient of 1 in 7.

A83			***Inveraray** ..	76¼
..	6	6	*Auchindrain ..	70¼
..	8	2	*Furnace ..	68¼
..	10	2	*Crarae	66¼
..	11½	1½	*Minard ..	64¾
..	17	5½	*Lochgair ..	59¼
..	24½	7½	*Lochgilphead ..	51¾
..	26½	2	***Ardrishaig** ..	49¾
..	38¼	11¾	*Tarbert ..	38
..	39¾	1½	Rd to Tarbert West Pier	36½
..	44¼	4½	Whitehouse ..	32
..	49¼	5	Clachan ..	27
..	57¼	8	*Tayinloan ..	19
..	58¼	1	*Killean	18
..	63¾	5½	*Glenbarr ..	12½
..	66¾	3	Bellochantuy ..	9½
..	76¼	9½	*Campbeltown	

122. CAMPBELTOWN to OBAN via the East Coast of Kintyre. A fine scenic tour along the east coast of *Kintyre, later touching the west coast of Argyll with its numerous islands off-shore. A narrow, winding and hilly road to West Loch Tarbert, particularly hilly between Saddell and Carradale, where there are gradients of 1 in 7, with hairpin bends. Fine views of the Isle of Arran across Kilbrennan Sound. A short detour can be made from Claonaig to visit *Skipness (2½ miles). The main road to Tarbert is by the west coast of Kintyre, see Iter 121. Beyond Tarbert a level road along the shore of *Loch Fyne is followed to Ardrishaig, then inland to Kilmartin. In *Knapdale a hilly road (B8024) provides a loop from Tarbert to Ardrishaig, passing by West Loch Tarbert and Loch Killisport. Approaching Kintraw the road becomes hilly (maximum gradient 1 in 8). Later the road follows the edge of Loch Melfort and then through the wooded Pass of Melfort to Kilninver, after which there is a pleasant stretch along Loch Feochan. Between Ardrishaig and Kilmichael, a detour can be made along the Crinan Canal via *Cairnbaan to visit *Crinan, with possible extensions by Loch Sween to *Kilmory Knap and *Tayvallich. Another detour can be made at Kilninver for *Clachan Bridge leading to the slate-quarrying island of Seil.

B842			*Campbeltown ..	89½
..	10	10	*Saddell	79½
..	15	5	*Carradale (PO)	74½
..	19½	4½	*Grogport ..	70
B8001	29	9½	*Claonaig ..	60½
A83	33¾	4¾	Junc B8001/A83	55¾
..	37¾	4	Rd to Tarbert West Pier ..	51¾
..	39¼	1½	*Tarbert ..	50¼
..	51	11¾	***Ardrishaig** ..	38½
A817	52½	1½	Junc A83/A817 ..	37
A816	53	½	Junc A817/A816	36½
..	56	3	*Kilmichael Glassary ..	33½
..	60½	4½	*Kilmartin ..	29
..	66	5½	*Kintraw ..	23½
..	74¼	8¼	*Kilmelford ..	15¼
..	81¼	7	*Kilninver ..	8¼
..	89½	8¼	***Oban**	

123. CAMPBELTOWN to MACHRIHANISH and MULL OF KINTYRE. Two independent routes covering the southern extremity of the *Kintyre peninsula. A level road is followed to Machrihanish on the Atlantic coast. The road to Southend is hilly, then follows the coast to Carskey, after which it is only a rough private track (gradient 1 in 7).

A83			*Campbeltown	5¾
B843	1¾	1¾	Stewarton ..	4
..	4	2¼	Drumlemble ..	1¾
..	5¾	1¾	*Machrihanish	
			OR	
A83			*Campbeltown	18½
B842	1¾	1¾	Stewarton ..	16¾
Uncl	9½	7¾	*Southend ..	9
..	13	3½	Carskey	5½
..	18½	5½	*Mull Lighthouse (Mull of Kintyre)	

124. OBAN to FORT WILLIAM via Connel Bridge. A coast route, with fine mountain and loch scenery, and utilizing the bridge across Loch Etive at Connel. *Dunstaffnage Castle lies just north of the road before reaching Connel, and *Barcaldine Castle is to the west beyond Benderloch. A side road to *Port Appin is passed before reaching the coast at Portnacroish, with a view of Castle Stalker, on its island, and there are extensive prospects across *Loch Linnhe towards the *Ardgour Hills. At Ballachulish, the road turns inland to encircle *Loch Leven, with some fine views of the Glencoe Hills. There is some industrial development at Kinlochleven, and if preferred the journey around Loch Leven can be avoided by crossing the ferry at Ballachulish, saving 19¼ miles. The latter part of the route is by a shore road alongside Loch Linnhe to Fort William, at the foot of *Ben Nevis, the highest mountain in Great Britain. A detour can be made from Connel North along the north shore of Loch Etive passing the ruined priory of *Ardchattan, and thence by B845 over the hill and by Glen Salach to rejoin the main road around Loch Creran. For an alternative touring route through Glencoe and avoiding Connel Bridge, see Iter 125.

A85			***Oban**	68
A828	4¾	4¾	Junc A85/A828 ..	63¼
			*Connel Br	
..	5¼	½	Connel North	62¾
..	7½	2¼	Ledaig	60½
..	8	½	*Benderloch ..	60
..	20½	12½	*Creagan ..	47½
..	23½	3	*Appin (PO) ..	44½
..	24	½	*Portnacroish ..	44
..	29¾	5¾	*Duror	38¼
..	33½	3¾	*Kentallen ..	34½
..	36¼	2¾	†*Ballachulish Hotel	31¾
..	37½	1¼	*Ballachulish ..	30½
A82	39¾	2¼	*Carnach ..	28¼
..	46¼	6½	*Kinlochleven ..	21¾
..	55¾	9½	*N Ballachulish	12¼
..	57¾	2	*Onich	10¼
..	59¼	1½	Rd to *Corran Ferry	8¾
..	68	8¾	***Fort William**	
	†		OR	
A828	36¼		***Ballachulish Hotel Ferry to Loch Leven Hotel**	
A82	36½	¼	*N Ballachulish	
..	38½	2	*Onich	
..	40	1½	Rd to *Corran Ferry	
..	48¾	8¾	***Fort William**	

125. OBAN to FORT WILLIAM via the Pass of Glencoe. Magnificent mountain and loch scenery throughout. *Dunstaffnage Castle lies just north of the road before passing under Connel Bridge, after which a pleasant road is followed along the shore of Loch Etive, on which *Bonawe is situated, just off the road from Taynuilt. Views of Ben Cruachan before reaching the Pass of Brander, then a shore road alongside Loch Awe, later passing *Kilchurn Castle. Easy to Tyndrum, then for 30 miles follows the reconstructed *Glencoe road, carefully graded and with an excellent surface. The direct road (B8074) from Dalmally by Glen Orchy to Bridge of Orchy is an attractive valley road, with fine views, but has a rough surface in places and is rather narrow, with numerous passing bays. Beyond Bridge of Orchy, Loch Tulla is attractive, and contrasts with the bleaker aspect of the Black Mount, which is skirted to reach a height of 1,143 feet on the open Moor of Rannoch. Part of the old road is seen leading past the *Kingshouse Hotel on the right, while another road to the left through Glen Etive ends at Loch Etive head. There are magnificent views of the Three Sisters of Glencoe as the road enters the rugged and historic Pass of Glencoe and descends, past Loch Triochatan to sea level at *Loch Leven. See Iter 142 for an alternative from this point using the Ballachulish ferry to avoid Kinlochleven and the circuit of the loch thus saving 12¼ miles The main road then circles Loch Leven, passing some industrial development at Kinlochleven, afterwards continuing along the shores of *Loch Linnhe, with extensive views towards the *Ardgour hills, to reach Fort William, at the foot of *Ben Nevis, the highest mountain in Great Britain. The direct road from Oban is given in Iter 124.

A85			***Oban**	95¼
..	5¼	5¼	*Connel	90
..	12¼	7	*Taynuilt ..	83
..	14¾	2½	Bridge of Awe ..	80½
..	18¼	3½	*Falls of Cruachan	77
..	21¾	3½	*Loch Awe Hotel	73½
..	24¾	3	*Dalmally ..	70½
A82	36¾	12	*Tyndrum ..	58½
..	43¼	6½	*Bridge of Orchy	52
..	67	23¾	*Carnach ..	28¼
..	73½	6½	*Kinlochleven ..	21¾
..	83	9½	*N Ballachulish	12¼
..	85	2	*Onich	10¼
..	86½	1½	Rd to *Corran Ferry ..	8¾
..	95¼	8¾	***Fort William**	

126. KIRKCALDY to DUNDEE. Through open agricultural country. The ruined *Balmerino Abbey can be reached by turning left before Kilmany. Crosses the Tay Road Bridge between Newport-on-Tay and Dundee.

A92			***Kirkcaldy** ..	29¾
..	1½	1½	Sinclairtown ..	28¼
..	2	½	Gallatown ..	27¾
..	4½	2½	*Thornton ..	25¼
..	6¼	1¾	*Glenrothes ..	23½
..	7¼	1	Cadham	22½
A914	9¼	2	Junc A92/A914	20½
..	22¾	13½	*Kilmany ..	7
A92	26¾	4	Junc A914/A92 ..	3
..	27½	¾	*Newport-on-Tay (Bypass) ..	2¼
..			Tay Road Bridge (Toll)	
..	29¾	2¼	***Dundee**	

127. KIRKCALDY to DUNDEE via Cupar. Pleasant, open agricultural country for the greater part. Hilly between Windygates and Cupar, with an ascent of 1 in 9 at Kennoway. Crosses the Tay Road Bridge between Newport-on-Tay and Dundee. The normal route is given in Iter 126 and a better way to Cupar is by Iter 93.

A92			***Kirkcaldy** ..	31¼
..	1½	1½	Sinclairtown ..	29¾
..	2	½	Gallatown ..	29¼
A915	2½	½	Junc A92/A915 ..	28¾
A916	7¾	5¼	*Windygates ..	23½
..	9¼	1½	Kennoway ..	22
..	15¼	6	*Craigrothie ..	16
A92	17½	2¼	Junc A916/A92 ..	13¾
A91	18¼	¾	***Cupar**	13
..	21¼	3	*Dairsie ..	10
A92	21½	¼	Junc A91/A92 ..	9¾
..	25¼	3¾	St Michael's Hotel	6
..	29	3¾	*Newport-on-Tay (Bypass)	2¼
			Tay Road Bridge (Toll)	
..	31¼	2¼	***Dundee**	

128. KIRKCALDY to ST ANDREWS via Leven. Colliery developments on the coast road to Lundin Links. Between Dysart and Coaltown there is a side road leading to *West Wemyss. Hilly, agricultural country on the latter part. The quickest way to Lundin Links is by Windygates, Iter 94, and to St Andrews the quickest is by Cupar, see Iter 93.

A92			***Kirkcaldy** ..	24
A955	1¼	1¼	Junc A92/A955 ..	22¾
..	2	¾	*Dysart ..	22
..	4½	2½	Coaltown of Wemyss	19½
..	5¾	1¼	*East Wemyss	18¼
..	7¼	1½	*Buckhaven	16¾
..	8¼	1	*Methil ..	15¾
..	9¼	1	*Leven ..	14¾
A915	10	¾	*Scoonie ..	14
..	12	2	*Lundin Links	12
..	13	1	*Upper Largo	11
..	17¼	4¼	Largoward	6¾
..	18¼	1	Lathones ..	5¾
..	24	5¾	***St Andrews**	

129. KIRKCALDY to ST ANDREWS via Ceres. Pleasant agricultural country. Hilly between Windygates and Ceres, with an ascent of 1 in 9 at Kennoway. Utilizes secondary roads from Craigrothie.

A92			***Kirkcaldy** ..	24¾
..	1½	1½	Sinclairtown ..	23¼
..	2	½	Gallatown ..	22¾
A915	2½	½	Junc A92/A915 ..	22¼

A916	7¾	5¼	*Windygates ..	17
..	9¾	1½	Kennoway ..	15½
B939	15¼	6	*Craigrothie ..	9½
..	16¾	1½	*Ceres	8
..	18¼	1½	*Pitscottie ..	6½
..	24¾	6½	***St Andrews**	

130. KIRKCALDY to PERTH. An easy road, with varied scenery, mainly through agricultural country, with views of the Lomond and Ochil Hills. Pretty in Glenfarg near the Bein Inn.

A92			***Kirkcaldy** ..	28¼
..	1½	1½	Sinclairtown ..	26¾
..	2	½	Gallatown ..	26¼
..	4½	2½	*Thornton ..	23¾
..	6¼	1¾	*Glenrothes ..	22
..	7¼	1	Cadham ..	21
A912	9¼	2	Junc A92/A912 ..	19
..	11½	2¼	*Falkland ..	16¾
..	15	3½	*Strathmiglo ..	13¼
A91	15¼	¼	Junc A912/A91 ..	13
A912	17	1¾	Gateside	11¼
A90	20	3	Junc A912/A90 ..	8¼
..	24¼	4¼	*Bridge of Earn ..	4
..	28¼	4	***Perth**	

131. ST ANDREWS to PERTH. Pretty scenery, with fine views of the River Tay on the latter part.

A91			***St Andrews** ..	31¼
..	4	4	*Guardbridge ..	27¼
..	6½	2½	*Dairsie ..	24¾
A913	9½	3	***Cupar**	21¾
..	17¾	8¼	*Lindores ..	13½
..	20	2¼	*Newburgh ..	11¼
..	23½	3½	*Abernethy ..	8
A90	25	1½	Junc A913/A90 ..	6¼
..	27¼	2¼	*Bridge of Earn ..	4
..	31¼	4	***Perth**	

132. PERTH to CRAIL or ELIE. Pretty scenery, with views of the River Tay on the first part. Hilly from Cupar to Crail and also from Cupar to Elie.

A90			***Perth**	39¼
..	4	4	*Bridge of Earn ..	35¼
A913	6¼	2¼	Junc A90/A913 ..	33
..	8	1¾	*Abernethy ..	31¼
..	11¼	3¼	*Newburgh ..	28
..	13½	2¼	*Lindores ..	25¾
B940	21¾	8¼	***Cupar**	17½
..	24¾	3	*Pitscottie ..	14½
..	28¼	3½	†Peat Inn ..	11
A918	38¾	10½	Junc B940/A918	½
..	39¼	½	*Crail	
	†		OR	
B941	28¼		Peat Inn	
..	30	1¾	Largoward	
..	34½	4½	*Kinconquhar	
A917	35¼	¾	Junc B941/A917	
..	36¼	1	*Elie	

133. STIRLING to KIRKCALDY via Dunfermline. A pleasant, easy road with views of the Ochil Hills on the first part.

A9	1¾	1¾	***Stirling**	35
A91	1¾	1¾	*Causewayhead	33¼
A907	2¾	1	Junc A91/A907 ..	32¼
..	5¼	2½	Cambus ..	29¾
..	7½	2¼	***Alloa**	27½
..	9¼	1¾	*Clackmannan ..	25¼
..	16¾	7½	*Oakley ..	18¼
..	18	1¼	Carnock	17
..	21½	2½	***Dunfermline** ..	13½
..	23¼	2¼	Halbeath.. ..	11¼
..	25	1¼	*Crossgates ..	10
..	26½	1½	Donibristle ..	8½
..	35	8½	***Kirkcaldy**	

134. STIRLING to KIRKCALDY via Culross. Views of the Ochil Hills at first, and beyond Kincardine some fine scenery along the shores of the River Forth, including a detour to visit Culross (NT Scot) and views of the Forth Bridges. Hilly beyond Aberdour, where there is an ascent of 1 in 6½. A shorter route (by 1½ miles) to Kincardine is by the south side of the River Forth, then across Kincardine Bridge. The direct road from Kincardine to Newmills is shown in Iter 97 and the coast road through Burntisland and Kinghorn can be avoided by proceeding via B923 from Kirkton. The quickest route from Stirling to Kirkcaldy is by Dunfermline (Iter 133).

A9			***Stirling**	39¼
A91	1¾	1¾	*Causewayhead	37½
A907	2¾	1	Junc A91/A907 ..	36½
..	5¼	2½	Cambus ..	34
..	7½	2¼	***Alloa**	31¾
..	9¼	1¾	*Clackmannan ..	30
A985	10½	1¼	Junc A907/A985	28¾
A977	11	½	Junc A985/A977	28¼
Uncl	12¼	1¼	Junc A977/Uncl	27
..	12¾	½	*Kincardine-on-Forth ..	26½
..	16¾	4	*Culross ..	22½
B9037	17¾	1	Junc Uncl/B9037	21½
..	18½	¾	*Newmills ..	20¾
..	19¼	¾	*Torryburn ..	20
A985	20¾	1½	Junc B9037/A985	18½
..	21	¼	Crombie	18¼
..	25¾	4¾	*Rosyth ..	13½
A92	26¾	1	*Inverkeithing Bypass ..	12½
..	27¾	1	Hillend	11½
..	29	1¼	Rd to *Dalgety Bay ..	10¼
..	30½	1½	*Aberdour ..	8¾
..	33¼	2¾	Kirkton	6
..	33¾	½	***Burntisland** (WM) ..	5½
..	36¼	2½	*Kinghorn ..	3
..	39¼	3	***Kirkcaldy**	

135. STIRLING to PERTH. An easy main road through fine country, with views of the Ochil Hills at first. Carsebreck Pond lies to the north of the road between Greenloaning and Blackford. Extensive views of the Perthshire hills on the latter part. Causewayhead and Bridge of Allan may be avoided by using M9 Motorway.

A9			***Stirling**	34½
..	1¾	1¾	*Causewayhead	32¾
..	3¼	1½	*Bridge of Allan	31¼
..	6	2¾	*Dunblane ..	28½
..	11½	5½	*Greenloaning ..	23
..	16	4½	*Blackford ..	18½
..	18	2	Loaninghead X-rds ..	16½
..	18¾	¾	*Gleneagles (Sta)	15¾
..	20¼	1½	*Auchterarder ..	14¼
..	23	2¾	*Aberuthven ..	11½
..	33	10	Cherrybank ..	1½
..	34½	1½	***Perth**	

136. STIRLING to ST ANDREWS. Fine scenery along the foot of the Ochil Hills to Milnathort, with views of Castle Campbell at Dollar. Later, a pleasant, easy road with pretty scenery, through agricultural country. Milnathort may be avoided by using the M90 Motorway.

A9			***Stirling**	51½
A91	1¾	1¾	*Causewayhead	49¾
..	4¼	2½	*Blairlogie ..	47¼
..	5¾	1½	Menstrie ..	45¾
..	7¾	2	*Alva	43¾
..	10	2¼	*Tillicoultry ..	41½
..	13	3	*Dollar ..	38½
..	16½	3½	*Yetts of Muckhart ..	35
..	20	3½	Carnbo ..	31½
..	24¼	4¼	*Milnathort ..	27¼
..	29	4¾	Gateside ..	22½
..	31	2	*Strathmiglo ..	20½
..	33	2	*Auchtermuchty	18½
..	38¼	5¼	Bow of Fife ..	13¼
..	42	3¾	***Cupar**	9½
..	45	3	*Dairsie	6½
..	47½	2½	*Guardbridge ..	4
..	51½	4	***St Andrews**	

137. STIRLING to DUNOON. Traverses a variety of agricultural, loch, woodland and mountain scenery. A broad level road for the first ten miles, with views of the Campsie Fells to the south, and passing close to the villages of *Gargunnock and *Kippen. Through pleasant, open agricultural districts to Balloch, after which the road follows the shore of *Loch Lomond to Tarbet, with views of Ben Lomond. Pleasant at Arrochar, on Loch Long, where there is a fine view of Ben Arthur (The Cobbler), before the gradual ascent by the reconstructed road in Glen Croe to the summit at Rest and be Thankful. An undulating descent leads to the shore of *Loch Fyne, which is followed for several miles before turning inland through the *Cowal district of Argyll. Very pretty along the shore road beside *Loch Eck, and shortly passes the well-wooded Benmore Estate of the Argyll National Forest Park, later touching the shore of the Holy Loch near Sandbank.

A811			***Stirling**	88½
..	12¼	12¼	Arnprior ..	76¼

..	14¾	2½	*Buchlyvie ..	73¾
..	18¼	3½	Ballat X-rds ..	70¼
..	22	3¾	*Drymen ..	66½
..	26¼	4¼	*Gartocharn ..	62
A813	29¾	3½	Junc A811/A813	58¾
..	30¼	½	*Balloch ..	58¼
A82	30½	¼	Junc A813/A82 ..	58
..	33	2½	Arden	55½
..	38½	5½	*Luss	50
A83	47	8½	***Tarbet**	41½
..	48¾	1¾	*Arrochar ..	39¾
..	55½	6¾	*Rest and be Thankful ..	33
A815	60	4½	Junc A83/A815 ..	28½
..	65	5	*St Catherine's ..	23½
..	69	4	Creggans Inn ..	19½
..	70	1	*Strachur (By-pass) ..	18½
..	81½	11½	*Benmore Estate	7
..	83½	2	Cothouse Bridge	5
A885	85¾	2¼	*Sandbank ..	2¾
..	88½	2¾	***Dunoon**	

138. A tour from STIRLING to AVIEMORE via Loch Earn, the Tummel Valley and Speyside. A tour through the lochs and mountains of the Perthshire Highlands, later crossing the Grampian mountains to skirt *Rothiemurchus Forest. Views of the Ochil hills at first, and passing the great Roman Station of Ardoch near Braco, then a pleasant road over the hills to Comrie, afterwards following the north shore of Loch Earn. There is also a narrow and hilly road along the south shore of the loch leading past Ardvorlich House and the Edinample Falls, while other routes to Lochearnhead are given in Iters 141 and 142. A gradual ascent through Glen Ogle leads over the ridge to Glen Dochart and Killin. Views of Ben Lawers from the road along the north shore of *Loch Tay, while after Fearnan a pleasantly wooded valley leads to Coshieville. A long climb over moorlands, reaching an altitude of 1,263 feet just beyond White Bridge, affords a view of Schiehallion, before a similar descent to the hydro-electric power station at Tummel Bridge. Picturesque by the wooded Loch Tummel to Queen's View, after which there is some development in connection with the hydro-electric power scheme. The road becomes hilly and winding to Bridge of Garry, where the main road is joined close by the historic Pass of Killiecrankie. Beyond Blair Atholl, desolate moorland country in the Grampians is traversed as the road climbs gradually to the summit of Drumochter Pass (1,506 feet). After the long descent, a narrow by-road is followed on the south side of well-timbered Strath Spey and finally skirts Rothiemurchus Forest.

A9			***Stirling**	136¼
..	1¾	1¾	*Causewayhead	134½
..	3¼	1½	*Bridge of Allan	133
..	6	2¾	*Dunblane ..	130¼
A822	11½	5½	*Greenloaning ..	124¾
..	13¼	1¾	*Braco	123
B827	13¾	½	Junc A822/B827	122½
A85	24¼	10½	*Comrie	112
..	29¾	5½	*St Fillans ..	106½
..	36¾	7	*Lochearnhead ..	99½
A827	41¾	5	Lix Toll ..	94½
..	44¼	2½	*Killin	92
..	52¾	8½	*Lawers	83½
Uncl	57	4¼	*Fearnan ..	79¼
..	59¼	2¼	*Fortingall ..	77
B846	62¼	3	*Coshieville ..	74
..	65½	3¼	*White Bridge ..	70¾
B8019	70½	5	*Tummel Bridge	65¾
..	77	6½	*Queen's View ..	59¼
..	78¾	1¾	*Fincastle PO ..	57½
..	81	2¼	*Bridge of Garry	55¼
A9	81¼	¼	Junc B8019/A9 ..	55
..	82¼	1	*Killiecrankie ..	54
..	85½	3¼	***Blair Atholl** ..	50¾
..	95¾	10¼	*Dalnacardoch ..	40½
..	101¼	5½	*Dalnaspidal ..	35
..	103	1¾	*Drumochter Pass (summit) ..	33¼
..	109	6	*Dalwhinnie ..	27¼
B970	118½	9½	Junc A9/B970 ..	17¾
..	122¼	3¾	*Ruthven ..	14
..	124	1¾	*Tromie Bridge ..	12¼
..	126	2	*Insh	10¼
..	129¾	3¾	*Feshie Bridge ..	6½
A951	135¼	5½	Inverdruie ..	1
..	136¼	1	*Aviemore	

139. A tour from STIRLING to PITLOCHRY via the Trossachs and the Tay Valley. A tour embracing the Trossachs and the loch, mountain and woodland scenery of the Perthshire Highlands. Open country, passing the Lake of Menteith to Aberfoyle, then climbs over the hills by a picturesque, winding road, with magnificent views of the Trossachs and Loch Vennachar. Returning from Loch Katrine, the tour passes the edge of Lochs Achray and Vennachar before reaching Callander. For alternative routes to Callander see Iters 141 and 142. An attractive stretch between Kilmahog and Strathyre by the Falls of Leny, where the road winds through the Pass of Leny to the shores of pretty Loch Lubnaig. Views of Loch Earn approaching Lochearnhead, after which there is a gradual ascent through Glen Ogle over the ridge to descend to Glen Dochart and Loch Tay. The wooded road along the south side of the loch is narrow and hilly, but there are splendid views of Ben Lawers. The main road by Killin and the north side of the loch (Iter 120) has a better surface, but is less scenic. Pleasant along Strath Tay through Aberfeldy to the delightful, well-timbered district around Dunkeld, where the river is crossed, and the tour doubles back to follow the opposite side of the valley to Ballinluig, and afterwards by the banks of the Tummel to Pitlochry.

A84			***Stirling**	107¾
A873	6	6	Junc A84/A873 ..	101¾
..	9¾	3¾	Thornhill ..	98
A81	13¾	4	Junc A873/A81 ..	94
..	15	1¼	*Port of Menteith	92¾
A821	18½	3½	Junc A81/A821 ..	89¼
..	19½	1	*Aberfoyle ..	88¼
..	26	6½	*Loch Katrine Pier	81¾
..	27¼	1¼	*Trossachs Hotel	80½
..	29	1¾	*Brig o' Turk ..	78¾
A892	33½	4½	Junc A821/A892	74¼
A81	35	1½	Junc A892/A81 ..	72¾
A84	35¼	¼	***Callander** ..	72½
..	36½	1¼	Kilmahog ..	71¼
..	44	7½	*Strathyre ..	63¾
..	46	2	(road to) *Balquhidder ..	61¾
..	48¾	2¾	*Lochearnhead ..	59
A827	53¾	5	Lix Toll	54
Uncl	55¾	2	Junc A827/Uncl	52
..	62¼	6½	Ardeonaig ..	45½
..	65¾	2½	Ardtalnaig ..	42
..	70½	4¾	Acharn	37¼
A827	72	1½	Junc Uncl/A827	35¾
..	78	6	***Aberfeldy** ..	29¾
B898	83	5	*Grandtully ..	24¾
A9	95	12	Junc B898/A822/A9 ..	12¾
..	95¼	¼	***Dunkeld** ..	12½
..	103¼	8	Ballinluig ..	4½
..	107¾	4½	***Pitlochry**	

140. STIRLING to INVERNESS via the Sma' Glen. During the summer months this is recommended as a through route across the Grampian mountains to the north, since this picturesque way to Dunkeld is also the shortest. For the winter months, and in periods of bad weather, the best way is by Perth (Iter 135 and 150). Views of the Ochil hills at first, and passing the great Roman Station of Ardoch near Braco, then pleasant, though rather winding in Strath Earn to Crieff, after which there is fine Highland scenery as the road ascends the *Sma' Glen to Amulree. Later descends by Strath Bran to the well-wooded district around Dunkeld, afterwards following parts of the valleys of the Tay, Tummel and Garry, then through the wooded Pass of Killiecrankie. Beyond Blair Atholl, desolate moorland country is entered as the road climbs gradually to the summit of Drumochter Pass (1,506 feet), then descends, later by the well-timbered Strath Spey, to about 700 feet at Aviemore, after which another gradual climb over the open moorlands leads to Slochd Summit (1,333 feet). Rather winding as Strath Dearn and Strath Nairn are crossed on the long gradual descent to sea level at Inverness.

A9			***Stirling**	144½
..	1¾	1¾	*Causewayhead ..	142¾
..	3¼	1½	*Bridge of Allan	141¼
..	6	2¾	*Dunblane ..	138½
A822	11½	5½	*Greenloaning ..	133
..	13¼	1¾	*Braco	131¼
..	19½	6¼	*Muthill	125
A85	23	3½	***Crieff**	121½
A822	25	2	*Gilmerton ..	119½
..	31½	6½	*Newton Bridge	113
..	35¼	3¾	*Amulree ..	109¼
..	37	1¾	*Milton	107½
..	41	4	Trochry	103½
A9	44½	3½	Junc A822/A9 ..	100
..	44¾	¼	***Dunkeld** ..	99¾
..	52¾	8	Ballinluig ..	91¾
..	57¼	4½	***Pitlochry** ..	87¼
..	61	3¾	*Killiecrankie ..	83½

..	64¼	3¼	***Blair Atholl** ..	80¼
..	74½	10¼	*Dalnacardoch ..	70
..	80	5½	*Dalnaspidal ..	64½
..	81¾	1¾	*Drumochter Pass (summit) ..	62¾
..	87¾	6	*Dalwhinnie ..	56¾
..	98½	10¾	*Newtonmore ..	46
..	101¼	2¾	***Kingussie** ..	43¼
..	107	5¾	*Kincraig ..	37½
..	110¾	3¾	*Lynwilg	33¾
..	113¼	2½	*Aviemore ..	31¼
..	120¼	7	*Carrbridge ..	24¼
..	126	5¾	*Slochd Summit	18½
..	128½	2½	*Tomatin ..	16
..	133¼	4¾	*Moy	11¼
..	138¾	5½	*Daviot	5¾
..	144½	5¾	***Inverness**	

141. A tour from STIRLING to GRANTOWN-ON-SPEY via Lochearnhead, Dunkeld and Balmoral. A scenic tour of the lochs, valleys and hills of Perthshire, afterwards crossing the Grampian mountains to Braemar in the Dee Valley, then skirting the Cairngorm mountains by way of Strathdon and the Lecht Road. Very high altitudes are attained and the road is liable to be blocked by snow during the winter months particularly at the Devil's Elbow beyond Spittal of Glenshee and also between Cock Bridge and Tomintoul. At first traverses pleasant agricultural country with views of the hills approaching Callander, the main road to which is shown in Iter 142. An attractive stretch between Kilmahog and Strathyre by the Falls of Leny, where the road winds through the Pass of Leny to the shores of pretty Loch Lubnaig. Follows the north shore of Loch Earn, although just before reaching Lochearnhead a narrow and hilly road, leading along the south shore, could be followed past Edinample Falls and Ardvorlich House. Fine scenery ascending the *Sma' Glen to Amulree, afterwards descending by Strath Bran to the wooded district around Dunkeld, the direct route to which is given in Iter 140. Pretty along the foot of the hills, where several lochs and the village of *Clunie lie adjacent to the road, then at Blairgowrie turns northwards into the hills by a long gradual ascent of Glen Shee. Between Spittal of Glenshee and Cairnwell summit the road becomes steeper until at Devil's Elbow the general gradient is 1 in 9, with a maximum of 1 in 5 on the awkward S bends. This summit (2,199 feet) is the highest altitude reached by any classified motoring road in Great Britain. After a gradual descent to wooded *Deeside, the Royal residence of *Balmoral Castle is passed. Leaving the Dee Valley at Cambus o'May the road passes close to Lochs Kinord and Davan, then by the Don Valley to Cock Bridge beyond which the road is narrow with a 1 in 5 ascent leading to the summit of the Lecht Road (2,090 feet), followed by a long descent to Tomintoul. After several ascents and descents (maximum gradient 1 in 7) between Bridge of Avon and the summit beyond Bridge of Brown, a gradual descent leads to the wooded Strath Spey. For the direct road between Braemar and Cock Bridge see Iter 160.

A9			***Stirling**	186
..	1¾	1¾	*Causewayhead ..	184¼
..	3¼	1½	*Bridge of Allan	182¾
A820	6	2¾	*Dunblane ..	180
A84	10¼	4¼	*Doune	175¾
..	17¾	7½	***Callander** ..	168¼
..	19	1¼	Kilmahog ..	167
..	26½	7½	*Strathyre ..	159½
..	28½	2	(road to) *Balquhidder	157½
A85	31¼	2¾	*Lochearnhead ..	154¾
..	38¼	7	*St Fillans ..	147¾
..	43¾	5½	*Comrie	142¼
..	50½	6¾	***Crieff**	135½
A822	52½	2	*Gilmerton ..	133½
..	59	6½	*Newton Bridge	127
..	62¾	3¾	*Amulree ..	123¼
..	64½	1¾	*Milton	121½
..	68½	4	Trochry	117½
A9	72	3½	Junc A822/A9 ..	114
..	72¼	¼	***Dunkeld** ..	113¾
A923	72¾	½	Junc A9/A923 ..	113¼
..	76¼	3½	*Butterstone ..	109¾
A93	83¾	7½	***Blairgowrie** ..	102¼
..	84¼	½	*Rattray	101¾
..	89¾	5½	*Bridge of Cally	96¼
..	97¾	8	*Lair	88¼
..	102¾	5	*Spittal of Glenshee ..	83¼
..	108¼	5½	*Cairnwell Pass (summit) ..	77¾
..	117¾	9½	***Braemar** ..	68¼
..	127	9¼	*Crathie Ch ..	59
..	133	6	Bridge of Gairn ..	53
..	134½	1½	*Ballater	51½
..	138	3½	*Cambus o' May	48
A97	139	1	Junc A93/A97 ..	47
Uncl	141½	2½	Junc A97/Uncl ..	44½
A97	143	1½	Junc Uncl/A97 ..	43
..	143¾	¾	Logie Coldstone ..	42¼
B973	151¼	7½	Junc A97/B973 ..	34¾
..	153¾	2½	*Strathdon ..	32¼
A939	159¾	6	Colnabaichin ..	26¼
..	161¼	1½	*Corgarff ..	24¾
..	165½	1¼	*Cock Bridge ..	23½
..	172¼	9¾	*Tomintoul ..	13¾
..	174¼	2	*Bridge of Avon	11¾
..	176½	2¼	*Bridge of Brown	9½
A95	184½	8	Junc A939/A95 ..	1½
..	186	1½	***Grantown-on-Spey**	

142. STIRLING to FORT WILLIAM via Ballachulish Ferry. Pleasant agricultural country at first, with views of the hills approaching Callander, whence the road passes through the heart of the Highlands, traversing splendid mountain loch and moorland scenery. An attractive stretch between Kilmahog and Strathyre, by the Falls of Leny, where the road winds through the Pass of Leny to the shores of pretty Loch Lubnaig. Views of Loch Earn approaching Lochearnhead, after which the road ascends to the ridge through Glen Ogle and then descends to Glen Dochart, which is traversed under the slopes of Ben More to Crianlarich. For 30 miles from Tyndrum follows the reconstructed *Glencoe road, which is carefully graded and has an excellent surface. Beyond Bridge of Orchy, Loch Tulla is attractive, and contrasts with the bleaker aspect as the Black Mount is skirted to cross the open Moor of Rannoch at a height of 1,143 feet, where part of the old road is seen leading past the *Kingshouse Hotel on the right. There are magnificent views of the Three Sisters of Glencoe as the road enters the Pass of Glencoe and descends past Loch Triochatan to sea level, then by the shores of *Loch Leven to the Ballachulish Ferry. (If desired the ferry can be avoided by following the main road encircling Loch Leven by Kinlochleven, 12¼ miles farther, see Iter 100.) Afterwards the shore of *Loch Linnhe is followed, with extensive views towards the *Ardgour hills, to reach Fort William, at the foot of *Ben Nevis, the highest mountain in Great Britain.

A84			***Stirling**	97¼
..	6¼	6¼	*Kincardine Ch ..	91
..	8¼	2	*Doune	89
..	15¾	7½	***Callander** ..	81½
..	17	1¼	Kilmahog ..	80¼
..	24½	7½	*Strathyre ..	72¾
..	26½	2	(road to) *Balquhidder	70¾
A85	29¼	2¾	*Lochearnhead ..	68
..	34¼	5	Lix Toll	63
A82	45½	11¼	*Crianlarich ..	51¾
..	51	5½	*Tyndrum ..	46¼
..	57½	6½	*Bridge of Orchy	39¾
A828	81¼	23¾	*Carnach ..	16
..	83½	2¼	*Ballachulish ..	13¾
..	84¾	1¼	*Ballachulish Hotel Ferry to Loch Leven Hotel	12½
A82	85	¼	*N Ballachulish ..	12¼
..	87	2	*Onich	10¼
..	88½	1½	Rd to *Corran Ferry	8¾
..	97¼	8¾	***Fort William**	

143. PITLOCHRY to FORT WILLIAM. Fine mountain and moorland scenery, at first through the wooded Pass of Killiecrankie to Blair Atholl, then across the desolate Grampian mountains by a gradual ascent, reaching the summit at Drumochter Pass (1,506 feet). Leaves the main road near Dalwhinnie, and reaches the Upper Spey valley at Drumgask, then follows the shores of Loch Laggan and through pretty Glen Spean to Roy Bridge and Spean Bridge. Open country on the latter part, with views of *Ben Nevis.

A9			***Pitlochry** ..	76
..	3¾	3¾	*Killiecrankie ..	72¼
..	7	3¾	***Blair Atholl** ..	69
..	17¼	10¼	*Dalnacardoch ..	58¾
..	22¾	5½	*Dalnaspidal ..	53¼
..	24½	1¾	*Drumochter Pass (summit) ..	51½
..	30½	6	*Dalwhinnie ..	45½
A899	31¼	¾	Junc A9/A889 ..	44¾
A86	37¾	6½	*Drumgask ..	38¼
..	44½	6¾	*Loch Laggan Inn ..	31½

..	57¾	13¼	Rd to *Tulloch Sta	18¼
..	63¼	5½	*Roy Bridge ..	12¾
A82	66½	3¼	***Spean Bridge** ..	9½
..	73¾	7¼	Lochy Bridge (near side)	2¼
..	76	2¼	***Fort William**	

144. STIRLING to OBAN. Pleasant agricultural country at first, with views of the hills approaching Callander, whence the road passes through the heart of the Highlands traversing splendid mountain, loch and moorland scenery. An attractive stretch between Kilmahog and Strathyre by the Falls of Leny, where the road winds through the Pass of Leny to the shores of pretty Loch Lubnaig. Views of Loch Earn approaching Lochearnhead, after which there is a gradual ascent through Glen Ogle over the ridge to descend into Glen Dochart, which is then followed under the slopes of Ben More to Crianlarich and on to Tyndrum. There is a fine view of Ben Cruachan approaching Dalmally, before crossing Loch Awe by the new bridge near *Kilchurn Castle, and there are more extensive views as the road follows the lochside towards the narrowing Pass of Brander. Pleasant along the shore road of Loch Etive before passing beneath Connel Bridge, after which *Dunstaffnage Castle lies just north of the road.

A84			***Stirling**	87¾
..	6¼	6¼	*Kincardine Ch.. ..	81½
..	8¼	2	*Doune	79½
..	15¾	7½	***Callander** ..	72
..	17	1¼	Kilmahog ..	70¾
..	24½	7½	*Strathyre ..	63¼
..	26½	2	(road to) *Balquhidder	61¼
A85	29¼	2¾	*Lochearnhead ..	58½
..	34¼	5	Lix Toll	53½
A82	45½	11¼	*Crianlarich ..	42¼
A85	51	5½	*Tyndrum ..	36¾
..	63	12	*Dalmally ..	24¾
..	66	3	*Loch Awe Hotel	21¾
..	69½	3½	*Falls of Cruachan	18¼
..	73	3½	Bridge of Awe ..	14¾
..	75½	2½	*Taynuilt ..	12¼
..	82½	7	*Connel	5¼
..	87¾	5¼	***Oban**	

145. PERTH to OBAN. Beautiful scenery, by way of Strath Earn and the shores of Loch Earn to the Highlands, with views of the Perthshire hills. An alternative narrow and hilly road along the south shore of Loch Earn leads past Ardvorlich House and the Edinample Falls. After Lochearnhead, there is a gradual ascent through Glen Ogle over the ridge to descend into Glen Dochart, which is then followed under the slopes of Ben More to Crianlarich and on to Tyndrum. There is a fine view of Ben Cruachan approaching Dalmally, before crossing Loch Awe by the new bridge near *Kilchurn Castle, and there are more extensive views as the road follows the lochside towards the narrowing Pass of Brander. Pleasant along the shore of Loch Etive before passing beneath Connel Bridge, after which *Dunstaffnage Castle lies just north of the road.

A85			***Perth**	95¼
..	2¾	2¾	*Huntingtower ..	92½
..	6½	3¾	*Methven ..	88¾
..	12¾	6¼	*New Fowlis ..	82½
..	15½	2¾	*Gilmerton ..	79¾
..	17½	2	***Crieff**	77¾
..	24¼	6¾	*Comrie	71
..	29¾	5½	*St Fillans ..	65½
..	36¾	7	*Lochearnhead ..	58½
..	41¾	5	Lix Toll	53½
A82	53	11¼	*Crianlarich ..	42¼
A85	58½	5½	*Tyndrum ..	36¾
..	70½	12	*Dalmally ..	24¾
..	73½	3	*Loch Awe Hotel	21¾
..	77	3½	*Falls of Cruachan	18¾
..	80½	3½	Bridge of Awe ..	14¾
..	83	2½	*Taynuilt ..	12½
..	90	7	*Connel ..	5¼
..	95¼	5¼	***Oban**	

146. PERTH to CALLANDER. A pleasant, undulating road in Strath Earn, with views of the Ochil hills on the middle part. Carsebreck Pond lies to the north of the road between Blackford and Greenloaning. There is a descent of 1 in 9 at Dunblane, after which it is pleasant open country giving views of the hills approaching Callander.

A9			***Perth**	40¼
..	1½	1½	Cherrybank ..	38¾
..	11½	10	*Aberuthven ..	28¾
..	14¼	2¾	*Auchterarder ..	26
..	15¾	1½	*Gleneagles (Sta)	24½
..	16½	¾	Loaninghead X-rds	23¾
..	18½	2	*Blackford ..	21¾
..	23	4½	*Greenloaning ..	17¼
A820	28½	5½	*Dunblane ..	11¾
A84	32¾	4¼	*Doune	7½
..	40¼	7½	***Callander**	

147. A tour from PERTH to AVIEMORE via the Sma' Glen and Loch Rannoch. A tour through the Perthshire Highlands to Loch Rannoch, afterwards crossing the Grampian mountains to Strath Spey. After passing Huntingtower, a pretty by-road is followed along the valley of the River Almond passing Trinity College, Glenalmond, before reaching the *Sma' Glen. At Milton, a long climb over the hills by Glen Cochill is succeeded by a similar descent to Aberfeldy, where there are extensive views. Beyond Coshieville, ascends across moorland country, skirting the mountain of Schiehallion. Care on the winding descent three miles before Kinloch Rannoch. If desired, the circuit of Loch Rannoch can be omitted, but there are some very fine views from the lochside. Leaving Kinloch Rannoch, a moorland road is followed by Trinafour in Glen Erochy passing near the village of *Struan just before joining the main road at Calvine. (The direct way from Trinafour to the main road at Dalnacardoch has a rough surface, with awkward hairpin bends and a steep ascent of 1 in 5.) Traverses desolate moorland country on the long, gradual ascent to the summit at Drumochter Pass (1,506 feet), and also on the descent, until reaching the wooded Strath Spey, near Newtonmore.

A85			***Perth**	130
..	2¾	2¾	*Huntingtower ..	127¼
Uncl	6	3¼	Junc A85/Uncl ..	124
B8063	13½	7½	Buchanty ..	116½
A822	15¼	1¾	Junc B8063/A822 ..	114¾
..	18	2¾	*Newton Bridge	112
..	21¾	3¾	*Amulree ..	108¼
A826	23½	1¾	*Milton	106½
B846	32¾	9¼	***Aberfeldy** ..	97¼
..	33¾	1	*Weem	96¼
..	38	4¼	*Coshieville ..	92
..	41¼	3¼	*White Bridge ..	88¾
Uncl	41¾	½	Junc B846/Uncl	88¼
B846	50½	8¾	***Kinloch Rannoch**	79½
..	58¼	7¾	Killichonan ..	71¾
Uncl	61¼	3	Junc B846/Uncl	68¾
..	61½	¼	Bridge of Gaur ..	68½
B846	72¾	11¼	***Kinloch Rannoch**	57¼
B847	75¼	2½	Junc B846/B847	54¾
..	79¼	4	*Trinafour ..	50¾
A9	85¼	6	Junc B847/A9 ..	44¾
..	91¼	6	*Dalnacardoch ..	38¾
..	96¾	5½	*Dalnaspidal ..	33¼
..	98½	1¾	*Drumochter Pass (summit) ..	31½
..	104½	6	*Dalwhinnie ..	25½
..	115¼	10¾	*Newtonmore ..	14¾
..	118	2¾	***Kingussie** ..	12
..	123¼	5¾	*Kincraig ..	6¼
..	127½	3¾	*Lynwilg ..	2½
..	130	2½	*Aviemore ..	

148. PERTH to RANNOCH STATION via Stanley. Follows the Tay and Tummel valleys throughout, with extensive views in places. As far as Dunkeld this forms a pleasant alternative to the main road (Iter 150) through mainly agricultural country, becoming well-wooded around Dunkeld. Leaves the main road near Bridge of Garry to follow a hilly, winding road to Queen's View, after which an easier, undulating road follows the shores of Loch Tummel and Loch Rannoch, with views of Schiehallion. Open moorland on the latter part. There are a number of developments in connection with hydro-electric power schemes on the second half of this route.

A9			***Perth**	66
..	4½	4½	*Luncarty ..	61½
B9099	5¼	¾	Junc A9/B9099 ..	60¾
..	7¼	2	*Stanley	58¾
..	10¾	3½	*Murthly ..	55¼
A984	12¼	1½	*Caputh	53¾
A9	17	4¾	***Dunkeld** ..	49
..	25	8	Ballinluig ..	41
..	29½	4½	***Pitlochry** ..	36½
B8019	32¼	2¾	Junc A9/B8019 ..	33¾
..	32½	¼	*Bridge of Garry	33½

..	34¾	2¼	*Fincastle (PO)	31¼
..	36½	1¾	*Queen's View	29½
B846	43	6½	*Tummel Bridge	23
..	50	7	***Kinloch Rannoch**	16
..	57¾	7¾	Killichonan	8¼
..	66	8¼	*Rannoch Sta	

149. PERTH to GRANTOWN-ON-SPEY via Aberfeldy and the Rothiemurchus Forest. Well wooded at first and utilising secondary roads beyond Aberfeldy, crossing moorland country in the Grampian mountains before reaching Strath Spey and the *Rothiemurchus Forest. Leaving the main road at Birnam, the wooded Strath Tay is followed to Coshieville, after which there is a long climb over moorlands, reaching an altitude of 1,263 feet just beyond White Bridge, affording a view of Schiehallion, before a similar descent to the hydro-electric power station at Tummel Bridge. Ascends again to over 1,000 feet near Trinafour. Continuing by Glen Erochy, the road passes close to *Struan, just before rejoining the main road at Calvine. (The direct way from Trinafour to the main road at Dalnacardoch has a rough surface, with awkward hairpin bends and a steep ascent of 1 in 5.) Desolate moorland country is traversed as the road climbs gradually over the Grampians to the summit of Drumochter Pass (1,506 feet). After the descent to the wooded Strath Spey, a rough, narrow by-road is followed on the south side of the valley, and one mile before Inverdruie a short detour can be made to Loch-an-Eilean, in Rothiemurchus Forest, after which the road improves.

A9			***Perth**	117¼
..	4½	4½	*Luncarty	112¾
..	8¾	4¼	*Bankfoot	108½
..	14	5¼	*Birnam	103¼
B898	14½	½	Junc A9/A822/B898	102¾
A827	26½	12	*Grandtully	90¾
B846	31½	5	***Aberfeldy**	85¾
..	32½	1	*Weem	84¾
..	36¾	4¼	*Coshieville	80½
..	40	3¼	*White Bridge	77¼
..	45	5	*Tummel Bridge	72¼
Uncl	45¾	¾	Junc B846/Uncl	71½
B847	49¼	3½	Junc Uncl/B847	68
..	49¾	½	*Trinafour	67½
A9	55¾	6	Junc B847/A9	61½
..	61¾	6	*Dalnacardoch	55½
..	67¼	5½	*Dalnaspidal	50
..	69	1¾	*Drumochter Pass (summit)	48¼
..	75	6	*Dalwhinnie	42¼
B970	84½	9½	Junc A9/B970	32¾
..	88¼	3¾	*Ruthven	29
..	90	1¾	*Tromie Bridge	27¼
..	92	2	*Insh	25¼
..	95¾	3¾	*Feshie Bridge	21½
A951	101¼	5½	Inverdruie	16
B970	102¼	1	*Coylumbridge	15
..	112	9¾	*Nethybridge	5¼
A95	116¼	4¼	Junc B970/A95	1
..	117¼	1	***Grantown-on-Spey**	

150. PERTH to INVERNESS. This main route to the north is a valley road on the early part, afterwards crossing the desolate Grampian mountains, partly relieved by a well-wooded stretch in Strath Spey. At first follows the valleys of the Tay, Tummel and Garry through agricultural scenery, with well-wooded districts around Dunkeld and in the famous Pass of Killiecrankie. Beyond Blair Atholl, desolate moorland country is entered as the road climbs gradually to the summit at Drumochter Pass (1,506 feet), then descends through the well-timbered Strath Spey to about 700 feet at Aviemore, after which another gradual climb over the open moorlands leads to Slochd Simmit (1,333 feet). Rather winding as Strath Dearn and Strath Nairn are crossed on the long gradual descent to sea level.

A9			***Perth**	114½
..	4½	4½	*Luncarty	110
..	8¾	4¼	*Bankfoot	105¾
..	14	5¼	*Birnam	100½
..	14¾	¾	***Dunkeld**	99¾
..	22¾	8	Ballinluig	91¾
..	27¼	4½	***Pitlochry**	87¼
..	31	3¾	*Killiecrankie	83½
..	34¼	3¼	***Blair Atholl**	80¼
..	44½	10¼	*Dalnacardoch	70
..	50	5½	*Dalnaspidal	64½
..	51¾	1¾	*Drumochter Pass (summit)	62¾
..	57¾	6	*Dalwhinnie	56¾
..	68½	10¾	*Newtonmore	46
..	71¼	2¾	***Kingussie**	43¼
..	77	5¾	*Kincraig	37½
..	80¾	3¾	*Lynwilg	33¾
..	83¼	2½	*Aviemore	31¼
..	90¼	7	*Carrbridge	24¼
..	96	5¾	*Slochd Summit	18½
..	98½	2½	*Tomatin	16
..	103¼	4¾	*Moy	11¼
..	108¾	5½	*Daviot	5¾
..	114½	5¾	***Inverness**	

151. PERTH to ABERDEEN. An easy main road through pleasant, open agricultural country, with views of the Sidlaw hills and passing Glamis Castle before Forfar. Fine views on the coast road beyond Stonehaven, after which the village of *Muchalls lies just off the main road. The old road (B9134) from Forfar to Brechin via *Aberlemno is 1½ miles shorter, but is narrow in places and not suitable for fast travel.

A94			***Perth**	82¼
..	2	2	*New Scone	80¼
..	5¼	3¼	*Balbeggie	77
..	10¼	5	Burrelton	72
..	12½	2¼	*Coupar Angus	69¾
..	17¾	5¼	*Meigle	64½
..	22	4¼	*Eassie	60¼
..	24½	2½	*Glamis	57¾
..	29¾	5¼	***Forfar**	52½
..	35¾	6	*Finhaven	46½
..	42½	6¾	***Brechin**	39¾
..	53½	11	*Laurencekirk	28¾
..	57	3½	*Fordoun	25¼
..	60¼	3¼	Mondynes Bridge	22
A92	67½	7¼	***Stonehaven**	14¾
..	80¼	12¾	*Bridge of Dee	2
..	82¼	2	***Aberdeen** (See town plan for Bypass)	

152. PERTH to ABERDEEN via Braemar and Deeside. A splendid touring route, contrasting the crossing of the bare Grampian mountains with the delightful, wooded *Deeside. Pleasant, open country in the Tay Valley at first, passing the famous *Meikleour beech hedge a little beyond Bridge of Isla, then gradually ascends, by Glen Shee into the hills. Between Spittal of Glenshee and Cairnwell summit, the road becomes steeper, until, at the Devil's Elbow, the general gradient is 1 in 9, with a maximum of 1 in 5 on the awkward S bends. The summit at Cairnwell (2,199 feet) is the highest altitude reached by any classified motoring road in Great Britain and is liable to become blocked by snow during winter months. Glen Clunie is traversed to reach Braemar, after which the picturesque Dee Valley is followed to Aberdeen. Ballater can be avoided by a short cut (B972) through the pretty Pass of Ballater, and the road on the south side of the river can be reached by several connecting bridges. The Royal residence of *Balmoral Castle is seen between Braemar and Crathie Church, and Loch Kinord lies just off the road near Cambus o'May. Crathes Castle, near Banchory, is interesting.

A93			***Perth**	108
..	2¼	2¼	*Old Scone	105¾
..	5¾	3½	Guildtown	102¼
..	10¾	5	*Bridge of Isla	97¼
..	15¼	4½	***Blairgowrie**	92¾
..	15¾	½	*Rattray	92¼
..	21¼	5½	*Bridge of Cally	86¾
..	29¼	8	*Lair	78¾
..	34¼	5	*Spittal of Glenshee	73¾
..	39¾	5½	*Cairnwell Pass (summit)	68¼
..	49¼	9½	***Braemar**	58¾
..	58½	9¼	*Crathie Church	49½
..	64½	6	Bridge of Gairn	43½
..	66	1½	*Ballater	42
..	69½	3½	*Cambus o' May	38½
..	73	3½	*Dinnet	35
..	77½	4½	*Aboyne	30½
..	82¼	4¾	*Kincardine o' Neil	25¾
..	90	7¾	*Banchory	18
..	93½	3½	*Crathes	14½
..	96¾	3¼	*Drumoak	11¼
..	100½	3¾	*Peterculter	7½
..	108	7½	***Aberdeen** (See town plan for Bypass)	

153. PERTH to MONTROSE. Pleasant, open agricultural country, with views of the Sidlaw hills to Forfar, and passing Glamis Castle. The direct road (B9113) from Forfar past the ruins of *Restenneth Priory is 1½ miles shorter, but it somewhat narrow.

A94			*Perth ..	.. 49
..	2	2	*New Scone	.. 47
..	3¼	5¼	*Balbeggie	.. 43¾
..	10¼	5	Burrelton	.. 38¾
..	12½	2¼	*Coupar Angus ..	36½
..	17¾	5¼	*Meigle	.. 31¼
..	22	4¼	*Eassie ..	.. 27
..	24½	2½	*Glamis ..	.. 24½
A932	29¾	5¼	*Forfar ..	.. 19¼
..	37	7¼	*Guthrie ..	.. 12
A933	38¼	1¼	*Friockheim	.. 10¾
A934	40¾	2½	Junc A933/A934	8¼
A92	48	7¼	Junc A934/A92 ..	1
..	49	1	*Montrose	

154. PERTH to DUNDEE. A fast, level road across the open *Carse of Gowrie, with the village of *Kinnaird to the north of the road at the foot of the Sidlaw hills. There is an alternative by-road through *Errol (B958) branching off before Glencarse and rejoining near Dundee.

A85			*Perth ..	.. 21¾
..	6	6	*Glencarse	.. 15¾
..	12¾	6¾	*Inchture	.. 9
..	15¼	2½	*Longforgan Bypass	.. 6½
..	17½	2¼	*Invergowrie	.. 4¼
..	21¾	4¼	*Dundee (See town plan for Bypass)	

155. DUNDEE to ABERDEEN. An easy main road through open country along the coast, with fine views in places, although not touching the shore. The alternative includes the coast resorts and golfing district between Dundee and Carnoustie. *Auchmithie and *Johnshaven lie east of the road, the former just beyond Arbroath, and the latter between St Cyrus and Inverbervie. *Dunnottar Castle is passed before reaching Stonehaven, beyond which *Muchalls is adjacent to the main road. Approaching Aberdeen, a detour can be made to include the rocky coastline from *Cove to Girdle Ness.

A92			*Dundee ..	.. 67
..	11	11	Muirdrum	.. 56
..	16¾	5¾	*Arbroath	.. 50¼
..	19	2¼	Marywell	.. 48
..	22½	3½	*Inverkeilor	.. 44½
..	29¾	7¼	*Montrose	.. 37¼
..	35	5¼	*St Cyrus	.. 32
..	42½	7½	*Inverbervie	.. 24½
..	52¼	9¾	*Stonehaven	.. 14¾
..	65	12¾	*Bridge of Dee ..	2
..	67	2	*Aberdeen (See town plan for Bypass)	

Alternative via Carnoustie

A930			*Dundee
..	3½	3½	*Broughty Ferry
..	6¼	2¾	*Monifieth
..	9	2¾	*Barry
..	10¾	1¾	*Carnoustie
A92	13	2¼	Muirdrum
..	18¾	5¾	*Arbroath

156. DUNDEE to ABERDEEN via Edzell. Undulating at first, on the edge of the Sidlaw hills to Forfar, then flat open country. The direct road (B9134) from Forfar to Brechin via *Aberlemno is not so fast, but is 1½ miles shorter. Leaves the main road beyond Brechin to follow by-roads along the foot of the hills, later rejoining the main road to Stonehaven. Fine coast scenery on the latter part, and passes the edge of *Muchalls, 4 miles beyond Stonehaven. Approaching Aberdeen a detour can be made to include the rocky coastline from *Cove to Girdle Ness.

A929			*Dundee ..	.. 69¼
..	6	6	Todhills ..	.. 63¼
A94	14	8	*Forfar ..	.. 55¼
..	20	6	*Finhaven	.. 49¼
..	26¾	6¾	*Brechin ..	.. 42½
B966	29	2¼	Junc A94/B966 ..	40¼
..	30¾	1¾	Inchbare ..	.. 38½
..	32¾	2	*Edzell ..	.. 36½
..	34	1¼	*Gannochy Bridge	35¼
..	37½	3½	*Fettercairn	.. 31¾
A94	45¼	7¾	Junc B966/A94 ..	24
..	47¼	2	Mondynes Bridge	22
A92	54½	7¼	*Stonehaven	.. 14¾
..	67¼	12¾	*Bridge of Dee ..	2
..	69¼	2	*Aberdeen (See town plan for Bypass)	

157. DUNDEE to ABERFELDY via Dunkeld. Rather winding on the crossing of the Sidlaw hills, with an easy descent of Tullybaccart Hill. Joins the Tay Valley at Meikleour, becoming wooded at Dunkeld, where the river is crossed.

A923			*Dundee ..	.. 47
..	5¼	5¼	*Muirhead	.. 41¾
..	12	6¾	*Pitcur ..	.. 35
..	14¾	2¾	*Coupar Angus ..	32¼
A984	16¼	1½	Junc A923/A984	30¾
..	19¾	3½	*Meikleour	.. 27¼
..	25	5¼	*Caputh ..	.. 22
A9	29¾	4¾	*Dunkeld	.. 17¼
B898	30	¼	Junc A9/A822/B898	17
A827	42	12	*Grandtully	.. 5
..	47	5	*Aberfeldy	

158. DUNDEE to PITLOCHRY or ABERFELDY. Rather winding on the crossing of the Sidlaw hills, with an easy descent of Tullybaccart Hill, afterwards a rather undulating road. Passes several lochs between Blairgowrie and Butterstone, and *Clunie village is adjacent to the road. Joins the well-wooded Tay Valley just north of Dunkeld, and shows divergent routes to either Pitlochry or Aberfeldy.

A923			*Dundee ..	.. 42½
..	5¼	5¼	*Muirhead	.. 37¼
..	12	6¾	*Pitcur ..	.. 30½
..	14¾	2¾	*Coupar Angus ..	27¾
..	18	3¼	Rosemount	.. 24½
..	19½	1½	*Blairgowrie	.. 23
..	27	7½	*Butterstone	.. 15½
A9	30½	3½	Junc A923/A9	12
..	38	7½	†Ballinluig	.. 4½
..	42½	4½	*Pitlochry	
	†		OR	
A827	38		Ballinluig	
..	38¾	¾	*Logierait	
..	43	4¼	*Grandtully	
..	48	5	*Aberfeldy	

159. DUNDEE to PITLOCHRY via Kirkmichael. Rather winding on the crossing of the Sidlaw hills, with an easy descent of Tullybaccart Hill. Ascends gradually into the hills from Blairgowrie, with pleasant scenery in Glen Brerachan, and views from the summit (1,260 feet) before the long descent to Pitlochry and the Tummel Valley. The quickest way is by Ballinluig, Iter 158.

A923			*Dundee ..	.. 45
..	5¼	5¼	*Muirhead	.. 39¾
..	12	6¾	*Pitcur ..	.. 33
..	14¾	2¾	*Coupar Angus ..	30¼
..	18	3¼	Rosemount	.. 27
A93	19½	1½	*Blairgowrie	.. 25½
..	20	½	*Rattray ..	.. 25
A924	25½	5½	*Bridge of Cally	19½
..	32½	7	*Kirkmichael	.. 12½
..	34½	2	Enochdhu	.. 10½
..	44¼	9¾	*Moulin ..	.. ¾
..	45	¾	*Pitlochry	

160. DUNDEE to GRANTOWN-ON-SPEY via Glen Isla and Tomintoul. A very hilly, scenic route, utilizing narrow roads in Glen Isla and on the Lecht Road crossing of the north-eastern Grampians. Very high altitudes are attained and the road is liable to be blocked by snow during the winter, particularly in the Grampians, at the Devil's Elbow beyond Spittal of Glenshee and again between Braemar and Tomintoul. An easy road is first followed from Dundee through a gap in the Sidlaw hills to Newtyle; 3 miles beyond Meigle, a detour can be made to *Alyth before joining the hilly road leading to Glen Isla. There are several gradients of 1 in 7 along the picturesque valley, and the road is narrow over the hill to the main road at Lair in Glen Shee.

Between Spittal of Glenshee and Cairnwell summit the road becomes steeper, until, at the Devil's Elbow, the general gradient is 1 in 9, with a maximum of 1 in 5 on the awkward S bends. The summit at Cairnwell (2,199 feet) is the highest altitude reached by any classified motoring road in Great Britain. Glen Clunie is traversed to reach Braemar, thence along wooded *Deeside, passing the Royal residence of *Balmoral Castle before turning off by a narrow, hilly road across the mountains. After the climb from the Dee Valley, there is a 1 in 5 descent before Gairnshiel Bridge. Afterwards, a climb to 1,800 feet (maximum gradient 1 in 5) is followed by a long descent to Strath Don (see Iter 141 for an alternative route via Ballater and Strathdon to Cock Bridge). There is a 1 in 5 ascent from Cock Bridge leading to the summit of the Lecht Road (2,090 feet), and another long descent follows to Tomintoul. After several ascents and descents (maximum gradient 1 in 7) between Bridge of Avon and the summit beyond Bridge of Brown, a gradual descent leads to the wooded Strath Spey.

A923			***Dundee**	100
A927	5¼	5¼	*Muirhead	94¾
..	11¼	6	*Newtyle	88¾
..	13½	2¼	*Meigle	86½
B954	16½	3	Junc A927/B954	83½
..	21	4½	*Bridge of Craig	79
B951	23¾	2¾	*Dykend	76¼
..	26¾	3	*Kirkton of Glenisla	73¼
A93	33½	6¾	*Lair	66½
..	38½	5	*Spittal of Glenshee	61½
..	44	5½	*Cairnwell Pass (summit)	56
..	53½	9½	***Braemar**	46½
A939	62¼	8¾	Junc A93/A939	37¾
..	67½	5¼	*Gairnshiel Bridge	32½
..	73¾	6¼	Colnabaichin	26¼
..	75¼	1½	*Corgarff	24¾
..	76½	1¼	*Cock Bridge	23½
..	86¼	9¾	*Tomintoul	13¾
..	88¼	2	*Bridge of Avon	11¾
..	90½	2¼	*Bridge of Brown	9½
A95	98½	8	Junc A939/A95	1½
..	100	1½	***Grantown-on-Spey**	

161. DUNDEE to GLEN CLOVA. Crosses the Sidlaw hills and passes Glamis Castle before Kirriemuir, then a hilly, but delightful by-road in picturesque Glen Clova. At Dykehead, a branch road diverges westwards to traverse Glen Prosen, while 3 miles up Glen Clova the road divides, and either side of the valley can be followed, but these roads are not through ways.

A929			***Dundee**	35¼
A928	6	6	Todhills	29¼
..	12	6	*Glamis	23¼
A926	17	5	***Kirriemuir**	18¼
B955	17½	½	Junc A926/B955	17¾
..	22¼	4¾	*Dykehead	13
Uncl	32¼	10	*Clova Church	3
..	35¼	3	*Braedownie	

162. CARNOUSTIE to PITLOCHRY via Glen Isla. Pleasant, wooded, agricultural districts to Kirriemuir, then following a hilly, secondary road passing Loch Lintrathen before reaching Dykend. There are several gradients of 1 in 7 along the picturesque Glen Isla, and the road is narrow over the hill to the main road at Lair in Glen Shee. Traverses moorland country on the latter part, with views from the summit (1,260 feet) beyond Glen Brerachan, before the long descent through Moulin to Pitlochry in the Tummel Valley. A faster route is via Dundee, Iters 155 and 158.

A930			*Carnoustie	60¼
A958	2¼	2¼	Muirdrum	58
..	10	7¾	Craichie	50¼
..	12	2	Kingsmuir	48¼
A94	14	2	***Forfar**	46¼
A926	14¾	¾	Junc A94/A926	45½
..	20	5¼	***Kirriemuir**	40¼
B951	20¾	¾	Junc A926/B951	39½
..	23¾	3	Kirkton of Kingoldrum	36½
..	30½	6¾	*Dykend	29¾
..	33½	3	*Kirkton of Glenisla	26¾
A93	40¼	6¾	*Lair	20
B950	43¾	3½	Junc A93/B950	16½
A924	47½	3¾	Junc B950/A924	12¾
..	47¾	¼	*Kirkmichael	12½
..	49¾	2	Enochdhu	10½
..	59½	9¾	*Moulin	¾
..	60¼	¾	***Pitlochry**	

163. ARBROATH to BANCHORY via Cairn o' Mouth. Pleasant, open country to Fettercairn, then a difficult cross-country road, with fine panoramic views, crossing Cairn o' Mouth to the Dee Valley. From Clattering Bridge, the road is narrow, with frequent passing bays, and there are several steep gradients, especially the long ascent to Cairn o' Mouth (maximum gradient 1 in 5½) and at Bridge of Dye (maximum gradient 1 in 6). The summit of the Cairn o' Mouth road is at 1,475 feet, and the road between Fettercairn and Strachan is frequently blocked by snow during the winter months, the easiest way being via Stonehaven and the Slug Road (Iter 190).

A933			***Arbroath**	42½
..	3½	3½	Gowanbank	39
..	6½	3	*Friockheim	36
A94	14¼	7¾	***Brechin**	28¼
B966	16½	2¼	Junc A94/B966	26
..	18¼	1¾	Inchbare	24¼
..	20¼	2	*Edzell	22¼
..	21½	1¼	*Gannochy Bridge	21
B974	25	3½	*Fettercairn	17½
..	28½	3½	*Clattering Bridge	14
..	30½	2	*Cairn o' Mouth (summit)	12
..	34½	4	*Bridge of Dye	8
..	39¼	4¾	*Strachan	3¼
A943	41¾	2½	*Bridge of Feugh (near side)	¾
..	42½	¾	*Banchory	

164. MONTROSE to LOCHLEE CHURCH (GLEN ESK). A flat main road to Brechin, then a by-road ascending into the hills. After Gannochy Bridge, becomes winding, as the beautiful valley of the North Esk is followed to the road end at Lochlee Church, finely situated amongst the eastern Grampian mountains.

A92			***Montrose**	30½
A935	½	½	Junc A92/A935	30
A94	8½	8	***Brechin**	22
B966	10¾	2¼	Junc A94/B966	19¾
..	12½	1¾	Inchbare	18
..	14½	2	*Edzell	16
..	15¾	1¼	*Gannochy Bridge	14¾
Uncl	16	¼	Junc B966/Uncl.	14½
..	26¼	10¼	*Tarfside	4¼
..	30½	4¼	*Lochlee Church	

165. MONTROSE to HUNTLY via Cairn o' Mouth. Pleasant open country to Fettercairn, then a difficult cross-country road, with fine panoramic views crossing the Cairn o' Mouth to the Dee Valley at Potarch Bridge, thereafter an easy, but twisting road through moorland and agricultural districts passing *Craigievar Castle about 4 miles from Lumphanan. The summit at Cairn o' Mouth is at 1,475 feet, and the road between Fettercairn and Feughside Inn is frequently blocked by snow during the winter months. From Clattering Bridge the road is narrow, with frequent passing bays, and there are several steep gradients, especially the long ascent to Cairn o' Mouth (maximum gradient 1 in 5½) and at Bridge of Dye (maximum gradient 1 in 6). There are two small fords on the unclassified road between Bridge of Dye and Feughside. A faster route is via Aberdeen (Iter 155 and 175). The direct road from Bridge of Alford to Huntly via *Tullynessle and *Kennethmont is hilly, narrow and winding.

A92			***Montrose**	68¼
A937	1	1	Junc A92/A937	67¼
B974	6	5	*Marykirk	62¼
..	11¾	5¾	*Fettercairn	56½
..	15¼	3½	*Clattering Bridge	53
..	17¼	2	*Cairn o' Mouth (summit)	51
..	21¼	4	*Bridge of Dye	47
Uncl	23¼	2	Junc B974/Uncl.	45
..	25¾	2½	*Feughside Inn	42½
A93	29¾	4	*Potarch Bridge	38½
B993	31	1¼	Junc A93/B993	37¼
A980	33¾	2¾	*Torphins	34½
..	37¼	3½	*Lumphanan	31
A944	47½	10¼	Junc A980/A944	20¾
..	48	½	*Bridge of Alford	20¼
A97	54	6	Junc A944/A97	14¼
..	55½	1½	*Lumsden	12¾
..	59½	4	*Rhynie	8¾
..	68¼	8¾	***Huntly**	

166. DUNKELD to MONTROSE. An undulating cross-country route through open agricultural districts, along the edge of the hills at first. Passes several lochs between Dunkeld and Blairgowrie, and *Clunie village is adjacent to the road. Rather narrow between Blairgowrie and Finhaven. *Alyth lies to the north of the road near New Alyth.

A9			***Dunkeld** ..	50
A923	½	½	Junc A9/A923 ..	49½
..	4	3½	*Butterstone ..	46
A93	11½	7½	***Blairgowrie** ..	38½
A926	12	½	*Rattray	38
..	16¼	4¼	*New Alyth ..	33¾
B957	26¾	10½	***Kirriemuir** ..	23¼
..	33¼	6½	*Tannadice ..	16¾
A94	34¾	1½	*Finhaven ..	15¼
A935	41½	6¾	***Brechin**	8½
A92	49½	8	Junc A935/A92 ..	½
..	50	½	***Montrose**	

167. PITLOCHRY to HUNTLY. A tour across the bare Grampian mountains to the delightful, wooded *Deeside, and later a part of the upper Don valley. A long climb from Pitlochry across moorland country, reaching the summit at 1,260 feet, then a gradual descent through Glen Brerachan to Kirkmichael, afterwards ascending by way of Glen Shee. Beyond Spittal of Glenshee the road becomes steeper until, at the Devil's Elbow, the general gradient is 1 in 9, with a maximum of 1 in 5 on the awkward S bends. The summit at Cairnwell (2,199 feet) is the highest altitude reached by any classified motoring road in Great Britain, and during winter months this road is liable to become blocked by snow. Moorland scenery through Glen Clunie to Braemar, then a picturesque road along the Dee valley, passing the Royal residence of *Balmoral Castle. Ballater can be avoided by the short cut (B972) through the pretty Pass of Ballater. Leaving the Dee valley at Cambus o' May, the road passes close to Lochs Kinord and Davan, then traverses moorland and agricultural country, including several miles along the Don valley to Kildrummy.

A924			***Pitlochry** ..	97½
..	¾	¾	*Moulin	96¾
..	10½	9¾	Enochdhu ..	87
..	12½	2	*Kirkmichael ..	85
B950	22¾	¼	Junc A924/B950..	84¾
A93	16½	3¾	Junc B950/A93 ..	81
..	20	3½	*Lair	77½
..	25	5	*Spittal of Glenshee ..	72½
..	30½	5½	*Cairnwell Pass.. (summit) ..	67
..	40	9½	***Braemar** ..	57½
..	49¼	9¼	*Crathie Church	48¼
..	55¼	6	Bridge of Gairn..	42¼
..	56¾	1½	*Ballater.. ..	40¾
..	60¼	3½	*Cambus o' May	37¼
A97	61¼	1	Junc A93/A97 ..	36¼
Uncl	63¾	2½	Junc A97/Uncl ..	33¾
A97	65¼	1½	Junc Uncl/A97 ..	32¼
..	66	¾	Logie Coldstone	31½
..	78	12	*Glenkindie ..	19½
..	81½	3½	*Kildrummy ..	16
..	84¾	3¼	*Lumsden ..	12¾
..	88¾	4	*Rhynie	8¾
..	97½	8¾	***Huntly**	

168. PITLOCHRY to ABERDEEN via Deeside. A tour across the bare Grampian mountains to the delightful, wooded Royal *Deeside. A long climb from Pitlochry across moorland country reaching the summit at 1,260 feet, then a gradual descent through Glen Brerachan to Kirkmichael, afterwards ascending by way of Glen Shee. Beyond Spittal of Glenshee the road becomes steeper, until, at the Devil's Elbow, the general gradient is 1 in 9, with a maximum gradient of 1 in 5 on the awkward S bends. The summit at Cairnwell (2,199 feet) is the highest altitude reached by any classified motoring road in Great Britain and during winter months this road is liable to become blocked by snow. Moorland scenery through Glen Clunie to Braemar, where the route crosses to the south side of the picturesque Dee valley as far as Potarch Bridge, where the river is re-crossed. Beyond Banchory, the tour reverts to the south bank, shortly crossing the pretty, but narrow Bridge of Feugh, and continues by the open valley to Aberdeen. Between Braemar and Aberdeen there are several connecting bridges between the parallel roads on opposite banks of the river, the main road being given in Iter 152.

A924			***Pitlochry** ..	98¼
..	¾	¾	*Moulin	97½
..	10½	9¾	Enochdhu ..	87¾
..	12½	2	*Kirkmichael ..	85¾
B950	12¾	¼	Junc A924/B950..	85½
A93	16½	3¾	Junc B950/A93 ..	81¾
..	20	3½	*Lair	78¼
..	25	5	*Spittal of Glenshee ..	73¼
..	30½	5½	*Cairnwell Pass (summit) ..	67¾
..	40	9½	***Braemar** ..	58¼
A973	49	9	Junc A93/A973 ..	49¼
..	49¼	¼	*Balmoral Castle (gates)	49
..	57¼	8	*Ballater Bridge (near side) ..	41
..	59¼	2	*Pannanich Wells	39
..	64	4¾	*Dinnet Bridge (near side) ..	34¼
..	67	3	*Bridge of Ess ..	31¼
..	68¼	1½	Birsemore ..	29¾
A93	74	5½	*Potarch Bridge	24¼
A943	80	6	*Banchory ..	18¼
..	80¾	¾	*Bridge of Feugh	17½
..	85	4¼	*Durris	13¼
..	91¼	6¼	*Maryculter ..	7
..	92¾	1½	*Blairs	5½
..	95	2¼	Banchory Devenick ..	3¼
A92	96¼	1¼	*Bridge of Dee ..	2
..	98¼	2	***Aberdeen** (See town plan for Bypass)	

169. AVIEMORE to CULLEN via Tomintoul. Undulating and well-wooded in Strath Spey for the first 15 miles, then a narrow, hilly, moorland road, with views of the Cairngorm mountains. There are several ascents and descents from near Bridge of Brown to Tomintoul, with a maximum gradient of 1 in 7. Later passes near the famous *Glenlivet distillery, near Tomnavoulin. Then follows an attractive run through Glen Rinnes to Dufftown. Pretty at Drummuir, in Strath Isla, and afterwards traverses agricultural country.

A9			*Aviemore ..	70½
A95	4¼	4¼	Junc A9/A95 ..	66¼
Uncl	5	¾	Junc A95/Uncl ..	65½
..	6¼	1¼	*Boat of Garten	64¼
B970	7	¾	Junc Uncl/B970..	63½
..	10½	3½	*Nethybridge ..	60
A95	14¾	4¼	Junc B970/A95 ..	55¾
A939	15¼	½	Junc A95/A939 ..	55¼
..	23¼	8	*Bridge of Brown	74¼
..	25½	2¼	*Bridge of Avon	45
..	27½	2	*Tomintoul ..	43
B9008	27¾	¼	Junc A939/B9008	42¾
..	32¼	4½	Knockandhu ..	38¼
..	34	1¾	*Tomnavoulin ..	36½
B9009	35¾	1¾	Achbreck (Church)	34¾
..	41¼	5½	*Glenrinnes ..	29¼
A941	46¼	5	*Dufftown ..	24¼
A920	46¾	½	Junc A941/A920	23¾
..	51¼	4½	*Drummuir ..	19¼
..	54¼	3	Auchindachy ..	16¼
A96	56¾	2½	Junc A920/A96 ..	13¾
A95	57¼	½	*Keith	13¼
B9018	59¼	2	Junc A95/B9018..	11¼
..	66¼	7	*Deskford ..	4¼
..	69	2¾	Lintmill	1½
A98	69¾	¾	Junc B9018/A98..	¾
..	70½	¾	***Cullen**	

170. AVIEMORE to BANFF. Attractive in Strath Spey to Craigellachie, well wooded on the earlier part. An undulating agricultural district beyond Keith. A better route to Craigellachie is via Grantown-on-Spey. Iters 172 and 195 (in reverse).

A9			*Aviemore ..	69¾
A95	4¼	4¼	Junc A9/A95 ..	65½
Uncl	5	¾	Junc A95/Uncl ..	64¾
..	6¼	1¼	*Boat of Garten	63½
B970	7	¾	Junc Uncl/B970..	62¾
..	10½	3½	*Nethybridge ..	59¼
A95	14¾	4¼	Junc B970/A95 ..	55
..	17¾	3	*Cromdale ..	52
..	27¾	10	*Delnashaugh Inn	42
..	35½	7¾	*Aberlour ..	34¼
..	37½	2	***Craigellachie** ..	32¼
..	40	2½	*Maggieknockater	29¾
A96	48¼	8¼	Junc A95/A96 ..	21½
A95	49½	1¼	*Keith	20¼
..	61½	12	*Cornhill ..	8¼
A98	65	3½	Junc A95/A98 ..	4¾
..	69¾	4¾	***Banff**	

171. AVIEMORE to SPEY BAY via Strath Spey. A touring route using secondary roads. At first through the Spey Valley, well wooded on the earlier part, then open agricultural country beyond Rothes.

A951			*Aviemore	56½
..	1	1	Inverdruie	55½
B970	2	1	*Coylumbridge	54½
..	11¾	9¾	*Nethybridge	44¾
A95	16	4¼	Junc B970/A95	40½
A939	17	1	***Grantown-on-Spey**	39½
B9102	17½	½	Junc A939/B9102	39
..	33½	16	*Knockando Church	23
..	36½	3	*Archiestown	20
A941	40¾	4¼	Junc B9102/A941	15¾
..	42¾	2	*Rothes	13¾
B9015	43¼	½	Junc A941/B9015	13¼
..	46½	3¼	*Orton	10
A96	51¼	4¾	*Mosstodloch	5¼
B9104	52¼	1	Junc A96/B9104	4¼
..	56½	4¼	*Spey Bay	

172. AVIEMORE to FORRES. Well wooded in Strath Spey to Grantown, then crosses Dava Moor and joins the Findhorn Valley at Logie.

A9			*Aviemore	36¼
A95	4¼	4¼	Junc A9/A95	32
..	11¾	7½	*Dulnain Bridge	24½
A939	14¾	3	***Grantown-on-Spey**	21½
A940	22¼	7½	*Dava	14
..	29	6¾	Dunphail	7¼
..	30¾	1¾	*Logie	5½
..	36¼	5½	***Forres**	

173. AVIEMORE to FORRES via Ferness. Beyond Carrbridge, a narrow moorland road, passing a little to the west of the lonely *Lochindorb. Before Ferness, a short detour can be made to the picturesque valley of the River Findhorn, threading a rocky gorge at *Dulsie Bridge. Between Ferness and Logie the River Divie is crossed near the beauty spot of Randolph's Leap and the grounds of Relugas House. Beyond Logie, the Findhorn flows through another fine gorge, both road and river later passing between Darnaway Forest and the Altyre woods. The easiest way is via Grantown, Iter 172.

A9			*Aviemore	33¾
A938	7	7	*Carrbridge	26¾
B9007	8¾	1¾	Junc A938/B9007	25
..	22¼	13½	*Ferness	11½
A940	28	5¾	Junc B9007/A940	5¾
..	28¼	¼	*Logie	5½
..	33¾	5½	***Forres**	

174. ABERDEEN to TOMINTOUL via Deeside. Mainly follows the south bank of the wooded Dee Valley to Ballater, afterwards continuing to Tomintoul by a narrow, hilly road which is liable to be blocked by snow during the winter months. Pretty at the narrow Bridge of Feugh, where a diversion is made beside the Feugh Water to rejoin Deeside near Birsemore. From Gairnshiel Bridge there is a long ascent and descent to Colnabaichin in the Don Valley. At Cock Bridge, a 1 in 5 ascent leads to the summit of the Lecht Road (2,090 feet), from which there is a long descent to Tomintoul. The main road to Ballater is given in Iter 152. The quickest way being by Huntly, Iters 175, 195 and 177.

A92			***Aberdeen**	67¾
A943	2	2	*Bridge of Dee	65¾
..	3¼	1¼	Banchory Devenick	64½
..	5½	2¼	*Blairs	62¼
..	7	1½	*Maryculter	60¾
..	13¼	6¼	*Durris	54½
B974	17¾	4½	*Bridge of Feugh	50
B976	20¼	2½	*Strachan	47½
..	22¼	2	*Feughside Inn	45½
..	25	2¾	Finzean (PO)	42¾
..	27¼	2¼	Marywell	40½
A973	27¾	½	Junc B976/A973	40
..	30¾	3	Birsemore	37
..	32¼	1½	*Bridge of Ess	35½
..	35¼	3	*Dinnet Bridge (near side)	32½
..	40	4¾	*Pannanich Wells	27¾
B971	42	2	Ballater Bridge	25¾
A93	42¼	¼	*Ballater	25½
..	43¾	1½	Bridge of Gairn	24
B972	44	¼	Junc A93/B972	23¾
A939	49	5	*Gairnshiel Bridge	18¾
..	55¼	6¼	Colnabaichin	12½
..	56¾	1½	*Corgarff	11
..	58	1¼	*Cock Bridge	9¾
..	67¾	9¾	*Tomintoul	

175. ABERDEEN to INVERNESS. A pleasant, easy main road through agricultural country.

A96			***Aberdeen**	104
..	8¾	8¾	*Blackburn	95¼
..	12¼	3½	*Kintore	91¾
..	14½	2¼	Port Elphinstone	89½
..	15¾	1¼	*Inverurie	88¼
..	19½	3¾	*Inveramsay	84½
..	21	1½	*Pitcaple	83
..	38¾	17¾	***Huntly**	65¼
..	49½	10¾	*Keith	54½
..	57¼	7¾	*Fochabers	46¾
..	58¾	1½	*Mosstodloch	45¼
..	62½	3¾	*Lhanbryde	41½
..	66¼	3¾	***Elgin**	37¾
..	71½	5¼	*Alves	32½
..	78	6½	***Forres**	26
..	82	4	*Brodie	22
..	86	4	*Auldearn	18
..	88¼	2¼	***Nairn**	15¾
A9	103	14¾	Junc A96/A9	1
..	104	1	***Inverness**	

176. A tour from ABERDEEN to INVERNESS via the Lecht Road and Grantown-on-Spey. Agricultural districts at first, passing near Dunecht House and *Castle Fraser, which lie on opposite sides of the road beyond Skene. Follows the Don Valley from Alford to Cock Bridge, whence the narrow road to Tomintoul is liable to be blocked by snow during the winter months. At Cock Bridge an ascent of 1 in 5 leads to the summit of the Lecht Road (2,090 feet), followed by a long descent to Tomintoul. After several ascents and descents (maximum gradient 1 in 7) between Bridge of Avon and the summit beyond Bridge of Brown, there is a gradual descent to the wooded Strath Spey. Beyond Grantown, Dava Moor is crossed to Ferness, in the pretty Findhorn Valley, to reach Nairn, on the Moray Firth. Flat agricultural country on the latter part.

A944			***Aberdeen**	116
..	8	8	*Skene	108
..	20	12	*Tillyfourie	96
..	25¼	5¼	*Alford	90¾
..	26¾	1½	*Bridge of Alford	89¼
A97	32¾	6	Junc A944/A97	83¼
..	34½	1¾	*Kildrummy	81½
..	38	3½	*Glenkindie	78
B973	42½	4½	Junc A97/B973	73½
..	45	2½	*Strathdon	71
A939	51	6	Colnabaichin	65
..	52½	1½	*Corgarff	63½
..	53¾	1¼	*Cock Bridge	62¼
..	63½	9¾	*Tomintoul	52½
..	65½	2	*Bridge of Avon	50½
..	67¾	2¼	*Bridge of Brown	48¼
A95	75¾	8	*Junc A939/A95	40¼
A939	77¼	1½	***Grantown-on-Spey**	38¾
..	84¾	7½	*Dava	31¼
..	90	5¼	*Ferness	26
A96	99¾	9¾	Junc A939/A96	16¼
..	100¼	½	***Nairn**	15¾
A9	115	14¾	Junc A96/A9	1
..	116	1	***Inverness**	

177. A tour from ABERDEEN to INVERNESS via Grantown-on-Spey and the Findhorn Valley. An alternative to the direct road as far as Tillyfourie, mostly following the River Don, through agricultural country. *Castle Fraser lies to the south of the road beyond Kemnay. Winding and hilly across moorlands, ascending from Rhynie to Cabrach, then by the Glacks of Balloch Pass (1,197 feet) to Dufftown. The direct road (B9002) from north of Lumsden to Cabrach avoids Rhynie. Pretty in Glen Rinnes, leading to Tomnavoulin, near the famous *Glenlivet distillery, then becomes hilly beyond Tomintoul, with several ascents and descents (maximum gradient 1 in 7) between Bridge of Avon and the summit beyond Bridge of Brown, after which there is a gradual descent to the wooded Spey Valley. Beyond Grantown, crosses Dava Moor, then leaves the main road to visit the delightful Findhorn valley at Dulsie Bridge, thence by Cawdor Castle to Culloden Moor. Between Dava and Inverness, a narrow, winding and hilly road is followed. See Iter 176 for the main road via Nairn. A short detour can be made along the banks of *Lochindorb, by turning off just before reaching Dava, and proceeding uphill by a narrow moorland road, rejoining the main route before Dulsie Bridge.

A96			***Aberdeen** ..	127¾
..	8¾	8¾	*Blackburn ..	119
B994	11½	2¾	Junc A96/B994 ..	116¼
B993	14¾	3¼	Junc B994/B993..	113
..	15¾	1	*Kemnay ..	112
..	18¾	3	*Monymusk ..	109
A944	22	3¼	*Tillyfourie ..	105¾
..	27¼	5¼	*Alford	100½
..	28¾	1½	*Bridge of Alford	99
A97	34¾	6	Junc A944/A97 ..	93
..	36¼	1½	*Lumsden ..	91½
A941	40¼	4	*Rhynie	87½
..	48¼	8	*Cabrach ..	79½
B9009	58¾	10½	*Dufftown ..	69
..	63¾	5	*Glenrinnes ..	64
B9008	69¼	5½	Achbreck (Church)	58½
..	71	1¾	*Tomnavoulin ..	56¾
..	72¾	1¾	Knockandhu ..	55
A939	77¼	4½	Junc B9008/A939	50½
..	77½	¼	*Tomintoul ..	50¼
..	79½	2	*Bridge of Avon ..	48¼
..	81¾	2¼	*Bridge of Brown	46
A95	89¾	8	Junc A939/A95 ..	38
A939	91¼	1½	***Grantown-on-Spey**	36½
..	98¾	7½	*Dava	29
Uncl	101¼	2½	Junc A939/Uncl..	26½
..	104¾	3½	*Dulsie Bridge ..	23
B9090	113½	8¾	Junc Uncl/B9090	14¼
..	113¾	¼	*Cawdor.. ..	14
B9091	115¾	2	Junc B9090/B9091	12
B9006	117¼	1½	*Croy	10½
..	122¼	5	*Culloden Cairn ..	5½
A9	125	2¾	Junc B9006/A9 ..	2¾
..	127¾	2¾	***Inverness**	

178. ABERDEEN to BUCKIE via Insch. Through pleasant agricultural districts and following an alternative to the main road (Iter 175) between Pitcaple and Huntly.

A96			***Aberdeen** ..	65
..	8¾	8¾	*Blackburn ..	56¼
..	12¼	3½	*Kintore.. ..	52¾
..	14¾	2½	Port Elphinstone	50½
..	15¾	1¼	*Inverurie ..	49¼
..	19½	3¾	*Inveramsay ..	45½
..	21	1½	*Pitcaple.. ..	44
A979	23	2	Junc A96/A979 ..	42
..	24¼	1¼	*Oyne	40¾
..	27¼	3	*Insch	37¾
..	33¼	6	*Kennethmont ..	31¾
A97	36	2¾	Junc A979/A97 ..	29
A96	41½	5½	***Huntly**	23½
..	52¼	10¾	*Keith	12¾
B9016	54¾	2½	Junc A96/B9016..	10¼
..	55½	¾	Aultmore ..	9½
..	61	5½	*Tynet	4
A98	61½	½	Junc B9016/A98..	3½
A942	64	2½	Junc A98/A942 ..	1
..	65	1	*Buckie	

179. ABERDEEN to BRAEMAR and LINN OF DEE via Tarland. Pleasant, rural country at first, passing *Midmar Castle 2 miles beyond Echt, while Lochs Davan and Kinord are adjacent to the road between Tarland and Cambus o' May. Ballater can be avoided by the short cut (B972) through the pretty Pass of Ballater. Delightful in wooded *Deeside, with a view of the Royal residence of *Balmoral Castle after Crathie Church. Narrow and winding along the secluded valley to Linn of Dee, where the motoring road doubles back along the opposite bank of the river to Linn of Quoich, but there is no through way. The main road from Aberdeen to Braemar is given in Iter 152 and a further alternative appears in Iter 168.

A944			***Aberdeen** ..	65¼
A974	5¾	5¾	Junc A944/A974	59½
..	9¾	4	Garlogie	55½
..	12½	2¾	*Echt	52¾
..	31	18½	*Tarland.. ..	34¼
A97	34	3	Junc A974/A97 ..	31¼
A93	37½	3½	Junc A97/A93 ..	27¾
..	38¾	1	*Cambus o' May	26¾
..	42	3½	*Ballater.. ..	23¼
..	43½	1½	Bridge of Gairn..	21¾
..	49½	6	*Crathie Church	15¾
Uncl	58¾	9¼	***Braemar** ..	6½
..	63¾	5	*Inverey	1½
..	65¼	1½	*Linn of Dee	

180. ABERDEEN to BANFF or MACDUFF. An undulating road through flat agricultural country.

A96			***Aberdeen** ..	45¾
A947	3¾	3¾	Junc A96/A947 ..	42
..	6	2¼	*Dyce	39¾
..	10¼	4¼	Newmachar ..	35½
..	17½	7¼	*Old Meldrum ..	28¼
..	25¼	7¾	*Fyvie	20½
..	30	4¾	*Auchterless ..	15¾
..	34¼	4¼	*Turriff	11½
..	40¼	6	*King Edward (PO)	5½
A98	45¼	5	†Banff Bridge ..	½
..	45¾	½	***Banff**	
			† OR	
A98	45¼		Banff Bridge (near side)	
..	46¼	1	*Macduff	

181. ABERDEEN to BANFF via Peterhead and Fraserburgh. An undulating main road connecting Aberdeen, Peterhead, Fraserburgh and Banff through mainly agricultural country, with glimpses of the North Sea.

A92			***Aberdeen** ..	77½
..	8	8	Balmedie.. ..	69½
..	16¾	8¾	*Ellon	60¾
A952	21¼	4½	Junc A92/A952 ..	56¼
..	24¾	3½	Hatton	52¾
..	31	6¼	*Boddam ..	46½
..	32¾	1¾	*Burnhaven ..	44¾
..	34¼	1½	***Peterhead** ..	43¼
..	39¼	5	St Fergus ..	38¼
..	43½	4¼	*Crimond ..	34
..	46½	3	*Lonmay ..	31
A92	47¼	¾	Junc A952/A92 ..	30¼
A98	52¼	5	***Fraserburgh** ..	25¼
..	57¾	5½	Tyrie	19¾
..	73¼	15½	Longmanhill ..	4¼
..	76	2¾	*Macduff ..	1½
..	77	1	Banff Bridge ..	½
..	77½	½	***Banff**	

182. ABERDEEN to BANFF via the Coast. A touring route, mainly through agricultural country, with fine coast views in places, especially between Fraserburgh and Banff, where the road is hilly and winding, with a steep descent and ascent near Pennan (maximum gradient 1 in 6). *Collieston lies on an alternative narrow road nearer the coast between Newburgh and Cruden Bay, whilst *Old Rattray and *St Combs lie to the east of the road between Peterhead and Fraserburgh. Approaching Rosehearty, the road passes near *Pitsligo Castle and beyond Protstonhill detours can be made to visit the picturesque fishing villages of *Crovie and *Gardenstown.

A92			***Aberdeen** ..	78
..	8	8	Balmedie.. ..	70
A975	11	3	Junc A92/A975 ..	67
..	13¾	2¾	*Newburgh ..	64¼
..	23¼	9½	***Cruden Bay** ..	54¾
A952	26½	3¼	Junc A975/A952	51½
..	29	3	*Boddam ..	49
..	30¾	1¾	*Burnhaven ..	47¼
..	32¼	1½	***Peterhead** ..	45¾
..	37¼	5	St Fergus ..	40¾
..	41½	4¼	Crimond ..	36½
..	44½	3	*Lonmay ..	33½
B9033	46	1½	Junc A952/B9033	32
..	47¼	1¼	Crofts of Savoch	30¾
..	51½	4¼	*Bridge of Philorth	26½
A92	53	1½	Junc B9033/A92	25
A98	54	1	***Fraserburgh**	24
B9031	54¾	¾	Junc A98/B9031	23¼
..	56½	1¾	*Sandhaven ..	21½
..	58½	2	*Rosehearty ..	19½
..	63¼	4¾	*New Aberdour ..	14¾
..	66½	3¼	*Pennan	11½
A98	75¼	8¾	Junc B9031/A98 ..	2¾
..	76½	1¾	*Macduff ..	1½
..	77½	1	Banff Bridge ..	½
..	78	½	***Banff**	

183. ABERDEEN to BANFF via Ellon. A cross-country alternative to the main road by Turriff (Iter 180). Through rural districts, hilly between New Deer and New Byth, with a descent of 1 in 8.

A92			***Aberdeen** ..	50
..	8	8	Balmedie. ..	42
A948	16¾	8¾	*Ellon	33¼
..	24½	7¾	Auchnagatt ..	25½
..	29	4½	*New Deer ..	21
Uncl	34¾	5¾	Junc A948/Uncl	15¼
B9027	35	¼	Junc Uncl/B9027	15
..	37½	2½	*New Byth ..	12½

Uncl	38½	1	Junc B9027/Uncl	11½
A98	39¼	¾	Junc Uncl/A98 ..	10¾
..	45¾	6½	Longmanhill ..	4¼
..	48½	2¾	*Macduff ..	1½
..	49½	1	Banff Bridge ..	½
..	50	½	***Banff**	

184. ABERDEEN to CULLEN. A rural cross-country route, utilizing undulating secondary roads between Inverurie and Portsoy. The recommended route is by Banff (Iters 180 and 198).

A96			***Aberdeen** ..	57¾
..	8¾	8¾	*Blackburn ..	49
..	12¼	3½	*Kintore ..	45½
..	14½	2¼	Port Elphinstone	43¼
..	15¾	1¼	*Inverurie ..	42
B9001	17	1¼	Junc A96/B9001	40¾
..	26¼	9¼	*Rothie Norman	31½
..	36½	10¼	*Forgue ..	21¼
A97	37½	1	Junc B9001/A97	20¼
..	43	5½	*Aberchirder ..	14¾
B9025	45½	2½	Blacklaw (PO) ..	12¼
A98	49¾	4¼	Junc B9025/A98	8
..	52¼	2½	*Portsoy ..	5½
..	57¾	5½	***Cullen**	

185. ABERDEEN to FRASERBURGH. An easy main road through open agricultural country.

A92			***Aberdeen** ..	42¾
..	8	8	Balmedie.. ..	34¾
..	16¾	8¾	*Ellon ..	26
..	30½	12¾	*Mintlaw ..	12¼
..	42¾	12¼	***Fraserburgh**	

186. ABERDEEN to FRASERBURGH via Tarves. Utilizes secondary roads through rural countryside for the greater part.

A92			***Aberdeen** ..	46¼
B999	4¼	4¼	Junc A92/B999 ..	42
..	8½	4¼	Whitecairns ..	37¾
..	15	6½	*Pitmedden ..	31¼
..	18¼	3¼	*Tarves ..	28
A981	20½	2¼	Junc B999/A981	25¾
..	23¼	2¾	*Methlick ..	23
..	30	6¾	*New Deer ..	16¼
..	37½	7½	*Strichen ..	8¾
..	42¾	5¼	Memsie	3½
..	46¼	3½	***Fraserburgh**	

187. PETERHEAD to LOSSIEMOUTH via Cruden Bay. A secondary route through agricultural country. The quickest way from Peterhead to Huntly is by Turriff (Iters 189 and 196), while the direct road from Peterhead to Ellon is given in Iter 181.

A952			***Peterhead** ..	84½
..	1½	1½	*Burnhaven ..	83
..	3¼	1¾	*Boddam ..	81¼
A975	5¾	2½	Junc A952/A975	78¾
..	9	3¼	***Cruden Bay** ..	75½
Uncl	9¼	¼	Junc A975/Uncl	75¼
A952	11¼	2	Junc Uncl/A952	73¼
..	12¼	1	Hatton	72¼
A92	15½	3¼	Junc A952/A92 ..	68¾
B9004	20¼	4¾	*Ellon ..	64¼
B999	25¼	5	Junc B9004/B999	59¼
B9000	26	¾	*Pitmedden ..	58½
A947	30¾	4¾	Junc B9000/A947	53¾
A981	31½	¾	*Old Meldrum ..	53
B9000	31¾	¼	Junc A981/B9000	52¾
..	42½	10¾	*Culsalmond ..	42
A96	43	½	Junc B9000/A96	41½
..	53	10	***Huntly**	31½
..	63¾	10¾	*Keith	20¾
..	71½	7¾	*Fochabers ..	13
..	73	1½	*Mosstodloch ..	11½
..	76¾	3¾	*Lhanbryde ..	7¾
B9103	77¾	1	Junc A96/B9103	6¾
..	79¼	1½	Calcots	5¼
A941	83½	4¼	Junc B9103/A941	1
..	84½	1	***Lossiemouth**	

188. PETERHEAD to BANFF. An easy road through agricultural country, flat at first, later becoming undulating.

A950			***Peterhead** ..	35¼
..	6½	6½	Longside ..	28¾
..	9	2½	*Mintlaw ..	26¼
..	19	10	*New Pitsligo ..	16¼
A98	20¼	1¼	Junc A950/A98 ..	15
..	31	10¾	Longmanhill ..	4¼
..	33¾	2¾	*Macduff ..	1½
..	34¾	1	Banff Bridge ..	½
..	35¼	½	***Banff**	

189. PETERHEAD to ELGIN via Turriff. A cross-country route mainly utilizing secondary roads through agricultural districts. *Old Deer can be included by following B9029 from beyond Mintlaw to Maud, but the route shown is easier to follow. Pretty scenery in places, especially in the Deveron Valley between Aberchirder and Keith, where *Rothiemay lies just off the road, and again the Spey Valley near Orton. The quickest way from Peterhead to Elgin is by Banff (Iters 188 and 198) and from Keith to Elgin is by Fochabers (Iter 175).

A950			***Peterhead** ..	71¾
..	6½	6½	Longside ..	65¼
..	9	2½	*Mintlaw ..	62¾
B9106	13	4	Junc A950/B9106	58¾
B9029	14¼	1¼	Maud	57½
A981	16¼	1¾	Junc B9029/A981	55½
A948	17¼	1	*New Deer ..	54½
..	23½	6¼	Cuminestown ..	48¼
A947	28	4½	Junc A948/A947	43¾
B9025	30	2	*Turriff	41¾
A97	37	7	Junc B9025/A97	34¾
..	37½	½	*Aberchirder ..	34¼
B9117	40	2½	Junc A97/B9117	31¾
..	40¾	¾	Marnoch.. ..	31
A95	48	7¼	Junc B9117/A95	23¾
A96	53¼	5¼	*Keith	18½
A95	54½	1¼	Junc A96/A95 ..	17¼
B9103	58½	4	Junc A95/B9103	13¼
B9015	61½	3	Junc B9103/B9015	10¼
..	62	½	*Orton	9¾
B9103	63½	1½	Junc B9015/B9103	8¼
A96	69	5½	Junc B9103/A96	2¾
..	71¾	2¾	***Elgin**	

190. STONEHAVEN to ELGIN. A useful cross-country link, forming a pleasant alternative to the main road by Aberdeen and Huntly (Iters 155 and 175). Although winding and hilly in places, the roads are good and there is little traffic. At first a steady climb across the moors by the Slug Road and over the pretty Bridge of Feugh to Banchory in the Dee Valley. *Craigievar Castle is passed 4 miles from Lumphanan, and later the Don Valley is traversed for several miles. Winding and hilly across moorland, ascending from Rhynie to Cabrach, then by the Glacks of Balloch Pass (1,197 feet) to Dufftown. The direct road (B9002) from north of Lumsden to Cabrach avoids Rhynie. Moorland and agricultural on the latter part, with pretty scenery around Craigellachie in the Spey Valley.

A957			***Stonehaven** ..	85
A943	14	14	Junc A957/A943	71
..	15½	1½	*Bridge of Feugh	69½
A93	16¼	¾	*Banchory ..	68¾
A980	16¾	½	Junc A93/A980 ..	68¼
..	23¾	7	*Torphins ..	61¼
..	27¼	3½	*Lumphanan ..	57¾
A944	37½	10¼	Junc A980/A944	47½
..	38	½	*Bridge of Alford	47
A97	44	6	Junc A944/A97 ..	41
..	45½	1½	*Lumsden ..	39½
A941	49½	4	*Rhynie ..	35½
..	57½	8	*Cabrach ..	27½
..	68	10½	*Dufftown ..	17
..	72¼	4¼	***Craigellachie** ..	12¾
..	75	2¾	*Rothes ..	10
..	84¼	9¼	New Elgin ..	¾
..	85	¾	***Elgin**	

191. STONEHAVEN to TOMINTOUL. At first a steady climb across the moors by the Slug Road and over the pretty Bridge of Feugh to the River Dee at Banchory. Continuing with *Deeside to Dinnet, moorland and agricultural country is traversed to the Don Valley, which is followed to Cock Bridge, beyond which the road is narrow with a 1 in 5 ascent leading to the summit of the Lecht Road (2,090 feet) followed by a long descent to Tomintoul. This road from Cock Bridge is liable to be blocked by snow during the winter months.

A957			***Stonehaven** ..	66
A943	14	14	Junc A957/A943	52
..	15½	1½	*Bridge of Feugh	50½

A93	16¼	¾	*Banchory ..	49¾
..	24	7¾	*Kincardine o' Neil	42
..	28¾	4¾	*Aboyne ..	37¾
B9119	33½	4½	*Dinnet	32¾
..	35¼	2	Ordie	30¾
A97	35½	¼	Junc B9119/A97	30½
..	37½	2	Logie Coldstone	28½
B973	45	7½	Junc A97/B973 ..	21
..	47½	2½	*Strathdon ..	18½
A939	53½	6	Colnabaichin ..	12½
..	55	1½	*Corgarff ..	11
..	56¼	1¼	*Cock Bridge ..	9¾
..	66	9¾	*Tomintoul	

192. TOMINTOUL to LOSSIEMOUTH. Moorland to Tomnavoulin, passing near the famous *Glenlivet distillery. If preferred, the alternative road (B9136) through Strath Avon to Downan can be used, although there is little to choose. Follows the wooded Strath Spey from Delnashaugh to Rothes, and traverses a flat agricultural district on the latter part. The ruined *Spynie Palace is adjacent to the road between Elgin and Lossiemouth.

A939			*Tomintoul ..	42¼
B9008	¼	¼	Junc A939/B9008	42
..	4¾	4½	Knockhandhu ..	37½
..	6½	1¾	*Tomnavoulin ..	35¾
..	8¼	1¾	Achbreck (Church)	34
..	10½	2¼	*Downan ..	31¾
A95	14	3½	*Delnashaugh Inn	28¼
..	21¾	7¾	*Aberlour ..	20½
A941	23¾	2	***Craigellachie** ..	18½
..	26½	2¾	*Rothes ..	15¾
..	35¾	9¼	New Elgin ..	6½
..	36½	¾	***Elgin** ..	5¾
..	37¼	¾	Bishopmill ..	5
..	42¼	5	*Lossiemouth	

193. HUNTLY to CULLEN. Pleasant open agricultural land, with coastal views between Portsoy and Cullen. *Rothiemay lies to the east of the road half way between Huntly and Glenbarry.

A96			***Huntly** ..	23¾
B9022	1	1	Junc A96/B9022	22¾
A95	10¾	9¾	Glenbarry ..	13
B9022	12	1¼	Junc A95/B9022	11¾
A98	17¾	5¾	Junc B9022/A98	6
..	18¼	½	*Portsoy ..	5½
..	23¾	5½	***Cullen**	

194. HUNTLY to BANFF. A pleasant undulating road through agricultural country.

A96			***Huntly**	20¾
A97	1	1	Junc A96/A97 ..	19¾
..	11¾	10¾	*Aberchirder ..	9
..	14¼	2½	Blacklaw (PO) ..	6½
..	20¾	6½	***Banff**	

195. HUNTLY to INVERNESS via Grantown-on-Spey. A picturesque alternative to the main road by Elgin Iter 175. Pretty in the Deveron Valley at first, then hilly across the moors to Dufftown. Attractive in Strath Spey between Craigellachie and Grantown, changing to moorland after Carrbridge, where the road gradually ascends to Slochd summit (1,333 feet), later becoming rather winding as Strath Dearn and Strath Nairn are crossed on the long, gradual descent to sea level.

A96			***Huntly**	75¾
B9014	½	½	Junc A96/B9014	75¼
..	11½	11	*Auchindown ..	64¼
A941	12¾	1¼	Junc B9014/A941	63
..	13¾	1	*Dufftown ..	62
A95	18	4¼	***Craigellachie** ..	57¾
..	20	2	*Aberlour ..	55¾
..	27¾	7¾	*Delnashaugh Inn	48
..	37¾	10	*Cromdale ..	38
..	42	4¼	***Grantown-on-Spey**	33¾
A938	45	3	*Dulnain Bridge	30¾
..	49½	4½	Duthil ..	26¼
A9	51½	2	*Carrbridge ..	24¼
..	57¼	5¾	*Slochd Summit	18½
..	59¾	2½	*Tomatin ..	16
..	64½	4¾	*Moy	11¼
..	70	5½	*Daviot	5¾
..	75¾	5¾	***Inverness**	

196. HUNTLY to FRASERBURGH. A pleasant cross-country route through agricultural districts, rather winding in places to Aberchirder.

A96			***Huntly**	41½
A97	1	1	Junc A96/A97 ..	40½
..	11¾	10¾	*Aberchirder ..	29¾
B9025	12¼	½	Junc A97/B9025	29¼
A947	19¼	7	***Turriff**	22¼
B9105	21¼	2	Junc A947/B9105	20¼
A98	27	5¾	Junc B9105/A98	14½
..	36	9	Tyrie	5½
..	41½	5½	***Fraserburgh**	

197. BANCHORY to FRASERBURGH via Inverurie. A cross-country route utilizing secondary roads through pleasant rural scenery.

A93			*Banchory ..	56½
A980	½	½	Junc A93/A980 ..	56
B977	2¾	2¼	Junc A980/B977	53¾
..	8¾	6	*Echt	47¾
A96	16½	7¾	Junc B977/A96	40
..	17	½	*Kintore ..	39½
..	19¼	2¼	Port Elphinstone	37¼
A981	20½	1¼	*Inverurie ..	36
A947	25¾	5¼	*Old Meldrum ..	30¾
A981	26½	¾	Junc A947/A981	30
..	33½	7	*Methlick ..	23
..	40¼	6¾	*New Deer ..	16¼
..	47¾	7½	*Strichen ..	8¾
..	53	5¼	Memsie	3½
..	56½	3½	***Fraserburgh**	

198. BANFF to INVERNESS via Culloden. Follows an inland route parallel to the coast through pleasant countryside. See Iter 199 for alternatives including the seaside resorts. *Fordyce lies to the south of the road between Portsoy and Cullen. Between Elgin and Forres there are quiet alternatives (uncl) to the south of the main road, passing *Pluscarden Priory and *Dallas (B9010) respectively. From Forres to Inverness a diversion is made to pass Cawdor Castle and the historic battlefield at Culloden.

A98			***Banff**	74½
..	8	8	*Portsoy ..	66½
..	13½	5½	***Cullen**	61
..	22½	9	*Tynet Bridge ..	52
A96	25½	3	Junc A98/A96 ..	49
..	25¾	¼	*Fochabers ..	48¾
..	27¼	1½	*Mosstodloch ..	47¼
..	31	3¾	*Lhanbryde ..	43½
..	34¾	3¾	***Elgin**	39¾
..	40	5¼	*Alves	34½
..	46½	6½	***Forres**	28
..	50½	4	*Brodie	24
B9101	54½	4	*Auldearn ..	20
B9090	57¾	3¼	Junc B9101/B9090	16¾
..	60½	2¾	*Cawdor ..	14
B9091	62½	2	Junc B9090/B9091	12
B9006	64	1½	*Croy	10½
..	69	5	*Culloden Cairn	5½
A9	71¾	2¾	Junc B9006/A9 ..	2¾
..	74½	2¾	***Inverness**	

199. BANFF to INVERNESS via the Coast. This touring route embraces most of the sandy seaside resorts in the counties of Banff, Moray and Nairn, the main road to Elgin being given in Iter 198 and Elgin to Inverness in Iter 175. Some other places of interest to the south of the main road are also mentioned in Iter 198. Just off the coast road there are a number of places which can be visited, if desired, including *Whitehills, between Banff and Portsoy, *Spey Bay beyond Portgordon, and also *Garmouth and *Kingston from Mosstodloch. A detour can be made (Iter 187) through *Lossiemouth on the coast north of Elgin, then via B9040 to Hopeman. An excursion which can be made, is from Kinloss to *Findhorn.

A98			***Banff**	85¾
B9139	1¼	1¼	Junc A98/B9139	84½
A98	6½	5¼	*Portsoy ..	79¼
..	12	5½	***Cullen** ..	73¾
A942	13¼	1¼	Junc A98/A942 ..	72½
..	14¼	1	*Portknockie ..	71½
..	16¾	2½	*Findochty ..	69
..	18½	1¾	*Portessie ..	67¼
A990	19½	1	*Buckie	66¼
Uncl	22	2½	*Portgordon ..	63¾
B9104	24¾	2¾	Junc Uncl/B9104	61
A96	26¾	2	Junc B9104/A96	59
..	27¾	1	*Mosstodloch ..	58
..	31½	3¾	*Lhanbryde ..	54¼
A941	35¼	3¾	***Elgin**	50½
B9012	36	¾	Bishopmill ..	49¾
..	40½	4½	*Duffus	45¼
..	42½	2	*Hopeman	43¼
..	43½	1	Cummingstown ..	42¼

..	45	1½	***Burghead**	40¾
B9089	45½	½	Junc B9012/B9089	40
..	52¼	6¾	***Kinloss**	33½
A96	54¼	2	Junc B9011/A96	31½
..	55	¾	***Forres**	30¾
..	59	4	*Brodie	26¾
..	63	4	*Auldearn	22¾
..	65¼	2¼	*Nairn	20½
B9092	67¼	2	Junc A96/B9092	18½
B9006	71½	4¼	Junc B9092/B9006	14¼
..	72	½	*Ardersier	13¾
..	73½	1½	*Fort George	12½
			Return to:	
B9039	75	1½	*Ardersier	10¾
A96	80¼	5¼	Junc B9039/A96	5½
A9	84¾	4½	Junc A96/A9	1
..	85¾	1	***Inverness**	

200. INVERNESS to JOHN O' GROATS. The main road to the far north of Scotland. Follows an inland route parallel to the coast through agricultural country, with moorland in places, and is level for the greater part. At first skirts Beauly Firth and then alongside Cromarty Firth beyond Dingwall. During the winter months, when the direct road over the hills by Aultnamain is affected by bad weather conditions, the longer, but level coast road by Tain (Iter 201) is recommended. After circling Dornoch Firth by Bonar Bridge, *Skibo Castle is passed between Spinningdale and Clashmore and the coast is regained by Golspie, shortly afterwards passing *Dunrobin Castle. Hilly and winding between Helmsdale and Latheron, with a steep descent and ascent (maximum gradient 1 in 9) at Berriedale, thereafter becoming level again. Undulating on the latter part, keeping a little inland but with some fine seascapes in places, especially to the east of John o' Groats.

A9			***Inverness**	140¼
..	2¼	2¼	*Clachnaharry	138
..	11½	9¼	*Lovat Bridge	128¾
..	12¾	1¼	*Beauly	127½
..	15¼	2½	*Muir of Ord	125
..	19	3¾	*Conon Bridge	121¼
..	20	1	Maryburgh	120¼
..	21½	1½	***Dingwall**	118¾
..	28	6½	*Evanton	112¼
A836	30	2	Junc A9/A836	110¼
..	39¾	9¾	*Aultnamain Inn	100½
A9	44¾	5	Junc A836/A9	95½
..	47¾	3	*Ardgay	92½
..	48¾	1	***Bonar Bridge**	91½
..	51¼	2½	*Creich	89
..	53¾	2½	*Spinningdale	86½
..	58¼	4½	*Clashmore	82
..	65¾	7½	*The Mound	74½
..	70	4¼	*Golspie	70¼
..	75	5	*Brora	65¼
..	82	7	*Loth	58¼
..	84¼	2½	*Portgower	55¾
..	86½	2	***Helmsdale**	53¾
..	96½	10	*Berriedale	43¾
..	102	5½	*Dunbeath	38¼
..	106½	4½	*Latheron	33¾
..	110	3½	*Lybster	30¼
..	111¼	1¼	*Occumster	29
..	114	2¾	*Mid Clyth	26¼
..	116¼	2¼	*Ulbster	24
..	119½	3¼	*Thrumster	20¾
..	123½	4	***Wick**	16¾
..	126¾	3¼	*Reiss	13½
..	131¼	4½	*Keiss	9
..	135½	4¼	*Freswick	4¾
..	140¼	4¾	***John o' Groats**	

201. INVERNESS to BONAR BRIDGE via Strathpeffer and Tain. Mainly through agricultural country, at first skirting Beauly Firth, then making a diversion from the main road to include Strathpeffer. A level coast road is followed from Dingwall, alongside Cromarty Firth to Barbaraville, and by the edge of Dornoch Firth beyond Tain. During the winter months this route from Dingwall to Bonar Bridge is recommended in preference to the direct road via Aultnamain (Iter 200) which is 13¼ miles shorter, but liable to be affected by bad weather.

A9			***Inverness**	68¾
..	2¼	2¼	*Clachnaharry	66½
..	11½	9¼	*Lovat Bridge	57¼
..	12¾	1¼	*Beauly	56
A832	15¼	2½	*Muir of Ord	53½
..	19½	4¼	*Marybank	49¼
Uncl	21¼	1¾	Junc A832/Uncl	47½
A834	21¾	½	Junc Uncl/A834	47
..	23½	1¾	***Strathpeffer**	45¼
A9	28¼	4¾	***Dingwall**	40½
..	34¾	6½	*Evanton	34
..	38½	3¾	*Alness	30¼
..	42	3½	*Invergordon	26¾
..	43¼	1¼	*Saltburn	25½
..	45½	2¼	Barbaraville	23¼
..	48½	3	*Logie Easter	20¼
..	53½	5	***Tain**	15¼
..	59	5½	*Edderton	9¾
..	67¾	8¾	*Ardgay	1
..	68¾	1	***Bonar Bridge**	

202. INVERNESS to DINGWALL via Kessock Ferry. A direct route, utilizing the Kessock Ferry, and thence by a secondary road through an agricultural district.

B9161			***Inverness**	13½
..	1¾	1¾	*South Kessock Ferry to *North Kessock	11¾
B9162	3¾	2	Junc B9161/B9162	9¾
	6¼	2½	Tore	7¼
A9	11	4¾	*Conon Bridge	2½
..	12	1	Maryburgh	1½
..	13½	1½	***Dingwall**	

203. INVERNESS to DINGWALL via Cromarty. A tour through the *Black Isle, with an alternative utilizing the Kessock Ferry to avoid the long detour around Beauly Firth. Pleasant, wooded agricultural country, with attractive coastal views and following the shore in several places.

A9			***Inverness**	60¾
..	2¼	2¼	*Clachnaharry	58½
..	11½	9¼	*Lovat Bridge	49¼
..	12¾	1¼	*Beauly	48
B9169	14½	1¾	Junc A9/B9169	46¼
A832	15¼	¾	Junc B9169/A832	45½
..	20¼	5	Tore	40½
..	26¾	6½	*Avoch	34
..	28½	1¾	*Fortrose	32¼
..	29½	1	*Rosemarkie	31¼
B9163	38¼	8¾	***Cromarty**	22½
..	45¼	7	Balbair	15½
..	49¼	4	*Cullicudden	11½
B9162	58	8¾	Junc B9163/B9162	2¾
A9	58¼	¼	*Conon Bridge	2½
..	59¼	1	Maryburgh	1½
..	60¾	1½	***Dingwall**	
			Alternative via Kessock Ferry	
B9161			***Inverness**	
..	1¾	1¾	*South Kessock Ferry to *North Kessock	
	6¾	5	Munlochy	
A832	7	¼	Junc B9161/A832	
..	10½	3½	*Avoch	

204. INVERNESS to ULLAPOOL. Skirts Beauly Firth at first, then follows a valley road to Loch Garve, passing the *Falls of Rogie near the Achilty Inn. Beyond Garve, the road crosses the open moorlands of the Dirrie More to reach the Falls of Measach at Braemore Junction. Beautiful mountain and loch scenery on the latter part, the last few miles being through Strath More and then along the shores of Loch Broom.

A9			***Inverness**	60¾
..	2¼	2¼	*Clachnaharry	58½
..	11½	9¼	*Lovat Bridge	49¼
..	12¾	1¼	*Beauly	48
A832	15¼	2½	*Muir of Ord	45½
..	19½	4¼	*Marybank	41¼
..	22	2½	*Contin	38¾
..	22¾	¾	*Achilty Inn	38
..	28¼	5½	*Garve	32½
A835	29	¾	Junc A832/A835	31¾
..	38¼	9¼	*Altguish Inn	22½
..	48½	10¼	*Braemore Junction	12¼
..	60¾	12¼	***Ullapool**	

205. INVERNESS to GAIRLOCH. Skirts Beauly Firth at first, then follows a valley road to Loch Garve, passing the *Falls of Rogie near the Achilty Inn. Crosses moorland country beyond Garve, with beautiful loch and mountain scenery, particularly after descending Glen Docherty to Kinlochewe, where the Ben Eighe National Nature Reserve is situated. Thence an attractive, winding road follows the banks of Loch Maree for several miles, with the peak of Slioch dominating the farther shore. Later descends by the wooded Kerrysdale to Gairloch.

A9			***Inverness** ..	73¾
..	2¼	2¼	*Clachnaharry ..	71½
..	11½	9¼	*Lovat Bridge ..	62¼
..	12¾	1¼	*Beauly	61
A832	15¼	2½	*Muir of Ord ..	58½
..	19½	4¼	*Marybank ..	54¼
..	22	2½	*Contin	51¾
..	22¾	¾	*Achilty Inn ..	51
..	28¼	5½	*Garve	45½
..	44¾	16½	***Achnasheen** ..	29
..	54¼	9½	*Kinlochewe ..	19½
..	64	9¾	*Loch Maree Hotel	9¾
..	73¾	9¾	*Gairloch	

206. A tour from INVERNESS to GAIRLOCH via Cannich (for Glen Affric) and Gruinard Bay. A touring route, embracing some of the finest north-west Highland scenery, but utilizing narrow and hilly roads in places. At first along the shore of *Loch Ness, then by Glen Urquhart to Cannich, where picturesque detours can be made along the richly-wooded Glen Affric and Glen Cannich. Here there are some hydro-electric power scheme developments. Strath Glass is followed to the main road at Beauly, turning off at Dingwall through Strathpeffer, and passing the *Falls of Rogie near Achilty Inn. Beyond Garve the road becomes narrow, with frequent passing places, and crosses open moorland to the Falls of Measach near Braemore Junction. Beautiful coast and mountain scenery, with excellent views on the remainder of the tour, but the road is narrow and hilly, including the 1 in 7 ascent of Gruinard Hill. Fine views of the An Teallach peaks on the descent from the so-called Destitution Road to Dundonnell, then follows Little Loch Broom to Gruinard Bay and the ascent of Gruinard Hill. *Aultbea, on Loch Ewe, lies just off the road between Laide and Poolewe. Fine views of Loch Maree and the Gair Loch on the latter part.

A82			***Inverness** ..	131½
A831	14¾	14¾	*Drumnadrochit	116¾
..	27¼	12½	*Cannich ..	104¼
..	34¼	7	*Struy Bridge ..	97¼
..	39¼	5	*Crask of Aigas	92¼
..	41¾	2½	*Kilmorack ..	89¾
A9	43¼	1½	Junc A831/A9 ..	88¼
..	44½	1¼	*Beauly	87
..	47	2½	*Muir of Ord ..	84½
..	50¾	3¾	*Conon Bridge ..	80¾
..	51¾	1	Maryburgh ..	79¾
A834	53¼	1½	***Dingwall** ..	78¼
..	58	4¾	***Strathpeffer** ..	73½
A832	60½	2½	*Contin	71
..	61¼	¾	*Achilty Inn ..	70¼
..	66¾	5½	*Garve	64¾
A835	67½	¾	Junc A832/A835	64
..	76¾	9¼	*Altguish Inn ..	54¾
A832	87	10¼	*Braemore Junction ..	44½
..	100½	13½	*Dundonnell ..	31
..	112¼	11¾	*Gruinard Bay ..	19¼
..	116½	4¼	*Laide	15
..	125½	9	*Poolewe ..	6
..	131½	6	*Gairloch	

207. INVERNESS to KYLE OF LOCHALSH (for the Isle of Skye) or GLENELG and ARNISDALE. At first along the *Caledonian Canal through the Great Glen or *Glen More, later passing the ruined Urquhart Castle beyond Drumnadrochit, on the shore of *Loch Ness, which is followed to Invermoriston. A gradual ascent is then made through the wooded Glen Moriston to Cluanie, afterwards descending (maximum gradient 1 in 8) by the lonely Glen Shiel along the route of one of the 'Roads to the Isles,' with magnificent mountain scenery. Fine views of the Kintail hills, including the Five Sisters, as the road follows the shore of *Loch Duich past Eilean Donan Castle, before crossing Loch Long by the fine modern bridge at Dornie. Hilly between Inverinate and Dornie as the road climbs high above the loch, with an ascent and descent of 1 in 6, while beyond Balmacara, on the shore of Loch Alsh, there is another ascent of 1 in 10, after which the hills of Skye come into view. On the alternative to Arnisdale there are fine panoramic views from the winding ascent of Mam Rattachan (maximum gradient 1 in 6, hairpin bends), where an altitude of 1,116 feet is reached, followed by an easier descent. The road then divides. One branch leads through Glenelg to reach Glen Beag, where a visit can be made to the remarkable Pictish Brochs; thereafter a narrow and hilly road is followed high above the Sound of Sleat and along the shore of picturesque *Loch Hourn to the road end at Arnisdale. The other branch road diverges before Glenelg village and leads to a ferry which operates during the summer months to Kylerhea (Isle of Skye). From Kylerhea there is a long climb (maximum gradient 1 in 5) by a narrow road through Glen Arroch, followed by a long descent to the main road halfway between Kyleakin and Broadford (Shiel Bridge to Broadford is 20¾ miles).

A82			***Inverness** ..	83½
..	14¾	14¾	*Drumnadrochit	68¾
..	15½	¾	*Lewiston ..	68
A887	27¼	11¾	*Invermoriston ..	56¼
..	35¾	8½	*Torgyle Bridge..	47¾
A87	51¾	16	*Cluanie ..	31¾
..	63½	11¾	†*Shiel Bridge ..	20
..	66	2½	*Croe Bridge ..	17½
..	69¼	3¼	*Inverinate ..	14¼
..	73	3¾	*Dornie ..	10½
..	73¾	¾	*Ardelve ..	9¾
..	76	2¼	*Auchtertyre ..	7½
..	77½	1½	*Balmacara ..	6
..	83½	6	*Kyle of Lochalsh	
		†	OR	
Uncl	63½		*Shiel Bridge	
..	66¾	3¼	*Mam Rattachan (summit)	
..	72	5¼	*Glenelg	
..	82	10	*Arnisdale	

208. FORT WILLIAM to AVIEMORE. Passes through a variety of mountain, moorland, loch and woodland scenery, with views of *Ben Nevis from the open country on the earlier part. Beyond Spean Bridge, the pretty Glen Spean is traversed, afterwards passing along the shores of Loch Laggan. Attractive woodland scenery in the Upper Spey Valley from Drumgask.

A82			***Fort William** ..	61¼
..	2¼	2¼	Lochy Bridge (near side) ..	59
A86	9½	7¼	***Spean Bridge** ..	51¾
..	12¾	3¼	*Roy Bridge ..	48½
..	18¼	5½	Rd to *Tulloch Sta	43
..	31½	13¼	*Loch Laggan Inn	29¾
..	38¼	6¾	*Drumgask ..	23
..	38¾	½	*Laggan Bridge	22½
A9	46½	7¾	*Newtonmore ..	14¾
..	49¼	2¾	***Kingussie** ..	12
..	55	5¾	*Kincraig ..	6¼
..	58¾	3¾	*Lynwilg.. ..	2½
..	61¼	2½	*Aviemore	

209. FORT WILLIAM to MALLAIG (for Isle of Skye). This 'Road to the Isles' is scenically one of the very finest in the Highlands. A variety of loch, mountain and woodland scenery is traversed at first along the shores of Loch Eil, then passing the Prince Charles Edward Monument on the edge of *Loch Shiel near Glenfinnan. Later along the shores of picturesque Loch Eilt, and afterwards passing the heads of Loch Ailort and *Loch Nan Uamh, before reaching the silver sands and Falls of Morar. A good surfaced two-lane road to west of Corpach followed by a narrow road with passing places to Glenfinnan. A good surfaced two-lane road to Lochailort thence a narrow winding and hilly road (1 in 7) to Mallaig.

A82			***Fort William** ..	47¾
A830	2¼	2¼	Lochy Bridge ..	45½
..	3½	1¼	*Banavie ..	44¼
..	4½	1	*Corpach ..	43¼
..	12¼	8	*Kinlocheil ..	35¼
..	18¾	6¼	*Glenfinnan ..	29
..	28¼	9½	*Lochailort ..	19½
..	38½	10¼	*Arisaig ..	9¼
..	45	6½	*Morar	2¾
..	47¾	2¾	***Mallaig**	

210. FORT WILLIAM to INVERNESS. A delightful main road following the line of the Great Glen, or *Glen More, threaded by the *Caledonian Canal, which joins a series of lochs to form a continuous waterway between the Atlantic Ocean and the North Sea. There are fine views of *Loch Lochy, *Loch Oich and *Loch Ness as the road keeps near to the waterside for most of the way, and passes the ruined Urquhart Castle before Lewiston. The alternative detour by Glen Urquhart and Strath

Glass can be extended by excursions from Cannich along the beautiful Glen Affric and Glen Cannich, where there are some hydro-electric power scheme developments.

A82			***Fort William**	65¾
..	2¼	2¼	Lochy Bridge (near side) ..	63½
..	9½	7¼	***Spean Bridge** ..	56¼
..	21	11½	*Laggan Locks ..	44¾
..	24¾	3¾	***Invergarry** ..	41
..	27¼	2½	*Oich Bridge ..	38½
..	32	4¾	*Fort Augustus ..	33¾
..	38½	6½	***Invermoriston** ..	27¼
..	50¼	11¾	*Lewiston ..	15½
..	51	¾	†*Drumnadrochit	14¾
..	65¾	14¾	***Inverness**	
			† OR	
			via Cannich	
A831	51		*Drumnadrochit	
..	63½	12½	*Cannich	
..	70½	7	*Struy Bridge	
..	75½	5	*Crask of Aigas	
..	78	2½	*Kilmorack	
A9	79½	1½	Junc A831/A9	
..	79¾	¼	*Lovat Bridge	
..	89	9¼	*Clachnaharry	
..	91¼	2¼	***Inverness**	

211. FORT WILLIAM to INVERNESS via Errogie or Foyers. There are several routes between Fort Augustus and Inverness, the main road by Invermoriston being shown in Iter 210, but there are fine views from the more winding, hilly and less frequented roads on the east side of *Loch Ness, which are indicated below. Leaving Fort Augustus, there is a steep ascent (maximum gradient 1 in 9) to Glen Doe, afterwards gradually rising to reach the summit at 1,275 feet, followed by a long descent to Whitebridge. There is a choice of routes from here, the best road, by Errogie, having a steep descent to Loch Ness at Dores, although there is a narrow secondary road which branches off 3 miles from Torness and follows a more gradual descent. The alternative, but narrow and hilly, road from Whitebridge goes by way of the Falls of Foyers before reaching the shores of Loch Ness which is then followed to Dores. Thereafter it is an easy level road to Inverness.

			***Fort William** ..	65½
			By Iter **210** to:	
A862	32	32	*Fort Augustus ..	33½
..	41¼	9¼	*Whitebridge ..	24¼
..	45¼	4	Gorthleck ..	20¼
..	47½	2¼	*Errogie	18
..	51½	4	*Torness ..	14
..	57½	6	*Dores	8
..	65½	8	***Inverness**	
			OR	
			via Foyers	
			***Fort William**	64¼
			By Iter **210** to:	
A862	32	32	*Fort Augustus ..	32¼
..	41¼	9¼	*Whitebridge ..	23
B852	42¼	1	Junc A862/B852	22
..	45¼	3	*Foyers	19
..	47¾	2½	*Inverfarigaig ..	16½
A862	56¼	8½	*Dores	8
..	64¼	8	***Inverness**	

212. FORT WILLIAM to NAIRN via Cawdor Castle. From Fort Augustus this is a cross-country route utilizing secondary roads, with a steep ascent (maximum gradient 1 in 9) leading to Glen Doe, afterwards rising to the summit at 1,275 feet, followed by a long descent to Whitebridge, and then follows the south side of Strath Nairn. On reaching the main Aviemore-Inverness road a detour can be made to *Culloden through *Daviot and thence by road B851 along the north side of Strath Nairn. The fastest route is by Inverness, Iters 210 and 175.

			***Fort William** ..	81¼
			By Iter **210** to:	
A862	32	32	*Fort Augustus	49¼
..	41¼	9¼	*Whitebridge ..	40
..	45¼	4	Gorthleck ..	36
..	47½	2¼	*Errogie	33¾
B851	49½	2	Junc A862/B851	31¾
..	55	5½	Aberarder ..	26¼
..	59½	4½	Farr	21¾
..	60¼	¾	*Dalvourn ..	21
A9	63¾	3½	Junc B851/A9 ..	17½
Uncl	64¼	½	Junc A9/Uncl ..	17
B9090	73¾	9½	Junc Uncl/B9090	7½
..	75	1¼	*Cawdor ..	6¼
..	81¼	6¼	***Nairn**	

213. FORT WILLIAM to DINGWALL. Beyond Fort Augustus, follows the shore of *Loch Ness through the Great Glen, or *Glen More, threaded by the *Caledonian Canal, and passing the ruined Urquhart Castle before Lewiston, near Drumnadrochit. It then utilizes a cross-country link, with a 1 in 6 ascent from Milton, giving extensive views from the summit before descending wooded Glen Convinth. Agricultural on the latter part.

			***Fort William** ..	74
			By Iter **210** to:	
..	32	32	*Fort Augustus	42
..	38½	6½	***Invermoriston** ..	35½
..	50¼	11¾	*Lewiston ..	23¾
A831	51	¾	*Drumnadrochit	32
A833	52	1	Junc A831/A833	22
..	59	7	Glackbea ..	15
A9	62	3	Junc A833/A9 ..	12
..	64	2	*Lovat Bridge ..	10
..	65¼	1¼	*Beauly	8¾
..	67¾	2½	*Muir of Ord ..	6¼
..	71½	3¾	*Conon Bridge ..	2½
..	72½	1	Maryburgh	1½
..	74	1½	***Dingwall**	

214. FORT WILLIAM to KINLOCH HOURN via Loch Arkaig. A touring route at first through the Great Glen, or *Glen More, and following the banks of the *Caledonian Canal to *Loch Lochy, and then by the 'Dark Mile' to Loch Arkaig. Returning by Loch Lochy, the Falls of Mucomer are passed before joining the main road to Invergarry. Pretty in Glen Garry past Loch Garry to Tomdoun. Grand mountain and loch scenery by *Loch Quoich, with the fine peak of Gairich rising to the south, and onwards to *Loch Hourn, but there is a descent (maximum gradient 1 in 6) for the last 2½ miles. There is no through road along either Loch Arkaig or Loch Hourn.

A82			***Fort William** ..	66½
A830	2¼	2¼	Lochy Bridge ..	64½
B8004	3½	1¼	*Banavie ..	63
B8005	9½	6	Junc B8004/B8005	57
..	15	5½	*Loch Arkaig ..	51½
			Return to:	
B8004	20½	5½	Junc B8005/B8004	46
..	20¾	¼	*Gairlochy ..	45¾
A82	23¼	2½	Junc B8004/A82	43¼
..	36¼	13	*Laggan Locks ..	30¼
A87	40	3¾	***Invergarry** ..	26½
Uncl	44½	4½	Junc A87/ Uncl..	22
..	50½	6	*Tomdoun Hotel	16
..	60½	10	*Quoich Bridge ..	6
..	66½	6	***Kinloch Hourn**	

215. FORT WILLIAM to ARDGOUR. Fine mountain and loch scenery, with views of *Ben Nevis as the route circles round Loch Eil to reach the west shore of *Loch Linnhe. The road is level, but beyond Kinlocheil becomes narrow and winding. The long detour can be avoided by following A82 southwards from Fort William and utilizing the *Corran Ferry to Ardgour.

A82			***Fort William** ..	35½
A830	2¼	2¼	Lochy Br ..	33¼
..	3½	1¼	*Banavie ..	32
..	4½	1	*Corpach ..	31
..	12½	8	*Kinlocheil ..	23
A861	13¾	1¼	Junc A830/A861	21¾
..	24	10¼	*Camusnagaul ..	11½
..	35½	11½	*Ardgour Hotel	

216. ARDGOUR to KILCHOAN (for Ardnamurchan Point). Fine mountain and loch scenery, although the road is narrow and winding, particularly beyond Salen, where the surface deteriorates and passing places are infrequent. At first along the edge of *Loch Linnhe, then from Strontian to Glenborrodale follows the wooded shore of *Loch Sunart, dominated to the north by Ben Resipol. After a short deviation inland, the ruins of Mingary Castle are passed before reaching Kilchoan. A road continues for 6 miles beyond Kilchoan to *Ardnamurchan Point, the most westerly extremity of the Scottish mainland. There is a passenger ferry from Mingary Pier, near Kilchoan, to Tobermory, Isle of Mull.

A861			*Ardgour Hotel..	44½
..	6½	6½	*Inversanda ..	38
..	14½	8	*Strontian ..	30
B8007	24½	10	Junc A861/B8007	20
..	24¾	¼	*Salen	19¾
..	32¼	7½	Glenborrodale Castle	12¼
..	44½	12¼	*Kilchoan	

217. ARDGOUR to MALLAIG via Kinlochmoidart. Fine mountain and loch scenery. Mainly a single track road with passing places to Kinlochmoidart and from Lochailort to Mallaig. Between Kinlochmoidart and Lochailort an excellent modern two-lane road. Follows the shores of *Loch Linnhe, and for 10 miles beyond Strontian, the wooded shores of *Loch Sunart dominated by Ben Resipol. *Loch Shiel is touched at Acharacle and the shores of Loch Moidart and *Loch Ailort are followed. The head of *Loch Nan Uamh is passed before reaching the silver sands and Falls of Morar.

A861			*Ardgour Hotel..	66½
..	6½	6½	*Inversanda ..	60
..	14½	8	*Strontian ..	52
B850	24½	10	Junc A861/B850	42
..	26½	2	*Acharacle ..	40
..	30¾	4¼	(road to) *Dalilea	35¾
..	34	3¼	*Kinlochmoidart	32½
..	38¾	4¾	*Glenuig ..	27¾
A830	47	8¼	*Lochailort ..	19½
..	57¼	10¼	*Arisaig ..	9¼
..	63¾	6½	*Morar	2¾
..	66½	2¾	***Mallaig**	

218. ARDGOUR to LOCHALINE or DRIMNIN. Fine mountain and loch scenery in the lonely *Morven district of Argyll, the road being narrow and hilly. Follows the shore of *Loch Linnhe to Inversanda, and by Glen Tarbert to the south shore of *Loch Sunart, thence a long climb over the hills. A narrow alternative road B8043 from Inversanda continues by Loch Linnhe to *Camasnacroise, joining the road from Loch Sunart (A884). Just before Lochaline, a branch road leads off along the Sound of Mull to Drimnin. There is a car-ferry service from Lochaline to Oban which calls at Craignure, Isle of Mull.

A861			*Ardgour Hotel	32½
..	6½	6½	*Inversanda ..	26
A884	13	6½	Junc A861/A884	19½
..	29¼	16¼	†*Larachbeg ..	3¼
..	32½	3¼	*Lochaline	
		†	OR	
A884	29¼		*Larachbeg	
B849	31¼	2	Junc A884/B849	
..	42½	11¼	*Drimnin	

219. STROME to APPLECROSS. Follows the shore of Loch Carron to Lochcarron, whence narrow and hilly roads are used. There is a 1 in 6 ascent from the main road, followed by a gradual descent, with views across Loch Kishorn. After Tornapress, the road climbs the well-known Pass of the Cattle, which is one of the most difficult roads in the country. It is narrow, without passing bays, and has several hairpin bends. On the 6 mile ascent the gradient steepens to a maximum of 1 in 4, with magnificent views from the summit at 2,054 feet. On the long descent to the sea at Applecross the road and gradients are similar but easier. This road is liable to be blocked by snow during the winter months.

A890			***Strome**	29½
	7½	7½	*Strathcarron Sta	22
A896	8½	1	Junc A890/A896	21
	11½	3	*Lochcarron ..	18
..	16¼	4¾	*Kishorn ..	13¼
Uncl	18	1¾	*Tornapress ..	11½
..	24	6	*Pass of the Cattle (summit) ..	5½
..	29½	5½	*Applecross	

220. FORT WILLIAM to KYLE OF LOCHALSH (for Isle of Skye) or STROME. At first through open country to the wooded shores of *Loch Lochy and *Loch Oich. Beyond Invergarry, the road has been mainly reconstructed and forms an alternative 'Road to the Isles.' Beautiful loch and mountain scenery by Loch Garry and Glen Garry then a long gradual ascent and descent to Loch Cluanie. There are important hydro-electric developments in this area. After Cluanie there is a long descent through the lonely Glen Shiel, a magnificent mountain defile. Fine views of the Kintail hills, including the Five Sisters as the road follows the shore of *Loch Duich past Eilean Donan Castle, before crossing Loch Long by the fine modern bridge at Dornie. Beyond Balmacara, on the shore of Loch Alsh, the hills of Skye come into view. The alternative to Strome is hilly with ascents and descents up to 1 in 6, but affords more fine views of Loch Duich and the Five Sisters of Kintail from Auchtertyre Hill.

A82			***Fort William** ..	78½
..	2¼	2¼	Lochy Bridge (near side) ..	76¼
..	9½	7¼	***Spean Bridge** ..	69
..	21	11½	*Laggan Lochs ..	57½
A87	24¾	3¾	***Invergarry** ..	53¾
..	46¾	22	*Cluanie ..	31¾
..	58½	11¾	*Shiel Bridge ..	29
..	61	2½	*Croe Bridge ..	17½
..	69¼	3¼	*Inverinate ..	14¼
..	68	3¾	*Dornie ..	10½
..	68¾	¾	*Ardelve ..	9¾
..	71	2¼	†*Auchtertyre ..	7½
..	72½	1½	*Balmacara ..	6
..	78½	6	***Kyle of Lochalsh**	
		†	OR	
A890	71		*Auchtertyre	
..	76½	5½	*Achmore	
..	77¾	1¼	***Strome**	

221. KYLE OF LOCHALSH to INVERNESS via Achnasheen. Hilly to Strome, with a 1 in 10 descent approaching Balmacara on Loch Alsh, and an ascent and descent of 1 in 6 before Strome, with fine views of Loch Duich and the Five Sisters of Kintail from Auchtertyre Hill. Then through mountain and loch scenery and across moorlands to Garve, the country becoming agricultural on the latter part. The road follows Beauly Firth for the last few miles. The *Falls of Rogie are passed near Achilty Inn. A quicker route to Inverness is via Invermoriston (Iter 207).

A87			***Kyle of Lochalsh**	86
..	6	6	*Balmacara ..	80
A890	7½	1½	*Auchtertyre ..	78½
..	13	5½	*Achmore ..	73
..	14¼	1¼	***Strome** ..	71¼
..	21¾	7½	*Strathcarron Sta	64¼
..	26¾	5	Balnacra ..	59¼
..	28½	1¾	*Achnashellach ..	57½
A832	41¼	12¾	Junc A890/A832	44¾
..	41½	¼	***Achnasheen** ..	44½
..	57¾	16¼	*Garve ..	28¼
..	63¼	5½	*Achilty Inn ..	22¾
..	64	¾	*Contin	22
..	66½	2½	*Marybank ..	19½
A9	70¾	4¼	*Muir of Ord ..	15¼
..	73¼	2½	*Beauly	12¾
..	74½	1¼	*Lovat Bridge ..	11½
..	83¾	9¼	*Clachnaharry ..	2¼
..	86	2¼	***Inverness**	

222. A tour from KYLE OF LOCHALSH to ULLAPOOL via Loch Maree and Gairloch. A picturesque tourist route through beautiful mountain, loch and coast scenery, with magnificent views, but utilizing some hilly and narrow roads provided with passing places. Hilly to Strome, with a 1 in 10 descent approaching Balmacara on Loch Alsh, and descent of 1 in 8 before Strome, with fine views of Loch Duich and the Five Sisters of Kintail from Auchtertyre Hill. 2 miles from Kyle, a secondary road (with gradients up to 1 in 5) branches off through Drumbuie and Duirinish to reach the coast at the picturesquely situated village of *Plockton. The road from Duirinish by Duncraig Castle to Strome is hilly, and becomes narrow and rough on the latter part. Then through beautiful loch and mountain scenery. After the long descent through Glen Docherty (maximum gradient 1 in 9) to Kinlochewe, where the Ben Eighe National Nature Reserve is situated, an attractive road follows the winding shore of Loch Maree, with views of Slioch rising from the opposite bank. Later descends through wooded Kerrysdale to Gairloch on the coast, after which a climb inland leads to Poolewe on Loch Ewe. *Aultbea lies just off the road between Poolewe and Laide. The road onwards to Braemore Junction is narrower and has gradients of 1 in 8, in addition to the 1 in 7 descent of Gruinard Hill (care required), but there are some magnificent coast and mountain views at Gruinard Bay and along Little Loch Broom, where the Ardessie Falls are passed before Dundonnell. Views of An Teallach on the long ascent over the so-called Destitution Road to the Falls of Measach near Braemore Junction, and finally after descending through Strath More, follows the shores of Loch Broom to Ullapool.

A87			***Kyle of Lochalsh**	126¾
..	6	6	*Balmacara ..	120¾
A890	7½	1½	*Auchtertyre ..	119¼
..	13	5½	*Achmore ..	113¾
..	14¼	1¼	***Strome**	112½
..	21¾	7½	*Strathcarron Sta	105
..	26¾	5	Balnacra ..	100
..	28½	1¾	*Achnashellach ..	98¼
A832	41¼	12¾	Junc A890/A832	85½
..	50½	9¼	*Kinlochewe ..	76¼
..	60¼	9¾	*Loch Maree Hotel ..	66½
..	70	9¾	*Gairloch ..	56¾
..	76	6	*Poolewe ..	50¾
..	85	9	*Laide ..	41¾
..	89¼	4¼	*Gruinard Bay	37½
..	101	11¾	*Dundonnell ..	25¾
A835	114½	13½	*Braemore Junction ..	12¼
..	126¾	12¼	***Ullapool**	

223. A tour from STROME to GAIRLOCH via Shieldaig and Torridon. A picturesque route through beautiful mountain, loch and coast scenery, with magnificent views, but utilizing some hilly and narrow roads provided with passing places. The route follows the shore of Loch Carron to Lochcarron then narrow and hilly roads are used. There is a 1 in 6 ascent, followed by a gradual descent, with views across Loch Kishorn and later passes through the wild and lovely Glen Shieldaig. Splendid loch scenery is then seen, and magnificent views of the Torridon mountains through Glen Torridon. From Kinlochewe, where the Ben Eighe National Nature Reserve is situated, an attractive road follows the winding shore of Loch Maree, with views of Slioch rising from the opposite bank. Later the tour descends through wooded Kerrysdale to Gairloch.

A890			***Strome**	64¾
..	7½	7½	*Strathcarron Sta	57¼
A896	8½	1	*Junc A890/A896	56¼
..	11½	3	*Lochcarron ..	53¼
..	16¼	4¾	*Kishorn ..	48½
..	18	1¾	*Tornapress ..	46¾
..	26½	8½	*Shieldaig ..	38¼
..	34½	8	*Torridon ..	30¼
A832	45¼	10¾	*Kinlochewe ..	19½
..	55	9¾	*Loch Maree Hotel ..	9¾
..	64¾	9¾	*Gairloch	

224. ULLAPOOL to LAIRG. Generally a good Highland road which has been reconstructed in parts. Fine views of the mountains of Wester Ross and the Assynt peaks of Sutherland on the first part, including Ben More Coigach, Cul Mor and Cul Beag. The peaks of Stack Polly and Canisp are prominent, while the sharp eastern cone of Suilven comes into view near Elphin. Crosses open moorland country from Ledmore, following Strath Oykell by way of Rosehall.

A835			***Ullapool** ..	45½
..	3¼	3¼	*Ardmair Bay ..	42¼
..	7¾	4½	*Strathkanaird ..	37¾
..	13	5¼	*Knockan ..	32½
..	16	3	*Elphin	29½
A837	18¼	2¼	Ledmore Fork ..	27¼
..	19¾	1½	*Altnacealgach Hotel ..	25¾
..	30¼	10½	*Oykell Bridge ..	15¼
A839	37	6¾	*Rosehall (WM)	8½
A836	45¼	8¼	Junc A839/A836	¼
..	45½	¼	***Lairg**	

225. A tour from ULLAPOOL to TONGUE via Kylesku Ferry. A tour through the Northern Highlands, touching the coast at several places. A good Highland road at first but beyond Kylesku there are hilly and narrow roads (maximum gradient 1 in 7) with frequent passing places. There are certain restrictions on the use of the ferry at Kylesku (see ferry details), which can be avoided by proceeding via **Lairg, Iter 224 and 229 or 230.** Fine views of the mountains of Wester Ross and Sutherland on the first part, including Ben More Coigach, Cul Mor and Cul Beag. The peaks of Stack Polly and Canisp are prominent, while Suilven comes into view near Elphin. Passes the ruins of Ardvreck Castle on the shore of *Loch Assynt beyond Inchnadamph (with views of Ben More Assynt and Quinag), where a detour can be made to *Lochinver on the coast, 11 miles away. The tour continues through a wild landscape of bare gneiss dotted with innumerable lochans. Touches the coast in several places to Rhiconich, with fine views of the peaks of the Reay Forest to the south-west and later passing close to the Cape Wrath Hotel, the nearest motoring point to Cape Wrath. From Durness, the indented north coastline is first followed past Smoo Cave, after which *Rispond lies just off the road before encircling Loch Eriboll. After passing the northern end of Loch Hope, there are views of Ben Hope and Ben Loyal as the road crosses the head of the Kyle of Tongue. A by-road along the western shore of the Kyle of Tongue leads to *Melness and *Port Vasco.

A835			***Ullapool** ..	107¾
..	3¼	3¼	*Ardmair Bay ..	104½
..	7¾	4½	*Strathkanaird ..	100
..	13	5¼	*Knockan ..	94¾
..	16	3	*Elphin	91¾
A837	18¼	2¼	Ledmore Fork ..	89½
..	24¼	6	*Inchnadamph ..	83½
A894	26½	2¼	Junc A837/A894	81¼
..	32½	6	*Unapool ..	75¼
..	34	1½	***Kylesku** Ferry to ..	73¾
..	34¾	¾	*Kylestrome ..	73
..	42½	7¾	*Eddrachillis Church ..	65¼
..	45	2½	*Scourie	62¾
A838	51¾	6¾	*Laxford Bridge	56
..	56¾	5	*Rhiconich ..	51
..	69¼	12½	Rd to *Cape Wrath Hotel	38½
..	71	1¾	***Durness** ..	36¾
..	72¾	1¾	*Smoo Cave ..	35
..	87¼	14½	*Eriboll	20½
..	90¼	3	*Heilim	17½
..	92	1¾	*Hope Lodge ..	15¾
..	107¾	15¾	***Tongue**	

226. ULLAPOOL to LOCHINVER or ACHILTIBUIE. Wild loch and mountain scenery, with views of Ben More Coigach and Cul Beag before turning off by a narrow road along the lonely shores of *Loch Lurgain, close by the splintered peak of Stack Polly. Beyond Baddagyle, very narrow, winding and hilly, with gradients up to 1 in 6, but giving splendid views of Enard Bay and the fantastic peaks of Stack Polly and Suilven. The main road from Ullapool to Lochinver is by Inchnadamph, Iter 225 and 228. The alternative from Baddagyle reaches the coast near Achiltibuie, where there are fine views of the Summer Isles.

A835			***Ullapool** ..	30
..	3¼	3¼	*Ardmair Bay ..	26¾
..	7¾	4½	*Strathkanaird ..	22¼
Uncl	10	2¼	Junc A835/Uncl	20
..	18¼	8¼	†*Baddagyle (Rd junc) ..	11¾
..	27	8¾	*Inverkirkaig ..	3
..	28¾	1¾	Strathan	1¼
..	30	1¼	***Lochinver**	
		†	OR	
Uncl	18¼		*Baddagyle (Rd junc)	
..	24¾	6½	*Achiltibuie	

227. LOCHINVER to KYLESKU FERRY or INCHNADAMPH via Drumbeg. A hilly and winding by-road following the coastline through wild desolate country, with fine views of the Assynt mountains of Sutherland, especially of Suilven and the Quinag. Magnificent mountain and loch scenery on the latter part, with a maximum descent and ascent of 1 in 4 between Drumbeg and A894. The alternative to Inchnadamph follows a good Highland road, where the shores of *Loch Assynt are followed past the ruins of Ardvreck Castle, with views of Ben More Assynt. The easiest way from Lochinver to Inchnadamph is by the direct road A837 and to Kylesku via A837 and A894.

A837			***Lochinver** ..	25
B869	¾	¾	Junc A837/B869	24¼
..	6½	5¾	*Stoer	18½
..	8½	2	Clashnessie ..	16½
..	14	5½	*Drumbeg ..	11
..	15¼	1¼	Nedd	9¾
A894	22¾	7½	†Junc B869/A894	2¼
..	23½	¾	*Unapool ..	1½
..	25	1½	***Kylesku Ferry**	
	†		OR	
A894	22¾		Junc B869/A894	
..	30¼	7½	*Inchnadamph	

228. BONAR BRIDGE to LOCHINVER. Open moorland country, following Strath Oykell to Altnacealgach, where there are extensive views of the mountains of Wester Ross and the Assynt peaks, including Cul Beag, Cul Mor, Suilven and Canisp. Narrow beyond Inchnadamph, following the shore of *Loch Assynt, and passing the ruins of Ardvreck Castle, with views of Quinag, and afterwards following the River Inver to the coast at Lochinver.

A836			***Bonar Bridge** ..	49¾
..	3¼	3¼	*Invershin (Sta)	46½
A837	4	¾	Junc A836/A837	45¾
..	4¾	¾	*Inveran Bridge..	45
..	11¾	7	*Rosehall (WM)	38
..	18½	6¾	*Oykell Bridge ..	31¼
..	29	10½	*Altnacealgach Hotel	20¾
..	30½	1½	Ledmore Fork ..	19¼
..	36½	6	*Inchnadamph ..	13¼
..	49¾	13¼	***Lochinver**	

229. BONAR BRIDGE to DURNESS or KINLOCHBERVIE. Follows the main road to Lairg, an alternative by the River Shin and the Shin Falls being given in Iter 232. Beyond Lairg, crosses open moorland country, passing Lochs Shin, Merkland, More and Stack. Ben Stack and the Reay Forest mountains are well seen before reaching Laxford Bridge, beyound which the road is hilly. Crosses open moorland after Rhiconich, later passing close to the Cape Wrath Hotel, the nearest motoring point to Cape Wrath. The alternative traverses a narrow road (with a descent of 1 in 8) along the shore of Loch Inchard to Kinlochbervie. This road continues for another 4 miles to Sheigra, near the open sea, from which the remote, but beautiful Sandwood Bay can be reached on foot.

A836			***Bonar Bridge** ..	66¾
..	3¼	3¼	*Invershin ..	63½
..	10¾	7½	***Lairg**	56
A838	12¾	2	Junc A836/A838	54
..	26½	13¾	*Overscaig ..	40¼
..	30¾	4¼	*Merkland Lodge	36
..	41	10¼	*Achfary.. ..	25¾
..	47½	6½	*Laxford Bridge	19¼
..	52½	5	†*Rhiconich ..	14¼
..	65	12½	Rd to *Cape Wrath Hotel	1¾
..	66¾	1¾	***Durness**	
	†		OR	
B801	52½		*Rhiconich	
..	56¾	4¼	*Kinlochbervie	

230. BONAR BRIDGE to TONGUE. Follows the main road to Lairg, an alternative by the River Shin and Shin Falls being given in Iter 232. Beyond Lairg, crosses open moorland country by the Pass of Crask and Strath Bagastie, with distant views of the Sutherland mountains to the west, to reach Altnaharra. Later follows the shore of Loch Loyal, with views of Ben Loyal. From Altnaharra a narrow, rough and hilly by-road leads along the shore of Loch Hope to Hope Lodge on A838.

A836			***Bonar Bridge** ..	48
..	3¼	3¼	*Invershin ..	44¾
..	10¾	7½	***Lairg**	37¼
..	23¾	13	*Crask	24¼
..	31½	7¾	*Altnaharra ..	16½
..	48	16½	***Tongue**	

231. BONAR BRIDGE to HELMSDALE via Dornoch. A fine coast run along the Dornoch Firth passing *Skibo Castle between Spinningdale and Clashmore, afterwards diverging from the main road to visit Dornoch. The coast is regained at Golspie where shortly afterwards *Dunrobin Castle is passed.

A9			***Bonar Bridge** ..	40¼
..	2½	2½	*Creich ..	37¾
..	5	2½	*Spinningdale ..	35¼
..	9½	4½	*Clashmore ..	30¾
B9167	11	1½	Junc A9/B9167..	29¼
B9168	13	2	***Dornoch** ..	27¼
A9	15¼	2¼	*Junc B9168/A9	25
..	19½	4¼	The *Mound ..	20¾
..	23¾	4¼	*Golspie ..	16½
..	28¾	5	*Brora	11½
..	35¾	7	*Loth	4½
..	38¼	2½	*Portgower ..	2
..	40¼	2	***Helmsdale**	

232. BONAR BRIDGE to THURSO via Strath Naver. A touring route, at first following the River Shin past the Shin Falls to Lairg, the main road being given in Iter 230. Afterwards crosses open moorland country by the Pass of Crask and Strath Bagastie, with distant views of the Sutherland mountains to the west, to reach Altnaharra, then follows a narrow, undulating road along the shores of Loch Naver and by Strath Naver to the coast at Bettyhill. Fine coast scenery on the latter part, but the road is narrow, winding and hilly to Melvich. A number of crofting villages, including *Farr, *Armadale and *Portskerra lie just off the road. See Iters 200 and 236 for the recommended route, via Helmsdale.

A836			***Bonar Bridge** ..	86½
..	3¼	3¼	*Invershin	83¼
A837	4	¾	Junc A836/A837	82½
B864	4¾	¾	*Inveran Bridge..	81¾
..	8¾	4	Gruids Mill ..	77¾
A839	9¾	1	Junc B864/A839	76¾
A836	10½	¾	Junc A839/A836	76
..	10¾	¼	***Lairg**	75¾
..	23¾	13	*Crask	62¾
..	31½	7¾	*Altnaharra ..	55
B873	32	½	Junc A836/B873	54½
B871	43½	11½	*Syre Church ..	43
..	46	2½	*Strath Naver (PO)	40½
A836	52¾	6¾	Junc B871/A836	33¾
..	55¾	3	*Bettyhill ..	30¾
..	66	10¼	*Strathy.. ..	20½
..	68¾	2¾	*Melvich.. ..	17¾
..	75¾	7	*Reay	10¾
..	77½	1¾	Rd to *Dounreay	9
..	81	3½	*Bridge of Forss	5½
..	86½	5½	***Thurso**	

233. LAIRG to HELMSDALE. Moorland country at first, the coast being reached at Golspie, where shortly afterwards *Dunrobin Castle is passed.

A839			***Lairg** ..	35¼
..	10½	10½	*Rogart (WM) ..	24¾
A9	14½	4	The *Mound ..	20¾
..	18¾	4¼	*Golspie ..	16½
..	23¾	5	*Brora	11½
..	30¾	7	*Loth	4½
..	33¼	2½	*Portgower ..	2
..	35¼	2	***Helmsdale**	

234. HELMSDALE to TONGUE or THURSO via Strath Halladale. A desolate, narrow moorland road by Strath Ullie and Strath Halladale to the coast at Melvich. Fine coast views on the latter part, but the road is hilly and winding, with a maximum gradient of 1 in 7 at Borgie Bridge. *Portskerra, *Armadale and *Farr lie just off the road between Melvich and Bettyhill. This route to Thurso avoids the hills of the main coast road by Berriedale (Iter 236), but is longer and narrower.

A897			***Helmsdale** ..	66¼
..	9	9	*Kildonan Church	57¼
..	17¼	8¼	*Kinbrace ..	49
..	24½	7¼	*Forsinard ..	41¾
..	32¾	8¼	*Dalhalvaig (PO)	33½
A836	38	5¼	†Junc A897/A836	28¼
..	40	2	*Melvich.. ..	26¼

..	42¾	2¾	*Strathy	23½
..	53	10¼	*Bettyhill	13¼
..	59	6	*Borgie Bridge ..	7¼
..	63¼	4¼	Coldbackie ..	3
..	66¼	3	***Tongue**	
		†	OR	
A836	38		Junc A897/A836	
..	43	5	*Reay	
..	44¾	1¾	Rd to *Dounreay	
..	48¼	3½	*Bridge of Forss	
..	53¾	5½	***Thurso**	

235. HELMSDALE to TONGUE via Strath Naver. A narrow, undulating cross-country route through loch and moorland scenery to Strath Naver. Hilly on the latter part, with a maximum gradient of 1 in 7 at Borgie Bridge.

A897			***Helmsdale** ..	52½
..	9	9	*Kildonan Church	43½
B871	17½	8½	*Kinbrace ..	35½
..	21¾	4¼	Baddanloch ..	30¾
..	32¾	11	*Syre Church ..	19¾
..	35¼	2½	*Strath Naver (PO)	17¼
A836	42	6¾	Junc B871/A836	10½
..	45¼	3¼	*Borgie Bridge ..	7¼
..	49½	4¼	Coldbackie ..	3
..	52½	3	***Tongue**	

236. HELMSDALE to THURSO and SCRABSTER (for Orkney). A pleasant, hilly and winding coast road to Latheron, with a steep descent at Berriedale (maximum gradient 1 in 9). Open moorland on the latter part, reaching the coast again at Thurso. For alternative see Iter 234.

A9			***Helmsdale** ..	45½
..	10	10	*Berriedale ..	35½
..	15½	5½	*Dunbeath ..	30
A895	20	4½	*Latheron ..	25½
A882	37½	17½	Junc A895/A882	8
A836	43½	6	***Thurso**	2
A882	44½	¾	Junc A836/A882	1¼
..	45½	1¼	***Scrabster**	

237. WICK to THURSO. An easy road through flat country.

A882			***Wick**	20¾
..	8¼	8¼	*Watten	12½
..	20¾	12½	***Thurso**	

238. WICK to THURSO via CASTLETOWN. Through flat, open country. An alternative to the main road given in Iter 237 with little to choose.

A9			**Wick**	20¾
B876	3¼	3¼	*Reiss ..	17½
..	7	3¾	Kirk ..	13¾
..	11¼	4¼	Bower (PO) ..	9½
A836	15½	4	Junc B876/A836	5¼
..	15¾	¼	*Castletown ..	5
..	20¾	5	***Thurso**	

239. WICK to THURSO via Halkirk. A secondary route through flat country, and going parallel to the main road given in Iter 237, but includes a diversion to Halkirk.

A9			***Wick**	23¾
B874	1¼	1¼	Junc A9/B874 ..	22½
..	11¾	10½	Gillock ..	12
..	17½	5¾	*Halkirk ..	6¼
..	23¾	6¼	***Thurso**	

240. TONGUE to JOHN O' GROATS. An undulating coast road, with fine seascapes in places, especially near Dunnet, where a short detour (B855) can be made to the most northerly point of the mainland at Dunnet Head, a bold promontory affording fine views of the Orkneys. *Farr, *Armadale and *Portskerra lie just off the road between Bettyhill and Melvich.

A836			***Tongue** ..	64
..	3	3	Coldbackie ..	61
..	7¼	4¼	*Borgie Bridge ..	56¾
..	13¼	6	*Bettyhill ..	50¾
..	23½	10¼	*Strathy ..	40½
..	26¼	2¾	*Melvich ..	37¾
..	33½	7¼	*Reay ..	30¾
..	35	1½	Rd to *Dounreay	29
..	38½	3½	*Bridge of Forss	25½
..	44	5½	***Thurso** ..	20
..	49	5	*Castletown ..	15
..	52½	3½	*Dunnet ..	11½
..	56¾	4¼	*Mey ..	7¼
..	58	1¼	*East Mey ..	6
..	62	4	*Huna ..	2
A9	63½	1½	Junc A836/A9	½
..	64	½	***John o' Groats**	

THE ISLANDS OF SCOTLAND

The itineraries tabulated below indicate the extent and nature of the main roads on the more important islands; the road mileage on the other islands is insufficient to warrant taking a vehicle for a short period.

Road conditions are extremely variable, and, in general, main roads on the islands are narrow with fair surfaces, although they are often winding and hilly. Side roads are usually inferior.

Particulars of the car-carrying services to the islands will be found at the end of the book.

Except on the smaller islands, bus services are usually provided to connect with the steamer sailings and cars are normally available for hire. Regular air services are also operated to many of the islands and particulars will be supplied by any office of British European Airways or by most travel agencies.

BUTE

The island is only 15 miles long and 5 miles broad, so that the road mileage is limited, but in its small compass the island offers a variety of attractive scenery, including moorland and lochs, and there are many delightful coastal views and sandy bays. The route given below utilizes the ferry from the mainland across the *Kyles of Bute, but alternative services are available between Rothesay and Wemyss Bay.

241. COLINTRAIVE to ROTHESAY and KILCHATTAN BAY. The road follows the east coast of the island with views of the Kyles of Bute, the Firth of Clyde and the twin Cumbraes. A number of excursions from the route can be made to places on the west coast, including Kilmichael, Etterick Bay, St Ninian's Bay, Scalpsie Bay and St Blane's Chapel.

A844			*Colintraive Ferry to *Rhubodach	17½
..	6¾	6¾	*Port Bannatyne	10¾
..	8¾	2	*Rothesay	8¾
..	9¾	1	*Craigmore	7¾
..	11½	1¾	*Ascog	6
B881	16	4½	Kingarth	1½
..	17½	1½	*Kilchattan Bay	

ARRAN

This delightful island has a wide variety of scenery, including rugged mountains, wild glens, rolling hills and farmlands. The coastline offers attractive views of the Firth of Clyde to the east and Kilbrennan Sound to the west. In addition to the circular tour described below, there is a link from Brodick to the west coast by way of the String Road, which later divides, one branch going past the Standing Stones of Tormore to Machrie, and the other to Blackwaterfoot. The only other motoring road is that leading south-west from Lamlash through the Monamore Glen and Glen Scorrodale to the coast road at Bennecarrigan Church, near Lagg. Passenger steamship services are available on weekdays from certain Clyde ports to Brodick and Lochranza; vehicles are conveyed between Brodick and Ardrossan.

242. A TOUR OF THE ISLE OF ARRAN. The winding coast road passes through a variety of scenery, with extensive views at first north-east across the Clyde to the islands of Bute and the Cumbraes, and then north to the Cowal hills. Later, on the west side, the views extend to the Kintyre peninsula. Between Lagg and Dippin, on the south side, a short detour can be made to the ruined *Kildonan Castle. There are fine views of Holy Island and the granite peak of Goat Fell on the latter part.

A841			*Brodick	55¼
..	6¼	6¼	*Corrie	49
..	7¾	1½	*Sannox	47½
..	14½	6¾	*Lochranza	40¾
..	16½	2	*Catacol	38¾
..	21	4½	*Pirnmill	34¼
..	23½	2½	Imachar	31¾
..	26	2½	Dougrie Lodge	29¼
..	27½	1½	*Machrie	27¾
..	32	4½	*Blackwaterfoot	23¼
..	36¼	4¼	Corriecravie	19
..	37	¾	*Sliddery	18¼
..	38	1	Bennecarrigan Ch	17¼
..	39	1	*Lagg (Kilmory PO)	16¼
..	45	6	Dippin (*Kildonan PO)	10¼
..	47¾	2¾	*Whiting Bay	7½
..	51¾	4	*Lamlash	3½
..	55¼	3½	*Brodick	

ISLAY

There is no road right round the island, but there are a number of roads linking the main villages, which are all situated on the coast. Although not very hilly, some of these roads afford extensive views and also give access to the many fine sandy beaches of the island. The car-carrying services operate from the mainland ports of Tarbert West and Kennacraig, West Loch Tarbert to Islay. Connections are provided to the islands of Gigha, Jura and Colonsay. A ferry also operates from Port Askaig across the Sounds of Islay to Feolin Ferry in Jura. Air services are operated from Glasgow to Glenegedale Airport.

243. PORT ELLEN to PORT ASKAIG via Bowmore. This route follows a straight, level road to Bowmore, known as the 'Low Road,' the shortest way to Bridgend and Port Askaig being described in Iter 246. Not far from Port Ellen, a side road leads to the extensive Machrie Sands, another approach being indicated in Iter 244. Wooded around Bridgend, otherwise mainly moorland country is traversed. Near Port Askaig, a short detour, affording splendid views of Jura and Mull, can be made northwards along a narrow, hilly road beside the Sound of Islay to Bonahaven Bay.

A846			*Port Ellen	21½
..	3¼	3¼	Rd to *Machrie	18¼
..	5	1¾	*Glenegedale Airport	16½
..	10½	5½	*Bowmore	11
..	13½	3	*Bridgend	8
..	18¼	4¾	Ballygrant	3¼
..	21½	3¼	*Port Askaig	

244. PORT ELLEN to MULL OF OA. This short route provides some extensive views beyond Cragabus, but becomes narrow and winding as it crosses the high moorlands. There are some fine sands and an American memorial at Kilnaughton Bay, about 1½ miles from Port Ellen. Here a side road leads off to the extensive Machrie Sands on the west coast. The magnificent cliff scenery at the Mull of Oa well repays the twenty-minute walk to reach the American soldiers' monument erected at this point.

A846			*Port Ellen ..	7
Uncl	¼	¼	Junc A846/Uncl	6¾
..	1½	1¼	Rd to *Machrie ..	5½
..	3	1½	Cragabus ..	4
..	4¼	1¼	Oa Church ..	2¾
..	7	2¾	Killeyan (for *Mull of Oa)	

245. PORT ELLEN to CLAGGAIN BAY. Traverses a variety of scenery, with fine stretches of rocky coast, later passing through the Kildalton estate, where the road becomes narrow. Fine views of Kintyre to the east, and of Jura to the north, and also of Beinn Bheigeir (1,609 feet), the highest point of the island.

A846			*Port Ellen ..	9¼
..	1½	1½	Laphroaig ..	7¾
..	2¾	1¼	*Lagavulin ..	6½
Uncl	3½	¾	Ardbeg ..	5¾
..	5	1½	*Kildalton (Castle Lodge) ..	4¼
..	9¼	4¼	*Claggain Bay	

246. PORT ELLEN to SANAIGMORE or KILCHOMAN (for Machir Bay). This direct road from Port Ellen to Bridgend is known as the 'High Road,' the alternative by Bowmore being shown in Iter 243. About 7 miles from Port Ellen, the narrow 'Glen Road' strikes north-east and forms the most direct way between Port Ellen and Port Askaig, although the best way is by Bridgend. After following the shore of Loch Indaal beyond Bridgend, the road turns inland across agricultural and moorland country and shortly divides, one branch leading to the rocky coast at Sanaigmore, and the other leading to Kilchoman and the sandy Machir Bay. An alternative loop road (B8017) to Sanaigmore turns off 2½ miles from Bridgend and crosses Gruinart Flats, where an excursion can be made along Loch Gruinart to Loch Ardnave. Beyond Sanaigmore there is a narrow road linking it with Kilchoman by way of Saligo Bay.

A846			*Port Ellen ..	22
B8016	1¼	1¼	Junc A846/B8016	20¾
A846	10½	9¼	Junc B8016/A846	11½
A847	11¼	¾	*Bridgend	10¾
B8018	15½	4¼	†Junc A847/B8018	6½
..	22	6½	*Sanaigmore	
			† OR	
B8018	15½		Junc A847/B8018	
Uncl	17½	2	Junc B8018/Uncl	
..	20¼	2¾	*Kilchoman (Coastguard Sta)	

247. PORT ASKAIG to PORTNAHAVEN, Moorland country, wooded around Bridgend, after which the shore of Loch Indaal is followed. At Port Charlotte there is a narrow side road which crosses the Rhinns of Islay to the rocky coast at Kilchiaran Bay, whence a rough, narrow road ascends over moorlands to Portnahaven.

A846			*Port Askaig ..	23¼
..	3¼	3¼	Ballygrant ..	20
A847	8	4¾	*Bridgend ..	15¼
..	14	6	*Bruichladdich	9¼
..	16	2	*Port Charlotte	7¼
..	23¼	7¼	*Portnahaven	

MULL

The island is well known for its picturesque scenery, but there are few roads apart from those detailed in the following itineraries. With the exception of the Tobermory-Salen road, all are narrow and winding and follow the coast for the greater part, affording fine mountain and loch views. The main access to the island is by the week-day steamer which operates from Oban and Lochaline (Morven) to Craignure.

248. A TOUR OF THE ISLAND OF MULL (Northern). This tour covers the northern half of the island, following narrow roads for the greater part. Crosses moorlands at first and passes the Mishnish Lochs, then descends by hairpin bends to Dervaig, beyond which woodland country is traversed to Calgary, where there is an excellent sandy bay. There are more hairpin bends on the descent before reaching Kilninian, and the Laggan Falls are passed some distance before the short side road leading to the passenger ferry to the island of Ulva. The road then winds high above the rocks along Loch na Keal, with views of Ben More, the highest mountain on Mull. From Gruline, a narrow neck of land is crossed to Salen, where the main road along the Sound of Mull is followed.

B8073			*Tobermory ..	43¾
..	7¾	7¾	*Dervaig ..	36
..	12¼	4½	*Calgary ..	31½
..	18¾	6½	*Kilninian ..	25
..	24½	5¾	*Ulva Ferry ..	19¼
B8035	31¼	6¾	Gruline Church	12½
A848	33¾	2½	*Salen	10
..	43¾	10	*Tobermory	

249. A TOUR OF THE ISLE OF MULL (Southern). This tour covers the southern part of the island, at first following the most direct road to the *Iona passenger ferry at Fionnphort. Upon leaving Craignure there are extensive views of Loch Linnhe with Ben Nevis in the distance, the Isle of Lismore, and the Appin Hills. The road then skirts Loch Don and Loch Spelve before ascending and descending the wild Glen More to Loch Scridain. From this point the tour can be shortened by omitting the excursion to Iona which follows the southern shore of Loch Scridain to Fionnphort and returns by the same road. (At Pennyghael a side road leads to *Carsaig Bay on the south coast.) From the head of Loch Scridain there are fine views of Ben More to the north and the road later follows the shore of Loch na Keal with many fine views of the western isles of Gometra, Ulva, and Staffa. From Gruline to Salen is the narrowest part of Mull and is a pretty run with woodland and moorland. The final stretch alongside the Sound of Mull gives delightful views of the mainland hills of Morven.

A849			*Craignure ..	87¼
..	2¼	2¼	*Lochdonhead ..	85
..	20¾	18½	*Pennyghael ..	66½
..	30¾	10	*Bunessan ..	56½
..	36¾	6	*Fionnphort ..	50½
			(Passenger ferry to Iona) Return to:	
..	42¾	6	*Bunessan ..	44½
..	52¾	10	*Pennyghael ..	34½
B8035	55¾	3	Junc A849/B8035	31½
..	59½	3¾	*Kilfinichen Church ..	27¾
..	64½	5	*Gribun	22¾
	73¼	8¾	Gruline Church	14
A848	75¾	2½	*Salen	11½
..	87¼	11½	*Craignure	

250. TOBERMORY to LOCHBUIE. This alternative way to Salen follows a hilly, winding road, past the Mishnish Lochs, with hairpin bends on the descent to Dervaig, then by Glen Aros to Salen. Extensive views from the coast road along the Sound of Mull, including the mainland hills of Morven, the Isle of Lismore and the Appin hills. Near Craignure there is a distant view of Ben Nevis at the head of Loch Linnhe. After Lochdonhead, the main road is left near Loch Spelve, and winds over Ardura Hill (gradient 1 in 8) to follow the attractive shore road beside Lochs Spelve and Uisg, with the peaks of Ben Buie and Creach Bheinn to the north.

B8073			*Tobermory ..	44½
Uncl	7¾	7¾	*Dervaig ..	36¾
A848	18	10¼	Junc Uncl/A848	26½
A849	19½	1½	*Salen ..	25
..	31	11½	*Craignure ..	13½
..	33¼	2¼	*Lochdonhead ..	11¼
Uncl	37	3¾	Junc A849/Uncl	7½
..	44½	7½	*Lochbuie	

SKYE

The island of Skye is some 50 miles long and provides a striking variety of scenery, with open moorlands, charming lochs, a rocky coastline affording lovely seascapes, the whole being dominated from most points by the serrated peaks of the Black Coolins, while there is also considerable historic interest, notably in the island's associations with Prince Charles Edward and Flora Macdonald. There are few roads other than those detailed in the following itineraries, which keep mainly to the indented coastline.

Most of the roads included are narrow and winding, with variable surfaces, and become hilly in places, although there are no serious gradients. The island is easily reached on weekdays, by the ferries from Kyle of Lochalsh to Kyleakin, and from Mallaig to Armadale. During the summer an additional ferry service is operated between Glenelg and Kylerhea. **There are no Sunday services,** except from Kyle of Lochalsh where there is a limited service during the summer.

251. KYLE OF LOCHALSH to PORTREE. Utilizes the ferry service across Kyle Akin, and then follows the main coast road to Sligachan, passing the Red Hills beyond Broadford, and with a fine view of Blaven before Loch Ainort. Striking views of the Black Coolin peak of Sgurr nan Gillean at Sligachan, after which the road keeps inland across the moors through Glen Varragill.

			*Kyle of Lochalsh	36¼
			Ferry to	
A850			*Kyleakin	
..	5½	5½	Breakish ..	30¾
..	8¼	2¾	*Broadford ..	28
..	13	4¾	*Dunan	23¼
..	23¾	10¾	*Sconser ..	12½
..	26¾	3	*Sligachan ..	9½
A855	36	9¼	Junc A850/A855	¼
..	36¼	¼	*Portree	

252. ELGOL to GLENBRITTLE. At Elgol there is an impressive view of the Coolins across *Loch Scavaig. The wild and picturesque *Loch Coruisk in the secluded heart of the Coolins can be reached by motor boat or on foot from Elgol. The narrow and hilly road between Elgol and Torrin passes the head of Loch Slapin and there are fine views of the Red Hills and the Coolin peak of Blaven. Thereafter an easier road is followed around the Red Hills and passes through Broadford and along the main coast road to Loch Ainort, where the Island of Scalpay is seen across the narrow channel. There is a striking view of Sgurr nan Gillean from Sligachan, after which the road passes over moorland country and winds through Glen Drynoch. A narrow, rough by-road is then followed to the climbing centre of Glenbrittle. Another branch road continues westwards along the west side of Loch Harport to the *Talisker distillery at *Carbost, from which two by-roads diverge. One leads to the splendid cliffs of Talisker Bay and the other to *Port na Long, well known for its weaving industry.

A881			*Elgol	45½
..	9	9	*Torrin	36½
A850	14½	5½	*Broadford ..	31
..	19¼	4¾	*Dunan	26¼
..	30	10¾	*Sconser	17¼
A863	33	3	*Sligachan ..	14¼
B8009	38¼	5¼	Junc A863/B8009	9
Uncl	39¾	1½	Junc B8009/Uncl	7½
..	47¼	7½	*Glenbrittle	

253. MALLAIG to PORTREE and UIG. Utilizes the ferry to Armadale then follows the Sound of Sleat to Isle Ornsay where the road turns inland as far as Broadford. The main coast road is followed passing the Red Hills and with a fine view of Blaven before Loch Ainort. At Sligachan there is a striking view of the Black Coolin peak of Sgurr nan Gillean after which the road keeps inland across the moors through Glen Varragil to Portree. A further stretch of moorland is crossed before reaching Loch Snizort and Uig Bay.

			***Mallaig** ..	60
			Ferry to	
A851			*Armadale	
..	4¼	4¼	*Teangue ..	55¾
..	7½	3¼	*Isle Ornsay ..	52½
A850	15	7½	Junc A851/A850	45
..	16¾	1¾	*Broadford ..	43¼
..	21½	4¾	*Dunan	38½
..	32¼	10¾	*Sconser ..	27¾
..	35¼	3	*Sligachan ..	24¾
..	44½	9¼	*Portree	15½
A856	48¼	3¾	Junc A850/A856	11¾
..	52½	4¼	*Snizort Church	7½
..	58	5½	Earlish	2
..	60	2	*Uig	

254. A tour from PORTREE via DUNTULM CASTLE and THE QUIRAING. A tour through the Trotternish district in the north-west corner of Skye, crossing moorlands to Loch Snizort and Uig Bay, on the north side of which there is a sharp turn up Idrigil Hill, near the summit of which a road branches off direct to Staffin. It is narrow and hilly, with a sharp 1 in 9 descent and hairpin bends, giving a panoramic view of Staffin Bay, but goes closer to the jagged mass of the Quiraing than the main tour, which continues by the easier road round the north coast by Kilmuir, passing the ruined Duntulm Castle and Flodigarry. The fantastic rock pinnacles of the Quiraing lie to the right near Staffin, while beyond are the Mealt Falls. After Culnaknock, the Lealt Falls are passed, as the precipitous Storr, the culminating point of the long Trotternish ridge, and noted for the detached pinnacle known as the Old Man of Storr, comes into view. The road then passes the Storr Lochs, now harnessed to the new hydro-electric power scheme inaugurated in 1952.

A855			*Portree	50
A850	¼	¼	Junc A855/A850	49¾
A856	4	3¾	Junc A850/A856	46
..	8¼	4¼	*Snizort Church	41¾
..	13¾	5½	Earlish	36¼
..	15¾	2	*Uig	34¼
A855	16¾	1	Junc A856/A855	33¼
..	20¾	4	*Kilmuir ..	29¼
..	24¾	4	*Duntulm ..	25¼
..	25¾	1	*Kilmaluag ..	24¼
..	28¾	3	*Flodigarry ..	21¼
			*Quiraing (to rt)	
..	32½	3¾	*Staffin ..	17½
..	36	3½	*Culnaknock ..	14
			*Storr (to rt)	
..	50	14	*Portree	

255. A tour from PORTREE via DUNVEGAN CASTLE. Follows the main road southwards across the moorlands of Glen Varragill, with fine views of the peak of Sgurr nan Gillean in the Black Coolins approaching Sligachan, where the tour turns westwards through Glen Drynoch. Continues along the east side of Loch Harport and round the head of little Loch Beag to Bracadale, where there is a rough, narrow road (B885) to Portree (11 miles). The tour then proceeds close by Loch Bracadale, branching off to visit the famous Dunvegan Castle, on the loch of that name, with views of the twin flat-topped Macleod's Tables to the south-west. The return is then made by way of Edinbain and the heads of Loch Greshornish and Loch Snizort Beag. 3¾ miles beyond Dunvegan a branch road (B886) leads to *Trumpan.

A855			*Portree	55½
A850	¼	¼	Junc A855/A850	55¼
A863	9½	9¼	*Sligachan ..	46
..	15	5½	*Drynoch Br ..	40½
..	23¾	8¾	*Bracadale (Struan PO)	31¾
..	26¾	3	*Ose (PO) ..	28¾
..	30¾	4	Roskhill (PO) ..	24¾
A850	33¾	3	*Dunvegan ..	21¾
..	37¼	3½	*Fairy Br ..	18¼
..	42	4¾	*Edinbain ..	13½
..	43¾	1¾	Arnisort	11¾
..	48¼	4½	Bernisdale ..	7¼
..	50¼	2	*Skeabost Bridge	5¼
A855	55¼	5	Junc A850/A855	¼
..	55½	¼	*Portree	

OUTER HEBRIDES

The Outer Hebrides group comprises the chain of islands stretching from the Butt of Lewis to Barra Head, but for the motorist the main interest lies in the largest island of Lewis and Harris, since the islands of North Uist, Benbecula, South Uist and Barra, which lie to the south, have a much smaller road mileage. Benbecula and North and South Uist are connected by bridges and causeways. The roads are gradually being improved, and, in general, main roads are fair, but great care must be exercised, as they are often narrow and tortuous, while side roads are inferior. One of the features of the islands is the variety of prehistoric cairns, duns, brochs and forts, which include the famous group of Standing Stones at Callernish. A comprehensive article dealing with the islands as a whole, and at the same time describing the various places of interest, will be found in the gazetteer under the heading of **Hebrides, Outer.**

There is a ferry connection from Uig (Skye) to Lochmaddy (North Uist) and Tarbert (Harris).

The airports situated at Stornoway and also on Benbecula and Barra are served from Glasgow, and in addition there is a direct service from Inverness to Stornoway.

256. TARBERT to STORNOWAY. Follows the shore of West Loch Tarbert to Ardhasig Bridge, where a side road (B887) leads off to Husinish Bay passing Amhuinnsuidhe Castle. The road then ascends round a shoulder of Clisham, the highest peak in the Outer Hebrides, followed by a long gradual descent to Loch Seaforth. To Laxay the road is generally hilly with delightful scenes of mountain moor and loch. Finally open moorland is crossed to reach Stornoway. *For * places see Hebrides, Outer, in gazetteer.*

A859			*Tarbert	36½
..	3¼	3¼	Ardhasig Bridge	33¼
..	12½	9¼	*Aline (Harris-Lewis Boundary)	24
..	22	9½	Balallan (PO)	14½
..	24¾	2¾	Laxay	11¾
..	33¾	9	Creed Lodge	2¾
A858	34¾	1	Junc A859/A858	1¾
A857	35½	¾	Junc A858/A857	1
..	36½	1	*Stornoway	

257. TARBERT to RODEL. From Tarbert, the main road follows Glen Laxdale to the west coast, and then traverses pastoral country, passing several sandy bays on the shores of the Sound of Harris on the way to Leverburgh and Rodel, with its famous church. 4½ miles from Tarbert there is a twisting and undulating road along the east coast through Finsbay to Rodel. *For * places see Hebrides, Outer, in gazetteer.*

A859			*Tarbert	24
..	13½	13½	Borve Lodge	10½
..	20½	7	*Obbe	3½
..	21¼	¾	*Leverburgh	2¾
..	24	2¾	*Rodel	

258. STORNOWAY to UIG or ARDROIL SANDS. As far as Garynahine pleasant moorland country is traversed, with some pretty loch scenery near Achmore. A narrow road is then followed between the hills and round the lochs, with many lovely views. Beyond Meavig, Glen Valtos is followed to the fork roads where one branch leads to Uig and the other to the fine sandy bay at Ardroil. *For * places see Hebrides, Outer, in gazetteer.*

A857			*Stornoway	35
A858	1	1	Junc A857/A858	34
..	9½	8½	Achmore	25½
B8011	14¼	4¾	*Garynahine	20¾
..	27	12¾	Eneclate	8
..	30½	3½	Carashader	4½
..	32	1½	Meavig	3
Uncl	34	2	†Junc B8011/Uncl	1
..	35	1	*Uig	
		†	OR	
Uncl	34		Junc B8011/Uncl	
..	36½	2½	*Ardroil Sands	

259. STORNOWAY to THE EYE PENINSULA (for Tiumpan Head). The road crosses the narrow isthmus linking the main part of the island to the Eye peninsula, with the sandy shores of Broad Bay to the north, and the open seas of the North Minch to the south. Beyond the isthmus stands the old church of Eye, noted for the Macleod tombs. From Tiumpan Head there are extensive views north towards Tolsta Head and north-east towards Cape Wrath on the mainland. *For * places see Hebrides, Outer, in gazetteer.*

A866			*Stornoway	11½
..	1½	1½	Sandwick	10
..	6¼	4¾	Garrabost	5¼
..	6¾	½	*Eye Church	4¾
..	8	1¼	Shulishader	3½
..	10	2	Portnaguran	1½
..	11½	1½	*Tiumpan Head (Lighthouse)	

260. A tour from STORNOWAY via CALLANISH. Crosses open moorland country dotted with sparkling lochs, and with extensive views of the Harris hills to the south-west. A short detour may be made to visit the famous Standing Stones of Callanish (second only in interest to the better known Stonehenge), after which the road continues within sight of the west coast, at first by East Loch Roag, and later by the Atlantic Ocean, passing near Carloway Broch. The main tour continues close by a number of crofting villages to Barvas. From here A857 continues northwards to *Shader and *Port of Ness where a secondary road (B8014) leads to the Butt of Lewis, the most northerly point of the island. From Laxdale, there is a secondary road (B895) along the east coast of the island past several sandy bays to Gress (noted for its caves), and Tolsta (12 miles), with fine coast scenery. *For * places see Hebrides, Outer, in gazetteer.*

A857			*Stornoway	46¾
A858	1	1	Junc A857/A858	45¾
..	9½	8½	Achmore	37¼
..	14¼	4¾	*Garynahine	32½
..	16¼	2	*Callanish	30½
..	17	¾	Breasclete	29¾
..	23	6	*Carloway	23¾
..	28½	5½	Shawbost	18¼
..	30½	2	Bragair	16¼
..	31¾	1¼	Arnol	15
A857	34¾	3	*Barvas	12
..	45½	10¾	Laxdale	1¼
..	46¾	1¼	*Stornoway	

261. A TOUR IN NORTH UIST. North Uist seems to consist more of water than of land, so numerous are the lochs and arms of the sea running into it. *For * places see Hebrides, Outer, in the gazetteer.*

A865			*Lochmaddy	34¼
..	8¾	8¾	Grenetote	25½
..	10	1¼	Sollas	24¼
..	18	8	Tighary	16¼
..	20¾	2¾	Bayhead	13½
A867	25¾	5	Clachan	8½
A865	33¼	7½	Junc A867/A865	1
..	34¼	1	*Lochmaddy	

262. LOCHMADDY (North Uist) to LOCHBOISDALE (South Uist). This route traverses the islands of North Uist, Benbecula and South Uist which are linked by the North and South Ford Causeways.

The Balivanich Airport is situated on road B892 2 miles west of Gramisdale, Benbecula.

From Daliburgh in South Uist there is a branch road (B888) leading south to *Pollachar, the nearest point to the islands of Eriskay and Barra.

3¼ miles north of Daliburgh, Flora Macdonald's birthplace at Milton lies just off the road. *For * places see Hebrides, Outer, in gazetteer.*

A865			Lochmaddy	42¼
A867	1	1	Junc A865/A867	41¼
A865	8½	7½	Clachan	33¾
..	11¼	2¾	*Carnish	31
			North Ford Causeway	
..	15¼	4	*Gramisdale	27
..	21	5¾	*Creagorry	21¼
			South Ford Causeway	
..	22	1	*Carnan	20¼
..	27¾	5¾	Stilligarry	14½
..	29¼	1½	Howmore	13
..	39¼	10	*Daliburgh Church	3
..	42¼	3	*Lochboisdale	

ORKNEY

The Orkney group consists of numerous islands some 20 miles north from the mainland port of Scrabster (Thurso).

The motorist is chiefly interested in the island called Mainland, or Pomona, on which there are about 150 miles of motoring roads, about half of them being of good surface, and the remainder mainly fair, although subsidiary roads are poor. There are no gradients of any consequence and road widths are sufficient to permit passing without difficulty. The second largest island, called Hoy, is notable for its cliff scenery, and is reached by steamer from Stromness, but there are few motoring roads.

During the last war the Churchill Barriers, linking Mainland to the islands of Lamb Holm, Glimps Holm, Burray and South Ronaldsay, were completed. Steamer and motor boat services are available to many of the other islands. The Orkneys are noted for fine seascapes and magnificent cliff scenery, although the latter is best viewed from the water. There is also much of antiquarian interest, notably the famous Standing Stones of Stenness and the prehistoric village of Skara Brae. A comprehensive article dealing with the islands as a whole and describing the various places of interest will be found in the gazetteer under the heading of **Orkney.**

Air services are available from Glasgow, Aberdeen and Inverness to Grimsetter Airport near Kirkwall and also to Sumburgh Airport, Shetland.

263. A tour from KIRKWALL via STROMNESS and BIRSAY. Follows the direct road to Stromness across moorland and agricultural country, passing near the gallery grave of Rennibister, on the shores of the Bay of Firth, while beyond Finstown is the notable Maeshowe cairn. The south shores of the Loch of Stenness are followed to Stromness, and returning from there the tour keeps to the west sides of the Lochs of Stenness and of Harray. Later there is a distant view of the Kitchener Memorial on Marwick Head. The tour continues round the north-east coast past Evie, where a side road leads to the large, ruined broch of Aikerness, to reach Finstown. Between Finstown and Kirkwall there is an alternative secondary road skirting the viewpoint of Wideford Hill. *For * places see Orkney, in gazetteer.*

A965			*Kirkwall ..	52
..	6¾	6¾	*Finstown ..	45¼
..	9½	2¾	*Maeshowe ..	42½
..	10½	1	*Stenness (PO) ..	41½
..	15	4½	*Stromness ..	37
			Return to:	
A967	16	1	Junc A965/A967	36
..	25½	9½	Twatt Church ..	26½
A966	28	2½	Junc A967/A966	24
..	28½	½	*Birsay (Earl's Palace) ..	23½
..	37½	9	*Evie Church ..	14½
..	42	4½	Rendall (PO) ..	10
A965	45¼	3¼	*Finstown ..	6¾
..	52	6¾	*Kirkwall	

264. A tour from KIRKWALL via SKARA BRAE. Follows the coast road to the Loch of Stenness, with views of Scapa Flow, and later crosses the Bridge of Brogar, which separates Stenness Loch from Harray Loch, to reach the Standing Stones of Stenness and Ring of Brogar. A detour is then made to the prehistoric Skara Brae, near Aith, on the west coast, and later the Kitchener Memorial on Marwick Head comes into view. On the return route, a diversion can be made by B9057 from Dounby to Klick Mill, afterwards continuing either by Evie and Iter 263, or by returning to Dounby. There are alternative roads between Finstown and Kirkwall, a secondary road skirting the view point of Wideford Hill. *For * places see Orkney, in gazetteer.*

A963			***Kirkwall** ..	47
A964	½	½	Junc A963/A964	46½
..	8	7½	*Orphir (PO) ..	39
A965	14¼	6¼	Junc A964/A965	32¾
..	15¾	1½	*Stenness (PO)	31¼
B9055	16	¼	Junc A965/B9055	31
..	16½	½	Bridge of Brogar	30½
..	21½	5	*Aith	25½
B9056	22¾	1¼	*Skara Brae ..	24¼
..	23	¼	Bay of Skaill ..	24
..	24¼	1¼	Scarwell	22¾
..	26¼	2	*Marwick ..	20¾
A967	28½	2¼	Junc B9056/A967	18½
..	30¼	1¾	Twatt Church ..	16¾
A986	30½	¼	Junc A967/A986	16½
..	33¼	2¾	*Dounby ..	13¾
..	36	2¾	Harray (PO) ..	11
A965	38¾	2¾	Junc A986/A965	8¼
..	40¼	1½	*Finstown ..	6¾
..	47	6¾	*Kirkwall	

265. A tour from KIRKWALL via DEERNESS. This short drive covers the area known as the East Mainland, and is mainly through pleasant country, with occasional moorland. Just beyond Toab, a narrow neck of land is crossed, with Deer Sound on the one side and the North Sea on the other. On the north of the Deerness peninsula is a Covenanters' monument at Scarva Taing, accessible on foot. Returning to Toab, moorland country is crossed before reaching the coast at Holm Sound, with views of the islands to the south, while the latter part to Kirkwall is mainly through agricultural districts. *For * places see Orkney, in gazetteer.*

A960			*Kirkwall ..	28½
..	7	7	Toab (PO) ..	21½
B9050	9¾	2¾	Junc A960/B9050	18¾
..	10	¼	Deerness (PO)	18½
..	12	2	*Deerness Church (Sandside Bay)	16½
			Return to:	
A960	17	5	Toab (PO) ..	11½
B9052	17¼	¼	Junc A960/B9052	11¼
A961	21	3¾	Junc B9052/A961	7½
..	21¾	¾	*St Mary's Holm	6¾
A960	27¾	6	Junc A961/A960	¾
..	28½	¾	*Kirkwall	

266. KIRKWALL to BURWICK (South Ronaldsay) via Churchill Barriers. Crosses agricultural country to St Mary's Holm, then utilizes the Churchill Barriers, which link Mainland with the islands of Lamb Holm, Glimps Holm, Burray and South Ronaldsay, to terminate at Burwick, on the Pentland Firth. The Barriers are liable to be closed from time to time for maintenance work. *For * places see Orkney, in gazetteer.*

A960			*Kirkwall ..	22¾
A961	¾	¾	Junc A960/A961	22
..	6¾	6	*St Mary's Holm	16
..	8¼	1½	Lamb Holm ..	14½
..	9¼	1	Glimps Holm ..	13½
..	12¾	3½	Burray	10
B9040	16½	3¾	*St Margaret's Hope .. .. (South Ronaldsay)	6¼
..	22¾	6¼	*Burwick	

SHETLAND

The 100 or so islands in the Shetland group lie 185 miles north of Aberdeen. For the motorist the largest island, called Mainland, claims chief attention. The road mileage on the other islands, with the exception of Unst and Yell, is limited and the road conditions rather poor. The coastline is broken by innumerable sea lochs, or 'Voes' as they are called in Shetland, so that no part of the Islands is more than three miles from the sea. Along the coast there is some magnificent scenery, most of it within easy reach of roads.

A comprehensive article dealing with the Islands as a whole and describing the various places of interest will be found in the gazetteer under the heading of **Shetland.**

The roads on the Mainland are generally in good condition and the main roads from the airport at Sumburgh to Lerwick and from Lerwick to Walls and Hillswick are excellent. The roads are generally undulating with no severe gradients, but care must be taken on narrow stretches and blind corners. The other large Islands, Yell and Unst, possess quite serviceable roads, but in each of these there are waterbound stretches, although these are gradually being tar sprayed.

Communication with Shetland (Mainland) is by steamer from Aberdeen direct to Lerwick,. There are air services from Aberdeen, Edinburgh, Glasgow, Inverness and Wick to Sumburgh.

A steamer connects Lerwick with the North Isles of Shetland three times a week. A bus and ferry route is also in operation leaving Lerwick every morning, but passengers cannot return the same day. In the summer season a tour is operated every Tuesday returning the same day. This covers a considerable portion of the Mainland and also large stretches of Yell and Unst.

267. LERWICK to HILLSWICK, ESHANESS or ISBISTER. Most of this route to the northern part of the Mainland lies through moorland country with low-lying hills, and the road is seldom out of sight of either an inland loch, a sea loch or the open sea. Mavis Grind, which is situated at the head of Sullom Voe, is a narrow neck of land separating the Atlantic Ocean from the North Sea by something like fifty yards or so. About six miles to the north of this, the road divides, the left-hand branch leading to the sandy bay and rocky coast at Hillswick, an excellent centre for trout fishing. Just before reaching Hillswick, a narrow secondary road leads to Eshaness, and while here an opportunity should be taken to visit the Grind of the Navir, a huge breach in the cliff face made by the force of the stormy sea. Another sight worth seeing is the Holes of Scraada, so called because there were at one time two of these holes, but the connecting bridge fell down about half a century ago and one hole now remains.

The other branch of the main road continues northward to Isbister.

A number of detours from the direct road are indicated in Iter 270.

*For places of interest marked * see Shetland, in gazetteer.*

A970			*Lerwick.. ..	35½
..	3¾	3¾	Bridge of Fitch ..	31¾
..	6	2¼	Gott (PO) ..	29½
..	9¾	3¾	Girlsta	25¾
..	18¾	9	*Voe (PO) ..	16¾
..	23¾	5	Brae	11¾
..	25½	1¾	§*Mavis Grind	10
..	33½	8	†Urafirth ..	2
..	35½	2	*Hillswick	
		†	OR	
A970	33½		Urafirth	
B9078	34¾	1¼	Junc A970/B9078	
Uncl	40	5¼	Junc B9078/Uncl	
..	40¾	¾	*Eshaness (Lighthouse)	
		§	OR	
A970	25½		*Mavis Grind	
..	35½	10	Collafirth	
..	39¾	4¼	North Roe (PO)	
..	41¼	1½	*Isbister	

268. LERWICK to WALLS or SANDNESS. This route to the western part of the Mainland crosses the usual Shetland moorland country through the fertile valley of Weisdale to the head of Weisdale Voe, then up the incline to the top of the road which now slopes down to Tresta. The view from the top of this hill, looking towards the south, is one of the finest in the Islands. After the head of Bixter Voe is passed at Parkhall, a secondary road leads in a southerly direction to Reawick with its nice sandy bay (6 miles). Two roads diverge at the Bridge of Walls, the left-hand one leading to Walls and the right-hand one to Sandness, with views of Papa Stour and St Magnus Bay. The other divergent road on this itinerary is just after Bixter is passed, and runs in a somewhat north-easterly direction to the township of Aith, continuing round the head of Aith Voe via Gonfirth to Voe.

*For places of interest marked * see Shetland, in gazetteer.*

A970			*Lerwick.. ..	24¾
	3¾	3¾	Bridge of Fitch ..	21
A971	5	1¼	Junc A970/A971	19¾
..	8¾	3¾	Whiteness ..	16
..	12¾	4	Weisdale	12
..	15¾	3	Tresta	9
..	17¾	2	Bixter	7
..	19	1¼	Twatt	5¾
..	23	4	†Bridge of Walls	1¾
..	24¾	1¾	*Walls	
		†	OR	
A971	23		Bridge of Walls	
..	29½	6½	*Sandness	

269. LERWICK to SUMBURGH. This route follows the east coast to the southern part of the Mainland, passing through Quarff with the Cunningsburgh hills to the west and fine views of the coastline. After passing the head of the Voe of Quarff, a loop road leads through the old-fashioned village of Fladdabister, which, in recent years, has been greatly modernized. The loop road continues through the fertile valley of Cunningsburgh and rejoins the main road at Mail. A mile or so farther on another detour can be made through Leebotten, where a boat can be hired to convey passengers to Mousa, where the best preserved specimen of a so-called Pictish broch can be examined. Continuing through Sandwick, the road splits just before Levenwick; the right-hand branch going in a westerly direction through Scousburgh and down to the Voe of Spiggie. It continues round the west side of Spiggie Loch, a very good trout loch (permission to fish must be obtained from the proprietor). The road rejoins the main road close to Boddam and continues down to Sumburgh. While there the opportunity should not be missed to visit the remarkable archaeological sites at Jarlshof, comprising the remains of three prehistoric and protohistoric village settlements dating from the Stone Age, and the Iron Age, and also a Viking House.

*For places of interest marked * see Shetland, in gazetteer.*

A970			*Lerwick.. ..	25¼
..	6½	6½	Quarff (PO) ..	18¾
..	10½	4	Cunningsburgh ..	14¾
..	13	2½	Rd to *Sandwick	12¼
..	17½	4½	Levenwick (PO)..	7¾
..	21½	4	*Dunrossness ..	3¾
..	25¼	3¾	*Sumburgh Airport (for Sumburgh Head)	

270. A TOUR FROM LERWICK. This tour covers the central part of the Mainland, making several detours from the main roads. Going first towards Scalloway, it then branches to the right through the very fertile valley of Tingwall before circling round Weisdale Voe, with very fine views at the top of the hill between Weisdale and Bixter. Here a branch road, running in a northerly direction, crosses the moors to reach the sea at Aith. Passing Gonfirth, the road connects with the north main road at Voe, where, still continuing northwards, a detour is made to Toft's Voe, near Mossbank, where there is a ferry service to the Island of Yell. A return to the main road at Voe is made by a high road overlooking Dales Voe, and then a narrow. winding coast road is followed through the parish of Nesting, with views of the Island of Whalsay, rejoining the main road to Lerwick before Girlsta.

*For places of interest marked * see Shetland, in gazetteer.*

A970			*Lerwick.. ..	83¾
..	3¾	3¾	Bridge of Fitch ..	80
..	7¼	3½	*Scalloway ..	76½
			Return to:	
B9074	8¼	1	Junc A970/B9074	75½
..	10¾	2½	*Tingwall Church	73
A971	11½	¾	Junc B9074/A971	72¼
..	14¾	3¼	Whiteness ..	69
..	18¾	4	Weisdale	65
..	21¾	3	Tresta	62
..	23¾	2	Bixter	60
B9071	24	¼	Junc A971/B9071	59¾
..	26¾	2¾	Aith	57
..	31¾	5	Gonfirth Church	52
..	34½	2¾	*Voe	49¼
A970	35	½	Junc B9071/A970	48¾
..	35½	½	Voe (PO) ..	48¼
..	40½	5	Brae ..	43¼
B9076	40¾	¼	Junc A970/B9076	43
..	42¼	1½	Voxter	41½
A968	47¾	5½	Junc B9076/A968	36
..	49½	1¾	*Mossbank ..	34¼
			Return to:	
A970	59¼	9¾	Voe (PO) ..	24½
B9071	60	¾	Junc A970/B9071	23¾
B9075	62¼	2¼	*Laxo	21½
..	67¼	5	South Nesting Bay ..	16½
..	69¼	2	Skellister (PO) ..	14½
..	70¼	1	Catfirth ..	13½
A970	71¾	1½	Junc B9075/A970	12
..	74	2¼	Girlsta ..	9¾
..	77¾	3¾	Gott (PO) ..	6
..	80	2¼	Bridge of Fitch ..	3¾
..	83¾	3¾	*Lerwick	

GAZETTEER

The county is given after each place name. This is followed by the population figures, taken mainly from the 1971 census and other sources. The following abbreviations are used: LB for Large Burgh; SB for Small Burgh; C of C for County of City.

The map square reference number appears on the right-hand side at the top of each entry, *eg* Map 10, **NT 27.** This reference is fully explained on pages ii and iii of the Atlas. It gives the major square letter, and the numbers of the smaller square. The scale of the map does not allow every place name to be shown, but this system enables the approximate position of a place to be ascertained whether or not it is marked on the map.

Early Closing and Market Days are indicated by the abbreviations E.C. and M.D. Where there is a golf course in the vicinity, this is shown by the word GOLF.

The times of opening for places of interest are included. These are correct up to the time of going to press, but members are strongly advised to verify the times, either locally or through the nearest AA Office. An annual publication, *Britain's Heritage*, is issued, giving up-to-date opening times for more than 2,000 places and is available to Members price 40p. (post free).

Gaelic spelling is not standardized, and there is considerable variation in the spelling of place names. No authority is therefore claimed in this difficult question, and it may also be found that the spelling of certain places in the Gazetteer differs from that shown on the map.

The numbers of the itineraries in which the places are mentioned are printed in the text in italics and should not be confused with page numbers.

Features of special interest referred to in the text are printed in italics.

The abbreviations used in the gazetteer are as follows:

A.M. ..	Ancient Monument (*such as building, earthwork, etc., generally under Government care, usually accessible to the public*)	C of C ..	County of City
		Iter. ..	Itinerary
		LB. ..	Large Burgh
		N.T. Scot.	Property or land in the care of The National Trust for Scotland (see article on page 32)
c. ..	circa		
cent. ..	century	SB. ..	Small Burgh

Many places mentioned in this book do not warrant their own separate Gazetteer entry—such places are listed alphabetically on page 278 with the indication of the particular Gazetteer entry under which they are to be found.

A combined glossary of technical terms and Gaelic and Norse words will be found at the end of the Gazetteer.

Town Plans appear in or near their appropriate places throughout the Gazetteer. Reconstruction is taking place in many city centres and may necessitate local detours or the closing of streets. These temporary diversions may contradict the details shown on the plans. One-way streets, or the alteration of traffic flow, may also conflict with the information given, and fresh parking meter zones may have been instituted since the preparation of the town plans.

The following markings are used on the various types of plans throughout the book. Members should in their own interests watch the road for signs.

Recommended Route .. ..

Congested Route .. ..

One-Way Street .. ..

Signposted Ring Road .. ..

Traffic Roundabout .. ..

Official Car Park (Free) .. ..

Parking available on Payment .. ..

Multi-Storey Car Park .. ..

Toilet (Conveniences) .. ..

Toilet (Conveniences) open always .. ..

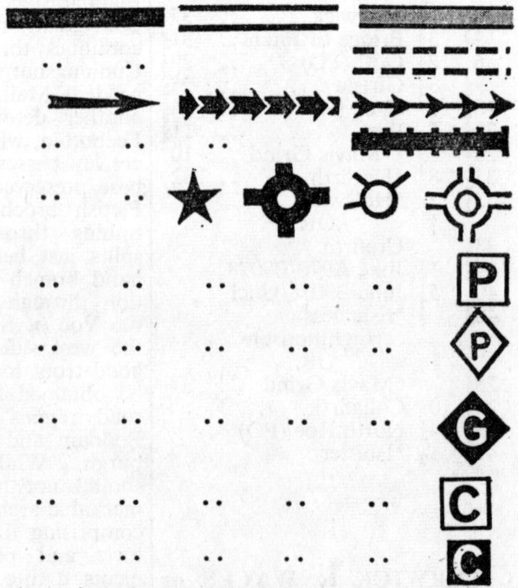

An exit name printed in brackets indicates that there is a better route by another exit.

AA

ILLUSTRATED ROAD BOOK OF SCOTLAND

GAZETTEER

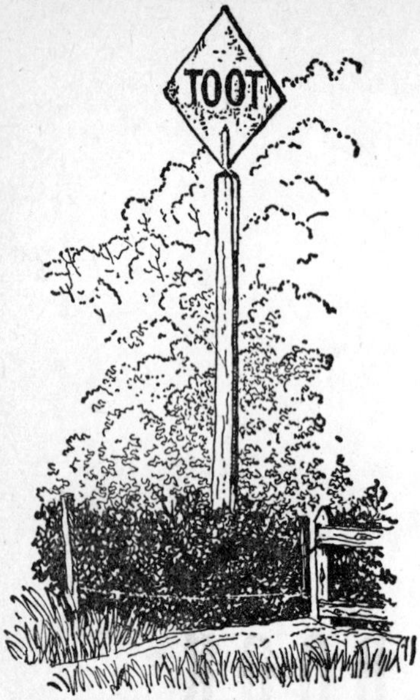

Abbey St. Bathans, Berwick. An unusual warning sign, situated on an unclassified road to the south of the village

Abbotsford House, Roxburgh. Sir Walter Scott's 19th century home, most of which he himself designed, having changed the name to Abbotsford from Clarty Hole, when he purchased the estate in 1811. It stands near the River Tweed, off B6360

Aberdeen, Aberdeen. The 14th century Auld Brig O'Don, or Bridge of Balgownie, the work of Bishop Cheyne. The bridge is mentioned in Byron's '*Don Juan*'

Abercorn, West Lothian. One of the many quaintly carved tombstones in the churchyard. Bishop Trumuini established an Anglian bishopric here in the 7th century

Aberchirder, Banff. Kinnairdy Castle, once a Crichton stronghold. It stands 3 miles to the south-west, on an unclassified road

Aberdeen, Aberdeen. Provost Ross's House, dating from 1593, the oldest in the city. It has been restored by the National Trust for Scotland

PLATE 1

[For ABERDEEN see also following plate
[For ABERCORN see also under BINNS (Plate 17)

ABBEY ST. BATHANS, Berwick. 468 with Bunkle. Map 11, NT 7 6. Situated on the Whiteadder Water in the region of the *Lammermuir* hills. In the Parish Church is preserved the tomb of a prioress, portraying her pet dog, from the former 12th cent. Abbey Church. The Holy Well of *St. Bathans* is in the nearby grounds of the manor house. To the south, on the slopes of *Cockburn Law*, 1,065 ft., is the ancient Pictish tower, or broch, known as *Edinshall* (A.M.), one of the very few examples known outside the Northern Highlands. (See **Glenelg.**) North-westwards of Abbey St. Bathans rises the long ridge of *Monynut Edge*, with *Heart Law* attaining 1,283 ft.

ABBOTSFORD HOUSE, Roxburgh. Map 10, NT 5 3. This last and most famous of Sir Walter Scott's homes, where he died in 1832, stands in a delightful, wooded setting near the banks of his beloved River Tweed, and was designed largely by Scott himself, while many of the trees on the estate were planted by his hand. The house dates from 1817 to 1824, and contains a collection of personal memorials and also historical Scottish relics. In the library is a bust of Scott by Chantrey, and the drawing-room contains interesting portraits. The armoury has a notable collection of weapons of all ages, and the study remains much as the author left it. Abbotsford is shown weekdays, 10 to 5; Sun., 2 to 5, from April to Oct. (See note page 98.) To the south-east rise the triple-peaked *Eildon* hills, a prominent landmark in the Scott country, with a view-indicator. See **Ashiestiel, Darnick, Dryburgh Abbey and Smailholm.** *Iter. 13, 41, 43.*

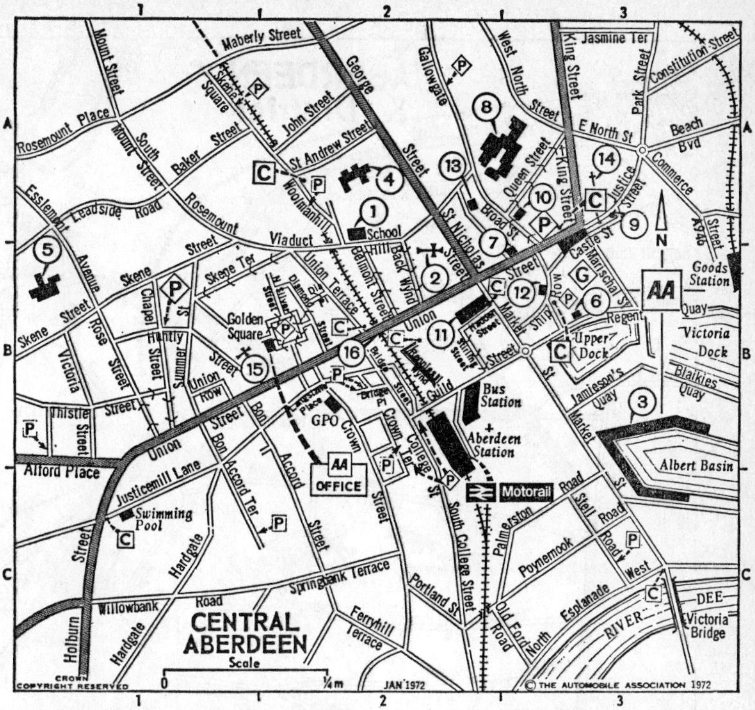

AA OFFICE: Fanum House, 19 Golden Square, Aberdeen, AB9 1JN. Telephone: 0224 51231.

Art Gallery, War Memorial and Cowdray Hall	1 (A2)	Harbour Offices	6 (B3)	Provost Skene's House (Museum)	13 (A2)
East and West Churches	2 (B2)	Marischal College, University	8 (A2/3)	St. Andrew's Episcopal Cathedral	14 (A3)
Fishmarket	3 (B3)	Mercat Cross, 1686	9 (A3)	St. Mary's R.C. Cathedral	15 (B1)
Gordon's College	4 (A2)	Municipal Buildings	10 (A3)	Tourist Information Centre	7 (B3)
Grammar School and Byron Statue	5 (B1)	New Markets	11 (B2)	Union Bridge	16 (B2)
		Provost Ross's House	12 (B3)		

ABBOTSINCH, Renfrew. **Map 8, NS 4 6.** See **Renfrew** (for **Glasgow Airport**). *Iter. 59, 65.*

ABERCHIRDER, Banff. 861. SB. **Map 27, NJ 6 5.** The smallest Royal Burgh, founded in 1764. About **3 m. S.W.,** where the River Deveron is joined by the Auchintoul Burn, stands the fine old *Kinnairdy Castle*, a former Crichton stronghold. *Iter. 184, 189, 194, 196.*

ABERCORN, West Lothian. 612. **Map 16, NT 0 7.** A little village by the Firth of Forth, on the opposite shore of which is the naval base of *Rosyth* (*q.v.*). The Church, restored in 1597 and 1838, contains retiring rooms and an elaborate laird's pew, designed by Sir William Bruce, the builder of the nearby *Hopetoun House* (*q.v.*). The curious *Binns* aisle is of note. Some ancient carved stones are preserved. There is also a pre-Reformation pulpit, and the Celtic cross-shafts are notable. **½ m. S.W.** is *Midhope Tower*, dating from the 16th cent. **3 m. W.S.W.** is the mansion of *The Binns* (N.T. Scot.), of 1478 and later, with 17th cent. plaster ceilings. Open daily, 2 to 5, mid-June to mid-Sept. On Sat. and Sun. all the year. (See note page 98.) General Tam Dalyell, who defeated the Covenanters at Rullion Green in 1666, raised the Royal Scots Greys here in 1681. *Iter. 96.*

ABERDEEN, Aberdeen. 182,006. C of C. Map 21, **NJ 9 0. E.C.** Wed., Sat. **M.D.** Fri. GOLF. An important Royal Burgh, Cathedral, University and maritime city, in the district of Mar, on the estuaries of the Rivers Dee and Don, the former flowing into the harbour, and the latter entering the sea to the north of Aberdeen Bay, beyond *Old Aberdeen.* The city, which is the third largest in Scotland, is built almost entirely of the granite for which it is perhaps best known, and presents a remarkably clean and solid picture to the eye. Its watchword is the phrase "Bon Accord." From the harbour are shipped granite, fish and cattle, and as a resort Aberdeen is noted for its fine, sandy bathing beach in the bay. The charters of the city date back to c. 1179, but the former Castle has entirely vanished. In 1296, Edward I came here, and Bruce was a refugee after the battle of *Methven* (*q.v.*) in 1306. Edward III burned Aberdeen in 1337, and Montrose thrice occupied it, the last time in 1644 After the burning of 1337, the city was rebuilt, and consisted of Aberdeen and Old Aberdeen, the latter including the Cathedral precincts, and being made a Burgh of Barony in 1498, but in 1891 the two were united.

Union St. is a splendid modern thoroughfare, off which stands the Church of *St. Nicholas*, divided at the Reformation into the *East* and *West* Churches. They were later reconstructed, the former being a rebuilding of the 19th cent., and the latter, a design of James Gibbs, dating from 1763, and forming the best example of Scottish ecclesiastical architecture of that period. Of the original structure remain the 12th to 13th cent. transepts, and the 15th cent. crypt below the apse, in which much woodwork of the period has been preserved. A rare Scottish brass is to be seen in the south transept, or "Drum's" aisle. West of the Union Bridge, in Huntly St., is the R.C. Cathedral. Near *Robert Gordon's Colleges*, founded in 1739, is the interesting Art Gallery and Museum. A statue of Byron stands in front of the Grammar School. The 17th cent. *Provost Skene's House* has been restored as a museum. The Duke of Cumberland stayed here in 1746. *Provost Ross's House*, built 1593, one of the oldest in Aberdeen, has been restored by the Scottish National Trust. It is open Mon. and Fri., 2.30 to 4.30 (See note page 98.) In Castle St. is the Mercat Cross, dating from 1686, built for the sum of £100, paid out of the guild wine funds, and not on its original site. A statue of the 5th Duke of Gordon, Scott's

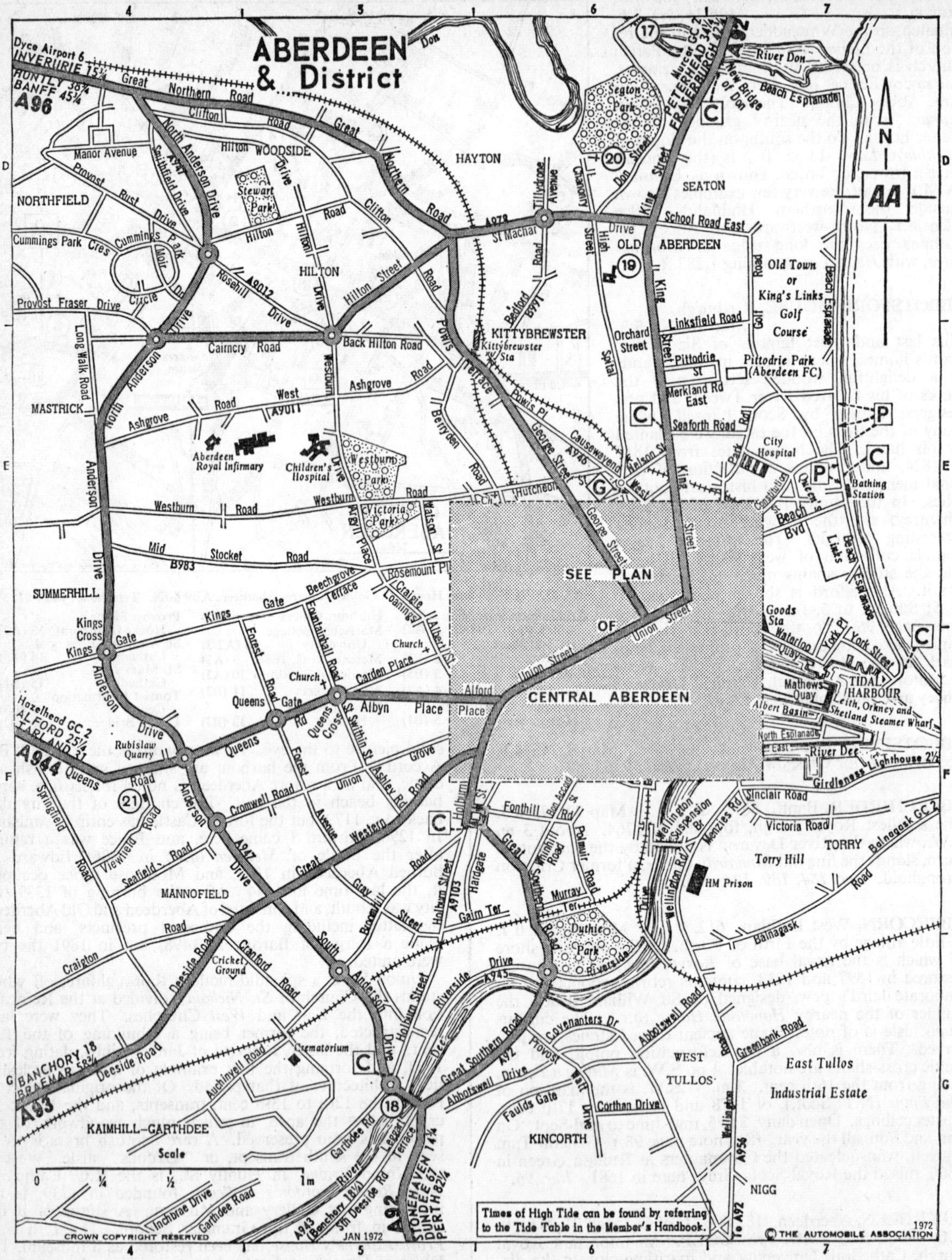

For Central Aberdeen Plan see page 99.

Auld Brig O'Don (Bridge of Balgownie) 17 (D6) | Bridge of Dee 18 (G5) | Gordon Highlanders Regimental Museum 21 (F4) | King's College, University 19 (D6) | St. Machar's Cathedral 20 (D6)

The 17th century Provost Skene's House, now a museum. The Duke of Cumberland occupied this house in 1746

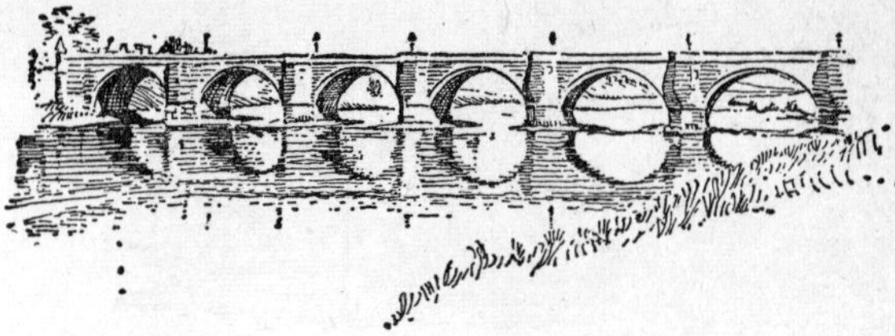
The seven-arched Bridge of Dee, built 1520–27 by Bishop Gavin Dunbar, and decorated with coats of arms

The Chapel (c.1500) and tower of the old University building. The 'crown' at the top of the tower was rebuilt after a storm in 1633

The Mercat Cross of 1686. It cost £100 to build, which was paid out of the Guild wine funds

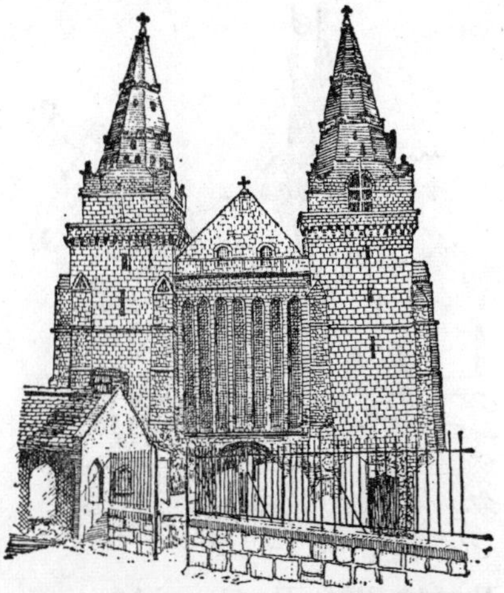
St. Machar's Cathedral in Old Aberdeen, mainly the work of Bishop Lichtoun in the mid-15th century and Bishop Gavin Dunbar between 1519 and 1532

The 19th century buildings of Marischal College, It was founded in 1593 by George Keith, the Earl Marischal

[For ABERDEEN see also preceding plate

Abergeldie Castle, Aberdeen. Abergeldie Castle, near Crathie, on Royal Deeside, where King Edward VII stayed at times when Prince of Wales. The Castle was garrisoned by Mackay in 1689. It stands off A973, on the south bank of the river.

Aberdour, Fife. The ruined 17th century and earlier Castle, the latest additions having been the work of the eighth Earl of Morton

Aberfoyle, Perth. 'Bailie Nicol Jarvie's poker,' the plough coulter hanging from a tree, which recalls a scene from Sir Walter Scott's '*Rob Roy*'

Aberlady, East Lothian. The old mounting stone, or 'loupin-on-stane' outside the Church

Aberfeldy, Perth. General Wade's bridge, spanning the River Tay, erected in 1733 at a cost of £4,095 5s. 10d.

Aberfeldy, Perth. The Memorial, erected in Queen Victoria's Jubilee Year (1887) to commemorate the enrolling of the Black Watch Regiment in October, 1739

PLATE 3

"Cock o' the North," is in Golden Square. The Municipal Buildings, in Castle Street, incorporate the tower and spire of the 14th cent. Tolbooth, and preserve the so-called "Aberdeen Maiden," the ancient executioner's weapon, on which was modelled the infamous French guillotine. In the near vicinity stands the modern *St. Andrew's* Cathedral. The *Marischal College*, part of the University, and an imposing granite structure of the 19th cent., was founded originally in 1593, being housed in the former buildings of the old *Greyfriars* Monastery. From the 233-ft. high *Mitchell* tower of the College, a splendid view can be obtained. The *Gordon Highlanders* Regimental Museum is of interest.

Smeaton and Telford both shared in the construction of the harbour and the Fish-market is a scene of much interest in the early morning. James Gibbs, the eminent 18th cent. architect, was born in Aberdeen in 1682. In *Old Aberdeen* stands the Cathedral of *St. Machar*, built of granite, and founded c.1136, though the earliest part of the present building goes back only to the mid-14th cent. (A.M.). The main part of the structure is a century later in date, and, apart from the spires, all the nave stonework is of granite. The choir has completely vanished. Of particular note are the west front, with its twin towers; the painted wooden nave ceiling of 1540; the 17th cent. monument to Bishop Scougal, and also the one to Bishop Dunbar; and the "Nuns" library. There is a very fine series of heraldic, wooden nave bosses, dating from the early 16th cent. In the High St. is *King's College*, also part of the University, founded in 1494, preserving the 16th cent. Chapel and the notable "crown" tower of the 17th cent. from the old buildings, the remainder being mostly 19th cent. reconstruction. The Chapel is famous for its rich woodwork, the screen having a wide rood-loft, and the carved stalls being canopied. The "crown" tower resembles those of *St. Giles*' at *Edinburgh* (*q.v.*) and the Tolbooth at *Glasgow* (*q.v.*), but is surmounted by a fine Renaissance crown, added in 1634. The Library, with some fine MSS., and also the Senators' Room are of interest.

Beyond the Cathedral is the picturesque "Auld Brig o' Don," or Bridge of Balgownie, a single span of early 14th cent. date, in a wooded setting. **2 m. S.S.W.** of the city centre is the even finer, widened Bridge of Dee, built 1520–1527, and showing seven fine arches decorated with coats of arms. Nearby is the similarly embellished Ruthriston packhorse bridge of 1693/4. **6 m. N.N.W.**, on the Turriff road, is *Dyce* (*q.v.*), where the airport for the city is situated. See **Blairs, Cove** and **Culter** (Aberdeen). For "Through Routes," see page 43. *Iter. 151, 152, 155, 168, 174, 175, 176, 177, 178, 179, 180, 181, 182, 183, 184, 185, 186,*

ABERDOUR, Fife. 4,230 with Dalgety. Map 17, **NT 1** 8. **E.C.** Wed. GOLF. A small Firth of Forth resort, with sands and bathing. The restored Church is Norman and 16th cent., and has a leper window blocked by what is known as the Pilgrim's Stone. There is a ruined 14th to 17th cent. Castle, neighboured by an old doocot (A.M.). In Dalgety Bay, to the west, is the mansion of *Donibristle House*, the surviving portion dating from c. 1720. It has fine wrought-iron entrance gates. In the vicinity, to the north-east, is the ruined Church (A.M.) of *St. Bridget*, at *Dalgety*, dating from the 12th cent., the burial place of the early Bishops of *Dunkeld* (*q.v.*). Near Donibristle took place, in 1592, the murder of the Earl of Moray by the Earl of Huntly, which is commemorated in an old ballad. East of the Bay is Braefoot Point, looking out towards *Inchcolm Island* (*q.v.*). See **Dalgety Bay.** *Iter. 134.*

ABERFELDY, Perth. 1,539. SB. Map 19, **NN 8** 4. **E.C.** Wed. **M.D.** Alt. Thurs. GOLF. A touring centre in Strath Tay, on the south bank of the river, which is spanned, to the north-west, by one of General Wade's finest bridges, dating from 1733. The cost of building the bridge is said to have amounted to £4,095 5*s.* 10*d.*. Near the bridge is the Black Watch Monument, the regiment having been enrolled in 1739. The poem by Burns entitled "The Birks of Aberfeldy" is thought to refer probably to a place by the name of Abergeldie, in Aberdeenshire. (See **Crathie.**) Some distance to the north of Aberfeldy, beyond the lochs of Glassie and Derculich, rises *Farragon Hill*, 2,559 ft., a fine viewpoint. **1 m. S.**, reached by footpath from Bank St., and situated on the Moness Burn, are the three **Falls** of

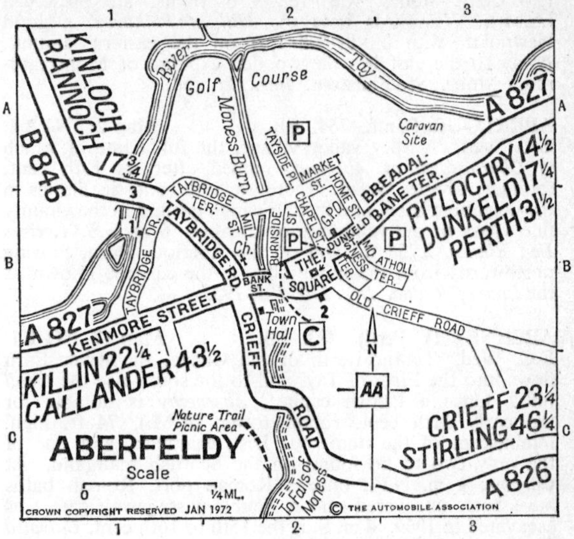

Black Watch Monument 1 (B1) Information Bureau 2 (B2) Wade Bridge 3 (A/B1)

Moness. The Amulree road goes south through Glen Cochill, and climbs to a height of over 1,400 ft., among lonely moors, with *Meall Dearg*, 2,258 ft., to the south. See **Amulree, Dull, Grandtully, Wade Roads** and **Weem.** *Iter. 89, 107, 120, 139, 147, 149, 157, 158.*

ABERFOYLE, Perth. 2,110 with Menteith. Map 15, **NN 5** 0. GOLF. This small holiday resort (pony-trekking), which is situated to the east of Loch Ard, is known as the "Gateway to the Trossachs." The former clachan of Aberfoyle, associated with Scott's "Rob Roy," lay **1 m. E.** of the present village. The well-known *Bailie Nicol Jarvie* Hotel is the successor to the inn made famous by Scott in "Rob Roy," and a plough coulter hanging from a tree opposite recalls a scene from the book. Two mortsafes in the churchyard recall the horrible exploits of the early 19th cent. body-snatchers, Burke and Hare, who were finally brought to trial at Edinburgh. The well-known *Duke's Road* to the *Trossachs* (*q.v.*) goes due north, giving fine views, notably towards Loch Drunkie and the larger Loch Vennachar, backed by *Ben Ledi*, 2,875 ft. To the west is the road through the Pass of Aberfoyle to Loch Ard, in its picturesque setting, and near the west end of the loch are two waterfalls on the Ledard Burn, described in Scott's "Waverley." In the vicinity is *Duchray Castle*, mainly 16th cent. Eastwards and westwards stretches Loch Ard Forest, part of the extensive Queen Elizabeth Forest Park. The road continues to Loch Chon, and terminates at *Stronachlachar* (*q.v.*), on the shores of Loch Katrine, another branch going westwards to *Inversnaid* (*q.v.*) on *Loch Lomond* (*q.v.*). To the east of the village rise the grassy *Menteith* hills, 1,289 ft. See **Port of Menteith.** *Iter. 105, 106, 111, 139.*

ABERGELDIE CASTLE, Aberdeen. Map 20, **NO 2** 9. See **Crathie.**

ABERLADY, East Lothian. 1,088. Map 10, **NT 4** 7. GOLF. A quiet holiday resort on the Firth of Forth, with a sandy beach, bathing, and the *Myreton* motor museum. The Church has a 15th cent. tower and the 1762 monument to Lady Elibank by Canova is notable. Aberlady Bay, a local Nature Reserve, is a haunt of sea-birds. On its shores stands *Luffness House*, late 16th cent., with modern additions, ornate chimneys, and preserving a fine 16th cent. circular dovecote. See **Gosford House** and **Gullane.** *Iter. 2, 36, 37.*

ABERLEMNO, Angus. 983 with Oathlaw. Map 21, **NO 5** 5. In the churchyard stands a notable cross-slab with Pictish symbols (A.M.), and at *Flemington* farm, in the vicinity, two Celtic stones, with reliefs of fights, are preserved (A.M.). Westwards rises the *Hill of Finhaven*, a good viewpoint, with a vitrified fort on the eastern summit. Away to the east lies the wooded expanse of Montreathmont Moor. See **Finhaven.** *Iter. 151, 156.*

ABERLOUR, Banff. 764. SB. Map 26, **NJ 2** 4. **E.C.** Wed. A Spey valley village, the full name of which is *Charlestown of Aberlour*, named after its 19th cent. founder, Charles Grant. There are 19th cent. distilleries in the neighbourhood, and from the high ground in the vicinity fine views of the valley are obtainable. **6 m. S.S.W.** rises *Ben Rinnes*, 2,755 ft., and on the Aberlour Burn, flowing northwards from the mountains, is the cascade known as the *Linn of Ruthie*. *Iter. 170, 192, 195.*

ABERNETHY, Perth. 783. SB. Map 17, **NO 1** 1. **E.C.** Wed. To the north of the village, the River Earn flows into the Firth of Tay, and to the south rise the *Ochil* hills. Once a Pictish capital, *Abernethy* is notable for the early 12th cent. round tower (A.M.), 74 ft. high, reminiscent of the numerous Irish examples, and one of the only two to be found on the Scottish mainland. At *Carpow*, **1 m. N.E.,** once a Roman port, Roman baths have been uncovered and a double-passageway gate was excavated in 1969. **4 m. S.** is the 15th to 16th cent. *Balvaird Castle*. See **Brechin.** *Iter. 131, 132.*

ABERUTHVEN, Perth. Map 16, **NN 9** 1. Lies in Strath Earn, to the north of the *Ochil* hills. Near the ruined old Parish Church of *St. Kattan* stands the mausoleum of the Dukes of Montrose. About **4 m. N.N.E.,** beyond Dalreoch Bridge, across the River Earn, and to the north of *Gask House* (1801), is a five-mile stretch of Roman road, where excavation has taken place at various points from time to time, notably in 1770 by Pennant, and again in 1890. In the grounds of the mansion, which preserves relics of Prince Charles Edward, is a fragment of the 17th cent. house in which the Prince spent several hours on his way to Edinburgh, in 1745. See **Braco** and **Forteviot.** *Iter. 135, 146.*

ABINGTON, Lanark. 250. Map 9, **NS 9** 2. **E.C.** Thurs. Attractively situated in Clydesdale in a ring of Lowland hills. To the former coaching inn came Prince Louis Napoleon, in 1839, on his way to the tournament at *Eglinton Castle* near *Kilwinning* (*q.v.*). There is a memorial on A.73 to a local postmaster and fisherman, Matthew McKendrick (1848–1926). In the valley of the Glengonnar Water, to the south-west, where gold has been found, the road through the valley climbs gradually to over 1,400 ft., the summit being reached near the mining village of *Leadhills* (*q.v.*). See **Crawford, Crawfordjohn** and **Elvanfoot.** *Iter. 25, 29, 48, 50, 51, 56.*

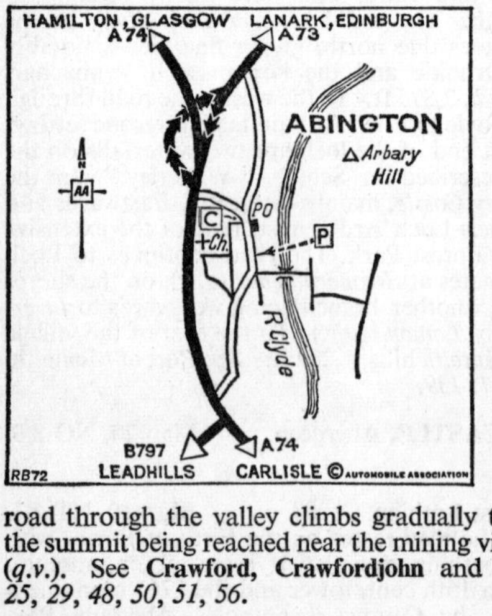

ABOYNE, Aberdeen. 2,269. Map 21, **NO 5** 9. **E.C.** Thurs. **M.D.** Alt. Mon. GOLF. A well-known *Deeside* (*q.v.*) resort, bordered to the south by the Forest of Birse, in the eastern Grampians, and backed by the *Hill of Cat*, 2,435 ft. The important annual Highland Gathering takes place in the first week of September. *Aboyne Castle*, a Gordon stronghold, to the north of the village, is mainly modern, but the west side is a rebuilding of 1671. In the private grounds is a megalithic circle. South-west of the village, the long, wooded valley of Glen Tanner (See **Bridge of Ess**), stretches into the hills to Glen Tanner Forest and the lofty peak of *Mount Keen*, 3,077 ft. Two well-known walkers' tracks leave Glen Tanner at different points. The Fir Mounth road leads from the Church in the glen and crosses the hills east of the *Hill of Cat* to reach Glen Esk near *Tarfside* (*q.v.*), while the Mounth road diverges much higher up the glen, and after crossing a shoulder of *Mount Keen*, reaches Glen Mark near *Lochlee* (*q.v.*). A third track, known as the Fungle Road, proceeds southwards from Aboyne, and penetrates deep into the Forest of Birse. *Iter. 152, 191.*

ABRIACHAN, Inverness. Map 25, **NH 5** 3. The village is situated near the western shores of *Loch Ness* (*q.v.*), and a steep and winding descent leads down to the pier. A poor and narrow road goes north-westwards from Abriachan into the hills, passing the tiny Loch Laide, and descending later into Glen Convinth. See **Lovat Bridge.**

ACHARACLE, Argyll. 500. Map 12, **NM 6** 6. A little anglers' resort, situated at the western extremity of the 18-mile long *Loch Shiel* (*q.v.*), and the terminal point for the steamer from *Glenfinnan* (*q.v.*) which plies on the loch. The neighbouring countryside and hills are associated with Prince Charles Edward. To the east rises *Ben Resipol*, 2,774 ft., a notable landmark in the Sunart district, from the summit of which the view is remarkable. Northwards from Acharacle, a road parallels the Shiel River, past Shiel Bridge, to its outlet in Loch Moidart near *Dorlin*, in a richly-wooded setting, opposite which is the large island of Eilean Shona. Offshore, but linked to the mainland, except at high spring tides, stands the picturesque, ruined 14th cent. *Castle Tioram* of the MacDonalds of Clanranald, which was burnt in 1715. To the west of Acharacle, a by-road leads across Kentra Moss to *Ardtoe*, in the delightful Kentra Bay, in the Ardnamurchan district, from which the Hebridean islands of Eigg and Rum are well seen. See **Dalilea, Kinlochmoidart, Loch Sunart** and **Salen** (Argyll). *Iter. 217.*

ACHFARY, Sutherland. Map 28, **NC 2** 3. Situated between Loch Stack and Loch More, two of the chain of lochs which give character to the road leading from Lairg to Loch Laxford, on the wild coast of Sutherland. *Ben Stack*, 2,364 ft. is a shapely cone. To the north rise the lonely hills of the great Reay Forest. See **Laxford Bridge.** *Iter. 229.*

ACHILTIBUIE, Ross and Cromarty. Map 29, **NC 0** 0. A remote little *Wester Ross* resort, providing fine maritime scenery, and most beautifully situated on the sandy shores of Baden Bay, in which lie the delightful Summer Islands. The largest of these is Tanera More, and to the south-east is Horse Island. On the mainland, farther to the south-east, rises *Ben More Coigach*, 2,438 ft., a splendid viewpoint in the Coigach district, overlooking the whole length of *Loch Broom* (*q.v.*). Northwards extends the Rhu More peninsula, with Rhu Coigach at its northern tip, looking over Enard Bay and the Minch. The lonely Sutherland peaks of *Stack Polly*, 2,009 ft., *Suilven*, 2,399 ft., and *Canisp*, 2,779 ft., dominate the country to the north-east. See **Baddagyle** and **Loch Lurgain.** *Iter. 226.*

ACHILTY INN, Ross and Cromarty. Map 25, **NH 4** 5. An old coaching inn, situated in a wooded setting on the Blackwater River. To the west is the little Loch Achilty, beyond which are the Conon Falls, on the river of that name, reached by paths which lead to the south-eastern extremity of Loch Luichart. See **Contin, Falls of Rogie** and **Marybank.** *Iter. 204, 206, 221.*

Aberlemno, Angus. A churchyard cross-slab, probably 8th-century, inscribed with Pictish symbols on the reverse face

Abernethy, Perth. One of the only two examples of an Irish-type round Church tower on the Scottish mainland. It is probably early 12th century. See Brechin (Plate 22)

Acharacle, Argyll. The wooded shores of Loch Moidart, with a distant view of the 14th century Castle Tioram, on its island. The loch lies on an unclassified road to the north-west

Abington, Lanark. The Memorial on A73, overlooking the River Clyde, to Matthew McKendrick, a local postmaster and angler (1848–1926)

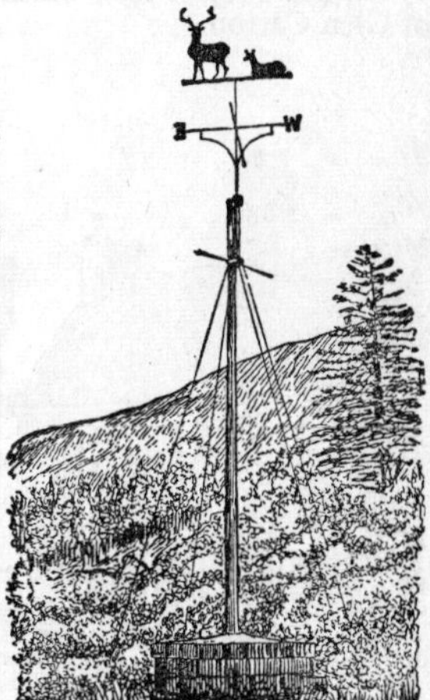

Achfary, Sutherland. A 'stag and hind' weather-vane by the entrance to Loch More Lodge, near the shores of Loch More, off A838, in a deer-stalking district

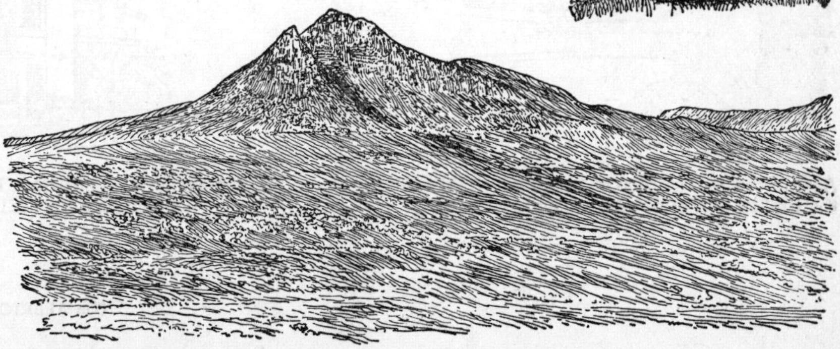

Achiltibuie, Ross and Cromarty. The peak of Ben More Coigach, seen from an unclassified road on Outer Loch Broom, a little to the south-east

Achmore, Ross and Cromarty. A view towards Loch Carron, as seen from A890, to the south of Strome Ferry

Achnacarry, Inverness. The ' Dark Mile ' of trees, near which Bonnie Prince Charlie hid in 1746. It lies to the north of the Achnacarry estate, on B8005, leading to Loch Arkaig. Commandos were trained here during the Second World War

Achnashellach, Ross and Cromarty. The mountain of Fuar Tholl, nearly 3,000 feet, which overlooks the whole length of Glen Carron

Affric, Inverness. A view of Loch Benevean, in the richly wooded Glen Affric, to the south-west of Inverness, on an unclassified road off A831. A large hydro-electric scheme is in operation here

Airth, Stirling. The Mercat Cross, which displays the Elphinstone arms and is dated 1697

Alexandria, Dunbarton. The old house of Dalquharn, the birthplace in 1721 of Tobias Smollett, the novelist

[For AFFRIC see also under GLEN AFFRIC (Plate 74)

ACHMORE, Isle of Lewis, Ross and Cromarty. *Iter. 258, 260.* Map 32, **NB 3 2.**

ACHMORE, Ross and Cromarty. Map 23, **NG 8 3.** Lies in the level valley of Strath Ascaig, on the picturesque road leading from *Strome* (*q.v.*) to the shores of Loch Alsh by way of the fine viewpoint of *Auchtertyre* (*q.v.*) hill. See **Plockton** (for *Duncraig Castle*). *Iter. 220, 221, 222.*

ACHNACARRY, Inverness. Map 18, **NN 1 8.** See **Loch Arkaig.**

ACHNASHEEN, Ross and Cromarty. Map 24, **NH 1 5.** **E.C.** Wed. Situated between Strath Bran and Glen Carron, dominated to the north by the peak of *Fionn Bhein*, 3,060 ft., beyond which lies the lonely Loch Fannich, with the *Fannich* peaks in the background. A large hydro-electric scheme in the Fannich district is now in operation. To the west, on the road to *Loch Maree* (*q.v.*), is Loch a' Chroisg, or Rosque, beyond which a climb is made to the head of Glen Docherty, from which a magnificent distant view of Loch Maree is obtained. The road to *Kyle of Lochalsh* (*q.v.*) crosses the Drum Alban watershed west of Loch Gowan, to the south-west of which rises *Moruisg*, 3,033 ft., in Glencarron Forest. To the south-east of Achnasheen is *Sgurr Vuillin*, 2,845 ft., overlooking the lonely Glen Conon, with the remote Loch Beannachan. See **Kinlochewe.** *Iter. 205, 221.*

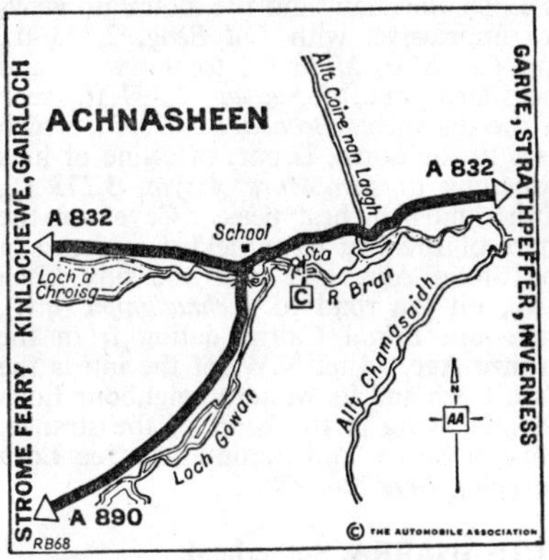

ACHNASHELLACH, Ross and Cromarty. Map 24, **NH 0 4.** In Glen Carron and Achnashellach Forest, by Loch Doule, dominated by the peaks of *Fuar Tholl*, 2,968 ft., and *Sgurr Ruadh*, 3,142 ft., to the north-west, while away to the east rises *Moruisg*, 3,033 ft., in Glencarron Forest. A most beautiful private road goes from here over the Coulin Pass in a north-easterly direction, past Lochs Coulin and Clair, to Glen Torridon and *Kinlochewe* (*q.v.*), but the public motoring road is by way of *Achnasheen* (*q.v.*). *Iter 221, 222.*

ACHUVOLDRACH, Sutherland. *Iter. 225.* Map 28, **NC 5 5.**

AE BRIDGE, Dumfries. Map 4, **NY 0 8.** This bridge spans the Water of Ae, flowing eastwards to join the Annan in the vicinity of *Lochmaben* (*q.v.*). The Ae rises on the 2,285-foot high *Queensberry Hill*, away to the north, near the Lanark border. **2½ m. N.W.,** in a newly-planted forest, is the village of *Ae*, created by the Forestry Commission in 1947. *Iter. 24, 46.*

AFFLECK CASTLE, Angus. See **Monikie.** Map 17, **NO 5 3.**

AFFRIC, Inverness. See **Cannich.** Map 24, **NH 1 2** and **NH 2 2.**

AILSA CRAIG, Ayr. See **Girvan.** Map 2, **NX 0 9** and **NS 0 0.**

AIRDRIE, Lanark. 37,736. LB. Map 9, **NS 7 6.** GOLF. A large town with coal mines and ironworks in the vicinity. *Iter. 16, 50, 87.*

AIRLIE CASTLE, Angus. Map 20, **NO 2 5.** See **Alyth.**

AIRTH, Stirling. 1,726. Map 16, **NS 8 8.** **E.C.** Wed. Lies near the southern extremity of the Kincardine road bridge spanning the Forth. In the 15th cent. a Royal dockyard was situated here. There is an old Mercat Cross, dated 1697, with two sundials, and displaying the Elphinstone arms, with their motto: "Doe well let them say." *Airth Castle*, modernized, incorporates Wallace's tower, of 14th cent. origin. To the north is *Dunmore Park* (1820), in the grounds of which is the curious 'Pineapple' garden conceit. *Iter. 96.*

AITH, Orkney. Map 33, **HY 2 1.** See **Orkney Islands** (Mainland). *Iter. 264.*

ALEXANDRIA, Dunbarton. 3,285. Map 15, **NS 3 8.** **E.C.** Wed. GOLF. One of a group of three neighbouring bleaching and manufacturing towns, the others being *Renton* and *Bonhill*, lying along the River Leven, which flows from the south end of *Loch Lomond* (*q.v.*) into the Clyde. Tobias Smollett, the novelist, was born at the old house of *Dalquharn*, in 1721, and is commemorated by a monument at *Renton* (*q.v.*). Scottish Argyll cars were formerly made at Alexandria. See **Balloch.** *Iter. 88, 100, 101, 110.*

ALFORD, Aberdeen. 1,754 Map 27, **NJ 5 1.** **E.C.** Wed. **M.D.** Tues. The River Don flows to the north of the village through the fertile Howe of Alford, with the *Correen* hills to the north-west and *Bennachie*, 1,733 ft., rising to the north-east. A Civil War battle was fought here in 1645, when the Marquis of Montrose defeated General Baillie, and relics of the fight have been dug up from time to time. The scene of the battle was near the Church, **2 m. W.,** and in the vicinity is the ruined *Asloun Castle*. To the north-east of the church is Bridge of Alford, where the Huntly road crosses the Don. **1 m. S.E.** of Alford is the decayed *Balfluig Castle*, dating from 1556. See **Craigievar Castle and Kildrummy.** *Iter. 176, 177.*

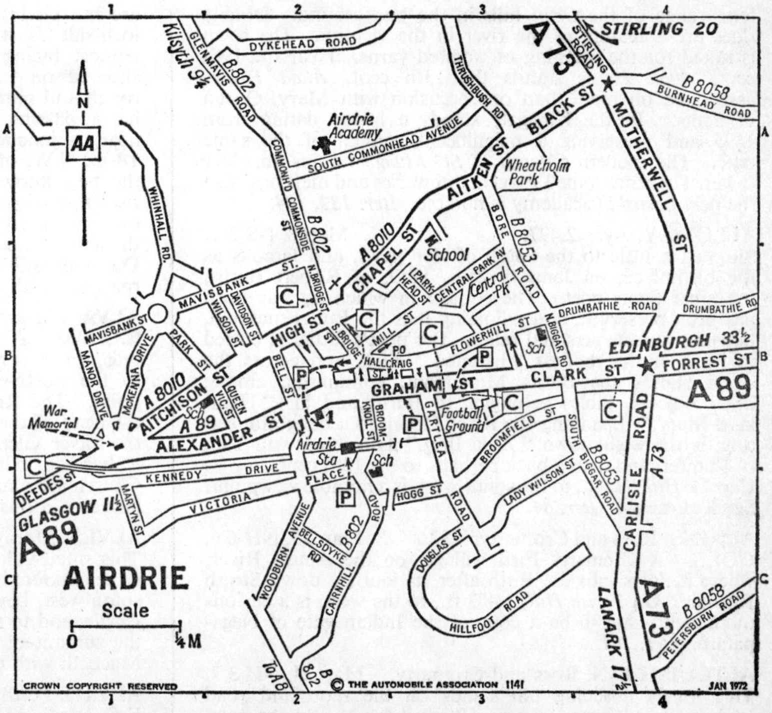

Town Hall: Information Bureau 1 (B2)

ALINE, Isle of Lewis (Harris), Inverness; Ross and Cromarty. Map 32, **NB 1 1.** Here, facing Seaforth Island, in Loch Seaforth, the road from Lewis enters the district of Harris. See **Hebrides, Outer** (Lewis). *Iter. 256.*

ALLARDYCE CASTLE, Kincardine. Map 21, **NO 8 7.** See **Inverbervie.**

ALLOA, Clackmannan. 14,296. SB. Map 16, **NS 8 9.** E.C. Tues. GOLF. The largest town in Scotland's smallest county, standing just north of the River Forth, with the

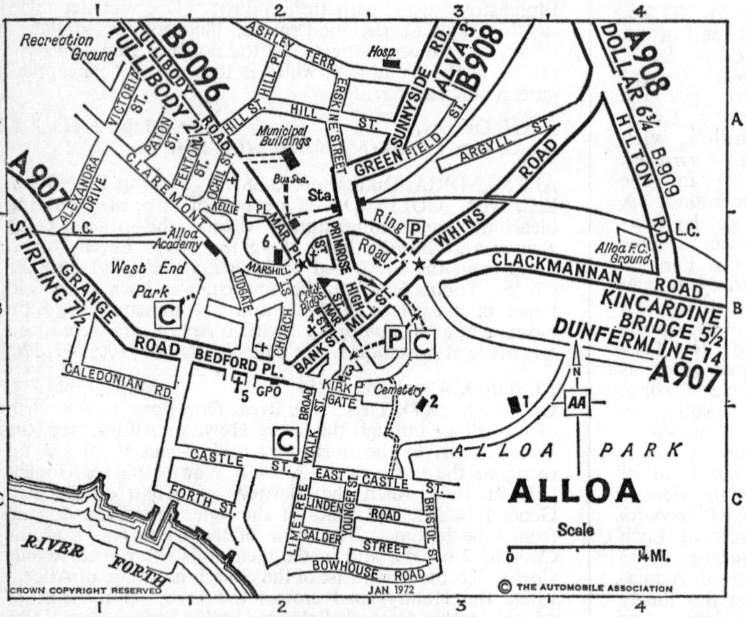

Alloa House	1 (B3)	House with sundial, 1695	3 (B2)	St. Mungo's Church	5 (B2)		
Alloa Tower	2 (B3)	Public Library	4 (B2)	Town Hall	6 (B2)		

long range of the *Ochil* hills in the background. Double tides are a feature of the river in the vicinity. The town is noted for the spinning of worsted yarns. Near the 19th cent. *Alloa House* stands the 13th cent. *Alloa Tower,* associated on more than one occasion with Mary, Queen of Scots. In the Kirkgate stands a house dating from 1695 and preserving a magnificent sundial of the same date. The modern Church of *St. Mungo* retains an older tower. There are some 19th cent. breweries and maltings, also the new *Lornshill* academy is notable. *Iter. 133, 134.*

ALLOWAY, Ayr. 2,497. Map 8, **NS 3 1.** Situated a little to the south of *Ayr* (*q.v.*), and famous as the birthplace, on January 25th, 1759, of Robert Burns, the great Scots poet. The cottage in which he was born has been preserved, and adjoining it is the Burns museum, housing various personal relics. The poet's father is buried in front of the roofless " haunted " Kirk, and across the street stands the Burns Monument, containing, among other objects, Bibles belonging to Burns and his " Highland Mary." Spanning the River Doon, in a delightful setting, is the well-known " Auld Brig," associated with Tam o' Shanter, and dating back perhaps to the 13th cent. *Brown Carrick Hill,* 912 ft., to the south-west, is a notable viewpoint. See **Kirkoswald.** *Iter. 84.*

ALNESS, Ross and Cromarty. 232. Map 25, **NH 6 6.** GOLF. A Cromarty Firth village, on the Alness River, where it flows into the Firth after its journey down Strath Rusdale. On *Fyrish Hill,* 1,483 ft., to the west, is a curious monument, said to be a copy of the Indian gate of Negapatam. *Iter. 201.*

ALTGUISH INN, Ross and Cromarty. Map 24, **NH 3 7.** This lonely coaching inn stands on the moorland road leading from *Garve* (*q.v.*) to *Ullapool* (*q.v.*). By the road flows the Glascarnoch River, to be joined by other streams before flowing into Loch Garve to the south-east. Nearby, on A.835, is a new revervoir (Loch Glascarnoch) part of the Fannich hydro-electric scheme. Away to the east rises *Ben Wyvis,* 3,429 ft., and westwards are the lonely *Fannichs,* the highest of which is *Sgurr Mor,* 3,637 ft. **5 m. W.N.W.** is Loch Droma, at a height of 915 ft., on the desolate stretch known as the Dirrie More. *Iter. 204, 206.*

ALTNACEALGACH, Sutherland. Map 29, **NC 2 1.** To the east, a thin wedge of Ross and Cromarty projects into Sutherland, and is said to have been claimed for the first-named county by men who walked the ground with Ross soil in their boots. A lonely inn stands here, on the shores of Loch Borralan, and the mountain views are impressive, with *Cul Beag,* 2,523 ft., and *Cul Mor,* 2,786 ft., to the west, and the sharp cone of *Suilven,* 2,399 ft., seen in the distance. *Breabag,* 2,670 ft., which rises to the north, is part of a line of hills extending to *Ben More Assynt,* 3,273 ft., Sutherland's highest peak. Caves on the spurs of Breabag have yielded evidence of the Stone Age, and near the tiny Loch Awe, on the road to *Inchnadamph* (*q.v.*), there are Burial Cairns dating from the Bronze Age. **4 m. N.W.** of the inn is the Cam Loch and its western neighbour Loch Veyatie, lying in the heart of the strange, isolated Sutherland mountains. See **Loch Lurgain.** *Iter. 224, 228.*

ALTNAHARRA, Sutherland. Map 28, **NC 5 3.** **E.C.** Fri. An angling resort, situated at the western extremity of Loch Naver, in *Strath Naver* (*q.v.*), and dominated by the schist peak of *Ben Klibreck,* 3,154 ft., which rises to the south. On the farther side of the mountain lies the lonely Loch Choire. Near *Klibreck* farm, at the south-western extremity of Loch Naver, there are hut circles and a Celtic Cross, and farther along the loch-side is a Pictish broch known as *Dun Creagach.* Almost facing it, across Loch Naver, is another broch, situated on the road traversing Strath Naver. A very rough and narrow road leads north-westwards from Altnaharra, passing Loch na Meadie, and reaching Strath More near its junction with Glen Golly. In Strath More, and **10 m. N.W.** of Altnaharra, stands *Dun Dornadilla,* one of the best known brochs on the mainland. To the north rises *Ben Hope,* 3,040 ft., a splendid viewpoint. This is the most northerly Scottish peak of over 3,000 ft., overlooking the narrow Loch Hope. A little farther to the north beyond Dun Dornadilla is the Allt-na-Caillich waterfall, east of the road in Strath More. *Iter. 230, 232.*

ALVA, Clackmannan. 4,118. SB. Map 16, **NS 8 9.** **E.C.** Wed. A small weaving town at the base of the *Ochil* hills, whose principal summit, *Ben Cleuch,* 2,363 ft., rises to the north-east of the town, and is a notable viewpoint. The River Devon flows to the south of Alva. At the head of the Alva Glen is the Craighall waterfall, and in the Silver Glen a silver mine was worked from 1712 until it became exhausted. Two Communion Cups in Alva Church are made of the local silver. Records of the woollen industry in this district go back to 1550. *Iter. 136.*

ALVES, Moray. 820. Map 26, **NJ 1 6.** This small village lies in the fertile Laigh of Moray, and is neighboured by the hamlet of *Crook of Alves.* To the south-west, beyond Alves Wood, stands the ruined *Asliesk Castle,* and to the north-east is the modern *York Tower,* on the summit of the *Knock,* the traditional meeting-place of Macbeth with the " Weird Sisters." *Iter. 175, 198.*

ALYTH, Perth. 1,701. SB. Map 20, **NO 2 4.** **E.C.** Wed. **M.D.** Sat. GOLF. A small linen-manufactur-

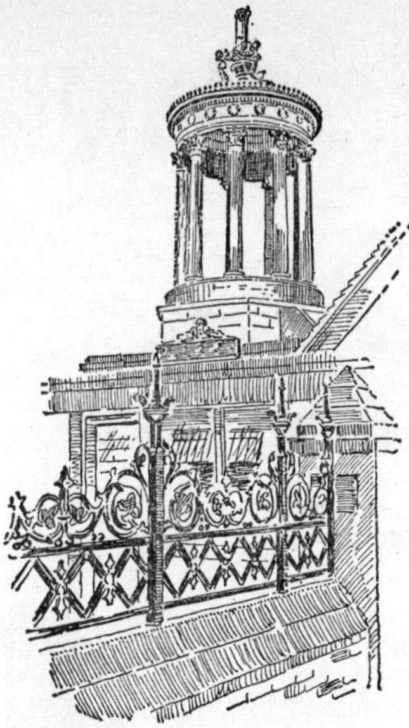

Alloway, Ayr. The Burns Monument, built in 1820, which contains many relics of the poet, including the Bible which he gave to his ' Highland Mary '

Alloa, Clackmannan. The ornate sundial of 1695 on a house in Kirkgate. It was built by Thomas Beauchop, the master mason of Kinross House and the Mid Steeple of Dumfries

Alves, Moray. The modern York Tower, on the Knock, off A96. On this hill Macbeth is said to have met the ' Weird Sisters '

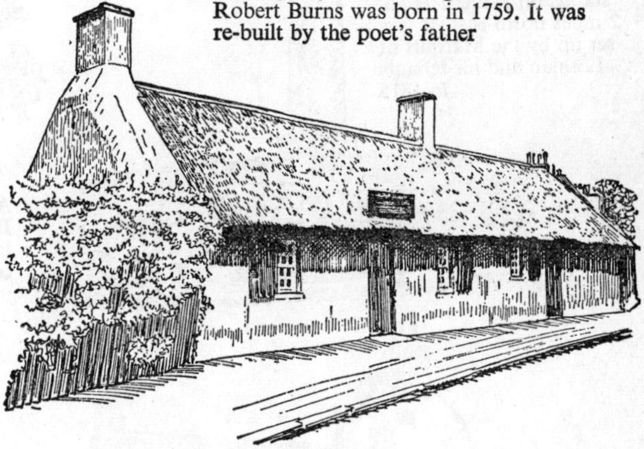

Alloway, Ayr. The cottage in which Robert Burns was born in 1759. It was re-built by the poet's father

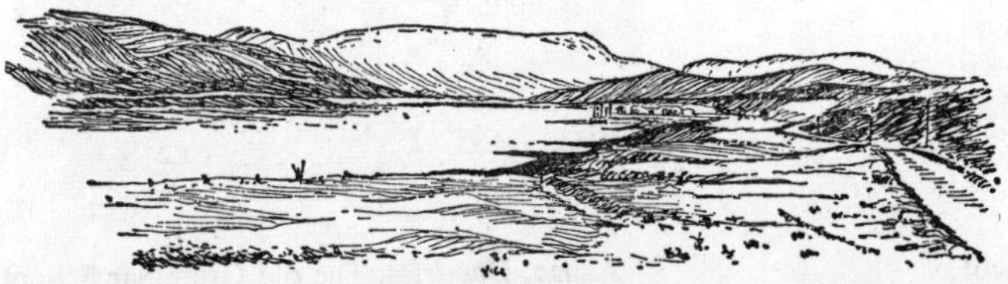

Altguish Inn, Ross and Cromarty. The reservoir on the Garve to Ullapool road (A835) in connection with the Fannich hydro-electric scheme

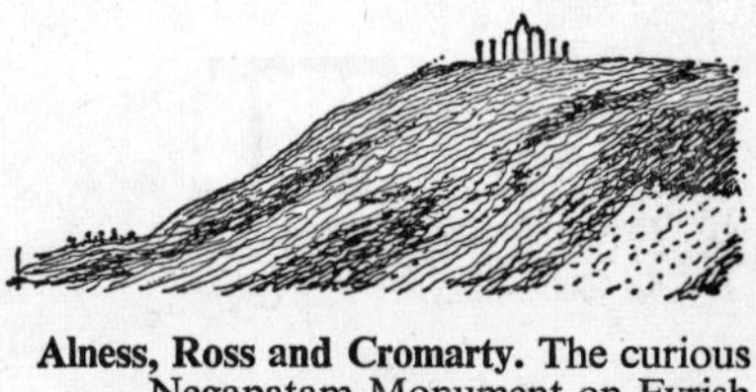

Alness, Ross and Cromarty. The curious Negapatam Monument on Fyrish Hill, as seen from A9. It was set up by Sir Hector Munro of Novar (1726–1805), who helped to capture the Indian town of that name

PLATE 6

Amisfield, Dumfries. The 16th century Amisfield Tower, one of the finest of its period in Scotland. It has been associated with the Charteris family since the 12th century

Appin, Argyll. The car ferry across Loch Leven at Ballachulish, at the northern extremity of the Appin country

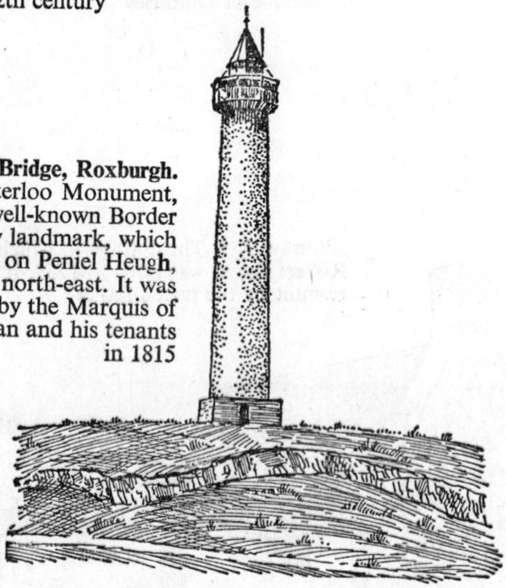

Ancrum Bridge, Roxburgh. The Waterloo Monument, a well-known Border Country landmark, which stands on Peniel Heugh, 2 miles north-east. It was set up by the Marquis of Lothian and his tenants in 1815

Applecross, Ross and Cromarty. Cottages facing Applecross Bay, in a remote village accessible by road only over the famous 2,054-foot high Pass of the Cattle. An illustration of this appears under Tornapress (Plate 163)

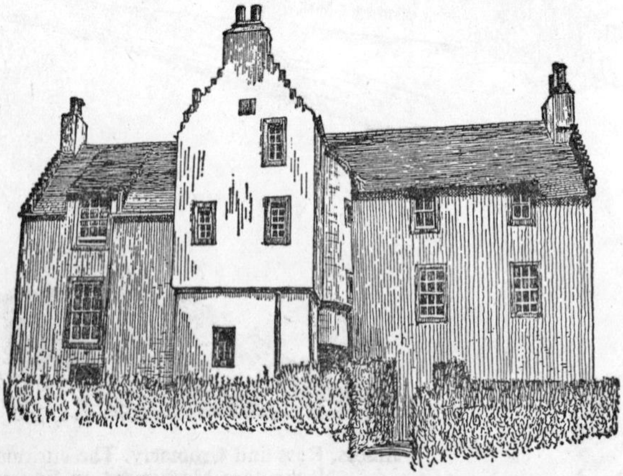

Anstruther, Fife. The old manse, or minister's house, of Anstruther Easter, which carries the date 1590, and is said to be the oldest inhabited manse in Scotland

Annan, Dumfries. The old Grammar School at which Thomas Carlyle was educated

[For **ARBROATH** see following plate

ing town in *Strathmore* (*q.v.*), overlooked by the *Hill of Alyth*, to the east of which is *Barry Hill*, preserving a British fort. The Auld Brig is of 16th cent. date. The town lies a little to the north of the Blairgowrie to Kirriemuir road. **4 m. N.E.**, beyond the River Isla is *Airlie Castle*, of which only part of the old building, burnt in 1640, has survived. Nearby is a rare Pict's house with a rudely sculptured roof. **4 m. N.** is *Bamff House*, mainly 16th cent. See **Bridge of Craig, Kirkton of Glenisla** and **Meigle.** *Iter. 160, 166.*

AMISFIELD, Dumfries. Map 4, **NX 9** 8.
Another name for this village is *Amisfield Town.* **1 m. N.W.** is *Amisfield Tower*, an ancient seat of the Charteris family. It is one of the best preserved and most picturesque of the ancient towers of Scotland, and was built largely in the latter half of the 16th cent., the date 1600 being inscribed on some heraldic panels. An oak door, with carvings, formerly in the tower, is now preserved in the National Museum of Antiquities at Edinburgh. **3 m. S.W.**, beyond the village of *Kirkmahoe*, is *Carnsalloch House*, dating from 1759, with its walled gardens. *Iter. 24, 46.*

AMULREE, Perth. Map 16, **NN 9** 3.
Situated at the western extremity of Strath Bran, and a good centre for exploring Glen Quaich, with Loch Freuchie, and also for Glen Cochill and Glen Almond. (See **Newton Bridge.**) The road through Glen Cochill, leading to *Aberfeldy* (*q.v.*), is partly on the line of one of General Wade's old roads, and southwards from Amulree the Wade road goes through the delightful *Sma' Glen* (*q.v.*). Another road goes north-westwards through Glen Quaich, and climbs to a height of 1,672 ft., before descending very steeply (1 in 4) with a poor surface and sharp bends, to *Kenmore* (*q.v.*), on *Loch Tay* (*q.v.*). To the south-west, beyond beautiful Glen Almond, rises *Ben Chonzie*, 3,048 ft. In 1715, the Clans met at Amulree, and were armed for the Jacobite rising. *Iter. 89, 140, 141, 147.*

ANCRUM BRIDGE, Roxburgh. 794. Map 10, **NT 6** 2.
The bridge spans the Teviot, and a little to the north-west is the village of *Ancrum*, on the Ale Water, which flows southwards to join the larger river. Part of a 13th cent. Cross stands on the village green. *Ancrum House* lies in a fine wooded setting, and nearby, on the banks of the Ale, are a number of old caves, used perhaps in ancient Border warfare. *Chesters House* dates from 1790. Away to the north of the village is Ancrum Moor, or Lilliard's Edge, the scene of one of the last major Border conflicts, fought in 1545, a Roman road threading the site. **2 m. N.E.** of Ancrum, on *Peniel Heugh*, 774 ft., is the Waterloo Monument, erected in 1815. *Iter. 4, 36, 43, 52.*

ANNAN, Dumfries. 5,723. SB. Map 4, **NY 1** 6.
E.C. Wed. **M.D.** Fri. GOLF. A small Solway Firth town, on the River Annan, looking across to Bowness in Cumberland and the distant peak of Skiddaw in the Lake District. The river is tidal and noted for its fish. Robert Stevenson built the bridge in 1826. Thomas Carlyle was educated at the old Grammar School, described later by the author as "Hinterschlag Gymnasium" in his "Sartor Resartus." The inscribed *Brus Stone* in the Town Hall may possibly be associated with Robert the Bruce. A nuclear power station has been built on the outskirts of the town at *Chapelcross*. Annandale extends northwards from the Firth, and the scenery in the dale becomes gradually hillier, the finest parts being reached beyond *Moffat* (*q.v.*). **3 m. N.E.** of the town is *Stapleton Tower*, dating from the 16th cent. See **Dunscore, Kirtlebridge, Powfoot** and **Rithwell.** *Iter. 26, 27, 28, 42, 47, 67.*

ANNIESLAND (GLASGOW), Lanark. Map 8, **NS 5** 6.
Iter. 100, 101, 102, 104, 105, 106, 108.

ANSTRUTHER, Fife. 3,036. SB with Kilrenny.
Map 17, **NO 5** 0.
E.C. Wed. GOLF. The ancient Royal Burghs of *Anstruther Easter* and *Anstruther Wester* lie on either side of the harbour, which has become an important herring fishing port. The foreshore is rocky, with sand at the Hynd. The manse of Anstruther Easter dates from 1590. Both burghs have Churches with unbuttressed 16th cent. towers, showing picturesque outlines, while the Church at *Kilrenny*, a little inland, has a similar tower. *St. Ayles House*, now a Fisheries Museum, is associated with the monks who once occupied *Balmerino Abbey* (*q.v.*). Adjacent to Anstruther Easter, on the north-east side, is *Cellardyke*, another Royal Burgh, these being now united under Kilrenny. Out to sea is the tiny Isle of May, with its bird-watching station and lighthouse, one of the earliest sites for a lighthouse off the coast of Scotland. It is now a National Nature Reserve, where more than 200 species of birds have been recorded. *Iter. 94, 98.*

ANTONINE WALL, Dunbarton; Lanark; Stirling; West Lothian. Map 8, **NS 4** 7 etc., and 16 **NT 0** 8 etc.
See **Roman Wall.**

ANWOTH, Kirkcudbright. 629. Map 3, **NX 6** 5.
The ruined Church here, built in 1627, retains a medieval bell and a remarkable 8-ft. high inscribed 17th cent. *Gordon* tomb. Samuel Rutherford was minister here in the 17th cent. and is commemorated by an obelisk on a hill.

APPIN, Argyll. 636 with Lismore. Map 14, **NM 9** 4.
Situated on the fine Oban to Ballachulish road, and near the point of divergence of the by-road leading westwards to the village of *Port Appin* (*q.v.*), which faces the island of *Lismore* (*q.v.*). The name *Appin* is applied generally to the stretch of picturesque country lying between Loch Creran and the confluence of Loch Leven and *Loch Linnhe* (*q.v.*), and is really part of the land of *Lorne* (*q.v.*). Included in the district is the massif of *Ben Vair*, with its two peaks of over 3,000 ft., stretching in a semi-circle from Glen Duror to *Ballachulish* (*q.v.*), and forming a magnificent viewpoint. R. L. Stevenson described the country in his novel "Kidnapped," which treats also of the celebrated Appin murder in 1752, when Colin Campbell, known as the Red Fox, was shot. Later, James Stewart (James of the Glen) was brought to trial at *Inveraray* (*q.v.*) as the alleged murderer, and, after a trial considered to have been unfair, was hanged at Ballachulish. See **Duror** and **Portnacroish** (for *Castle Stalker*). *Iter. 124.*

APPLECROSS, Ross and Cromarty. 578. Map 22, **NG 7** 4.
A remote West Highland village at the foot of wild hills, situated on Applecross Bay, facing the island of Raasay in the Inner Sound, beyond which lies Skye. The patron saint, named Maelrubha, or Maree, founded a monastery here in A.D. 673, being later buried in the little Church north of the village. Motor boats from Kyle of Lochalsh serve *Toscaig*, which lies some 4 miles to the south, at the head of the small inlet of Loch Toscaig. By road, the only approach is over the famous 2,054-ft. high Pass of "Bealach nam Bo," the Pass of the Cattle, a most difficult route, described under *Tornapress*, and liable to be blocked by snow in winter. The descent from the summit of the pass to Applecross Bay is without serious difficulty. Beyond Loch Toscaig lie the three small Crowlin Islands. A walkers' track goes northwards from Applecross to the mouth of Outer Loch Torridon, giving splendid views, and continuing in an easterly direction to *Shieldaig* (*q.v.*), on the loch of that name, looking towards the splendid *Torridon* (*q.v.*) mountains. *Iter. 219.*

ARBIGLAND, Kirkcudbright. Map 4, **NX 9** 5.
See **Kirkbean.**

ARBIRLOT, Angus. 1,297 with Carmyllie. Map 21, **NO 6** 4.
On the Elliot Water. A little to the south-east is *Kelly Castle*, 16th cent. and later.

ARBROATH, Angus. 22,585. LB. Map 17, **NO 6** 4.
E.C. Wed. **M.D.** Thurs. GOLF. A fishing port, Royal Burgh, industrial town and resort, the name being a contraction of *Aberbrothock*. The town is associated with Scott's novel "The Antiquary," under the name of "Fairport." There are sands and a bathing pool, and the coastal stretch away to the north-east is noted for its cliffs and caves, among the latter being Dickmont's Den, Mason's and the Forbidden Cave. A curious rock

stack is known as the Pint Stoup. The Brothock Water flows through the town to enter the North Sea. The notable, ruined Abbey Church of Arbroath (A.M.), dedicated to St. Thomas à Becket, is in the style of the early 13th cent., the most impressive portions being the South transept gable and the West front, with its tower and portal. In the South transept is the circular window known as the "O" of Arbroath, formerly lit up and used as a beacon for mariners. In 1951, the Stone of *Scone* (*q.v.*), after having been removed from Westminster Abbey, found a temporary resting place in the Abbey before being returned to

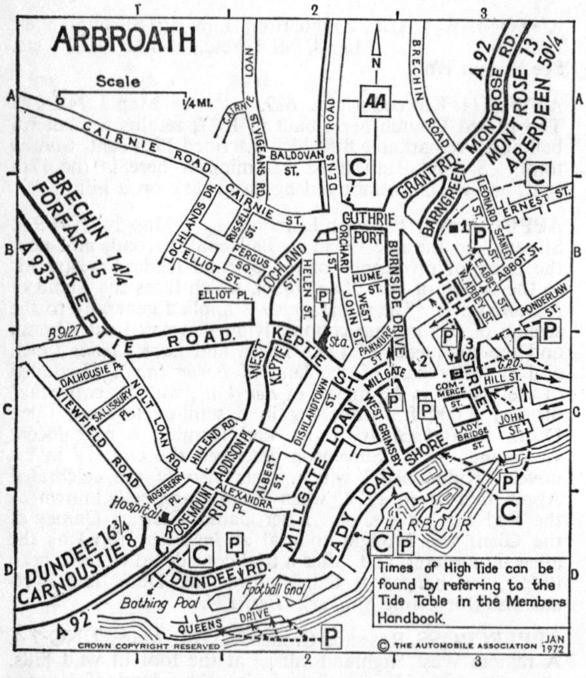

Abbey 1 (B3) Information Bureau 2 (C3) Town Hall 3 (C3)

England. The Sacristy contains the tomb of William the Lion, who founded the Abbey in 1176, and the Abbot's House, with its 12th cent. vaulted kitchen, has a Folk Museum, and is associated with Robert Bruce. In 1320, the Declaration of Independence was signed by Robert Bruce in the Abbey. The Arbroath Abbey Pageant has been held in most years during the summer since 1947, and takes place in the Abbey precincts. The fine old restored mansion of *Hospitalfield*, to the west of the town, is associated with Jonathan Oldbuck in Scott's "The Antiquary," and now contains a collection of Scottish pictures. The house is open from 2 to 5 on Fri. July and Aug. (see note page 98). There are several 19th cent. mills in the town. The Court House (Trades Hall) was built in 1814. Out to sea, some 11 miles south-east, is the *Bell Rock*, or Inchcape Rock lighthouse, marking a dangerous reef. The lighthouse (1808/11) is considered the outstanding achievement of Robert Stevenson, an ancestor of Robert Louis Stevenson. A well-known Scottish ballad tells how the Bell Rock received its name. See **Arbirlot, Auchmithie, Carnoustie** and **St. Vigeans.** *Iter. 155, 163.*

ARBUTHNOTT, Kincardine. 497. Map 21, **NO 8 7.**
This remotely situated place in the valley of the Bervie Water possesses a very interesting Church, where the Arbuthnott Missal was written in 1491. The Church was Collegiate, and shows 13th and 15th cent. work, being especially notable for the Arbuthnott Aisle, heavily buttressed outside and vaulted inside. *Arbuthnott House* is an old mansion, dating back to the 16th cent., and contains fine 17th cent. plaster ceilings.

ARCHIESTOWN, Moray. Map 26, **NJ 2 4.**
In the vicinity lies *Elchies Forest. Iter. 171.*

ARDBEG, Isle of Islay, Argyll. Map 6, **NR 4 4.**
Iter. 245.

ARDCHATTAN, Argyll. 1,322. Map 14, **NM 9 3.**
Iter. 124. See **Connel.**

ARDCLACH CHURCH, Nairn. Map 25, **NH 9 4.**
Near this Church is an unusual detached bell tower (A.M.), perhaps of 17th cent. date and situated high above the River Findhorn.

ARDELVE, Ross and Cromarty. Map 23, **NG 8 2.**
E.C. Wed Picturesquely situated at the junction of *Loch Alsh* (*q.v.*) with *Loch Duich* (*q.v.*), in a setting of North-West Highland mountains. From the west side of the road bridge at *Dornie* (*q.v.*), lying a little to the south-east, a passenger ferry connects with *Totaig*, across Loch Duich, from which there are fine views up the loch towards the *Five Sisters of Kintail.* A by-road goes north-eastwards from Ardelve, at first following the shores of Loch Long, and passing Killilan. *Ben Killilan*, 2,466 ft., and *Sguman Coinntich*, 2,881 ft., both very fine viewpoints, dominate this part of the valley, which leads into Glen Elchaig. From the western end of the little Loch na Leitreach access is then gained by means of a stiff climb on foot to the lofty *Falls of Glomach* (*q.v.*), which can also be approached from quite a different direction, for which see under *Croe Bridge.* By means of long-distance walkers' paths from the head of Glen Elchaig, it is possible to reach Glen Cannich, farther to the east, which is described under *Cannich. Iter. 207, 220.*

ARDEN, Dunbarton. Map 15, **NS 3 8.**
Iter. 88, 100, 101, 110, 114, 137.

ARDENTINNY, Argyll. Map 14, **NS 1 8.**
The terminal point of a fine road from *Dunoon* (*q.v.*) in the land of *Cowal* (*q.v.*). Traversing the shores of Loch Long, the road looks towards the Rosneath peninsula, on which stands, facing Ardentinny, the village of *Coulport* (*q.v.*). There is also a hilly and narrow road continuing up Glen Finart to the shores of *Loch Eck* (*q.v.*), dominated to the west by *Beinn Mhor*, 2,433 ft. This connects with a better road towards *Strachur* (*q.v.*) near the shores of *Loch Fyne* (*q.v.*). *Iter. 102.*

ARDERSIER, Inverness. 1,441. Map 25, **NH 7 5.**
An Inner Moray Firth fishing village, known also as *Campbelltown. Iter. 199.*

ARDGARTAN (Argyll Forest Park), Argyll.
See **Arrochar.** Map 14, **NN 2 0.**

ARDGAY, Ross and Cromarty. Map 29, **NH 6 9.**
E.C. Wed. Lies on the Inner Dornoch Firth. In the market square is the White Stone of Kincardine, marking the annual winter market, and formerly built into the walling of what was once an inn. To the west extends Strath Carron, with its river, and roads along both banks, which terminate on the outskirts of Amat Forest, in a setting of lonely hills farther to the west, with the extensive Diebidale and Freevater Forests in the background. *Iter. 200, 201.*

ARDGOUR, Argyll. Map 18, **NN 0 6.**
The village is situated where the Corran Narrows almost divide *Loch Linnhe* (*q.v.*) into two parts, and *Corran* (*q.v.*) car ferry connects with the opposite shore for *Fort William* (*q.v.*) and the south. This avoids the detour around Loch Eil to the north, which adds some 25 miles to the journey along a narrow and winding road. The Corran lighthouse guards the narrows at this point and dominating the scene in the background rises *Sgurr na h'Eanchainne*, 2,397 ft. The name Ardgour is generally applied to the whole district lying between Loch Linnhe and *Loch Shiel* (*q.v.*), and its finest mountain, though not the highest, is *Garbh Bheinn*, 2,903 ft., which is described under *Inversanda.* About **3 m. S.W.** of Ardgour, on Loch Linnhe, is the entrance to Glen Gour, which has no road,

Arbroath, Angus. The ruined 13th century Abbey, the circular south transept window of which is known as the ' O ' of Arbroath. It was formerly lit up as an aid to shipping off the coast

Arbroath, Angus. The entrance to the old mansion of Hospitalfield, which houses a collection of Scottish pictures

Ardelve, Ross and Cromarty. An old heather-thatched crofter's house, of a type now almost vanished. It stands by Loch Alsh, and was used in the filming of R. L. Stevenson's '*Master of Ballantrae*'

Ardgour, Argyll. A view of the Ardgour hills across Loch Linnhe, at the Corran narrows, which are crossed by a car ferry

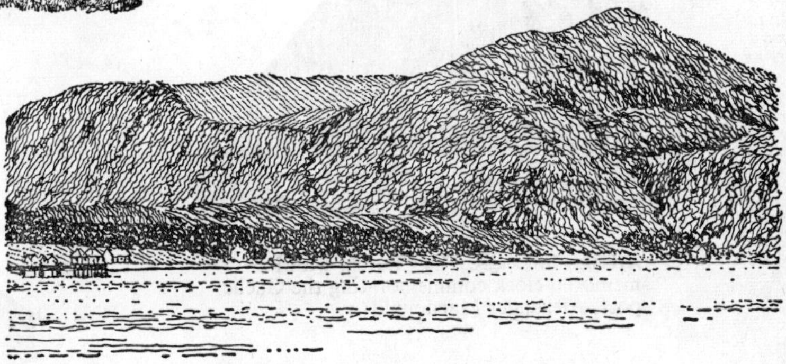

Arbuthnott, Kincardine. The 13th to 15th century Church, which is noted for the heavily buttressed Arbuthnott Aisle

Ardclach, Nairn. The detached bell tower of the Church, which is considered to be of 17th century date

[For ARDGOUR (Loch Linnhe) see also Plate 113

Ardmair Bay, Ross and Cromarty. A view across Loch Kanaird towards the Coigach mountains

Ardnamurchan Point, Argyll. The lonely lighthouse at Ardnamurchan Point, the most westerly place on the mainland of Scotland, its name meaning ' Cape of the Great Seas '

Arisaig, Inverness. The Church, with its memorial clock commemorating the Gaelic poet, Alexander Macdonald

Ardrossan, Ayr. The modern Roman Catholic Church of St. Peter-in-Chains, built in Swedish style

Armadale, Isle of Skye, Inverness. The modern Castle (c. 1815), which replaces a former house where Dr. Johnson and Boswell were entertained during their tour of the Hebrides in 1773

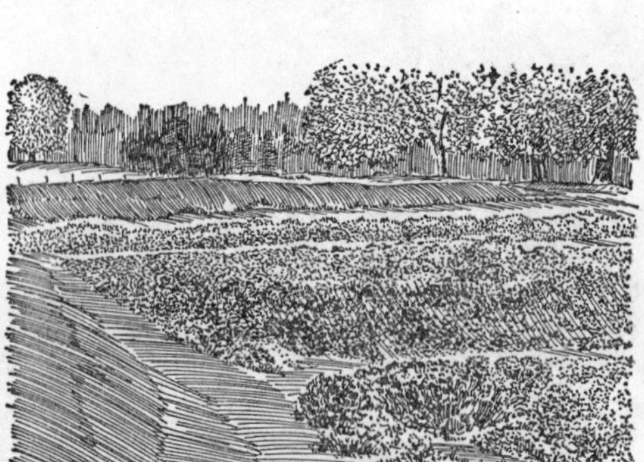

Ardoch Roman Camp, Perth. Part of the well-preserved defences of the extensive Roman fort, one of the largest in Great Britain. It is situated near Braco, off A822

and is overlooked at its far end by *Sgurr Dhomhail*, 2,915 ft., the highest peak in Ardgour. **4 m. N.W.** of Ardgour, on the same loch, is *Inverscaddle Bay*, where Glen Scaddle and Cona Glen, both roadless, converge. From here, the views into *Lochaber* (*q.v.*) over Loch Linnhe, looking towards *Ben Nevis* (*q.v.*), are very fine. See **Camusnagaul.** *Iter. 215, 216, 217, 218.*

ARDHASIG BRIDGE (Isle of Lewis), Harris, Inverness. *Iter. 256.* Map 32, **NB 1 0.**

ARDLUI, Dunbarton. Map 15, **NN 3 1.** Picturesquely situated among mountains, dominated by *Ben Vorlich*, 3,092 ft., to the south-west, and at the northern extremity of *Loch Lomond* (*q.v.*). It is the terminal place of call for the loch steamers. In the vicinity is a curious pulpit, hewn out of the solid rock-face, from which sermons have been delivered. The road which has traversed the western shores of Loch Lomond continues northwards from here through lovely Glen Falloch, in Perthshire, towards *Crianlarich* (*q.v.*), with *Beinn Oss*, 3,374 ft., rising away to the west, and *Cruach Ardran*, 3,428 ft., to the east. See **Inveruglas.** *Iter. 100, 110, 111.*

ARDLUSSA, Isle of Jura, Argyll. Map 13, **NR 6 8.** See **Jura.**

ARDMAIR BAY, Ross and Cromarty. Map 29, **NH 1 9.** Faces Loch Kanaird, an offshoot of Loch Broom, and looks out across Isle Martin towards the *Coigach* mountains. There is a pebbly foreshore. *Iter. 224, 225, 226.*

ARDNADAM, Argyll. Map 14, **NS 1 8.** On the south shore of the Holy Loch and noted for yachting. *Iter. 102.*

ARDNAMURCHAN POINT, Argyll. Map 12, **NM 4 6.** The most westerly point on the Scottish mainland, on which stands a lonely lighthouse, built by Alan Stevenson in 1848, from where the views extend northwards out to sea towards the islands of Muck, Eigg and *Rum* (*q.v.*), and westwards to the islands of Coll and *Tiree* (*q.v.*). A rough road connects the lighthouse with *Kilchoan* (*q.v.*). To the north-east of the Point is Sanna Bay, with its white sands, overlooked by Sanna Point. The name Ardnamurchan is also given to the whole of the peninsula which stretches westwards to the Point, and is bounded to the east by the sea lochs of Loch Moidart and *Loch Sunart* (*q.v.*). The last-named is traversed on its northern shores by the road which links Ardnamurchan with the head of the loch. See **Acharacle.** *Iter. 216.*

ARDOCH ROMAN CAMP, Perth. Map 16, **NN 8 0.** See **Braco.** *Iter. 138, 140.*

ARDRISHAIG, Argyll. 1,058. Map 14, **NR 8 8.** **E.C.** Wed. Lies on Loch Gilp, a shingly inlet of *Loch Fyne* (*q.v.*). Here is the eastern end of the 9-mile long *Crinan Canal*, linking Loch Fyne with the Sound of Jura, and terminating at *Crinan* (*q.v.*). The road leading southwards from Ardrishaig forks within 2½ miles, the rather hilly western branch leading through the *Knapdale* (*q.v.*) hills towards Loch Killisport, and the main road continuing along the shores of Loch Fyne to *Tarbert* (*q.v.*). See **Cairnbaan** and **Lochgilphead.** *Iter. 119, 121, 122.*

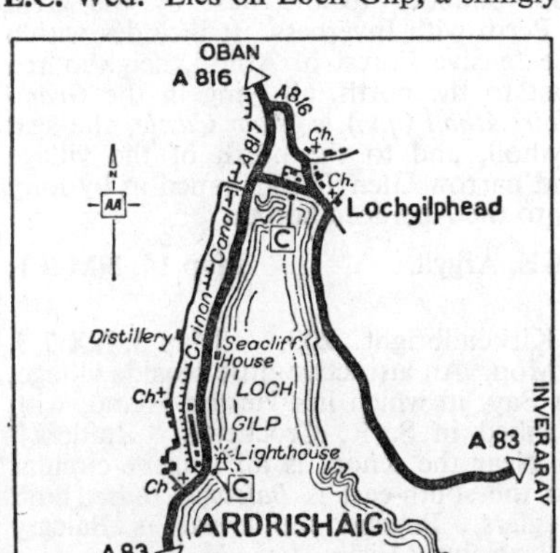

ARDROIL SANDS, Isle of Lewis, Ross and Cromarty. *Iter. 258.* See **Hebrides, Outer** (Lewis). Map 32, **NB 0 3.**

ARDROSSAN, Ayr. 10,569. SB. Map 8, **NS 2 4.** **E.C.** Wed. GOLF. A holiday resort with sands and bathing, and also a port of departure in summer for steamers to the island of *Arran* (*q.v.*). The harbour dates from 1806. On the

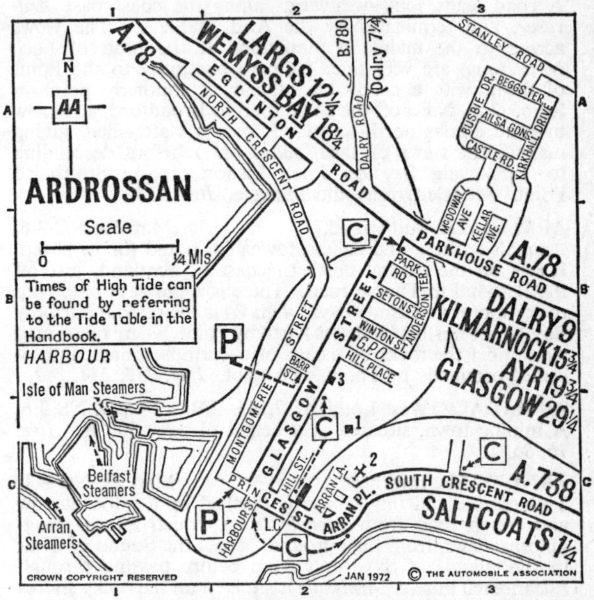

Castle ruins 1 (C2) St. Peter-in-Chains Church 2 (C2) Town Hall 3 (B2)

old Customs House are the Royal Arms. The modern Church of St. Peter-in-Chains (R.C.) is a striking building in the Swedish style. There are slight remains of a 12th cent. Castle of the Montgomerys. The town, which was planned in 1806, stands between the North and South Bays, and beyond the last-named lies *Saltcoats* (*q.v.*), a well-known resort. Horse Island, a bird sanctuary, lies off-shore in the North Bay. There are magnificent views to be obtained of the granite peaks of Arran, 15 miles across the Firth of Clyde. *Iter. 57, 63, 69, 88.*

ARDWELL, Wigtown. Map 2, **NX 1 4.** On the western shores of Luce Bay, in the narrow Rhinns of Galloway peninsula, which extends southwards to the *Mull of Galloway* (*q.v.*). *Ardwell* is a restored late 17th cent. house, with fine gardens. See **Port Logan.** *Iter. 82.*

ARGYLL FOREST PARK, Argyll. Map 14, **NS 1 9** etc. See **Arrochar** (for *Ardgartan*) and **Benmore Estate.**

ARISAIG, Inverness. 847. Map 12, **NM 6 8.** **E.C.** Tues. Situated in the green landscape of South Morar, amid rocks and sand. There is a wonderful outlook from the romantic " Road to the Isles " across Loch nan Cilltean to the islands of Eigg and Rum, and also northwards towards the distant Coolins of Skye. The tower of the Catholic Church is a local landmark, and near a ruined 16th cent. Chapel, in the burial ground, are some old sculptured slabs. In the Church is a memorial clock to Alexander Macdonald, or Alasdair MacMhaigstir Alasdair, the famous Gaelic poet. *Arisaig House* is noted for its rhododendron and shrub gardens, and in the vicinity is a cave in which Prince Charles Edward hid before escaping to France in 1746. Southwards lies the Sound of Arisaig, with the inlet of *Loch nan Uamh* (*q.v.*), noted for its associations with the Prince. Across the water rise the hills of *Moidart* (*q.v.*), culminating in *Fros Beinn*, 2,876 ft. See **Dalilea, Lochailort** and **Morar.** *Iter. 209, 217.*

ARMADALE, Isle of Skye, Inverness. Map 23, **NG 6 0.** Lies in the fertile peninsula of Sleat, in the far south of the island, its shores washed by the Sound of Sleat and the waters of Loch Eishort. There is a steamer service, carrying cars, to *Mallaig* (*q.v.*) on the mainland. Sleat has been called the "Garden of Skye," and has numerous trees, which were admired by Dr. Johnson and Boswell during their visit in 1773. The house where they stayed is now *Armadale Castle*, built by Gillespie Graham, c. 1819. A road leads south-westwards along the coast past *Ardvasar*, and terminates by the Aird of Sleat. The views across to the mainland mountains at the head of *Loch Nevis* (*q.v.*) are very fine. A path continues to the Point of Sleat, with a sandy bay, the most southerly point in Skye. **2 m. N.E.**, off the coast road to Broadford, a narrow by-road climbs north-westwards over a water-shed, giving magnificent views of the *Coolins* (*q.v.*) before descending to Tarskavaig Bay on Loch Eishort, facing Strathaird Point. See **Isle Ornsay** and **Teangue.** *Iter. 253.*

ARMADALE, Sutherland. Map 30, **NC 7 6.**
A small crofting and fishing township, noted for its sheep. It lies on the stormy northern coast of Scotland, just off the Bettyhill to Thurso road. There is a pleasant bay, with rocky shores and sandy bays. **4 m. W.** is the remote Kirtomy Bay, to the north of which is Kirtomy Point, where boats may pass under the rocks by means of a curious tunnel, as described originally by Thomas Pennant. *Iter. 232, 234, 240.*

ARMADALE, West Lothian. 7,165. SB. Map 9, **NS 9 6.**
A mining town, situated at a height of over 500 ft. *Iter. 16, 86.*

ARNISDALE, Inverness. Map 23, **NG 8 1.**
This remote and tiny village is reached by a hilly, narrow and rough road from *Glenelg* (*q.v.*), which affords magnificent views, from high ground, across the Sound of Sleat to the islands of Skye and Rum before passing through Eileanreach Forest. *Arnisdale* is situated on the rocky shores of Outer *Loch Hourn* (*q.v.*), in a picturesque mountain setting. West of the village are the Rassaidh Islands in the loch. Behind the village rises the steep, twin-peaked *Ben Sgriol*, 3,196 ft., and across the loch is *Ladhar Bheinn*, 3,343 ft., the most westerly of the 3,000-ft. peaks on the mainland, both being exceptionally fine viewpoints. A poorly-defined path leads south-eastwards from Arnisdale, and the clachan of *Corran*, where the Arnisdale River flows into Loch Hourn from Glen Arnsidale and Glen Dubh, under the slopes of *Druim Fada*, 2,401 ft. This path gives access to the magnificent fjord-like scenery of Inner Loch Hourn, facing Barrisdale Bay on the south side of the loch. See **Kinloch Hourn.** *Iter. 207.*

ARNPRIOR, Stirling. Map 16, **NS 6 9.**
Garden is a fine Georgian mansion in a setting of trees. *Iter. 108, 112, 137.*

ARRAN, ISLE OF, Bute. Map 7, **NR 9 3** etc.
The picturesque island of *Arran* lies in the Firth of Clyde, some 14 miles from the mainland coast. Its attractive western shores are washed by the Kilbrennan Sound, less than 4 miles in width at its narrowest point, and separating it from the narrow *Kintyre* (*q.v.*) peninsula. Arran is some 20 miles long and 10 miles wide, the finest scenery being concentrated in the northern half. Here, the fine Highland ridges of granite, interesting geologically, are dominated by *Goat Fell*, 2,866 ft. (N.T. Scot.), the highest, though not the wildest peak, and are bitten into from west to east by Glen Iorsa, Glen Rosa and Glen Sannox. Robert Bruce is said to have crossed from the island, in 1307, to *Turnberry* (*q.v.*), where he commenced his struggle to achieve Scotland's independence. A good road, 56 miles in length, encircles the island, and two others cross it from east to west, the best known being the so-called "String" road, linking Brodick with the south-west coast. There are a number of resorts and villages, with bathing, fishing and other amenities, all of which are described under separate headings. The most important approaches from the mainland are by steamer from *Ardrossan* and *Fairlie*, both (*q.v.*) to *Brodick*. The view from the summit of *Goat Fell* is one of the most extensive in Scotland. In addition, fine panoramic views of Arran are obtained from a number of points on the mainland, notably the Kintyre peninsula, the Ayrshire coast, and also from the island of *Bute* (*q.v.*). See **Blackwaterfoot, Brodick, Corrie, Kildonan, Lagg, Lamlash, Lochranza, Machrie, Pirnmill, Sannox** and **Whiting Bay.** *Iter. 242.*

ARROCHAR, Dunbarton. 740. Map 15, **NN 2 0.**
E.C. Wed. (Winter). Situated at the northern end of the sandy and narrow *Loch Long* (*q.v.*), with a steamer pier, and only 2 miles distant from the western shores of *Loch Lomond* (*q.v.*). Wordsworth and his sister, with Coleridge, came here in 1803. To the north-west of the village are some of Argyll's finest peaks, notably *Ben Arthur*, familiarly known as *The Cobbler*, 2,891 ft., from the Gaelic "An Gobaileach," *Ben Narnain*, 3,036 ft., and *Ben Ime*, 3,318 ft., the two first-named being famous for rock-climbing, and all being notable *Cowal* (*q.v.*) viewpoints. **2 m. S.W.** is *Ardgartan*, in the extensive Argyll Forest Park, covering some 37,000 acres, developed largely by the Forestry Commission, and overlooked to the west by the rocky peak of *The Brack*, 2,580 ft. The park includes also *The Cobbler* and the neighbouring peaks. From here the road climbing westwards through Glen Croe passes *Rest and Be Thankful* (*q.v.*) before descending to *Loch Fyne* (*q.v.*). To the south-west of Glen Croe is the Ardgoil Estate of the Forest Park, in which rises *Ben Donich*, 2,774 ft. There are camping grounds in the Park both at Arrochar and Ardgartan. See **Benmore Estate** and **Tarbet.** *Iter. 88, 101, 102, 103, 117, 137.*

ASCOG, Bute. Map 7, **NS 1 6.**
On the eastern shore of the island, with Loch Ascog to the west. *Iter. 241.*

ASHIESTIEL, Selkirk. Map 10, **NT 4 3.**
Ashiestiel (or *Ashiesteel*) *House* lies on the south bank of the Tweed, and here Scott lived, as sheriff of the county, from 1804 to 1812, while during this period were written "The Lay of the Last Minstrel," "The Lady of the Lake" and "Marmion." Mungo Park, the explorer, visited Scott at Ashiestiel. See **Abbotsford House.**

ASSYNT, Sutherland. Map 29, **NC 1 2**
See **Inchnadamph, Loch Assynt** and **Lochinver.** and **2 2.**

ATHELSTANEFORD, East Lothian. 982.
Map 17, **NT 5 7.**
The rebuilt Church dates originally from c. 1100. Nearby is a very fine example of a stone-built and crow-stepped gabled doocot. John Home, the writer of "Douglas," produced at Covent Garden, London, in 1757, was at one time minister here. Athelstaneford is associated with a 10th cent. battle fought by the Saxon King Athelstan against the Picts and Scots, which is said to have originated the St. Andrew's Cross as the Scottish flag.

ATHOLL, Perth. Map 19, **NN 6 7** etc.
This district includes most of northern Perthshire, a mountainous region, bounded to the west by the great trunk road linking Perth with Inverness. It includes within its boundaries the extensive Forest of Atholl, neighboured by the Gaick Forest to the north, all lying in the *Grampians* (*q.v.*). At *Blair Atholl* (*q.v.*) is *Blair Castle*, the seat of the Duke of Atholl, and to the north of the village extends the long and narrow Glen Tilt, hemmed in by lofty hills, and extending to the Aberdeen border.

ATLANTIC BRIDGE, Argyll. Map 14, **NM 7 1.**
See **Clachan Bridge.**

AUCHENCAIRN, Kirkcudbright. 200. Map 3, **NX 7 5.**
E.C. Thurs. **M.D.** Mon. An attractive little seaside village, facing Auchencairn Bay, in which lies Hestan Island, with its lighthouse, described in S. R. Crockett's "Raiders" as "Isle Rathan." Near the school is an ancient circular burial cairn, and to the south-east is *Balcary House*, built originally by smugglers. Beyond the house is Balcary Point, overlooking the Solway Firth. *Iter. 73.*

AUCHENCROW, Berwick. Map 11, **NT 8 6.**
This small village, below the 860-ft. high *Horseley Hill*, is associated with gruesome stories of the 18th cent. practices of dealing with witches.

Arran, Isle of, Bute. The peak of Goat Fell, 2,866 feet (N.T. Scot.), the highest point in the island. It rises above Brodick Bay, and the first recorded ascent was in 1628

Arrochar, Dunbarton. A bridge on A83, in the heart of the Macfarlane country, in which, at one time, the new moon is said to have been known as ' Macfarlane's Lantern '

Assynt, Sutherland. The mountain of Quinag, which forms a long ridge to the west of A894, between Loch Assynt and Kylesku, in the district of Assynt. On a spit of land stands the ruined 16th century Ardvreck Castle, illustrated also under Inchnadamph (Plate 86)

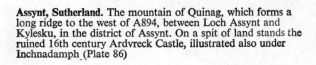

Athelstaneford, East Lothian. A notable example of an old stone-built dovecote, showing a crow-stepped gable. It stands behind the church

Atholl, Perth. A toll cottage on A9, at Edendon Bridge, to the north-west of Dalnacardoch, on the edge of the vast Forest of Atholl in the Grampian mountains

[For ARRAN, ISLE OF, see also under LAMLASH (Plate 105)

Auchmithie, Angus. Sandstone cliff scenery at a village which is associated with Sir Walter Scott's novel, '*The Antiquary*,' under the name of 'Musselcrag'

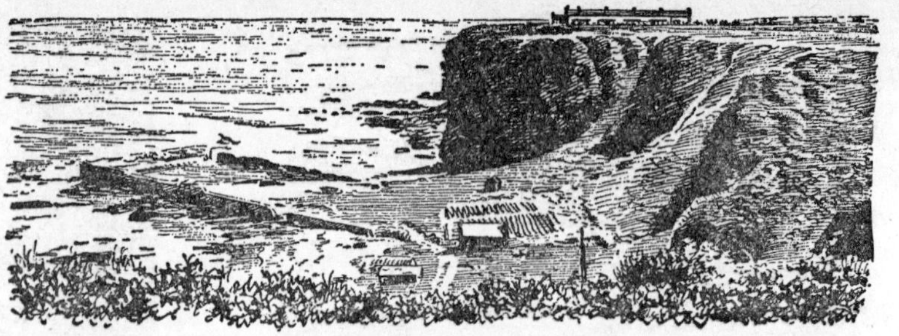

Auchindoun, Banff. The remains of the Castle, built partly by Thomas Cochrane, the favourite of James III. It stands on an unclassified road beyond Parkhead Farm, some 2 miles south-east of Dufftown, off A941

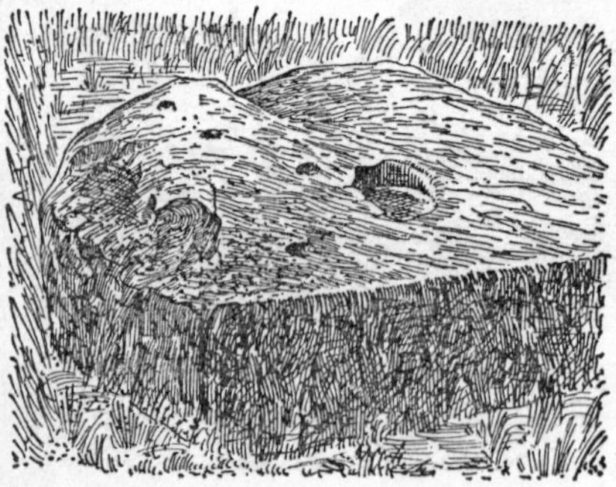

Auchtermuchty, Fife. The 'Thirlestane,' a stone block used formerly for the beam holding the wool-scales. It stands some 3 miles north-west of the village, on the Mournipea road (unclassified) leading westwards off A983

Auldearn, Nairn. The 17th century Boath dovecote (N.T. Scot.). Here, the Royal Standard was raised by Montrose in 1645, when he defeated the Covenanters

Auldgirth, Dumfries. The late 18th century bridge across the River Nith, which Thomas Carlyle's father helped to build

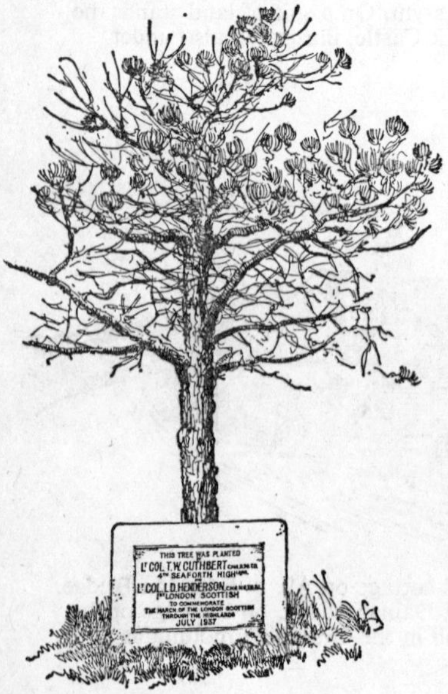

Aultnamain Inn, Ross and Cromarty. A tree, planted in July 1937, to commemorate the march of the London Scottish through the Highlands. It is situated 3 miles north, on A9

[For AVIEMORE see following plate]
[For AUCHTERMUCHTY see also Plate 175
[For AUCHTERTYRE see under KINTAIL (Plate 100)

AUCHENDINNY, Midlothian. Map 9, **NT 2** 6.
See **Penicuik.** *Iter. 14.*

AUCHENLOCHAN, Argyll. Map 7, **NR 9** 7.
See **Tighnabruaich.** *Iter. 102.*

AUCHINBLAE, Kincardine. Map 21, **NO 7** 7.
See **Fordoun Church.** *Iter. 151.*

AUCHINCRUIVE, Ayr. Map 8, **NS 3** 2.
Auchincruive House and its extensive grounds lying in a wooded setting on the River Ayr, with its sandstone cliffs, now houses a West of Scotland Agricultural College, and was presented to the nation in 1930. There are associations with both Burns and Wallace, the latter having reputedly hid in woods in the vicinity. *Iter. 35.*

AUCHINDOIR CHURCH, Aberdeen. Map 26, **NJ 4** 2.
See **Lumsden.**

AUCHINDOUN, Banff. Map 26, **NJ 3** 3.
The Castle (A.M.) stands **2 m. S.**, on an eminence surrounded by prehistoric earthworks overlooking the Fiddich River. It is said to have been founded in the 11th cent., and includes a 15th cent. tower, much of the structure having been destroyed c. 1600. *Iter. 195.*

AUCHINDRAIN, Argyll. Map 14, **NN 0** 0.
Here is an interesting museum of farming life. *Iter. 118, 121.*

AUCHINEDEN, Stirling. Map 15, **NS 5** 8.
Queen's View (1171 ft.), from which Queen Victoria had her first glimpse of Loch Lomond in 1869, is now an AA viewpoint. See **Stockiemuir.** *Iter. 104, 106.*

AUCHINLECK, Ayr. 8,111. Map 8, **NS 5** 2.
Auchinleck House, known locally as *Place Affleck*, lies **3 m. W.**, near the banks of the River Lugar, and was built by the father of the famous James Boswell, the biographer of Dr. Johnson. The house is partly the work of the brothers Adam, dating from c. 1780, and nearer the river are the remains of the former Castle. Boswell was buried in Auchinleck Church in 1795. *Iter. 67.*

AUCHMITHIE, Angus. Map 21, **NO 6** 4.
Little village, with a sandy beach, high on a rocky part of the Angus coast, with its sandstone cliffs, which extend north-eastwards towards the impressive Red Head and Lang Craig, overlooking Lunan Bay. Both Auchmithie and Red Head are associated with Scott's " The Antiquary." A picturesque stretch of foreshore also lies to the south, with the caves of Dickmont's Den, Mason's and the Forbidden Cave, and also the detached stack of the Pint Stoup *Iter. 155.*

AUCHTERARDER, Perth. 2,440. SB. Map 16, **NN 9** 1.
E.C. Wed. GOLF. This Royal Burgh consists mainly of a single street over a mile in length, situated to the north of the *Ochil* hills. In 1716, the old town was burnt by the Earl of Mar. **1 m. S.**, near the Ruthven Water, is the ancient *Kincardine Castle*, dismantled in 1645, while in the vicinity stands the modern Castle. **2½ m. N.W.**, near the Machany Water, is *Strathallan Castle*. See **Blackford, Gleneagles Hotel** and **Tullibardine.** *Iter. 135, 146.*

AUCHTERDERRAN, Fife. 2,957. Map 17, **NT 2** 9.
A village on the winding River Ore, with an 18th cent. Church which preserves a doorway dated 1676. The large *Bowhill* colliery is in the vicinity. **2½ m. N.E.**, at *Dogton* farm, is the inscribed, Celtic *Dogton Stone* (A.M.).

AUCHTERLESS, Aberdeen. 981. Map 27, **NJ 7** 4.
A little to the south-west, and just off the Fyvie to Turriff road, stands *Towie-Barclay* farm, incorporating the remains of *Tolly Castle*, an erstwhile Barclay residence, and of which the 14th cent. hall is of note. See **Kirktown of Auchterless.** *Iter. 180.*

AUCHTERMUCHTY, Fife. 1,344. SB. Map 17, **NO 2** 1.
Once a Royal Burgh, this little town stands on the edge of the fertile Howe of Fife, looking north-westwards to the *Ochil* hills. On the Perth road is the *Thirlestane*, a stone block once used for the beam holding the wool-scales. An old Tolbooth still remains, dating from 1728, and in the town are several weavers' houses with thatched roofs, unusual in Scotland. *Myres Castle* is 16th cent. and later. *Iter. 92, 136.*

AUCHTERTOOL, Fife. 1,203. Map 17, **NT 2** 9.
The ruined *Knockdavie Castle* stands some **2½ m. S.**, on the farther side of A907.

AUCHTERTYRE, Ross and Cromarty. Map 23, **NG 8** 2.
From Auchtertyre Hill, to the north-east, on the hilly road leading towards *Strome* (*q.v.*), there is a magnificent view towards the lofty mountains at the head of *Loch Duich* (*q.v.*), notably the picturesque *Five Sisters of Kintail*, dominated by *Scour Ouran*, 3,505 ft. Below the peak, in Glen Udalain, a small hydro-electric scheme is in operation. *Iter. 207, 220, 221, 222.*

AULDEARN, Nairn. 556. Map 25, **NH 9** 5.
A pleasant village, situated a little inland from the Moray Firth. The circular 17th cent. *Boath* dovecote (N.T. Scot) stands on the spot where *Montrose* raised the Royal Standard before the battle in 1645, in which he decisively routed a force of Covenanters. **½ m. E.** is the ruined Parish Church. Cairns and cists from the Bronze Age are to be found in the neighbourhood. **2 m. N.E.** is *Inshoch Tower*, now in ruins. **3 m. E.**, off the Forres road, is the *Hardmuir*, a wooded stretch, supposedly the scene of the encounter of Macbeth and Banquo with the witches. *Iter. 175, 198, 199.*

AULDGIRTH, Dumfries. Map 4, **NX 9** 8.
The River Nith flows through a picturesque gorge below the bridge, dating from c. 1780, which Carlyle's father helped to build. **2 m. S.E.**, near the river, is *Ellisland* farm, where Burns composed Tam o'Shanter among other works. Beyond the river is the small *Dalswinton* Castle loch, where, in 1788, Patrick Millar experimented with a steam-driven vessel, with Burns as a passenger. **2 m. W.** is the ruined 16th cent. tower of *Lag.* **3 m. S.E.** is *Isle Tower*, dated 1587, in a good state of preservation, situated on the west bank of the Nith. See **Dunscore.** *Iter. 27, 48, 56, 67.*

AULTBEA, Ross and Cromarty. 500. Map 22, **NG 8** 8.
E.C. Wed. **M.D.** Tues./Fri. This crofting village is situated in a remote part of *Wester Ross*, on Loch Ewe, facing the Isle of Ewe, and lies just off the Poolewe to Ullapool road. In both the World Wars Loch Ewe was of considerable naval importance. Northwards extends the peninsula of Rudha Mor, terminated by Greenstone Point. The road continuing northwards towards *Gruinard Bay* (*q.v.*) passes the curiously-named clachans of *First Coast* and *Second Coast*. See **Poolewe.** *Iter. 206, 222.*

AULTNAHARRIE, Ross and Cromarty.
Map 29, **NH 1** 9.
Lies on the south side of Loch Broom, facing *Ullapool* (*q.v.*), to which it is connected by passenger ferry. *Ben Goleach*, 2,052 ft., a good viewpoint, is the prominent hill rising to the west, overlooking Loch Broom and Little Loch Broom. A track leads southwards, climbing steeply over the hills, with fine views of the great *Teallach* mountains, before descending to *Dundonnell* (*q.v.*). Near Aultnaharrie are two examples of ruined brochs.

AULTNAMAIN INN, Ross and Cromarty.
Map 31, **NH 6** 8.
Stands on the fine moorland road linking *Evanton* (*q.v.*) and *Bonar Bridge* (*q.v.*), an alternative to the longer route by way of *Tain* (*q.v.*). The inn was formerly a resting-place for drovers on their southward journey. Away to the south-west rises *Beinn Tharsuinn*, 2,270 ft. On the descent of *Struie Hill* (AA viewpoint), **3 m. N.**, a fine view is obtained over Dornoch Firth. *Iter. 200.*

AVIEMORE, Inverness. 650. Map 25, **NH 8** 1.
E.C. Wed. A well-known and newly-developed Highland resort in a wooded stretch of Strath Spey, dividing the *Monadhliath* and *Cairngorm* (*q.v.*) mountains, and on the western fringe of the great forests of *Rothiemurchus*

(*q.v.*) and Glenmore, between the Spey and the lofty Cairngorm summits. The last-named forest is reached by way of *Coylumbridge* (*q.v.*), on the road to *Nethybridge* (*q.v.*), which keeps to the east of the Spey. Climbing, walking, and winter sports, notably ski-ing, are all practised here. To the south-west rises the *Rock of Craigellachie*, which gave its name to the well-known slogan of the Grants: "Stand fast—Craigellachie." A 600-acre National Nature Reserve is situated here. In the Queen's Forest of Glenmore is one of the newly-created Forest Parks, extending to

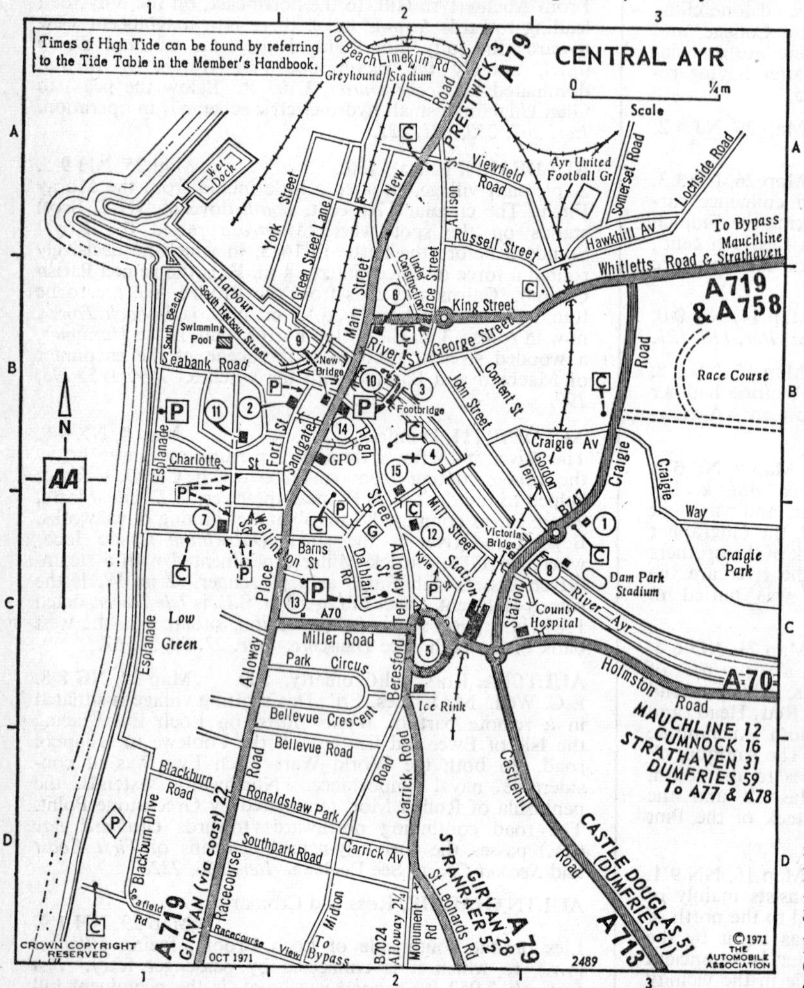

Ayr Technical College	1 (C3)	County Buildings	7 (C1)	Tam o'Shanter Inn	12 (C2)
Academy, founded 1233	2 (B2)	Dam Park Hall	8 (C3)	Tourist Inform. Centre	13 (C2)
Auld Brig	3 (B2)	Loudoun Hall, 16th-century	9 (B2)	Town Hall, Town Buildings and Information Bureau	14 (B2)
Auld Kirk (1655)	4 (B2)	New Brig, 1788	10 (B2)	Wallace Tower	15 (B2)
Burns Statue	5 (C2)	St. John's Tower	11 (B1)		
Carnegie Library	6 (B2)				

12,500 acres, in which *Glenmore Lodge*, at the eastern end of lovely *Loch Morlich* (*q.v.*), backed by *Cairn Gorm*, 4,084 ft., and *Cairn Lochan*, 3,983 ft., is now a training centre for mountaineering. Nearby is a public camping ground. Excellent ski-ing takes place here (See **Rothiemurchus**). A path from here climbs over the Ryvoan Pass, with the picturesque Green Loch, and leads eventually to Nethybridge through the Forest of Abernethy, another way being by means of the Sluggan Pass, farther to the west. The views of the Cairngorms are very fine as seen from Aviemore, and the cleft of the well-known *Lairig Ghru* (*q.v.*) Pass is seen in the distance. See **Kincraig** and **Lynwilg**. *Iter. 138, 140, 147, 150, 169, 170, 171, 172, 173, 208.*

AVOCH, Ross and Cromarty. 1,252. Map 25, **NH 7 5.** **E.C.** Thurs. A fishing village, situated in the *Black Isle* (*q.v.*), on the sandy shores of the Inner Moray Firth. The original early 19th cent. harbour works were by Telford. To the south, on Ormond Hill, are traces of the former *Avoch Castle*. *Iter. 203.*

AYR, Ayr. 47,884. **LB.** Map 8, **NS 3 2.** **E.C.** Wed. **M.D.** Tues. GOLF. An attractive resort, seaport and industrial Royal Burgh, in the Kyle division of the county, on Ayr Bay in the Firth of Clyde, with a sandy beach and forming a convenient centre for the *Burns Country* (*q.v.*). The neighbouring resorts of *Prestwick* (*q.v.*), with its important airport, and *Troon* (*q.v.*) are both well-known golfing centres. Ayr is famous for its Burns associations, notably the old thatched "*Tam o'Shanter*" Inn, and the "*Twa Brigs*," of which the "Auld Brig" dates back possibly to the 13th cent. (See **Alloway.**) A slender spire surmounts the Town Buildings (1828) and the Academy is a 13th cent. foundation. *Wallace's* tower, built in 1832, has a statue of Wallace, and near the station is the Burns statue. The *Auld Kirk* dates from 1655, with Cromwellian associations, and in it Burns was baptized. The *Fort Castle* is the tower of the old Greyfriars Church of *St. John*, in which Bruce's Parliament met in 1315, and forms a splendid viewpoint, including within its orbit the island of Arran. The 16th cent. *Loudoun Hall*, of much architectural interest, has been restored. The Hall is the oldest building in the town, the original owner having been James Tait, a burgess of Ayr, while later owners, the Campbells, enlarged the house. In the late 18th cent. the fortunes of Loudoun declined rapidly, until the commencement of its restoration in 1938. John Macadam, the well-known maker of roads, was born at Ayr, in 1756. There is a racecourse to the east of the town. **2½ m. S.**, on the coast, is the ruined *Greenan Castle*, and beyond it is the cape known as the *Heads of Ayr*. See **Auchincruive, Culzean Castle, Dunure, Kirkoswald, Maybole** and **Tarbolton.** *Iter. 20, 21, 27, 35, 49, 55, 60, 66, 75, 76, 77, 79, 80, 84, 88.*

AYTON, Berwick. 614. Map 11, **NT 9 6.** **E.C.** Thurs. Stands on the north bank of the Eye Water, whose wooded reaches are here spanned by a single-arched bridge. There is a modern Castle. The church lodge was once a toll-house. The ruined old Church, has been replaced by a modern structure. See **Eyemouth.** *Iter. 1, 41.*

BADDAGYLE, Ross and Cromarty. Map 29, **NC 0 1.** Situated at the western extremity of Loch Baddagyle, in the district known as the Aird of Coigach. Here, the road from Ullapool forks, the left branch going westwards past Loch Owskeich to *Achiltibuie* (*q.v.*), dominated by *Ben More Coigach*, 2,438 ft., and the right fork climbing by means of a reverse turn on to moorland, to continue its tortuous way towards *Inverkirkaig* and *Lochinver* (both *q.v.*). From the summit, a magnificent panoramic view of the distant, isolated Sutherland peaks to the north, dominated by the long ridge of *Suilven*, 2,399 ft., is gained. To the south-east of Loch Baddagyle is the beautiful mountain-encircled *Loch Lurgain* (*q.v.*) on the road to *Ullapool* (*q.v.*). **2½ m. N.** of Baddagyle, after crossing the River Polly, the strangely-shaped Loch Sionascaig is seen to the right in Inverpolly Forest, now part of a 27,000-acre National Nature Reserve. The 50 mile long Inverpolly Motor Trail covers the area, commencing at the *Knockan* AA viewpoint (*q.v.*). *Iter. 226.*

Aviemore, Inverness. A view from Strath Spey across Rothiemurchus Forest towards Carn Eilrig, in the foothills of the Cairngorm mountains. To the east of this hill goes the long-distance walkers' path through the rugged Lairig Ghru pass, leading through a cleft of the Cairngorms towards the upper reaches of the River Dee in Glen Dee

Ayton, Berwick. The church lodge, which was at one time used as a toll house on the Berwick to Edinburgh road until tolls were abolished

Ayr, Ayr. The Auld Kirk of 1655, in which Robert Burns was baptized. The building was restored in 1952, and the interior contains three lofts, known as the Merchants', Sailors' and Traders' Lofts

Ayr, Ayr. The 'Tam O'Shanter' Inn, associated with Robert Burns. It was bought for the town in 1943

Ayr, Ayr. The late mediaeval Auld Brig, now used for foot passengers only. It is one of the famous 'Twa Brigs' of the town, the other being a modern replacement of a bridge first erected in 1788

Badenoch, Inverness. Ruthven Barracks, to the east of the River Spey, at Kingussie, off B970. They were built in 1716 and enlarged by General Wade in 1734. The Highlanders destroyed them after the '45 Rising

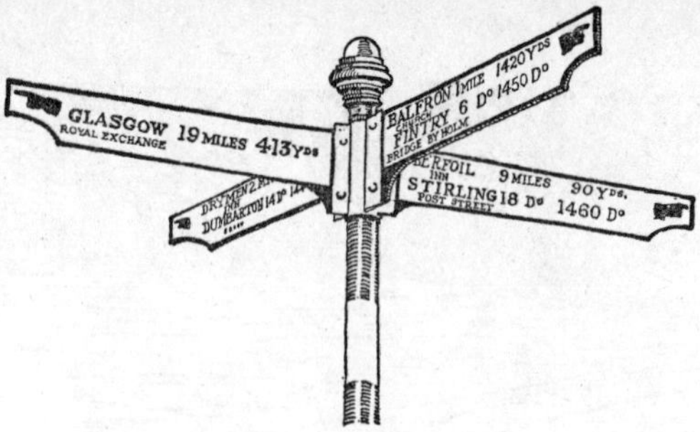

Balfron, Stirling. A signpost near the station, which gives distances in miles and yards

Ballachulish, Argyll. The Monument to James of the Glens, who was hanged for allegedly shooting Colin Roy Campbell of Glenure, known as the 'Red Fox,' on 14th May, 1752, a crime he never committed. The white stone at the top of the monument is visible from the ferry when in mid-stream

Ballantrae, Ayr. The ruined stronghold of Ardstinchar, once held by the Bargany Kennedys. Robert Louis Stevenson came here in 1876, but the scene of his '*Master of Ballantrae*' is not laid here

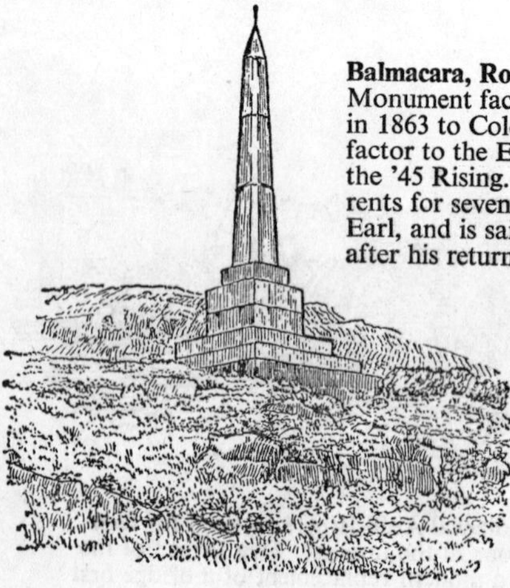

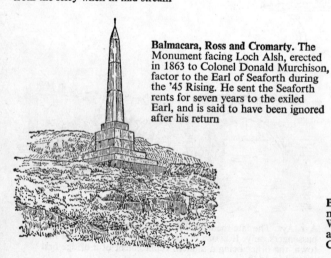

Balmacara, Ross and Cromarty. The Monument facing Loch Alsh, erected in 1863 to Colonel Donald Murchison, factor to the Earl of Seaforth during the '45 Rising. He sent the Seaforth rents for seven years to the exiled Earl, and is said to have been ignored after his return

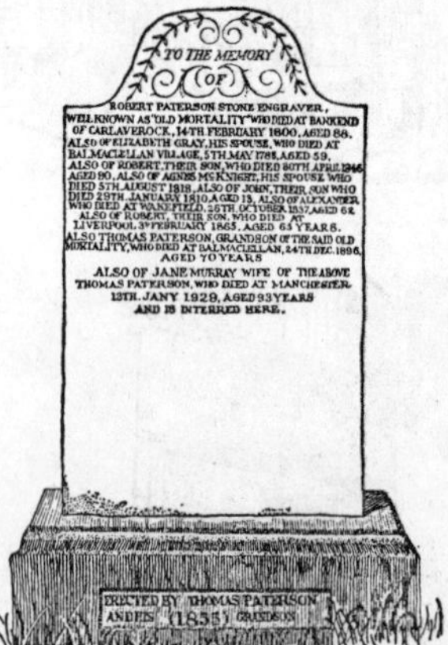

Balmaclellan, Kirkcudbright. The churchyard monument to Robert Paterson, famous as Sir Walter Scott's 'Old Mortality.' His wife kept a school here for 20 years, while he repaired Covenanters' tombstones all over Scotland

[For BALLATER see Plate 172

BADENOCH, Inverness. Map 19, **NN 5 8** etc. This mountainous district in the *Grampians* (*q.v.*) stretches roughly from the neighbourhood of *Loch Laggan* (*q.v.*) and the lonely head-waters of the Upper Spey valley to the lofty *Cairngorms* (*q.v.*). A good centre for its exploration is *Kingussie* (*q.v.*), where the ruins of *Ruthven Barracks* are associated with the notorious Wolf of Badenoch, whose former stronghold stood on the site. Prior to that, Badenoch was Comyn country, passing, after their annihilation, to the Earls of Moray. At the western extremity of Loch Laggan is Glen Spean, where Badenoch meets the district of *Lochaber* (*q.v.*). See **Lochindorb.**

BAILLIESTON, Lanark. 6,380. Map 8, **NS 6 6.** A town engaged in the coal and iron industry. *Iter. 16.*

BALBEGGIE, Perth. Map 17, **NO 1 2.** To the north-east rise the *Sidlaw* hills, with the prominent *Dunsinane Hill*, 1,012 ft., on the summit of which is an ancient fort, said to have been Macbeth's castle. *Iter. 151, 153.*

BALERNO, Midlothian. 1,726. Map 9, **NT 1 6.** *Malleny House* (N.T. Scot.), early 17th cent., has a fine old doocot. See **Currie.**

BALFRON, Stirling. 1,393. Map 15, **NS 5 8.** An attractively situated village near the Endrick Water, with the *Campsies* and the *Fintry* hills rising away to the south and east. See **Killearn.** *Iter. 108.*

BALINTORE, Ross and Cromarty. 349. Map 31, **NH 8 7.** A fishing village on the Moray Firth, once known as *Abbotshaven.* A little to the north is *Hilton of Cadboll*, where a sculptured 7th cent. stone was found, and is now in the Edinburgh Museum of National Antiquities. See **Shandwick** (for beach).

BALLACHULISH, Argyll. 1,254. Map 18, **NN 0 5.** **E.C.** Wed. A straggling village, situated about a mile east of the busy car ferry over Loch Leven to *North Ballachulish* (*q.v.*). Roofing slates are quarried in the neighbourhood. Behind the village rises *Ben Vair*, with its two 3,000-ft. peaks, and away to the north, beyond the loch, are the mountains of *Mamore Forest* (*q.v.*). Near the ferry is the monument marking the spot where James of the Glen was hanged, in 1752, after the famous *Appin* (*q.v.*) murder trial at *Inveraray* (*q.v.*). The identity of the real murderer has never been solved, and R. L. Stevenson has graphically portrayed the events in his novel "Kidnapped." The views from here across Loch Linnhe towards the Ardgour Hills, dominated by *Garbh Bheinn*, 2,903 ft. (See **Inversanda**) are exceptionally fine, and gorgeous sunsets are a feature at times. Equally fine are the views looking up Loch Leven towards the entrance to the famous pass of *Glencoe* (*q.v.*), dominated from this end by the conical *Pap of Glencoe*, 2,430 ft. The ferry avoids the long detour around Loch Leven for motorists proceeding from Glencoe towards *Fort William* (*q.v.*). South-westwards from Ballachulish, the road to *Oban* (*q.v.*) through the *Appin* (*q.v.*) country traverses the shores of Outer Loch Linnhe amid delightful scenery below the massif of *Ben Vair*, with its peaks of *Sgurr Dhearg*, 3,362 ft., and *Sgurr Dhonuill*, 3,284 ft., both fine viewpoints. See **Ardgour, Duror** and **Kentallen.** *Iter. 124, 142.*

BALLANTRAE, Ayr. 1,566 with Colmonell. Map 2, **NX 0 8.** A pleasant little holiday resort in the *Carrick* (*q.v.*) district, on Ballantrae Bay, north of the estuary of the River Stinchar, with a sand and shingle beach. The view out to sea is dominated by the 1,114-ft. high rock of *Ailsa Craig.* Near the bridge over the Stinchar is the ruined *Ardstinchar Castle*, an ancient Kennedy stronghold, and up the delightful river valley are two further Kennedy castles, those of *Knockdolian* and *Kirkhill.* South of Ballantrae, on the road to *Stranraer* (*q.v.*), is the beautifully wooded Glen App, in which stands a small mid-19th cent. Church, restored in the present century in memory of the Hon. Elsie Mackay, lost when flying the Atlantic in 1928. To the north, on the *Girvan* (*q.v.*) road, is *Kennedy's Pass*, the highlight of one of the finest coastal drives in southern Scotland. R. L. Stevenson used the name of Ballantrae for his well-known novel "The Master of Ballantrae." See **Colmonell.** *Iter. 55, 80, 84.*

BALLATER, Aberdeen. 1,663. SB. Map 20, **NO 3 9.** **E.C.** Thurs. GOLF. A well-known holiday resort on Royal *Deeside* (*q.v.*), at a height of nearly 700 ft., surrounded by wooded hills (Alltcailleach Forest), and dominated by *Lochnagar*, 3,786 ft. (*q.v.*), rising far to the south-west. *Craig-an-Darroch*, 1,250 ft., is a good viewpoint, below which the pretty pass of Ballater is threaded by the old Deeside road, on which stands the ruined Kirk of *St. Nathalan of Tullich*, preserving some sculptured Celtic stones. South-west of the town is the long valley of Glen Muick, with picturesque Loch Muick, dominated by the *Broad Cairn*, 3,268 ft., and beloved of Queen Victoria. It gives access for long-distance walkers to the *White Mounth* plateau and *Lochnagar*, and by the long Capel Mounth track to *Braedownie* (*q.v.*), at the head of Glen Clova. In Glen Muick is *Birkhall*, dating from 1715, a Royal home, bought by King Edward VII when Prince of Wales. A motoring road extends for some 9 miles down the glen, but the loch is accessible only on foot. Eastwards of Glen Muick lies the Forest of Glen Tanner, with *Mount Keen*, 3,077 ft. The narrow road linking the Dee valley with the upper valley of the Don, to the north, goes through the hills by way of *Gairnshiel Bridge* (*q.v.*), the lofty section beyond being liable to become snow-bound in winter. **1½ m. N.E.** of Ballater, on the main Aboyne road, is Bridge of Tullich, a noted viewpoint, from which Lochnagar is prominent. See **Balmoral, Cambus o' May, Crathie** and **Pannanich Wells.** *Iter. 141, 152, 167, 168, 174, 179.*

BALLINDALLOCH CASTLE, Banff. Map 26, **NJ 1 3.** See **Delnashaugh Inn.**

BALLINGRY, Fife. Map 17, **NT 1 9.** Lies below *Benarty Hill*, its partly ancient Church preserving a bell inscribed "Malcolme of Lochore, 1658." Scotland's first pre-fabricated school (1950) stands here. There are coal mines in the vicinity.

BALLINLUIG, Perth. Map 20, **NN 9 5.** *Iter. 120, 139, 140, 148, 150, 158.*

BALLOCH, Dunbarton. 1,719. Map 15, **NS 3 8.** **E.C.** Wed. Here is the pier from which steamers start on their journey up picturesque *Loch Lomond* (*q.v.*). The town stands actually on the River Leven, which flows southwards from the loch into the Clyde. In the park is the mound of the vanished Castle associated with both Wallace and Bruce. To the north of Balloch, on the eastern shores of Loch Lomond, are the modern houses of *Balloch Castle* and, farther north, *Boturich Castle.* *Iter. 114, 137.*

BALMACARA, Ross and Cromarty. 50. Map 23, **NG 8 2.** **E.C.** Thurs. The 8,000-acre *Balmacara* estate, extending over most of the peninsula which includes *Kyle of Lochalsh* (*q.v.*) and *Plockton* (*q.v.*), incorporates *Balmacara House*, now a school, and belongs to the N.T. Scot. There are fine views over Loch Alsh and Kyle Rhea, beyond which lies the island of Skye, in which *Beinn na Caillich*, 2,396 ft., faces Balmacara across the waters of *Loch Alsh* (*q.v.*). See **Auchtertyre.** *Iter. 207, 220, 221, 222.*

BALMACLELLAN, Kirkcudbright. 487. Map 3, **NX 6 7.** A delightful hillside village in *Galloway* (*q.v.*), in the churchyard of which is a monument to Robert Paterson, Scott's "Old Mortality." There is also a Covenanter's tombstone with an inscription. Another tombstone shows weapons used in the Crimean War. Celtic relics have been excavated in the vicinity and are preserved in one of the Edinburgh museums. See **Caerlaverock.** *Iter. 71, 75.*

BALMAGHIE, Kirkcudbright. 659. Map 3, **NX 7 6.** See **Laurieston.**

BALMAHA, Stirling. Map 15, **NS 4 9.** A calling-place for the *Loch Lomond* (*q.v.*) steamers. A picturesque group of wooded islands lies in the loch at this point. The road along the loch-side continues north-westwards through the Pass of Balmaha towards *Rowardennan* (*q.v.*). *Iter. 104, 115.*

BALMANNO, Perth. Map 17, **NO 1 1.**
See Bridge of Earn.

BALMERINO ABBEY, Fife. 533. Map 17, **NO 3 2.**
This ruined Cistercian Abbey (N.T. Scot.), founded in 1229, stands in a delightful setting on the south shore of the Firth of Tay. The beautiful Chapter House dates from the 15th cent. Monks from Melrose built the Abbey, which was burnt in 1547 and sacked in 1559. (Not open.) *Naughton House* has a fine old doocot. Each one of a block of modern houses facing the Firth carries an inscription giving the last words addressed to his troops by Lt.-Col. David Scrymgeour-Wedderburn before the Anzio battle in the Second World War. *Iter. 126.*

BALMORAL CASTLE, Aberdeen. Map 20, **NO 2 9.**
The Highland residence of Her Majesty, the Queen, situated on a curve of the river in Royal *Deeside* (*q.v.*), in the district of Mar, and faced by the wooded *Craig Gowan*, 1,319 ft., a viewpoint crowned by a cairn. Balmoral Castle was first mentioned in 1484, and was at that time known as *Bouchmorale*. In 1848 it was first visited by Queen Victoria, and in 1852 the estate was purchased by the Prince Consort, who had it rebuilt in the present " Scottish Baronial " style, the new structure being first occupied by the Royal Family in 1855. Later, Queen Victoria added the Ballochbuie Forest to the property, and it has ever since remained a Royal residence. The grounds are generally open to the public from 10 to 5, daily, except Sun., from May to end of July, in the absence of the Royal Family (see note page 98). This is Clan Farquharson country, and a mile west of Balmoral is a mound known as Carn na Cuimhne, associated with the clan. To the south of the Castle is Glen Gelder, leading to Balmoral Forest and the lofty *White Mounth* (*q.v.*) group, and it was by this route that Queen Victoria and the Prince Consort climbed *Lochnagar* (*q.v.*) on ponies, in 1848. To the north-west of Balmoral, beyond Invercauld Forest, rises *Ben Avon*, 3,843 ft., one of the loftiest of the *Cairngorm* (*q.v.*) peaks. See **Ballater, Braemar** and **Crathie.** *Iter. 152, 160, 167, 168, 179.*

BALNAGOWN CASTLE, Ross and Cromarty.
See **Logie Easter.** Map 31, **NH 7 7.**

BALQUHIDDER, Perth. 671. Map 15, **NN 5 2.**
E.C. Wed. Beautifully situated to the east of Loch Voil, about **2 m. W.** of Balquhidder station on the Callander to Lochearnhead road, in the country of the MacGregors, and upon which looks down the lofty ridge known as the *Braes of Balquhidder*. In the churchyard of the roofless old Kirk is buried Rob Roy, the famous freebooter and hero of Scott's well-known novel of that name. Three sculptured stones mark the grave of Rob Roy and some of his family, and one stone is carved with the MacGregor arms. Another stone commemorates members of the Clan Laurin, murdered in 1588 by incendiarists from Glen Dochart. The Church contains an ancient font and a sculptured stone associated with St. Angus. *Edinchip*, the present seat of the MacGregors, lies **3 m. E.**, near Loch Earn and Glen Kendrum. South of Balquhidder, the short Glen Buckie penetrates into the green hills. **7 m. W.**, beyond Loch Voil and its continuation Loch Doine, reached by a rough and narrow by-way, is *Inverlochlaraig*, where Rob Roy died in 1734. *Stobinian*, 3,821 ft., and *Beinn Tulachan*, 3,099 ft., overlook this lonely place. *Iter. 107, 111, 139, 141, 142, 144.*

BALVENIE CASTLE, Banff. Map 26, **NJ 3 3.**
See **Dufftown.**

BANAVIE, Inverness. Map 18, **NN 7 7.**
Stands on the road from *Corpach* (*q.v.*) to *Gairlochy* (*q.v.*), and provides a splendid view of *Ben Nevis*, 4,406 ft. (*q.v.*). **2 m. N.E.**, on the west bank of the River Lochy, is *Tor Castle*, near which stands a ruined tower of the Clan Chattan. Two miles farther, in the same direction, to the west of the road, is the entrance to the roadless Glen Loy, down which Prince Charles Edward marched in 1745. *Iter. 209, 214, 215.*

BANCHORY, Kincardine. 2,353. SB. Map 21, **NO 6 9.**
E.C. Thurs. **M.D.** Alt. Wed. **GOLF.** A pleasant holiday resort on Royal *Deeside* (*q.v.*), near the point where the Water of Feugh, here spanned by the narrow Bridge of Feugh, carrying the date 1799, but probably earlier, and lying in a picturesque Blackhall Forest setting, joins the Dee. Away to the north rises the *Hill of Fare*, 1,545 ft., on the slopes of which a battle was fought in 1562. From Banchory a road leads southwards, following the Water of Feugh through Glen Dye towards the *Cairn o' Mounth Pass* (*q.v.*). The road leading south-eastwards to Stonehaven, which rises to nearly 800 ft., with fine views, is known, when crossing the hills, as the *Slug Road.* To the south of this road, and about **4 m.** from Banchory, lies the 16th cent. *Tilquhillie Castle*, now a farmhouse. **8 m. E.** is the 17th cent. and later Durris House. See **Crathes Castle.** *Iter. 152, 163, 168, 190, 191, 197.*

BANCHORY DEVENICK, Kincardine. 1,263.
Map 21. **NJ 9 0.**
Findon corn-mill is late 18th cent. *Iter. 168, 174.*

BANFF, Banff. 3,723. SB. Map 27, **NJ 6 6.**
E.C. Wed. **GOLF.** An ancient seaport, Royal Burgh and resort, with sands and bathing, on Banff Bay at the mouth of the River Deveron. On the opposite shore of the river stands *Macduff* (*q.v.*). Banff has fragmentary remains of the former Castle. The later Castle was built in

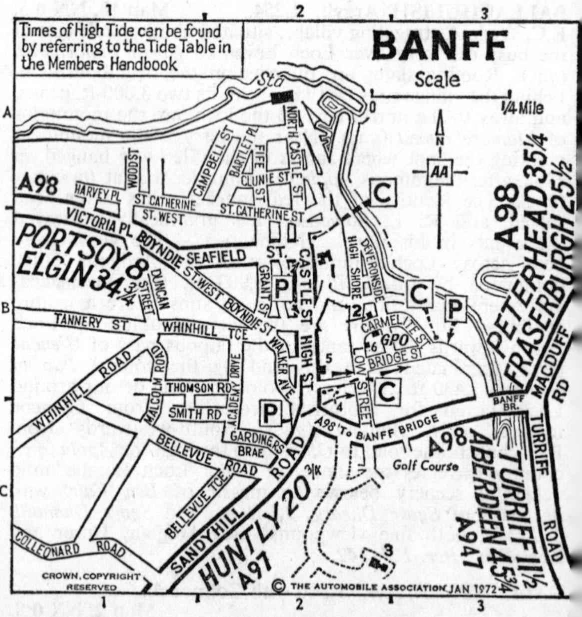

Castle remains	1 (B2)	Information Bureau	4 (B2)
Church remains and old churchyard	2 (B2)	Library and Museum	5 (B2)
Duff House	3 (C2)	Town House, the Biggar Fountain and Old Cross	6 (B2)

1750. *Duff House* (A.M.), William Adam's masterpiece, dating from c. 1735, has fine grounds, which are now a public park belonging to the town. The shaft of an old Cross stands at the Planestanes. The Town House dates from 1796, with an earlier tower. There are some remains of the old Church, and a few 17th cent. houses have survived. On the site of the former gallows is the *Biggar* fountain. Southey, Byron and Doctor Johnson all have associations with the

Balmerino Abbey, Fife. The inscribed portico in a block of houses built by Mr. Henry J. Scrymgeour-Wedderburn, Hereditary Standard Bearer of Scotland. They are in memory of his brother, a colonel of the Scots Guards, who died of wounds at Anzio, in Italy, in 1944

Balquhidder, Perth. The grave of Rob Roy, the famous freebooter, who died on December 28th, 1734

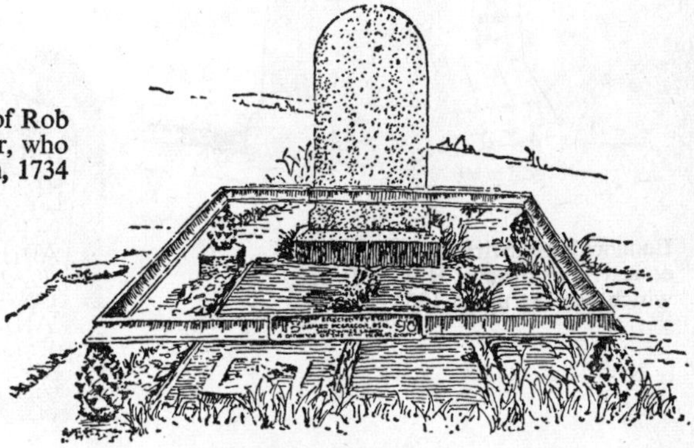

Banchory, Kincardine. A memorial fountain, dated 1870, on A93

Balvenie Castle, Banff. The ruined 15th century Atholl castle of Balvenie, which retains its original 'yett,' or iron gate. Earlier owners were the Comyns, followed by the Douglases. It stands near Dufftown station, off A941

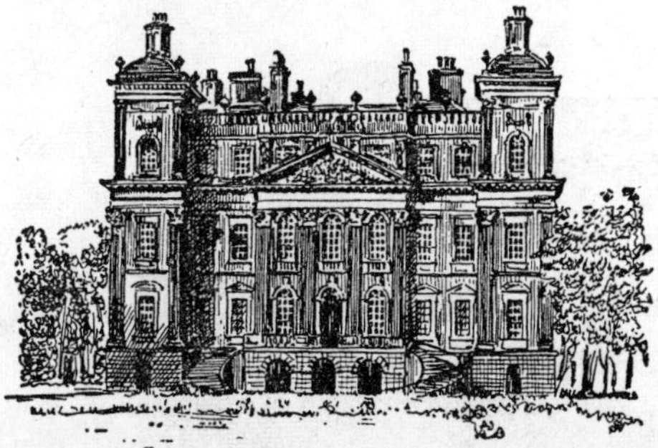

Banff, Banff. Duff House, built c. 1735, and considered to be William Adam's masterpiece. It was donated to the town by the Duke of Fife

Banff, Banff. The Biggar Fountain, on the site of the former gallows, where, in 1701, James Macpherson, the outlaw and fiddler, offered his instrument to the crowd before going to his death

Bannockburn, Stirling. The equestrian statue of Robert Bruce, which was set up in 1964

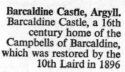

Barcaldine Castle, Argyll. Barcaldine Castle, a 16th century home of the Campbells of Barcaldine, which was restored by the 10th Laird in 1896

Bargrennan, Kirkcudbright; Wigtown. The Martyrs' Stone, at the south-west extremity of Loch Trool, in the large Glen Trool Forest Park. It lies about 4 miles north-east of Bargrennan, off an unclassified road

Barnton (Edinburgh), Midlothian. Lauriston Castle, mainly modern, but incorporating 16th century work by Sir Archibald Napier, father of the inventor of logarithms. It was once the home of Sir John Law, who sponsored the disastrous 'Mississippi Scheme' of 1720

Bass Rock, East Lothian. The Bass Rock, which stands out to sea some 3 miles north-east of North Berwick. It was used as a Covenanters' prison after 1671

town. **2½ m. W.N.W.**, on a rocky piece of coast, is the village of *Whitehills* (*q.v.*), sheltered by Knock Head. **3 m. S.**, off the Huntly road, is *Kirktown of Alvah* (*q.v.*). See **Boyndie Bay.** *Iter. 170, 180, 181, 182, 183, 188, 194, 198, 199.*

BANKFOOT, Perth. 726. Map 16, **NO 0 3.**
E.C. Thurs. A *Strathmore* (*q.v.*) village, on the Garry Burn, with the level Cornleith Moss and beyond it the Muir of Thorn, both lying to the north-east. *Iter. 149, 150.*

BANNOCKBURN, Stirling. 3,090. Map 16, **NS 8 9.**
E.C. Wed. A coal-mining village, on the Bannock Burn, a mile to the north of which, and nearer to *St. Ninian's* (*q.v.*), is the famous battlefield where Bruce defeated the English under Edward II in 1314. The *Borestone* (N.T. Scot.), nearby, is, by tradition, where Bruce displayed the Scottish Royal Standard. As an immediate result of the battle, Stirling surrendered, Edward II fled to Dunbar, and Scotland achieved her independence. Scott's " Lord of the Isles " describes the conflict between Bruce and De Bohun. An open-air rotunda together with an equestrian statue of Bruce has now been set up. In the vicinity was fought also the battle of Sauchieburn, in 1488, when James III was defeated and afterwards fatally stabbed. Prince Charles Edward made *Bannockburn House*, to the south, his headquarters in January, 1746. The house displays fine carvings. The Royal George Mill is early 19th cent. *Iter. 95.*

BARASSIE, Ayr. Map 8, **NS 3 3.**
GOLF. See **Troon.** *Iter. 88.*

BARCALDINE CASTLE, Argyll. Map 14, **NM 9 4.**
This old castle is situated on a level piece of land which juts out from the main *Benderloch* (*q.v.*) district, and is bounded on three sides by Ardmucknish Bay, the Lynn of Lorne and Loch Creran. The castle is a typical example of the 16th cent. Scottish baronial style (1579) and has been restored. A by-road leads to the castle, diverging from the main Oban to Ballachulish road at Benderloch station, and terminating on the shores of Loch Creran opposite the small island of Eriska.

BARGRENNAN, Kirkcudbright; Wigtown. 280.
Map 2, **NX 3 7.**
From *Bargrennan* Church, near the River Cree, a road turns north-eastwards, leading shortly to *Loch Trool* (*q.v.*) in lovely Glen Trool with the extensive Forest Park one of the most beautiful pieces of country in *Galloway* (*q.v.*). Beyond rises the *Merrick*, 2,764 ft., the loftiest mountain in the Lowlands, and farther east is *Corserine*, 2,668 ft., the monarch of the *Rhinns of Kells*. Westwards from Bargrennan are three small lochs, those of Ochiltree, Dornal and Maberry. **10½ m. N.**, on the narrow and winding moorland road leading towards Maybole, is the lonely Nick o' the Balloch Pass, 1,280 ft., in a fine, hilly setting, looking eastwards to *Shalloch on Minnoch*, 2,520 ft., beyond which lies the remote Loch Macaterick. Before the pass is reached, the road crosses into Ayrshire, with Loch Moan to the west, and *Kirriereoch Hill*, 2,562 ft., away to the east, facing *Mullwharchar*, 2,270 ft. See **Rowantree.** *Iter. 71, 79.*

BARNTON (Edinburgh), Midlothian. Map 9, **NT 1 7.**
A little to the north-east stands *Lauriston Castle*, late 16th cent., attached to a modern house, now public property, and once the home of John Law, author of the disastrous early 18th cent. Mississippi scheme. Open in summer, daily, except Fri., 11 to 1 and 2 to 5; winter, Sat. and Sun. only, 2 to 5 (see note page 98). See **Cramond Bridge.** *Iter. 17, 89, 90, 92, 93, 94, 96.*

BARR, Ayr. 1,186 with Barrhill. Map 2, **NX 2 9.**
A little anglers' resort of the *Carrick* (*q.v.*) district, in the valley of the Upper Stinchar River looking south-eastwards to *Polmadie Hill*, 1,852 ft. **6 m. E.S.E.**, on a narrow, winding moorland road leading from Maybole in a southerly direction towards *Bargrennan* (*q.v.*), is the Nick o' the Balloch Pass, at a height of 1,280 ft., with views towards *Shalloch on Minnoch*, 2,520 ft., and the *Merrick*, 2,764 ft., the monarch of the *Galloway* (*q.v.*) Highlands. South of Barr is Changue Forest, and farther to the east is Carrick Forest, both being part of the fine Glen Trool Forest Park. See **Loch Trool.** *Iter. 78, 84.*

BARRA CASTLE, Aberdeen. Map 27, **NJ 7 2.**
See **Old Meldrum.**

BARRA, ISLE OF, Inverness. Map 32, **NF 6 0** etc.
See **Hebrides, Outer** (Barra).

BARRHEAD, Renfrew. 18,281. **SB.** Map 8, **NS 4 5.**
E.C. Tues. GOLF. A manufacturing town, with bleach-works and remains of old textile mills. *Cross Arthurlic* mill (18th cent.) of three storeys, is well preserved. It stands on

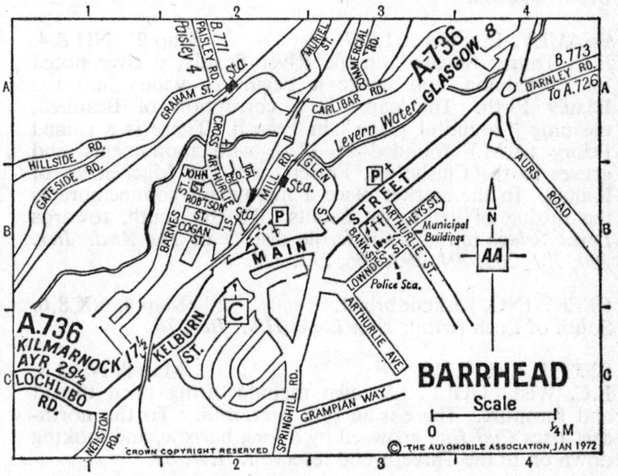

the Levern Water, with an extensive and lofty moorland area lying to the south, in which a number of reservoirs are situated. John Davidson, the poet, was born here in 1857. See **Clarkston** and **Neilston.** *Iter. 57, 60, 62.*

BARRHILL, Ayr. 1,186 with Barr. Map 2, **NX 2 8.**
E.C. Tues. Situated in the Duisk valley, with moorland country to the west and east. The road leading southwards towards *New Luce* (*q.v.*), in Wigtownshire, traverses lonely moorlands threaded by the Cross Water of Luce. This road is gated, narrow and hilly. See **Bargrennann.** *Iter. 71, 78.*

BARROGILL CASTLE, Caithness. Map 30, **ND 2 7.**
See **East Mey.**

BARRY, Angus. 1,600 with Penbride. Map 17, **NO 5 3.**
GOLF. See **Carnoustie.** *Iter. 155.*

BARVAS, Isle of Lewis, Ross and Cromarty.
Iter. 260. Map 32, **NB 3 4.**

BASS ROCK, East Lothian. Map 10, **NT 6 8.**
See **North Berwick.** *Iter. 2, 38.*

BATHGATE, West Lothian. 1,4233. **SB.** Map 9, **NS 9 6.**
E.C. Wed. **M.D.** Mon. GOLF. There are iron and steel foundries. The town is also engaged in the shale oil industry. A silver mine was formerly worked in the neighbourhood. Sir James Simpson, who introduced chloroform into midwifery, was born at Bathgate in 1811. To the north are situated the *Bathgate* hills, with *The Knock* attaining 1,017 ft. See **Torphichen.** *Iter. 16.*

BEARSDEN, Dunbarton. 25,017. **SB.** Map 8, **NS 5 7.**
GOLF. On the Antonine, or *Roman Wall* (*q.v.*), some of the best preserved portions of which are to be found to the north-west and north-east of the town, which is also known as *New Kilpatrick*. *Iter. 104, 106, 113.*

BEATTOCK, Dumfries. Map 9, **NT 0 0.**
On the Evan Water, in Upper Annandale, in a hilly setting. Above the station there are four prehistoric forts, notably

one on Beattock Hill. **1 m. N.N.W.** is *Auchen Castle*, late 13th cent., and farther north, in the Evan valley, leading to Beattock summit, 1,025 ft., which is situated some 10 miles from the village, are the ruined towers of *Blacklaw*, *Mellingshaw* and *Raecleuch*. **4 m. S.** of Beattock is *Lochwood Tower*, 15th cent., in a wooded setting, once a Johnstone seat. See **Beattock Summit** and **Moffat.** *Iter. 10, 13, 24, 29, 46, 50, 51.*

BEATTOCK SUMMIT, Lanark. Map 9, **NS 9 1.**
The highest point (1,029 ft.) on the road from Beattock to the Clyde valley at Elvanfoot. It is situated some 10 miles north-west of Beattock. See **Beattock.** *Iter. 29, 49, 50, 51.*

BEAUFORT CASTLE, Inverness. Map 25, **NH 5 4.**
See **Kilmorack.**

BEAULY, Inverness. 1,387. Map 25, **NH 5 4.**
E.C. Thurs. Situated on the River Beauly, a river noted for its salmon, and where it begins to widen into the Beauly Firth. The name is a corruption of Beaulieu, meaning "beautiful place" in French. There is a ruined Priory (A.M.), founded in 1230, with monuments and graves to the Chisholms, Frasers, and the Mackenzies of Kintail. In the market place a monument commemorates the raising of the Lovat Scouts. To the south, towards *Lovat Bridge* (*q.v.*), is the fertile district of *The Aird. Iter. 200, 201, 203, 204, 205, 206, 213, 221.*

BEESWING, Kirkcudbright. Map 4, **NX 8 6.**
South of Loch Arthur rises *Lotus Hill. Iter. 76.*

BEITH, Ayr. 6,712. Map 8, **NS 3 5.**
E.C. Wed. GOLF. A town manufacturing linen thread and furniture. There is an 18th cent. mill. To the north-east rises *Cuff Hill*, crowned by a long barrow, and looking down on to the Threepwood reservoir. *Iter. 63.*

BELLSHILL, Lanark. 17,844. Map 9, **NS 7 6.**
E.C. Wed. GOLF. A mining town, situated to the north-east of the Clyde valley. *Iter. 18, 54.*

BEMERSYDE, Berwick. Map 10, **NT 5 3.**
Bemersyde House is famous as the hereditary home of the Haigs, and was presented by the nation in 1921 to Field-Marshal Earl Haig, who lies buried in *Dryburgh Abbey* (*q.v.*). It incorporates an ancient, but restored tower which was burnt in a raid in 1545. Sir Walter Scott was a frequent visitor to the house, and delighted in the splendid viewpoint of *Bemersyde Hill* (AA viewpoint), with its panorama of the winding Tweed, backed by the triple-peaked *Eildon* hills to the west. See **Scott's View** and **Smailholm.** *Iter. 13, 43.*

BENBECULA, ISLE OF, Inverness. Map 32, **NF 7 5.**
See **Hebrides, Outer** (Benbecula). *Iter. 262.*

BENDERLOCH, Argyll. Map 14, **NM 9 3** etc.
Near *Benderloch* station, on the shores of Ardmucknish Bay, rises a low twin-peaked hill, crowned by a vitrified fort, and forming a good viewpoint. The name *Beregonium*, by which it is sometimes known, would appear to have been given to it in error. The hilly district lying between Loch Etive and Loch Creran, dominated by *Beinn Sguliaird*, 3,059 ft., is generally known as Benderloch, which is really a part of the much larger district of *Lorne* (*q.v.*). A by-road leads north-westwards from Benderloch station to *Barcaldine Castle* (*q.v.*). *Iter. 124.*

BEN EIGHE NATIONAL NATURE RESERVE, Ross and Cromarty. See **Kinlochewe.** Map 24, **NG 9 6.**

BEN MACDHUI, Aberdeen; Banff. Map 20, **NN 9 9.**
See **Cairngorms.**

BENMORE ESTATE, Argyll. Map 14, **NS 1 8.**
This estate forms part of the extensive Argyll Forest Park, and *Benmore House* is now the Forester Training School. The *Younger Botanic Garden* (A.M.) is open daily, 10 to 6, April to September. (See note page 98.) The sector of the Park to the north includes the forests of *Glenbranter* and *Glenfinart*. There is magnificent mountain and loch scenery in this *Cowal* (*q.v.*) district, notably around *Loch Eck* (*q.v.*) and Loch Long. Glen Masson, to the north-west of the Holy Loch, and the picturesque little *Puck's Glen*, just beyond the head of the loch, are of special note, the latter incorporating a fine viewpoint. The highest peak in the district is *Beinn Mhor*, 2,433 ft., west of Loch Eck. See **Arrochar.** *Iter. 137.*

BEN NEVIS, Inverness. Map 18, **NN 1 7.**
The highest mountain in Great Britain, a conglomerate of granite, schists and lavas, rising to a height of 4,406 ft., and dominating *Fort William* (*q.v.*) and the district of *Lochaber* (*q.v.*), at the south-west extremity of the Great Glen, or *Glen More* (*q.v.*). Around its western and southern flanks extends *Glen Nevis*, one of the loveliest of Scottish glens, with the finely-wooded gorge of the River Nevis near its farther end. A narrow, switchback road traverses the glen for much of its length, keeping to the west side of the river, and passing near *Glen Nevis House*, the headquarters of Lochiel when besieging Fort William in 1746. *Dun Deardurl*, a hill on the west side of the road, has remains of a vitrified fort, and within a few miles the road reaches the Polldubh waterfall. After this point the road turns east and deteriorates, and at its termination the slopes of the Ben tower 4,000 ft. above at an angle of 35 degrees. The Allt Coire Eaghainn water falls a great height from a hidden corrie. At the end of the glen, reached on foot only, is seen the lofty Steall waterfall, in its wild setting below *An Gearanach*, among the peaks of the *Mamores*, at the commencement of the long and lonely track leading towards Loch Treig. (See **Tulloch** and **Rannoch Moor.**)

Although the Ben is often considered to be unshapely, the stupendous range of cliffs, about two miles in length, which fall away on its northern flanks, can only be seen properly from the remote Mhuilinn Glen leading to Coire Leis, at its foot, or from the upper slopes of *Carn Mor Dearg*, 4,012 ft., linked to the Ben by a spectacular, narrow arête overlooking upper Glen Nevis. Snow lingers generally until late in the summer, or even all the year round, in the remote corries of these great cliffs. On the summit of Ben Nevis, an exposed wilderness of massive boulders, stood formerly an observatory, first erected in 1883, but this is now in ruins, having been closed down in 1904, while a hotel, or hostel, which also once stood here was shut in 1915. A mountain indicator gives particulars of the wide view which can be enjoyed in clear weather, ranging over the whole country from the Cairngorms to the Hebrides, as well as taking in occasionally the far distant Irish coast. The fine *Mamore Forest* (*q.v.*) group, seen almost in its entirety, forms a prominent feature in the aspect across Glen Nevis to the south, with the white quartzite peak of *Sgurr a' Mhaim*, 3,601 ft., dominating the lesser heights. The upper reaches of the glen are dominated by *Aonach Beag*, 4,060 ft., and *Aonach Mor*, 3,999 ft., which form a ridge over 3 miles in length.

The ascent of Ben Nevis is usually made along a well-defined, but rough and stony path commencing at *Achintee* farm in Glen Nevis, this being reached by road from Fort William by crossing the River Nevis a little to the north-east of the town, and then keeping to the east bank of the river. Halfway up the mountain is the little Lochan Meall-an-t-Suidhe, near which a descent can be made over moorland into the Mhuilinn Glen, in order to see the precipices on the north side rising above Coire Leis. When the observatory was in operation, supplies were taken up the track, up which in 1911 a car was driven to the mountain top. In the course of time the track has gradually degenerated into the present narrow foot-track. Nevertheless, in 1961 and later, cars have again reached the summit. A 15-mile long pipeline for the Lochaber Power Scheme has been driven through the Ben from Loch Treig, near *Tulloch* (*q.v.*), in order to feed the power house on the outskirts of Fort William. East of the Ben, beyond *Carn Mor Dearg* and the *Aonach* peaks, are the seldom visited *Grey Corries*, 3,858 ft.

Beauly, Inverness. The remains of the Priory, founded by Sir John Bisset of Lovat in 1230. Abbot Reid erected the façade after 1530. The restored north transept is the burial place of the Mackenzies of Kintail

Bemersyde, Berwick. Bemersyde House, the home of the Haigs, presented to Field-Marshal Earl Haig by the nation in 1921. An old prophecy by Thomas the Rhymer says:

'Tide, 'tide, what'er betide,
There'll aye be Haigs of Bemersyde.

Ben Eighe National Nature Reserve, Ross and Cromarty. The northern spurs of Ben Eighe, seen from Grudie Bridge, on A832, near Loch Maree. On its slopes is situated Britain's first National Nature Reserve

Benmore Estate, Argyll. Newly-afforested hill slopes overlooking Loch Eck, between Loch Fyne and Loch Long, in the Argyll National Forest Park. A road follows the eastern shores of the loch for the whole of its length

Ben Nevis, Inverness. The highest mountain in Great Britain, 4,406 feet, as seen from Corpach across the head of Loch Linnhe. In the great northern corries of the Ben, snow lies sometimes all the year round

[For BENDERLOCH see Plate 175

Berriedale, Caithness. The smithy, decorated with stags' antlers, at the foot of Berriedale Hill

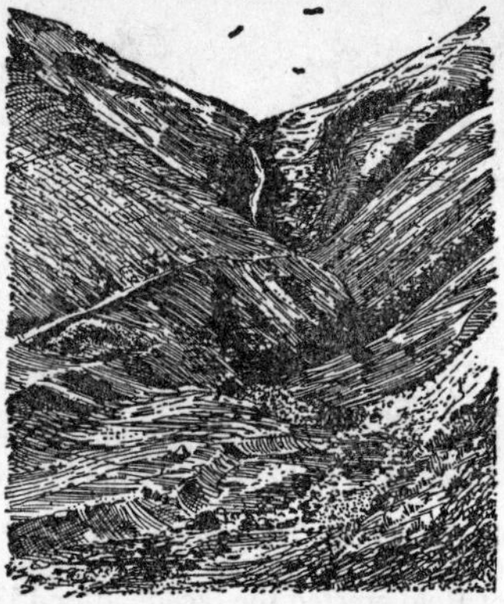

Birkhill, Dumfries. The 200-foot high waterfall known as the 'Grey Mare's Tail', which is situated a mile to the south-west, off A708

Berriedale, Caithness. Stones near the bridge over the Berriedale Water, marking the height of flood waters in 1896 and 1912

Bettyhill, Sutherland. A view of the estuary of the River Naver, where it flows into Torrisdale Bay, to the north-west of Bettyhill

Biggar, Lanark. The 'Cadger's Brig' in the main street

Binns, West Lothian. The 15th to 17th century house of The Binns (N.T. Scot.), where General Tam Dalyell raised the Royal Scots Greys in 1681. It stands off A904 between Blackness and Abercorn.

overlooking Glen Spean and *Roy Bridge* (*q.v.*) See **Corpach.** *Iter. 100, 124, 125, 142, 143, 208, 215.*

BENTPATH, Dumfries. Map 4, **NY 3 9.**
See **Westerkirk.**

BERNERAY, ISLE OF, Inverness. Map 32, **NL 5 7**
See **Hebrides, Outer** (Barra). and **5 8.**

BERRIEDALE, Caithness. 322. Map 31, **ND 1 2.**
The Berriedale Water flows here into the sea from its long valley, the last part of which is richly wooded. The stream is joined near its mouth by the Langwell Water, which rises on the distant slopes of the conical peak of *Morven*, 2,313 ft. Nearer to the village is the long ridge of *Scaraben*, 2,054 ft., overlooking the bare expanse of Langwell Forest. There are scanty remains of the 14th cent. *Berriedale Castle.* The Post Office is decorated with stags' antlers, as is also the old smithy. The main road to the south is steep and winding, skirting a number of deep ravines on its way to the Ord of Caithness. To the north, the coast is wild and rocky, and features in the novels of Neil Gunn. *Iter. 200, 236.*

BERVIE, Kincardine. 910. Map 21, **NO 8 7.**
See **Inverbervie.**

BERWICK-UPON-TWEED, Northumberland (England). 11,440. Map 11, **NT 9 5.**
E.C. Thurs. **M.D.** Sat. GOLF. The ancient border town of *Berwick-upon-Tweed* has a long history, and changed hands

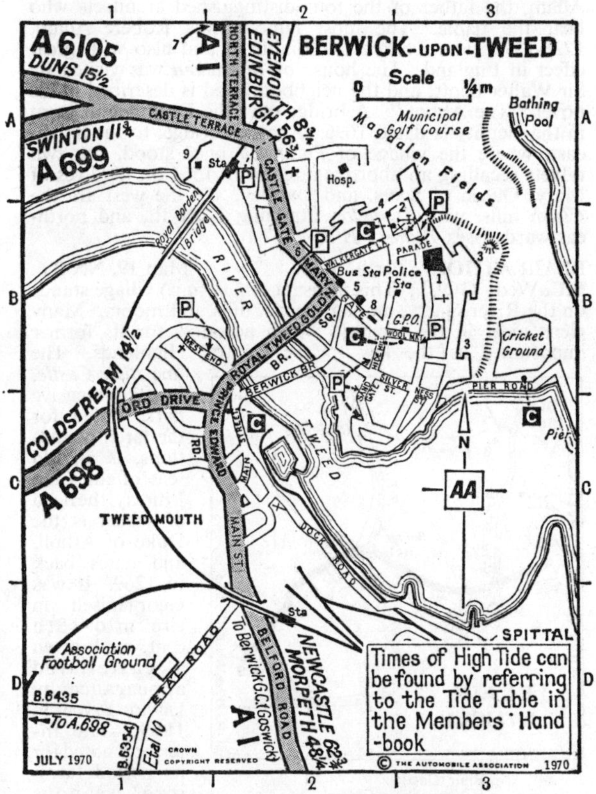

Barracks, designed by Vanbrugh	1 (B3)	Scotch Gate, rebuilt 1815	6 (B2)
Church, 17th cent.	2 (B3)	Tourist Information Centre	7 (A2)
Elizabethan Walls	3 (B3)	Town Hall, 18th cent.	8 (B2)
Municipal Buildings	4 (B2)	Town Walls and traces of Castle	9 (A2)
Museum and Art Gallery	5 (B2)		

on numerous occasions in medieval times, reverting finally to England in 1482, when it became a bastion against the Scots, with a government of its own. At one period it was an important Scottish port, and was frequently visited by the early kings of the country, who were given hospitality by the town's merchants. Berwick is today a fishing port and resort, with good sands, while both sea and river fishing are available, the Tweed being especially famous for its salmon. The river is one of the most important in Scotland, being nearly 100 miles long, and forming the boundary between the two countries for some 16 miles of its course. Three bridges span its waters at Berwick: the early 17th cent. fifteen-arched **Old Bridge**; the **Royal Tweed Bridge** of 1928 carrying the Great North Road; and the **Royal Border Bridge** (1850) of the railway. Of the town walls, there remain slight traces of those built in the 13th cent., together with larger stretches of those constructed in Elizabethan times, which are of much interest. Near the station are situated scanty remains of the former Norman Castle. The Parish Church is of the 17th cent., and the Town Hall carries the date 1754. The fine barracks (closed) are the work of the great architect Vanbrugh, and date from 1717 to 1721. There is still a regimental museum. A number of late Georgian houses stand in the town, some of the finest being found along the Quay Walls. **2 m. N.W.** of the town is *Halidon Hill*, the scene of a Scottish defeat by the English in 1333. See **Burnmouth, Ladykirk, Lamberton** and **Paxton.** *Iter. 1, 2, 3, 8, 9, 30, 33, 46, 47.*

BETTYHILL, Sutherland. 600. Map 30, **NC 7 6.**
E.C. Wed. Once known as *Bettyhill of Farr*, and founded originally as a fishing and agricultural centre. It is now a touring and fishing resort on Torrisdale Bay, with bathing from good, though exposed sands, and is noted for sea birds and alpine plants and the *Invernaver* National Nature Reserve. Beyond the bay, to the north-west, are the islands of Eilean Co'omb and the precipitous Roan Island. The River Naver flows here into the sea from *Strath Naver* (*q.v.*), in which many prehistoric remains, tumuli, hut circles and cairns are to be found. **4 m. S.**, on a by-road to the east of the River Naver, are some horned burial cairns near *Skelpick Lodge.* See **Farr** and **Syre.** *Iter. 232, 234, 240.*

BIGGAR, Lanark. 1,636. SB. Map 9, **NT 0 3.**
E.C. Wed. **M.D.** Thurs. GOLF. Lies in the broad vale of the Biggar Water, a tributary of the Tweed, but whose waters reach the Clyde, to the west, in times of flood. There are slight traces of the former *Boghall Castle*, south of the town. At the end of the wide main street is the restored bridge, or " Cadger's brig." The restored, cruciform Church was commenced in 1545, and has in its churchyard a tomb in which lie the ancestors of Gladstone. A bust in the School recalls the fact that Dr. John Brown, author of " Rab and his Friends," was born in the nearby manse in 1810. *Culter House*, 17th cent. has a mile-long avenue of trees. See **Symington** (Lanark). *Iter. 25, 35, 53.*

BINNS, THE, West Lothian. Map 9, **NT 0 7.**
See **Abercorn.** *Iter. 96.*

BIRGHAM, Berwick. Map 11, **NT 7 3.**
A Tweed-side village on the edge of the fertile plain of the *Merse* (*q.v.*). The Treaty of Birgham, signed in 1290, established the details of Scotland's independence. The fine gardens of *Springhill House* are of note. *Iter. 30, 32.*

BIRKHALL, Aberdeen. Map 20, **NO 3 9.**
See **Ballater.**

BIRKHILL, Dumfries. Map 9, **NT 1 1.**
Surrounded by green Lowland hills, *Birkhill*, which stands at the 1,105-ft. high summit of the Birkhill Pass, is overshadowed by *White Coomb*, 2,695 ft., and lies almost on the Selkirk border. In the near vicinity is Dob's Linn, formerly a refuge for the persecuted Covenanters. **1 m. S.W.** is the well-known 200 ft. high waterfall, known as the *Grey Mare's Tail* (N.T. Scot.), where the Tail Burn joins the Moffat Water, while beyond the junction, to the north, is the wild Loch Skene, in its lonely setting under *Lochcraig Head*, 2,625 ft. See **Moffat** and **St. Mary's Loch.** *Iter. 13, 46.*

BIRNAM, Perth. 629. Map 16, **NO 0 4.**
E.C. Thurs. The village lies in a delightful wooded setting

between *Birnam Hill*, 1,324 ft., and the River Tay, the narrow Birnam Pass being the traditional " Mouth of the Highlands," having been traversed by both Montrose and Prince Charles Edward. " Duncan's Castle," a hill fort on Birnam Hill, is associated with Shakespeare's King Duncan, and the " Birnam Oaks," actually an oak and a sycamore, standing on the south bank of the Tay behind Birnam Hotel, are thought to be the survivors of Shakespeare's " Great Birnam Wood." **4 m. S.E.** is *Murthly Castle*, in fine wooded grounds in a bend of the Tay, and beyond it is Caputh Bridge. See **Dunkeld.** *Iter. 149, 150.*

BIRNIE, Moray. Map 26, **NJ 2** 5.
The little Kirk, dating from the 12th cent., has chancel windows and a font of Norman date, and preserves a Celtic bell, known as the " Ronnel Bell." Other points of interest are an 18th cent. sundial and a Druid stone in the kirkyard. To the west flows the little River Lossie.

BIRSAY, Orkney. Map 33, **HY 2 2.**
See **Orkney Islands** (Mainland). *Iter. 263.*

BISHOPBRIGGS, Lanark. 20,428. SB. Map 8, **NS 6 7.**
GOLF. Lies on the northern outskirts of Glasgow, in the vicinity of the Forth and Clyde canal and the line of the *Roman Wall* (*q.v.*). *Iter. 98, 107.*

BISHOPTON, Renfrew. 1,620. Map 8, **NS 4 7.**
E.C. Wed. GOLF. On the Glasgow to Gourock road and to the north-west of which a view is opened up of *Dumbarton* (*q.v.*) Castle, backed by the distant peak of *Ben Lomond*, 3,192 ft., on the farther side of the Clyde estuary. *Bishopton House* was once the home of the Brisbanes. **1½ m. S.** is the 16th cent. and modernized *Dargavel House*, an old Maxwell possession, a gable carrying their arms, with the date 1584. **2 m. S.W.** is the modern mansion of *Formakin*, built by Sir Robert Lorimer. *Iter. 59, 65.*

BLACKBURN, Aberdeen. Map 27, **NJ 8 1.**
On Tyrebagger Hill, 823 ft., to the east, is *Kirkhill Forest. Iter. 175, 177, 178, 184.*

BLACKFORD, Perth. 1,426. Map 16, **NN 8 0.**
E.C. Wed. Situated on the Allan Water. In the vicinity, about **4 m. W. N.W.,** is the *Carsebreck* Curling pond, where the annual match between North and South Scotland formerly took place. **1 m. S.E.** of Blackford stand the remains of *Ogilvie Castle*, backed by the ridges of the *Ochil* hills. See **Gleneagles Hotel.** *Iter. 135, 146.*

BLACKHALL (Edinburgh), Midlothian. Map 9, **NT 2 7.**
Iter. 17, 89, 90, 92, 93, 94, 96.

BLACK ISLE, Ross and Cromarty. Map 25, **NH 6** 5 etc.
The name given to the broad and fertile strip of land which lies between the Firth of Cromarty and the Beauly and Inner Moray Firths, terminating in the South Sutor headland beyond the town of *Cromarty* (*q.v.*). In the centre of the Black Isle is a wooded ridge, known as *Millbuie*, or Ardmeanach. the lordship of which was granted originally to Darnley by Mary, Queen of Scots. It forms a notable viewpoint. See **Fortrose** and **Rosemarkie.** *Iter. 203.*

BLACK MOUNT, Argyll. Map 18, **NN 2** 4.
The name given to the bleak and hilly moors between Loch Tulla and Rannoch Moor. The present Glencoe road traverses its eastern border, the old road having taken a higher course farther west. On this western side rise the fine peaks of *Stob Ghabhar*, 3,565 ft., *Clachlet*, 3,602 ft. and *Meall a Bhuiridh*, 3,636 ft. Corrie Ba, between the two first-named, is one of 'Scotland's largest'. See **Inveran and Kingshouse.**

BLACKNESS, West Lothian. Map 16, **NT 0 7.**
Once the third port of Scotland, and now but a small village. The Castle (A.M.) dates from the 15th cent. and later. After having been used as a prison in Covenanting times, it became at a later date a powder magazine. There are views across the Firth of Forth, and eastwards to the Forth Bridges. *Iter. 96.*

BLACKSHIELS, Midlothian. 100. Map 10, **NT 4 6.**
E.C. Wed. *Blackshiels* and *Fala* lie below *Soutra Hill* (*q.v.*), an outlier of the extensive *Lammermuirs*, a sparsely populated area devoted to sheep. **2½ m. S.W.,** by the Cakemuir Burn, is *Cakemuir Castle*, 16th to 18th cent., associated with Mary, Queen of Scots, and Bothwell. The chamber in which the Queen is said to have changed her page's clothes after escaping from *Borthwick Castle* (*q.v.*), in 1567, is on the first floor. *Iter. 4, 5, 13.*

BLACKWATERFOOT, Isle of Arran, Bute. Map 7, **N R 8 2.**
GOLF. A small village on Drumadoon Bay, with some cliff scenery and views over Kilbrennan Sound to the *Kintyre* (*q.v.*) peninsula. Here, the String Road from *Brodick* (*q.v.*) links up with the coast road following the western shores of the island. **2 m. N.E.,** off the Brodick road, is *Shiskine* Church, in which a carved tombstone is preserved. See **Lagg** and **Machrie.** *Iter. 242.*

BLADNOCH, Wigtown. Map 2, **NX 4** 5.
This little village stands on the Bladnoch Water, here spanned by a bridge, the river flowing eastwards past an old quay to enter Wigtown Bay north of the Baldoon Sands. About a mile to the south-east of the village lie the remains of *Baldoon Castle*, associated with Scott's " Bride of Lammermoor," and once the home of David Dunbar, the original of the bridegroom in the novel. *Iter. 78, 82.*

BLAIRADAM, Kinross. Map 17, **NT 1 9.**
Once known as *Maryburgh*, and the birthplace of William Adam, the father of the four distinguished architects who bear the name. The most famous was Robert Adam, 1728-1792, who worked in Edinburgh and also with great effect in England. The house of *Blairadam* was visited by Sir Walter Scott, and the neighbourhood is described in his novel " The Abbot." A bridge over the Drumnagoil Burn in the vicinity is dated 1696. Another bridge, to the north-east, where the village of *Paranwell* once stood, has two tablets recalling an abortive attempt in 1564 on the lives of Mary, Queen of Scots, and Darnley. To the west are the *Cleish* hills, with *Dumglow* attaining 1,241 ft., and north-eastwards rises *Benarty Hill*, 1,167 ft.

BLAIR ATHOLL, Perth. 1,386. Map 19, **NN 8** 6.
E.C. Wed. GOLF. This pleasant *Atholl* (*q.v.*) village stands on the River Garry, among woods, hills and moors. Many glens meet in the vicinity, which accounts for its former importance as the key to the Central Highlands. The fine *Blair Castle*, in its extensive park, noted for the larch plantations, is an old seat of the Clan Murray, the head of which is the Duke of Atholl, and dates back to 1269. It was Georganised in the mid-18th cent. and given a castellated appearance by David Bryce in 1869. The interior is noted for its period furniture, weapons and other relics.

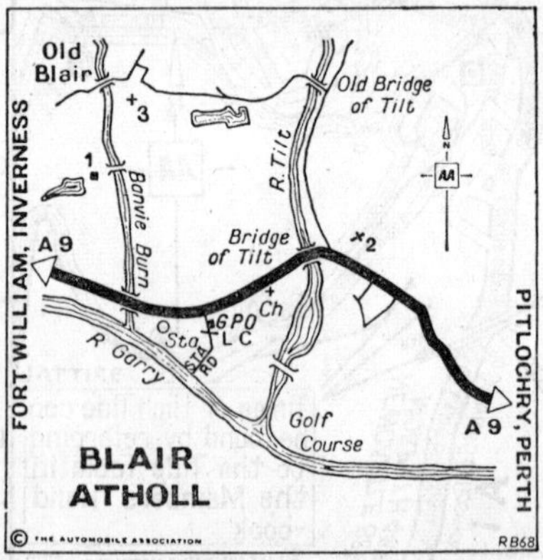

Blair Castle	1
Kilmaveonaig Church	2
St. Bride's Church	3

There are associations with James V, Mary, Queen of Scots, Montrose and Prince Charles Edward, and the castle at one period held a Cromwellian garrison. It is said to be the last castle in Britain to have withstood a siege. The oldest part of the castle is the *Cumming's* Tower. It is shown weekdays, 10 to 6 (Sun., 2 to 6), early May to early Oct. Also on Sun. and Mon. in April. (See note page 98.) The 16th cent. Parish Church of *Kilmaveonaig* was rebuilt in 1794. In *St. Bride's* Churchyard at *Old Blair* is buried Claverhouse of Dundee, slain in 1689 at the battle

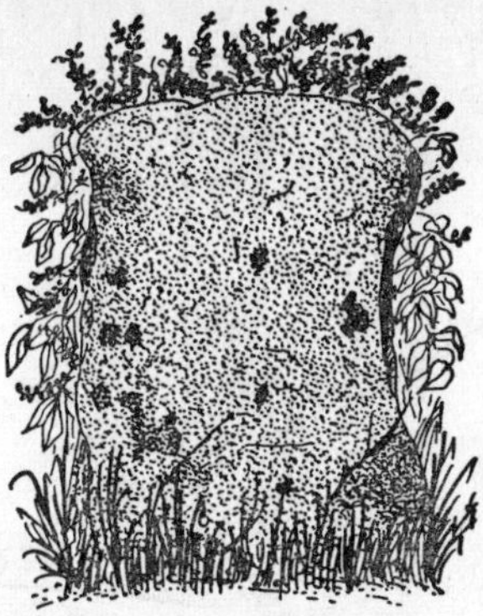

Birnie, Moray. The ' Druid Stone ' in the churchyard

Black Isle, Ross and Cromarty. The 16th century Castle Craig, a former Black Isle residence of the Bishops of Ross. It faces Cromarty Firth, beyond B9163, from which it is hidden from view, and can be seen from A9, on the farther shores of the Firth

Blackness, West Lothian. The Castle, of the 15th century and later. It was once used as a prison for Covenanters, and in more recent times as an ordnance depot

Blackshiels, Midlothian. Cakemuir Castle, some 2½ miles south-west, on a by-road off B6458. Here Mary, Queen of Scots, is said to have changed from her page's clothes after her escape from Borthwick Castle in 1567

Bladnoch, Wigtown. Baldoon Castle, off an unclassified road to the south-east, which has associations with Sir Walter Scott's '*Bride of Lammermoor*'

Blair Atholl, Perth. Blair Castle, the ancient seat of the Clan Murray. It was Georgianised in the mid-18th century and given its present castellated appearance in 1869

Blantyre, Lanark. Shuttle Row, where David Livingstone was born in 1813. It is now a Livingstone Memorial

Boddam, Aberdeen. The lighthouse at Buchan Ness, Scotland's most easterly point

Blyth Bridge, Peebles. An example of a whalebone archway in the village

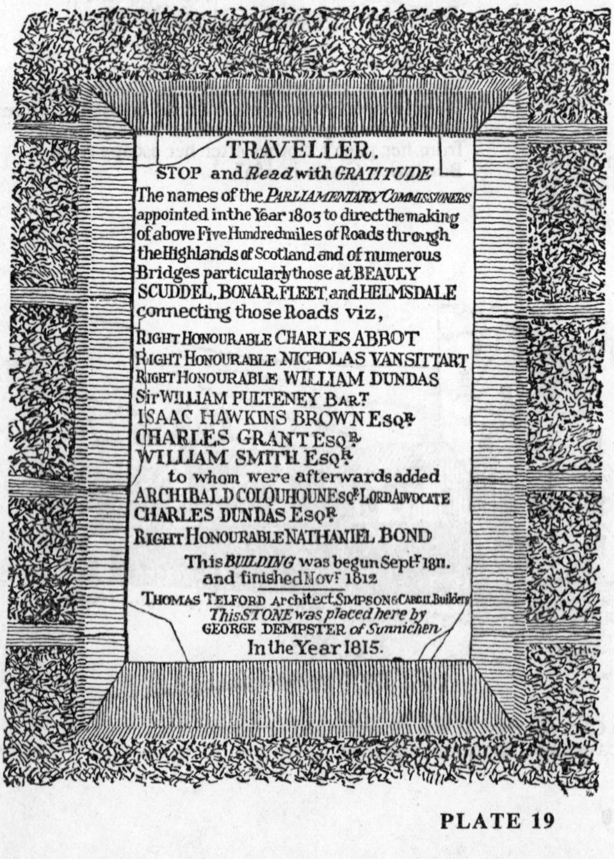
TRAVELLER.
STOP and Read with GRATITUDE
The names of the PARLIAMENTARY COMMISSIONERS
appointed in the Year 1803 to direct the making
of above Five Hundred miles of Roads through
the Highlands of Scotland and of numerous
Bridges particularly those at BEAULY
SCUDDEL, BONAR, FLEET, and HELMSDALE
connecting those Roads viz,
RIGHT HONOURABLE CHARLES ABBOT
RIGHT HONOURABLE NICHOLAS VANSITTART
RIGHT HONOURABLE WILLIAM DUNDAS
SIR WILLIAM PULTENEY BART.
ISAAC HAWKINS BROWN ESQR.
CHARLES GRANT ESQR.
WILLIAM SMITH ESQR.
to whom were afterwards added
ARCHIBALD COLQUHOUN ESQR. LORD ADVOCATE
CHARLES DUNDAS ESQR.
RIGHT HONOURABLE NATHANIEL BOND
This BUILDING was begun Septr. 1811.
and finished Novr. 1812
THOMAS TELFORD Architect, SIMPSON & CARGILL Builders
This STONE was placed here by
GEORGE DEMPSTER of Sunnichen
In the Year 1815.

Bonar Bridge, Sutherland. A tablet on the bridge recording the building of the original structure by Telford (1811–12)

Bolton, East Lothian. The well near the Gifford Water, where Robert Burns's mother drew water. The well is inscribed: 'Drink of the pure crystals and not only be ye succoured but also refreshed in mind. Agnes Broun, 1732–1820'

of *Killiecrankie* (*q.v.*). To the north of the village is Glen Tilt, extending far into the mountains of the Forest of Atholl, with *Ben-y-Gloe*, 3,671 ft., to the east. At the commencement of the glen, near the Old Bridge of Tilt, are the Falls of Fender. Farther north, the glen is hemmed in by steep hills, and extends for some six miles in an almost dead straight line, the river meanwhile flowing through a granite dyke. Later the Tarf Water, with its numerous falls, joins the Tilt amid a wilderness of lonely hills. Beyond the meeting of the rivers lie the remote Aberdeenshire deer forests of Glen Ey and Mar, with *Beinn Bhrotain*, 3,797 ft., in the *Cairngorm* range, dominating the latter. See **Struan** (for *Falls of Bruar*). *Iter. 138, 140, 143, 150.*

BLAIRGOWRIE, Perth. 5,554. SB. with Rattray. Map 20, **NO 1 4.**
E.C. Thurs. **M.D.** Tues. GOLF. On the River Ericht, and linked by the 19th cent. Brig o' Blair to *Rattray*, on the edge of *Strathmore* (*q.v.*). By the bridge is a fish pass, built in 1958. Part of the lay-out around the spinning mill of Lornty (1755) is still extant and there are other mills in the district. It is noted as the centre of a raspberry and strawberry growing district. The whitewashed Z-plan *Newton Castle*, partly 17th cent., stands on high ground above the town. The main road leading northwards from the town crosses the river twice within a few miles, and then enters the

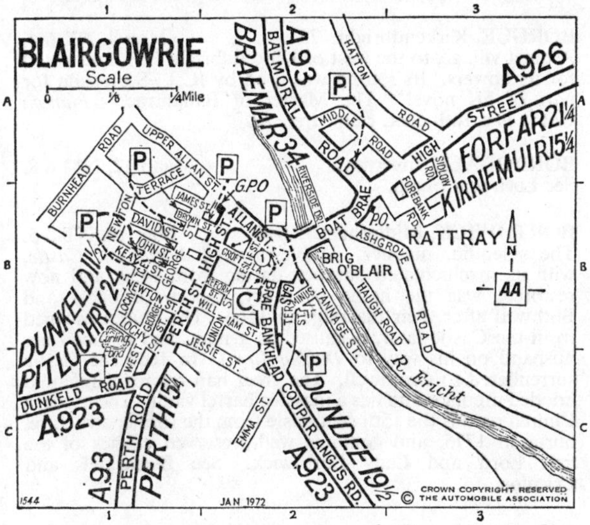

Information Bureau 1 (B2)

fine Ericht gorge, where the river flows between cliffs 200 ft. high. Nearby, on high ground to the right, stands the rebuilt mansion of *Craighall Rattray* (1832), which has claims to be the original of Scott's " Tully-Veolan " in his novel " Waverley." The road continues by way of *Bridge of Cally* (*q.v.*) and climbs through Glen Shee to the lofty *Cairnwell* (*q.v.*) Pass and Braemar. Off the Dunkeld road, to the west of the town, are Lochs Ardblair and Marlee, with the 16th cent. mansion of *Ardblair Castle* near the first-named. **2 m. N.W.** of Blairgowrie stands the ruined *Glasclune Castle* of the Blairs. A battle was fought here in 1392. See **Clunie, Meikleour, Stobhall** and **Traquair.** *Iter. 141, 152, 158, 159, 166.*

BLAIRLOGIE, Stirling. Map 16, **NS 8 9.**
A village under the *Ochil* hills, with *Dumyat*, 1,375 ft., a viewpoint, rising in the background. Sir William Alexander Stirling, founder of Nova Scotia, once worshipped in the former old church. *The Blair* is 16th cent. and later. This is Scotland's first conserved village. In the 18th cent. it was a goat-milk spa. *Powis House* (mid-18th cent.) contains Adam features. *Iter. 136.*

BLAIRMORE, Argyll. Map 14, **NS 1 8.**
GOLF. See **Strone.** *Iter. 102.*

BLAIRS, Kincardine. Map 21, **NJ 8 0.**
Here is *Blairs House*, now a R.C. College, in which is preserved a splendid portrait of Mary, Queen of Scots, one of the very few considered to be authentic. It was originally found concealed at Douai after the French Revolution. See **Knockandhu.** *Iter. 168, 174.*

BLANTYRE, Lanark. 7,075. Map 8, **NS 6 5.**
The Clyde flows a little to the north, in a wooded setting. Situated in *Shuttle Row* (1780) is the one-time tenement where Livingstone was born in 1813, and which has been restored as a National Memorial, housing relics. On the tower of the *Livingstone* memorial church is the explorer's statue. There are slight remains of *Blantyre Priory*, **2 m. N.,** near the river. The district is largely devoted to coal-mining. A little to the west of Blantyre, near the Rotten Calder Water, stands *Crossbasket Castle*, 16th cent., with large modern additions. See **Bothwell.** *Iter. 18, 19.*

BLYTH BRIDGE, Peebles. Map 9, **NT 1 4.**
On the Tarth Water, in a setting of Lowland hills. See **Romanno Bridge.** *Iter. 10, 35, 37, 52, 53.*

BOAT OF GARTEN, Inverness. 480. Map 25, **NH 9 1.**
E.C. Thurs. A Strath Spey resort, on the fringe of the extensive Forest of Abernethy, to the east, with its many paths, and sheltering the tiny Loch Garten. Ospreys have nested in the vicinity. The name Boat of Garten refers to the former ferry, by means of which the river was crossed prior to the construction of the bridge in 1898. Away to the south rise the peaks of the *Cairngorms* (*q.v.*), reached by a track over the Sluggan Pass, at the foot of *Craiggowrie*, 2,237 ft., to the east of the road from Nethybridge to Aviemore. See **Aviemore, Carrbridge** and **Nethybridge.** *Iter. 169, 170.*

BODDAM, Aberdeen. Map 27, **NK 1 4.**
Buchan Ness, with its lighthouse, the most easterly point in Scotland, shelters this little pink granite fishing village, lying just off the Peterhead road, and to the south of which stands the ruined 14th cent. Castle. To the south-west are the large Peterhead granite quarries. See **Cruden Bay.** *Iter. 181, 182, 187.*

BOGSIDE, Ayr. Map 8, **NS 3 3.**
A racecourse was formerly here. *Iter. 66, 69, 85, 88.*

BOLTON, East Lothian. 562. Map 10, **NT 5 7.**
In the churchyard lie buried Burns's mother, sister and brother. A well near the Gifford Water, which Burns's mother used, was restored in 1932. **2 m. S.W.** is *Pilmuir House*, a delightful, gabled mansion, built in 1624 by the Cairns family, and retaining a contemporary dovecote. **2 m. N.** is *Lennoxlove*, a mansion of several dates, the nucleus a fine 15th cent. tower. The great hall, and also two sundials, dated 1644 and 1679 respectively, are of interest, while above the entrance door, which still preserves its iron yett, is an inscription with the date 1626. The house was formerly known as *Lethington Tower*, and was associated with William Maitland, the " Mr. Secretary Lethington " to Mary, Queen of Scots. *Iter. 36.*

BONAR BRIDGE, Sutherland. 288. Map 29, **NH 6 9.**
E.C. Wed. This bridge, which spans the channel connecting the Inner Dornoch Firth with the Kyle of Sutherland, replaces one built originally by Telford. Before its construction occurred the Meikle Ferry disaster, in 1809, when 99 lives were lost. Hut circles and stone-age burial cairns are to be found in the vicinity, and on *Duncreich*, **4 m. S.E.,** is a vitrified fort. Strath Carron to the west, and Strath Oykell to the north-west, are two picturesque glens, the latter traversed by the road leading to *Oykell Bridge* (*q.v.*) and the mountains of the west coast. A little to the east of

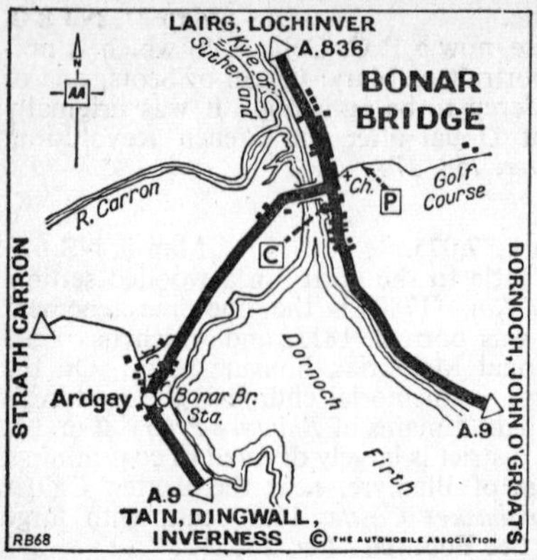

Bonar Bridge lies the small Loch Migdale, in a wooded setting. *Iter. 200, 201, 228, 229, 230, 231, 232.*

BONAWE, Argyll. Map 14, **NN 0 3.** Lies on Airds Bay, near the point where the River Awe flows into *Loch Etive* (*q.v.*), dividing it into the lower and upper lochs, the latter dominated by *Ben Starav*, 3,541 ft. *Inverawe House*, partly 16th cent., and associated with a curious ghost story, stands on the east bank of the river. Beyond the north side of the loch, and reached by ferry, are the Bonawe granite quarries. *Ben Cruachan*, 3,689 ft., with its twin peaks, rises to the south-east of the village, and below the northern flanks of the mountain lies the lonely Glen Noe, hemmed in by lofty hills. See **Falls of Cruachan.** *Iter. 125.*

BONCHESTER BRIDGE, Roxburgh. Map 5, **NT 5 1.** The bridge is over the Rule Water, flowing in a northerly direction to join the Teviot, and is overlooked by *Bonchester Hill*, 1,059 ft. *Greenriver House*, late Georgian, was renamed after a place in Jamaica. Roads fork here for Jedburgh and Hawick, and to the south is another fork. Here, the road climbing south-eastwards towards *Carter Bar* (*q.v.*) leaves the fine Liddesdale road which goes south-westwards into the hills, and reaches a height of 1,250 ft. at Note o' the Gate, below the main *Cheviot* (*q.v.*) range dominated here by *Peel Fell*, 1,975 ft. and *Carter Fell*, 1,815 ft. This is the Wauchope Forest area, which, together with *Newcastleton* (*q.v.*) Forest, forms part of the Border Forest Park, extending across the English border. See **Southdean.** *Iter. 44, 47.*

BO'NESS, West Lothian. 13,636. SB. Map 16, **NS 9 8.** The name is a contraction of *Borrowstounness*. An industrial town and port on the Forth estuary, Bo'ness is associated with Henry Bell, who launched an early steamboat, the "Comet," on the Clyde in 1812, and also with James Watt, who experimented, in 1764, with his steam engine on the nearby *Kinneil* estate, now a public park. Mid-16th cent. wall paintings, perhaps Flemish or French work, and illustrating the story of the Good Samaritan, have been discovered on one of the walls of a room in *Kinneil House* (A.M.), which is open weekdays, 10 to 7 or 12 to 4; Sunday, 2 to 4 or 7 (see note page 98). Bo'ness Hill climb for cars takes place in the grounds. The *Antonine* or *Roman Wall* (*q.v.*) terminated just to the east of Bo'ness, and in 1868, a Distance Slab, now in the National Museum of Antiquities at Edinburgh was unearthed. A copy of this has been erected, set in a framework of Roman stones, and situated near *Bridgeness Tower*, at the east end of the town. **1½ m. E.** is the modernised *Carriden House*, the old portion of which is dated 1602. See **Bowling** and **Falkirk.** *Iter. 17.*

BONHILL, Dunbarton. 4,005. Map 15, **NS 3 7.** On the River Leven, between the Clyde estuary and the southern extremity of *Loch Lomond* (*q.v.*) and engaged in bleaching. See **Alexandria.** *Iter. 88, 100, 101, 109, 110, 112.*

BONNYBRIDGE, Stirling. 7,192. Map 16, **NS 8 8.** GOLF. An industrial town on the Forth and Clyde canal and also on the line of the *Roman Wall* (*q.v.*). *Iter. 17, 113, 115.*

BONNYRIGG, Midlothian. 7,110. SB. with Lasswade. Map 10, **NT 3 6.** A colliery town. See **Lasswade.** *Iter. 37.*

BORDER COUNTRY, THE. Maps 4, 5, 9, 10, and 11. The term Border Country is generally applied to the Lowland counties of Roxburgh, Peebles, Selkirk and also parts of Berwick and Dumfries, though the essence of true Border scenery is confined mainly to the first three counties. This land of rounded green hills, delightful glens and dales, together with numerous ruined castles and peel towers, is separated from England by the long line of the *Cheviot* (*q.v.*) hills, and is impregnated with legends and stories of Border warfare and raids in medieval times. Above all, the district is associated with the life and works of Sir Walter Scott, whose last and most famous home of *Abbotsford* (*q.v.*) is situated in the very heart of the Border Country, in which are also to be found the four great ruined Abbeys of *Melrose*, *Jedburgh*, *Dryburgh* and *Kelso* (all *q.v.*). See **Lowlands** and **Scott Country.** *Iter. 30, 47.*

BORDER FOREST PARK, Roxburgh. Map 5, **NY 4 8** and **NT 5 1** etc. See **Bonchester Bridge** and **Newcastleton.**

BORGIE BRIDGE, Sutherland. Map 28, **NC 6 5.** The bridge spans the River Borgie, which flows northwards from here into Torrisdale Bay. A by-road follows the river towards the coast before veering north-westwards for the crofting township of *Skerray* (*q.v.*). *Iter. 234, 235, 240.*

BORGUE, Kirkcudbright. 752. Map 4, **NX 6 4.** A quiet village, to the west of Kirkcudbright Bay, and noted for its flowers. Its setting was used by R. L. Stevenson for part of his novel "The Master of Ballantrae." *Plunton Castle* is a 16th cent. ruin. *Iter. 73.*

BORRODALE, Inverness. Map 12, **NM 6 8.** See **Loch nan Uamh.**

BORTHWICK, Midlothian. 2,046 Map 10, **NT 3 5.** The splendid, massive, double-towered *Borthwick Castle*, with its machicolated parapet, dating from 1430, and now restored, was the home of Mary, Queen of Scots and Bothwell after their marriage in 1566. The Queen escaped from the Castle later, disguised as a man, and rejoined her husband on his way to *Dunbar* (*q.v.*). In 1650 the Castle surrendered to Cromwell. The great hall retains a splendid hooded fireplace and has a massive barrel vault. The modern Church retains the 15th cent. aisle from the former structure, burnt in 1775, and contains well-preserved effigies of the first Lord and Lady Borthwick. See **Blackshiels** and **Crichton.**

BOTHWELL, Lanark. 9,167 with Uddingston. Map 8, **NS 7 5.** E.C. Wed. In 1679 was fought near here the battle of Bothwell Brig, ending in the defeat of the Covenanters. The prisoners, to a number of 1,200, were confined for 5 months in the Greyfriars churchyard at *Edinburgh* (*q.v.*). The bridge over the Clyde, built originally c. 1400, was modernized in 1826. *Bothwell Castle* (A.M.), belonging to the Douglas family, is one of the most impressive ruined strongholds in Scotland, dating from the 13th and 15th cents., and situated in a picturesque setting above the Clyde Valley to the north-west of the town. The great hall was formerly one of the finest in the country, but the whole structure has suffered many vicissitudes. The great tower resembles its prototype at Coucy, in France. Sir Walter Scott wrote "Young Lochinvar" at Bothwell. The Castle is open weekdays 10 to 4.30 or 7; Sun., 2 to 4.30 or 7 (see note page 98). The Collegiate Church of Bothwell dates partly from 1398, and contains 18th cent.monuments to the Douglas family, being noted architecturally for its pointed barrel vault. Joanna Baillie, the poetess, was born at Bothwell in 1762. *Iter. 51.*

BOWDEN, Roxburgh. 428. Map 10, **NT 5 3.** The restored Church dates mainly from the 17th cent. and contains a laird's loft. A church was founded here in the 12th cent. The 16th cent. Market Cross has been restored as a

Border Country, The. The 'Capon Tree' at Jedburgh, Roxburghshire, a survivor of the ancient Jed, or Jethart Forest, which formerly covered the region. It stands south of the town, to the right of A68

Bo'ness, West Lothian. A copy of a distance slab, set up in 1868, marking the terminal point of the Antonine, or Roman Wall. The original, which was excavated here, is now in the National Museum of Antiquities at Edinburgh

Bothwell, Lanark. The Monument commemorating the defeat of the Covenanters at Bothwell Brig in 1679

Bothwell, Lanark. The ruined 13th to 15th century Castle, incorporating the Douglas tower, which took 36 years to complete, and was probably built by French craftsmen

Borthwick, Midlothian. Borthwick Castle, 15th century and restored, once the home of Mary, Queen of Scots and Bothwell

Border Country, The. The iron 'yett', or gate, of the 15th century Comlongon Castle, which stands on an unclassified road west of Clarencefield, in Dumfries-shire, not far from the English border

[For BOWDEN see following plate
[For BONAWE see under LORNE (Plate 117)

Braemar, Aberdeen. Invercauld Bridge, carrying A93 across the River Dee to the east of Braemar

Bowden, Roxburgh. The mainly 17th century Church, which contains an example of a laird's loft. A church was founded here originally in the 12th century

Bowden, Roxburgh. The restored 16th century village Cross, now a War Memorial

Braemar, Aberdeen. Braemar Castle, built in 1628 and partly re-built c.1748

Braemar, Aberdeen. The Old Bridge of Dee, some 3 miles east of the resort

Bracadale, Isle of Skye, Inverness. The flat-topped twin hills known as Macleod's Tables, seen from A863, near the shores of Loch Bracadale, on the way to Dunvegan

War Memorial. Bowden's market dates from 1571, the first non-burghal Scottish one to be licensed. To the north rise the prominent triple-peaked *Eildon* hills, and from the high ground in the vicinity the view extends southwards towards the distant *Cheviots* (*q.v.*). *Iter. 46.*

BOWER, Caithness. Map 30, **ND 2 6.**
Iter. 238.

BOWHILL, Selkirk. Map 10, **NT 4 2.**
See **Selkirk.**

BOWLAND, Midlothian; Selkirk. Map 10, **NT 4 4.**
On the Gala Water. To the south is the road to the Tweed valley, between Knowes Hill and the Torwoodlee Woods, among which stands the old Castle of *Torwoodlee*, near the Georgian house, dating from c. 1783. Nearby is *Crosslee Hill*, where, within a British Camp, are the foundations of a broch known as " The Rings." *Iter. 11.*

BOWLING, Dunbarton. 622. Map 8, **NS 4 7.**
E.C. Wed. The point where the Forth and Clyde Canal, 38 miles long, crossing the narrow waist of Scotland, and built by Smeaton in 1790, enters the Clyde. The first practical steamboat, Symington's " Charlotte Dundas," was tried out here in 1802, and in 1812, Bell launched here the famous " Comet," the first Clyde passenger steamer. The western terminus of the Antonine, or *Roman Wall* (*q.v.*) was near Bowling. Farther to the west, by the Clyde, at Dunglass Point, is a ruined Castle, near which stands an obelisk to Henry Bell. In the background rise the *Kilpatrick hills*, attaining 1,313 ft., with their numerous small reservoirs. See **Bo'ness, Helensburgh, Leadhills, Neilston** and **Torphichen.** *Iter. 88.*

BOWMORE, Isle of Islay, Argyll. Map 6, **NR 3 5.**
A large fishing village on Loch Indaal, noted for the curious circular Parish Church of *Kilmarrow*, on the tower of which an inscribed panel records its construction in 1767 by Daniel Campbell, " Lord of this island." From 1718 to 1843 the Islay Parliament met at Bowmore. There are alternative roads leading southwards towards *Port Ellen* (*q.v.*), the " low " road keeping near the shores of Laggan Bay, and the " high " road following an inland course. *Iter. 243.*

BOW OF FIFE, Fife. Map 17, **NO 3 1.**
Fernie Castle, to the north, is a 16th cent. and later house. *Iter. 136.*

BRACADALE, Isle of Skye, Inverness. 835.
(Struan P.O.) Map 23, **NG 3 3.**
On Loch Beag, an inlet of Loch Harport, and the junction of a very rough hill road from *Portree* with a better road linking *Sligachan* (*q.v.*) to the Vaternish peninsula away to the north-west. A little to the west of the village is the ruined *Dun Beag*, one of the best preserved brochs in the island. Farther to the west is Loch Bracadale, with the islands of Wiay, Harlosh and Tarner, beyond which lies the Duirinish peninsula, dominated by the flat-topped, twin *Macleod's Tables.* See **Dunvegan.** *Iter. 255.*

BRACO, Perth. 273. Map 16, **NN 8 0.**
To the east of the old bridge over the Knaik Water is the great Roman station of *Ardoch*, in the grounds of *Ardoch House*. The earthworks are of great strength, and are among the most striking of their kind in Great Britain. Coins excavated here date from the period of Hadrian. A little farther to the north-west is another Roman Camp, known as the Great Camp, adjacent to which is another and smaller example, the two camps together being considered to have had space for nearly 40,000 troops at a time. *Braco Castle* is 16th cent. and later. See **Forteviot.** *Iter. 138, 140.*

BRACORA, Inverness. Map 23, **NM 7 9.**
Beautifully situated on the north shores of the mountain-girdled Loch Morar.

BRAE, Shetland. Map 33, **HU 3 6.**
Iter. 267, 270.

BRAEDOWNIE, Angus. Map 20, **NO 2 7.**
Beautifully situated in the Braes of Angus mountains at the head of the long valley of Glen Clova, where the road ends, and two roadless valleys fork north-westwards into the high hills, the more easterly of which gives access to the lofty *White Mounth* (*q.v.*) plateau, and *Lochnagar* (*q.v.*), lying to the north. A branch track, known as the Capel Mounth (2,275 ft.), diverges to the north, and leads to Loch Muick, in Glen Muick, giving access to *Ballater* (*q.v.*). The westerly valley of Glen Doll Forest is traversed by a track leading to the curiously named Jock's Road, later becoming a path which climbs high (2,863 ft.) above the White Water below *Broad Cairn*, 3,268 ft. and *Tolmount*, 3,143 ft. The hills of *Driesh*, 3,105 ft., to the south, and *Craig Mellon*, 2,815 ft., to the north, overshadow this glen, overlooked near its head by the crags of *Craig Rennet*, 2,442 ft. See **Clova.** *Iter. 161.*

BRAEMAR, Aberdeen. 1,018 with Crathie. Map 20, **NO 1 9.**
E.C. Thurs. GOLF. This famous Royal *Deeside* (*q.v.*) summer and winter resort in the Highlands, at an altitude of 1,100 ft., consists actually of *Castleton of Braemar* and *Auchindryne*, situated on either side of the Clunie Water, which flows into the Dee a little to the north of the village. The scenery is some of the most notable in Scotland, with heather-clad hills rising all round, dominated by the *Cairngorm* (*q.v.*) massif of *Cairn Toul*, 4,241 ft., away to the west, and to the south-east by the peak of *Lochnagar*, 3,786 ft. (*q.v.*), in the lofty *White Mounth* (*q.v.*) group, reached by way of Glen Callater. The neighbourhood was popularized originally by Queen Victoria, who spent many holidays at the Royal Castle of *Balmoral* (*q.v.*). On a mound, on which stands now the *Invercauld Arms* Hotel, the Earl of Mar raised the Jacobite Standard in 1715. *Braemar Castle*, dating from 1628, was largely rebuilt c. 1748, and is situated to the north of the resort, near the Dee. Open daily, 10 to 6, May to mid-Oct. (See note page 98.) R. L. Stevenson wrote part of " Treasure Island " in a cottage at the south end of Castleton Terrace. The annual Braemar Gathering, held in September, is an important social event, and takes place in the Princess Royal Park.

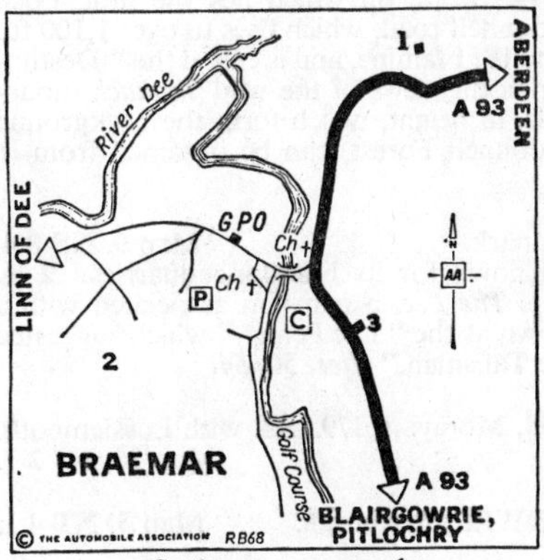

Castle	1
Princess Royal Park	2
Stevenson Cottage	3

Below Invercauld Bridge, **3 m. E.**, is the Old Bridge of Dee (1753). Access is sometimes possible from the lodge here to the Garbh-Allt Falls in the Royal Forest of Ballochbuie. *Invercauld House*, north of the river, is partly 15th cent., and the view of Lochnagar from Invercauld Bridge over the Dee is extremely fine. Some **4 m. W.** of Braemar, and north of the river, is the modern *Mar Lodge*, where winter sports developments have taken place. *Morrone Hill*, 2,819 ft., to the south-west of Braemar, is a splendid viewpoint, looking north-westwards towards the Cairngorms. The main road leading southwards from Braemar climbs through Glen Clunie, and over the *Cairnwell* (*q.v.*) Pass, prior to descending over the famous *Devil's Elbow* (frequently blocked by snow in winter) to reach Spittal of *Glenshee* (*q.v.*). The continuation along Glen Shee leads to lower-lying country watered by the River Ericht, and gives access to Blairgowrie. Private roads leave the main Deeside road (A93) to the east of Braemar, from points near Invercauld Bridge and Inver; these roads later unite and lead northwards to the remote *Loch Builg*, on the eastern fringe of *Ben Avon*, in the Cairngorms. At one point this road reaches a height of 2,391 ft., making it one of the highest in Great Britain, but in addition to being private it is at the present time completely unserviceable for motor vehicles. A steep and narrow road, linking the Dee valley with the upper valley of the Don, leaves Deeside near Balmoral Castle, climbing into the hills by way of *Gairnshiel Bridge* (*q.v.*), in Glen Gairn. The lofty section beyond this point attains 1,805 ft., and is liable to become snow-bound in winter. From a point approaching Gairnshiel Bridge, a by-road diverges to the west, following the River Gairn, but becoming private beyond Daldownie. The continuation of this road gives access to Loch Builg by an easier route. See **Crathie** and **Inverey** (for *Linn of Dee* and *Mar Lodge*). *Iter. 141, 152, 160, 167, 168, 179.*

BRAEMORE JUNCTION, Ross and Cromarty. Map 29, **NH 2 7.**
Here, the roads from *Dundonnell* (*q.v.*) and *Ullapool* (*q.v.*) converge on their way eastwards to Inverness. On the former, just before the junction, is the very impressive *Corrieshalloch Gorge* (N.T. Scot), well seen from a fragile bridge spanning the deep and narrow chasm, below which lie the spectacular *Falls of Measach*, some of the finest in Scotland. The road descending to Ullapool, on Loch Broom, goes through the beautiful fertile valley of Strath More, and in the background, to the east, are the lofty peaks of *Beinn Dearg*, 3,547 ft., and *Cona Mheall*, 3,200 ft., the latter sheltering the wild little Loch Choire Ghranda, in its precipitous setting. The remote, vertical cliffs of *Seana Bhraigh*, 3,041 ft., rise away to the north between the Inverlael and Freevater Forests. To the south of Braemore Junction is the large *Fannich* group, in which *Sgurr Mor*, 3,637 ft., overlooks the lonely Loch Fannich. The road leading south-eastwards towards Inverness traverses the bleak moorland known as the Dirrie More, on which lies the little Loch Droma. The Dundonnell road, which rises to over 1,100 ft., was made during the 1851 famine, and is called the " Destitution Road." Magnificent views of the wild *Teallach* mountains nearly 3,500 ft. in height, which form the background to the lonely Dundonnell Forest, can be obtained from it. *Iter. 204, 206, 222.*

BRAIDWOOD, Lanark. Map 9, **NS 8 4.**
E.C. Wed., Sat. Known for its limestone quarries. **2 m. S.S.E.,** in a park, is *The Lee*, a mansion associated with a famous amulet known as the " Lee Penny," which suggested Scott's novel " The Talisman." *Iter. 50, 54.*

BRANDERBURGH, Moray. 6,379. SB. with Lossiemouth. See **Lossiemouth.** Map 26, **NJ 2 7.**

BRANXHOLM TOWER, Roxburgh. Map 5, **NT 4 1.**
See **Hawick.**

BREADALBANE, Perth. Maps 15, **NN 3 3** etc.
The name given to a large part of north-west Perthshire, extending from the Inverness border to the basin of the rivers Earn and Forth, lying to the south towards the Stirling border. The *Grampian* (*q.v.*) mountains cover most of the area, which includes also Loch Rannoch and Glen Lyon, one of the longest and finest of Scottish glens. The view from the summit of *Ben Lawers*, 3,984 ft. (N.T. Scot.) gives a far-reaching panorama over the tangled ranges of the Breadalbane hills, which include the lofty *Forest of Mamlorn* group. See **Bridge of Balgie, Fortingall, Kinloch Rannoch** and **Lawers.**

BRECHIN, Angus. 6,575. SB. Map 21, **NO 6 6.**
E.C. Wed. **M.D.** Tues. GOLF. Stands on the South Esk River, facing the valley of *Strathmore* (*q.v.*), with a background of hills rising gradually to the eastern Grampians. The old town, with its steep streets, is well seen from the river bridge on the Arbroath road. Parts of the Cathedral, now the Parish Church, are of 12th cent. date. After partial demolition in 1807, the building was restored in 1902. The spired tower dates from c. 1360, and the prominent Round Tower (A.M.), 87 ft. high, one of the two examples on the Scottish mainland, is held to be 10th or 11th cent. work, and recalls similar examples in Ireland. In the town stands a fragment of the 13th cent. Maison Dieu Chapel (A.M.). **5 m. W.** is *Careston Castle*, a 15th and

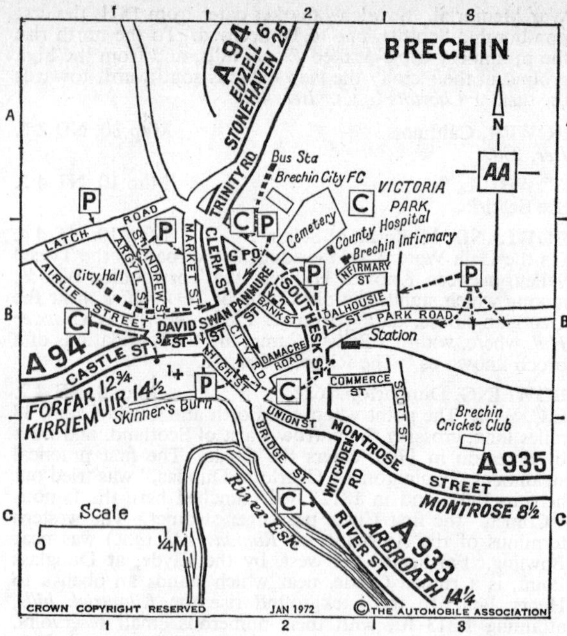

Cathedral with Round Tower 1 (B1) Museum 3 (B1)
Municipal Buildings; Information Bureau 2 (B2)

18th cent. structure. **6 m. N.W.** are two prehistoric hill forts (A.M.), known as the Black Caterthun and the White Caterthun, situated on a ridge commanding extensive views over the Howe of the Mearns and towards the eastern Grampians. **5 m. S.E.,** in a deer-park of 1,300 acres, is *Kinnaird Castle*, a 19th cent. structure with a portion dating from 1405. Away to the south-west lies Montreathmont Forest. Farther south-east is *Farnell Castle*, late 16th cent. See **Aberlemno, Abernethy** and **Edzell.** *Iter. 151, 156, 163, 164, 166.*

BRESSAY, Shetland. Map 33, **HU 4 3** etc.
See **Shetlands Islands** (Mainland).

BRIDGEND, Isle of Islay, Argyll. Map 6, **NR 3 6.**
At the head of Loch Indaal, in a wooded setting, and a junction of roads proceeding westwards and south-westwards along its shores. *Islay House* stands in wooded grounds. **2½ m. W.,** on the coast at *Blackrock*, is a sandy bathing beach. A road leads northwards from here across Gruinart Flats to the head of Loch Gruinart, where a clan battle took place in 1598. A branch road follows the west shores of the loch as far as Ardnave, beyond which lie Ardnave Point and Nave Island, on a rocky stretch of coast. See **Bowmore.** *Iter. 243, 246, 247.*

BRIDGEND, Perth. Map 17 **NO 1 2.**
See **Perth.**

BRIDGE OF ALFORD, Aberdeen. Map 26, **NJ 5 1.**
See **Alford.** *Iter. 165, 176, 177, 190.*

BRIDGE OF ALLAN, Stirling. 4,311. SB. Map 16, **NS 7 9.**
E.C. Wed. This pleasant watering-place and touring centre, on the Allan Water, which unites with the Forth to the south of the town, stands in a wooded setting at the foot of the *Ochil* hills, with *Dumyat*, 1,375 ft., a good viewpoint, rising to the east. There is a modern Pump Room and baths. Stirling University has been founded here. R. L. Stevenson was a frequent visitor to the resort. **2 m. N.W.** is *Keir*, with fine gardens, where Chopin was a guest in 1848. *Iter. 135, 138, 140, 141.*

BRIDGE OF AVON, Banff. Map 26, **NJ 1 2.**
Here, the road leading northwards from *Tomintoul* (*q.v.*) forks, the left branch going over the hills by way of *Bridge*

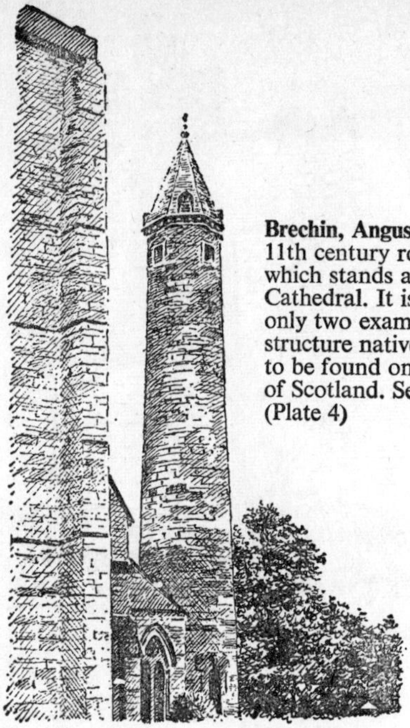

Brechin, Angus. The 10th or 11th century round tower, which stands apart from the Cathedral. It is one of the only two examples of a structure native to Ireland to be found on the mainland of Scotland. See Abernethy (Plate 4)

Braemore Junction, Ross and Cromarty. The deep Corrieshalloch ravine, belonging to the National Trust for Scotland, in which lie the impressive Falls of Measach

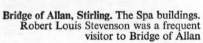

Bridge of Allan, Stirling. The Spa buildings. Robert Louis Stevenson was a frequent visitor to Bridge of Allan

Breadalbane, Perth. A bridge over the River Lyon at Fortingall, north of Loch Tay, at the entrance to Glen Lyon, among the Breadalbane hills of north-west Perthshire

Bridge of Avon, Banff. Here, the Tomintoul to Grantown-on-Spey road (A939) crosses the River Avon

Brig O'Doon, Ayr. The Auld Brig at Alloway, immediately to the south of Ayr, on B7024. It is of late mediaeval date, and is associated with Robert Burns's '*Tam O'Shanter*'

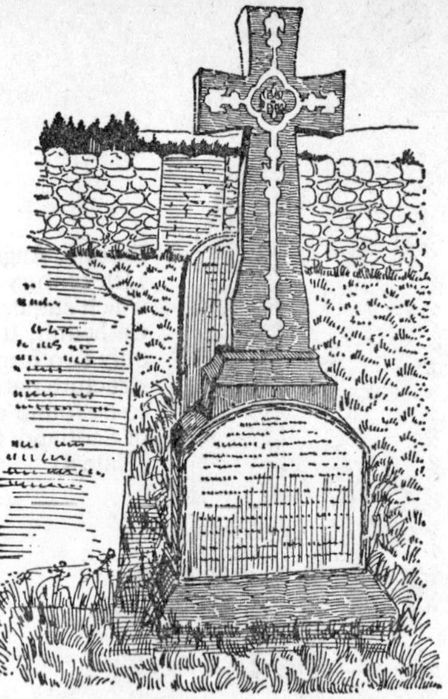

Bridge of Ess, Aberdeen. The tomb of Byron's 'Mary,' who died at Aberdeen in 1887. It is situated in the churchyard of Glentanner, on an unclassified road some 2 miles west

Bridge of Forss, Caithness. The remains of the 16th century Brims Castle, now part of a farm, on Crosskirk Bay, to the north

Bridge of Orchy, Argyll. A curious forestry workers' 'bucket bridge' over the River Orchy, operated by a hand rope. It is situated 3 miles south-west, in Glen Orchy, on B8074

Bridge of Orchy, Argyll. This old bridge on A82 stands at the entrance to Glen Orchy, where the new Glencoe road leaves the line of the old road

Bridge of Brown, Banff; Moray. A moorland bridge carrying A939 across a stream in Glen Brown, on the Banff–Moray border

[For BRIDGE OF FEUGH see under DEESIDE (Plate 44)
[For BROADFORD see under SKYE, ISLE OF (Plate 151)

of Brown (*q.v.*) to Strath Spey, and the right branch following the River Avon northwards, with the *Cromdale* hills to the west. *Iter. 141, 160, 169, 176, 177.*

BRIDGE OF AWE, Argyll. Map 14, **NN 0 2.**
Iter. 110, 117, 125, 144, 145.

BRIDGE OF BALGIE, Perth. Map 15, **NN 5 4.**
Situated in beautiful Glen Lyon, one of the longest in Scotland, and at the point of divergence of the steep (1 in 6), narrow and poorly surfaced mountain road leading southwards to *Loch Tay* (*q.v.*) over a 1,805-ft. high shoulder of *Ben Lawers*, 3,984 ft., and passing the little Lochan na Lairige. To the south-east of the lochan rise the peaks of the *Tarmachan* group, 3,421 ft. There are hydro-electric developments in this district. The narrow road continuing westwards from Bridge of Balgie into the bare and lonely hill country of Upper Glen Lyon soon passes near the picturesque *Meggernie Castle*, by the River Lyon, which dates partly from c. 1582. To the west, in the hills, Lochs Giorra and Dhamh have been united to form a new reservoir. The road eventually reaches Loch Lyon, now greatly extended, near which a large new dam has been constructed. The head of the glen is surrounded by lofty, green hills, dominated by *Ben Achallader*, 3,404 ft., to the north-west, on the Argyll border, and *Ben Heasgarnich*, 3,530 ft., to the south. The latter is the highest peak of the Forest of Mamlorn group in the *Breadalbane* (*q.v.*) country. See **Fortingall, Innerwick Church** and **Lawers.** *Iter. 107.*

BRIDGE OF BROWN, Banff; Moray. Map 26, **NJ 1 2.**
The bridge stands at the county boundary, on the lofty moorland road from *Tomintoul* (*q.v.*) to *Grantown-on-Spey* (*q.v.*). To the south lies Glen Brown. The Grantown road climbs to more than 1,400 ft., before commencing the descent towards the wooded Strath Spey, and there are views of the lofty *Cairngorm* (*q.v.*) mountains away to the south-west, in which *Ben Avon*, 3,843 ft., is prominent. To the north rise the nearer, but lower *Cromdale* hills. *Iter. 141 160, 169, 176, 177.*

BRIDGE OF CALLY, Perth. 300. Map 20, **NO 1 5.**
This bridge spans the River Ardle, flowing through Strath Ardle, the stream being joined a short distance away by the Black Water, coming down from Glen Shee, the two forming the River Ericht. Westwards lies the moorland area of Clunie Forest, and to the east is the Forest of Alyth. The main road from Blairgowrie divides at Bridge of Cally, the left fork leading to Pitlochry, and the right fork climbing through Glen Shee to the lofty *Cairnwell* (*q.v.*) Pass on its way to Braemar. *Iter. 141, 152, 159.*

BRIDGE OF CRAIG, Angus. Map 20, **NO 2 5.**
The bridge spans the River Isla, and a little to the east are the fine falls known as the Reekie Linn. Still farther east is the waterfall of the Slug of Auchrannie. To the north is Loch Lintrathen, a reservoir for Dundee's water supply. See **Dykend.** *Iter. 160.*

BRIDGE OF DEE, Aberdeen. Map 27, **NJ 9 0.**
See **Aberdeen.** *Iter. 151, 155, 156, 168, 174.*

BRIDGE OF DYE, Kincardine. Map 21, **NO 6 8.**
See **Cairn o' Mounth.** *Iter. 163, 165.*

BRIDGE OF EARN, Perth. 2,794. Map 17, **NO 1 1.**
E.C. Thurs. M.D. Fri. Part of the medieval bridge may still be seen. **1 m. W.** are *Pitkeathly Wells*, once well known. **2½ m. S.E.** is the fine old mansion of *Balmanno*, well restored by Sir Robert Lorimer. See **Abernethy.** *Iter. 90, 91, 130, 131, 132.*

BRIDGE OF ESS, Aberdeen. Map 21, **NO 5 9.**
At the entrance to the wooded valley of Glen Tanner in which stands *Glentanar House*, in Glentanar Forest. In the churchyard of *Glentanner*, some **2 m. W.,** on the south bank of the Dee, is buried Byron's " Mary." (See **Cambus o' May.**) The various hill-paths which lead out of the valley into the eastern Grampian mountains are described under *Aboyne*. *Iter. 168, 174.*

BRIDGE OF FEUGH, Kincardine. Map 21, **NO 7 9.**
The bridge and toll-house are late 18th cent. See **Banchory.** *Iter. 163, 168, 174, 190, 191.*

BRIDGE OF FITCH, Shetland. Map 33, **HU 4 4.**
Iter. 267, 268, 270.

BRIDGE OF FORSS, Caithness. Map 30, **ND 0 6.**
An old tree-surrounded mill stands here near the rapids of the Forss Water, flowing towards Crosskirk Bay, on the eastern arm of which is Brims Ness, sheltering the ruined 16th cent. *Brims Castle*, now incorporated in a farm. To the north-west is the little chapel of *St. Mary*, perhaps of 12th cent. date. *Iter. 232, 234, 240.*

BRIDGE OF GAIRN, Aberdeen. Map 20, **NO 3 9.**
Iter. 141, 152, 167, 174, 179.

BRIDGE OF GARRY, Perth. Map 20, **NN 9 6.**
A little to the south, the River Garry flows into the Tummel, a path leading to the junction of the rivers. In the vicinity is the Linn of Tummel (N.T. Scot.). Bridge of Garry is sometimes considered to stand almost in the exact centre of Scotland. The hydro-electric developments in the vicinity are part of the Tummel-Garry scheme, and are described under *Pitlochry*. The falls are accessible by road from that resort by means of the new Aldour Bridge and road built in connection with the scheme, and leading past the newly-created Loch Faskally, near the west bank of the Tummel. The road continues westwards from Bridge of Garry towards Loch Tummel and passes the famous *Queen's View* (*q.v.*) at the eastern end of the loch. See **Killiecrankie.** *Iter. 138. 148.*

BRIDGE OF ISLA, Perth. Map 17, **NO 1 3.**
See **Meikleour** and **Stobhall.** *Iter. 152.*

BRIDGE OF ORCHY, Argyll. 50. Map 15, **NN 2 3.**
E.C. Wed. The old and the new roads to *Glencoe* (*q.v.*) diverge here, the new road, completed in 1935, continuing northwards round the eastern side of Loch Tulla, where old pine trees, relics of the former extensive Caledonian Forest, are still standing. This road avoids the exposed climb over the *Black Mount* which the old road was forced to take, the new alignment merely skirting the *Mount*, attaining a height of 1,143 ft. on *Rannoch Moor*, and passing near Loch Ba. *Ben Dorain*, 3,524 ft., dominates the surrounding country, its steep, furrowed slopes rising in a continuous sweep to the summit. Farther to the north, on the east side of Loch Tulla, in the Drum Alban ridge, and near the country's main watershed, is *Ben Achallader*, 3,404 ft. Below stands the ruined *Achallader Castle*, on a rough by-road in Glen Tulla, in which are the ancient pine trees of Crannach. Glen Orchy extends south-westwards from Bridge of Orchy, and is traversed by a narrow and rather rough road, which is later joined by the main Oban road through Glen Lochy, the two roads converging on *Dalmally* (*q.v.*). See **Inveroran** and **Kingshouse.** *Iter. 100, 125, 142.*

BRIDGE OF PHILORTH, Aberdeen. Map 27, **NK 0 6.**
See **Inverallochy.** *Iter. 182.*

BRIDGE OF WALLS, Shetland. Map 33, **HU 2 5.**
Iter. 268.

BRIDGE OF WEIR, Renfrew. 1,837. Map 8, **NS 3 6.**
E.C. Wed. GOLF. A residential and golfing district on the Gryfe Water. Tanning is an important local industry. *Ranfurly Castle* was formerly the home of John Knox's ancestors. To the north-west lie the well-known *Quarrier's Orphan Homes.* See **Houston.** *Iter. 64.*

BRIG O' DOON, Ayr. Map 8, **NS 3 1.**
See **Alloway.** *Iter. 84.*

BRIG O' TURK, Perth. Map 15, **NN 5 0.**
See **Trossachs.** *Iter. 106, 111, 139.*

BROADFORD, Isle of Skye, Inverness. 900.
Map 23, **NG 6 2.**
E.C. Wed. A small tourist resort on Broadford Bay,

looking to the little island of Pabay, known for its fossils, and beyond it to the Applecross mountains on the mainland. *Beinn na Caillich*, 2,403 ft., and *Beinn Dearg Mhor*, 2,323 ft., in the Broadford group of *Red* hills, dominate the village to the west. At the foot of the hills is the ruined *Coire Chatachan*, a former Mackinnon home, where Dr. Johnson and Boswell were entertained in 1773. The coast road leading north-westwards towards *Sligachan* (*q.v.*) provides superb views of mountain and sea, and makes the complete circuit of the sea loch of *Loch Ainort*, at the mouth of which is the island of Scalpay. The finest excursion from Broadford is a visit to the magnificent scenery of *Lochs Scavaig* and *Coruisk* (both described under their own headings), the hilly and narrow road proceeding by way of Loch Slapin, dominated by the great peak of *Blaven*, 3,042 ft., an outlier of the *Coolins* (*q.v.*). It then crosses the low Strathaird peninsula to reach the village of *Elgol* (*q.v.*), the remainder of the journey having to be made by motor boat on Loch Scavaig. See **Dunan, Kyleakin, Kylerhea** and **Torrin.** *Iter. 251, 252, 253.*

BROADMEADOWS, Selkirk. Map 10, **NT 4** 3.
Beautifully situated in the pastoral Vale of Yarrow, threaded by the Yarrow Water. An old drovers' track, the *Minch* road, goes over the hills in a north-easterly direction from here towards *Traquair* (*q.v.*). **1 m. S.E.** is *Newark Castle*, an impressive 15th cent. ruin, the retreat of the widowed Anne, Duchess of Buccleuch, to whom Scott made the "Last Minstrel" address his "Lay," and visited by Scott and Wordsworth together. On the opposite side of the river is Mungo Park's birthplace, a small cottage at *Foulshiels*, where the explorer was born in 1771. The Yarrow flows here through a most picturesque wooded reach. **1 m. W.** of Broadmeadows is *Hangingshaw*, on the Yarrow, here joined by the Hangingshaw Burn. There are remains of an old Castle of the outlaw Murray. See **Ettrick Bridge End** and **Yarrow Church.** *Iter. 13, 46.*

BRODICK, Isle of Arran, Bute. 1,227 with Corrie. Map 7, **NS 0** 3.
E.C. Wed. Finely placed on the sandy Brodick Bay, with a pier served by the Clyde steamers, one of the most important approaches being from *Ardrossan* (*q.v.*), on the mainland across the Firth of Clyde. The real name of the village is *Invercloy*. *Brodick Castle* (N.T. Scot.), once the home of the Dukes of Hamilton, is open, with its fine gardens, daily, May to Sept. (except Sun.), 1 to 5 p.m. (See note page 98.) Parts of the Castle date from the 14th cent. and it was enlarged by Cromwell's garrison. The western end and the tower were built in 1844. The National Trust for Scotland now also owns *Goat Fell*, 2,866 ft., the highest of Arran's mountains, in addition to some 7,000 acres above the 750-ft. level. This includes Glen Rosa and *Cir Mhor*, 2,618 ft., whose south-west ridge and the Rosa pinnacle, together with the nearby *a'Chir* ridge, provide some of Scotland's finest rock climbing and ridge walking. There are, however, a number of easy routes to the summits, all of which are magnificent viewpoints. *Caisteal Abhail* (Peak of the Castles), 2,817 ft., *Beinn Tarsuinn* (N.T. Scot.) and *Beinn Nuis* (N.T. Scot.) also offer splendid climbing. A road, known as the String Road, proceeds south-west from Brodick through Glen Shurig, affording fine views from high ground, and reaching the west coast at *Blackwaterfoot* (*q.v.*). A branch from this road leads to *Machrie* (*q.v.*) higher up the coast, and passes within sight of the Standing Stones of Tormore, with remains of some 10 circles, situated to the south of the Machrie Water, nearing the shores of Kilbrennan Sound. The Glen Rosa valley, north-west of Brodick, offers some of the finest scenery in the neighbourhood, and from its head, a climb over a col gives access for walkers to Glen Sannox and *Sannox* (*q.v.*). South of Brodick, the *Lamlash* (*q.v.*) road goes inland, but a path circles the low *Clauchland* hills, keeping near the coast, affording fine views. See **Corrie.** *Iter. 242.*

BRODIE, Moray. Map 25, **NH 9** 5.
E.C. Sat. The imposing *Brodie Castle* stands a little to the north, with the Muckle Water flowing to the east on its way to Findhorn Bay. *Iter. 175, 198, 199.*

BROOMHALL, Fife. Map 16, **NT 0** 8.
See **Charlestown.**

BRORA, Sutherland. 1,074. Map 31, **NC 9** 0.
E.C. Wed. GOLF. A small resort, with a harbour, sands and bathing, on the River Brora, noted for salmon. Here the river enters the sea after flowing through Loch Brora, over which, a few miles inland, hangs the *Carrol Rock*, nearly 700 ft. high. To the west of the loch is Strath Brora. Brora Bridge was the only one in the county prior to Telford's 19th cent. road-making. A coal mine, first opened at Brora in 1598, is said to be the sole example in the north of Scotland. There are a number of Pictish brochs in the vicinity, including *Cole Castle*, near the head of Loch Brora, and *Kintradwell*. The latter, a particularly notable example, is situated **3 m. N.E.** of Brora, off the Helmsdale road. **3 m. S.W.** is *Uppat House*, dating from the 18th cent. See **Loth.** *Iter. 200, 231, 233.*

BROUGHTON, Peebles. 732 Map 9, **NT 1** 3.
E.C. Wed. Here, Biggar Water and the Broughton Burn unite to flow together into the Tweed to the south-east of the village. Beside the ruined old church, in the cemetery, is a restored vault, thought to be the remains of a cell, founded in the 7th cent. by St. Llolan, a Pictish saint. There are numerous hill-forts on the surrounding hills. The village is associated with John Buchan (Lord Tweedsmuir) who spent many holidays here. The modern mansion of *Broughton Place* has fine gardens. The former house was the home of Murray of Broughton, who was secretary to Prince Charles Edward in 1745, and was later captured, subsequently turning King's Evidence and eventually dying in England. See **Drumelzier** and **Lyne.** *Iter. 10.*

BROUGHTY FERRY, Angus. 11,380. Map 17, **NO 4** 3.
E.C. Wed. GOLF. A pleasant resort and suburb of Dundee, with sands and bathing. Opposite, across the Firth of Tay, stands Tayport. *Broughty Castle*, 15th cent. (A.M.), was restored in 1860, and has a battlemented top. *Claypotts Castle* (A.M.), built between 1569 and 1588, is a quaint example of its period, notably the angle towers, with their crow-stepped gables. Claverhouse of Dundee once owned the castle. It is partly a museum and is open weekdays (except Fri.) 11 to 1 and 2 to 5; Sun. 2 to 5 (museum only June to Sept. (See note page 98.) See **Monifieth.** *Iter. 155.*

BROW, Dumfries. Map 3, **NY 0** 6.
On an inlet of the Solway Firth, and once a small watering-place, visited in 1796 by Robert Burns, a week prior to his death. The Brow Well recalls the visit.

BROXBURN, East Lothian. Map 10, **NT 6** 7.
Just off the Great North Road, to the south-east, is the site of the battle of *Dunbar* (*q.v.*), fought in 1650, in which Cromwell defeated Leslie and the Covenanters. A stone was erected in 1950 to commemorate the fight. To the east, on the coast, are white sands and the Barn's Ness lighthouse. *Iter. 1, 2, 38, 39.*

BROXBURN, West Lothian. 7,555. Map 9, **NT 0** 7.
E.C. Wed. A mining village. At *Kirkhill* farm, to the north-west, is a curious, inscribed "solar" stone, erected by the 11th Earl of Buchan in the 18th cent. See **Uphall.** *Iter. 16.*

BRUAR FALLS, Perth. Map 19, **NN 8** 6.
See **Struan.**

BRUICHLADDICH, Isle of Islay, Argyll. Map 6, **NR 2** 6.
A small port on the western shores of Loch Indaal. There are distilleries in the neighbourhood. *Iter. 247.*

BUCCLEUCH, Selkirk. Map 10, **NT 3** 1.
Near *Buccleuch* farm stood formerly a tower, which gave its name to the title of the Dukes of Buccleuch. *Iter. 34.*

BUCHAN, Aberdeen. Map 27, **NJ 8** 5 etc.
The name given to the north-eastern and rather bleak sector of the county, which includes the fishing ports of Fraserburgh and Peterhead, and a long, mainly undeveloped stretch of coastline north and south of Rattray Head. The land is almost entirely flat, a notable land-

Brora, Sutherland. The broch of Kintradwell, situated some 3 miles to the north-east, off A9

Broughton, Peebles. An inscribed gate on the Rachan estate

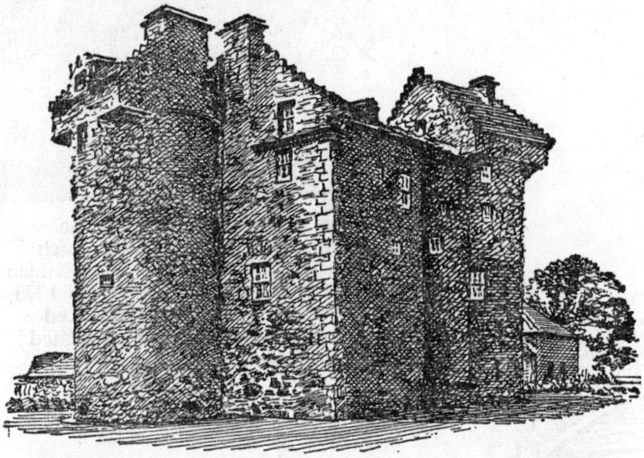

Broughty Ferry, Angus. The 16th century Claypotts Castle. It was allegedly once the home of a mistress of Cardinal Beaton, and Claverhouse of Dundee lived there for a time

Brow, Dumfries. The Brow Well, visited by Robert Burns a week before his death in 1796. It stands on B725, a mile south-west of Ruthwell Church

Broxburn, East Lothian. A stone, placed just off the Great North Road (A1), commemorating the Battle of Dunbar, fought in 1650. The inscription quotes words written by Thomas Carlyle

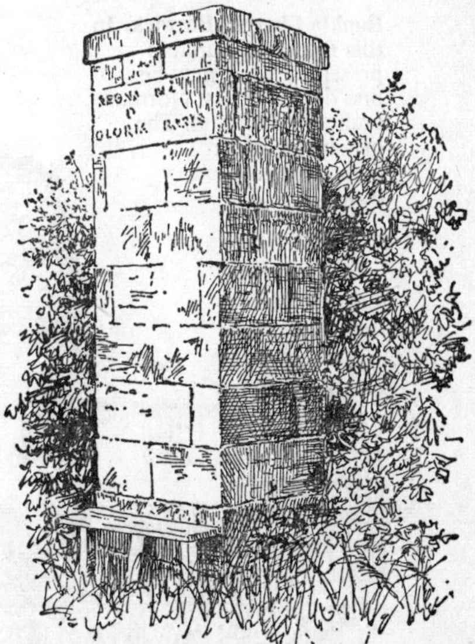

Broxburn, West Lothian. The curious inscribed 'Solar Stone' at Kirkhill Farm. It was set up in the 18th century by the 11th Earl of Buchan, who founded the Society of Antiquaries of Scotland

[For BUCHAN see following plate
[For BRODICK see under ARRAN (Plate 10)
[For BROADMEADOWS see under NEWARK CASTLE (Plate 127)

Buchan, Aberdeen. The Town House of 1788 at Peterhead, a fishing port in the Buchan, or north-east corner of the county

Bullers of Buchan, Aberdeen. The strange, rocky amphitheatre, which lies a mile to the north-east of Cruden Bay. Dr. Johnson, in his tour of 1773, visited it by boat, and pronounced it a 'rock perpendicularly tubulated'

Bunkle Church, Berwick. In this re-built Church is preserved what may be one of the earliest Norman arches in Scotland. The original Norman Church was taken down in 1820

Burns Country, Ayr; Dumfries. The late 19th century Burns Memorial Tower, which stands to the north of Mauchline, an Ayrshire town, on A76. In the vicinity is Mossgiel Farm, where his early poems were written

Burntisland, Fife. The Church, built in 1592, probably to a Dutch design. The tower was added in 1759

[For BUTE see following plate

mark being the low *Mormond Hill*, with its two carved animals, a white horse and a stag, situated near *Strichen* (*q.v.*). The River Deveron forms the western boundary of Buchan for a short distance, and along the southern boundary flows the less-important Ythan, on the banks of which is situated the splendid castle of *Fyvie* (*q.v.*). On the Buchan coast is *Buchan Ness* the most easterly point in Scotland, situated to the south of Peterhead. Its powerful lighthouse dates from 1827.

BUCHANTY, Perth. Map 16, **NN 9** 2.
Iter. 147.

BUCHLYVIE, Stirling. 349. Map 15, **NS 5** 9.
E.C. Wed. A hand-weaving industry is established here. **2 m. W.** is *Auchentoig*, a house dating from 1702, which is associated with Rob Roy. *Iter. 108, 112, 137.*

BUCKHAVEN, Fife. 18,689. SB. with Methil. Map 17, **NT 3** 9.
E.C. Thurs. Once a ferry-port and fishing centre, this quaint little place has " streets " of steps and also old-world corners, common to many Fife villages. It is now united with *Methil* (*q.v.*). The Church was brought here in sections from St. Andrews by boat by the local fishermen and then re-erected. *Iter. 128.*

BUCKIE, Banff. 7.914. SB. Map 26, **NJ 4** 6.
E.C. Wed. GOLF. An important fishing town, with a good harbour, situated on Spey Bay. Along the coast, to the east, are a number of small fishing villages nestling in the cliffside, among which, beyond Craig Head, *Findochty* (*q.v.*) and *Portnockie* (*q.v.*) are the most attractive. See **Portessie.** *Iter. 178, 199.*

BULLERS OF BUCHAN, Aberdeen. Map 27, **NK 1** 3.
See **Cruden Bay.**

BUNESSAN, Isle of Mull, Argyll. Map 13, **NM 3** 2.
Lies in the peninsula of the Ross of Mull, noted for granite quarries, and on the road which links the eastern part of the island with *Fionnphort*, some five miles to the west, from where a passenger ferry connects with *Iona* (*q.v.*). Away to the south is the small island of *Erraid*, associated with R. L. Stevenson's " Kidnapped," and out to sea are the Torran Rocks. North of Bunessan is the sea loch of Na Lathaich, and to the south-east is Loch Assapol. *Iter. 249.*

BUNKLE CHURCH, Berwick. Map 11, **NT 8** 5.
See **Preston.**

BURGHEAD, Moray. 1,369. SB. Map 26, **NJ 1** 6.
A fishing village, with a harbour and lighthouse, on the eastern horn of Burghead Bay overlooking the Moray Firth. There are extensive sands in the bay. The past is recalled by a rampart known as the " Broch Bailies," and also by a rock-cistern (A.M.) called the " Roman Bath." Ptolemy's " Alata Castra " may be identified with the village. The 505-ft. high mast of the B.B.C. radio transmitter, erected in 1936, is a notable local landmark. A curious old custom, still kept up on Old Yule Night, January 11th, is " Burning the Clavie," a tar-filled barrel being set alight and rolled down Dorrie Hill in order to ward off evil spirits. See **Duffus** and **Hopeman.** *Iter. 199.*

BURNBANK, Lanark. Map 8, **NS 7** 5.
Iter. 19, 53.

BURNHAVEN, Aberdeen. Map 27, **NK 1** 4.
Dates from the 19th cent. and lies adjacent to *Peterhead* (*q.v.*) prison. The village is situated between Peterhead and Sandford Bays and looks south-eastwards to Buchan Ness. *Iter. 181, 182, 187.*

BURNHOUSES, Berwick. Map 11, **NT 7** 5.
Above the hamlet, to the north, rises *Cockburn Law*, 1,065 ft., and to the east are the curves of the Whiteadder Water. See **Abbey St. Bathans.** *Iter. 3.*

BURNMOUTH, Berwick. 512. Map 11, **NT 9** 6.
A delightful little fishing village, at the foot of sandstone cliffs, sheltered by Ross Point, to the south. Northwards, beyond Ross Bay, is a rocky stretch of coast leading to Nestends, facing Hare Point across the Eye estuary. Two treaties between Scotland and England, in 1384, and again in 1497, were signed at Burnmouth. See **Eyemouth and Lamberton.** *Iter. 2.*

BURNS COUNTRY, THE, Ayr; Dumfries.
Map 3, **NX 9** 7 etc. and 8, **NS 3** 2 etc.
Ayrshire is the county most intimately connected with the works of the great poet Robert Burns, and the town of *Ayr* itself, together with its neighbour *Alloway*, the birthplace of Burns, makes an admirable centre for visits to those places which are most associated with his life and works. Outside the county, the town of *Dumfries* is very closely connected with Burns, he having lived and worked there for five years, and being buried, together with members of his family, in *St. Michael's* churchyard. In the vicinity of Dumfries, near Auldgirth, is *Ellisland*, a farm, where Burns composed " Tam o'Shanter." Outside Mauchline, an Ayrshire town, is the farmhouse of *Mossgiel*, where some of his earliest works were written. See **Alloway, Auldgirth, Ayr, Catrine, Dumfries, Kilmarnock, Kirkoswald, Mauchline, Moffat** and **Tarbolton.**

BURNTISLAND, Fife. 5,422. SB. Map 17, **NT 2** 8.
E.C. Wed. GOLF. This Royal Burgh and coaling port on the Firth of Forth is overlooked by the hill known as *The Binn*, 632 ft. Bathing is from sands. The Church, modelled perhaps on the North Church at Amsterdam, dates from 1592, the tower having been built in 1749. An outside staircase gives access to the Sailors' Loft. It has a magistrate's pew, constructed in 1606, and there are seats especially marked for the various town guilds. Some characteristic 17th cent. houses line Somerville Street. In the Civil War, Burntisland was occupied by Cromwell. The town faces *Granton* (*q.v.*), some five miles across the Firth of Forth. See **Aberdour, Inchcolm** and **Inchkeith.** *Iter. 134.*

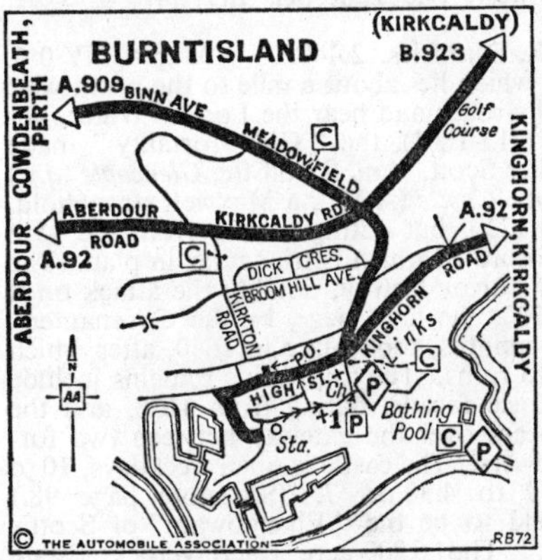

Church (1592) 1

BURRAY, Orkney. Map 33, **ND 4** 9.
Iter. 266.

BURRELTON, Perth. Map 17, **NO 2** 3.
Iter. 151, 153.

BURWICK, Orkney. Map 33, **ND 4** 8.
See **Orkney Islands** (South Ronaldsay). *Iter. 266.*

BUSBY, Lanark; Renfrew. 5,333. Map 8, **NS 5** 5.
GOLF. *Iter. 18, 29.*

BUTE, ISLE OF, Bute. Map 7, **NS 0** 6 etc.
The island is situated off the *Cowal* (*q.v.*) coast, from which it is separated by the picturesque *Kyles of Bute* (*q.v.*). To the south, the Sound of Bute, in which lies the tiny island of *Inch Marnock*, divides it from the larger island of *Arran* (*q.v.*), well seen from various points. These islands, together with the smaller *Cumbraes* (See **Millport**), in the Firth of Clyde to the east, constitute the county of Bute. The island of Bute itself is about 15 miles long, averaging 3 to 5 miles in width, and, except in the northern sector, it is well provided with roads. The only high ground is in the north, beyond *Port Bannatyne*. The resort of *Rothesay* is one of the best known in Scotland, and in the south-eastern extremity of the island is *Kilchattan Bay*, the nearest point to the Cumbraes. Access to the island, which has a number of

sandy bays for bathing, is gained by steamer services connecting Rothesay with various Clyde ports, and also by means of the car ferry linking *Rhubodach* with *Colintraive* (*q.v.*), on the Kyles of Bute. See **Kilchattan Bay, Port Bannatyne, Rothesay** and **Rhubodach.** *Iter. 241.*

BUTTERSTONE, Perth. Map 20, **NO 0** 4.
To the south is the little Loch Butterstone, and almost adjoining it is the Loch of the Lowes, with the tiny Loch Craignish to the north. Away to the north lie the lofty moorlands of the Forest of Clunie, with the lonely lochs of Ordie and Benachally. See **Clunie.** *Iter. 141, 158, 166.*

CABRACH, Banff. Map 26, **NJ 3** 2.
Stands about 1,000 ft. high, on a fine road leading north-westwards over the hills towards *Dufftown* (*q.v.*), crossing first the Deveron valley and then the 1,197-ft. high Glacks of Balloch pass. East of the village, the road to Rhynie attains 1,350 ft. on the Aberdeenshire border. To the south-east of Cabrach, on the Aberdeen border, rises the *Buck o, Cabrach*, 2,368 ft., away to the west of which the Deveron has its lonely source among the hills. *Iter. 177, 190.*

CADDONFOOT, Selkirk. 411. Map 10, **NT 4** 3.
Situated in the wooded Tweed valley, between *Craig Hill*, 1,252 ft., to the south, and *Meigle*, 1,387 ft., and its neighbours, to the north-east. The Caddon Water flows into the river a little to the west. See **Ashiestiel.** *Iter. 14.*

CAERLAVEROCK, Dumfries. 2,440. Map 4, **NY 0** 6.
In the churchyard, which lies about a mile to the north-west of *Bankend*, off a by-road, and near the Lochar Water, lies Robert Paterson (1715-1801), the "Old Mortality" made famous by Sir Walter Scott. **4 m. S.,** off the *Glencaple* (*q.v.*) road, is *Caerlaverock Castle* (A.M.), a Maxwell stronghold, first mentioned in 1220, but dating mainly from the 15th cent., and the enclosure of which is triangular in plan. The building has had a stormy history, notably the attack on it by Edward I in 1300. Its final siege, by the Covenanters, which lasted three months, took place in 1640, after which it fell gradually into ruins. The impressive remains include a notable Renaissance façade, dating from 1638, and the Maxwell crest appears over the gateway between two formidable circular towers. The castle is open weekdays, 10 to 4.30 or 7; Sun., 2 to 4.30 or 7. (See note page 98.) Caerlaverock is held to be the "Ellangowan" of Scott's "Guy Mannering." The 6,200-acre Caerlaverock Estate is now a Nature Reserve. To the north is *Wardlaw Hill*, crowned by a prehistoric fort, with views over the Solway Firth and across the estuary of the Nith to *Criffell*, 1,866 ft., overlooking the Solway Firth. See **Balmaclellan** and **Dunnottar Castle.** *Iter. 28.*

CAIRNBAAN, Argyll. Map 14, **NR 8** 9.
Situated midway along the Crinan Canal, on which the summit level is a little to the west. At Cairnbaan is a series of nine locks on the canal. Some 200 yards north of the hotel are two cup and ring-marked rocks (A.M.), relics of the prehistoric age. See **Crinan** and **Kilmichael.** *Iter. 122.*

CAIRNDOW, Argyll. Map 14, **NN 1** 1.
Stands at the western end of Glen Kinglas a little below the re-aligned main road and on the shores of upper *Loch Fyne* (*q.v.*), overlooked by *Binnein an Fhidhleir*, 2,658 ft. To the north, the River Fyne flows into the loch from Glen Fyne, to the east of which, at a height of 1,278 ft., are the impressive, but not so well-known Eagle's Falls. **1 m. S.W.** is *Ardkinglas House*, a modern mansion, built by Sir Robert Lorimer. See **Rest and be Thankful.** *Iter. 88, 101, 102.*

CAIRNGORMS, Aberdeen; Banff; Inverness.
Map 20, **NH 9** 0 etc.
The *Cairngorms* form an extensive group of lofty flat-topped mountains, broken by lonely corries, and stretching from *Deeside* (*q.v.*) to Speyside, to the north-east of the main *Grampian* (*q.v.*) range. Their outlook across the Dee Valley is towards the famous peak of *Lochnagar* (*q.v.*), the monarch of the *Mounth* group. In the Cairngorms lies the largest area of ground in Scotland over the 4,000-ft. level, including the four well-defined peaks of *Ben Macdhui*, 4,296 ft., the second highest of Scottish mountains, with a view-indicator on the summit; *Braeriach*, 4,248 ft., on the two-mile long Garbh Choire cliffs on which is the source of the River Dee, and which overlooks the well-known pass of the *Lairig Ghru* (*q.v.*), used by long-distance walkers; *Cairn Toul*, 4,241 ft., prominent in the westerly view from *Braemar* (*q.v.*); and lastly *Cairn Gorm*, 4,084 ft., the most northerly of the quartet, which has given its name to the entire range. Near *Cairn Gorm* is *Cairn Lochan*, 3,983 ft., on the edge of the wild Coire an t-Sneachda, overlooked by the spectacular Fiacaill Ridge. Below *Cairn Gorm* lies the remote and gloomy Loch Avon, in its wild mountain setting, with the Shelter Stone at the western extremity. *Beinn Mheadoin*, 3,883 ft., also overlooks the loch, and to the south-west lies the tiny Loch Etchachan, at a height of more than 3,000 ft. This loch to said to remain frozen over for more than half the year. Another wild loch, that of Einich, deep below the great cliffs of *Sgoran Dubh*, 3,658 ft., on the western fringe of the range, is overlooked by the bare and lofty plateau known as the Great Moss, or Am Moine Mhor, sheltering the tiny Lochan nan Cnapan. In 1859, Queen Victoria climbed to the summit of *Ben Macdhui*, once considered to be Britain's highest peak.

Among the lesser peaks are *Ben Avon*, 3,843 ft., in the extreme east, overlooking the great Slochd Mor rift, and the waters of the Upper Avon; *Bheinn a'Bhuird*, 3,924 ft., and 3,860 ft., rising above Glen Quoich; *Derry Cairngorm*, 3,788 ft., between Glen Derry and Glen Lui Beg; and *Beinn Bhrotain*, 3,797 ft., to the west of Glen Dee, and on the edge of Mar Forest. Owing to their great bulk, the Cairngorms can be seen at a distance from many parts of Scotland, while some of the best of the nearer views are those obtainable from parts of the Spey valley, in particular near *Aviemore* (*q.v.*). The two main passes through the hills linking Deeside and Speyside, the *Lairig Ghru*, and the less well-known *Lairig an Laoigh*, are ancient rights-of-way, and were formerly much used by cattle drovers. They are, however, only suitable for very strong walkers, as the distances are long and the going very difficult in places, while bad weather can turn the crossings into hazardous expeditions.

The Cairngorms are composed mainly of granite, and in some places quartz crystals, known as "Cairngorms," are to be found, and are often mounted in articles of jewellery. On the lower slopes of the hills large expanses of heather give a vivid colouring to the scene. The old name for the Cairngorms is the *Monadruadh*, or Red Mountains, as opposed to the much lower *Monadhliath*, or Grey Mountains, which rise west of the Spey valley. Snow lies to a great depth for many months on certain of the peaks and also in the remote corries, notably on *Braeriach*. Winter sports can be enjoyed from some of the well-known resorts on the fringe of the high hills, such as Aviemore, Kingussie, Braemar and Tomintoul. (See **Rothiemurchus.**) All of these are described under their own headings, and the first-named is convenient for the fine Glen More Forest Park, east ot *Rothiemurchus* Forest, in which are scanty remains of the former Caledonian Forest once covering much of the Highlands. The Cairngorm district forms one of the proposed Scottish National Parks, which is expected to cover some 180 square miles. The Cairngorm National Nature Reserve is over 60,000 acres in extent and is rich in local fauna and flora, notably of arctic-alpine type. Bird life includes the greenshank, dotterel and snow bunting. See **Inverey, Loch Morlich** and **Nethybridge.**

CAIRN O' MOUNTH, Kincardine. Map 21, **NO 6** 8.
One of the best known of the passes traversing the lower, or eastern *Grampians* (*q.v.*), linking *Banchory* (*q.v.*) with *Fettercairn* (*q.v.*), and liable to be blocked by snow in winter. The summit of the pass, at a height of 1,475 ft., a fine viewpoint, is **5 m. N.** of Fettercairn, gradients on the ascent reaching 1 in 5½, and on the subsequent descent 1 in 6½. Far to the west is *Mount Battock*, 2,555 ft., and to the north is *Clachnaben*, 1,944 ft. Eastwards, the view

Bute, Isle of, Bute. The remains of the mainly 13th century Castle at Rothesay, the most important resort on the island.

Caerlaverock, Dumfries. The impressive, ruined Maxwell stronghold, invested by Edward I in 1300, and attacked by the Covenanters in 1640. It stands 3 miles to the south, off B725

Cairnbaan, Argyll. Examples of prehistoric cup and ring marked rocks

Cairngorms, Aberdeen; Banff; Inverness. Alvie Church, on Loch Alvie, near Lynwilg, as seen from A9. To the north-west rises Geal Charn Mor, 2,702 feet, from which the view of the Cairngorms is perhaps the finest in Strath Spey

Cairngorms, Aberdeen; Banff; Inverness. The Cairngorm mountains, seen from the unclassified road from Aviemore to Loch Morlich, in the Glen More Forest Park

Cairn O'Mounth, Kincardine. A footbridge and ford near Glen Dye (B974), on the descent from the pass towards Deeside

[For CAIRNBAAN see also under KNAPDALE (Plate 103)

Cairn Ryan, Wigtown. White-harled houses on Loch Ryan. Part of the 'Mulberry' harbour used for the invasion of Normandy during the Second World War was constructed here

Cairnwell Pass, Aberdeen; Perth. Near the summit of the pass in the Grampian mountains, where A93 attains 2,199 feet, the highest altitude of any main road in Great Britain

Caledonian Canal, Inverness. The series of eight locks at Corpach, near Fort William, off A830, which are known as 'Neptune's Staircase'

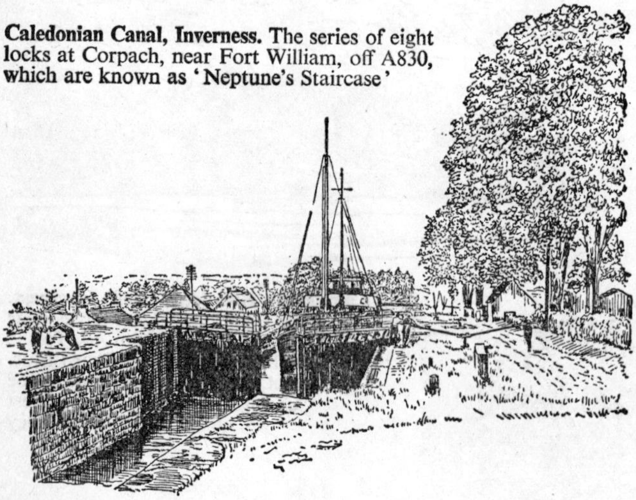

California, Stirling. The surprising village sign

Callander, Perth. The sundial of 1753, which stands in South Church Street, near the River Teith. The inscription reads:

"I mark not the hours
unless they bring light,
I mark not the hours of
darkness and night,
My promise is solely to
follow the sun,
And point out the course
his chariot doth run"

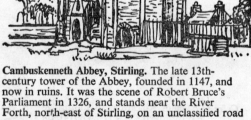

Cambuskenneth Abbey, Stirling. The late 13th-century tower of the Abbey, founded in 1147, and now in ruins. It was the scene of Robert Bruce's Parliament in 1326, and stands near the River Forth, north-east of Stirling, on an unclassified road

ranges over the fertile Howe of the Mearns and the distant Kincardine coast. The names of Macbeth, Edward I, Montrose and Claverhouse, are all associated with the Pass, the first-named having fled northwards to *Lumphanan* (*q.v.*) across the Dee. The bridge over the Dye Water, **4 m. N.** of the summit, in the heart of the delightfully wooded Glen Dye, dates from 1680, and was one of the earliest bridges in the district. *Iter. 163, 165.*

CAIRNPAPPLE HILL, West Lothian. Map 9, **NS 9 7.** See **Torphichen.**

CAIRN RYAN, Wigtown. Map 2, **NX 0 6.** Once known as *Macherie* this little village of whitewashed houses is situated on the eastern shores of Loch Ryan, sheltered by Cairn Point. *Lochryan*, a house of 1701, has fine gardens. To the north, on Leight Moor, is the so-called "Taxing Stone," said to mark the tomb of a Scottish King, murdered in 741. Beyond the Moor is lovely Glen App, traversed by the Water of App, flowing into Loch Ryan at Finnart Bay. See **Ballantrae.** *Iter. 55, 80, 84.*

CAIRNWELL PASS, Aberdeen; Perth. Map 20, **NO 1 7.** The summit of the pass, at 2,199 ft., is the highest main road altitude reached in Great Britain, and forms part of the original military road linking Coupar Angus with Braemar, first constructed in the mid-18th cent. by General Caulfeild, one of Wade's successors. The *Devil's Elbow* section was not, however, on the line of the original road, and probably dates from the early 19th cent. The road over the pass is liable to be blocked by snow in winter. The *Cairnwell*, 3,059 ft., to the west, and *Glas Maol*, 3,502 ft., to the east, the latter across the Angus border, dominate the Cairnwell Pass, and below the summit, on the road leading southwards to *Blairgowrie* (*q.v.*), is the well-known *Devil's Elbow*, described under *Glenshee*. Excellent ski-ing (chairlift) can be enjoyed in the vicinity when conditions are suitable. The northerly descent from the summit of the pass gives access through Glen Clunie to *Braemar* (*q.v.*). A path, essentially for long-distance walkers, crosses the eastern shoulder of *Glas Maol*, and is known as the *Monega Pass.* It attains 3,318 ft., the highest right-of-way in the country, and gives access to the head of Glen Isla and *Kirkton of Glenisla* (*q.v.*). An unbroken chain of lofty hills stretches north-eastwards from *Glas Maol* by way of *Cairn na Glasha*, 3,484 ft. to *Lochnagar* (*q.v.*) in the *White Mounth* (*q.v.*) group. *Iter. 141, 152, 160, 167, 168.*

CALDERCRUIX, Lanark. 2,917. Map 9, **NS 8 6.** To the east is the large Hillend reservoir. *Iter. 16.*

CALEDONIAN CANAL, Inverness. Map 18, **NN 1** 7 etc. and 25, **NH 6** 4 etc. Thomas Telford began, in 1803, the construction of this artificial waterway through the Great Glen of Alban, or *Glen More* (*q.v.*), which virtually splits Scotland into two portions. The work, which cost more than £1,250,000, was completed after 44 years, at the end of which sailing vessels were enabled to pass from the North Sea to the Atlantic and the West Coast of Scotland, avoiding the stormy journey around Cape Wrath. The advent of steam has since made the canal largely unnecessary. By means of the canal, the towns of *Inverness* (*q.v.*), on the Inner Moray Firth, and *Fort William* (*q.v.*), on Loch Linnhe, were brought into touch, utilising the waters of Loch Ness, Loch Oich, and Loch Lochy, which are links in the canal proper. The latter extends in length to some 22 miles out of a total length of 60½ miles along the glen, and no fewer than 29 locks had to be constructed, the most notable being the series known as "Neptune's Staircase" near *Corpach* (*q.v.*). See **Loch Lochy, Loch Ness, Loch Oich** and **Westerkirk.** *Iter. 207, 210, 213, 214.*

CALGARY, Isle of Mull, Argyll. Map 12, **NM 3 5.** Lies in the north-western extremity of the island, on Calgary Bay, with fine sands for bathing. Emigrants from here founded a Calgary in Canada. Away to the north, near the lonely Callach Point, the poet Campbell once lived as a tutor, and here some of his works were composed. From Calgary there are views of the scattered Treshnish Islands away to the south-west, while almost due westwards lie the larger islands of Coll and *Tiree* (*q.v.*). *Iter. 248.*

CALIFORNIA, Stirling. Map 16, **NS 9 7.** A village on high ground in a mining district.

CALLANDER, Perth. 1,769. SB. Map 15, **NN 6 0.** **E.C.** Wed. GOLF. A well-known touring centre and "Gateway of the Highlands," especially convenient for the *Trossachs* (*q.v.*). Sir Walter Scott was a frequent visitor to the district, which he has depicted in the "Lady of the Lake." The *Roman Camp* Hotel has associations with J. M. Barrie. In South Church Street is an inscribed sundial dated 1753. The town stands on the River Teith, which is joined to the west by the Leny, flowing through the beautiful Pass of Leny from Loch Lubnaig. In the Pass are the picturesque Falls of Leny. *St. Bride's Chapel*, partly restored as a memorial to Sir Walter Scott, stands beyond the Pass, on the way to Loch Lubnaig. North-west of Callander is *Ben Ledi*, 2,875 ft., the monarch of the district, a noted viewpoint, and on its northern slopes lies the tiny Lochan nan Corp, with which is associated the tragedy of a burial party due to breaking ice. To the north-east of the town are the Falls of Bracklinn, on the Keltie Water, from which a path continues through the hills to lonely Glen Artney, by means of which the town of *Comrie* (*q.v.*) can be reached. The road leading westwards from Callander traverses the northern shores of Loch Vennachar, described in Scott's "Lady of the Lake," and later reaches the *Brig o' Turk*, for which see under *Trossachs*. Callander is the "Tannochbrae" of the television series "Dr. Finlay's Casebook." See **Balquhidder, Doune** and **Strathyre.** *Iter. 106, 107, 109, 139, 141, 142, 144, 146.*

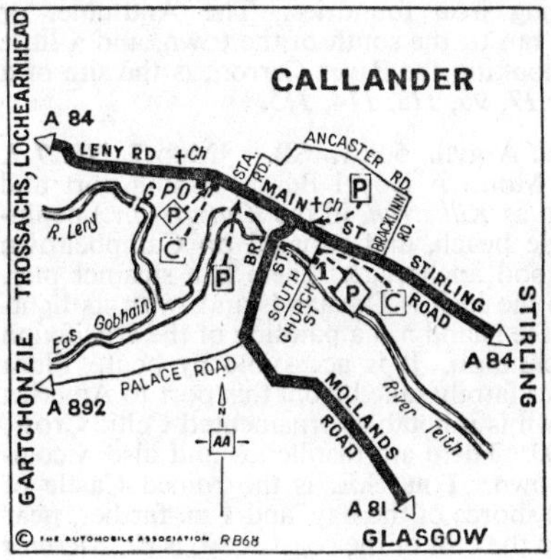

Sundial (1753) 1

CALLANISH, Isle of Lewis, Ross and Cromarty. Map 32, **NB 2 3.** See **Hebrides, Outer** (Lewis). *Iter. 260.*

CAMASNACROISE, Argyll. Map 18, **NM 8 5.** Situated on a small inlet of *Loch Linnhe* (*q.v.*), with the smaller Loch a' Choire lying a little to the west. In the background rises *Creach Bheinn*, 2,800 ft., at the head of Glenalmadale. The views across Loch Linnhe from Camasnacroise are very fine, and extend from the island of *Lismore* (*q.v.*) along the picturesque *Appin* (*q.v.*) coast towards the distant *Lochaber* (*q.v.*) mountains. The road leading north-eastwards into the hills forks after about six miles, the northern branch giving access to the shores of *Loch Sunart* (*q.v.*), and the south-western branch continuing through Gleann Geal towards the *Morven* (*q.v.*) country and the shores of the Sound of Mull at *Lochaline* (*q.v.*). *Iter. 218.*

CAMBUSKENNETH ABBEY, Stirling. Map 16, **NS 8 9.** See **Stirling.**

CAMBUSLANG, Lanark. 15,905 Map 8, **NS 6 6.** **E.C.** Wed. GOLF. Has extensive iron and steel works. To the south-west lies the attractive, wooded public park of Cathkin Braes, at a height of 646 ft., with wide views. The 17th century house of *Gilbertfield* stands off the Hamilton road, to the south-east. *Iter 53.*

CAMBUS O'MAY, Aberdeen. 40. Map 20, **NO 4 9.** **E.C.** Thurs. Nearby flows the Dee in a richly wooded stretch, and to the north-east are the two small lochs of Kinord and Davan. On the latter is an ancient "crannog," or lake-dwelling. Across the Dee, to the south, is the farm-house of *Ballaterach*, where Byron spent part of his youth (See **Bridge of Ess**). On *Culblean Hill*, 1,567 ft., to the north of Cambus o' May, where a battle was fought in 1335, is a curious rock-chamber called the "Vat," and beyond rises *Morven*, 2,862 ft., the highest mountain in the district. *Iter 141, 152, 167, 179.*

CAMELON, Stirling. 9,398. Map 16, **NS 8 8.** **E.C.** Wed. Situated on the site of a former Roman town, and now possessing iron foundries. The Antonine, or *Roman* (*q.v.*) Wall ran to the south of the town, and a little to the north, overlooking the River Carron, is the site of a double camp. *Iter 17, 95, 113, 114, 115.*

CAMPBELTOWN, Argyll. 5,961. SB. Map 7, **NR 7 2.** **E.C.** Wed. **M.D.** Mon. A Royal Burgh, fishing port and resort, once known as *Kilkerran*, in the *Kintyre* (*q.v.*) peninsula, with a shingle beach, and situated on Campbeltown Loch, forming a good anchorage. There is a steamer pier. At the entrance to the loch is Davaar Island, with its lighthouse. A cave on the island has a painting of the crucifixion by Archibald Mackinnon. It is accessible by boat. Flora MacDonald and her family sailed from this port to America in 1774. In the town is a notable, ornamented Celtic Cross, dating from c. 1500. There are distilleries and also a coal-mine at Campbeltown. **1 m. S.E.** is the ruined Castle of *Kilkerran*, near the shores of the bay, and **1 m.** farther, near Achinhoan Head to the east of the coast road, is *St. Kieran's Cave*, 25 ft. above high water, which may be the earliest Christian Chapel in Scotland. A car ferry links with Red Bay, Co. Antrim, in Northern Ireland. To the west of the town is the *Machrihanish* (*q.v.*) airport, with services to Glasgow (Renfrew airport), and Islay, and still farther west is Machrihanish itself, famous for golf. See **Mull of Kintyre, Saddell** and **Southend.** *Iter 121, 122, 123.*

CAMPSIE GLEN, Stirling. Map 15, **NS 6 7.** Stands at the foot of the well-known glen in the *Campsie Fells*, through which climbs the Crow Road, leading from *Lennoxtown* (*q.v.*) to *Fintry* (*q.v.*), reaching a height of 1,154 ft., with good views. *Earl's Seat*, 1,896 ft., away to the west, is a noted viewpoint. *Iter. 107, 115.*

CAMUSNAGAUL, Argyll. Map 18, **NN 0 7.** At the head of *Loch Linnhe* (*q.v.*) on its western shore, and near the meeting with Loch Eil, *Camusnagaul* stands on the narrow, winding road linking *Kinlocheil* (*q.v.*) with *Ardgour* (*q.v.*). It gives a view across Loch Linnhe to Fort William, backed by the great bulk of *Ben Nevis*, 4,406 ft., which from this point dominates the town. The hill-ridge rising west of Camusnagaul attains 2,527 ft. with *Stob Choire a' Chearcail*, a fine viewpoint, overlooking the junction of the Cona Glen with Glen Scaddle. *Iter. 215.*

CANISBAY, Caithness. 846. Map 30, **ND 3 7.** The Church here is the most northerly on the mainland and overlooks Gills Bay. Much of the structure is early 18th cent. work and a slab on the south wall is the actual gravestone of the original John de Groot, whose famous house stood formerly at *John O'Groats* (*q.v.*). There is also an old mill.

CANNA, ISLE OF, Inverness. Map 23, **NG 2 0.** See **Rum.**

CANNICH, Inverness. 243. Map 24, **NH 3 3.** **E.C.** Wed. Situated in a beautiful, wooded setting, at the south-western extremity of the picturesque and long valley of Strath Glass (See **Struy Bridge**), and in the immediate vicinity of the confluence of the Rivers Cannich and Glass. Two of Scotland's loveliest and most famous glens, those of Affric and Cannich, noted especially for their richly-wooded scenery, extend westwards from Cannich into the bare and lonely mountain country on the borders of Ross and Cromarty, but neither glen provides a throughway for motor traffic. The proposed Affric National Park will eventually cover the area contiguous to the two glens. A large hydro-electric scheme, inaugurated by the Duke of Edinburgh, in October 1952, now operates in the Cannich district, and has changed touring conditions to some extent. The power station for the whole scheme is situated at Fasnakyle, some **2½ m. S.W.** of Cannich, on the Glass. The new road to Glen Affric leads south-westwards from Cannich, passing near Fasnakyle, in the woods around which Prince Charles Edward wandered as a fugitive in 1746. It then traverses the picturesque Chisholm's Pass, with the Dog Fall, to emerge later by the shores of Loch Benevean, in a rich setting of birch and pine trees. The level of this loch has been raised, resulting in the formation of many tiny wooded islets, and a dam has been constructed at the eastern end, beyond which, to the south, lies the extensive Guisachan Forest. The road follows the northern shores of the loch, amid scenery of increasing grandeur, and finally reaches Loch Affric, above which rises the peak of *Sgurr na Lapaich*, 3,401 ft. In the background are the still higher summits of *Mam Sodhail*, 3,862 ft. and *Carn Eige*, 3,877 ft., the highest, though by no means the wildest mountains north of the Great Glen of Scotland, both forming notable viewpoints. Lonely tracks continue westwards beyond Loch Affric, passing under the slopes of the remote peak of *Sgurr nan Ceathreamhnan*, 3,771 ft., and giving access for long-distance walkers to *Croe Bridge* (*q.v.*) near Loch Duich.

Glen Cannich is reached by a re-made road leading first north-westwards from Cannich under *Beinn Acharain*, 2,119 ft., and then penetrating westwards through rugged, densely-wooded hills, later passing the tiny Loch Car, and then following the River Cannich to Loch Mullardoch. At the eastern end of this loch the main dam for the hydro-electric scheme has been built. The waters of the loch have been taken by tunnel to Loch Benevean. Lofty, bare hills rise to the north-west of the loch, *Sgurr na Lapaich*, 3,773 ft. (Ross-shire), and *An Riabhachan* 3,730 ft., being the principal summits. Long distance walkers' tracks continue westwards beyond Loch Mullardoch, passing Loch Lungard, and eventually reaching Glen Elchaig and Loch Long, in Wester Ross (See **Ardelve**). The peaks of *Mam Sodhail* and *Sgurr na Lapaich* (Ross-shire) were chosen as key-points in the principal triangulation of the Ordnance Survey of Great Britain in the years 1846 and 1848.

The road which links Cannich through Glen Urquhart to *Drumnadrochit* (*q.v.*), on Loch Ness, was constructed by Telford. Although the coming of the hydro-electric scheme to the Cannich district has brought in its train undoubted advantages, there are nevertheless many who will regret the need to have tampered with the magnificent scenery with which the area was endowed by nature, while the feeling of peace and solitude formerly associated with these two exceptionally lovely glens may never again be recaptured in its entirety. *Iter. 206, 210.*

CANONBIE, Dumfries. 1,609 Map 4, **NY 3 7.** **E.C.** Wed. The pleasant village of *Canonbie*, with its old coaching inn, stands on the river Esk, at the southern extremity of Eskdale. The river is joined, a little to the south, near the Liddel Moat, by the Liddel Water, traversing the long valley of *Liddesdale* (*q.v.*), which is associated with Dandie Dinmont in Scott's "Guy Mannering." The Esk, flowing towards the Solway Firth, was formerly the boundary between England and Scotland, and the tract between the Esk and the Sark became the so-called "debatable land," which deteriorated gradually into an area of lawlessness, until, in 1552, the *Scots Dyke* was constructed across the district to form a new territorial boundary. The former Priory of Canonbie was destroyed by the English in 1542. **2 m. N.**, to the east of the Esk, is a Roman Camp, situated to the north of Gilnockie station. **2 m. N.N.W.**, beyond Gilnockie Bridge, on the main Langholm road, stands *Hollows Tower*, dating from the 16th cent. and preserving walls 6 ft. thick. It was once the home of the 16th cent. Border reiver, Johnny Armstrong, whose other home of *Gilnockie* stood formerly near Gilnockie Bridge. See **Langholm** and **Teviothead.** *Iter. 11, 12, 30, 31, 47.*

CAPE DIFFICULTY, Isle of Lewis (Harris), Inverness. See **Hebrides, Outer** (Harris). Map 32, **NF 9 9.**

Canonbie, Dumfries. The 16th century Hollows Tower, where Johnny Armstrong, the celebrated Border 'reiver,' or freebooter, once lived. It stands 2 miles north-west of Canonbie, off A7

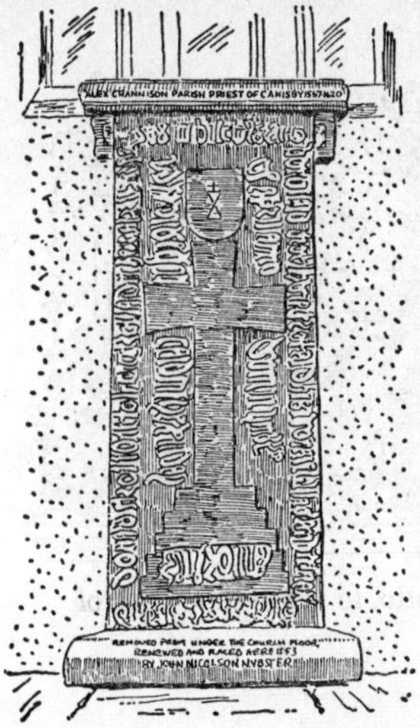

Canisbay, Caithness. The gravestone in the Church of the original John de Groot, whose house gave the name of John O' Groat's to the lonely outpost a little to the east

Cambus O'May, Aberdeen. The stone recalling the battle of Culblean (1335), fought on Culblean Hill. It was erected in 1956 by the Deeside Field Club and is situated 2 miles north, on A97

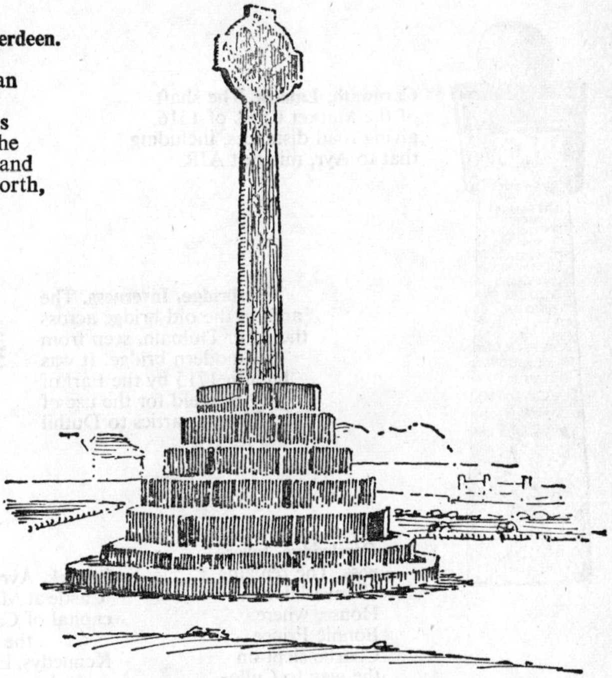

Campbeltown, Argyll. The richly-decorated Celtic Cross

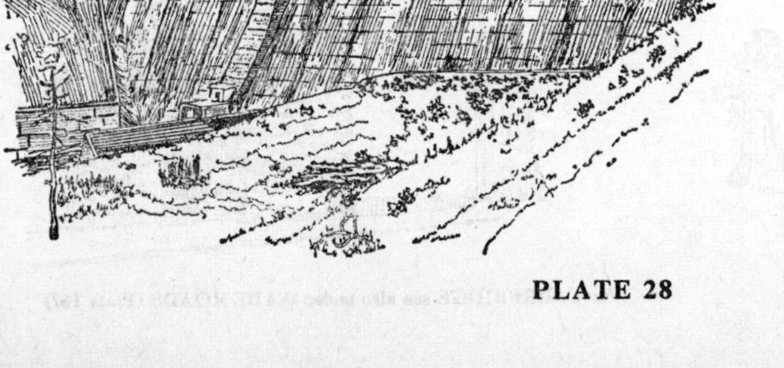

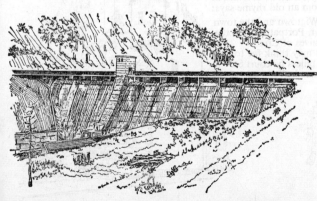

Cannich, Inverness. The dam on Loch Benevean, erected in connection with a large hydro-electric scheme operating in Glen Affric and Glen Cannich

Carfin, Lanark. The famous Grotto, to which thousands of pilgrims come each year

Carluke, Lanark. The plaque at the site of Miltonhead, the birthplace of Major-General William Roy, 1726–90, known as the 'father' of the Ordnance Survey. Out of his military map of Scotland, drawn between 1747 and 1755, grew the Ordnance Survey of Great Britain. It is situated on an unclassified road 2 miles west, near Milton Lockhart farm

Carnwath, Lanark. The shaft of the Market Cross of 1516, giving road distances, including that to Ayr, misspelt AIR

Carrbridge, Inverness. The arch of the old bridge across the River Dulnain, seen from the modern bridge. It was built in 1715 by the Earl of Seafield for the use of funeral parties to Duthil

Carrbridge, Inverness. The remains of Inverlaidnan House, where Bonnie Prince Charlie slept on the way to Culloden in 1746. It stands on an unclassified road near the River Dulnain, some 3½ miles west

Carrick, Ayr. The 17th century Castle at Maybole, the former capital of Carrick. It was once the town house of the Kennedys, Earls of Cassillis, of whom an old rhyme says:
"Twixt Wigtown and the town of Ayr, Portpatrick and the Cruives of Cree,
No man may think for to bide there unless he court St. Kennedie"

[For CARRBRIDGE see also under WADE ROADS (Plate 167)

CAPE WRATH, Sutherland. Map 28, **NC 2 7.**
This wild, cliff-bound headland, the most northerly point of Scotland's north-west seaboard, cannot be reached by car, as only a passenger ferry is available for crossing the narrow Kyle of Durness. This ferry connects in summer only (weather permitting) with a minibus service to the cape. The lighthouse is 11 miles distant, over a stretch of lonely moorland known as The Parph, which is overlooked to the north by *Scrishven,* 1,216 ft., and to the south by *Fashven,* 1,498 ft. This lighthouse was constructed in 1828, and provides distant views across the Minch to the island of Lewis in the Outer Hebrides. The wild *Clo Mor* cliffs to the east attain some 800 ft., the highest sheer mainland cliffs. The remote Atlantic islands of *North Rona* and *Sula Sgeir,* some 50 miles to the north-west, are now National Nature Reserves. They are the home of the rare Atlantic grey seal, and the equally rare Leach's fork-tailed petrel breeds there. See **Durness** and **Kinlochbervie.** *Iter. 225, 229.*

CAPUTH, Perth. 1,357. Map 16, **NO 0 3.**
Lies just to the north of the River Tay, here spanned by a bridge. **3 m. E.** is the Roman Camp of *Inchtuthil,* situated in the private grounds of *Delvine House.* Recent excavation brought to light a 7-ton hoard of Roman nails, the largest 16 inches in length. Across the river, to the west, is *Murthly Castle,* 16th cent. and later, in a fine, wooded setting. A Sitka spruce tree in the park is some 160 feet tall, and a Douglas fir has grown to 172 feet. *Iter. 148, 157.*

CARBERRY HILL, Midlothian. Map 10, **NT 3 6.**
Famous for the skirmish, fought in 1567, when Mary, Queen of Scots, after Bothwell had fled, surrendered to the Lords of the Congregation, and was taken thence to *Loch Leven Castle* (*q.v.*). A little to the west is *Carberry Tower,* rebuilt in 1830, but keeping an old tower. See **Pinkie House.**

CARBISDALE CASTLE, Ross and Cromarty.
See **Invershin.** Map 29, **NH 5 9.**

CARBOST, Isle of Skye, Inverness. Map 23, **NG 3 3.**
To the south, a road leads through Glen Eynort to the loch of that name, where recent afforestation is changing the face of the landscape. See **Talisker.** *Iter. 252.*

CARDROSS, Dunbarton. 1,466. Map 8, **NS 3 7.**
E.C. Thurs. GOLF. Here, in a castle now vanished, Robert Bruce died in 1329. The Parish Church was destroyed in the Second World War. The grandfather of Macaulay, the historian, was at one period minister at Cardross. In *Ardoch House,* an 18th cent. mansion facing the Clyde, lived R. B. Cunninghame-Graham, the author and explorer. To the north of Cardross is the ruined *Kilmahew Castle.* The 15th cent. *Kilmahew* Chapel was restored in 1955. See **Dumbarton.** *Iter. 102, 111.*

CARFIN, Lanark. 1,795. Map 9, **NS 7 5.**
A mining village, with a population largely of Irish extraction. A grotto, dedicated to Our Lady of Lourdes in 1922, is the yearly venue of thousands of pilgrims. Two fragments of rock from Lourdes are inset in a marble block from Iona above the pool of holy water. There are several shrines in a well-designed garden setting. *Iter. 87.*

CARFRAEMILL, Berwick. Map 10, **NT 5 5.**
Situated in Lauderdale, with the *Lammermuir* hills rising away to the north-east. From here the Leader Water flows southwards between the main roads leading to Lauder and Greenlaw. To the north-west of Carfraemill, the Edinburgh road climbs steadily towards the viewpoint of *Soutra Hill* (*q.v.*). See **Oxton.** *Iter. 4, 5, 6, 8, 13, 36.*

CARINISH, North Uist, Inverness. Map 32, **NF 8 6.**
See **Hebrides, Outer** (North Uist). *Iter. 261.*

CARLISLE, Cumberland (England). 71,410.
For " Through Routes " see page 44. Map 5, **NY 4 5.**
E.C. Thurs. **M.D.** Wed./Sat. GOLF. *Iter. 10, 11, 12, 13, 26, 27, 28, 29, 30, 31, 42, 50, 51.*

CARLOPS, Peebles. Map 9, **NT 1 5.**
A *Pentland* hills village, on the North Esk river, well known as a small inland holiday resort. A curious rock outcrop overshadows the northern extremity of the village. There are associations with Allan Ramsay, author of the pastoral play " The Gentle Shepherd." A path follows the river into the hills past the North Esk reservoir to the Bore Stone, from which *East Cairn Hill,* 1,839 ft., a good viewpoint, is reached. See **Penicuik** and **Polwarth.** *Iter. 25.*

CARLOWAY, Isle of Lewis, Ross and Cromarty.
See **Hebrides, Outer** (Lewis). *Iter. 260.* Map 32, **NB 2 4.**

CARLUKE, Lanark. 11,929. Map 9, **NS 8 5.**
E.C. Wed. GOLF. Stands at an altitude of over 600 ft., above the fertile Clyde valley, and with moors to the east. The tower of the former 18th cent. Church still stands. The growing of fruit in the valley dates back as fai as the 12th cent. **2 m. S.W.** is the 16th to 17th cent. house of *Waygateshaw.* See **Braidwood.** *Iter. 50, 52, 54.*

CARNACH, Argyll. Map 18, **NN 0 5.**
At the western end of *Glencoe* (*q.v.*) on Loch Leven, and the point of divergence of the picturesque road circling Loch Leven to North Ballachulish from the direct road to *Ballachulish* (*q.v.*). The latter route, by utilising the ferry over Loch Leven, shortens the distance to Fort William considerably. Across the glen rises the *Pap of Glencoe,* 2,430 ft., a conical peak, being an outlier of the long ridge of *Aonach Eagach,* with its 3,000-ft. high summits, facing *Bidean nam Bian,* 3,766 ft., across the deep rift of Glencoe. See **Kinlochleven.** *Iter. 100, 124, 125, 142.*

CARNAN, South Uist, Inverness. Map 32, **NF 7 4.**
See **Hebrides, Outer** (South Uist). *Iter. 262.*

CARNOUSTIE, Angus. 6,234. SB. Map 17, **NO 5 3.**
E.C. Tues. GOLF. A well-known golfing resort on the North Sea cost, with a fine, sandy beach and bathing. To the south-west are the Barry links, extending to Buddon Ness, a military training area. See **Arbroath** and **Monikie.** *Iter. 155, 162.*

CARNWATH, Lanark. 3,392. Map 9, **NS 9 4.**
E.C. Wed. GOLF. Only the aisle remains from the old Church, built c. 1424. The shaft of the Market Cross gives road distances. The road leading north-eastwards towards Edinburgh traverses the lower slopes of the *Pentland* hills, and is known as the " Lang Whang," once much used as a drove road. **2 m. N.W.** of Carnwath are slight remains of *Cowthally Castle,* a Somerville stronghold, consisting once of three separate towers. James IV, V and VI were entertained here at different periods. *Iter. 21, 23, 37, 52.*

CARRADALE, Argyll. Map 7, **NR 8 3.**
A small *Kintyre* (*q.v.*) resort, with a fishing harbour, on Kilbrennan Sound facing the Isle of Arran, and about **1½ m. E.** of the Campbeltown road. Near the pier is the ruined *Aird Castle,* and on the west side of the sandy bay is a vitrified fort. Carradale Bay, sheltered by Carradale Point, lies to the south. Farther inland rises *Beinn an Tuirc,* 1,491 ft., the highest point in Kintyre. See **Saddell.** *Iter. 122.*

CARRBRIDGE, Inverness. 233. Map 25, **NH 9 2.**
E.C. Thurs. GOLF. A pleasant Highland resort, on the River Dulnain, here spanned by a modern bridge, beside which the arch of a much older one is still in position. The new Landmark Centre (1970) contains exhibitions relating to the Highlands among other features. **2½ m. W.,** on the river, is Wade's old *Sluggan Bridge,* on one of his military roads. In the vicinity is the ruined *Inverlaidnan House,* where Prince Charles Edward spent the night on the way to Culloden. **1½ m. N.E.,** a narrow moorland road diverges northwards from the Grantown-on-Spey road towards Forres, and a right fork after another seven miles gives access to the lonely *Lochindorb* (*q.v.*), with its romantic island castle. See **Boat of Garten** and **Slochd Summit.** *Iter. 140, 150, 173, 195.*

CARRICK, Ayr. Map 2, **NX 2 9** etc.
The name given to the southernmost division of the county, lying to the south of the River Doon, and formerly part of

the district of *Galloway* (*q.v.*), which was, until 1747, administered by hereditary stewards. The scenery is at its best in the south-east, where the foothills of the "Galloway Highlands" of Kirkcudbright extend over the border, and of which *Kirriereoch Hill*, 2,562 ft., and *Shalloch on Minnoch*, 2,520 ft., are perhaps the best known Carrick hills. The two narrow and hilly moorland roads which lead northwards from *Rowantree* (*q.v.*) towards *Maybole* (*q.v.*) wind through the heart of the hills of Carrick, the more westerly road climbing over the Nick o' the Balloch Pass, which attains nearly 1,300 ft. Between *Ballantrae* (*q.v.*) and *Girvan* (*q.v.*) is a particularly fine stretch of coastline, which includes the picturesque Kennedy's Pass. See **Barr.**

CARRINGTON, Midlothian. 2,052 with Cockpen. Map 10, **NT 3 6.**
The little cruciform Church, with its ogee-capped tower, dates from 1710.

CARRONBRIDGE, Dumfries. Map 3, **NX 8 9.**
A Nithsdale village, where the Carron Water joins the River Nith a little to the south-west. From here, a fine road forks north-eastwards leading to the picturesque, winding Dalveen Pass, the summit of which is at a height of 1,140 ft., near the Lanark border, above which rises *Comb Head*, 1,998 ft., an outlier of the *Lowther* hills. West of the village, across the Nith, are scanty remains of *Tibbers Castle*. **2½ m. N.E.** is the ruined *Morton Castle*, perhaps 15th cent., in a glen overlooking Morton Loch. See **Drumlanrig Castle, Durisdeer** and **Enterkinfoot.** *Iter. 25, 27, 48, 56, 67.*

CARSAIG BAY, Isle of Mull, Argyll. Map 13, **NM 5 2.**
On the wild, rocky southern shores of the island, with cliffs rising to nearly 1,000 ft. in places. *Carsaig Bay* is reached by a narrow road leading southwards through Glen Leidle from the road which traverses the southern shores of Loch Scridain. The film "I Know Where I'm Going" was shot in the vicinity. Away to the south-west, on the coast, not accessible by road, are the remarkable Carsaig Arches, basalt tunnels in the rock, and farther to the east is the Nun's Cave, with carvings supposed to be the original designs of a Cross on Iona. To the east of Carsaig Bay is the seaward end of Loch Buie, dominated at its head by *Ben Buie*, 2,354 ft. See **Pennyghael.** *Iter. 249.*

CARSE OF GOWRIE, Perth. Map 17, **NO 2 2** and **3 2.**
The name given to the strip of fertile, level country which lies between the *Sidlaw* hills and the Firth of Tay, and is especially noted for the cultivation of strawberries. See **Errol, Kinnaird** and **Longforgan.** *Iter. 154.*

CARSETHORN, Kirkcudbright. Map 3, **NX 9 5.**
A small harbour on Carse Bay. With 18th and 19th cent. fishermen's houses.

CARSPHAIRN, Kirkcudbright. 670 Map 3, **NX 5 9.**
E.C. Wed. A small *Galloway* (*q.v.*) village situated on the Water of Deugh, between two ranges of lofty hills, *Cairnsmore of Carsphairn*, 2,612 ft., to the north-east, and *Corserine*, 2,688 ft., and *Carlins Cairn*, 2,650 ft., to the south-west. North-west of the village is *Lagwine*, a ruined tower, belonging formerly to the Macadams. *Cairn Avel*, south of the village, is a prehistoric chambered cairn. East of the village is *Knockgray Park*, where a cairn indicates the place where the last wild deer in the Lowlands is said to have been slain. A track goes westwards from Carsphairn past the Woodhead lead mines to the shores of *Loch Doon* (*q.v.*), and its former island-castle, to the south of *Dalmellington* (*q.v.*). Away to the west of Carsphairn is Carrick Forest, part of the extensive Glen Trool Forest Park, included in which are the lonely Lochs Recar and Macaterick, situated deep in the Galloway hills. **3 m. S.E.** of the village, in the Glenkens district, on the more easterly of the two roads leading towards New Galloway, is the newly-created Kendoon Loch, connected with the Galloway Power Scheme. In this loch, the gorge known as the Tinkler's Loup has been engulfed. Beyond here the High Bridge of Ken spans the Water of Ken. Farther to the south is the large Carsfad dam. See **Loch Trool.** *Iter. 74, 75, 76, 77.*

CARSTAIRS, Lanark. 3,826. Map 9, **NS 9 4.**
E.C. Thurs. To the south, beyond the Roman fort of *Castledykes*, are the many windings of the Clyde, flowing through a broad and fertile valley. To the north is the Mouse Water, which joins the Clyde above *Lanark* (*q.v.*). In the Parish Church is preserved a rare 15th cent. Crucifixion stone. To the east lies the White Loch noted for curling. *Iter. 21, 23, 37.*

CARTER BAR, Roxburgh. Map 5, **NT 6 0.**
Situated on the summit ridge of the *Cheviots* (*q.v.*), where the main road from Newcastle enters Scotland and divides into two, the right fork descending to *Jedburgh* (*q.v.*) and the left fork to *Bonchester Bridge* (*q.v.*) and *Hawick* (*q.v.*). The view from the 1,371-ft. high Carter Bar is famous, and extends towards the Cheviot itself and well into the Lowlands, with the triple-peaked *Eildon* hills appearing in the distance to the north-west. The last Border battle, the Redeswire Raid, took place here, in 1575. Away to the east, on the crest of the hills, near the source of the River Coquet, are the notable camp and earthworks of *Chew Green*, situated just inside Northumberland, across the English border. Here, the earliest of the Roman roads into Scotland, the Dere Street, of Agricola, crosses the border at a height of some 1,500 ft., and later descends towards *Oxnam* (*q.v.*). *Iter. 4, 43, 44, 52.*

CASTLEBAY, Isle of Barra, Inverness. Map 32, **NL 6 9.**
See **Hebrides, Outer** (Barra).

CASTLE CAMPBELL, Clackmannan. Map 16, **NS 9 9.**
See **Dollar.** *Iter. 136.*

CASTLECARY, Stirling. Map 16, **NS 7 7.**
One of the forts of the *Roman Wall* (*q.v.*) is situated in the vicinity. Castlecary takes its name from a former square tower, which was largely destroyed in 1715; the remaining portion is 15th to 16th cent. The Forth and Clyde Canal reaches its highest elevation at this point. *Iter. 17, 50, 87, 97, 99.*

CASTLE DOUGLAS, Kirkcudbright. 3,311 SB. Map 3, **NX 7 6.**
E.C. Thurs. **M.D.** Mon. **GOLF.** A market town and commercial capital of the *Stewartry* (*q.v.*) of Kirkcudbright, the name of the town having at one time been *Carlingwark*, the title of the loch situated immediately to the south. Castle Douglas has associations with S. R. Crockett, the novelist, and is noted for fishing. **1½ m. S.W.** is the *Threave* Estate with a 19th cent. mansion (N.T. Scot.). **The gardens** are noted for their wealth of daffodils and rhododendrons, and are shown daily, 9 to 5. There is a wildfowl refuge. **3 m.** farther to the north-west, and reached after having first crossed the River Dee, stands the ancient *Threave Castle* (N.T. Scot.), situated on an island in the river. This Douglas stronghold dates from the 14th cent., with a 15th cent. courtyard, and is open weekdays (except Thurs.), 10 to 7; Sun., 2 to 7, April to end of Sept. (see note page 98). In 1640, the interior of the castle was wrecked by the Covenanters. The main road leading north-westwards from the town to *New Galloway* (*q.v.*). passes by the shores of Loch Ken for some miles, the loch having been extended considerably to the south-east in connection with the Galloway Power Scheme (See **Crossmichael**). Away to the south of Castle Douglas rises *Bengairn*, which attains 1,250 ft. See **Galloway, Laurieston** and **Palnackie.** *Iter.* 26, *70, 76.*

CASTLE FRASER, Aberdeen. Map 27, **NJ 7 1.**
See **Kemnay.** *Iter. 176, 177.*

CASTLE GRANT, Moray. May 26, **NJ 0 3.**
See **Grantown-on-Spey.**

CASTLE KENNEDY, Wigtown. Map 2, **NX 1 6.**
Between the Black and White Lochs, to the north, stands the modern *Lochinch Castle*, famous for its magnificent grounds, laid out on landscape lines. Facing it, to the east, is the ivy-clad ruin of *Castle Kennedy*, dating from the early 17th cent., and burnt in 1715. The gardens are shown daily, 9 to 5, April to end of Sept. (See note page 98.) *Iter. 25, 26, 80.*

Carsphairn, Kirkcudbright. The remains of Lagwine Tower, of the Macadams, which was burnt down before the birth of John Loudon Macadam, famous in the history of road-making. It stands to the north-west of the village, off A713

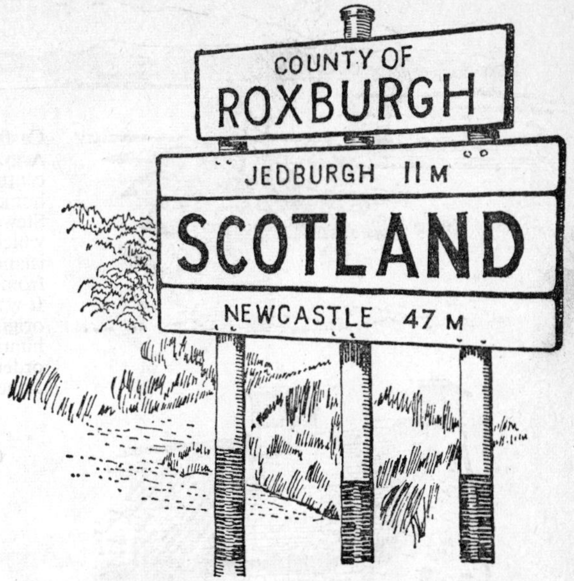

Carter Bar, Roxburgh. The Border between Scotland and England, at the summit ridge of the Cheviot Hills, on A68

Castle Kennedy, Wigtown. The ruined Kennedy stronghold, built by the 5th Earl of Cassillis in 1607 and burnt in 1715. It stands in the famous Lochinch gardens, laid out originally by the second Earl of Stair, Commander-in-Chief to George II. They have since been re-created. The present mansion of Lochinch dates from 1867

Castle Campbell, Clackmannan. A ruined 14th to 16th century stronghold, built by the first Earl of Argyll, and once known as Castle Gloume. Montrose burnt it in 1645. It stands below the Ochil Hills, in the Dollar Glen, on an unclassified road off A91

Carrington, Midlothian. The Church dates from 1710

Castle Stalker, Argyll. The 16th century former home of the Stewarts of Appin, which stands on an island off-shore from Portnacroish. It was built originally as a hunting lodge in order to entertain James IV

Ceres, Fife. A carving of the last Provost of Ceres (1578) on a wall in the village

Ceres, Fife. The carving of a bale being weighed on the old iron scales, above the door of the former 17th century weigh-house. The inscription reads: 'God bless the just'

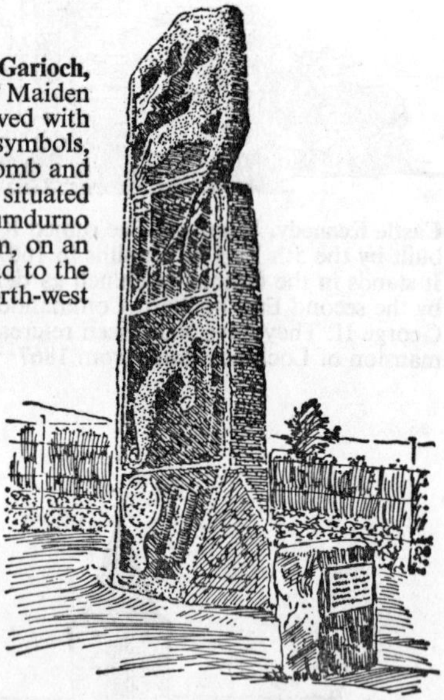

Chapel of Garioch, Aberdeen. The 'Maiden Stone,' carved with Pictish symbols, including a comb and mirror. It is situated near Drumdurno Farm, on an unclassified road to the north-west

Castle Semple, Renfrew. The remains of the Collegiate Church, founded by the first Lord Sempill, who was killed at Flodden Field in 1513

Castletown, Caithness. An example of fencing utilising the local flagstones

CASTLE OF MEY, Caithness. Map 30, **ND 2 7.**
See **East Mey.**

CASTLE SEMPLE, Renfrew. Map 8, **NS 3 6.**
Near Castle Semple Loch is the Collegiate Church (A.M.), which has a three-sided apse, and a monument dated 1513 in memory of John, Lord Semple, killed at Flodden.

CASTLE STALKER, Argyll. Map 14, **NM 9 4.**
See **Portnacroish.** *Iter. 124.*

CASTLE STEWART, Inverness. Map 25, **NH 7 4.**
See **Inverness.**

CASTLETOWN, Caithness. 804. Map 30, **ND 1 6.**
E.C. Thurs. **GOLF.** Noted formerly for its flagstones, an industry founded in 1837. These are also used locally for fencing. A brooch, found in a burial cist here in 1786, is now in the National Museum of Antiquities in Edinburgh. The wide expanse of Dunnet Bay lies to the north of the village. *Iter. 238, 240.*

CASTLE SWEEN, Argyll. Map 6, **NR 7 7.**
See **Kilmory Knap.**

CATACOL, Isle of Arran, Bute. Map 7, **NR 9 4.**
See **Lochranza.** *Iter. 242.*

CATRAIL, Roxburgh; Selkirk. Map 5, **NT 5 0**
See **Galashiels** and **Shankend.** and 10, **NT 4 3.**

CATRINE, Ayr. 2,672. Map 8, **NS 5 2.**
A village on the River Ayr, with a mill once noted for its huge water-wheel. *Ballochmyle House*, a little to the north-west, forms the setting for two well-known songs of Burns, while at *Catrine House*, to the south-west of Catrine, Burns dined with Professor Dugald Stewart before visiting Edinburgh in 1786. *Howford* Bridge to the west (A.76), spans the River Ayr by means of Scotland's largest concrete arch. See **Mauchline** and **Sorn.**

CAUSEWAYEND, Midlothian. Map 9, **NT 0 6.**
A little to the east is the Harper Rig reservoir, with slight remains of *Cairns Castle*, and near the shores of which goes the old drove road known as the Cauld Stane Slap, with *East Cairn Hill*, 1,839 ft., one of the loftiest *Pentland* hills rising beyond. About **6 m. S.W.** of Causewayend, to the west of the Lanark road, is the larger Cobbinshaw reservoir. *Iter. 21, 23.*

CAUSEWAYHEAD, Stirling. 1,000. Map 16, **NS 8 9.**
Powis House, to the east, dates from c. 1746. See **Stirling.** *Iter. 133, 134, 135, 136, 138, 140, 141.*

CAWDOR, Nairn. 249. Map 25, **NH 8 4.**
A pleasant village, the Church having an unusual tower and a Norman doorway. To the south is Cawdor Wood, threaded by the Hermitage Burn. *Cawdor Castle*, one of the finest and most picturesque of Scotland's medieval buildings, retains a central tower dating from 1454, a drawbridge with its gateway and iron yett, and preserves some 16th cent. portions, which have been altered at a slightly later period. There are also notable gardens surrounding the castle. Shakespeare's Macbeth was Thane of Cawdor, and the castle is traditionally the scene of the murder of Duncan. To the south-west of Cawdor there are roads on both sides of the River Nairn leading towards *Daviot* (*q.v.*), that on the north bank going by way of *Culloden* (*q.v.*). **3 m. W.** of Cawdor, across the Nairn, stands *Kilravock Castle*, described under *Croy*. **8 m. S.E.**, in the valley of the Findhorn, is some very attractive scenery around *Dulsie Bridge* (*q.v.*), reached by means of a road traversing the line of one of the former military roads. *Iter. 177, 198, 212.*

CELLARDYKE, Fife. Map 17, **NO 5 0.**
See **Anstruther.**

CERES, Fife. 1,827. Map 17, **NO 3 1.**
A most attractive little village, with an old bridge, known as the Bishop's Bridge. Adjoining the Parish Church is the medieval mausoleum of the Crawfords. On a wall in the village is a carving of the last Provost of Ceres, who received this office in 1578. Annual games take place on the last Saturday in June, in commemoration of the return of the villagers in 1314, after fighting in Robert Bruce's army. An obelisk in the Bow Butts has an inscription recording the association with Bannockburn. Above the doorway of the 17th cent. weigh-house is an interesting carving of a bale being weighed, with an inscription. Nearby hang the medieval jougs. The 18th cent. *St. John's Lodge* has been restored. **1 m. S.E.** is the ruined 17th cent. *Craighall Castle. Iter. 129.*

CHANNELKIRK CHURCH, Berwick. Map 10, **NT 4 5.**
See **Oxton.**

CHAPELCROSS, Dumfries. Map 4, **NY 1 6.**
See **Annan.**

CHAPELHALL, Lanark. 2,497. Map 9, **NS 7 6.**
Iter. 50, 87.

CHAPEL OF GARIOCH, Aberdeen. 1,694 with Daviot. Map 27, **NJ 7 2.**
A little to the north-west, by *Drumdurno* farm, is the *Maiden Stone*, a remarkable 10-ft. high carved slab, carrying Pictish characters, and depicting a comb and mirror. **1 m. S.E.** of Chapel of Garioch is the ruined *Balquhain Tower*, dating from 1530. **1 m. W.** is *Pittodrie House*, 17th cent.

CHAPELTON, Lanark. Map 8, **NS 6 4.**
E.C. Wed. *Iter. 29, 56.*

CHAPELTOWN OF GLENLIVET, Banff.
See **Knockandhu.** Map 26, **NJ 2 2.**

CHARLESTOWN, Fife. Map 16, **NT 0 8.**
A small Forth estuary coal port. A little to the east is *Limekilns*, associated with R. L. Stevenson's "Kidnapped." In the vicinity stands the fine mansion of *Broomhall.*

CHARLESTOWN OF ABERLOUR, Banff. 1,153. Map 26, **NJ 2 4.**
E.C. Wed. See **Aberlour.** *Iter. 170, 192, 195.*

CHARTERHALL, Berwick. Map 11, **NT 7 4.**
Here is a motor racing track.

CHEVIOT HILLS, Roxburgh. Map 5, **NY 5 9** etc. and 11, **NT 8 1** etc.
This range of lonely, grassy hills forms the boundary with England for much of its length, its highest point, *The Cheviot*, 2,676 ft., being over the Northumberland border, part of the range being included within the Northumberland National Park. Other prominent heights are *Peel Fell*, 1,964 ft., and *Carter Fell*, 1,815 ft., both rising to the south-west of the viewpoint of *Carter Bar* (*q.v.*), 1,371 ft. high, where the road from Hawick and Jedburgh to Newcastle crosses the border to the west of the line followed by the Roman Dere Street. Away to the south-west of *Peel Fell*, the road from *Riccarton* (*q.v.*) cuts through the hills at a comparatively low altitude, and gives access to the lonely North Tyne valley across the Northumberland border. Many of the hill slopes are grazed by the characteristic Cheviot and black-faced sheep. *Iter. 6, 7, 47.*

CHIRNSIDE, Berwick. 1,111. Map 11, **NT 8 5.**
E.C. Wed. A village affording wide southerly views. The Parish Church has a Norman south doorway with tympanum. In the churchyard is the grave and memorial of the racing driver, Jim Clark, killed in Germany in 1968. The junction of the Whiteadder Water with that of the Blackadder takes place a little to the south. To the east are slight remains of *Edington Castle*, and also a fine old crow-step-gabled dovecote. See **Duns** and **Edrom Church.** *Iter. 41.*

CHURCHILL BARRIERS, Orkney. Map 33, **ND 4 9**
See **Orkney Islands** (Mainland and South Ronaldsay). *Iter. 266.*

CLACHAIG INN, Argyll. Map 18, **NN 1 5.**
See **Glencoe.**

CLACHAN BRIDGE, Argyll. Map 14, **NM 7** 1.
This picturesque single-arched bridge, designed by Telford in 1792, which links the mainland with the island of *Seil*, has achieved fame as being probably the only bridge to "span the Atlantic." The waters are actually those of the narrow Seil Sound, which joins the Firth of Lorne to Outer Loch Melfort, but they can, nevertheless, with some justification, claim to be an arm of the Atlantic. On Seil there are slate quarries at *Balvicar*, while off the west coast lies the smaller island of *Easdale*, also noted for its slates. The Cuan Sound, crossed by the *Cuan* ferry, separates Seil from *Luing*, yet another slate-quarrying island, on the coast of which is the little port of *Cullipool*. The Luing Sound separates this island from Lunga, hilly Scarba, and the smaller Garvellach group, among which is Eileach an Naoimh, which retains a ruined chapel, associated with *St. Brendan* and *St. Columba*. Nearby are the remains of a double beehive house. To the south of Scarba is the Gulf of Corryvreckan, with its treacherous tide-race, the noise of which can be heard from a great distance. The island of *Scarba* attains almost 1,500 ft. at one point and is noted for its deer. **3 m. S.** of Clachan Bridge on the mainland, and situated close to Seil Sound, is the ancient seat of *Ardmaddy Castle*, overlooking the bay of that name. See **Kilninver.** *Iter. 122.*

CLACHNAHARRY, Inverness. Map 25, **NH 6** 4.
Situated on the south side of the Beauly Firth, at the point where the *Caledonian Canal* (*q.v.*), after its journey across the Highlands by way of the Great Glen, or *Glen More* (*q.v.*), enters the Firth with the aid of six locks. On *Craig Phadraig*, 550 ft., a little to the south, there is a notable vitrified fort. *Iter. 200, 201, 203, 204, 205, 210, 221.*

CLACKMANNAN, Clackmannan. 3,000. Map 16, **NS 9** 9.
E.C. Tues. This name town of the smallest Scottish county lies on the Black Devon River, which flows southwards into the estuary of the Forth, to the south, at *Clackmannan Pow*. In the town is an old Tolbooth, neighboured by the ancient Stone of Manau. *Clackmannan Tower* (A.M.), 79 ft. high, on a hill to the west, is 14th or 15th cent. work, with 17th cent. additions, and is finely machicolated. Tradition has it that Robert Bruce built the tower. See **Culross.** *Iter. 133, 134.*

CLADICH, Argyll. Map 14, **NN 0** 2.
Here the road from Dalmally along the shores of *Loch Awe* (*q.v.*) divides into two, the westerly fork continuing along the loch-side, and the southerly fork climbing over the hills, with fine views of *Ben Cruachan*, 3,689 ft., away to the north. The subsequent descent through the delightful wooded Glen Aray leads towards *Inveraray* (*q.v.*). See **Kilchurn Castle** and **Portsonachan.** *Iter. 117, 119, 120.*

CLAGGAIN BAY, Isle of Islay, Argyll. Map 6, **NR 4** 5.
This rocky and sandy bay is overlooked from the west by *Beinn Bheigeir*, 1,609 ft., the highest point on the island. The road from *Port Ellen* (*q.v.*) along the south-east coast of the island terminates here. There are views of the island of Jura and of the *Kintyre* (*q.v.*) peninsula. *Iter. 245.*

CLARENCEFIELD, Dumfries. Map 4, **NY 0** 6.
A little to the west is *Comlongon Castle*, a well preserved 15th cent. tower, with walls 10 to 13 ft. in thickness, and retaining an iron yett. A modern building is now joined to the tower. See **Caerlaverock** and **Ruthwell.** *Iter. 47.*

CLARKSTON, Renfrew. 3,547. Map 8, **NS 5** 5.
E.C. Tues. About **2 m. N.**, on the White Cart River, are the remains of *Cathcart Castle*, partly demolished in the 15th cent., and later replaced by the nearby *Cathcart House*. The ruined castle is associated with Mary, Queen of Scots, who is said to have watched the battle of Langside, in 1568, from the so-called "Queen Mary's Window." The result of the battle was fatal to the Queen's cause, and from here she fled to *Dundrennan* (*q.v.*), before finally departing from Scottish shores. *Iter. 18, 29.*

CLASHMORE, Sutherland. Map 31, **NH 7** 8.
See **Skibo Castle.** *Iter. 200, 231.*

CLASHNESSIE, Sutherland. Map 28, **NC 0** 3.
Fishing and bathing from sand. *Iter. 227.*

CLATTERING BRIDGE, Kincardine. Map 21, **NO 6** 7.
At the foot of the fine moorland road over the *Cairn o' Mounth* (*q.v.*) leading to the Dee valley at *Banchory* (*q.v.*). A little to the north is the Slack Burn, in its deep gorge, overlooked by *Finella Hill*, 1,358 ft., which is encircled by the road leading towards *Fordoun* (*q.v.*) by way of *Drumtochty Castle*, now a school. *Iter. 163, 165.*

CLATTERINGSHAWS DAM, Kirkcudbright.
Map 3, **NX 5** 7.
This large dam was erected across the Black Water of Dee, thus creating a new inland reservoir, the water being then taken through a tunnel to a hydro-electric station of the *Galloway* (*q.v.*) power scheme. The district has associations with Robert Bruce, and is now part of the Cairn Edward Forest, belonging to the Glen Trool Forest Park. A boulder on Moss Raploch (N.T. Scot.) marks the site of one of Bruce's early fights. **4½ m. S.W.**, off the Newton Stewart road, is the prominent *Murray Monument*, commemorating a late 18th cent. professor. Away to the south-west, beyond the remote Loch Grennoch, rises *Cairnsmore of Fleet*, 2,331 ft., in the Galloway hills, associated with John Buchan's "The Thirty-nine Steps." To the north is *Meikle Millyea*, 2,446 ft., the most southerly peak in the fine *Rhinns of Kells* range, and beyond it lies the lonely Loch Dungeon. South-west of Meikle Millyea is Loch Dee, in the vicinity of which is the lonely area of bog known as the Silverflowe Nature Reserve. See **Dalry** (Kirkcudbright) and **Loch Trool.** *Iter. 25, 71.*

CLEISH, Kinross. 415. Map 16, **NT 0** 9.
A rare burial boundary stone is set into the churchyard wall. *Cleish Castle* is a restored 16th cent. house. **4 m. W.** is the restored *Aldie Castle*, of 16th and 17th cent. date.

CLOCH LIGHTHOUSE, Renfrew. Map 8, **NS 2** 7.
This notable landmark stands at Cloch Point, and overlooks the outer Clyde estuary, opposite which lies the famous resort of *Dunoon* (*q.v.*) on the *Cowal* (*q.v.*) coast. The white-painted lighthouse was constructed in 1797. *Iter. 65, 66, 88.*

CLOSEBURN, Dumfries. 1,174. Map 3, **NX 8** 9.
The massive 14th cent. *Closeburn Tower*, visited by Burns, still preserves its iron yett. **2½ m. N.**, in a ravine, is *Crichope Linn*, described in Scott's "Old Mortality." To the east rise lonely moors and hills, culminating in *Queensberry* 2,285 ft., a good viewpoint. *Iter. 27, 48, 56, 67.*

CLOVA, Angus. 402 with Cortachy. Map 20, **NO 3** 7.
E.C. Thurs. Situated in the lonely and picturesque Glen Clova, threaded by the South Esk River, and forming one of the fine Braes of Angus glens, which lead into the heart of the eastern Grampian, or *Benchinnan* mountains. The tiny village is known as *Milton of Clova*, and to the north-west are scanty remains of the former castle. A walkers' track leads northwards from a point near the church, and penetrates into the hills to reach the mountain-encircled Loch Brandy, at a height of 2,098 ft., overlooked by a sharp ridge known as the "Snub of Clova," with *Boustie Ley*, 2,868 ft., rising to the west. The road continuing towards the lonely head of the glen, near *Braedownie* (*q.v.*), traverses scenery of increasing wilderness as the hills close in on either side. Near Clova Church, the road through the glen divides into two branches, one on each bank of the river, with *Finbracks*, 2,478 ft. and *Dog Hillock*, 2,369 ft., rising to the east. The roads reunite after some six miles and lead to *Dykehead* (*q.v.*). *Iter. 161.*

CLOVENFORDS, Selkirk. 150. Map 10, **NT 4** 3.
E.C. Thurs. On the Caddon Water, flowing southwards from lonely hill country to its junction with the Tweed. Scott once lodged at an inn here, as sheriff of Selkirk, before moving to *Ashiestiel* (*q.v.*). In 1803, Dorothy and William Wordsworth came to Clovenfords. There is a monument

Clackmannan, Clackmannan. The old Tolbooth, neighboured by the ancient Stone of Manau and the stepped Town Cross

Cleish, Kinross. A rare example of a burial boundary stone, set in the churchyard wall

Clashmore, Sutherland. A standing stone, traditionally believed to commemorate the killing of a Danish chief of the name of Ospis. It stands some 2 miles west, by the side of A9

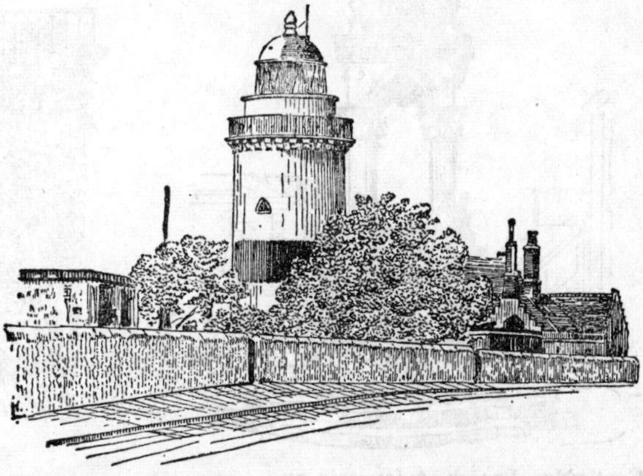

Cloch Lighthouse, Renfrew. The white-painted lighthouse at Cloch Point, a notable Clyde estuary landmark

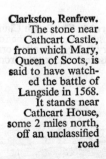

Clarkston, Renfrew. The stone near Cathcart Castle, from which Mary, Queen of Scots, is said to have watched the battle of Langside in 1568. It stands near Cathcart House, some 2 miles north, off an unclassified road

Clachan Bridge, Argyll. This is often described as the only bridge to 'span the Atlantic.' It crosses the narrow Seil Sound, which is, in fact, an arm of the Atlantic Ocean

[For CLOVENFORDS see following plate
[For CLARENCEFIELD see under BORDER COUNTRY (Plate 20)
[For CLATTERINGSHAWS DAM see under GALLOWAY (Plate 70)
[For CLOSEBURN see Plate 175

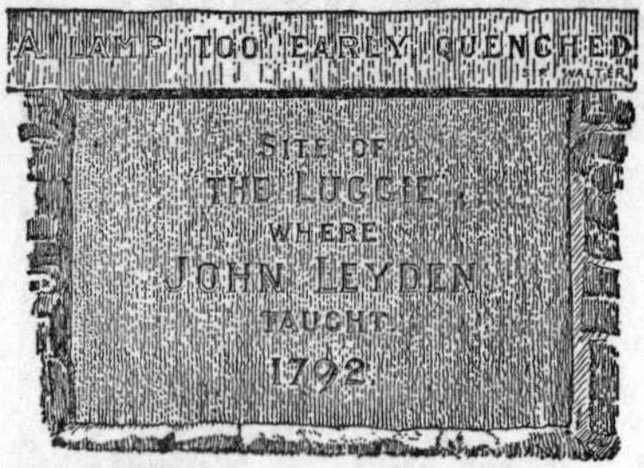

Clovenfords, Selkirk. The inscribed tablet to John Leyden, the poet and orientalist, who was a schoolmaster here in 1792

Cock Bridge, Aberdeen. The Well of the Lecht, some 4 miles north-west, which records the construction of the well known Lecht road (A939) by the 33rd regiment under Lord Charles Hay, in 1754

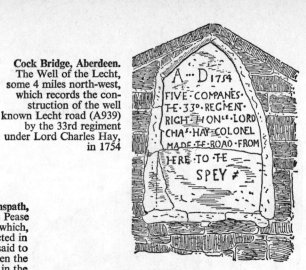

Cockburnspath, Berwick. Pease Bridge, which, when erected in 1837, is said to have been the highest in the world (124 feet)

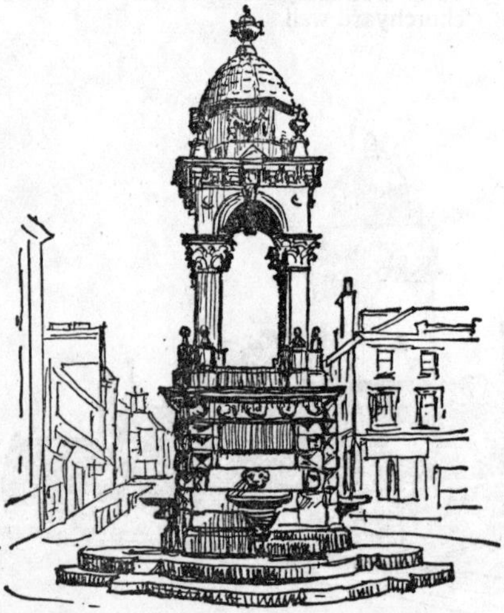

Coatbridge, Lanark. A fountain on the site of the track of the Monkland and Kirkintilloch railway (1824–72), on which an experimental form of traction by wind power using umbrellas was first used. For travel to windward, the services of a Clydesdale horse were utilised

Coldingham, Berwick. The Parish Church, which incorporates the remains of the former 12th century Priory, colonised originally by Benedictine monks from Durham

Coigach, Ross and Cromarty. The peaks of Stack Polly, Cul Beag and Ben More Coigach, seen from an unclassified road along Loch Baddagyle, in the Coigach district, near Achiltibuie

to John Leyden, who taught here in 1792. The Tweed Vineries are situated here, having been commenced in 1868 by the Duke of Buccleuch's head gardener. *Iter. 32, 33, 52.*

CLUANIE, Ross and Cromarty. Map 24, **NH 0 1.** Here, in a grand setting of lonely hills overlooking Glen Cluanie, the road to *Kyle of Lochalsh* (*q.v.*), for the island of Skye, commences the long descent through picturesque *Glen Shiel* (*q.v.*). The road to the south, which formerly went over the hills to *Tomdoun* (*q.v.*), is now unusable where it crossed Loch Loyne, a new hydro-electric scheme having necessitated the construction of a large reservoir here. A new road has been built, turning southwards to the east of Loch Cluanie (also now forming a reservoir), and crossing some low hills to reach the shores of Loch Garry, from which Tomdoun can be reached by following the enlarged loch towards the west. The grassy peaks around Cluanie are well known to hill-walkers. The highest point is *A'Chralaig*, 3,673 ft., which rises to the north, on the Inverness border, and gives a fine view of the remote peak of *Sgurr nan Ceathreamhnan*, 3,771 ft., to the north-west. *Iter. 207, 220.*

CLUNIE, Perth. Map 20, **NO 1 4.** Lies south of the Blairgowrie to Dunkeld road, and immediately west of the Loch of Clunie, on an island of which stands the ruined 16th cent. *Clunie Castle*, perhaps the early home of the "Admirable Crichton," born in 1560. **2½ m. E.** of Clunie, on the Blairgowrie road, is the Loch of Marlee. See **Mennock.** *Iter. 141, 158, 166.*

CLYDEBANK, Dunbarton. 48,296. LB. Map 8, **NS 5 6.** **E.C.** Wed. GOLF. An important Clyde shipbuilding centre, with docks and factories. Among many great ships built here are the liners "Queen Mary," "Queen Elizabeth" and "Queen Elizabeth 2". Bomb damage in the Second World War was severe. To the south-east is *Yoker* (*q.v.*), with a car ferry giving access to *Renfrew* (*q.v.*) and the south.

CLYDE FALLS, Lanark. Map 9, **NS 8 4.** See **Lanark.**

COATBRIDGE, Lanark. 54,688. LB. Map 8, **NS 7 6.** **E.C.** Wed. GOLF. An industrial town, noted especially for its large ironworks. Birthplace of Lord Reith, first head of B.C.C. **4 m. N.W.** is the 16th and 17th cent. *Bedlay House. Iter. 16.*

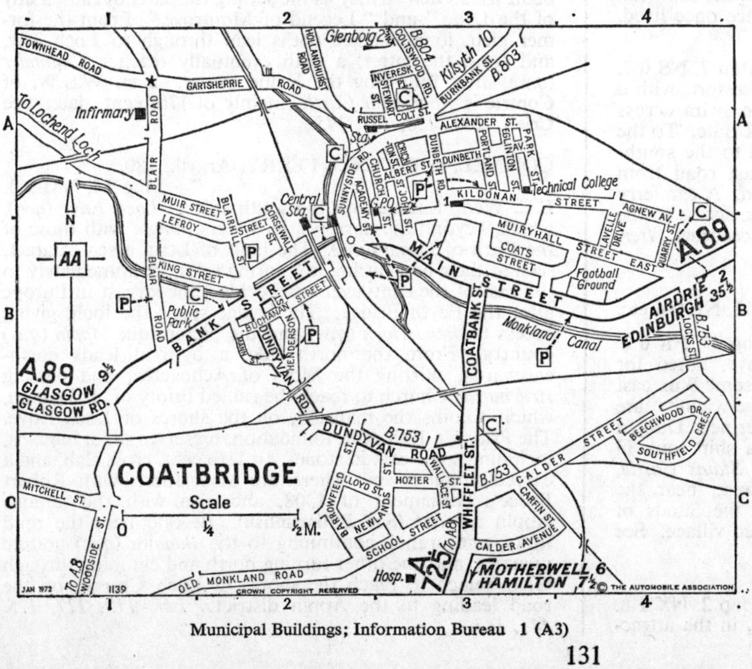

Municipal Buildings; Information Bureau 1 (A3)

COCK BRIDGE, Aberdeen. Map 26, **NJ 2 0.** Situated at a height of more than 1,300 ft., on the River Don, and the starting-point of the well-known *Lecht* road, crossing the north-eastern *Grampians* (*q.v.*), known here as the *Ladder Hills*, in which *Carn Mor* attains 2,636 ft. This road forms part of a military road of 1754, the date being carved on the Well of the Lecht, some **4 m. N.N.W.** of Cock Bridge. The road continues together with the Conglass Water in a gradual descent to *Tomintoul* (*q.v.*), and later descends still farther to reach the valley of the Spey. The Lecht road, once the terror of motorists, with its steep gradients and sharp bends, has been reconstructed, but remains one of the loftiest roads in the kingdom, the summit, **2½ m.** N. of Cock Bridge, being at a height of 2,090 ft., with hills on either side rising to more than 2,600 ft. The steepest section, gradient 1 in 5, is on the ascent out of Cock Bridge over the Hill of Allargue, and the whole road is liable to become snow-bound in severe weather. To the west stretches the long valley of Glen Avon, dominated by *Ben Avon*, 3,843 ft., at the eastern extremity of the great *Cairngorm* (*q.v.*) range. Some **2½ m. E.** of Cock Bridge, a road turns southwards off the *Strathdon* (*q.v.*) road and climbs into the hills, reaching a height of over 1,800 ft. in the steep and narrow Glas Choille section, sometimes blocked by snow. This road leads to *Gairnshiel Bridge* (*q.v.*), in the lonely Glen Gairn, giving access thence to the various resorts on *Deeside* (*q.v.*). See **Corgarff.** *Iter. 141, 160, 174, 176, 191.*

COCKBURNSPATH, Berwick. 635. Map 11, **NT 7 7.** **E.C.** Thurs. Near the point where the long range of the *Lammermuir* hills slopes down to the rocky North Sea coast stands this village. To the south-east is a deep, wooded valley, traversed both by the Great North Road, and the main Edinburgh to London railway line. The ruined *Cockburnspath Tower* stands near the junction of the road through the valley with the road to *Coldingham* (*q.v.*), the latter crossed by the lofty Pease Bridge, built c. 1780, and 300 ft. in length. In the village is an old thistle-crowned Mercat Cross, which is early 17th cent. The Church is partly 14th cent., with a curious round tower. **2 m. E.,** near the sandy shores of Pease Bay, is the ruined Norman Church of *St. Helen.* **6½ m. E.,** on a farm road leading eastwards off the Great North Road, is the ruined clifftop *Fast Castle*, associated with Scott's "Bride of Lammermoor." See **Abbey St. Bathans** and **Dunglass.** *Iter. 1, 2, 38, 39.*

COCKENZIE, East Lothian. 3,549. SB. with Port Seton. Map 10, **NT 4 7.** A little Firth of Forth fishing village, where, in the autumn, the picturesque custom of the "Fishermen's Walks" is still kept up. See **Prestonpans** and **Seton.** *Iter. 2.*

COCKPEN, Midlothian. 2,052 with Carrington. Map 10, **NT 3 6.** The small Church, set on rising ground, is the burial place of the Marquis of Dalhousie, who was Viceroy of India at the time of the mutiny. *Dalhousie Castle*, near the west bank of the South Esk River, and dating originally from the 12th cent., has been much modernized, but retains its original drawbridge grooves in the old entrance.

COIGACH, Ross and Cromarty. Map 29, **NC 1 0.** See **Achiltibuie, Loch Lurgain, Strathkanaird** and **Ullapool.**

COIRE CAS (Cairngorms), Inverness. See **Rothiemurchus.** Map 25, **NH 9 0.**

COLDINGHAM, Berwick. 946. Map 11, **NT 9 6.** **E.C.** Wed. This pleasant mainly 18th cent. village is situated a little inland from the sandy shores of Coldingham Bay. Here, a Priory was founded c. 1147, which was later burnt and plundered, being finally partially blown up by Cromwell in 1648. In 1854, the remains were restored and added to, and now form the Parish Church, much 12th and 13th cent. work having been preserved. The discovery, in the 19th cent., of a female skeleton embedded upright in the south transept, was turned to account by Scott in "Marmion." The underwater rocks near Coldingham are well known to sub-aqua clubs. See **St. Abb's**. *Iter. 2.*

COLDSTREAM, Berwick. 1,242. SB. Map 11, **NT 8** 3. **E.C.** Thurs. The River Tweed flows between the village and Cornhill, on the English side of the water. The ford here, used by Edward I entering Scotland in 1296, was used also for many later invasions. Smeaton designed the bridge, first opened in 1766, and up to 1856 marriages were frequently performed at the former toll-house at the Scottish end of the bridge. A tablet, placed on the bridge in 1926, records the fact that on May 7th, 1787, Robert Burns first visited England by this route. A tall, fluted column commemorates Charles Marjoribanks, a former M.P. for Berwick. General Monk originally raised the famous Coldstream Guards here in 1659. A house in the Market Square has a plaque recalling the regimental headquarters. **2 m. N.W.** is the mansion of *The Hirsel*, in its splendid grounds, with a small loch. See **Ladykirk.** *Iter. 5, 30, 32, 38.*

COLINSBURGH, Fife. Map 17, **NO 4** 0. A village founded by Colin, third Earl of Balcarres, in 1705. It is noted for its cattle shows. A little to the north-west is the fine mansion of *Balcarres House*, which dates partly from 1595, and is a seat of the Lindsays. A "folly" tower stands on Balcarres Crag. *Iter. 94, 98.*

COLINTON (Edinburgh), Midlothian. 26,874. Map 9, **NT 2** 6. GOLF. On the Water of Leith. The imposing modern Church preserves an old mortsafe in the churchyard. R. L. Stevenson, in his youth, was a frequent visitor at the Manse. The new buildings of *Merchiston* School are situated at Colinton, and here are also the *Redford* Barracks. The old Castle of *Merchiston*, dating from the 16th cent., where John Napier, the inventor of logarithms, was born in 1550, lies to the north-east on the road leading back into the city. Nearby stands *George Watson's* College, a well-known school. Away to the south, in the foothills of the *Pentlands*, is *Bonaly Tower*, formerly the home of the well-known judge, Lord Cockburn. Nearby stands *Dreghorn Castle*, where lived the 18th cent. author of the ballad "William and Margaret." Westwards, beyond *Juniper Green*, lies *Baberton House*, 1622-23, in which Charles X of France once lived. See **Swanston.**

COLINTRAIVE, Argyll. 173. Map 7, **NS 0** 7. A small *Kyles of Bute* (*q.v.*) and *Cowal* (*q.v.*) resort, with a shingle beach. Cattle were formerly made to swim across the strait near this point to reach the island of Bute. To the north-west is the inlet of Loch Riddon, and to the south-east, beyond Strone Point, linked by a coast road from Colintraive, is the larger inlet of Loch Striven. A car ferry connects with *Rhubodach* (*q.v.*) in Bute, giving access to the well-known resort of *Rothesay* (*q.v.*). See **Glendaruel.** *Iter. 102, 103, 241.*

COLL, ISLE OF, Argyll. 1,143 with Tiree. See **Tiree.** Map 13, **NL 9** 4 etc.

COLLIESTON, Aberdeen. 147. Map 27, **NK 0** 2. An attractive little fishing village, in a cove, noted for "speldings," or small haddock, and situated some **5 m.** east of the Aberdeen to Peterhead road. In the vicinity are smugglers' caves in the cliffs. In St. Catherine's Dub, a deep creek to the north, a Spanish Armada ship sank in 1588. **2 m. N.E.** are slight remains of *Old Slains Castle*, demolished in 1594. Away to the south-west, near the Ythan estuary, facing *Newburgh* (*q.v.*), are the Sands of Forvie, beyond Forvie Ness, covering a buried village. See **Cruden Bay.** *Iter. 182.*

COLMONELL, Ayr. 1,566 with Ballantrae. Map 2, **NX 1** 8. **E.C.** Tues. Lies inland from Ballantrae Bay, in the attractive valley of the River Stinchar. In the churchyard is a Covenanter's memorial. *Kirkhill Castle* dates from 1589, and has received modern additions. Across the stream is the ruined 13th cent. *Craigneil Castle*, and farther west, on the opposite side, stands the 17th cent. *Knockdolian Tower*, under the hill of that name. *Iter. 84.*

COLNABAICHIN, Aberdeen. Map 26, **NJ 2** 0. *Iter. 141, 160, 174, 176, 191.*

COLONSAY, ISLE OF, Argyll. 417 with Jura. Map 13, **NR 3** 9. The two small Inner Hedridean islands of *Colonsay* and *Oronsay* lie to the west of *Jura* (*q.v.*), and Colonsay is linked by steamer to *Tarbert* (*q.v.*), on the mainland, by way of *Islay* (*q.v.*). The islands are separated from each other by a narrow strait, which is dry at low tide for a period of three hours. Colonsay has a pier at *Scalasaig*, and on the island is good pasture land. *Colonsay House*, situated near Kiloran, inland to the north, has sub-tropical gardens. Oronsay possesses the interesting remains of a 14th cent. Priory, in the churchyard of which is a notable sculptured Cross, and other sculptured stones have also been preserved. Out to sea, to the north-west of Colonsay, stands the lonely *Dubh Heartach* lighthouse, on an isolated reef. It was the work of David and Thomas Stevenson.

COLVEND, Kirkcudbright. 901. Map 3, **NX 8** 5. GOLF. The little White Loch lies immediately to the north, and farther to the north-west are the smaller Clonyard and Barean Lochs. A short by-road leads south-westwards from Colvend to *Rockcliffe* (*q.v.*), on Rough Firth. *Iter. 73.*

COMRIE, Perth. 1,811. Map 16, **NN 7** 2. **E.C.** Wed. GOLF. A small summer resort, on the River Earn, in Strath Earn, within easy reach of the attractive Loch Earn, at the eastern end of which lies *St. Fillan's* (*q.v.*). At Hogmanay, a midnight torch procession takes place, featuring mummers with quaint costumes. *Dunmore Hill*, 837 ft., crowned by the Melville monument, is a good viewpoint. Comrie Church dates from 1805, the steeple being by John Stewart. To the north of Comrie is Glen Lednock, with its falls, and to the south is Glen Artney, the two glens facing each other across the Highland "fault," which has given rise at various times, notably in 1839, to minor earthquake shocks in this district. Near Drumearn is the tiny *Earthquake House* (1869), where quakes were recorded. Scott used Glen Artney as the setting for parts of the "Lady of the Lake" and "Legend of Montrose." From the former glen, long-distance paths lead through to Loch Tay, and from the latter, a path eventually reaches *Callander* (*q.v.*), after following the Keltie Water. **2 m. W.S.W.** of Comrie is *Aberuchill Castle*, mainly of 17th cent. date. See **Crieff.** *Iter. 138, 141, 145.*

CONNEL, or CONNEL FERRY, Argyll. 180. Map 14, **NM 9** 3. **E.C.** Wed. Situated on the south side of *Loch Etive* (*q.v.*), where, beyond the narrows, its waters mingle with those of the Firth of *Lorne* (*q.v.*). The Falls of Lora, a sea cataract, seen at their best during low spring tides, lie immediately to the east of the cantilever road bridge, the largest in Europe after the Forth Bridge. The bridge spans the loch, giving access to *Benderloch* (*q.v.*) and the picturesque *Appin* (*q.v.*) country. From the north side, a by-road leads north-eastwards, skirting the Moss of Achnacree, and passing *Ardchattan* Church to reach the ruined Priory of *Ardchattan*, which adjoins the mansion, on the shores of Loch Etive. The Priory, a 13th cent. foundation, preserves slight remains, including some carved stones, an 11th cent. cross slab, and a carved coffin-cover. There are associations with Robert Bruce's Parliament of 1308, and also with the famous Appin murder (See **Ballachulish**). Beyond here the road forks, one branch continuing to the *Bonawe* (*q.v.*) granite quarries, and the other turning north and climbing through Glen Salach to reach the shores of Loch Creran, on the road leading to the Appin district. *Iter. 110, 117, 125. 144, 145.*

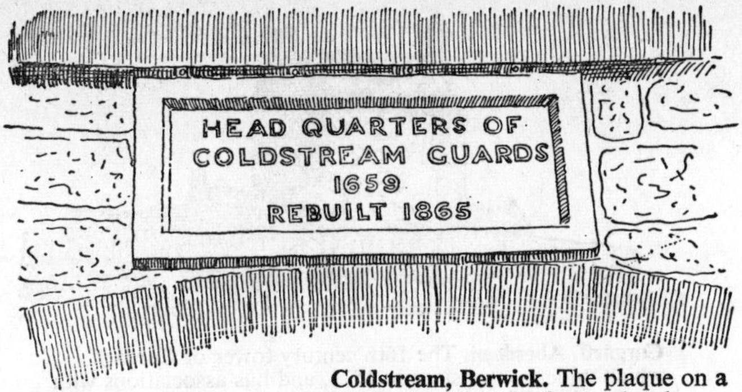

Coldstream, Berwick. The plaque on a house recording the former head-quarters of the Coldstream Guards in 1659, which General Monk raised here

Colinsburgh, Fife. A 'folly' tower on Balcarres Crag, to the north-west. It was erected in the 19th century

Colmonell, Ayr. Kirkhill Castle, built originally in 1589 as a Kennedy stronghold

Colnabaichin, Aberdeen. An unusual warning sign, 2 miles south of Colnabaichin, on A939

Connel, Argyll. The road bridge spanning the mouth of Loch Etive, with the Falls of Lora below. It is the largest cantilever bridge in Europe after the Forth Bridge

Comrie, Perth. The Melville Monument, on the summit of Dunmore Hill. It was set up in 1812 in memory of Viscount Melville, who died the previous year

[For COLDSTREAM see also under MERSE (Plate 121)]

Corgarff, Aberdeen. The 16th century tower of Corgarff, which underwent a siege in 1571, and has associations with the Jacobite Risings of 1715 and 1745

Corstorphine, Midlothian. Clermiston Tower, on Corstorphine Hill, erected in 1872 to commemorate the centenary of Sir Walter Scott

Corrieyairack Pass, Inverness. General Wade's 18th century Garva, or St. George's Bridge, which spans the Upper Spey on the way to his famous road over the Pass, now unusable

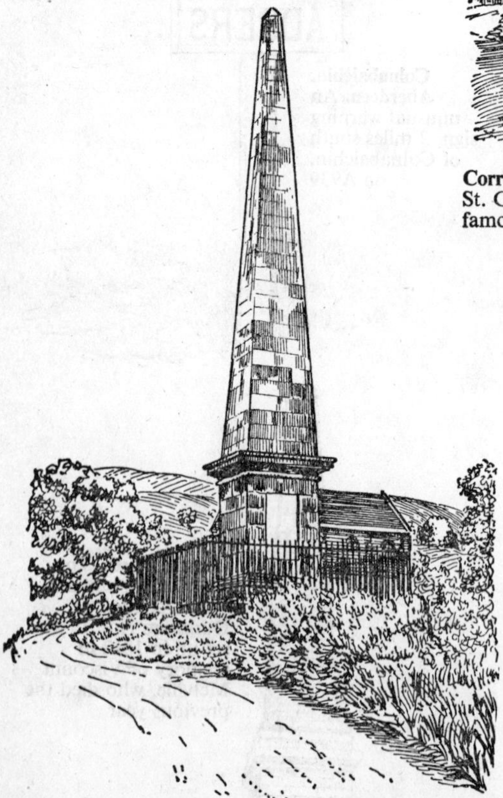

Corpach, Inverness. The obelisk at Kilmallie Church to Colonel John Cameron, who fell at the battle of Quatre Bras during the Waterloo campaign of 1815. It stands to the west, off A830

Conon Bridge, Ross and Cromarty. The former toll house on the bridge over the River Conon

[For CORPACH see also under CALEDONIAN CANAL (Plate 27)

CONON BRIDGE, Ross and Cromarty. 339. Map 25, **NH 5 5.**
E.C. Thurs. An attractive village, at the eastern extremity of the wooded Strath Conon and lying on the River Conon, which flows almost immediately into the Firth of Cromarty to the north-east. On the bridge over the river stands the former toll-house. A hydro-electric scheme is to operate in the Conon valley. North-eastwards of Conon Bridge, a road traverses the shores of Cromarty Firth, with the *Black Isle* (*q.v.*) lying to the east, and later reaches Udale and Cromarty Bays, beyond which stands the town of *Cromarty* (*q.v.*). **2 m. S.** of Conon Bridge, near the river, is *Conon House*, in the grounds of which is a beech tree 25 ft. in girth. *Iter. 200, 202, 203, 206, 213.*

CONTIN, Ross and Cromarty. 1,129. Map 25, **NH 4 5.**
A meeting-place of two roads from *Dingwall* (*q.v.*). The River Blackwater here forms two channels, the Church standing in the island formed by the branches of the river. *Iter. 204, 205, 206, 221.*

COOLINS, Isle of Skye, Inverness. Map 23, **NG 4 2.**
This grand range of mountains, the most precipitous and striking in Great Britain, is known also as the *Cuillin*, or the *Cuchullins*, the last-named referring to its possible association with an Ossianic hero. The main Coolin ridges, sometimes known as the Black Coolins in order to distinguish them from the much less impressive Red Coolins, extend in an irregular semi-circle, some 6 miles in length, overlooking the spectacular Loch Coruisk in the south-western sector of the island, and are composed of black gabbro, a rock particularly suitable for climbing. The highest peak is *Sgurr Alasdair*, 3,309 ft., but the finest is perhaps *Sgurr nan Gillean*, 3,167 ft., which rises dramatically above the village of Sligachan. The Coolins are of much interest to geologists, and are noted for the misty conditions with which they are often affected, a danger to inexperienced climbers. The views from the summit ridges are superb, and quite unequalled elsewhere in Scotland. The Red Coolins, or Red Hills, face the main ridge from the opposite side of Glen Sligachan, and their chief peaks, *Glamaig*, 2,537 ft., and *Marsco*, 2,414 ft., are rounded and smooth, being composed of a crumbly pink granite. Beyond them, to the south, rises *Blaven*, 3,042 ft., a magnificent outlier of the Black Coolins, noted for the rock traverse of *Clach Glas*, and overlooking Loch na Creitheach and Loch Slapin, both in the Strathaird peninsula. The main Coolin ridge is essentially for expert climbers, but it is possible to reach the peak of *Bruach na Frithe*, 3,143 ft., from the famous climbing centre of Sligachan, without serious difficulty, and the view of the fantastically curved summit ridge and wild corries from this belvedere is most impressive. From the mainland, the serrated Coolin ridge can be seen from the summits of some of the loftiest of the Ross-shire and Inverness-shire peaks, and from points on the coast between the Kyle of Lochalsh and Gairloch districts. Nearer views of their splendour can be obtained from a boat on Loch Scavaig, above which rises *Gars Bheinn*, 2,934 ft., the most southerly of the Coolins. John Mackenzie, Scotland's most famous guide in the 19th cent. made numerous Coolin ascents and a peak bears his name. See **Broadford, Dunan, Elgol, Glenbrittle, Loch Coruisk, Loch Scavaig and Sligachan.**

CORGARFF, Aberdeen. Map 26, **NJ 2 0.**
The old tower of *Corgarff* was besieged in 1571, and played a part in the Jacobite risings of 1715 and 1745. Later it became a barracks, and was used as a military depot against smugglers until c. 1830. See **Cock Bridge.** *Iter. 141, 160, 174, 176, 191.*

CORNHILL, Banff. Map 27, **NJ 5 5.**
Park House, 16th cent., has fine gardens. *Iter. 170.*

CORNHILL, Northumberland (England). Map 11, **NT 8 3.**
E.C. Thurs. *Iter. 5, 30, 32.*

CORPACH, Inverness. 209. Map 18, **NN 0 7.**
E.C. Wed. Here, near the shores of Loch Linnhe, looking across to *Fort William* (*q.v.*), are large new paper mills, and the eight locks on the Caledonian Canal which are known as "Neptune's Staircase." A little to the west is *Kilmallie* Church, where an obelisk to the memory of Col. John Cameron, with whom Prince Charles Edward once stayed, has an inscription thought to be by Sir Walter Scott. The "Road to the Isles" leads westwards from here by the shores of Loch Eil towards *Glenfinnan* (*q.v.*). See **Banavie** and **Kinlocheil.** *Iter. 209, 215.*

CORRAN FERRY (NETHER LOCHABER), Inverness. Map 18, **NN 0 6.**
On the east side of the Corran Narrows, which almost divide *Loch Linnhe* (*q.v.*) into two parts, and situated just off the main Ballachulish to Fort William road. This car ferry connects with *Ardgour* (*q.v.*), on the opposite shore, and gives access to the beautiful Ardgour district, which can also be visited by continuing along the eastern shore of Loch Linnhe as far as *Fort William* (*q.v.*), and then making the complete circuit of Loch Eil before reaching Ardgour village across the narrows. By this means the ferry crossing is avoided, but an addition of some 25 miles will have to be reckoned with on the journey, along a narrow and winding road. Nether Lochaber is the name given to this whole district, which is Cameron country, stretching from Loch Leven to Fort William and *Ben Nevis* (*q.v.*), as opposed to Brae Lochaber, which lies beyond the Ben in the direction of Glen Spean. *Iter. 100, 124, 125, 142.*

CORRIE, Isle of Arran, Bute. 1,227 with Brodick. Map 7, **NS 0 4.**
A delightful little coastal village, at the foot of *Goat Fell*, 2,866 ft., Arran's loftiest mountain. White posts on the nearby hillside as far north as Sannox Bay indicate the well-known "Measured Mile" for large vessels on speed trials. Farther north, on the coast, a path leads to the picturesque Fallen Rocks. See **Sannox** and **Skelmorlie.** *Iter. 242.*

CORRIESHALLOCH GORGE, Ross and Cromarty. (Falls of Measach). Map 29, **NH 2 7.**
See **Braemore Junction.**

CORRIEYAIRACK PASS, Inverness. Map 19, **NN 4 9.**
This famous Pass, which carried the road built by General Wade in 1735 in order to link *Kingussie* (*q.v.*) with *Fort Augustus* (*q.v.*), has deteriorated to such an extent that it is now quite impassable for vehicles, but long-distance walkers can still make the crossing. Prince Charles Edward crossed in 1745 from west to east, and droves of sheep made the journey regularly over the pass until 1899. The summit, approached from the east by a series of 13 zig-zags, is at a height of 2,507 ft., the *Corrieyairack* itself attaining 2,922 ft. immediately to the north. The view is very extensive, and ranges from the Moray Firth to the distant Coolins of Skye. The east side of the pass from *Drumgask* (*q.v.*) is paralleled by the River Spey, while the descent on the north-west side goes through Glen Tarff. Neil Munro, in his "New Road," has described the construction of the road. Although little remains today of the road over the pass, it ranks as one of the greatest achievements of Wade. See **Wade Roads.**

CORSTORPHINE (Edinburgh), Midlothian. 21,543. Map 9, **NT 1 7.**
Here is the Edinburgh Zoological Park, situated on the slopes of *Corstorphine Hill*, 530 ft., on which is the viewpoint of *Rest and be Thankful*, associated with R. L. Stevenson's "Kidnapped." On the summit of the hill stands the *Clermiston Tower*, commemorating Sir Walter Scott. Corstorphine Church, of 15th cent. date, became collegiate in 1429, and is noted for the Forrest memorials, the separate gabled roofs, and the coats of arms on the exterior. To the east of the hill is the early 17th cent. *Craigcrook Castle*, with later alterations and additions. **2 m. E.** is the famous Rugby

Football ground of *Murrayfield*, the home of Scotland's international matches, and near it stands *Roseburn House*, 1562 and later, in which Cromwell is said to have passed the night in 1650. See **Gogar.** *Iter. 15, 16, 91, 95.*

CORTACHY, Angus. 402 with Clova. Map 20, **NO 3 5.**
The Church retains a 15th cent. window. *Cortachy Castle*, a seat of the Earl of Airlie, the head of Clan Ogilvie, has a well known herd of cattle. To the north-west rises *Cat Law*, 2,196 ft.

COSHIEVILLE, Perth. Map 19, **NN 7 4.**
A road junction in the Strath of Appin, where the road to *Fortingall* (*q.v.*) and beautiful Glen Lyon diverges from that linking *Aberfeldy* (*q.v.*) with Lochs Rannoch and Tummel. A little to the north is the restored 14th cent. *Garth Castle.* Farther north still, off the road which mounts steadily over moorlands towards *White Bridge* (*q.v.*), a walkers' track diverges westwards, by which the graceful peak of *Schiehallion*, 3,547 ft., may be climbed. *Iter. 89, 107, 138, 147, 149.*

COULPORT, Dunbarton. Map 14, **NS 2 8.**
On the east shores of *Loch Long* (*q.v.*), facing *Ardentinny* (*q.v.*) across its waters. At Coulport terminates the road which almost encircles the narrow Rosneath peninsula. *Iter. 116.*

COUPAR ANGUS, Perth. 1,964. SB. Map 17, **NO 2 3.**
E.C. Wed. The centre of a fruit-growing district, situated in the valley of *Strathmore* (*q.v.*), immediately to the south of the winding Tay. There are slight remains of a Cistercian Abbey, founded in 1164, standing in a corner of the churchyard. Away to the south are the *Sidlaw* hills, with *King's Seat*, 1,235 ft., and *Dunsinane Hill*, 1,012 ft. (See **Balbeggie**). At *Lintrose*, **2 m. S.**, are the outlines of an extensive Roman Camp. Off the Blairgowrie road, to the north-west of the town, lies the Stormont Loch. See **Meikleour, Pitcur** and **Stobhall.** *Iter. 151, 153, 157, 158, 159.*

COVE, Dunbarton. 1,286. SB. with Kilcreggan.
See **Kilcreggan.** *Iter. 116.* Map 14, **NS 2 8.**

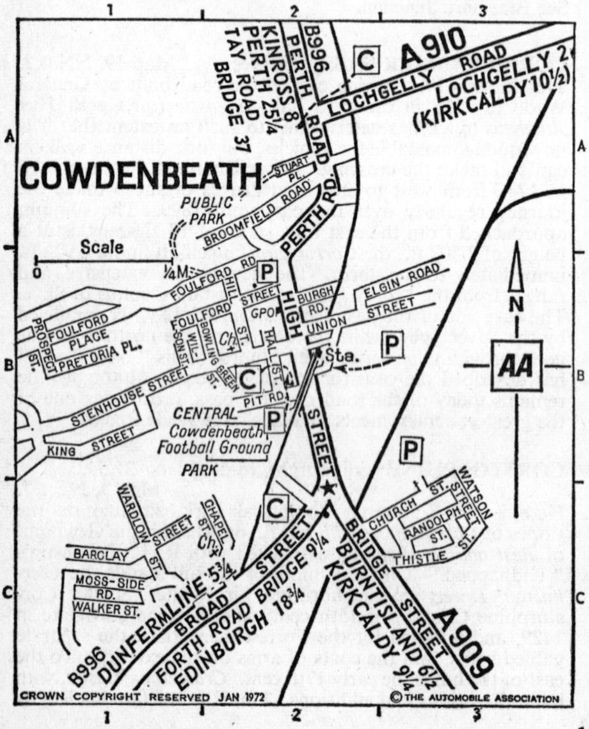

COVE, Kincardine. Map 21, **NJ 9 0.**
A small village, off the Aberdeen to Stonehaven road, and on an interesting stretch of coastline, with the rocky shores of Nigg Bay lying **2½ m. N.N.E.**, sheltered by Girdle Ness, with its lighthouse. A road traverses the shores as far as the Ness, and continues towards Aberdeen Bay. See **Findon.** *Iter. 155, 156.*

COVESEA, Moray. Map 26, **NJ 1 7.**
Covesea Skerries lighthouse (1844) is a notable example of Alan Stevenson's work. See **Lossiemouth.**

COWAL, Argyll. Map 14, **NS 0 8** etc.
The name given to the extensive tract of hilly country, forming a peninsula, which lies between *Loch Fyne* (*q.v.*) and the Clyde estuary. It is indented by a number of picturesque sea lochs, notably Loch Striven and Loch Goil. To the east of the last-named is Loch Long, at the head of which stands *Arrochar* (*q.v.*), in a setting of lofty hills, most of which form part of the Argyll Forest Park. To the south of Cowal, and separated from it by the *Kyles of Bute* (*q.v.*), is situated the island of Bute, access to which is gained by car ferry from *Colintraive* (*q.v.*). See **Ardentinny, Benmore Estate, Dunoon** (*for Cowal Highland Gathering*), **Kilmun, Lochgoilhead, Rest and be Thankful, Strachur** and **Tighnabruaich.** *Iter. 102, 103, 137.*

COWDENBEATH, Fife. 10,460. SB. Map 17, **NT 1 9.**
E.C. Wed. The principal town on the Fife coalfield. To the east of the town lies Loch Gelly, and away to the west is Loch Fitty, backed by the low *Roscobie* hills. See **Blairadam.** *Iter. 90.*

COWIE, Kincardine. Map 21, **NO 8 8.**
A small fishing village, on a rocky bay, with a ruined chapel.

COXTON TOWER, Moray. Map 26, **NJ 2 6.**
See **Lhanbryde.**

COYLTON, Ayr. 2,295. Map 8, **NS 4 1.**
Lies in a coal-mining area. A little to the east are the many windings of the Water of Coyle. **2½ m. S.W.** is Martnaham Loch. See **Drongan.** *Iter. 21, 27, 68.*

COYLUMBRIDGE, Inverness. Map 25, **NH 9 1.**
A developing ski resort on the outskirts of *Rothiemurchus* (*q.v.*) Forest, on the road leading to the Glenmore Forest Park. Coylumbridge is also on the walkers' track leading to the well-known *Lairig Ghru* (*q.v.*) pass in the *Cairngorms* (*q.v.*). A little to the west, beyond *Inverdruie*, a short by-road gives access to Loch an Eilean, described under Rothiemurchus. A road leads northwards from Coylumbridge by way of the attractive little Loch Pityoulish, and later passes *Kincardine* Church on the way to the Forest of Abernethy and *Nethybridge* (*q.v.*). See **Aviemore.** *Iter. 149, 171.*

CRAIGELLACHIE, Banff. 400. Map 26, **NJ 2 4.**
E.C. Thurs. A village beautifully situated in the wooded

Strath Spey, near the point where the Fiddich joins the larger river. The bridge over the Spey leading into Morayshire was designed by Telford. This district is well known for its distilleries. The village is sometimes known as *Lower Craigellachie*, to avoid confusion with the well-known *Rock of Craigel-*

Coshieville, Perth. The statue to Major-General David Stewart (1788–1829), erected by the Stewart Society in 1925

Coupar Angus, Perth. Remains of the Cistercian Abbey, founded by Malcolm IV in 1164 and destroyed in 1559

Cowal, Argyll. Hunter's Quay, a Clyde yachting rendezvous, at the mouth of the Holy Loch

Cowal, Argyll. The obelisk to J. Duncan, at Kilmun, on the north shore of the Holy Loch. His chemical research in the 19th century is said to have revolutionised the British sugar refining industry

Coxton Tower, Moray. The white-harled tower of 1641, the work of the Innes family of Invermarkie. It stands on an unclassified road off A96, south of Lhanbryde

Craigellachie, Banff. The old Spey Bridge, constructed by Thomas Telford

Cramond Bridge, Midlothian; West Lothian. The 'Cramond' Inn, where Robert Louis Stevenson once cut his initials on a table. It stands at Cramond village, 2 miles north, on the Firth of Forth

Crail, Fife. The Mercat Cross, topped by a unicorn

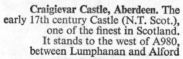

Cramond Bridge, Midlothian; West Lothian. A pillar in the churchyard of Cramond village, near the Firth of Forth

Craigievar Castle, Aberdeen. The early 17th century Castle (N.T. Scot.), one of the finest in Scotland. It stands to the west of A980, between Lumphanan and Alford

Craigmillar Castle, Midlothian. The 14th century Castle of the Prestons, where, in 1566, Mary, Queen of Scots, in company with Bothwell, plotted the murder of Darnley

[For CRAIL see also under EAST NEUK (Plate 56) and also Plates 172 and 175
[For CRANSHAWS see under LAMMERMUIR HILLS (Plate 105)

lachie at *Aviemore* (*q.v.*). **3½ m. E.S.E.**, above Glen Fiddich, is the old mansion of *Kininvie*. **2½ m. N.E.** is *Ben Aigan*, 1,544 ft., from which a remarkable view of the Spey Valley can be obtained. See **Aberlour.** *Iter. 170, 190, 192, 195.*

CRAIGENDORAN, Dunbarton. 1,101. Map 15, **NS 3 8.** One of the most important railhead centres for steamers on the Clyde coast, situated on the south-east outskirts of the resort of *Helensburgh* (*q.v.*). *Iter. 102, 111.*

CRAIGENPUTTOCK, Dumfries. Map 3, **NX 7 8.** See **Dunscore.**

CRAIGHOUSE, Isle of Jura, Argyll. Map 6, **NR 5 6.** E.C. Tues. See **Jura.**

CRAIGIEVAR CASTLE, Aberdeen. Map 27, **NJ 5 0.** One of the loveliest of Scottish Castles (N.T. Scot.), built to an L-plan in the baronial style, and situated north of the Aberdeen to Tarland road on high ground above the Leochel Burn, with views across the Don valley. The structure dates from 1610 to 1624, with a fine show of turrets and high-pitched roofs, while the interior is noted for its splendid Renaissance ceiling in the Hall. Over a four-poster bed is the inscription " Doe not vaiken sleeping dogs." Open 2 to 7, Wed., Thurs. and Sun., May to Sept. (See note page 98.) *Iter. 165, 190.*

CRAIGMILLAR CASTLE (Edinburgh), Midlothian. Map 10, **NT 2 7.** This fine, ruined Castle (A.M.), with its massive 14th cent. keep, a noted viewpoint, has been added to at later periods, and was a favourite residence of Mary, Queen of Scots, who, within its walls, in 1566, plotted with Bothwell to murder Darnley. Earlier, in 1477, the Castle was the prison of the Earl of Mar, who is said to have been bled to death here. It is open weekdays, 10 to 4 or 7; Sun., 2 to 4 or 7. (See note page 98.) In the vicinity, on the road to Dalkeith, are some old houses known as *Little France*, where some of the Queen's French attendants once lived.

CRAIGNURE, Isle of Mull, Argyll. Map 12, **NM 7 3.** Stands at the meeting of the waters of the Sound of Mull and *Loch Linnhe* (*q.v.*), with a steamer pier. *Craignure* faces the flat island of *Lismore* (*q.v.*), and looks to the mainland mountains of Appin and also the distant peak of Ben Nevis. **3½m. S.E.**, at Duart Point, is the famous, restored *Duart Castle*, the ancestral home of the chiefs of the Macleans, the 26th of whom died in 1937 at the age of 101. Open Suns., 2.30 to 6, July and Aug. (See note page 98.) The road leading southwards from Craignure, by way of the head of Loch Don, traverses later the shores of the almost land-locked Loch Spelve, in the midst of fine mountain and cliff scenery, dominated by *Creach Bheinn*, 2,289 ft. A branch from this road penetrates the lonely Glen More, backed by wild hills, with *Ben Buie* attaining 2,354 ft., and later reaches the shores of Loch Scridain. Another range of hills, exceeding 2,500 ft. in height, dominates the road which leads north-westwards from Craignure along the shores of the Sound of Mull past Scallastle Bay in the direction of *Salen* (*q.v.*). See **Lochbuie.** *Iter. 249, 250.*

CRAIGROTHIE, Fife. Map 17, **NO 3 1.** To the south are scanty remains of the one-time palatial *Struthers Castle*, which, in 1547 was known by the name of *Auchtervthyrstruthyr*. It was occupied by Cromwell in 1653. See **Ceres.** *Iter. 127, 129.*

CRAIL, Fife. 1.072. SB. Map 17, **NO 6 0.** E.C. Wed. GOLF. A most picturesque fishing town and ancient Royal Burgh, the oldest in the East Neuk, with a number of old crow-stepped and red-tiled houses, notably near the harbour. The Tolbooth dates from the early 16th cent., displaying a fish weather-vane, and a coat of arms with the date 1602. There have been 18th and early 19th cent. additions. The Collegiate Church is a 13th cent. structure, with later alterations, and retains a plain short-spired tower. There is some 17th cent. woodwork, an ancient carved cross, and in the chancel is a picture of a sailor taking a bearing with a sextant. The churchyard is rich in carved memorials. Near the shore stands an ancient doocot and in the Victoria Gardens is the ancient *Sauchope Stone.* The Town Cross displays a unicorn. On the Isle of May, out to sea to the south-east, and once a place of pilgrimage, is a powerful lighthouse. **2 m. N.E.**, on the coast, is the tower of *Balcomie Castle*, where Mary of Guise, the mother of Mary, Queen of Scots, was entertained in 1538. Beyond the Castle is Fife Ness, in the " East Neuk of Fife," facing the North Carr lighthouse, marking the perilous Carr Rocks. Away to the north-east, visible in clear weather, is the lonely Bell Rock lighthouse. **2 m. S.W.** of the town are the caves of *Caiplie*, the largest being 40 ft. long. *Iter. 94, 98, 132.*

CRAILING, Roxburgh. 302. Map 10, **NT 6 2.** *Crailing House*, dating from 1803, is a fine Regency mansion. *Iter. 30, 47.*

CRAMOND BRIDGE, Midlothian; West Lothian. 500. Map 17, **NT 1 7.** The present bridge (1820) spanning the Almond, built by Rennie, stands in sight of the old bridge, in its wooded setting, and dated 1619, a little way to the north. Beyond here, the river flows into the Firth of Forth at the village of *Cramond*, with Cramond Island lying on the edge of the Drum Sands. A predecessor of the old bridge figures in Rossetti's " The King's Tragedy," which describes the warning of impending tragedy given by a prophetess to James I, in 1436, when journeying from Edinburgh to Perth, where he was murdered. Another legend of the bridge tells of the rescue of James V from footpads in the 16th cent. (See **Fenwick**), while some years later the bridge figured in an incident with which Mary, Queen of Scots was associated. Cramond Church stands on the site of a Roman fort, and the village was described in R. L. Stevenson's " St. Ives." *Cramond House* dates from the 17th and 18th cents. *Inchmickery* Island is a small bird sanctuary. See **Barnton** (Edinburgh) and **Dalmeny.** *Iter. 17, 89, 90, 92, 93, 94, 96.*

CRANSHAWS, Berwick. 338 Map 10, **NT 6 6.** A tiny village in a picturesque, lonely setting on the Whiteadder Water in the *Lammermuir* hills. Near the remains of the old Church stands *Cranshaws Tower*, a fine Border peel, still inhabited, and once a Douglas stronghold. The arms of James VI, once in the old Church, have been transferred to the inner north door of the present Church. The narrow and hilly road leading north-westwards into the hills towards *Gifford* (*q.v.*) crosses the " Hungry Snout," and reaches an altitude of well over 1,000 ft., with *Spartleton Edge* rising away to the east. A right fork from this road gives access, below *Clints Dod*, 1,307 ft., a good viewpoint, to the village of *Garvald* (*q.v.*). See **Abbey St. Bathans.** *Iter. 3.*

CRARAE, Argyll. Map 14, **NR 9 9.** A pleasant village on *Loch Fyne* (*q.v.*). *Crarae Lodge* has notable gardens, shown all day, March to end of Oct. The *Crarae Forest Garden* is accessible regularly (see note page 98). *Iter. 118, 121.*

CRASK, Sutherland. Map 28, **NC 5 2.** A little to the north is the low road pass of *The Crask*, 828 ft., a watershed, from which the view extends to *Ben Klibreck*, 3,154 ft., to the east, and *Ben More Assynt*, 3,273 ft., the highest mountain in the county, to the west. Below the first-named mountain, to the east of Crask, lies the remote Loch Choire. *Iter. 230, 232.*

CRASK OF AIGAS, Inverness. Map 25, **NH 4 4.** The Beauly River, in a very beautiful wooded setting, flows here, dividing at one point into two arms, which encircle *Eilean Aigas* house, a refuge of Lord Lovat, in 1697, and once the home of Sir Robert Peel. The house is also associated with the two brothers known as the Sobiéski Stuarts, who claimed to be descendants of Prince Charles Edward, and were well known as sportsmen and naturalists. The gardens are of especial note. Farther to the north-east is the low Druim Pass, with richly wooded cliffs. *Iter. 206, 210.*

CRATHES CASTLE, Kincardine. Map 21, **NO 7 9.** To the north of the River Dee stands this fine Castle, or double square tower, presented in 1952 to the Scottish National Trust, and open daily, 2 to 7, May to Sept. In Oct. and Apr., on Wed. and Sun. only. Gardens daily, all the year, 9.30 to dusk. (See note page 98.) The structure was commenced in 1553 and completed between 1596 and 1600, forming a notable example of the Scottish baronial style, rich in turrets and gables. It is famous for its woodwork, and several painted ceilings, which date from 1599, considered to be the finest in Scotland. There are also beautiful walled gardens, including some massive yew hedges. Among the rare antiquities preserved in the Castle is the jewelled "Horn of Leys," of 1324, possibly connected with Robert Bruce. Crathes has belonged to the Burnetts of Leys since 1323. *Iter. 152.*

CRATHIE, Aberdeen. 1,018 with Braemar. Map 20, **NO 2 9.** The small Royal *Deeside* (*q.v.*) Church here is attended by the Royal Family when in residence at *Balmoral Castle* (*q.v.*). The Church is built of granite, and dates from 1895. Queen Victoria laid the foundation stone, and in the graveyard of the ruined Old Church is buried John Brown, her personal attendant for many years. **1 m. E.,** on the south side of the Dee, is *Abergeldie Castle*, an old tower, with modern additions, where King Edward VII lived when Prince of Wales. See **Aberfeldy.** *Iter. 141, 152, 167, 179.*

CRAWFORD, Lanark. 1,238. Map 9, **NS 9 2.** **E.C.** Thurs. A Clydesdale resort, surrounded by green Lowland hills, and well suited for walking. There is an old stone pillar, associated with the owners of the local hotel who ran the last mail coach. *Tower Lindsay* is a fragment of an old castle, visited by both James IV and James V. The Camps Water, issuing from the Camps reservoir, in its amphitheatre of hills to the east, flows into the Clyde at Crawford. See **Elvanfoot.** *Iter. 25, 29, 50, 51, 56.*

CRAWFORDJOHN, Lanark. 1,536. Map 9, **NS 8 2.** The village stands at the foot of *Mountherrick Hill*, 1,400 ft., and on a narrow road linking Clydesdale with Nithsdale, in Dumfriesshire, the latter part of the road following the winding valley of the Crawick Water. *Iter. 48.*

CREAGAN, Argyll. Map 14, **NM 9 4.** On the shores of Loch Creran, around the head of which winds the picturesque road linking Benderloch with Appin. Beyond extend Glens Creran and Ure, dominated by *Beinn Sguliaird*, 3,059 ft., and *Beinn Fhionnlaidh*, 3,139 ft. *Iter. 124.*

CREAGORRY, Isle of Benbecula, Inverness. Map 32, **NF 7 4.** See **Hebrides, Outer** (Benbecula). *Iter. 262.*

CREETOWN, Kirkcudbright. 887. Map 2, **NX 4 5.** **E.C.** Wed. Stands on Wigtown Bay, near the widening estuary of the Cree. Until 1785 it was named *Ferrytown.* From the local granite quarries came the stone for part of Liverpool's docks. The clock tower commemorates Queen Victoria's Diamond Jubilee. The neighbourhood is associated with Scott's "Guy Mannering," notably the mansion of *Cassencary*, to the south. The old road to *Gatehouse of Fleet* (*q.v.*) went inland, but the present road follows the curve of Wigtown Bay, and is one of the most beautiful coast roads in southern Scotland. The ruined castles of *Carsluith* and *Barholm*, the latter once a hiding place of John Knox, lie off the road between Creetown and Ravenshall Point, to the west of which is *Dirk Hatteraick's Cave.* Near Barholm, up the valley of the Kirkdale Burn, are the long cairns at *Cairnholy*, relics of the New Stone Age. North of Creetown rises the lonely mass of *Cairnsmore of Fleet*, 2,331 ft., a prominent landmark, associated with John Buchan's "The Thirty-nine Steps." See **Newton Stewart.** *Iter. 26, 72, 73.*

CREICH, Sutherland. 1,218. Map 31, **NH 6 8.** Near the Church stands the 7-ft. high *St. Demhan's* Cross. *Dun Creich*, to the south-east, is a vitrified fort on the Dornoch Firth, with chambered cairns nearby. *Iter. 200, 231.*

CRIANLARICH, Perth. 400. Map 15, **NN 3 2.** **E.C.** Wed. A centre for climbing, walking and winter sports, in the *Breadalbane* (*q.v.*) country, situated at the meeting-place of Strath Fillan, Glen Dochart and Glen Falloch, and in the midst of some of the finest mountain scenery in the Highlands. The road leading south-eastwards by way of Glen Falloch to *Ardlui* (*q.v.*), at the head of *Loch Lomond* (*q.v.*), is very picturesque. In Glen Dochart, the Dochart River flows through Loch Dochart and Loch Iubhair, backed by the well-known twin peaks of *Ben More*, 3,843 ft., and *Stobinian*, 3,821 ft., while a little to the west rises *Cruach Ardran*, 3,428 ft. On a small wooded island in Loch Dochart are scanty remains of an old castle where Iver Campbell of Strachur was besieged in 1597. **3 m. N.W.,** in Strath Fillan, east of the Fillan Water, are slight remains of *St. Fillan's* Chapel, dating from 1314, and dedicated by Bruce as a thanks-offering for the victory of Bannockburn. St. Fillan's bell is now preserved in the National Museum of Antiquities at Edinburgh. To the west of Crianlarich rises *Beinn Oss*, 3,374 ft., almost on the Argyll border. See **Tyndrum.** *Iter. 100, 110, 111, 120, 142, 144, 145.*

CRICHTON, Midlothian. 1,338. Map 10, **NT 3 6.** Above the steep, wooded banks of the Tyne Water stands the little Collegiate Church, dating from 1449, notable for its tower and barrel vaulting, and a quaint bell-cote. To the south is the fine Castle (A.M.), 14th to 16th cent., showing a curious Italianate north wing, with numerous projecting bosses in the courtyard walls. The building was originally composed of a single tower, but developed into a three-sided enclosure, and finally received the unique north wing. The dungeon is known as the "Massie More." The Castle was visited by Mary, Queen of Scots in 1562, and is associated with Scott's "Marmion." Open weekdays (except Fri.): summer 10 to 7, winter 10 to 4; Sun., 2 to 7 or 4. (See note page 98.) See **Borthwick.**

CRIEFF, Perth. 5,604. SB. Map 16, **NN 8 2.** **E.C.** Wed. **M.D.** Tues. GOLF. A good touring centre in Strath Earn. To the north of Crieff, the Earn is joined by the Turret Water flowing from the picturesque Loch Turret with its falls, in the remote glen of that name, lying at the base of *Ben Chonzie*, 3,048 ft. Outside the Town Hall are the

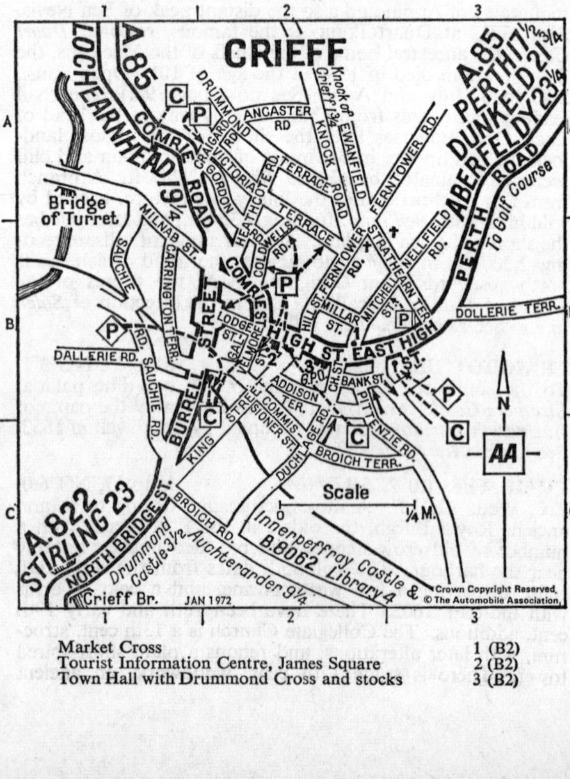

Market Cross	1 (B2)
Tourist Information Centre, James Square	2 (B2)
Town Hall with Drummond Cross and stocks	3 (B2)

Crathes Castle, Kincardine. The late 16th century Castle of the Burnetts of Leys (N.T. Scot.). It stands to the north of A93, east of the Deeside resort of Banchory

Crathie, Aberdeen. The Church, built in 1895, of which Queen Victoria laid the foundation stone. The Royal Family worship here when in residence at Balmoral Castle

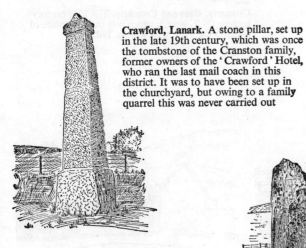

Crawford, Lanark. A stone pillar, set up in the late 19th century, which was once the tombstone of the Cranston family, former owners of the 'Crawford' Hotel, who ran the last mail coach in this district. It was to have been set up in the churchyard, but owing to a family quarrel this was never carried out

Creich, Sutherland. The 7-foot high St. Demhan's Cross

Creetown, Kirkcudbright. The ruined Barholm Castle, situated about half-way to Gatehouse of Fleet, on A75. It was once a hiding-place of John Knox

Crichton, Midlothian. The 14th to 16th century Castle, associated with Sir Walter Scott's '*Marmion.*' The north wing, the work of the Earl of Bothwell, was probably copied from a Veronese palace

[For CRIEFF see following plate
[For CRATHIE see also Plate 3

Crieff, Perth. A cross slab, re-used as a Market Cross, probably 10th century

Cromarty, Ross and Cromarty. The 17th century cottage (N.T. Scot.), which was the birthplace of Hugh Miller, the geologist, in 1802

Crieff, Perth. The Drummond Cross of 1688. The iron stocks below were in use until 1816

Crook Inn, Peebles. A well known posting inn of coaching days, now rebuilt and enlarged. A former Jacobite landlord, captured at Culloden, in 1746, saved his life by dashing down the steep slopes of the Devil's Beef Tub (see Plate 45), near Moffat, when on his way to be tried at Carlisle

Crossford, Lanark. The 16th century Craignethan Castle, which may be the 'Tillietudlem' of Sir Walter Scott's '*Old Mortality*'

Crossmichael, Kirkcudbright. The tombstone to William Graham, a Covenanter martyr of 1682

old stocks, and nearby is the octagonal *Drummond Cross*, dated 1688. The old Market Cross, ornamented with runic knots, is perhaps 10th cent. work. Crieff was burnt in 1716, being further damaged in 1745. Prince Charles Edward held a council of war in the "*Drummond Arms*" Hotel in 1746. To the north of the town is the *Knock o, Crieff*, 911 ft., surmounted by an indicator, and forming a fine viewpoint. It overlooks the mansion of *Ochtertyre*, with its small loch, visited by Burns in 1787. **3 m. W.** is *Tomachastle Hill*, crowned by a monument to Sir David Baird, the hero of Seringapatam. **3½ m. S.S.W.** is *Drummond Castle*, once bombarded by Cromwell, and partially dismantled in 1745. An old tower, now an armoury, still remains, but the rest of the structure is mostly rebuilt. The multiple sundial is dated 1630, and there are notable gardens, which are shown 2 to 6, Wed. and Sat., April to mid Aug. (See note page 98.) **4 m. S.E.** is the ruined *Innerpeffray Castle*, dated 1610. Nearby is the second oldest library in Scotland, founded in 1691, and housed in a late 18th cent. building. The library is open to the public on week-days. (See **Orkney Islands; Mainland**). The adjoining burial-chapel of the Drummonds was once a Collegiate Church, dating from 1508, and has quaint tombs. See **Fowlis Wester, Gilmerton** (Perth), **Sma' Glen** and **Muthill.** *Iter. 89, 140, 141, 145.*

CRIMOND, Aberdeen. 1,083 with St. Fergus.
See **Old Rattray.** *Iter. 181, 182.* Map 27, **NK 0 5.**

CRINAN, Argyll. 40. Map 14, **NR 7 9.**
A small village, situated at the foot of a remarkable rock garden on Crinan Loch. Here, the Crinan Canal terminates its journey from *Ardrishaig* (*q.v.*) and flows into the Sound o Jura. This 9-mile long waterway dates from 1793 to 1801, but it is now comparatively little used. The purpose of its construction was to enable ships to reach the Atlantic from Loch Fyne, without having to make the long and often stormy circuit of the Kintyre peninsula away to the south. Queen Victoria traversed the canal in both directions by barge in 1847. **3 m. S.W.,** to the north of the canal, is the Moss of Crinan, or Moine Mhor. Away to the south, in the *Knapdale* (*q.v.*) district, is the well-wooded Loch Sween, with roads along both east and west shores, which terminate with views over the Sound of Jura to the island of Jura. See **Cairnbaan, Kilmartin, Kilmory Knap** and **Tayvallich.** *Iter. 122*

CROCKETFORD, Kirkcudbright. 115. Map 3, **NX 8 7.**
E.C. Thurs. About halfway between the little lochs of Auchenreoch and Milton, and slightly to the north, stands the village, which was founded by a religious sect, known as the Buchanites. On the hills to the north-west are a tombstone and monument to four Covenanting martyrs, shot in 1685. See **Irvine and Shawhead.** *Iter. 26, 70, 71, 75.*

CROE BRIDGE, Ross and Cromarty. Map 24, **NG 9 2.**
Situated near the head of picturesque *Loch Duich* (*q.v.*), on the lovely road leading towards *Kyle of Lochalsh* (*q.v.*). A long-distance walkers' path goes 7 miles through the hills from here, by way of Dorusduain, and over the rough and steep 2,000-ft. high Bealach na Sroine towards the magnificent *Falls of Glomach* (*q.v.*). These can also be approached from quite a different direction, for which see under *Ardelve*. Another path goes south-eastwards, through Glen Lichd, under the slopes of *Ben Attow*, or *Beinn Fhada*, 3,383 ft., and follows the River Croe and the Allt Granda over the Inverness border to the headwaters of the Affric River, giving access for hardy walkers to Glen Affric. (See **Cannich.**) West of Croe Bridge, on the way to *Inverinate* (*q.v.*), is the little Church and manse of *Kintail* (*q.v.*). See **Shiel Bridge.** *Iter. 207, 220.*

CROFTER COUNTIES
The collective name for the Highland and Island counties of Caithness, Ross and Cromarty, Sutherland, Inverness, Argyll, Orkney and Shetland. Their 9,000,000 acres constitute almost half of Scotland, with a population of only 275,000, a density of only 20 per square mile.

CROMARTY, Ross and Cromarty. 480. SB.
Map 25, **NH 7 6.**
E.C. Wed. A small *Black Isle* (*q.v.*) seaport of Easter Ross, guarding the narrows of Cromarty Firth, with the North Sutor headland over the water, and the South Sutor headland to the east of the town, looking out towards the Moray Firth. The two are known together as the Sutors of Cromarty. Cromarty was the birthplace of Hugh Miller, the geologist, and his cottage, dating from c. 1650 (N.T. Scot.), contains a geological collection. Open week-days only, 10 to 12 and 2 to 5, Apr. to Oct.; Sun, 2 to 5, June to Sept. (See note page 98.) A statue to him is on a hill above the town. Among the 17th to 18th cent. houses in the town is *Albion House*, in Church Street. The Parish Church is of interest for its interior furnishings. On the site of the former Castle, to the south-east of the town, stands the 18th cent. *Cromarty House*. A passenger ferry crosses the Firth to *Dunskeath* (*q.v.*) on the opposite shore. *Iter. 203.*

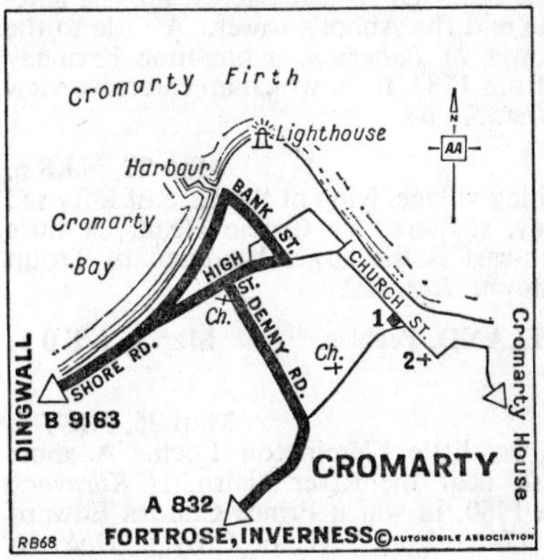

Hugh Miller's birthplace (N.T. Scot.) 1
Parish Church 2

CROMDALE, Moray. 607. Map 26, **NJ 0 2.**
To the south-east rise the *Cromdale* hills, several of whose summits top the 2,000-ft. mark, the highest being *Carn Eachie*, 2,136 ft., and along the crest of which goes the Banff county boundary. The long, winding course of the River Spey is a little to the north of the village. **2 m. E.,** in the Haughs of Moray, is the site of a battle fought and lost by the Jacobites in 1690. *Iter. 170, 195.*

CROOK INN, Peebles. Map 9, **NT 1 2.**
At a height of nearly 750 ft., in a setting of hills, this inn was once a famous posting house on the Edinburgh to Dumfries road. By following the Hearthstane Burn it is possible to climb south-eastwards and reach the flat summit of *Broad Law*, 2,754 ft., rising to the east of the lonely Talla Reservoir. Farther to the north is *Dollar Law*, 2,680 ft. *Iter. 10, 24.*

CROOK OF ALVES, Moray. Map 26, **NJ 1 6.**
See **Alves.** *Iter. 175, 198.*

CROOK OF DEVON, Kinross. Map 16, **NO 0 0.**
The River Devon, flowing southwards through a picturesque defile, makes a sharp bend, or "crook" here on its way to *Rumbling Bridge* (*q.v.*). It would appear that the flow was formerly in an easterly direction, along the course of the present Gairney Water. Away to the south-east rise the *Cleish* hills, with *Dumglow* attaining 1,241 ft. **1 m. E.N.E.** is *Tullibole Castle*, an old tower, dated 1608. *Iter. 91, 98.*

CROSSFORD, Lanark. 618. Map 9, **NS 8 4.**
A Clydesdale village, in a district of orchards, near which the River Nethan flows into the main stream. **1 m. W.S.W.,** overlooking the Nethan, is *Craignethan Castle*, now a ruin, preserving two towers and portions of the walls, and dating from the 16th cent. (A.M.). It is supposed to be the "Tillietudlem Castle" of Scott's "Old Mortality." **1 m. N.E.,** situated in a ravine of the Fiddler's Burn, is the 16th cent. *Hallbar Tower*. See **Kirkfieldbank.** *Iter. 53, 69.*

CROSSGATES, Fife. 1,771. Map 17, **NT 1 8.**
A little to the south-east are the low, wooded *Cullalo* hills, overlooking the Burntisland reservoir. *Iter. 90, 97. 133.*

CROSSMICHAEL, Kirkcudbright. 1,010. Map 3, **NX 7 6.**
E.C. Wed. Situated on the River Dee, where it broadens

out into a reservoir which has been constructed by means of the Glenlochar barrage, and the waters of which are united with those of Loch Ken, to the north-west. In the Kirkyard is a Covenanter's gravestone of 1682. **2 m. N.E.** of Crossmichael, and on high ground, is the tiny Loch Roan. See **Laurieston.** *Iter. 76.*

CROSSRAGUEL ABBEY, Ayr. Map 8, **NS 2 0.**
This Cluniac Abbey (A.M.), founded in the 12th cent., is now an interesting ruin, most of the present structure dating from the 15th cent. Of special interest are the gatehouse, the dove-cote and the Abbot's tower. A little to the north-east is the tower of *Baltersan*, a one-time Kennedy stronghold, dating from 1584, from which an extensive view can be obtained. *Iter. 55, 68.*

CROVIE, Banff. Map 27, **NJ 8 6.**
A secluded little fishing village, lying at the base of lofty red cliffs in Gamrie Bay, sheltered by Crovie Head. A little farther to the north-east is the larger headland of Troup Head. See **Gardenstown.** *Iter. 182.*

CROWN OF SCOTLAND, Peebles. Map 4, **NT 0 1.**
See **Tweeddale.**

CROY, Inverness. Map 25, **NH 7 4.**
To the north lies the little Flemington Loch. A short distance to the east, near the River Nairn, is *Kilravock Castle*, dating from 1460, in which Prince Charles Edward was entertained in 1746. **2 m. S.W.** of Croy is *Dalcross Castle*, built in 1621, and later modernized. See **Cawdor.** *Iter. 177, 198.*

CROY BRAE, Ayr. Map 8, **NS 2 1.**
See **Dunure.** *Iter. 49, 80.*

CRUACHAN, Argyll. Map 14, **NN 0 2.**
See **Falls of Cruachan.**

CRUDEN BAY, Aberdeen. 1,987. Map 27, **NK 0 3.**
E.C. Thurs. GOLF. A well-known resort, with fine sands, and noted for golf. The Bishop's Bridge, spanning the Cruden Water, dates from 1697. A little to the east is the ruined *Slains Castle*, built in 1664 to replace the old Castle near *Collieston* (*q.v.*), and visited in 1773 by Dr. Johnson. To the south of the castle, on a headland, is the fishing village of *Port Erroll*, overlooking the waters of Cruden Bay. Some **2 m. N.E.** of the resort are the well known *Bullers of Buchan*, a great rock amphitheatre, 200 ft. deep and 50 ft. wide, particularly impressive in rough weather, and once described by Dr. Johnson. To the south-east of the Bullers is the Dun Buy, or Yellow Rock, associated with Scott's "The Antiquary." *Iter. 182, 187.*

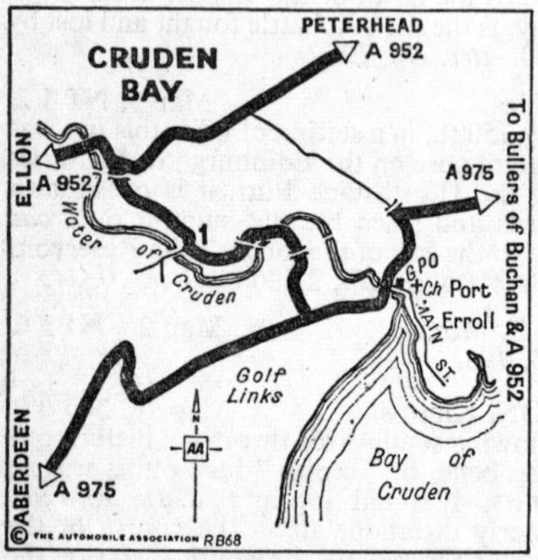

Bishop's Bridge (1697) 1

CRUGGLETON, Wigtown. Map 2, **NX 4 4.**
Here is a little Norman Church, the chancel arch, doors and windows dating from the 12th cent. Near the shore are the remains of *Cruggleton Castle*, and farther to the north, beyond Sliddery Point, is Cruggleton, or Rigg Bay. *Iter. 82.*

CUAN FERRY, Argyll. Map 14, **NM 7 1.**
See **Clachan Bridge.**

CUILLIN, Isle of Skye, Inverness. Map 23, **NG 4 2.**
See **Coolins.**

CULBIN SANDS, Moray. Map 25, **NH 9 6** and **NJ 0 6.**
These famous former sands lay to the west of Findhorn Bay, facing the Moray Firth. They extended to over 3,600 acres and have been afforested with Scots and Corsican pine. In 1694, a disastrous sandstorm overwhelmed what was at that time an exceptionally fertile district. The Barony of Culbin had already previously been affected by sandstorms, and in the final storm the mansion of *Culbin*, a former home of the Kinnairds, was completely engulfed.

CULLEN, Banff. 1,210. SB. Map 26, **NJ 5 6.**
E.C. Wed. GOLF. A resort and fishing town, formerly known as *Invercullen*, with a sandy beach and bathing, situated on Cullen Bay, between Scar Nose to the west, and Logie Head to the east. On the shore are three rocks known as the "Three Kings of Cullen." In the square is a Mercat Cross. Behind the town is the fine mansion of *Cullen House*, partly 16th cent. The house enjoys fine views out to sea, and is situated where the Old Town formerly stood, before being demolished in 1822. Near the house is the cruciform *St. Mary's* Church, 16th cent., but much altered. It was founded by Bruce, and became Collegiate in 1543. In the Chancel are Sacrament House, the prominent Ogilvie monument and the fine laird's pew of the Seafield family of Clan Grant, with its 17th cent. woodwork. The churchyard has many fine table tombs. Some **2 m. E.**, on the coast, is the picturesque, ruined *Findlater Castle.* **3 m. S.W.** is the *Bin of Cullen*, 1,050 ft., a good viewpoint. See **Deskford, Fordyce** and **Portknockie.** *Iter. 169, 184, 193, 198, 199.*

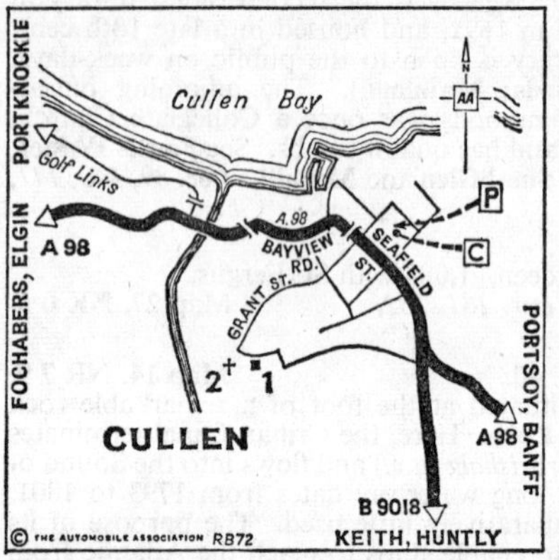

Cullen House, 16th cent. 1
St. Mary's Church, 16th cent. 2

CULLICUDDEN, Ross and Cromarty. Map 25, **NH 6 6.**
About **2 m. W.**, on the shores of Cromarty Firth, are the remains of the 16th cent. *Castle Craig*, at one time a residence of the Bishops of Ross. *Iter. 203.*

CULLODEN, Inverness. Map 25, **NH 7 4.**
A great cairn (N.T. Scot.) marks the site of the famous battle, fought in 1746 on Culloden, or Drummossie, Muir, where Prince Charles Edward lost for ever all hope of restoring the fortunes of the Stuarts, when his army of some 5,000 Highlanders was crushed by the Duke of Cumberland's forces. *Old Leanach* Farmhouse (N.T. Scot.) survived the battle which was fought around it. "Cumberland's Stone" was used by the general to survey the ground. Near the Graves of the Clans is the Well of the Dead. (All N.T. Scot.) *Culloden House*, late 18th cent., **2 m. N.W.**, stands on the site of the former mansion where the Prince spent some hours before the fight. **1 m. S.E.**, across the River Nairn, are the *Stones of Clava* (N.T. Scot.), cairns and standing stones from the Bronze Age, some of the most extensive in the country. *Iter. 177, 198, 212.*

CULNAKNOCK, Isle of Skye, Inverness. Map 22, **NG 5 6.**
On the east coast of the Trotternish peninsula, and a little to the south of which are the Lealt Falls, the river Lealt having issued from the wild and lonely range of hills in the background which culminate farther south in *The Storr* (*q.v.*). Out to sea is the island of South Rona, with the larger island of Raasay to the south. *Iter. 254.*

Crossraguel Abbey, Ayr. The old dovecote of the Abbey, which has 240 nesting boxes. The monks of Crossraguel formerly minted their own pennies and farthings

Cruggleton, Wigtown. The little Norman Church, which dates back to the 12th century

Cruden Bay, Aberdeen. The remains of Slains Castle (1664), which Dr. Johnson and Boswell visited in 1773

Culbin Sands, Moray. Afforestation on the wastes of the Culbin Sands. A great sandstorm took place here in 1694 and devastated the area

Cullen, Banff. Rocks on the foreshore known as the 'Three Kings of Cullen'

Culloden, Inverness. The 'Cumberland Stone,' from which the Duke of Cumberland watched the battle of 1746 which marked the end of the Jacobite Rising

[For CROSSRAGUEL ABBEY see also Plate 172
[For CULLODEN see also under STONES OF CLAVA (Plate 156) and Plate 173
[For CRUDEN BAY see also under BULLERS OF BUCHAN (Plate 25)

Culross, Fife. The Tolbooth, dating from 1626, with a tower added after some 57 years

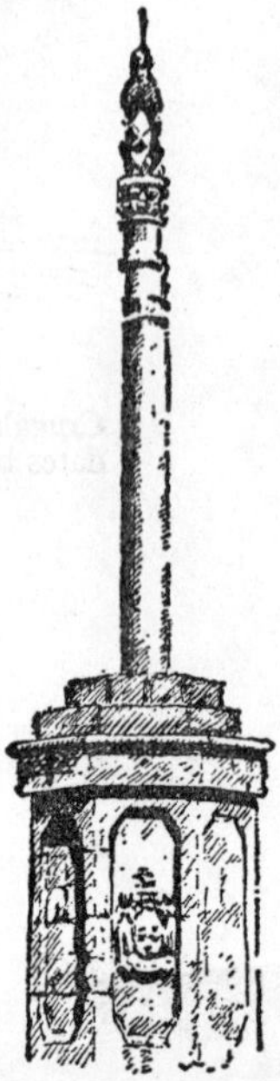

Cupar, Fife. The Mercat Cross, brought back to the town from Wemysshall Hill in 1897. It is surmounted by a unicorn

Culross, Fife. The old Palace, dated 1597 and 1611, once the home of Sir George Bruce of Carnock. In the vicinity is the 'snuffmaker's' house, of 1673, inscribed 'Who would have thocht it, noses would have bocht it'

Culter, Aberdeen. The statue of Rob Roy, the famous freebooter, which stands above the Leuchar Burn, at Peterculter, on A93

Culross, Fife. The paved road known as the 'Crown o' the Causey', the raised crown of which was for the use of the 'upper classes' only

Culzean, Ayr. Robert Adam's late 18th century mansion (N.T. Scot.), built for the 10th Earl of Cassillis. The top flat has been given to President Eisenhower as his Scottish residence

[For CURRIE see following plate
[For CULROSS see also Plate 173

CULROSS, Fife. 491. SB. Map 16, **NS 9 8.**
This picturesque little Royal Burgh, associated with both St. Serf and St. Kentigern, stands in Torry Bay, on the estuary of the River Forth, and well justifies its reputation as the loveliest of the old Fife Burghs. It has the supreme benefit of being largely under the control of the Scottish National Trust, who have admirably preserved many of the old buildings, among which are some typical 16th and 17th cent. houses with crow-stepped gables and red pantiled roofs. The famous "Palace," dated 1597 and 1611, the work of George Bruce (Lord Carnock), and once visited by James VI, is notable for the panelled and painted rooms, and also the curious terraced and walled gardens (A.M.). It is open weekdays, 10 to 7 in summer, 10 to 4 in winter; Sundays, 2 to 7 or 4. The delightful Tolbooth, facing the estuary, dates from 1626, and the 'snuffmaker's' house, dated 1673, carries the inscription, "Who would have thocht it, noses would have bocht it." In the village are the attractive 17th cent. house of "The Study," with the panelled Culross Room, open weekdays, 10 to 12.30 and 2 to 4 or 7; Sun. 2 to 4 or 7. (See note page 98.) *Parleyhill House;* the Manse; and the Hospital, founded in 1637. The modern Mercat Cross, on the original steps, is approached by the 'Crown o' the Causey,' the raised crown of which was for the use of the "upper classes." The Abbey (A.M.), on the hillside to the north, was founded in 1217, and the 13th cent. Church preserves the choir and central tower, the latter built over the rood-screen and pulpitum, but the nave of the Church is ruined. There are interesting 17th cent. alabaster effigies to the Bruce family. The Abbey House, 17th and 19th cent., and latterly reduced in size, stands near the Church, and was built partly from stones belonging to the former monastic buildings. The town was formerly noted for "girdles," and James VI visited its salt-pans. A little to the west of Culross stands *Dunimarle Castle*, open daily, 2 to 6, April to Oct. (See note page 98.) *Iter. 134.*

CULSALMOND, Aberdeen. Map 27, **NJ 6 3.**
The full name of the village is *Kirkton of Culsalmond.* To the north-west, threaded by the main road from Aberdeen to Huntly, is Glen Foudland, above which rises the *Hill of Foudland*, 1,529 ft. A little to the south of Culsalmond is *Williamston House* with fine gardens. *Iter. 187.*

CULTER, Aberdeen. 2,997. Map 21, **NJ 8 0.**
GOLF. A village on the River Dee, known more generally as *Peterculter*. The paperworks on the Leuchar Burn, which flows here into the Dee, date from 1751. Above the burn is a statue of Rob Roy. To the south-west of the village are the *Normandykes* earthworks. Near the modern *Maryculter* Church, across the Dee in Kincardine, is the Corbie Linn, a wild ravine. See **Blairs** and **Drumoak.** For *Iter.* see *Maryculter* and *Peterculter.*

CULTER, Lanark. Map 9, **NT 0 3.**
An attractive village on the Culter Water, near its junction with the Clyde. *Culter House* is a white-harled building of the 17th cent., with a mile-long avenue of trees. Away to the west is *Tinto Hill*, 2,335 ft., and to the south-east is *Culter Fell*, 2,454 ft. *Iter. 25.*

CULZEAN CASTLE, Ayr. Map 8, **NS 2 1.**
This splendid pile (N.T. Scot.), situated in a commanding position facing Culzean Bay, and about a mile to the west of the Ayr to Girvan road, is one of Robert Adam's most notable creations, and dates mainly from 1777, though an earlier tower is incorporated in the structure. The Castle has long been a Kennedy stronghold, they having succeeded the Earls of Carrick, and becoming later Earls of Cassillis. Interesting Kennedy relics are preserved, and the top flat in the Castle was presented to the late General Eisenhower as a Scottish residence. The splendid grounds and Castle are shown 10 to 6.30 or 7.30, March to end of Oct. The newly-restored aviary dates from c. 1800. (See note page 98.) Below the Castle are rock caves known as the Coves of Culzean. *Iter. 80.*

CUMBERNAULD, Dunbarton. 31,787 incl. New Town. Map 16, **NS 7 7.**
GOLF. Lies in a detached portion of the county. A New Town has been developed and acclaimed as one of the finest of its type. There are late 18th cent. locks and a bridge on the Forth and Clyde canal. To the south-east is Fannyside Muir and the small loch, once part of the extensive former Caledonian Forest. *Iter. 17, 50, 87, 97, 99.*

CUMBRAE ISLANDS, GREAT AND LITTLE, Bute.
See **Millport.** Map 7, **NS 1 5.**

CUMMERTREES, Dumfries. 1,152. Map 4, **NY 1 6.**
E.C. Tues. A Solway Firth village from which the notorious spring tides of the Firth can be observed. The Church is said to have been founded by Robert Bruce. The district is described in Scott's "Redgauntlet." Some **3 m. N.** is *Kinmount*, replacing a Queensberry mansion burnt in the 18th cent., and said, until recently, to have contained no wood of any description. See **Powfoot** and **Ruthwell.** *Iter. 28, 47.*

CUMNOCK, Ayr. 5,714. SB. Map 8, **NS 5 1.**
E.C. Wed. **M.D.** Thurs. Stands on the Lugar Water, and is the centre of a mining district. There is a restored Mercat Cross, erected in 1703. Snuff-boxes were once manufactured here. Near the Town Hall is a bust of Keir Hardie, who lived at Cumnock. **2 m. N.E.** is *Lugar* (*q.v.*), where the great ironworks were built in 1845. Between Cumnock and Lugar, the river is spanned by a viaduct 150 ft. high, overlooking a deep gorge. **2 m. W.** is *Dumfries House*, a very fine and unspoilt Adam mansion; within its grounds is the ruined *Terrenzean Castle.* See **New Cumnock.** *Iter. 21, 27, 67, 68.*

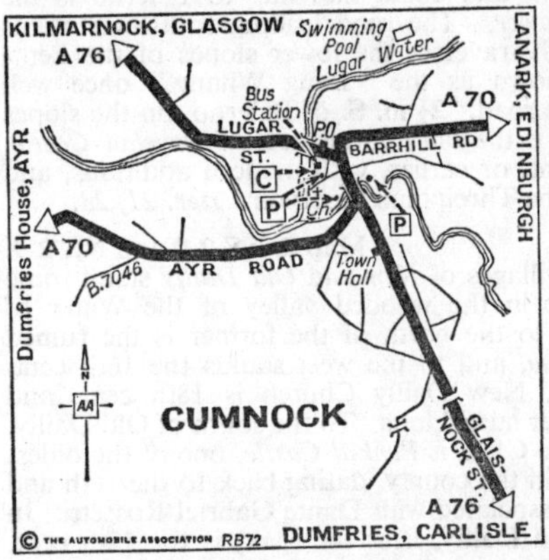

CUPAR, Fife. 6,601. SB. Map 17, **NO 3 1.**
E.C. Thurs. **M.D.** Tues. GOLF. This Royal Burgh has a charter dating back to 1363. Outside the town, to the south, flows the Eden, coming from the Howe of Fife, and entering the sea in St. Andrews Bay, to the north-east. The Parish Church tower dates from 1415, but the spire is two centuries later. A 17th cent. gravestone carved with two

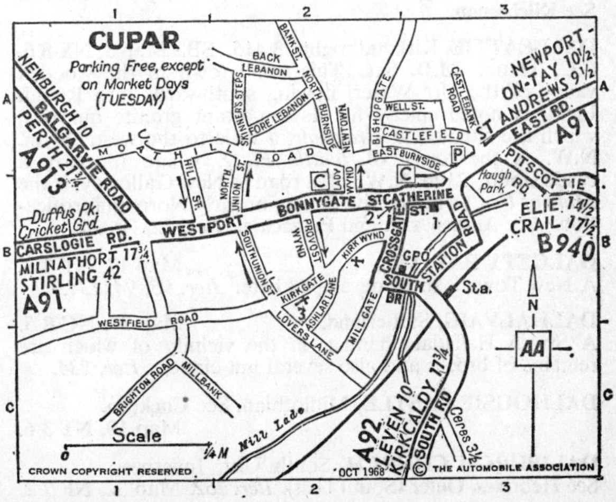

County Offices 1 (B3) Mercat Cross 2 (B2) Parish Church 3 (B2)

heads and a hand records the murder of martyrs of the period. The Mercat Cross is topped by a unicorn, which stood once on Wemysshall Hill; the hill is associated with a treaty of 1559 between the Queen Regent and the Lords of the Congregation, as a result of which French troops were to leave Fife. **2 m. S.** is the fine *Scotstarvit Tower*, dating partly from 1627, and standing on the *Hill of Tarvit* estate (N.T. Scot.), in which the mansion, open Wed. and Sun., 2 to 6, from May to the end of Sept. (see page 98), was restored in 1906 by Sir Robert Lorimer. It contains art treasures and overlooks the Howe of Fife. **3 m. N.W.**, off the Newburgh road, an obelisk to the 4th Earl of Hopetoun stands on *Mount Hill*. Farther to the north-west stands the ruined 16th cent. *Collairnie Castle*. See **Ceres, Dairsie** and **Monimail.** *Iter. 93, 127, 131, 132, 136.*

CURRIE, Midlothian. 4,649. Map 9, **NT 1** 6. GOLF. Through the village flows the Water of Leith, in its deep valley, and southwards is the long range of the *Pentland* hills. Both here and at *Balerno*, the neighbouring village to the south-west, paper-mills are an important industry. An ancient bridge crosses the river near the little 18th cent. Church, and about half-way to Balerno is the ruined *Lennox Tower*. The road leading south-westwards towards Carnwath traverses the lower slopes of the Pentlands, and is known as the "Lang Whang," once well known as a drove road. **2½ m. S.** of Balerno, on the slopes of the Pentlands, is the old hunting seat of *Bavelaw Castle*, probably 17th cent. or earlier, with modern additions, and situated beyond the Threipmuir reservoir. *Iter. 21, 23.*

DAILLY, Ayr. Map 2, **NS 2** 0 and **NX 2** 9. E.C. Wed. The villages of *New* and *Old Dailly* stand some three miles apart in the wooded valley of the Water of Girvan. A little to the north of the former is the ruined *Dalquharran Castle*, and to the west stands the 16th cent. *Brunston Castle*. New Dailly Church is 18th cent. and contains the former lairds' lofts. To the south of Old Dailly, in the Penwhapple Glen, is *Penkill Castle*, one of the oldest inhabited houses in the county, dating back to the 16th and 17th cents., and associated with Dante Gabriel Rossetti. In the vicinity of Old Dailly, near the river, is the 17th cent. house of *Bargany*, with its very notable gardens. See **Straiton.** For Iter. see *New Dailly and Old Dailly.*

DAIRSIE, Fife. 492. Map 17, **NO 4** 1. **E.C.** Thurs. The village is situated three miles east of Cupar, on the main Cupar-St. Andrews road. A mile south, on the Pitscottie road, the River Eden is spanned by a bridge dating from 1522. On a height is the ruined *Dairsie Castle*. The little Church dates from 1621. Southwards from the bridge, the road traverses the charmingly wooded *Dura Den*, where fossilized fishes have been discovered. To the north is the 16th cent. *Pitcullo Castle. Iter. 93, 127, 131, 136.*

DALAVICH, Argyll. Map 14, **NM 9** 1. See **Kilchrenan.**

DALBEATTIE, Kirkcudbright. 3,415. SB. Map 3, **NX 8** 6. **E.C.** Thurs. **M.D.** Sat. This small town in the wooded valley of the Urr Water, flowing southwards into Rough Firth, is noted chiefly for its important granite quarries, which are situated at *Craignair*, a little to the west. **1½ m. N.W.** is the tower of *Buittle Place*, where formerly a castle stood. **2½ m. N.W.**, off a road to New Galloway, is the *Mote of Urr*, an impressive Saxon, or early Norman fortification. See **Auchencairn** and **Palnackie.** *Iter. 72, 73, 76.*

DALGETY BAY, Fife. Map 17, **NT 1** 8. A New Town is to be developed here. *Iter. 93, 94, 134.*

DALHALVAIG, Sutherland. Map 30, **NC 8** 5. A Strath Halladale hamlet, in the vicinity of which are remains of brochs and also several hut circles. *Iter. 234.*

DALHOUSIE CASTLE, Midlothian. See **Cockpen.** Map 10, **NT 3** 6.

DALIBURGH CHURCH, South Uist, Inverness. See **Hebrides, Outer** (South Uist). *Iter. 262.* Map 32, **NF 7** 2.

DALILEA, Inverness. Map 12,**NM 7** 6. A stopping-place for the little *Loch Shiel* (*q.v.*) steamer, and a resort of anglers, in the historic *Moidart* (*q.v.*) district, reached by way of *Acharacle* (*q.v.*), to the south-west. *Dalilea* has two associations of note: Alexander Macdonald, the earliest, and perhaps the best-known of Gaelic Jacobite bards, once lived here, and in 1745, Prince Charles Edward and his Clanranald followers sailed up the loch from here in three boats to Glenaladale, a lonely, roadless glen, leading northwards into the hills farther up the loch, where they received hospitality. Across the loch, to the south-east, is *Ben Resipol*, 2,774 ft. a notable landmark and viewpoint in the district of Sunart. See **Arisaig.** *Iter. 217.*

DALKEITH, Midlothian. 9,529. SB. Map 10, **NT 3** 6. **E.C.** Tues. **M.D.** Mon. GOLF. This market town lies on high ground between the North and South Esk rivers, which unite beyond the park of *Dalkeith Palace*, to the north-east. The original stronghold dates from the 12th cent., but the present Palace was built c. 1700 by Vanbrugh for Anne, Duchess of Buccleuch, who married the unfortunate Duke of Monmouth, executed in London in 1685, and is associated with Scott's "Lay of the Last Minstrel." Among the famous visitors to the Palace have been James IV, James VI and Prince Charles Edward. Queen Victoria stayed here in 1842. *St. Nicholas'* Church, restored in 1852, contains, in the roofless eastern apse, the tomb of Monmouth's widow, who lived for some years at *Newark Castle* near *Broadmeadows* (*q.v.*) in the Vale of Yarrow. See **Cockpen, Dundee, Hawick, Lasswade** and **Newbattle.** *Iter. 4, 5, 13, 37.*

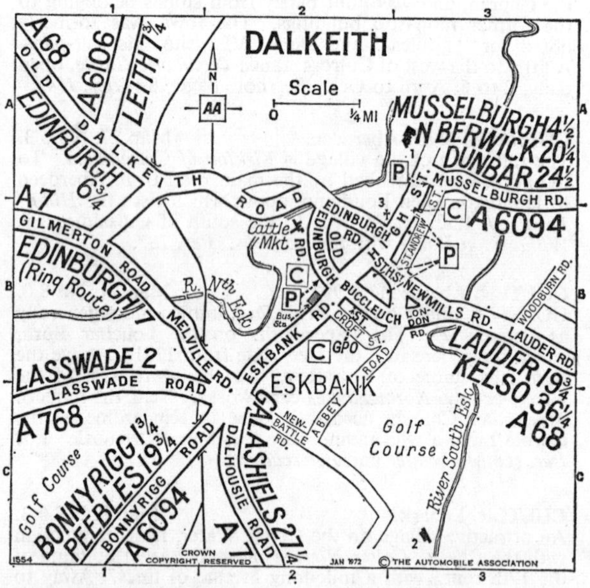

Dalkeith Palace 1 (A3) St. Nicholas' Church 3 (B2) Newbattle Abbey 2 (C3)

DALLAS, Moray. 421. Map 26, **NJ 1** 5. *Dallas Lodge*, built in 1680 and circular in style, has fine gardens.

DALMALLY, Argyll. 1,000. Map 14, **NN 1** 2. E.C. Wed. The River Orchy flows here through Strath Orchy into *Loch Awe* (*q.v.*), to the west, the road to the lochside and Taynuilt now utilizing a new bridge over an inner reach of the loch, and passing near *Kilchurn Castle* (*q.v.*), with views of *Ben Cruachan*, 3,689 ft. Nearly **2 m. S.W.** of Dalmally, off the old road to Inveraray, and on high ground, forming a good viewpoint, stands a monument to the famous bard, Duncan Ban MacIntyre. (See **Inveroran.**) Beyond Glen Strae, to the north, rises *Ben Eunaich*, 3,242 ft. **6 m. E.** of Dalmally, overlooking Glen Orchy and Glen

Currie, Midlothian. The road to Carnwath, across the Pentland foothills, which follows the line of an old drove road, known as the 'Lang Whang'

Dailly, Ayr. The 16th to 17th century Penkill Castle, associated with Dante Gabriel Rossetti, who composed poetry here in 1869. It is situated near Old Dailly

Dailly, Ayr. A roadside stone, a mile to the east of New Dailly, recording the death at this spot of a local road man

Dailly, Ayr. The shell of the 17th century Dalquharran Castle, which stands near New Dailly. In the vicinity stands the newer castle of 1790, designed by Robert Adam

Dairsie, Fife. The old bridge over the River Eden, which dates from 1522

Dalkeith, Midlothian. St. Nicholas' Church, with its roofless eastern apse, in which is the grave of Anne, Duchess of Buccleuch, who had married the Duke of Monmouth, beheaded in 1685

Dalmally, Argyll. The Monument to the bard, Duncan Ban MacIntyre, some 2 miles south-west, on the old unclassified road to Inverarary. He has been described as the 'Burns of the Highlands'

Dalmeny, West Lothian. One of the finest Norman churches in Scotland. The tower is modern, its predecessor having collapsed in the 15th century

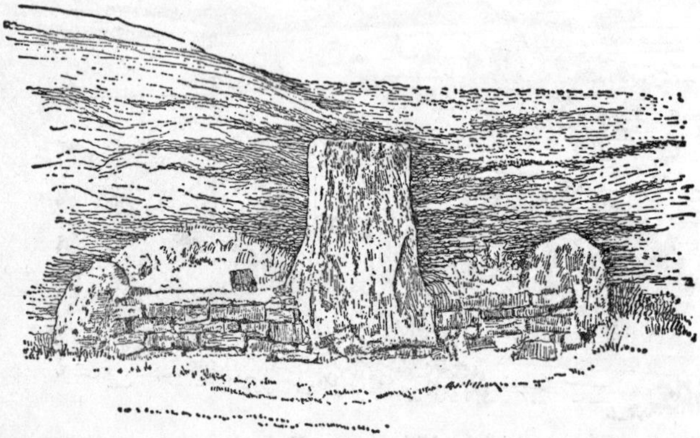

Dalnacardoch, Perth. The 8-foot high Wade Stone, dated 1729, situated off A9, some 2 miles north-west. General Wade is said to have placed a coin on the top and found it still in position a year later

Darnick, Roxburgh. Darnick Tower, first erected in 1425. After being burnt by the English under Hertford, it was re-built in 1569 by Andrew Heiton

Daltulich Bridge, Moray; Nairn. Randolph's Leap, named after Randolph, first Earl of Moray, whose opponent jumped the river during a combat. It is situated on the River Findhorn, off B9007, some 7 miles south of Forres

Dalry, Kirkcudbright. The ancient St. John's Stone, recalling the dedication name of John the Baptist, given originally to the Church by the Knights Templars

[For DALNACARDOCH see also under ATHOLL (Plate 10) and WADE ROADS (Plate 167)

[For DALWHINNIE see under GRAMPIANS (Plate 78)

Lochy, rises *Ben Lui*, 3,708 ft., one of Argyll's highest mountains, situated in a National Nature Reserve. Eastwards from Dalmally, a rather rough and narrow road leaves the *Tyndrum* (*q.v.*) road and traverses Glen Orchy, surrounded by lofty hills. *Iter. 110, 120, 125, 144, 145.*

DALMELLINGTON, Ayr. 8,946. Map 8, **NS 4 0.**
E.C. Wed. A small iron-working town at a height of 800 ft., to the west of which is Bogton Loch, with the waterfall of Dalcairnie Linn, and threaded by the River Doon, which has its source in the long and narrow *Loch Doon* (*q.v.*), to the south. This loch lies in the shadow of the *Rhinns of Kells*, dominated by *Corserine*, 2,668 ft., and *Carlins Cairn*, 2,650 ft. At its northern end is the picturesque Ness Glen. *Benbeoch*, 1,521 ft., a hill to the north of Dalmellington, is a good viewpoint. See **Barr, Loch Trool** and **Straiton.** *Iter. 49, 74, 75, 76, 77.*

DALMENY, West Lothian. 1,510. Map 10, **NT 1 7.**
The little 12th cent. Parish Church is perhaps the finest example of the Norman style in the whole of Scotland. Of special interest are the richly carved south doorway, and also the chancel and semi-circular vaulted apse, with their fine arches. Some of the carvings represent curious mythological wild beasts. The Church has been restored, and the tower is of recent date. East of the village is the park of the modern *Dalmeny House*, with the restored *Barnbougle Castle* in the vicinity, looking towards the Drum Sands on the Firth of Forth. The Royal Elizabeth naval victualling yard dates from 1948. See **Queensferry, South.** *Iter. 96.*

DALNACARDOCH, Perth. Map 19, **NN 7 7.**
Here, the Wade road, now a rough track, dating from 1730, and striding across the hills from *Trinafour* (*q.v.*), joins the present main highway through Glen Garry leading to Inverness, itself also largely one of Wade's roads. General Wade had a hut at Dalnacardoch, which later became an inn, and here Prince Charles Edward spent a night in 1745. Beyond the junction, about **2 m. N.W.**, in a lonely setting of hills, is the *Wade Stone*, an 8-foot high pillar, carrying the date 1729, marking the completion of that particular sector of the road. Wade, a man of great stature, is said to have placed a coin on the pillar, and to have found it still there when re-visiting the site in a year's time. To the north is the vast hill and moorland area known as the Forest of Atholl. See **Tromie Bridge** and **Wade Roads.** *Iter. 138, 140, 143, 147, 149, 150.*

DALNASPIDAL, Perth. Map 19, **NN 6 7.**
At this lonely spot in the *Grampian* (*q.v.*) moorlands, the main road and railway from Perth to Inverness leave Glen Garry to traverse the bleak and lofty Pass of *Drumochter* (*q.v.*), the road reaching a height of 1,507 ft. A little to the south is Loch Garry, which is now joined by a tunnel to Loch Ericht, a larger loch to the west, in connection with a big hydro-electric scheme. *Ben Alder*, 3,757 ft., dominates Loch Ericht from the west, while on the eastern shores rises *Beinn Udlaman*, 3,306 ft. To the north-west of Dalnaspidal are two prominent hills known as the *Sow of Atholl* and the *Boar of Badenoch*, and away to the east are the desolate 3,000-ft. high hills of the Forest of Atholl, stretching northwards to the great Gaick Forest. See **Dalnacardoch** and **Dalwhinnie.** *Iter. 138, 140, 143, 147, 149, 150.*

DALNESS FOREST, Argyll. Map 18, **NN 1 5.**
See **Glencoe** and **Kingshouse.**

DALRY, Ayr. 6,506. Map 8, **NS 2 4.**
E.C. Wed. An iron-working town in the Ayrshire coalfield, standing on the River Garnock. **1½ m. S.E.** is *Blair House*, a fine mansion, retaining two 17th cent. doorways and incorporating a 14th cent. keep. Through the park flows the Dusk Water, and in the glen is a stalactite cave. *Iter. 63, 85.*

DALRY, Kirkcudbright. 752. Map 3, **NX 6 8.**
E.C. Thurs. Properly named *St. John's Town of Dalry*, this little *Galloway* (*q.v.*) village, in the Glenkens district of the county, is well situated for touring the Galloway Highlands. *St. John's Stone* is the name given to an ancient block in the village street. There are distant views of the lofty *Rhinns of Kells* to the north-west, dominated by *Corserine*, 2,668 ft., and *Carlins Cairn*, 2,650 ft. James IV rested here in 1507, and returned in the following year. The Water of Ken circles the churchyard, in which a Covenanter's Stone is to be seen. Across the river valley, to the west, is the Glenlee power station of the Galloway Power Scheme, supplied from the *Clatteringshaws* (*q.v.*) loch. **4½ m. N.E.** is *Lochinvar*, with slight remains of an island castle, the home of the "Young Lochinvar" of the famous ballad. **2 m. N.N.E.**, on the road to Carsphairn, which proceeds along the west bank of the Water of Ken, is Earlston Linn, where the Ken is joined by the Polharrow Burn. To the east stands *Earlston Tower*, dating from 1655, now replaced by the later *Earlston Lodge* in the near vicinity. *Iter. 75, 76.*

DALRYMPLE, Ayr. 2,895. Map 8, **NS 3 1.**
Iter. 68.

DALTULICH BRIDGE, Moray; Nairn. Map 25, **NH 9 4.**
See **Ferness and Logie.**

DALVEEN PASS, Dumfries; Lanark.
Map 4, **NS 8 0 and 9 0.**
See **Carronbridge** and **Elvanfoot.** *Iter. 25, 26.*

DALVOURN, Inverness. Map 25, **NH 6 3.**
Lies in Strath Nairn, with *Culloden* (*q.v.*), or Drummossie Muir rising to the north-east, and crossed by a road leading northwards towards Inverness. **3 m. S.W.** of Dalvourn, off a by-road, is *Dunlichity* Church, built in 1758 to replace an earlier structure, of which some walls remain. On two stones there are cuts remaining, said to have been made by clansmen sharpening their weapons before Culloden fight, in 1746. A watchtower, near the entrance to the Church, was used as a means of preventing the theft of corpses by body-snatchers in the 19th cent. *Iter. 212.*

DALWHINNIE, Inverness. 180. Map 19, **NN 6 8.**
E.C. Wed. Situated on the River Truim, on the great trunk road linking Perth with Inverness, and convenient for winter sports in the *Grampian* (*q.v.*) hills of the Drumochter Forest area, lying away to the south-east. Westwards, on the fringe of *Badenoch* (*q.v.*), stretches the lonely Loch Ericht, 15 miles in length, the waters of which are used in connection with a big hydro-electric scheme. At the far western extremity rises the remote peak of *Ben Alder*, 3,757 ft., and facing it across the loch is *Beinn Udlaman*, 3,306 ft. Wade's road to Inverness and his road to Fort Augustus over the *Corrieyairack Pass* (*q.v.*) fork just north of the village, which stands at a height of 1,200 ft., and here Sir John Hope failed to intercept Prince Charles Edward in 1745. A year later the Prince was a fugitive in this same district, one of his hiding-places being the so-called "Cluny's Cage," below the southern slopes of Ben Alder, and described by R. L. Stevenson in "Kidnapped." To the north of the village, the Inverness road descends gradually through Glen Truim, past the Falls of Truim, into less desolate country. To the east is the extensive and wild Gaick Forest. See **Drumgask, Drumochter Pass** and **Wade Roads.** *Iter. 138, 140, 143, 147, 149, 150.*

DARNAWAY CASTLE, Moray Map 25, **NH 9 5.**
See **Forres.**

DARNICK, Roxburgh. Map 10, **NT 5 3.**
The fine old *Darnick Tower*, rebuilt in 1569, on the site of an earlier structure, retains its iron entrance yett, and was much coveted by Sir Walter Scott. It stands in a picturesque setting near the River Tweed, a little to the west of *Melrose* (*q.v.*). Between the tower and the river is *Skirmish Hill*, where a Border battle took place in 1526, described in Scott's "The Monastery." To the south-east rise the triple-peaked *Eildon* hills and southwards lies the attractively

wooded "Rhymer's Glen," with Cauldshiels Loch to the west. In the glen is *Chiefswood*, once the home of J. G. Lockhart, the biographer of Scott. Some **2 m. N.W.** of Darnick, off the Galashiels road, is the entrance to the lonely valley of the Allan Water, in which are situated in close proximity, among the hills to the north, the three Border peel towers of *Glendearg*, *Colmslie* and *Langshaw*, the first-named associated with Scott's "The Monastery." See **Earlston.** *Iter. 13, 43.*

DARVEL, Ayr. 3,180. SB. Map 8, **NS 5** 3.
E.C. Wed. A lace-making town, and the birthplace in 1881 of Sir Alexander Fleming, the discoverer of penicillin. The prehistoric *Dragon Stone* stands in Burn Road. *Iter. 20, 69.*

DAVA, Moray. Map 26, **NJ 0** 3.
The lofty Dava Moor lies between the valleys of the Spey and the Findhorn, giving wide views in the direction of the Moray Firth to the north, and southwards towards the distant *Cairngorm* (*q.v.*) range. A little to the north is the hill known as the *Knock of Braemoray*, 1,493 ft., and to the east is a lonely area of hill and moor culminating in *Cairn Kitty*, 1,711 ft. See **Dulsie Bridge** and **Lochindorb.** *Iter. 172, 176, 177.*

DAVIOT, Inverness. Map 25, **NH 7** 3.
The village is situated in a dip of Strath Nairn, which lies between the high ground of the Glen of Moy to the south-east and Drummossie Moor to the north-west. The Church, with its unusual steeple, is a landmark. Wade's old military road follows a course parallel to the main Daviot to Inverness road, but keeps about a mile to the west, along the west side of the wooded *Dunmore Hill.* To the north-east of Daviot, there are roads on both sides of the River Nairn leading towards *Cawdor* (*q.v.*), that on the north bank going by way of *Culloden* (*q.v.*). *Iter. 140, 150, 195, 212.*

DAWYCK, Peebles. Map 9, **NT 1** 3.
See **Stobo.**

DECHMONT, West Lothian. Map 9, **NT 0** 7.
Iter. 16

DEERNESS, Orkney. Map 33, **HY 5** 0.
See **Orkney Islands** (Mainland). *Iter. 265.*

DEESIDE, Aberdeen; Kincardine.
Map 20, **NO 1** 9 etc. and 21, **NO 6** 9 etc.
The long and picturesque wooded valley of the River Dee, famous for its salmon, extends westwards from Aberdeen across the Mar division of the county, with a brief intrusion into Kincardineshire in the vicinity of the pleasant resort of *Banchory* (*q.v.*) and *Crathes Castle* (*q.v.*). From here its finest and most typical reaches may be said to commence. The valley, to which has been given the proud title of "Royal Deeside," now becomes increasingly lovely, with rich woodlands near the river banks. Nearing *Aboyne* (*q.v.*), views are opened up of lofty hills to the south-west in the extensive Forest of Birse, dominated by the *Hill of Cat*, 2,433 ft., and *Mount Battock*, 2,555 ft. The most famous stretch of Deeside is that lying between the well-known Highland resorts of *Ballater* (*q.v.*) and *Braemar* (*q.v.*). Here are situated the Royal Castle of *Balmoral* (*q.v.*) and the little Church of *Crathie* (*q.v.*) where the Royal Family worship when in residence at the Castle. Queen Victoria did much to introduce this district to the public, and in the course of her numerous visits with the Prince Consort made many excursions into the surrounding mountains, including the ascent by pony of the great peak of *Lochnagar* (*q.v.*). This famous peak dominates the country across the Royal Forest of Ballochbuie from its position at the northern extremity of the extensive, elevated plateau of the *White Mounth* (*q.v.*). Many of the heather-clad moors on Deeside are shot over for grouse during the season. Along the whole stretch of the Dee between Aboyne and Balmoral there are good motoring roads on both sides of the river, from each of which there are attractive views to be obtained of this beautiful part of the Scottish Highlands, much of which is given over to deer.

Braemar, a summer and winter resort, famed for its annual September Gathering, presents Deeside in its most characteristic vein, the surrounding hill country being rich in forest and heather. Fine views may be obtained from many points towards the lofty ridges of the great *Cairngorm* (*q.v.*) range, which rises away to the north-west, and includes a larger area of ground over the 4,000-ft. level than any other part of Scotland, the highest point reached being *Ben Macdhui*, which attains 4,296 ft. The Dee is much wilder and swift-flowing to the west of Braemar, and beyond *Inverey* (*q.v.*) is the well-known Linn of Dee, a rocky cleft, in which Byron once nearly lost his life. Beyond the *Devil's Point*, 3,303 ft. and *Cairn Toul*, 4,241 ft., far up Glen Dee, in the fastnesses of the Cairngorms, are the Pools of Dee, situated in the wild and lonely pass of the *Lairig Ghru* (*q.v.*). The actual source of the Dee, known as the Wells of Dee, is located high up near the summit of the 4,248-ft. high peak of *Braeriach.* Deeside is linked to the upper valley of the Don, to the north, in the vicinity of *Cock Bridge* (*q.v.*), by narrow roads leading into the hills from points near Braemar and Ballater respectively. These roads converge at *Gairnshiel Bridge* (*q.v.*), and continue over the narrow and steep Glas Choille section, liable to be snowbound in winter. *Iter. 141, 152, 160, 167, 168, 174, 179.*

DELGATIE CASTLE, Aberdeen. Map 27, **NJ 7** 4.
See **Turriff.**

DELNASHAUGH INN, Banff. Map 26, **NJ 1** 3.
To the north, on the Grantown-on-Spey road, the fine old Bridge of Avon, in a picturesque, wooded setting, spans the river which flows northwards to join the Spey beyond the lovely grounds of *Ballindalloch Castle.* This 16th cent. tower is linked to a modern building, and approached from the Craigellachie road. Beyond the junction of the two rivers rises the *Hill of Delnapot*, 1,001 ft., in Moray. Southwards from Delnashaugh Inn, a road follows the Avon to its junction with the Livet Water by *Downan* (*q.v.*), near the famous *Glenlivet* (*q.v.*) distillery. *Iter. 170, 192, 195.*

DENHOLM, Roxburgh. 365. Map 10, **NT 5** 1.
On the River Teviot, with a pleasant green. This village was the birthplace of John Leyden, the 18th cent. poet and friend of Scott, and also of Sir James Murray, who edited the Oxford English Dictionary. An obelisk was set up in Leyden's memory in 1861, and a tablet on a thatched cottage records his birth in 1776. *Westgate Hall* is 17th cent. **2 m. N.E.,** beyond the river, on the summit of the steep *Minto Crags*, is the ruined *Fatlips Castle*, dating from the 16th cent. Westwards lies *Minto House*, now a hospital. To the south of Denholm rises "dark" *Ruberslaw*, 1,392 ft., of old a Covenanters' retreat, and to the east flows the Rule Water. Alexander Peden preached formerly from a rock known as "Peden's Pulpit" near the summit of Ruberslaw. See **Sorn.** *Iter. 30, 36.*

DENNY, Stirling. 8.951 SB. with Dunipace.
Map 16, **NS 8** 8.
E.C. Wed. A small paper manufacturing town, together with *Dunipace*, to the north, on the River Carron, and situated to the east of the *Kilsyth* hills. *Quarter*, to the north, is a small Georgian house. A narrow and hilly moorland road leads westwards from Denny to follow the Carron and later the Endrick Water between the *Campsie Falls* and *Fintry* hills towards *Fintry* (*q.v.*). See **St. Ninian's.** *Iter. 50, 87, 99, 114.*

DENNYLOANHEAD, Stirling. 3,136. Map 16, **NS 8** 8.
A small mining town. *Iter. 17, 113, 115.*

DERE STREET (Roman Road), Roxburgh.
Map 5, **NT 7** 0 etc.
See **Carter Bar** and **Oxnam.**

DERVAIG, Isle of Mull, Argyll. Map 12, **NM 4** 5.
At the head of the narrow Loch Cuan, in Glen Bellart, in a picturesque setting. To the south-east, the inland road

Delnashaugh Inn, Banff. The entrance lodge and gate of the 16th century and later Ballindalloch Castle, which carries the arms of the Macpherson-Grants

Daviot, Inverness. The Church, as seen from A9. From points in the vicinity there are distant views of Ben Wyvis, in Easter Ross

Deeside, Aberdeen. The Bridge of Feugh, dated 1799, though probably of earlier date. It spans the river near its junction with the Dee, on the outskirts of the resort of Banchory

Darvel, Ayr. The prehistoric Dragon Stone, in Burn Road, around which New Year's Day processions were once held

Denholm, Roxburgh. The 'Text House,' embellished with exhortations, erected by a local eccentric, Dr. Haddon

Devil's Beef Tub, Dumfries. A view of the deep Annandale hollow off the Moffat to Edinburgh road (A70). It was used by Annandale raiders to secrete stolen cattle. See Crook Inn (Plate 39)

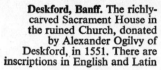

Deskford, Banff. The richly-carved Sacrament House in the ruined Church, donated by Alexander Ogilvy of Deskford, in 1551. There are inscriptions in English and Latin

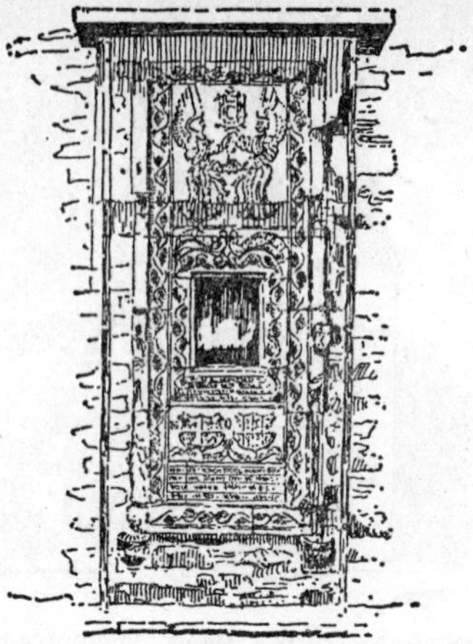

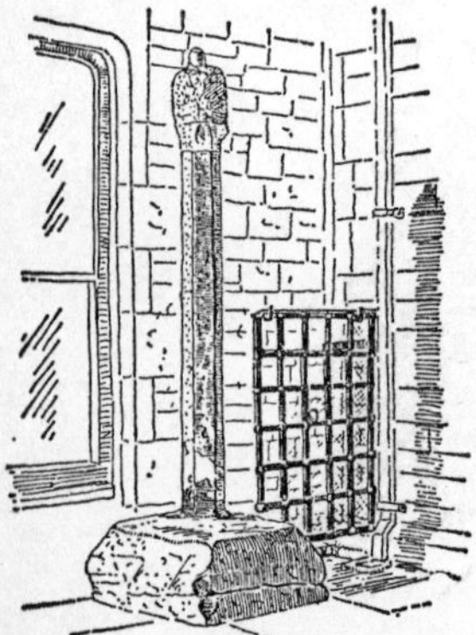

Dingwall, Ross and Cromarty. The shaft of the old Mercat Cross, neighboured by the iron 'yett,' or gate from the former town gaol

Dirleton, East Lothian. The 13th century de Vaux Castle, captured by the Bishop of Durham for Edward I. Later it resisted Cromwell's troops, before falling to General Monk, who dismantled it in 1650. In the foreground is an old dovecote

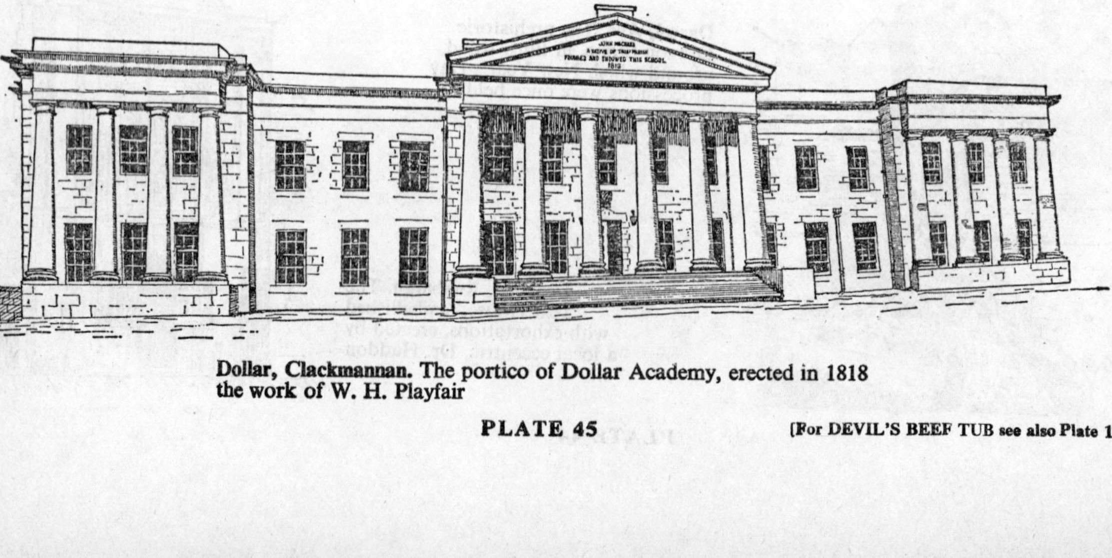

Dollar, Clackmannan. The portico of Dollar Academy, erected in 1818 the work of W. H. Playfair

[For DEVIL'S BEEF TUB see also Plate 173

to *Salen* (*q.v.*) goes near Loch Frisa on the way to Glen Aros. The road leading eastwards towards *Tobermory* (*q.v.*) is narrow, with hairpin bends, in the vicinity of the Mishnish Lochs. See **Calgary**. *Iter. 248, 250.*

DESKFORD, Banff. 541. Map 26, **NJ 5 6.**
Kirktown of Deskford is the full name of this village, which lies on the Burn of Deskford. The Church (A.M.), not now in use, is noted for its Sacrament House, dating from 1551, with an inscription in English as well as in the usual Latin, and is one of the best examples of this Church fitting, which is peculiar to certain parts of Scotland. Away to the north-west of the village rises the *Bin of Cullen*, 1,050 ft. See **Fordyce**. *Iter. 169.*

DEVIL'S BEEF TUB, Dumfries. Map 9, **NT 0 1.**
See **Moffat**. *Iter. 10, 24.*

DEVIL'S DYKE, Dumfries. Map 9, **NS 7 0.**
See **Sanquhar.**

DEVIL'S ELBOW, Perth. Map 20, **NO 1 7.**
See **Glenshee**. *Iter. 141, 152, 160, 167, 168.*

DEVIL'S MILL, Kinross, Perth. Map 16, **NT 0 9.**
See **Rumbling Bridge.**

DEVIL'S POINT, Aberdeen. Map 20, **NN 9 9.**
See **Inverey.**

DEVIL'S STAIRCASE, Argyll. Map 18, **NN 2 5.**
See **Kingshouse.**

DINGWALL, Ross and Cromarty. 4,233. SB. Map 25, **NH 5 5.**
E.C. Thurs. **M.D.** Wed. A busy little Easter Ross town, with a long main street, created a Royal Burgh in 1226, and situated on Cromarty Firth. Slight remains of the former castle are preserved. The harbour was constructed by Telford. The Tolbooth dates from 1730 and shows the Town Arms, a starfish. The shaft of the former Cross stands near the iron yett of the old town gaol. Near the church is a statue (1714) to the 1st Earl of Cromarty. On a hill south of the town is a tower commemorating the birth of General Sir Hector Macdonald. *Tulloch Castle*, to the north of the town, was for many years a seat of the Davidsons. Far away to the north-west is *Ben Wyvis*, 3,426 ft., a landmark for many miles around. See **Conon Bridge, Evanton and Strathpeffer**. *Iter. 200, 201, 202, 203, 206, 213.*

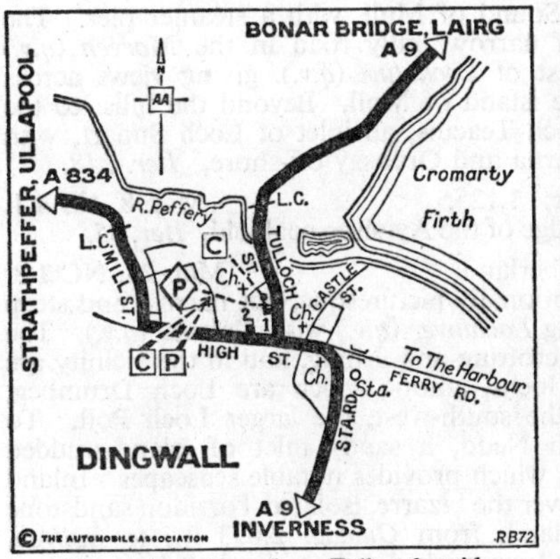

Cromarty statue 1 Tolbooth, with cross-shaft and iron yett, from gaol 2

DINNET, Aberdeen. 93. Map 21, **NO 4 9.**
The road leading northwards towards Huntly crosses Dinnet Moor, on which prehistoric remains are to be found. To the south, beyond Dinnet Bridge across the Dee, lie Glen Tanner and Glen Tanar Forest. See **Aboyne, Bridge of** Ess and **Cambus o'May**. *Iter. 152, 168, 174, 191.*

DIRK HATTERAICK'S CAVE, Kirkcudbright.
See **Creetown**. Map 2, **NX 5 5.**

DIRLETON, East Lothian. 2,768. Map 10, **NT 5 8.**
The attractive village of *Dirleton* lies almost exactly halfway between the famous golfing resorts of *Gullane* (*q.v.*) and *North Berwick* (*q.v.*), and has a Church dating from the early 17th cent., the interior having been modernized. The massive remains of *Dirleton Castle* (A.M.), situated on its rock, date largely from the 13th cent., the structure having been partly dismantled by General Monk in 1650. There is a three-storey Renaissance portion still standing. By the garden is a bowling green of the 17th cent. In 1298, the stronghold was invested by Edward I, and was a home of the de Vaux family. To the west is *Archerfield House*, which took the place of the Castle as a residence, and a 16th cent. circular dovecote has survived nearby. The surroundings of the house are associated with R. L. Stevenson's " Pavilion on the Links." To the north, beyond the expanse of the North links, is the tiny island of *Fidra*, with a lighthouse. *Iter. 2, 36, 37.*

DOLLAR, Clackmannan. 2,279. SB. Map 16, **NS 9 9.**
E.C. Thurs. GOLF. This residential town near the River Devon stands at the foot of the *Ochil* hills, and is noted for its Academy, the buildings of which date from 1818. About a mile to the north, between the Burn of Sorrow and the Burn of Care, the former flowing through the narrow and steep Windy Pass, stands the ruined *Castle Campbell*, in the wooded Dollar Glen (A.M. and N.T. Scot.). Its setting is one of the most romantic in Scotland, being protected by deep ravines, with a view extending southwards over the windings of the Devon towards the Firth of Forth and the distant *Pentland* hills. The structure, which was once known as *Castle Gloume*, or *Gloom*, has a fine 14th cent. square tower joined to a 16th cent. wing, and is open weekdays, 10 to 4 or 7; Sun. 2 to 4 or 7. (See note page 98.) In 1645 it was sacked by Montrose, and was at one time associated with John Knox and also Mary, Queen of Scots. To the north-west of the Castle, in the Ochils, is *King's Seat*, 2,111 ft., behind which rises *Ben Cleuch*, 2,363 ft., the highest point in the range, forming a splendid viewpoint. **2 m. N.E.** of Dollar, off the Milnathort road, are the remains of *Cowden House*. *Iter. 136.*

DOLPHINTON, Lanark; Peebles. 184. Map 9, **NT 1 4.**
Outside the door of the small and ancient church is the grave of a Covenanter. On *Kippit Hill*, to the north-east, a sandstone cist, perhaps 2,000 years old, was uncovered in 1920.

DONIBRISTLE (near Cowdenbeath), Fife. Map 17, **NT 1 8.**
Iter. 97, 133.

DONIBRISTLE (near Inverkeithing), Fife. Map 17, **NT 1 8.**
See **Aberdour.**

DORES, Inverness. 512. Map 25, **NH 5 3.**
A *Loch Ness* (*q.v.*) village, at the south-western extremity of Strath Dores. A little to the east is Loch Ashie, and beyond it, to the south, is the larger Loch Duntelchaig, both at a height of over 700 ft. **2 m. N.**, where Loch Ness begins to narrow, is the 18th cent. *Aldourie Castle*. To the south of Dores there is a choice of routes to Fort Augustus, the more westerly road following the shores of Loch Ness, and the easterly road climbing steeply on to moorland by way of *Errogie* (*q.v.*). *Iter. 211.*

DORNIE, Ross and Cromarty. Map 24, **NG 8 2.**
E.C. Wed. Here, in a beautiful North-West Highland setting of mountain and loch, where *Loch Duich* (*q.v.*) meets Loch Long, is a road bridge, spanning the last-named loch, and replacing the former ferry which linked the small crofting village with *Ardelve* (*q.v.*), on *Loch Alsh* (*q.v.*). A little to the north-east of Dornie, on Loch Long, is the clachan of *Bundalloch*, where byres of several old crofters' cottages, once known as " black houses," are still to be found. Facing Loch Duich, with a view towards Totaig, on the opposite side of the loch, is the picturesque *Eilean Donan Castle*, an ancient structure, once surrounded by water, but now completely restored and linked to the mainland by a causeway. The Castle incorporates a War Memorial to the Clan Macrae, and is open Easter to Oct. weekdays, 10 to 12.30 and 2 to 6. (See note page 98.) In 1719, during an abortive Jacobite rising, a British frigate bombarded the structure. **2 m. S.E.** of Dornie, on the road to *Shiel Bridge* (*q.v.*), the road climbs above Loch Duich to a height of more than 500 ft. at Carr Brae, or Keppoch, a splendid viewpoint, looking towards the *Five Sisters of Kintail*, dominated by *Scour Ouran*, 3,505 ft., which form part of the *Kintail* (*q.v.*) estate. *Iter. 207, 220.*

DORNOCH, Sutherland. 838. SB. Map 31, **NH 7 8.** **E.C.** Thurs. GOLF. A small golfing resort and Royal Burgh, with a good bathing beach and sands, looking over the Dornoch Firth, into which a narrow spit of land projects terminating at Dornoch Point. Only the lofty tower is still standing from the Bishop's Castle, destroyed in 1570. The Cathedral dates from 1224, the choir having been probably completed c. 1539. After severe damage in 1570, and later much neglect, considerable restorations took place, first in 1835 to 1837, and latterly in 1924. No fewer than 16 Earls of Sutherland are said to be buried in the Cathedral, and there is a statue by Chantrey of the first Duke. Dornoch was the scene, in 1722, of the last judicial execution for witchcraft to take place in Scotland, the Witch's Stone on the golf course recalling the event. **2 m. N.** is the late 18th cent. mansion of *Embo House. Iter. 231.*

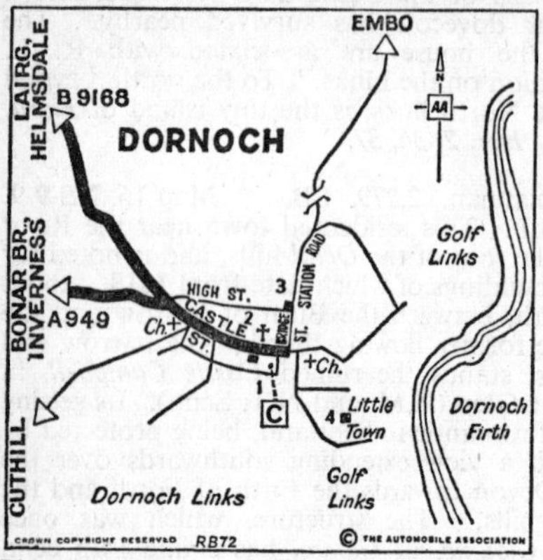

Bishop's Castle 1 Cathedral 2 Town Clerk's Office, Information Bureau 3 Witch's Stone 4

DORNOCK, Dumfries. 693. Map 4, **NY 2 6.** In the vicinity are remains of a stone circle and also two ancient towers. *Iter. 26, 27, 28, 42, 67.*

DOUGLAS, Lanark. 5,045. Map 9, **NS 8 3.** This little town, in the valley of the Douglas Water, lies in a coal-mining district, and colliery operations were responsible for the demolition of *Douglas Castle,* which had been rebuilt by Adam in 1759. Only the Chapel and porch remain, and nearby is a fragment of Scott's "Castle Dangerous." The restored chancel of *St. Bride's* Church (A.M.) stands in the churchyard and contains the tomb of the Earl of Angus, known as "Bell-the-Cat," who died in 1514. There is also a notable range of Douglas tombs, and some 13th and 15th cent. French stained glass. Near the building stands a tower, built in 1618, in which is a clock dated 1565, said to be the gift of Mary, Queen of Scots. Facing the tower is a monument to commemorate the raising of the Cameronian Regiment in 1689. The "*Sun*" and *Cross Keys* are old inns, the former dating from 1621. A house in Main Street has an inscribed panel of 1695 recalling an atrocity perpetrated on James Gavin, a Covenanter. See **Lauder.** *Iter. 21, 35.*

DOUGLAS HALL, Kirkcudbright. Map 3, **NX 8 5.** A small resort on Sandyhills Bay, overlooking the waters of the Solway Firth, with *Criffell,* 1,866 ft., rising away to the north-east. In the vicinity are two natural rock archways on a delightful stretch of coast, with Sandyhills Bay facing Craigneuk Point and the Mersehead Sands. *Iter. 73.*

DOUNE, Perth. 741. SB. Map 16, **NN 7 0.** **E.C.** Wed. The River Teith is crossed here by a picturesque bridge, built originally in 1535. The builder was James Spittal, the wealthy tailor to James IV, who, when arriving at the former ferry without any money, was refused a passage by the ferryman, and built the bridge out of spite in order to deprive the ferryman of a living. In the small town, once noted for the manufacture of fine metal pistols, as shown by the crossed pistols on a sign, stands a good Mercat Cross. *Doune Castle,* situated between the Teith and the smaller Ardoch, and open daily, 10 to 6, Mar. to end of Nov. Closed Thu., Mar. to end of May and in Oct. and Nov. (see note page 98), is a splendid, though mixed example of its period, and overlooks the swift-flowing rivers. The building dates from the early 15th cent., the work of the Regent Albany. Subsequent to his execution in 1424 it passed to the Crown. The castle has two fine towers, between which is the hall, and has been well restored. In 1745, the castle was held for Prince Charles Edward, and the hero of Scott's "Waverley" was confined within. Home the author of "Douglas," once escaped from the castle, using a rope of bedclothes. In the attractive Doune Park gardens is a motor museum. See **Callander** and **Dunblane.** *Iter. 141, 142, 144, 146.*

DOUNREAY, Caithness. Map 30, **NC 9 6.** Situated on the far northern coast. Here stands Scotland's first experimental nuclear power station, commenced in 1954. Its silver sphere is noteworthy. The United Kingdom Atomic Energy Authority's Exhibition is a feature. A second reactor should be completed in 1972.

DOWNAN, Banff. Map 26, **NJ 1 3.** A road junction in the vicinity of the famous *Glenlivet* (*q.v.*) distillery. At Downan, the River Avon is joined by the Livet Water, and there is a choice of alternative routes to *Tomintoul* (*q.v.*), the more westerly road traversing Strath Avon, backed by the *Cromdale* hills, and the easterly road going by way of the Braes of Glenlivet. *Iter. 192.*

DREGHORN, Ayr. 4,093. Map 8, **NS 3 3.** **E.C.** Wed. The town stands on the Annick Water, which, to the west, is joined by the River Irvine, on its way to Irvine Bay. John Dunlop, inventor of the pneumatic tyre, was born here in 1845. There is an early 19th cent. corn-mill. *Iter. 66, 69, 85.*

DREM, East Lothian. Map 10, **NT 5 7.** At *East Fortune,* some **2½ m. E.,** is a monument commemorating the start of the first two-way crossing of the Atlantic in 1919 by the airship R34.

DRIMNIN, Argyll. Map 12, **NM 5 5.** Situated on the Sound of Mull, with a steamer pier. The village lies on a narrow, hilly road in the *Morven* (*q.v.*) district north-west of *Lochaline* (*q.v.*), giving views across the Sound to the island of Mull. Beyond the hills, to the north-east, is Loch Teacuis, an inlet of Loch Sunart, with the islands of Carna and Oronsay off-shore. *Iter. 218.*

DRONGAN, Ayr. 1,125. Map 8, **NS 4 1.** Situated on the edge of the Ayrshire coalfield. *Iter. 85.*

DRUMBEG, Sutherland. Map 28, **NC 1 3.** Lies on the exceptionally picturesque, but narrow and steep coast road linking *Lochinver* (*q.v.*) with *Kylesku* (*q.v.*). The district is one of crofting and fishing, and in the vicinity are numerous small lochs, among which are Loch Drumbeg, and, farther to the south-west, the larger Loch Poll. To the east is Loch Nedd, a sandy inlet of island-studded Eddrachillis Bay, which provides notable seascapes. Inland the view ranges over the bizarre, isolated Torridon sandstone peaks of Sutherland, from *Quinag,* 2,653 ft., to *Suilven,* 2,399 ft., with its twin-peaked mile and a half long summit ridge. To the north-west of Drumbeg, off the coast, lies the island of Oldany. See **Stoer.** *Iter. 227.*

DRUMCLOG, Lanark. Map 8, **NS 6 3.** See **Loudounhill.** *Iter. 20, 69.*

DRUMELZIER, Peebles. 732 Map 9, **NT 1 3.** The Drumelzier Burn comes down from its wooded dell to join the Tweed near the reputed burial place of Merlin, the wizard of Arthurian legend. Of the 16th cent. Castle, only fragments remain, situated near the Tweed, about a mile to the south-west. The Church preserves the ancient burial vault of the Tweedies, and away to the east, is the ruined *Tinnis* or *Thanes Castle,* with *Pykestone Hill,* 2,414 ft., rising in the background. *Iter. 24.*

DRUMGASK, Inverness. Map 19, **NN 6 9.** Here, in the lonely valley of the Upper Spey, roads from *Dalwhinnie* (*q.v.*) and *Newtonmore* (*q.v.*) meet on their way through Strath Mashie to *Loch Laggan* (*q.v.*). **½ m. W.,** the old Wade road to Fort Augustus over the *Corrieyairack Pass* (*q.v.*) diverges to the north, and **6 m. W.,** along the track, beyond Loch Crunachan, is Wade's *Garva,* or *St. George's* Bridge, dating from 1732, over the Upper Spey. Beyond this point the river leaves the track and its source is farther to the west near the small Loch Spey. **2 m. N.E.,** beyond *Laggan* Church and bridge, is *Cluny Castle,* the

Dornoch, Sutherland. The Witch's Stone, on the golf course, where, in 1722, the last judicial execution for witchcraft took place in Scotland. This witch was said to have changed her daughter into a pony, which was then shod by the Devil

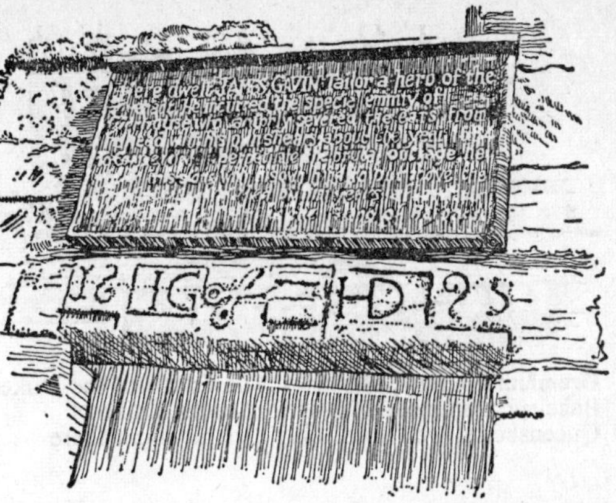

Douglas, Lanark. A house in Main Street, its inscription recalling the atrocity perpetrated in 1695 on James Gavin, a Covenanter

Doune, Perth. The original bridge of 1535 was built by the wealthy tailor to James IV. He was refused a passage by the ferryman, as he had no money with him, and built the bridge out of spite in order to ruin him

Douglas, Lanark. The Monument which commemorates the raising of the Cameronian Regiment in 1689

Drem, East Lothian. The Monument marking the start of the first Atlantic double crossing by air, by the British airship R34, in July 1919. It stands 2½ miles east, at East Fortune, on B1377

Drumgask, Inverness. A stone, near Mains of Glentruim, on a by-road on the south bank of the River Spey. It is said to mark the geographical centre of Scotland

[For DOUNE see also Plate 174

Drumlanrig Castle, Dumfries. The Castle of the Dukes of Buccleuch, erected 1676–89 for the 1st Duke of Queensberry, who spent only a single night there

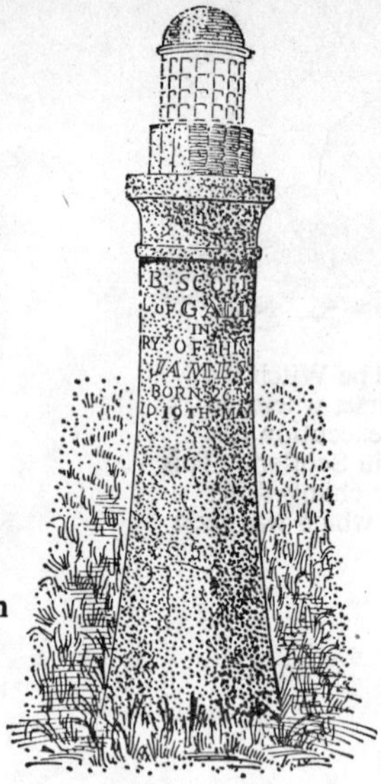

Drummore, Wigtown. A churchyard gravestone in the form of a lighthouse

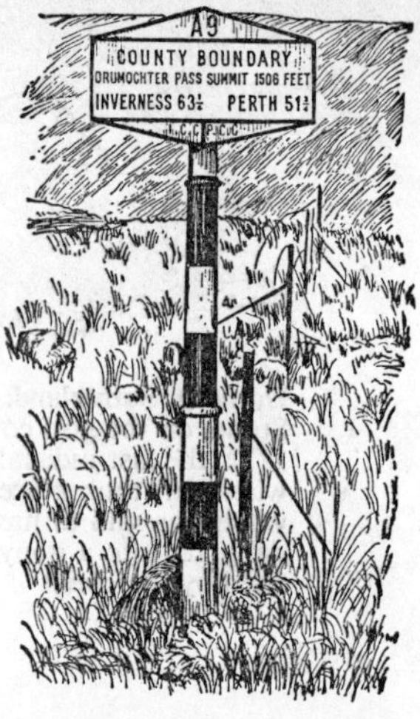

Drumochter Pass, Inverness; Perth. A sign at the summit of the Pass which carries A9 through the Grampian mountains

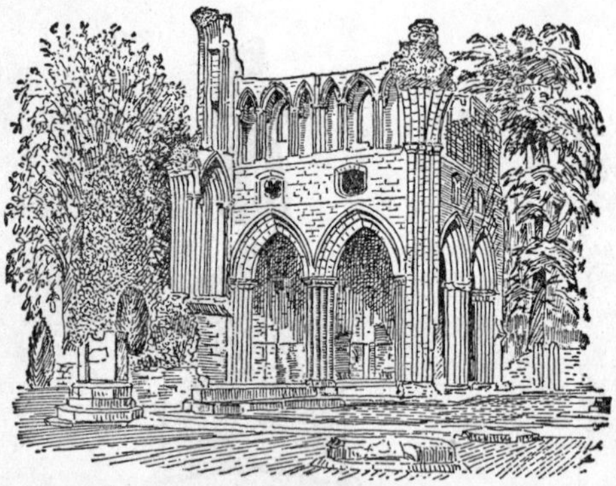

Dryburgh Abbey, Berwick. Founded in 1150 by monks from Alnwick, in Northumberland, but many times destroyed and rebuilt, the Abbey is now the burial-place of Field-Marshal Earl Haig and Sir Walter Scott

Drumlithie, Kincardine. The bell tower of 1777, the bell of which was rung to regulate weavers' working hours

Drynoch Bridge, Isle of Skye, Inverness. This bridge across a mountain burn issuing into Loch Harport is said to be the highest masonry road bridge in Scotland

Duddingston, Midlothian. The jougs, or iron collar for malefactors, hanging outside the 12th and 17th century Church, partially renewed

[For DUFFTOWN see following plate

ancient home of Cluny Macpherson, with whom Prince Charles Edward hid in a cave after Culloden, in 1746. In the background, to the north, rise the lonely *Monadhliath* mountains, with *Carn Dearg* attaining 3,093 ft. On a by-road on the south side of the Spey, near the Glen Truim estate, a little to the south-east of Cluny Castle, is a stone with some arrow markings, situated by the road, at an altitude of some 950 ft. This is said to mark the geographical centre of Scotland. See **Wade Roads.** *Iter. 143, 208.*

DRUMLANRIG CASTLE, Dumfries. Map 3, **NX 8 9.**
This magnificent house, containing much fine woodwork, and belonging to the Duke of Buccleuch, stands in a lovely wooded setting in Nithsdale, a little to the west of the river. Its construction dates from 1676 to 1689, the designer being Sir William Bruce, and it was occupied in 1745 by Prince Charles Edward. The first Duke of Queensberry, for whom the house was built, lived in it for one day only. In the park is the ruined *Tibber's Castle*, destroyed by Bruce in 1311.

DRUMLITHIE, Kincardine. Map 21, **NO 7 8.**
Lies a little to the north-east of the fertile Howe of the Mearns, and just off the Brechin to Stonehaven road. There is a slender 18th cent. weavers' bell tower. *Glenbervie House*, to the west, is an old mansion, with fine gardens. **3½ m. E.,** off the Stonehaven road, to the south, is the charming little *Fiddes Castle*.

DRUMMOND CASTLE, Perth. Map 16, **NN 8 1.**
See **Crieff.**

DRUMMORE, Wigtown. 352. Map 2, **NX 1 3.**
The small fishing port of *Drummore*, in the Rhinns of Galloway, facing Luce Bay, stands in the parish of *Kirkmaiden* (*q.v.*), the most southerly in Scotland. The Church dates from 1639, the old Church having been situated some **3 m. S.,** near Mull Farm. A gravestone in the churchyard is in the form of a lighthouse. Beyond here, at the foot of the cliffs, are fragments of *St. Medan's* Chapel, the oldest in *Galloway* (*q.v.*). See **Mull of Galloway, Port Logan** and **Port William.** *Iter. 82.*

DRUMMOSSIE MUIR, Inverness. Map 25, **NH 7** 4.
See **Culloden.**

DRUMMUIR, Banff. Map 26, **NJ 3 4.**
Prettily situated in a wooded part of Strath Isla, with the small Loch Park, its banks thickly clothed with trees, lying a little to the south-west, on the road to Dufftown. Nearer the village, in a park, stands *Drummuir Castle*, while in the background rise *Knockan*, 1,219 ft., to the north, and *Carran Hill*, 1,366 ft., to the south. *Iter. 169.*

DRUMNADROCHIT, Inverness. Map 25, **NH 5 3.**
E.C. Wed. The green and fertile Glen Urquhart, in which lies the little Loch Meiklie, extends between bare moorlands, with the extensive Balmacaan Forest to the south, while the eastern extremity of the glen opens out to the shores of Urquhart Bay, on *Loch Ness* (*q.v.*). Here stands the village of *Drumnadrochit*, on the River Enrick, which traverses the glen before flowing into the loch. The road through Glen Urquhart was constructed by Telford, and gives access to the grand scenery of Glens Affric and Cannich, described under *Cannich*. A little to the south of Drumnadrochit is the clachan of *Lewiston* (*q.v.*), beyond which a footpath leads to the picturesque Divach Falls. On the south side of Urquhart Bay is Strone Point, and here is situated the picturesque, ruined 13th to 16th cent. *Urquhart Castle* (A.M.), which was destroyed before 1715 and was built possibly by the Lords of the Isles. It is accessible weekdays, 10 to 4 or 7; Sun., 2 to 4 or 7 (see note page 98). **1 m. W.** of Drumnadrochit, a road leaves Glen Urquhart in a northerly direction to ascend steeply over moorland, with good views, and descend later into Glen Convinth in the direction of *Lovat Bridge* (*q.v.*). *Iter. 206, 207, 210, 213.*

DRUMOAK, Aberdeen. 1,407 with Peterculter.
Map 21, **NO 7 9.**
To the north-east is *Drum Castle*, a mansion of the 17th cent., joined to a much older tower, which has walls 12 to 15 ft. in thickness. It is shown Sundays, 2.30 to 6, late June to end of Aug. (See note page 98.) *Iter. 152.*

DRUMOCHTER PASS, Inverness; Perth.
Map 19, **NN 6 7.**
The main Inverness road, accompanied by the railway, on its way from Blair Atholl to Speyside, traverses this lofty and desolate pass in the *Grampians* (*q.v.*), an altitude of 1,506 ft. being reached near the point where the counties of Perth and Inverness meet. The *Sow of Atholl* and the *Boar of Badenoch* are strangely-named hills rising to the west, while eastwards are the 3,000-ft. summits of the vast Forest of Atholl, with the Gaick Forest farther north. In Drumochter Forest, which lies on both sides of the northern end of the pass, *Beinn Udlaman*, 3,306 ft., rises to the west, and *Chaoruinn*, 3,004 ft., to the east, winter sports being sometimes possible in this area. Wade built the original road through the pass in 1729, and it was traversed in 1745 by Prince Charles Edward. In 1829, Telford redesigned the road, on a slightly different course, though the original Wade road, with its derelict bridges, may still be seen in places on the hillsides. See **Dalnaspidal, Dalwhinnie, Drumgask** and **Wade Roads.** *Iter. 138, 140, 143, 147, 149, 150.*

DRYBURGH ABBEY, Berwick. Map 10, **NT 5 3.**
The situation of this Abbey (A.M.), standing in a loop of the River Tweed, is one of great beauty. It has become a place of pilgrimage for many thousands who come to visit the *St. Mary's Aisle*, burial-place of Sir Walter Scott and members of his family, together with J. G. Lockhart, his biographer, and also of Field-Marshal Earl Haig. The Abbey was founded in 1150, but in 1322, 1385, and finally in 1544, it was badly damaged by English forces. In 1918, the remains were presented to the nation by Lord Glenconner. The west front, with its 13th cent. portal, and parts of the nave, transepts, and chapter house, are still standing, showing 12th to 15th cent. work. Much of the cloistral buildings can also be seen, notably the refectory, with its rose window, and the calefactory, retaining a large fireplace. To the north of the Abbey, on the slopes of *Bemersyde Hill*, is the lofty *Wallace* statue. See **Bemersyde** and **Smailholm.** *Iter. 13, 43.*

DRYMEN, Stirling. 1,153. Map 15, **NS 4 8.**
E.C. Wed. GOLF. The *Buchanan Arms* Inn has fine gardens, from which *Loch Lomond* (*q.v.*) is well seen. Drymen Bridge, spanning the Endrick Water, was built in 1765 and widened in 1929. In extensive grounds, bordered by the Endrick Water, to the west of the village, stood formerly the 19th cent. *Buchanan Castle*, a seat of the Duke of Montrose, the head of Clan Graham. See **Balmaha.** *Iter. 104, 106, 109, 112, 115, 137.*

DRYNOCH BRIDGE, Isle of Skye, Inverness.
Map 23, **NG 4 3.**
A bridge spanning a burn here is said to be the highest masonry road bridge in Scotland. *Iter. 255.*

DUART CASTLE, Isle of Mull, Argyll. Map 13, **NM 7** 3.
See **Craignure.**

DUDDINGSTON (Edinburgh), Midlothian.
Map 10, **NT 2 7.**
Picturesquely situated below the Queen's Drive and *Arthur's Seat*, 822 ft., a magnificent viewpoint with an indicator, overlooking Edinburgh and the Firth of Forth. Duddingston Loch is now a bird sanctuary. The Church, much altered in the 17th cent., has a Norman chancel arch and south doorway and also the medieval jougs. An old mounting block (louping-on-stane) is preserved outside. The *Sheep's Heid* Inn is an ancient hostelry. There are several interesting houses in the neighbourhood, among which is *Duddingston House*, built by Sir William Chambers, in 1768, a good example of its period. The delightful *Peffermill House* dates from 1636, and *Prestonfield House* was designed in 1687 by Sir William Bruce. This latter house was visited by Dr. Johnson and Boswell in 1773 as guests of the Dick family.

DUFFTOWN, Banff. 1,528. SB. Map 26, **NJ 3 3.**
Outside the town, in the vicinity of which are situated several well-known distilleries, the River Fiddich is joined by the Dullan Water, which flows along the attractive Glen Rinnes, to the south-west, under the slopes of *Ben Rinnes*, 2,755 ft.

To the north, near the station, stands the picturesque, ruined *Balvenie Castle* (A.M.), an ancient Atholl stronghold, perhaps of 15th cent. date, and preserving a good example of a yett. It was visited by Edward I in 1304 and by Queen Mary in 1562. The Castle is open weekdays, 10 to 7 in summer and 10 to 4 in winter; Sun., 2 to 4 or 7 (see note page 98). The *Glenfiddich* Distillery, north of the town, incorporates a whisky museum. The fine road leading south-eastwards from Dufftown towards Alford and Rhynie ascends over the Glacks of Balloch Pass, 1,197 ft. The pass leads from the Fiddich, issuing from the lonely glen of that name, and backed by *Cooks Cairn*, 2,478 ft., to the more important Deveron, which flows north-eastwards into the Strathbogie district of Aberdeenshire. Almost adjoining Dufftown, to the south, is the modernised 12th cent. Church of *Mortlach*, attractively situated near the Dullan Water. The churchyard preserves a " Battle Stone " recalling a victory over the Danes in 1010. The road to *Keith* (*q.v.*) leaves Dufftown in a north-easterly direction to traverse the pleasantly wooded Strath Isla, with the tiny Lock Park, beyond which lies *Drummuir* (*q.v.*). See **Auchindoun, Craigellachie** and **Glenlivet.** *Iter. 169, 177, 190, 195.*

DUFFUS, Moray. 806. Map 26, **NJ 1 6.**
St. Peter's Kirk has a curious porch, and faces the shaft of the old Parish Cross (A.M.), dating probably from the 14th cent. The Church was founded by a member of the Freskyn family, ancestors of several notable Scottish families, among which are the Murrays. **1½ m. S.E.** is a mound on which stand the remains of *Duffus Castle* (A.M.), with walls of great thickness, and also considerable outer defences. A little to the north-east of Duffus is *Gordonstoun School*, founded in 1934, and occupying a 17th and 18th cent. mansion. The Duke of Edinburgh was formerly a pupil, and the Prince of Wales also studied here. The fishing villages of *Hopeman* (*q.v.*) and *Burghead* (*q.v.*), on its sandy bay, lie a little to the north-west. *Iter. 199.*

DULL, Perth. 609 with Weem. Map 19, **NN 8 4.**
A Strath Appin hamlet, with an old Cross. Prehistoric cairns, standing stones and remains of stone circles are in the vicinity. Adamnan, or Eonan, the biographer of St. Columba, is said to have been buried near Dull, and a college was founded here in his memory. The ruined *Comrie Castle* stands a little to the west.

DULNAIN BRIDGE, Moray. Map 25 **NH 9 2.**
Roads from *Aviemore* (*q.v.*) and *Carrbridge* (*q.v.*) converge here, near the point where the River Dulnain flows into the Spey. **1 m. W.** is the old tower of *Muckerach*, dating from 1598. *Iter. 172, 195.*

DULSIE BRIDGE, Nairn. Map 25, **NH 9 4.**
The River Findhorn, after having traversed the lonely Streens valley of Strath Dearn, overlooked by hills rising to more than 2,000 ft., flows here through a narrow and rocky gorge, spanned by a single-arched 18th cent. bridge, in a richly wooded setting, one of the most picturesque spots in the country. The great Moray floods of 1892 came near to damaging the bridge, the river rising to 40 ft. above normal. To the north, in the grounds of *Glenferness House*, is the " Princess Stone," a sculptured tablet, situated near a cairn supposed to mark the grave of a Celtic princess. Dulsie Bridge is approached from the Carrbridge to Forres road by using a short link, while to the north-west, one of the former military roads leads towards *Cawdor* (*q.v.*) and the Moray Firth. See **Ferness.** *Iter. 173, 177.*

DUMBARTON, Dunbarton. 25,640. LB. Map 8, **NS 3 7.**
E.C. Wed. GOLF. An important shipbuilding town and Royal Burgh, standing at the point where the River Leven, flowing southwards from *Loch Lomond* (*q.v.*), joins the Clyde. Dumbarton was, in medieval times, the capital of the ancient kingdom of Strathclyde, which extended from the Clyde as far as Lancashire. St. Patrick is said to have been born here, and was later taken by raiders to Ireland. The *College Bow*, an arch from *St. Mary's* Collegiate Church, founded 1453, has been re-erected in Church St. The Castle (A.M.) stands in a commanding situation on the summit of a 240-ft. high rock, and consists mainly of modern barracks, while a 12th cent. gateway, and a sundial, the gift of Mary, Queen of Scots, have been preserved. The view from the Castle is very notable. In 1548, the ill-fated Queen, at the age of 6

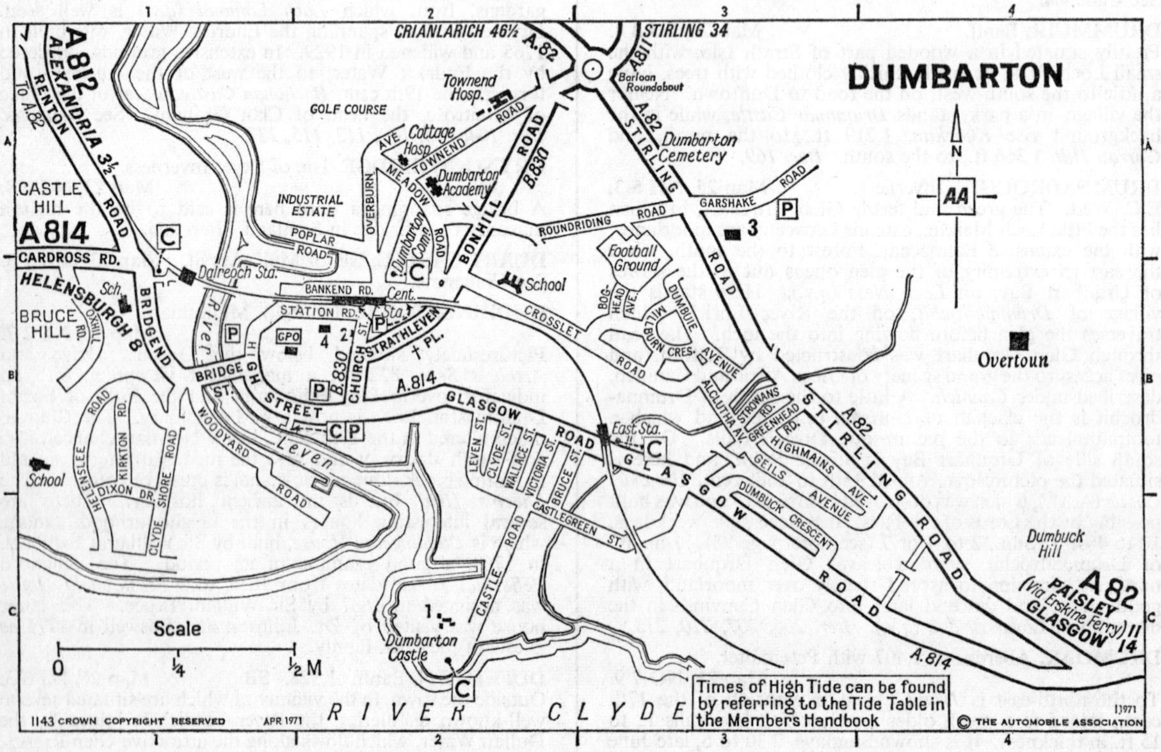

Castle 1 (C2) College Bow 2 (B2) Town Hall 4 (A3)

Dull, Perth. The old Church, near which one of the three former Crosses of the Abbey still stands, in a mutilated condition

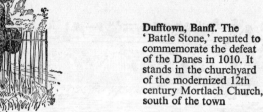

Dufftown, Banff. The 'Battle Stone,' reputed to commemorate the defeat of the Danes in 1010. It stands in the churchyard of the modernized 12th century Mortlach Church, south of the town

Dulnain Bridge, Moray. The bridge spanning the River Dulnain at the junction of A95 and A938

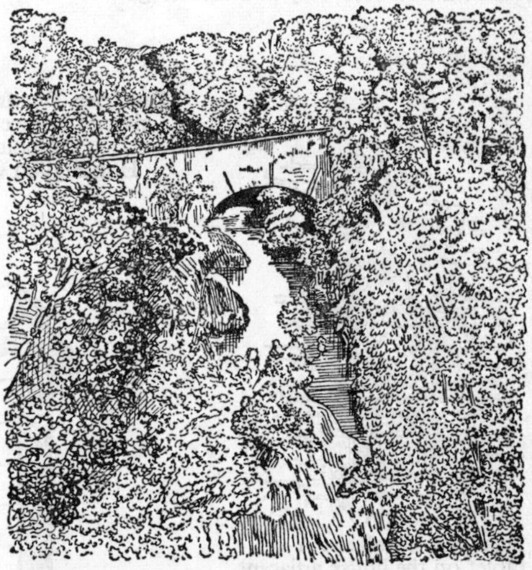

Dulsie Bridge, Nairn. The 18th century bridge, which spans the River Findhorn in what is considered its most picturesque reach

Duffus, Moray. The shaft of the ancient Parish Cross facing the ruined Church

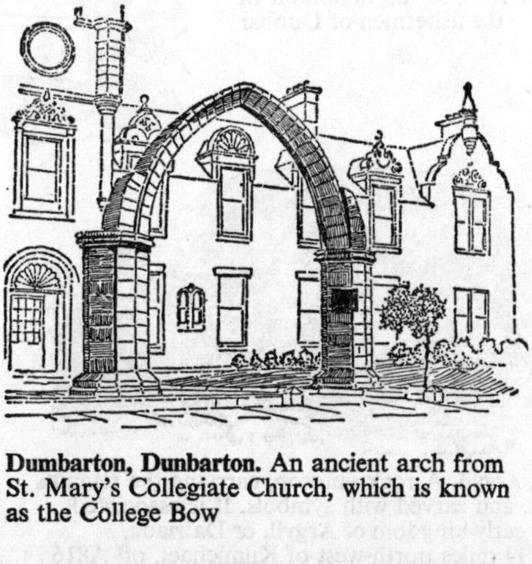

Dumbarton, Dunbarton. An ancient arch from St. Mary's Collegiate Church, which is known as the College Bow

[For DUFFTOWN see also under BALVENIE CASTLE (Plate 14)

Dumfries, Dumfries. The 13th century Old Bridge across the River Nith, which is now used only as a footbridge

Dumfries, Dumfries. A panel on the Mid Steeple giving distances to Scottish and English towns, including Huntingdon. The Earldom of Huntingdon was held by three early Kings of Scotland

Dumfries, Dumfries. A tablet on the house adjacent to that in which Robert Burns died in 1796

Dunbar, East Lothian. The carved Victorian 'barometer' monument of 1856, set up in honour of the fishermen of Dunbar

Dunadd, Argyll. A rock outcrop, carrying the remains of a fort, and carved with symbols. It is associated with the early kingdom of Argyll, or Dalriada, and lies 1½ miles north-west of Kilmichael, off A816

Dunbar, East Lothian. The great monument in the Parish Church to the 1st Earl of Dunbar, who died in 1610

[For DUNBAR see also Plate 51

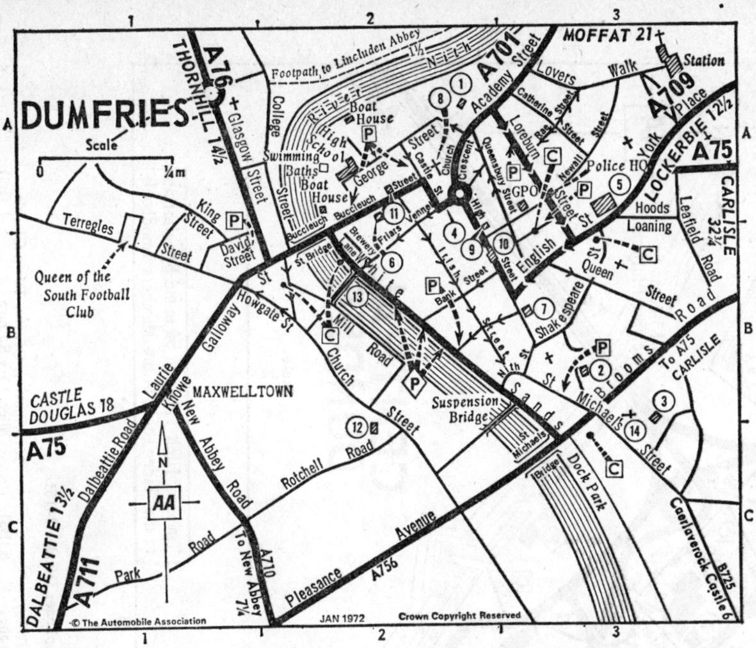

Academy	1 (A2)	Court House	6 (A2)	Municipal Chambers, Information Bureau	11 (A2)
Burns House	2 (B3)	Globe Inn	7 (B3)	Observatory	12 (C2)
Burns Mausoleum	3 (B3)	Greyfriars Church	8 (A2)	Old Bridge (footbridge)	13 (B2)
Burns Statue	4 (A2)	" Hole in the Wa' "	9 (B2)	St. Michael's Church	14 (B3)
County Buildings; Information Bureau	5 (A3)	Mid Steeple	10 (B3)		

was sent from here to France, and in 1571, under cover of night, the Castle was captured from her followers. Dumbarton Castle is open summer 10 to 7, winter 10 to 4; Sun., 2 to 4 or 7 (see note page 98). *Glencairn House* (A.M.) dates from 1623. *Castlehill* (N.T. Scot.) consists of two wooded mounds. Nearby is the Cunninghame-Graham Memorial (N.T. Scot.). The Royal Scots, the oldest British regiment, has for its regimental march 'Dumbarton's Drums.' See **Cardross, Old Kilpatrick** and **Port of Menteith.** *Iter. 102, 111.*

DUMFRIES, Dumfries. 29,384. LB. Map 4, **NX 9** 7. **E.C.** Thurs. **M.D.** Wed. GOLF. The important town of *Dumfries* stands about 7 miles inland from the Solway Firth and Nith estuary. The river divides Dumfries from Maxwelltown, in the county of Kirkcudbright, but the two towns were amalgamated in 1929. In the 12th cent. Dumfries became a Royal Burgh, but it suffered many vicissitudes, and was badly treated by Prince Charles Edward in 1745. Robert Burns came to the town in 1791, and did much of his work there. Among the buildings with which he is associated are the *Burns House,* in which he died in 1796, now preserving personal relics, and *St. Michael's* Church (see below). In the churchyard is the mausoleum in which Burns, his wife and several of his children lie buried. The *Hole in the Wa'* and *Globe* taverns, or " howffs," contain Burns relics, and in front of the modern *Greyfriars* church is the poet's statue. *St. Michael's* Church dates from 1744-54, later restored, and has, on the south wall of the interior, a tablet recording the gratitude of Norwegians who took refuge in Scotland during the Second World War. A tablet marks the pew formerly used by Robert Burns. In the former Greyfriars Monastery Church, in 1306, Robert Bruce stabbed the " Red Comyn," an action which is said to have altered the course of Scottish history. A plaque on a building in Castle Street marks the supposed place of the murder. The picturesque *Mid Steeple,* or old Town Hall, dates from 1707. It shows distances to important Scottish towns, and in addition to Huntingdon, in England, the earldom of which was held by three successive early Kings of Scotland. On the south face is sculptured the old Scots " ell " measure of 37 inches. Sir James Barrie was a pupil at the Academy. The Guid Nychburris Festival is held generally in the early summer. Four bridges link the town with Maxwelltown, of which the Old Bridge, for foot passengers only, dates back to the 13th cent., and was built by Devorgilla, who endowed Balliol College, Oxford. The Town Museum in Maxwelltown contains Burns relics. There is also an observatory with a camera obscura. **2 m. N.W.** is the mansion of *Terregles,* rebuilt in 1789, and said to have been Mary, Queen of Scots' last resting-place before her final journey to England, though this was more likely *Dundrennan (q.v.).* The 18th cent. *Terregles* Church has a restored choir, dating from 1583, with several interesting tombs and stalls, and also a notable medieval painting on wood. **4 m. S.** is the Kirkconnel Flow National Nature Reserve. See **Amisfield, Auldgirth, Brow, Caerlaverock, Irongray, Lincluden Abbey, Lochfoot, New Abbey, New Bridge, Ruthwell** and **Shawhead.** *Iter. 24, 26, 27, 28, 45, 46, 47, 48, 56, 67, 70, 71, 72, 73, 74, 75, 76.*

DUNADD, Argyll. Map 14, **NR 8** 9. See **Kilmichael.**

DUNAN, Isle of Skye, Inverness. Map 23, **NG 5** 2. Faces Loch na Cairidh, which separates Skye from the small island of Scalpay, beyond which lie Longay and the three Crowlin Islands. To the north-west of Dunan, the *Sligachan (q.v.)* road makes a circuit of Loch Ainort, backed by the Red *Coolins (q.v.),* or Red Hills, in Lord Macdonald's Forest, and giving views of *Blaven,* 3,042 ft., the great Black Coolin peak to the south-west of the roadless Strath Mor. *Iter. 251, 252, 253.*

DUNBAR, East Lothian. 4,586. SB. Map 10, **NT 6** 7. **E.C.** Wed. GOLF. An old fishing port, Royal Burgh and resort, with a beach of sand and pebbles. It is situated on the edge of rich farming country, notable for its reddish soil, in which the famous " Dunbar Red " potatoes flourish. The town is bordered to the south by the *Lammermuir* hills, and looks north-westwards out to sea to the lonely *Bass Rock* near *North Berwick (q.v.),* and south-

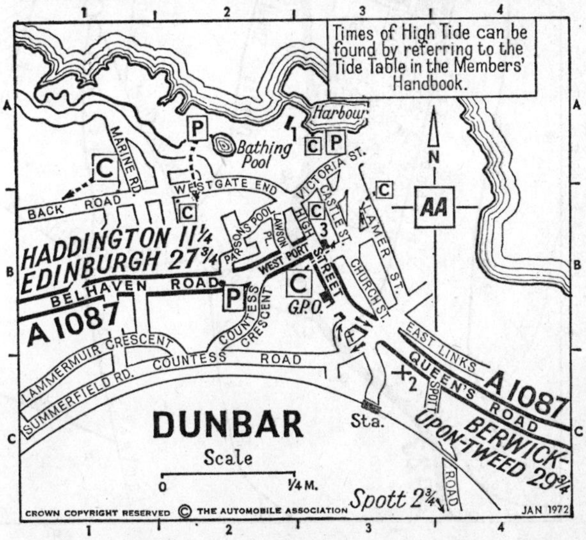

Castle	1 (A2)	Church, with Home monument	2 (C3)
Old Town House, Tourist Information Centre and Market Cross	3 (B3)		

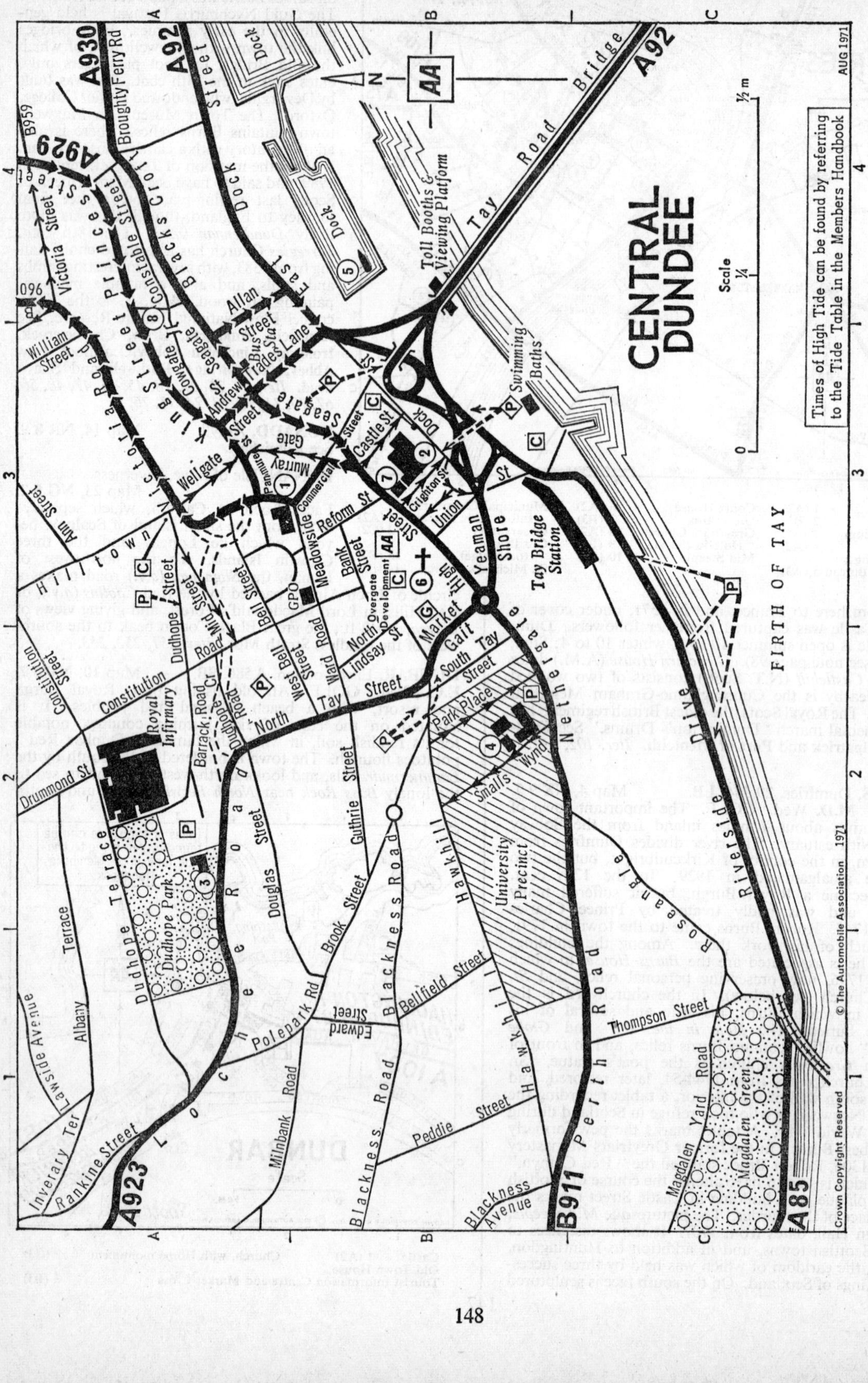
CENTRAL DUNDEE
FIRTH OF TAY
Tay Road Bridge
Toll Booths & Viewing Platform
Tay Bridge Station
University Precinct
Royal Infirmary
Dudhope Park
Magdalen Green
A TOWNPOINT: Royal Exchange Buildings, Albert Square. Telephone: Dundee 24161.
AA Service Centre (B3)
Albert Institute 1 (A3)
Caird Hall 2 (B3)
Dudhope Castle 3 (A2)
Dundee University 4 (B2)
HMS Unicorn 5 (B4)
St. Mary's Tower, City Churches 6 (B3)
Information Centre, Town Clerk's Office, City Square 7 (B3)
Wishart Arch 8 (A3)
Times of High Tide can be found by referring to the Tide Table in the Members Handbook
Scale 0 ¼ ½ m
AUG 1971
Crown Copyright Reserved
© The Automobile Association 1971

The 15th century Old Steeple of the City Churches, whose defenders surrendered to General Monck (or Monk) in1651, after being threatened with burning

The restored Dudhope Castle, once the seat of the Scrymgeours, Hereditary Constables of Dundee, and later the home of Graham of Claverhouse, Scott's 'Bonnie Dundee'. It is now a technical school

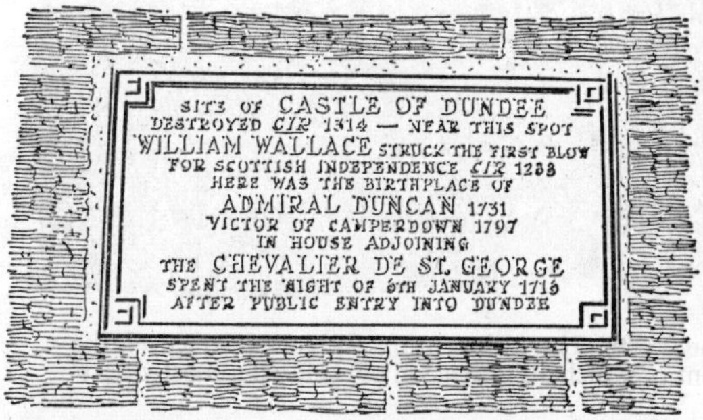

The plaque on the wall of St. Paul's Episcopal Cathedral, in the High Street, recording the site of the vanished castle

The tablet on an old house, now a shop, the birthplace in 1651 of Anna (or Anne) Scott, wife of the Duke of Monmouth, who was executed in 1685. They were created Duke and Duchess of Buccleuch in 1663. Sir Walter Scott's '*Lay of the Last Minstrel*' is associated with the Duchess

The ruined Mains of Fintry Castle, dating from 1582, a former home of the Grahams

[For DUNDEE see also following plate

Dundonald, Ayr. The ruined Castle, in which Robert II died in 1309. Dr. Johnson came here during his tour of 1773

Dundee, Angus. The East Port, where George Wishart is said to have preached in 1544 during an outbreak of plague

Dundrennan, Kirkcudbright. A 13th century monument to a former Abbot at the ruined Abbey. He may have been murdered by the man on whose effigy he stands

Dunblane, Perth. The 13th century and later Cathedral, the west front of which John Ruskin considered a masterpiece

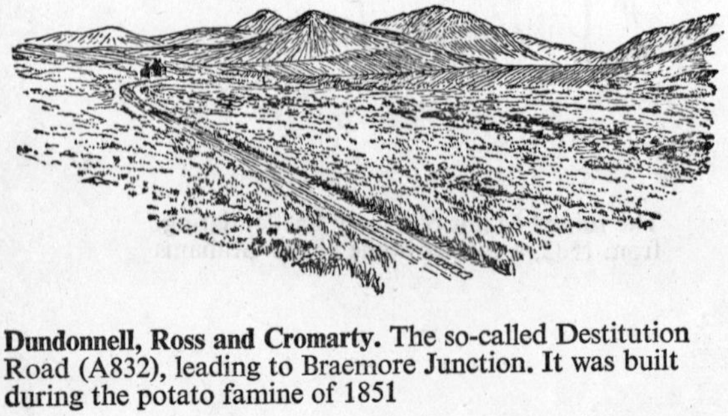

Dundonnell, Ross and Cromarty. The so-called Destitution Road (A832), leading to Braemore Junction. It was built during the potato famine of 1851

Dunbar, East Lothian. The old Town House, dating from 1620

[For DUNBAR see also Plate 49
[For DUNDEE see also preceding plate

eastwards along a long stretch of coastline towards the distant St. Abb's Head. There is a quaint old Town House, with a six-sided tower, dating from c. 1620. Close to it is the old Market Cross. The Parish Church has a 108-ft. high tower, visible out to sea, and a notable sight is the great *Home* monument, dated 1611. The ruined Castle stands on a rock above the harbour, and has a long history, including a notable siege in 1339, and was associated with Mary, Queen of Scots, in 1556 and 1567, after which it was destroyed. The battle of Dunbar, fought in 1650, in which Cromwell defeated the Covenanters under General Leslie, took place a little to the south-east of the town off the Great North Road, close to *Broxburn* (*q.v.*), where a stone was erected, in 1950, to commemorate the fight. See **East Linton, St. Monance, Spott, Stenton** (for *Biel House*) and **Whittinghame.** *Iter. 2, 39, 40.*

DUNBEATH, Caithness. 402. Map 30, **ND 1 2.** **E.C.** Thurs. A fishing village, situated on the Dunbeath River, where it flows into the narrow bay. The name is said to have been taken from the broch of *Dun Beath*, which stands in the angle formed by the river and the Burn of Houstry, to the north-west of the village. The Castle, captured by Montrose in 1650, is situated **1 m. S.**, on a lofty promontory off the *Berriedale* (*q.v.*) road, preserving a 15th cent. keep, and having been enlarged in the 19th cent. West of the village, on the moors inland, near the Berriedale Water, is a granite cross marking the place where the Duke of Kent was killed in a flying accident in 1942. The coast road leading south-westwards from Dunbeath gives an excellent picture of the lofty Caithness plateau, which has been carved out in places by its rivers. *Iter. 200, 236.*

DUNBLANE, Perth. 4,499. SB. Map 16, **NN 7 0.** **E.C.** Wed. GOLF. Situated on the Allan Water, at the south-western extremity of Strath Allan, and forming a good touring centre for the *Ochil* hills to the east, and the Perthshire Highlands to the west and north. This old-world city, with its narrow streets containing a few good 17th cent. houses, is best known for the Cathedral (A.M.), which is a building dating chiefly from the 13th cent., but retaining a Norman tower, probably of the 11th cent. The West front, with its central doorway and tall lancet windows, was greatly praised by Ruskin, and is one of the finest compositions in Scottish church architecture. The nave roof collapsed in the 16th cent., but a restoration took place in 1893, and the choir was restored in 1914. In the south aisle of the nave are the six very finely carved 15th cent. Ochiltree stalls, recalling Bishop Ochiltree, who died in 1447. The north aisle contains a stone with curious carvings and a Celtic Cross. Three blue slabs in the pavement of the choir are in memory of the three Drummond sisters, associated with James IV, and all poisoned in 1501. There are scanty remains of the Bishop's Palace; in the 17th cent. Dean's House is a small museum; and the Leighton Library is housed in a building dated 1687, near the churchyard gate. **2½ m. E.**, on the moors, is the site of the indecisive battle of *Sheriffmuir*, fought in 1715, between the Pretender's forces under the Earl of Mar and the Royal troops under the Duke of Argyll. The "Gathering Stone" of the clans commemorate the fight. See **Bridge of Allan** and **Doune.** *Iter. 135, 138, 140, 141, 146.*

DUNDEE, Angus. 182,084. C. of C. Map 17, **NO 3 3.** **E.C.** Wed. **M.D.** Tues., Fri. GOLF. The fourth largest city in Scotland, situated on the Firth of Tay, to the north-east of the fertile *Carse of Gowrie* (*q.v.*), and overlooking the coast of Fife. The famous two-mile-long Tay Bridge, built 1883-1888, carries the main railway line from Edinburgh to Aberdeen, and is the successor to the ill-fated earlier structure, which was blown down in a gale in 1879 while a train was making the crossing, with heavy loss of life. A fine new road bridge has now been opened. *Dundee* is essentially a modern city, its best known industry being jute, but engineering, shipbuilding and preserve-manufacturing are all of considerable importance, and the docks cover more than 35 acres. In 1190, Dundee became a Royal Burgh, and later it suffered severely in wars with the English. Montrose stormed the city in 1645, and General Monk captured it in 1651, while there are also associations with both the Old and the Young Pretenders, in 1715 and 1745 respectively.

The most notable building is the splendid Old Steeple, or Tower of *St. Mary*, belonging to the *City Churches*, which formerly comprised four separate Churches. The Churches were almost destroyed by fire in 1841, but were later restored. This Old Steeple, 156 ft. high, is of 15th cent. date, and considered the largest and finest of its kind in Scotland. It surrendered to General Monk, in 1651, only after burning straw had been piled at its base. The University was combined with that of *St. Andrews* (*q.v.*) from 1897 to 1967. A house in the High Street was the birth-place, in 1651, of Anne Scott, Duchess of Buccleuch (See **Dalkeith** and **Hawick**), and in the same building General Monk stayed. Among the many fine modern buildings the *Caird Hall* is outstanding. From the *East Port*, or *Wishart Arch*, George Wishart is said to have preached during the plague of 1544. The Museum and Art Gallery in the *Albert* Institute are of much interest, and in the old cemetery, known as the *Howff*, are many quaint gravestones. William Wallace was educated at the Grammar School, and Hector Boece, the historian, was born in the city, c. 1465 (See **Grampians**). *Dundee Law*, 571 ft., a good viewpoint, is surmounted by a War Memorial. *Dudhope Castle*, 15th cent., restored, is used as a technical school, and *Mains of Fintry Castle*, a ruin, dating from 1582, stands in *Caird* Park. The *Mills* Observatory is situated in *Balgay* Park. To the north-west of the city is *Camperdown House* (partly a Golf Museum), built by the son of Lord Duncan, victor of the battle of Camperdown in 1797, and farther away to the north rise the *Sidlaw* hills, with the high point of *Craigowl Hill*, 1,493 ft. **3 m. N.**, off the Forfar road, is the ruined *Pourie Castle*. See **Broughty Ferry, Fowlis Easter, Glamis, Longforgan** and Newtyle. For "Through Routes" see page 45. *Iter. 92, 94, 126, 127, 154, 155, 156, 157, 158, 159, 160, 161.*

DUNDONALD, Ayr. 2,791. Map 8, **NS 3 3.** The Church was built in 1803. On a height, a little to the west, is the ruined *Dundonald Castle*, where Robert II died, in 1390. This castle was visited by Dr. Johnson in 1773, who also went to the 17th cent. *Auchans House*, situated to the north-west of the castle, where he was received by the Countess of Eglinton. *Iter. 85.*

DUNDONNELL, Ross and Cromarty. Map 29, **NH 1 8.** This remote *Wester Ross* village stands at the head of Little Loch Broom, in the green valley of Strath Beg. At *Ardessie*, **2½ m. W.N.W.**, and also near *Corryhallie*, **3 m. S.E.**, in a picturesque gorge on the road to *Braemore Junction* (*q.v.*), there are fine waterfalls. The road to Braemore climbs to a height of over 1,100 ft. at Fain Hill along the so-called "Destitution Road," which was built during the potato famine of 1851. There are magnificent views of the grand red Torridon sandstone peaks of *An Teallach*, nearly 3,500 ft. high, some of the wildest mountains on the Scottish mainland, situated to the north-west above Dundonnell Forest and the remote valley of Strath na Sheallag. In the heart of the *Teallach* range, at a height of about 2,000 ft., is the tiny loch *Toll an Lochain*, in a spectacular rocky setting, overlooked by an extraordinary ridge of white quartzite slabs facing the great cliffs of *Sgurr Fiona*, 3,474 ft. This loch, which is one of the most remarkable sights in the Scottish Highlands, can be reached by a climb on foot from a point on the Braemore Junction road about **2 m. S.E.** of Dundonnell. The 18th cent. *Dundonnell House*, to the south-east, has Chinese and Japanese gardens. East of the village, in Straith Beg, is *Dundonnell Lodge*, and from here a hill track goes north to *Aultnaharrie* (*q.v.*), on Loch Broom, facing *Ullapool* (*q.v.*), to which it is linked by a passenger ferry. Beyond the track, above Little Loch Broom, rises *Ben Goleach*, 2,052 ft. See **Gruinard Bay.** *Iter. 206, 222.*

DUNDRENNAN, Kirkcudbright. 89. Map 3, **NX 7 4.** This village, in an attractive setting on the Abbey Burn, which flows into the Solway Firth near Abbey Head to the south, is partly built of stones from its Abbey. On the coast, near the outflow of the river, is *Abbey Burnfoot*, sheltered

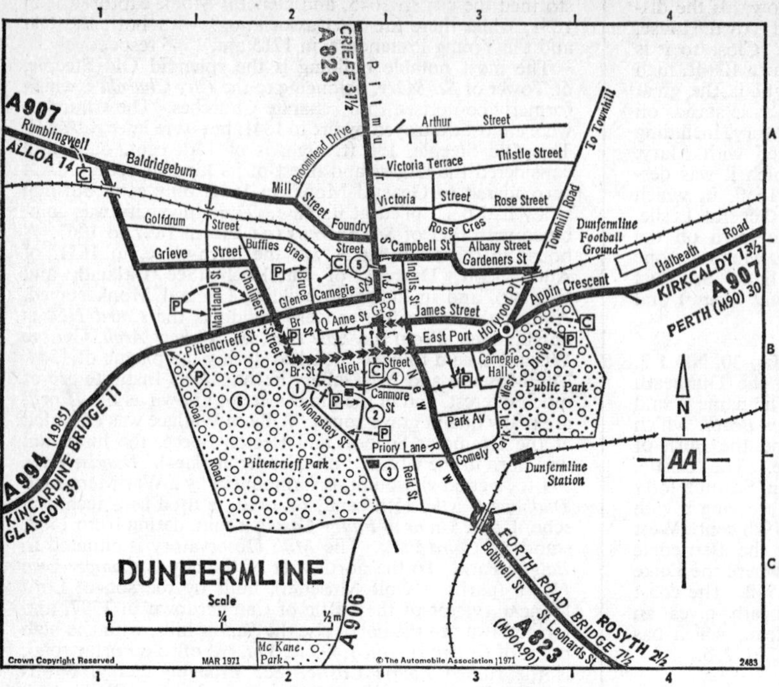

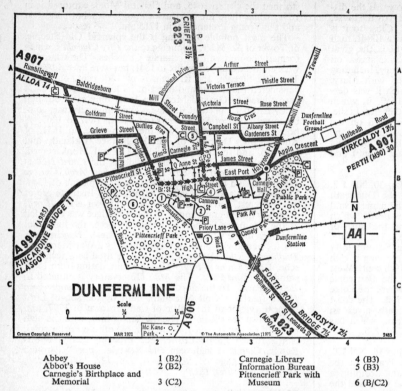

Abbey	1 (B2)	Carnegie Library	4 (B3)
Abbot's House	2 (B2)	Information Bureau	5 (B3)
Carnegie's Birthplace and Memorial	3 (C2)	Pittencrieff Park with Museum	6 (B/C2)

by Abbey Head, and to the east is *Port Mary*, where stands the rock from which Mary, Queen of Scots stepped on to the boat which took her, after her last night in Scotland, probably at the Abbey, to Workington in England. *Dundrennan Abbey* (A.M.), Cistercian, dates from 1142, and was annexed to the Chapel Royal at *Stirling* (*q.v.*), in 1621. Much of the building is irretrievably ruined, but the 13th cent. Chapter House remains are of interest, and parts of the 13th cent. transepts of the Church can be seen. There are some incised slabs; the Cellarer's Monument, dated 1480; and a fine 13th cent. monument to an abbot. See **Clarkston** and **Dumfries.** *Iter. 73.*

DUNECHT, Aberdeen. Map 27, **NJ 7 0.**
Off the *Echt* (*q.v.*) road, to the south, stands *Dunecht House*, in its park, once well known for its observatory, and possessing fine gardens. **2½ m. N.W.** is *Castle Fraser,* described under **Kemnay. 5 m. W.** is the mainly 16th cent. *Corsindae House*. For *Iter*. see *Waterton-Dunecht*.

DUNFERMLINE, Fife. 49,882. LB. Map 17, **NT 0 8.**
E.C. Wed. **M.D.** Tues. GOLF. A Royal Burgh and modern linen-manufacturing town, noted for its magnificent Abbey Church, in which Robert Bruce is buried. The town has had an historic past, and was the birthplace of James I in 1394 and also of Charles I in 1600 and his sister Elizabeth. Andrew Carnegie was born in a small cottage, in 1835, and the Carnegie Trusts have benefited the town to a very great extent. The first of the numerous Carnegie libraries was founded here in 1881 and contains many treasures. A memorial building adjoins his birthplace. The attractive Pittencrieff Glen, with its splendid flower gardens, was presented to the town by Carnegie in 1903, and in the 17th cent. mansion is a museum. There are slight remains of the Royal Palace, which was built out of the former monastery, notably a 200-ft. long buttressed wall, and also a mound with the remains of *Malcolm's Tower*. The Pends archway links the Palace with the Abbey. The Abbey Church (A.M.), founded soon after 1070, and associated with Queen Margaret, contains a magnificent Norman nave, reminiscent of Durham Cathedral, and dating from 1150, the finest of its period in Scotland. The original steeple and south-western tower fell in 1753 and 1807 respectively. The choir was rebuilt in 1817-1822. The West front, with its fine door and twin towers, has been much rebuilt, and of special note are the massive 16th cent. buttresses against the north and south sides of the nave. A brass plate marks the burial-place of Robert Bruce in 1329 in the choir. The battlemented 100-ft. high square tower has the words: " King Robert the Bruce " cut out in stone around the four sides. The Abbot's House dates from the 16th cent., and an inscription on its door lintel was made use of by Scott in his " Fair Maid of Perth." *Hill House*, south of the town, is 16th and 17th cent. To the north-east of the town is the tiny Town Loch, and still farther in the same direction lies the larger Loch Fitty. **2½ m. S.W.** is *Pitfirraine Castle*, which retains a 15th cent. tower. See **Charlestown,** retains a 15th cent. tower. **3 m. S.E.** is *Pitreavie* now the HQ of the RAF Rescue Co-ordination Services. See **Charlestown, Culross** and **Melrose.** *Iter. 89, 97, 133.*

DUNGLASS, East Lothian. Map 11, **NT 7 7.**
In the grounds of the modern *Dunglass House* is a fine, partially restored cruciform 14th cent. Collegiate Church, preserving notable sedilia. (A.M.)

DUNINO, Fife. 1,294. Map 17, **NO 5 1.**
Near the Church is a very ancient carved stone, topped by a sundial of 1698. In the vicinity is a picturesque small glen.

DUNKELD, Perth. 1,064. Map 16, **NO 0 4.**
E.C. Thurs. GOLF. This ancient little Cathedral city is beautifully situated in the richly wooded valley of the Tay, where it is crossed by a bridge erected in 1809 by Telford. A house in The Square has on it the delineation of a Scottish " ell " (37 inches), dated 1706. The first church here was founded in 849. The ancient Cathedral (A.M.) dates from the 12th to the 15th cents., but was desecrated in 1560, and although the 14th cent. choir, now used as the Parish Church, was restored in 1815 and 1908, much of the structure is still roofless. Some of the damage was caused in 1689, in the Battle of Dunkeld, when the Highlanders were defeated. The nave, with its fine window tracery, was begun in 1406, and the massive tower is late 15th cent. work, and contains some wall paintings. In the choir is a tomb, believed to be that of the Wolf of Badenoch, the destroyer of *Elgin Cathedral* (*q.v.*). The 15th cent. Chapter House is now the Atholl tomb-chapel. Cathedral Street and The Cross have been the scene of an ambitious group-restoration project, where the " little houses " have been given new life by the National Trust for Scotland. In the grounds of *Dunkeld House*,

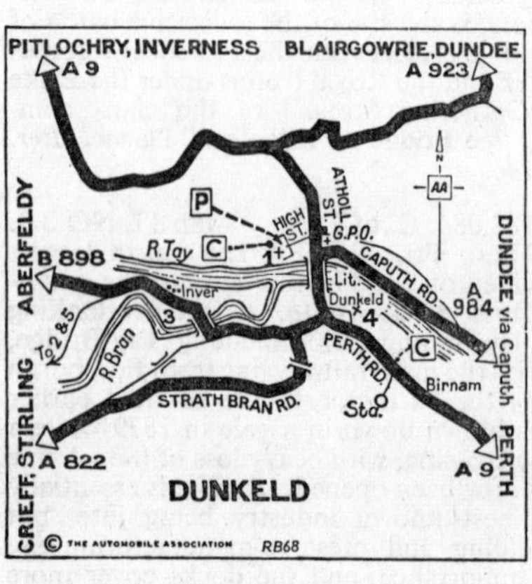

Cathedral	1	Little Dunkeld Church	4
Hermitage	2	Ossians Hall	5
Inver Village	3		

Dunfermline, Fife. The Abbey Church, with its massive buttresses. A brass plate in the choir marks the resting place of Robert Bruce

Dunfermline, Fife. The inscription over the door of the 16th century Abbot's House, which Sir Walter Scott used in his '*Fair Maid of Perth*'

Dunkeld, Perth. The Scottish 'ell' (37 inches), portrayed on a house in The Square, dating from 1706

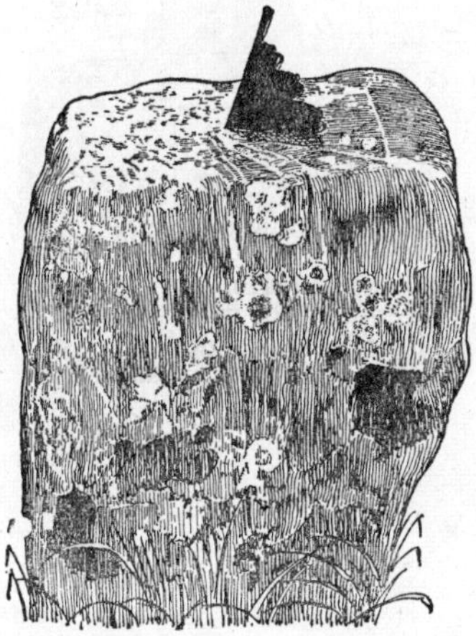

Dunino, Fife. An ancient carved stone, topped by a sundial of 1698. It stands near the south wall of the church

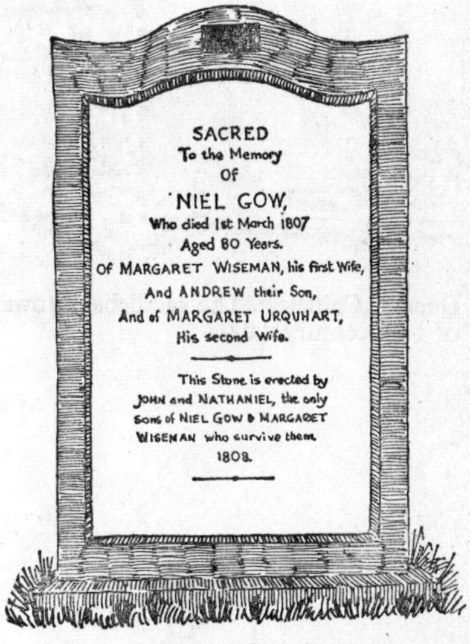

Dunkeld, Perth. The tomb of Niel Gow, the famous fiddler, who died in 1807. It stands in the church-yard of Little Dunkeld, across the River Tay

Dunkeld, Perth. The gate-way to Dunkeld House, in the grounds of which are the remains of a prehistoric fort

Dunnottar Castle, Kincardine. The ruined 14th to 16th century Castle, in which the Scottish regalia were kept for safety for a period during the Commonwealth Wars in the 17th century. See Kinneff (Plate 100)

Dunrobin, Sutherland. The Castle, built originally in the 13th century, but greatly altered during the Victorian period

Dunnet, Caithness. The saddleback tower of the Church, which may be of 14th century date

Dunning, Perth. The Memorial recording the burning here in 1657 of Maggie Wall as a witch. It stands a mile to the west, on B9062

Dunoon, Argyll. The statue to Robert Burns's 'Mary,' who was born at Auchnamore Farm near the town. It was unveiled by Lady Kelvin in 1896

Dunlichity, Inverness. The watch-tower of the 18th century Church, used in the 19th century for preventing the theft of corpses. It stands 3 miles south-west of Dalvourn, in Strath Nairn, on an unclassified road off B851

[For DUNS see under MERSE (Plate 121)

to the west, are the remains of a prehistoric fort. Fine Japanese larches grow on the estate. Across the Tay is *Little Dunkeld*, where, in the churchyard, is the grave of Niel Gow, the famous fiddler, born **1 m.W.** at *Inver*. Nearby, in Strath Bran, is *The Hermitage, Ossians Hall* (N.T. Scot.), a restored 18th cent. "folly," with views of the River Bran. To the south is the *Hermitage Bridge* (N.T. Scot.) below the Falls of Bran. Beyond the falls is *Rumbling Bridge*, in Craigvinean Forest, where the river enters a picturesque chasm. North-west of Inver is the hill of *Craig Vinean*, from which Dunkeld and its Cathedral are well seen. The wooded hill of *Craigiebarns*, 1,106 ft., above the river north-west of the town, is also an excellent viewpoint. See **Aberdour, Amulree, Birnam, Caputh** (for *Murthly Castle*) and **Butterstone.** *Iter. 139, 140, 141, 148, 150, 157, 166.*

DUNLICHITY CHURCH, Inverness. Map 25, **NH 6 3.**
See **Dalvourn.**

DUNLOP, Ayr. 553. Map 8, **NS 4 4.**
E.C. Wed. The district is noted for "Dunlop" cheeses. The Laigh Kirk of 1835 contains the *Dunlop* aisle of 1641 and has also much stained glass. The adjacent mausoleum and Church hall were erected by Viscount Clandeboyes. *Iter. 62.*

DUNMORE PARK, Stirling. Map 16, **NS 8 8.**
See **Airth.**

DUNNET, Caithness. 681. Map 30, **ND 2 7.**
E.C. Thurs. **M.D.** Tues. Overlooks Dunnet Bay, with a sandy beach. To the north is St. John's Loch, and **3 m. N.N.W.** of the loch is Dunnet Head, a bold promontory, with a lighthouse, on the most northerly point of the mainland, forming a magnificent viewpoint. Across the waters of the stormy Pentland Firth can be seen the detached *Old Man of Hoy*. (See **Orkney.**) The little early Presbyterian Church of Dunnet, with a saddleback tower, may be of 14th cent. date. Timothy Pont, an early cartographer, was minister here from 1601 to 1608, and his revised surveys were incorporated in Blaeu's atlas, published in 1654, at Amsterdam. See **John o' Groats.** *Iter.* **240.**

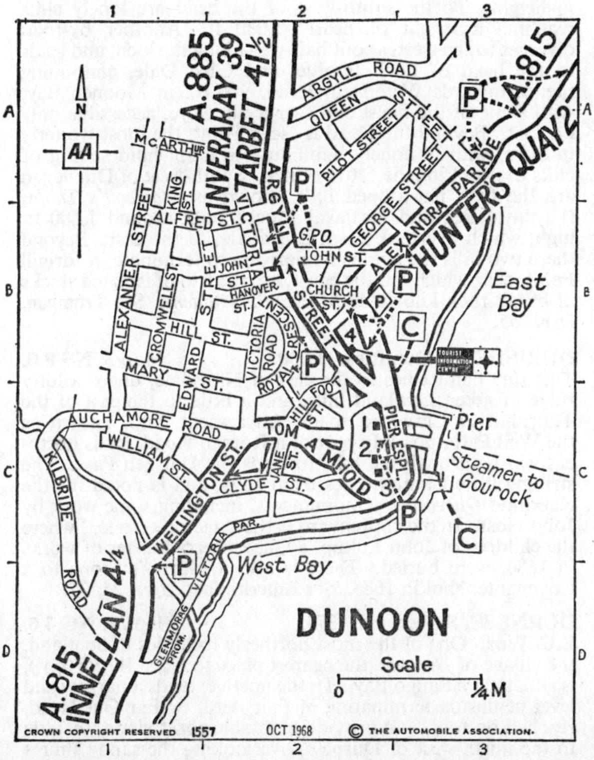

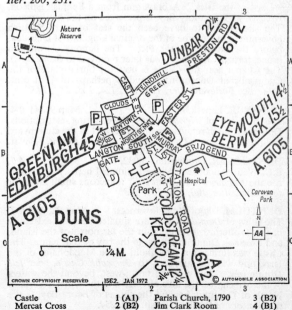

Castle House	1 (C2)	Statue of "Highland Mary"	3 (C2)
Old Castle ruins	2 (C2)	Tourist Information Centre	4 (B2)

DUNNING, Perth. 1,030. Map 16, **NO 0 1.**
Situated to the north of the *Ochil* hills, overlooking Strath Earn. The rebuilt Church, dedicated to St. Serf, retains its fine 13th cent. tower. A standing stone recalls the legendary battle of Duncrub. *Keltie Castle,* **1 m. W.,** is late 16th cent. See **Forteviot.** *Iter. 86.*

DUNNOTTAR CASTLE, Kincardine. Map 21, **NO 8 8.**
The ruins of this great Castle stand in a picturesque setting on a rocky headland overlooking the North Sea. The oldest parts are the tower and chapel, dating from c. 1392, and the fine gate-house dates from c. 1575. Montrose besieged the castle in 1645, and during the Commonwealth Wars the Scottish regalia were kept here, being removed in 1652 and hidden in the pulpit of the Church at *Kinneff* (*q.v.*). In 1685, no less than 167 Covenanters were confined in the dungeon, and when Scott visited the old churchyard, **2 m.** inland, near the Carron Water, he met "Old Mortality" cleaning the headstones of the graves. To the south of the castle, the coast is rocky, with magnificent cliff scenery. See **Caerlaverock.** *Iter. 155.*

DUNOON, Argyll. 9,824. **SB.** Map 14, **NS 1 7.**
E.C. Wed. **GOLF.** The largest and best known of the *Cowal* (*q.v.*) resorts. It is situated on the Firth of Clyde, facing Cloch Point in Renfrewshire, and forms a splendid centre for yachting and excursions by steamer in the neighbouring waters. The Cowal Highland Gathering takes place here at the end of August, and the Clyde Yachting Fortnight in July is also associated with the town. The modern castle dates from 1822, but traces of an ancient castle can be seen on a rock above the pier, and at the foot is a statue of Burns's "Highland Mary," who was born at a farm near the town. A coast road goes southwards for Toward Point, giving fine views, and inland to the west are lofty moorlands rising to *Bishop's Seat*, 1,651 ft., looking across Loch Striven to the *Kyles of Bute* (*q.v.*). See **Benmore Estate, Hunter's Quay, Innellan and Kirn.** *Iter. 102, 137.*

DUNROBIN, Sutherland. Map 31, **NC 8 0.**
The magnificent *Dunrobin Castle*, belonging to the Duke of Sutherland, stands in a great park overlooking the sea. The original structure dates back to c. 1275, but some extensive additions were made in 1856. An old yett is preserved and in the grounds is a museum. The house has become a boys' public school. It is shown daily (except Sun.), 11 to 6, early July to end of Aug. Gardens and museum only from early Jun. (See note page 98.). A private railway was formerly situated on the estate. See **Golspie** (for *Dunrobin Glen*). *Iter. 200, 231.*

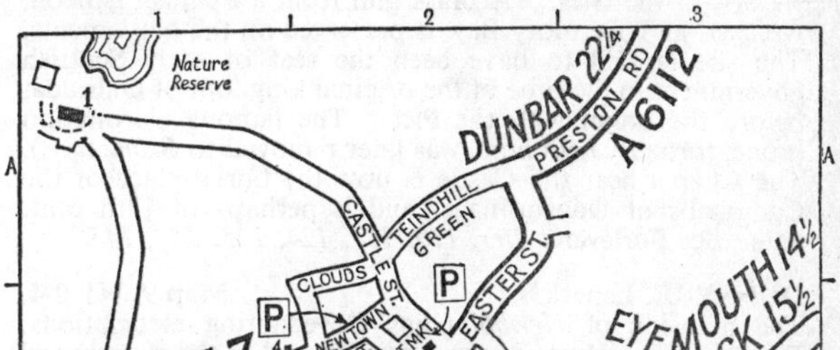

Castle	1 (A1)	Parish Church, 1790	3 (B2)
Mercat Cross	2 (B2)	Jim Clark Room	4 (B1)

DUNROSSNESS, Shetland. Map 33, **HU 3 1.**
See **Shetland Islands** (Mainland). *Iter. 269.*

DUNS, Berwick. 1,767. SB. Map 11, **NT 7 5.**
E.C. Wed. **M.D.** Mon. A pleasant little market town, lying at the foot of *Duns Law*, 713 ft., on which the town was at one time situated, before being destroyed by the English in 1545. On the summit of the hill is a "Covenanters' stone," recalling the presence of General Leslie's army in 1639. The Parish Church dates from 1880, and the Mercat Cross stands in a public park. There is a 19th cent. Town Hall. The Jim Clark Room (Burgh Chambers) contains racing trophies won by the famous driver, killed in Germany in 1968. The modern *Duns Castle*, by Gillespie Graham, to the north-west retains an ancient tower. In the grounds is a fine lime avenue, and nearby is a tiny loch, known as the *Hen Poo*. To the north-west of Duns rise the foothills of the *Lammermuirs*, through which penetrate two narrow roads, the westerly of which gives access to *Longformacus* (*q.v.*), and the easterly goes by the valley of the Whiteadder Water to *Cranshaws* (*q.v.*). **2 m. S.** of Duns is *Nisbet House*, dating from the 17th and 18th cents., and notable for its wealth of gun loops, unusual at so late a period. **2 m. E.** of the town is *Manderston House*, with its fine gardens. See **Abbey St. Bathans, Chirnside** and **Preston.** *Iter. 3, 9, 33, 38, 39, 41.* For Town Plan see preceding page.

DUNSCORE, Dumfries. Map 3, **NX 8 8.**
Lies in the fertile valley of the Cairn Water. **6 m. W.**, under *Bar Hill*, on the Kirkcudbright border, is *Craigenputtock* farm, where Carlyle wrote "Sartor Resartus." **1½ m. N.E.** is the ruined tower of *Lag*, associated with Sir Robert Grierson, a noted persecutor of the Covenanters in the 17th cent. See **Auldgirth** and **Ringford.** *Iter. 74.*

DUNSKEATH, Ross and Cromarty. Map 31, **NH 7 7.**
On the north shore of the Cromarty Firth narrows, with a passenger ferry to *Cromarty* (*q.v.*). To the east is the cave-riddled North Sutor.

DUNSTAFFNAGE CASTLE, Argyll. Map 14, **NM 8 3.**
This isolated Campbell stronghold stands on a promontory guarding Dunstaffnage Bay, where the waters of Loch Etive join those of the Firth of Lorne, and is easily reached from the Oban to Connel road. The four-sided structure has a gatehouse and two round towers, and dates probably from the 13th cent., some of the walls being 10 ft. thick. In 1746, Flora Macdonald was imprisoned here, and Scott introduced the Castle into his "Legend of Montrose" and "Lord of the Isles." A brass gun from a Spanish galleon, wrecked in Tobermory Bay, is preserved on the battlements. The site is said to have been the seat of early Scottish government in the time of the original kingdom of Dalriada, before the union with the Picts. The famous Coronation Stone, formerly held here, was later removed to *Scone* (*q.v.*). The Chapel near the Castle is now the burial-place of the Campbells of Dunstaffnage, and is perhaps of 13th cent. date. See **Forteviot.** *Iter. 110, 117, 124, 125, 144, 145.*

DUNSYRE, Lanark. Map 9, **NT 0 4.**
The mansion of *Newholm* has Covenanting associations. Dunsyre Church retains the old jougs and in the churchyard are old gravestones. To the south rises *Black Mount*, 1,689 ft.

DUNTOCHER, Dunbarton. 3,032. Map 8, **NS 4 7.**
E.C. Wed. An ancient bridge is situated here. Northwards rise the *Kilpatrick* hills, with their numerous small lochs, or reservoirs. *Iter. 100, 101, 102, 113.*

DUNTULM, Isle of Skye, Inverness. Map 22, **NG 4 7.**
The ruins of *Duntulm Castle* are situated near the extremity of the Trotternish peninsula, in the far north of the island, and overlook Duntulm Island, in the bay of that name. The Castle was formerly a stronghold of the Macdonalds of the Isles, and was the successor to *Dunscaith Castle*, near *Isle Ornsay* (*q.v.*). Away to the north-west, beyond the waters of the Minch, rise the hills of Harris, in the Outer Hebrides. North of Duntulm, beyond the shores of Score Bay, is the promontory of Rudha Hunish. *Iter. 254.*

DUNURE, Ayr. Map 8, **NS 2 1.**
A small fishing village and resort with a sand and shingle foreshore to the south-west of the Heads of Ayr, and slightly to the west of the Ayr to Girvan road. There are fragmentary remains of the former Castle on the cliffs, and an old dovecote is preserved. In the background, inland, is *Brown Carrick Hill*, 940 ft., a good viewpoint. **2 m. S.**, on the Girvan road, is *Croy Brae*, better known as the "Electric Brae," where a curious optical illusion is created that the road descends, whereas, in effect, it is ascending, this being due to certain factors in the configuration of the land on either side of the road. A car which is stopped on this stretch of road will start to roll backwards, although appearing to be facing a descent. Away to the south-west are *Croy* sands, at the northern extremity of *Culzean* (*q.v.*) Bay. *Iter. 49.*

DUNVEGAN, Isle of Skye, Inverness. Map 22, **NG 2 4.**
The famous Castle of *Dunvegan* stands at the head of the island-studded Loch Dunvegan, between the Vaternish and Duirinish peninsulas. Near it, to the south, is the pleasant village, to the south-east of which lies the ruined Church of *Duirinish*. The Castle, which is shown Mon. to Sat., 2 to 5, April to mid-Oct. (see note page 98), is entered by a bridge spanning the former moat, and dates from the 15th to 19th cents., much of it having been restored. It has long been the seat of the Macleod of Macleod. In the 15th cent. tower is the dungeon, while the south tower, of early 16th cent. date, contains the Fairy Room, the towers having been linked in the 17th cent. by the 12th Chief, known as Rory More. Among the Castle's treasures are Rory More's drinking horn; a richly carved Irish Communion Cup; relics of Prince Charles Edward; letters from Dr. Johnson and Scott; and, most priceless of all, the "Fairy Flag" of Dunvegan. Some **4 m. N.E.** is *Fairy Bridge*, to which a legend is attached.

A memorial Cairn to the MacCrimmons, the hereditary pipers to the Macleods, stands **8 m. N.W.**, at *Boreraig*, where a piping College once stood. This clachan lies on a by-road traversing the western shores of Loch Dunvegan, beyond which is Dunvegan Head, with black cliffs 100 ft. in height. To the south-west of the head are lonely cliffs reaching a height of nearly 1,000 ft. Another by-road diverges to the west, about half-way along the loch, and leads to the head of Loch Pooltiel and Glen Dale, continuing thence towards Waterstein Head, 966 ft., in Moonen Bay, with some of the finest cliff scenery in Skye, accessible only on foot. Beyond the Head is Neist Point, the most westerly in Skye, with its lonely lighthouse in a splendid setting of cliffs overlooking the Little Minch. South-west of Dunvegan are the twin flat-topped hills known as *Macleod's Tables* (Healaval Beg and Healaval More), both around 1,600 ft. high, which overlook Loch Bracadale, to the east. Beyond these two hills the peninsula narrows to terminate in Idrigill Point, near which, off the coast, are the trio of isolated stacks of basalt rock known as *Macleod's Maidens.* See **Trumpan.** *Iter. 255.*

DURISDEER, Dumfries. 1,030. Map 3, **NS 8 0.**
This tiny hamlet lies to the east of Nithsdale, under a lofty ridge of green Lowland hills, and a little to the east of the Thornhill to Crawford road. An ancient path, known as the Well Path, possibly part of a Roman Road, leads north-eastwards through the hills towards the Dalveen Pass. The striking little Church dates from 1699, and is noted for the elaborate *Queensberry* monuments, including some work by John Nost. In the churchyard is the "factor's stone," where the children of John Lukup, a Queensberry master of works in 1684, were buried. There is also a Martyr's Stone to a Covenanter shot in 1685. See **Enterkinfoot.** *Iter. 25, 26.*

DURNESS, Sutherland. 374. Map 28, **NC 4 6.**
E.C. Wed. One of the most northerly localities in Scotland, the village of *Durness*, the nearest place to *Cape Wrath* (*q.v.*), is situated on Sango Bay. To the north extends a narrow and level peninsula terminating in Fair Aird, or Far Out Head, reached on foot, and providing notable coast views. A little to the north-west of Durness, overlooking the sandy shores of Balnakeil Bay, is *Balnakeil* which became a craft village in 1964, and has a roofless old *Balnakeil* Church, dating from

Dunstaffnage Castle, Argyll. Remains of the mainly 15th century Castle, where Flora Macdonald was imprisoned for a period of 10 days during 1746 before she was taken to London

Duntocher, Dunbarton. The old twin-arched bridge, in its wooded setting

Dunure, Ayr. The ancient dovecote by the ruined Castle. The Commendator of Crossraguel Abbey was twice nearly roasted to death in the castle by the fourth Earl of Cassillis, in 1570, before surrendering his lands

Durisdeer, Dumfries. The notable Queensberry monument in the Church. It was designed by John Nost, early in the 18th century

Dunvegan, Isle of Skye, Inverness. The restored 15th to 19th century Castle of the Macleods, in which is kept the famous 'Fairy Flag' of Dunvegan. Dr. Johnson and Boswell came here during their tour of 1773

Dunvegan, Isle of Skye, Inverness. Fairy Bridge, which in the old days had an evil reputation. It was said that no horse would cross the bridge without shying. The bridge is situated 4 miles north-east, on A850

[For DUNTOCHER see also under ROMAN WALL (Plate 142)
[For DUNTULM see under SKYE (Plate 151)
[For DUNSYRE see Plate 173

Dyce, Aberdeen. The ruined Church, in the churchyard of which is a watch-house erected to prevent body-snatchers rifling the graves. It lies 1½ miles north-west, on an unclassified road between the River Don and the railway

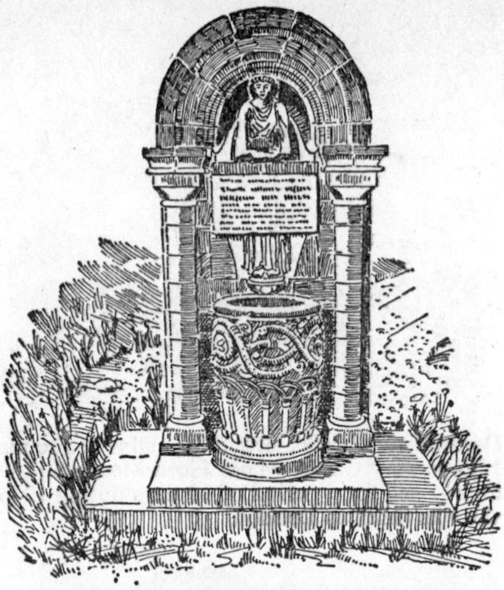

Dykehead, Angus. The fountain in memory of the Antarctic explorers, Captain Scott and Dr. Wilson, who reached the South Pole in 1912. It stands in Glen Prosen, on an unclassified road to the north-west

Eaglesham, Renfrew. The Church, which was built in 1790, and has an eagle for a weather-cock

East Kilbride, Lanark. An old mounting stone by the churchyard

Dysart, Fife. The doorway of a house, dated 1583, inscribed: ' My hoip is in the Lord '

[For EAST LINTON see following plate

1619, and preserving the quaintly-carved monument of Donald Makmurchou. Also buried here is Robert Donn, the illiterate "Burns of the North." A nearby 18th cent. house, now a farm, was once a residence of the Bishops of Caithness. In the vicinity of Durness are several small lochs noted for fishing. South-west of the village, the road to *Rhiconich* (*q.v.*) reaches the shores of the Kyle of Durness, and from the *Cape Wrath* Hotel, just off the road, a passenger ferry crosses the narrow Kyle to the Cape Wrath side, and a minibus service, in summer only, links with the Cape (weather permitting). There is an 11-mile stretch of moorland, known as The Parph, which must be traversed to reach the lonely Cape Wrath lighthouse, where the striking reddish cliffs exhibit rugged scenery. See **Smoo Cave.** *Iter. 225, 229.*

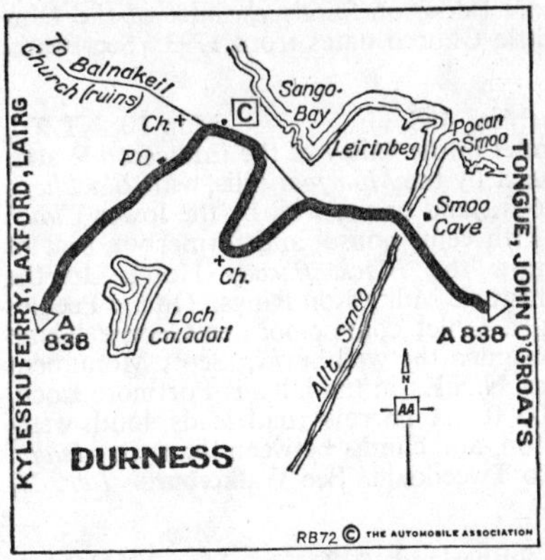

DUROR, Argyll. Map 18, **NM 9** 5.
A small *Appin* (*q.v.*) clachan, in the vicinity of which the famous Appin murder was committed, in 1752, for which James Stewart, whose home was at the nearby farm of Acharn, was tried at *Inveraray* (*q.v.*), and unjustly hanged at *Ballachulish* (*q.v.*). **2 m. S.W.**, on the shores of *Loch Linnhe* (*q.v.*), is the ruined kirk of *Keil*, where James Stewart lies, and is commemorated by a tablet. *Iter. 124.*

DURRIS, Kincardine. Map 21, **NO 7** 9.
The grounds of *Durris House* contain notable trees which have grown to great heights. *Iter. 168, 174.*

DYCE, Aberdeen. 3,287 with Kinellar. Map 27, **NH 8** 1.
The airport for Aberdeen is situated here. The village lies west of the River Don, and farther away to the west is *Tyrebagger Hill*, 823 ft., a good viewpoint, with indicators. There are prehistoric remains on the slopes of the hill. **1½ m. N.W.**, on the west bank of the river, is the ruined Church, in the churchyard of which are preserved two sculptured stones (A.M.). A watchhouse, erected a century ago, was used to prevent body-snatchers entering the precincts. *Iter. 180.*

DYKEHEAD, Angus. Map 20, **NO 3** 6.
Situated where two roads fork, each of which proceeds northwards up one of the long and picturesque Angus glens. The right fork follows the South Esk River, and later divides into two branches, one on each side of the river, to reach *Clova* (*q.v.*) in Glen Clova. The left fork proceeds into Glen Prosen Forest, and about a mile up the glen is a fountain, commemorating Captain Scott and Dr. Wilson, the Antarctic explorers, which is overlooked by *Tulloch Hill*, 1,230 ft., on which stands the prominent Airlie monument. The road continues up the beautiful glen, shortly afterwards accompanied by the Prosen Water, for about seven miles, before terminating near Glen Prosen Lodge, beyond which a path leads into the lonely eastern Grampians in the Braes of Angus, dominated by *Mayar*, 3,043 ft. See **Cortachy** and **Kirriemuir.** *Iter. 161.*

DYKEND, Angus. Map 20, **NO 2** 5.
Here, roads from Alyth and Kirriemuir converge at the entrance to the delightful Glen Isla, with the River Isla flowing a little to the west. *Creigh Hill*, 1,630 ft., rises to the north-east, and **2½ m. S.E.**, on the Kirriemuir road, is Loch Lintrathen, a reservoir for Dundee's water supply. See **Bridge of Craig.** *Iter. 160, 162.*

DYSART, Fife. Map 17, **NT 2** 9.
E.C. Wed. This picturesque little Royal Burgh, with its old houses, is now united with *Kirkcaldy* (*q.v.*). The Tolbooth dates from 1576, and was damaged by Cromwell's soldiers. The ruined Church of *St. Serf* carries the date 1570, and has a fortress-like tower. In the vicinity of the church stands an old house, with a courtyard, carrying an inscription and the date 1583. *The Towers* is a 16th-cent. house. The foreshore is rocky. See **Kirkcaldy** (for Town Plan) and **Pathhead** (Fife). *Iter. 128*

EAGLESHAM, Renfrew. 2,860. Map 8, **NS 5** 5.
GOLF. An 18th cent. village, the creation of the 12th Earl of Eglinton, with a number of houses dating from late in the period. The Parish Church of 1790 has an eagle on the spire. In the churchyard is a Covenanter's monument. *Eaglesham* achieved fame during the Second World War, when Rudolf Hess, the deputy German Fuehrer, made his sensational 1941 landing from the air in the vicinity. To the south-west, traversed by the Kilmarnock road, is Eaglesham Moor, over 900 ft. high, providing wide views. Beyond the Lochgoin reservoir, across the Ayrshire border, is a Covenanter's monument to John Howie, erected in 1896. The nearby farmhouse contains Covenanting relics. *Iter. 19.*

EARLSFERRY, Fife. 774. SB. with Elie. Map 17, **NO 4** 0.
See **Elie.**

EARLSHALL, Fife. Map 17, **NO 4** 2.
See **Leuchars.**

EARLSTON, Berwick. 1,829. Map 10, **NT 5** 3.
E.C. Wed. Lies in the pleasant Lauderdale valley, threaded by the Leader Water, and was once named *Ercildoune*. To the south of the town stands part of the ancient *Rhymer's Tower*, associated with the almost legendary "Thomas the Rhymer," a 13th cent. poet and prophet. In Earlston Church is a stone inscribed "Auld Rymer's Tace lies in this place." **1 m. S.** of the town, near the Leader Water, is the 16th cent. and later house of *Cowdenknowes*, associated with the Border family of Home in old ballads. *Iter. 4, 7, 13, 33, 36, 41, 43.*

EAS-COUL-AULIN WATERFALL, Sutherland.
See **Kylesku.** Map 28, **NC 2** 2.

EASDALE, ISLE OF, Argyll. Map 13, **NM 7** 1.
See **Clachan Bridge.**

EASSIE, Angus. 1,169 with Glamis. Map 17, **NO 3** 4.
In the churchyard is a fine example of a sculptured stone, inscribed with a cross and some Pictish symbols (A.M.). *Iter. 151, 153.*

EAST CALDER, Midlothian. 1,374 Map 9, **NT 0** 6.
E.C. Wed. Some **2 m. N.W.** is *Illieston House*, 16th or 17th cent. *Iter. 18, 19, 20, 22.*

EASTER ROSS, Ross and Cromarty. Map 25, **NH 5** 6 etc.
The name given to the rather flat, eastern part of the county, between the Dornoch and Cromarty Firths and once known as Cromarty. It forms a striking contrast to the wilder and more picturesque *Wester Ross* (*q.v.*) district. See **Cromarty, Dingwall** and **Dornoch.**

EAST KILBRIDE, Lanark. 63,505. LB. incl. New Town.
Map 8, **NS 6** 5.
E.C. Wed. GOLF. One of the best-planned New Towns, incorporating extensive research laboratories. It is noted also for dairy-farming. In the vicinity were born the brothers Hunter, 18th cent. anatomists, now commemorated by a monument. The first Scottish Society of Friends meeting took place here, in 1653. The Church has a 19th cent. "crown" tower and the date 1774 is above the tower entrance. A covered Olympic length swimming pool has been built. There is an 18th cent. *Stuart* mausoleum. At *Mount Cameron* farm lived Jean Cameron, associated with Prince Charles Edward and the '45. **1 m. N.** is the restored *Mains Castle*, probably early 13th cent. *Iter. 18, 19, 29, 56.*

EAST LINTON, East Lothian. 888. SB. Map 10, **NT 5 7.** **E.C.** Wed. An old-world village on the River Tyne, which flows here through a miniature gorge, and is crossed by a 16th cent. bridge. John Rennie, the famous engineer and bridge builder, was born in 1761 in the mansion of *Phantassie,* to the east. The Rennie memorial is situated beside the East Linton by-pass road. To the north of the village is the little Church of *Prestonkirk,* erected in 1770, but retaining the interesting 13th cent. square-ended chancel from its predecessor, and now used as a mortuary Chapel. There is also a 17th cent. tower. **2 m. S.W.,** near the Tyne, is the ruined 13th to 15th cent. *Hailes Castle* (A.M.), preserving its original water-gate and dungeons, and associated with Mary, Queen of Scots. It was dismantled by Cromwell in 1650. Open summer 10 to 7, winter 10 to 4; Sun., 2 to 7 or 4. (See note page 98.) To the south of the Castle rises *Traprain Law,* 724 ft., where excavations, in 1919, revealed a hoard of Roman silver, now in the National Museum of Antiquities, Edinburgh. *Preston Mill* (N.T. Scot.), on the river bank near East Linton, dates from the 17th cent., and can be inspected. See **Athelstaneford, Whitekirk** and **Whittinghame.** *Iter. 1, 40.*

EAST MEY, Caithness. Map 30, **ND 3 7.** Near Mey Bay, to the north-west, is *Castle of Mey,* formerly Barrogill Castle, dated 1606, and now the property of Her Majesty, Queen Elizabeth, the Queen Mother. To the north of East Mey is St. John's Point and the dangerous reef known as the " Merry Men of Mey," overlooking the Pentland Firth, with Stroma Island lying off-shore beyond the Inner Sound. See **Canisbay.** *Iter. 240.*

EAST NEUK, Fife. Map 17, **NO 6 1.** The name given to the extreme eastern corner of the county, around Fife Ness. It includes several of the picturesque, small coastal Royal Burghs and villages of Fife. See **Crail, Pittenweem** and **St. Monance.**

EASTRIGGS, Dumfries. 1,323. Map 4, **NY 2 6.** **E.C.** Wed. *Iter. 26, 27, 28, 42, 67.*

EAST SALTOUN, East Lothian. 141. Map 10, **NT 4 6.** At *Saltoun Hall,* to the north-west, was born, in 1653, Andrew Fletcher of Saltoun, the well-known Scottish patriot. The Hall is mainly modern, but retains a 17th cent. nucleus. The village was the first place in Britain to weave fine hollands, and the first in Scotland to produce pot barley. Saltoun Mill, near the station, is of late 17th cent. date. See **Pencaitland.** *Iter. 3.*

EAST WEMYSS, Fife. 3,037. Map 17, **NT 3 9.** GOLF. A small coal-port on a rocky stretch of coast, with caves, or " weems," including the Glass Cave, situated to the south-west in the direction of *West Wemyss* (*q.v.*). Just beyond East Wemyss, to the north-east, is the massive ruin of *Macduff's Castle,* with an old dovecote nearby. *Iter. 128.*

ECCLEFECHAN, Dumfries. 611. Map 4, **NY 1 7.** **E.C.** Thurs. The birthplace, in 1795, of Thomas Carlyle, who described the village in his " Sartor Resartus " under the name of " Entepfuhl." The house (N.T. Scot.) in which he was born, known as the " Arched House," is built over a pend, and contains personal relics. Open weekdays, 10 to 6, Mar. to Oct. (See page 98.) A Carlyle statue stands in the village, and in the churchyard are the graves of the author and his parents. Archibald Arnott, who was doctor to Napoleon at St. Helena, is also buried in the churchyard. See **Dunscore, Hoddom Bridge, Kirtlebridge** and **Lockerbie.** *Iter. 10, 13, 29, 50, 51.*

ECCLES, Berwick. 485. Map 11, **NT 7 4.** There are slight remains of a Cistercian convent, burnt in 1545. The church dates from 1779. A tall Cross stands by the road to the south-west of Crosshall Farm. *Iter. 39, 46.*

ECHT, Aberdeen. 2,138 with Skene. Map 21, **NJ 7 0.** To the north-west is the Barmekin of Echt, an isolated hill, crowned by prehistoric fortifications. **1½ m. W.,** near *Sunhoney* farm, is the stone circle of *Cullerlie* (A.M.), dating probably from the late Bronze Age. See **Dunecht** and **Midmar Castle.** *Iter. 179, 197.*

ECKFORD, Roxburgh. 494. Map 11, **NT 7 2.** Stands on the east bank of the River Teviot. The Church still preserves the jougs of 1718, and also the old watch-house in the churchyard. The Kale Water joins the Teviot at this point. See **Morebattle** and **Oxnam.** *Iter. 30, 47.*

EDDERTON, Ross and Cromarty. Map 31, **NH 7 8.** To the north-east are Edderton Sands, an inlet of the Dornoch Firth. The little Church dates from 1793. See **Fearn.** *Iter. 201.*

EDDLESTON, Peebles. 488. Map 10, **NT 2 4.** **E.C.** Thurs. A hamlet in the valley of the Eddleston Water, overlooked to the east by the *Moorfoot* hills, with *Blackhope Scar* rising to 2,136 ft., and to the west by the lower *Cloich* hills. *Darnhall* a 17th cent. house and formerly a seat of the Murrays, is now the *Black Barony* Hotel. In the vicinity are the prehistoric Milkieston Rings. On the Peebles road, to the south, a tablet commemorates George Kemp (1795-1844) who designed the well known Scott Monument at Edinburgh. **2½ m. N.N.E.,** in the hills, is Portmore Loch, at a height of 1,000 ft. A narrow road leads south-westwards from Eddleston, and climbs between the twin *Meldon* hills to descend into Tweeddale. See **Walkerburn.** *Iter. 24, 40.*

EDDRACHILLIS, Sutherland. 738. Map 28, **NC 1 4.** Overlooks Badcall Bay, an inlet of the larger island-studded Eddrachillis Bay. Inland, across a landscape of many tiny lochans, rises the sharp gneiss cone of *Ben Stack,* 2,364 ft. The rough and hilly road leading south-eastwards towards the ferry at *Kylesku* (*q.v.*) passes near the shores of the little Calva Bay, with its two islands off-shore, and then turns inland by Loch Allt nan Airbhe. See **Scourie.** *Iter. 225.*

EDINBAIN, Isle of Skye, Inverness. Map 22, **NG 3 5.** By the head of Loch Greshornish, at the southern extremity of the Vaternish peninsula, with a background of lonely moors. **4 m. N.E.,** on the Portree road, are the shores of Loch Snizort Beag. *Iter. 255.*

EDINBURGH, Midlothian. 453,422. Map 10, **NT 2 7.** **E.C.** Tues./Wed./Sat. **M.D.** Tues./Wed. GOLF. The capital of Scotland, and the second largest in population, a city whose beauty, interest and historic associations are alike famous, the Royal Burgh of *Edinburgh* owes not a little to its superb natural setting, overlooked by the dominating mass of Arthur's Seat, a mountain in miniature, with the prominent Salisbury Crags on its lower flanks. To the south of the city's outskirts, and well seen from Arthur's Seat, is the long range of the Pentland Hills, approaching 2,000 ft. in height, and providing a splendid playground for the citizens of Edinburgh. The waters of the Firth of Forth wash the outer boundaries of the city, and here is situated the important port of *Leith,* incorporated since 1920 within the administration of the parent city. Edinburgh itself has been not inaptly described as the modern Athens, while the name " Auld Reekie," by which it is sometimes affectionately known, is a reference to the smoke curling upwards from its chimneys. The city is a great centre of education, noted for the University, and a number of well-known schools, among them the Royal High School, the Academy, Fettes, Loretto, George Heriot's and Donaldson's Hospitals, and George Watson's, Stewart's and Merchiston Colleges. Its varied industries include both printing and brewing, but it is essentially as a showpiece that the fame of Edinburgh has resounded throughout the world. The outline of the historic Castle, on its rocky site 445 ft. high above the former Nor' Loch, now drained and occupied by pleasant gardens, through which runs the railway to the great Waverley Station. The North Bridge (1772 and later) may be said to divide the historic Old Town from the New Town, the latter of which dates mainly from the 18th cent.

The Old Town descends eastwards along the ridge from the Castle, its most noteworthy feature being the historic " Royal Mile," now mainly restored, commencing with Castle Hill and the Lawnmarket. This is continued by the longer High Street and Canongate, with their picturesque multi-storeyed houses and quaint Closes, or Wynds. At the foot

East Linton, East Lothian. The memorial to the engineer and architect, John Rennie. He was born at the mansion of Phantassie near here in 1761

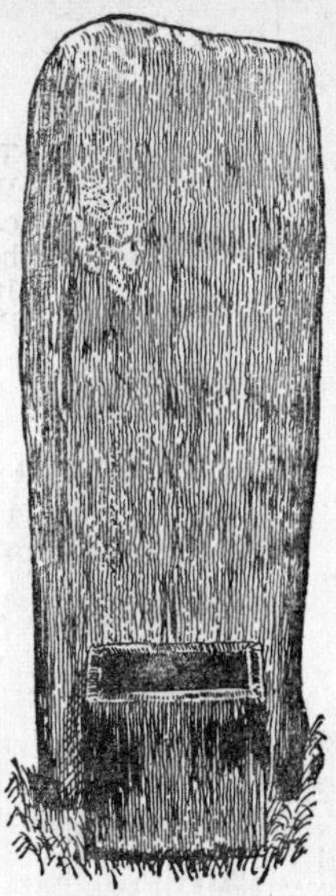

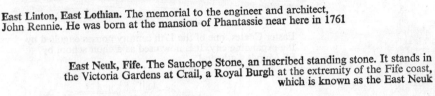

East Neuk, Fife. The Sauchope Stone, an inscribed standing stone. It stands in the Victoria Gardens at Crail, a Royal Burgh at the extremity of the Fife coast, which is known as the East Neuk

East Saltoun, East Lothian. The 17th century mill, commenced by Fletcher of Saltoun, the Scottish patriot

Ecclefechan, Dumfries. The birthplace (N.T. Scot.) in 1785 of Thomas Carlyle

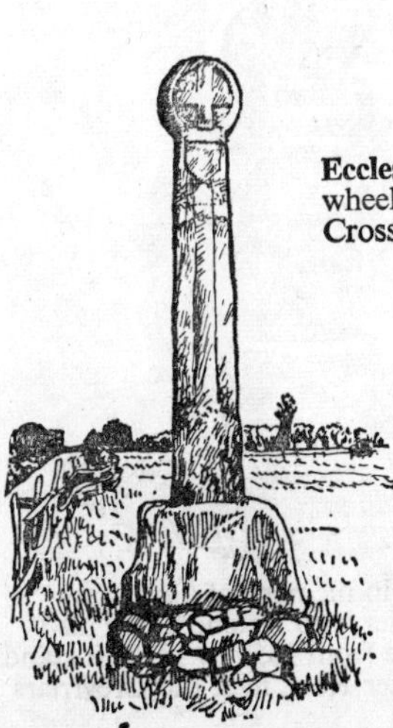

Eccles, Berwick. An ancient wheel-headed Cross near Crosshall Farm

Eddleston, Peebles. The memorial on A703, to the south, in memory of George Kemp, who served as an apprentice here. He later designed the Scott Monument (1840–44) in Edinburgh (*see following plate*)

[For EDINBURGH see PLATES 57 to 61 and also 174
[For EAST LINTON see also under LOTHIANS (Plate 117)
[For EDDRACHILLIS see under HIGHLANDS (Plate 84)

The Monument to Sir Walter Scott, the work of George Kemp between 1840 and 1844. It stands in Princes Street Gardens See Eddleston (Plate 56)

Easter Coates, one of the 17th century houses engulfed by the expanding city. It is now used as a choir school by St. Mary's Cathedral

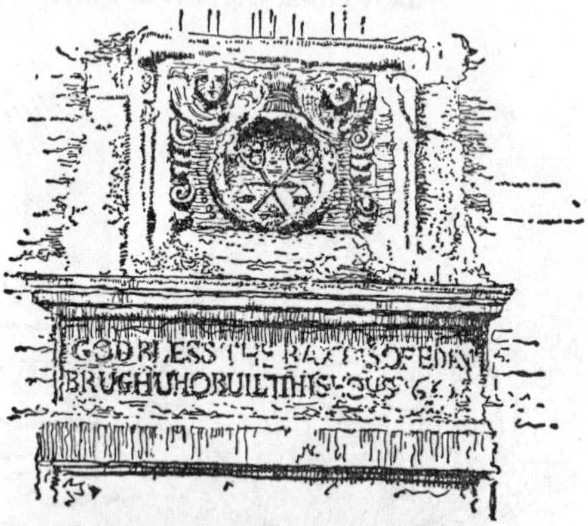

A tablet on the 'Old Tolbooth' of the former Water of Leith village. The inscription reads: 'God Bless the Baxters of Edinbrugh uho built this hous 1675'

The tower (1495) of St. Giles' Church, with its 'crown' steeple, the finest of the three examples to be found in Scotland

A boy's head and scroll at the entrance to Paisley Close, High Street. The boy was the sole survivor when the original house fell in 1861. The scroll reads: 'Heave awa chaps, I'm no dead yet'

The fountain in memory of Greyfriars Bobby, a terrier who watched over his master's grave from 1858 to 1872. It stands in Candlemaker Row, near the Greyfriars Church

[For EDINBURGH see also Plates 58 to 61 and 174

are the portals of the Palace of Holyroodhouse, backed by the Salisbury Crags below Arthur's Seat.

The late 18th cent. New Town is dignified by broad and stately streets and squares, among which George Street and Charlotte Square are perhaps the finest, and some of the most characteristic buildings of the great Georgian architect Robert Adam grace the district. In George Street are the Assembly Rooms of 1787 and Music Hall of 1843, in which Paderewski and Pachmann gave piano recitals; Dickens and Thackeray lectured; and Gladstone addressed political meetings. Most famous of all is the splendid avenue of *Princes Street*, with its array of shops, clubs and hotels on the north side. Its south side is noted for the unique vista over the beautifully-tended Princes Street Gardens, with the prominent *Scott Monument*, the Scottish-American War Memorial, and the well-known *Floral Clock*, with the guardian bastion of the Castle rising in the background. Away beyond the eastern end of Princes Street lies Calton Hill, with its notable group of buildings, dominated by the unfinished *National Monument*.

Among the city's parks, that of Blackford, the oldest, lies on the 300-ft. high Blackford Hill, where the Royal Observatory is situated. The view from here was described by Scott in his " Marmion." The Royal Botanic Garden and Arboretum, which contains an attractive Rock Garden, lies on the way to Granton, and to the west of the Arboretum is Inverleith Park. Farther to the south-west, in the Corstorphine direction, are the *Murrayfield* Rugby Football Ground and the Zoological Park, the latter on the slopes of Corstorphine Hill.

Although Holyrood Abbey was already founded in 1128, the early history of Edinburgh is bound up mainly with that of its ancient Castle, which is described separately below. The city superseded Perth as Scotland's capital in 1437, and was ravaged both in 1544 and 1547 by Henry VIII. In the 17th cent., it played a part in the religious and civil struggles of the period, among the events which took place in Edinburgh being the occupation of the city in 1650 by Cromwell, and the executions, in 1650 and 1661, of the Marquis of Montrose and the Marquis of Argyll. The Scottish Parliament ceased to function after the amalgamation of Scotland with England in 1707, and the unfortunate Porteous Riots of 1736 reflected this loss of privilege. Prince Charles Edward held a gay, but brief, court at Holyroodhouse in 1745, while later in the century, and during the commencement of the one following, the limelight became focused principally on Edinburgh's literary activities. Many famous names are associated with the city, both Sir Walter Scott and Robert Louis Stevenson having been born within its boundaries. Of Scott's several Edinburgh homes, perhaps the best known is 39 Castle Street, where many of the Waverley novels were written. A modern development, which has added increased lustre to the city's world-wide renown, is the establishment, since 1947, of the Edinburgh International Festival of Art, Drama and Music, which takes place annually in the late summer, the concerts being held in the Usher Hall and the Freemasons' Hall. Opera, ballet, plays and a military tattoo are other features of the Festival. The splendid new *Meadowbank* Sports Centre and Stadium was built for the 1970 Commonwealth games. The city airport lies some **7 m. W.**, at *Turnhouse*, off the road to Glasgow. In order to appreciate fully the many places of interest in Edinburgh outstanding among which are the Castle, the Palace of Holyroodhouse, the Church of St. Giles and the picturesque Royal Mile in the Old Town, the purchase of a detailed guide-book, of which many are available, is strongly advised. The majority of the principal buildings are described briefly below, together with times of admission where available (see note page 98). The race-course is situated **6 m. E.**, at *Musselburgh* (*q.v.*).

The most notable nearby physical feature of Edinbugh is the 822-ft. high *Arthur's Seat*, together with the Salisbury Crags on its lower slopes, which rises almost directly above Holyroodhouse, and is easily climbed from various points. The view from the summit is superb, and includes the city itself, the *Pentland* hills, and also the distant coast of Fife. On the lower slopes of the hill are St. Margaret's Well, the remains of St. Anthony's Chapel, and also the tiny St. Margaret's and Dunsappie Lochs. The hill is encircled by Holyrood Park, around the perimeter of which extends the beautiful Queen's Drive, which, itself, provides beautiful views across *Duddingston* loch and village, and also towards *Craigmillar Castle*. The Water of Leith flows along the western side of the city and is spanned by the Dean Bridge, built by Telford in 1831. Farther upstream is the picturesque village of *Dean*. Downstream, near *Stockbridge*, is a curious Doric temple covering *St. Bernard's Well*, which was erected in 1789. Some of the more interesting of the outer districts of the city have been described separately in the gazetteer, these being: *Barnton, Colinton, Corstorphine, Craigmillar Castle, Duddingston, Fairmilehead, Granton, Hillend, Leith, Liberton, Newhaven* and *Portobello*. The two famous *Forth Bridges*, situated some **8 m. W.N.W.** of the city centre, are described under *Queensferry, South*.

CATHEDRALS AND CHURCHES

CHURCH OF ST. GILES. The finest of the city's Churches, erected largely in the 14th and 15th cents., the tower dating from c. 1495 and being surmounted by the famous " Crown " steeple, the finest of the three ancient examples in Scotland. The others are the Tolbooth at *Glasgow* (*q.v.*) and King's College Chapel, *Aberdeen* (*q.v.*). Many of the Church's altars and precious relics were destroyed in 1556, and in 1559 John Knox became minister of St. Giles, the building being later subdivided at one period into as many as four Churches. Under Charles I, in 1663, St. Giles obtained for a short period Cathedral status, and in 1637 occurred the notorious incident of a stool being thrown at the Dean for reading the service from Laud's book. Again under Charles II St. Giles became a Cathedral, but lost the rank finally in 1688. Considerable and damaging restorations took place in the 19th cent. The latest addition is Sir Robert Lorimer's fine, ornate Thistle Chapel, which dates from 1911. In the Chepman aisle lie the remains of the great Marquis of Montrose, and both the Moray and Albany aisles are of considerable interest. The colours of the Scottish regiments hang in the nave, and by the Preston aisle is the Royal pew. There is a monument to R. L. Stevenson, who is buried in Samoa, and in St. Elio's Chapel is a monument to the Covenanter Marquis of Argyll.

ST. MARY'S CATHEDRAL. This imposing, three-towered structure, carrying a 276-ft. high spire, was designed by Sir Gilbert Scott and commenced in 1874, though not finally completed until 1917. Nearby stands the attractive small mansion of *Easter Coates*, built in c. 1615 by John Byres, and probably the oldest house in the New Town. It is now used as the choir school.

GREYFRIARS CHURCH. This Church was built originally in 1612, and was altered a century later, being for long divided into two parts. In 1936, the building was restored and made into a single Church. Copies of Covenanters' flags hang above the pillars. The Greyfriars Churchyard has historic associations, the National Covenant having been signed here in 1638, while, in 1679, some 1,200 Covenanter prisoners were confined here after the battle of *Bothwell Brig* (*q.v.*), and are commemorated by the Martyrs' Memorial. Captain Porteous, Regent Morton and Allan Ramsay are buried in the churchyard. Nearby, in Candlemaker Row, is a fountain in memory of " Greyfriars Bobby," a faithful Edinburgh terrier of 1858, who lingered near his master's grave for 14 years.

TRON CHURCH. Dates from 1637 to 1663, and owes its name to a public " tron," or weighing beam, situated nearby. The stone steeple, erected in 1824, replaced the former wooden one which was burnt. Hogmanay, or New Year, is celebrated annually outside the Church.

MAGDALEN CHAPEL. Founded in 1547, under the patronage of the guild of Hammermen, and preserving the founder's tomb. Outstanding in the Chapel is the notable pre-Reformation stained glass, while the little steeple dates

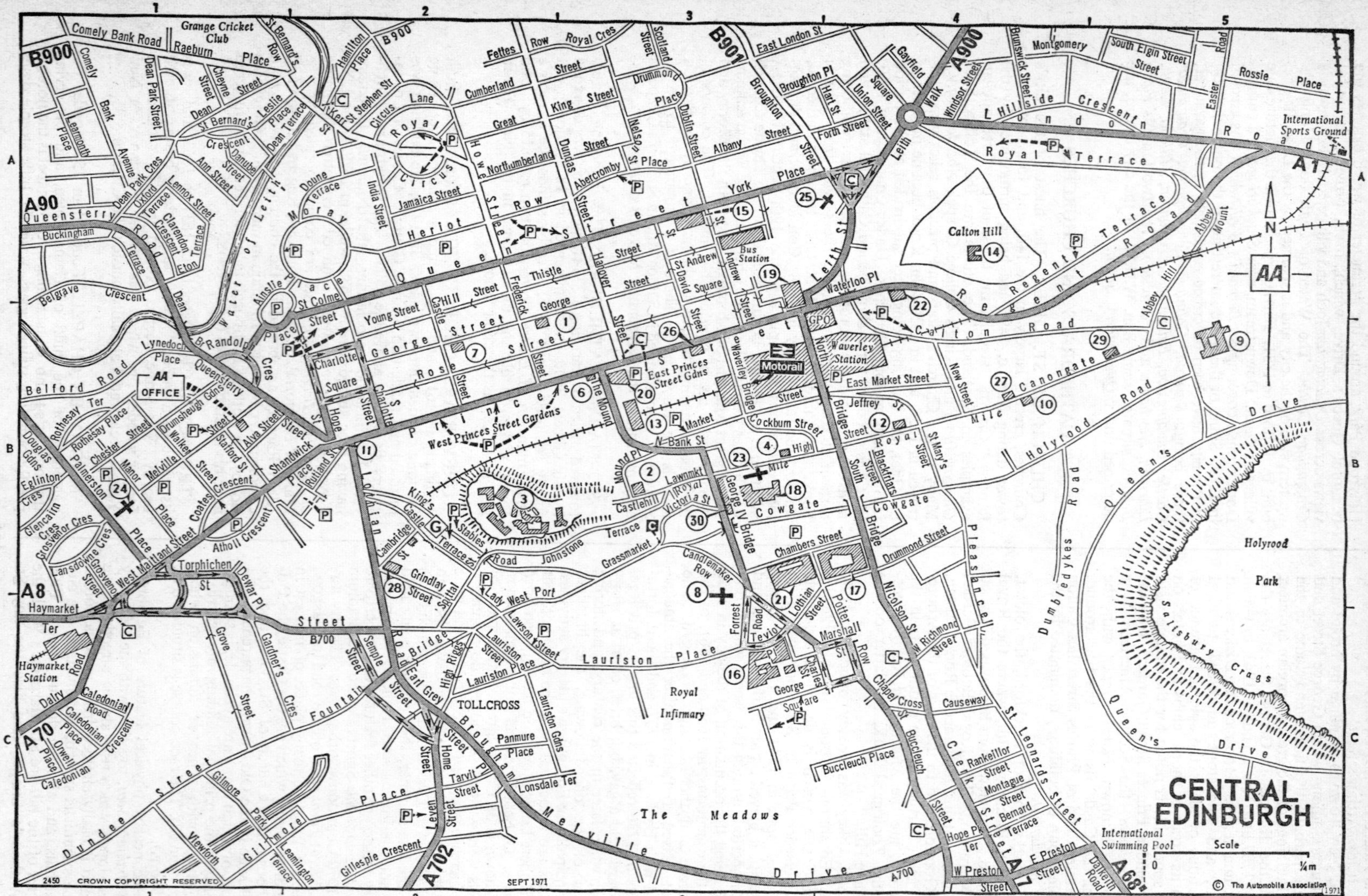

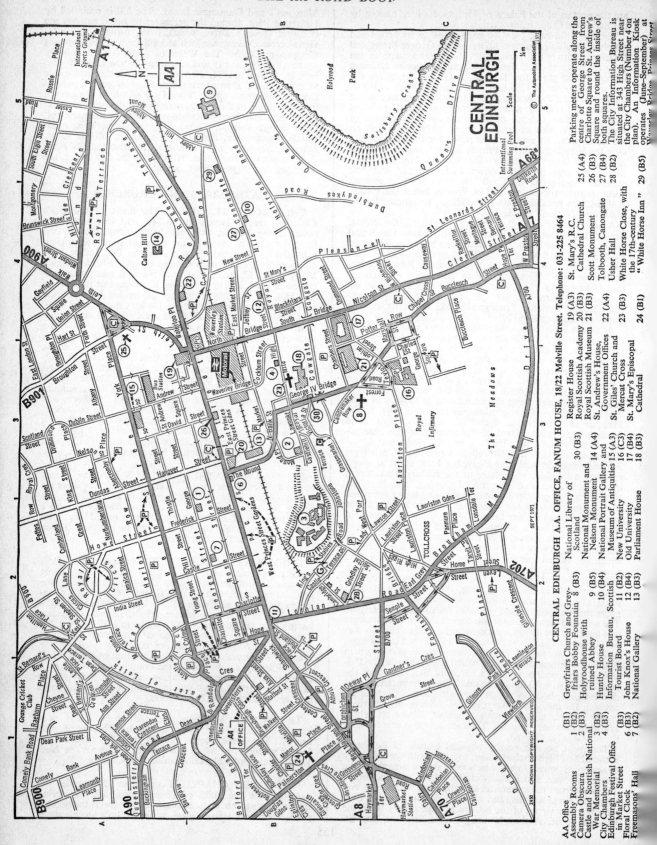

CENTRAL EDINBURGH A.A. OFFICE, FANUM HOUSE, 18/22 Melville Street. Telephone: 031-225 8464

AA Office	(B1)
Assembly Rooms	1 (B2)
Camera Obscura	2 (B3)
Castle and Scottish National War Memorial	3 (B2)
City Chambers	4 (B3)
Edinburgh Festival Office in Market Street	(B3)
Floral Clock	6 (B3)
Freemasons' Hall	7 (B2)
Greyfriars Church and Greyfriars Bobby Fountain	8 (B3)
Holyroodhouse with ruined Abbey	9 (B5)
Huntly House	10 (B4)
Information Bureau, Scottish Tourist Board	11 (B2)
John Knox's House	12 (B4)
National Gallery	13 (B3)
National Library of Scotland	30 (B3)
National Monument and Nelson Monument	14 (A4)
National Portrait Gallery and Museum of Antiquities	15 (A3)
New University	16 (C3)
Old University	17 (B4)
Parliament House	18 (B3)
Register House	19 (A3)
Royal Scottish Academy	20 (B3)
Royal Scottish Museum	21 (B3)
St. Andrew's House, Government Offices	22 (A4)
St. Giles' Church and Mercat Cross	23 (B3)
St. Mary's Episcopal Cathedral	24 (B1)
St. Mary's R.C. Cathedral Church	25 (A4)
Scott Monument	26 (B3)
Tolbooth, Canongate	27 (B4)
Usher Hall	28 (B2)
White Horse Close, with the 17th-century "White Horse Inn"	29 (B5)

Parking meters operate along the centre of George Street from Charlotte Square to St. Andrew's Square and round the inside of both squares.

The City Information Bureau is situated at 343 High Street near the City Chambers (Number 4 on plan). An Information Kiosk operates (June–September) at [illegible]

George Heriot's Hospital School (1628–93), founded by George Heriot, the 'Jingling Geordie' of Sir Walter Scott's '*Fortunes of Nigel*'

The Canongate Tolbooth, in the 'Royal Mile,' dating from 1591 and once used as a prison. It is an interesting survival of contemporary municipal architecture.

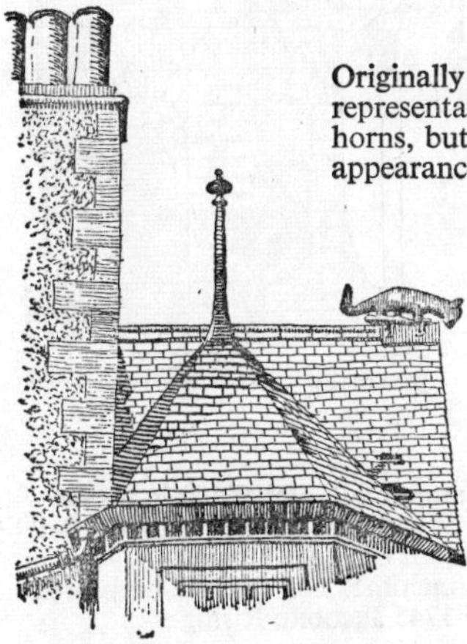

Originally this figure on a roof in Ramsay Gardens was a representation of 'Auld Nick' complete with wings and horns, but erosion has eaten these away to give now the appearance of a cat

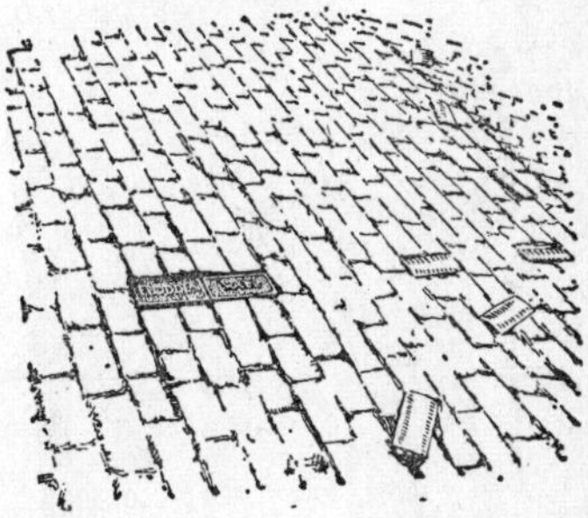

Metal plates, marking where the Flodden Wall once stood, let into the roadway at the crossing of High Street, Jeffrey's Street and St. Mary's Street

The so-called John Knox's House, 16th century, built reputedly by the goldsmith to Mary, Queen of Scots

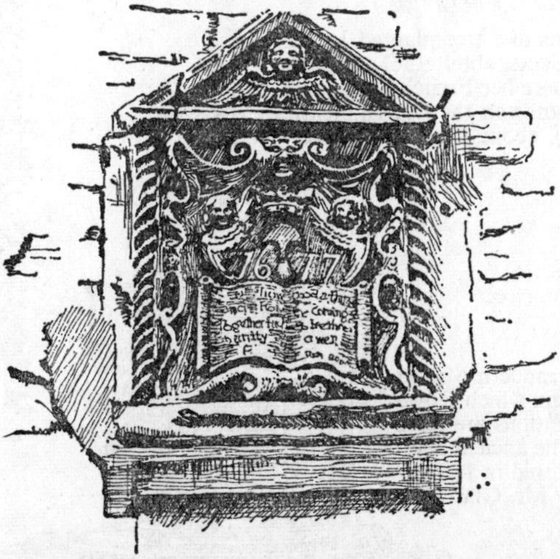

The tablet on a 17th century house in Bible Land (187–197 Canongate), facing Moray House

[For EDINBURGH see also Plates 57, 59 to 61 and 174

The site of the Old Tolbooth, the 'Heart of Midlothian,' which was stormed in the 1736 Porteous Riots, and demolished in 1817. It is situated near the Mercat Cross in the High Street of the Old Town (see below)

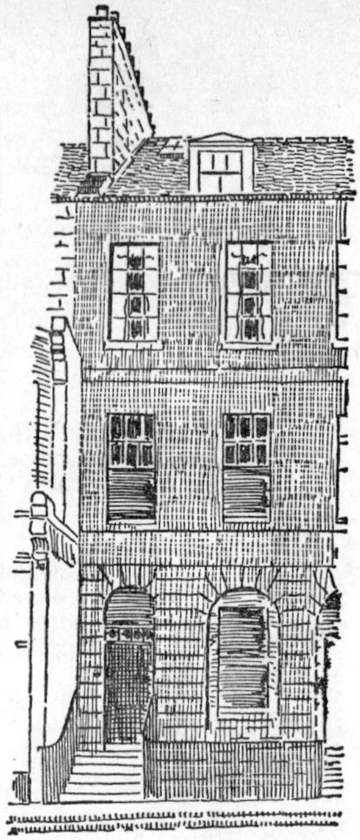

No. 11 Picardy Place, where Sir Arthur Conan Doyle, the creator of 'Sherlock Holmes,' was born in 1859. The name Picardy recalls a settlement here of French weavers employed by the British Linen Company in the 18th century

The cannon ball embedded in a side gable of the 17th century Cannon Ball House, on Castle Hill, near the Castle. It is sometimes said to have been fired in the 1745 Jacobite Rising

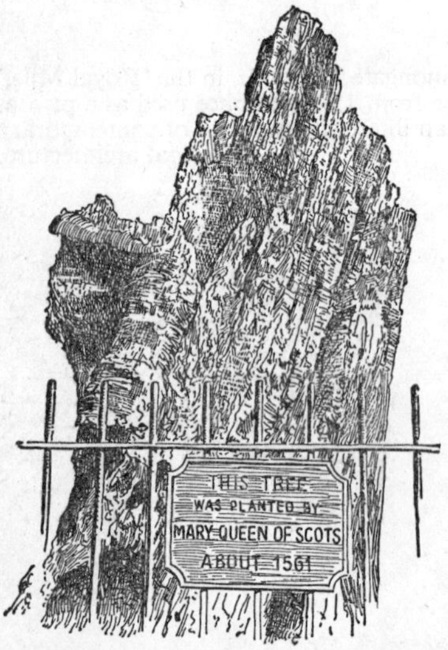

The remains of a tree planted by Mary, Queen of Scots, about 1561, at Little France, where her French attendants lived. It stands on the Old Dalkeith road (A68), about 3 miles from the city centre

The modern Mercat Cross, from which Royal Proclamations are read. Part of the ancient shaft was restored in 1885 by Mr. Gladstone

The Stevenson Memorial House, in Howard Place, where Robert Louis Stevenson was born in 1850. It contains relics and books associated with the writer.

[For EDINBURGH see also Plates 57, 58, 60, 61 and 174

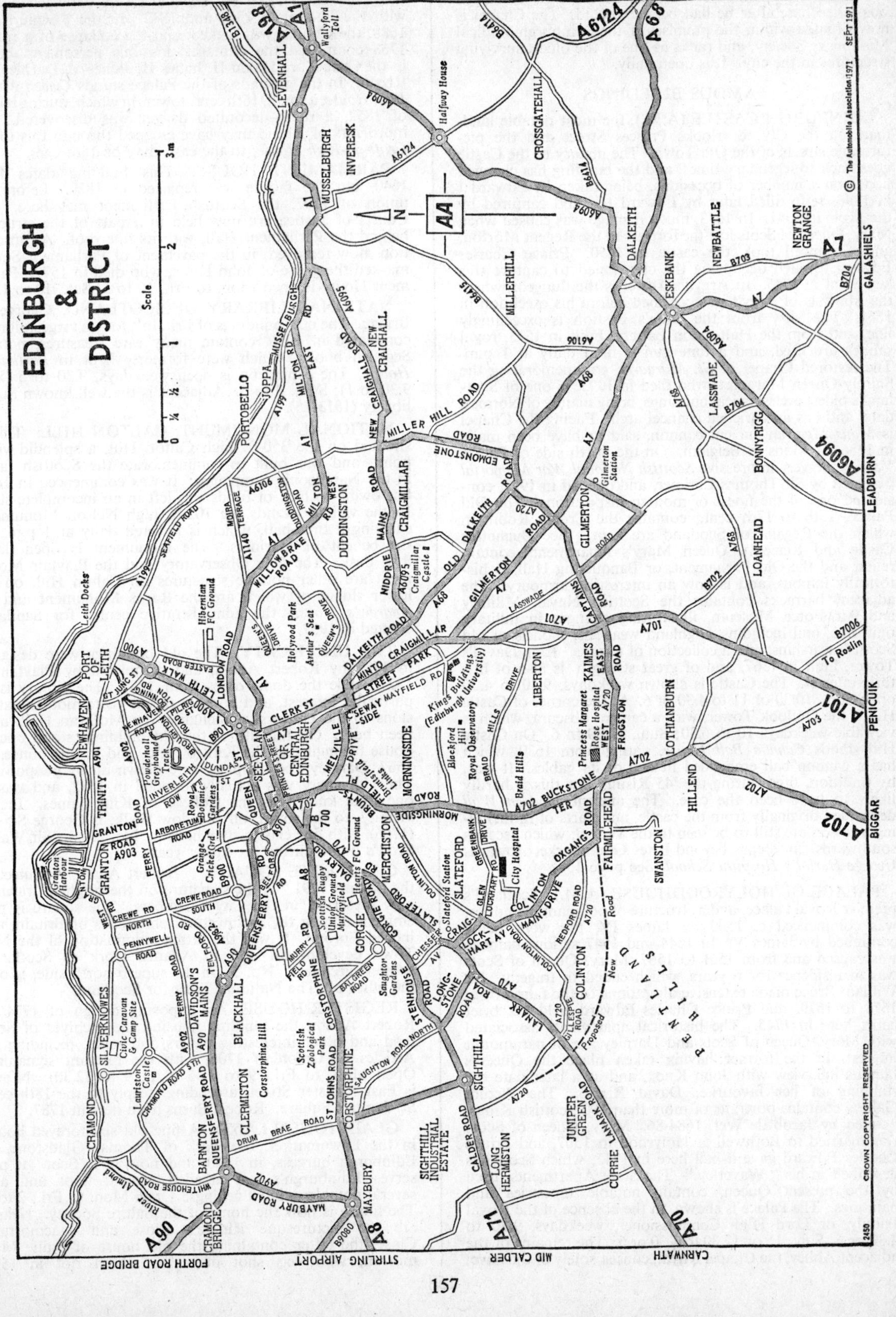
EDINBURGH & DISTRICT
Scale
0 ¼ ½ 1 2 3m
AA
N
NORTH BERWICK
BERWICK UPON TWEED
To A1
LAUDER
GALASHIELS
LEADBURN
PENICUIK
BIGGAR
CARNWATH
MID CALDER
STIRLING AIRPORT
FORTH ROAD BRIDGE
To Roslin
A198
A1
A6124
A68
A7
A6094
A701
A702
A70
A71
A8
A90
LEVENHALL
Wallyford Toll
Halfway House
INVERESK
MUSSELBURGH
CROSSGATEHALL
DALKEITH
ESKBANK
NEWBATTLE
NEWTON GRANGE
MILLERHILL
LASSWADE
BONNYRIGG
LOANHEAD
LOTHIANBURN
HILLEND
PORTOBELLO
JOPPA
NEW CRAIGHALL
CRAIGMILLAR
Craigmillar Castle
DUDDINGSTON
NIDDRIE
GILMERTON
Gilmerton Station
LIBERTON
KAIMES
FROGSTON
FAIRMILEHEAD
SWANSTON
Holyrood Park
Arthur's Seat
Hibernian FC Ground
Leith Docks
PORT OF LEITH
NEWHAVEN
TRINITY
GRANTON
Granton Harbour
Powderhall Greyhound Track
INVERLEITH
Royal Botanic Gardens
CENTRAL EDINBURGH
MORNINGSIDE
Royal Observatory
Blackford Hill
Kings Buildings (Edinburgh University)
Braid Hills
Princess Margaret Rose Hospital
City Hospital
MERCHISTON
Grange Cricket Grd
Scottish Rugby Union Ground Murrayfield
Hearts FC Ground
GORGIE
SLATEFORD
Saughton Gardens
STENHOUSE
CORSTORPHINE
Scottish Zoological Park
Corstorphine Hill
BLACKHALL
CLERMISTON
DAVIDSON'S MAINS
SILVERKNOWES
Civic Caravan & Camp Site
Lauriston Castle
CRAMOND
CRAMOND BRIDGE
BARNTON
River Almond
MAYBURY
SIGHTHILL
SIGHTHILL INDUSTRIAL ESTATE
LONGSTONE
COLINTON
JUNIPER GREEN
CURRIE
LONG HERMISTON
THE PENTLAND HILLS
Proposed New Road
© The Automobile Association 1971
SEPT 1971
CROWN COPYRIGHT RESERVED
2450

from 1618 to 1628. The building was at one period used as a mortuary, and in 1685 the body of the Earl of Argyll was taken here after he had been executed. The Chapel is now situated within the premises of the Edinburgh Medical Missionary Society, and ranks as one of the oldest surviving structures in the city. It is open daily.

FAMOUS BUILDINGS

EDINBURGH CASTLE (A.M.), the most notable landmark in the city, overlooks Princes Street and the picturesque streets of the Old Town. The history of the Castle goes back to legendary times, and the building has changed hands on a number of occasions, being taken by Edward I in 1296, re-fortified later by Edward III, and captured by the Scots in 1341. In 1573, much damage was caused when Mary, Queen of Scots lost the fortress to the Regent Morton, and Cromwell took the castle in 1650. Prince Charles Edward, though occupying the city, failed to capture this key-point in 1745. In Argyll's Tower is the dungeon where the Marquis of Argyll was confined before his execution in 1661. The view from the King's Bastion is exceedingly fine, and from the Half-moon Battery, built in 1573, royal salutes are fired, and a time gun is fired daily at 1 p.m. The restored Chapel of *St. Margaret*, commemorating the Saintly Queen Margaret, who died in 1093, is one of Scotland's oldest ecclesiastical buildings, being mainly of Norman date, and has an enriched chancel arch. Facing the Chapel is *Mons Meg*, an ancient cannon, said to have been made in 1486, at Mons in Belgium. On the north side of Palace Yard is the very impressive *Scottish National War Memorial* designed by Sir Thomas Lorimer, and opened in 1927, considered one of the finest of modern inspirations. The Old Palace, 15th to 17th cent., contains the Crown Room in which the Regalia of Scotland are kept. (See **Dunnottar Castle** and **Kinneff.**) Queen Mary's Apartments contain relics, and the Old Parliament, or Banqueting Hall, is historically famous, and is now an interesting armoury. The adjacent barracks contains the Scottish Naval, Military and Air Force Museum, illustrating changes in military uniforms, and including Highland weapons, models of old Scottish warships, and a collection of tartans. King David's Tower, built in 1367, and of great strength is also of historic interest. The Castle is shown weekdays, 9.30 to 4.30 or 6; Sun., 10.30 or 11 to 4.30 or 6. At the corner of Castle Hill is the Outlook Tower, with a camera obscura, which is viewable weekdays 10 to 6.30; Sun., 12.30 to 6. On Castle Hill stands *Cannon Ball House*, dating from 1630, which has a cannon ball embedded in one of its gables. It was, by tradition, fired during the '45 Rising, but this is hardly likely to have been the case. The ancient *Flodden Wall* descended originally from the castle, and parts of it, including a tower, are still to be seen in the Vennel, which ascends southwards in steps beyond the Grassmarket towards *George Heriot's Hospital School* (See page 159).

PALACE OF HOLYROODHOUSE (A.M.). Scotland's premier Royal Palace, and a structure of poignant memories, was commenced c. 1500 by James IV, the work being continued by James V. In 1544 and 1547 serious damage was caused and from 1561 to 1567, Mary, Queen of Scots was in residence for 6 years, which ended in tragedy. Sir William Bruce made extensive alterations to the fabric from 1670 to 1679, and Prince Charles Edward held his brief court here in 1745. The historical apartments associated with Mary, Queen of Scots and Darnley are of paramount interest, in the former having taken place the Queen's famous interview with John Knox, and at a later date the stabbing of her favourite, David Rizzio. The Picture Gallery contains portraits of more than 100 Scottish Kings, painted by Jacob de Wet, 1684-86. Mary, Queen of Scots was married to Bothwell at Holyrood in 1567, and Prince Charles Edward gave a ball here in 1745, which Scott has described in his "Waverley." The State Apartments, used by the present Queen, contain notable tapestries and paintings. The Palace is shown, in the absence of the Royal Family, or Lord High Commissioner, weekdays, 9.30 to 4.30 or 6; Sun., 11 or 12.30 to 4.30 or 6. The remains of the adjacent Abbey, the Chapel Royal, consist solely of the nave, the fine west front and the north-west tower. The Abbey was founded in 1128, but suffered severe damage, together with the Palace, in 1544 and 1547. In the Revolution of 1688, the Church was sacked, and the collapse of a roof in 1768 completed the damage. Famous personages buried in the Chapel are David II, James II, James V, Darnley and Rizzio. In the grounds of the Palace stands *Queen Mary's Bath House*, a small, 16th cent. tower, in which, during repairs of 1852, a richly-decorated dagger was discovered. The murderers of Rizzio may have escaped through this tower. *Croft-an-Righ House*, to the east, may be 16th cent.

PARLIAMENT HOUSE. This building dates from 1640, but the façade was replaced in 1829. Before the union of 1707, the Scottish Parliament met here. The Courts of Justice are now held in a part of the structure behind the Parliament Hall, with its fine roof. An inscription, now removed, in the pavement of Parliament Square marked the grave of John Knox, who died in 1572. Parliament House is open Mon. to Fri., 10 to 5; Sat., 10 to 1.

NATIONAL LIBRARY OF SCOTLAND, George IV Bridge. The new buildings of Britain's fourth largest library, completed in 1956, contain many rare treasures, notably Scottish books, which were formerly kept in *Parliament House*. The exhibition is open weekdays, 9.30 to 5 (Sat., 9.30 to 1); Sun., 2 to 5. Adjacent is the well known Signet library (1813/15).

NATIONAL MONUMENT, CALTON HILL. This is situated on the 350-ft. high Calton Hill, a splendid viewpoint, and was built to commemorate the Scottish fallen in the Napoleonic campaigns. It was commenced in 1822, but owing to lack of funds was left in an incomplete state. In the vicinity stands the 102-ft. high Nelson Monument, carrying a time-ball, which is lowered daily at 1 p.m. for the benefit of mariners. The monument is open daily, 8 to dusk. The City Observatory and the Playfair Monument are other notable structures on Calton Hill, on the lower slopes of which are the Burns Monument and *St. Andrew's House*, the administrative centre for Scotland, erected in 1937.

THE UNIVERSITY. The old buildings were designed in 1789 by Robert Adam, and completed by Playfair in 1827, while the dome dates from 1883. The library is of particular interest, and in more recent years modern extensions to the University, including the McEwan Hall, have been built. On the site of the old buildings stood once a house belonging to the Kirk o'Field, and in this house, in 1567, Darnley and his page were blown up by gunpowder. The University was actually founded in 1582, and was at one time known as the College of King James. In the vicinity, to the south, off Meadow Walk, is George Square (1766), with fine classic-style houses. No. 25 was Sir Walter Scott's home during his earlier years.

CHARLOTTE SQUARE. "Robert Adam, Architect to the Square, 1791," is the signature on the original drawings now preserved in the City Chambers. The square is pre-eminent among the architectural ensembles of Britain, and indeed Europe. It was the fitting culmination of the New Town development and to Adam's work as Scotland's greatest architect. No. 5, on the superb north side, is now the office of The National Trust for Scotland.

REGISTER HOUSE. An imposing design of 1774 by Robert Adam, the building housing the archives of Scotland and other interesting papers and relics, including the Articles of Union of 1706, with the relevant signatures. Open Mon. to Fri., 9 to 4.45 (Sat., 9 to 12.30). Nearby is East Register Street, ascending steeply to the 18th cent. St. James's Square. Robert Burns lived here in 1787.

GLADSTONE'S LAND. A fine old six-storeyed house, in the Lawnmarket, the work of Thomas Gladstone, an Edinburgh burgess, in 1620, and now N.T. Scot. It preserves Edinburgh's last arcaded ground floor and also several notable painted ceilings. Open Mon. to Fri., 2 to 5. The house is now the home of the Saltire Society. Nearby are the picturesque Riddle's Close and Macmorran's Close, the latter containing the old house of Bailie Macmorran, who was shot during a school riot in 1595.

The historic Castle, which was captured by Edward I in 1296 and re-taken by the Scots in 1314. The original name was 'Duneadain', meaning 'Fort on a slope.' It overlooks Princes Street and the Old Town

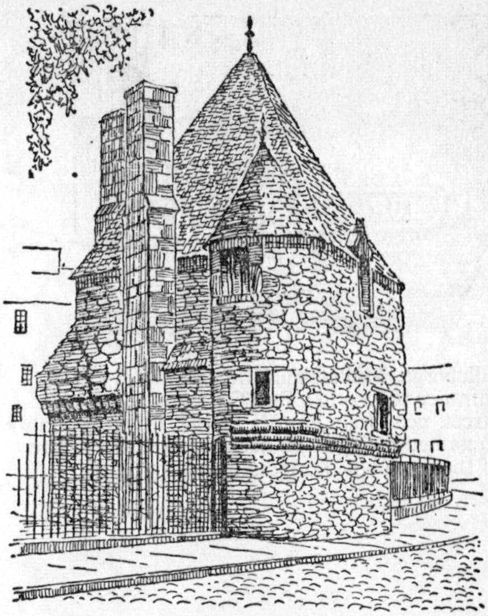

A small building, known as the Queen's Bath House, outside the Palace of Holyroodhouse. It was originally a lodge, or pavilion, and a richly decorated dagger was found here during restoration work in 1852

Remains of the Chapel Royal of Holyrood Abbey, which was sacked in 1688

The unfinished National Monument on Calton Hill, commenced in 1822 in honour of the Scottish dead in the Napoleonic campaigns

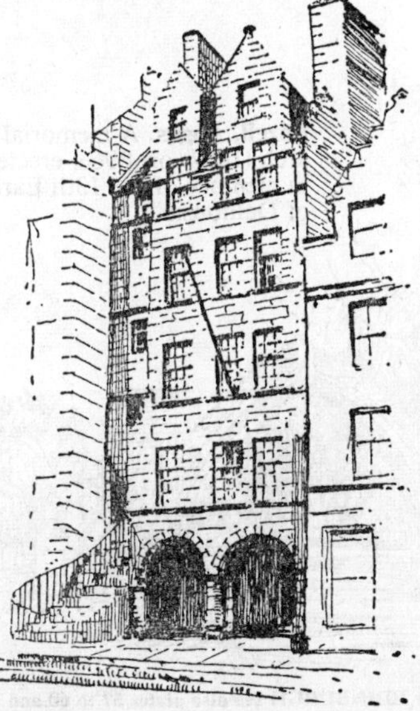

Gladstone's Land, a 16th and 17th century house in the Lawnmarket, which has been preserved by the National Trust for Scotland. It is the only building in Edinburgh to preserve its arcaded front.

The archway made from the jawbones of a whale, which stands on The Meadows, to the south of the Old Town

[For EDINBURGH see also Plates 57 to 59, 61 and 174

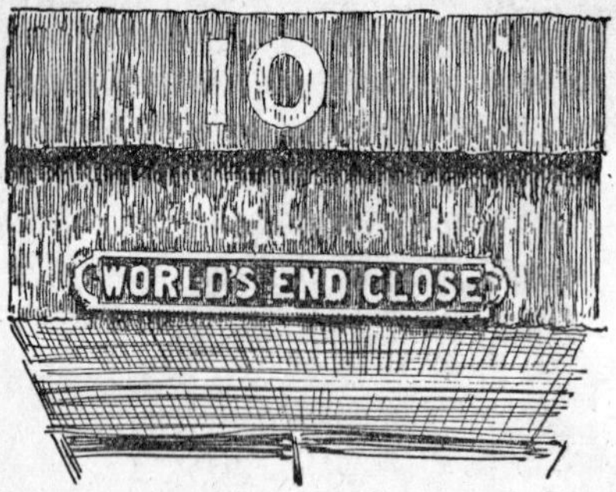

Edinburgh, Midlothian. The inscription at the entrance to World's End Close, off the High Street, near John Knox's House. It was probably so named owing to its distance from the centre of the town when originally built

Edinburgh, Midlothian. White Horse Close, a courtyard in the 'Royal Mile,' in which is situated the restored 17th century 'White Horse Inn,' associated with Sir Walter Scott's '*Waverley*'

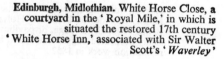

Edinburgh, Midlothian. The tablet on Huntly House, the former residence of the Marquis of Huntly, which dates from 1570 and is now a museum, including old panelling and manuscripts of Robert Burns and Sir Walter Scott

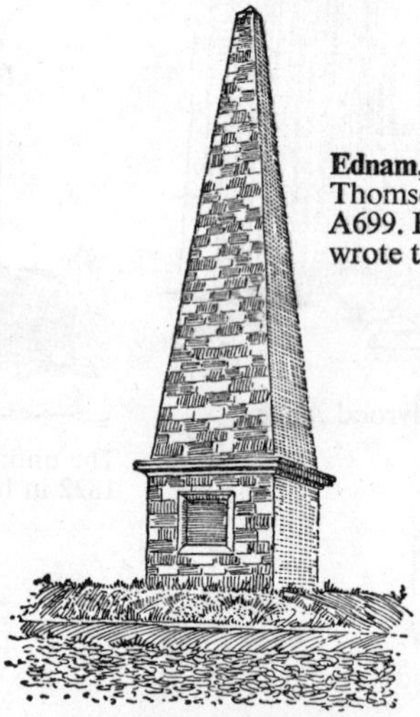

Ednam, Roxburgh. The obelisk to James Thomson, at Ferniehill, to the south, off A699. He was born at Ednam, in 1700, and wrote the words of '*Rule Britannia*'

Edzell, Angus. A memorial arch (1887) on B966, erected in memory of the 13th Earl of Dalhousie

Edrom, Berwick. The Norman entrance doorway to a burial vault at the church

[For EDINBURGH see also plates 57 to 60 and 174

MERCAT CROSS. This famous Cross, facing the City Chambers in the Royal Mile, is modern, but preserves part of the ancient shaft, having been restored in 1885 by Gladstone. Royal Proclamations are read from here. The former Cross was demolished in 1756. Nearby is the site of the old Tolbooth, Scott's " Heart of Midlothian," now marked by setts and a heart-shaped design in the causeway. The old building, built originally in 1466, became later a prison, and was stormed in the Porteous Riots of 1736, being finally demolished in 1817. The well-known Advocate's Close is nearby.

JOHN KNOX'S HOUSE. A picturesque 15th cent. building, thought to have been lived in by John Knox, and shown weekdays only, 10 to 5. The house preserves old wooden galleries, and was built by the goldsmith to Mary, Queen of Scots. Nearby stood the Netherbow, one of the city gates, associated with the'45 Rising, and removed in 1764.

CANONGATE TOLBOOTH. One of the most fascinating old landmarks of the Royal Mile, dating from 1591, and showing a curious projecting clock, the building having been used formerly as a prison and courthouse. It is open weekdays, 10 to 5. The restored *Canongate* Church, built in 1688, and with a stag's antlers supporting a cross on the gable, stands nearby, and in the churchyard is buried Adam Smith, the famous 18th cent. economist.

MORAY HOUSE and ACHESON HOUSE. Two interesting old houses in the Royal Mile, the former, which dates from 1628, and has historic associations, preserving fine ceilings, and being used as a school, while the latter, built in 1633, possesses a quaint courtyard, and has been well restored. It now houses a Scottish Craft Centre display. Facing Moray House are *Bible Land* and *Morocco Land*, both of 17th cent. date, showing interesting carvings. Adjacent is the old-world Bakehouse Close, and nearby is the site of *Panmure House*, once the home of Adam Smith.

WHITE HORSE CLOSE. Perhaps the most picturesque of the courtyards, or closes in the Royal Mile, and in which is situated the restored " *White Horse* " Inn, an early 17th cent. posting house, associated with Scott's " Waverley."

GEORGE HERIOT'S HOSPITAL SCHOOL. This splendid structure, commenced in 1628 by William Wallace, was not completed until 1693, and was at first used as a military hospital. It was founded by George Heriot, a wealthy jeweller, and the " Jingling Geordie " of Scott's " Fortunes of Nigel." The building, which possesses a fine quadrangle, is now a well-known school. Open Mon. to Fri., 9 to 5; Sat., 9 to 12. Between Heriot's Hospital and the Castle is the *Grassmarket*, the scene of execution of many Covenanters in the 17th cent., the site of the gallows being marked by a cross in the pavement. The Porteous Riots of 1736 ended here with the hanging of Captain Porteous by a furious mob.

ART GALLERIES AND MUSEUMS

NATIONAL GALLERY. A modern building, containing a large collection of paintings of various important schools. Open weekdays, 10 to 4 or 5; Sun., 2 to 5.

ROYAL SCOTTISH ACADEMY. Founded in 1823, and originally known as the Royal Institution. An exhibition is held annually from April to August, and other collections are on view weekdays only, 10 to 9 in summer; 10 to 5 in winter, when exhibitions are held.

ROYAL SCOTTISH MUSEUM. Opened in 1866, and containing the United Kingdom's greatest display under one roof of the decorative arts, natural history, geology and technology. There are art and sculpture collections from all over the world; animals in many habitat groups; an internationally famous collection of fossil fishes; and halls devoted to mining, shipping, aeronautics and power. Open weekdays, 10 to 5; Sun., 2 to 5.

NATIONAL PORTRAIT GALLERY. The exterior is embellished by statues of eminent Scotsmen by native artists. There are collections of historical portraits, and also statuary. (See below.) Open weekdays, 10 to 4 or 5; Sun., 2 to 5.

NATIONAL MUSEUM OF ANTIQUITIES. Housed in the same building as the National Portrait Gallery, described above. The exhibits consist of prehistoric and historic collections, illustrating the development of human life in Scotland. Among many interesting objects are relics associated with Mary, Queen of Scots, Prince Charles Edward, Sir Walter Scott, and Robert Burns. There is also a remarkable collection of antiquities excavated at Traprain Law near *East Linton* (*q.v.*), as well as a fine oak door from the tower of *Amisfield* (*q.v.*). Open weekdays, 10 to 5; Sun., 2-5. The annexe at 18 Shandwick Place, known as the *Museum Gallery*, is open weekdays only, 10 to 5.

HUNTLY HOUSE: CITY MUSEUM. This fine old house, once the town residence of the Marquis of Huntly, dates from 1570, and preserves a unique timbered front. There are collections of special interest to lovers of Edinburgh, including some relics of both Burns and Scott. Open weekdays, 10 to 5; on Wed., from June to Sept., open 6 to 9. Also on Sun., 2 to 5, during Festival.

LADY STAIR'S HOUSE. A severely restored old house, dating from 1622, and situated in Lady Stair's Close. It is now a branch of the City Museum, and contains relics of Burns, Scott and Stevenson. Open Mon. to Fri., 10 to 4; Sat., 10 to 1. During Festival period, 10 to 5 (Sun., 2 to 5).

MUSEUM OF CHILDHOOD. Situated in Hyndford's Close, in the Royal Mile, and containing an exhibition of children's toys, dress and books, made for and also by children. Open weekdays, 10 to 5. During Festival period also on Sun., 2 to 5.

TRANSPORT MUSEUM, Shrubhill, Leith Walk. Old trams and buses and a collection of uniforms. Open Mon. to Fri., 10 to 5; Sat., 10 to 1.

See also **Cramond Bridge, Currie, Dalkeith, Lasswade, Musselburgh, Pinkie House, Queensferry (South), Roslin** and **Swanston.** For " Through Routes " see page 46. *Iter. 1, 2, 3, 4, 5, 6, 7, 8, 9, 10, 11, 12, 13, 14, 15, 16, 17, 18, 19, 20, 21, 22, 23, 24, 25, 89, 90, 91, 92, 93, 94, 95, 96.*

EDNAM, Roxburgh. 568. Map 11, **NT 7 3.**
The birthplace, in 1700, of James Thomson, who wrote the words of " Rule Britannia," and to whom an obelisk has been erected at *Ferniehill*, to the south. The village stands on the Eden Water, here spanned by a bridge, on which, in 1952, a plaque was affixed, to commemorate Henry Francis Lyte, the hymnologist, and author of "Abide with me," who was born in a nearby house. **2 m. W.** of Ednam, across the Eden Water, is the mansion of *Newton Don*, partly 17th cent. *Iter. 39, 46.*

EDROM, Berwick. 748. Map 11, **NT 8 5.**
In the Church (A.M.), the *Blackadder* aisle has a tomb dated 1553. A Norman outside doorway is the entrance to a burial vault.

EDZELL, Angus. 1,034 with Lochlee. Map 21, **NO 6 6.**
E.C. Thurs. GOLF. This little inland resort lies between Strathmore and the Howe of the Mearns, and is situated just to the west of the North Esk River, which forms here the Kincardine boundary. The river flows through the attractive Glen Esk, to the north-west, which is threaded by a road penetrating as far as lonely *Lochlee* (*q.v.*) in the eastern Grampian, or Benchinnan mountains, with *Mount Keen*, 3,077 ft., rising in the background to the north. A little to the west of Edzell, near the West Water, a tributary of the North Esk, stands the ruined *Edzell Castle* (A.M.) of the Lindsays, preserving the fine Stirling tower, and the bower used by Mary, Queen of Scots. The most remarkable feature of the lay-out is the walled garden, dating from 1604, with its curious square recesses in the walls, perhaps unique. A turreted garden-house has also survived, and at the adjoining farm is a fine dovecote. Open 10 to 7, summer; 10 to 4, winter; Sun., 2 to 7 or 4. (See note page 98.) See **Fettercairn** and **Tarfside.** *Iter. 156, 163, 164.*

EGILSAY, ISLE OF, Orkney. Map 33, **HY 4** 2 and **4** 3. See **Orkney Islands** (Egilsay).

EIGG, ISLE OF, Inverness. Map 12, **NM 4** 8. See **Rum.**

EILDON HILLS, Roxburgh. Map 10, **NT 5** 3. The triple-peaked *Eildons*, attaining 1,385, 1,327 and 1,216 ft. respectively, with an indicator on the highest point, form a prominent feature in the landscape of the *Scott Country* (*q.v.*). The views from the summit are far-reaching and include a long stretch of the River Tweed. To Sir Walter Scott these hills were especially dear. See **Melrose** and **Scott's View.**

EILEAN DONAN CASTLE, Ross and Cromarty. See **Dornie.** *Iter. 207, 220.* Map 24, **NG 8** 2.

ELDERSLIE, Renfrew. 5,476. Map 8, **NS 4** 6. The town is the traditional birthplace of William Wallace. A modern memorial has been erected near an old house, perhaps on the site of the patriot's former home. *Iter. 58, 63.*

ELECTRIC BRAE, Ayr. Map 8, **NS 2** 1. See **Dunure.** *Iter. 49, 80.*

ELGIN, Moray. 16,401. SB. Map 26, **NJ 2** 6. **E.C.** Wed. **M.D.** Fri. GOLF. The windings of the River Lossie, in the fertile Laigh of Moray, almost encircle the Royal Burgh of *Elgin*, known best for its ruined Cathedral (A.M.), one of the finest ecclesiastical monuments in Scotland. Part of the town was burned in 1390 by the notorious Wolf of Badenoch, whose castle was *Lochindorb* (*q.v.*), and who treated the Cathedral likewise, while in 1452 Elgin again suffered severely. The town was visited by Prince

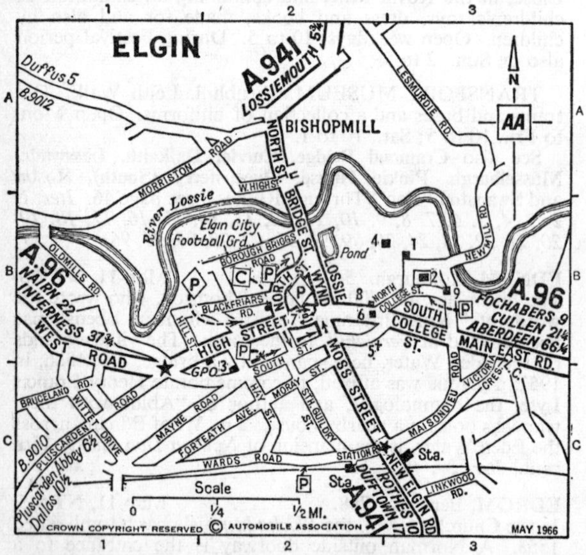

Bishop's Palace	1 (B3)	Greyfriars Chapel	5 (B2)
Cathedral	2 (B3)	Little Cross	6 (B2)
City Chambers. Information Bureau	3 (C2)	Muckle Cross	7 (B2)
		Museum	8 (B2)
Grant Lodge Library	4 (B2)	Panns Port	9 (B3)

Charles Edward before Culloden, and in 1773 Dr. Johnson and Boswell stayed there. Near *St. Giles'* Church, rebuilt in 1826, is the Muckle Cross, and in the High St. is the restored 17th cent. Little Cross. The 15th cent. *Greyfriars* Chapel has been restored. The Georgian *Grant Lodge* houses the Museum and Library, and the house of Duff of Braco, with its arches, dates from 1694. The domed *Gray's* Hospital dates from 1815. In *Thunderton House* (1650), now an hotel, Prince Charles Edward stayed prior to Culloden in 1746. On Lady Hill, where stood the former castle, is the Gordon Monument. The Cathedral, once known as the "Lantern of the North," had already suffered from a serious fire before the visitation of the Wolf of Badenoch, and in the 16th and 17th cents. more disasters befell it, culminating in the fall of the central tower in 1711, after which the building became a quarry until 1807. Of the surviving portions, much work of the 13th cent. can still be admired, notably the choir, in which is situated the founder's grave, while the nave and chapter house date from the 15th cent., the latter in a tolerably good state of preservation. A cross-slab, possibly of 6th cent. date, with strange Pictish symbols, can be seen in the choir. In the south choir aisle are several noteworthy tombs, and in the burial ground, south of the Cathedral, are numerous tombstones with quaint inscriptions. The Panns Port, or East Gate, is the sole surviving gate from the precincts, and a wing of the Bishop's Palace, dated 1406, is still standing. **5 m. N.E.** is *Innes House*, a fine mansion, built between 1640 and 1653, perhaps by the designer of *George Heriot's Hospital School, Edinburgh* (*q.v.*). **6 m. N.** is the well-known resort of *Lossiemouth* (*q.v.*), with its harbour of *Branderburgh.* See **Birnie, Duffus, Lhanbryde, Pluscarden** and **Spynie.** *Iter. 175, 189, 190, 192, 198, 199.*

ELGOL, Isle of Skye, Inverness. Map 23, **NG 5** 1. The terminal point of the narrow and hilly road which crosses the low Strathaird peninsula on its way from *Broadford* (*q.v.*). The situation of *Elgol*, on the eastern shore of *Loch Scavaig* (*q.v.*), is very fine, and from the 1,128-ft. high hill behind the village, known as *Ben Meabost*, the view of the *Coolins* (*q.v.*), grouped above Loch Scavaig, has been described as one of the finest in the world. A path goes northwards along the lochside from Elgol to *Camasunary*, from which Loch na Creitheach, under the fine peak of *Blaven*, 3,042 ft., can be reached. The path then turns westwards towards the rocky slopes of *Sgurr na Stri*, 1,623 ft., and fords a stream before reaching the notorious "Bad Step," which requires some care. Access is thus gained to the magnificent scenery of *Loch Coruisk* (*q.v.*), separated by a narrow ridge from Loch Scavaig. The usual approach to Loch Coruisk from Elgol is by motor boat to the head of Loch Scavaig. The island of Soay lies in Outer Loch Scavaig, and away to the south-west is the lofty mountain outline of the island of Rum. To the south of Elgol is Strathaird Point, and north-east of here is the curious Spar Cave, with its stalagmites, generally visited by boat. Curious eroded cliffs, showing deep fissures, overlook the scene. *Iter. 252.*

ELIE, Fife. 895. SB. with Earlsferry. Map 17, **NO 4** 0. **E.C.** Wed. GOLF. The twin resorts of *Elie* and *Earlsferry* stand on either side of a sandy bay between Chapel Ness, to the west, and Elie Ness, to the east. Good sands and bathing are available, and garnets have been found on the beach near Elie. *Gillespie House*, in South Street, Elie, has a fine carved door, dated 1682. The Parish Church is 17th cent., with an octagonal steeple. East of the town, near the sea, stands the *Lady's Tower*, built originally for Lady Janet Anstruther, whom Thomas Carlyle has described. The remains of *Ardross Castle* are not far distant. At Earlsferry is *Kincraig House*, dating from 1680. Westwards from Earlsferry is Kincraig Point, near which is Macduff's Cave. See **Kilconquhar** and **St. Monance.** *Iter. 94, 98, 132.*

ELLISLAND, Dumfries. Map 3, **NX 9** 8. See **Auldgirth.**

ELLON, Aberdeen. 2,263. SB. Map 27, **NJ 9** 3. **E.C.** Wed. **M.D.** Mon. GOLF. On the River Ythan, in the agricultural Formartine district. The Earl's Mount is an ancient mote-hill. **5 m. N.** is the late 16th cent. *Arnage Castle.* See **Collieston, Methlick** and **Tarves.** *Iter. 181, 183, 185, 187.*

ELPHIN, Sutherland. Map 29, **NC 2** 1. Lies almost on the Ross-shire border, on the fringe of the wild *Assynt* country, and in a lonely setting of mountain and loch. To the south rise the *Cromalt* hills, forming the boundary with Ross and Cromarty, and eastwards lies Loch Urigill. Westwards, in Drumrunie Forest, is *Cul Mor*, 2,786 ft., overlooking Loch Veyatie and the Cam Loch, a little to the north of Elphin. Beyond rises the spectacular double-topped peak of *Suilven*, 2,399 ft., the sharp eastern cone of which is well seen from Elphin. See **Inchnadamph.** *Iter. 224, 225.*

ELSRICKLE, Lanark. Map 9, **NT 0** 4. *Iter. 37, 52.*

Eilean Donan Castle, Ross and Cromarty. The restored Macrae stronghold, bombarded by the British frigate 'Worcester' in 1719, in order to dislodge a party of Spaniards supporting an abortive Jacobite Rising. It stands near the meeting point of Lochs Duich, Alsh and Long, south of Dornie Bridge, and is linked by a causeway to A87

Elderslie, Renfrew. The Memorial to William Wallace, who is said to have been born near here

CROY BRAE
(ELECTRIC BRAE)

Electric Brae, Ayr. This hill, known also as Croy Brae, is on the Girvan road (A719), 2 miles south of Dunure. Owing to certain configurations of the land, a car appears to be descending the hill when it is in fact ascending

Elgin, Moray. The ruined Cathedral, which has suffered many vicissitudes, including its sack by the Wolf of Badenoch in 1390

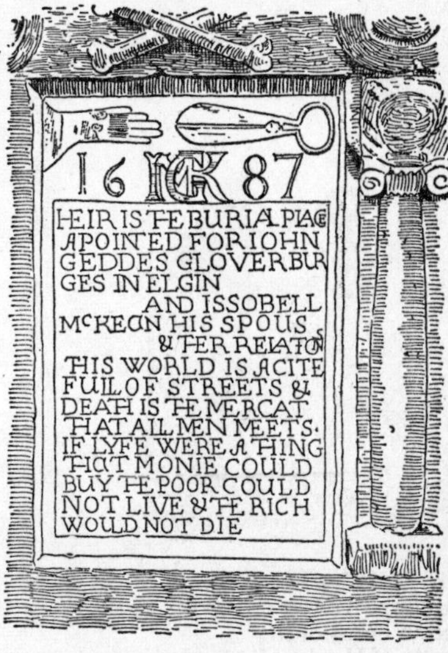
16 87
HEIR IS THE BURIAL PLACE
APOINTED FOR IOHN
GEDDES GLOVER BUR
GES IN ELGIN
AND ISSOBELL
MCKEAN HIS SPOUS
& THER RELATON
THIS WORLD IS A CITE
FULL OF STREETS &
DEATH IS THE MERCAT
THAT ALL MEN MEETS.
IF LYFE WERE A THING
THAT MONIE COULD
BUY THE POOR COULD
NOT LIVE & THE RICH
WOULD NOT DIE

Elgin, Moray. The inscription on a gravestone of 1687 in the Cathedral churchyard

Elie, Fife. The carved doorway of Gillespie House, in the High Street, which is dated 1682

[For ELGIN see also under LAIGH OF MORAY (Plate 104)

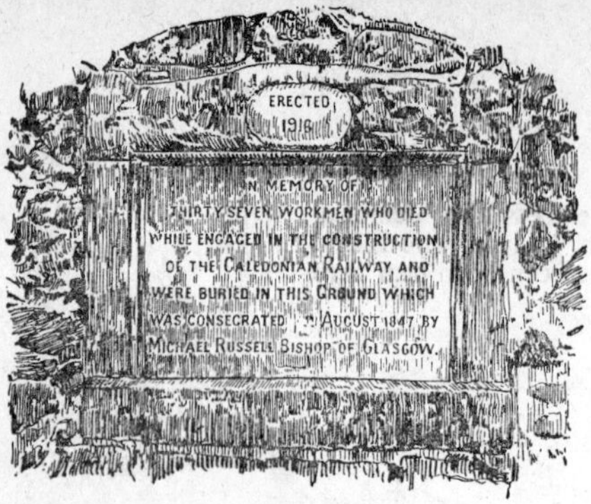

Elvanfoot, Lanark. Plaque in the burial ground near the bridge over the River Clyde. It records the death from cholera, in 1847, of 37 men working on the Caledonian Railway who were afterwards buried on the spot

Erskine, Renfrew. The tall Monument in memory of the 11th Lord Blantyre, who was killed in the Brussels riots of 1830. It stands off B815, some 2 miles to the west

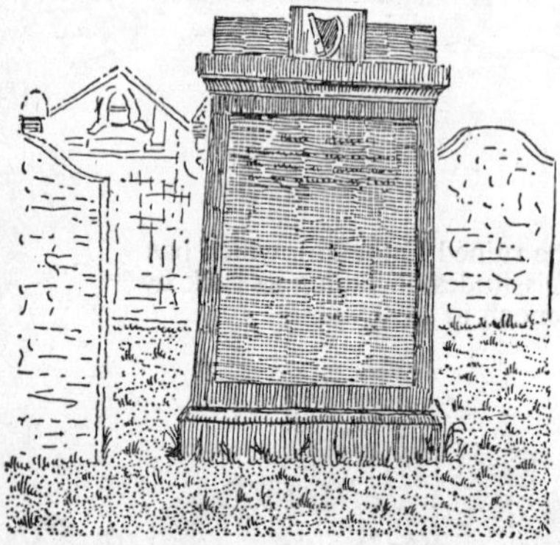

Ettrick, Selkirk. The grave of James Hogg, the poet, known as the 'Ettrick Shepherd,' who died in 1835. Nearby is the grave of Tibbie Shiel, who was hostess of the famous inn by St. Mary's Loch which bears her name

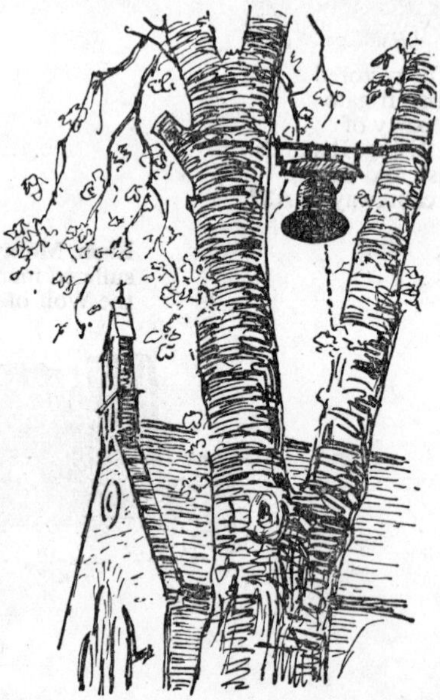

Ewes, Dumfries. The 300-year old church bell, which hangs in the fork of a tree

Eyemouth, Berwick. The early 17th century Linthill House, where, in 1751, the wealthy Mrs Patrick Hume is said to have been murdered by her butler. It stands 1½ miles to the south-west, on an unclassified road

Ettrick Bridge End, Selkirk. Kirkhope Tower, c. 1600, once a home of the Scotts of Harden. It stands on an unclassified road to the north-west

Eyemouth, Berwick. Gunsgreen House, a centre for smugglers' activities during the 18th century. The nearby tower is believed to have been erected by Cromwell in 1650

[For ETTRICK BRIDGE END see also Plate 173

ELVANFOOT, Lanark. Map 9, **NS 9** 1.
Here, in a setting of Lowland hills, the Elvan Water unites with the Clyde in the upper part of Clydesdale. The Telford bridge over the Clyde on A74 has been replaced by a new bridge. South of the village, the tiny Clydes Burn is joined by the combined streams of the Daer Water and the Potrail Water, Elvanfoot being the first place on the true Clyde river. To the north-west is *Harryburn Brae*, 1,629 ft., and to the east rise *Harleburn Head*, 1,776 ft., and *Clyde Law*, 1,789 ft., the latter forming the border with Peeblesshire. A road leading south-westwards towards the Nith Valley traverses the picturesque, winding Dalveen Pass, which attains a height of 1,140 ft. across the Dumfries border, and above which, to the north, rises *Comb Head*, 1,998 ft., an outlier of the *Lowther* hills. Another road also leads south-westwards, by way of *Leadhills* (*q.v.*), and reaches Nithsdale through the fine Mennock Pass. See **Beattock, Enterkinfoot** and **Mennock.** *Iter. 25, 49, 56.*

EMBO, Sutherland. Map 31, **NH 8** 9.
E.C. Thurs. A coastal village on the Outer Dornoch Firth, associated with " Granny's Heiland Hame."

ENTERKINFOOT, Dumfries. Map 3, **NS 8** 0.
A hamlet in Upper Nithsdale, from which an old track climbs through the hills to emerge near the northern extremity of the Mennock Pass, over 1,400 ft. in height, on the outskirts of *Leadhills* (*q.v.*). This track goes by way of the narrow and deep Enterkin Pass, overshadowed by *Green Lowther*, 2,403 ft., and where a party of dragoons was once trapped by the Covenanters, as described by Defoe. To the south-east of Enterkinfoot, a short link connects with the fine road traversing the Dalveen Pass, with *Comb Head*, 1,998 ft., an outlier of the *Lowthers*, rising to the west. This pass reaches a height of 1,140 ft. before descending to *Elvanfoot* (*q.v.*) in the valley of the Clyde. See **Carronbridge** and **Mennock.** *Iter. 27, 48, 67.*

ERIBOLL, Sutherland. Map 28, **NC 4** 5.
Situated on the road traversing the eastern shores of the wild and beautiful Loch Eriboll, a safe anchorage, which penetrates deep into the Sutherland mountains, with *Grann Stacach*, 2,630 ft., and *Beinn Spionnaidh*, 2,537 ft., to the west at its head. Away to the south-east, beyond Loch Hope, is *Ben Hope*, 3,040 ft., the most northerly peak of over 3,000 ft. in Scotland. South-westwards, beyond Strath Beag, rises *Foinaven*, 2,980 ft., with the lonely Loch Dionard at its foot. See **Heilim** and **Hope Lodge.** *Iter. 225.*

ERISKAY, ISLE OF, Inverness. Map 32, **NF 7** 0.
See **Hebrides, Outer** (South Uist).

ERROGIE, Inverness. Map 25, **NH 5** 2.
A hamlet on the west shores of Loch Mhor, situated at an altitude of over 600 ft., a few miles east of *Loch Ness* (*q.v.*). Near the east shores of Loch Mhor is the estate of *Easter Aberchalder*, noted for its fine rock gardens. Loch Mhor is now a reservoir, uniting the waters of Lochs Garth and Farraline, and feeding the Foyers river for use in the aluminium works near *Foyers* (*q.v.*). Beyond Loch Mhor, to the east, stretch bare and lonely moorlands culminating in *Carn Odhar*, 2,618 ft. See **Inverfarigaig.** *Iter. 211, 212.*

ERROL, Perth. 1,833. Map 17, **NO 2** 2.
E.C. Thurs. A village in the fertile *Carse of Gowrie* (*q.v.*), near the Firth of Tay, facing the Fife coast. The Earls of Errol take their title from the name. **2 m. N.** is *Megginch Castle*, dating partly from 1575. Farther north is *Fingask Castle*, 16th cent. and later. *Iter. 154.*

ERSKINE, Renfrew. Map 8, **NS 4** 7.
The former car-ferry has been replaced by a fine new bridge opened in 1971. It by-passes Glasgow and takes traffic to *Old Kilpatrick* (*q.v.*), Dunbartonshire. The 19th cent. *Erskine House*, now a hospital, was built for Lord Blantyre, to whom a tall obelisk stands in the vicinity. The Parish Church of Erskine was built in 1813. See **Bishopton.** *Iter. 88, 109, 110, 111, 112, 113.*

ESHANESS, Shetland. Map 33, **HU 2** 7.
See **Shetland Islands** (Mainland). *Iter. 267.*

ESKBANK, Midlothian. Map 10, **NJ 3** 6.
See **Newbattle.** *Iter. 9, 11, 12, 37.*

ESKDALEMUIR, Dumfries. 794 Map 4, **NY 2** 9.
Roads from Lockerbie and Langholm converge here, at the northern end of picturesque Eskdale. The continuation northwards through lonely hill country, with *Ettrick Pen*, 2,269 ft., to the west, leads towards the valley of the Ettrick Water, reaching a height of nearly 1,100 ft., near the Selkirk border. To the north of the Church is the Roman Camp of *Raeburnfoot*. **3 m. N.** of the road junction is the well-known *Eskdalemuir* observatory, erected in 1908, and situated at a height of nearly 700 ft. Prehistoric remains are to be found in the district in various places, and **4 m. S.** of Eskdalemuir Church, in the angle formed by the White Esk and Black Esk Rivers before their junction, is the notable hill-fort of *Castleoer*, on a lofty ridge. *Iter. 12, 42.*

ETTRICK, Selkirk. 487. Map 10, **NT 2** 1.
The little Church of *Ettrick* stands about a mile to the west of the Selkirk to Eskdalemuir road, on the Ettrick Water, which emerges from a valley hemmed in by lofty hills, dominated by the remote and lonely *Ettrick Pen*, 2,269 ft. In the churchyard lies James Hogg, the " Ettrick Shepherd," who died in 1835, and also the well-known Tibbie Shiel (See **Tibbie Shiel's Inn**), who died in 1878 at the age of 96. A little to the east of the Church stands the Hogg monument, on the site of the former cottage where he was born in 1770. The Eskdalemuir road follows the valley of the Tima Water southwards, climbing to a height of more than 1,000 ft. nearing the Dumfries border. See **Ettrick Bridge End, St. Mary's Loch** and **Tushielaw Inn.** *Iter. 12, 42.*

ETTRICK BRIDGE END, Selkirk. Map 10, **NT 3** 2.
On the Ettrick Water, and in the extensive Ettrick Forest, formerly a Royal hunting-ground, and which once gave its name to the county. The old river bridge was washed away in 1777, but a stone from it, bearing the Harden coat of arms, and associated with Sir Walter Scott, has been built into the present structure. A by-road leads north-westwards over the hills to *Yarrow* (*q.v.*), passing near the 16th cent. tower of *Kirkhope*, once a home of the Scotts. **2 m. N.E.,** near the river, in a picturesque setting, is *Oakwood Tower*, the home of Scott's grandfather, having been built by Robert Scott in 1602. In the vicinity are remains of the Roman fort of *Oakwood*. **5 m. S.W.,** off the road to *Tushielaw* (*q.v.*), is *Deloraine*, the home of William of Deloraine, in Scott's " Lay of the Last Minstrel." *Iter. 42.*

EVANTON, Ross and Cromarty. 372. Map 25, **NH 6** 6.
E.C. Thurs. Stands just inland from the waters of Cromarty Firth, where the Allt Grand river flows into the Firth. The river, known farther west as the Glass, emerges from Loch Glass, **5 m. N.W.,** in the foothills of *Ben Wyvis*, 3,429 ft. To the north of Loch Glass is the smaller Loch Morie, below *Meall Mor*, 2,419 ft. A little to the west of Evanton, a path leads near the stream to the remarkable ravine known as the Black Rock of Novar. **2½m. S.W.** of Evanton is the 18th cent. Clan Munro seat of *Foulis Castle*, the original structure having been burnt. *Iter. 200, 201.*

EVIE, Orkney. Map 33, **HY 3** 2.
See **Orkney Islands** (Mainland). *Iter. 263.*

EWES CHURCH, Dumfries. Map 4, **NY 3** 9.
The Church bell, 300 years old, hangs outside, high up in the fork of a lime tree. On Sorbie Bridge, in the vicinity, a tablet commemorates the Rev. Henry Scott Riddell, the author of " Scotland Yet."

EYE CHURCH, Isle of Lewis, Ross and Cromarty.
Map 32, **NB 5** 3.
See **Hebrides, Outer** (Lewis). *Iter. 259.*

EYEMOUTH, Berwick. 2,529. SB. Map 11, **NT 9** 6.
E.C. Thurs. GOLF. A busy little fishing town and resort, on the Eye Water, where it flows into the sea between Hare

Point and Nestends. The breakwater by Smeaton dates from 1770. The jagged *Hurkers* rocks protect the harbour. The beach is partly sandy, with bathing. In 1881 a gale destroyed much of the fishing fleet, with heavy loss of life. The coast scenery, both to the north and to the south, is rocky and picturesque, with caves and caverns once used for smuggling, and at Hare Point are remains of a fort. *Netherbyres* was at one time the home of Sir Samuel Brown, who, in 1820, built the Union Suspension Bridge across the Tweed near *Paxton* (*q.v.*). **1½ m. S.W.** is *Linthill House*, early 17th cent. This house is said to have been the scene of a gruesome tragedy in the 18th cent. see **Burnmouth** and **Coldingham.** *Iter. 2, 41.*

FAILFORD, Ayr. Map 8, **NS 4 2.**
Here, the Water of Fail flows into the River Ayr. A monument commemorates the parting of Robert Burns from his "Highland Mary," an Argyllshire dairymaid by the name of Mary Campbell. *Iter. 35.*

FAIR ISLE, Shetland. Map 33, **HZ 2 7.**
See **Shetland Islands** (Fair Isle).

FAIRLIE, Ayr. 975. Map 8, **NS 2 5.**
E.C. Wed. A small Firth of Clyde resort, with a sandy beach and a pier used by the *Arran* (*q.v.*) steamers. In *St. Margaret's* Church is the ancient Fairlie Stone. The resort is situated opposite the island of *Great Cumbrae*, on which stands *Millport* (*q.v.*). South of the island is *Little Cumbrae*, which is separated by a narrow channel from the much larger island of *Bute* (*q.v.*). Away to the south-west rise the mountains of Arran. In a glen to the east is the ruined *Fairlie Castle*, dated 1521, and to the north of the town is *Kelburne Castle*, a late 16th cent. tower, joined to a house dating from 1700. **3 m. S.S.W.** of Fairlie is *Hunterston Castle*, an old tower, with modern additions. *Iter. 66, 88.*

FAIRMILEHEAD (Edinburgh), Midlothian.
Map 9, **NT 2 6.**
A little to the west, on the road to *Colinton* (*q.v.*), is the cottage known as the *Hunter's Tryst*, associated with R. L. Stevenson's "St. Ives." Nearby is the *Caiy Stone* (N.T. Scot.), a prehistoric monolith. *Iter. 14, 25.*

FAIRNILEE, Selkirk. Map 10, **NT 4 3.**
On the River Tweed, with the mansion of *Yair House*, built in 1788, situated west of Yair Bridge over the river, and having as a background the hill known as *Three Brethren*, 1,523 ft. *Fairnilee House*, and its ruined tower, stand high above the Tweed, among trees, and in the tower Alison Cockburn wrote in the 18th cent., her version of the "Flowers of the Forest." *Iter. 14.*

FALKIRK, Stirling. 27,587. LB.
Map 16, **NS 8 7.**
E.C. Wed. GOLF. A town of importance for its coal-mining and the great Carron iron works, but once noted as a collecting-place, or trust for cattle, brought to *Stenhousemuir*, about three miles to the north-west, along numerous drove roads from all parts of the Highlands. Two battles were fought near Falkirk, in 1298 and 1746, in the former of which Wallace was defeated, while in the latter Prince Charles Edward was victorious. The Prince spent the night in a bootmaker's shop opposite the new Falkirk Steeple. In the High Street is the *Cross Keys* Inn, visited by Burns. In Dollar Park is a museum. The town house dates from 1813. There are some 19th cent. brewery buildings. Near the town flow the Forth and Clyde and Union Canals, with locks on the former. The Scottish Railway Preservation Centre has an interesting depot at Wallace St. In the private grounds of the fine mansion of *Callender House*, east of the town, are some well-preserved portions of the Antonine, or *Roman Wall* (*q.v.*). Mary, Queen of Scots visited the house on several occasions between 1562 and 1567. Other sections of the wall (N.T. Scot.) lie to the west of Falkirk, towards Bonnybridge, including the fort known as "Rough Castle." See **Glenelg, Grangemouth, Polmont** and **Westerglen.** *Iter. 17, 95, 113, 114, 115.*

FALKLAND, Fife. 941. SB. Map 17, **NO 2 0.**
E.C. Thurs. This picturesque little Royal Burgh, with its cobbled streets and old weaver's cottages, is best known for *Falkland Palace* (N.T. Scot.), a favourite seat of the Scottish Court from the time of James V, who died here, after having done much to improve its amenities. His daughter, the future Mary, Queen of Scots, used to hunt from the Palace. Both Charles I and Charles II visited Falkland, and Rob Roy occupied it in 1715, after the battle of Sheriffmuir. The Royal Tennis court of 1539 still exists. The buildings are in the Renaissance style, dating from 1530-1540, with a fine façade to the south wing, and containing a banqueting-hall, now a Chapel, showing a good screen and 17th cent. tapestries. In 1654, the east wing was burnt when occupied by Cromwell's troops. Scott, in his "Fair Maid of Perth," has introduced the story of the Duke of Rothesay, who is said to have been starved to death in one of the dungeons. The palace is open weekdays, 10 to 6; Sun., 2 to 6, April to Oct. (See note page 98.) The Town House, with its spire, dates from 1805. A house in the square carries an inscribed panel to Richard Cameron, a Covenanter martyr, born in 1648, who is associated with the raising of the Cameronian regiment. On Green Hill stands a monument to O. Tyndall-Bruce, an Englishman, who, in 1849, restored the Palace and built the Church. To the south rise the *Lomond* hills, with *East Lomond*, 1,471 ft., in the immediate background, and *West Lomond*, 1,713 ft., the highest point in the range, to the west, overlooking *Loch Leven* (*q.v.*). See **Linlithgow.** *Iter. 130.*

FALLS OF CRUACHAN, Argyll. Map 14, **NN 0 2.**
These falls are situated at the eastern end of the dark and gloomy Pass of Brander, overlooking the waters of Loch Awe. In 1308, Robert Bruce routed the MacDougalls of Lorne in the pass. In the background is *Ben Cruachan*, 3,689 ft., with its twin summits, which can be climbed from a point west of the falls, and which forms a magnificent

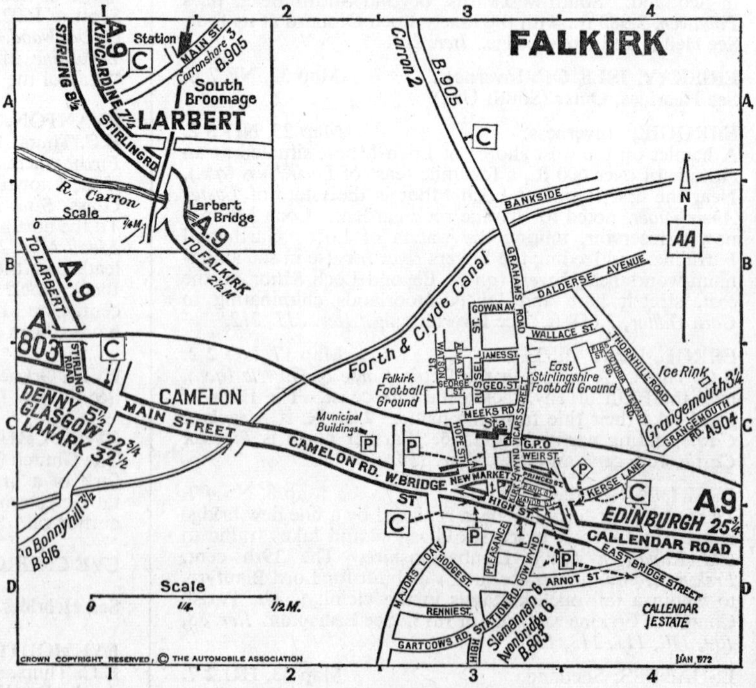

Bootmaker's shop where Prince Charles Edward spent a night in 1746 1 (D3)

Failford, Ayr. The Monument which commemorates Robert Burns's parting from his 'Highland Mary,' on May 14th, 1786

Fairlie, Ayr. The entrance to the 16th century and later Kelburne Castle, a seat of the Earl of Glasgow

Fairmilehead, Midlothian. The Caiy Stone (N.T. Scot.), a prehistoric monolith

Falkirk, Stirling. The bootmaker's shop on the site of a house in which Prince Charles Edward spent a night during the '45 Rising

Falkland, Fife. The entrance to the 16th century Palace, from which Mary, Queen of Scots, used to hunt. It is now the property of the National Trust for Scotland

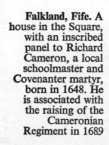

Falkland, Fife. A house in the Square, with an inscribed panel to Richard Cameron, a local schoolmaster and Covenanter martyr, born in 1648. He is associated with the raising of the Cameronian Regiment in 1689

(For FAIRY BRIDGE see under DUNVEGAN (Plate 54)

Farr, Sutherland. An ancient sculptured stone in the churchyard

Fearn, Ross and Cromarty. The restored Abbey Church, which was moved here in 1338 from its original site at Edderton, near the Dornoch Firth

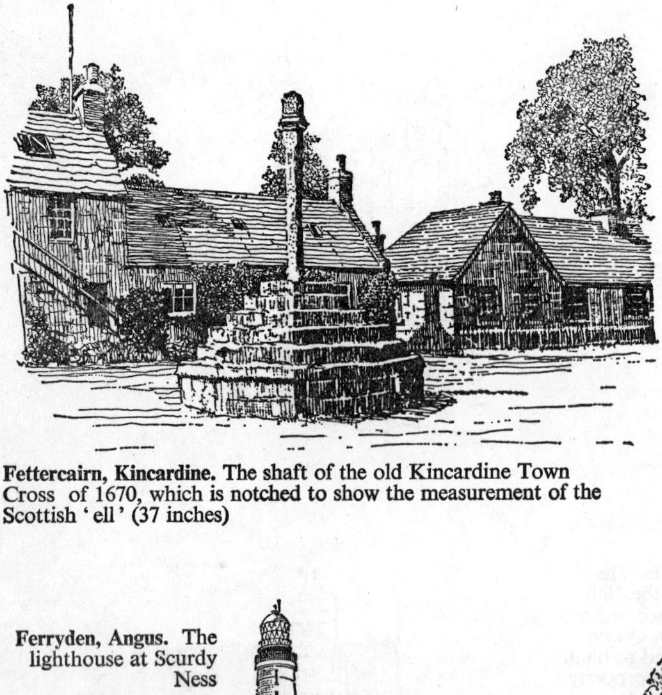

Fettercairn, Kincardine. The shaft of the old Kincardine Town Cross of 1670, which is notched to show the measurement of the Scottish 'ell' (37 inches)

Fenwick, Ayr. One of a number of Covenanter monuments in the churchyard

Ferryden, Angus. The lighthouse at Scurdy Ness

Ferniehirst Castle, Roxburgh. The late 16th century Castle, which is now used as a Youth Hostel. It was a seat of the old Border family of Ker

[For FALLS OF MEASACH see under BRAEMORE JUNCTION (Plate 22)

viewpoint, the prospect embracing the picturesque *Lorne* (*q.v.*) country. including Loch Etive and *Loch Linnhe* (*q.v.*). In the Pass of Brander is a river barrage that is part of the Loch Awe hydro-electric scheme. See **Kilchurn Castle** and **Loch Awe.** *Iter. 110, 117, 125, 144, 145.*

FALLS OF GLOMACH, Ross and Cromarty. Map 24, **NH 0** 2.
These lofty falls, with a drop of over 350 ft., are situated in an estate of more than 2,000 acres (N.T. Scot.), and are some of the highest in Britain, but are somewhat difficult of access. They can be approached from *Ardelve* (*q.v.*) by means of a road along Loch Long, which continues through Glen Elchaig. The falls themselves can be reached only on foot, from the western end of Loch na Leitreach in Glen Elchaig, and by means of a rough and arduous climb of some 1½ hours on a steep and narrow unfenced path (care necessary in wet conditions) along the west bank of the stream descending from the hills. Another method of approach is from the head of *Loch Duich* (*q.v.*), at *Croe Bridge* (*q.v.*), a long-distance walkers' path leading for about 7 miles through the hills to the falls by way of Dorusduain and the rough and steep 2,000-ft. high Bealach na Sroine. South-east of the falls rises the remote and massive peak of *Sgurr nan Ceathreamhnan*, 3,771 ft. See **Kintail** and **Kylesku.**

FALLS OF LENY, Perth. Map 15, **NN 5** 0.
See **Callander.** *Iter. 107, 111, 139, 141, 142, 144.*

FALLS OF MEASACH, Ross and Cromarty. Map 29, **NH 2** 7.
See **Braemore Junction.** *Iter. 204, 206, 222.*

FALLS OF ROGIE, Ross and Cromarty. Map 25, **NH 4** 5.
These picturesque falls, on the River Blackwater, have an attractive wooded background, and can be reached from the road near *Achilty Inn* (*q.v.*). *Iter. 204, 205, 206, 221.*

FALLS OF SHIN, Sutherland. Map 29, **NH 5** 9.
See **Inveran Bridge.**

FARR, Sutherland. 552. Map 30, **NC 7** 6.
A little to the south of the village, which lies just off the Bettyhill to Thurso road, is the delightful little Farr Bay, and northwards is Farr Point, overlooking the stormy waters of the Pentland Firth. The little 18th cent. Church, south of Farr Bay is described under *Bettyhill* (*q.v.*). *Iter. 232, 234, 240.*

FASKALLY, Perth. Map 20, **NN 9** 5.
See **Pitlochry.**

FASLANE, Dunbarton. Map 14, **NS 2** 8.
Near the head of the Gare Loch. In a local graveyard are buried men from the submarine K.13, which sank in the loch in 1917. Large vessels are broken up here for scrap, these having included the battleships "Malaya" and "Renown," and also the famous Cunard liner "Aquitania." Faslane is now a Polaris submarine base. *Iter. 102, 111, 116.*

FEARN, Ross and Cromarty, 1,261. Map 31, **NH 8** 7.
Lies in the fertile stretch of country between the Cromarty and Dornoch Firths. The restored Abbey Church was originally situated at *Edderton* (*q.v.*), but was moved to its present site in 1338. In 1742, the Chapel roof collapsed, killing a number of people. An interesting tomb may be seen in the South Chapel, near the Shandwick burial-place. **2½ m. N.E.**, near the shores of Loch Eye, is the ruined *Lochslin Castle.* **4½ m.** N.E. is *Geanies House*, with fine gardens and views of the Moray Firth. See **Balintore.**

FEARNAN, Perth. Map 16, **NN 7** 4.
A small *Loch Tay* (*q.v.*) resort, to the west of the wooded *Drummond Hill.* It is convenient for visiting the beautiful Glen Lyon, which can be reached by way of *Fortingall* (*q.v.*), along a short piece of road crossing the River Lyon a mile to the north of Fearnan. See **Kenmore.** *Iter. 120, 138.*

FENWICK, Ayr. Map 8, **NS 4** 4.
Situated on the Fenwick Water, with a moorland area to the east. The restored Church, built originally in 1643, contains a post-Reformation pulpit and the jougs are preserved. There are Covenanter monuments in the churchyard, and one inscription recalls Scott's "Old Mortality." **2 m. S.** stands the seat of *Crawfurdland Castle*, given to the Hewison-Crawfurds by James V as a reward for his rescue from footpads at *Cramond Bridge* (*q.v.*). *Iter. 19, 55, 61.*

FEOLIN FERRY, Isle of Jura, Argyll. Map 6, **NR 4** 6.
See **Jura.**

FERNESS, Nairn. Map 25, **NH 9** 4.
On the River Findhorn, which, to the south, enters upon one of its loveliest reaches, in a setting of woods and high rocky banks, culminating in what is perhaps the finest scenery of its entire length at *Dulsie Bridge* (*q.v.*). **4 m. N.E.** of Ferness, near *Daltulich Bridge*, off the *Forres* (*q.v.*) road, is the Morayshire beauty spot known as "Randolph's Leap," reached on foot, and situated in the Findhorn Glen at a point near the confluence of the Findhorn and the Divie, another most picturesque scene. Nearby are the fine grounds of *Relugas House.* A stone, near the meeting of the two rivers, commemorates the record height of the waters reached during the great floods of 1829. See **Ardclach Church** and **Logie.** *Iter. 173, 176.*

FERNIEHIRST CASTLE, Roxburgh. Map 10, **NT 6** 1.
This fine late 16th cent. Castle, now a Youth Hostel, stands a little to the east of the Jed Water, in a lovely wooded setting, and replaced an earlier structure, destroyed in 1571. It played its part in the many fierce Border fights throughout the years, and was many times besieged and frequently changed hands. The castle is L-shaped, and carries the Ker arms on several panels, while the great hall is of note and contains a huge fireplace. See **Jedburgh.** *Iter. 4, 43, 52.*

FERRYDEN, Angus. Map 21, **NO 7** 5.
On the estuary of the South Esk River, facing *Montrose* (*q.v.*). *Craig House* dates from 1637 and earlier. East of the village is Sandy Ness, with its lighthouse.

FESHIE BRIDGE, Inverness. Map 25, **NH 8** 0.
The bridge crosses the fine gorge of the River Feshie, to the east of the little village, which stands at the mouth of the picturesque, wooded Glen Feshie, extending deep into the *Cairngorms* (*q.v.*), rising north of Glen Feshie Forest. (See **Kincraig.**) Wade planned to build a road through the glen, in order to link Speyside with Deeside, reaching the latter near the *Linn of Dee* by *Inverie* (*q.v.*), but the road was never constructed. Apart from the walkers' track through the wild *Lairig Ghru Pass* (*q.v.*), the only means of proceeding from the Spey valley to that of the Dee is by making the long road detour by way of *Tomintoul* (*q.v.*). See **Insh** and **Rothiemurchus.** *Iter. 138, 149.*

FETLAR, ISLE OF, Shetland. Map 33, **HU 6** 9.
See **Shetland Islands** (Yell).

FETTERCAIRN, Kincardine. 1,115. Map 21, **NO 6** 7.
E.C. Thurs. An attractive village, on the edge of the fertile Howe of the Mearns, with the heights of the eastern Grampians in the background. In the square is the shaft of the old Kincardine Town Cross, dating from 1670, and notched to show the measurements of the Scottish "ell." An arch commemorates the visit of Queen Victoria and the Prince Consort in 1861. At *Fettercairn House*, interesting letters and papers relating to the Boswell family were discovered in 1931. **2 m. N.E.**, off the Stonehaven road, are the ruins of *Kincardine Castle,* on the site of the former county town of Kincardine, and once a Royal residence. This Castle is associated with Macbeth, whose head was brought here to the waiting Malcolm, after the defeat of the former at *Lumphanan* (*q.v.*). **1 m. S.W.** is *Balbegno Castle*, which dates partly from the 16th cent. See **Cairn o' Mounth** and **Clattering Bridge.** *Iter. 156, 163, 165.*

FEUGHSIDE INN, Kincardine. Map 21, **NO 6** 9.
Situated near the Water of Feugh, almost on the Aberdeen border, and on the road linking the *Cairn o' Mounth* (*q.v.*) with Deeside in the vicinity of *Kincardine o' Neil* (*q.v.*). An

alternative road to the main Deeside road, linking Aboyne with Banchory, also passes by the Feughside Inn. Away to the west extends the great Forest of Birse. *Iter. 165, 174.*

FIFE KEITH, Banff. Map 26, **NJ 4** 5.
See **Keith.**

FINCASTLE, Perth. Map 19, **NN 8** 6.
To the north-west is *Old Fincastle*, a 17th cent. house, with a small loch. *Iter. 138, 148.*

FINDHORN, Moray. 480. Map 26, **NJ 0** 6.
E.C. Thurs. A little resort and fishing village, situated on the east side of the sandy Findhorn Bay, facing the Moray Firth. The two previous villages have both vanished, the first being engulfed by the *Culbin Sands* (*q.v.*), and the second by the floods of 1701. Findhorn was once one of the chief exporting towns of Moray. To the south, across the bay, into which flows the River Findhorn, can be seen the distant town of *Forres* (*q.v.*). See **Kinloss.** *Iter. 199.*

FINDOCHTY, Banff. 1,227. SB. Map 26, **NJ 4** 6.
A quaint little fishing village with sands, situated between Craig Head and Long Head, on a rocky part of the coast, with Spey Bay to the west. See **Portessie** and **Portknockie.** *Iter. 199.*

FINDON, Kincardine. Map 21, **NO 9** 9.
A fishing village (stone and shingle foreshore) known also as Finnan, a name which is associated with smoked haddocks.

FINGAL'S CAVE, Isle of Staffa, Argyll. Map 13, **NM 3** 3.
See **Staffa.**

FINHAVEN, Angus. Map 21, **NO 4** 5.
On the River South Esk, and known alternatively as *Finavon*. The ruined *Finhaven Castle* (c. 1500), to the south of the river, was a former Crawford stronghold. Beyond the Castle rises the *Hill of Finhaven*, a viewpoint with a vitrified fort on the eastern summit. *Iter. 151, 156, 166.*

FINNART, Dunbarton. Map 14, **NS 2** 9.
An ocean terminal oil-port on the eastern bank of *Loch Long* (*q.v.*), north of the Gare Loch. *Iter. 102, 111.*

FINSTOWN, Orkney. Map 33, **HY 3** 1.
See **Orkney Islands** (Mainland). *Iter. 263, 264.*

FINTRY, Stirling. 1,983 with Killearn. Map 15, **NS 6** 8.
The village is set in a hollow, threaded by the Endrick Water, between the *Fintry* hills to the north, and the more extensive and slightly higher *Campsie Fells* to the south, in the heart of what is known as the *Lennox* country. *Culcreuch Tower*, an ancient structure, with 17th cent. additions, lies a little to the north. The Crow Road, leading south-eastwards to *Lennoxtown* (*q.v.*), crosses the *Campsies*, and reaches a height of 1,154 ft., with fine views over the Clyde valley. **3 m. E.** of Fintry, near the Walton reservoir, is the Loup of Fintry, a waterfall on the Endrick Water, the fall being over a 100-ft. high ledge of rock. The narrow and hilly moorland road continues eastwards from here, passing near the site of the former *Sir John de Graham's Castle*, and keeping to the north of the *Kilsyth* hills to reach the flat, industrial area of the county at *Denny* (*q.v.*). *Iter. 107, 114.*

FIONNPHORT, Isle of Mull, Argyll. Map 13, **NM 3** 2.
See **Bunessan.** *Iter. 249.*

FIRTH OF CLYDE, Argyll; Ayr; Bute; Renfrew.
Map 7, **NS 1 5** etc.
The name given to the stretch of water separating the Ayrshire and Renfrewshire coasts from the islands of Arran and Bute and the Cowal shores of the Argyll mainland. The Firth is noted particularly for yachting, and regattas are held both here and in the more confined waters of the Kyles of Bute, which lie farther to the north-west. Among the well-known resorts on the Firth are Ardrossan, Largs, Wemyss Bay and Dunoon, all of which are described individually. *Rothesay* (*q.v.*), in the island of Bute, is associated particularly with the Clyde Yachting fortnight.

FLODIGARRY, Isle of Skye, Inverness. Map 22, **NG 4** 7.
Famous as the early home of Flora Macdonald, who married Allan Macdonald of Kingsburgh, in 1750. The old house is now neighboured by an hotel. In 1746, Flora Macdonald escorted Prince Charles Edward, who was disguised as her maid, from *Benbecula* in the *Outer Hebrides* (*q.v.*) to *Portree* (*q.v.*) in Skye. Dr. Johnson and Boswell were entertained here in 1773, and later her family emigrated to North Carolina, but they returned, and in 1790 Flora Macdonald was buried at *Kilmuir* (*q.v.*). Off-shore, opposite Flodigarry, is the little Eilean Flodigarry, while a little inland are the rocks and pinnacles of *Leac na Fionn*, rising above Loch Langaid near the fantastic *Quiraing* (*q.v.*). *Iter. 254.*

FLOORS CASTLE, Roxburgh. Map 10 **NT 7** 3.
This magnificent house, in its great park, near the River Tweed, stands immediately to the north-west of *Kelso* (*q.v.*). It was designed, in 1718, by Vanbrugh, but was altered later by Playfair, and shows Tudor-style work. The palatial "golden" entrance gates to Roxburgh St. in Kelso were set up in 1929. A holly-tree in the grounds is said to mark the spot where, in 1460, James II, while laying siege to the castle of *Roxburgh* (*q.v.*), met his end through the bursting of a cannon. The grounds and gardens are shown with a permit Wed., 10 to 4, in summer (see note page 98). *Iter. 32, 46.*

FOCHABERS, Moray. 1,193. Map 26, **NJ 3** 5.
E.C. Wed. Lies to the east of the River Spey, on the edge of *Speymouth Forest*, where erosion of the soil has taken place. The great park of *Gordon Castle* lies to the north. The Castle, with the exception of one tower, was demolished in 1955. The village stood formerly nearer the Castle, but was removed in the 18th cent., only the Market Cross and jougs remaining. The 19th cent. Church has a pillared portico. Across the Spey, to the west of Fochabers, is *Mosstodloch* (*q.v.*), the bridge over the river being the successor to that destroyed in the floods of 1829. See **Methlick** and **Spey Bay.** *Iter. 175, 187, 198.*

FOGO, Berwick. 350 with Polwarth. Map 11, **NT 7** 4.
The Church has two laird's lofts, dated 1671 and 1677 respectively, one having an outside staircase.

FORD, Argyll. Map 14, **NM 8** 0.
A small anglers' resort, with a steamer pier, between the south-western extremity of *Loch Awe* (*q.v.*), and the little Loch Ederline. The road along Loch Awe follows the south shores, and passes, after two miles, the ruined *Fincharn Castle*, which is faced across the loch by Inverliver Woods. Another road parallels the north shores of the loch and leads to Dalavich and *Kilchrenan* (*q.v.*). See **Kilmartin** and **Portinnisherrich.** *Iter. 119.*

FORDOUN CHURCH, Kincardine. 1,347. Map 21, **NO 7** 7.
This is situated **3 m. N.N.W.** of the Brechin to Stonehaven road, on the edge of Drumtochty Forest. In the churchyard of the small Church, standing on a steep bank above the River Luther, is a fragment of the ancient Chapel of *St. Palladius*, an Irish Bishop. Almost adjacent to the church is the village of *Auchinblae*. A road goes north-westwards from here, circling round *Finella Hill*, 1,358 ft., and passing *Drumtochty Castle*, now a school, before reaching *Clattering Bridge* (*q.v.*). **1½ m.** N.E. of Auchinblae stands *Monboddo House*, once the home of the 18th cent. judge, Lord Monboddo, and visited by Dr. Samuel Johnson in 1773. *Iter. 151.*

FORDYCE, Banff. 1,419. Map 26, **NJ 5** 6.
Delightfully situated a little to the south of the Portsoy to Cullen road. In the centre of the village stands the small late 16th cent. *Fordyce Castle*, with some fine corbelling, dormer windows, and an angle tower overlooking the street. **1½ m. N.W.** is the mansion of *Birkenbog*, with a fine walled garden. Here, in 1645, Thomas Nicholson, the first Vicar-Apostolic of Scotland, was born. See **Deskford.** *Iter. 198.*

FOREST PARKS
Argyll, See **Arrochar** (for Ardgartan) and **Benmore Estate.**
Border, See **Bonchester Bridge** and **Newcastleton.**
Glenmore, See **Aviemore, Loch Morlich** and **Rothiemurchus.**
Glen Trool, See **Loch Trool** and also **Barr, Clatteringshaws Dam** and **Newton Stewart.**
Queen Elizabeth, See **Aberfoyle, Rowardennan** and **Trossachs.**

FORFAR, Angus. 10,500. SB. Map 21, **NO 4** 5.
E.C. Thurs. **M.D.** Mon./Fri. GOLF. The Royal Burgh of *Forfar* stands in flat country between the two little lochs of Forfar and Fithie, lying respectively to the west and east,

Findon, Kincardine. A scene at the village, which has given its name to smoked haddocks, known as ' Finnan haddies.' They were at one time cured here in the local peat-reek

Fintry, Stirling. The Loup of Fintry waterfall, which lies 3 miles to the east, off B818

Floors Castle, Roxburgh. The 18th century and later Castle, designed originally by Vanbrugh. It stands just outside Kelso, to the north-west, off A6089. In Roxburgh Street, Kelso, are the so-called ' golden gates ' leading to the castle drive, which were erected in 1929, and display ornate wrought-iron work overlaid with gold-leaf

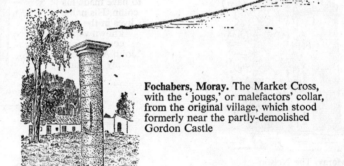

Fochabers, Moray. The Market Cross, with the ' jougs,' or malefactors' collar, from the original village, which stood formerly near the partly-demolished Gordon Castle

Fogo, Berwick. The Church, which has an outside staircase giving access to the private laird's loft of the Trotters of Charterhall, dating from 1671

Fordyce, Banff. The small 16th century Castle, which is still lived in, and overlooks the village street

[For FORFAR see following plate

Forfar, Angus. The Town Hall, in which is kept the Forfar ' bridle ' or gag, used for witches

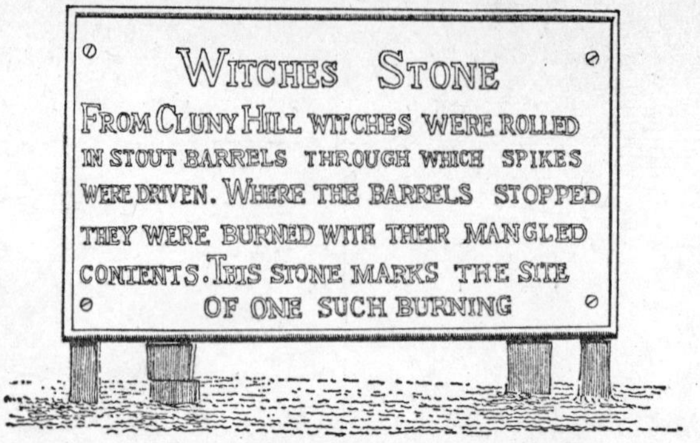
WITCHES STONE
FROM CLUNY HILL WITCHES WERE ROLLED
IN STOUT BARRELS THROUGH WHICH SPIKES
WERE DRIVEN. WHERE THE BARRELS STOPPED
THEY WERE BURNED WITH THEIR MANGLED
CONTENTS. THIS STONE MARKS THE SITE
OF ONE SUCH BURNING

Forres, Moray. The Witches Stone inscription. It is situated near the police station

Fort Augustus, Inverness. The grave of John Anderson, a carpenter, who died here in 1832. He was an old friend of Robert Burns, and is said to have made his coffin. His name lives in the well known verses commencing: ' John Anderson, my jo John '

Forres, Moray. The Nelson Monument, on Cluny Hill, to the east of the town, off A96

Fort Augustus, Inverness. The Benedictine Monastery of 1876, on the site of the former castle, which was built after the Jacobite Rising of 1715, and taken by the Highlanders during the 1745 Rising

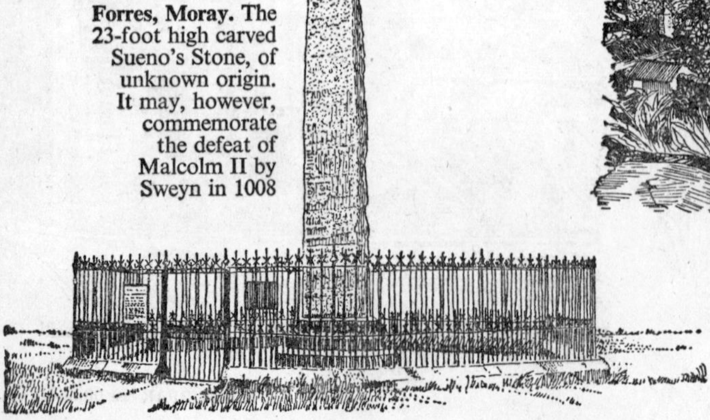

Forres, Moray. The 23-foot high carved Sueno's Stone, of unknown origin. It may, however, commemorate the defeat of Malcolm II by Sweyn in 1008

[For FORTEVIOT see following plate

and at the north-eastern extremity of the fertile Vale of *Strathmore* (*q.v.*), here known as the Howe of Angus. Near the Forfar Loch was once fought a battle between the Scots and the Picts. In the Town Hall is preserved the Forfar "bridle," or gag. The site of the Castle is marked by an octagonal turret, once the Town Cross. A track, known as the "King's Codger's Road," formerly led to the coast at *Usan* (*q,v,*), along which fresh fish was brought to the former

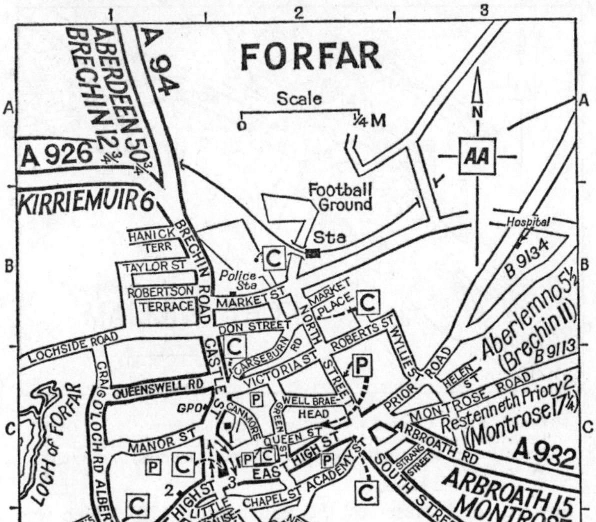

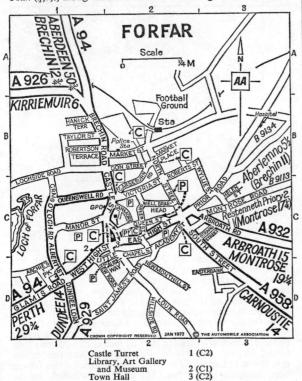

Castle Turret	1 (C2)
Library, Art Gallery and Museum	2 (C1)
Town Hall	3 (C2)

Royal Castle. To the north-east, between the two roads leading towards Brechin, is the *Hill of Finhaven*, a fine viewpoint, crowned by a vitrified fort. (See **Finhaven.**) **2 m. N.E.** of Forfar, near Loch Fithie, is the ruined *Restenneth Priory* (A.M.), with a very early tower, the remainder of the work being mainly of the 12th cent., though the broach spire dates probably from the 15th cent. **4 m. S.E.**, and to the east of the Carnoustie road, is *Dunnichen*, once known as *Nectan's Mere*, near which was the scene, in 685, of a great battle, when Ecgfrith, King of the Angles, was defeated and slain. As a result of this battle Scotland's future as an independent country was at the time assured. See **Glamis** and **Kirriemuir.** *Iter. 151, 153, 156, 162.*

FORGUE, Aberdeen. 980. Map 27, **NJ 6** 4.
Lies on the Burn of Forgue, a tributary of the Deveron, which flows a few miles to the north of the village. The Church preserves what is said to be the oldest silver communion cup (1629) in Scotland. *Iter. 184.*

FORRES, Moray. 4,710. SB. Map 26, **NJ 0** 5.
E.C. Wed. **M.D.** Tues. GOLF. The town, which is of great antiquity, stands a little to the right of the widening River Findhorn, near the point where it enters Findhorn Bay. Shakespeare, in "Macbeth," has mentioned it under the name of "Fores." A little to the east, where the roads to *Findhorn* (*q.v.*) and *Elgin* (*q.v.*) diverge, stands the well-known *Sueno's Stone* (A.M.)., a remarkable carved pillar, of unknown origin. Near the police station is the "Witches' Stone," where local witches were once burnt. On *Cluny Hill*, to the east of the town, is the Nelson Monument, a good viewpoint. **6 m. S.W.**, to the south of the road to *Auldearn* (*q.v.*), and on the west bank of the Findhorn, is Darnaway Forest, in which stands the modern *Darnaway*

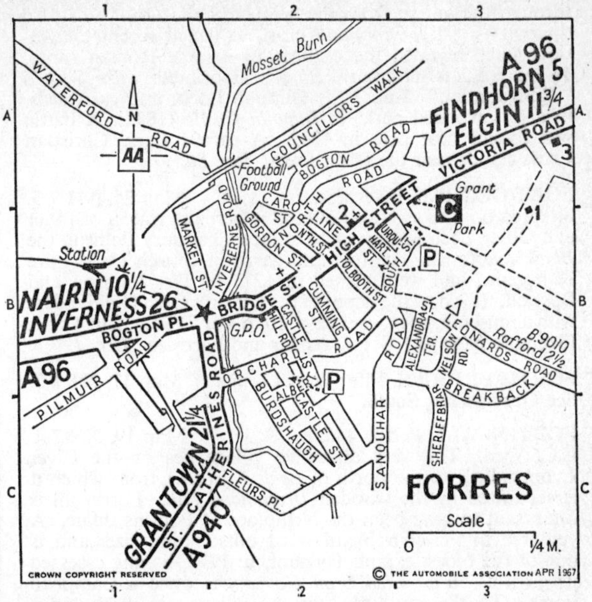

Nelson Monument 1 (B3) Town Hall 2 (B2) Witches' Stone 3 (A3)

Castle, retaining the 15th cent. hall of an earlier structure, and belonging to the Earls of Moray. Mary, Queen of Scots stayed here in 1562. The scenery in the valley to the south, where the river flows between the forest and the woods of *Altyre*, is of exceptional beauty. See **Brodie, Culbin Sands, Ferness, Findhorn, Kinloss, Lochindorb** and **Logie.** *Iter. 172, 173, 175, 198, 199.*

FORSINARD, Sutherland. Map 30, **NC 8** 4.
An anglers' resort, lying between Strath Halladale and Achintoul Forest, with *Ben Griam Beg*, 1,803 ft., and *Ben Griam Mhor*, 1,936 ft., to the west. **4 m. S.** is Loch an Ruathair, off the Helmsdale road. *Iter. 234.*

FORT AUGUSTUS, Inverness. 887. Map 24, **NH 3** 0.
E.C. Wed. GOLF. The village of *Fort Augustus*, once known as *Kilcummin*, or *Killichiumen*, stands on the fine modern highway, partly on the line of General Wade's road of 1725-26, linking Fort William with Inverness by way of *Glen More* (*q.v.*). Fort Augustus is well known to anglers, and is situated in a setting of hills and woods, at the south-western extremity of *Loch Ness* (*q.v.*), near the point where it is entered by the *Caledonian Canal* (*q.v.*), with its six locks. The former fort, which took its name from Augustus, Duke of Cumberland, was built after the 1715 rising, and Wade enlarged it in 1730. In 1745, the Highlanders took it, but the government regained it after the battle of Culloden, and in 1876 a Benedictine Abbey was built on the remains of the fort. Wade linked Fort Augustus with Speyside by means of his famous road over the lofty *Corrieyairack Pass* (*q.v.*), but the crossing is no longer possible, except for hardy long-distance walkers. Neil Munro, in his "New Road," has described the making of the road. From Fort Augustus, a military road went formerly north-westwards over the hills to reach Glen Moriston, and was used in 1773 by Dr. Johnson and Boswell, who stayed at Fort Augustus. The former declared he spent there his best night for 20 years. The old Wade road to Inverness climbs steeply eastwards from Fort Augustus, crossing the wooded Glen Doe, and passing Loch Tarff, before ascending to 1,275 ft., with good views, on the way to *Whitebridge* (*q.v.*). There are Forestry Commission developments on the western shores of Loch Ness, including the recently-founded village of *Inchnacardoch*. See **Invergarry** and **Wade Roads.** *Iter. 210, 211, 212, 213.*

FORTEVIOT, Perth. 894. Map 16, **NO 0** 1.
A pleasant Strath Earn village, once a Pictish capital, as was also *Dunstaffnage* (*q.v.*). The river is a little to the north, where it is joined by the Water of May, flowing

through the village from the heights of the *Ochil* hills. To the south-west is *Broomhill* farm, at which recent excavations have revealed the outlines of a large Roman camp. **1½ m. S.E.** is *Invermay House*, associated with Scott's "Redgauntlet." **2 m. N.** is Dupplin Loch, and eastwards, in a fine wooded park, is *Dupplin Castle* (1832). A battle was fought near here in 1332. A carved Early Christian Cross stands near the River Earn. *Iter. 86.*

FORT GEORGE, Inverness. Map 25, **NH 7 5.** Situated on a narrow spit of land, where the waters of Inner and Outer Loch Moray unite to face Chanonry Point in the *Black Isle* (*q.v.*). The fort and garrison church (A.M.) are 18th cent., and were visited in 1773 by Dr. Johnson and Boswell. It is now the depot of the Queen's Own Highlanders with a museum, open weekdays, 10 to 4 or 7; Sun., 2 to 4 or 7. (See note page 98.) See **Ardersier** and **Fortrose.** *Iter. 199.*

FORTH BRIDGES, Fife; West Lothian. Map 17, **NT 1 7.** See **Queensferry, South.**

FORTINGALL, Perth. 446. Map 19, **NN 7 4.** **E.C.** Wed. This very attractive village lies on the River Lyon, a little to the north of *Loch Tay* (*q.v.*), from which it is separated by the wooded *Drummond Hill.* Fortingall is often said to have been the birthplace of Pontius Pilate. A yew-tree in the churchyard is of outstanding size, and is one of the oldest extant, Pennant, in 1772, having assessed its girth as 56 ft. *Glen Lyon House* was once a Campbell home. To the south-west of the village are earthworks, perhaps once a Roman outpost, and to the east, for some five miles, flows the River Lyon, prior to its confluence with the more important Tay, which has issued from the loch of that name near *Kenmore* (*q.v.*). Westwards from Fortingall stretches Glen Lyon, 25 miles long, in the *Breadalbane* (*q.v.*) country, one of the loveliest of Scottish glens, approached by the richly wooded Pass of Lyon, in which is situated the romantic "Macgregor's Leap." **2 m. W.** in the glen, and to the south of the road, are the Allt do Ghob Falls, after which the road continues westwards, between the peaks of *Cairn Mairg*, 3,419 ft., to the north, and *Ben Lawers*, 3,984 ft., and its satellites, to the south. See **Bridge of Balgie** and **Fearnan.** *Iter. 107, 138.*

FORTROSE, Ross and Cromarty. 1,037. SB. Map 25, **NH 7 5.** GOLF. A quiet *Black Isle* (*q.v.*) resort and Royal Burgh, facing the Inner Moray, or Inverness Firth, and separated by a narrow neck of land, terminating in Chanonry Point, from the Outer Moray Firth. On the opposite shore, facing the Point, is *Fort George* (*q.v.*). The ruined Cathedral (A.M.) is in the styles of the 14th and 15th cents., and the most interesting portion is the vaulted south aisle, in which are several monuments and an old font. The detached Chapter House is now used as a Court House. Cromwell is thought to have used some of the stones of the already derelict building to raise his fortress at *Inverness* (*q.v.*). Inland, to the north-west, is the elevated, wooded ridge known as *Millbuie*, the lordship of which Mary, Queen of Scots bestowed on Darnley. See **Rosemarkie.** *Iter. 203.*

FORT WILLIAM, Inverness. 4,195. SB. Map 18, **NN 1 7.** **E.C.** Wed. A very important touring centre for *Lochaber* (*q.v.*) and the Western Highlands, situated near the western extremity of the Great Glen, or *Glen More* (*q.v.*), by the head of *Loch Linnhe* (*q.v.*), and at the foot of *Ben Nevis* (*q.v.*), 4,406 ft., the highest mountain in the British Isles. For the ascent the town makes a very convenient base. The Ben itself is not visible from the streets of Fort William, but is a landmark for many miles around, and can be well seen from the summit of *Cow Hill*, 942 ft., which rises behind the town. The view includes, in addition, the lower reaches of the beautiful Glen Nevis (See **Ben Nevis**), backed by *Sgurr a' Mhaim*, 3,601 ft., in the *Mamores* (*q.v.*), with its white quartzite top. The entrance to Glen Nevis is near Bridge of Nevis, at the north-east end of the town. The east side of the glen is traversed for the commencement of the long ascent of Ben Nevis. The original Fort was built in 1655 by General Monk, and was rebuilt under William III, when, for a short time, the town was called Maryborough. Both in 1715, and again in 1745, the Jacobites failed to capture the fort. It had been strengthened by General Wade after the first siege. A garrison occupied the fort until 1855, soon after which it was dismantled. The very interesting West Highland Museum exhibits relics, which include the well-known "secret portrait" of Prince Charles

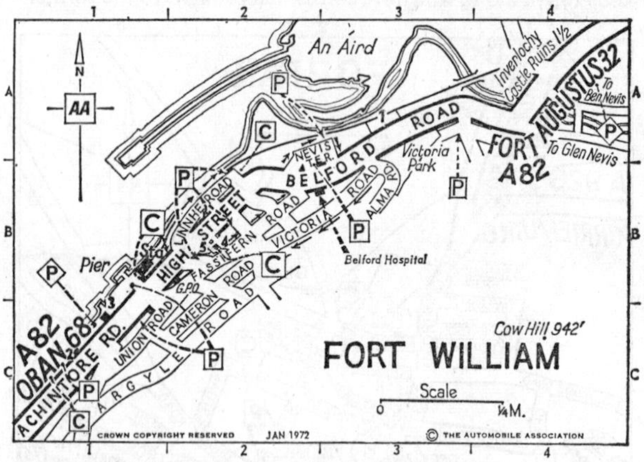

Craig's Burial Ground with gateway from old fort	1 (A3)
Lochaber Tourist Association (Tourist Information Centre)	2 (C1)
Scottish Arts and Crafts Exhibition (Summer months)	3 (C1)
Town Hall	4 (B2)
West Highland Museum	5 (B2)

Edward, and preserves the panelling of 1707 which was formerly in the house of the governor of the Fort. The gateway from the Fort was re-erected in 1896 at *The Craigs*, the old cemetery. From The Rock, west of the gateway, cannons fired on the fort in 1746. The Lochaber Gathering takes place usually during the latter half of August.

To the north-east of the town is a large aluminium factory and power house, fed by the waters of the Lochaber Power Scheme, which are brought here by means of a 15-mile long tunnel through Ben Nevis. Fort William was one of the first towns in Great Britain to be lit by electricity, this having been inaugurated in 1896. Still farther north-east, by the shores of the River Lochy, is the ruined *Inverlochy Castle*, probably dating from the 15th cent. Comyn's Tower, the largest of its circular towers had walls 10 feet thick and rooms 20 feet across. In 1431, the Earls of Mar and Caithness were defeated here in a battle. Another battle was fought near the Castle in 1645, in which the great Marquis of Montrose, of Clan Graham, after some remarkable forced marches through the Lochaber mountains, defeated the Covenanters. The fight has been described in Scott's "Legend of Montrose," and also in Neil Munro's "John Splendid." The modern *Inverlochy Castle* stands about **2 m. N.E.**, in a loop of the little River Lundy, being known also as *Torlundy Castle.* In the vicinity of the castle the rearing of cattle is being carried on in a large way. The main road leading north-eastwards from here towards the Great Glen, on the line of General Wade's original road, gives access beyond *Loch Lochy* (*q.v.*) to *Invergarry* (*q.v.*). From here commences the fine road to *Cluanie* (*q.v.*), Glen Shiel and *Kyle of Lochalsh* (*q.v.*), the terminal point of one of the "Roads to the Isles."

South-westwards from Fort William, the road to *Kinlochleven* (*q.v.*) follows the shores of Loch Linnhe and Loch Leven, but the old road went inland over the lonely hills past Loch Lundavra. Westwards from the town stretch the waters of *Loch Linnhe* (*q.v.*), and to the north-west is Loch Eil, paralleled by the romantic Road to the Isles, "By Ailort and by Morar to the Sea," leading to *Mallaig* (*q.v.*), in a land poignant with memories of Prince Charles Edward and the '45. This road was originally constructed, as far as Arisaig, by Thomas Telford, in 1800-04. The waters of Loch Eil mingle with those of Loch Linnhe beyond the narrows near *Corpach* (*q.v.*), where the *Caledonian Canal* (*q.v.*) has its western terminus. By rounding the head of Loch Eil, and utilizing a narrow and winding road, access

Forteviot, Perth. A splendidly carved Early Christian Cross, situated near Bankhead Farm, off B9112, on a hill near the River Earn

Forth Bridge, Fife; West Lothian. The famous late 19th century railway bridge neighboured by the 20th century road bridge, which was opened in 1964

Fortingall, Perth. The large churchyard yew, which is perhaps the oldest in Great Britain

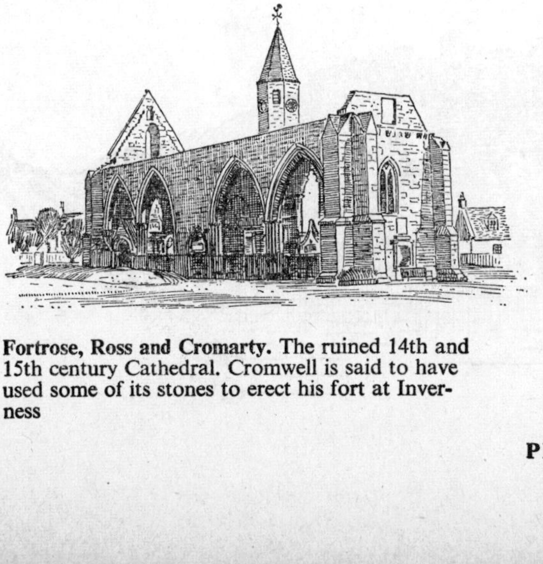

Fortrose, Ross and Cromarty. The ruined 14th and 15th century Cathedral. Cromwell is said to have used some of its stones to erect his fort at Inverness

Fort William, Inverness. The secret portrait mirror of 'Bonnie Prince Charlie,' which is kept in the West Highland Museum

[For FORTINGALL see also under BREADALBANE (Plate 22)

Foulden, Berwick. The two-storeyed tithe barn

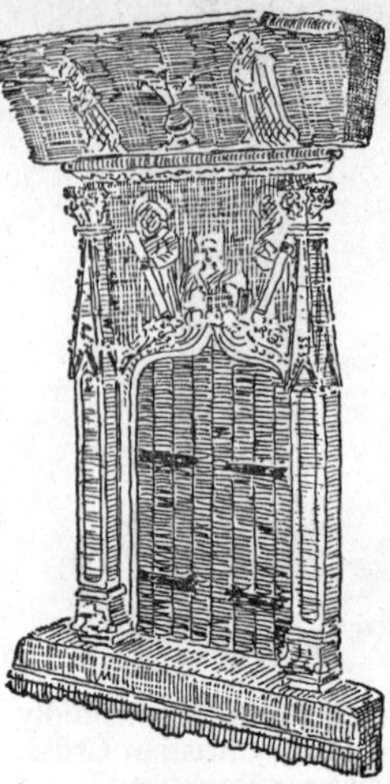

Fowlis Easter, Angus. The richly carved Sacrament House inside the 15th century Church

Fowlis Wester, Perth. The lych-gate of the Church, the inscription above which carries the date 1644

Foyers, Inverness. A stone on B852, near Loch Ness, some 5 miles north-east. It records the site of a 'Change House' (for horses), visited by Dr. Johnson and Boswell during their Highland tour of 1773

Fraserburgh, Aberdeen. The Mercat Cross of 1736 in the fishing port which Sir Alexander Fraser founded in the mid-16th century

Freswick, Caithness. The ruined 15th century Bucholly Castle of the Mowats. It stands near Ness Head

PLATE 69

is gained to the beautiful *Ardgour* (*q.v.*) district, but this journey can be shortened by some 25 miles by following the shores of Loch Linnhe from Fort William, and then utilizing the ferry at *Corran* (*q.v.*). The proposed new name for the communities of Fort William, Inverlochy, Banavie, Corpach and Caol is *Nevisburgh*. See **Ballachulish, Glenfinnan, Kinlocheil, North Ballachulish, Roy Bridge** and **Spean Bridge.** *Iter. 100, 124, 125, 126, 142, 143, 208, 209, 210, 211, 212, 213, 214, 215, 220.*

FOULA, ISLE OF, Shetland. Map 33, **HT 9** 3.
See **Shetland Islands** (Mainland).

FOULDEN, Berwick. 538. Map 11, **NT 9** 5.
Here is an unusual two-storeyed and crow-stepped tithe barn (A.M.). An inscribed churchyard gravestone is dated 1592. *Iter. 3, 9, 33.*

FOWLIS EASTER, Angus. Map 17, **NO 3** 3.
The restored Church, dedicated to *St. Marnan*, dates from 1453, and is of much interest. There is a bell dated 1508, a well-carved font and also a series of notable Pre-Reformation painted panels. The Sacrament House is one of the finest in Scotland, and is elaborately carved. Beside the south door still hang the jougs. *Fowlis Castle* is early 17th. cent.

FOWLIS WESTER, Perth. 896. Map 16, **NN 9** 2.
A quaint little village, lying a short distance to the north of the Crieff to Perth road, with a restored 15th cent. Church, and a Celtic cross, having the jougs attached. There is a lych-gate dated 1644, and a 10-ft. high cross-slab preserves Pictish symbols and Celtic sculpture (A.M.). A little to the north-west, on the moors, are some prehistoric standing stones.

FOYERS, Inverness. 250. Map 25, **NH 4** 2.
E.C. Wed. Overlooking *Loch Ness* (*q.v.*), and best known for its Falls, in a lovely, wooded setting, the upper one being 30 ft. high and the lower 90 ft. high. The volume of water has been much reduced, owing to the demands of the now closed aluminium works which were fed from the Loch Mhor reservoir, on the banks of which stands the little hamlet of *Errogie* (*q.v.*). This hydro-electric scheme, the first in Britain, was completed in 1896. Across Loch Ness rises *Mealfuarvonie*, 2,284 ft., the highest point in the extensive Balmacaan Forest. Foyers is on the line of Wade's road linking Fort Augustus with Inverness, and here the General built for himself a shelter, called the General's hut, the exact location of which is not known today. See **Inverfarigaig** and **Wade Roads.** *Iter. 211.*

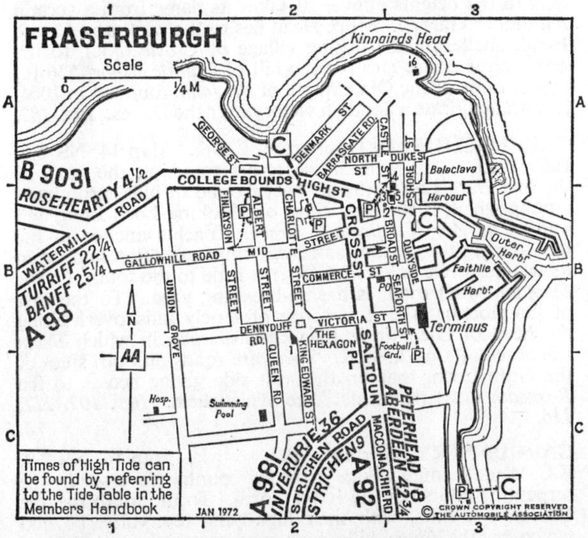

Library	1 (B2)	Old Town House	4 (A3)
Mercat Cross	2 (B3)	Information Bureau	5 (B3)
Old Parish Church	3 (B3)	Wine Tower	6 (A3)

FRASERBURGH, Aberdeen. 10,605. SB. Map 27, **NJ 9** 6.
E.C. Wed. **M.D.** Tues. GOLF. An important *Buchan* (*q.v.*) herring port and resort, situated on Fraserburgh Bay, with fine sands, and sheltered to the west by Kinnaird's Head, which was mentioned originally by Ptolemy. The town was founded in the 16th cent. under the original name of *Farthlie*. The Mercat Cross dates from 1736. The Parish Church was rebuilt in 1899. The lighthouse on Kinnaird's Head, overlooking the North Sea, stands on the remains of a tower built in 1574. Nearby is the *Wine Tower*, probably dating from the 15th cent., built above a 100-ft. long cave called the Scalch's Hole. **3 m. S.E.,** near the Water of Philorth, is the restored *Cairnbulg Castle*. See **Inverallochy, Rosehearty** and **Sandhaven.** *Iter. 181, 182, 185, 186, 196, 197.*

FRESWICK, Caithness. Map 30, **ND 3** 6.
Situated a little inland from Freswick Bay, which is sheltered to the north by Skirsa Head, and to the south by Ness Head. Beyond the latter are remains of the 15th cent. *Bucholly Castle*. There are various prehistoric sites in the neighbourhood. **2 m. N.,** on the *John o' Groats* (*q.v.*) road, is the low Warth Hill, from which the distant Orkneys can be glimpsed. *Iter. 200.*

FRIOCKHEIM, Angus. 585. Map 21, **NO 5** 4.
This curious name is said to be derived from Freke, a one-time bailie of Forfar, and "heim," meaning home, the suffix having been added in 1830 by one John Andson, who had been domiciled in Germany. See **Guthrie.** *Iter. 153, 163.*

FURNACE, Argyll. Map 14, **NS 0** 9.
A *Loch Fyne* (*q.v.*) village, known for its large granite quarry. Smelting-works were formerly situated here. *Iter. 118, 121.*

FUSHIEBRIDGE, Midlothian. Map 10, **NT 3** 6.
See **Carrington, Crichton and Temple.** *Iter. 9, 11, 12.*

FYVIE, Aberdeen. 2,669. Map 27, **NJ 7** 3.
The magnificent *Fyvie Castle*, one of the most imposing in Scotland, stands in a finely wooded park, threaded by the River Ythan. The rich south front, dating from the 15th and 16th cents., was added to in the 17th cent., and the four old turreted towers are named after their builders, Gordon, Meldrum, Preston and Seton. In 1644, Montrose evaded capture here by **Argyll.** Inside the Castle is an exceptionally fine spiral stone staircase. Lord Dunfermline, who completed the 17th cent. alterations, later worked at *Pinkie House* (*q.v.*) in Midlothian. *Iter.* 180.

GAILES, Ayr. Map 8, **NS 3** 3.
See **Troon.**

GAIRLOCH, Ross and Cromarty. 758. Map 22, **NG 8** 7.
E.C. Wed. GOLF. Overlooks the lovely Gair Loch of *Wester Ross*, in which lie the islands of Eilean Horrisdale and Longa. The small resort of *Gairloch* boasts one of the loveliest settings in the Scottish Highlands, and has sandy shores providing good bathing and fishing. Away to the south-west, across the Inner Sound, there are distant views of the *Coolin* hills in the southern part of the island of Skye. Southwards, the view ranges over the Flowerdale Forest peaks, in which *Baeshven*, 2,869 ft., is the highest, while still farther south rises *Beinn Alligin*, 3,232 ft., one of the splendid, wild Torridon peaks overlooking lonely *Torridon* (*q.v.*). The road leading south-eastwards to *Loch Maree* (*q.v.*) passes through the beautifully wooded Kerrysdale, in which a hydro-electric scheme is in operation. A branch off this road gives access to the coast between Opinan and Red Point. Another road leads north-westwards from Gairloch along the coast as far as *Melvaig*, beyond which lies the lonely Rudha Reidh, with its lighthouse. See **Gruinard Bay** and **Poolewe.** *Iter. 205, 206, 222, 223.*

GAIRLOCHY, Inverness. Map 18, **NN 1** 8.
Here, the *Caledonian Canal* (*q.v.*) is raised to the level of *Loch Lochy* (*q.v.*) by means of two locks. The River Lochy formerly flowed into the loch at this point, but its waters have been diverted over the picturesque Mucomer Falls into those of the River Spean, which itself joins the loch a little farther east. **2½ m. S.W.,** to the north of the road to *Corpach* (*q.v.*), along which magnificent views of *Ben Nevis* (*q.v.*), 4,406 ft., and its lofty neighbours can be obtained, is

the entrance to the roadless Glen Loy, down which Prince Charles Edward marched in 1745. In the glen are slight remains of the old Caledonian Forest. See **Loch Arkaig.** *Iter. 214.*

GAIRNEYBRIDGE, Fife. Map 17, **NT 1 9.**
Lies to the south of *Loch Leven (q.v.)*, with *Benarty Hill*, 1,167 ft., rising to the east. A monument here commemorates the foundation, in 1733, of the first Secession Presbytery. See **Blairadam.** *Iter. 90, 92.*

GAIRNSHIEL BRIDGE, Aberdeen. Map 20, **NJ 2 0.**
Situated amid lofty hills and moors, in Glen Gairn, at the junction of roads coming from Braemar and Ballater in the Dee valley. To the north-east, beyond Glen Finzie, rises *Morven*, 2,862 ft. The continuation northwards leads over the hills along the narrow and steep Glas Choille section, rising to over 1,800 ft., and liable to be blocked by snow in winter, before descending towards the fertile valley of the Don in the vicinity of *Cock Bridge (q.v.)*. *Iter. 160, 174.*

GALASHIELS, Selkirk. 12,605. SB. Map 10, **NT 4 3.**
E.C. Wed. GOLF. A busy Border manufacturing town, noted especially for tweeds and woollen hosiery. There is a well-known Woollen Technical College, and the Mercat Cross dates from 1695. The War Memorial includes a

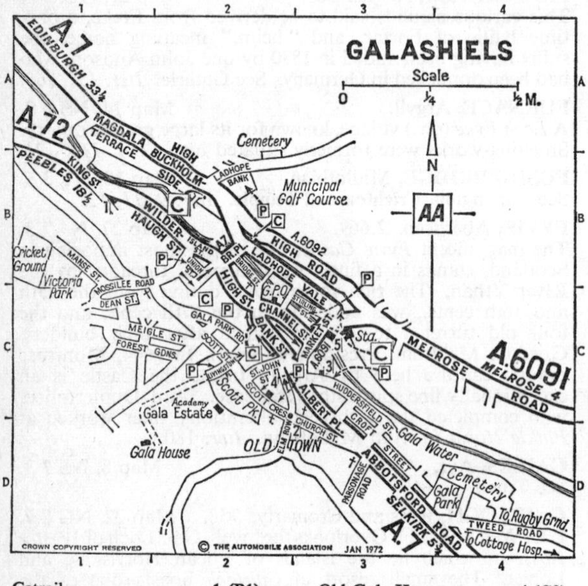

Catrail	1 (B1)	Old Gala House	4 (C2)
Mercat Cross	2 (C2)	Scottish Woollen Technical College	5 (C3)
Municipal Buildings with town crest	3 (C3)		

Clock Tower by Sir Robert Lorimer, in front of which is a representation of a Border " Reiver," or moss-trooper. *Old Gala House* dates from the 15th and 17th cents., with modern alterations, and is now an art centre, open on weekdays (see note page 98). The granting of a charter in 1599 is celebrated in early summer by the " Braw Lads " Gathering. The town crest, with its motto " Sour Plums," as depicted on the Municipal Buildings, recalls the deaths of some English soldiers in a Border foray of 1337, after gathering plums. An old track, known as the " Catrail," or Pict's Ditch, passes westwards of the town, on high ground, and is thought to have extended for more than 50 miles in a southerly direction, another stretch being visible near *Shankend (q.v.)*, on the Hawick to Newcastleton road. On the slopes of *Buckholm Hill*, to the north of Galashiels, stands the well-preserved *Old Buckholm Tower*. About **1½ m. S.E.** of the town, on the Melrose road, near *Langlee*, is an inscribed tablet recording Sir Walter Scott's last journey to *Abbotsford (q.v.)* on his return from Italy in 1832 shortly before his death. See **Bowland, Darnick** and **Melrose.** *Iter. 11, 32, 33, 52.*

GALLOWAY, Kirkcudbright; Wigtown. Map 2, **NX 1 5** etc. and 3, **NX 5 7** etc.
Within this area, which consists of the counties of Kirkcudbright and Wigtown, is included some of the wildest, but least known scenery in Scotland, particularly in the so-called " Galloway Highlands." The mountains here, dominated by the 2,764-ft. high peak of the *Merrick*, and the fine *Rhinns of Kells* range, are bare and lonely, sheltering remote little lochs containing pike. Perhaps the loveliest parts are in the neighbourhood of *Loch Trool (q.v.)*, where an extensive Forest Park is situated. Galloway was administered in the 14th and 15th cents. by the Douglas family, and afterwards by hereditary stewards under the Crown until 1747. The district was later to a large extent bound up with the Covenanters. At one time Galloway also included *Carrick (q.v.)*, which is however now part of the county of Ayr. An extensive power scheme has been developed in Galloway, harnessing the local water resources, and the large *Clatteringshaws Dam (q.v.)* was constructed in connection with the project, while there are also a number of power-houses. (See **Carsphairn** and **Tongland.**) The " belted " Galloway cattle are well known, and the breed of horses known as " Galloways " is thought to have originated partly from animals which swam ashore from wrecked Spanish Armada galleys. S. R. Crockett's " Raiders " introduces the country of the Merrick, in wildest Galloway, and the lofty hill of *Cairnsmore of Fleet*, near *Creetown (q.v.)*, is associated with John Buchan's " The Thirty-Nine Steps." See **Mull of Galloway** and **Stewartry.**

GALSTON, Ayr. 4,094. SB. Map 8, **NS 4 3.**
E.C. Wed. The town stands in a pleasant wooded setting in the valley of the River Irvine. *Barr Castle* is an old tower. To the north are the remains of *Loudoun Castle*, dating mainly from 1811 and burnt in 1941. **1½ m. S.E.**, near the Burn Anne, is *Cessnock Castle*, mainly modern, but preserving an old tower. *Iter. 20, 69.*

GANNOCHY BRIDGE, Angus; Kincardine. Map 21, **NO 5 7.**
The North Esk, flowing here through a picturesque, rocky and wooded defile, forms the boundary between Angus and Kincardine. North-westwards is the beautiful valley of the river, traversed by a road leading to *Tarfside (q.v.)* and *Lochlee (q.v.)*. The hills to the north-west include the *Hill of Wirren*, 2,220 ft., and *Bulg*, 1,986 ft. *Iter. 156, 163, 164.*

GARDENSTOWN, Banff. 986. Map 27, **NJ 8 6.**
Under lofty red cliffs in Gamrie Bay lies this picturesque fishing village, with a small harbour, and houses rising in tiers to the heights above. It takes its name from a certain Alexander Garden. More Head lies to the west, and Crovie Head, sheltering the fishing village of *Crovie (q.v.)*, to the east. Near More Head is the hill of *Gamrie Mhor*, 536 ft., by the ruins of the Old Church of *St. John*, founded in 1004, to commemorate a Scottish victory over the Danes. *Iter. 182.*

GARELOCHHEAD, Dunbarton. 2,276. Map 14, **NS 2 9.**
E.C. Wed. This well-known resort stands at the head of the fine Gare Loch, with its background of hills, prominent among which is the long ridge overlooking Loch Long and known as *Argyll's Bowling Green.* Yachts anchor in the loch during the season, and large ships are often laid up in its waters, while at *Faslane (q.v.)*, a little to the south, on the *Shandon (q.v.)* road, is a ship-breaking yard. To the east of Garelochhead rises a range of lonely hills overlooking the head of Glen Fruin (See **Helensburgh**), in which *Beinn Chaorach* attains 2,338 ft. There are roads on both sides of the Gare Loch, that on the west side giving access to the *Rosneath (q.v.)* peninsula. See **Whistlefield.** *Iter. 102, 111, 116.*

GARGUNNOCK, Stirling. 619. Map 16, **NS 7 9.**
E.C. Wed. A small village in the flat country traversed by the serpentine course of the River Forth. To the south rise the *Gargunnock* hills, with their high-lying reservoirs, beyond which are the *Fintry* hills, both ranges attaining a height of about 1,500 feet. Eastwards from Gargunnock lie the lower *Touch* hills, threaded by the Touch Burn. *Gargunnock House*

Gairneybridge, Fife. The Monument commemorating the founding of the first Secession Presbytery, on the 6th December, 1733. It was erected in 1883

Galashiels, Selkirk. The Town Crest, on the Municipal Buildings, with its motto: ' Sour Plums,' commemorating a Border foray of 1337, when some English soldiers were caught picking plums and afterwards slain

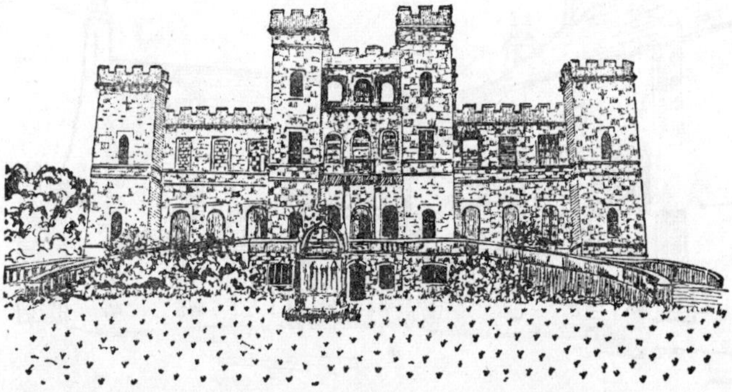

Galston, Ayr. Loudoun Castle, mainly 19th century, but retaining a 15th century tower. The structure was partially burnt in 1941. It stands to the north of Galston, off A719

Galloway, Kirkcudbright; Wigtown. The Monument to the 18th century Professor Alexander Murray, a celebrated linguist, who began as a shepherd boy in the hills of Galloway. It stands 4½ miles south-west of the Clatteringshaws Dam, on the Newton Stewart to New Galloway road (A712)

Gannochy Bridge, Angus; Kincardine. The bridge over the North Esk River, forming the boundary between Angus and Kincardine. It was erected in 1732 by James Black, a local farmer, who is said to have built the parapet with his own hands

Gardenstown, Banff. The cliff-bound fishing village, which was founded by Alexander Garden of Troup

[For GALASHIELS see also under SCOTT COUNTRY (Plate 148)

Garmouth, Moray. Charles II landed near this village in 1650, and signed the Solemn League and Covenant in the cottage which carries this plaque

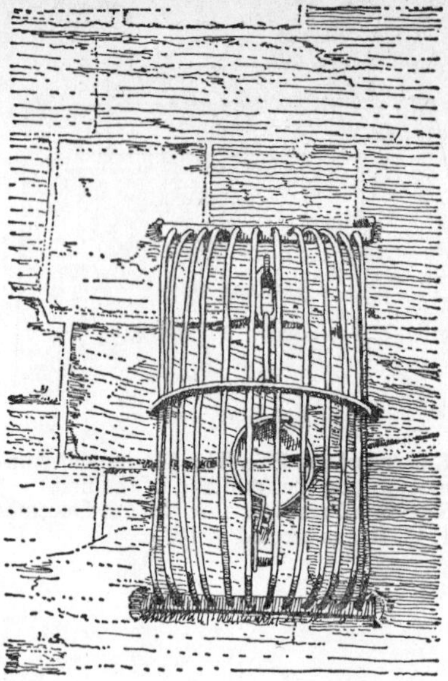

Garvald, East Lothian. The jougs, or iron collar for wrongdoers, on the west gable of the Church

Gatehouse of Fleet, Kirkcudbright. The ruined 15th century Cardoness Castle, overlooking Fleet Bay. It was once the home of the McCullochs and later of the Gordons of Lochinvar

Gatehouse of Fleet, Kirkcudbright. The 'Murray Arms' Inn, where Robert Burns is said to have written down the words of '*Scots wha ha'e*'

Gifford, East Lothian. The early 18th century Church. Its predecessor stood formerly near Yester House

is a 16th to 18th cent. mansion, situated to the east of the village. **4 m. E.** of Gargunnock is the notable 15th to 18th cent. *Touch House* displaying fine carving. **1½ m. W.** is the 16th cent. *Old Leckie House*. *Iter. 108, 112, 137.*

GARLIESTON, Wigtown. Map 2, **NX 4** 4.
A small port on the sandy Garlieston Bay, with Eggerness Point to the north-east, near which are slight remains of *Eggerness Castle*. To the south of Garlieston, on the coast near Rigg Bay, stands *Galloway House* (1740), once the seat of the Earls of Galloway, and noted for its wealth of trees and shrubs. It is now a school. See **Cruggleton.** *Iter. 82.*

GARLOGIE, Aberdeen. Map 21, **NJ 7** 0.
Iter. 179.

GARMOUTH, Moray. Map 26, **NJ 3** 6.
Now a quaint little village, but once a port, near which Charles II landed in 1650. The revived Maggie Fair, held last Sat. in June, recalls Lady Margaret Ker, a 17th cent. Royalist. See **Kingston** and **Mosstodloch.** *Iter. 199.*

GARTOCHARN, Dunbarton. 773. Map 15, **NS 4** 8.
E.C. Wed. A small resort near the south-eastern shores of *Loch Lomond* (*q.v.*) and its numerous wooded islands. To the north-west, by the lochside, is *Ross Priory*, with its lovely grounds, notably the yew avenue. It was once visited by Sir Walter Scott. *Iter. 109, 112, 114, 137.*

GARVALD, East Lothian. 508. Map 10, **NT 5** 7.
A tiny village on the northern slopes of the *Lammermuir* hills, with *Clints Dod*, 1,307 ft., a good viewpoint, rising to the south-east. The Church dates partly from the 12th cent., and retains a sundial dated 1633, and also the ancient jougs, attached to the west gable. To the south-east is the mansion of *Nunraw*, mainly 19th cent., but preserving a late 16th cent. tower. It is now occupied by Cistercian monks who commenced the building of a new Abbey in 1952. Eastwards of Garvald lies a wooded glen in which stands the ruined tower of *Stoneypath*. A narrow and hilly road threads its way south-eastwards from Garvald into the hills below *Spartleton Edge*, and later crosses the " Hungry Snout," before descending to the Berwickshire valley of the Whiteadder Water near *Cranshaws* (*q.v.*).

GARVE, Ross and Cromarty. 149. Map 24, **NH 3** 6.
E.C. Tues. Situated between Loch Garve, a little to the south-east, and the entrance to Strath Garve, which is traversed by the lonely road leading towards Ullapool. The main road westwards continues along Strath Bran, passing Loch Luichart, to the south, and giving views of the distant *Fannich* peaks away to the north-west, beyond Kinlochluichart Forest. A large hydro-electric scheme now operates in the Fannich district. Beyond Loch Luichart, and to the south of the road, are the smaller Lochs a'Chuilinn and Achanalt, with *Sgurr Vuillin*, 2,845 ft., rising in the background. To the north-east of Garve is *Little Wyvis*, 2,497 ft., backed by the larger mass of *Ben Wyvis*, 3,429 ft. *Iter. 204, 205, 206, 221.*

GARVELLACH ISLANDS, Argyll. Map 13, **NM 6** 1.
See **Clachan Bridge.**

GARYNAHINE, Isle of Lewis, Ross and Cromarty. Map 32, **NB 2** 3.
See **Hebrides, Outer** (Lewis). *Iter. 258, 260.*

GATEHOUSE OF FLEET, Kirkcudbright. 837. SB. Map 3, **NX 6** 5.
E.C. Thurs. **M.D.** Sat. GOLF. A pleasant little *Galloway* (*q.v.*) town, the " Kippletringan " of Scott's " Guy Mannering," situated on the Water of Fleet, which flows southwards into Fleet Bay, an inlet of Wigtown Bay. On the moors in the vicinity Burns composed " Scots wha ha'e," and the room in the *Murray Arms* Hotel in which he wrote it down is still pointed out. To the south of the town, which is well known to anglers, is *Cally House*, designed by Robert Mylne in 1763, in its fine grounds. **1 m. S.W.,** on a rocky height overlooking Fleet Bay, are the remains of the late 15th cent. *Cardoness Castle* (A.M.), a former home of the McCullochs of Galloway, and retaining its original stairway. **3 m. N.W.,** in the beautiful valley of the Fleet Water, is the ruined, but imposing *Rusco Castle*, dating from c. 1500, once the home of an old Galloway family, the Gordons of Lochinvar. Farther east rises *Bengray*, 1,203 ft., below which lies Loch Whinyeon. Beyond Fleet Bay, to the south-west, are the *Murray Isles* (N.T. Scot.), in Wigtown Bay. The old road to *Creetown* (*q.v.*) went inland, where the lonely Gatehouse of Fleet station once stood, some **6 m. N.W.** of the town. The present road follows the curve of Wigtown Bay, and is one of the loveliest coast roads in southern Scotland, passing *Dirk Hatteraick's Cave* beyond Ravenshall Point, and also the ruined castles of *Barholm* and *Carsluith*. The hills in the background include *Cairnharrow*, 1,497 ft. See **Anwoth Church** and **Kirkcudbright.** *Iter. 26, 72, 73.*

GATESIDE, Fife. Map 17, **NO 1** 0.
Iter. 130, 136.

GATTONSIDE, Roxburgh. Map 10, **NT 5** 3.
Iter. 33.

GIFFNOCK, Renfrew. 11,597 Map 8, **NS 5** 5.
E.C. Tues. GOLF. Situated on the south-western fringes of Glasgow. Away to the east, over the Lanark border, is the attractive, wooded public park of Cathkin Braes. See **Clarkston.** *Iter. 18, 29, 55, 61.*

GIFFORD, East Lothian. 338. Map 10, **NT 5** 6.
E.C. Wed. This delightful 18th cent. village, retaining its Mercat Cross, is situated on the Gifford Water, with views to the south of the *Lammermuir* hills. These are given over largely to sheep, and to the south, near the Berwick border, rises *Lammer Law*, 1,733 ft., a fine viewpoint. The Church at Gifford dates from 1708. Its predecessor stood near *Yester House*. In it is preserved a late medieval bell, and also a 17th cent. pulpit. South-east of the village, in a woodland setting, threaded by the Hopes Water, is *Yester House*, a fine Adam mansion, dating from 1745. Beyond it lie the remains of *Yester Castle*, best known for the remarkable underground chamber known as the " Goblin Ha'," which dates perhaps from 1267. Scott has introduced the scene in his " Marmion." A beech tree in the park is 142 ft. in height. Near the mansion is the small, restored 15th cent. Collegiate *Bothan's* Church, the burial-place of the Tweeddales since 1710, with a number of old monuments. A narrow, hilly and winding road climbs south-eastwards from Gifford into the *Lammermuirs*, attaining some 1,400 ft., and passing later over the " Hungry Snout " to descend to the Berwickshire valley of the Whiteadder Water near *Cranshaws* (*q.v.*), on the way to *Duns* (*q.v.*). See **Garvald** and **Whittinghame.** *Iter. 3.*

GIGHA, ISLE OF, Argyll. Map 6, **NR 6** 4.
This small island lies a little way off the west coast of Kintyre, from which it is separated by the Sound of Gigha. It is only about 6 miles in length, and is flat, with rocky shores. The ruined Church of *Kilchattan* is of 13th cent. date. The fine gardens of *Achamore* contain flowering shrubs. The well-known " Songs of the Hebrides " include verses written by Dr. Kenneth MacLeod, the Gaelic scholar, of Gigha parish. To the south is the tiny island of *Cara*. Access to Gigha is by steamer from West Loch Tarbert (See **Tarbert**; Argyll), or by passenger ferry from *Tayinloan* (*q.v.*) in *Kintyre* (*q.v.*).

GILMERTON, Midlothian. Map 10, **NT 2** 6.
A little to the east is the fine mid-18th cent. mansion known as *The Drum*, built by William Adam, the father of the even more famous Robert Adam. *Iter. 4, 5, 9, 11, 12, 13.*

GILMERTON, Perth. Map 16, **NN 8** 2.
A by-road proceeding north-westwards, and later leading to *Crieff* (*q.v.*), circles the fine park of *Monzie Castle*, 17th to

19th cent., threaded by the Shaggie Burn. To the south-east, and south of the Perth road, are the mansions of *Cultoquhey* and *Inchbrackie*. **4 m. N.** of Gilmerton is the very beautiful *Sma' Glen (q.v.)*. **5½ m. E.,** off the Perth road, are slight remains of the 13th cent. *Inchaffray Abbey*. See **Fowlis Wester.** *Iter. 89, 140, 141, 145.*

GIRVAN, Ayr. 7,405. SB. Map 2, **NX 1 9.** **E.C.** Wed. GOLF. A well-known resort in the *Carrick (q.v.)* division of the county, with a sandy beach and bathing. The Town House, moved from its original site in 1828, was at one time used as a gaol. About ten miles out to sea is the lonely, rocky *Ailsa Craig*, 1,114 ft. high and two miles

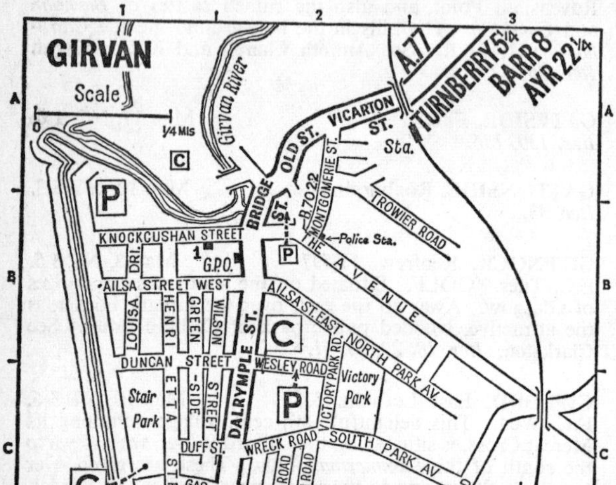

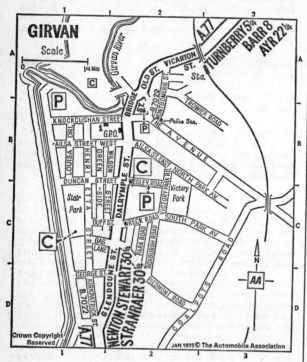

Town House, Information Bureau 1 (B1)

in circumference, a breeding-place for birds, and noted for its granite quarries, which supply material for the manufacture of curling-stones. A lighthouse and an ancient ruined Castle are also situated on Ailsa Craig, which is known as " Paddy's Milestone," owing to its position about half-way between Glasgow and Belfast. **3 m. N.E.,** in the valley of the Water of Girvan, is the picturesque *Killochan Castle*, dating from c. 1586. **4 m. S.S.W.** is *Kennedy's Pass*, perhaps the finest piece of scenery on the lovely coastal road to *Ballantrae (q.v.)*. **2 m. S.** is *Ardmillan House*, 16th cent. and restored, where Mary, Queen of Scots once stayed. See **Barr, Culzean Castle, Dailly, Kirkoswald** and **Turnberry.** *Iter. 55, 68, 71, 74, 78, 80, 85.*

GLAMIS, Angus. 1,169 with Eassie. Map 20, **NO 3 4.** Famous for *Glamis Castle*, one of the most notable of its period in Scotland, and standing in fine grounds, bordered by the Dean Water. Shakespeare's " Macbeth " was Thane of Glamis, but the events the poet has described lack historical foundation. In 1715, the Old Pretender lodged for a short period in the Castle, which is the ancestral home of the Earl of Strathmore, father of H.M. Queen Elizabeth, the Queen Mother, and was the birthplace, in 1930, of Her Royal Highness Princess Margaret. The greater part of the structure dates from 1675-1687, but an older tower, with 15-ft. thick walls, survives. The drawing-room, with its plaster ceiling of 1621, and the panelled Chapel are notable, and in the Castle is preserved the " lion-cup " of Glamis, associated with Scott's " Waverley." The Castle is reputedly ghost-haunted. Open from 2 to 5 or 5.30, Wed. and Thurs. in May and June; Wed., Thurs. and Sun. in July, Aug. and Sept. (See note page 98.) From the battlements there are splendid views. The great sundial in the grounds is over 21 ft. in height and has 84 dials. In the village, the old jougs hang near the churchyard gate. The incised *Glamis* churchyard stone at the manse is notable. *Kirk Wynd* cottages (N.T. Scot.) contain the Angus folk museum, open daily, 1 to 6, Easter to Sept. (See note page 98.) **2½ m. N.E.,** beyond the station, near *Cossans* farm, is the richly-carved *St. Orland's Stone* (A.M.), of the Early Christian period. *Iter. 151, 153, 161.*

GLASGOW, Lanark. 896,958. C. of C. Map 8, **NS 5 6.** **E.C.** Tues. **MD.** Wed. GOLF. The largest city and seaport of Scotland, and the third largest in population of the British Isles, *Glasgow* has grown with enormous rapidity within the last 150 years, due largely to the enterprise of Glaswegians in developing the River Clyde and establishing large docks and shipbuilding yards. Among other important industries established on Clydeside are chemicals, textiles, and both engineering and iron-works, these being made possible by the proximity of the important Lanarkshire coalfield. The patron saint of the city is St. Kentigern, or St. Mungo, who began his missionary work here in the 6th cent. The first Cathedral was finished in 1136, on the site of the early Church of *St. Kentigern*. The University was founded in 1450, and 4 years later Glasgow became a Royal Burgh. In 1650, and also in the following year, Cromwell was in the city, and Prince Charles Edward, on his retreat from England in 1745, levied toll on Glasgow. He had been proclaimed Regent at the 17th cent. Glasgow Cross. This was later demolished and replaced by the present Cross, erected in 1929. On Glasgow Green, where the Prince reviewed his troops after the retreat, stands the prominent Nelson obelisk. In the vicinity is the *People's Palace*, containing the *Old Glasgow Museum*. A great Empire Exhibition was held at Bellahouston Park in 1938.

Among the various parks, the best known are perhaps Glasgow Green, Kelvingrove Park and Queen's Park, the last-named having a memorial to mark the site of the battle of Langside, in 1568, after which Mary, Queen of Scots commenced her flight from Scotland. (See **Clarkston.**) South-east of Queen's Park is the famous *Hampden Park* football ground. Rouken Glen Park contains a waterfall and lake, and to the south-east of the city, near Calderpark, is the Zoological Park. In Victoria Park, Whiteinch, is a notable fossil grove. The old-established Glasgow Fair holidays take place in the 2nd or 3rd week of July. Many Clyde pleasure steamers start from the *Broomielaw*, on the north bank, adjacent to the George V bridge. The new airport lies **2 m. S.** of *Renfrew (q.v.)*. The most important structure in the city is the very fine 13th cent. Cathedral, and among the places of interest are the Universities, the splendid Art Gallery and Museum, and Provand's Lordship and Provan Hall, two interesting old houses. All these are described in detail below, together with other buildings, and admission times are given if available (see note page 98). In George Square stands an 80-ft. high column crowned by a statue to Sir Walter Scott, and the nearby Cenotaph is by Sir John Burnet. The mid-18th cent. *St. Andrew's* Church, in St. Andrew's Square, has a notable interior of the period. The imposing *St. Vincent Street* Church, and also the stone-built terraces in Great Western Road, are the work of the Glasgow architect Alexander Thomson (1817-1875), known as 'Greek' Thomson. The notable School of Art (1896) is by Charles Rennie Mackintosh. Near Provanhill (to the NE) are 28 and 31 storey flats, some of Europe's tallest. The Forth and Clyde and Monkland Canals (partly drained) flow near the city and there are old bridges and warehouses in addition to the *Kelvin* aqueduct at Maryhill. Glasgow is exceptionally fortunate in the country by which it is surrounded, more particularly to the west and north. Within easy reach are such world-famous districts as the *Kyles of Bute (q.v.)*, *Loch Lomond (q.v.)* and the *Trossachs (q.v.)*, while almost on the city's doorstep, to the north, are the *Kilpatrick*, *Campsie* and *Kilsyth* hills. To the south-east,

Girvan, Ayr. The 16th century Killochan Castle, an ancient stronghold of the Cathcarts of Carleton. It stands some 3 miles north-east, off B741

Glamis, Angus. The great sundial, with its 84 dials, which stands in the grounds of the 17th century Castle, situated in large policies to the north of the village

Glasgow, Lanark. The statue of Sir Walter Scott, which dominates George Square

Glamis, Angus. The Kirk Wynd cottages, restored by the National Trust for Scotland, and now housing the Angus Folk Museum.

Girvan, Ayr. A stone in memory of Alexander Ross, a special constable, who was shot here in 1831. It stands at the junction of A77 and B734, to the north-east

[For GLASGOW see also Plates 73 and 74

The Cathedral, partly the work of Bishop Bondington in the 13th century. It is noted for the crypt, or 'Laigh Kirk,' consecrated by Bishop Jocelin in 1197

Provand's Lordship, of 15th century date, probably the oldest house in the city. It was once part of the Hospital of St. Nicholas, and was built by Bishop Muirhead

The 'crown' steeple of the former 17th century Tolbooth, which Sir Walter Scott has portrayed in his '*Rob Roy*'

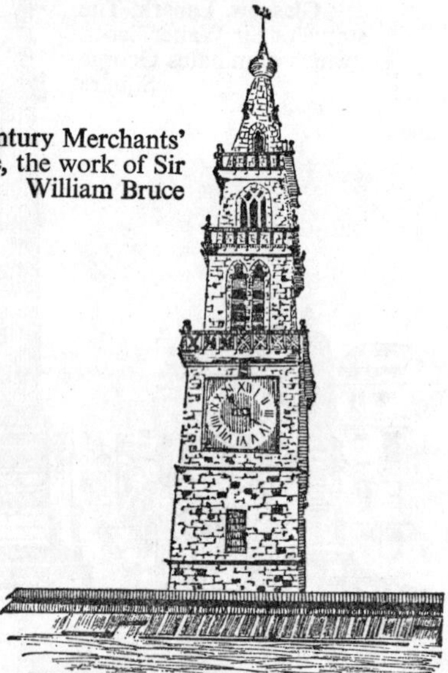

The 17th century Merchants' Hall steeple, the work of Sir William Bruce

The Memorial in Queen's Park commemorating the battle of Langside, in 1568, which was fatal to the cause of Mary, Queen of Scots

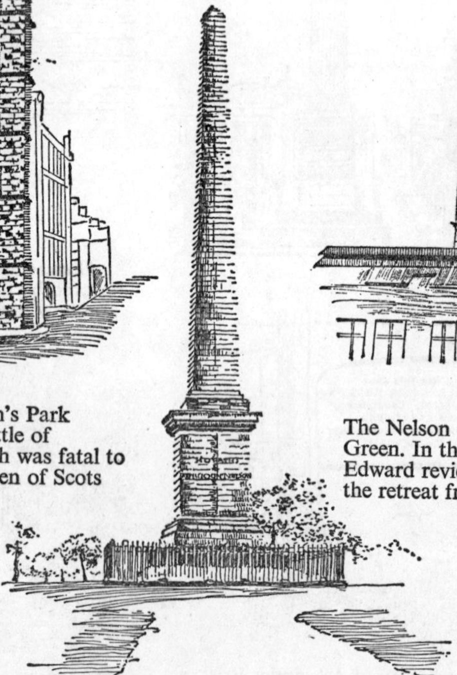

The Nelson obelisk on Glasgow Green. In the vicinity Prince Charles Edward reviewed his forces after the retreat from England in 1745

[For GLASGOW see also Plates 72 and 74

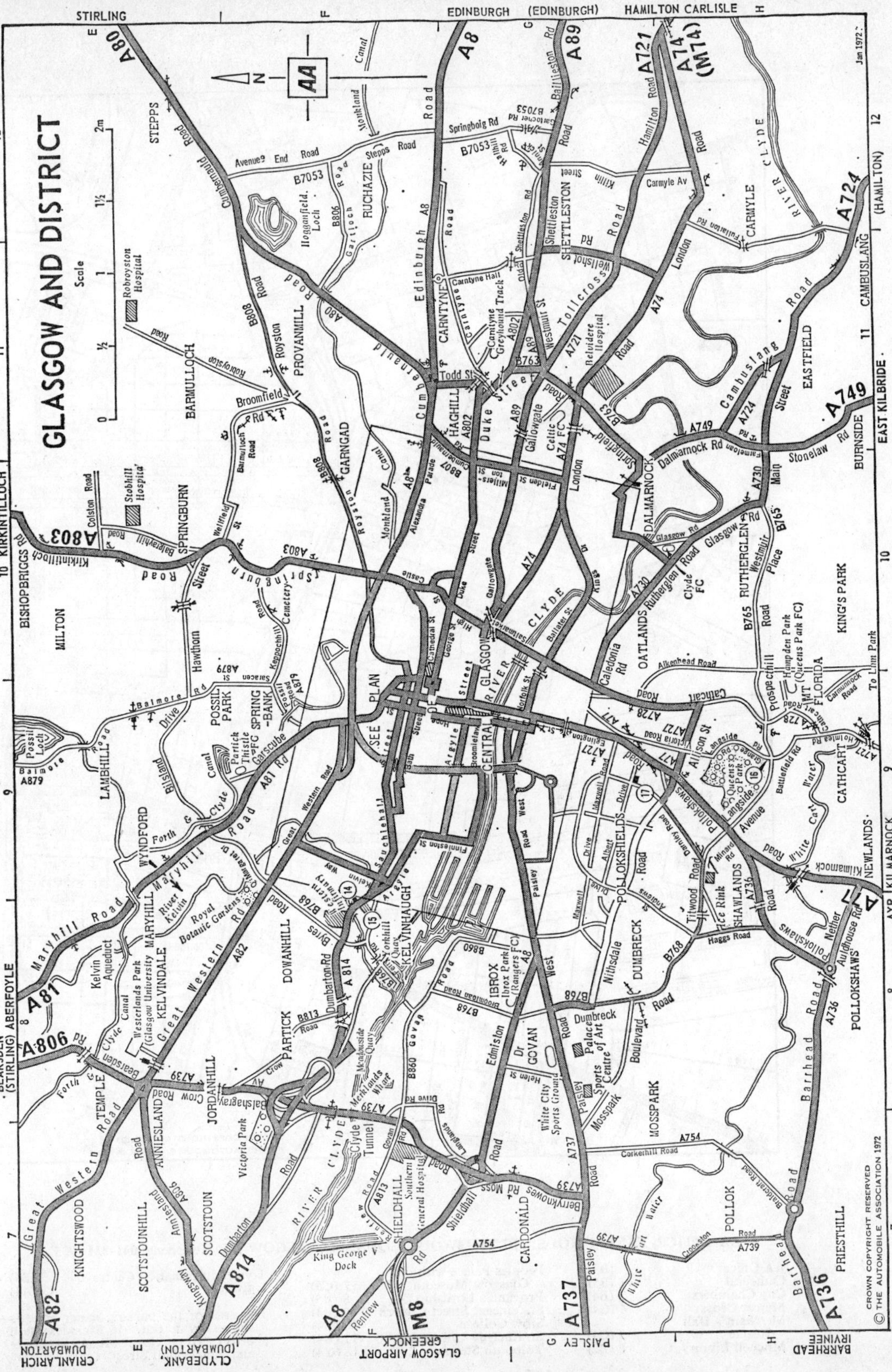

DOCKS
For Queen's Dock Area, follow YELLOW arrows.
Meadowside Quay (F8)
Merklands Wharf (F8)
Yorkhill Quay (F8)

For King George V Dock (F7) follow BLUE arrows.

Art Gallery and Museum	14	(F8)
Kelvin Hall	15	(F8)
Langside Memorial	16	(H9)
Transport Museum	17	(G9)

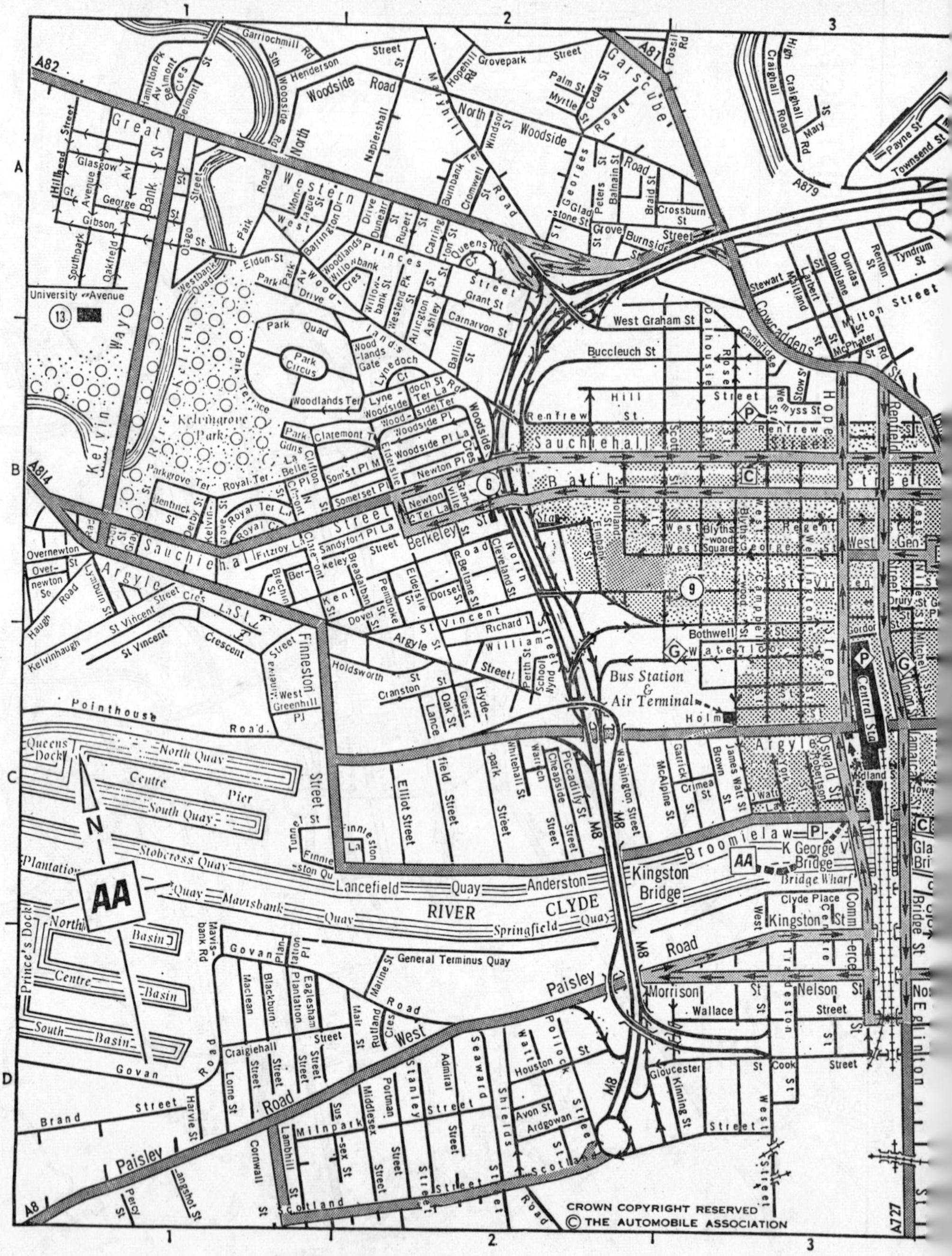

AA OFFICE, FANUM HOUSE, BLYTHSWOOD SQUARE, GLASGOW C2. Telephone: 041-221 8755

AA Office	(B3)	Peoples Palace with old Glasgow Museum	7 (C5)	Tourist Information Centre	3 (B4)
Cathedral	1 (B5)	Provand's Lordship	8 (B5)	University	13 (A1)
City Chambers	2 (B4)	St. Vincent Street Church	9 (B3)		
Mercat Cross	4 (C4)	Stow College	10 (B4)		
Merchant's Hall Steeple	5 (C4)	Strathclyde University	11 (B4)		
Mitchell Library	6 (B2)	Tolbooth Steeple	12 (C4)		

The area of the parking meter zone is shown by a tint. It excludes Bath Street, Hope Street, Renfield Street and Sauchiehall Street.

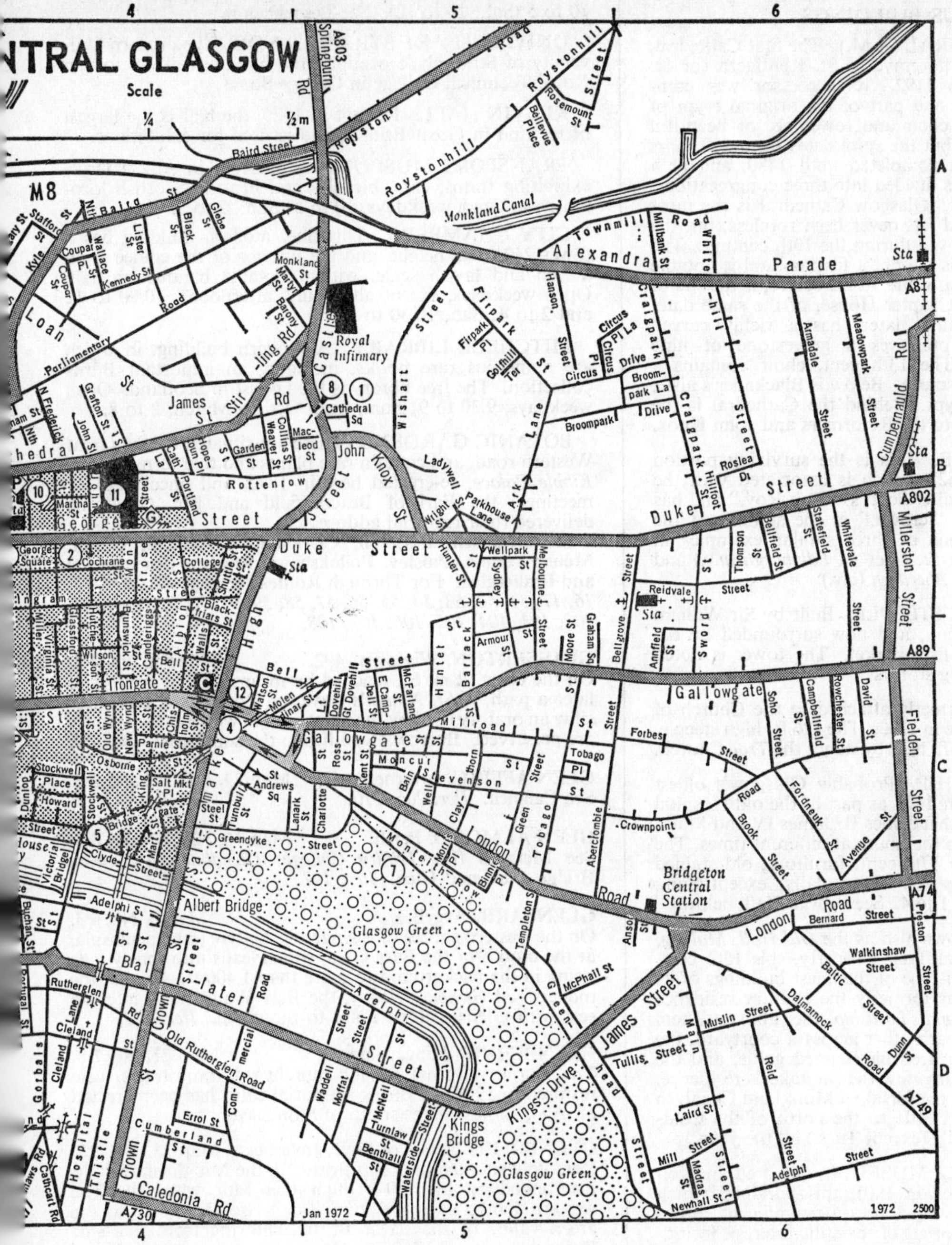

DOCKS

For Queen's Dock Area follow YELLOW arrows		For Prince's Dock Area follow RED arrows	
Anderston Quay	(C2)	Bridge Wharf, River Steamers	(C3)
Broomielaw	(C3)	Mavisbank Quay	(C1)
Lancefield Quay	(C2)	Plantation Quay	(C1)
Queen's Dock	(C1)	Prince's Dock	(D1)
Stobcross Quay	(C1)	Springfield Quay	(C2)

beyond *Hamilton* (*q.v.*), the Clyde flows through increasingly attractive orchard country, with a series of notable waterfalls near *Lanark* (*q.v.*).

FAMOUS BUILDINGS

GLASGOW CATHEDRAL (A.M.). The first Cathedral, built in 1123-1136 over the grave of St. Kentigern (or St. Mungo), was burned in 1192. Its successor was commenced soon afterwards, and part of the original crypt of 1197 has survived. The choir and tower are of beautiful 13th cent. workmanship, but the spire dates from 200 years later. The nave was not completed until 1480, and at a later date the building was divided into three congregations, the nave, choir and crypt. Glasgow Cathedral is the most complete in Scotland, and has never been roofless, but the western towers were removed during the 19th century. The crypt, or " Laigh Kirk," is the finest feature, and is notable for the pillars and vaulting, while, in the centre, is the site of St. Mungo's tomb. The Chapter House, of the same date, though not completed until later, has a richly carved entrance doorway and preserves a gravestone of nine martyred Covenanters. The 13th cent. choir contains a splendid 15th cent. stone screen. Below is Blackader's aisle, an interesting vaulted crypt. Behind the Cathedral is the Necropolis, with a statue to the Reformers and John Knox.

TOLBOOTH STEEPLE. This is the surviving portion of the Tolbooth of c. 1628, which is associated with the prison described in Sir Walter Scott's " Rob Roy," and has been reconditioned. The " crown," at the summit of the 113-ft. high steeple, is one of three similar examples in Scotland, the others being *St. Giles*' at *Edinburgh* (*q.v.*) and King's College Chapel in *Aberdeen* (*q.v.*).

MERCHANTS' HALL STEEPLE. Built by Sir William Bruce in the late 17th cent., and now surrounded by the buildings of the modern fish market. The tower is noted for its effect of diminishing storeys.

TRON STEEPLE. Formerly attached to the Church of *St. Mary*, destroyed by fire in 1793. The 126 ft. high steeple, 126ft. high, dates from 1637. Nearby stands the *Tron* Church.

PROVAND'S LORDSHIP. Probably Glasgow's oldest house, having been built in 1471 as part of the old Hospital of *St. Nicholas*. It is said that James II, James IV and Mary, Queen of Scots all lived in the house at different times. The rooms now contain much 17th cent. furniture, old stained glass, portraits and tapestries. Open daily, except Sun., summer, 10 to 5; winter, 11 to 4. See **Provan Hall**, below.

PROVAN HALL. Known also as the *Old Hall*, *Mailing*, and now Scottish National Trust property, this 15th cent. house, very well restored, is one of the finest buildings of its period in Scotland. It was formerly the country residence of the Prebendary of *Provand's Lordship*. (See above.) There are two buildings, facing each other across a courtyard, the original structure showing a corbie-stepped gable, and the 17th to 18th cent. wing being now the caretaker's residence. The house is situated near the forsaken Monkland Canal, to the east of the city, and a little to the north of the Coatbridge road. It is open daily (except Tues.) all the year.

ART GALLERY AND MUSEUM. Situated in Kelvingrove Park, and opened in 1901, this building, which received war damage in 1941, houses a magnificent collection of works of art and objects of scientific interest, including the famous Burrell collection. The paintings form one of the most comprehensive collections in Great Britain, and are representative of the Dutch, French and Scottish schools. Open weekdays, 10 to 5; Sun., 2 to 5.

GLASGOW UNIVERSITY. Founded in 1450, the University is no longer housed in its old building, but occupies a commanding site on Gilmorehill, the structure having been designed in 1868-1870 by Sir Gilbert Scott, and incorporating a tower and spire 300 ft. high. The imposing Bute Hall was added in 1882. The Old Lodge, which stands near the entrance, is built of stones from the Old College. In the *Hunterian* Museum and Library, open weekdays, 10 to 5 (Sat., 10 to 12), are valuable collections bequeathed by Dr. William Hunter, who died in 1783. The University library contains many rare volumes, and is open weekdays, 10 to 5 (Sat., 10 to 12). See **Lesmahagow.**

UNIVERSITY OF STRATHCLYDE. The modern University of Strathclyde occupies the buildings of the former Royal Technical College in George Street.

KELVIN HALL. Rebuilt in 1926, the hall is the largest of its kind in Great Britain, and is used for exhibitions.

TRANSPORT MUSEUM. A museum in Albert Drive exhibiting trams, cars, bicycles and historic Scottish locomotives. Open weekdays, 10 to 5; Sun., 2 to 5.

CITY CHAMBERS. This fine, modern building has a tower 240 ft. in height, and the interior of the edifice is on a rich and lavish scale, with a notable banqueting hall. Open weekdays, except alt. Thurs. afternoons, 10.30 to 12 and 2 to 4; Sat., 10.30 to 12.

MITCHELL LIBRARY. A modern building, in which are numerous rare books, including an important Burns collection. The free library is the largest in Scotland. Open weekdays, 9.30 to 9; Sun., from Oct. to March, 2 to 8.

BOTANIC GARDENS. These are situated off the Great Western road, and contain rare plants and tree-ferns. In the *Kibble Palace*, re-erected here in 1872, and once used for meetings, the Earl of Beaconsfield and Mr. Gladstone delivered their rectorial addresses.

See **Bearsden, Bothwell, Clarkston, Clydebank, Govan, Mount Vernon, Paisley, Pollokshaws, Renfrew** (for airport) and **Rutherglen.** For Through Routes see page 47. *Iter. 15, 16, 17, 51, 52, 53, 54, 55, 56, 57, 58, 59, 97, 98, 99, 100, 101, 102, 103, 104, 105, 106, 107, 108,*

GLASSERTON, Wigtown. 492. Map 2, **NX 4** 3.
On the coast, **2 m. S.,** reached by means of a by-road, and later a path, is *St. Ninian's* Cave, on Port Castle Bay, possibly an oratory used by the Saint, and in which carved stones are preserved. Burrow Head lies to the south-east. *Iter. 82.*

GLEN AFFRIC, Inverness. Map 24, **NH 1** 2 and **2** 2.
See **Cannich.** *Iter. 206, 210.*

GLEN ALMOND, Perth. Map 16, **NN 7** 3 and **8** 3.
See **Methven** (for *Trinity College; Glenalmond*), **Newton Bridge** and **Sma' Glen.** *Iter. 147.*

GLENBARR, Argyll. Map 6, **NR 6** 3.
On the western shores of the narrow *Kintyre* (*q.v.*) peninsula, at the mouth of the Barr Glen, which leads into lonely hills rising in the background to more than 1,400 ft. Beyond the modernised *Glenbarr Abbey*, the Barr Water flows into the sea, with Glenacardoch Point to the north. *Iter. 121.*

GLENBERVIE, Kincardine. Map 21, **NO 7** 8.
The Burnes (Burns) family churchyard tombstones were restored in 1968. A Burns memorial cairn has been erected on A94, some 3 miles south of Stonehaven.

GLENBRITTLE, Isle of Skye, Inverness. Map 23, **NG 4** 2.
Remotely situated on Loch Brittle, in the Minginish district, overlooked by the 150-ft. high Eas Mor waterfall. The western flanks of the *Coolins* (*q.v.*) rise steeply from the green valley of the River Brittle, showing from this side Coire Lagan and Coir' a Ghrunnda, two of their finest corries, the first-named being dominated by the great precipices of *Sron na Ciche*. *Sgurr Alasdair*, 3,309 ft., the highest point in the range, with its well-known " Stone Shoot," is usually climbed from here, Glenbrittle being best known as a climbers' rendezvous. A very narrow and rough road leads northwards through the upper part of the glen, now partly afforested by the Forestry Commission, and continues over high ground to reach the shores of Loch Harport. Turning eastwards, access is gained to the better road through Glen Drynoch to *Sligachan* (*q.v.*), near the northern extremity of the main Coolin ridge. A path leads south-

Glasgow, Lanark. Provan Hall, a 15th century house, cared for by the National Trust for Scotland. It stands near the Monkland Canal, off B806, to the east of the city

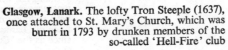

Glasgow, Lanark. The lofty Tron Steeple (1637), once attached to St. Mary's Church, which was burnt in 1793 by drunken members of the so-called 'Hell-Fire' club

Glasgow, Lanark. The Old Lodge, which forms part of Glasgow University. It is built of stones from the old college, founded originally in 1450

Glasgow, Lanark. The spacious Kelvin Hall (1926), used for exhibition purposes

Glasgow, Lanark. The 19th century University Buildings, seen from Kelvingrove Park

Glen Affric, Inverness. The westerly view from Loch Benevean. Hydro-electric developments have taken place in the vicinity. The loch lies on an unclassified road south-west of Cannich

[For GLASGOW see also Plates 72 and 73
[For GLEN AFFRIC see also under AFFRIC (Plate 5)

Glencaple, Dumfries. A village associated with Sir Walter Scott's '*Guy Mannering*,' under the name of 'Portanferry'

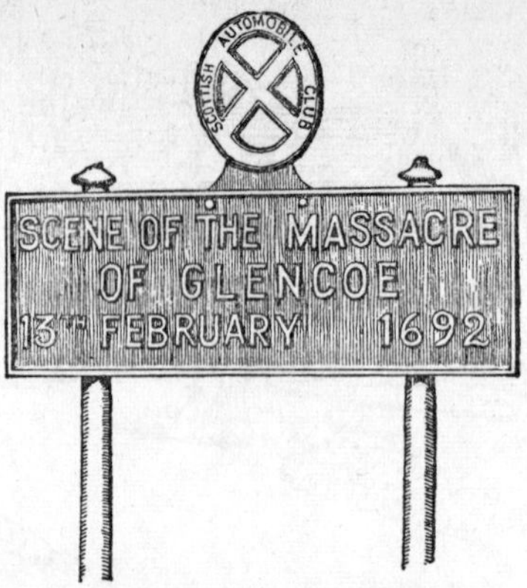

Glencoe, Argyll. The site of the 1692 massacre of Glencoe, when Government troops treacherously slew more than 40 Macdonalds, whose Chieftain had been a few days late tending allegiance to William III. The order for the savage massacre is sometimes said to have been written on a playing card, the Nine of Diamonds, a card known since as the 'Curse of Scotland'

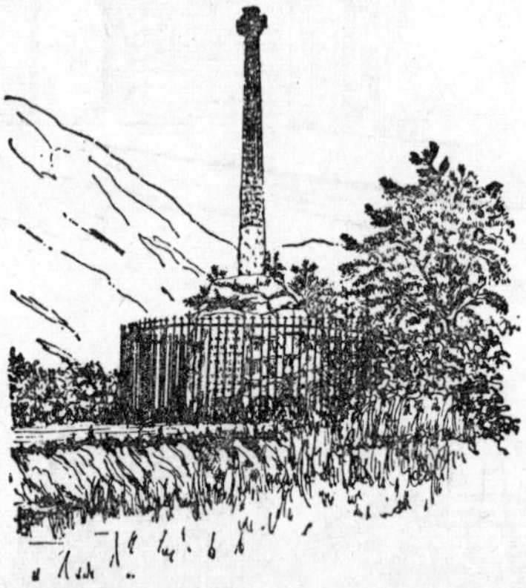

Glencoe, Argyll. The monument to the Macdonald Chief, who was slain in the massacre of 1692, and is buried on an island in Loch Leven

Glenelg, Inverness. The remains of the early 18th century Bernera Barracks, which fell into disuse after 1790. They lie to the north-west, facing Skye across the narrow and fast-flowing strait of Kyle Rhea

Glencorse, Midlothian. The entrance to the barracks of the Royal Scots, Britain's oldest regiment, whose regimental march is '*Dumbarton's Drums.*' The Earl of Dumbarton was appointed their Colonel by Charles II

Glenelg, Inverness. One of the two well preserved brochs which stand in Glen Beag, on an unclassified road to the south

wards from Glenbrittle, along the shores of the loch, towards the picturesque headland of Rudh'an Dunain, from which the views are very fine. *Iter. 252.*

GLENBUCHAT CASTLE, Aberdeen. Map 26, **NJ 3 1.**
See **Glenkindie.**

GLEN CANNICH, Inverness. Map 24, **NH 1 3**
See **Cannich.** *Iter. 206, 210.* and **2 3.**

GLENCAPLE, Dumfries. Map 4, **NX 9 6.**
A small bathing place on the estuary of the River Nith, associated with Scott's "Guy Mannering." It is known locally as *The Auld Quay*. Robert Burns, when working as an exciseman, once composed a poem here. *Iter. 28.*

GLENCARSE, Perth. Map 17, **NO 1 2.**
Pitfour Castle is a late 18th cent. mansion, and *Inchyra House* is of the same period. *Iter. 154.*

GLEN CLOVA, Angus. Map 20, **NO 3 7** and **3 6.**
See **Braedownie** and **Clova Church.** *Iter. 161.*

GLENCOE, Argyll. Map 18, **NN 1 5.**
The famous pass through Glen Coe, in Gaelic the "narrow glen," but also known as "glen of weeping," is perhaps the best known in all Scotland. This is due as much to its grim historical associations as to the magnificent and wild mountain setting of north-east *Lorne* (*q.v.*) in which it lies. Some 13,000 acres in the neighbourhood are now the property of the Scottish National Trust, including the site of the main part of the Glencoe massacre, and also the lofty peak of *Bidean nam Bian*, 3,766 ft., Argyll's highest mountain. Contiguous with this property are the mountains of *Dalness* Forest, facing Glen Etive, and including the twin *Buchaille Etive* peaks, separated by the lonely Lairig Gartain pass, this district having been acquired by the Trust in 1937. The new road, dating from 1935, leading through Glen Coe from the east, which attains just over 1,000 ft. in height, has been constructed at a lower level than the old one. In the heart of the defile, above the road, is a rock platform known as the "Studdie," or "Study," which provides perhaps the finest view of the savage, bare mountains which overhang the pass.

On the south side are the *Three Sisters of Glencoe*, known as *Beinn Fhada, Gearr Aonach* and *Aonach Dubh*, all around 2,500 to 3,000 ft. high, and being outliers of the peaks of *Stob Coire nan Lochan*, 3,657 ft. and *Bidean nam Bian*. High up on *Aonach Dubh*, overlooking Loch Triochatan, is Ossian's Cave, a deep cleft. On the north side of the glen extends the pinnacled ridge of *Aonach Eagach*, with a number of 3,000-ft. summits, overlooking Loch Leven and the *Mamore Forest* (*q.v.*) mountains of *Lochaber* (*q.v.*) beyond its shores. At the western end of this ridge is the conical *Pap of Glencoe*, 2,430 ft., which is a conspicuous feature in the view from the neighbourhood of Loch Leven and *Ballachulish* (*q.v.*). Lower down the glen, beyond Loch Triochatan, the old and new roads part company, the latter keeping to the south of the river and looking across its waters to the little "*Clachaig*" Inn. From the Signal Rock, in the vicinity, came, on a midwinter's dawn in 1692, the signal for the hideous massacre of the Macdonalds of Glencoe by Campbell of Glen Lyon, more than 40 being slain, while others fled into the hills to die of want and exposure. All the hamlets in the glen were burnt down by the soldiers. A monument has been set up to the memory of the murdered chief, who is buried on the island of *Eilean Munde*, in Loch Leven, near the entrance to the glen. R. L. Stevenson, in his novel "Kidnapped," has described Glencoe. See **Bridge of Orchy, Carnach** and **Kingshouse** (for *Buchaille Etives* and *Meall Bhuiridh* ski tow). *Iter. 100, 125, 142.*

GLENCORSE, Midlothian. 1,059. Map 10, **NT 2 6.**
GOLF. Here are the barracks of the Royal Scots (now part of the Lowland Brigade), the oldest regiment in Britain, the nucleus having been the companies formed by Louis XIII in 1633, with which were incorporated the famous Scots brigade from the Swedish army. The old Kirk, to the north of Milton Bridge, was described by R. L. Stevenson in his "Weir of Hermiston." Farther north, in the foothills of the Pentlands, is Glencorse reservoir, at a height of 740 ft., with *Black Hill*, 1,628 ft., in the background. In the vicinity is *Rullion Green*, where the Covenanters were defeated by General Tom Dalyell in 1666. An inscribed stone, set up in 1738, recalls the fight and a service is held annually in a field at *Flotterstane*, to the north-east. Farther north rises *Castle Law*, 1,595 ft., with a small Iron Age hill fort (A.M.). See **Swanston** and **West Linton.** *Iter. 10, 24.*

GLEN CROE, Argyll. Map 14, **NN 2 0.**
See **Rest and be Thankful.** *Iter. 88, 101, 102, 103, 137.*

GLENDARUEL, Argyll. Map 14, **NR 9 8.**
A pleasant glen, stretching from the head of Loch Riddon, an inlet of the *Kyles of Bute* (*q.v.*), and extending to the hills bordering *Loch Fyne* (*q.v.*). In *Kilmodan* Church is a memorial to Colin Maclaurin, the mathematician, who organized Edinburgh's defences during the '45. A little to the south of Glendaruel, a narrow, winding and hilly (1 in 4) road, attaining 1,026 ft., leads to *Otter Ferry* (*q.v.*) on Loch Fyne and a new road along Loch Riddon gives access to *Tighnabruaich* (*q.v.*). *Iter. 103.*

GLENDEVON, Perth. 630. Map 16, **NN 9 0.**
In the heart of the picturesque, winding Glen Devon, which penetrates the *Ochil* hills, and merges to the north into Glen Eagles. The highest point of the road in Glen Devon attains nearly 900 ft., giving a fine northerly view over Strath Earn towards the distant Perthshire mountains. To the south-east rises *Innerdownie*, 2,004 ft., with several large reservoirs in the vicinity. *Iter. 89.*

GLENEAGLES HOTEL, Perth. Map 16, **NN 9 1.**
E.C. Wed. GOLF. This famous golfing resort, one of the best known in Scotland, is situated on the moors between Strath Earn and Strath Allan, and a little beyond the northern extremity of Glen Eagles, with views of the *Ochil* hills away to the south. **2 m. S.,** off the road through the glen, stands *Gleneagles House*, dating from 1624, and in the near vicinity are remains of the former castle. *St. Mungo's* Chapel (1149) contains Haldane memorials. *Iter. 89, 135, 146.*

GLENEGEDALE AIRPORT, Isle of Islay, Argyll.
See **Port Ellen.** *Iter. 243.* Map 6, **NR 3 5.**

GLENELG, Inverness. 413. Map 23, **NG 8 1.**
This little village on Glenelg Bay lies in a picturesque, remote situation on the Sound of Sleat, noted for its exceptionally strong currents. The Sound separates the mainland from the island of Skye, and to the north is less than half a mile wide. Glenelg is accessible by one road only, this crossing a high ridge west of *Loch Duich* (*q.v.*) by means of the well-known pass of *Mam Rattachan* (*q.v.*). Dr. Johnson and Boswell reached Glenelg over the pass on their Highland tour, in 1773. A curious point, not often realized, is that the name of Glenelg is a palindrome, reading the same both backwards and forwards. On the north side of Glenelg Bay are the remains of Bernera Barracks, erected c. 1722, soldiers having been quartered there continuously until after 1790. A carved stone in the churchyard, dated 1730, is in memory of one of the garrison officers. Opposite the barracks are the narrows of Kyle Rhea, facing *Kylerhea* (*q.v.*), in Skye, which is overlooked by *Beinn na Caillich*, 2,396 ft., and *Sgurr na Coinnich*, 2,401 ft. Cattle were formerly ferried from Skye across these narrow waters, being driven over the Mam Rattachan Pass and thence down through the Highlands to the great cattle trysts near *Falkirk* (*q.v.*). A car ferry, operated during the summer, connects with Kylerhea in Skye. **1 m. S** of Glenelg is the entrance to the lovely Glen Beag, in which are situated two notable Pictish brochs, *Dun Telve* and *Dun Troddan* (A.M.), perhaps the most complete on the mainland; farther east is another example, *Dun Grugaig*, near which is a waterfall. To the south rises *Ben Sgriol*, 3,196 ft., a splendid viewpoint. The narrow, rough and hilly coast road from Glenelg around Outer *Loch Hourn* (*q.v.*) to *Arnisdale* (*q.v.*) is one of the loveliest in Scotland, providing exquisite views from the high ground above the Sound of Sleat towards the islands of Skye and Rum. On the south side of Loch Hourn rises *Ladhar Bheinn*, 3,343 ft., one of the highest of the remote *Knoydart* (*q.v.*) peaks. *Iter. 207.*

GLENFARG, Perth. 295. Map 17, **NO 1 1.** **E.C.** Thurs. Situated at the southern end of the delightful and narrow defile of Glen Farg, which winds through the outliers of the main *Ochil* range towards the flat country near the estuary of the River Earn. where it flows into the inner Firth of Tay. *Iter. 90, 91.*

GLENFINNAN, Inverness. Map 18, **NM 8 8.** One of the most beautiful and romantic places in the Western Highlands, where the well-known " Road to the Isles " passes the head of *Loch Shiel* (*q.v.*) on its way to *Morar* (*q.v.*) and *Mallaig* (*q.v.*), on the picturesque north-west coast. At the head of the loch, in its superb mountain setting, near the point where the little River Finnan flows down from Glen Finnan into the loch, stands the prominent *Prince Charles Edward* monument (N.T. Scot.), set up in 1815, to commemorate the Highlanders who followed the Prince in the '45, the Royal Standard having been raised here on August 19th, 1745. In the R.C. Church, standing in the grounds of *Glenfinnan House*, a little to the west, a tablet recalls the Prince. The Church bell carries the delineation of an Irish wolfhound and is placed at ground level. Westwards from Glenfinnan, the road follows a valley between lofty hills, notable for their steep rock-strewn flanks, with *Beinn Odhar Mhor*, 2,853 ft., to the south, and *Fraoch Bheinn*, 2,489 ft., to the north. In about three miles this road begins to descend, and on the right, by climbing a small bluff on foot, a magnificent view is opened up, extending over Loch Eilt to the Sound of Arisaig and the islands of Eigg and Rum. There is a steamer service along the whole 18-mile length of Loch Shiel. terminating at *Acharacle* (*q.v.*). North of Glenfinnan, behind the railway viaduct, is the lonely Glen Finnan, beyond which rise the bare and stony peaks of *Sgurr Thuilm*, 3,164 ft., and the twin *Streaps*, 2,988 ft., and 2,916 ft. See **Kinlocheil, Lochailort** and **Spean Bridge.** *Iter. 209.*

GLEN ISLA, Angus. Map 20, **NO 1 6** and **2 5.** See **Kirkton of Glenisla** and **Lair.**

GLENKINDIE, Aberdeen. Map 26, **NJ 4 1.** Situated in the upper Don valley. Near *Glenkindie House* is a remarkable weem, or Pict's House. **1 m. S.S.W.,** across the river, is *Towie* Church, with an ancient sculptured Cross in the churchyard, while nearby are the remains of *Towie Castle.* **3 m. W.N.W.,** beyond the Bridge of Buchat, is the ruined *Glenbuchat Castle* (A.M.), dating from c. 1590. John Gordon, the last laird, fought in the 1715 and 1745 Risings and escaped after the battle of Culloden, in 1746. See **Kildrummy.** *Iter. 167, 176.*

GLENLIVET, Banff. Map 26, **NJ 2 2.** Lies a little west of the Tomintoul to Dalnashaugh Inn road by way of Tomnavoulin, and is best known for the famous distillery, founded in 1824. Glen Livet extends south-eastwards from here towards the *Ladder Hills* (*Carn Mor*, 2,636 ft.), and James VI fought a battle in the glen in 1594. There are scanty remains of *Blairfindy Castle* (A.M.). At *Bridgend*, a little to the north, near the Livet Water, is a picturesque, ruined bridge. Farther west, near the River Avon, here joined by the Livet Water, stands the ancient *Drumin Tower*, situated on an alternative road to Tomintoul by way of Strath Avon and the *Cromdale* hills. North-east of Glenlivet, overlooking the Dufftown road traversing Glen Rinnes, rises *Ben Rinnes*, 2,755 ft. *Iter. 169, 177, 192.*

GLENLUCE, Wigtown. 750. Map 2, **NX 1 5.** **E.C.** Wed. GOLF. A short way inland from the sandy shores of Luce Bay stands this *Galloway* (*q.v.*) village, to the west of which flows the Water of Luce on its way to the bay. The remains of *Luce Abbey* (A.M.), founded in 1191, are near the river, north of the village on the road to *New Luce* (*q.v.*), but are slight, though the chapter house shows good 15th cent. work. Part of the adjoining land is N.T. Scot. **1 m. S.W.** is the restored *Castle of Park* (A.M.), a fine castellated house, dating from 1590, as shown by the inscription above the main entrance. **2 m. N.E.,** off the Newton Stewart road, is the ruined 17th cent. *Carscreuch Castle*, built by the first Lord Stair, and associated with Scott's " Bride of Lammermoor." See **Castle Kennedy** and **Kirkcowan.** *Iter. 25, 26, 78, 80, 81, 82.*

GLEN LYON, Perth. Map 15, **NN 5 4** and **6 4.** See **Bridge of Balgie** and **Fortingall.** *Iter. 107.*

GLEN MORE, Inverness. Map 18, **NN 2 9** etc. and **2 4, NH 3 0** etc. Known also as the " Great Glen of Alban," or simply the " Great Glen," this well-known trough extends diagonally in a straight line across north-west Scotland, from *Inverness* (*q.v.*) in the north-east, to *Fort William* (*q.v.*) in the south-west. It forms a remarkable physical feature, dividing the mainland into two unequal portions. A chain of lochs, the largest of which is *Loch Ness* (*q.v.*), is situated in the glen, and these are linked together by the famous *Caledonian Canal* (*q.v.*), by means of which small vessels coming from the North Sea can reach the Atlantic without having to navigate the stormy waters off the north coast of Scotland. For much of the distance lofty hills look down upon the glen, these increasing in height towards the west, and culminating in *Ben Nevis*, 4,406 ft. (*q.v.*), the highest mountain in the British Isles. The Glen More Forest Park will be found in a different Glen More, situated in the same county, but to the east of *Aviemore* (*q.v.*), in the foothills of the *Cairngorms* (*q.v.*). General Wade's road through the Great Glen, linking Inverness with Fort William, traverses the glen almost from end to end, the line of the present fine road being, however, only partly on the line of the original Wade road. See **Fort Augustus, Loch Lochy, Loch Oich** and **Wade Roads.** *Iter. 207, 210, 213, 214.*

GLEN MORE FOREST PARK, Inverness. Map 25, **NH 9 1.** See **Aviemore, Loch Morlich** and **Rothiemurchus** (for ski road).

GLEN NEVIS, Inverness. Map 18, **NN 1 6** and **1 7.** See **Ben Nevis.**

GLEN PROSEN, Angus. Map 20, **NO 2 6** and **3 6.** See **Dykehead.**

GLENRINNES, Banff. Map 26, **NJ 2 3.** Situated in the heart of the pleasant valley of Glen Rinnes, with *Ben Rinnes*, 2,755 ft., rising to the north-west, and *Corryhabbie*, 2,563 ft., to the south. *Iter. 169, 177.*

GLENROTHES, Fife. 29,000, incl. New Town. Map 17, **NO 2 0.** **E.C.** Tues., Wed. A New Town, in course of development, situated on the Fife coalfield. *Iter. 93, 126, 130.*

GLENSHEE, SPITTAL OF, Perth. Map 20, **NO 1 6.** GOLF. Lies in the heart of the *Grampians* (*q.v.*), at a height of 1,125 ft., in Glen Shee, on the fine hill road linking Blairgowrie and the south with Braemar on Royal Deeside. In former days a travellers' hospice stood at this point. Climbing and ski-ing can be enjoyed, with a rope tow on *Ben Gulabin*, 2,641 ft., and both a ski lift (on *Meall Odhar*, 3,019 ft.), and a chair lift, to the north, at the *Cairnwell Pass* (see below). A little to the east of the Spittal is a stone circle, and also a tumulus, known as the Tomb of Diarmid, associated with the ancestors of the Clan Campbell. **5 m. S.E.** stands the modern *Dalnaglar Castle*, beyond the Shee Water. **5 m. N.N.E.,** on the Braemar road, beyond Gleann Beag, is the *Devil's Elbow*, 1,950 ft., notorious in the early days of motoring, with a gradient of 1 in 5, with double bends, now being eased. The road reaches 2,199 ft. at the nearby *Cairnwell Pass* (*q.v.*) summit, on the Aberdeenshire border, the highest main road in Great Britain, and liable to be blocked by snow in winter. To the west is the *Cairnwell* itself, 3,059 ft., and to the east rises *Glas Maol*, 3,502 ft., the highest of an extensive group of 3,000-ft peaks, culminating far to the north-east in *Lochnagar* (*q.v.*). The long descent northwards leads along Glen Clunie, with the lofty mass of the *White Mounth* (*q.v.*) rising to the east, and a range of lesser hills guarding Glen Ey forest away to the west. *Iter. 141, 152, 160, 167, 168.*

GLEN SHIEL, Ross and Cromarty. 612 with Kintail. Map 24, **NG 9 1.** One of the loveliest of Scottish glens, traversed by one of the two well-known " Roads to the Isles," and considered by many good authorities to exceed even *Glencoe* (*q.v.*) in scenic grandeur. It extends for nearly 10 miles from Glen

Glenfinnan, Inverness. The Monument (N.T. Scot.) to the Highlanders who followed Prince Charles Edward in the '45. It was erected in 1815 by Macdonald of Glenaladale, a grandson of one of the Prince's original supporters

Glenfinnan, Inverness. The bell of the Church, with its delineation of a wolf. It lies at ground level

Glenlivet, Banff. The well-known distillery, which was founded in 1824

Glenrothes, Fife. Part of the shopping centre in one of Scotland's New Towns, now in course of development

Glenluce, Wigtown. The remains of Luce Abbey, which was founded by the Lord of Galloway in 1191, and was lived in during the 13th century by Michael Scott, the 'Wizard'

[For GLENMORE FOREST PARK see under CAIRNGORMS (Plate 26)
[For GLENSHEE, SPITTAL OF, see under SPITTAL OF GLENSHEE (Plate 153) and GRAMPIANS (Plate 78)

Gordon, Berwick. Greenknowe Tower (1581), once the home of the Covenanter, William Pringle. It stands a little to the north, off A6105

Gorebridge, Midlothian. The ornate gateposts at the entrance to the Palladian mansion of Arniston. The house stands to the south-west, off B6372

Glen Torridon, Ross and Cromarty. The peak of Liathach, 3,456 feet. It rises above B858, dominating Upper Loch Torridon, to the south-west of Kinlochewe

Golspie, Sutherland. The inscribed memorial to the Clan Sutherland on a bridge in the village

Gourock, Renfrew. Granny Kempock's Stone, on Tower Hill, probably of prehistoric origin. In 1622, Mary Lamont was burnt as a witch on a charge of intending to throw the stone into the sea to cause shipwrecks

Gosford House, East Lothian. The entrance gateway to the 18th century Gosford House, a seat of the Earls of Wemyss. The house is partly the work of Robert Adam and stands in a park off A198

[For GLEN TORRIDON see also under TORRIDON (Plate 163)

Cluanie to the head of *Loch Duich* (*q.v.*) at *Shiel Bridge* (*q.v.*). High mountains (N.T. Scot. 15,000 acres) overhang the glen, and in the lower reaches Bonnie Prince Charlie hid after the '45. On the east side, overlooking Loch Duich, are the famous *Five Sisters of Kintail*, with *Scour Ouran*, 3,505 ft., rising direct from the road-side. To the west is a line of hills culminating in the serrated ridge of *The Saddle*, 3,317 ft., with its sharp-pointed outlier of *Faochag*, 3,010 ft. In the heart of the glen, at Bridge of Shiel, spanning the River Shiel, is the site of a skirmish with Spanish troops who landed from frigates in Loch Duich during a Jacobite rising of 1719. *Sgurr nan Spainteach*, 3,129 ft., one of the Five Sisters, thus obtained its name. Dr. Johnson and Boswell traversed the glen on horseback in 1773 during their Highland tour, and the scenery in Glen Shiel determined the Doctor to write his classic "Journey to the Western Isles." A boulder in the glen, known as "Clach Johnson," is still pointed out as one under which he rested. The reconstructed road is on the line of one of the former military roads. During wet weather waterfalls in full spate descend from hills on both sides of the road. See **Kintail** and **Mam Rattachan Pass.** *Iter. 207, 220.*

GLEN STRATHFARRAR, Inverness. Map 24, **NH 2 4.**
See **Struy Bridge.**

GLEN TORRIDON, Ross and Cromarty. Map 24, **NG 9 5.**
See **Kinlochewe** and **Torridon.** *Iter. 223.*

GLEN TROOL FOREST PARK, Ayr; Kirkcudbright. Map 2, **NX 4 6** etc.
See **Loch Trool** (for main portion), **Barr, Clatteringshaws Dam** and **Newton Stewart.**

GLENUIG, Inverness. Map 12, **NM 6 7.**
See **Kinlochmoidart** and **Lochailort.** *Iter. 217.*

GLENWHILLY, Wigtown. Map 2, **NX 1 7.**
On the narrow, hilly and gated road traversing the moors between New Luce and Barrhill, the Cross Water of Luce flowing beside the road for some distance. *Iter. 78.*

GLOMACH, Ross and Cromarty. Map 24, **NH 0 2.**
See **Falls of Glomach.**

GOAT FELL, Isle of Arran, Bute. Map 7, **NR 9 4.**
See **Brodick.**

GOGAR, Midlothian. Map 9, **NT 1 7.**
GOLF. A little to the north-west stands the picturesque old *Gogar House*, which dates from 1625, and has angle turrets and a balustraded roof. Away to the north lies the Edinburgh airport at *Turnhouse*. *Iter. 15, 16.*

GOLSPIE, Sutherland. 1,614. Map 31, **NH 8 9.**
E.C. Wed. GOLF. A resort and fishing village, with a sandy beach, in an arable stretch of the county having a background of lofty moors culminating in *Beinn Lundie*, 1,464 ft. On a bridge in the village is an inscribed Sutherland clan memorial. Nearer to the village is *Beinn a' Bhragie*, 1,256 ft., on which stands a statue by Chantrey to the first Duke of Sutherland. To the north-west of Golspie is the pretty Dunrobin Glen, with its burn, overlooked to the north by *Ben Horn*, 1,706 ft. A bridge spanning the burn carries a rare Gaelic, or Ogham, inscription. See **Dunrobin.** *Iter. 200, 231, 233.*

GORDON, Berwick. 642. Map 10, **NT 6 4.**
The village is associated with the "Gay Gordons," who moved to Aberdeenshire in the 14th cent. (See **Huntly.**) A circular clock tower stands in the main street. To the north of the village is *Greenknowe Castle* (A.M.), dating from 1581, and retaining its yett, above which is inscribed the date, between two carved shields. The castle was the 16th cent. home of the Covenanter Walter Pringle. See **Mellerstain.** *Iter. 6, 33, 41.*

GORDON ARMS HOTEL, Selkirk. Map 10, **NT 3 2.**
A fishing inn and junction of roads, situated on Yarrow Water, in the heart of Ettrick Forest, within easy reach of the charming *St. Mary's Loch* (*q.v.*). Here, in 1830, Sir Walter Scott and James Hogg, the "Ettrick Shepherd," parted for the last time. A little to the north is the farm of *Mountbenger*, once tenanted by Hogg, and to the south is *Eldinhope*, formerly *Altrive Lake* farm, where he died in 1835. The road leading northwards through the hills into Peeblesshire towards *Traquair* (*q.v.*) is known as the "Paddy Slacks." **3 m. N.W.**, in the valley of the Douglas Burn, leading off the road to St. Mary's Loch, is the ruined *Blackhouse Tower*, associated with both Scott and Hogg, and the birthplace, in 1780, of Willie Laidlaw, the friend and amanuensis of Scott. *Iter. 12, 13, 34, 46.*

GORDONSTOUN, Moray. Map 26, **NJ 1 6.**
See **Duffus.**

GOREBRIDGE, Midlothian. 1,364. Map 10, **NT 3 6.**
E.C. Wed. A short distance to the south-west is the fine Palladian mansion of *Arniston*, the seat of the Dundas family. The entrance to the house has gateposts showing a lion and an elephant, and there are lovely walled gardens. See **Borthwick Castle.** *Iter. 40.*

GORTHLECK, Inverness. Map 25, **NH 5 2.**
Iter. 211, 212.

GOSFORD HOUSE, East Lothian. Map 10, **NT 4 7.**
This magnificent 18th cent. house, partly by Robert Adam, and one of the best examples of his work, stands in a park overlooking Gosford Bay in the Firth of Forth. *Iter. 2, 37.*

GOURDON, Kincardine. Map 21, **NO 8 7.**
A small hand-line fishing port with a shingle and stone foreshore, sheltered by Doolie Ness.

GOUROCK, Renfrew. 10.922. SB. Map 8, **NS 2 7.**
E.C. Wed. GOLF. One of the best known of the Firth of Clyde resorts, with a pier and a pebble beach. Its situation,

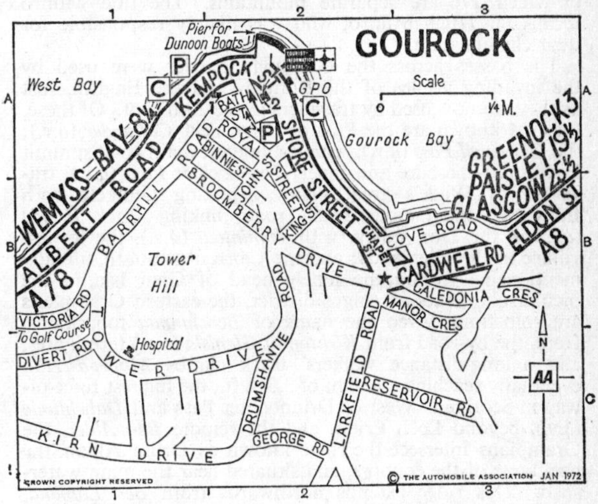

Granny Kempock's Stone 1 (A2) Tourist Information Centre 2 (A2)

on a bay facing *Kilcreggan* (*q.v.*) in the Rosneath peninsula, and looking north-westwards towards Loch Long and the Holy Loch, backed by the hills of *Cowal* (*q.v.*), is one of great natural beauty. Gourock is a good centre for yachting and for steamer trips in the waters of the Firth, and also in the *Kyles of Bute* (*q.v.*). The ancient *Granny Kempock's* Stone is probably prehistoric. **2½ m. S.W.**, on the coast, beyond the suburb of Ashton, is the ruined *Levan Castle*, in a wooded setting, near which stands the white *Cloch* (*q.v.*) lighthouse, a notable landmark. See **Inverkip.** *Iter. 59, 65, 66, 85, 88, 112, 113.*

GOVAN (Glasgow), Lanark. 35,969. Map 8, **NS 5 6.**
E.C. Tues. Now part of Glasgow, in the industrial Clydeside district, but, until 1856, a village composed largely of handloom weavers. The modern Church, on the site of an ancient monastery, stands among early Christian monuments, and in the chancel is a sarcophagus, which may have been raised over the tomb of St. Constantine, the founder, who undertook missionary work at the request of St. Mungo, the patron saint of Glasgow. *Haggs Castle*, to the south-east, an old home of the Maxwells, although altered and restored, carries the date 1585 on a door enriched by orna-

mental panels. A road tunnel under the Clyde connects with Partick. *Iter. 59.*

GRAMISDALE, Isle of Benbecula, Inverness. Map 32, **NF 0** 5. See **Hebrides, Outer** (Benbecula). *Iter. 262.*

GRAMPIANS. Map 18, **NN 1** 4, etc. The name *Grampians* is essentially a literary one, having been first used, in 1520, by Hector Boece, the historian (See **Dundee**), who found, and misread, the name " Mons Graupius," which Tacitus gave as the scene of Agricola's victory over the Picts, c. A.D. 84. Modern research places the scene of this battle at some distance to the north of the River Tay. The grass-and-heather-covered mountains which stretch across the *Highlands* (*q.v.*), from Argyll, in the west, across Perthshire to Aberdeenshire, in the north-east, are generally termed the Grampians. The range was known earlier as the Mounth, a name still preserved in the well-known pass of the *Cairn o' Mounth* (*q.v.*) in Kincardineshire, and in the great plateau of the *White Mounth* (*q.v.*), south of the Dee valley, of which the highest point is the famous granite peak of *Lochnagar* (*q.v.*). Across the valley is the even higher mass of the *Cairngorms* (*q.v.*), with their lonely lochs and corries, and a large area of flat tops exceeding 4,000 ft., a height surpassed in Scotland only by *Ben Nevis* (*q.v.*) and several of its neighbours. A considerable number of the Grampian summits exceed 3,000 ft. in height, and are known generally as " Munros," the name given to all the tops in Scotland of 3,000 ft. and over, numbering in all 543, of which 276 are separate mountains. The title Munro recalls Sir Hugh Munro, who was mainly responsible for their classification.

The passes across the Grampian barrier were used by the invading armies of the Romans and the English, just as they are now used by travellers in the 20th cent. Of these, the best known are the Pass of Leny, near *Callander* (*q.v.*); the *Cairnwell Pass* (*q.v.*), with the highest main road summit in Britain; the bare and lonely *Drumochter Pass* (*q.v.*), traversed by Wade's great highway linking Dunkeld with Inverness; the famous Lecht road, linking *Cock Bridge* (*q.v.*) in the Don valley, with *Tomintoul* (*q.v.*), the loftiest village in the Highlands; and the Cairn o' Mounth, already mentioned. Around the lonely head of Glen Isla, in the picturesque Braes of Angus district, the eastern Grampians are sometimes given the name of *Benchinnan* mountains. Here, the by-road from *Kirkton of Glenisla* (*q.v.*) terminates, and a long-distance walkers' track climbs *Monega Hill*, eventually reaching a height of 3,318 ft., the highest right-of-way in Scotland. West of Drumochter Pass and *Dalwhinnie* (*q.v.*), beyond Loch Ericht and the remote *Ben Alder*, the Grampians intersect the ridge known as Drum Alban, the backbone of the country, and situated near the main watershed. This ridge extends northwards from *Ben Lomond*, above *Loch Lomond* (*q.v.*), and finally reaches *Ben Hope*, the most northerly 3,000-ft. peak in the country, situated beyond *Altnaharra* (*q.v.*), in Sutherland. Many of the high moors in the Grampians are shot over for grouse during the season, and deer-stalking takes place in the hills, which carry snow in the winter months and provide opportunities for ski-ing in places. See **Glenshee, Spittal of.**

GRANDTULLY, Perth. 500. Map 20, **NN 9** 5. **E.C.** Wed. A small village in Strath Tay, where a bridge over the river links the roads traversing the north and south shores. **2 m. S.W.,** off the Aberfeldy road, is *Grandtully Castle*, dating from 1560, with enlargements of 1626 and 1893. It is one of those castles which Scott may have had in mind when describing " Tullyveolan " in " Waverley." A little to the south is the old Church of *St. Mary* (A.M.), which is notable for its 17th cent. painted ceiling. In the background, beyond the river to the north, rises *Farragon Hill*, 2,559 ft., below which is Loch Derculich, from which flows the Derculich Burn to join the Tay. *Iter. 120, 139, 149, 157, 158.*

GRANGEMOUTH, Stirling. 24,572. SB. Map 16, **NS 9** 8 **E.C.** Wed. A Forth estuary port (stony foreshore) and oil-refining town, with important docks, situated at the point of convergence of the River Carron and the Forth and Clyde Canal. The latter, which is 38 miles long, was the work of Smeaton, in 1790, and crosses the narrow waist of Scotland to enter the Clyde at *Bowling* (*q.v.*). Scotland's first power bridge was opened here in 1880. Grangemouth is to-day Scotland's largest complex of oil installations, refineries and ancillary works. *Iter. 17.*

GRANTON (Edinburgh), Midlothian. Map 17, **NT 2** 7. The harbour dates from 1835, and faces *Burntisland* (*q.v.*), some five miles across the Firth of Forth. On the southern outskirts of Granton is the beautiful old mansion of *Caroline Park*, commenced in 1685, the picturesque south front, with its ogee-shaped tower roofs, dating from 1696. There is some notable ironwork in the house. Farther to the west lies *Drylaw*, another house from about the same period, also with good ironwork.

GRANTOWN-ON-SPEY, Moray. 1,581. SB. Map 26, **NJ 0** 2. **E.C.** Thurs. **M.D.** Sat. GOLF. A well-known Highland summer and winter resort, at a height of nearly 700 ft., beautifully situated in Strath Spey, and having been founded in 1776. It is built almost entirely of granite, and makes an excellent touring centre for Strath Spey and the fine mountain country in the district. There are good distant views of the lofty *Cairngorms* (*q.v.*) away to the south, while eastwards rise the nearer *Cromdale* hills, over 2,000 ft. high in places.

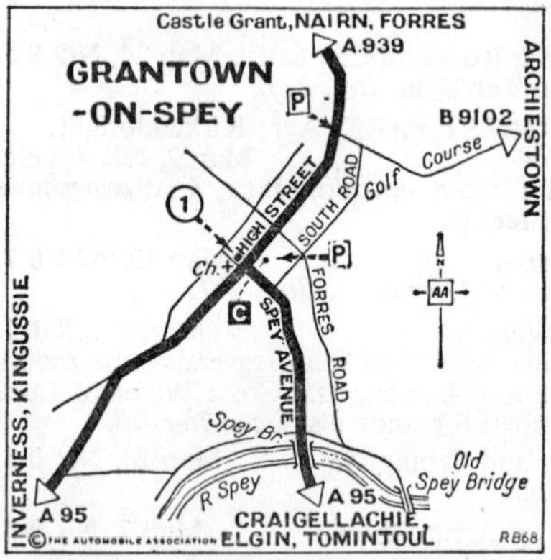

Tourist Information Centre 1

The bridge over the Spey, on the Craigellachie road, has a concrete arch of 240 ft., and a little farther east is the older three-span bridge, dating from 1754. This rapid-flowing river is the second longest in Scotland, and is famous for its salmon. The road leading south-eastwards from the Spey into the hills towards *Tomintoul* (*q.v.*) climbs to more than 1,400 ft., with fine views, on the way to *Bridge of Brown* (*q.v.*). **2½ m. N.** of Grantown is the fine old mansion of *Castle Grant*, 16th to 18th cent. See **Dulnain Bridge** and **Lochindorb.** *Iter. 141, 149, 160, 171, 172, 176, 177, 195.*

GRANTSHOUSE, Berwick. Map 11, **NT 8** 6. Situated on the Eye Water. **3 m. S.E.,** off the Great North Road, is the old mansion of *Houndwood*, with its fine gardens. *Iter. 1, 38, 39.*

GREAT GLEN, Inverness. Map 18, **NN 2** 9 etc. and 24, **NH 3** 0 etc. See **Glen More.** *Iter. 207, 210, 213, 214.*

GREENLAW, Berwick. 778. Map 10, **NT 7** 4. **E.C.** Wed. This little town, on the Blackadder Water, in the foothills of the *Lammermuirs*, takes its name from a low " green law," or isolated hill, a little to the south-east, where the village was formerly situated. Greenlaw was between 1696 and 1853 the county town of Berwickshire until replaced by Duns. The Mercat Cross by the Church dates from 1696, but is not on the original site. The tower of the Church dates from 1712, though built in the style of the late 15th cent., and was built for use as a gaol. **3 m. S.** is the ruined *Hume Castle*, at a height of some 600 ft., having been captured by Cromwell in 1651, and to a certain extent restored in 1794. The Castle makes a fine viewpoint, and was at one period a seat of the Earls of Home. **3 m. S.E.** is the mansion of *Rowchester*, with its attractive gardens. **4 m. E.N.E.,** off the Berwick road, is the motor-racing track of *Charterhall.* See **Gordon** and **Polwarth.** *Iter. 5, 8, 33, 41.*

Grampians, Argyll; Perth. An old bridge, at a height of 1,125 feet, at the Spittal of Glenshee, on the Blairgowrie to Braemar road (A93), in the Grampian mountains. Near this point a hospice once stood

Grampians, Argyll; Perth. The point north of Dalwhinnie, on A9, in the Grampian mountains, where General Wade's road to Inverness diverges from his famous road over the Corrieyairack Pass, leading to Fort Augustus, now derelict

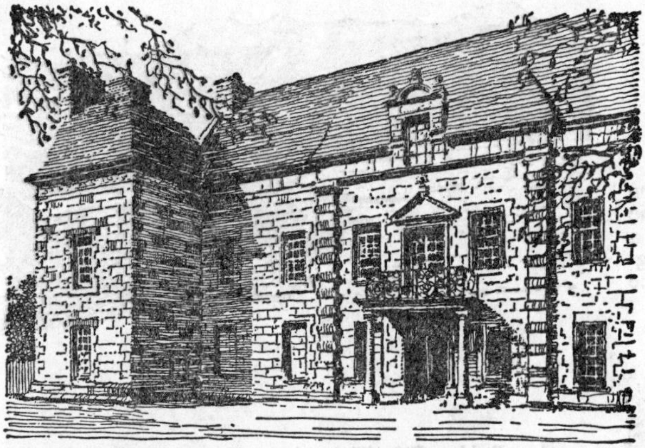

Granton, Midlothian. The south front of Caroline Park, a house built in 1685–96 by George Mackenzie, first Viscount Tarbat

Greenlaw, Berwick. The Market Cross of 1696, which has been moved from its original site

Greenlaw, Berwick. The restored Hume Castle, the predecessor of which was captured by Cromwell in 1651. In 1804, as the result of a false alarm, a beacon was lit here to give warning of an impending Napoleonic invasion. It stands 3 miles south, off B6364

Grantown-on-Spey, Moray. The Old Spey Bridge (1754), now closed to traffic

PLATE 78

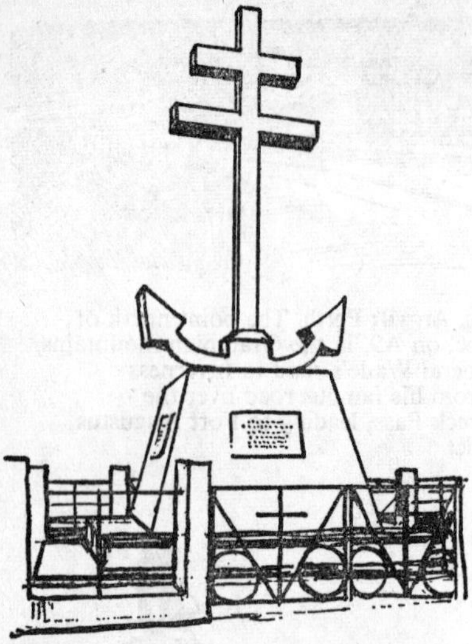

Greenock, Renfrew. The Cross on Lyle Hill, in memory of Free French sailors who gave their lives during the Second World War battle of the Atlantic

Gretna, Dumfries. Gretna Hall, built in 1710. Between 1825 and 1855, some 1,134 runaway marriages were performed in Gretna according to records preserved at the Hall

Gruinard Bay, Ross and Cromarty. The view towards the great Teallach peaks. On the west side of the bay, in the Rudha Mor peninsula, is the little Loch na Beiste, where a monster is said to have been destroyed by the throwing-in of 14 barrels of lime

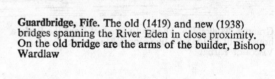

Guardbridge, Fife. The old (1419) and new (1938) bridges spanning the River Eden in close proximity. On the old bridge are the arms of the builder, Bishop Wardlaw

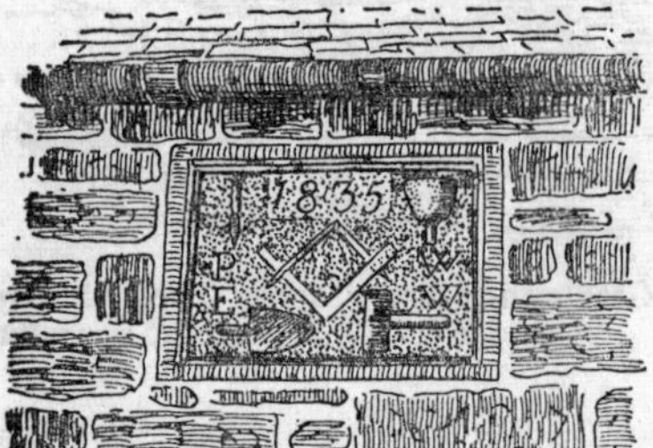

Guildtown, Perth. An inscription of 1835 on the wall of a cottage, probably commemorating a local marriage, and depicting a mason's tools

Gullane, East Lothian. The remains of the 12th century Church. James VI dismissed the last vicar for smoking tobacco, and the building was destroyed in 1631

[For GRETNA see also under SOLWAY FIRTH (Plate 152)

GREENLOANING, Perth. Map 16, NN 8 0.
In Strath Allan, and a junction of roads leading from Dunblane to Crieff and Perth. The Allan Water is joined here by the Knaik Water, the latter flowing down from *Braco* (*q.v.*), noted for its great Roman earthworks. See **Blackford.** *Iter. 135, 138, 140, 146.*

GREENOCK, Renfrew. 69,004. LB. Map 8, NS 2 7.
E.C. Wed. **M.D.** Tues. GOLF. An important industrial and shipbuilding town on the Clyde estuary, damaged by bombs in the Second World War. The oldest shipyard dates from 1711 and the last sizable wooden ship was built here in 1859. East of the town is the new Clydeport Container Terminal. The well-known roadstead in the river off Greenock is known as the " Tail of the Bank." The town was the birtplace in 1736, of James Watt, and a statue of him by Chantrey is in the Watt Library and Institution. In the cemetery is the Watt Cairn, and nearby is the tombstone of Burns's " Highland Mary," which has been removed from the old North Kirk. A Cross on the viewpoint of Lyle Hill is a monument to Free French sailors who lost their lives in the Battle of the Atlantic during the Second World War. Behind the town are moors, on which the waterworks are situated, commanding good views of the Clyde estuary and its mountain background. See **Gourock** and **Tarbolton.** *Iter. 59, 64, 65, 85, 88, 112, 113.*

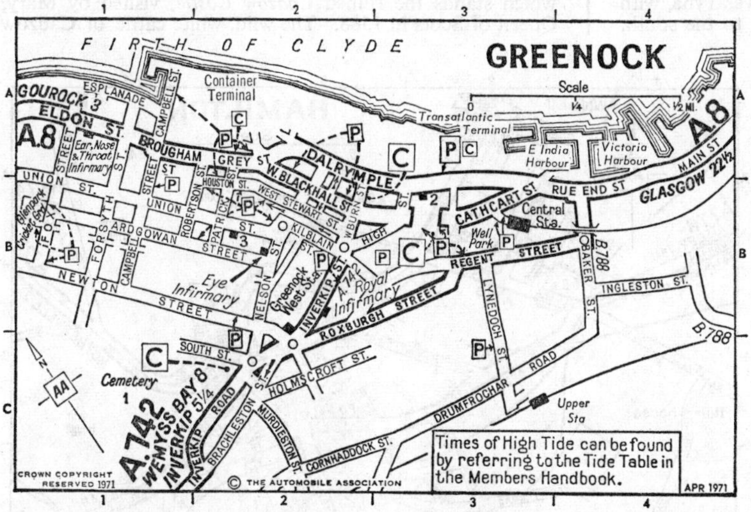

Cemetery (Watt Cairn) 1 (C1)
James Watt's Birthplace 2 (B3)
Watt Library and Institute 3 (B2)

GRETNA, Dumfries. 1,930. Map 4, NY 3 6.
E.C. Wed. Famous as the place where runaway couples from England formerly came to be married, the ceremony being performed in accordance with 18th cent. Scots law by means of a declaration before witnesses. These took place at the Sark Toll Bar (See **Sark Bridge**); in local inns; at *Gretna Hall*; and in the well-known smithy at *Gretna Green*, interesting records having been kept at the two latter places. In 1856, an Act was passed necessitating three weeks residence north of the Border before a marriage could take place. The bridge over the River Sark is the actual Border, and a little to the south-west the river flows into the Solway Firth, noted for its dangerous tides, which occasionally form a " bore " nearly 4 ft. in height. About **3 m. N.E.** is the site of the battle of Solway Moss, in 1542, where the Scots were defeated. **1 m. S.**, near the Solway Firth shore, is the *Lochmaben Stone*, 7 ft. high and weighing 10 tons, probably having formed part of a stone circle. The stone has been on various occasions a meeting place for conferences, and in 1398 details of a truce between Scotland and England were discussed here. See **Canonbie, Lamberton, Sark Bridge** and **Springfield.** *Iter. 10, 13, 26, 27, 28, 29, 42, 50, 51.*

GRETNA GREEN, Dumfries. Map 4, NY 3 6.
See **Gretna.** *Iter. 10, 13, 29, 50, 51, 67.*

GREY MARE'S TAIL, Dumfries. Map 4, NT 1 1.
See **Birkhill** and **Moffat.** *Iter. 13, 46.*

GRIBUN, Isle of Mull, Argyll. Map 13, NM 4 3.
Situated on Loch na Keal, with a remarkable range of lofty cliffs, below which lies the road from *Salen* (*q.v.*) to Loch Scridain. Off-shore is the island of *Inch Kenneth*, where Dr. Johnson and Boswell were once entertained. Farther out are the islands of Ulva, Gometra, Little Colonsay and *Staffa* (*q.v.*). In the background, to the east, rises *Ben More*, 3,169 ft., the monarch of the island, and a splendid viewpoint. To the west of the Gribun cliffs is the almost roadless Ardmeanach peninsula, showing notable cliff scenery, and with the experimental farm of *Burg* (N.T. Scot.) facing Loch Scridain (See **Kilfinichen Church**). The road linking Gribun with the south-west corner of Mull goes east of the hilly Ardmeanach country by way of Glen Seilisdeir, and then rounds the head of Loch Scridain. *Iter. 249.*

GROGPORT, Argyll. Map 7, NR 8 4.
Lies in a small bay of the Kilbrennan Sound, looking across its waters to *Beinn Bharrain*, 2,345 ft., one of the Arran peaks. *Iter. 122.*

GRUDIE BRIDGE, Ross and Cromarty.
See **Loch Maree.** Map 24, NG 9 6.

GRUINARD BAY, Ross and Cromarty.
Map 29, NG 9 9.
One of the loveliest bays of *Wester Ross* in the North-West Highlands, having fine sands and picturesque outcrops of grey rock in a background of low, rugged hills. The bay is approached from the west by descending the once-notorious Gruinard Hill (1 in 6), from the summit of which the view is remarkably fine, taking in the great *Teallach* range, and also the *Coigach* hills away to the north-east. A little to the west of the summit are the curiously-named clachans of *Second Coast* and *First Coast*. Two rivers, the Little Gruinard and the Gruinard, flow into the bay, in which is situated Gruinard Island. *Gruinard House*, behind which the Gruinard River flows through a gorge, is situated on the shores of the bay. The course of the river is south-eastwards towards the lonely Loch na Sheallag, above which rise the Torridon sandstone peaks of *An Teallach*, nearly 3,500 ft. high, best visited from *Dundonnell* (*q.v.*). To the south of Gruinard Bay lies the lonely Fisherfield Forest, dominated by *Beinn Dearg Mhor*, 2,974 ft. *Iter. 206, 222.*

GUARDBRIDGE, Fife. 977. Map 17, NO 4 1.
The old bridge over the River Eden dates from c. 1420, and carries on one of the keystones a shield of arms and a pastoral staff recalling its building by Bishop Wardlaw, an early Bishop of St. Andrews. A new bridge, situated alongside, now carries the traffic. To the north is a large paper mill. The Eden flows into St. Andrews Bay, on the north shore of which is the lonely and extensive Tents Moor, with its forestrv plantations. See **Tayport.** *Iter. 93, 94, 131 136.*

GUILDTOWN, Perth. Map 17, NO 1 3.
See **Stobhall.** *Iter. 152.*

GULLANE, East Lothian. 1,482. Map 10, NT 4 8.
E.C. Wed. GOLF. A well-known resort and golfing centre on the Firth of Forth, with excellent sands and bathing. The championship course at *Muirfield*, the headquarters of the Hon. Company of Edinburgh Golfers, situated a little to the north-east, is world-famous. The roofless Old Church at Gullane retains a little Norman work. *Saltcoats Castle*, to the south, is of 16th cent. date, and preserves its old

dovecote. R. L. Stevenson's novel "Catriona" contains local colour. There are fine views over the Firth towards the Fife coast, backed by the distant *Lomond* and *Ochil* hills. See **Aberlady** and **Dirleton.** *Iter. 2, 36, 37.*

GUTHRIE, Angus. 1,072 with Kirkden. Map 21, NO 5 5. The square *Guthrie Tower* dates largely from 1468, and the gardens are picturesque. It is open Sun., 2 to 6, mid-May to Aug. (see note page 98). *Gardyne Castle* is 16th, 18th and 19th cent. To the west, off the Forfar road, are the small Balgavies Loch and the larger Rescobie Loch. *Iter. 153.*

HADDINGTON, East Lothian. 6,505. SB. Map 10, NT 5 7. **E.C.** Thurs. **M.D.** Mon. GOLF. A Royal Burgh, noted for its grain market, situated on the River Tyne, with the *Lammermuir* hills as a background away to the south. It is now by-passed by the Great North Road. The town was burnt on several occasions by the English in the middle ages, and its name was at one time given to the county as a whole. Alexander II was born here in 1198, and John Knox is thought to have been born in the town in 1505. The Town House (1748), with its curfew bell, is the work of William Adam, the tower having been added in 1831 by Gillespie Graham. The Mercat Cross is topped by a goat. The town library includes the valuable 17th cent. collection amassed by John Gray, born in the town in 1646. Both *Haddington House* and *Moat House*, Eastgate, date from the 17th cent. The fine, restored Church (A.M.), known as the "Lamp of Lothian," dating mainly from the 15th cent., is a cruciform structure, but the choir and transepts are ruined. The splendid central tower was once surmounted by a crown, as at *St. Giles* in *Edinburgh* (*q.v.*). The west front of the nave is impressive, with a good double doorway, and in the choir is the tomb of Jane Welsh, the wife of Thomas Carlyle. The ruined Church of *St. Martin*, nearby, is of 12th cent. date. Two fine old bridges span the Tyne, the *Nungate Bridge*, 16th cent., from which criminals were hanged, and the *Abbey Bridge*, about a mile to the east of the town, a structure of the early 16th cent. **2 m. N.**, near the *Garleton* hills, are remains of the 16th cent. *Barnes Castle.* A monument to the 4th Earl of Hopetoun is situated on the hills. **2 m. N.E.** of the town is the restored 16th and 18th cent. *Stevenson House*, near the River Tyne. **3 m. E.** of Haddington, situated off a by-road, stands the lonely little Church of *Morham*, dating from 1685 and 1724, and preserving a bell dated 1681, which was probably cast in Holland. See **Aberlady, Bolton** (for *Lennoxlove*), **Garvald** and **Gifford.** *Iter. 1, 36, 40.*

HALKIRK, Caithness. 1,474. Map 30, ND 1 5. **E.C.** Wed. A village laid out in symmetrical fashion, and situated on the River Thurso, noted for its fishing. The main Wick to Thurso road passes a little to the east of Halkirk. Across the river, to the north, is the ancient *Brawl Castle*, with walls 8 to 10 feet thick, perhaps 14th cent. work. A modern house adjoins the old tower. **4 m. W.** is Loch Calder, with numerous prehistoric remains in the vicinity, and to the east are Loch Scarmelett (4 m.) and the larger Loch Watten (6½ m.), the latter noted for trout fishing. *Iter. 239.*

HAMILTON, Lanark. 46,347. LB. Map 8, NS 7 5. **E.C.** Wed. **M.D.** Fri. GOLF. A Royal Burgh and centre of a mining district, with some of the pleasantest wooded stretches of the River Avon to the south-east. To the east of the town, the Avon has its junction with the more important Clyde. Beyond the meeting of the waters, away to the south-east, the Clyde flows through attractive orchard country in the direction of *Crossford* (*q.v.*). Mary, Queen of Scots rested at Hamilton after escaping from *Loch Leven Castle* (*q.v.*), and in 1651 Cromwell made his headquarters in the town. The octagonal Parish Church was designed in 1732 by William Adam. Facing it is the Celtic *Netherton* Cross. A Covenanters' monument, with four heads in relief, is in the churchyard. A late 17th cent. house is intended to become a museum. The palatial *Hamilton Palace*, now demolished, owing to subsidences caused by mining, stood formerly in the *Low Parks*, to the north-east. In the parks are the racecourse, and the Hamilton Mausoleum, which cost some £150,000 to build around 1850 and was designed by David Bryce. South of Hamilton are the *High Parks*, in which stands the ruined *Cadzow Castle*, visited by Mary, Queen of Scots in 1568. The wild, white cattle of Cadzow

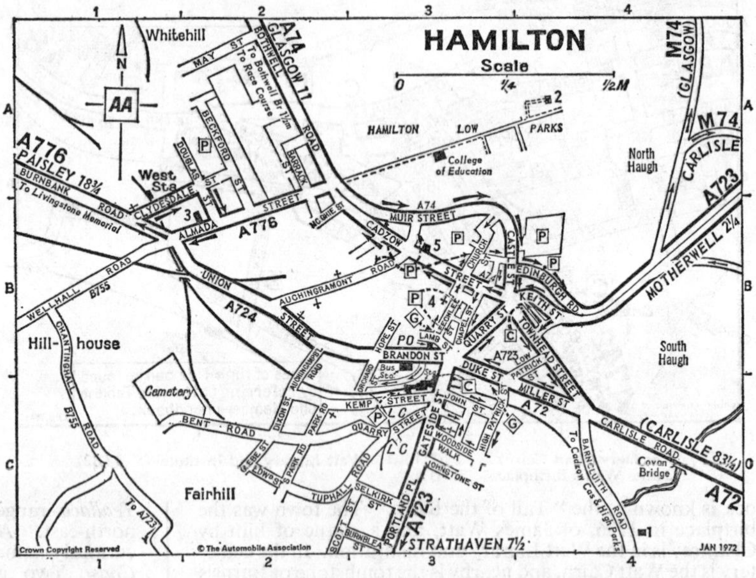

Barncluith House, 16th cent. 1 (C4)
Hamilton Mausoleum 2 (A4)
Hamilton County Office 3 (B2)
Parish Church, 1732 and Netherton Cross 4 (B3)
Town Hall; Information Bureau 5 (B3)

3 m. N.W. by exit A724 (A1), is the Livingstone Memorial at Blantyre

Park are probably unique in Scotland. *Chatelherault Lodge* is an 18th cent. design by William Adam. Above the Avon stands the 16th cent. house of *Barncluith*, with its fine gardens, both house and gardens being constructed in a series of terraces. See **Blantyre** (for *Livingstone Memorial*) and **Bothwell.** *Iter. 19, 51, 53, 87.*

HAMPDEN PARK (Glasgow), Lanark. Map 8, NS 5 6. See **Glasgow.**

HANDA, ISLE OF, Sutherland. Map 28, NC 1 4. This tiny island lies a little to the north-west of *Scourie* (*q.v.*) Bay, and is separated from the mainland by the narrow Sound of Handa. On the island, which is reached by boat from Scourie, there are red Torridon sandstone cliffs 400 ft. high, which command a fine view of the mainland mountains in the lonely Forest of Reay. Handa is preserved as a sanctuary for sea-fowl.

HARDGATE, Dunbarton. 1,904. Map 8, NS 5 7. *Iter. 113.*

HARLAW, Aberdeen. Map 27, NJ 7 2. See **Inveramsay.**

Haddington, East Lothian. The Mercat Cross, which is surmounted by the figure of a goat

Haddington, East Lothian. The Town House, designed originally in 1748 by William Adam

Halkirk, Caithness. Massive walls of the 14th century Brawl Castle, which stands on the farther side of the River Thurso

Harlaw, Aberdeen. The Monument, erected in 1911, to commemorate the battle of Harlaw (1411), ending in the defeat of the Highlanders under Donald, Lord of the Isles. It stands north of the River Urie, off B9001

Hamilton, Lanark. The octagonal Parish Church, the work of William Adam in 1732. In front of it stands the Celtic Netherton Cross

Hawick Mote, the mound of a Norman Castle, which was probably 12th century work by one of the Lovels who then held Hawick

The Horse Monument, which recalls the defeat of English marauders at Hornshole Bridge in 1514, by the local 'callants,' or youths, the grown men having been practically wiped out at Flodden a year earlier

The Monument in Wilton Lodge Park to the well known racing motor-cyclist, Jimmie Guthrie, who was killed in Germany in 1937

A pillar near Hornshole Bridge, over the River Teviot (off A698), some 2 miles north-east, commemorating the victory of the Hawick youths in 1514 (see above)

Branxholm Tower (1571), an old home of the Scott family. It stands some 3 miles south-west, in Teviotdale, off A7

[For HEBRIDES, OUTER, see two following plates

HARRIS, Inverness. Map 32, **NG 0 9** etc.
(Part of Isle of Lewis, Ross and Cromarty.)
See **Hebrides, Outer** (Harris and Lewis). *Iter. 256.*

HARTHILL, Lanark. 4,152. Map 9, **NS 9 6.**
E.C. Wed. A small mining town, on the edge of moorland country. *Iter. 15, 18.*

HASSENDEAN, Roxburgh. Map 10, **NT 5 1.**
A village associated with the song "Jock o' Hazeldean." The old Church was demolished in 1690.

HAWICK, Roxburgh. 16,760. SB. Map 10, **NT 5 1.**
E.C. Tues. **M.D.** Thurs. GOLF. One of the most important of the Border towns, situated in the heart of Teviotdale, at the confluence of the River Teviot and the Slitrig Water, and noted especially for woollens, yarn and hosiery. In 1570, the town was almost completely burnt down, one of the few earlier buildings still remaining being part of what is now the "*Tower*" Hotel. Anne, the widow of the executed Duke of Monmouth, and with whom Scott's "Lay of the Last Minstrel" is associated, lived here once, while the building was visited also by Wordsworth and Scott. *St. Mary's* Church, consecrated in 1214, was rebuilt in 1763. In the churchyard is buried John Hardie, the founder, in 1771, of the town's woollen industry. The extensive

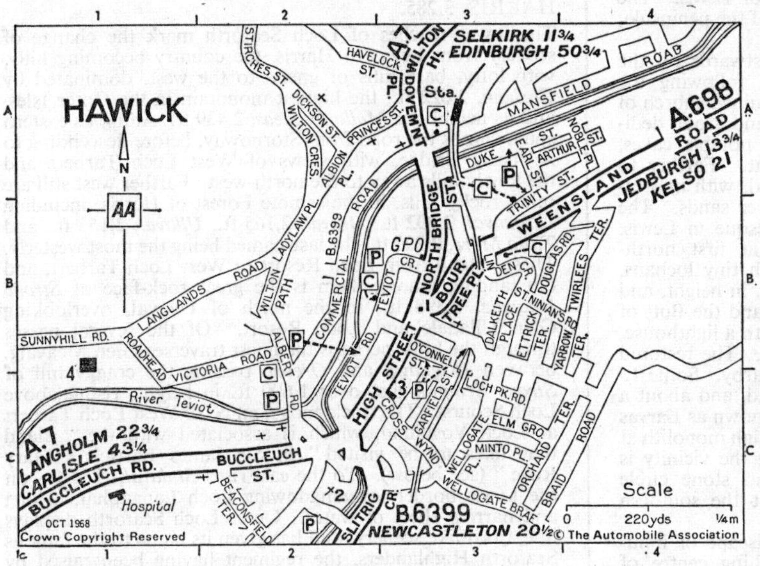

Horse Monument 1 (B3) Town Hall; Information Bureau 3 (C3)
St. Mary's Church, 1763 2 (C2) Wilton Lodge Park, Museum and War Memorial 4 (B1)

Mote Hill, 30 ft. high and 300 ft. round, nearby, is the mound of a Norman Castle. Hawick is well known for the picturesque ceremony known as the "Common Riding" which takes place annually early in June, and commemorates a victory over the English in 1514. The Horse Monument in the town recalls the event, and a pillar, dated 1514, stands **2 m. N.E.,** near a bridge over the Teviot at Hornshole. *Wilton Lodge* is now a museum of much interest, open regularly. (See note page 98.) **2 m. S.W.,** in Teviotdale, is the ancient tower of *Goldielands*, owned formerly by a branch of the Scott family. A mile farther is *Branxholm Tower*, an old home of the Scotts, dated 1571 and later, the original tower having been blown up in 1570. It is associated with Sir Walter Scott's "Lay of the Last Minstrel." **4½ m.W.,** beyond the valley of the Borthwick Water, is the much-restored *Harden House*, 16th or 17th cent., associated with Scott's ancestors. See **Bonchester Bridge** (for *Border Forest Park*), **Dalkeith, Denholm, Dundee, Hassendean, Hermitage Castle, Roberton** and **St. Mary's Loch.** *Iter. 11, 30, 31, 34, 36, 44, 45.*

HAWTHORNDEN, Midlothian. Map 10, **NT 2 6.**
See **Lasswade.**

HAZELBANK, Lanark. Map 9, **NS 8 4.**
Iter. 53.

HEBRIDES, INNER, Argyll; Inverness.
(Western Isles.) Maps 6, 12, 13, 22 and 23.
The islands of this group lie off the much-indented west coast. They extend from Skye, the most northerly, which is separated from the *Outer Hebrides* (*q.v.*) by the waters of the Little Minch, to Islay, in the south, which lies off the narrow Kintyre peninsula, and is at one point only some 25 miles distant from the coast of Northern Ireland. The largest and most picturesque island is Skye, famous for the precipitous Coolin mountains, while Iona and Staffa, two of the smallest, are both of unique interest, the former for its Cathedral and associations with St. Columba, and the latter for its strange basaltic rocks and the well-known Fingal's Cave. The principal islands are fully described individually, and, in addition, all places of interest on Skye, Mull and Islay have their own separate entries. See **Colonsay, Iona, Islay, Jura, Mull, Rum** (also for **Eigg**), **Skye, Staffa** and **Tiree** (also for **Coll**). *Iter. 243 to 255.*

HEBRIDES, OUTER, Inverness; Ross and Cromarty.
(Western Isles.) Map 32.
The chain of islands 130 miles in length, known as the *Outer Hebrides*, or *Long Island*, is separated from the Scottish mainland by the Minch, and from the nearer island of Skye, in the Inner Hebrides, by the Little Minch. The much-indented and sandy western Hebridean seaboard, with its many small islands off-shore, receives the full force of the great Atlantic breakers. In the extreme north is the Butt of Lewis, and the most southerly point is the small island of Berneray, where a lighthouse is situated on Barra Head. The largest of the group is *Lewis*, which belongs to Ross and Cromarty, but its southern quarter, *Harris*, forms part of Inverness-shire, as do all the smaller islands to the south, chief among which are North and South Uist, Benbecula, and Barra. Except in Harris, where there are bare and lonely mountains over 2,500 ft. high, the surface of the islands is almost universally flat, with lonely moors and a multiplicity of small lochans. The soil is mainly of poor quality and lacking in trees. Some of the primitive, thatched "black" houses in which the Gaelic-speaking inhabitants live are still to be seen, though in rapidly diminishing numbers. Roads on the large island of Lewis are fair, but many are narrow and winding, more particularly in the district of South Harris. There are altogether about 170 miles of good motoring roads in Lewis and Harris. On the smaller islands the road mileage is very limited, but a viaduct links Benbecula with South Uist. A new causeway now connects Benbecula and North Uist. Excellent fishing and shooting are available in the islands, and manufacture of the famous handwoven Harris Tweed is of great importance.

In the 11th cent. the Norsemen settled in the islands, but after their defeat at *Largs* (*q.v.*) in Ayrshire, in 1263, the Scottish supremacy was established. In the 14th cent., John of Islay, a supporter of Robert Bruce, became the first Lord of the Isles. Prehistoric remains, such as cairns, brochs and forts, notably the famous standing stones of *Callanish*, as well as numerous small ruined churches, are a feature of the Outer Hebrides, which are described individually below. A number of ports in the islands, from *Stornoway*, in Lewis, to *Castlebay*, in Barra, are linked by steamer to various mainland ports, for which see details in the steamship communications section at the end of the book. A map of the **Western Isles** appears on pages 34 and 35 of the atlas. There are air services to Barra and Benbecula from Glasgow (Renfrew airport), and Stornoway is linked by air to both Glasgow and Inverness.

LEWIS. 16,708.
Known also as *The Lews*, this island, together with its southern extension of Harris (see below), is some 60 miles long and 18 to 28 miles wide. It was for a time, after 1918, a possession of Lord Leverhulme, whose efforts to modernise the islands' trade failed owing to the indifference of the inhabitants. The largest town in the Outer Isles is the important herring fishing port and tweed-spinning town of **Stornoway** (5,282. SB), situated on the east coast, with a fine natural harbour, an airport, and linked by a narrow neck of land to the **Eye** peninsula. There is a GOLF course. In *St. Peter's* Church is an ancient font, and Livingstone's Prayer Book is preserved. The modern *Stornoway*, or *Lewis Castle*, in its fine, wooded grounds, donated by Lord Leverhulme, is now a technical college. South of the town, on Arnish Moor, beyond the Creed estate, a cairn and a loch commemorate the night spent by Prince Charles Edward in a local farm after the battle of Culloden, in 1746. At the north-east extremity of the Eye peninsula, looking over the sandy Broad Bay to Vatisker Point and Tolsta Head on the main part of the island, is *Tiumpan Head*, with rock scenery and a lighthouse, giving views extending across the Minch towards the distant cliffs of Cape Wrath. The ruined 14th cent. or earlier *Eye* Church of *St. Columba* contains monuments of interest, including the Macleod tombs, one of which may be of Roderick Macleod VIII of Lewis. The building stands in the south-western corner of the peninsula, near the Stornoway road.

On the secondary road leading north-eastwards on the main part of the island from Stornoway, following the sandy bays of the coast, is *Gress*, where the ruined church of *St. O af* is said to be the only one in the island group dedicated to a Norse saint. There are some notable caves, including the Seal Cave, accessible by boat. Farther to the north-east, beyond *Tolsta*, is Tolsta Head, with impressive, rocky cliffs, a lighthouse, and fine silver sands. The bay of *Geiraha* is one of the most picturesque in Lewis. Another road from Stornoway proceeds at first north-westwards by way of moorland, dotted with tiny lochans, passing near the *Barvas* hills, nearly 1,000 ft. in height, and then follows the west coast to **Port of Ness** and the Butt of Lewis, at the northern extremity of Lewis, with a lighthouse, some wild rock scenery and extensive views. The restored 12th cent. Teampull of *St. Molua* stands nearby. Some 15 miles distant from Stornoway along this road, and about a mile from the Atlantic coast in the district known as **Barvas** (4,331), a left turn leads to the notable 18-ft. high monolith at **Shader** known as the *Clach an Trushal*. In the vicinity is the ruined *Steinacleit* chambered cairn and stone circle (A.M.) of the Neolithic period, situated at the southern extremity of Loch an Duin.

Some **16 m. W.** of Stornoway, in a landscape of innumerable tiny lochans, and beyond the fishing centre of **Garynahine,** is the famous group of Standing Stones at **Callanish** (A.M.), situated just off the main road, and forming the most remarkable antiquity in the Western Isles, being exceeded in importance only by Stonehenge. There is a well-marked megalithic avenue, comprising 19 monoliths, ending in a circle of 13 stones, with rows of other stones fanning out, and forming probably remains of additional circles. A great cairn, 40 ft. in diameter, stands within the circle. Nearby stood formerly a typical crofter's "black house." Opposite Callanish is the island of *Great Bernera*, now accessible by means of a road bridge, with Loch Roag to the west and East Loch Roag to the east. About **7 m. N.W.** of Garynahine, on Loch Carloway, an inlet of the larger East Loch Roag, is the well-known and exceptionally well-preserved **Carloway** broch (A.M.). A road leads north-eastwards from here, along a coastline dotted with crofting communities, notably *Shawbost* and *Bragor*, the last-named still having thatched roof "black" houses. It links up with the direct Stornoway to Port of Ness road. Another road can be followed from Garynahine in a south-westerly direction, through remote country with many lochans, beyond which lies the large expanse of Loch Langabhat. This road traverses some of the farthest west parts of Lewis by way of Little Loch Roag, and goes through the picturesque trough of Glen Valtos to reach **Uig** (2,431), near which are large stretches of silver sands and fine cliff scenery, with Gallen Head overlooking the island-studded Loch Roag, to the north. On Loch Bharabhat is an example of a defensive dun on a small island, linked to the shore by a narrow causeway. Far out to sea, to the north-west, are the lonely *Flannan* islands, known also as the "Seven Hunters." Some **4 m. S.W.** of Uig are *Ardroil Sands*, backed to the south by a range of remote and rocky hills, in which rises *Mealasbhal*, 1,885 ft. Beyond its eastern flanks and the hill of *Tarain* extends the long and narrow Loch Suainaval, over 200 ft. deep in places, the greatest depth reached in the Lews. South of the hills in a roadless district, is the headland of Gearraidh na h-Airde Moire, with its collection of beehive houses near the mouth of Loch Resort, opposite which rises the precipitous, rocky hill of *Tarran Mor*, in Harris.

South-westwards from Stornoway, the road to Harris passes near many small lochs, and also the heads of Lochs Luirbost and Erisort, to reach the very picturesque Loch Seaforth and the county boundary at **Aline**, facing Seaforth Island. This south-east corner of Lewis is known as **Park** (797), with a high point of 1,874 ft. at *Beinn Mhor*, and off its shores, beyond the inlet of Loch Shell, lie the tiny *Shiant* islands.

HARRIS. 3,285.
The lower reaches of Loch Seaforth mark the change of scenery from Lewis to Harris, the country becoming hilly, with lofty, bare hills of gneiss to the west, dominated by *Clisham*, 2,622 ft., the highest mountain in the Outer Isles, and its neighbour *Mulla fo dheas*, 2,439 ft. Along its eastern spurs climbs the road from Stornoway, before descending to Ardhasig Bridge, with views of West Loch Tarbert and the lonely hills away to the north-west. Farther west still are other rocky hills, in the remote Forest of Harris, including *Uisgnaval*, 2,392 ft., *Oreval*, 2,165 ft., *Ullaval*, 2,153 ft., and *Tirga More*, 2,227 ft., the last-named being the most westerly. These extend from Loch Resort to West Loch Tarbert, and outstanding among them is the great rock-face of *Strone Ulladale*, 1,398 ft., to the north of Ullaval, overlooking Glen Ulladale and Loch Resort. Of the several passes through the hills perhaps the finest traverses Glen Meavaig. between *Uisgnaval* and *Oreval*, passing the craggy hill of *Strone Scourst*, just over 1,600 ft. in height, rising above Loch Scourst. The track ends **4 m. N.** of West Loch Tarbert at Loch Voshimid, which is associated with the "island that likes to be visited" in Sir James Barrie's "Mary Rose" (see below). To the east rises *Stulaval*, 1,887 ft., on the Lewis border, overshadowing Loch Langabhat, a long and narrow sheet of water. Outer Loch Seaforth displays fine, fjord-like scenery, and has given its name to the famous Seaforth Highlanders, the regiment having been raised by the Mackenzie who hunted in the *Park* district, to the east of the loch. **Tarbert**, the principal village of Harris, is situated on the narrow isthmus dividing West and East Loch Tarbert, and has a steamer pier on the latter. Away to the west rises *Ben Luskentyre*, over 1,600 ft. high, overlooking the island of Taransay.

About **10 m. N.W.** of Tarbert, on an attractive, narrow road along West Loch Tarbert, beyond Ardhasig Bridge, is *Amhuinnsuidhe Castle*, where Barrie wrote much of "Mary Rose." Still farther west is *Husinish Bay*, with fine scenery, and to the north-west lies the small island of Scarp. South of Tarbert, and looking across East Loch Tarbert towards *Scalpay*, a calling-place for steamers, a road leads through the delightful district of South Harris, turning westwards by way of Glen Laxdale, noted for its funeral cairns, to reach Luskentyre Bay, with its silver sands. Beyond lies the Sound of Taransay with Taransay Island. The road continues past sandy bays, with views of the Toe Head peninsula, on which is situated *Cape Difficulty*, one of the only three "capes" in Great Britain. It then traverses Glen Coishletter, near the shores of the Sound of Harris, to reach the most southerly part of Harris at **Leverburgh, or Obbe,** where Lord Leverhulme tried unsuccessfully to create a fishing station. **3 m. S.E.,** on Rodel Bay, is **Rodel,** where the well-known, restored cruciform Church of *St. Clement* (A.M.)

The remarkable collection of Standing Stones, amounting to nearly 50 in all, which are to be found at Callanish, on A858, some 16 miles west of Stornoway

Rodel Church, dating from 1500, which contains some notable Macleod tombs. It stands on A859, in the extreme south of Harris, near Obbe

A primitive, thatched crofter's ' black house,' near Daliburgh, on the island of South Uist

Stornoway, or Lewis Castle, built in the 19th century, and now a technical college. Lord Leverhulme presented it to the town

The Memorial cairn on the site of the former birthplace (1722) of Flora Macdonald, which stands at Milton, on the island of South Uist

The new bridge across an ' arm of the Atlantic,' which links the islands of South Uist and Benbecula

[For HEBRIDES, OUTER, see also following plate

PLATE 82

Hebrides, Outer, Inverness; Ross and Cromarty. The remains of Kishmul, or Kiessimul Castle, 15th century and later, an ancient MacNeil stronghold, on an island facing Castlebay, in the island of Barra. At one period a retainer is said to have announced daily from the castle walls: " MacNeil has dined, the Kings, Princes and others of the earth may now dine "

Helensburgh, Dunbarton. The obelisk to Henry Bell, who, in 1812, designed the ' Comet,' Europe's first steam-driven craft

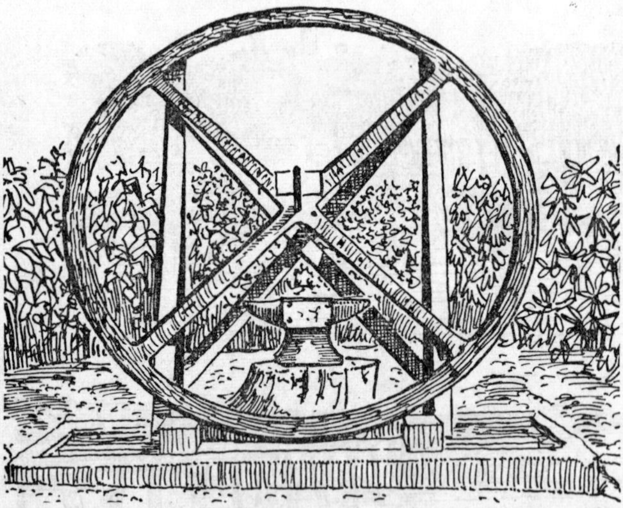

Helensburgh, Dunbarton. The flywheel of the ' Comet,' the first steam-driven craft in Europe, and also the anvil used by Henry Bell, its designer, which are both preserved in Hermitage Park

Helensburgh, Dunbarton. The Cross set up by Sir James Colquhoun, to celebrate the centenary of the Burgh (1802–1902)

[For HEBRIDES, OUTER, see also proceeding plate

dates from 1500, and has some curious sculptures on the tower. The church was built by the eighth Macleod chief of Dunvegan Castle in Skye. Of particular note is the fine, recessed *Macleod* tomb, dated 1528, and in the churchyard is the tomb of a Macleod of Berneray who once fought for Prince Charles Edward. There are also some good examples of Highland grave slabs. Overlooking the village is *Roneval*, 1,506 ft., rising away to the north and forming a fine viewpoint. **4 m. N.E.** of Rodel is the small port of *Finsbay*, on the loch of that name, and reached by a very narrow and winding road, with blind corners and acute bends. This road continues along the east coat, passing the head of Loch Stockinish, with a steamer calling-place at *Stockinish*, and linking up with the main road leading back to Tarbert.

NORTH UIST. 1,925.
This island, in which many standing-stones, stone circles and chambered cairns are to be found, is separated from Lewis and Harris by the Sound of Harris, in which lie the fair-sized islands of Berneray and Pabbay, together with many smaller ones. North Uist consists almost of more water than land, and a road encircles the northern portion of the island, giving a picture, more especially in the east and south, of myriads of tiny lochans and inlets of the sea. Loch Scadavay is the largest inland loch, and its innumerable indentations give it a length of shore out of all proportion to its actual size. The western side of the island includes the *Paible* district, and farther to the north-west is Hoglan Bay, on the exposed Atlantic coast. Far out to sea lie the remote *Haskeir* islands. The most important centre is **Lochmaddy,** having a pier on Loch Maddy, with its numerous islets. *South Lee*, 920 ft., to the south of Lochmaddy, gives a comprehensive panorama of the loch-studded landscape to the west. Farther south still rises *Eaval*, 1,138 ft., the highest point on the island, overlooking Loch Obisary and Loch Eport, with its narrow entrance, to the north, and also the tidal island of Grimsay, to the south. The road to the west coast of the island goes south-west from Lochmaddy, to pass, after 5 miles, the notable chambered cairn of *Langass Barp*. Some 3 miles farther, a branch road to the south gives access to *Carinish*, from which the *North Ford* is crossed by a new causeway connecting with *Grimsay* island and the larger island of *Benbecula* (see below). The ruined *Teampull na Trionaid*, or *Temple of Carinish*, stands on a small eminence, and is of massive 14th or 16th cent. construction. Away to the west lies *Baleshare* island, and farther west still are the *Monach* isles, (National Nature Reserve), separated from North Uist by the Sound of Monach.

BENBECULA. 1,390.
This small island, the surface of which is literally a maze of small lochs, lies between North and South Uist, and is linked to the former by means of a new causeway from **Gramisdale.** The island of South Uist is reached by a viaduct commencing at **Creagorry.** A road links both these points, but apart from this there are only a few very narrow roads on the island. Benbecula is perhaps best known for its associations with Prince Charles Edward, who sailed from here, in 1746, with Flora Macdonald, to Port Kilbride near *Uig* (*q.v.*), in Skye. **2 m. N.W.** of Creagorry stands the ruined *Borve Castle*, a former stronghold of the chiefs of Benbecula. **2 m. W.** of Gramisdale is the airport of *Balivanich.*

SOUTH UIST. 3,995 and ERISKAY.
A road traverses the entire length of this large island, commencing at **Carnan,** in the extreme north, at the end of the viaduct which links the island with Benbecula. It then crosses the expanse of Loch Bee by means of a narrow, raised causeway. This road, from points on which *St. Kilda* (*q.v.*), 60 miles out in the Atlantic, can be seen at times, is a little over 20 miles in length and terminates at **Pollachar** near Kilbride, in the extreme south, on the Sound of Eriskay. From here there are views looking south-eastwards to the island of *Eriskay*, where Prince Charles Edward first set foot on Scottish soil, in 1745, and which is noted for its charming folksongs. The ship " Politician," carrying a large export cargo of whisky, went aground off Eriskay in 1941. On the east coast of South Uist is an area of high ground, dominated by the peaks of *Beinn Mhor*, 2,034 ft., and *Hecla*, 1,988 ft., the latter overlooking outer Loch Skiport, to the north. Between these hills the Prince sheltered in a forester's hut for three weeks, in 1746. In the vicinity is the National Nature Reserve of Loch Druidibeg. Farther south, beyond Loch Eynort, rises *Stulaval*, 1,227 ft., with Loch Snigisclett below its northern slopes. **5 m. N.** of Pollachar, at **Daliburgh** Church, a short branch from the north to south road leads eastwards to **Lochboisdale** (1,770). This is the chief centre of the island, and is noted for fishing. It has a pier on Loch Boisdale. **4 m. N.** of Daliburgh Church, and to the west of the main road from Benbecula, are the remains of Flora Macdonald's early home at *Milton*, near the shores of Loch Kildonan. **2½ m.** farther north, a by-road leads north-westwards to the ruined castle of *Ormaclett*, dating from c. 1701 and burnt in 1715.

BARRA. 1,467.
This is the most southerly island of importance in the chain of the Outer Islands. Barra, separated from South Uist by the Sound of Barra and the island of Eriskay, is mainly sterile, and has a busy herring fishing station and pier at **Castlebay,** in the south, situated on Castle Bay. On an island in the bay stands the picturesque, ruined *Kishmul Castle*, dating from c. 1427, the largest in the Outer Hebrides, and the ancient home of the MacNeils of Barra. It is shown Sat., 3 to 6, May to Sept. (See note page 98.) The island of Barra is noted for its pure Gaelic, and also for the native Hebridean folk-songs and lore. In the southern half rises *Heaval*, 1,260 ft., a fine viewpoint. A road about 12 miles in length encircles Barra, giving access to the sandy *Traigh Mor*, or Great Cockle Shore, in the north, where aircraft landings are made. At the north point rises *Ben Eoligarry*, 338 ft., a good viewpoint. The ruined *Cille-bharra*, where several carved slabs are still to be seen, was once the church of St. Barr. Beyond is a narrow peninsula, extending past the old burial-ground of Kilbar and the former MacNeil dwelling of *Eoligarry House* to Scurrival Point, washed by the waters of the Sound of Fuday. To the south of Barra are the islands of Vatersay, Sandray, Pabbay, and *Mingulay*, the last-named with some very remarkable heights on the west side known as the *Biulacraig* cliffs. Finally, *Berneray* terminates the long chain, and has a lighthouse on the 580-ft. high Barra Head, the southernmost point in the Outer Hebrides. See **St. Kilda.**

HEILIM, Sutherland. Map 28, **NC 4** 5.
Lies on the north-east shore of Loch Eriboll, a sheltered anchorage from storms, in a rugged setting, with a fine mountain background. A little to the south of Heilim is a ruined broch by the loch-side. To the north-west, on the road to *Tongue* (*q.v.*), is the head of Loch Hope, at the southern end of which rises *Ben Hope*, 3,040 ft., the most northerly of the 3,000-ft. peaks of Scotland. See **Eriboll** and **Hope Lodge.** *Iter. 225.*

HELENSBURGH, Dunbarton. 12,874 SB. Map 15, **NS 2** 8.
E.C. Wed. GOLF. A well-known resort and centre for steamer trips and yachting, situated at the point where the beautiful Gare Loch merges into the broadening estuary of the Clyde. The main steamer pier is at *Craigendoran* (*q.v.*). An obelisk in the town commemorates Henry Bell, designer of the " Comet," one of the earliest steamboats. J. Logie Baird, the inventor of television, was born here in 1888. A road leading north-eastwards gives access to the shores of *Loch Lomond* (*q.v.*), and a left fork, a mile and a half from Helensburgh, leads into Glen Fruin, with *Beinn Chaorach*, 2,338 ft., rising to the north. In this glen was fought, in 1603, a savage clan battle between the Macgregors and Colquhouns, which gave the glen its name meaning " glen of sorrow." See **Bowling, Rhu** and **Torphichen.** *Iter. 102, 111, 114, 116.*

HELL'S GLEN, Argyll. Map 14, **NN 1** 0.
See **Lochgoilhead** and **Rest and be Thankful.** *Iter. 102.*

HELMSDALE, Sutherland. 732. Map 31, **ND 0** 1.
E.C. Wed. GOLF. Where the green valley of Strath Ullie, with the Helmsdale River and noted for its fishing, reaches

the sea between ridges of elevated moorland, stands the little fishing port of *Helmsdale*, with its safe anchorage. There is also bathing from a sandy beach. The ruined Castle, demolished in 1971, was the scene of a double murder, in 1567, when the Earl of Sutherland and his wife were poisoned. To the north, the road to *Berriedale* (*q.v.*) winds through the picturesque Navidale ravines to enter Caithness near the rocky Ord of Caithness, at a height of more than 700 ft., with fine views towards the bare hills in the background to the north-west. See **Kildonan** (Sutherland) and **Portgower.** *Iter. 200, 231, 233, 234, 235, 236.*

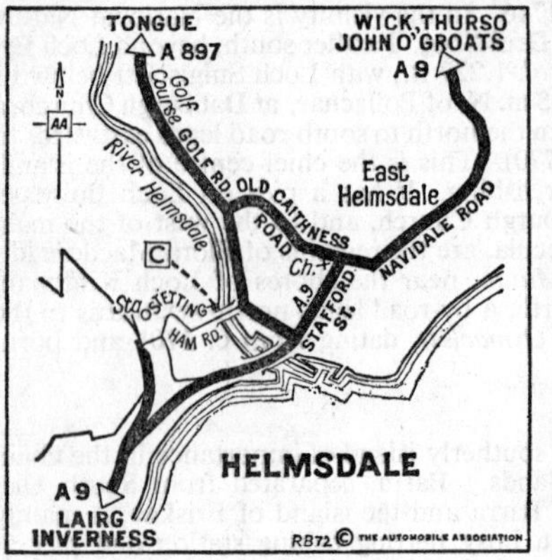

HERIOT, Midlothian. 1,404 with Stow. Map 10, **NT 4 5.** Lies in a pleasant and lofty setting on the main Carlisle to Edinburgh road, with the *Moorfoot* hills to the west. The Church stands **2 m. S.W.,** on the delightful road following the Heriot Water and the Dewar Burn through the hills, and reaching a height of about 1,200 ft. where the counties of Midlothian and Peebles meet. The descent later follows the Leithen Water towards Tweeddale, with *Windlestraw Law*, 2,161 ft., to the east. See **Crichton.** *Iter. 9, 11.*

HERMISTON, Midlothian. Map 9, **NT 1 7.** GOLF. The estates of *Riccarton* and *Dalmahoy*, to the south of the road leading to Mid-Calder, are both noted for their trees. A little to the north stands the restored Church of *Ratho*, of 12th cent. dedication, where the last Earl of Lauderdale, who lived at *Hatton House*, now demolished after a fire, is buried. *Iter. 18, 19, 20, 22.*

HERMITAGE CASTLE, Roxburgh. Map 5, **NY 4 9.** This famous, restored 13th cent. Liddesdale Castle (A.M.), a stronghold of the Douglases, stands on a height surrounded by moorlands overlooking the Hermitage Water, a little to the west of the Newcastleton to Hawick road, and is a structure of immense strength, dating from the 14th cent. Its history is long and particularly cruel, and the castle was visited in 1566 by Mary, Queen of Scots, who nearly died as the result of a fever caught there after riding from *Jedburgh* (*q.v.*), and returning in a single day, some 40 miles in all. Swinburne has described the castle in one of his poems. The building consists of four towers and connecting walls, outwardly almost perfect, and the interior contains remains of the original tower. Open summer, 10 to 7, winter, 10 to 4; Sun., 2 to 7 or 4. (See note page 98.) To the east, beyond the Whitterhope Burn, is *Ninestane Rig*, 943 ft., on which is a stone circle. *Iter. 31.*

HIGH BLANTYRE, Lanark. 5,291. Map 8, **NS 6 5.** See **Blantyre.**

HIGHLANDS, THE

Scotland is traditionally divided into two distinct areas, known as the *Highlands* and the *Lowlands* (*q.v.*) respectively, but no definite line of demarcation exists between the two, and the junction is essentially an artificial one, created by the geological structure of the land itself. It is often said that the Highlands can be taken to consist of the entire district of hills, glens, lochs and islands lying to the north and west of, and including the grassy and heather-clad *Grampian* (*q.v.*) mountains. The rather scanty population is largely of Celtic extraction, and to some extent still employs the Gaelic speech. The Northern Highlands were at one time mainly Pictish territory, while Argyll, in the Southern Highlands, formed the ancient kingdom of Dalriada. The rock formation of the Highland mountains, with their 543 tops of more than 3,000 ft., including seven well-defined peaks exceeding 4,000 ft., tends to make them rugged and precipitous in many places. Their most notable features are the granite of Arran and the plateau of the Cairngorms, the latter range including an extensive National Nature Reserve; the wild hills around Glencoe, including also Ben Nevis and the Mamores; the black gabbro of the serrated Coolins of Skye, the finest rock peaks in Britain, which form a paradise for the mountaineer and hill walker; the Archaean gneiss rock of the remote Assynt district; and finally the grand Torridon red sandstone and white quartzite of Wester Ross and Sutherland. All these form a striking contrast compared with the more softly rounded contours of the green Lowland hills.

The *Highland Line*, or geological boundary between the two areas, may be said to commence in the Firth of Clyde, thence skirting the Cowal coast of Argyll to cross the mouth of the Gare Loch, and pass later over the lower reaches of Loch Lomond. It then follows, approximately, a line linking Aberfoyle with Callander and Comrie, where, at the last-named place, occasional earth tremors occur as the result of the so-called Highland "fault" being situated in the vicinity. Continuing past the entrance to the Sma' Glen, the line reaches the Tay to the south of Dunkeld, and then stretches north-eastwards through central Angus towards the Dee valley at Dinnet. From here it traverses Banffshire and Moray in a north-westerly direction to reach the Moray Firth at *Nairn* (*q.v.*). Across the Firth, to the north, lies the remote county of Caithness, which exhibits however characteristics entitling it to be regarded more as a Lowland than as a Highland county. A remarkable topographical feature of the Highlands is the deep rift, known as the Great Glen, or *Glen More* (*q.v.*), stretching across the country to link Fort William with Inverness, and in which lies a chain of lochs, the largest being *Loch Ness* (*q.v.*), threaded by the *Caledonian Canal* (*q.v.*). It is overlooked near its western extremity by the great bulk of *Ben Nevis* (*q.v.*), 4,406 ft., the highest mountain in the whole of Great Britain, together with its lesser satellites.

That part of the Highlands lying to the west of the rift is known generally as the North-West Highlands, and includes what is considered to be the finest and most memorable of the wild mountain and loch scenery for which Scotland is renowned. The picturesque Hebridean island of *Skye* (*q.v.*) is outstanding, and along the much-indented shores of the mainland, several of the great sea lochs, notably those of *Hourn* and *Nevis* (both *q.v.*), can be compared with the Norwegian fjords. Among the inland lochs, those of *Shiel*, *Morar*, *Duich*, *Quoich* and *Maree* (all *q.v.*) are perhaps the most memorable. The mountains of the North-West Highlands include the great hills on both sides of picturesque *Glen Shiel* (*q.v.*), extending as far as *Loch Duich*; the little-known peaks dominating Glens Affric and Cannich (See **Cannich**); Suilven and the other strange, isolated summits of the lonely Assynt district; the great cirque of the Teallachs, near *Dundonnell* (*q.v.*) in Wester Ross; and the grand Torridon peaks of Liathach and Ben Eighe near *Kinlochewe* (*q.v.*), where the Ben Eighe National Nature Reserve, the first of its kind in the British Isles, is to be found. Much of the mountain area in the Highlands is given over to deer-forest, and grouse-shooting takes place on some of the moors. Fishing can be enjoyed in many of the lochs and rivers, and pony-trekking is now a popular sport (See **Kingussie** and **Newtonmore**). Ski-ing takes place in the Glencoe, Grampian and Cairngorm mountains, a notable centre for the last-named range being *Aviemore* (*q.v.*), which is convenient for visiting the *Glen More Forest Park* and the ski road to the peak of Cairn Gorm (See **Rothiemurchus**).

A recent and much-debated feature of the Highlands is the advent of hydro-electric schemes in certain areas. (See **Cannich, Inveruglas, Pitlochry** and **Tomdoun.**) As a result, the villages and lonely crofts now enjoy the benefit of electric power, but the effect on the scenery is questionable, and though the construction of new roads is often of considerable help to the tourist, the primeval beauty of the scenery must inevitably suffer to some degree by the introduction of immense dams and other ancillary works, how-

Hermitage Castle, Roxburgh. The restored 14th century Douglas stronghold. Mary, Queen of Scots, nearly died here from a fever in 1566 after riding from Jedburgh to visit Bothwell

Highlands. A view of Loch Katrine, in Perthshire, which has associations with Sir Walter Scott's '*Lady of the Lake.*' This loch forms part of the richly wooded Trossachs district

Highlands. The Sutherland peaks of Stack Polly and Cul Beag, in the lonely Assynt country, seen from a point on A835, between Ullapool and Inchnadamph

Highlands. Ben Lomond, the highest mountain in Stirlingshire, rising above the northern reaches of Loch Lomond, and prominent in the view from Tarbet, on its western shores

Highlands. A view of the islands in the lonely bay of Eddrachillis, on the north-west Sutherland coast, as seen from A894 between Kylesku Ferry and Scourie

Highlands. The ruined 16th century Carnasserie Castle, erected by a Bishop of the Isles, who is said to have had printed Knox's liturgy in Gaelic. It was burnt in 1685, and stands $1\frac{1}{2}$ miles north of Kilmartin, in Argyll, on an unclassified road off A816

Hoddom Bridge, Dumfries. The 16th century Trailtrow, or ' Repentance ' Tower. The name recalls John Maxwell, who repented of his decision to use his forces against his compatriots in the 16th century, and later defeated the English

Houston, Renfrew. The Mercat Cross, which was restored in 1713

Hopetoun House, West Lothian. A magnificent Scottish country house, commenced in 1696 by Sir William Bruce and completed by the Adams, father and son. It stands on an unclassified road off A904, near the Firth of Forth

Howwood, Renfrew. The ancient Clochodrich Stone, its name taken perhaps from an early ruler of Strathclyde. It stands on the Lochwinnoch road (unclassified), to the north-west

Humbie, East Lothian. A village associated with the Edinburgh Children's Holiday Fund. During the Second World War, the first German bomber to crash on British soil fell near Humbie

[For HUNTLY see following plate
[For HUNTER'S QUAY see under COWAL (Plate 36)
[For HUNTINGTOWER see under STRATHMORE (Plate 157)
[For HUNA see Plate 172
[For HOLY LOCH see under COWAL (Plate 36)

ever carefully these may be planned. See **Arran, Ben Nevis, Cairngorms, Kintail, Knoydart, Lochaber, Mamore Forest, Moidart, Morven, Mull, Rum, Skye** and **Tomintoul.**

HIGHTAE, Dumfries Map 4, **NY 0 7.**
On the River Annan. To the south-west stands the fine mansion of *Rammerscales*, 1763-73, built by Dr. James Mounsey, at one time chief physician to the Russian Imperial Court.

HILLEND (Edinburgh), Midlothian. Map 10, **NT 2 6.**
Situated on the outskirts of the *Pentland* hills, looking westwards towards the *Caerketton Crags* and the summit of *Allermuir Hill*, 1,617 ft. **2 m. S.S.W.** is *Woodhouselee House*, visited frequently by Sir Walter Scott. *Iter. 14, 25.*

HILLSWICK, Shetland. Map 33, **HU 2 7.**
See **Shetland Islands** (Mainland). *Iter. 267.*

HODDOM BRIDGE, Dumfries. 1,259. Map 4, **NY 1 7.**
The bridge spans the River Annan, and a little to the west, on the south side of the Annan, stood *Hoddom Castle*, demolished in 1953. On a hill above stands the 16th cent. *Trailtrow*, or *Repentance Tower*, taking its name from the word " Repentance " which appears in raised lettering on the door lintel. Hoddom Church, on the Ecclefechan road, was once the See of St. Mungo. *Iter. 42.*

HOLY LOCH, Argyll. Map 14, **NS 1 8.**
A small inlet of the Clyde estuary, near the entrance to Loch Long, now a Polaris Submarine base. The Forestry Commission owns a 166-acre Forest Garden here planted with exotic trees, including eucalyptus. At *Sandbank* (*q.v.*) was launched, in 1958, the yacht " Sceptre," Britain's losing challenger for the America's Cup. See **Hunter's Quay, Kilmun** and **Kirn.** *Iter. 102, 137.*

HOLYROODHOUSE, Midlothian. Map 10, **NT 2 7.**
See **Edinburgh.**

HOLYTOWN, Lanark. 6,615. Map 9, **NS 7 5.**
Lies to the east of the Clyde valley, in a mining area. Keir Hardie was born near here in 1856. See **Carfin.** *Iter. 18.*

HOPE LODGE, Sutherland. Map 28, **NC 4 6.**
Finely situated at the northern extremity of the long and narrow Loch Hope, with *Ben Hope*, the most northerly 3,000-ft. peak in Scotland, rising beyond the head of the loch. Westwards lies Loch Eriboll, and to the east is the Kyle of Tongue, at the far end of the lonely moors of A'Mhoine. To the north, not accessible by road, is the cave-ridden Whiten Head, with fine cliff scenery. See **Melness.** *Iter. 225.*

HOPEMAN, Moray. 1,126. Map 26, **NJ 1 6.**
GOLF. A fishing village and small resort, with a harbour and lighthouse. See **Duffus.** *Iter. 199.*

HOPETOUN HOUSE, West Lothian. Map 16, **NT 0 7.**
This splendid mansion, rich in treasures, including a museum, is one of the finest of its period in Scotland, and stands in a park overlooking the estuary of the Forth. It was commenced in 1696 by Sir William Bruce, but left unfinished, and the completion of the house was by the hands of William Adam, and his more famous son Robert. The house is shown daily (exc. Thurs. and Fri.), 1.30 to 5.30, May to end of Sept. (See note page 98.) *Iter. 96.*

HOSPITALFIELD, Angus. Map 17, **NO 6 4.**
See **Arbroath.**

HOUNAM, Roxburgh. 711. Map 11, **NT 7 1.**
On the Kale Water. *Heatherhope Loch*, noted for its heather-clad surroundings, lies to the south-east, and is now a reservoir for Kelso. The main *Cheviot* range rises beyond here, and farther east is *The Cheviot*, 2,676 ft., in Northumberland. The *Auchopecairn*, 2,382 ft., on its western slopes, is a fine viewpoint, and lies actually on the Scottish border.

HOUSTON, Renfrew. 3,038. Map 8, **NS 4 6.**
The Mercat Cross was restored in 1713. North of the town is *St. Peter's Well*, and on a hill farther north stands the 11-ft. high Celtic *Barochan* Cross (A.M.), moved from its original site. *Houston House* is mainly 19th cent.

HOWE OF FIFE, Fife. Map 17, **NO 2 1.**
The fertile area to the north-east of the *Lomond Hills.*

HOWGATE, Midlothian. Map 9, **NT 2 5.**
Known for its associations with Dr. John Brown's " Rab and his Friends." **4 m. S.E.,** on the slopes of the *Moorfoot* hills, is the large *Gladhouse* reservoir. See **Carrington, Penicuik** and **Temple.** *Iter. 14, 37.*

HOWWOOD, Renfrew. Map 8, **NS 3 6.**
To the west is Castle Semple Loch, near which stands *Castle Semple* Church (*q.v.*). To the north-west, on the Lochwinnoch road, is the ancient *Clochodrich* Stone. *Iter. 58, 63.*

HOY, ISLE OF, Orkney. Map 33, **ND 2 9.**
See **Orkney Islands** (Hoy).

HUMBIE, East Lothian. 399. Map 10, **NT 4 6.**
At the foot of the *Lammermuir* hills and noted as a " Children's Village," being associated with the Edinburgh Children's Holiday Fund early in this century. To the south is *Johnstounburn House*, with its fine gardens. *Iter. 36.*

HUME CASTLE, Berwick. Map 10, **NT 7 4.**
See **Greenlaw.**

HUNA, Caithness. Map 30, **ND 3 7.**
Situated about halfway between St. John's Point and Duncansby Head, on the Inner Sound of the Pentland Firth, facing the island of Stroma. Farms in the vicinity display the characteristic Caithness flagstones, used in place of fences. See **Canisbay** and **John o' Groats.** *Iter. 240.*

HUNTER'S QUAY, Argyll. Map 14, **NS 1 7.**
This little Firth of Clyde resort is the headquarters of the Royal Clyde Yachting Club. The annual Clyde Yachting Fortnight, held in July, is based on Hunter's Quay, which takes its name from the Hunters of *Hafton House* (1828), to the north-west. Across the mouth of the Holy Loch, to the north, is Strone Point and the small resort of *Strone* (*q.v.*). See **Kirn** and **Sandbank.** *Iter. 102.*

HUNTERSTON, Ayr. Map 7, **NS 1 5.**
There is a large nuclear power station in the vicinity.

HUNTINGTOWER, Perth. Map 16, **NO 0 2.**
Huntingtower Castle (A.M.), formerly called *Ruthven Castle*, has associations with James VI and the so-called " Ruthven Raid," in 1582, as a result of which, two years later, the Earl of Gowrie was executed. The restored 15th cent. buildings include two towers joined by lower buildings, the space between the towers being known as the " Maiden's Leap." Open summer, 10 to 7, winter, 10 to 4; Sun., 2 to 7 or 4. (See note page 98.) See **Pitcairngreen.** *Iter. 145, 147.*

HUNTLY, Aberdeen. 3,643. SB. Map 26, **NJ 5 3.**
E.C. Thurs. **M.D.** Wed. GOLF. Immediately to the north of this important market town, which is situated in Strathbogie, the River Bogie is joined by the better-known Deveron, which has come from the higher ground to the west, overlooked by *Clashmach Hill*, 1,229 ft. The town makes a pleasant summer resort, and is noted for its good fishing facilities. The imposing, ruined Castle (A.M.), noted for the elaboration of the topmost storey, was once the home of the Gordon Marquesses of Huntly, the " Gay Gordons," one of whom bore the title of the " Cock o' the North." It was formerly known as the *Palace of Strathbogie*, and dates from 1602, the medieval structure having been burnt 8 years previously. In the 18th cent., the structure gradually became derelict, and some of the stones were used in the construction of *Huntly Lodge*, now an hotel, which stands to the north of the town. The castle is open weekdays, 10 to 7 in summer; 10 to 4 in winter. Sun., 2 to 7 or 4. (See note page 98.) **8 m. W.** is the early 17th cent. *Beldorney Castle*. See **Gordon** and **Rhynie.** *Iter. 165, 167, 175, 178, 187, 193, 194, 195, 196.*

(See page 186 for Town Plan of **HUNTLY.**)

HURLFORD, Ayr, 4,147. Map 8, **NS 4 3.**
A small town with iron and fireclay works. The house of *Carnell* has a 15th cent. peel tower. *Iter. 67, 69.*

Castle 1 (A3) **Town Clerk's Office, Information Bureau** 2 (C2)

HUTTON, Berwick. 484. **Map 11, NT 9 5.**
On the Whiteadder Water stands *Hutton Castle*, a modern structure incorporating an ancient pele tower. Sir William Burrell, its former owner, donated the famous Burrell Art Collection to Glasgow in 1944.

HYNDFORD BRIDGE, Lanark. **Map 9, NS 9 4.**
The bridge (1773) spans the River Clyde, and is overlooked by *Cairngrufe Hill*, 1,131 ft., to the east. To the north-west of Hyndford Bridge, on Lanark Moor, is the *Lanark* (*q.v.*) racecourse. *Iter. 21, 35, 48, 50, 53.*

INCHCOLM ISLAND, Fife. **Map 17, NT 1 8.**
This little island lies a mile and a half out to sea, to the south of *Aberdour* (*q.v.*). On it stands the very interesting ruined Abbey of *St. Columba* (A.M.), founded in 1123, and comprising some of the most complete monastic remains in Scotland. Much of the existing structure dates from the 13th and 15th cents., the tower on the octagonal Chapter House being of note, while remains of frescoes have been discovered in the choir. The island is mentioned in Shakespeare's "Macbeth."

INCHINNAN CHURCH, Renfrew. **Map 8, NS 5 6.**
See **Renfrew.**

INCHKEITH ISLAND, Fife. **Map 17, NT 2 8.**
The fortified island of *Inchkeith*, with its powerful lighthouse, stands three miles out to sea off the Fife coast, to the south-east of *Kinghorn* (*q.v.*). Between 1549 and 1567 it was held by the French. In 1773 it was visited by Dr. Johnson and Boswell, and in 1817 by Carlyle.

INCHMAHOME PRIORY, Perth. **Map 15 NN 5 0.**
See **Port of Menteith.**

INCHNADAMPH, Sutherland. **Map 29, NC 2 2.**
This small fishing resort is situated in the remote *Assynt* district of the North-West Highlands, in the heart of some of the strangest and most notable mountain scenery in Great Britain. Geologically, this part of Sutherland is of the greatest interest, many of the surrounding peaks being composed of Torridon sandstone, topped in places by gleaming white quartzite. Much of the land to the north-west is composed of Archaean gneiss rock, some of the oldest formation known to exist in the world, found elsewhere only in the Outer Hebrides, and near the St. Lawrence River in Canada. Small lochs abound in the sterile country around Inchnadamph, and in one loch is found the very rare gilaroo trout. Picturesque *Loch Assynt* (*q.v.*) stretches north-westwards for some 7 miles, and on its northern shore stands the ruin of the late 16th cent. *Ardvreck Castle*, where, in 1650, the great Marquis of Montrose, of the Clan Graham, was betrayed by the laird after his last battle, fought at *Carbisdale* near *Invershin* (*q.v.*). In the vicinity stands the ruined 17th cent. *Calda House*, once a home of the Mackenzies. Near Inchnadamph is a National Nature Reserve of 3,200 acres, which includes an area of limestone country containing caves and under-ground streams. The Allt nan Uamh bone caves show traces of occupation by early man. **4 m. S.E.** of the village stands *Ben More Assynt*, 3,273 ft., the highest mountain in the county, and composed mainly of gneiss, being linked to the subsidiary height of *Conaveall*, 3,234 ft., on the slopes of which rises the Traligill, a partly subterranean stream. To the south-west of Inchnadamph are *Canisp*, 2,779 ft., and the sharp cone of *Suilven*, 2,399 ft., a remarkable Torridon sandstone hill, described sometimes as Scotland's "Matterhorn." These are separated from each other by the lonely Loch Gainimh. Northwards from Loch Assynt, the road to *Kylesku* (*q.v.*) climbs under the slopes of *Glasven*, 2,541 ft., to the east and the long and many-peaked ridge of *Quinag*, 2,653 ft., to the west. See **Altnacealgach** and **Lochinver** (for *Suilven*). *Iter. 225, 227, 228.*

INCHTURE, Perth. 695. **Map 17, NO 2 2.**
In the heart of the fertile district known as the *Carse of Gowrie* (*q.v.*), between the *Sidlaw* hills and the Firth of Tay, and noted for the cultivation of strawberries. To the north is *Rossie Priory*, in its fine grounds, situated below *Rossie Hill*, 567 ft. See **Kinnaird** and **Longforgan.** *Iter. 154.*

INCHTUTHIL, Perth. **Map 16, NO 0 3.**
See **Caputh.**

INNELLAN, Argyll. 1,306. **Map 7, NS 1 7.**
E.C. Wed. GOLF. A Firth of Clyde and *Cowal* (*q.v.*) resort, with a steamer pier, facing Wemyss Bay on the Renfrew coast. **2½ m. S.S.W.** is Toward Point, with a lighthouse, and a modern Castle to the west. A road continues westwards, passing the ruined *Castle Toward*, and proceeding thence along the east shore of Loch Striven, with views up the *Kyles of Bute* (*q.v.*), and across to the bay of *Rothesay* (*q.v.*) in the island of Bute. The road comes to an end shortly beyond *Inverchaolin* (*q.v.*) Church, with its background of lonely hills, dominated by *Bishop's Seat*, 1,651 ft. *Iter. 102.*

INNER HEBRIDES, Argyll; Inverness.
See **Hebrides, Inner.** **Maps 6, 12, 13, 22 and 23.**

INNERLEITHEN, Peebles. 2,233. SB. **Map 10, NT 3 3.**
E.C. Tues. A woollen town, with mineral springs, situated on the Leithen Water, near its confluence with the Tweed a little to the south-east. The summer Cleikum Ceremony is associated with the 7th cent. St. Ronan, and the town may be the original of Sir Walter Scott's "St. Ronan's Well." There are numerous hill-forts in the vicinity. Northwards lie the Leithen Water and Glentress Water valleys, in a delightful setting of hills, and with *Windlestraw Law* rising to 2,161 ft. near the point where the counties of Peebles, Selkirk and Midlothian meet. To the south of Innerleithen, across the Tweed, is situated the famous old mansion of *Traquair* (*q.v.*). **2 m. N.W.,** across the Tweed, is the ancient tower of *Cardrona.* See **Walkerburn.** *Iter. 12, 14, 32, 33, 34, 52.*

INNERMESSAN, Wigtown. **Map 2, NX 0 6.**
The Roman site of "Rericonium" is thought to have been a little to the north, where stands the isolated *Craigcaffie Castle*, overlooking Loch Ryan, and dating from c. 1570, a good example of its period. *Iter. 55, 80, 84.*

INNERPEFFRAY, Perth. **Map 16, NN 9 1.**
See **Crieff.**

INNERWICK, East Lothian. 705 **Map 11, NT 7 7.**
The ruined Castle was destroyed in the English invasion of 1547. There are also some remains of *Thornton Castle.* The Church dates from 1784. A school of 100 whales came ashore near here in 1950. To the south is *Monynut Edge*, with *Heart Law*, near the Berwick border, attaining 1,283 ft.

Huntly, Aberdeen. The ruined Castle, known formerly as the Palace of Strathbogie, and once the home of the Gordon Marquesses of Huntly, the 'Gay Gordons,' one of whom was nicknamed the 'Cock o' the North'

Inchnadamph, Sutherland. The 16th century Ardvreck Castle, by Loch Assynt, off A837, to the north-west. In 1650, the great Marquis of Montrose was brought here as a prisoner and later betrayed by the laird, it is said for £20,000. See Invershin (Plate 89)

Innerpeffray, Perth. The second oldest library in Scotland, founded in 1691. It stands 4 miles east of Crieff, on a by-road off B8062, near the River Earn

Innerpeffray, Perth. The Faichney Stone (1707), carved by a mason during his life-time, with the dates of birth of his 10 children. It is situated on a by-road off B8062, near the River Earn, 4 miles east of Crieff

Innermessan, Wigtown. The late 16th century Craigcaffie Castle, to the north, off A77. Its foundations are said to have been strengthened with bags of wool to counteract the danger of sinking in the marshy sub-soil

[For INCHNADAMPH see also under HIGHLANDS (Plate 84)
[For INCHMAHOME PRIORY see under LAKE OF MENTEITH (Plate 105)

Insh, Inverness. The Church by Loch Insh, which is reputed to stand on an Early Christian site

Inverallochy, Aberdeen. The ancient stronghold of the Comyns, situated some 2 miles south, off B9033

Inveraray, Argyll. A Celtic Cross brought from Iona

Inveraray, Argyll. The 18th century Castle of the Duke of Argyll, the head of the Clan Campbell. In 1773, Dr. Johnson was entertained here by the 5th Duke during his tour of the Highlands

Inverbervie, Kincardine. The white-harled and richly-corbelled early 17th century Allardyce Castle, near the Bervie Water, to the north-west, off B967

Inveresk, Midlothian. The loftily situated Parish Church, erected in 1805. A mound in the churchyard is said to have served Cromwell as a battery site

[For INVEREY see following plate
[For INVERARAY see also under Loch Fyne (Plate 112)
[For INVERAN BRIDGE (Falls of Shin) see frontispiece

INNERWICK CHURCH, Perth. Map 15, **NN 5** 4.
This lonely little church, in its setting of green hills in Glen Lyon, preserves an ancient bell. *Iter. 107.*

INSCH, Aberdeen. 1,421. Map 27, **NJ 6** 2.
E.C. Thurs. **M.D.** Mon. A large village, to the west of which is the conical hill of *Dunnideer,* crowned by a vitrified fort, on which stands a ruined 16th cent. Castle. The hill of *Christ's Kirk,* 1,021 ft., faces it across the Shevock Burn. To the north-west rise the *Foudland* hills, attaining over 1,500 ft. On their southern side, at *Mireton,* some 2½ miles from Insch, is the inscribed Pictish *Picardy Stone* (A.M.). See **Leslie** (Aberdeen) and **Oyne.** *Iter. 178.*

INSH, Inverness. Map 19, **NH 8** 0.
On the shores of the tiny Loch Insh, in the upper Spey valley. The Church, which stands on a hillock close to the bridge over the River Spey, is said to be the sole example of a Scottish Church on a site used continuously since the 6th cent. An ancient Celtic hand-bell has been preserved. See **Feshie Bridge.** *Iter. 138, 149.*

INVERALLOCHY, Aberdeen. Map 27, **NK 0** 6.
A coastal village, situated to the east of Fraserburgh Bay, with its fine sands. The Castle, which lies inland, some **2 m. S.,** was built by the Comyns, as was also the restored *Cairnbulg Castle,* standing **2 m. S.W.** of Inverallochy, on the Water of Philorth. See **St. Combs.**

INVERAMSAY, Aberdeen. Map 27, **NJ 7** 2.
Lies on the River Urie. Beyond the river, to the south-east, is *Harlaw House,* and the tall monument commemorating the battle of Harlaw, fought in 1411, with great loss of life, and which is associated with Scott's " The Antiquary." As a result of this important battle, the southward progress of the Highlanders under Donald, the Lord of the Isles, was checked, and the predominance of the Lowlanders made certain. *Iter. 175, 178.*

INVERAN BRIDGE, Sutherland. Map 29, **NH 5** 9.
Noted for fishing on the turbulent River Shin, here spanned by a three-arched bridge. The Falls of Shin lie about a mile to the north. To the south, the Shin meets the Kyle of Sutherland near *Invershin* (*q.v.*). *Iter. 228, 232.*

INVERARAY, Argyll. 438. SB. Map 14, **NN 0** 0.
E.C. Wed. This pleasant little Royal Burgh stands in a richly wooded setting on *Loch Fyne* (*q.v.*) facing Strone Point, at the eastern extremity of the small inlet known as Loch Shira. The well-known *Inveraray Castle* is the seat of the Duke of Argyll, the head of Clan Campbell, and known in Gaelic as " MacCailean Mor." (See **Glenshee.**) The Campbells have a long history, in which the Earls and Dukes of Argyll had their full share. The eighth Earl and his son were executed in Edinburgh, in 1661 and 1685 respectively, and Scott has introduced the former into his " Legend of Montrose," while in the " Heart of Midlothian " is portrayed the second Duke. The town, which stood formerly near the ancient castle, was moved to its new site in the mid-18th cent. The present Castle is shown weekdays (except Fri), 10 to 12.30 and 2 to 6; Sun., 2 to 6, April to June; then daily 10 to 6 (Sun., 2 to 6) to early Oct. (See note page 98.) It was designed c. 1780 by Roger Morris and Robert Mylne, and has a large park, through which flows the River Aray. A silver fir in the park may be the bulkiest tree in Great Britain. A cannon, taken from the wreck of the sunken galleon Florida, of the Armada fleet, has been brought here from *Tobermory* (*q.v.*) in Mull. The hill of *Duniquoich,* 850 ft., surmounted by a tower, rises near the park, and was described in the " Legend of Montrose." In the town stands the Church, built in 1794 by Robert Mylne, in which services in English and Gaelic are held in separate divisions. A Celtic Cross from Iona stands at the junction of Front Street and Main Street. R. L. Stevenson's novel " Catriona " contains much local colour towards the end. The famous Appin murder trial was held at Inveraray, in the old Courthouse, in 1752. Dr. Johnson visited the Castle in 1773, and tasted whisky for the first time at an inn. At the head of Loch Shira, the little River Shira, which has descended through Glen Shira, overlooked by *Beinn Bhuidhe,* 3,106 ft., is spanned by a fine 18th cent. ornamental bridge. Below the Ben, to the north-west, hydro-electric works are situated. North of the town, the road traversing Glen Aray, with its falls, is richly wooded, before climbing on to the open moors. In the glen, on an eminence, is a memorial to Neil Munro, the author, who was a native of Inveraray. **4 m. N.E.,** on the road to Glen Croe, and overlooking Loch Fyne, is the well-restored *Dundarave Castle,* dating from 1598, and described under the name of " *Doom Castle* " in Neil Munro's " John Splendid." See **Auchindrain, Ballachulish, Cladich, Duror, Kilchrenan** and **Oban.** *Iter. 88, 101, 102, 117, 118, 119, 120, 121.*

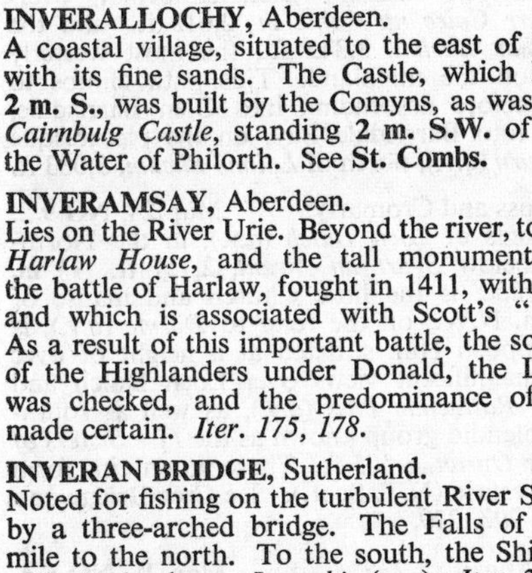

Castle 1 Cross 3
Church 2 Old Court House 4

INVERASDALE, Ross and Cromarty. Map 22, **NG 8** 8.
See **Poolewe.**

INVERBERVIE, Kincardine. 881. SB. Map 21, **NO 8** 7.
E.C. Wed. A little flax-spinning Royal Burgh, known also as *Bervie,* and situated on Bervie Bay, where the Bervie Water has its outlet into the sea. John Coutts, the father of Thomas Coutts, the famous London banker, was born here in 1699. To the south of the town is a picturesque stretch of rocky coastline, with caves and gullies. **½ m. S.** stands *Hallgreen Castle.* **1 m. N.W.,** standing in a bend of the Bervie Water, is the delightful little *Allardyce Castle,* dating from c. 1600, with its fine corbelling and white-harled walls. See **Arbuthnott** and **Kinneff.** *Iter. 155.*

INVERCANNICH, Inverness. Map 24, **NH 3** 3.
See **Cannich.**

INVERCHAOLIN, Argyll. Map 7, **NS 0** 7.
Shortly beyond the Church, the road following the eastern shores of Loch Striven comes to an end. *Bishop's Seat,* 1,651 ft., rises in the background, and farther to the north-west are higher hills overlooking Glen Lean. *Iter. 102.*

INVERESK, Midlothian. 5,505. Map 10, **NT 3** 7.
Pleasantly situated on the River Esk, and almost adjoining *Musselburgh* (*q.v.*). It was once a Roman station, numerous remains having been excavated, and is now best known for its paper mills. The Parish Church is set on a height, from which the view ranges over a large extent of country. It replaced an older church in 1805, and has a tall spire and an exceptionally lovely churchyard. There are some Georgian houses, including *Halkerston* and the Manor House. *Inveresk Lodge* (N.T. Scot.), a 17th cent. house, has fine gardens, which are open Mon. to Fri., 10 to 4.30, all the year. On Sun., 2 to 5, from May to Sept. (See note page 98.) Roman remains have been excavated at *Inveresk House.* See **Carberry Hill** and **Pinkie House.**

INVEREWE, Ross and Cromarty. Map 22, **NG 8** 8.
See **Poolewe.**

INVEREY, Aberdeen. Map 20, **NO 0** 8.
A *Deeside* (*q.v.*) hamlet, where the main stream is joined by the Ey Water, in a beautiful, wooded setting on the road leading westwards from *Braemar* (*q.v.*) towards the *Cairngorm* (*q.v.*) foothills. A memorial tablet recalls John Lamont (1805-79), who became Johann von Lamont, Astronomer Royal of Bavaria. Eastwards, off the Braemar road, is the Linn of Corriemulzie, a picturesquely situated waterfall. Away to the south, up the rugged valley of the Ey Water, is a deep chasm, known as the " Colonel's Bed," thought to have been the hiding place of Colonel John Farquharson, who fought in 1689 at *Killiecrankie* (*q.v.*) North-west of

Inverey, beyond the Dee, a path leads through Glen Lui and Glen Derry into the Cairngorms, under the slopes of *Derry Cairngorm* 3,788 ft. and farther north below *Beinn Mheadoin*, 3,883 ft., which overlooks the remote Loch Avon. This path is known as the Lairig an Laoigh, and gives access for long-distance walkers to *Nethybridge* (*q.v.*), on the edge of the Forest of Abernethy. Another pass leads westwards from Glen Lui through Glen Lu Beg, giving access to Glen Dee and the *Lairig Ghru* (see below). **2 m. W.** of Inverey by road is the well-known *Linn of Dee*, a wild and rocky cleft through which the river cascades, situated on the edge of the extensive Mar Forest. It was here that Byron was once nearly drowned.

Farther to the west, along the valley of the Upper Dee, in surroundings which become progressively wilder, the path leading towards the southern Cairngorms, accompanied by the river, turns northwards into Glen Dee. From here onwards it is known as the *Lairig Ghru* (*q.v.*), the most famous of the walkers' passes in the Cairngorms, dominated to the west by *Beinn Bhrotain*, 3,797 ft., and later by the *Devil's Point*, 3,303 ft. Where the path diverges into Glen Dee, the river is spanned by the White Bridge, and a short distance to the east of the bridge is the rock cataract and pool known as the Chest of Dee.

At the Linn of Dee, a road crosses the river and doubles back to the east, crossing the Lui Water, and passing by the modern *Mar Lodge*, where ski-ing developments have taken place. The road terminates near the Linn of Quoich, a deep, wooded ravine, where the Quoich Water flows down from Glen Quoich, backed by *Bheinn a'Bhuird*, 3,924 ft. and 3,860 ft., one of the loftiest Cairngorm peaks. A very rough track has recently been cut almost to the summit of this peak, but should not be attempted. It attains some 3,900 ft., by far the highest in Britain. *Iter. 179.*

INVERFARIGAIG, Inverness. Map 25, **NH 5 2.**
Lies in a richly-wooded setting on *Loch Ness* (*q.v.*), with a pier. The narrow and wooded Pass of Inverfarigaig is picturesque, and leads in an easterly direction towards *Errogie* (*q.v.*) on Loch Mhor. The Black Rock section of the original 18th cent. Wade road, at the foot of the pass, near Loch Ness, had to be blasted by miners. See **Foyers** and **Wade Roads.** *Iter. 211.*

INVERGARRY, Inverness. Map 18, **NH 3 0.**
E.C. Thurs. Here, on the west side of *Loch Oich* (*q.v.*), is the commencement of a magnificent road through the West Highland glens and mountains, by way of *Cluanie* (*q.v.*) and *Glen Shiel* (*q.v.*). It forms one of the famous "Roads to the Isles," and terminates at *Kyle of Lochalsh* (*q.v.*), on the *Wester Ross* coast facing the island of Skye. The River Garry flows into the loch to the north of the ruined *Invergarry Castle* where Prince Charles Edward slept before and after Culloden, and which was afterwards burnt by the Duke of Cumberland. The Castle belonged to the Macdonells of Glengarry, many of whose descendants emigrated in 1803 to Canada and founded a new Glengarry. The Kyle of Lochalsh road climbs westwards through the richly wooded Glen Garry on the first stage of its journey, traversing after a few miles the lovely tree-lined shores of Loch Garry, beyond the opposite shores of which rises *Ben Tee*, 2,956 ft. A hydro-electric scheme now operates in this district. See **Loch Lochy** and **Tomdoun.** *Iter. 210, 214, 220.*

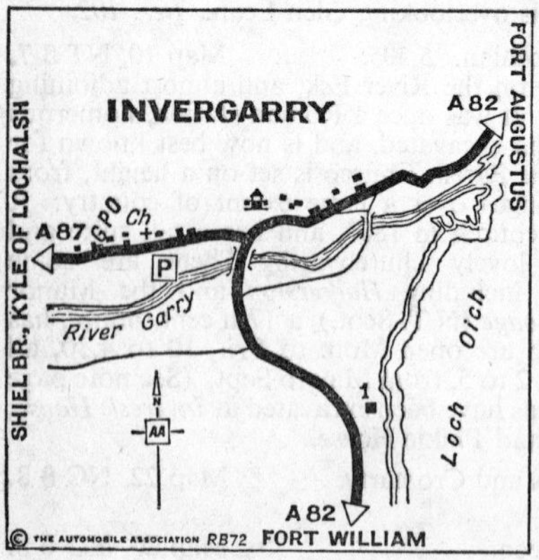

Castle 1

INVERGORDON, Ross and Cromarty. 2,240. SB. Map 25, **NH 7 6.**
E.C. Wed. GOLF. A former naval base, with a fine harbour, on the Inner Cromarty Firth, facing Udale Bay and Cromarty Bay in the *Black Isle* (*q.v.*). The view eastwards is over the Bay of Nigg, and across to *Cromarty* (*q.v.*), guarded by the twin Sutors of Cromarty. See **Logie Easter** and **Saltburn.** *Iter. 201.*

INVERGOWRIE, Angus. Map 17, **NO 3 3.**
In the Church wall is an interesting sculptured stone. St. Boniface landed here c. 715. *Invergowrie House* is 16th to 19th cent. *Iter. 154.*

INVERIE, Inverness. Map 23, **NG 7 0.**
This remote little place is situated in the *Knoydart* (*q.v.*) district, on Inverie Bay, an inlet of Outer *Loch Nevis* (*q.v.*), in a beautiful setting of mountain and loch. It is not approachable by road, access being gained by motor-launch from *Mallaig* (*q.v.*). A bridle path leads north-eastwards from Inverie through Glen Dulochan, over-shadowed by *Sgurr Coire na Coinnich*, 2,612 ft., and the fine peak of *Ladhar Bheinn*, 3,343 ft., the most westerly 3,000-ft. summit on the mainland. This path climbs to nearly 1,100 ft., before descending into Glen Barrisdale, which debouches into Barrisdale Bay, on the picturesque shores of *Loch Hourn* (*q.v.*), north of *Luinne Bheinn*, 3,083 ft.

INVERINATE, Ross and Cromarty. Map 24, **NG 9 2.**
On the lovely shores of *Loch Duich* (*q.v.*), in the North-West Highlands, below *Sgurr an Airgid*, 2,757 ft. **1½ m. S.E.**, on the lochside, is the little Church and manse of *Kintail* (*q.v.*). **2 m. N.W.**, on the road to *Dornie* (*q.v.*), is Carr Brae, or Keppoch Hill, situated at a height of over 500 ft. It gives magnificent views over Loch Duich and towards the *Mam Rattachan Pass* (*q.v.*), as well as south-eastwards to the splendid group known as the *Five Sisters of Kintail*, with *Scour Ouran*, 3,505 ft. These mountains form part of the *Kintail* estate (N.T. Scot.). See **Croe Bridge** and **Shiel Bridge.** *Iter. 207, 220.*

INVERKEILOR, Angus. 1,235. Map 21, **NO 6 4.**
The Church contains the 17th cent. *Northesk* pew. To the east is Lunan Bay, with some "singing" sands, stretching between Boddin Point and Lang Craig, while to the south of the latter, is the fine promontory of Red Head, associated with Scott's "The Antiquary." At Lunan Bay is the ruined *Red Castle*, destroyed in 1579. Farther north, at Boddin Point, is the curious Rock of St. Skeagh. **3 m. S.E.** of Inverkeilor is the 15th cent. and later *Ethie Castle*. See **Usan.** *Iter. 155.*

INVERKEITHING, Fife. 5,860. SB. Map 17, **NT 1 8.**
E.C. Wed. A Royal Burgh, on the Firth of Forth, retaining a 16th cent. Mercat Cross, with carved armorial bearings, surmounted by a unicorn, added in 1688. The Old Town House, dated 1770, and also the 15th cent. Greyfriars Hospital, now a public library, are of interest. The Church has an old font, but only the tower remains from the original 15th cent. structure. In 1651, a battle was fought to the north, in which the forces of Cromwell were victorious, defeating a Royalist army led by a Maclean of Duart. The town is now best-known as a centre for ship-building and shipbreaking. **2 m. N.** is the 16th cent. *Fordell Castle*, on the estate of which a private railway once took coal to the coast. See **Rosyth.** *Iter. 93, 94, 134.*

INVERKIP, Renfrew. 1,190. Map 8, **NS 2 7.**
Situated a little inland from the sandy coast of the Firth of Clyde, with moors to the south-east. *Ardgowan House*, built in 1798, and the 15th cent. *Inverkip Castle*, stand in a park facing Lunderston Bay. On high ground, to the east, are large reservoirs for Greenock. **2½ m. N.**, at Cloch Point, on the fine coast road to *Gourock* (*q.v.*), is the white *Cloch* (*q.v.*) lighthouse. *Iter. 59, 64, 65, 66, 68.*

INVERKIRKAIG, Sutherland. Map 29, **NC 0 1.**
The River Kirkaig, forming the border between Ross and Cromarty and Sutherland, and on which are situated some falls, flows here into Loch Kirkaig. The stream has its

Inverey, Aberdeen. The memorial to John Lamont (1805–79), born at Corriemulzie, who became Johann von Lamont, Astronomer Royal of Bavaria

Invergarry, Inverness. The ruined Castle, burnt by the Duke of Cumberland after Prince Charles Edward had slept there both before and after the battle of Culloden, in 1746

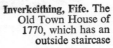

Inverkeilor, Angus. The remains of Red Castle, burnt and sacked in 1579 by a son of Lord Gray, who for this action was declared an outlaw. It stands in Lunan Bay, to the north-east, on an unclassified road off A92

Inverkeithing, Fife. The 16th century Mercat Cross, topped by a unicorn placed there in 1688

Inverkeithing, Fife. The Old Town House of 1770, which has an outside staircase

Inverkirkaig, Sutherland. The isolated Sutherland peaks of Suilven, Cul Mor, Cul Beag and Ben More Coigach, seen from a point just south of Inverkirkaig, on an unclassified road

[For INVEREY see also under LINN OF DEE (Plate 109)

Inverlochy Castle, Inverness. The ruined 15th century Castle, near which the Marquis of Montrose defeated the Covenanters in 1645. It stands off A82, to the north-east of Fort William

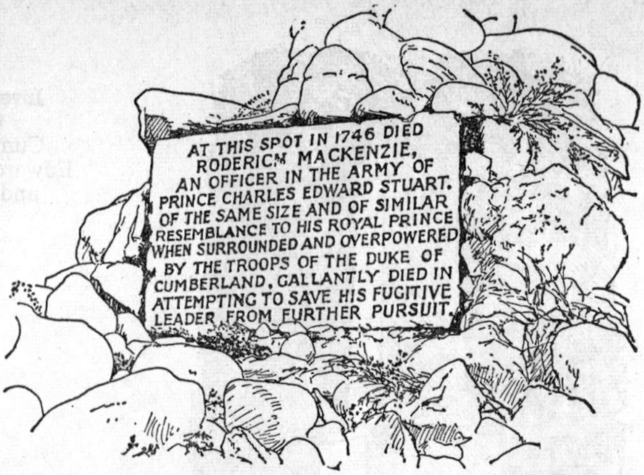

Invermoriston, Inverness. The inscribed cairn in memory of Roderick Mackenzie, who was killed during the '45 Rising, after he had feigned to be the fleeing Prince Charles Edward. It stands 13 miles to the west, on the south side of A887, near the meeting of the Rivers Moriston and Doe in Glen Moriston

Inverness, Inverness. The Mercat Cross, incorporating the 'Stone of the Tubs,' on which women drawing water from the river used to rest their tubs

Inverness, Inverness The inscription over the doorway of Dunbar's Hospital, dated 1668

Invershin, Sutherland. The modern Carbisdale Castle, on a height to the south, near which Montrose's last battle was fought in 1650

Inveruglas, Dunbarton. The power station of the Loch Sloy hydro-electric scheme, which was inaugurated in 1950

[For INVERNESS see also following plate

source in the Fionn Loch, lying to the south-east, and dominated by *Suilven*, 2,399 ft., one of the strange, isolated Torridon sandstone peaks of Sutherland. The picturesque, narrow and hilly road leading southwards from *Lochinver* (*q.v.*) into Ross-shire by way of Inverkirkaig has been called the " mad little road of Sutherland." It pursues a tortuous and hilly course, first along the steep, island-studded shores of Enard Bay, and later inland towards Loch Sionascaig, passing numerous little rocky lochans, and giving magnificent views, but demanding great care in driving. See **Achiltibuie** and **Baddagyle.** *Iter. 226.*

INVERMORISTON, Inverness. 160. Map 24, **NH 4 1.** **E.C.** Tues. Lies at the eastern end of the long Glen Moriston, bordered to the north by the heights of Invermoriston Forest, and faces *Loch Ness* (*q.v.*), near the point where the River Moriston enters the Loch. The road through Glen Moriston is part of the through route from Loch Ness to the north-west coast, joining the road from Invergarry and the south near *Cluanie* (*q.v.*). From Invermoriston, the first part of the glen is well wooded, the road later emerging on to bare moors, and being joined by the track of an old military road from *Fort Augustus* (*q.v.*), over the mountains through Inchnacardoch Forest. By means of this route, Dr. Johnson and Boswell travelled on their Highland tour in 1773, staying the night at Invermoriston, where the Doctor presented the landlord's daughter with a text-book on arithmetic. At a point **13 m. W.** of Invermoriston, the river is joined by the Doe, flowing from the north-west, and a few miles up its glen is *Corriedoe* cave, a hiding-place used by Prince Charles Edward in the '45, when he was guarded by the " Eight Men of Glenmoriston." A cairn, situated near the meeting of the rivers, commemorates Roderick Mackenzie, who feigned to be the Prince, and was killed by the soldiers searching for him. Developments in connection with a hydro-electric scheme have taken place in Glen Moriston. **5 m. N.E.,** above Loch Ness, rises the prominent hill of *Mealfuarvonie*, 2,284 ft. *Iter. 207, 210, 213.*

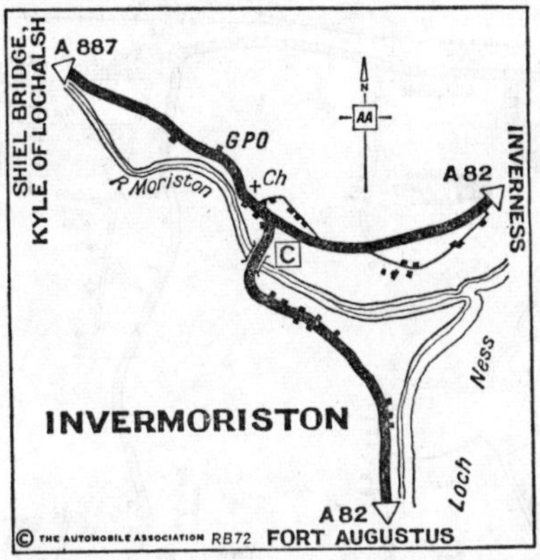

INVERNESS, Inverness. 34,870. LB. Map 25, **NH 6 4.** **E.C.** Wed. **M.D.** Tues./Fri. GOLF. Known as the " Capital of the Highlands," and finely situated on the Ness at the north-eastern extremity of *Glen More* (*q.v.*) and the *Caledonian Canal* (*q.v.*). Here, the waters of the Beauly Firth and the Inner Moray, or Inverness Firth, unite at the narrows which are overlooked to the north by Craigton Point. In 1652-57, Cromwell erected a fort, known as " The Sconce," on the right bank of the Ness, but of this only slight traces now remain, though the clock tower still stands on the site. *Inverness* was the terminal point of the two great military roads built in the 18th cent. by General Wade, commencing at Dunkeld and Fort William respectively. Wade's barracks, on the site of the old Castle, which surrendered to Mary, Queen of Scots in 1562, were named by him *Fort George*, and after their destruction by Prince Charles Edward, in 1746, a new *Fort George* (*q.v.*) was built away to the north-east. In the town are the late 13th and 18th cent. *High* Church; *Dunbar's* Hospital, dating from 1668; the Mercat Cross, enclosing the so-called " Clach-na-Cudainn " or " Stone of the Tubs "; the Museum, housing Jacobite relics; the modern Castle: *St. Andrew's* Cathedral of 1866-71; the Tolbooth Steeple of 1791. The 16th cent. *Abertarff House* (N.T. Scot.) has an ancient turnpike stair. The view from Castle Hill extends over a large expanse of Highland country, and to the north-west rises *Ben Wyvis*, 3,429 ft. To the west of the town is *Tomnahurich Hill*, another good viewpoint, and a little to the north is *Craig Phadraig*, 550 ft., crowned by a vitrified fort. The town is associated with Shakespeare's " Macbeth." The Northern Piping Competition, which takes place annually in September, is an important event. **6 m. N.E.,** on the road to Fort George, near *Dalcross* airport, is *Castle Stewart*, dating from 1625, and restored, a good example of the Scottish baronial style. See **Cawdor, Clachnaharry, Croy, Culloden, Loch Ness, South Kessock** and **Wade Roads.** For "Through Routes" see page 48. *Iter. 140, 150, 175, 176, 177, 195, 198, 199, 200, 201, 202, 203, 204, 205, 206, 207, 210, 211, 221.*

(See page 190 for Town Plan of **INVERNESS.**)

INVERORAN, Argyll. Map 14, **NN 2 4.** At the western end of Loch Tulla, on the line of the old Glencoe road, and at the foot of the *Black Mount*, looking to *Stob Ghabhar*, 3,565 ft. Near Inveroran was born, in 1724, Duncan Ban MacIntyre, the famous bard, whose monument stands at *Dalmally* (*q.v.*).

INVERPOLLY MOTOR TRAIL, Sutherland. Map 29, **NC 0 1.** See **Baddagyle.**

INVERSANDA, Argyll. Map 18, **NM 9 5.** Faces Inversanda Bay, on *Loch Linnhe* (*q.v.*), on the picturesque road through the *Ardgour* (*q.v.*) country, and near the eastern end of Glen Tarbert, which leads towards *Loch Sunart* (*q.v.*). **1 m. W.** up this glen is the wild Coire an Iubhair, leading off to the north, and giving access on foot to the splendid rock scenery of *Garbh Bheinn*, 2,903 ft., the finest peak of Ardgour, well-known to cragsmen. **To** the south of the glen rises *Creach Bheinn*, 2,800 ft., a notable viewpoint. The road through Glen Tarbert leads south-westwards round the head and southern side of Loch Sunart to *Lochaline* (*q.v.*), on the Sound of Mull, and an alternative route to Lochaline can also be followed from Inversanda along the shores of Loch Linnhe by way of *Camasnacroise* (*q.v.*). See **Strontian.** *Iter. 216, 217, 218.*

INVERSHIN, Sutherland. 90. Map 29, **NH 5 9.** **E.C.** Wed. Here, the River Shin meets the Kyle of Sutherland, and nearby, on an eminence beyond the combined streams, is the modern *Carbisdale Castle.* It is situated actually in Ross and Cromarty, and is famous for its proximity to the scene of Montrose's last battle, fought in 1650, after which he fled, before being betrayed by the laird at *Ardvreck Castle* near *Inchnadamph* (*q.v.*). Farther to the south-east, the widening Kyle is known at this point as the Maikle Pool. *Iter. 228, 229, 230, 232.*

INVERSNAID, Stirling. Map 15, **NN 3 0.** Finely situated on the eastern shores of *Loch Lomond* (*q.v.*), facing a splendid group of mountains on the opposite shore of the loch, including *Ben Ime*, 3,318 ft., *Ben Vane*, 3,004 ft., and *Ben Vorlich*, 3,092 ft. A fort to repress the Macgregors was constructed here in 1713 and was at one time under the command of General Wolfe, of Quebec fame. The road from *Aberfoyle* (*q.v.*) terminates at this point, and the loch steamers call here. Nearby are the Arklet Falls, on the Arklet Water flowing from Loch Arklet, a little to the east, at the far end of which is *Stronachlachar* (*q.v.*) on the beautiful Loch Katrine. The Falls are associated with Wordsworth's " Highland Girl," and a path going northwards by Loch Lomond leads to Rob Roy's Cave, described by Dorothy Wordsworth. Robert Bruce is believed to have sheltered here in 1306. South-east of the falls rises *Cruachan*, 1,762 ft., a good viewpoint. On the western shore of Loch Lomond is the power house at *Inveruglas* (*q.v.*), which forms part of the Loch Sloy hydro-electric scheme. *Iter. 105.*

INVERUGLAS, Dunbarton. Map 15, **NN 3 0.** Here, on the western shores of *Loch Lomond* (*q.v.*), is the power station of the Loch Sloy hydro-electric scheme, opened by Her Majesty Queen Elizabeth, the Queen Mother, in October, 1950. Loch Sloy itself lies away to the north-

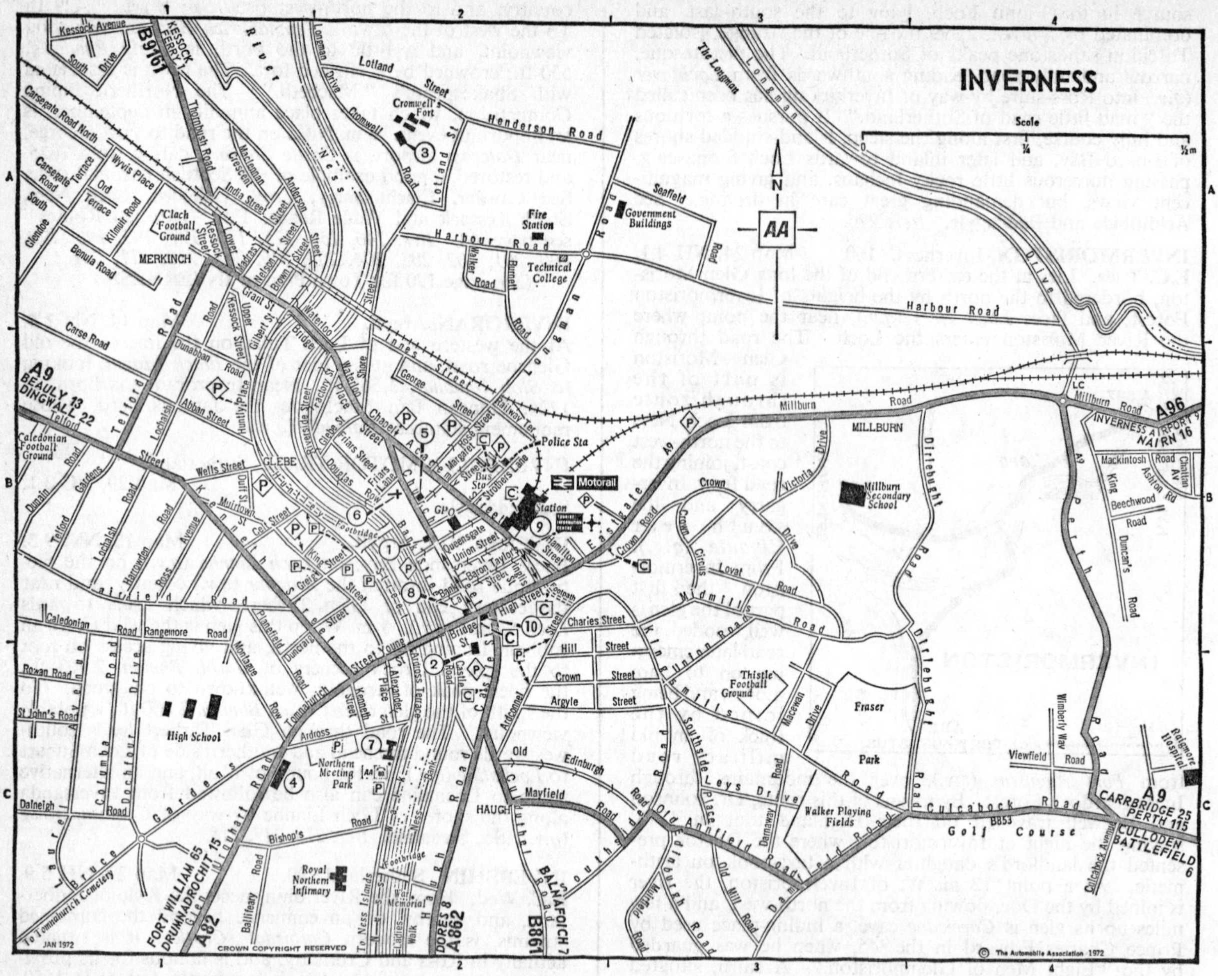

Abertarff House, 16th-cent. (N.T.) 1 (B2)
Castle, incorporating the Sheriff's Court House 2 (C2)
Clock Tower 3 (A3)
County Buildings 4 (C1)
Dunbar's Hospital, 1668 5 (B2)
Old High Church, 13th cent. 6 (B2)
St. Andrew's Cathedral 7 (B2)
Queen Mary's House, Bridge Street (B2)
Tolbooth Steeple, 1791-8 8 (B2)
Tourist Board Information Centre 9 (B2)
Town Hall, facing is the Mercat Cross with the Clach-na-Cudainn, or Stone of the Tubs 10 (B5)

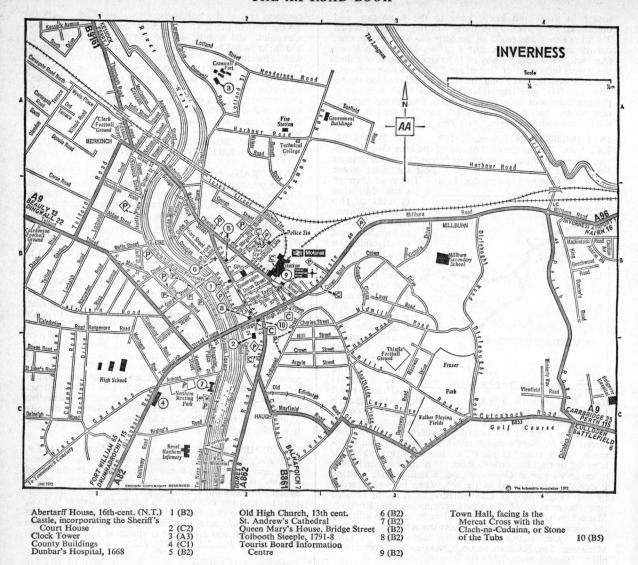

west, beyond Glen Sloy, and is overlooked by *Ben Vane*, 3,004 ft., from the south, and by *Ben Vorlich*, 3,092 ft., from the north. The surrounding country was MacFarlane property, their ancient rallying cry being "Loch Sloy." *Iter. 100, 110, 111.*

INVERURIE, Aberdeen. 5,438. SB. Map 27, NJ 7 2. E.C. Wed. M.D. Thurs. GOLF. Immediately to the south of the town, which is situated in the Garioch district, is the confluence of the Rivers Urie and Don, and in the vicinity is situated a 50-ft. high natural mound known as the "Bass," the site of an ancient stronghold, and visited by Mary, Queen of Scots in 1562. In the nearby churchyard is an inscribed Pictish Stone. Another ancient stone, carrying an Ogham inscription, and known as the *Brandsbutt Stone* (A.M.), stands ½ m. N.W. of the town. Inverurie has long been a Royal Burgh, and contains railway workshops. *Keith Hall* stands on the farther bank of the River Urie. Away to the west rises the *Mither Tap of Bennachie*, 1,698 ft., a notable local landmark. **2 m. S.**, near the Don, is the ruined *Kinkell* Church (A.M.), rebuilt in 1528, and preserving one of the rare Sacrament Houses. **2 m. M.E.** is *Bourtie House*, built in 1754. See **Chapel of Garioch, Inveramsay, Kintore and Old Meldrum.** *Iter. 175, 178, 184, 197.*

IONA, ISLE OF, Argyll. Map 13, NM 2 2. This famous Inner Hebridean island, only 3 miles long by 1½ miles broad, is separated by the narrow Sound of Iona from *Fionphort*, near *Bunessan* (*q.v.*), in the south-western tip of *Mull* (*q.v.*), to which it is connected by passenger ferry. *Iona*, which has no motoring roads, is generally visited from *Oban* (*q.v.*) by steamer. Its associations stretch back through the centuries to the coming of *St. Columba* from Ireland in 563. The Saint founded a small monastery here, and for 34 years carried on his great work of introducing Christianity to the Scottish mainland and islands until his death, in 597. Although buried in Iona, his remains were later removed to Ireland. The island became for many years a resort of pilgrims, and also the burial place of early Scottish Kings and Chieftains. The Norsemen ravaged Iona time and again, the monastery suffering severely, and having to be constantly rebuilt. In 1203, the Benedictines founded a new monastery, but the buildings were destroyed in 1561. Near the landing place are remains of a nunnery, founded in 1203, and in the Chapel adjoining the nave is the tomb of the last Prioress, who died in 1543. *McLean's Cross*, richly-carved and possibly of 15th cent. date, stands on the road which parallels the ancient "Road of the Dead," leading to *St. Oran's* Cemetery. This is the oldest Christian burial ground in

Inverurie, Aberdeen. The ancient Brandsbutt Stone, which bears Pictish symbols and an Ogham inscription. It stands just to the north-west of the town

Inverness, Inverness. The Clock Tower, on the site of The Sconce, the fort erected by Cromwell in 1652–57

Inverness, Inverness. The Tolbooth, or Town Steeple, dating from 1791

Inverness, Inverness. The Monument to Flora Macdonald, which stands on the terrace south of the modern Castle. The old Castle was blown up by Bonnie Prince Charlie in 1745

Inverness, Inverness. Castle Stewart, built by the 3rd Earl of Moray, in 1625. It stands 6 miles north-east of the town, off B9039, near the Inner Moray Firth

[For INVERNESS see also preceding plate
[For IONA see following plate

Iona, Argyll. The restored Cathedral, mainly of 15th or 16th century date, which is faced by the ancient St. Martin's Cross, nearly 17 feet in height. Adjoining the Cathedral are the newly-restored monastic buildings, including the chapter house, refectory, undercroft and cloister

Irvine, Ayr. The 14th century remains of Seagate Castle. In 1297, the Treaty of Irvine was signed here, and Mary, Queen of Scots, came to the castle in 1563

Irongray, Kirkcudbright. A Covenanter's tomb of 1685, situated on a mound to the west. Near Irongray is Skeogh Hill, where, in 1678, a great gathering of Covenanters took place. An obelisk, set up on the moors in 1870, marks the spot

Irvine, Ayr. The 120-foot high Town House. Between 1781 and 1783, Robert Burns worked in the town as a flax-dresser

Isle of Whithorn, Wigtown. The ruined 13th century Chapel. The site is traditionally associated with St. Ninian (4th century), the first Christian missionary in Scotland

Scotland, and contains the graves of many Kings, among them 48 Scottish, the last being Duncan, said to have been murdered by Macbeth in 1040. Among many carved Celtic slabs are those of former Clan Chiefs, bearing the designs of their galleys. In 1932, the ashes of Margaret Kennedy-Fraser, the transcriber of Gaelic songs, were buried here.

The restored, Romanesque *St. Oran's* Chapel, thought to have been built originally in 1080 by Queen Margaret, is the oldest of the island's surviving buildings, and is entered by a carved Norman doorway. In the chapel is the tomb of Scott's " Lord of the Isles." The granite *Great Cross of Iona*, or *St. Martin's* Cross, 16 ft. 8 in. high, boldly carved with Runic ornament, and possibly dating from the 9th or 10th cent., stands facing the Cathedral. This was founded in the 13th cent., but is mainly the work of two or more centuries later, and has been much added to and restored. The present cruciform structure of granite has a low square tower, and inside the Church are pier capitals carved with a variety of birds, animals and flowers. There are a number of tombs of interest, and below the east window is preserved the so-called *St. Columba's* pillow. Fragments of the monastery, which adjoins the Cathedral, are in process of restoration. The 9th cent. Celtic *St. John's* Cross has been blown down by a gale and awaits re-erection. At the southern extremity of *Iona* is *Port na Curaich*, where St. Columba is thought to have landed. On the west coast is a " spouting " cave, and in the northern part of the island is *Dun I*, 332 ft., a good viewpoint, overlooking beautiful sands. The colouring of the scenery and the profusion of wild flowers and sea-shells give added interest to Iona. At the time of Dr. Johnson's visit, in 1773, the island was known as *Icolmkill*, ant the Doctor referred to it as " that luminary of the Caledonian regions." See **Staffa.** *Iter. 249.*

IRONGRAY, Kirkcudbright. 912. Map 4, **NX 9 7.** Lies in the pleasant valley of the Cluden Water. In the churchyard is a tombstone erected by Scott in memory of Helen Walker, said to be the original of Jeannie Deans in the " Heart of Midlothian," which was first published in 1818. **¼ m. W.,** on a knoll, is a Covenanter's inscribed tomb, dating from 1685. A little to the north, across the Cluden Water, is *Fourmerkland Tower*, dated 1590. **4 m. W.,** beyond the Cairn Water, is *Skeogh Hill*, 1,286 ft., reached by way of Routin Bridge. An obelisk, on the south-eastern slopes of the hill, marks the Communion Stones, where John Welsh, the local minister in 1678, and a great-grandson of John Knox, gave the Sacrament to a body of 3,000 Covenanters. *Iter. 74.*

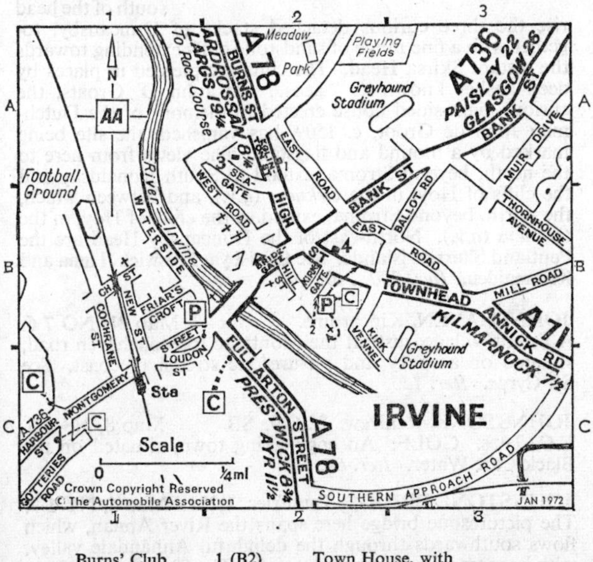

Burns' Club 1 (B2)	Town House, with
Parish Church 2 (B2)	Information Bureau and
Seagate Castle 3 (A2)	Mercat Cross 4 (B2)

IRVINE, Ayr. 23,011. SB. Map 8, **NS 3 3.** E.C. Wed. GOLF. A Royal Burgh, manufacturing town and port, on the Ayrshire coast, where the waters of the River Irvine and the Annick Water flow into the sea by the estuary of the Garnock. Burns lived in the town between 1781 and 1783, and a plaque on a cottage in Glasgow Vennel records his sojourn as a flax-dresser. Irvine is noted for its Burns Club and on the Town Moor is a statue of the poet. John Galt, the novelist, was born here in 1779. The Academy was founded in 1572 from the revenues of a former monastery. The ruined 14th cent. *Seagate Castle* was visited by Mary, Queen of Scots, in 1563. Facing the exotic 120-ft. high Town House is the old Mercat Cross. The Buchanite Sect originated in the *Relief* Church, in 1783. Marymass Week, an annual summer event, includes some Riding of the Marches. Irvine, together with the smaller *Kilwinning* (*q.v.*) to the north, is to become a New Town. See **Crocketford** and **Kilwinning.** *Iter. 60, 66, 69, 85, 88.*

ISBISTER, Shetland. Map 33, **HU 3 9.** See **Shetland Islands** (Mainland). *Iter. 267.*

ISLAY, ISLE OF, Argyll. 3,869. Map 6, **NR 2** 6, etc. Lying off the west coast of *Kintyre* (*q.v.*), and separated by the narrow Sound of Islay from its smaller, but hillier Inner Hebridean neighbour *Jura* (*q.v.*), the island of *Islay* is the most southerly of the Hebrides, and has for industries, agriculture, fishing and distilleries. In size, 25 miles long and some 20 miles broad, and enjoying a mild climate, it is gaining in popularity, being reached by steamer, calling at Port Ellen or Port Askaig, from West Loch Tarbert (See **Tarbert;** Argyll). There are also regular air services to Glenegedale airport, near Port Ellen, from Glasgow airport. On the west side of the island, Lochs Indaal and Gruinart are separated by only a narrow neck of land, the fine coastal district to the south-west being known as the Rhinns of Islay. Away to the south-east, beyond Laggan Bay. is the Mull of Oa peninsula, with lofty cliffs, accessible by road from Port Ellen, to the north-east of which are hills rising to more than 1,500 ft. There are a number of sculptured stones, Celtic Crosses and caves on the island. No road encircles Islay, but there are some well-surfaced, classified roads linking the coastal villages, the others being mostly poor and very narrow. Some 75 miles of road can be traversed by car. See **Bowmore, Bridgend, Bruichladdich, Claggain Bay, Kilchoman, Kildalton, Mull of Oa, Port Askaig, Port Charlotte, Port Ellen, Portnahaven** and **Sanaigmore.** *Iter. 243 to 247.*

ISLE OF WHITHORN, Wigtown. Map 2, **NX 4 3.** This tiny mainland port is situated on rocky shores, sheltered by Isle Head, while away to the south-west is Burrow Head. The ruined Chapel (A.M.), possibly of 13th cent. date, is traditionally associated with St. Ninian, the first Christian missionary in Scotland, who worked in the 4th cent. *St. Ninian's* Shrine at Whithorn became an important place of pilgrimage, and was visited regularly by James IV. *Isle Tower* is a 17th cent. building. Away to the west on the shores of Luce Bay, and reached by a track off the Port William road nearing *Glasserton* (*q.v.*), is *St. Ninian's Cave* (A.M.) in Port Castle Bay. This is perhaps an oratory used by the Saint, and contains sculptured stones and Crosses. In the vicinity, to the east, is the 17th cent. house of *Tonderghie*. See **Whithorn.** *Iter. 82.*

ISLE ORNSAY, Isle of Skye, Inverness. Map 23, **NG 6 1.** A small coastal and fishing resort in the fertile peninsula of Sleat, facing an island in the Sound of Sleat, on which are situated a lighthouse and the remains of a small nunnery. **2 m. S.W.,** off the *Armadale* (*q.v.*) road, a rough and hilly by-road goes north-westwards to *Ord* (*q.v.*) on *Loch Eishort*. South-west of Ord, on the coast, is the ruined *Dunscaith Castle*, on an isolated rock, and once the home of the Macdonalds of Sleat, before they removed to *Duntulm* (*q.v.*). See **Teangue.** *Iter, 253.*

JAMESTOWN, Dunbarton. 5,692. Map 15, **NS 3 8.** *Iter. 109, 112.*

JARLSHOF, Shetland. Map 33, **HU 4 0.** See **Shetland Islands** (Mainland).

JEANTOWN, Ross and Cromarty. Map 24, **NG 9 3.** See **Lochcarron.**

JEDBURGH, Roxburgh. 3,785. SB. Map 10, **NT 6 2.** **E.C.** Thurs. **M.D.** Fri. GOLF. One of the most famous of the well known border Abbeys is situated here, in the delightful valley of the Jed Water, which flows northwards to join the Teviot beyond Bonjedward. The former Castle, once a residence of Scottish Kings, has vanished, but the modern castle, built as a gaol in 1823, stands at the top of Castlegate. In this Royal Burgh is preserved *Queen Mary's House*, now a museum, where she may have lain ill in 1566 after her ride to *Hermitage Castle* (*q.v.*). The house, restored after its partial destruction in 1523, is now a museum. *Blackfriars* Church, built in 1746, was reconstructed in 1818, and has an ornate iron lantern set in the portico.

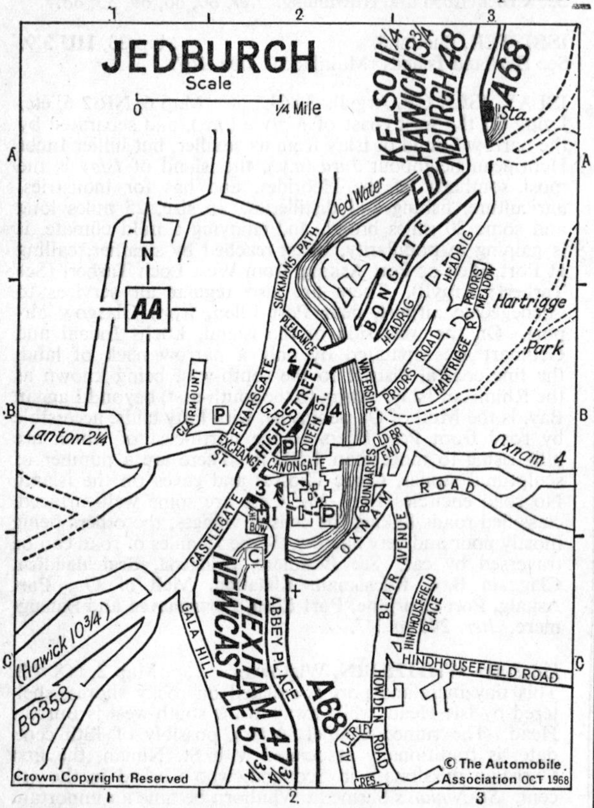

Abbey 1 (B2) New Gate 3 (B2)
Blackfriars Church 2 (B2) Queen Mary's House (Museum) 4 (B2)

The *New Gate*, surmounted by a tall steeple, carries the dates 1720, 1755 and 1761. Sir Walter Scott was an advocate here in 1793 and his associations with the town are recalled by a bronze tablet on the County Buildings. A quaint old custom perpetuated is the Candlemas Ba', on February 2nd, when the " Uppies " play the " Doonies," while the Callants' Festival, in early summer, dates from 1947. The very interesting and imposing remains of the Abbey (A.M.), founded in c. 1118, and sacked on numerous occasions in medieval times, are built of red sandstone, and are noted for the splendid nave, dating from the Transitional period, with beautiful detail-work. The west front has a fine rose window, known as *St. Catherine's Wheel*, and there is a richly-carved Norman doorway. The central tower has been many times restored, and the choir is much rebuilt, but the fine north transept of the 14th cent. is in good condition, and contains interesting monuments. The three-arched 16th cent. bridge off Canongate is of interest. The town has many houses displaying characteristic crow-stepped gables and is one of the most attractive in the Lowlands. Burns once lodged in a house in Canongate; Prince Charles Edward stayed in Blackhills Close in 1745; and Wordsworth and his sister visited a house in Abbey Close. A tablet marks the house where Sir David Brewster, founder of the British Association, was born. Among earlier names for the town are Jeddart and Jethart, both derived from the original Geddewrd. **1 m. S.,** near the river, and to the right of the A68, is the " Capon Tree," a lone survivor of the former Forest of Jethart. To the south-west of Jedburgh rise *Dunian Hill*, 1,095 ft., and *Black Law*, 1,110 ft., overlooking a wide stretch of country. **1½ m. N.W.** of the town, on Lanton Moor, are the ancient earthworks and ruined 17th cent. tower of *Timpendean*. See **Ancrum Bridge, Denholm** and **Ferniehirst Castle.** *Iter. 4, 43, 47, 52.*

JERICHO, Angus. Map 20, **NO 4 4.** A strangely-named, tiny village, lying just to the south of the main Glamis to Forfar road. There are several hand-loom weavers' cottages.

JOHN O' GROATS, Caithness. 140. Map 30, **ND 3 7.** **E.C.** Wed. **M.D.** Thurs. This well-known place is situated near the extreme north-eastern tip of the Scottish mainland. It is 873 miles distant by road from Land's End in Cornwall, and 280 miles from Kirkmaiden, Scotland's most southerly parish, associated with Burns's " Frae Maidenkirk to Johnny Groats'." John O' Groats overlooks the stormy waters of the Pentland Firth, with Stroma Island lying offshore beyond the Inner Sound. On the beach are found small shells called " Groatie Buckies." Farther to the east is the imposing headland of Duncansby Head, the " Vervedrum " of Ptolemy, with its lighthouse, a notable viewpoint. To the south of the head rise the three curious detached stacks of Duncansby, together with a fine range of sandstone cliffs extending towards the distant Skirsa Head. The cliffs are pierced in places by deep gashes known as " geos." At John O' Groats, the curious eight-sided house erected in memory of the Dutchman John de Groot, c. 1509, has vanished, the site being marked by a mound and flagstaff. The views from here to the north, beyond Stroma, extend to South Ronaldsay and the cliffs of Hoy, in the *Orkneys* (*q.v.*), and between which, the north, beyond Stroma, extend to the cliffs of Hoy, in the *Orkneys* (*q.v.*). North-east of the Duncansby Head are the Pentland Skerries islands. See **Canisbya, Freswick, Huna** and **Kirkmaiden.** *Iter. 200, 240.*

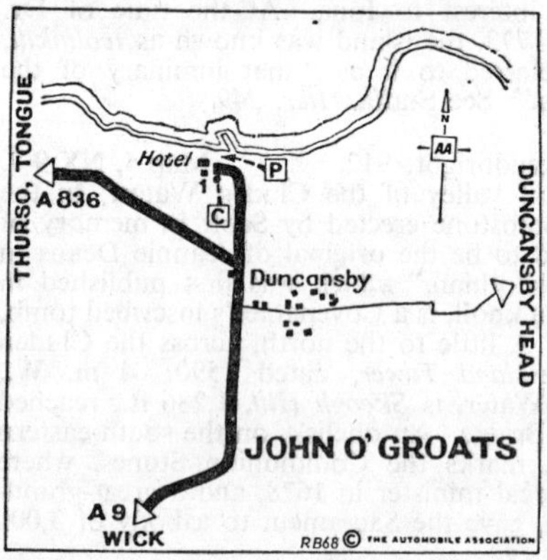

Site of John O'Groats House 1

JOHNSHAVEN, Kincardine. Map 21, **NO 7 6.** A fishing village, just off the Montrose to Stonehaven road, situated on a rocky and picturesque stretch of coast. See **St. Cyrus.** *Iter. 155.*

JOHNSTONE, Renfrew. 22,629. SB. Map 8, **NS 4 6.** **E.C.** Tues. GOLF. An engineering town, situated on the Black Cart Water. *Iter. 64.*

JOHNSTONE BRIDGE, Dumfries. 1,221. Map 4, **NY 1 9.** The picturesque bridge here spans the River Annan, which flows southwards through the delightful Annandale valley, with its memories of Border warfare. The Church dates from 1733. See **Lockerbie.** *Iter. 10, 13, 29, 50, 51.*

Jedburgh, Roxburgh. 'Queen Mary's House,' a late 16th century bastel-house. Mary, Queen of Scots, is said to have lain ill at Jedburgh in 1566, after riding to visit Bothwell at Hermitage Castle

Jedburgh, Roxburgh. The New Gate, which dates from the 18th century, and carries a lofty steeple. It gives access to the Abbey precincts

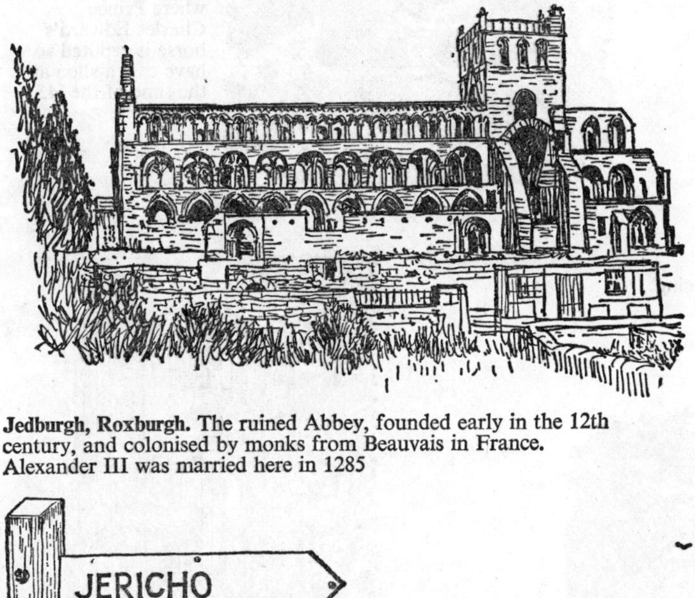

Jedburgh, Roxburgh. The ruined Abbey, founded early in the 12th century, and colonised by monks from Beauvais in France. Alexander III was married here in 1285

John O'Groats, Caithness. The mound and flagstaff on the site of the former house lived in by the Dutchman John de Groot, in the 16th century. This house was octagonal with eight entrances, and each of his eight descendants entered by his own door and sat at the 'head' of an octagonal table, to assert his claim to the estate

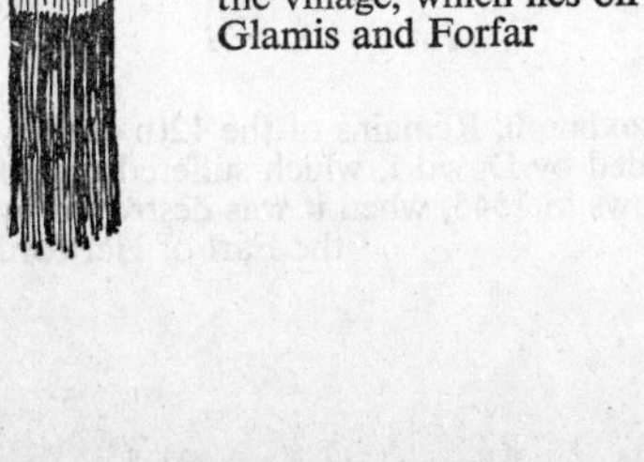

Jericho, Angus. The sign pointing to the village, which lies off A94, between Glamis and Forfar

[For JEDBURGH see also under BORDER COUNTRY (Plate 20)

Keills, Argyll. The carved Celtic Cross at the Chapel

Kelso, Roxburgh. John Rennie's bridge across the River Tweed, erected in 1803. This is virtually a model of old Waterloo Bridge, in London, which he built in 1811, and the demolition of which was begun in 1934

Keiss, Caithness. The remains of the old Castle, facing the sea near the modern building

Kelso, Roxburgh. The mark in Roxburgh Street where Prince Charles Edward's horse is reputed to have cast a shoe at the time of the '45 Rising

Keith, Banff. A bridge across the River Isla, built in 1609, linking Keith with Fife-Keith

Kelso, Roxburgh. Remains of the 12th century Abbey, founded by David I, which suffered one of its worst blows in 1545, when it was destroyed by the Earl of Hertford

JUNIPER GREEN, Midlothian. Map 9, **NT 1** 6.
See Colinton.

JURA, ISLE OF, Argyll. 417 with Colonsay.
Map 6, **NR 5** 7 and 13, **NR 5** 8.
This picturesque Inner Hebridean island is separated from *Knapdale* (*q.v.*), on the mainland coast, by the Sound of Jura, and from the neighbouring island of *Islay* (*q.v.*), by the Sound of Islay. It is perhaps best known for the three *Paps of Jura*, all about 2,500 ft. in height, forming notable viewpoints, and being prominent objects in the view from many points on the mainland. The island is some 28 miles long and 8 miles broad, but it is comparatively little visited, due mainly to lack of accommodation. Jura is linked by passenger ferry from *Feolin Ferry*, on the Sound of Islay, to *Port Askaig* (*q.v.*), in Islay, and there is a pier at *Craighouse* (**E.C.** Tues.) for the steamers serving *Tarbert* (*q.v.*). A fair, waterbound road extends from Feolin Ferry along the eastern shores of the island for 24 miles as far as *Ardlussa*. The sea lock of Tarbert divides Jura almost into half, and in the southern sector rise the well-known *Paps*. O ffthe north coast is the strait of Corryvreckan, noted as a whirlpool, the noise of which is audible from afar. The strait separates Jura from Scarba. See **Colonsay.**

KAMES, Argyll. 297. Map 7, **NR 9** 7.
E.C. Wed. **M.D.** Wed. A small *Cowal* (*q.v.*) resort on the *Kyles of Bute* (*q.v.*), with a pier. A little to the west, near the large powder-mills, a by-road branches southwards and continues almost as far as Ardlamont Point, with views towards the island of Bute and also to the northern tip of Arran across the Sound of Bute. **1½ m. S.W.** of Kames is the little village of *Millhouse*, from which a road leads northwestwards to *Kilfinan* (*q.v.*), while a branch road goes southwestwards to the shores of *Loch Fyne* (*q.v.*), from which the wooded Glenan Bay can be reached on foot. *Iter. 103.*

KEIG, Aberdeen. Map 27, **NJ 6** 1.
A little to the east, near *My Lord's Throat* Pass, by a winding stretch of the River Don, is the modern *Forbes Castle*, with *Cairn William*, 1,469 ft., rising away to the south-east.

KEILLS, Argyll. Map 13, **NR 6** 8.
Situated between the Sound of Jura and the southern reaches of Loch Sween. A ruined chapel here has a notable Celtic Cross. Loch na Cille lies to the south.

KEIR, Dumfries. 1,076. Map 3, **NX 8** 9.
See **Penpont** (for *Courthill*).

KEISS, Caithness. 495. Map 30, **ND 3** 6.
This little fishing village lies on Sinclair's Bay. A little to the north, on the coast, is the ruined *Keiss Castle*, near the modern castle. Beyond, to the left of the road, is a Baptist chapel in memory of Sir William Sinclair founder of the country's first Baptist church. The main road leading southwards towards Wick crosses the wide Keiss Links, with the Loch of Wester to the west. *Iter. 200.*

KEITH, Banff. 4,178. SB. Map 26, **NJ 4** 5.
E.C. Wed. **M.D.** Tues. An agricultural centre in Strath Isla, on the river of that name, and once famous for its fair. The town consists of the regularly-planned Keith, and also Fife-Keith, to the west of the river, which is linked to the former by two bridges one of which dates from 1609. In the R.C. Church is a notable altarpiece. *Milton Tower*, in ruins, was formerly a castle of the Oliphants. To the south-east of the town is a hill known as the *Balloch*, 1,199 ft., a good viewpoint. See **Deskford** and **Drummuir.** *Iter. 169, 175, 178, 187, 189.*

KELLIE CASTLE, Fife. Map 17, **NO 5** 0.
See Pittenween. *Iter. 94, 98.*

KELLS CHURCH, Kirkcudbright. Map 3, **NX 6** 7.
See New Galloway.

KELSO, Roxburgh. 4,854. SB. Map 11, **NT 7** 3.
E.C. Wed. **M.D.** Fri. GOLF. A most attractive Border town on the River Tweed, with a wide square, in which stands

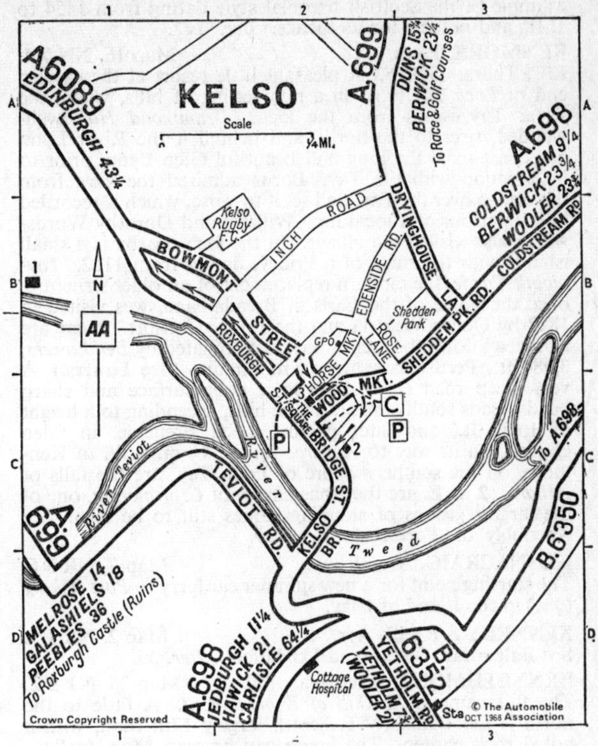

Floors Castle 1 (B1) Kelso Abbey 2 (C2)
Town Clerk's Office, Information Bureau 3 (C2)

the Court House of 1816, where a nightly curfew is sounded. Just outside the town, best known for its ruined Abbey, the Tweed is joined by the Teviot. *Kelso* has many historical associations, including visits from Mary, Queen of Scots, and Prince Charles Edward. Scott lived here for 6 months, in 1783, as a school-fellow at the former grammar school, staying at *Garden Cottage*, now *Waverley Lodge*. At the same school were the brothers Ballantyne, who later printed and published his works. Among these, the first edition of his "Minstrelsy of the Scottish Border" was printed in Kelso. The Abbey (A.M.) was founded in 1128, but only a small portion is still to be seen of what was perhaps the greatest of the Border Abbeys. In 1545, the building was almost totally destroyed, after having been besieged. All that now remains are the west façade and transepts, part of the tower and two of the nave bays, showing some fine Norman and early Gothic detail, notably on the north transept. From the fine 5-arched bridge over the river, built by Rennie in 1803, to replace one destroyed by the floods of 1797, there is a fine view of *Floors Castle* (*q.v.*). On the bridge are two lamp-posts from Rennie's demolished Old Waterloo Bridge in London. To the south-west is the Teviot bridge, modelled perhaps on Rennie's structure at Kelso. *Wooden House*, early 19th cent., is a fine house. *Ednam House*, above Kelso Bridge, dates from 1761. **6 m. N.W.** is *Mellerstain House* (*q.v.*), a notable old Berwickshire mansion, by William and Robert Adam. **See Ednam, Roxburgh** and **Yetholm.** *Iter. 6, 7, 30, 32, 39, 46.*

KELTY. Fife. 7,750. Map 17 **NT 1** 9.
Situated on the edge of the Fife coal-field.

KEMNAY, Aberdeen. 1,992. Map 27, **NJ 7** 1.
The wooded curves of the Don lie to the west of the village, and beyond its banks stands *Fetternear House*, once the country seat of the Bishops of Aberdeen. *Kemnay* is best known for its granite quarries, some of the material having been used in the construction of the Forth Bridge, and also the Thames Embankment, in London. **3 m. S.S.W.**, off the *Monymusk* (*q.v.*) road, is *Castle Fraser*, a very fine

example of the Scottish baronial style dating from 1454 to 1618, and notable for its turrets. *Iter. 177.*

KENMORE, Perth. 718. Map 16, **NN 7 4.**
E.C. Thurs. GOLF. A pleasant little resort at the eastern end of *Loch Tay* (*q.v.*) in a rich setting of hills, where the River Tay issues from the loch. *Drummond Hill,* well-wooded, rises to the north, and behind it the River Lyon has come from the long and beautiful Glen Lyon, prior to its junction with the Tay. Burns admired the view from the bridge over the Tay, and set it to verse, which is recorded in the parlour of a local inn. William and Dorothy Wordsworth also visited the village. In the loch nearby is a small island, with the ruins of a Priory, dating from 1122. *Taymouth Castle,* the modern replacement of an older structure, once the home of the Earls of Breadalbane, was visited in 1842 by Queen Victoria and the Prince Consort. There are fine views down the loch, which is dominated by *Ben Lawers,* 3,984 ft., Perthshire's highest mountain. (See **Lawers.**) A very steep road (1 in 4), with a poor surface and sharp bends, leads southwards over the hills, ascending to a height of 1,672 ft., and later passing Loch Freuchie, in Glen Quaich, on its way to *Amulree* (*q.v.*). **1½ m. S.W.** of Kenmore, on the southern shore of Loch Tay, are the falls of *Acharn.* **2 m. E.** are the stone circles of *Croftmoraig,* one of the largest groups of standing stones still to be seen. See **Aberfeldy** and **Fortingall.** *Iter. 120.*

KENNACRAIG, Argyll. Map 7, **NR 8 6.**
The starting point for a new summer car ferry to *Port Askaig* (*q.v.*) in the Island of Islay.

KENNEDY'S PASS, Ayr. Map 2, **NX 1 9.**
See **Ballantrae, Girvan** and **Lendalfoot.** *Iter. 55.*

KENNETHMONT, Aberdeen. 750 Map 26, **NJ 5 2.**
The full name is *Kirkhill of Kennethmont.* A little to the north is *Leith Hall* (N.T. Scot.), largely 17th cent., with a noted rock garden. The house can be seen Mon. to Sat., 11 to 6; Sun., 2.30 to 6, May to Sept. (See note page 98.) *Iter. 178.*

KENTALLEN, Argyll. Map 18, **NN 0 5.**
E.C. Sat. On Kentallen Bay, an inlet of *Loch Linnhe* (*q.v.*), with the great horseshoe curve of *Ben Vair,* 3,362 ft., in the background. From the summit of this fine peak, the Glencoe mountains provide a wonderful spectacle, with *Bidean nam Bian,* 3,766 ft., Argyll's highest mountain, dominating the scene. To the south of Kentallen is the wooded but roadless Glen Duror. There are fine views from the Ballachulish road over Loch Linnhe towards the Ardgour mountains, the best known of which is *Garbh Bheinn,* 2,903 ft. *Iter. 124.*

KENTRA BAY, Argyll. Map 12, **NM 6 6.**
See **Acharacle.**

KERRERA, ISLE OF, Argyll. Map 14, **NM 8 2.**
See **Oban.**

KERRYCROY, Bute. Map 7, **NS 1 6.**
See **Kilchattan Bay.**

KESSOCK, Inverness; Ross and Cromarty. Map 25, **NH 6 4.**
See **North Kessock** and **South Kessock.** *Iter. 202, 203.*

KILBARCHAN, Renfrew. 3,910. Map 8, **NS 4 6.**
E.C. Wed. On a building now used as an Old Folks' Hall is the statue of a well-known local piper of the 17th cent. An 18th cent. Weaver's Cottage is preserved (N.T. Scot.), and is open 2 to 5, Tues., Thurs., Sat.; also Sun. from May to Oct. (See note page 98). A fountain has been erected in memory of Robert Allan, a local weaver poet.

KILBIRNIE, Ayr. 8,713. Map 8, **NS 3 5.**
E.C. Wed. GOLF. On the River Garnock, with Kilbirnie Loch to the east. The Church dates from 1654, and contains a carved pulpit and the grandiose *Garnock* gallery of the Crawford family. *Kilbirnie Place,* an ancient mansion situated to the west, was damaged by fire in the 18th cent. *Ladyland* and *Glengarnock Castle* are two other ruined structures in the vicinity. *Iter. 58, 85.*

KILCHATTAN BAY, Bute. 333. Map 7, **NS 1 5.**
A quiet resort, with a steamer pier and a sandy bay, facing the twin Cumbraes across the Firth of Clyde. **3 m. S.W.,** on a narrow road, and reached by way of Kingarth, beyond which are the Standing Stones of Lubas, is the ruined Chapel of *St. Blane.* Near it, to the west, on the sandy Dunagoil Bay, is a vitrified fort. Southwards lies Garroch Head, looking towards the island of Arran. To the north of Kilchattan, some four miles distant, on the coast, is the palatial modern mansion of *Mount Stuart,* a seat of the Marquis of Bute, beyond which lies the model village of *Kerrycroy.* Another road leads north-westwards from the resort, and gives access to the sandy bays of Scalpsie and St. Ninian's, the latter facing the island of Inch Marnock, in the Sound of Bute. *Iter. 241.*

KILCHOAN, Argyll. Map 12, **NM 4 6.**
This remote village is situated on the picturesque, rocky Ardnamurchan coast, and has a pier, known as *Mingary* from which there is a service to *Tobermory* (*q.v.*) in Mull. The pier lies on a by-road about **1 m. S.E.,** looking eastwards across the water to the impressive, but ruined *Mingary Castle,* where James IV held his court in 1495, and which was taken for Montrose in 1644. The castle, described in Scott's "Lord of the Isles," was the ancient home of the MacIains, a sept or branch of the Clan Macdonald, Beyond the castle rises *Ben Hiant,* 1,729 ft., a very fine viewpoint, looking eastwards towards *Loch Sunart* (*q.v.*). To the north-west of Kilchoan and its bay, a rough, gated road gives access to the most westerly point of the Scottish mainland at *Ardnamurchan Point* (*q.v.*), with its lonely lighthouse. To the west of this road, some 2 miles from Kilchoan, is the low hill of *Beinn na Seilg,* 1,123 ft. From its rocky summit the panorama is wide and beautiful, and on the eastern slopes is a stone circle. **6 m. N.E.** of Kilchoan, off the Salen road, and reached partly by means of a by-road and partly on foot, are the silver sands of Kilmory Bay, with Ockle Point lying to the east. *Iter. 216.*

KILCHOMAN, Isle of Islay, Argyll. 910. Map 6, **NR 2 6.**
The Church, situated a little to the south of the road, contains a notable example of a sculptured Celtic cross. To the north-east is Loch Gorm, with the remains of an ancient castle of the Macdonalds. There are good sands at Machir Bay, in the Rhinns of Islay, to the west, and also at Saligo Bay, to the north, the latter reached by a narrow road. Near the former are the graves of some of those drowned in the sinking of the "Otranto," in 1918, and there are also several standing stones in the vicinity. See **Port Ellen** and **Sanaigmore.** *Iter. 246.*

KILCHRENAN, Argyll. Map 14, **NN 0 2.**
E.C. Wed. Situated a little to the north of *Loch Awe* (*q.v.*), and facing *Portsonachan* (*q.v.*). In the churchyard is a block of granite commemorating Mac Cailean Mor, killed in 1294, the founder of the Argyll fortunes. Near the shores of the loch, away to the south-west, are Forestry Commission developments, including the newly-founded village of *Dalavich,* the road continuing by the loch to reach *Ford* (*q.v.*). Through the wooded Glen Nant, to the north of Kilchrenan goes the road to *Taynuilt* (*q.v.*).

KILCHURN CASTLE, Argyll. Map 14, **NN 1 2.**
This romantic, ruined Castle (A.M.), the keep of which was built by Sir Colin Campbell, the founder of the Breadalbane family, dates originally from 1440, and was garrisoned by Hanoverian troops in 1746. It stands most picturesquely in upper Loch Awe, on a site which was once an island. The south and north sides of the building are of 16th and 17th cent. date respectively, and in 1879, the great gale which at the same time wrecked the Tay Bridge, blew down one of the castle's tower tops. The Rivers Orchy and Strae enter the loch at this point, and behind Loch Awe, to the north-west rises *Ben Cruachan* 3,689 ft., the monarch of the surrounding country, with new hydro-electric works nearby. The Dalmally to Taynuilt road passes near the castle by means of a bridge over an inner reach of Loch Awe. *Iter. 110, 117, 125, 144, 145.*

KILCONQUHAR, Fife. 1,338. Map 17, **NO 4 0.**
An attractive village, on the shore of Kilconquhar Loch. *Kilconquhar House* has a 16th cent. tower. In the churchyard are carved gravestones. See **Colinsburgh.** *Iter. 132.*

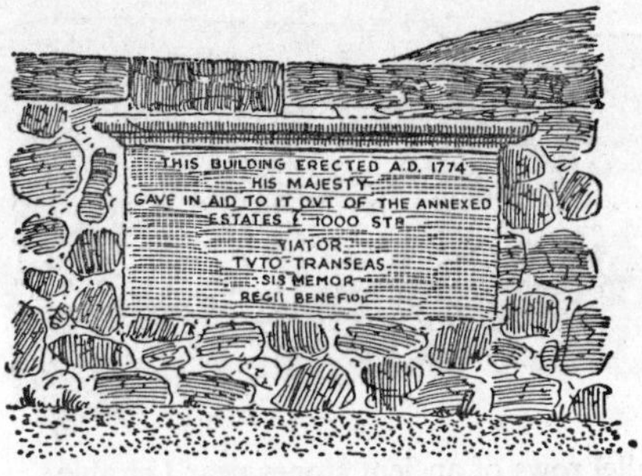

Kenmore, Perth. The tablet on the bridge over the River Tay, which dates from 1774

Kenmore, Perth. The entrance to the modern Taymouth Castle, seen from A827, to the north-east. The former 16th century structure was the work of Colin Campbell of Glenorchy and became later a home of the Breadalbanes

Kilbarchan, Renfrew. The inscription above the door of an 18th century Weaver's Cottage, now under the guardianship of the National Trust for Scotland

Kilbarchan, Renfrew. The statue of Habbie Simpson, a local piper of the 17th century, which stands on the Church steeple

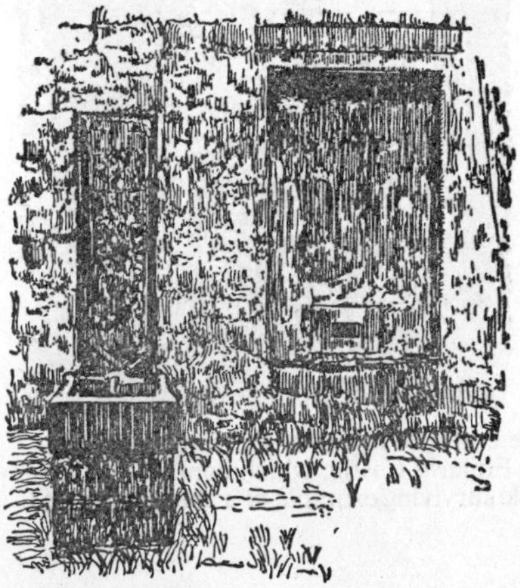

Kilchrenan, Argyll. A granite block, showing what is said to be a carving of a claymore, set up in 1866, and commemorating MacCailean Mor, the ancestor of the Clan Argyll, killed in 1294

Kilchurn Castle, Argyll. The 15th to 17th century Castle, built by the Breadalbanes, whose ancestor, Sir Colin Campbell, Knight of Rhodes, erected the keep. The gale which destroyed the Tay Bridge in 1879 blew down one of the tower tops

PLATE 94

[For KILCHOAN see under MINGARY CASTLE (Plate 122)

Kilcreggan, Dunbarton. Knockderry Castle, the 'Knock Dunder' of Sir Walter Scott's '*Heart of Midlothian.*' It stands some 3 miles to the north, on the Coulport road (B833)

Kildonan, Sutherland. Parallel rows of ancient stones near Leirable Hill, to the north-west, off A897

Kildrummy, Aberdeen. The ruined Castle of the Earls of Mar, defended by Sir Nigel Bruce in 1306, and besieged in 1404 by the son of the Wolf of Badenoch. It was dismantled after the 1715 Jacobite Rising

Killearn, Stirling. The obelisk to George Buchanan, born here in 1506, who became tutor to James VI

Killin, Perth. The entrance tower of the former Breadalbane stronghold of Finlarig Castle, which contains what is reputed to be the sole surviving example of a 'beheading pit'

Killiecrankie, Perth. Scenery in the gorge of Killiecrankie (part N.T. Scot.), famous for the battle which was won by the Highlanders in 1689

[For KILMACOLM see following plate

KILCREGGAN, Dunbarton. 1,343. SB. with Cove. Map 14, **NS 2** 8.
At the southern extremity of the Rosneath peninsula, with a pier, overlooking the mouth of Loch Long and the Holy Loch. The resort faces *Gourock* (*q.v.*), on the opposite shores of the Firth of Clyde. Beyond Baron's Point, west of Kilcreggan, is *Cove*, also with a pier. A little farther to the north, on the road to *Coulport* (*q.v.*), is the Castle of *Knockderry*, standing on the dungeons of an old tower, and associated with Scott's " Heart of Midlothian " under the name of " Knock Dunder." See **Rosneath.** *Iter. 116.*

KILDALTON, Isle of Islay, Argyll. 1,150. Map 6, **NR 4** 4.
In the churchyard are two finely sculptured Celtic crosses. Inland, to the north-west, rises *Beinn Sholum*, 1,136 ft., the most southerly in a long line of hills extending towards the Sound of Islay. The Kildalton estate extends towards the shores of Loch a' Chnoic, with numerous small islands offshore. *Iter. 245.*

KILDONAN, Isle of Arran, Bute. Map 7, **NS 0** 2.
Here, situated on a loop off the main road, are remains of *Kildonan Castle*, on a rocky stretch of coast looking seawards towards the tiny island of Pladda, with its lighthouse. To the north-east is Dippin Head, near Dippin rocks, from which magnificent marine views may be obtained. *Iter. 242.*

KILDONAN, Sutherland. 1,209. Map 31, **NC 9** 2.
The tiny village lies in Strath Ullie, which is threaded by the Helmsdale River, noted for its fishing. Gold was discovered in the Kildonan Burn in 1868. There are numerous prehistoric remains in the neighbourhood, notably on *Leirable Hill*, to the north-west, and some examples of parallel rows of ancient stones are to be found. In the vicinity stands *Suisgill Lodge*, with its fine gardens. To the north and south of the Strath rise moorlands and bare hills. See **Lybster.** *Iter. 234, 235.*

KILDRUMMY, Aberdeen. 924. Map 26, **NJ 4** 1.
The imposing ruins of the great castle of *Kildrummy* (A.M.), accessible always (see note page 98), lie a little to the south-west, at a height of nearly 800 ft., in a picturesque setting, guarded on two sides by a ravine, and overlooking the valley of the Upper Don. The castle is of 13th century date, added to at various times later, having the usual stormy history common to so many Scottish castles. It was gallantly defended by Sir Nigel Bruce in 1306. One of its two round towers, the *Snow* Tower, is almost equal in size to the outstanding example at *Bothwell* (*q.v.*). There are also remains of the Chapel, with a triple lancet window. The castle Garden Trust is open daily, 9 to 6, Mar. to Oct. (See note page 98). **1 m. N.E.** of the castle, and a little to the east of the main road, near the modern Kildrummy Church, are remains of the older Kirk, retaining a Norman wall, and also a vault containing monuments, known as the Elphinstone aisle, dating from 1605 and restored in 1862. Farther to the north, and to the left of the Huntly road, is Drumnahive Wood, in which lies *Lulach's Stone*, traditionally associated with the slaying of Lady Macbeth's son. *Iter. 167, 176.*

KILFINAN, Argyll. 1,092. Map 14, **NR 9** 7.
Lies a little to the east of Kilfinan Bay, on *Loch Fyne* (*q.v.*), with the heights of Knapdale beyond the farther shore of the loch. The road leading southwards from here, passing Loch Melldalloch, continues as far as *Tighnabruaich* (*q.v.*), on the *Kyles of Bute* (*q.v.*). See **Kames.** *Iter. 102.*

KILFINICHEN CHURCH, Isle of Mull, Argyll. Map 13, **NM 4** 2.
Situated on the northern shores of Loch Scridain. A by-road leads westwards along the shores of the loch and gives access to the 2,000-acre Scottish National Trust farm property known as *Burg*, with lofty cliffs rising farther west, at the extremity of the lonely and hilly Ardmeanach peninsula. On the shore is preserved *McCulloch's Tree*, a noted geological specimen. The road which leaves Kilfinichen in a northerly direction proceeds through Glen Seilisdeir towards the remarkable *Gribun* (*q.v.*) cliffs. To the north-east of Kilfinichen rises *Ben More*, 3,169 ft., the highest point in the island, and a splendid viewpoint, the Outer Hebrides being visible at times. *Iter. 249.*

KILLEAN, Argyll. Map 6, **NR 6** 4.
Near the modern Church are remains of an earlier structure, which retains a good double window. *Iter. 121.*

KILLEARN, Stirling. 1,983 with Fintry. Map 15, **NS 5** 8.
E.C. Wed. A pleasant village, situated to the north-west of the *Campsie Fells*, among which *Earl's Seat*, 1,896 ft., is the principal summit, and *Dumgoyne*, 1,401 ft., is prominent with its conical top. In the village stands an obelisk in memory of George Buchanan, the historian, scholar and tutor to James VI, who was born at Killearn, in 1506. To the west and north are the windings of the Endrick Water. **1½ m. S.W.** is *Killearn House* (1816). In the vicinity is the fine modern hospital. **2 m. N.W.**, near the small village of *Gartness*, is the *Pot of Gartness*, a cascade and ravine on the Endrick Water. *Iter. 108, 114.*

KILLIECRANKIE, Perth. Map 20, **NN 9** 6.
E.C. Thurs. This defile, through which pass the road, the railway with its viaduct, and the River Garry, is best known for the battle, fought in 1689, about **1 m. N.** of the head of the pass. In the fight, won for James VII and II by the Highlanders, Graham of Claverhouse, Viscount Dundee, defeated General Mackay, but was himself slain in the moment of victory, a stone now marking the spot where he fell. Both Scott in his " Bonnie Dundee," and Macaulay, have graphically portrayed the battle. In the heart of the pass is the Soldier's Leap (N.T. Scot.), where two rocks almost bridge the gorge. At the south end is *Bridge of Garry* (*q.v.*), where the roads leading to Loch Tummel and Pitlochry diverge. Much of the pass was given to the Scottish National Trust in 1947, and adjoins the Trust's Linn of Tummel property, which can be reached on foot from Bridge of Garry, or by road from *Pitlochry* (*q.v.*). See **Blair Atholl** and **Queen's View.** *Iter. 138, 140, 143, 150.*

KILLIN, Perth. 1,265. Map 15, **NN 5** 3.
E.C. Wed. GOLF. A delightful little summer and winter sports resort, overlooking *Loch Tay* (*q.v.*), and situated at the eastern extremity of the mountain-encircled Glen Dochart and Glen Lochay. Through the former flows the River Dochart, with its picturesque falls, and the river is joined by the Lochay, flowing through Glen Lochay, also graced by beautiful falls, before the combined streams enter the loch. Near the Dochart bridge, built in 1760 and repaired in 1830, are two small islands, on one of which, *Inch Buie*, was the burial place of the Clan MacNab. At the head of the loch is the ruined *Finlarig Castle*, preserving sculptured stones and an ancient beheading pit which may possibly be the only surviving example. The castle is described in Scott's " Fair Maid of Perth." At *Kinnell House*, to the south of the Dochart, is a famous vine, one of the largest in Europe. The views across Loch Tay towards *Ben Lawers* (N.T.), 3,984 ft., Perthshire's highest mountain, are very fine. Nearer to Killin rise the peaks of the *Tarmachan* group, 3,421 ft., now a National Nature Reserve of 1,142 acres. West of the village is *Stronachlachan*, 1,708 ft. and 1,977 ft., a good viewpoint. **2½ m. S.W.**, in Glen Dochart, is the entrance to the gloomy defile of Glen Ogle, between steep slopes, the road attaining a height of nearly 1,000 ft. on the way to *Lochearnhead* (*q.v.*). See **Lawers.** *Iter. 107, 120, 138.*

KILMACOLM, Renfrew. 4,558. Map 8, **NS 3** 6.
E.C. Wed. GOLF. A pleasant resort in Strath Gryfe, with good views from some of the low hills in the neighbourhood. Adjoining the modern Church is the aisle from an older structure. In the church are buried the Earls of Glencairn. **2 m. S.E.**, on a by-road leading towards Houston, is the ruined Church of *St. Fillan*, with a doorway

dated 1635. **2 m. S.W.** are scanty remains of *Duchall Castle*, which has ghostly associations. See **Bridge of Weir.** *Iter. 64, 85.*

KILMAHOG, Perth. Map 15, **NN 6 0.**
Iter. 106, 107, 111, 139, 141, 142, 144.

KILMALUAG, Isle of Skye, Inverness. Map 22, **NG 4 7.**
Away to the north-west is Rudha Hunish, a narrow promontory, at the tip of the Trotternish peninsula, forming the northern extremity of Skye, and looking across to Eilean Trodday, a tiny island. The Kilmaluag River flows northwards through the village to the bay of that name. See **Flodigarry.** *Iter. 254.*

KILMANY, Fife. Map 17, **NO 3 2.**
The Church, built in 1768, is associated with Dr. Thomas Chalmers, a famous 19th cent. preacher. *Goales Den* is pretty. *Mountquhanie* is a ruined 16th cent. castle. *Iter. 92, 126.*

KILMARNOCK, Ayr. 48,785. **LB.** Map 8, **NS 4 3.**
E.C. Wed. **M.D.** Fri. **GOLF.** An important manufacturing town, noted for whisky, Kilmarnock "bonnets," carpets and boots. There are numerous Burns associations, including the "*Angel*" Hotel, the former Laigh Kirk, and an epitaph by the poet on "Tam Samson" in the churchyard, in which are also several Covenanters' monuments. The steeple of the old Kirk, dating from 1410, survived the fire of 1668. The present Laigh Kirk dates from 1802. In Kay Park, is an interesting Burns museum, contained within a monument. In 1786, the first edition of Burns's poems was published from the town. The Dick Institute contains an interesting museum of rural life. Johnnie Walker, a grocer in King Street founded, in 1820, what has become the largest whisky bottling concern in the world. **1 m. N.**, near the Fenwick Water, is *Dean Castle*, early and late 15th cent. preserving two towers. *Craigie Hill*, 500 ft., south of the town, is a notable viewpoint, with an indicator, erected in 1915 by the Glenfield Ramblers. See **Fenwick** (for *Crawfurdland Castle*), **Kilmaurs** and **Symington** (Ayr). *Iter. 19, 55, 61, 62, 66, 67, 69.*

KILMARTIN, Argyll. 581 with Craignish. Map 14, **NR 8 9.**
Situated in an attractive glen, and famous for its various groups of Bronze Age cup and ring marked rocks, in particular those at *Balvachraig* (A.M.). Of even greater note are the chambered cairns, notably those of *Nether Largie* (A.M.), which are attributed to the Bronze Age. In Kilmartin Churchyard are several richly-sculptured slabs, while inside the War Memorial gateway is the well-known *Kilmartin* Cross, and nearby is a notable, though mutilated, Crucifixion (all A.M.). A ruined Castle is situated near the village. **1½ m. N.**, on an eminence, are the remains of the 16th cent. *Carnasserie Castle* (A.M.) overlooking the Kilmartin valley. This stronghold was built by a Bishop of the Isles, who had printed Knox's liturgy in the Gaelic language, in 1567. **4 m. S.W.** of Kilmartin, on the shores of the Crinan Loch, stands the modernized *Duntroon Castle. Iter. 118, 119, 122.*

KILMAURS, Ayr. 5,692. Map 8, **NS 4 4.**
E.C. Wed. This old burgh, once well known for its cutlery, retains its Tolbooth, on which the jougs are still hanging. **2 m. N.E.** is *Rowallan Castle* (A.M.), an interesting old structure, parts of which date back to 1560 and earlier. There are two impressive circular towers, and a Renaissance doorway leads into the forecourt. *Iter. 62.*

KILMELFORD, Argyll. 279. Map 14, **NM 8 1.**
E.C. Wed. A small angling resort, situated at the head of Loch Melfort. It is sheltered from the open sea by numerous islands, large and small, including those of *Luing* and *Shuna*, which are separated by the Sound of Luing from the more mountainous island of *Scarba*. Eastwards from Kilmelford, a very rough and narrow road climbs towards Loch Avich, giving a fine distant view of *Ben Cruachan*, 3,689 ft. Northwards, on the *Kilninver* (*q.v.*) road, is the picturesque, wooded Pass of Melfort, above the valley of the River Oude. The road through part of the pass has been reconstructed. **4 m. S.W.**, on the shores of Loch Melfort, and off the Ardrishaig road, is *Arduaine House*, which has attractive gardens. *Iter. 118, 119, 122.*

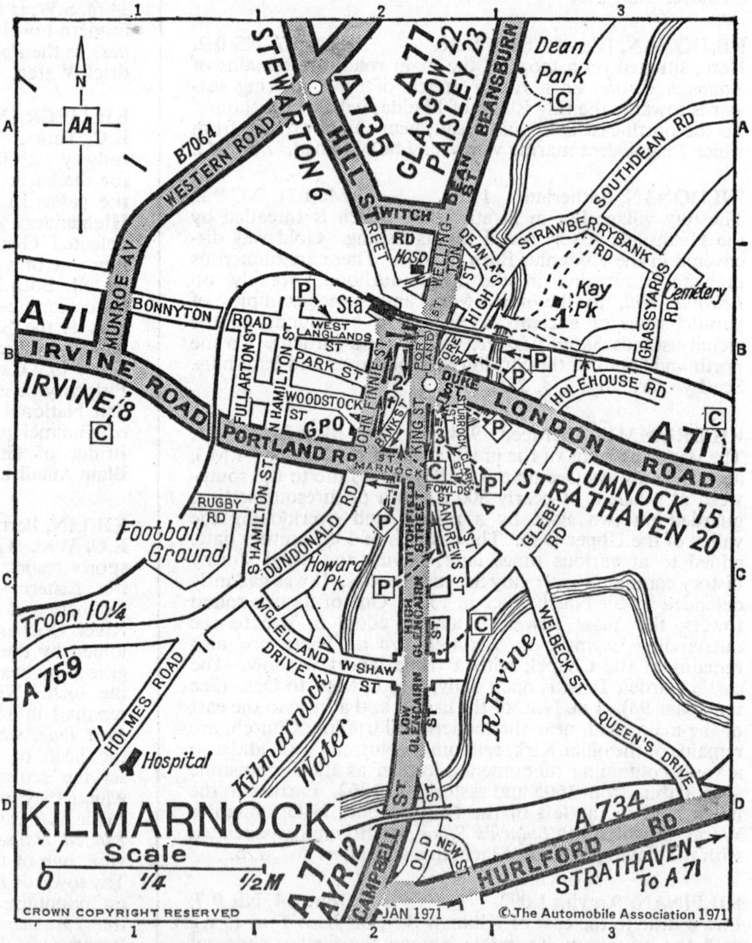

Burns Monument and Museum	1 (B3)	Town Hall;	
Laigh Kirk	2 (B2)	Information Bureau	3 (B2)

When approaching Kilmarnock from the north and making for Irvine, and the coast, the town can be avoided by turning right along B7064 and joining A71, the Irvine road, 1 m. west of the town centre.

KILMICHAEL, Bute. Map 7, **NR 9 7.**
See **Port Bannatyne.**

KILMICHAEL GLASSARY, Argyll. Map 14, **NR 8 9.**
This village, on the River Add, situated on the edge of the Moine Mhor, or Great Moss of Crinan, was once known for its cattle fairs. Prehistoric standing stones are in the vicinity.

Kilmacolm, Renfrew. The Holy Well of St. Fillan, where children were formerly brought to be cured of rickets. It is situated on an unclassified road some 2 miles to the south-east

Kilmacolm, Renfrew. The rock on which St. Fillan sat when baptising children. It is situated on an unclassified road some 2 miles to the south-east

Kilmany, Fife. The remains of the 16th century Mountquhanie Castle, whose 17th century owner, Robert Lumsden, refused to give up Dundee to General Monk, and was later executed

Kilmartin, Argyll. The ancient carved Cross of Kilmartin

Kilmarnock, Ayr. The Burns Museum in Kay Park. In it is preserved the announcement of the poet's death on July 21st, 1796, as printed in the '*Kilmarnock Standard*'

Kilmaurs, Ayr. The partly 16th century Rowallan Castle, off B751, to the north-east. It bears the arms of the Mures of Rowallan, and is the home of Lord Rowallan, the former Chief Scout

[For KILMARNOCK see also Plate 174
[For KILMARTIN see also under Highlands (Plate 84)

Kilmory Knap, Argyll. Castle Sween, a 13th century stronghold, facing Loch Sween, on an unclassified road some 2½ miles north-north-east. It was largely destroyed by Colkitto Macdonald in 1645

Kilmuir, Isle of Skye, Inverness. The Celtic Cross, inscribed with lines by Dr. Johnson in memory of Flora Macdonald, who died in 1790

IN MEMORY OF
ARCHIBALD CLARK.
WHO DIED AT ARDTARIC 2º SEP. 1854
AGED 20 YEARS.
DEEPLY REGRETTED
BY HIS SORROWING RELATIONS.

Kilmun, Argyll. A carved tombstone in the churchyard to a shepherd boy, who was found frozen to death on a hillside more than 100 years ago

Kilsyth, Stirling. The rebuilt Colzium House, which adjoins the site of Montrose's defeat of the Covenanters in 1645. It is now partly a museum

Kilwinning, Ayr. A rare example of a wooden Cross, surmounting the Mercat Cross

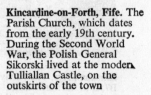

Kincardine-on-Forth, Fife. The Parish Church, which dates from the early 19th century. During the Second World War, the Polish General Sikorski lived at the modern Tulliallan Castle, on the outskirts of the town

[For KINCARDINE-ON-FORTH see also Plate 174
For KILMUN see under COWAL (Plate 36)

1½ m. N.W. is *Dunadd*, where a fort-crowned rock (A.M.), carved with symbols of sovereignty, is associated with the first dynasty of the Kings of Scotland, the ancient kingdom of Argyll, known once as Dalriada. *Iter. 118, 119, 122.*

KILMORACK, Inverness. 1,391. Map 25, **NH 4** 4.
Lies on the Beauly River, in the district known as The Aird. A hydro-electric scheme has caused the disappearance of the former falls. To the south-east, beyond the river, is the late 19th cent. *Beaufort Castle*, damaged by fire in 1937, and situated in fine grounds. The Castle is the seat of Lord Lovat, the Chief of Clan Fraser. The older castle is now a ruin. See **Crask of Aigas.** *Iter. 206, 210.*

KILMORY KNAP, Argyll. Map 6, **NR 7** 7.
Situated in *Knapdale* (*q.v.*), on a narrow neck of land separating the attractively wooded Loch Sween from Loch Killisport, and known for the carved Celtic slabs and the *MacMillan Cross* (A.M.), which are preserved in the churchyard. There are fine views over the Sound of Jura towards the conical Paps of Jura. **2½ m. N.N.E.** is *Castle Sween* (A.M.), incorporating *MacMillan's Tower*, and being one of the earliest stone castles in Scotland, dating from the 12th cent. Much of the structure was destroyed by Colkitto Macdonald in 1647. See **Tayvallich.** *Iter. 122.*

KILMUIR, Isle of Skye, Inverness. 912. Map 22, **NG 3** 7.
Lies on Score Bay, and on the road leading round the northern tip of the island linking *Uig* (*q.v.*) with *Flodigarry* (*q.v.*), and is famous as the burial-place of Flora Macdonald, who died in 1790. A tall Celtic cross marks her grave, on which is inscribed Dr. Johnson's tribute. The graveyard lies a little to the north-east of the road. There is a small cottage museum. **2 m. S.** of Kilmuir, and off the Uig road, facing the sea, is Loch Chaluim Cille, now drained, and on an island of which stood a Celtic monastery, the remains of which still show the original plan. *Iter. 254.*

KILMUN, Argyll. 1,473. Map 14, **NS 1** 8.
On the north shore of the Holy Loch, in the *Cowal* (*q.v.*) peninsula, and retaining the tower of the Collegiate Church, founded in 1442. The Marquis of Argyll, executed in 1661, is buried in the vault. In the churchyard are interesting carved tombstones. Artistic sea stones, set in stucco, are a feature of garden gates in the village. There are fine woods and rhododendrons in the vicinity. To the south-east is Strone Point, overlooking the Firth of Clyde. **2 m. N.W.** of Kilmun is the delightful little *Puck's Glen*, incorporating a fine viewpoint, and beyond it, to the north-west, stretches Glen Masson, ringed by high hills. See **Ardentinny, Benmore Estate** and **Sandbank.** *Iter. 102.*

KILNINIAN, Isle of Mull, Argyll. Map 12, **NM 4** 4.
In the churchyard are some stones with carved Celtic inscriptions. The road to the north-west climbs over moors, with hairpin bends, to reach *Calgary* (*q.v.*). **4½ m. S.E.**, of Kilninian are the Laggan Falls, facing Loch Tuath and the island of *Ulva*, described under *Ulva Ferry*. *Iter. 248.*

KILNINVER, Argyll. Map 14, **NM 8** 2.
Stands on Loch Feochan, an inlet of the Firth of Lorne, with views of the mountainous island of *Mull* (*q.v.*) to the west. The road leading south-eastwards to *Kilmelford* (*q.v.*) goes through the wooded Glen Callon on the way to the picturesque Pass of Melfort, with a small hydro-electric dam. **4 m. S.E.**, beyond Glen Euchar, is the attractive, hill-enriched *Loch Scamadale*. See **Clachan Bridge.** *Iter. 118, 119, 122.*

KILRENNY, Fife. 2,799. SB. with Anstruther.
See **Anstruther.** *Iter. 94, 98.* Map 17, **NO 5** 0.

KILSYTH, Stirling. 10,168. SB. Map 15, **NS 7** 7.
E.C. Wed. GOLF. A mining town at the foot of the *Kilsyth* hills, the highest point of which, *Meikle Bin*, 1,870 ft., rises away to the north-west. Montrose defeated the Covenanters here, in 1645. Relics of the fight are preserved in the mansion of *Colzium*, which has become partly a museum, open weekdays, except Thurs., 2 to 5 and 7 to dusk (see note page 98). *Iter. 98, 113, 115.*

KILWINNING, Ayr. 8,291. SB. Map 8, **NS 2** 4.
E.C. Wed. An iron-working town, known formerly as *Segdoune*, on the River Garnock. It claims to be the earliest home of Freemasonry in Scotland. There are very scanty remains of the former Priory, and the present Church is 18th cent. and later. The Mercat Cross is a shaft topped by a rare wooden Cross. Kilwinning has for many years been associated with archery contests and together with *Irvine q.v.*, to the south is to become a New Town. **1½ m. S.E.** is *Eglinton Castle*, dating from 1798, and now roofless. The Eglinton Tournament was held here in 1839. See **Abington.** *Iter. 5763, 66, 69, 85, 88.*

KINBRACE, Sutherland. Map 30, **NC 8** 3.
A lonely crofting village, with a number of chambered cairns in the vicinity, especially near the Kinbrace Burn, to the south. Land reclamation schemes were attempted here by the 3rd Duke of Sutherland. *Iter. 234, 235.*

KINCARDINE, Perth. 1,043. Map 16, **NS 7** 9.
The early 19th cent. Church contains Drummond monuments and also a rare example of a Scottish brass, of 17th cent. date. To the north-east is *Blair Drummond House*. Open Sat, Sun 12–6, Easter to Sep. Safari Park daily all year.

KINCARDINE BRIDGE, Fife; Stirling. Map 16, **NS 9** 8.
This bridge which dates from 1936, spans the Forth some 10 miles south-east of Stirling. It is the last bridge before the estuary widens and by using it traffic proceeding from Glasgow and the south to Fife and the adjacent counties can avoid passing through Stirling. See **Kincardine-on-Forth.** *Iter. 86, 91, 97, 98.*

KINCARDINE O'NEIL, Aberdeen. 2,248. Map 21, **NO 5** 9.
Formerly of importance as the Dee bridgehead of the road leading over the *Cairn o' Mounth Pass* (*q.v.*), the erstwhile bridge, and at a later date a ferry, being utilized. The modern bridge over the river stands **2 m. S.E.** at Potarch, the road towards the pass proceeding thence by way of *Feughside Inn* (*q.v.*). At Kincardine o'Neil there are remains of the Auld Kirk, and a fair was at one time held in the village. **1½ m. W.**, the Dee is joined by the Dess Burn, on which is the picturesque Slug of Dess waterfall, near a road leading northwards to the small Loch of Auchlossan and *Lumphanan* (*q.v.*). See **Deeside** and **Midmar Castle.** *Iter. 152, 191.*

KINCARDINE-ON-FORTH, Fife. 2,900. Map 16, **NS 9** 8.
E.C. Tues. GOLF. A small port, on the estuary of the River Forth, spanned here by the fine Kincardine Bridge (see above). The town has a notable 17th cent. Mercat Cross with the arms of the Earl of Kincardine. Sir John Dewar, inventor of the vacuum flask, was born here in 1842. Many houses in the little town carry date inscriptions. The ruined *Tulliallan* Church dates from 1675. Behind the Church is the ruined late 15th cent. *Tulliallan Castle*, of much architectural interest, notably the ground floor vaulting. In the background lies Tulliallan Forest, now in the hands of the Forestry Commission. The former *Kilbagie* distillery was once the largest in Scotland. See **Culross.** *Iter. 86, 91, 97, 98, 134.*

KINCRAIG, Inverness. 400. Map 25, **NH 8** 0.
E.C. Wed. On the north side of Loch Insh, through which flows the River Spey. It is joined, after leaving the loch, by the Feshie, emerging from the long glen of that name, finely wooded in its deeper recesses beneath the western outliers of the lofty *Cairngorms* (*q.v.*). In the Glen Feshie Forest, the Feshie is joined by the Eidart, from the Great Moss on the lofty Cairngorm plateau. See **Feshie Bridge, Insh** and **Rothiemurchus.** *Iter. 140, 147, 150, 208.*

KING EDWARD, Aberdeen. 1,476. Map 27, **NJ 7** 5.
The name King Edward is a corruption through Kinedart of the Gaelic Ceann-eador. The ruined *Kinedart Castle* lies **1 m. S.**, on the road to *Turriff* (*q.v.*). **2 m. N.W.**, near the River Deveron, are the ruins of *Eden Castle*. The modern mansion, in its fine grounds, stands in the vicinity. *Iter. 180.*

KINGHORN, Fife. 2,088. SB. Map 17, **NT 2 8.**
E.C. Thurs. A small Royal Burgh and resort on the Firth of Forth, with good sands, associated with King Alexander III, who died in 1286 as a result of a fall, and is commemorated by a monument erected on the King's Crag on the *Pettycur* promontory. There are fine views obtainable from this promontory, notably towards *Inchkeith Island* (*q.v.*). Pettycur was at one time the terminal point of a ferry across the Firth, which explains the various milestones in the district which carry its name. **1½ m. N.E.**, on the coast, is the old tower of *Seafield. Iter. 134.*

KINGLASSIE, Fife. Map 17, **NO 2 9.**
A village once known by the name of *Goatmilk*, a corruption of Gaytmylkschire. On *Redwells Hill*, 605 ft., stands the unfinished 52-ft. high tower known as "Blythe's Folly," erected in 1820.

KINGSBARNS, Fife. Map 17, **NO 5 1.**
Stands a little inland from a stretch of coast between Babbet Ness and Cambo Ness. The Church has a tall and slender spire. **2 m. S.E.**, off the Crail road, is the 17th cent. *Randerston House*, now a farm. *Iter. 94.*

KINGSBURGH HOUSE, Isle of Skye, Inverness.
See Uig (Isle of Skye). Map 22, **NG 3 5.**

KINGSHOUSE, Argyll. Map 18, **NN 2 5.**
This well-known climbing venue near the *White Corries* ski-ing centre lies a little to the east of the new Glencoe road, and stands actually on a section of the former road through the glen. At the inn here, the soldiers under Captain Campbell are said to have gathered before the massacre of *Glencoe* (*q.v.*). The setting is magnificent, with the great rock peak of *Buchaille Etive Mor*, 3,345 ft., the "Shepherd of Etive," towering to the west. To the south rise the peaks of the *Black Mount*, outstanding among which are *Sron na Creise*, 2,952 ft., *Meall Bhuiridh*, 3,636 ft., noted for ski-ing (chair lift and ski tow available), *Clachlet*, 3,602 ft., and still farther south, *Stob Ghabhar*, 3,565 ft. Buchaille Etive is famous among rock climbers, and its sensational Crowberry Ridge is one of the best known in Scotland. The wild Lairig Gartain pass separates the peak from *Buchaille Etive Bheag*, 3,129 ft., to the west. Kinghouse is described in Neil Munro's "John Splendid." Glen Etive stretches away to the south-west, and the mountains dividing it from Glencoe are part of *Dalness* Forest, acquired by the National Trust for Scotland in 1937. The narrow road diverging from the main Glencoe road and traversing Glen Etive comes to an end at the picturesque head of *Loch Etive* (*q.v.*), where there is a steamer pier. *Ben Starav*, 3,541 ft. high, dominates the loch at this point.

On the Glencoe road, **3 m. N.W.** of Kingshouse, is *Altnafeadh*, from which point commenced the former military road to *Kinlochleven* (*q.v.*) over the so-called "Devil's Staircase," rising to 1,754 ft. The old road from Kingshouse to the south, over the exposed *Black Mount*, which climbed to about 1,450 ft., and is now disused, was built by soldiers under General Caulfeild, in 1757, using Kingshouse as a rest-house. The present road, re-aligned farther to the east, crosses part of the vast and desolate *Rannoch Moor*, passing by the shores of Loch Ba, and is easily graded all the way. This region has been graphically described in R. L. Stevenson's "Kidnapped." On the watershed, at a height of 1,143 ft., a cairn marks the division of waters flowing eastwards to the North Sea and westwards to the Atlantic. Beyond Rannoch Moor, away to the east, is *Rannoch* (*q.v.*) station, but there is no road link across the ten desolate miles of moorland. See **Bridge of Orchy, Glencoe** and **Kinloch Rannoch.** *Iter. 100, 125, 142.*

KINGSTON, Moray. Map 26, **NJ 3 6.**
Near the Spey estuary. Charles II landed at *Garmouth* (*q.v.*) near here in 1650. The name Kingston is derived from Kingston-upon-Hull, and was given to the village in 1784 by two Yorkshiremen, who came here to purchase timber.

KINGUSSIE, Inverness. 1,006. SB. Map 19, **NH 7 0.**
E.C. Wed. GOLF. A well-known *Badenoch* (*q.v.*) resort, in the wooded *Strath Spey* (*q.v.*), with fine views of the lofty *Cairngorm* (*q.v.*) range away to the east. *Craig Beg*, 1,593 ft., is a good viewpoint, and overlooks the attractive golf course. Kingussie was the birthplace of James Macpherson, the 18th cent. translater of the Ossianic poems. The Highland Folk Museum, known as *Am Fasgadh*, was originally founded in Iona in 1935, and contains exhibits of much interest. Pony-trekking is a sport recently-introduced to this district. Westwards lie the little-visited *Monadhliath* mountains, with several tops over 3,000 ft. high, including *Carn Dearg*, 3,093 ft., and *Carn Mairg*, 3,087 ft. Near the lonely headwaters of the Findhorn one of Scotland's last wolves was reputedly slain in 1743. The former fortress of the Wolf of Badenoch stood on a site across the Spey, on a minor road leading north-eastwards towards *Rothiemurchus* (*q.v.*) Forest, and where are now the ruins of Wade's *Ruthven Barracks*, a grim reminder of the '45. These barracks were built in 1716, and added to by Wade in 1734, but were destroyed by the Highlanders in 1746, after the failure of the '45. General Wade's military road from the south reached the barracks over the hills from Glen Truim. To the south-east of Kingussie, across the Spey, and east of the barracks, is *Tromie Bridge* (*q.v.*), leading to the long valley of Glen Tromie, which penetrates into the great Gaick Forest, where Loch an't Seileich lies amid lofty hills. The wild Minigaig Pass, for long-distance walkers only, leads out of the glen to the south-east, and crosses the hills at a high altitude, before descending into Glen Bruar, north of *Struan* (*q.v.*). **3 m. N.E.** of Kingussie, off the Aviemore road, is the mansion of *Balavil*, built by James Macpherson, who is commemorated by an obelisk at the point where the Raitts Burn passes under the road on its way to join the nearby Spey. See **Corrieyairack Pass, Drumgask, Feshie Bridge, Kincraig, Newtonmore** and **Wade Roads.** *Iter. 140, 147, 150, 208.*

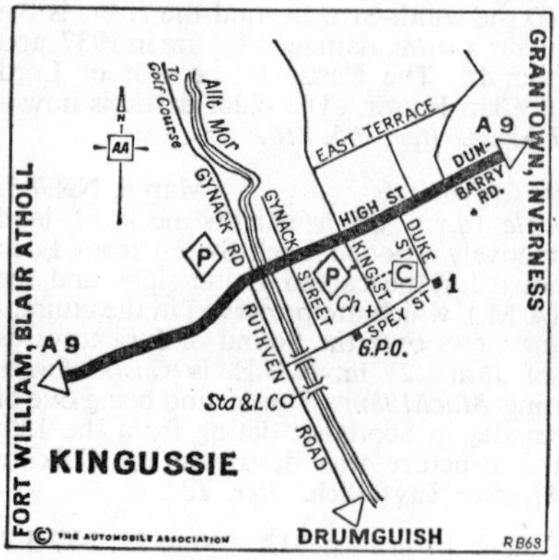

Highland Folk Museum 1

KINKELL CHURCH, Aberdeen. Map 27, **NJ 7 1.**
See **Inverurie.**

KINLOCHBERVIE, Sutherland. Map 28, **NC 2 5.**
Beautifully situated on Loch Inchard, on a narrow and winding road leading north-westwards from *Rhiconich* (*q.v.*), with splendid views towards the lonely mountains of the Reay Forest, dominated by *Foinaven*, 2,980 ft. The fisheries at Kinlochbervie are of increasing importance. The road continues for some four miles towards the open sea, giving fine views, and terminating beyond Balchrick at the little fishing village of *Sheigra.* From here it is possible to follow the coast on foot to the remote *Sandwood Bay*, which has been described as almost the loveliest in all Scotland, and where, in the present century, a mermaid is said to have been seen. Lofty cliffs, with detached stacks of red Torridon sandstone, overlook the reddish sands of this little-visited bay. Far away to the north, at the extremity of a cliff-bound stretch of coast, is the lonely lighthouse at *Cape Wrath* (*q.v.*). *Iter. 229.*

KINLOCHEIL, Inverness. Map 18, **NM 9 7.**
Near the western extremity of Loch Eil, which forms the boundary between Inverness and Argyll. Here, the road to *Ardgour* (*q.v.*) and Ardnamurchan leaves the "Road to the Isles" and continues along the south shore of the loch in the opposite direction. There are associations with Prince Charles Edward, who halted at Kinlocheil a few days after

Kingussie, Inverness. The Highland Folk Museum of Am Fasgadh, which was founded in 1935 in the island of Iona

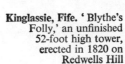

Kinghorn, Fife. The Monument (1886) on the Pettycur promontory to Alexander III, who died here from a fall in 1286

Kinglassie, Fife. 'Blythe's Folly,' an unfinished 52-foot high tower, erected in 1820 on Redwells Hill

Kinlochbervie, Sutherland. The view up Loch Inchard, a lonely sea loch penetrating some 3 miles inland towards Rhiconich, with the mountains of the Reay Forest in the background

Kingshouse, Argyll. The 'Kingshouse' Inn, situated just off the new road through Glencoe. Soldiers, commanded by Captain Campbell, are said to have met here in 1692 prior to the massacre of Glencoe. The great rock peak of Buchaille Etive Mor rises a short distance to the west

[For KINLOCHEIL see following plate
[For KINGUSSIE see also under BADENOCH (Plate 13)

PLATE 98

Kinlocheil, Inverness. Fassifern House, which gave shelter to Prince Charles Edward for a night in 1745 at the commencement of the Jacobite Rising. It stands 3 miles to the east, on A830

Kinlochewe, Ross and Cromarty. Sgurr Ban, at the south-eastern extremity of the Ben Eighe ridge. On its slopes lies the first National Nature Reserve to be formed in Great Britain

Kinlochleven, Argyll; Inverness. The westerly view down Loch Leven towards the conical Pap of Glencoe

Kinlochmoidart, Inverness. The row of beech trees commemorating the 'Seven Men of Moidart,' who defended Prince Charles Edward faithfully during the '45 Rising

Kinloch Rannoch, Perth. The mansion of The Barracks, erected originally for soldiers after the '45 Rising. It stands west of Loch Rannoch, on an unclassified road south of B846

[For KINLOCHEWE see also under BEN EIGHE NATIONAL NATURE RESERVE (Plate 36)
[For KINLOCHLEVEN see also under LOCHABER (Plate 110)
[For KINLOCH RANNOCH see also under SCHIEHALLION (Plate 148)

the raising of his Standard at *Glenfinnan* (*q.v.*), in 1745. *Ben Nevis*, 4,406 ft. is seen in the distance, and to the west rise the lofty hills guarding *Loch Shiel* (*q.v.*). **3 m. E.**, on the Fort William road, is *Fassifern House*, encircled by trees, where, in 1745, the Prince spent a night as the guest of John Cameron. See **Corpach.** *Iter. 209, 215.*

KINLOCHEWE, Ross and Cromarty. 140. Map 24, **NH 0 6. E.C.** Thurs. A centre in *Wester Ross* for some of the very finest mountain scenery on the mainland of Scotland. Here, the road having descended Glen Docherty divides, the south-western branch entering Glen Torridon, and the north-western branch continuing towards the nearby head of beautiful *Loch Maree* (*q.v.*), dominated by *Slioch*, 3,217 ft., rising steeply above its eastern shores. Beneath its south-eastern flanks access is gained on foot through Glen Bannisdail to the solitary *Lochan Fada*, to the north-west of which lie the great cliffs of Glen Tulacha, part of *Ben Lair*, 2,817 ft., with *A'Mhaigdhean*, 3,060 ft., a splendid rock peak, rising to the east above the lonely *Dubh* and *Fionn Lochs*. To the north is *Beinn Dearg Mhor*, 2.974 ft., towering above Loch na Sheallag. This is one of the most spectacular, but remote and least-known mountain districts in Scotland, due mainly to lack of roads and paths. South-west of Kinlochewe, the *Torridon* (*q.v.*) road skirts the base of *Ben Eighe*, with its array of 3,000-ft. high white quartzite peaks, and passes Loch Clair, where the beautiful private road to *Achnashellach* (*q.v.*) by way of Loch Coulin is joined. The scenery in Glen Torridon is wild and rocky, and to the north, overhanging the road, rises *Liathach*, 3,456 ft., one of the finest peaks in Scotland, built up of parallel ledges of red Torridon sandstone, most difficult to climb. Behind the peak are wild corries, notably Coire na Caime. Between *Liathach* and *Ben Eighe* lies a deep cleft, which gives access to the stupendous cliffs of *Coire Mhic Fhearchair*, rising above a tiny lochan, and reached only by means of a long and arduous walk. A little to the north of Kinlochewe, on the west bank of Loch Maree, are the woodlands of Coille na Glas-Leitire, which, with the lofty slopes of Kinlochewe Forest and Ben Eighe in the background, now form the *Ben Eighe National Nature Reserve*, the first of its kind to be formed in Great Britain. Scots pine and birch flourish in the woods, while the wild life in the area, which is more than 10.000 acres in extent, includes deer, wild cats and eagles. A new Mountain Trail leads to spectacular viewpoints. *Iter. 205, 222, 223.*

KINLOCH HOURN, Inverness. Map 18, **NG 9 0.** Situated in a green hollow, sheltering a grove of eucalyptus trees, at the head of *Loch Hourn* (*q.v.*), perhaps the finest of the great sea lochs of the Western Highlands. Access is by means of a road from *Tomdoun* (*q.v.*), first along the shores of *Loch Quoich* (*q.v.*) where a hydro-electric scheme now operates. The narrow and very rough road later descends steeply (1 in 6) on the final 600 ft. to the loch, amid a wilderness of glaciated, grey rocks on the rugged slopes of *Sgurr nan Eugallt*, 2,933 ft., to the west, and *Sgurr a'Mhoraire*, 3,365 ft., to the east. The view from the summit of the last-named peak is one of the loveliest in the Highlands, taking in the whole length of Loch Hourn, and extending towards the *Coolins* (*q.v.*) of Skye. A path leads for a short distance along the south shore of the Inner Loch, giving good views of the wooded northern shores under the slopes of *Druim Fada* 2,327 ft. Prince Charles Edward wandered in these lonely mountains after his defeat at *Culloden* (*q.v.*), in 1746, and narrowly missed the sentries posted on the slopes of *Sgurr a'Mhoraire.* The superb mountain scenery at the head of Inner Loch Hourn is reminiscent of the Norwegian fjords, and is probably the finest of its kind in Great Britain, its only rival being the freshwater *Loch Coruisk* (*q.v.*) in Skye. *Iter. 214.*

KINLOCHLEVEN, Argyll; Inverness. 616. Map 18, **NN 1 6. E.C.** Wed. A busy industrial centre, at the head of the beautiful *Loch Leven*, in a fine mountain setting. The power for the aluminium works is supplied by means of the water stored in the great Blackwater Reservoir, away to the east of the town. Loch Leven is traversed by picturesque roads on both shores, giving splendid views of mountain and water. To the north rises the grand *Mamore Forest* (*q.v.*) group, with *Binnein Mor* attaining 3,700 ft., and to the south are the ridges of *Aonach Eagach*, 3,168 ft., overlooking *Glencoe* (*q.v.*) on their far side. The old military road over the " Devil's Staircase " from *Kingshouse* (*q.v.*), which rises to 1,745 ft., reached Kinlochleven from the south-east, and continued inland over the hills to the north-west past Loch Lundavra towards *Fort William* (*q.v.*). The modern road goes by way of Loch Leven and the shores of Loch Linnhe. See **Ballachulish, Carnach** and **North Ballachulish.** *Iter. 100, 124, 125.*

KINLOCHMOIDART, Inverness. Map 12, **NM 7 7.** Lies at the head of Loch Moidart, in the historic *Moidart* (*q.v.*) district, with fine woodlands on the shores of the loch. The River Moidart, issuing from the lonely glen of that name, flows here into the loch. Prince Charles Edward was given hospitality here, in 1745, by the Macdonalds, before the raising of his Standard at *Glenfinnan* (*q.v.*). A line of beeches in a meadow commemorates the " Seven Men of Moidart," who were among the most faithful of the Prince's companions. North of Glen Moidart rise lofty hills, culminating in *Fros Bheinn*, 2,876 ft., a fine viewpoint, looking towards Rum and Skye beyond the Sound of Arisaig. A path leads westwards from Kinlochmoidart along the northern shores of the loch, and reaches the coast by way of Glen Uig, at the little village of *Glenuig*, on the Sound of Arisaig, and associated with the Prince. The path continues eastwards towards Loch Ailort, eventually reaching *Lochailort* (*q.v.*), on the " Road to the Isles," the seaward views all the way being magnificent. A new road now links Kinlochmoidart with Lochailort. See **Acharacle** (for *Castle Tioram*) and **Dalilea.** *Iter. 217.*

KINLOCH RANNOCH, Perth. 300. Map 19, **NN 6 5. E.C.** Wed. This little fishing resort lies on the River Tummel, at the eastern end of *Loch Rannoch* (*q.v.*), in the *Breadalbane* (*q.v.*) country. The river flows eastwards through a reservoir, which is part of the extensive Tummel-Garry hydro-electric scheme, while power-houses are situated at the far western end of the loch, and also at *Tummel Bridge* (*q.v.*). To the south-east of Kinloch Rannoch, is *Dalchoisnie*, where English invaders are said to have fought Robert Bruce in 1306, and farther south extends Glen Sassunn, beyond which rise the various 3,000-ft. peaks of the extensive *Carn Mairg* group. Loch Rannoch has well-wooded roads on both north and south shores, these roads converging some five miles east of the remote *Rannoch* (*q.v.*) station, which lies almost on the Argyll border. Near the point where the roads meet, a mansion, known as *The Barracks*, was erected for the troops after the '45. The desolate expanse of *Rannoch Moor* stretches westwards from the railhead, and contains Loch Laidon and Loch Ba. Beyond the ridge of the Black Corries are the large Blackwater Reservoir and the small Lochan a Chlaidheimh, the latter associated with a sword thrown into its waters by a 15th cent. Earl of Atholl in connection with a land claim against the Camerons. From the Moor, views of the lofty *Black Mount*, the *Glencoe* (*q.v.*) and the *Grampian* (*q.v.*) mountains may be obtained. This country has been graphically described in R. L. Stevenson's " Kidnapped." Northwards from Loch Rannoch, and linked by a tunnel aqueduct, lies the lonely Loch Ericht, overlooked by the fine peak of *Ben Alder*, 3,757 ft., but not accessible by road except at the far north-east extremity near *Dalwhinnie* (*q.v.*). To the south-east of Kinloch Ran-

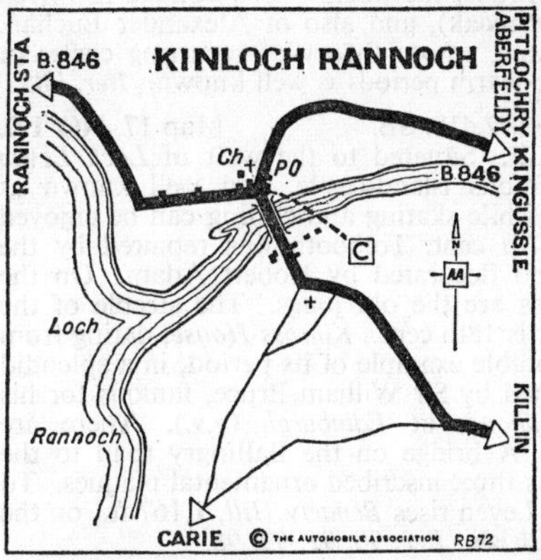

noch rises the sharp quartzite cone of *Schiehallion*, 3,547 ft., one of the best known landmarks and viewpoints in the Central Highlands, and the focal point in the panorama from the famous *Queen's View* (*q.v.*) near Loch Tummel, away to the east. Beyond Schiehallion, to the west, is *Geal Charn*, 2,593 ft., which rises at the head of Gleann Mor. From the south shores of Loch Rannoch, on the edge of the picturesque Black Wood of Rannoch, where the native Caledonian pine is still to be seen growing, a path leads over the hills giving access to Glen Lyon. Beyond the reservoir, to the east of the village, a road diverges northwards, climbing to over 1,000 ft., and later descending through Glen Erochy to reach *Struan* (*q.v.*) in Glen Garry. Another road climbs steeply on to the moors to the south-east of Kinloch Rannoch, and after passing the ruined *St. Blane's* Chapel at *Lassentulich*, goes close to the lower slopes of Schiehallion on the way to the little Loch Kinardochy near *White Bridge* (*q.v.*). See **Trinafour.** *Iter. 89, 147, 148.*

KINLOSS, Moray. Map 26, **NJ 0** 6.
The once-famous *Kinloss Abbey* was founded in 1150, but little is now left, the scanty remains including the foundations and two fine round-headed arches. **2½ m. N.E.** is *Milton Brodie*, with an old Abbey garden and retaining a hexagonal tower. *Iter. 199.*

KINNAIRD, Perth. Map 17, **NO 2** 2.
Situated on the slopes of the *Sidlaw* hills, overlooking the fertile *Carse of Gowrie* (*q.v.*), beyond which lies the Firth of Tay. The 12th to 15th cent. *Kinnaird Castle*, built of red stone, has been well restored. *Iter. 154.*

KINNEFF, Kincardine. 719. Map 21, **NO 8** 7.
The legend is that to the little Church of Kinneff the Scottish regalia were brought, in 1652, from *Dunnottar Castle* (*q.v.*). The jewels were hidden behind the pulpit, until the Restoration, by a Mrs. Grainger, to whom a monument has been erected.

KINNESSWOOD, Kinross. Map 17, **NO 1** 0.
GOLF. Lies in an attractive setting east of *Loch Leven* (*q.v.*), and at the foot of *Bishop Hill* and *White Craigs*, 1,492 ft., in the *Lomonds*. It is noted as the birthplace, in 1746, of Michael Bruce, the poet, whose cottage has been preserved (See **Portmoak**), and also of Alexander Buchan, of weather-lore fame, whose theory of recurring cycles of five cold and three warm periods is well known. *Iter. 98.*

KINROSS, Kinross. 2,418. SB. Map 17, **NO 1** 0.
E.C. Thurs. GOLF. Situated to the west of *Loch Leven* (*q.v.*), with its famous island-castle, and well known as an angling resort, while skating and curling can be enjoyed in winter. The 17th cent. Tolbooth was repaired by the Crown in 1771 and decorated by Robert Adam. On the carved Town Cross are the old jougs. The steeple of the former Town Kirk is 18th cent. *Kinross House*, dating from 1685 to 1692, a notable example of its period, in a splendid setting, was designed by Sir William Bruce, famous for his work at *Holyroodhouse* at *Edinburgh* (*q.v.*). There are beautiful gardens. A bridge on the Ballingry road to the south, off A.90, has three inscribed ornamental plaques. To the south of Loch Leven rises *Benarty Hill*, 1,167 ft., on the Fife border. See **Cleish.** *Iter. 90, 91, 92, 98.*

KINTAIL, Ross and Cromarty. 612 with Glen Shiel.
Map 24, **NG 9** 1.
The *Kintail* district of Wester Ross lies around the head of *Loch Duich* (*q.v.*), and includes some of the grandest mountain scenery in Scotland. About 15,000 acres are now the property of the Scottish National Trust, and among the mountains on the estate are the well-known *Five Sisters of Kintail*, of which *Scour Ouran*, 3,505 ft., is the highest, and shows on its western flanks what is said to be the longest continuous grass slope in the Highlands, dropping steeply from the summit almost to the roadside in picturesque *Glen Shiel* (*q.v.*). A smaller, contiguous estate belonging to the Trust contains the famous, but very remote *Falls of Glomach* (*q.v.*). The little Church and manse of Kintail stand on the eastern shore of Loch Duich, near *Inverinate* (*q.v.*). One of the finest views of the loch is that obtained from the summit of the lofty *Mam Rattachan* (*q.v.*) Pass, on the road to Glenelg, which gives a wonderful picture of the Kintail peaks in the background beyond Loch Duich. See **Shiel Bridge.**

KINTORE, Aberdeen. 794. SB. Map 27, **NJ 7** 1.
E.C. Wed. GOLF. A tiny Royal Burgh, with a Tolbooth dating from 1740. The Church retains one of the rare Sacrament Houses, a feature peculiar to churches in some parts of Eastern Scotland. In the churchyard is the carved *Ichthus* stone. In the vicinity there are prehistoric remains, such as hill forts and stone circles. *Balbithan House* is 17th cent. **1½ m. S.W.** is *Hallforest*, a ruined tower, entirely without staircases, inhabited until 1639, and said to have been visited by Mary, Queen of Scots, in 1562. See **Inverurie.** *Iter. 175, 178, 184, 197.*

KINTRAW, Argyll. Map 14, **NM 8** 0.
Lies at the head of Loch Craignish. Just north of the village, a by-road to the south-west diverges for *Craignish* Church, on the shores of the loch. Beyond lie *Craignish Castle* and Craignish Point, looking towards the turbulent channel known as the Dorus Mor, or Great Door, near which lie several tiny islands. The road leading south-eastwards from Kintraw climbs high over moorland, with sharp curves, before descending to *Kilmartin* (*q.v.*). *Iter. 118, 119, 122.*

KINTYRE, Argyll. 5,147. Map 6, **NR 6** 1 etc.
The long and narrow Kintyre peninsula, an appendage of the Argyllshire Highlands, stretches southwards towards the Atlantic and the Northern Irish coast, from which it is some 12 miles distant, and has an average width of not much over 5 miles. It is traversed for most of its length by roads on both west and east sides, the former providing fine views towards Islay, Jura, and the distant Irish shores, and the latter looking across Kilbrennan Sound to the mountainous outline of the island of Arran. Only a few miles from the western shores of Kintyre is the small island of Gigha, which is reached from *Tayinloan* (*q.v.*). The northern boundary of Kintyre is formed by West Loch Tarbert, with steamer services from *Tarbert* (*q.v.*) to the large island of Islay. Beyond here lies the district of *Knapdale* (*q.v.*). The most southerly point of the peninsula is the *Mull of Kintyre* (*q.v.*), where a lighthouse is situated. A ridge of hills extends down the peninsula for most of its length, in which *Beinn an Tuirc*, near *Saddell* (*q.v.*), attains 1,491 ft. See **Campbeltown, Gigha** and **Machrihanish.** *Iter. 121, 122, 123.*

KIPPEN, Stirling. 1,400. Map 15, **NS 6** 9.
An attractive village, lying to the south of the winding River Forth, and with the *Gargunnock* and *Fintry* hills forming a lofty background. To the north of the river, across the Perthshire border, is the treacherous Flanders Moss, perhaps the remains of a former forest. A vine in Kippen, planted in 1891, and said to be the largest in existence, was removed in 1964 to make way for a housing project. There is a fine old dovecote (N.T. Scot.). The modern Church, built in 1825, is considered to be one of the finest of its kind Scotland, and its 20th cent. renovation is associated with Sir David Cameron, the Scottish artist. **1½ m. S.S.W.** is *Wrightpark*, dating from 1750. See **Killin.** *Iter. 107, 108, 112, 137.*

KIPPFORD, Kirkcudbright. Map 3, **NX 8** 5.
A small yachting resort, off the main road, and pleasantly situated on Rough Firth, the estuary of the Urr Water, forming an inlet of the Solway Firth. The beach is rocky and stony, and care should be exercised when bathing. See **Rockcliffe.** *Iter. 73.*

KIRKANDREWS, Kirkcudbright. Map 3, **NX 5** 4.
The Church, farm and laundry together form a group of curious, modern castellated structures, the work of James Brown, a business man from Manchester. In Wigtown Bay lie the small Islands of Fleet.

KIRKBEAN, Kirkcudbright. 1,295 with New Abbey.
Map 3, **NX 9** 5.
Lies a little inland from the waters of the Solway Firth, and is dominated by *Boreland Hill*, 1,632 ft., and the bulky *Criffell*, 1,866 ft., a fine viewpoint. The font in the Church was presented in 1945 by the American Navy to commemorate Paul Jones (see below), who died in Paris in 1792. Off the Dalbeattie road is the ancient *Preston* Cross. **1½ m. S.E.** of

Kinneff, Kincardine. In this Church, the regalia of Scotland were temporarily hidden in 1652. A Monument has been erected to Mrs. Grainger, who secreted them behind the pulpit, where they remained until the Restoration. See Dunnottar Castle (Plate 53)

Kinross, Kinross. The old jougs, or iron collar for wrongdoers, on the Town Cross, which was restored in 1886

Kippen, Stirling. The ancient dovecote, the property of the National Trust for Scotland.

Kintail, Ross and Cromarty. The Five Sisters of Kintail peaks (N.T. Scot.), at the head of Loch Duich, seen from Auchtertyre Hill, on A890, between Kyle of Lochalsh and Strome Ferry

Kintore, Aberdeen. The Tolbooth of 1740, which has a dual outside staircase

Kirkandrews, Kirkcudbright. Castellated farm and laundry buildings, built by James Brown, a Manchester business man, early in this century.

[For KIRKBEAN see following plate
[For KINNAIRD see Plate 172
[For KINTORE see also Plate 173

Kirkbean, Kirkcudbright. The ancient Preston Cross, situated off the road to Dalbeattie (A710)

Kirkcaldy, Fife. Restored 17th century and earlier houses known as the 'Sailors' Walk' (N.T. Scot.)

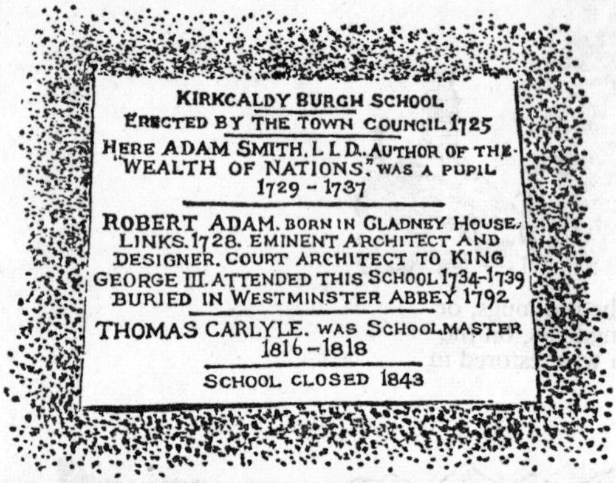

Kirkcaldy, Fife. A tablet on the former Burgh school, where both Adam Smith and Robert Adam were pupils, and Thomas Carlyle once taught.

Kirkconnell Church, Dumfries. The graves of 'Fair Helen of Kirkconnell Lee and her lover' in the churchyard of the ruined church. It lies 2½ miles north-east of Kirtlebridge, on an unclassified road off B722

Kirkcowan, Wigtown. The external stairway of the Church, giving access to the gallery

Kirkcudbright, Kirkcudbright. The 16th to 17th century Tolbooth, with the Mercat Cross of 1610. Witches were tried and imprisoned here, the last one to be put to death in the town being Elspeth McEwen, in 1698. Paul Jones, the 'founder' of the American navy, to whom the Tolbooth is now a memorial, was also once held prisoner here

[For KIRKCALDY see also Plate 175)
[For KIRKCUDBRIGHT see also under STEWARTRY (Plate 154)

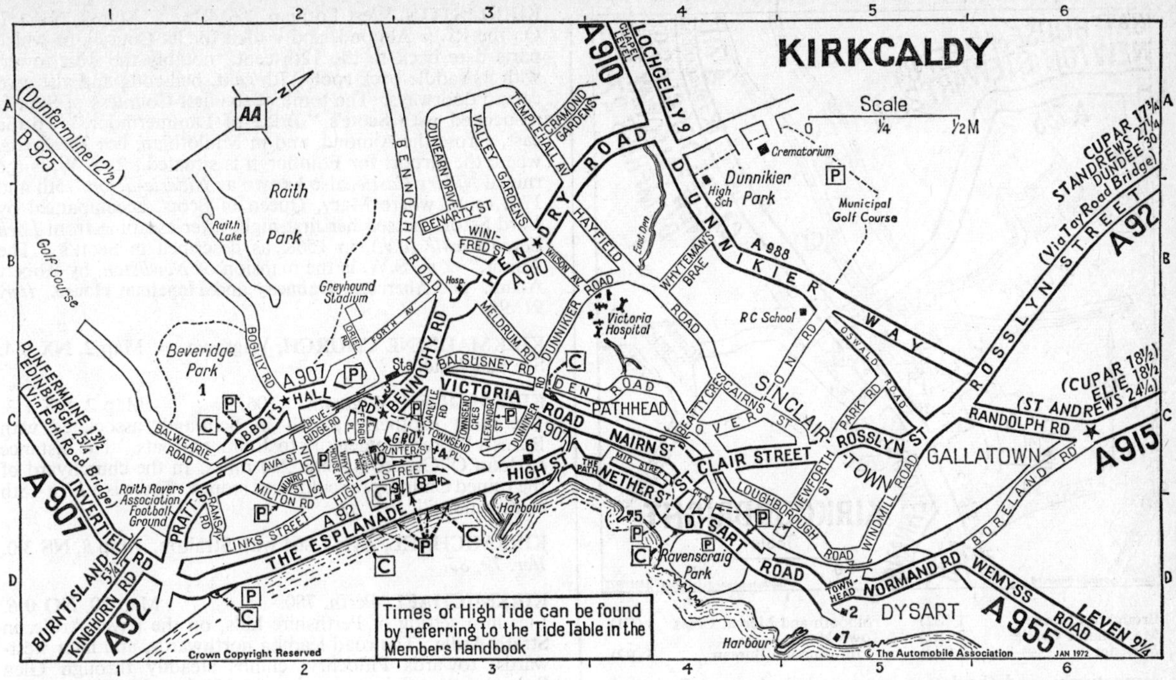

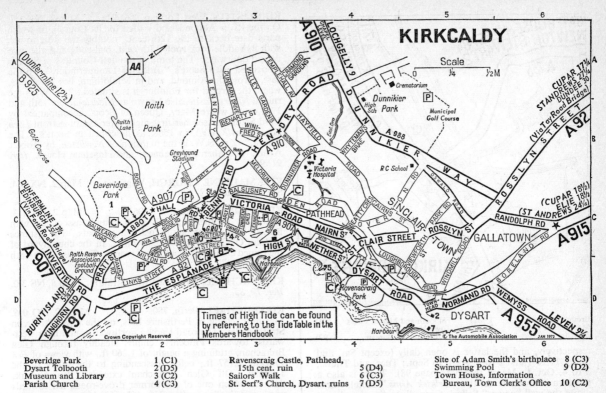

Beveridge Park	1 (C1)	Ravenscraig Castle, Pathhead, 15th cent. ruin	5 (D4)	Site of Adam Smith's birthplace	8 (C3)
Dysart Tolbooth	2 (D5)	Sailors' Walk	6 (C3)	Swimming Pool	9 (D2)
Museum and Library	3 (C2)	St. Serf's Church, Dysart, ruins	7 (D5)	Town House, Information Bureau, Town Clerk's Office	10 (C2)
Parish Church	4 (C3)				

Kirkbean is the estate of *Arbigland*, where Paul Jones, the privateer, sometimes described as the "father" of the American navy, was born in 1747. Here also was born Dr. Craik, Washington's personal medical assistant. The nearby *House on the Shore* has lovely gardens, and there are views across the rocky shores of the firth towards the Lake District mountains. See **Carsethorn** and **Southerness.** *Iter. 72, 73.*

KIRKCALDY, Fife. 50,338. LB. Map 17, **NT 2 9. E.C.** Wed. GOLF. An industrial town and coal port, well known for the manufacture of linoleum. The town has been a Royal Burgh since 1450. Its boundaries now include *Dysart (q.v.)*, lying beyond Pathhead, to the north-east, while the long main street, which extends for nearly 4 miles in this direction, has caused Kirkcaldy to become known as the "Lang Toun." In the predecessor of a house in the High St., marked by a tablet, was born, in 1723, Adam Smith, author of the "Wealth of Nations." Opposite stands the 17th cent. *Old Dunnikier House*, now used as shops. The Parish Church retains its 13th cent. tower. Thomas Carlyle and his friend Edward Irving were masters at the burgh school, the former having lived in Kirk Wynd, where a tablet has been set up. There are old cottages in this steep lane. Robert Adam, the famous architect, was born at Kirkcaldy, in 1728. Near the harbour are several fine 17th cent. houses, now restored, known as the *Sailors' Walk* (N.T. Scot.). The Links Market fair, held in the spring, is well known as the largest in Scotland. Behind the town is *Beveridge Park*, noted for motor cycle and small car racing, and giving access into the large park surrounding *Raith House.* **2 m. W.** of Kirkcaldy is *Balwearie Tower*, in ruins, with 7-ft. thick walls. See **Kinghorn** and **Pathhead** (Fife). *Iter. 93, 94, 97, 126, 127, 128, 129, 130, 133, 134.*

KIRKCOLM, Wigtown. 1,019. Map 2, **NX 0 6.** On the west side of Loch Ryan, in the Rhinns of Galloway peninsula, with Loch Connel to the west. Beyond the loch, to the west, is situated *Balsarroch House*, the birthplace, in 1777, of Sir John Ross, the Arctic explorer. **4 m. N.W.** of Kirkcolm is Corsewall Point, with a lighthouse of 1815 by Robert Stevenson. Nearby stands the ruined *Corsewall Castle. Iter. 83.*

KIRKCONNEL, Dumfries. 4,265. Map 9, **NS 7 1. E.C.** Thurs., Sat. A mining town, on the edge of the Ayrshire coalfield, and situated on the River Nith. To the south are slight remains of the ancient Devil's Dyke, the origin of which is not clear. (For *Kirkconnell* Church, see **Kirtlebridge.**) *Iter. 27, 49, 67.*

KIRKCONNELL CHURCH, Dumfries. Map 4, **NY 2 7.** See **Kirtlebridge.**

KIRKCOWAN, Wigtown. 695. Map 2, **NX 3 6. E.C.** Wed. The Tarf Water and the River Bladnoch unite to the south-east of the village. The Church has an external stair to the gallery. There are some remains of the old Church. **5 m. S.S.W.,** beyond the Tarf Water, is the fine, restored *Old Place of Mochrum*, or *Drumwalt Castle*, incorporating much 15th and 16th cent. work. The oldest part consists of two towers of picturesque appearance. Beyond the house is Mochrum Loch and to the west of it lies the Castle Loch. **6 m. N.W.** of Kirkcowan, in the district known as *The Moors*, lies Loch Ronald. See **Glenluce.** *Iter. 81.*

KIRKCUDBRIGHT, Kirkcudbright. 2,506. SB. Map 3, **NX 6 5. E.C.** Thurs. **M.D.** Fri. GOLF. A market town, Royal Burgh, and the most important town in the *Stewartry (q.v.)*, situated on the River Dee, with a small harbour at the head of Kirkcudbright Bay. The ruined *MacLellan's Castle* (A.M.) is a prominent feature in the town and dates from 1582. It was built by Sir Thomas MacLellan of Bombie, Provost of Kirkcudbright, whose Renaissance tomb is in the Old Greyfriars Kirk. Open summer, 10 to 7: winter, 10 to 4; Sun., 2 to 7 or 4. Two previous castles have both vanished. There is a fine 16th to 17th cent. Tolbooth preserving two old bells; the building is now a memorial to Paul Jones, founder of the American navy, who was at one time imprisoned here. (See **Kirkbean.**) The Mercat Cross dates from 1610 and stands on the outside stair of the Tolbooth, which has on its north-west wall the old jougs. There are a number of good 18th cent. houses in the town. *Auchengool House* and *Broughton House* date from the 17th and 18th cents.

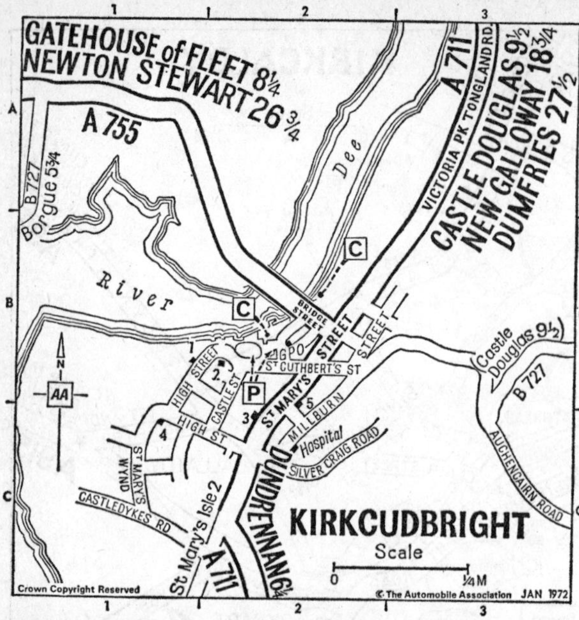

Broughton House	1 (B2)	Tolbooth and Mercat Cross	4 (C1)
MacLellan's Castle	2 (B2)	Town Hall:	
Museum	3 (C2)	Information Bureau	5 (B2)

respectively, and the latter is open daily (except Sat. and Sun.), 11 to 1 and 2 to 4, April to Sept.; Tues. and Thurs., 2 to 4, Oct. to March (see note page 98). There is also a museum of interest. At the " *Selkirk Arms* " Hotel, Burns wrote the well-known " Selkirk Grace." In the churchyard of *St. Cuthbert* are the graves of three Covenanters, executed in 1684-85, and also of William Marshall, a noted Galloway tinker, who died at the age of 120. Part of the former "yett," or town entrance, has been incorporated in the entrance. In Kirkcudbright Bay is *St. Mary's Isle*, a peninsula, on which is a heronry, situated in private grounds. Farther south, near the open sea, is *Little Ross Island*, on which stands a lighthouse, built by the father of R. L. Stevenson. See **Dundrenan** and **Tongland.** *Iter. 70, 72, 73, 77.*

KIRKFIELDBANK, Lanark. Map 9, **NS 8** 4.
Situated on the River Clyde, a little to the west of *Lanark* (*q.v.*), the pretty village of *Kirkfieldbank* has old (17th cent.) and new bridges spanning the river in close proximity. The district is noted for its orchard setting, the fruit-growing extending along the river valley. *Iter. 53, 69.*

KIRKGUNZEON, Kirkcudbright. 901. Map 3, **NX 8** 6.
Lies on a stream known as the Kirkgunzeon Lane. In the churchyard are numerous tall monuments. Two old towers, *Drumcoltran* (A.M.), **1½ m. N.E.,** and *Corra,* **1 m. S.,** stand in the vicinity, the former being a characteristic 16th cent. example. Away to the south-east rises *Criffell*, 1,866 ft., a landmark for many miles around. *Iter. 76.*

KIRKINNER, Wigtown. 857. Map 2, **NX 4** 5.
There is a Celtic Cross in the churchyard. About a mile and a half to the north, near the Bladnoch Water, are the remains of *Baldoon Castle*, described under *Bladnoch. Iter. 82.*

KIRKINTILLOCH, Dunbarton. 25,185. SB. Map 8, **NS 6** 7.
E.C. Wed. GOLF. An ancient town, adjacent to which, on the south side, is *Lenzie*. Both lie in a detached portion of the county, and are on the Forth and Clyde canal, which traverses the flat country to the south of the *Campsies* and the *Kilsyth* hills. The old name of the town was " Caerpentulach," recalling one of the forts on the *Roman Wall* (*q.v.*), which can still be traced in the neighbourhood. A corbie-stepped house in the town dates from 1644. The local museum is housed in a former church. *Iter. 98, 113.*

KIRKLAND, Dumfries. Map 3, **NX 8** 9.
See **Moniaive.** *Iter. 25, 74.*

KIRKLISTON, West Lothian. 1,614. Map 9, **NT 1** 7.
On the River Almond, and visited for its Church, of which parts date back to the 12th cent., notably the west tower. with its saddle-back roof, 17th cent. bell-cote, and also two carved doorways. The tomb of the first Countess of Stair is associated with Scott's " Bride of Lammermoor." To the east, across the Almond, and in Midlothian, lies *Turnhouse*, where the airport for Edinburgh is situated. **2 m. W.** is the ruined *Niddry Castle*, also known as *Niddrie-Seton*, 15th and 17th cent., where Mary, Queen of Scots, accompanied by Lord Seton, passed her first night after escaping from *Loch Leven Castle* (*q.v.*), in 1568, as described in Scott's " The Abbot." **2 m. S.W.** is the mansion of *Newliston*, by Robert Adam. See **Abercorn, Dalmeny** and **Hopetoun House.** *Iter. 91, 95.*

KIRKMADRINE CHURCH, Wigtown. Map 2, **NX 0** 4.
See **Sandhead.**

KIRKMAIDEN, Wigtown. 1,106. Map 2, **NX 1** 3.
The most southerly parish in Scotland, associated with Burns's " Frae Maidenkirk to Johnny Groats." The distance to John O' Groats is some 280 miles. In the churchyard of the ruined Church are sculptured stones. There is a 17th-18th cent. windmill. *Iter. 82.*

KIRKMICHAEL, Ayr. 1,864 with Straiton. Map 8, **NS 3** 0.
Iter. 79, 85.

KIRKMICHAEL, Perth. 780. Map 20, **NO 0** 6.
Lies in a setting of Perthshire hills, on the River Ardle, in Strath Ardle. The road leading northwards, and later westwards, towards Pitlochry, climbs steadily through Glen Brerachan, attaining a height of 1,260 ft., with views of *Ben Vrackie*, 2,757 ft., before descending to the valley of the Tummel. Off Glen Brerachan extends Glen Fernalt, through which one of the former drove-roads led towards north-east Scotland. *Iter. 159, 162, 167, 168.*

KIRK OF MOCHRUM, Wigtown. Map 2, **NX 3** 4.
The Church contains a fine pulpit of carved oak.

KIRK O'SHOTTS, Lanark. 2,390. Map 9, **NS 8** 6.
A tall Scottish Television mast is situated here. To the south-east lies the Lanark coalfield. *Iter. 15, 18.*

KIRKOSWALD, Ayr. 1,915. Map 8, **NS 2** 0.
A pleasant village, famous for its Burns associations. In the churchyard are the graves of " Tam o'Shanter " and " Souter Johnnie," two of Burns's best known characters. The new Church was designed by Robert Adam in 1777. An 18th cent. thatched cottage (N.T. Scot.), the home of Souter Johnnie, contains Burns relics, and in the garden are stone figures of the Burns characters. Open weekdays, 2.30 to 8, April to Sept. (See note page 98.) To the south of the village are the farms of *Shanter* and *Jameston*, associated with " Tam " and " Johnnie." *Iter. 55, 68.*

KIRKPATRICK DURHAM, Kirkcudbright. 643.
Map 3, **NX 7** 7.
In the churchyard is a Covenanter's stone in memory of John Neilson, Laird of Corsock, martyred at Edinburgh in 1666.

KIRKPATRICK FLEMING, Dumfries. 1,157.
Map 4, **NY 2** 7.
To the west, beyond the Kirtle Water, on the *Cove* estate, is a cave said to have once sheltered Robert Bruce. See **Kirtlebridge.** *Iter. 10, 13, 29, 47, 50, 51.*

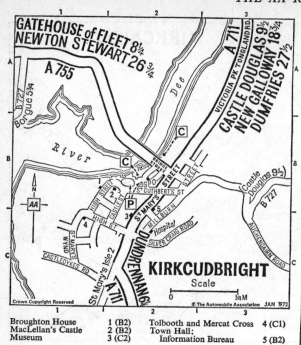

KIRKTON OF GLENISLA, Angus. Map 20, **NO 2** 6.
Lies on the River Isla, in Glen Isla Forest, in one of the long and picturesque glens of Angus, which thread their way into the remote fastnesses of the eastern Grampians, in the Braes of Angus district. The road up the glen continues northwards, and after four miles a fork to the right rejoins the River Isla, passing the ruins of *Forter Castle*, burnt in 1640. With a deteriorating surface, this road reaches, after five miles, the lodge of *Tulchan*, beyond which a track goes still farther northwards, climbing to the picturesque Caenlochan Glen, on the left, in a 9,000-acre National Nature Reserve, under the slopes of *Monega Hill*, 2,917 ft., and

Kirkfieldbank, Lanark. The 17th century bridge over the River Clyde, which has now been superseded by a modern bridge close by

Kirkgunzeon, Kirkcudbright. A tomb with a spire, one of several tall monuments in the churchyard

Kirkoswald, Ayr. Souter Johnnie's House (N.T. Scot.), dating from 1786, a thatched cottage associated with a famous poem by Robert Burns. In the garden are life-size figures of the Souter and his friend Tam o'Shanter (see below)

Kirkliston, West Lothian. Niddry Castle, where Mary, Queen of Scots, spent a night in 1568, after her escape from Loch Leven Castle. It lies 2 miles west, off an unclassified road

Kirkoswald, Ayr. The grave of 'Tam o'Shanter', made famous by Robert Burns, in the churchyard. Nearby is the grave of Tam's friend 'Souter Johnnie' (see above)

Kirkton of Glenisla, Angus. The remains of Forter Castle, perhaps the 'Bonnie Hoose o'Airlie' associated with the lines:

" Lady Ogilvie looks o'er her bower window,
And O, but she looks weary,
And there she spied the great Argyle,
Come to plunder the castle o' Airlie."

The castle was burnt by Argyle in 1640, and stands on B951, some 4 miles to the north-west

Kirktown of Tealing, Angus. The late 16th century dovecote

Kirriemuir, Angus. The birthplace (N.T. Scot.), in 1860, of Sir James Barrie

Kirtlebridge, Dumfries. The 15th century Merkland Cross, said to mark the spot where a Master of Maxwell was murdered in 1484. It stands to the south-east, on an unclassified road off A74

Knapdale, Argyll. Locks on the Crinan Canal, near the meeting of A816 and B841 at Cairnbaan, on the northern fringe of the district of Knapdale

Knockando, Moray. The Church, which has an internal gallery. The Grant brothers, made famous by Charles Dickens as the 'Cheeryble brothers' in '*Nicholas Nickleby*' lived in this parish

Kyleakin, Isle of Skye, Inverness. The remains of Castle Moil. It is said to have been built by the daughter of a Norwegian king, who installed a chain across the strait to extract a toll from passing ships, and became known as 'Saucy Mary'

[For KYLE OF LOCHALSH see following plate
[For KIRRIEMUIR see also under STRATHMORE (Plate 157)

Glas Maol, 3,502 ft. The *Monega Pass*, for long-distance walkers, formerly a drove road for cattle, attains 3,318 ft., probably the highest right-of-way in Scotland, the *Cairnwell Pass* (*q.v.*), on the Aberdeen-Perth border, can be reached this way. See **Lair**. *Iter. 160, 162.*

KIRKTOWN OF ALVAH, Banff. Map 27, **NJ 6** 5.
To the north is Bridge of Alvah, in a very beautiful wooded reach of the River Deveron. **2 m. N.W.** is *Inchdrewer Castle*, where, in 1713, the third Lord Banff was burnt to death.

KIRKTOWN OF AUCHTERLESS, Aberdeen. Map 27, **NJ 7** 4.
In the Howe of Auchterless, with some stone circles and earth-houses in the vicinity.

KIRKTOWN OF TEALING, Angus. Map 17, **NO 4** 3.
A late 16th cent. dove-cote and an earth-house of Iron Age date, both (A.M.) are of interest.

KIRKWALL, Orkney. 4,618. SB. Map 33, **HY 4** 1.
See **Orkney Islands** (Mainland). *Iter. 263, 264, 265, 266.*

KIRN, Argyll. Map 14, **NS 1** 7.
A Firth of Clyde resort (shingle beach), to the north-east of *Dunoon* (*q.v.*) to which it is contiguous. *Iter. 102.*

KIRRIEMUIR, Angus. 4.137. SB. Map 20, **NO 3** 5.
E.C. Thurs. **M.D.** Fri. GOLF. Famous as the birthplace, in 1860, of Sir James Barrie, and the " Thrums " of his novels. His birthplace, together with the washhouse behind, which Barrie used as a theatre, is now (N.T. Scot.), and is open weekdays 10 to 12.30 and 2 to 6 (Sun., 2 to 6), Apr. to Oct. Opposite stands the " Auld Licht Manse," and in the weavers' suburb of Southmuir is the cottage known as " A Window in Thrums." The gable of the " Auld Licht Kirk " is preserved in the new Church by Sir Ninian Comper, and in the pavilion behind the cemetery, where, in 1937, Barrie was buried, is a camera obscura, open Wed., Sat. and Sun., 2 to 6, June 1 to Sept. 30. (See note page 98.) Kirriemuir, which lies at the north-eastern extremity of the fertile valley of *Strathmore* (*q.v.*), or Howe of Angus, has picturesque narrow streets, and is to-day noted for jute manufacturing. The town makes a good centre for explorations of the beautiful Braes of Angus, which include Glen Glova, Glen Prosen and Glen Isla, all penetrating deep into the lonely eastern Grampian mountains. **1½ m. S.** is *Logie*, a mainly 17th cent. house, with fine gardens. **4 m. N.E.**, near the South Esk river, is *Inverquharity Castle*, a well-preserved four-storeyed tower, dating from c. 1450. *Iter. 161, 162, 166.*

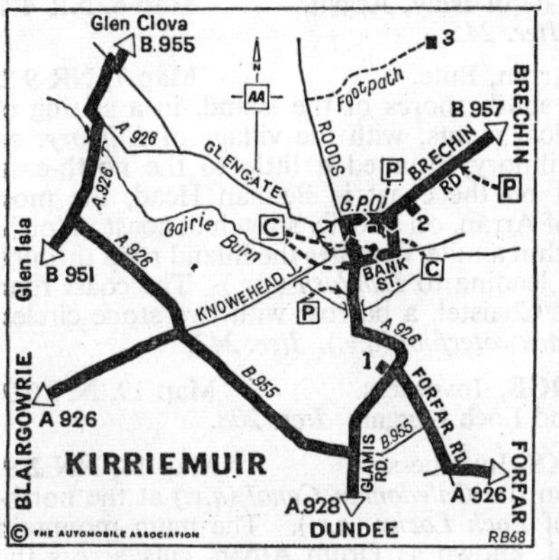

" A Window in Thrums " 1
Birthplace of Sir James Barrie 2
Camera Obscura 3

KIRTLEBRIDGE, Dumfries. Map 4, **NY 2** 7.
Near the Kirtle Water, a little to the south-east, stand the old towers of *Robgill*, *Woodhouse* and *Bonshaw*. The first-named, dating from the 16th cent., is now incorporated in a modern mansion, and the last-named, very well preserved is an ancient and long-inhabited Irving stronghold, retaining its 16th cent. clan bell. Here lived Sir Robert Irving, captain of the liner " Queen Mary," who died in 1954. **2½ m. N.E.**, by the Kirtle Water, is the ruined Church (A.M.) of *Kirkconnell*, which is visited for the graves of " Fair Helen of Kirkconnell Lee " and her lover. **1 m. S.E.**, off the Gretna road and on a by-road, stands the notable 15th cent. *Merkland Cross* (A.M.). *Iter. 10, 13, 29, 50, 51.*

KISHORN, Ross and Cromarty. Map 23, **NG 8** 4.
Known also as *Courthill*, and situated near the head of Loch Kishorn, an inlet of the larger Loch Carron. The view westwards, over the Inner Sound towards Skye, is very fine, and above the loch rise *Sgurr a'Charaochain*, 2,539 ft., and its rugged outlier *The Cioch*, in the *Applecross* hills of red Torridon sandstone. Near the head of the loch is *Rassall Ashwood*, now a Nature Reserve and forming the most northerly habitat of this tree in Great Britain. Through this tiny village passes the road leading to *Applecross* (*q.v.*), which makes the climb over the wild and lofty Pass of the Cattle, described under *Tornapress*. The miniature Pass of Kishorn is traversed by the road leading eastwards from Kishorn to *Lochcarron* (*q.v.*). See **Shieldaig**. *Iter. 219, 223.*

KNAPDALE, Argyll. Map 7, **NR 7** 6 etc.
A small district, consisting mainly of low hills, lying between the Sound of Jura and *Loch Fyne* (*q.v.*), and separated from the *Kintyre* (*q.v.*) peninsula, to the south, by West Loch Tarbert. Knapdale is almost encircled by roads around its perimeter, but only one road penetrates into the interior, that leading from Ardrishaig to the inner reach of Loch Killisport, on the west coast. The *Crinan* (*q.v.*) Canal, linking Loch Gilp and Loch Fyne with the Sound of Jura, lies on the northern fringe of Knapdale. See **Ardrishaig, Kilmory Knap** and **Tayvallich.** *Iter. 122.*

KNOCKAN, Sutherland. Map 29, **NC 2** 1.
Knockan Cliff is an AA viewpoint. See **Baddagyle** (for Inverpolly Motor Trail). *Iter. 224, 225.*

KNOCKANDHU, Banff. Map 26, **NJ 2** 2.
Some **3½ m. S.E.**, beyond Chapeltown, in the Braes of Glenlivet, is the old *Scalen* Seminary (R.C.), founded in the mid-17th cent., burnt in 1745, and later largely removed to *Blairs* (*q.v.*). *Iter. 169, 177, 192.*

KNOCKANDO, Moray. 928. Map 26, **NJ 1** 4.
The galleried Parish Church here has carved slabs in the churchyard. The village lies near the winding Spey, with *Ben Rinnes*, 2,755 ft., to the south-east beyond the wooded river valley. *Iter. 171.*

KNOYDART, Inverness. Map 23, **NG 7** 0 etc.
This very picturesque and mountainous tract of the Western Highlands, dominated by *Sgurr na Ciche*, 3,410 ft., and *Ladhar Bheinn*, 3,343 ft., lies between *Loch Hourn* (*q.v.*) and *Loch Nevis* (*q.v.*). It is sometimes referred to under the name of the " Rough Bounds," possibly due to its comparative inaccessibility, though the fringe of the area is traversed by the narrow and rough road leading from *Tomdoun* (*q.v.*) to *Kinloch Hourn* (*q.v.*). Cattle ranching on an extensive scale has been introduced into the district. Some of the finest mountain and loch scenery in Scotland is to be found in Knoydart, and has been somewhat affected as a result of a large new hydro-electric scheme in the district around *Loch Quoich* (*q.v.*). See **Inverie.**

KYLEAKIN, Isle of Skye, Inverness. Map 23, **18 7** 2.
The arrival point for the car ferry from *Kyle of Lochalsh* (*q.v.*), Kyleakin overlooks the narrow strait of Kyle Akin, the name being derived from an early King of Norway, who sailed through the narrows, in 1263, on his way to *Largs* (*q.v.*). The ruined *Castle Moil* stands on the shore to the east, with a fine view up Loch Alsh. In the background rises *Beinn na Cailleach*, 2,396 ft., a notable viewpoint. *Iter. 251.*

KYLE OF LOCHALSH, Ross and Cromarty. 1,650. Map 23, **NG 7** 2.
E.C. Thurs. Finely situated at the western extremity of Loch Alsh where the narrow strait of Kyle Akin (car ferry), separates the mainland from *Kyleakin* (*q.v.*) in Skye. Kyle of Lochalsh, the *Wester Ross* railhead of the line from Inverness, is sometimes known as the " Gateway to Skye," and is the terminal point of one branch of the " Road to the Isles." As well as being a fishing port, there are regular steamer services to Mallaig, Skye, and the Outer Hebrides. Motor boats provide a service to Loch Toscaig for *Applecross* (*q.v.*). From numerous points in the vicinity magni-

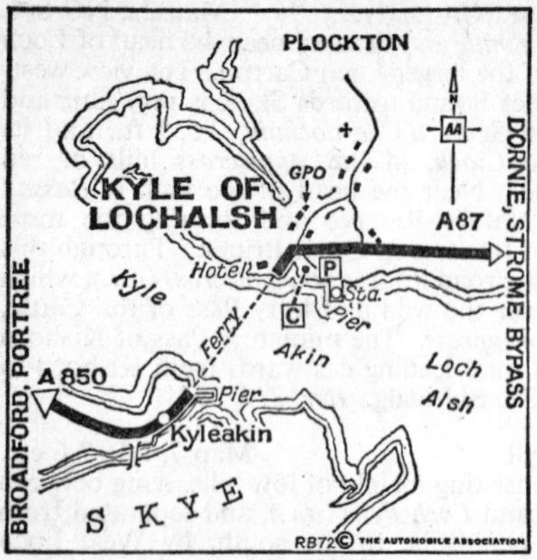

ficent views towards the Coolins of Skye, and over *Loch Alsh* (*q.v.*), Loch Carron and the Inner Sound, with the Crowlin Islands, can be obtained. Beyond the Crowlins rise the lofty *Applecross* hills and westwards lies the narrow island of Raasay. Kyle of Lochalsh is situated partly within the extensive N.T. Scot. estate of *Balmacara* (*q.v.*). See **Plockton.** *Iter. 207, 220, 221, 222, 251.*

KYLERHEA, Isle of Skye, Inverness. Map 23, **NG 7 2.** On the narrow strait of Kyle Rhea, facing Glenelg in Inverness-shire. From here, a narrow road, with good views, climbs very steeply (1 in 5) to over 900 ft. through Glen Arroch, before descending to the coast road linking *Kyleakin* (*q.v.*) with *Broadford* (*q.v.*). *Beinn na Cailleach*, 2,396 ft., rises to the north-west of Kylerhea and commands a fine prospect. To the south is *Ben Aslak*, 1,984 ft. A car ferry, operated in the summer, connects with *Glenelg* (*q.v.*), on the mainland.

KYLESKU, Sutherland. Map 28, **NC 2 3.** One of the most beautiful and remote places in the Northern Highlands, where the narrows of Loch Cairnbawn, an inlet of the picturesque Eddrachillis Bay, are guarded by several small islands. The waters are crossed by a car ferry to Kylestrome, opposite which is the small island of Garbh. To the east, the waters of Loch Glendhu and Loch Glencoul penetrate deep into the wild and roadless hills in the manner of Norwegian fjords. The distant peak of *Ben Leoid*, 2,597 ft., overlooks the latter, and beyond its head is the remote 658-ft. high waterfall of *Eas-coul-Aulin*, the highest in Britain, descending to a valley beyond Loch Beag. It is reached by boat from Kylesku and then on foot. It is considered to be about thrice the height of Niagara when in full spate. South of Kylesku, the road to *Inchnadamph* (*q.v.*) follows the pass between *Quinag*, 2,653 ft. and *Glasven*, 2,541 ft. Westwards goes the picturesque, but rough, hilly and narrow road along Loch Cairnbawn's southern shores leading towards *Drumbeg* (*q.v.*) and *Lochinver* (*q.v.*), providing magnificent views, both inland towards the mountains and out to sea for the whole of the distance. See **Scourie.** *Iter. 225, 227.*

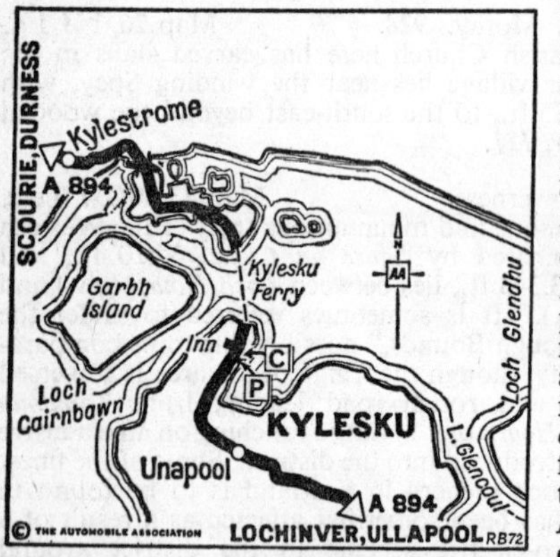

KYLES OF BUTE, Argyll; Bute. Map 7, **NR 9 7** etc. The name given to the picturesque, curved strait traversed by the Clyde steamers, which encircles the northern extremity of the island of *Bute* (*q.v.*), washing the shores of the *Cowal* (*q.v.*) peninsula of Argyll, on the mainland. The Kyles of Bute, and the wider expanse of the Firth of Clyde, to the east, are a favourite venue of yachtsmen and regattas are held in the summer. About halfway along the coast of Cowal, the inlet of Loch Riddon bites into the land, and farther east is Loch Striven, which penetrates even deeper, to the north, against a background of green hills. At the mouth of Loch Striven is Strone Point, to the west of which lies *South Hall*, where the woods have been so planted as to show the positions of the opposing armies at the battle of Waterloo. Between the two inlets stands *Colintraive* (*q.v.*), with a steamer pier, and also a ferry to *Rhubodach* (*q.v.*), in Bute. The small *Burnt* Islands almost block the channel to the west, facing the northern tip of Bute, where two standing stones, known as the " Maids of Bute," form prominent landmarks. See **Rothesay** and **Tighnabruaich.** *Iter. 102, 103, 241.*

KYLESTROME, Sutherland. Map 28, **NC 2 3.** Lies on the wild and lonely road leading to *Scourie* (*q.v.*), which passes several small lochans before reaching the sea at Calva Bay, an inlet of the larger, island-studded Eddrachillis Bay. See **Kylesku.** *Iter. 225.*

LADYBANK, Fife. 1,176. SB. Map 17, **NO 3 0.** GOLF. Stands in the fertile Howe of Fife, to the north-east of the *Lomond* hills. **3 m. N.** is the notable *Melville House*, now a school, described under *Monimail.*

LADYKIRK, Berwick. 480. Map 11, **NT 8 4.** On the River Tweed. The picturesque cruciform Church dates from 1500, but the tower was probably completed by William Adam in 1743. The building, built entirely of stone, in order to obviate the risk of damage by fire, is said to have been erected by James IV as a thanks-offering for his escape from drowning in the river nearby. On the Northumberland side of the river is the ruined Norham Castle. *Iter. 46.*

LAGAVULIN, Isle of Islay, Argyll. Map 6, **NR 4 4.** See **Port Ellen.** *Iter. 245.*

LAGG, Isle of Arran, Bute. Map 7, **NR 9 2.** Stands near the south shores of the island, in a setting of woods and tropical plants, with the village of *Kilmory*, on the Water of Kilmory, situated a little to the north-east. Still farther east on the coast is Bennan Head, the most southerly point of Arran, on a rocky stretch of coast. North-west of Lagg, within a mile, diverges the inland road through Glen Scorrodale leading to *Lamlash* (*q.v.*). The coast road continues to Tor Chaistel, a barrow with two stone circles, on the way to *Blackwaterfoot* (*q.v.*). *Iter. 242.*

LAGGAN BRIDGE, Inverness. Map 19, **NN 6 9.** See **Drumgask** and **Loch Laggan.** *Iter. 208.*

LAGGAN LOCKS, Inverness. Map 18, **NN 2 9.** These locks lie on the *Caledonian Canal* (*q.v.*) at the north-west extremity of *Loch Lochy* (*q.v.*). The main mountain ridge of Scotland, known as Drum Alban, cuts across the Great Glen, or *Glen More* (*q.v.*), at this point, forming an important watershed at a height of 115 ft., rivers to the west flowing into the Atlantic, and those to the east entering the North Sea. **1 m. S.W.,** on the north bank of Loch Lochy, is *Kilfinnan*, where the mausoleum is the burial ground of the Glengarry chiefs. *Iter. 210, 214, 220.*

LAG TOWER, Dumfries. Map 3, **NX 8 8.** See **Dunscore.**

LAIDE, Ross and Cromarty. Map 22, **NG 8 9.** Here are fine sands and views of Gruinard Bay. *Iter. 206, 222.*

LAIGH OF MORAY, Moray Map 26, **NJ 2** 6 etc. The name given to the fertile, flat countryside, watered by the River Lossie, bordering the Outer Moray Firth. In the centre of the district stands the town of *Elgin* (*q.v.*).

LAIR, Perth. Map 20, **NO 1 5.** Situated in Glen Shee, surrounded by hills, with *Mount Blair*, 2,441 ft., to the east. A road leads eastwards from here across the River Shee to enter Angus and reach, within a few miles, the beautiful valley of Glen Isla, which is traversed by a picturesque road for the greater part of its length. See **Kirkton of Glenisla.** *Iter. 141, 152, 160, 162, 167, 168.*

LAIRG, Sutherland. 1,050. Map 29, **NC 5 0.** **E.C.** Wed. In the cemetery is a quaint old tombstone portraying death. Lairg is an important junction for roads radiating west and north to the wild and beautiful country of the far North-West Highlands. The featureless Loch

Kyle of Lochalsh, Ross and Cromarty. The car ferry across Loch Alsh to Kyleakin, in the island of Skye

Kylesku, Sutherland. The meeting of Lochs Cairnbawn, Glencoul and Glendhu. The narrows here are crossed by a car ferry

Ladykirk, Berwick. The Church, which James IV had built c. 1500 as a thanks-offering for his escape from drowning in the River Tweed. It was built entirely of stone to avoid the risk of fire

Lag Tower, Dumfries. This ruined 16th century Nithsdale tower was once the seat of Sir Robert Grierson (1650–1736), a persecutor of the Covenanters. It stands on an unclassified road, 1½ miles north-east of Dunscore

Laigh of Moray, Moray. The rebuilt Muckle Cross (1888) at Elgin, in the flat country near the Outer Moray Firth. It is associated with the raising, in 1778, of the Macleod Highlanders, later the Highland Light Infantry

Kyles of Bute, Argyll; Bute. A view of the small resort of Tighnabruaich, facing the island of Bute. Its Gaelic name means 'House on the Brae,' and refers to the solitary house which once stood there

[For KYLE OF LOCHALSH see also under WESTER ROSS (Plate 169)
[For KYLESKU see also under ASSYNT (Plate 10)

Lamlash, Isle of Arran, Bute. Holy Island, in Lamlash Bay, which is associated with the naval battle of Largs against the Norwegians, in 1263

Lamberton, Berwick. The notice board on the former toll house at Lamberton Bar, where runaway marriages used to be performed

Lamington, Lanark. The Norman doorway of the old Church

Lake of Menteith, Perth. A view of the 13th century Inchmahome Priory, on an island in one of the only two ' lakes ' in Scotland. Mary, Queen of Scots, was sent here at the age of 5, attended by her servants, the Four Marys

Lammermuir Hills, Berwick; East Lothian. The former Douglas stronghold of Cranshaws Tower, in Berwickshire, which is still inhabited. It stands on B6355, the road which crosses the hills to link Gifford with Duns

Lammermuir Hills, Berwick; East Lothian. The old watch-house of the Church at Spott, erected as a protection against body snatchers. The village stands at the northern extremity of the hills, near Dunbar, in East Lothian

[For LANARK see following plate

Shin, where hydro-electric developments have taken place, extends north-westwards from the village, and in the distance rises *Ben More Assynt*, 3,273 ft., Sutherland's highest mountain. Lairg is well known to anglers, and is a busy centre for local bus routes. Important lamb sales take place here. Southwards from Loch Shin flows the turbulent River Shin, in a wooded setting. There are numerous remains of archaeological interest, especially hut circles and tumuli, in the neighbourhood, notably to the north of Lairg, where the Scourie and Tongue roads fork, the latter continuing northwards through Strath Tirry towards the low *Crask* (*q.v.*) Pass. See **Inveran Bridge, Overscaig** and **Rosehall.** *Iter. 224, 229, 230, 232, 233.*

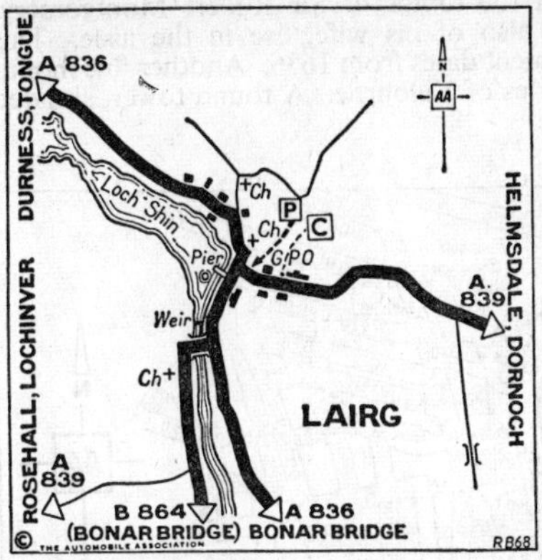

LAIRIG GHRU PASS, Aberdeen; Inverness. Map 20, **NH 9 0.**
This famous pass, essentially for hardy long-distance walkers only, links Speyside with Deeside by cutting through the heart of the great *Cairngorm* (*q.v.*) range, the distance from *Aviemore* (*q.v.*) to *Braemar* (*q.v.*) being about 28 miles. The northern extremity of the pass is overshadowed to the east by the great cliffs of *Cairn Lochan*, 3,983 ft., and also by the *Lurcher's Crag*, 3,448 ft., the path descending from this point into the woodlands of the great forest of *Rothiemurchus* (*q.v.*). The track reaches a height of more than 2,700 ft. between the shoulders of *Ben Macdhui*, 4,296 ft., and *Braeriach*, 4,248 ft., amid a wilderness of huge boulders, near which are situated the Pools of Dee. These are not, however, the source of the river, which rises high up in the remote fastnesses of Braeriach, at a height of more than 4,000 ft. On the descent towards Glen Dee and the extensive Mar Forest, to the south of the great peaks, rises the *Devil's Point*, 3,303 ft., to the west. Below it is situated the ruined Corrour bothy, well known as a shelter to walkers. The path then keeps near the Dee and follows the river to *Inverey* (*q.v.*). Another branch diverges south-eastwards from the bothy and goes through Glen Lui Beg and Glen Lui to reach Inverey. See **Coylumbridge.**

LAKE OF MENTEITH, Perth. Map 15, **NN 5 0** and **NS 5 9.** See **Port of Menteith.** *Iter. 109, 111, 139.*

LAMANCHA, Peebles. Map 9, **NT 2 5.**
Situated a little to the west is *Lamancha House*, dating from 1663. *Iter. 10, 14, 37.*

LAMBERTON, Berwick. Map 11, **NT 9 5.**
On the Great North Road, and at the Border between Scotland and England, situated a little to the north of *Berwick-upon-Tweed* (*q.v.*). At the former *Lamberton Bar*, the toll-keeper once performed runaway marriages similar to those which took place at *Gretna* (*q.v.*). The coastline in the vicinity is characterized by lofty cliffs. *Iter. 1, 2.*

LAMINGTON, Lanark. Map 9, **NS 9 3.**
A small Clydesdale village, looking towards *Tinto Hill*, 2,335 ft., a noted viewpoint to the west, and also to *Culter Fell*, 2,454 ft., situated among a network of lesser heights away to the east. The Church, once visited by Robert Burns, has a good Norman doorway, and retains the jougs. *Lamington Tower*, in ruins, to the north, carries the date 1589. *Iter. 25.*

LAMLASH, Isle of Arran, Bute. 687. Map 7, **NS 0 3.**
GOLF. The largest village in Arran, attractively situated on Lamlash Bay, with bathing, sheltered by Kingscross Point to the south and Clauchlands Point to the north. From the former, Bruce is said to have embarked for the mainland in 1307. In the bay, associated with the naval battle of *Largs* (*q.v.*) in 1263, when Haco of Norway rallied his defeated fleet, lies *Holy Island*, on which *Mullach Mor* attains 1,030 ft. Below the hill, facing the bay, is the cave of *St. Molus*, with Runic inscriptions. Inland from Lamlash, a road ascends through the Monamore Glen to nearly 1,000 ft., a steep, twisting climb, with a gradient of nearly 1 in 6, prior to descending through Glen Scorrodale towards the south-west coast, which is reached near *Lagg* (*q.v.*). The road to *Brodick* (*q.v.*) keeps inland, but a path goes round by the coast, affording fine views, and keeping near the low *Clauchland* hills to the west. See **Whiting Bay.** *Iter. 242.*

LAMMERMUIR HILLS, Berwick; East Lothian. Map 10, **NT 5 5** etc.
See **Cranshaws, Duns, Garvald, Gifford, Longformacus** and **Soutra Hill.** *Iter. 3.*

LANARK, Lanark. 8,701. SB. Map 9, **NS 8 4.**
E.C. Thurs. **M.D.** Mon. GOLF. This Clydesdale town, which is of considerable antiquity, though visible relics of its past are lacking, stands high above the banks of the winding River Clyde, which flows through what are perhaps its most picturesque reaches within a short distance of Lanark. The Parish Church dates from 1777, and has a large statue of Wallace, who is said to have lived in the town. There are slight remains of the 12th cent. *St. Kentigern's* Church. Pageants are held to celebrate Lanimer Day, or "Beating the Bounds," which is held on the Thursday following June 6. "Whuppity Scoorie," another local festival, possibly associated with ancient pagan rites, and including a children's race round the Parish Church, takes place annually on March 1. To the west of Lanark, the Mouse Water, spanned by an ancient bridge, possibly Roman, flows into the Clyde, and nearby are the lofty Cartland

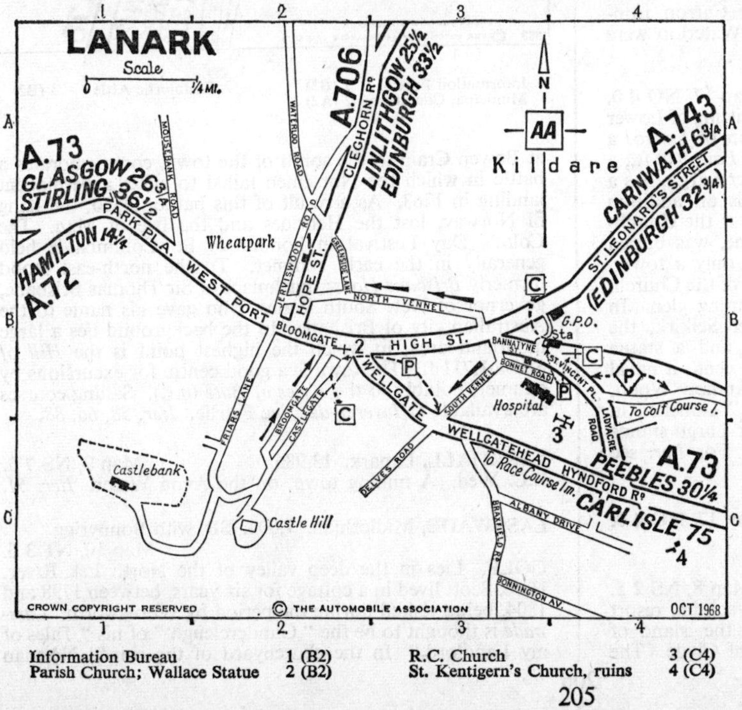

Information Bureau	1 (B2)	R.C. Church	3 (C4)
Parish Church; Wallace Statue	2 (B2)	St. Kentigern's Church, ruins	4 (C4)

Crags, overlooking a deep chasm. The race-course is situated on Lanark Moor, where there is a small loch. **1 m. S.** of the town is *New Lanark*, founded in 1784, with its textile mills, and complete planned community layout. This is perhaps Scotland's finest example of industrial archaeology and under Robert Owen became a European showplace by the early 19th cent. Beyond Lanark are the picturesque Falls of Clyde, including Cora Linn, the finest, and also the Bonnington Falls. The Stonebyres Linn Fall lies **2 m. W.** of Lanark, and nearby is *Blackhill* (N.T. Scot.), a fine viewpoint. All the various Falls have been affected by developments in hydro-electric schemes. *Braxfield House*, on the way to New Lanark, is associated with R. L. Stevenson's "Weir of Hermiston." A little to the west of Lanark, on the south bank of the Clyde, is the pretty village of *Kirkfieldbank* (*q.v.*). See **Crossford** and **Douglas.** *Iter. 22, 23, 37, 48, 50, 53, 54, 69, 86.*

LANGHOLM, Dumfries. 2,341. SB. Map 4, **NY 3 8.**
E.C. Wed. An Eskdale town, noted for woollens, and also an angling resort, situated on the wooded River Esk, where it is joined by the Wauchope Water from the south-west, and also by the picturesque Ewes Water from the north. A picturesque Border Riding ceremony is held annually, having been inaugurated in 1816, and the town is associated with the 16th cent. Border reiver, Johnny Armstrong. (See **Canonbie** and **Teviothead.**) The poet Hugh MacDiarmid was born in the town. *Whita Hill*, 1,162 ft., to the east, a splendid viewpoint, is crowned by a monument to General Sir John Malcolm, who is buried in Westminster Abbey. There are very scanty remains of *Langholm Castle*, on the Castle Holm. **2½ m. N.N.W.,** near a bend of the Esk, is the motte of the former *Barntalloch Castle. Iter. 11, 12, 30, 45.*

LARACHBEG, Argyll. Map 12, **NM 6** 4.
A tiny *Morven* (*q.v.*) clachan, situated in a valley between Loch Aline and Loch Arienas, where smallholdings were given to many of the inhabitants of the island of *St. Kilda* (*q.v.*) following its evacuation in 1930. At the head of Loch Aline is the 15th cent. *Kinlochaline Castle*, a square, turreted structure. The road leading north-eastwards towards *Loch Linnhe* (*q.v.*) climbs by way of Gleann Geal, and later divides into two branches, the main one traversing the south-east shores of *Loch Sunart* (*q.v.*). See **Lochaline.** *Iter. 218*

LARBERT, Stirling. 3,627. Map 16, **NS 8 8.**
E.C. Wed. GOLF. Known for the large Carron ironworks, at which guns used in the battle of Waterloo were cast. For plan, see **Falkirk.** *Iter. 95.*

LARGO, Fife. 9,775. Map 17, **NO 4** 0.
E.C. Wed. Situated on Largo Bay, and consisting of Lower Largo, on the coast, and Upper, or Kirkton of Largo, a little inland, dominated by the cone of *Largo Law*, 948 ft., a good viewpoint. The Parish Church, at Upper Largo, has a 16th cent. chancel and tower. The spire is an addition of 1623. There is also a Celtic cross-slab near the churchyard gate. Sir Andrew Wood, of naval fame, was buried here, in 1515, and of his once-great Castle, only a tower, with its conical cap, still remains. To the west of the Church, beyond Largo House, is Kiels Den, a charming glen. In Lower Largo was born, in 1676, Alexander Selkirk, the prototype of Defoe's "Robinson Crusoe," and a statue to him stands near the harbour. In the 15th cent., a naval victory over the English was gained by Sir Andrew Wood, among his ships being the "Great Michael," launched in 1507 at *Newhaven* (*q.v.*). **1 m. N.W.** of Upper Largo stands the old *Pitcruvie Castle*. See **Lundin Links.** For *Iter.* see *Upper Largo.*

LARGOWARD, Fife. Map 17, **NO 4** 0.
Iter. 128, 132.

LARGS, Ayr. 8,858. SB. Map 8, **NS 2** 5.
E.C. Wed. GOLF. A popular Clyde coast yachting resort on the Gogo Water and Largs Bay, facing the island of *Great Cumbrae* (See **Millport**), in the Firth of Clyde. The beach is pebble. The splendid mausoleum of the former Parish Church of *St. Columba* dates from 1636, and is known as the *Skelmorlie* Aisle (A.M.). There is a painted wooden roof, and the tombs of Sir Robert Montgomery, the founder, and also of his wife, are in the aisle. This remarkable monument dates from 1636. Another fine monument is to the Boyles of Kelburne. A round tower, situated

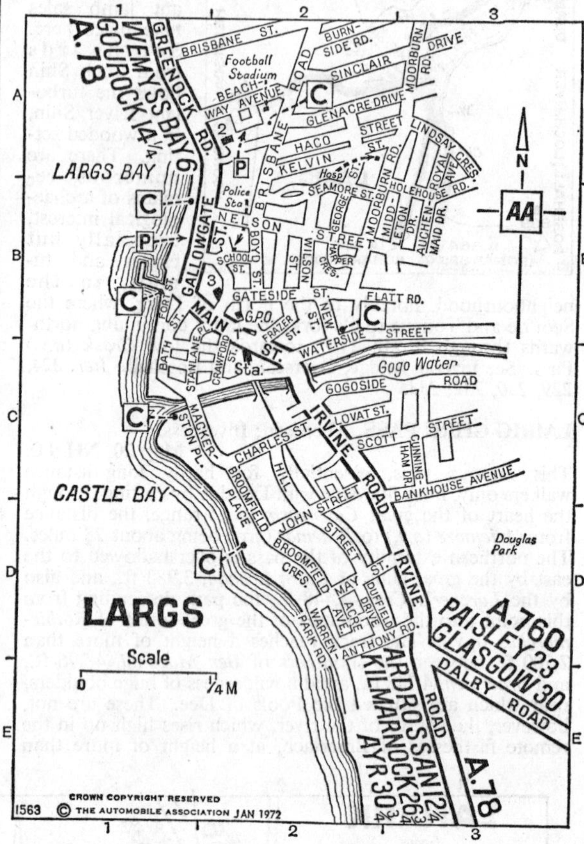

Information Bureau 1 (B2) Municipal Chambers 2 (A2) Skelmorlie Aisle 3 (B2)

at Bowen Craig to the south of the town, commemorates a battle in which the Norsemen failed to effect a permanent landing in 1263. As a result of this battle, Haco, the King of Norway, lost the Hebrides and the Isle of Man. The Colm's Day Festival in honour of St. Columba is held generally in the early summer. To the north-east stood formerly *Brisbane House*, birthplace of Sir Thomas Brisbane, governor of New South Wales, who gave his name to the Australian city of Brisbane. In the background lies a large moorland area, in which the highest point is the *Hill of Stake* 1,711 ft. The town is a good centre for excursions by steamer, notably to the *Kyles of Bute* (*q.v.*). Sailing courses are available at *Inverclyde*. See **Fairlie.** *Iter. 58, 66, 88.*

LARKHALL, Lanark. 13,986. Map 9, **NS 7** 5.
E.C. Wed. A mining town, on the Avon Water. *Iter. 51.*

LASSWADE, Midlothian. 7,004. SB. with Bonnyrigg. Map 10, **NT 3** 6.
GOLF. Lies in the deep valley of the North Esk River. Here, Scott lived in a cottage for six years, between 1798 and 1804, being visited during the period by Wordsworth. *Lasswade* is thought to be the "Gandercleugh" of his "Tales of my Landlord." In the churchyard of the ruined Norman

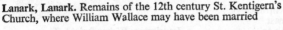

Lanark, Lanark. Remains of the 12th century St. Kentigern's Church, where William Wallace may have been married

Largo, Fife. The 'Robinson Crusoe' statue. Alexander Selkirk, the prototype of Daniel Defoe's hero, was born at Lower Largo, in 1676

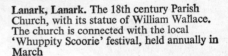

Largo, Fife. The tower of the former castle of Sir Andrew Wood, the 15th century naval commander of the 'Yellow Carvel'

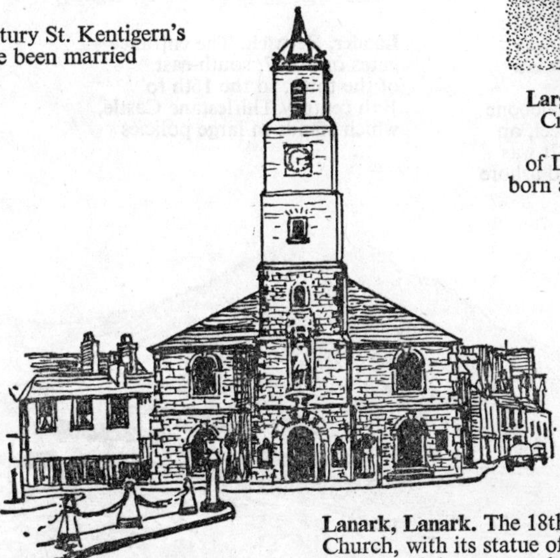

Lanark, Lanark. The 18th century Parish Church, with its statue of William Wallace. The church is connected with the local 'Whuppity Scoorie' festival, held annually in March

Largs, Ayr. The Skelmorlie Aisle of the old Parish Church, which contains the tomb of the founder, Sir Robert Montgomery, who died in 1639

Lasswade, Midlothian. Mavisbush, now De Quincey cottage, where Thomas de Quincey, the writer, lived between 1840 and 1859. It stands at Polton, 2 miles south-west of Lasswade, on an unclassified road

Latheron, Caithness. A whalebone archway near Latheronwheel, on the south-east side of A9. It was taken from a whale washed ashore in 1869

Lauder, Berwick. The entrance gates on A697, south-east of the town, to the 16th to 19th century Thirlestane Castle, which stands in large policies

Laurieston, Kirkcudbright. The monument to S. R. Crockett, the author, who died in 1914 at Tarascon, in France. He is buried in Balmaghie churchyard, near the shores of Loch Ken, to the east

Laxford Bridge, Sutherland. A view of the conical peak of Ben Stack, which rises to 2,364 feet beyond the western shores of Loch Stack

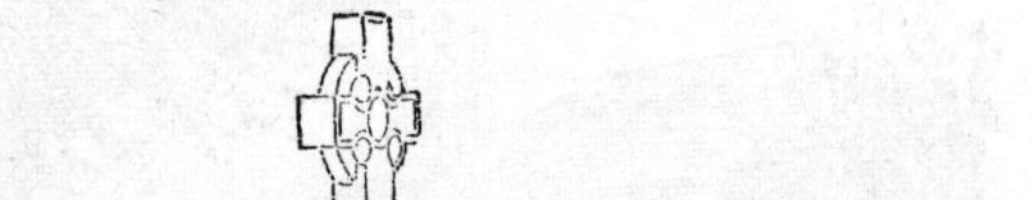

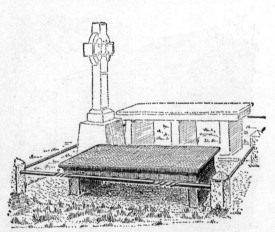

Leadhills, Lanark. A churchyard gravestone in memory of John Taylor, who lived to the age of 137

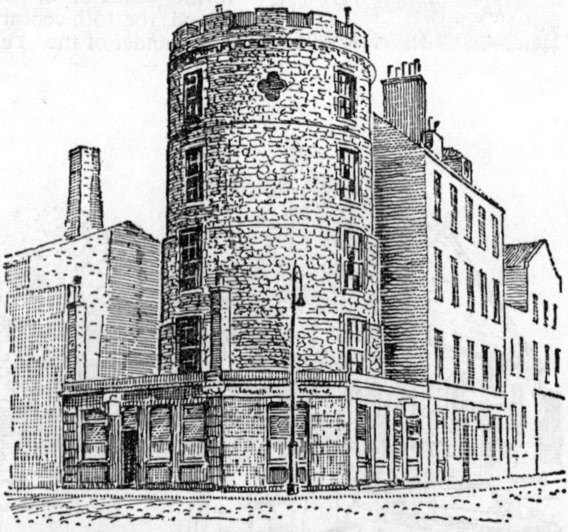

Leith (Edinburgh), Midlothian. The so-called Signal Tower, at the corner of Tower St. and The Shore, which Robert Mylne erected originally as a windmill in 1686

[For LEITH see also following plate
[For LATHERON see also Plate 175

Church are the graves of William Drummond, the poet, and Henry Dundas, 1st Viscount Melville, a famous late 18th cent. benevolent despot, and virtual ruler of the country, whose home was the nearby 19th cent. *Melville Castle*, now an hotel. **2 m. S.W.,** near the river, is *Mavisbush*, now De Quincey Cottage, where De Quincey lived between 1840 and 1859. **2½ m. S.W.,** also near the river, is *Hawthornden House*, rebuilt in 1638, by Drummond (see above), and beautifully situated on a height overlooking the North Esk, in a setting of lovely gardens. An ancient bell tower is incorporated in the house, and below are artificial caves of great age. In the grounds stands Ben Jonson's tree, recalling the poet's visit in 1618-19.

LATHERON, Caithness. 409. Map 30, **ND 1** 3.
On a hill above the Church stands a detached tower, in which the church bells were formerly hung. Near the Post Office is a large Standing Stone of great antiquity. The moorland road which links Latheron with Thurso, on the Pentland Firth, was built in the late 18th cent. There are numerous hut circles and Pictish remains in the neighbourhood. **1 m. S.S.W.** is *Latheronwheel*, or *Janetstown*, with a quaint little harbour. **2½ m. N.E.,** on the rock-bound coast, is the ruined *Forse Castle*, and farther inland are some recently excavated stone structures of very early date, known as *The Wag* (A.M.). *Iter. 200, 236.*

LAUDER, Berwick. 602. SB. Map 10, **NT 5** 4.
E.C. Thurs. A small Royal Burgh, the only example in the county, situated in Lauderdale, on the Leader Water, which flows southwards from the *Lammermuirs*, on the East Lothian border. It forms a good angling centre, and a Border Riding ceremony is still held annually. There is a curious little Tolbooth, approached by a flight of steps. The cruciform Church dating from 1673, may be partly the work of Sir William Bruce. In 1482, several favourites of James III were hanged from the former Lauder Bridge by the Earl of Angus, who earned for himself the soubriquet of " Bell-the-Cat." James Guthrie, minister at Lauder from 1642 to 1649, was the first Covenanter martyr to be recorded on the Greyfriars churchyard monument in Edinburgh. He was executed in 1661. Outside Lauder is the park of *Thirlestane Castle*, an imposing structure, dating from 1595, 1675 and 1841, with a fine west front by Sir William Bruce. The castle is associated with the ancient tower of *Thirlestane*, situated **2½ m. E.** of Lauder, off the Greenlaw road. A fine moorland road leads westwards from Lauder, attaining over 1,100 ft., and later descending to the Gala Water at *Stow* (*q.v.*). See **Douglas** and **Gordon.** *Iter. 4, 9, 13, 36.*

LAURENCEKIRK, Kincardine. 1,349. SB. Map 21, **NO 7** 7.
E.C. Wed. **M.D.** Mon. A small town, founded in 1779 by Lord Gardenstone. It was once noted for the manufacture of snuff-boxes, and is situated in the fertile Howe of the Mearns. To the south-east rises *Garvock Hill*, 915 ft., topped by the *Johnstone* Tower. **3 m. W.** is *Thornton Castle*, 15th to 16th cent. and later. See **Drumlithie.** *Iter. 151.*

LAURIESTON, Kirkcudbright. 122. Map 3, **NX 6** 6.
A *Galloway* (*q.v.*) village, to the north of which lies the little Woodhall Loch. Its name prior to the 18th cent. was *Clachanpluck*. There is a monument to S. T. Crockett, the author, whose novels introduced much local colour, and who lies buried in the churchyard at *Balmaghie*, situated **3 m. E.,** near the shores of Loch Ken. In the churchyard are also Covenanters' gravestones. *Iter. 77, 95.*

LAURISTON CASTLE, Midlothian. Map 9, **NT 2** 7.
See **Barnton.**

LAWERS, Perth. Map 15, **NN 6** 3.
E.C. Wed. Situated on *Loch Tay* (*q.v.*), at the foot of *Ben Lawers*, 3,984 ft. (N.T. Scot.), the highest mountain in the county, and noted especially for its botanical interest. It can be easily ascended from Lawers, while the view from the summit is very rewarding, including the whole of the *Breadalbane* (*q.v.*) country and much of the *Grampians* (*q.v.*). From the summit, a descent can be made westwards to the tiny Lochan na Lairige, on the steep, narrow and rough mountain road linking Loch Tay with *Bridge of Balgie* (*q.v.*), in Glen Lyon. The slopes of Ben Lawers and its satellites provide good ski-ing in suitable conditions, and Coire Odhar, on *Beinn Ghlas*, 3,657 ft., is used by the Scottish Ski Club. To the west of Lochan na Lairige rise the peaks of the *Tarmachan* group, reaching a height of 3,421 ft. *Iter. 120, 138.*

LAXFORD BRIDGE, Sutherland. Map 28, **NC 2** 4.
This remote place in the Northern Highlands is situated on the Laxford River, a famous salmon stream, which flows through Laxford Bay into the island-studded Loch Laxford, a little to the north-west. To the south-east rises the gneiss cone of *Ben Stack*, 2,364 ft., below which is Loch Stack, drained by the Laxford River, and along the south shore of which goes the picturesque road leading south-eastwards to *Lairg* (*q.v.*). North of the loch is *Arcuil*, 2,580 ft., with its rough quartzite scree slopes, and farther east rises *Meall Horn*, 2,548 ft., both in the great Reay Forest. The whole district is noted especially for a multiplicity of tiny lochans, forming a fisherman's paradise. From the summits of the mountains in the vicinity the view shows almost more water than land, the latter consisting largely of bare outcrops of Archaean grey gneiss, some of the oldest rocks in the world. **4 m. W.,** on the Scourie road, a by-road leads north to *Tarbet* in the wild and rocky *Fanagmore* district facing the island of Handa. See **Rhiconich.** *Iter. 225, 229.*

LAXO, Shetland. Map 33 **HU 4** 6.
See **Shetland Islands** (Mainland). *Iter. 270.*

LEADBURN, Midlothian. Map 9, **NT 2** 5.
Lies in a moorland district. **2 m. S.W.,** over the Peeblesshire border, is *Whim*, a fine 18th cent. Adam mansion. See **Lamancha.** *Iter. 10, 14, 24, 37.*

LEADHILLS, Lanark. 670. Map 9, **NS 8** 1.
E.C. Thurs. GOLF. This pleasant village was once noted especially for its lead, though gold and silver have also been extensively mined as long ago as the 12th cent. It is situated at a height of 1,350 ft., and is exceeded in height only by its near neighbour to the south-west, *Wanlockhead* (*q.v.*), the road linking the two villages attaining a height of 1,531 ft. on the Lanark-Dumfries boundary. A stone in the churchyard is in memory of John Taylor, who died at the age of 137 years. The '*Hopetoun Arms*' inn is the highest in Scotland. To the south-east rise the rounded *Lowther* hills, of which *Green Lowther*, 2,403 ft., and *Lowther Hill*, 2,377 ft., are the principal summits, commanding wide views over the Lowlands and into Cumberland. In the late 17th cent. these hills were a refuge for the persecuted Covenanters. The golf course, at an altitude of 1,500 ft., is said to be the highest in Britain. William Symington, a pioneer of steam navigation, was born at Leadhills in 1763, and is commemorated by a monument below the churchyard. Here also was born, in 1686, Allan Ramsay, author of the " Gentle Shepherd," and founder of an early Edinburgh theatre. See **Bowling** and **Mennock.** *Iter. 48, 49.*

LECHT ROAD, Aberdeen; Banff. Map 26, **NJ 2** 1.
See **Cock Bridge.** *Iter. 141, 160, 174, 176, 191.*

LEGERWOOD, Berwick. 257. Map 10, **NT 5** 4.
The Church has a Norman chancel arch and there is a 17th-century Ker monument. *Corsbie Tower* is a ruined 16th-century stronghold.

LEITH (Edinburgh), Midlothian. 51,378. Map 17, **NT 2** 7.
E.C. Wed. Known officially as the *Port of Leith*, the town has been, since 1920, incorporated within the Edinburgh boundaries. It suffered many attacks from the English, and was devastated in 1544 and 1547. Through the town flows the Water of Leith, dividing it into North and South Leith. The important harbour has well-equipped docks and shipyards. The shore was the old landing-place, and

the visit of George IV, in 1822, is recorded on a stone by the quay wall. Among the town's manufacturing interests are sawmills, biscuits and chemical works. In Kirkgate is the restored 15th cent. *St. Mary's* Church, and nearby is *Trinity House*, in which are some notable paintings. The fine 16th cent. and later Merchant's House in Water's Close, known as *Lamb's House* (N.T. Scot.), where Mary, Queen of Scots spent her first day after landing in 1561, has been restored as an Old Folks' Centre. Only scanty remains of the Citadel of 1650 now exist. The *Signal Tower*, built originally in 1686 as a windmill, still stands near the shore. On Leith Links, now a park, Charles I played golf in 1641.

LENDALFOOT, Ayr. Map 2, **NX 1** 9.
Situated on a fine stretch of coast, with Bennane Head to the south-west. There is a memorial recalling the drowning of some Arran men in 1711. The Lendal Water flows into the sea at Lendalfoot, and a little inland is the ruined *Carleton Castle*, associated with the legend of a baron, who pushed his first seven wives over the cliffs, but was himself thus disposed of by the eighth. On the way to Bennane Head is some fine rock scenery at *Gamesloup*, and beyond the Head is Bennane Cove, associated with Crockett's "Grey Man." To the north of Lendalfoot, on the coast road, one of the most picturesque in the country, is the delightful *Kennedy's Pass*. See **Ballantrae.** *Iter. 55, 80.*

LENNEL, Berwick. Map 11, **NT 8** 4.
Iter. 38.

LENNOXLOVE, East Lothian. Map 10, **NT 5** 7.
See **Bolton.**

LENNOXTOWN, Stirling. 3,161. Map 15, **NS 6** 7.
E.C. Wed. This town stands below the *Campsie Fells*, at the foot of the road leading over the hills to *Fintry* (*q.v.*) by way of the head of *Campsie Glen* (*q.v.*), at a height of 1,154 ft., and is noted for its nail-works and dye-works. The name *Lennox* was formerly applied to the county of Dunbarton, and included also parts of the adjacent counties, but is now only used to describe the various hill ranges in north-west Stirlingshire, which are known generally as the *Campsies* or the *Lennox* hills. *Iter. 107, 115.*

LENY FALLS, Perth. Map 15, **NN 5** 0.
See **Callander.** *Iter. 107, 111, 139, 141, 142, 144.*

LENZIE, Dunbarton. Map 8, **NS 6** 7.
See **Kirkintilloch.**

LERWICK, Shetland. 6,107. SB. Map 33, **HU 4** 4.
See **Shetland Islands** (Mainland). *Iter. 267, 268, 269, 270.*

LESLIE, Aberdeen. Map 27, **NJ 5** 2.
On the Gady Burn, looking towards the long ridge of *Bennachie*, to the south-east. The Castle dates from 1661. **2½ m. E.**, beyond *Auchleven*, is the restored mansion of *Lickleyhead*, built in 1629.

LESLIE, Fife. 3,273. SB. Map 17, **NO 2** 0.
E.C. Wed. A small industrial town, with some old houses and a green, which claims to be the scene of the 15th-cent. poem "Christ's Kirk on the Green." The "bull stone" on the green was formerly used to tether bulls when bull-baiting was in progress. *Leslie House*, two wings of which were burnt down in 1763, dates partly from 1670, and stands to the east of the town. **2 m. W.** is the restored *Strathendry Castle*, with a view over *Loch Leven* (*q.v.*). See **Markinch.** *Iter. 98.*

LESMAHAGOW, Lanark. 5,006. Map 9, **NS 8** 4.
E.C. Thurs. GOLF. Known also as *Abbey Green*, and situated on the edge of an extensive moorland area lying to the south-west. The River Nethan flows northwards through the town on its way to join the Clyde at *Crossford* (*q.v.*). The former Priory was famous for its orchards, and the monks may have pioneered the important fruit-growing industry of Clydesdale. In the Hunterian Museum at the University of *Glasgow* (*q.v.*) is preserved the bronze Lesmahagow Flagon, found here in 1810. Alexander Muir, associated with Canada's national anthem, was born at Lesmahagow in 1830. *Iter. 29, 50, 51, 56.*

LESWALT, Wigtown. 821. Map 2, **NX 0** 6.
Iter. 83.

LEUCHARS, Fife. 2,921. Map 17, **NO 4** 2.
E.C. Wed. GOLF. Famous for its Norman Church, one of the finest of its period in the country, noted especially for the chancel and apse, both interior and exterior being richly carved. A 17th cent. bell turret has been added to the structure above the apse. The two carved *Earlshall* stones (1584 and 1635) are of interest. To the east, on the borders of the lonely Tents Moor, with its forestry plantations, is the picturesque old mansion of *Earlshall*, dating from 1546 to 1607, with beautiful gardens, the house having been well restored by Sir Robert Lorimer. See **Guardbridge** and **Tayport.** *Iter. 94.*

LEVEN, Fife. 9,454. SB. Map 17, **NO 3** 0.
E.C. Thurs. GOLF. A Firth of Forth resort and coal port on Largo Bay, with fine sands. The River Leven flows here into the Firth. A re-erected Cross marks the jubilee of King George V. On the promenade is a curious "shell" house. See **Lundin Links.** *Iter. 128.*

LEVERBURGH (Isle of Lewis), Harris, Inverness.
Map 32, **NG 0** 8.
See **Hebrides, Outer** (Harris). *Iter. 257.*

LEWIS, ISLE OF, Ross and Cromarty
(includes **Harris,** Inverness). Map 32, **NB 0** 2, etc.
See **Hebrides, Outer** (Lewis and Harris). *Iter. 256 to 260.*

LEWISTON, Inverness. Map 25, **NH 5** 2.
A hamlet lying a little to the south of *Drumnadrochit* (*q.v.*), at the foot of Glen Urquhart. *Balmacaan House* is now the headquarters of the College of Celtic Art. To the south-west, and reached on foot, are the picturesque Divach Falls, on a tributary of the River Coiltie. *Iter. 207, 210, 213.*

LHANBRYDE, Moray. Map 26, **NJ 2** 6.
Lies in a wooded setting, with the little Loch na Bo to the south-east. **1 m. S.W.** is the well-preserved and white-harled *Coxton Tower*, with its characteristic iron yett, the building dating from 1644, a particularly fine example of its kind. *Iter. 175, 187, 198, 199.*

LIATHACH, Ross and Cromarty. Map 24, **NG 9** 5.
See **Torridon.**

LIBERTON (Edinburgh), Midlothian. 34,610.
Map 10, **NT 2** 6.
To the west rise the *Braid* hills, 698 ft., a public park. *Liberton House* is of early 17th-cent. date, a sundial bearing the date 1683. The house is the successor to the ruined 15th-cent. *Liberton Tower*, situated on a slight ridge, and forming a conspicuous landmark. **1 m. N.N.E.** is *The Inch*, an early 17th-cent. house, with modern additions. *Iter. 10, 24.*

LIDDESDALE, or LIDDISDALE, Roxburgh.
Map 5, **NY 4** 8, etc.
See **Canonbie, Hermitage Castle, Newcastleton and Riccarton.** *Iter. 31, 47.*

LILLIESLEAF, Roxburgh. 416. Map 10 **NT 5** 2.
The Church of 1771 has been enlarged. **2 m. S.W.** is the *Riddell* motte, crowned by a tower of 1885. The old house of *Riddell* was burnt down in 1942.

LIMEKILNS, Fife. Map 16, **NT 0** 8.
The restored 14th century *King's Cellar*, once a storage depot for the court at Dunfermline, is now a Freemasons' Lodge. See **Charlestown.**

LINCLUDEN ABBEY, Kirkcudbright. Map 3, **NX 9** 7.
The red sandstone remains of this Abbey, or College (A.M.),

Leith (Edinburgh), Midlothian. A stone in the quay wall recording the visit of George IV in 1822

Lendalfoot, Ayr. The Memorial recording the drowning of a number of men from the island of Arran in 1711

Leuchars, Fife. The richly carved Norman Church, perhaps the finest of its period in Scotland

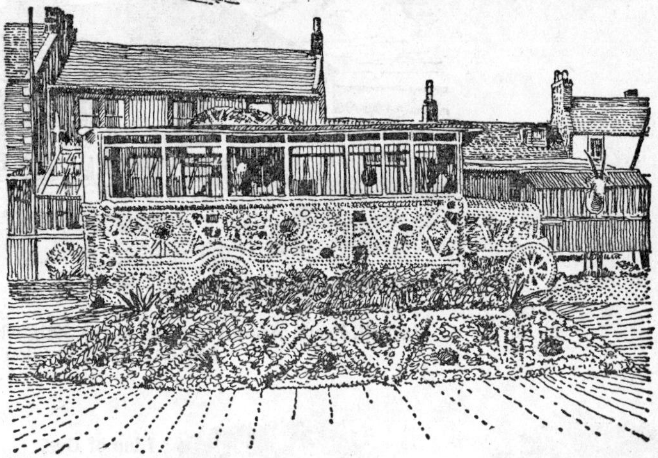

Leven, Fife. The curious 'shell' car on the promenade. A 'shell' house stands adjacent to it

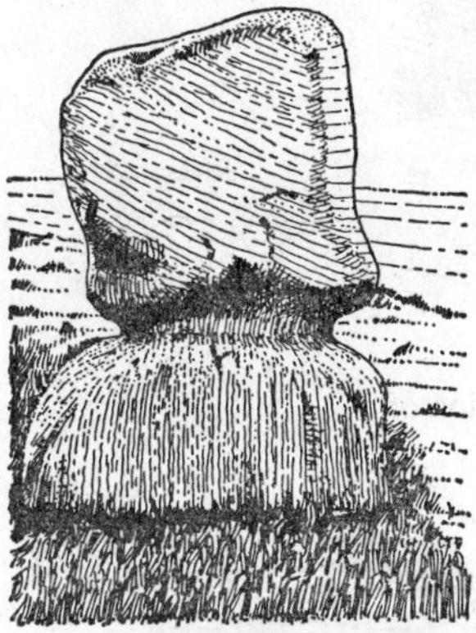

Leslie, Fife. The Bull Stone on the green, which was once used to tether bulls during bull-baiting

Liberton, Midlothian. The ruined 15th century Liberton Tower of the Dalmahoys

[For LEITH see also preceding plate
[For LENDALFOOT see also under **LOWLANDS** (Plate 118)

Linlithgow, West Lothian. The gateway of Linlithgow Palace, which was burnt down accidentally in 1746 by General Hawley's soldiers

Linlithgow, West Lothian. The Cross Well, a reconstruction of 1807. An earlier well was destroyed in 1659 by Cromwell's troops

Lix Toll, Perth. An old toll house, the 59th, which stands at the junction of A85 and A827, in Glen Dochart

Linn of Dee, Aberdeen. A view below the bridge. The poet Byron, as a boy, narrowly escaped drowning in this reach of the river

Linlithgow, West Lothian. The plaque facing the County Buildings, which records the shooting in the street of the Earl of Moray, in 1570

[For LOCHABER see following plate

lie in a lovely setting, near the meeting of the River Nith and the Cluden Water, a little to the north-west of Dumfries, off the Thornhill road. A Benedictine Convent was founded here in the 12th cent., and later it was rebuilt as a Collegiate Church, and still retains portions of the medieval domestic buildings. Of the Church, the richly decorated choir preserves the stone rood-screen, and a tomb of very great beauty to Princess Margaret, who died c. 1430. The arms of the Douglas family appear in various places. Lincluden was a favourite resort of Burns. See **Irongray.** *Iter. 27, 48, 56, 67, 74.*

LINDORES, Fife. Map 17, **NO 2 1.** Situated near the small and reed-surrounded Lindores Loch. About **$2\frac{1}{2}$ m. N.W.,** and to the east of *Newburgh (q.v.)*, lie the scanty remains of *Lindores Abbey* founded in 1178. The groined entrance arch, and a portion of the west tower are the sole substantial survivals of the former structure. In the vicinity is the ruined 16th cent. *Denmylne Castle. Iter. 131, 132.*

LINLITHGOW, West Lothian. 5,685. SB. Map 16, **NS 9 7. E.C.** Wed. **M.D.** Mon. GOLF. This ancient Royal Burgh, famous for its Palace and Church, stands on the south shore of Linlithgow Loch. Its name was at one time given to the county as a whole. In the town are some late 16th cent. houses (several N.T. Scot.), and the fountain of *St. Michael,* dated 1720, inscribed "Saint Michael is kind to strangers." The curious Cross Well, erected in 1807, with its thirteen water jets, is a reproduction of an earlier example. The Earl of Moray, Regent of Scotland, was shot in the street outside the present County Buildings, in 1510, and a plaque set up in 1875 recalls the fact. The last Scottish National Parliament met in the Palace in 1646, and Cromwell garrisoned the town between 1651 and 1659. A fine gateway,

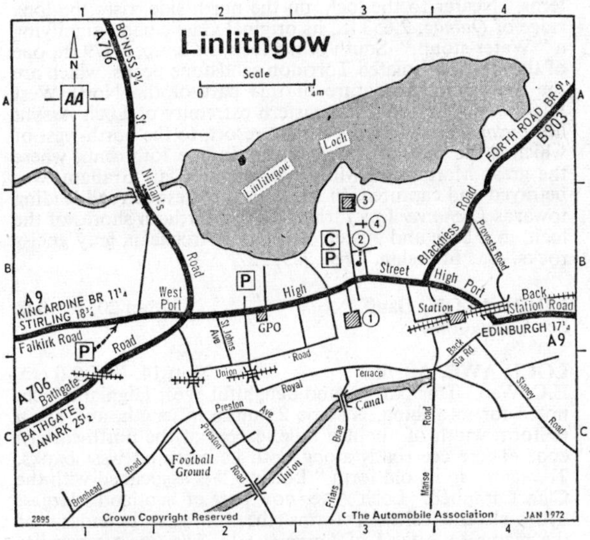

County Buildings	1 (B3)	Palace	3 (B3)
Cross Well	2 (B3)	St. Michael's Church, 1424	4 (B3)

erected by James V, leads to the precincts, in which the Palace and Church are situated. *St. Michael's* Church, one of the finest in Scotland, exhibits strong French characteristics, and was rebuilt after a fire in 1424, though the apse was not finished until 1531. The nave and choir are a fine composition, and in place of transepts there are two chapels, in the southerly of which James IV had the vision of his coming end at Flodden. The window tracery, notably in the Katherine's aisle, is partly in the flamboyant style, and is outstanding for its beauty. The splendid, ruined Palace (A.M.) overlooks the loch, and is the successor to an older building, burnt in 1424. The chapel and magnificent Great Hall are late 15th-cent. work and there is also notable work from the early 16th cent. A fine quadrangle inside the building contains a richly carved 16th cent. fountain. The Royal apartments are on the west side of the quadrangle, and on the 1st floor is the room, where, in 1542, Mary, Queen of Scots was born, while her father, James V, lay dying at *Falkland Palace (q.v.).* Queen Margaret's Bower is the little room in a turret where the Queen kept vigil while James IV fought at Flodden. Prince Charles Edward stayed in the Palace in 1745, but in 1746 it was burnt, probably by accident, by troops of General Hawley. In 1914, King George V held a court in the Lyon Chamber. The Palace is open weekdays, summer, 10 to 7, winter, 10 to 4; Sun., 2 to 7 or 4. (See note page 98.) **2 m. N.,** beyond Linlithgow Loch, on a hill 559 ft. high, is a monument to General Hope, a hero of the Indian Mutiny. **$2\frac{1}{2}$ m. W.** is the ruined 15th cent. *Almond Castle.* See **Abercorn, Blackness, Hopetoun House** and **Torphichen.** *Iter. 86, 91, 95, 96.*

LINN OF DEE, Aberdeen. Map 20, **NO 0 8.** See **Inverey.** *Iter. 179.*

LINWOOD, Renfrew. 2,503. Map 8, **NS 4 6.** A large motor car factory is situated here. *Iter. 64.*

LISMORE, ISLE OF, Argyll. 636 with Appin. Map 14, **NM 8 3** and **8 4.** This flat, green and treeless island lies in Outer *Loch Linnhe (q.v.)*, where its waters mingle with those of the Firth of Lorne and the Sound of Mull. Between Lismore and the nearest point on the mainland is the Lynn of Lorne, threaded by the steamers, whose calling-place is *Achnacroish* pier, on the east side of the island. Lismore was formerly the seat of the Argyll diocese, and the tiny Cathedral, now modernized, is used as the Parish Church. There are associations with St. Moluag, an early saint, who was contemporary with St. Columba. The ruined *Castle Coeffin* is situated on the west coast, in a picturesque setting, not far from the little village of *Clachan.* There are splendid views from points on the island, looking to the hills of *Morven (q.v.)*, and the rugged island of *Mull (q.v.)*. There is a steamer service from *Oban (q.v.)*, and a passenger ferry connects with *Port Appin (q.v.).*

LIVINGSTON, West Lothian. 11,300. Map 9, **NT 0 6.** Being developed as one of the New Towns. *Iter. 18.*

LIX TOLL, Perth. Map 15, **NN 5 3.** *Iter. 107, 111, 120, 138, 139, 142, 144, 145.*

LOANHEAD, Aberdeen. Map 27, **NJ 7 2.** See **Old Meldrum.**

LOANHEAD, Midlothian. 5,931 SB. Map 10, **NT 2 6.** Situated a little to the north of the North Esk River, with the *Pentland* hills rising away to the west.

LOCHABER, Inverness. 10,027. Map 18, **NN 1** 6, etc. The district of *Lochaber,* one of the loveliest in the Highlands, is inseparably bound up with the fortunes and wanderings of Prince Charles Edward. It stretches roughly east of the Great Glen, or *Glen More (q.v.)*, from Loch Leven and Loch Linnhe to *Loch Lochy (q.v.)* and Glen Spean, where it touches the borders of the almost equally lovely *Badenoch (q.v.)* country. The boundaries of Lochaber have varied at different times in the course of history, and at one time the district extended from the Atlantic as far as the country of *Strath Spey (q.v.)*. The name Lochaber is probably derived from a loch of that name, which has long since dried up. The district is divided into the Cameron country of Nether Lochaber, south of *Ben Nevis (q.v.)*, including the *Mamores (q.v.)*, and Brae, or Upper Lochaber, the original land of the MacDonnells of Keppoch, famous for their Gaelic bards, and which lies beyond the Ben. The head of Clan Cameron is Cameron of Locheil, whose ancestral home of *Achnacarry House* stands near the richly wooded shores of *Loch Arkaig (q.v.)*. *Fort William (q.v.)* is the scene of the annual Lochaber gathering. The Lochaber Power Scheme is described under *Ben Nevis, Fort William* and *Loch Laggan.* See **Corran Ferry, Gairlochy, Roy Bridge** and **Spean Bridge.**

LOCH ACHRAY, Perth. Map 15, **NN 5 0.**
See **Trossachs.** *Iter. 106, 111, 139*

LOCHAILORT, Inverness. 58. Map 12, **NM 7 8.**
Beautifully situated at the head of the sea loch of Loch Ailort, backed by a range of high hills, among which *Fros Bheinn*, 2,876 ft., a fine viewpoint, is the most prominent feature. At the seaward end of the loch is the tiny island of Eilean nan Gobhar, where the French ship bringing Prince Charles Edward anchored in July, 1745, at the start of the great, but hopeless adventure, which ended one year later where it had begun. The little River Ailort flows into the loch at Lochailort, having issued, **2 m. E.,** from the exceptionally beautiful *Loch Eilt*, with its picturesque tree-crowned islets, backed by steep rock-strewn hills. The well-known Road to the Isles, " By Ailort and by Morar to the sea," traverses the shores of Loch Eilt from end to end. From the western extremity of this loch, a path climbs northwards through the hills, reaching a height of over 1,000 ft. This path gives a superb view down the narrow and little-known *Loch Beoraid* in the South Morar country. The loch stretches away to the east, hemmed in by lonely mountains, some of which show outcrops of glaciated grey rocks. In the vicinity is a cave in which the Prince hid during his wanderings. The path descends by the Meoble River to the lonely clachan of Meoble, and eventually reaches the remote shores of Loch Morar (See **Morar**). From Lochailort, another path leads south-westwards into picturesque *Moidart* (*q.v.*), first along the shores of Loch Ailort, and later reaching the Sound of Arisaig. Here lies the tiny village of *Glenuig*, at which the Prince landed on his way from *Borrodale House*, near the head of *Loch nan Uamh* (*q.v.*), on his way to *Kinlochmoidart* (*q.v.*). The seaward views along the entire length of this path are splendid. A picturesque new road now links Lochailort with Kinlochmoidart. See **Arisaig.** *Iter. 209, 217.*

LOCHALINE, Argyll. Map 12, **NM 6 4.**
Lying at the seaward end of Loch Aline, with a steamer pier, overlooking the Isle of Mull beyond the Sound of Mull, and with a background of low hills, *Lochaline* is a small, but pleasant *Morven* (*q.v.*) village. Across the narrow mouth of Loch Aline is a flat, wooded stretch, terminating in Ardtornish Point, with the ruins of the 14th-cent. *Ardtornish Castle*, associated with Scott's " Lord of the Isles." Near the Church of Lochaline, at *Keil*, which has carved slabs of interest, one depicting what is perhaps the earliest portrayal of the wearing of the kilt, is an old Cross, which was formerly on the island of *Iona* (*q.v.*). There are important deposits of silica sand on the west shore of Loch Aline. See **Drimnin** and **Larachbeg** (for *Kinlochaline Castle*). *Iter. 218.*

LOCH ALSH, Ross and Cromarty. Map 23, **NG 7 2,** and **8 2.**
One of the finest of the sea lochs of *Wester Ross*, extending inland from the narrow strait of Kyle Akin, which separates Skye from the mainland, to the point where it joins Loch Duich and Loch Long at the *Dornie* (*q.v.*) bridge. The road from Dornie leading westwards towards *Kyle of Lochalsh* (*q.v.*) gives views of the loch and of *Beinn na Cailleach*, 2,396 ft., one of the Skye hills rising above the narrows of *Kyle Rhea*. See **Ardelve, Balmacara** and **Kyleakin.** *Iter. 207, 220, 221, 222.*

LOCHANS, Wigtown. Map 2, **NX 0 5.**
A small Rhinns of Galloway village, a little to the south-east of which is the ruined *Garthland Tower*. *Iter. 81, 83.*

LOCHARBRIGGS, Dumfries. Map 4, **NX 9 8.**
E.C. Thurs. *Iter. 24, 46.*

LOCH ARD, Perth. Map 15, **NN 4 0.**
See **Aberfoyle.**

LOCH ARKAIG, Inverness. Map 18, **NN 0 9.**
This beautiful loch is separated from *Loch Lochy* (*q.v.*), in the Great Glen, by the short length of the River Arkaig. Near the point where the river enters Loch Arkaig is *Achnacarry House*, among its woods, looking westwards to Glen Mallie. This is the ancestral home of Cameron of Lochiel, Chief of Clan Cameron, one of whose ancestors, known as the " gentle Lochiel," was associated with Prince Charles Edward in the '45. The estates were later forfeited by the family, and the original castle burnt in 1746, but in 1784 they were handed back. There are several magnificent tree-lined avenues, the best-known of which is the so-called " Dark Mile," traversed by the road leading from *Gairlochy* (*q.v.*) to Loch Arkaig, with the picturesque Cia-aig Falls on the right. A picturesque, narrow road, degenerating later into a path, leads west along the whole length of the loch, at first in a richly-wooded setting, and later in surroundings becoming gradually wilder, with the bare peaks of *Gulvain*, 3,224 ft., and the *Streaps*, 2,988 ft. and 2,916 ft., rising to the west. At the far end of the loch, paths continue through Glen Dessary and the rocky Glen Pean to the remote shores of *Loch Nevis* (*q.v.*) and Loch Morar respectively. In Glen Dessary lived Jenny Cameron, who was present when the standard of Prince Charles Edward was raised at *Glenfinnan* (*q.v.*), in 1745. A path leading from this glen to Loch Nevis traverses the very picturesque and rugged pass known as the Mam na Cloiche Airde. This wild country in the neighbourhood of Loch Arkaig is associated with the wanderings of Prince Charles Edward after the failure of the '45. *Iter. 214.*

LOCH ARKLET, Stirling. Map 15, **NN 3 0.**
See **Inversnaid.** *Iter. 105.*

LOCH ASSYNT, Sutherland. Map 29, **NC 1 2** and **2 2.**
A lonely and picturesque loch, situated in the heart of the wild, rocky Sutherland mountains, which are dominated to the east by *Ben More Assynt*, 3,273 ft., the highest peak in the county. The district is known for rare plants and ferns. Nearer to the loch, on the north side, rises the long ridge of *Quinag*, 2,653 ft., its original Gaelic name signifying a " Water-stoup." South of the loch is *Canisp*, 2,779 ft., one of the strange, isolated Torridon sandstone peaks, which are the most notable feature of this part of the North-West Highlands. At the south-eastern extremity of Loch Assynt lies *Inchnadamph* (*q.v.*), a fishing resort, to the north-west of which is the shell of *Ardvreck Castle*, late 15th cent., where the great Marquis of Montrose, of the Clan Graham, was betrayed and captured, in 1650. A picturesque road leading towards *Lochinver* (*q.v.*) traverses the northern shores of the loch, in a bare and austere setting of Archaean, grey gneiss rocks. See **Invershin.** *Iter. 225, 227, 228.*

LOCH AVON, Banff. Map 20, **NJ 0 0.**
See **Cairngorms.**

LOCH AWE, Argyll. Map 14, **NM 9 0** etc.
E.C. Wed. This narrow and delightful West Highland loch, noted for its fishing, is some 23 miles in length, and has a uniform width of about a mile, except at the north-eastern end. There are roads along both its east and west banks. The name, in its old form " Lochow," is associated with the Clan Campbell. Loch Awe, now part of Scotland's largest hydro-electric scheme, forms the southern boundary of the picturesque land of *Lorne* (*q.v.*). The finest reach lies under the shadow of the twin-peaked *Ben Cruachan*, where the loch is drained by the River Awe, flowing through the wild Pass of Brander towards *Taynuilt* (*q.v.*), near the shores of Loch Etive. (See **Kilchurn Castle.**) In the vicinity is the wooded island of Fraoch Eilean, with a romantic ruined 14th cent. castle, half-hidden by trees, having been erected by the McNaughtons. On the nearby island of Inishail stands an ancient burial-ground. To the south-west of Loch Awe station stands the beautiful modern Church of *St. Conan*, dedicated in its present form in 1930. See **Falls of Cruachan, Ford, Portinnisherrich** and **Portsonachan.** *Iter. 110, 117, 119, 125, 144, 145.*

LOCH BEORAID, Inverness. Map 12, **NM 8 8.**
See **Lochailort and Morar.**

Lochaber, Inverness. The view across the head of Loch Leven towards the Mamore Forest mountains from A82, near Kinlochleven, in the district of Nether Lochaber

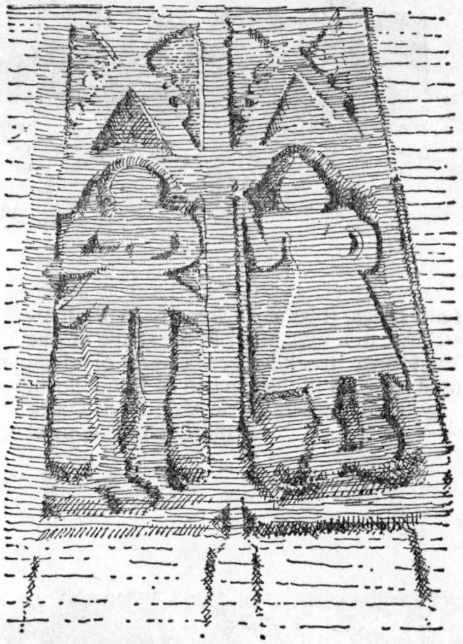

Lochaline, Argyll. A gravestone in Keil churchyard, which depicts what is considered to be perhaps the earliest portrayal of a kilt

Loch Arkaig, Inverness. The Cia-aig Falls, in the tree-lined avenue known as the ' Dark Mile ' (B8005), situated near the eastern end of Loch Arkaig, which is **said to contain treasure hidden by the Jacobites**

Loch Assynt, Sutherland. The remains of Calda House, a one-time home of the Mackenzies, situated off A837, near the south-eastern extremity of the loch. Ardvreck Castle, seen in the distance, is illustrated under Inchnadamph (Plate 86)

Loch Awe, Argyll. The notable modern Church of St. Conan (1881–1930), which stands near the station, on A85, at the northern end of the loch

PLATE 110

I.R.B.S.—12

Loch Doon, Ayr; Kirkcudbright. The ruined 14th century Loch Doon Castle, also known as Balliol's Castle. It stood formerly on an island in the loch and was re-erected on its banks

Loch Duich, Ross and Cromarty. A heather-thatched cattle byre, built in the shape of one of the former 'black houses,' several of which used to stand in the clachan of Bundalloch, by Dornie, where Loch Alsh, Loch Duich and Loch Long meet

Lochearnhead, Perth. The scanty remains of St. Blane's Chapel, at the south-western extremity of Loch Earn

Lochearnhead, Perth. The tombstone to a band of seven Glencoe men, killed when attempting to raid Ardvorlich House, in 1620. It is situated 4 miles east, off the unclassified road on the south shore of the loch, near the entrance to Glen Vorlich

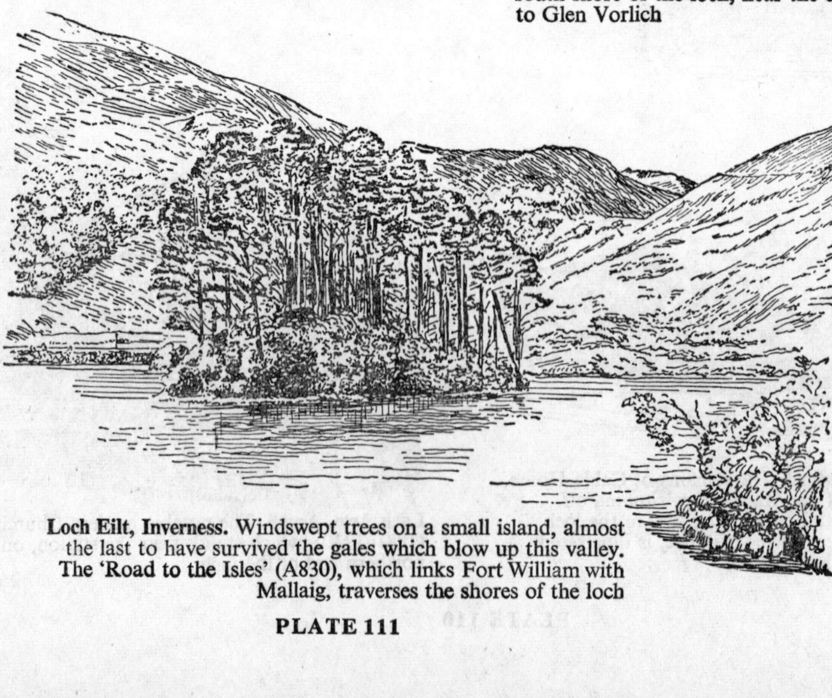

Loch Eilt, Inverness. Windswept trees on a small island, almost the last to have survived the gales which blow up this valley. The 'Road to the Isles' (A830), which links Fort William with Mallaig, traverses the shores of the loch

PLATE 111

LOCHBOISDALE, South Uist, Inverness. Map 32, **NF 7 1.** See **Hebrides, Outer** (South Uist). *Iter. 262.*

LOCH BROOM, Ross and Cromarty. Map 29, **NH 0 9.** This fine *Wester Ross* sea loch stretches south-eastwards from the *Coigach* district into the hills separating the Dundonnell and Inverlael Forests. Near its mouth stands the small fishing town and resort of *Ullapool* (*q.v.*). *Beinn Dearg*, 3,547 ft., dominates the Strath More valley at the head of the loch. To the west of Ullapool, across the loch, rises *Ben Goleach*, 2,082 ft., and beyond it lies Little Loch Broom, along the shores of which goes the road linking Ullapool with *Dundonnell* (*q.v.*), with the great *An Teallach* range dominating the landscape to the south.

LOCHBUIE, Isle of Mull, Argyll. Map 13, **NM 6 2.** On the south side of the island, on the shores of picturesque Loch Buie, overlooked by *Ben Buie*, 2,354 ft., to the north. The ruined *Moy Castle* was a former Maclaine stronghold, and was once visited by Dr. Johnson. To the east is the little Loch Uisg, near which stands a stone circle, and beyond lies the almost land-locked Loch Spelve, traversed by the road leading towards *Craignure* (*q.v.*). Above the road rises *Creach Bheinn*, 2,289 ft., and the cliff scenery in the neighbourhood is remarkable. At the entrance to Loch Buie, on the south-eastern shore, looking towards the Firth of Lorne, is Lovat's Cave, 300 ft., long and 150 ft. high, accessible only by boat. See **Carsaig Bay.** *Iter. 250.*

LOCHCARRON, Ross and Cromarty. 707. Map 24, **NG 9 3.** Known also as *Jeantown*, this attractive village lies on the shores of Inner Loch Carron, at the point of divergence of the road leading to the famous Pass of the Cattle, which gives access from *Tornapress* (*q.v.*) to *Applecross* (*q.v.*). There is a little fishing harbour at Slumbay, to the south-west of the village. On the Tornapress road, to the west, is the miniature Pass of Kishorn, which leads towards the shores of Loch Kishorn and the tiny village of *Kishorn* (*q.v.*). This loch leads into Outer Loch Carron, the widening waters of which merge into the Inner Sound facing Skye. North-west of the village is the thickly-wooded *Allt-nen-Carman* National Nature Reserve. Perhaps the prettiest spot on Loch Carron is the village of *Plockton* (*q.v.*). See **Shieldaig** and **Strome.** *Iter. 219, 223.*

LOCH CORUISK, Isle of Skye, Inverness. Map 23, **NG 4 2.** This wild and picturesque loch lies in what is considered to be the grandest mountain amphitheatre in Great Britain, and is separated from the sea loch of *Loch Scavaig* (*q.v.*) by a narrow neck of land. Access is generally gained by boat from *Elgol* (*q.v.*), but long-distance paths are also available, from Elgol by way of Camasunary and the notorious "Bad Step," and also from *Sligachan* (*q.v.*) by means of the low Drumhain ridge. By far the most impressive view of the loch is gained by climbing the steep and rocky little peak of *Sgurr na Stri*, 1,623 ft., which rises at the south-eastern extremity of Loch Coruisk. This hill faces directly towards the great cirque of the *Coolins* (*q.v.*) massed to the west, with a view, beyond the corrie of Coire-uisg, of the almost unapproachable "Inaccessible Pinnacle" perched near the rocky summit of *Sgurr Dearg*, 3,254 ft. Sir Walter Scott, in his "Lord of the Isles," has described the loch, and John Buchan's "Mr. Standfast" contains local colour, while Turner and countless others have essayed to portray the savage beauty of the scene in its deep-set mountain-girdled hollow. The grandeur of the mountain scenery of Loch Coruisk is rivalled only by *Loch Hourn* (*q.v.*), the finest of the great sea lochs of the Western Highlands. *Iter. 252.*

LOCH DOON, Ayr; Kirkcudbright. Map 2, **NX 4 9.** A long, narrow loch, surrounded by hills. At its northern extremity lies the picturesque Ness Glen. A road traverses the western shores, passing the 14th-cent. island-castle of *Loch Doon* (A.M.), now carefully re-erected by the road-side. The waters of the loch form part of the extensive Galloway Power Scheme. West of the loch is the Carrick Forest area, part of the Glen Trool Forest Park. The lonely Lochs Recar and Macaterick are situated here, with the waters of the Eglin Lane and the Gala Lane to the east. The hills rising to the south of Loch Doon include *Shalloch on Minnoch*, 2,520 ft., *Kirriereoch Hill*, 2,562 ft., *Corserine*, 2,668 ft. and *Carlin's Cairn* 2,650 ft., some of the best known of the *Galloway* heights. *Iter. 74, 75, 76, 77.*

LOCH DUICH, Ross and Cromarty. Map 24, NG **8 2.** A very beautiful North-West Highland sea loch, extending from *Shiel Bridge* (*q.v.*), at the northern extremity of the magnificent mountain-encircled defile of *Glen Shiel* (*q.v.*), to *Dornie* (*q.v.*). There it is joined by Loch Long, the combined waters then uniting to join Loch Alsh, which stretches as far as the shores of Skye. Beyond Shiel Bridge, there are roads on both sides of Loch Duich, that on the eastern shore proceeding towards Dornie and *Kyle of Lochalsh* (*q.v.*), forming part of one of the "Roads to the Isles," and considered one of the loveliest roads in Scotland. That on the western shore terminates at *Totaig*, which is linked by a passenger ferry to the *Ardelve* (*q.v.*) side of Dornie Bridge. A branch to the left off the road leading towards Totaig climbs over the steep and narrow *Mam Rattachan Pass* (*q.v.*) to *Glenelg* (*q.v.*). The outstanding feature of the views from Loch Duich is the fine ridge known as the *Five Sisters of Kintail*, dominated by *Scour Ouran*, 3,505 ft., which towers over Glen Shiel, away to the south-east of the loch, and forms part of the *Kintail* (*q.v.*) estate (N.T. Scot.). See **Croe Bridge, Dornie** (for *Eilean Donan Castle*) and **Inverinate.** *Iter. 207, 220.*

LOCHEARNHEAD, Perth. 300. Map 15, **NN 5** 2. **E.C.** Wed. A small touring centre, situated at the western extremity of the charmingly wooded Loch Earn (water skiing), which stretches eastwards for some six miles. Highland Games are held here in July. The resort of *St. Fillan's* (*q.v.*) lies at the far end of the loch. Near the south shore of the loch is the ruined *St. Blane's* Chapel, and a little farther east is the entrance to Glen Ample, with a waterfall, facing the old, castellated mansion of *Edinample*. The glen is associated with Scott's "Legend of Montrose," as is also *Ardvorlich House*, **2 m. E.,** by the lochside. In this house is preserved the Clach Dearg, a famous talisman of rock-crystal. By the road-side near the house is a stone recalling the slaying of seven Macdonalds of Glencoe, who were trying to raid Ardvorlich. North of the loch rise the hills of the *Breadalbane* (*q.v.*) country, and to the south are the lofty summits of *Ben Vorlich*, 3,224 ft., and *Stuc a' Chroin*, 3,189 ft. Roads traverse the shores of the loch on both sides, the main road on the north bank giving the best mountain views, while that to the south is narrow and hilly. To the north of Lochearnhead is the gloomy defile of Glen Ogle, leading towards Glen Dochart and *Killin* (*q.v.*), the road through the pass attaining a height of 948 ft. See **Balquhidder.** *Iter. 107, 111, 138, 139, 141, 142, 144, 145.*

LOCH ECK, Argyll. Map 14, **NS 1** 8 and **1 9.** This lonely and charming hill-encircled loch lies in the *Cowal* (*q.v.*) peninsula, which divides *Loch Fyne* (*q.v.*) from Loch Long and the Clyde estuary. To the south-west of the loch rises *Beinn Mhor*, 2,433 ft., one of the highest points in this district. The slopes of the hills overlooking Loch Eck are clothed with a forest of variegated spruces, an unusual and attractive picture. A delightful road traverses the eastern shores of the loch, linking *Strachur* (*q.v.*) with the inner waters of the Holy Loch and the resort of *Dunoon* (*q.v.*). *Iter. 102, 137.*

LOCH EILT, Inverness. Map 12, **NM 8 8.** See **Lochailort.** *Iter. 209.*

LOCH ERIBOLL, Sutherland. Map 28, **NC 4** 5 and **4** 6. See **Eriboll, Heilim** and **Rispond.** *Iter. 225.*

LOCH ERICHT, Inverness; Perth. Map 19, NN **5** 6 etc. See **Dalwhinnie** and **Kinloch Rannoch.**

LOCH ETIVE, Argyll. Map 14, **NM 9** 3 and **NN 0** 3. This narrow sea loch extends from the Firth of Lorne to the foot of Glen Etive, where there is a steamer pier, and a narrow road, bordered by the *Dalness* Forest (N.T. Scot.) mountains, leads towards *Kingshouse* (*q.v.*). *Ben Starav*, 3,541 ft., *Stob Coir'an Albannaich*, 3,425 ft. and *Ben Trillea-*

chan, 2,752 ft., dominate the head of the loch. Farther to the south, beyond Glen Kinglass and Glen Noe, rises the twin-peaked *Ben Cruachan*, 3,689 ft., and here the loch turns westwards to reach the narrows at *Connel* (*q.v.*), where the Falls of Lora are situated.

LOCHFOOT, Kirkcudbright. Map 3, **NX 8 7**.
A tiny village on the northern shores of the small Lochrutton Loch. **1½ m. S.E.** is the restored *Hills Castle*, mid-16th cent., joined to an early 18th cent. house, and preserving a rare gatehouse of the early 17th cent.

LOCH FYNE, Argyll. Map 7, **NR 8 7** and 14, **NR 9 9** etc.
One of the best-known of the Scottish sea lochs, famous for its herrings. It extends for about 40 miles from a little beyond *Inveraray* (*q.v.*), in the north, to the Sound of Bute, which separates the Island of Bute from the shores of the *Kintyre* (*q.v.*) peninsula. As with most of the sea lochs, the finest scenery is around the head, near *Cairndow* (*q.v.*), where the peaks of *Beinn Bhuidhe*, 3,106 ft., *Binnein an Fhidleir*, 2,658 ft., and *Beinn an Lochain*, 3,021 ft., overlook its waters. From here, a picturesque road climbs through Glen Kinglas, and descends past *Rest and be Thankful* (*q.v.*) to Glen Croe and the head of Loch Long at *Arrochar* (*q.v.*). Beyond *Otter Ferry* (*q.v.*), in the hilly *Cowal* (*q.v.*) country, the loch widens, with the heights of *Knapdale* (*q.v.*) as a background to the western shores. See **Ardrishaig** and **Tarbert** (Argyll). *Iter. 88, 101, 102, 103, 118, 121, 122, 137.*

LOCHGAIR, Argyll. Map 14, **NR 9 9**.
Situated on Loch Gair, a tiny inlet of *Loch Fyne* (*q.v.*). To the north-west is the little Loch Glashan. *Iter. 118, 121.*

LOCH GARTEN, Inverness. Map 25, **NH 9 1**.
See **Boat of Garten.**

LOCHGELLY, Fife. 8,772. SB. Map 17, **NT 1 9**.
A town situated on the Fife coalfield. The little Loch Gelly lies just to the south-east.

LOCHGILPHEAD, Argyll. 1,184. SB. Map 14, **NR 8 8**.
E.C. Tues. **M.D.** Mon. This small town stands at the head of Loch Gilp, an inlet of the larger *Loch Fyne* (*q.v.*). The Crinan Canal flows to the west on its way from *Crinan* (*q.v.*) to Loch Gilp at *Ardrishaig* (*q.v.*). There are views of the low *Knapdale* (*q.v.*) hills to the south-west. A little to the north is the chambered cairn of *Auchnahoish*, a notable prehistoric monument. See **Kilmartin, Kilmichael** and **Lochgair.** *Iter. 118, 121.*

LOCHGOILHEAD, Argyll. 300. Map 14, **NN 2 0**.
Situated in a hollow below lofty *Cowal* (*q.v.*) hills, with a pier at the shingly head of attractive Loch Goil, a stretch of water diverging from the larger Loch Long to the south-east. A steep and narrow road leads northwards from Lochgoilhead, dividing after about two miles, the eastern fork leading towards the well-known *Rest and be Thankful* (*q.v.*). The western branch traverses the rocky and lonely *Hell's Glen*, before debouching on to the eastern shores of *Loch Fyne* (*q.v.*) by means of steep zig-zags. On the western shores of Loch Goil, and well seen from the loch steamers, stands the ruined *Carrick Castle*, perhaps 14th cent., which was burnt down in 1685. A narrow road leads from Lochgoilhead along the shores of the loch as far as this point. Across the loch, and extending along the western shore of Loch Long, is a range of hills over 2,000 ft. high known as *Argyll's Bowling Green*. These form part of the Ardgoil estate (Argyll Forest Park), which has been donated to the city of Glasgow. See **Arrochar.** *Iter. 102.*

LOCH HOURN, Inverness. Map 18, **NG 8 1** and 23, **NG 7 1** etc.
Competent judges declare this loch, which lies in the remote district of *Knoydart* (*q.v.*), to be the grandest of the great sea lochs of the Western Highlands. Its mountain setting is certainly unequalled, the scenery providing a picturesque blending of savage, rocky slopes, together with stretches of woodland, consisting partly of Scots pines from the ancient forests, and partly of trees newly-planted by the Forestry Commission. The whole picture comes perhaps nearest in Great Britain to approximate in grandeur to the Norwegian fjords, especially in the land-locked inner reach around *Kinloch Hourn* (*q.v.*). Loch Hourn is divided by a narrow strait, known as Caolas Mor, into the Inner and Outer lochs, and each section has a poor and narrow road leading steeply to its shores. The magnificent Inner Loch is reached by a road commencing at *Tomdoun* (*q.v.*) in Glen Garry, and later passing *Loch Quoich* (*q.v.*) before descending steeply (1 in 6 and very rough) the 600 ft. to Kinloch Hourn, on its shores, amid a wilderness of glaciated grey rocks on the lofty mountain flanks. The Outer Loch can be reached from *Glenelg* (*q.v.*) by means of a rough road traversing the shores of the Sound of Sleat, facing across to Skye, and providing magnificent seaward views. This road bends round Outer Loch Hourn and terminates near *Arnisdale* (*q.v.*), dominated by *Ben Sgriol*, 3,196 ft. Across the loch rises *Ladhar Bheinn*, 3,343 ft., the most westerly 3,000-ft. peak on the mainland, forming a splendid viewpoint. The mountain can be climbed from *Inverie* (*q.v.*) on *Loch Nevis* (*q.v.*), which is linked to Loch Hourn by a path from Barrisdale Bay through Glen Dulochan below *Luinne Bheinn*, 3,083 ft., the track reaching a height of nearly 1,100 ft. Perhaps the finest of all views of the loch is that obtained by climbing the rock-strewn peak of *Sgurr a'Mhoraire*, 3,365 ft., which rises to the east of the Inner Loch, and can be approached from the steep road leading inland from Kinloch Hourn towards Loch Quoich. *Iter. 207, 214.*

LOCHINCH, Wigtown. Map 2, **NX 1 6**.
See **Castle Kennedy.**

LOCHINDORB, Moray. Map 25, **NH 9 3**.
This little loch, situated high up on the west side of the bleak *Dava Moor*, is best known for the ruins of the sinister *Lochindorb Castle*, on its island site, once occupied by Edward III, in 1303, and later becoming a stronghold of the notorious Wolf of Badenoch. In the reign of James II the structure was destroyed. A narrow road, diverging from the Grantown-on-Spey to Forres main road, climbs on to moorland to traverse the eastern shores of the loch, and then leads south-westwards towards a road which attains some 1,200 ft., linking Carrbridge with Forres. *Iter. 173, 177.*

LOCHINVAR, Kirkcudbright. Map 3, **NX 6 8**.
See **Dalry** (Kirkcudbright).

LOCHINVER, Sutherland. Map 29, **NC 0 2**.
One of the most beautiful small resorts on the wild, rocky coast of the *Assynt* district in the North-West Highlands, with a pier at the stony head of Loch Inver. Into the loch flows the River Inver, at the end of its short, but picturesque partly-wooded course from the western extremity of *Loch Assynt* (*q.v.*). *Lochinver* is well known for fishing, being surrounded by a maze of numerous tiny lochans in all directions. To the south-east lies the Glencanisp Forest, in which are situated the isolated Torridon sandstone peaks of *Canisp*, 2,779 ft., and *Suilven*, 2,399 ft. The latter, one of the most striking on the mainland, has been called the "Matterhorn" of Scotland. Its summit, a notable viewpoint, forms a ridge a mile and a half long, with a sharp eastern peak, well seen from the neighbourhood of *Altnacealgach* (*q.v.*). The better-known western peak resembles a gigantic sugarloaf, virtually unclimbable, and is a striking object when seen from various points on the coast around Lochinver, notably from the rocky shores of Loch Roe, which lies to the north-west, on

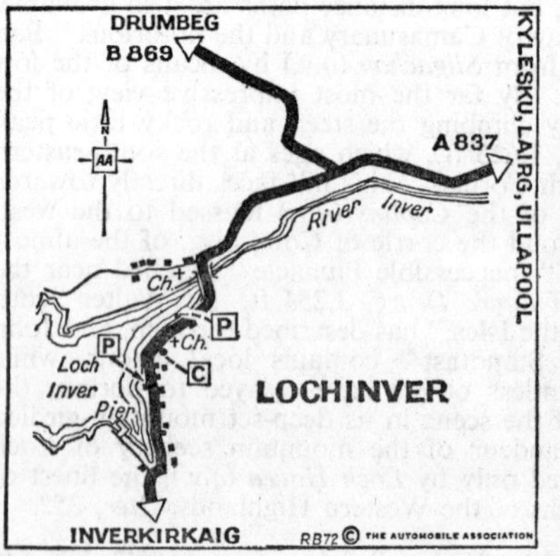

Lochinver, Sutherland. The 'sugar-loaf' double peak of Suilven, 2,399 feet high, seen from a point on A837, some 5 or 6 miles to the south-west. The view from the summit ranges over a barren landscape of isolated peaks interspersed with innumerable small lochs.

Lochgoilhead, Argyll. The remains of the 14th century Carrick Castle, of the Earls of Argyll, burnt in 1685. It stands 5 miles south, on an unclassified road on the west shore of Loch Goil

Loch Fyne, Argyll. An archway in the town of Inveraray, on Loch Fyne. It spans A819, leading northwards towards the richly wooded Glen Aray

Loch Fyne, Argyll. The 18th century bridge carrying A83 across the River Shira, where it enters Loch Shira, an inlet of Loch Fyne, a little to the north-east of Inveraray

Lochfoot, Kirkcudbright. Hills Castle, 16th to 18th century, which has its original 'yett,' or grated iron door. It stands on an unclassified road about $1\frac{1}{2}$ miles to the south-east

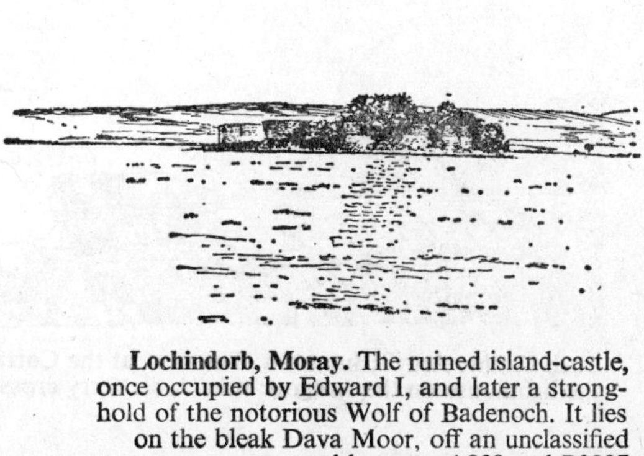

Lochindorb, Moray. The ruined island-castle, once occupied by Edward I, and later a stronghold of the notorious Wolf of Badenoch. It lies on the bleak Dava Moor, off an unclassified road between A939 and B9007

Loch Katrine, Perth. Ellen's Isle, facing the now submerged 'Silver Strand,' associated with Sir Walter Scott's poem, '*The Lady of the Lake*'

Lochlee, Angus. The ruined Invermark Castle of the Stirlings, which stands between the church and Loch Lee, on an unclassified road

Loch Leven, Kinross. The 15th century island-castle from which Mary, Queen of Scots, made her sensational escape in 1568. The notorious Wolf of Badenoch, and Patrick Grahame, Primate of Scotland, were also imprisoned here at different times

Loch Lochy, Inverness. The former 'Letterfinlay' Inn, which General Wade's soldiers used as a road-house during the construction of the road in the early 18th century. It stands on the east shore of the loch, on A82

Loch Lomond, Dunbarton; Stirling. A plinth, with the figure of a child, placed in the loch near Luss, a Dunbartonshire village on A82. It was erected by William Kerr, who made a fortune in England and returned to visit his boyhood home some 70 years ago

Loch Linnhe, Argyll; Inverness. The view at the Corran narrows, looking towards the lighthouse on the Ardgour side. A car ferry crosses the loch at this point

[For LOCH LEVEN (Argyll) see under LOCHABER (Plate 110)
[For LOCH KATRINE see also under HIGHLANDS (Plate 84) and TROSSACHS (Plate 165)
[For LOCH LINNHE see also under ARDGOUR (Plate 8)

the road to Stoer. It is also seen from points on the very wild and beautiful road leading southwards towards *Inverkirkaig* (*q.v.*) and the lovely Enard Bay. This narrow and hilly road has been described as the " mad little road of Sutherland." North-westwards from Lochinver, a most picturesque road, narrow and steep in places, follows the coast by way of *Stoer* (*q.v.*) to *Kylesku* (*q.v.*), giving magnificent views of the remarkable Sutherland peaks, and of the distant island of Skye beyond the Minch. See **Achiltibuie, Drumbeg, Inchnadamph** and **Loch Lurgain.** *Iter. 226, 227, 228.*

LOCH KATRINE, Perth; Stirling. Map 15, **NN 40 and 4 1.**
This Perthshire loch, the north-western extremity of which extends into Stirlingshire, is one of the loveliest in the Highlands, and is ringed with hills, the most prominent of which is the bare and rocky *Ben Venue*, 2,393 ft., which rises beyond the south-east corner. There are associations with the romantic works of Sir Walter Scott, notably the " Lady of the Lake," in which Ellen's Isle and the now-vanished " Silver Strand " appear. Steamers ply on the loch from Loch Katrine pier, but no roads encircle the shores, that on the north bank being private, though available for pedestrians who can reach *Glengyle*, the birthplace of Rob Roy. The waters of the loch are used in connection with Glasgow's water supply by means of a subterranean aqueduct. The richly-wooded *Trossachs* (*q.v.*) district, with *Ben A'an*, 1,750 ft., fringes the loch, and part of the Queen Elizabeth Forest Park is in the vicinity. See **Aberfoyle** and **Stronachlachar.** *Iter. 106, 111, 139.*

LOCH LAGGAN, Inverness. Map 19, **NN 4** 8 and **5** 8.
Works in connection with the Lochaber Power Scheme (See **Ben Nevis** and **Fort William**) have caused the appearance of wooded Loch Laggan to be greatly changed. A large reservoir is now situated to the south-west, at the far end of which is the great *Laggan Dam*, near the outflow to the River Spean, in *Glen Spean.* A tunnel connects with the waters of Loch Treig, away to the south. During works in connection with the scheme, several ancient dug-out canoes were taken from the loch. Lofty mountains rise above the north shore of Loch Laggan, and beyond *Aberarder* farm, about halfway along the loch, is the entrance to the wild Coire Ardair, with its remote lochan, above which rises *Creag Meaghaidh*, 3,700 ft., the highest point in a range of hills which falls but little below the 3,000-ft. level for nearly 10 miles. Beyond the dam, farther to the west, on the north side of the road, are " Parallel Roads," similar to the better-known examples to be found near *Roy Bridge* (*q.v.*). At the north-east extremity of the loch, the River Pattack, on which is situated the Linn of Pattack, flows near the Kingussie road in Ardverikie Forest prior to entering the loch. See **Dalwhinnie, Drumgask, Newtonmore** and **Tulloch.** *Iter. 143, 208.*

LOCHLEE, Angus. 1,034 with Edzell. Map 21, **NO 4** 8.
Beyond the Church, a little to the south-west, is situated the little Loch Lee, at the terminal point of the long and beautiful valley of Glen Esk, threaded by the North Esk River. The glen extends far into this corner of the eastern Grampian, or *Benchinnan* mountains from the neighbourhood of *Edzell* (*q.v.*). A short distance from the Church, to the east of the loch, where the Water of Mark comes down from Glen Mark, stand the remains of *Invermark Castle.* To the north rises *Mount Keen*, 3,077 ft., climbed by Queen Victoria and the Prince Consort in 1861, and away to the west is the *White Mounth* (*q.v.*) group, dominated by *Lochnagar*, 3,786 ft. (*q.v.*). On the path leading towards Mount Keen is the Queen's Well, commemorating the ascent by Queen Victoria, and along the western shoulder of the mountain goes the Mounth track, giving access for walkers through Glen Tanner to *Aboyne* (*q.v.*). See **Tarfside.** *Iter. 164.*

LOCH LEVEN, Argyll; Inverness. Map 18, **NN 1** 6 etc.
See **Ballachulish, Carnach, Kinlochleven** and **North Ballachulish.** *Iter. 100, 124, 125, 142.*

LOCH LEVEN, Kinross. Map 17, **NT 1** 9 and **NO 1** 0.
This attractive loch, now a Nature Reserve, lies east of *Kinross* (*q.v.*), and is famous for its pink-trout fishing and its historic associations. On *St. Serf's* island are the remains of an old Priory, and on Castle Island is the ruined 15th cent. *Loch Leven Castle* (A.M.), from which Mary, Queen of Scots made her celebrated escape, in 1568, after having spent nearly a year imprisoned in the tower. The Queen escaped with the help of William Douglas, a friend of George Douglas, the gaoler's son. William Douglas, after having stolen the castle keys and locked the building, threw them into the loch after the Queen had entered a boat. Scott's novel, " The Abbot," has immortalized the well-known story. To the east of the loch rise the *Lomond* hills, with *Bishop Hill* and *West Lomond*, the latter rising to 1,713 ft., while away to the south is *Benarty Hill*, 1,167 ft. See **Carberry Hill** and **Kirkliston.** *Iter. 90, 92, 98.*

LOCH LINNHE, Argyll; Inverness. Map 14, **NM 8** 4 and 18, **NN 0** 6 etc.
This fine sea loch extends for a distance of some 35 miles, from its meeting with Loch Eil at the western extremity of the Great Glen, or *Glen More* (*q.v.*), to Duart Point in the island of Mull, beyond the smaller island of Lismore in the Firth of *Lorne* (*q.v.*). Loch Linnhe falls naturally into two sub-divisions, an inner and an outer loch, which are separated by the Corran narrows, crossed by the car ferry at *Corran* (*q.v.*) linking the *Lochaber* (*q.v.*) and *Ardgour* (*q.v.*) districts. The inner stretch of the loch, to the north-east of the narrows, is dominated by *Ben Nevis* (*q.v.*) and the range of *Mamore Forest* (*q.v.*). To the north of *Fort William* (*q.v.*), the *Caledonian Canal* (*q.v.*) issues into Loch Linnhe and Loch Eil at *Corpach* (*q.v.*). Beyond the Corran narrows, after being joined by Loch Leven, the loch broadens out, and its waters are overlooked by the *Ben Vair* ridges of the *Appin* (*q.v.*) country, and also by the sharp peak of *Garbh Bheinn* in Ardgour, rising behind *Inversanda* (*q.v.*). There are roads on each shore of the inner loch, and also for some distance on both shores of the outer loch, but the best way to appreciate the splendid mountain scenery along its entire length is to make a journey on one of the regular steamers which link Fort William with Oban in the summer months. *Iter. 100, 124, 125, 142, 215, 216, 217, 218.*

LOCH LOCHY, Inverness. Map 18, **NN 2** 8 and **2** 9.
One of the chain of lochs in the Great Glen, or *Glen More* (*q.v.*), forming part of the waterway known as the *Caledonian Canal* (*q.v.*), and at the north-western extremity of which are situated the *Laggan Locks* (*q.v.*). The shores of Loch Lochy are for the most part hilly and sometimes wooded, the highest mountains being on the north side, in Glengarry Forest, where *Sron a'Choire Ghairbh* attains 3,066 ft., and the sharp cone of *Ben Tee* is 2,956 ft. in height. The main Fort William to Inverness road traverses the eastern shores of the loch, and about half-way along its length is the former "*Letterfinlay*" Inn, a road-house for General Wade's soldiers when the original road was being built, and once visited by Wordsworth and his sister. About **4 m. S.W.** of Letterfinlay is the entrance to Glen Gloy, a long, roadless valley leading into lonely hills, in which are situated some " Parallel Roads," similar to the better-known examples near *Roy Bridge* (*q.v.*). See **Gairlochy, Loch Arkaig** and **Loch Oich.** *Iter. 210, 214, 220.*

LOCH LOMOND, Dunbarton; Stirling. Map 15, **NS 3** 9 etc.
This famous and beautiful inland loch, known as the " Queen of Scottish Lakes," and noted for its fishing, is the largest in Great Britain. It is some 23 miles long and 5 miles broad at its widest point, though a long stretch in the north is less than a mile in width. The south-east corner has been declared a Nature Reserve. Steamers, calling at various points, traverse its full length, from *Balloch* (*q.v.*) in the south, to *Ardlui* (*q.v.*) in the north. The writings of Sir Walter Scott have done much to make the loch so well known, and Smollett admired it greatly, but both Dr. Johnson and Wordsworth were less enthusiastic. In the lower part of the loch are a number of wooded islands, and roads traverse both the east and west shores, but beyond *Rowardennan* (*q.v.*), on the eastern side, there is no road. On *Inchmurrin* island, to the north of Balloch, are situated the ruins of *Lennox Castle. Ben Lomond*, 3,192 ft., the most prominent feature in views of Loch Lomond, rises to the east of the loch, opposite *Tarbet* (*q.v.*), and is best climbed

from Rowardennan. The view from the summit is very extensive, extending from the Arran hills to Ben Cruachan. A narrow neck of land on the west side separates Loch Lomond from the northern extremity of Loch Long at *Arrochar* (*q.v.*). Later, lofty hills close in beyond the shores, the most notable being to the west, where *Ben Ime*, 3,318 ft., *Ben Vane*, 3 004 ft., and *Ben Vorlich*, 3,092 ft., make an impressive picture. Between the two last-named mountains lies Glen Sloy, sheltering Loch Sloy, its waters now harnessed to one of the hydro-electric schemes. The powerhouse at *Inveruglas* (*q.v.*) was opened by Her Majesty Queen Elizabeth, the Queen Mother, in October, 1950. The head of Loch Lomond, near Ardlui, is very beautiful, and the fine road along the whole length of the wooded western shores, traversed annually by thousands of tourists, continues northwards into Perthshire, through picturesque Glen Falloch, to reach *Crianlarich* (*q.v.*). See **Inversnaid** and **Luss.** *Iter. 88, 100, 101, 104, 105, 110, 111, 115, 137.*

LOCH LONG, Argyll; Dunbarton. Map 14, **NS 2** 8 etc. A long and narrow sea loch, extending for some 16 miles from its head at Arrochar to its mouth, where the waters are joined with those of the widening Clyde estuary. Near Arrochar rises the prominent rock peak of *Ben Arthur* (*The Cobbler*), 2,891 ft., and farther south is the line of hills known as *Argyll's Bowling Green*, which overlooks Loch Goil near its junction with Loch Long. At the mouth of Loch Long is Strone Point, where the Holy Loch also meets the Clyde estuary, into which at this point extends the *Rosneath* peninsula, dividing Loch Long from the Gare Loch. On the eastern bank, north of the Gare Loch, is the new oil-port of *Finnart*. See **Ardentinny, Arrochar, Coulport, Kilcreggan and Whistlefield.** *Iter. 88, 101, 102, 103, 111, 116, 137.*

LOCH LONG, Ross and Cromarty.
Map 24, **NG 8** 2 and **9** 2.
See **Ardelve, Dornie** and **Falls of Glomach.** *Iter. 207, 220.*

LOCH LURGAIN, Ross and Cromarty. Map 29, **NC 1** 0. This remote North-West Highland loch is comparatively little known, owing to its situation away from any main road, but its mountain setting is one of the finest in Scotland, and a visit would be eminently worth the extra trouble involved. A narrow road, leading off the Ullapool to Inchnadamph road, traverses its northern shores, above which rise *Cul Beag*, 2,523 ft., and later *An Stac*, or *Stack Polly*, 2,009 ft., an amazing little mountain, with a summit ridge of sharp and practically unclimbable rock pinnacles overlooking Inverpolly Forest. Behind these two peaks is the still higher *Cul Mor*, 2,786 ft., one of the isolated Torridon sandstone hills of the district. Beyond the roadless south shore of the loch is *Beinn Eun*, which faces *Ben More Coigach*, 2,438 ft., a magnificent viewpoint, overlooking Outer Loch Broom, and the Coigach district. Between these two hills lies the tiny Lochan Tuath, overlooked by the great crag of *Sgurr an Fhidhleir*, 2,285 ft. At the west end of Loch Lurgain lies Loch Baddagyle, along the shores of which the road continues towards *Baddagyle* (*q.v.*) and the picturesque, rocky seaboard at *Achiltibuie* (*q.v.*) and Enard Bay. *Iter. 226.*

LOCHMABEN, Dumfries. 1.250. SB. Map 4, **NY 0** 8. **E.C.** Thurs. A small Annandale Royal Burgh, which is situated between the Castle Loch, to the south-east, the Kirk and Mill Lochs, to the north-west, and the Brumel Loch, to the east. In the Castle Loch, and also in two other lochs in the vicinity, is found the vendace, a rare species of fish. Castle Loch and Hightae Loch are Nature Reserves. Lochmaben's Mercat Cross displays sundials on the faces of the top block. At the southern extremity of the Castle Loch stands the ruined *Lochmaben Castle* (A.M.), which may have been the birthplace of Robert Bruce, though *Turnberry* (*q.v.*) also claims this honour. To the north of Lochmaben, the Water of Ae is joined by the Kinnel Water, the combined streams shortly uniting with the River Annan, which flows to the east of the Castle Loch in a series of acute bends through Annandale. **2 m. N.N.W.** of Lochmaben, on the banks of the Water of Ae, stands the late 16th cent. *Elshieshields Tower*, partly modernized and joined to an 18th cent. house. **3 m. S.W.** is *Skipmyre*, the birthplace, in 1658, of William Paterson, who is associated with the founding of the Bank of England. See **Lockerbie** and **Torthorwald.** *Iter. 45.*

LOCHMADDY, North Uist, Inverness. Map 32, **NF 9** 6. See **Hebrides, Outer** (North Uist). *Iter. 261.*

LOCH MAREE, Ross and Cromarty.
Map 22, **NG 8** 7 and 24, **NG 9** 6 etc.
One of the loveliest of the North-West Highland lochs in *Wester Ross*. It is well known to fishermen, being some 12 miles in length, and separated by less than two miles of land, traversed by the short River Ewe, from the sea loch of Ewe, which may at one time have been joined to Loch Maree. The finest mountain scenery is at the south-east end of the loch, where *Slioch*, 3,260 ft., a notable landmark and a grand viewpoint, rises in steep, rocky slopes above the eastern shores. To the north-west of Slioch is *Ben Lair*, 2,817 ft., with its great cliffs, and farther away is *Beinn Airidh Charr*, 2,593 ft. The road along Loch Maree traverses the western shores. passing *Grudie Bridge*, from where a magnificent view is gained towards the grand Torridon peaks to the south, from *Beinn a Chearcaill*, 2,376 ft., to the much loftier *Ben Eighe*, 3,220 ft., and *Liathach* 3,456 ft. Beyond Grudie Bridge is situated the "*Loch Maree*" Hotel, opposite which lie a number of picturesque, wooded islands, one of which is *Isle Maree*, on which are slight remains of a chapel, the successor to an early hermitage of *St. Maelrubha*. South of the hotel rise *Beinn an Eoin*, 2,801 ft., and *Baeshven*, 2,896 ft., overlooking the remote Shieldaig and Flowerdale Forests. From the clachan of *Slattadale*, near which are the Victoria Falls, so named to commemorate a visit by Queen Victoria, the road bears away from the wooded shores of the loch on the way to *Gairloch* (*q.v.*), and passes through the narrow and beautiful Kerrysdale, in which a hydro-electric scheme is now operating. On the far side of Loch Maree, opposite the hotel, is *Letterewe*, where iron-smelting for cannons, using charcoal now exhausted, was in full swing until the mid-17th century. One of the best views of Loch Maree, seen from the north-western extremity, and looking towards Slioch, can be obtained from the southern outskirts of *Poolewe* (*q.v.*) on Loch Ewe. Another splendid view of the loch, from the south-east, can be had from the road leading to *Kinlochewe* (*q.v.*) and Glen Docherty. Here, above the south-west shore of the loch, in Kinlochewe Forest, on the slopes of Ben Eighe, is Britain's first National Nature Reserve, described under *Kinlochewe*. *Iter. 205, 222, 223.*

LOCH MORAR, Inverness. Map 23, **NM 7** 9. See **Morar.**

LOCH MORLICH, Inverness. Map 25, **NH 9** 0. This loch, with its sandy shores, at a height of 1,046 ft., lies in the heart of the Glen More Forest Park, to the south of the peak of *Cairngorm*, 4,084 ft., which has given its name to the range as a whole. *Glenmore Lodge* is now a mountaineering training centre. There is a camping ground in the vicinity, and the district is becoming well known for ski-ing. Swedish reindeer were introduced here as an experiment in 1952 and the herd has since increased. To the north-east of the loch is the extensive Abernethy Forest, reached by means of a track over the Ryvoan Pass, with the picturesque little Green Loch. North-west of Loch Morlich, the Sluggan Pass gives access by means of another track to the Spey valley near *Boat of Garten* (*q.v.*). See **Nethybridge** and **Rothiemurchus** (for ski road).

LOCHNAGAR, Aberdeen. Map 20, **NO 2** 8. This famous granite peak, with its twin summits of 3,786 ft., and 3,768 ft., respectively, is the culminating point of the extensive, high-lying *White Mounth* (*q.v.*) plateau. It rises near the meeting-point of Aberdeen and Angus, overlooking the Royal Forest of Balmoral, and is separated from the great *Cairngorm* (*q.v.*) range by the beautifully-wooded Dee Valley. Lochnagar is a prominent feature in the view from many points on Deeside, and is also well seen from places far afield in Angus. The ascent can be made from *Braemar* (*q.v.*) up Glen Callater; from *Ballater* (*q.v.*) up Glen Muick by way of Loch Muick, above which rises *Cuidhe Crom*, 3,552 ft., a

Loch Long, Argyll; Dunbarton. Ben Arthur, 2,891 feet high, better known as ' The Cobbler,' rising to the north-west of the loch

Loch Lurgain, Ross and Cromarty. A view of the mountain of Stack Polly, 2,009 feet, its curious, pinnacled summit having the appearance of a porcupine's quills

Lochmaben, Dumfries. The Mercat Cross, which has sundials on the faces of its upper portion

Loch Maree, Ross and Cromarty. A tablet with a Gaelic inscription, recording Queen Victoria's visit in October, 1877, to the ' Loch Maree ' Hotel, on the west side of the loch, on A832

Loch Maree, Ross and Cromarty. The peak of Slioch, 3,260 feet, dominating the head of the loch, as seen from A832 on its western shores

Loch Morlich, Inverness. Cairn Gorm, 4,084 feet, from which the Cairngorm range takes its name, seen across the loch. It forms the background to the Glen More Forest Park

[For LOCH MORLICH see also under CAIRNGORMS (Plate 26)

Loch Oich, Inverness. The Well of the Seven Heads, recording in four languages, Gaelic, English, French and Latin, the fate which overtook seven brothers who murdered the two sons of a 17th century Clan Keppoch chief

Loch Ness, Inverness. The Memorial to John Cobb, the racing motorist, who lost his life when his speedboat capsized in the loch in September, 1952. It is situated on A82, between Drumnadrochit and Invermoriston

Lochnaw Castle, Wigtown. The modernised 16th to 18th century Castle, now an hotel. It was the seat of the Agnews, formerly Sheriffs of Galloway

Loch Nan Uamh, Inverness. This loch saw the arrival, aboard a French ship, of Bonnie Prince Charlie at the start of the '45 Rising. A year later he fled to France by ship, departing from the same loch

Loch Nan Uamh, Inverness. The Memorial Cairn, set up in 1956 by the '45 Association, on the traditional spot from which Bonnie Prince Charlie left to set sail for France on the 20th September, 1746, after having wandered through the Highlands as a fugitive, with a price of £30,000 on his head

south-eastern buttress of Lochnagar; and also from *Braedownie* (*q.v.*) in Glen Clova. Queen Victoria and the Prince Consort made the ascent from *Balmoral* (*q.v.*) on ponies, in 1848, by way of Glen Gelder. The view from the summit, where there is an indicator, is exceptionally fine, and below the peak is a deep corrie overhung by tremendous cliffs surrounding a tiny lochan. One of Byron's best-known poems has portrayed the mountain.

LOCH NAN UAMH, Inverness. Map 12, **NM 6** 8. A picturesque West Highland sea loch, forming an offshoot of the Sound of Arisaig, and famous for its associations with Prince Charles Edward, who arrived on board a French frigate, on August 5th, 1745, and landed at Borrodale, where the tiny Borrodale Burn flows into the bay. *Borrodale House*, burnt after Culloden, but still preserving much of the original structure, has many associations with the Prince, and here took place the fateful interview with Lochiel, when the whole issue of the Jacobite Rising hung in the balance. The following year the Prince returned, this time as a fugitive, and was forced to hide in the nearby Glen Beasdale woods, before he was able to cross to the Outer Hebrides. Later, he returned to the mainland, and after again hiding in a cave near Borrodale, was taken on board the French frigate "*L'Heureux*," on September 20th, 1746, and left Scotland for the last time. A memorial cairn was set up on the shore in 1956 by the '45 Association. Behind the shores of the inner loch and the tiny Loch Beag is Gleann Mama, leading to Loch Mama, in the hills of South Morar. The views out to sea, towards Eigg and Rum are very noteworthy. See **Culloden, Glenfinnan, Kinlochmoidart, Lochailort** and **Morar.** *Iter. 209.*

LOCHNAW CASTLE, Wigtown. Map 2, **NW 9** 6. Situated in the northern half of the peninsula known as the Rhinns of Galloway, and about half-way between Loch Ryan and the North Channel, in a setting of woods and rhodododendrons. The Castle, 16th to 18th cent., and modernised, stands near a small loch, and is the ancient seat of the Agnews, once sheriffs of *Galloway* (*q.v.*). To the east of the castle lies the pretty *Aldouran Glen*, traversed by the Stranraer road. To the west is the ruined 16th-cent. *Galdenoch Castle*. *Iter. 83.*

LOCH NESS, Inverness. Map 25, **NH 4** 1 etc. Extending for 24 miles, from a point south-west of *Inverness* (*q.v.*) to *Fort Augustus* (*q.v.*), this narrow loch is over 700 ft. deep in parts, and has not yet been known to freeze. In recent years it has acquired notoriety due to the appearance of the famous "Loch Ness Monster," first reported in 1932, and reputedly seen by a number of people, though its possible existence is still a matter of considerable speculation. St. Adamnan, the 7th-cent. Abbot of Iona and biographer of St. Columba (See **Dull**), refers in his writings to a much earlier Loch Ness monster, which he describes as an "aquatilis bestia." The splendid Inverness to Fort William road traverses the wooded western shores of the loch, while on the eastern side a road extends south-westwards as far as *Foyers* (*q.v.*), after which it veers inland, and only reaches the loch again near Fort Augustus. This road follows partly the course of Wade's original Fort Augustus to Inverness military road. There are no high hills in the immediate vicinity of Loch Ness, but *Mealfuarvonie*, 2,284 ft., is a conspicuous feature rising above the western shores opposite Foyers. The *Caledonian Canal* (*q.v.*) traverses its length in progressing through the Great Glen, or *Glen More* (*q.v.*). One of the most picturesque views from the loch extends into Glen Urquhart, stretching westwards from its bay, and guarded by the ruins of *Urquhart Castle* near *Drumnadrochit* (*q.v.*). In September 1952, when attempting to beat the water speed record with his jet speedboat, John Cobb, the well-known racing motorist, lost his life when his craft capsized and sank. A cairn has been erected in his memory between Invermoriston and Drumnadrochit. See **Inverfarigaig, Invermoriston** and **Loch Oich.** *Iter. 206, 207, 210, 211, 123.*

LOCH NEVIS, Inverness. Map 23, **NM 7** 9 and **8** 9. This magnificent sea loch, inferior in grandeur perhaps only to *Loch Hourn* (*q.v.*), is divided, like its rival, into an Inner and Outer loch, separated by the narrow strait of Kylesknoydart. The mountain background is very impressive, with the rugged *Knoydart* (*q.v.*) hills to the north, and the lower hills of North Morar to the south dividing it from *Loch Morar* (See **Morar**). Finest of all are the lofty peaks at the head of Inner Loch Nevis, dominated by *Luinne Bheinn*, 3,083 ft., *Ben Aden*, 2,905 ft., and the sharp cone of *Sgurr na Ciche*, 3,410 ft. Unlike Loch Hourn, no roads give access to the shores of Loch Nevis, which is therefore almost isolated, and can only be visited by boat, or by long-distance walkers, and is reached by motor launch from *Mallaig* (*q.v.*) to *Inverie* (*q.v.*), on its north-west shores. From the head of the Inner Loch, a path traverses the wild pass of the Mam na Cloiche Airde, giving access for hardy walkers to *Loch Arkaig* (*q.v.*). Perhaps the finest view of the loch is that obtained from *Carn a' Ghobhair*, 1,794 ft., which can be climbed from Mallaig, the panorama from the summit including also the whole length of Loch Morar.

LOCH OICH, Inverness. Map 18, **NN 3** 9 and **NH 3** 0. A short but beautiful loch, forming one of the chain of lochs in the Great Glen, or *Glen More* (*q.v.*), through which penetrates the *Caledonian Canal* (*q.v.*), here reaching its highest point above sea-level. Along the western shores goes the fine Fort William to Inverness road, passing through *Invergarry* (*q.v.*), the gateway to some of the finest scenery in the North-West Highlands, while along the wooded eastern shores went Wade's former military road, now a minor road. At the northern end of the loch is *Aberchalder Lodge*, where Prince Charles Edward rallied his forces before crossing the *Corrieyairack Pass* (*q.v.*), in 1745, on his way to Edinburgh and England. On the west side of the loch, near its southern extremity, is the historic "Well of the Heads." This was erected to commemorate the fate which overtook seven brothers, who had killed the two sons of a 17th cent. Clan Keppoch chief, and whose gory heads were washed in the well by the avenger. The inscription on the monument is in four languages, Gaelic, English, French and Latin, the seven heads being carved around the top of the pillar, and surmounted by a hand clasping a dagger. See **Laggan Locks, Loch Lochy, Loch Ness** and **Roy Bridge.** *Iter. 210, 220.*

LOCH QUOICH, Inverness. Map 18, **NG 9** 0 and **NH 0** 0. A most beautiful loch, penetrating westwards from Glen Garry into the rocky *Knoydart* (*q.v.*) mountains, its northern shores being traversed by the road from *Tomdoun* (*q.v.*) to *Kinloch Hourn* (*q.v.*), very rough at the end. King Edward VII visited Glen Quoich Lodge for the shooting on numerous occasions. Half-way along the road is *Quoich Bridge*, where the River Quoich flows into the loch from Glen Quoich. This roadless glen is surrounded by lofty hills, *Sgurr a' Mhoraire*, 3,365 ft., to the west, and *Gleouraich*, 3,395 ft., and *Spidean Mialach*, 3,268 ft., to the east, and leads towards Glen Shiel, far to the north, having been traversed, in 1654, by General Monk and his troops. To the south of Loch Quoich rises the fine peak of *Gairich*, 3,015 ft., a notable landmark. From the south-western extremity of the loch, at Kinlochquoich, a walkers' track penetrates into the wild and lonely district known as the "Rough Bounds," dominated by *Sgurr na Ciche*, 3,410 ft., passing the very picturesque and tiny rock-girt Lochan nam Breac on the way to the distant shores of *Loch Hourn* (*q.v.*). Prince Charles Edward wandered in the district as a fugitive, in 1746, and had many narrow escapes from capture. There is much rugged scenery all around Loch Quoich, which is noted for the highest average annual rainfall in Scotland. A large hydro-electric scheme now operates in the district and the loch has been considerably enlarged. *Iter. 214.*

LOCH RANNOCH, Perth. Map 19, **NN 5** 5 and **6** 5. This inland sheet of water, 10 miles in length, extends westwards from *Kinloch Rannoch* to a point near Bridge of Gaur, on the road to the remote *Rannoch* (*q.v.* station. High hills rise south of the loch, from *Schiehallion*, 3,547 ft., and *Carn Mairg*, 3,419 ft., in the south-eastern corner, to *Garbh Mheall*, 3,054 ft., lying to the south-west. The southern shores of the loch are bordered by the Black Wood of Rannoch. The waters of Loch Rannoch now form part of the Tummel-Garry hydro-electric scheme and there is a large power station. See **Kinloch Rannoch.** *Iter. 147, 148.*

LOCHRANZA, Isle of Arran, Bute. 283. Map 7, NR **9 5**. GOLF. The most northerly resort on the island, with a steamer pier. It is situated on an attractive bay, at the foot of Glen Chalmadale, with the Cock of Arran away to the north-east, facing the Sound and Island of Bute, backed by the hills of Cowal. The picturesque, ruined double-towered Castle dates from the 16th cent., and overlooks Loch Ranza, where Bruce is said to have landed, in 1306, from Ireland. The fine road leading southwards towards *Pirnmill* (*q.v.*) hugs the coast at the foot of a range of hills for the whole of the distance, and passes, within two miles, the delightful bay of *Catacol*, on Kilbrennan Sound. From here, Glen Catacol extends southwards into the hills, with *Beinn Bhreac* and *Beinn Bharrain* both exceeding 2,300 ft., in height. They overlook the lonely Loch Tanna, which lies at an altitude of 1,051 ft., beyond the head of the glen. To the south of the loch extends the lengthy Glen Iorsa. Glen Diomhan is a small National Nature Reserve to the south-west, below *Meall nan Damh*, 1,870 ft., in Glen Catacol, and contains rare whitebeam trees. See **Sannox.** *Iter. 242.*

LOCH SCAVAIG, Isle of Skye, Inverness. Map 23, **NG 4 1** and **5 1**. The beautiful sea loch of *Scavaig* lies immediately to the south of the great *Coolin* (*q.v.*) range, and is crossed by the motor boats from *Elgol* (*q.v.*) on their way to its head. Beyond here, separated by a narrow barrier of land, lies the wild and impressive *Loch Coruisk* (*q.v.*), with the jagged peaks of the Coolins overhanging the far end. A little to the west, the so-called " Mad Burn " impressive when in spate, falls through its narrow ravine into the waters of Scavaig. *Gars Bheinn*, 2,934 ft., the most southerly Coolin peak, and a fine viewpoint, rises above the loch to the north-west, and off-shore is the flat island of *Soay*. Farther out to sea is the mountainous island of Rum, and also the smaller Eigg, with the curious Sgurr of Eigg. Perhaps the loveliest views of Scavaig, with its superb mountain background, are those which are to be obtained from the heights in the immediate neighbourhood of Elgol. *Iter. 252.*

LOCH SHIEL, Argyll; Inverness. Map 12, **NM 7 7** and 18 **NM 8 7**. A long and narrow fresh-water loch, in the romantic Clanranald country, stretching south-westwards from the Prince Charles Edward monument (N.T. Scot.) at *Glenfinnan* (*q.v.*) to *Acharacle* (*q.v.*). It forms the boundary between the *Argour* (*q.v.*) district of Argyll and the *Moidart* (*q.v.*) district of Inverness. For the whole of its 18 miles its breadth nowhere exceeds a mile. The setting of this loch is one of exceptional beauty, justifying its claim to be one of the very finest in the Western Highlands, while its historical associations with the '45 give it much added interest. (See **Dalilea** and **Kinlochmoidart.**) Lofty mountains look down on the loch for much of its length, the finest being to the north, where *Bheinn Odhar Bheag*, 2,895 ft., towering above the west shore, faces *Meall nan Creag Leac*, 2,784 ft. In the background, behind the Prince's monument, rise parallel ranges of rock-strewn hills guarding Glen Finnan. Farther down the loch, the mountains of Moidart recede, and interest turns to the eastern shore, where *Ben Resipol*, 2,774 ft. tapers to a sharp, rocky peak. Near its foot, in the narrows of Loch Shiel, is the little island of *Eilean Fhionain*, with an ancient burial-ground, preserving a very rare example of a Celtic bell. To the east, where the Polloch River flows into the loch from the tiny Loch Doilate, is an opening in the hills threaded by the lonely, wooded Glen Hurich. At the far end of Loch Shiel, the Shiel River connects with Outer Loch Moidart, in flat, mossy surroundings. Loch Shiel is difficult of access by road, except at the two extremities. A steamer links Glenfinnan with Acharacle, at its south-western extremity, and there are magnificent views from the boat journey. *Iter. 209, 217.*

LOCH SHIN, Sutherland. Map 29, NC **4 1** etc. See **Lairg** and **Overscaig.**

LOCH SLOY, Dunbarton. Map 15, NN **2 1**. See **Inveruglas** and **Loch Lomond.** *Iter. 100, 110, 111.*

LOCH SUNART, Argyll. Map 12, **NM 6 5** etc. A delightful sea loch, extending inland from the Ardnamurchan peninsula on the Sound of Mull for a distance of some 20 miles. Its head lies in an amphitheatre of hills, where the districts of *Ardgour* (*q.v.*) and *Morven* (*q.v.*) meet, and is dominated to the north-east by the fine rock peak of *Garbh Bheinn*, 2,903 ft., and to the south-east by *Creach Bheinn*, 2,800 ft. Both of these are notable viewpoints, and between them a road threads its way through Glen Tarbert, giving access to Loch Linnhe. This picturesque, though narrow and hilly road, traverses the northern shores of Loch Sunart, providing lovely views of the wooded southern shores, with some low hills beyond. It passes the small resorts of *Strontian* (*q.v.*) and *Salen* (*q.v.*), behind which rises the prominent cone of *Ben Resipol*, 2,774 ft., from the summit of which the panorama is one of the finest in the Western Highlands, overlooking the whole length of picturesque *Loch Shiel* (*q.v.*) and across the sea to the islands of Eigg and Rum. *Iter. 216, 217, 218.*

LOCH TAY, Perth. Map 15, **NN 6** 3 etc. This large and deep Highland loch, nearly 15 miles long, is noted for its salmon fishing, and is overlooked, to the north, by *Ben Lawers*, 3,984 ft. (N.T. Scot.), Perthshire's highest mountain. (See **Lawers.**) Facing Ben Lawers, to the west, are the peaks of the *Tarmachans*, 3,421 ft., the views from these mountains being very extensive, including almost the whole of the *Breadalbane* (*q.v.*) country and much of the *Grampians* (*q.v.*). Roads traverse both shores of Loch Tay, the main road being on the north side, but the views from the wooded south shore are more beautiful, though the road is somewhat narrow and hilly. From this side paths lead into the hills, that from Ardeonaig, with its mill and waterfall, giving access to Glen Lednoch, and that from Ardtalnaig, farther to the north-east, leading towards Glen Almond. Loch Tay has been well described in Scott's " Fair Maid of Perth." The River Tay, some 120 miles in length, and with the largest volume of water of any river in Britain, flows from the eastern extremity of Loch Tay towards *Aberfeldy* (*q.v.*). See **Kenmore, Killin** and **Tyndrum.** *Iter. 107, 120, 138, 139.*

LOCH TORRIDON, Ross and Cromarty. Map 22, NG **7** 6 etc. See **Torridon.** *Iter. 223.*

LOCH TROOL, Kirkcudbright. Map 2, NX **4 7**. This beautiful loch, in the heart of the remote *Galloway* (*q.v.*) Highlands, and reached from *Bargrennan* (*q.v.*), on the Girvan to Newton Stewart road, lies in a most picturesque setting in Glen Trool. It is now becoming better known, due mainly to the creation of the Glen Trool Forest Park. The Park has a total area of over 110,000 acres, and consists in all of five forests, several of which are contiguous. The Glen Trool Forest contains the finest scenery, and a camping site is situated near the loch, at Caldons Farm. (The remaining forests in the Park are described under **Barr, Clatteringshaws Dam** and **Newton Stewart.**) To the north of the loch rises the *Merrick*, 2,764 ft., the highest mainland mountain south of the Highlands proper. This, together with its lesser satellites, is included within the Park, and below its eastern and southern slopes lie Loch Enoch and Loch Neldricken, the latter incorporating the remote " Murder Hole." South-east of Loch Enoch are the remote Round and Long Lochs of the Dungeon. At the east end of Loch Trool is the Bruce Memorial, a fine viewpoint, the stone commemorating a victory over the English by Bruce in 1307. At the south-western extremity of the loch, near Caldons Farm, is an inscribed Martyrs' Stone, dominated in the background by *Muldonach* and *Lamachan Hill*, 2,349 ft., in the hills of the Minnigaff district. Away to the north-east rise the *Rhinns of Kells*, dominated by *Corserine*, 2,668 ft., and *Carlins Cairn*, 2,650 ft. Farther south are *Millfire*, 2,350 ft. and *Meikle Millyea*, 2,446 ft., between which lies the lonely Loch Dungeon. Much of the fine, wild mountain country of the Merrick district is described in S. R. Crockett's " Raiders." *Iter. 71, 79.*

LOCH TULLA, Argyll. Map 15, NN **2 4**. See **Inveroran.**

Loch Shiel, Argyll; Inverness. A view from Glenfinnan of the 18-mile long loch up which Prince Charles Edward sailed with some of his followers at the start of the '45 Rising. The monument to the Prince is visible in the foreground, and is illustrated also under Glenfinnan (Plate 76)

Loch Sunart, Argyll. Ben Resipol, 2,774 feet, seen from a point near Strontian, which lies on the northern shore of the loch

Loch Trool, Kirkcudbright. The Bruce Memorial, at the eastern end of the loch, which commemorates one of his victories, in 1307

Loch Tay, Perth. Ben Lawers, 3,984 feet (N.T. Scot.), Perthshire's highest mountain, and of great botanical interest, seen from the unclassified road along the south shore

Loch Tulla, Argyll. A view of the loch, which lies on the edge of the Black Mount, to the west of the new road leading to Glencoe. In the vicinity was born, in 1724, Duncan Ban MacIntyre, who has been described as the 'Burns of the Highlands'

Logierait, Perth. Examples of mortsafes in the churchyard, formerly used to prevent the the removal of corpses for sale as anatomical specimens

Longforgan, Perth. The 15th century Castle Huntly, on a rocky site to the south-west, off an unclassified road. It was erected by Lord Gray of Foulis, Master of the Household to James II, and was at one period known as Castle Lyon

Lorne, Argyll. Inverawe House, partly 16th century, which is associated with a ghost story. It stands north of the River Awe, at Bonawe, off A85, in the district of Lorne

Loth, Sutherland. The Monument commemorating the slaying by Hunter Polson, c. 1700, of the last wolf in Sutherland. It stands at the foot of Glen Loth, to the south-west, and on the north side of A9

Lothians. The remains of the 15th century Soutra Aisle, a one-time hospice and sanctuary. It stands just to the south-west of Soutra Hill, on B6368, in Midlothian

Lothians. Preston Mill, a 17th century water-mill (N.T. Scot.), perhaps the oldest in Scotland, at East Linton, an East Lothian village, situated between the Lammermuir Hills and the Firth of Forth

LOCH TUMMEL, Perth. Map 19, **NN 8** 5.
See **Queen's View** and **Tummel Bridge.** *Iter. 138, 148.*

LOCH VENNACHAR, Perth. Map 15, **NN 5** 0.
See **Callander** and **Trossachs.** *Iter. 106, 111, 139.*

LOCHWINNOCH, Renfrew. 3,885. Map 8, **NS 3** 5.
E.C. Wed. GOLF. A small textile and furniture manufacturing town, on Castle Semple Loch. At the south end of the loch are the remains of *Barr Castle* and *Peel Castle.* To the north-west lies an extensive and lofty moorland area, which rises to 1,663 ft. at *Misty Law*, and 1,711 ft. at the *Hill of Stake*, the former being a splendid viewpoint. Both of these hills are situated on the borders of Ayrshire. See **Howwood.** *Iter. 58, 85.*

LOCHY BRIDGE, Inverness. Map 18, **NN 1** 7.
Iter. 143, 208, 209, 210, 214, 215, 220.

LOCKERBIE, Dumfries. 2,999. SB. Map 4, **NY 1** 8.
E.C. Tues. **M.D.** Thurs. GOLF. An Annandale market town, noted for its August lamb fair, which dates back to the 17th cent. The Old Tower was formerly the town gaol. To the east flows the Water of Milk, near which stands the mansion of *Castle Milk* with its fine gardens, situated **3 m. S.** of Lockerbie. A Roman Camp, comprising a remarkable group of fortifications, is situated near the flat-topped *Birrenswark Hill*, to the south-east of the town. Recent excavations here have unearthed a circular oven, 6 ft. in diameter. **5 m. N.N.W.**, to the west of the Moffat road and beyond the River Annan, is *Spedlins Tower*, dated 1605, though some portions of the structure are 15th cent. work. See **Lochmaben.** *Iter. 10, 13, 29, 42, 45, 50, 51.*

LOGAN HOUSE, Wigtown. Map 2, **NX 0** 4.
See **Port Logan.**

LOGIE, Moray. Map 26, **NJ 0** 5.
Situated a little to the east of the River Findhorn, which flows here through a deep and picturesque gorge, with the Altyre Woods and Darnaway Forest to the north. (See **Forres.**) **1½ m. S.W.** of Logie is the beauty spot known as "Randolph's Leap," reached on foot, in the picturesque Findhorn Glen, near the confluence of the river with the Divie. The fine grounds of *Relugas House* lie nearby, and farther to the south-west, off the road to *Ferness* (*q.v.*) is *Daltulich Bridge*, spanning the Findhorn, on the Nairn border. See **Dulsie Bridge.** *Iter. 172, 173.*

LOGIE EASTER, Ross and Cromarty. 1,217.
Map 31, **NH 7** 7.
An agricultural village, well known for its herds of cattle. **1 m. S.W.**, beyond the Balnagown River, is the 13th to 16th cent. turreted *Balnagown Castle*, once the home of the Earls of Ross. The castle has fine gardens. **2 m. W.**, near the Balnagown River, lies *Marybank* churchyard, in which are preserved some ancient stones. See **Milton** (Ross and Cromarty) and **Nigg.** *Iter. 201.*

LOGIERAIT, Perth. 1,195. Map 20, **NN 9** 5.
Once famous for a Royal Castle, the seat of the Regality Courts of Atholl. From its gaol, Rob Roy made an escape in 1717. The village is situated in Strath Tay, and a little to the south-east the River Tay is joined by the Tummel. In the Church are preserved some sculptured stones, and there are mortsafes in the churchyard. Standing stones and remains of stone circles exist at various places on the east bank of the Tay. *Iter. 120, 158.*

LONGANNET POINT, Fife. Map 16, **NS 9** 8.
The site of a large new generating station.

LONGFORGAN, Perth. 2,684. Map 17, **NO 3** 2.
In the fertile *Carse of Gowrie* (*q.v.*), between the *Sidlaw* hills and the Firth of Tay. **1 m. S.W.**, on a rocky site, is the impressive *Castle Huntly*, once known as *Castle Lyon*, and dating from the 15th cent., with considerable additions from the latter half of the 17th cent. See **Fowlis Easter** and **Kinnaird.** *Iter. 154.*

LONGFORMACUS, Berwick. 338 with Cranshaws.
Map 10, **NT 6** 5.
A remote little place in the foothills of the *Lammermuirs*, situated on the Dye Water, not far from its junction with the Whiteadder Water away to the north-east. *Longformacus House* is Georgian. *Dirrington Great Law*, 1,309 ft., rises to the south, overlooking the Duns road. The hilly and winding road leading north-westwards from Longformacus into the hills gives access to the village of *Gifford* (*q.v.*). To the west of this road, on the Lammermuir heights, near the East Lothian border, are the so-called "Mutiny Stones," a relic of the Stone Age. *Iter 3.*

LONGNIDDRY, East Lothian. Map 10, **NT 4** 7.
GOLF. The village stands just inland from a stretch of flat, sandy and stony coast, where there is a golf course. Between 1643 and 1647, John Knox was a tutor here. **1½ m. N.E.**, is the ruined 16th to 17th cent. mansion of *Redhouse.* See **Gosford House** and **Seton.** *Iter. 2, 37.*

LONGTOWN, Cumberland (England). Map 4, **NY 3** 6.
E.C. Wed. **M.D.** Thurs. *Iter. 11, 12, 30, 31, 51, 67.*

LONMAY, Aberdeen. 1,471. Map 27, **NK 0** 5.
A little to the east is the Loch of Strathbeg, near Strathbeg Bay. **2½ m. N.E.** is *Cairness House*, dating from 1792. **3 m. N.N.W.**, near the village of *Rathen*, is the Bronze Age burial cairn of *Memsie* (A.M.). *Iter. 181, 182.*

LORNE, Argyll. Map 14, **NM 9** 2 etc.
The name given to the picturesque stretch of country lying between the Firth of Lorne, at the seaward end of *Loch Linnhe* (*q.v.*), and *Loch Awe* (*q.v.*), farther to the south. The eastern boundary of the district is formed by the mountains surrounding Loch Etive, beyond which, to the west, lie the districts of *Benderloch* and *Appin* (both *q.v.*). These are in reality a part of Lorne itself, which extends in a northerly direction as far as Loch Leven and the wild *Glencoe* (*q.v.*) country. *Oban* (*q.v.*) is the principal centre of Lorne, and is well placed for explorations in one of the loveliest parts of the Western Highlands. The Duke of Argyll takes one of his titles from the name Lorne. A magnificent panorama of the entire Lorne country can be obtained from the summit of *Ben Cruachan*, 3,689 ft., which may be climbed from a point near the *Falls of Cruachan* (*q.v.*), on the shores of Loch Awe, near the Pass of Brander.

LOSSIEMOUTH, Moray. Map 26, **NJ 2** 7.
5,681. SB. with Branderburgh.
E.C. Thurs. GOLF. A well-known resort on Spey Bay, at the mouth of the River Lossie, with good sands and bathing; there are extensive sandhills to the east beyond the river. The harbour, at *Branderburgh*, at the west end of the town, serves as the port of *Elgin* (*q.v.*). The Rt. Hon. Ramsay Macdonald was born in 1866 at Lossiemouth. To the west of the harbour, about two miles distant, is *Covesea* (*q.v.*), and also a number of caves showing fantastic rock formations. At *Kinnedar*, to the south-west of Lossiemouth, the Bishops of Moray formerly had a castle, of which there are but scanty remains still in existence. See **Duffus** and **Spynie Palace.** *Iter. 187, 192, 199.*

LOTH, Sunderland. 726. Map 31, **NC 9** 1.
A monument at the foot of Glen Loth, a little to the south-west, commemorates the slaying of the last wolf in the county. East of Lothbeg Bridge, at the foot of the glen, are remains of an early long cairn, and in Glen Loth itself are standing stones, while in the background rise *Beinn Dobhrain*, 2,060 ft., and *Ben Uarie*, 2,046 ft. **2 m. S.W.**, on the coast, is the ruined broch of Cinn Trolla. *Iter. 200, 231, 233.*

LOTHIANS. Map 9, **NS 9** 7 and 10, **NT 6** 7 etc.
The Lothian district now comprises a large expanse of country bordered by the Firth of Forth, and extending roughly from Dunbar, in the east, to Linlithgow, in the west, incorporating the greater part of the *Lammermuir*, *Moorfoot* and *Pentland* hills. It is divided into the counties

of East Lothian, Midlothian, which includes the city of Edinburgh, and West Lothian. In former times the Lothians extended as far south as the River Tweed, and were part of the ancient kingdom of Northumbria. The family of Kerr takes its title of Marquis from the name Lothian. An extensive panorama of much of the Lothian country can be obtained from the summit of *Soutra Hill* (*q.v.*), on the Edinburgh to Lauder road.

LOUDOUNHILL, Ayr. Map 8, **NS 6 3.**
Near *Loudoun Hill*, 1,043 ft., an isolated cone of rock, was fought, in 1307, a battle in which Robert Bruce defeated the English. A little to the north of the hill, in 1679, the battle of *Drumclog* was won by the Covenanters. To the east of Loudon Hill a successful skirmish was once fought by Sir William Wallace. This region is well depicted by Scott in " Old Mortality." *Loudon Castle* is described under **Galston.** *Iter. 20, 69.*

LOVAT BRIDGE, Inverness. Map 25, **NH 5 4.**
About a mile to the south-east of this bridge over the Beauly River, a road diverges southwards from the Inverness road, and leads by way of the fertile district of *The Aird*, through Glen Convinth, in the direction of Glen Urquhart. Another branch, narrow and poor, forks south-eastwards from the glen, and climbs towards the tiny Loch Laide. *Iter. 200, 201, 203, 204, 205, 210, 213, 221.*

LOWLANDS, THE
That part of Scotland known as the *Lowlands*, as distinct from the *Highlands*, and which includes also the tumbled Border Country, separated from England by the *Cheviots* (*q.v.*), is sometimes described as being the area lying to the south and east of the *Grampian* (*q.v.*) mountains. A rather more definite geological line of demarcation is often quoted, which has been given in detail in the separate article describing the *Highlands*. Broadly speaking, the Lowlands are perhaps best known as the country situated to the south of the Clyde estuary and the Firth of Forth, or simply to the south of a line linking Glasgow, Stirling and Edinburgh. The landscape is characterized by rounded green hills, pleasant valleys and some excellent farming country. Much of this area has become famous owing to its associations with Sir Walter Scott and Robert Burns, and the romantic Border Country is especially delightful. It must, however, not be forgotten that nearly all the country lying near the east coast between the Firth of Forth and the Moray Firth, and even the distant county of Caithness, beyond the latter, is true Lowland country. This area is often better described as the *North-East Lowlands*. A remarkable feature of the Lowlands in the south-west is the less well-known district of *Galloway*, where the lonely, rugged hills, dominated by the lofty *Merrick*, 2,764 ft., exhibit many of the features of real Highland mountains. Most of Scotland's industrial area is centred in the Lowlands, notably between the Clyde and Forth estuaries. See **Border Country, Burns Country, Galloway, Highlands, Scott Country** and **Wanlockhead.**

LUCE ABBEY, Wigtown. Map 2, **NX 1 5.**
See **Glenluce.** *Iter. 78.*

LUGAR, Ayr. 1,148. Map 8, **NS 5 2.**
A cave here was the scene of early experiments in coal-gas lighting by William Murdoch, who was born at Bello Mill in the village, in 1754. The large ironworks date from 1845. See **Muirkirk** (for *Airds Moss*). *Iter. 21, 68.*

LUGTON, Ayr. Map 8, **NS 4 5.**
GOLF. *Iter. 57, 60, 62.*

LUING, ISLE OF, Argyll. Map 14, **NM 7 0**
See **Clachan Bridge.** and **7 1.**

LUMPHANAN, Aberdeen. 2,248 with Kincardine O'Neil. Map 27, **NJ 5 0.**
E.C. Thurs. Situated a little to the north of the winding River Dee, beyond the Loch of Auchlossan. To the north is Macbeth's Cairn, where he made his last stand in 1057. After he had been killed, his head was taken to Malcolm at *Kincardine Castle*, near *Fettercairn* (*q.v.*). See **Craigievar Castle** and **Torphins.** *Iter. 165, 190.*

LUMSDEN, Aberdeen. Map 26, **NJ 4 2.**
Lies in a valley between the *Correen* hills, to the east, and the *Buck of Cabrach*, 2,368 ft., to the west. **2 m. N.**, off the Dufftown road, to the left, is the ruined *Auchindoir* Church, with a richly-carved 12th or 13th cent. doorway, and also a Sacrament House. Near the Church is a motte, on which stood formerly the Norman castle. To the west, on the Burn of Craig, stands the 16th cent. *Craig Castle. Iter. 165, 167, 177, 190.*

LUNCARTY, Perth. Map 16, **NO 0 2.**
Near the River Tay, on which is situated at this point a salmon hatchery. A battle is said to have been fought in the vicinity in 990, when the Danes were defeated, the Scots having been rallied by a peasant armed only with a plough-yoke. It is sometimes thought that the adoption of the thistle as the Scottish national emblem arose out of an incident in this battle. *Iter. 148, 149, 150.*

LUNDIE, Angus. Map 17, **NO 2 3.**
A *Sidlaw Hills* village, to the south of Loch Long. The Church contains Norman work.

LUNDIN LINKS, Fife. 400. Map 17, **NO 4 0.**
E.C. Thurs. GOLF. A golfing resort, on Largo Bay, with its good sands. Three standing stones are preserved near the station. A tall 14th cent. tower from a former mansion of the Lundins can still be seen. *Iter. 94, 98, 128.*

LUSS, Dunbarton. 456. Map 15, **NS 3 9.**
E.C. Wed. An exceptionally pretty village, at the mouth of Glen Luss, on the western shores of *Loch Lomond* (*q.v.*) facing a group of wooded islands, and looking northwards to *Ben Lomond*, 3,192 ft. The Church contains a 14th to 15th cent. effigy of the 6th cent. St. Kessog. There is a steamer pier. Coleridge, and also Wordsworth and his sister visited Luss, in 1803. **3 m. S.**, on a promontory facing Loch Lomond, is *Rossdhu House*, a seat of the Colquhouns. **3½ m. N.**, off the *Tarbet* (*q.v.*) road, is the entrance to Glen Douglas, set between lofty hills, and threaded by a road leading to the shores of Loch Long. At *Inverbeg*, **3 m. N.** of Luss, Loch Lomond is crossed in summer by a passenger ferry, giving access to *Rowardennan* (*q.v.*). *Iter. 88, 100, 101, 110, 137.*

LYBSTER, Caithness. 826. Map 30, **ND 2 3.**
E.C. Thurs. On Lybster Bay, situated on a wild and rocky stretch of coast, with Clyth Ness to the east, and of some importance for its fishing industry. The Church, built of dressed local flagstones, has a west door in the ancient native tradition, and the chancel entrance is in the same form. **3 m. N.E.** is the newly-planted Rumster Forest. See **Kildonan** (Sutherland) and **Mid Clyth.** *Iter. 200.*

LYNE, Peebles. Map 9, **NT 1 4.**
The Church, one of the smallest in Scotland, contains a pulpit and two canopied pews said to be of Dutch workmanship. Near the Church is a Roman camp. A little to the south, beyond Lyne station, and across the River Tweed near its junction with the Lyne Water, is *Barns Tower*, dating from 1488, and retaining its iron yett. It is associated with an early novel by John Buchan. In the vicinity is the white-harled *Barns House*. To the north of Lyne are the twin *Meldon* hills, facing each other across a narrow road leading to *Eddleston* (*q.v.*) Farther north, and to the west of this road, rises *Crailzie Hill*, 1,561 ft., with the interesting Harehope Rings and the prehistoric Harehope Fort. See **Broughton** and **Romanno Bridge.** *Iter. 14, 35, 52, 53.*

LYNWILG, Inverness. Map 25, **NH 8 0.**
On Loch Alvie, in a pleasant wooded setting, with a Waterloo cairn, and a monument to the last Duke of Gordon standing on *Tor of Alvie Hill*, to the south-east. From the summit, the view extends eastwards over the great *Rothiemurchus* (*q.v.*) forest towards the distant *Cairngorms* (*q.v.*). In Alvie churchyard, at the western extremity of the loch, is buried Sir George Henschel. To the north-west of Lynwilg rises *Geal Charn Mor*, 2,702 ft., from the summit of which the distant view of the Cairngorms has been described as one of the finest panoramas in the country. *Iter. 140, 147, 150, 208.*

MACDUFF, Banff. 3,708. SB. Map 27, **NJ 7 6.**
E.C. Wed. GOLF. An important herring-fishing town,

Luss, Dunbarton. The gateway, on A82, leading to the mansion of Rhos Dhu, the seat of the Colquhouns

Lundin Links, Fife. A trio of prehistoric standing stones, which are situated off the Leven road (A915)

Lumphanan, Aberdeen. Macbeth's Cairn, locally reputed to commemorate his last stand in 1057 before he was slain. It stands a little to the north, off A980

Lowlands. The remains of Carleton Castle, at Lendalfoot, on the Ayrshire coast. Its former baronial owner is said to have pushed his first seven wives over the cliff, but was himself thus disposed of by the eighth

Lugar, Ayr. A scene on the Lugar Water. Near this spot is a cave in which William Murdoch conducted experiments in coal-gas lighting during the 18th century

Lumsden, Aberdeen. Craig Castle, which stands off B9002, some 3½ miles to the north. Patrick Gordon, slain at Flodden Field in 1513, built the original tower three years previously

[For MACDUFF see following plate
[For LYNWILG see under CAIRNGORMS (Plate 26)
[For LYNE see under TWEEDDALE (Plate 166)

Macduff, Banff. Rock outcrops near the Howe of Tarlair, to the east

Mallaig, Inverness. The fishing port of Mallaig, which faces the island of Skye across the Sound of Sleat

Magus Muir, Fife. The gravestone of five Covenanters, taken prisoner at the battle of Bothwell Brig, in 1679, and later executed here. It is situated 3 miles north-east of Pitscottie, on B939. In a wood nearby is a cairn marking the spot where Archbishop Sharp was murdered in the same year

Manor, Peebles. The stone which David Ritchie, the original of the 'Black Dwarf,' or 'Bowed Davie' of Sir Walter Scott's novel, '*The Black Dwarf*,' is said to have carried here from the bed of the River Tweed, nearly a mile distant (see below)

Manor, Peebles. The cottage in which David Ritchie, the original of the 'Black Dwarf' of Sir Walter Scott's novel is said to have lived, showing the special 'dwarf' door

situated in Banff Bay, with a large harbour. Across the mouth of the River Deveron, to the west, is the town of *Banff* (*q.v.*). Macduff was formerly known as *Down*, the name being changed in 1783. On the *Hill of Down*, a viewpoint, is a lofty War Memorial. A little to the east is the Howe of Tarlair, with Tarlair Well, and some fantastic rock outcrops by the shore, where there is also a bathing pool. See **Crovie, Gardenstown** and **King Edward.** *Iter. 180, 181, 182, 183, 188.*

MACHRIE, Isle of Arran, Bute. Map 7, **NR 8** 3. GOLF. Situated on Machrie Bay, on the Kilbrennan Sound, facing the *Kintyre* (*q.v.*) peninsula. The Machrie Water flows into the bay at this point, and about **1½ m. E.,** on its south bank, are the Standing Stones of Tormore, with remains of some 10 circles. The coast road to the south leads inland to *Blackwaterfoot* (*q.v.*), and a path from it diverges to the coast for the King's Caves, in the largest of which Fingal and Bruce are traditionally said to have sheltered. North of Machrie, a road goes eastwards inland to link up with the String Road, leading to the east coast of the island at *Brodick* (*q.v.*). The coast road goes due north towards Dougrie Point, near which is the seaward end of the long and desolate Glen Iorsa, hemmed in by high hills at its head. *Iter. 242.*

MACHRIE, Isle of Islay. Argyll. Map 6, **NR 3** 4. GOLF. See **Port Ellen.** *Iter. 243, 244.*

MACHRIHANISH, Argyll. 130. Map 6, **NR 6** 2. **E.C.** Thurs. GOLF. A *Kintyre* (*q.v.*) resort on Machrihanish Bay, looking towards the open Atlantic, with good sands for bathing, and also extensive sand dunes to the north, on which is situated a very well-known golf course. The airport for *Campbeltown* (*q.v.*) lies between that town and Machrihanish. **4 m. S.S.W.** is *Cnoc Moy*, 1,462 ft., whose slopes overlook the sea, and are honeycombed with caves which contain stalactites. These are best reached by way of *Southend* (*q.v.*). *Iter. 123.*

MACMERRY, East Lothian. Map 10, **NT 4** 7. *Iter. 1.*

MAESHOWE, Orkney. Map 33, **HY 3** 1. See **Orkney Islands** (Mainland). *Iter. 263.*

MAGGIEKNOCKATER, Banff. Map 26, **NJ 3** 4. This tiny village is situated in a finely-wooded glen between the heights of *Ben Aigan*, 1,544 ft., to the north-west, and *Knockan*, 1,219 ft., to the north-east. *Iter. 170.*

MAGUS MUIR, Fife. Map 17, **NO 4** 1. See **Pitscottie.**

MAIDENS, Ayr. Map 8, **NS 2** 0. A small fishing village and resort on Maidenhead Bay, with a sandy beach. See **Culzean Castle, Kirkoswald** and **Turnberry.** *Iter. 80.*

MAINLAND, Orkney. Map 33, **HY 4** 1 etc. See **Orkney Islands** (Mainland).

MAINLAND, Shetland. Map 33, **HY 4** 4 etc. See **Shetland Islands** (Mainland).

MAINSRIDDLE, Kirkcudbright. Map 3, **NX 9** 5. See **Southerness.** *Iter. 72, 73.*

MALLAIG, Inverness. 921. Map 23, **NM 6** 9. **E.C.** Wed. A fishing harbour and port for the Inner and Outer Hebridean steamers lying in a splendid setting on the rocky shores of North Morar, looking towards Skye. It forms the terminal point of the romantic Road to the Isles. "By Ailort and by Morar to the sea." Steamers, carrying cars, maintain a service to *Armadale* (*q.v.*) in Skye. There are connections by motor launch to *Inverie* (*q.v.*), on the hill-girt inlet of *Loch Nevis* (*q.v.*), which lies on the threshold of the rugged *Knoydart* (*q.v.*) country, in which *Ladhar Bheinn*, 3,343 ft., rises to the south of *Loch Hourn* (*q.v.*). Prince Charles Edward landed at Mallaig, as a fugitive, in 1746, and after much wandering in the lonely hills in the vicinity finally reached *Loch nan Uamh* (*q.v.*). **3 m. E.** of Mallaig rises the pathless, wild and rocky hill of *Carn a'Ghobhair*, 1,794 ft., from the summit of which the view is one of the very finest in Scotland, taking

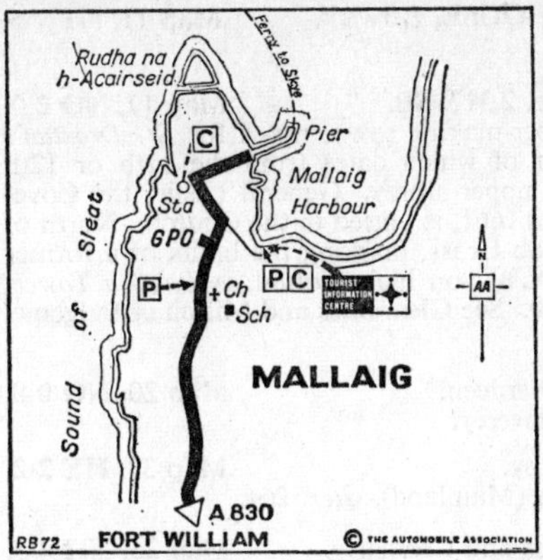

in the whole length of both Loch Morar and Loch Nevis, with their background of picturesque, rocky peaks. The panorama extends westwards over the sea to distant Ardnamurchan Point, and across towards the mountainous outline of Rum, and also Skye, in which the jagged Coolin peaks are the dominating feature. See **Morar.** *Iter. 209, 217, 253.*

MAMORE FOREST, Inverness. Map 18, **NN 1** 6 and **2** 6. The fine group of mountains known as the *Mamore Forest*, or simply the *Mamores*, lies in the heart of *Lochaber* (*q.v.*), between Glen Nevis and Loch Leven. The highest peak is *Binnein Mor*, 3,700 ft., rising above *Kinlochleven* (*q.v.*). The next highest is *Sgurr a'Mhaim*, 3,601 ft., with its white quartzite summit, neighboured by *Stob Ban*, 3,274 ft., both of which form a prominent feature in the view up Glen Nevis at the foot of *Ben Nevis* (*q.v.*). The ridges of the Mamores extend from east to west for a distance of 8 miles, the average height being rarely less than 3,000 ft., providing some of the finest ridge-walking to be found in Scotland. In winter, under snow conditions, they present an impressive sight from many points in the vicinity. A magnificent view of the entire group of hills can be obtained from the summit of Ben Nevis, or from the lofty peaks around *Glencoe* (*q.v.*).

MAM RATTACHAN (or **RATAGAN**) **PASS,** Inverness; Ross and Cromarty. Map 24, **NG 9** 1. This splendid pass, which rises to 1,116 ft., the summit being on the county boundary between Inverness and Ross and Cromarty, links the shores of *Loch Duich* (*q.v.*) with the remote village of *Glenelg* (*q.v.*), on the narrow strait separating the mainland from the island of *Skye* (*q.v.*). The climb is steep (1 in 6) and winding, with hairpin bends, while considerable recent afforestation has somewhat changed the magnificent views from the lower slopes. From the summit, Loch Duich, the jewel of *Kintail* (*q.v.*), is seen in all its beauty, backed by the famous *Five Sisters of Kintail*, dominated by *Scour Ouran*, 3,505 ft., overlooking the defile of *Glen Shiel* (*q.v.*). The whole picture is one of the grandest in Scotland. The descent to the west, following the Glenmore River, is more gradual, and to the south-west is seen the prominent *Ben Sgriol*, 3,196 ft., one of the rugged peaks which guard *Loch Hourn* (*q.v.*). Dr. Johnson and Boswell crossed the pass on horseback during their Highland Tour in 1773 on the way to Glenelg, and the Doctor described it as "a terrible steep to climb." See **Shiel Bridge.** *Iter. 207.*

MANOR, Peebles. 201. Map 9, **NT 2** 3. The little Church of *Manor* stands at the northern extremity of the long and beautiful valley of the Manor Water, which flows into the Tweed to the west of *Peebles* (*q.v.*). In the churchyard is the tombstone of the "Black Dwarf" (see below). The setting is one of green, rounded Lowland hills, becoming loftier as the valley is ascended, and culminating in *Dollar Law*, 2,680 ft. Once a centre of population, the valley is now only sparsely occupied, and several ruined towers, among them *Castlehill* and *Posso*, recall the past. Near the latter is the isolated *Woodhill*, on which stood traditionally a building known as *Macbeth's Castle*. To the south of the Church is *Hallyards Manor*, associated in 1797 with Sir Walter Scott, when visiting David Ritchie, the original of the "Black Dwarf." The present "Black Dwarf's Cottage" is situated a little to the south, and beyond it, to the south-east, rises *Canada Hill*, 1,713 ft. See **Lyne.**

MARCHMONT HOUSE, Berwick. Map 11, **NT 7 5.**
See **Polwarth.**

MARKINCH, Fife. 2,317. SB. Map 17, **NO 2 0.**
E.C. Wed. A paper-making town, noted for *St. Drostan's* Church, the tower of which dates from the 11th or 12th cent., with a later upper storey. General Leslie, the Covenanter, who died in 1661, is buried in the Church. North of the town is the Stob Cross, marking the limits of a former sanctuary. **2 m. N.W.,** on high ground, is *Bandon Tower,* dating from c. 1580. See **Glenrothes** and **Milton of Balgonie.** *Iter. 98.*

MAR LODGE, Aberdeen. Map 20, **NO 0 8.**
See **Braemar** and **Inverey.**

MARWICK, Orkney. Map 33, **HY 2 2.**
See **Orkney Islands** (Mainland). *Iter. 264.*

MARYBANK, Ross and Cromarty. Map 25, **NH 4 5.**
Situated at the eastern extremity of Strath Conon. The road through this wooded glen, backed by high hills, *Scuir Vuillin,* 2,845 ft. and *Bac an Eich,* 2,791 ft., at its farthest extremity where Loch Beannachan is situated, leaves the Beauly to Garve road at Marybank. A little to the south, beyond the windings of the River Orrin, and stretching away to the west, in a district of lonely hills, extends the picturesque but roadless Glen Orrin, on the Inverness border.

MARYBURGH, Ross and Cromarty. 830. Map 25, **NH 5 5.**
Iter. 200, 202, 203, 206, 213.

MARYCULTER, Kincardine. 813. Map 21, **NO 8 9.**
See **Culter** (Aberdeen). *Iter. 168, 174.*

MARYKIRK, Kincardine. 1,076. Map 21, **NO 6 6.**
A village on the North Esk River, situated on the edge of the Vale of *Strathmore* (*q.v.*), near the point where it merges into the country of the *Mearns* (*q.v.*). **3 m. N.W.** is *Inglismaldie Castle,* c. 1700 and later, once the seat of the Earls of Kintore. *Iter. 165.*

MARYWELL, Aberdeen. Map 21, **NO 5 9.**
Iter. 174.

MARYWELL, Angus. Map 21, **NO 6 4.**
Iter. 155.

MAUCHLINE, Ayr. 4,454. Map 8, **NS 4 2.**
E.C. Wed. GOLF. A town visited principally for its associations with Robert Burns, and formerly noted for the manufacture of wooden snuff-boxes. Some of Burns's children and friends, including Gavin Hamilton, are buried in the churchyard, the scene of the poet's "Holy Fair," but the Church itself was rebuilt in 1829. The "Burns House" is where he set up home with Jean Armour. Nearby is "Auld Nanse Tinnock's," now a hostel. In the house of Gavin Hamilton, once Burns's landlord, is the room in which the poet was married in 1788. "Poosie Nansie's" cottage, and the former "*Whitefoord Arms*" Inn both have well-known Burns associations. *Mauchline Castle,* or Abbot Hunter's Tower (A.M.) is of 15th cent. date, and contains a fine vaulted hall. An obelisk recalls five Covenanters hanged in 1685. About a mile to the north of the town is the *Burns Memorial Tower,* with a museum. A little farther west is *Mossgiel* farm, rented by Burns and his brother between 1784 and 1788, and where much of his first volume of poems was completed, before he visited Edinburgh, in 1786. The farm was rebuilt in 1859. To the north-west, about 2 miles distant, is *Lochlea* farm, where the Burns family lived from 1777 to 1784. South-east of the town is the great 19th cent. sandstone railway bridge of *Ballochmoyle,* spanning the Ayr valley. **3 m. W.S.W.** of Mauchline, on the Ayr road, is *Failford* (*q.v.*). See **Auchinleck, Catrine, Sorn, Stair** and **Tarbolton.** *Iter. 35, 67.*

MAUD, Aberdeen. Map 27, **NJ 9 4.**
Iter. 189.

MAVIS GRIND, Shetland. Map 33, **HU 3 6.**
See **Shetland Islands** (Mainland). *Iter. 267.*

MAXTON, Roxburgh. 581 with Roxburgh. Map 10, **NT 6 2.**
Near a loop of the River Tweed, and retaining an old cross shaft. The Church, of 12th cent. foundation, has been much altered. There is a ruined tower of the Kers. See **St. Boswells Green** (for *Mertoun House*). *Iter. 32, 46.*

MAXWELLTOWN, Kirkcudbright. Map 4, **NX 9 7.**
See **Dumfries.**

MAXWELTON HOUSE, Dumfries. Map 3, **NX 8 8.**
See **Moniaive.**

MAYBOLE, Ayr. 4,521. SB. Map 8, **NS 3 0.**
E.C. Wed. GOLF. This small town, once the capital of the *Carrick* (*q.v.*) district, now manufactures shoes and agricultural implements. The restored 17th cent. *Maybole Castle,* in the High St., formerly the town house of the Earls of Cassillis, has picturesque turrets with oriel windows. The partly ancient Tolbooth was formerly a mansion of the Kennedy family. The Collegiate Church (A.M.), founded in 1371, fell into disrepair, and became a burial chapel for the Earls of Cassillis. In a vanished Provost's house, John Knox and an Abbot of Crossraguel held a 3-day theological contest in 1561. A little to the north, near *Cargilston* farm, is a monument to six Covenanters drowned in a slave ship off the Orkney Islands after having been captured in the battle of *Bothwell* (*q.v.*) Brig in 1679. **3½ m. N.E.,** near the banks of the River Doon, is *Cassillis House,* incorporating an old peel tower, and associated with Burn's "Hallowe'en." **1 m. S.** is *Kilhenzie Castle,* 16th to 17th cent., and now a farm. **4 m. S.** is the late 17th cent. *Kilkerran House.* See **Crossraguel Abbey, Culzean Castle, Dunure** (for *Electric Brae*) and **Kirkoswald.** *Iter. 49, 55, 68, 84.*

MAY, ISLE OF, Fife. Map 17, **NT 6 9.**
See **Anstruther.**

MEARNS, Renfrew. Map 8, **NS 5 5.**
See **Newton Mearns.**

MEARNS, THE, Kincardine. Map 21, **NO 6 7** etc.
An alternative name for the county of Kincardine, one particular district of which, between the Rivers North Esk and Bervie Water, is known as the "Howe of the Mearns." This forms a north-eastern extension of the fertile valley of *Strathmore* (*q.v.*) in the counties of Perth and Angus. The "Men o' the Mearns" are supposed to be of particular strength and noted for their efficiency.

MEASACH FALLS, Ross and Cromarty.
Map 29, **NH 2 7.**
See **Braemore Lodge.** *Iter. 204, 206, 222.*

MEIGLE, Perth. 759. Map 17, **NO 2 4.**
To the north of the village, with its old houses, and situated in the *Strathmore* (*q.v.*) valley, flows the River Isla. There is a museum (A.M.) containing a very notable collection of ancient sculptured stones, and Meigle is said to be the place of burial of Queen Guinevere. In the churchyard lies Sir Henry Campbell-Bannerman, the politician, who died in 1908. *Drumkilbo,* a mansion to the east, has fine gardens. See **Alyth, Eassie** and **Newtyle.** *Iter. 151, 153, 160.*

MEIKLEOUR, Perth. Map 17, **NO 1 3.**
A little to the south, near the meeting of the Rivers Tay and Isla, is the famous beech hedge, bordering the grounds of the modern *Meikleour House.* This hedge, which was planted in 1746, is now 85 ft. high and borders the Perth to Blairgowrie road for more than 600 yards. In the village of Meikleour is a Cross, dating from 1698, and the joug stone is still standing. See **Caputh.** *Iter. 152, 157.*

MELLERSTAIN, Berwick. Map 10, **NT 6 3.**
This notable 18th cent. mansion, designed by William and Robert Adam, is associated with an old 17th cent. custom, that of giving a white rose to the reigning monarch when on a visit. There are fine walled gardens adjoining the house, which looks southwards across a lake to the distant Cheviots. Lady Grizel Baillie, a heroine of Covenanting times, is associated with the house. It is shown daily (exc. Sat.), May to end of Sept., 2 to 5.30. (See note page 98.) See **Pathhead** (Midlothian). *Iter. 6, 7.*

Meikleour, Perth. The 'joug' stone, or place of punishment, which stands opposite the Mercat Cross, to the left of the Dunkeld road (A984)

Meikleour, Perth. The famous beech hedge, now 85 feet high. It was first planted in 1746

Maxwelton House, Dumfries. The modernized 17th century home of 'Annie Laurie,' the subject of the famous song, written originally c.1700. It stands on an unclassified road off A702, near Moniaive

Maybole, Ayr. The Monument to six Covenanters, drowned in a slave ship off the Orkneys in 1679. It stands near Cargilston Farm, on an unclassified road a little to the north

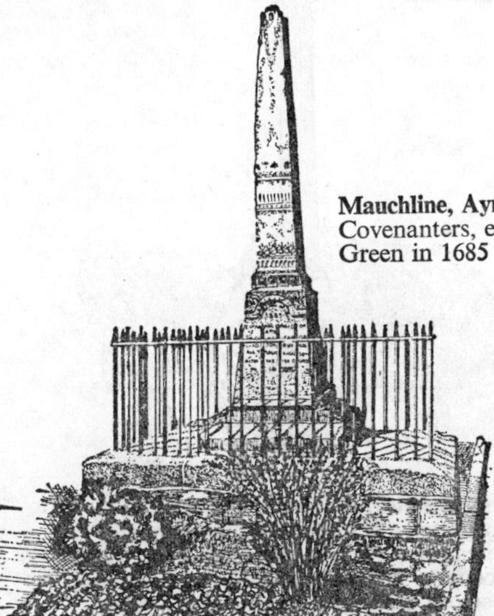

Mauchline, Ayr. The Memorial to five Covenanters, executed on the Loan Green in 1685

Markinch, Fife. The Stob Cross, reputed to be an old sanctuary stone, situated at the northern entrance to the town

[For MAUCHLINE see also under BURNS COUNTRY (Plate 25)

Melness, Sutherland. Moin House, situated off A838, on the moors to the west. It was built originally as a refuge when the road was being constructed in 1830

Methven, Perth. Millhaugh Old Bridge, built in 1619, which carries an unclassified road across the River Almond, some 3 miles north-west of Methven

Merse, Berwick. The Mercat Cross at Duns, which was removed to the park at the beginning of this century. The town stands at the northern edge of the Merse plain

Melrose, Roxburgh. The ruined Cistercian Abbey, founded by monks from Rievaulx, in Yorkshire, in 1136, and showing some of the finest 14th century work in Scotland. It was presented to the nation in 1918 by the Duke of Buccleuch

Methlick, Aberdeen. The remains of the Old Church

Merse, Berwick. A tall column at Coldstream, erected in 1832 in honour of Charles Marjoribanks, a former M.P. for the county. The village stands on the River Tweed, on the southern edge of the plain of the Merse

MELNESS, Sutherland. Map 28, **NC 5 6.** Situated at the mouth of the Kyle of Tongue, on Tongue Bay, overlooking the Rabbit Islands. A sloop, carrying French gold for Prince Charles Edward, ran aground here in 1745. Away to the north-west, not accessible by road, is Whiten Head, on a lonely rockbound stretch of coast, noted for its numerous caves, near the mouth of Loch Eriboll. Inland rises *Beinn Thutaig*, 1,340 ft., overlooking the moors of A'Mhoine, traversed by the road leading westwards towards the shores of Loch Eriboll. **6 m. S.W.** of Melness, on the moors, is *Moin House*, built in 1830 as a refuge while the road was being built. See **Port Vasco** and **Tongue.** *Iter. 225.*

MELROSE, Roxburgh. 2,188. SB. Map 10, **NT 5 3.** **E.C.** Thurs. GOLF. Here, beautifully situated near the River Tweed, famous for its salmon, and with the triple-peaked *Eildon Hills* (*q.v.*) rising just to the south, are the picturesque remains of what is perhaps the finest and best known ruined Scottish Abbey. *Melrose* itself is the "Kennaquhair" of Scott's "Abbot" and "Monastery," while the Abbey was described by him in the "Lay of the Last Minstrel." There are some old houses in the town, and the Cross, which carries the arms of Scotland, dates from 1642. The tower of the Parish Church dates from 1810.

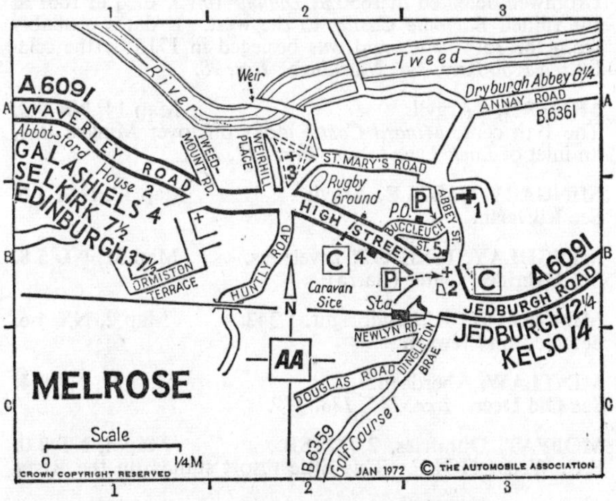

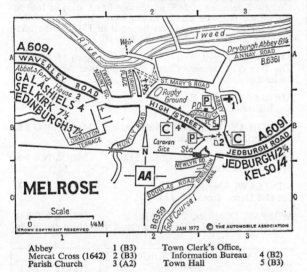

Abbey	1 (B3)	Town Clerk's Office, Information Bureau	4 (B2)
Mercat Cross (1642)	2 (B3)	Town Hall	5 (B3)
Parish Church	3 (A2)		

An old custom kept up is the "Masons' Walk" from the Cross to the Abbey and back by torchlight, on St. John's Day, December 27th. The Cistercian Abbey (A.M.) was founded in 1136, but was almost wrecked by the English during several invasions, more especially in 1322 and 1385, while in 1545 it suffered further serious damage. Parts of the nave and choir date from a rebuilding of 1385, and represent the best and most elaborate work of this period in Scotland. The flying buttresses, pinnacles and rich window tracery, wrought of red sandstone, are all of much interest. The five-light window in the south transept, with its flowing flamboyant tracery, is the finest in the Abbey. A gargoyle on the roof shows a pig with a set of bagpipes. On a west buttress of the south side are carved the Royal Arms. The heart of Robert Bruce is said to have been interred under the east window of the chancel, after it had been brought back from Spain (See **Dunfermline**). In the chancel is also the supposed tomb of Michael Scott, the Wizard, associated with Deloraine in "The Lay." The ground plan of the cloisters and other parts of the monastic buildings has been revealed by recent excavations. The Abbey museum is housed in a 15th to 16th cent. building, possibly the former Commendator's house. There are interesting tombs in the old graveyard, including those oi Scott's wood-forester, Tom Purdie, and of his coachman, Peter Matheson. The whole of the Melrose district is redolent with memories of Sir Walter Scott. See **Abbotsford, Ashiestiel, Darnick, Dryburgh, Earlston, Sandyknowe, Scott Country** and **Smailholm.** *Iter. 13, 32, 41, 43, 52.*

MELVICH, Sutherland. 500. Map 30, **NC 8 6.** **E.C.** Thurs. Lies at the seaward end of the long valley of Strath Halladale, on Melvich Bay. There is fine cliff scenery in the vicinity, notably at *Bighouse*, to the east of the Halladale River, and also at *Portskerra* (*q.v.*). *Iter. 232, 234, 240.*

MENNOCK, Dumfries. Map 9, **NS 8 0.** A tiny Nithsdale village, the starting point of the fine road which winds north-eastwards through the Mennock Pass, rising to more than 1,400 ft. in height. *Lowther Hill*, 2,377 ft. and *Green Lowther*, 2,403 ft., overlook the pass on the short descent to *Wanlockhead* (*q.v.*), Scotland's highest village, after which the road climbs again to a height of 1,531 ft. before reaching *Leadhills* (*q.v.*). Wordsworth and his sister journeyed over the pass in 1803. Across the Nith, to the west of Mennock, is *Eliock House*, which has claims to be the birthplace, in 1560, of the "Admirable Crichton." See **Clunie** and **Enterkinfoot.** *Iter. 27, 48, 49, 67.*

MENSTRIE, Clackmannan. 774. Map 16, **NS 8 9.** **E.C.** Wed. A small weaving and furniture-making town, at the foot of *Dumyat*, 1,375 ft., on the fringe of the *Ochil* hills. The restored 16th cent. Castle, where Sir William Alexander, a 17th cent. North American Colonist, was born, has a Nova Scotia exhibition room open 2.30 to 5, Wed., Sat. and Sun., May to Sept. (See note page 98.) Menstrie was also the birthplace, in 1734, of Sir Ralph Abercromby, the victor of the battle of Alexandria in the Napoleonic wars. *Iter. 136.*

MENTEITH, Perth. 2,110 with Aberfoyle.
See **Port of Menteith.** Map 15, **NN 5 0.**

MENZIES CASTLE, Perth. Map 19, **NN 8 4.**
See **Weem.**

MERCHISTON (Edinburgh), Midlothian. Map 9, **NT 2 6.**
See **Colinton.**

MERKLAND LODGE, Sutherland. Map 28, **NC 4 2.** On Loch Merkland, one of the chain of lochs whose shores are traversed by the road leading from Lairg to the wild north-western seaboard of Scotland, near Loch Laxford. To the north rises *Ben Hee*, 2,864 ft., in the great Reay deer forest, and to the west is *Ben Leoid*, 2,597 ft. *Iter. 229.*

MERSE, THE, Berwick. Map 11, **NT 8 5** etc. A name given to that part of the county of Berwickshire which lies near the valley of the Tweed, and extends in a north-easterly direction towards the Whiteadder Water. It forms the largest plain in Scotland, and contains some of the richest agricultural land. At one time, the Merse included all the flat country between the Cheviots and the Lammermuirs, and the name is still sometimes applied to the whole of Berwickshire. The main road linking Berwick-upon-Tweed with Kelso cuts right through the Merse.

MERTOUN HOUSE, Berwick. Map 10, **NT 3 6.**
See **St. Boswells Green.**

METHIL, Fife. 18,689. SB. with Buckhaven.
Map 17, **NT 3 9.**
E.C. Thurs. An important port for the Fife coalfield, and now linked with *Buckhaven* (*q.v.*), which lies to the south-west. *Iter. 128.*

METHLICK, Aberdeen. 1,254. Map 27, **NJ 8 3.** On the River Ythan, with a modern Church, near which, in the burial ground, is the ruined Old Church. **3½ m. N.W.,** near the river, are the remains of the ancient *Castle of Gight*, in a picturesque, wooded setting, having been besieged by Montrose in 1639. Lord Byron's mother, Catherine Gordon of Gight, was heiress to the estate, but was forced to sell it, in 1787, in order to pay her husband's debts. **2 m. S.S.E.,** in a fine park, is the 18th cent. Adam mansion of *Haddo House*, open on certain Sundays during the summer. (See note page 98.) **3 m. S.E.** is the fine old, restored *House of Schivas*. See **Fochabers, Fyvie** and **Tarves.** *Iter. 186, 197.*

METHVEN, Perth. 1,530. Map 16, **NO 0 2.** Lies at the south-western extremity of the fertile valley of *Strathmore* (*q.v.*). Only a fragment remains from the 15th cent. Church. In 1306, Robert Bruce was defeated by the

English in Methven Wood, and in 1644, near *Tibbermuir*, to the south-east, Montrose defeated the Covenanters. **1½ m. E.** is *Methven Castle*, mainly early 17th cent., in a splendid wooded park. Queen Margaret Tudor died here in 1541. **3 m. N.W.** is *Millhaugh* Old Bridge, built in 1619, and spanning the River Almond. **4½ m. N.W.,** near the River Almond, is *Trinity College, Glenalmond*, a well-known public school, situated in the eastern part of Glen Almond, the finest stretches of which lie beyond the *Sma' Glen* (*q.v.*). See **Huntingtower.** *Iter. 145.*

MEY, Caithness. Map 30, **ND 2 7.**
E.C. Sat. See **East Mey.** *Iter. 240.*

MID CALDER, Midlothian. 1,164. Map 9, **NT 0 6.**
E.C. Wed. Lies on the River Almond, in a district noted for its oil shales. The Church has an apsidal choir, which was rebuilt in 1541. There is some flamboyant 16th cent. window tracery, and also corbels carved with heraldic devices. The remainder of the building is modern. John Knox first administered the Communion under the Protestant rite, in 1556, at *Calder House*, a partly ancient mansion, and here also Chopin stayed in 1848. *Linhouse* is a 16th and 17th cent. house. **2½ m. S.W.** of Mid Calder is *Alderston*, a 17th cent. house, with modern additions, and preserving an old dovecote. *Iter. 18, 19, 20, 22.*

MID CLYTH, Caithness. Map 30, **ND 2 3.**
On the hill-slopes behind the village are 22 parallel rows of prehistoric stones, comprising 192 in all, the best examples in the county. **2 m. N.W.,** off the Wick road, is the picturesque sandstone inlet of *Whaligoe*. See **Ulbster.** *Iter 200.*

MIDDLETON, Midlothian. Map 10, **NT 3 5.**
A small village on the northern slopes of the *Moorfoot* hills. From here, a road deviates from the main Galashiels road to penetrate into the hills, attaining a height of over 1,200 ft., and later reaching Tweeddale at *Innerleithen* (*q.v.*). See **Borthwick Castle.** *Iter. 9, 11, 12.*

MIDMAR CASTLE, Aberdeen. Map 21, **NJ 7 0.**
This splendid example of a late 16th cent. or early 17th cent. Scottish castle in the baronial style is situated to the north of the *Hill of Fare*, 1,545 ft., just off the Aberdeen to Tarland road, and is notable for a characteristic display of turrets. The Castle is said to have been built originally by Sir William Wallace, and was formerly known as *Ballogie*. The garden is 17th cent. The old churchyard of Midmar, in the near vicinity, contains a slab, dated 1575, to the memory of George Bell, probably the master-mason of the castle. *Iter. 179.*

MILLHOUSE, Argyll. Map 7, **NR 9 7.**
See **Kames.** *Iter 102.*

MILLPORT, Great Cumbrae Island, Bute. 1,128. SB.
GOLF. Map 7, **NS 1 5.**
Faces Millport Bay, on the Island of *Great Cumbrae*, in the Firth of Clyde, and is reached by steamer from *Largs* (*q.v.*), *Fairlie* (*q.v.*) or *Wemyss Bay* (*q.v.*) on the mainland. There are good sands and bathing. The modern Collegiate Church was consecrated in 1876 as the Episcopal Cathedral of Argyll and the Isles. On the eastern shores of the island, adjacent to *Keppel* pier, is a Marine Biological Station and museum. The island is only about 10 miles in circumference, and a road encircles its shores, giving good views. To the south is *Little Cumbrae* island, on which stands a lighthouse. Off its eastern shores lies the tiny Castle Island, on which are the remains of a Castle, destroyed by Cromwell, in 1653.

MILNATHORT, Kinross. 1,139. Map 17, **NO 1 0.**
E.C. Thurs. **M.D.** Mon. GOLF. A small woollen-manufacturing town, standing a little to the north of *Loch Leven* (*q.v.*). To the east is the ruined *Burleigh Castle*, dated 1582 (A.M.), a former stronghold of the Balfours, and with which Scott's "Old Mortality" is associated. In the vicinity, a few miles to the south-east, are the standing stones of *Orwell*. *Iter. 90, 91, 92, 98, 136.*

MILNGAVIE, Dunbarton. 10,742. SB. Map 8, **NS 5 7.**
E.C. Tues. GOLF. A small town in a pleasant setting, with the Mugdock and Craigmaddie reservoirs to the north. Beyond the reservoirs, amid woodlands, stands *Mugdock Castle*, preserving an old tower. To the south of the town are faint traces of the former Antonine, or *Roman Wall* (*q.v.*). **2 m. E.** is the 16th cent. *Bardowie Castle*, facing its tiny loch. **2 m. N.E.** is *Craigmaddie Castle*, only the foundations remaining. To the east, on Blairskaith Muir, are the strange boulders known as the *Auld Wives' Lichts*. See **Strathblane.** *Iter. 105, 108.*

MILTON, Dunbarton. Map 8, **NS 4 7.**
Iter. 88, 100, 101, 102.

MILTON, Perth. Map 16, **NN 9 3.**
Lies in Strath Bran, which is here joined by Glen Cochill, traversed by the road leading to *Aberfeldy* (*q.v.*). To the north-west rises *Meall Dearg*, 2,258 ft. overlooking the lonely little Loch Fender. *Iter. 89, 140, 141, 147.*

MILTON, Ross and Cromarty. Map 31, **NH 7 7.**
An old-world village, known also as *Milntown*. *Tarbat House* faces the Bay of Nigg.

MILTON BRIDGE, Midlothian. Map 9, **NT 2 6.**
GOLF. See **Roslin.** *Iter. 10, 24.*

MILTON OF BALGONIE, Fife. Map 17, **NO 3 0.**
David Leslie, Lord Newark, the Covenanting general whom Cromwell defeated in 1650 at *Dunbar* (*q.v.*), died in 1661 at the ruined *Balgonie Castle*, to the west. It dates probably from the 15th cent., and was besieged in 1716 by the celebrated Rob Roy. See **Markinch.** *Iter. 98.*

MINARD, Argyll. Map 14, **NR 9 9.**
The 19th cent. *Minard Castle* looks out over Minard Bay, an inlet of *Loch Fyne* (*q.v.*). *Iter. 118, 121.*

MINGARY CASTLE, Argyll Map 12, **NM 4 6.**
See **Kilchoan.**

MINGULAY, ISLE OF, Inverness. Map 32, **NL 5 8.**
See **Hebrides, Outer** (Barra).

MINNIGAFF, Kirkcudbright. 1,342. Map 2, **NX 4 6.**
See **Newton Stewart.**

MINTLAW, Aberdeen. Map 27, **NJ 9 4.**
See **Old Deer.** *Iter. 185, 188, 189.*

MOFFAT, Dumfries. 2,034. SB. Map 4, **NT 0 0.**
E.C. Wed. GOLF. This little resort stands on the River

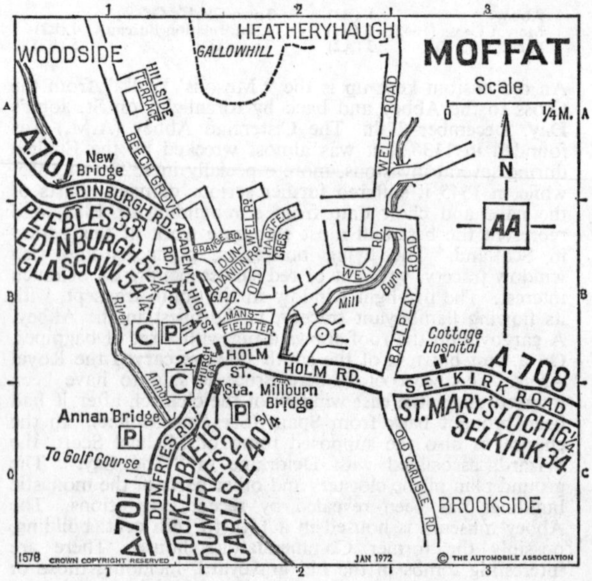

Colvin Fountain 1 (B1) Town Hall 3 (B1)
St. Andrew's Parish Church 2 (B1)

Mid Clyth, Caithness. Rows of prehistoric stones, nearly 200 in all, on the Hill of Clyth behind the village

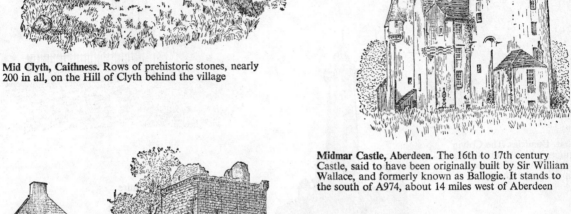

Midmar Castle, Aberdeen. The 16th to 17th century Castle, said to have been originally built by Sir William Wallace, and formerly known as Ballogie. It stands to the south of A974, about 14 miles west of Aberdeen

Milnathort, Kinross. The ruined Burleigh Castle, a former Balfour fortress, dated 1582. It stands to the east of the town, on A911

Milton of Balgonie, Fife. The ruined 15th century Balgonie Castle, to the west, off A911. It was besieged by Rob Roy in 1716, and became later the home of the Covenanter General Leslie

Mingary Castle, Argyll. The ruined Clan Macdonald fortress, visited by James IV in 1495, and captured for Montrose in 1644. It stands near Kilchoan, on an unclassified road off B8007

Millerston, Lanark. The Monument on the site of the house in which Sir John Menteith, the 'fause' Menteith, betrayed William Wallace and a copatriot in 1305. It stands 2 miles north-west, on an unclassified road

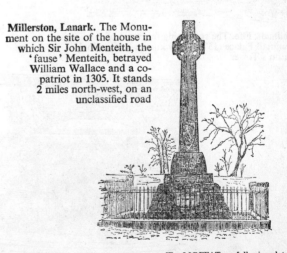

[For MOFFAT see following plate
[For MID CALDER see Plate 174

Moniaive, Dumfries. The Monument to James Renwick, the last of the Covenanter martyrs, who was executed at Edinburgh in 1688, at the age of 26

Moffat, Dumfries. The Colvin fountain, with its ram, signifying the importance of the local sheep farming industry

Monikie, Angus. The Panmure Monument, on a hillside to the south. It commemorates the first Lord Panmure of Brechin, who died in 1852

Monimail, Fife. The remaining fragment of Monimail Palace (1573), now known as Cardinal Beaton's Tower

Montrose, Angus. The Town Hall, erected in 1763. Dr. Johnson, after his visit in 1773, spoke of its " good dining-room and other rooms for tea drinking "

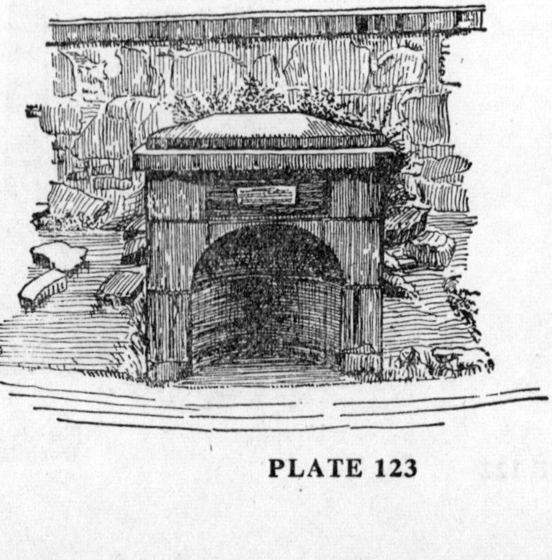

Montrose, Angus. The Medicine Well, well known as a spa during the 18th century

[For MONIAIVE see also under MAXWELTON HOUSE (Plate 120)

PLATE 123

Annan, in a delightful setting of Lowland hills. It makes a good centre for walks in Annandale, as well as being noted for angling. The *Colvin* fountain, surmounted by a ram, stands in the town, and signifies the importance of sheep-farming in this district. A sulphur spring, situated **1½ m. N.E.** of the town, was discovered in 1630, and brought some fame to Moffat as a spa, among the visitors for its waters being Boswell and Burns. From the 18th cent. *Moffat House*, now a hotel, James Macpherson published, in 1759, his " Ossianic Fragments." John Macadam, who lived at *Dumcrieff House*, on the Moffat Water to the south-east, was buried in the churchyard, in 1836. *St. Andrew's* Parish Church, the successor to an older building, dates from 1887. *Garpol Glen* (**2 m. S.W.**) and *Bell Craig Glen* (**4 m. S.E.**) are attractive glens. *Lochfell*, 2,256 ft., to the east, is a good viewpoint. The Edinburgh road, leaving the town in a northerly direction, climbs into the hills, and reaches, after five miles, the well-known *Devil's Beef Tub*, a spectacular Upper Annandale hollow by the side of the road at Ericstane Brae, over-shadowed by steep, green slopes, and associated with Scott's " Redgauntlet." There is a memorial stone (1935) to John Hunter, a Covenanter, shot on a nearby hill-side, in 1685. A little farther to the north-west, at a height of more than 1,300 ft., is the meeting point of the counties of Dumfries, Lanark and Peebles, near which is the watershed where the Rivers Annan, Clyde and Tweed (See **Tweedsmuir**) all have their sources. North-east from Moffat, the road towards *St. Mary's Loch* (*q.v.*) follows the Moffat Water past the *Burns Cottage*, near which is Craigieburn Wood, associated with the poet. Beyond this point, *Saddle Yoke*, 2,412 ft., *Hart Fell*, 2,651 ft., and *White Coomb*, 2,695 ft., rise to the west, and the road later reaches the notable waterfall known as the *Grey Mare's Tail*, some 200 ft. high. In the hilly background lies the lonely Loch Skene. See **Beattock** and **Birkhill.** *Iter. 10, 13, 24, 46, 49.*

MOIDART, Inverness. Map 12, **NM 7 7** etc.
The name applied to the wild and mountainous Clanranald country, lying between the western shores of *Loch Shiel* (*q.v.*) and the Sound of Arisaig, and associated very largely with Prince Charles Edward and the '45. Loch Ailort and *Loch nan Uamh* (*q.v.*) are two picturesque inlets of the Sound, the last-named having witnessed both the arrival and the departure of the Prince. At the western extremity of Moidart lies Loch Moidart, which divides the district from the remote Ardnamurchan peninsula. See **Acharacle, Dalilea, Kinlochmoidart** and **Lochailort.**

MONALTRIE, Aberdeen. Map 20, **NO 2 9.**
South-west of the ruined *Monaltrie House* is the Farquharson *Cairn-na-Cuimhne*, or Cairn of Remembrance, near the River Dee, off A93.

MONDYNES BRIDGE, Kincardine. Map 21, **NO 7 7.**
See **Drumlithie.** *Iter. 151, 156.*

MONIAIVE, Dumfries. 527. Map 3, **NX 7 9.**
E.C. Thurs. Three streams meet in the vicinity of this pleasant village to form the Cairn Water. The village Cross dates from 1638, and there is a monument to James Renwick, the last Covenanter martyr, who died in 1688. **3 m. E.S.E.** is *Maxwelton House*, carrying the date 1641, but altered and modernised, and long the seat of the Laurie family, being well known as the one-time home of the heroine of " Annie Laurie." To the south-west of the house is the little village of *Kirkland*, and also *Glencairn* Church, where Annie Laurie and her husband are said to be buried. **2½ m. W.** of Moniaive, off the Carphairn road, is *Craigdarroch*, built by William Adam in 1729, with its lovely gardens. It was once the married home of Annie Laurie, and where she died. See **Penpont.** *Iter. 25, 74.*

MONIFIETH, Angus. 6,333. SB. Map 17, **NO 4 3.**
E.C. Wed. GOLF. A small resort, with a sandy beach, to the east of which are the Barry Links, on which is situated a large military training-ground. Farther to the south-east is Buddon Ness. See **Broughty Ferry.** *Iter. 155.*

MONIKIE, Angus. 919. Map 17, **NO 5 3.**
Beyond the reservoirs, to the west of the station, stands the battlemented and turreted 15th cent. keep of *Affleck Castle* (A.M.), in which is a vaulted chapel and also a solar. The castle is usually viewable (weekdays only) on application. (See note page 98.) South of Monikie, in a prominent position on a hillside, is the *Panmure* monument.

MONIMAIL, Fife. Map 17, **NO 2 1.**
The Church has the Melville gallery and a notable Adam ceiling. *Melville House*, to the south-west, now a school, is a fine house of 1692, with an imposing lay-out and an interesting interior attributed to Sir William Bruce. *Monimail*, or *Beaton's Tower* dates from 1578 and is the surviving portion of an ecclesiastical palace.

MONKTON, Ayr. 3,134 with Symington. Map 8, **NS 3 2.**
M.D. Tues. Stands a little inland from Ayr Bay, its Church preserving a Romanesque doorway. See **Symington (Ayr),** and **Tarbolton.** *Iter. 60, 66, 88.*

MONREITH, Wigtown. Map 2, **NX 3 4.**
Situated on Monreith Bay, in the Machers peninsula, between Barsalloch Point and the Point of Lag. Near the latter is the ancient, restored Church of *Kirkmaiden-in-Fernis. Monreith House*, about **2 m. N.E.** of Barsalloch Point, is well known from the essays of Sir Thomas Maxwell, and possesses very notable woodland gardens, with magnificent rhododendrons. In the park is the White Loch of Myrton, and in the grounds of the mansion stands the carved, wheel-headed *Monreith Cross* (A.M.). In the vicinity is the ruined *Myrton Castle*. *Iter. 82.*

MONTROSE, Angus. 9,963. SB. Map 21, **NO 7 5.**
E.C. Wed. **M.D.** Fri. GOLF. A well-known resort, fishing port, and Royal Burgh, with excellent sands and bathing, situated on the estuary of the South Esk River. This flows through Montrose Basin, a tidal lagoon, some two miles square, behind the town. Montrose has a long history, and formerly possessed a strong castle, which was occupied in 1296 by Edward I, before Wallace destroyed it during the following year. The Old Pretender sailed from the harbour at the close of the 1715 rising, and at *Old Montrose*, beyond the Basin, was born, in 1612, the famous Marquis of

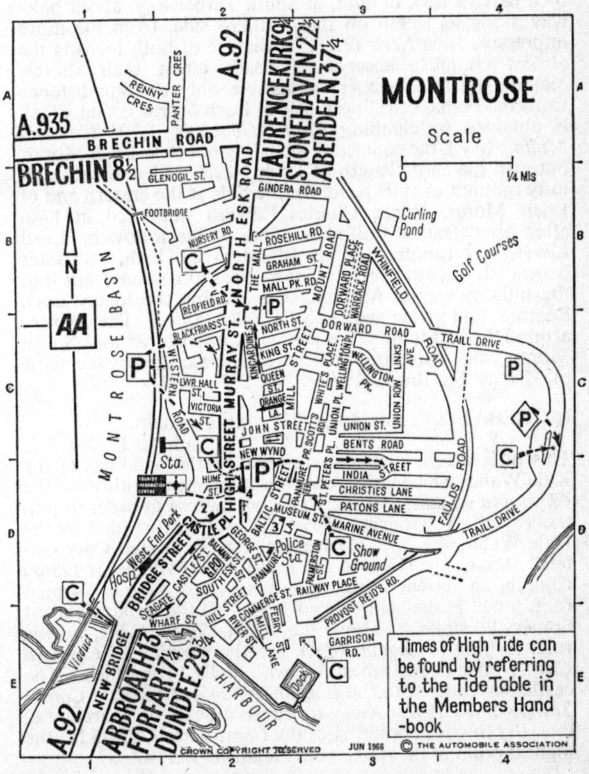

Church, 18th cent.	1 (D2)	Town Hall and Tourist Information Centre	4 (D2)
Library	2 (D2)		
Museum	3 (D2)		

Montrose. Both the Town Hall and the Church date from the late 18th cent., the spire of the latter being a 19th cent. addition by Gillespie Graham. The restored Medicine Well was much visited as a spa during the 18th cent. See **Ferryden, Inverkeilor,** and **Usan.** *Iter. 153, 155, 164, 165, 166.*

MONYMUSK, Aberdeen. 1,992. Map 27, **NJ 6 1.**
A village situated just off the Alford to Inverurie road, and which was formerly the site of a Priory and later of a monastery. The remains of the Priory Church, probably of Norman date, are incorporated in the present Parish Church. The well-known Monymusk Reliquary, a casket of the Celtic period, is now in the National Museum of Antiquities in Edinburgh. *Monymusk House* is of 16th-18th cent. date. To the north-west of the village rises *Cairn William*, 1,469 ft., and below its wooded eastern shoulder, known as *Pitfichie Hill*, is the ruined *Pitfichie Castle*, beyond which flows the River Don in a delightful, wooded gorge setting past Paradise Wood, which Queen Victoria visited in 1866 to see the larches planted in 1741 **1½ m. S.** of Monymusk is the modern *Cluny Castle*. See **Kemnay.** *Iter. 177.*

MOORFOOT HILLS, Midlothian. Map 10, **NT 3 5.**
See **Eddleston, Heriot** and **Temple.** *Iter. 12, 40.*

MORAR, Inverness. Map 23, **NM 6 9.**
E.C. Wed. Situated on the narrow neck of land separating Loch Morar from the outer waters of the Sound of Sleat, and through which flows the Morar River, with the Falls of Morar, now harnessed to a local hydro-electric scheme. The bay formed by the estuary is famous for its white sands, and looks across the sea to the picturesque outlines of the islands of Rum and Eigg. Loch Morar, a little to the east, has a depth of 180 fathoms, almost the deepest known hollow in Europe, and the scenery along its shores, notably at the east end, where the hills are highest, is of great beauty. On an island in the lake stood formerly an 18th cent. Catholic college, and also the residence of the Pope's Vicar Apostolic of Scotland. Loch Morar is separated by a narrow neck of land, at South Tarbet Bay, about halfway along its length on the northern side, from the more impressive *Loch Nevis* (*q.v.*). A feature of both lochs is the almost complete absence of roads along their shores, making the finest scenery accessible only to long-distance walkers. Perhaps the finest view of Loch Morar is that which is obtained by climbing *Carn a'Ghobhair*, 1,794 ft. from *Mallaig* (*q.v.*), the panorama including not only Loch Morar, but also the entire length of Loch Nevis, with the cirque of lofty mountains at its head. In the hills at the eastern end of Loch Morar, Prince Charles Edward wandered in 1746 after his defeat at Culloden. One of his followers, Lord Lovat, was captured on an island in the loch, and later beheaded. A path from a point on the south shore leads into the hills by way of Meoble, later passing the lonely Loch Beoraid, and giving access to *Lochailort* (*q.v.*). The country around Loch Morar is known as North Morar and South Morar, while the entire district is often described by the name of Morar. See **Bracora.** *Iter. 209, 217.*

MOREBATTLE, Roxburgh. 711 with Hounam.
Map 11, **NT 7 2.**
This little village is almost encircled by the windings of the Kale Water, which flows southwards from the outliers of the *Cheviot* (*q.v.*) hills, and then turns westwards in order to join the Teviot. The lonely valley to the south, threaded by the Kale Water, was once a refuge for the persecuted Covenanters. Across the river, to the north of the village, is *Linton* Church, an ancient structure, now restored, with a Norman font, a bell in the belfry dated 1697, and the notable carved Somerville stone set above the porch. **2½ m. S.W.,** on the road leading to *Oxnam* (*q.v.*), are the remains of *Cessford Castle*, built of reddish stone, with walls 14 ft. thick. The castle surrendered to the English in 1545. **1 m. S.** is *Corbet Tower*, dated 1592. Away to the south-east of Morebattle, over the English border, rises the *Cheviot* itself, 2,676 ft., the highest point of the range. See **Hounam.** *Iter. 47.*

MORTON LOCHS, Fife. Map 17, **NO 4 2.**
See **Tayport.**

MORVEN, Argyll. Map 12, **NM 6 5** etc.
The district of *Morven*, or *Morvern*, is bounded to the north by *Loch Sunart* (*q.v.*), and to the west and east by the Sound of Mull and *Loch Linnhe* (*q.v.*) respectively. It is mainly a country of low hills, though *Creach Bheinn*, in the north-eastern corner, attains 2,800 ft., and forms a very fine viewpoint. Some of the best views of Morven are those obtained from the steamers linking Fort William with Oban in summer. See **Drimnin, Laracheb g** and **Lochaline.** *Iter. 218.*

MOSCOW, Ayr. Map 8, **NS 4 4.**
A small village on the little River Volga. From its moorland setting there are westerly views towards the Firth of Clyde.

MOSSEND, Lanark. 5,200. Map 9, **NS 7 6.**
Iter. 18.

MOSSGIEL, Ayr. Map 8, **NS 4 2.**
See **Mauchline.**

MOSSTODLOCH, Moray. Map 26, **NJ 5 5.**
A pleasant village, situated immediately to the west of Fochabers Bridge across the Spey, the predecessor of the bridge having been destroyed in the floods of 1829. **3 m. N.** of Mosstodloch, and on the left bank of the Spey before it reaches the sea, stands *Garmouth* (*q.v.*), once a port. See **Fochabers** and **Spey Bay.** *Iter. 171, 175, 187, 198, 199.*

MOTHERWELL, with Wishaw, Lanark. 74,184. LB.
Map 9, **NS 7 5.**
GOLF. The centre of an important coal-mining area, forming, together with *Wishaw*, a single Burgh. It is noted for iron, steel and engineering works. The great Dalzell works were founded by David Colville in 1871. The site of the

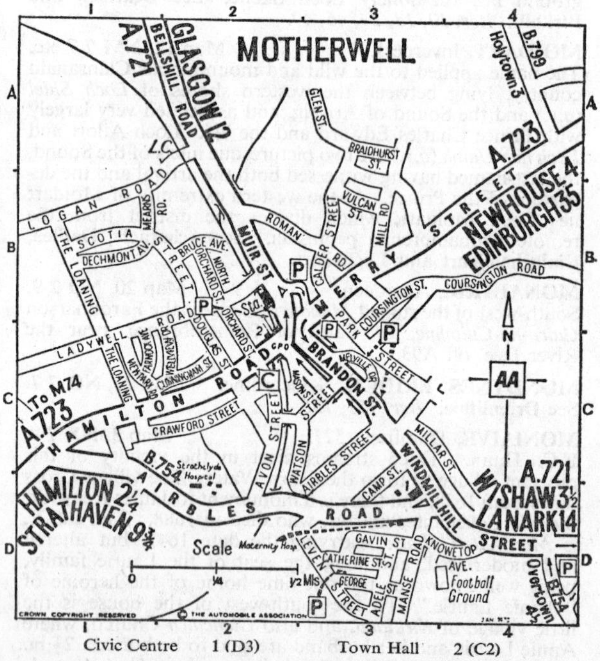

Civic Centre 1 (D3) Town Hall 2 (C2)

original " well " is marked by a plaque in Ladywell Road. North of the town is *Jerviston House*, the 16th cent. tower of the Baillie family. To the south-east of *Motherwell*, near the River Clyde is *Dalzell House*, 17th cent. and later, incorporating a 15th cent. tower. *Iter. 19, 54, 87.*

MOULIN, Perth. 597. Map 20, **NN 9 5.**
E.C. Thurs. A picturesque little village, in the vicinity of which are the remains of *Castle Dhu*. To the east is *Kinnaird Cottage*, where R. L. Stevenson lived and wrote, in 1881. *Craigour*, 1,300 ft., (N.T. Scot.), to the north-west, is a good viewpoint, and to the north rises *Ben Vrackie*, 2,757 ft. The

Morar, Inverness. The White Sands of Morar, which fringe the bay. Loch Morar, to the east, is 180 fathoms in depth, one of Europe's greatest hollows

Morar, Inverness. The Falls of Morar, its waters now used by a local hydro-electric scheme. This district is said to be the setting for L. A. G. Strong's novel, '*The Brothers*'

Morebattle, Roxburgh. The ruined Cessford Castle, which surrendered to the Earl of Surrey in 1545. It stands 2½ miles to the south-west, on an unclassified road

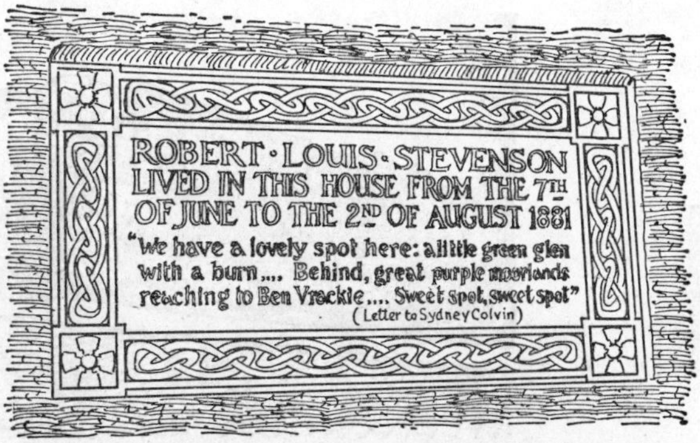

Moulin, Perth. The inscribed panel on Kinnaird Cottage, where Robert Louis Stevenson wrote several of his shorter works, including '*Thrawn Janet*,' during 1881

Moscow, Ayr. The sign at the small village of Moscow, which actually stands on the River Volga

Mound, Sutherland. Thomas Telford's embankment across Loch Fleet, built in 1815, at a cost of £9,600, in order to obviate the use of a ferry

Moy, Inverness. The obelisk to Sir Aeneas Mackintosh, who died in 1820. It stands on an island of Loch Moy, and is visible from A9

Muchalls, Kincardine. The 17th century Muchalls Castle, which was built by the Burnetts of Leys

Muir of Ord, Ross and Cromarty. The restored 17th century Kilcoy Castle of the Stewarts and later of the Mackenzies. It stands 4 miles east-north-east, off an unclassified road between A832 and B9162

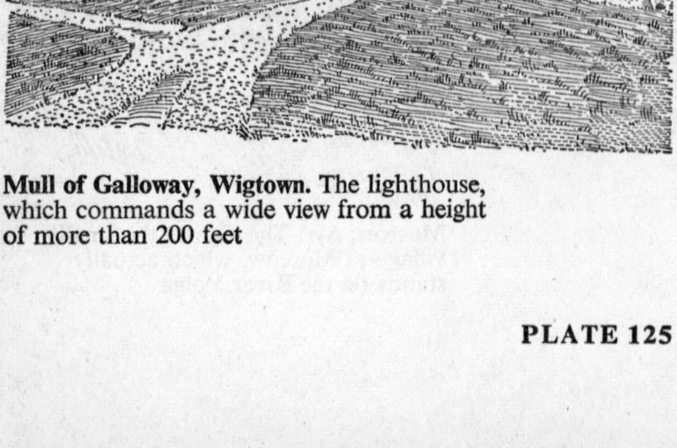

Mull of Galloway, Wigtown. The lighthouse, which commands a wide view from a height of more than 200 feet

Musselburgh, Midlothian. The mid-16th-century footbridge across the River Esk, for the repair of which an Act of Parliament was passed in 1597

[For MUSSELBURGH see also following plate

road leading north-eastwards towards Kirkmichael climbs to 1,260 ft. before descending into Glen Brerachan. See **Pitlochry.** *Iter. 159, 162, 167, 168.*

MOUND, THE, Sutherland. Map 31, **NH 7 9.**
The 1,000-yard long embankment, which here carries both the road and the railway across the waters of Loch Fleet, was constructed by Telford, in 1815, in order to reclaim some of the land and obviate the use of a ferry. The *Mound Alderwoods* National Nature Reserve covers 689 acres. *Iter. 200, 231, 233.*

MOUNT VERNON (Glasgow), Lanark. 5,819. Map 8, **NS 6 6.**
On the south-eastern outskirts of Glasgow, near the River Clyde, and adjacent to Calderpark, where the Zoological Park of *Glasgow* (*q.v.*) is situated. *Iter. 51, 54.*

MOUSA, Shetland. Map 33, **HU 4 2.**
See **Shetland Islands** (Mainland).

MOUSWALD, Dumfries. Map 4, **NY 0 7.**
A tall late 18th cent. tower windmill is still standing.

MOY, Inverness. 511. Map 25, **NH 7 3.**
To the east is Loch Moy, on an island of which are remains of a castle, and also an obelisk to the memory of Sir Aeneas Mackintosh. *Moy Hall*, at the north end of the loch, was commenced in 1955 to replace a former house, and is the seat of the chief of the Clan Mackintosh. An episode, known as the " Rout of Moy," took place in the vicinity during the '45, when a force under Lord Loudoun fled in disorder. **3 m. N.,** on the Inverness road, beyond the tiny Lochan a' Chaoruinn, a fine view is opened up over Strath Nairn, and towards the far-distant *Ben Wyvis*, 3,429 ft., to the north-west. *Iter. 140, 150, 195.*

MUCHALLS, Kincardine. 500. Map 21, **NO 9 9.**
E.C. Wed./Thurs. Situated just off the Stonehaven to Aberdeen road, on a picturesque stretch of coast, with cliffs and gullies. The Castle dates from the 17th cent. and belonged to the Burnetts of Leys. It is shown Tues. and Sun., 3 to 5.30, May to Sept., or by arrangement (see note page 98). To the north are the little fishing villages of Skateraw, Porthleven and *Findon* (*q.v.*). *Iter. 151, 155, 156.*

MUCK, ISLE OF, Inverness. Map 12, **NG 4 7.**
See **Rum.**

MUIRFIELD, East Lothian. Map 10, **NT 4 8.**
See **Gullane.** *Iter. 2, 36, 37.*

MUIRHEAD, Lanark. 3,229. Map 8, **NS 6 6.**
GOLF. The small lochs of Johnston, Bishop, Woodend and Lochend lie to the south-east. *Iter. 17, 97, 99.*

MUIRKIRK, Ayr. 3,652. Map 8, **NS 6 2.**
In a district of coal-mines and ironworks, and situated on the River Ayr. The Church was built in 1650. To the south-east rise *Cairn Table*, 1,944 ft., and *Stony Hill*, 1,843 ft., on the Lanark border, the former crowned with prehistoric cairns. Still farther south is *Three Shire Hill*, where a boulder marks the meeting of three counties: Ayr, Dumfries and Lanark. **5 m. S.W.** is Airds Moss, a barren expanse of moorland, where, in 1680, a fight took place between Royalists and Covenanters, in which Richard Cameron, who gave his name to a famous regiment, was slain. A monument commemorates the action. *Iter. 21, 25, 35, 68.*

MUIR OF ORD, Ross and Cromarty. Map 25, **NH 5 5.**
GOLF. Now the centre of a crofting district, and formerly noted for its cattle fairs. **2 m. S.E.,** near the Beauly Firth, is *Taradale House*, where Sir Roderick Murchison, the 19th cent. geologist, was born. **4 m. E.N.E.** is *Kilcoy Castle*, 17th cent., restored, a good example of the Scottish baronial style, with the Stuart arms carved on the west tower. See **Marybank.** *Iter. 200, 201, 204, 205, 206, 213, 221.*

MULL, ISLE OF, Argyll. 1,675. Map 13, **NM 5** 3 etc.
The picturesque, hilly island of *Mull*, one of the Inner Hebrides, lies in the approaches to *Loch Linnhe* (*q.v.*), and is separated from the mainland coast of *Morven* (*q.v.*) by the Sound of Mull, and from the coast of *Lorne* (*q.v.*) by the Firth of Lorne. Irregular in shape, and only about 30 miles in length, the rocky coastline, owing to its numerous sea-lochs and indentations, measures approximately 300 miles. The island is almost cut in two at one point opposite the Sound of Mull, where the inlet of Loch na Keal, on the west coast, is separated from the Sound by only 3 miles of land. Mull is accessible by steamers from Oban calling at Craignure, Salen or Tobermory. With the exception of the stretch between Salen and Tobermory, the chief centre on the island, the roads are narrow, winding and difficult for passing, while some of the surfaces are poor. About 120 miles of road are suitable for motoring. The road which goes round the north-western extremity of Mull, from Tobermory to the shores of Loch Tuath and thence to Loch na Keal, is winding and hilly (1 in 6), with hairpin bends, but is scenically of much interest. The shores of Loch na Keal, in which lies the small island of Forsa, are traversed for their entire length by a road providing fine scenery, and in the background, to the south, rises *Ben More*, 3,169 ft., the monarch of Mull, a fine viewpoint. The road along the loch is overlooked by the steep Gribun cliffs, facing the islands of Inch Kenneth and Ulva, and later turns south to reach the northern shore of Loch Scridain. The south-western peninsula of the island is known as the Ross of Mull, and is traversed by the road leading to Fionnphort west of Bunessan. From Fionnphort a passenger ferry plies to *Iona* (*q.v.*), to the north of which lies the island of *Staffa* (*q.v.*). In the south-east corner of Mull lie the picturesque Lochs Buie and Spelve, while near Craignure stands the well-known restored *Duart Castle*. The island was visited by Dr. Johnson during his Highland tour of 1773, and his comment was " O Sir! a most dolorous country." See **Bunessan, Calgary, Carsaig Bay, Craignure** (for *Duart Castle*), **Dervaig, Gribun, Kilninian, Lochbuie, Pennyghael, Salen** (Mull), **Tobermory** and **Ulva Ferry.** *Iter. 248, 249, 250.*

MULL OF GALLOWAY, Wigtown. Map 2, **NX 1 3.**
The most southerly point on the mainland of Scotland, at the extremity of the Rhinns of Galloway peninsula. The lighthouse stands at a height of 210 ft., and commands an extensive view. Nearby are ancient entrenchments, thought to have been the last defences of the Picts against the Scots. There are scanty remains of *St. Medan's* Chapel, near Mull Farm, overlooking Luce Bay. *Iter. 82.*

MULL OF KINTYRE, Argyll. Map 6, **NR 5 0.**
This wild headland, the terminal point of the long and narrow *Kintyre* (*q.v.*) peninsula, is approached by a rough and narrow road from *Southend* (*q.v.*), which descends about 1,000 ft. in a mile and a half. The last portion of the road is private. A lighthouse is situated near South Point, built originally in 1788, and having been remodelled by Robert Stevenson. The views from here are remarkable, and extend towards the open Atlantic and the coast of Northern Ireland, with Rathlin Island some 12 miles distant, the Mull being the nearest point in Scotland to the Irish coast. Behind the lighthouse rises *Beinn na Lice*, 1,405 ft. *Iter. 123.*

MULL OF OA, Isle of Islay, Argyll. Map 6, **NR 2 4.**
Situated in the extreme south of the island, in the Oa peninsula, with fine cliff scenery and caves. A little to the east is an American memorial to the soldiers drowned in the loss of the " Tuscania," in the First World War. (See **Port Ellen.**) The road from Port Ellen ends about a mile short of the Mull itself, accessible on foot only. *Iter. 244.*

MURRAYFIELD (Edinburgh), Midlothian. Map 9, **NT 2 7.**
See **Corstorphine.**

MUSSELBURGH, Midlothian. 16,853. SB. Map 10, **NT 3 7.**
E.C. Wed./Thurs. GOLF. Stands on the sandy estuary

of the River Esk, and looks out over the Firth of Forth to the distant coast of Fife, with the *Lomond* hills rising dimly in the background. *Musselburgh* has a number of local industries, and mussels are still gathered, a picturesque ceremony still observed being the annual autumn fishermen's "Walks of Thanksgiving," which take place in the town and in the adjoining village of *Fisherrow*, across the river. There is a Tolbooth, dating from c. 1591, in which an old clock, given by the Dutch, in 1496, is preserved. Nearby stands the Mercat Cross. A statue in the town commemorates David Moir, the "Delta" of Blackwood's Magazine. An old three-arched footbridge still spans the river upstream from Rennie's bridge of 1807. An Act of Parliament was passed in 1597 for its repair, and the structure may date from the mid-16th cent. Near the links, noted for golf, horse-racing and archery, and on which Cromwell camped after the battle of *Dunbar* (*q.v.*), in 1650, stands *Loretto College*, a well-known Public School A chapel of "Our Lady of Loretto" stood formerly on the site, and the stones are said to have been used in the building of the Tolbooth at Musselburgh. South of the town is *Monkton House*, 16th cent. and later. See **Carberry Hill, Inveresk, Pinkie House** and **Prestonpans.** *Iter. 1, 2.*

MUTHILL, Perth. 1,197. Map 16, **NN 8 1.**
E.C. Wed. GOLF. A Strath Earn village, in a wooded setting, on the outskirts of the park of *Drummond Castle.* (See **Crieff.**) The ancient Church, abandoned many years ago, was largely 15th cent. The fine Romanesque tower, 12th cent. or earlier, with a later gabled roof, is still standing, as is also the old chancel arch. *Iter. 89, 140.*

NAIRN, Nairn. 8,038. SB. Map 25, **NH 8 5.**
E.C. Wed. **M.D.** Thurs. GOLF. A well-known Royal Burgh, resort and golfing centre on the Moray Firth, with good sands and bathing, and a particularly dry and sunny climate. The town, once known as *Invernairn*, stands on the River Nairn, and makes an excellent centre for visiting the wooded country in the vicinity, as well as the exceptionally picturesque reaches of the River Findhorn near *Dulsie Bridge* (*q.v.*) and *Ferness* (*q.v.*). Dr. Johnson and Boswell visited Nairn during the course of their Highland tour of 1773. Near the harbour, built by Telford in 1820, but badly damaged in the great 1829 floods, is the Fishertown. An old Cross stands in the High St. The town is held to mark the division between the Highlands and the Lowlands; at one time it was said that Gaelic was spoken in the south-western and English in the north-eastern quarter. **3 m. S.** is *Rait Castle*, 16th to 17th cent., with a round tower. See **Auldearn** and **Cawdor.** *Iter. 175, 176, 199, 212.*

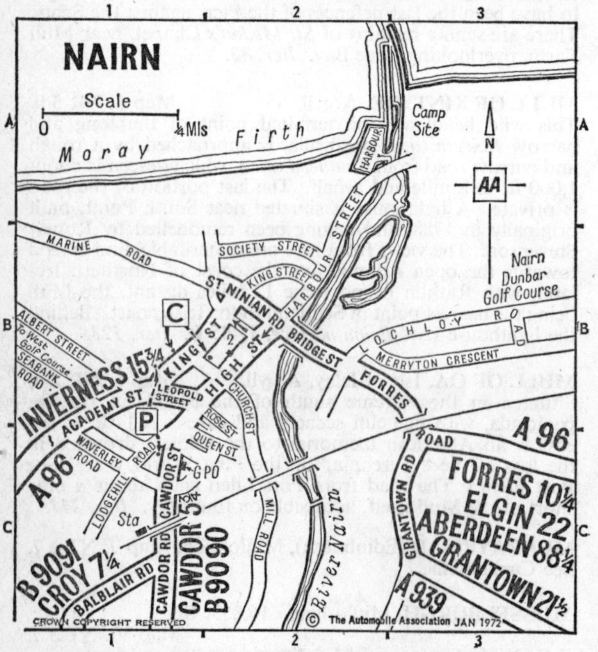

Information Bureau 1 (B1) Old Cross 2 (B2)

NATIONAL FOREST PARKS.
See **Forest Parks.**

NATIONAL OR LOCAL NATURE RESERVES.
These reserves, which are controlled by the Nature Conservancy (see page 31), are to be found at or near the following places which are described in the gazetteer. Those printed in black type have public access; those in italics require permits, obtainable locally. See **Aberlady,** *Anstruther* (*for Isle of May*), *Ardrossan, Aviemore,* **Baddagyle, Bettyhill,** *Caerlaverock,* **Cairngorms,** *Cape Wrath,* **Clatteringshaws Dam,** *Cramond Bridge,* **Dalmally,** *Dumfries, Hebrides, Outer* (*North Uist*), **Inchnadamph,** *Killin,* **Kinlochewe** (for **Ben Eighe), Kirkton of Glenisla,** *Kishorn, Lochcarron,* **Loch Leven** (Kinross), **Loch Lomond,** *Lochmaben,* **Lochranza,** *Mound, Newburgh* (*Aberdeen*), *North Berwick, Rannoch, Rum,* **St. Cyrus,** *St. Kilda, Shetland, Strathy, Strontian, Tayport and Tynron.*

NEIDPATH CASTLE, Peebles. Map 9, **NT 2 4.**
See **Peebles.**

NEILSTON, Renfrew. 3,340. Map 8, **NS 4 5.**
At the foot of the moors, with the Balgray reservoir to the east and the flat-topped *Neilston Pad* to the south. The Church is 18th cent., and nearby is a monument to John Robertson, who manufactured the engines for the "Comet," an early steamship, launched in 1812 at *Bowling* (*q.v.*) **4 m. S.W.,** above Loch Libo, stands the 15 cent. *Caldwell Tower.*

NENTHORN, Berwick. Map 10, **NT 6 3.**
About **2 m. E.** stands *Newton Don*, with fine 18th cent. furnishings and lovely gardens. *Iter. 6.*

NETHER LOCHABER, Inverness. Map 18, **NN 0 6.**
See **Corran Ferry** and **Lochaber.**

NETHYBRIDGE, Inverness, 387. Map 26, **NJ 0 2.**
E.C. Thurs. Lies on the River Nethy, which has its junction with the more important Spey a little to the north of the village. The village has become a centre for early spring ski-ing. To the north-east is *Abernethy* Church, near which stands the ruined *Castle Roy.* South of Nethybridge lies the great Forest of Abernethy, through which wander many paths, giving access by the Ryvoan Pass, with the picturesque little Green Loch, to *Loch Morlich* (*q.v.*) in the Glenmore Forest Park. (See **Aviemore.**) Other hill tracks lead southwards towards the Lairig an Laoigh, one of the two well-known passes in the *Cairngorms* (*q.v.*), in this case linking Speyside with *Inverey* (*q.v.*) on Deeside but suitable only for long-distance walkers. The road from Nethybridge to Aviemore traverses the fringe of Abernethy Forest, keeping east of the Spey, and passing the little Church of *Kincardine*, beyond which lies Loch Pityoulish. See **Boat of Garten.** *Iter. 149, 169, 170, 171.*

NEVIS, Inverness. Map 18, **NN 1 7.**
See **Ben Nevis** (for *Glen Nevis*) and **Fort William.**
See also **Loch Nevis.** Map 23, **NM 7 9.**

NEW ABBEY, Kirkcudbright. 1,295. Map 3, **NX 9 6.**
Beautifully situated on the Pow Burn, in a wooded setting, backed by *Meikle Hard Hill*, 1,300 ft. and the bulky *Criffell*, 1,866 ft. The village, in which stands the 16th to 18th cent. *Kirkconnell House*, is known chiefly for the ruined Cistercian *New Abbey*, or *Sweetheart Abbey* (A.M.), built of red sandstone, and founded, in 1273, by Devorgilla, who also endowed Balliol College at Oxford and built the 13th cent. bridge over the River Nith at *Dumfries* (*q.v.*). Devorgilla was buried in front of the high altar, together with the heart of her husband, the Abbey thus obtaining its name of "Dulce Cor" or Sweetheart. The picturesque, roofless remains, mainly 13th and 14th cent. work, include the 90-ft. high central tower, much of the nave and transepts, and a short aisleless choir. A little to the north-east stands the isolated Abbot's Tower, and a short distance beyond is the estuary of the River Nith, on the Solway Firth. A circular *Waterloo* tower crowns Glen Hill, to the west. **2 m. N.E.** is *Kirkconnel Tower*, 16th to 18th cent. **1 m. N.W.** is *Shambellie Wood*, which contains what are considered to be the finest Scots pines in the country. *Iter. 72, 73.*

Musselburgh, Midlothian. The Tolbooth of c. 1591, built of stones from the Chapel of Our Lady of Loretto. For this act the town was excommunicated for a period of two centuries

Muthill, Perth. A dog-headed drinking fountain on A822

Nairn, Nairn. The ancient Cross shaft, which stands in the High Street

Neilston, Renfrew. The Monument to John Robertson, who made the engines for the 'Comet,' the earliest steam-driven craft in Europe, launched on the Clyde in 1812

New Abbey, Kirkcudbright. A carved plaque on a house in the village, recalling the assistance given to Devorgilla (who founded the Abbey in 1273) by three women who helped to ferry the stones across the River Nith

Nethybridge, Inverness. Broomhill Bridge, across the River Spey, to the north of the village. It carries an unclassified road linking A95 and B970

[For MUSSELBURGH see also preceding plate
[For NETHYBRIDGE see also under STRATH SPEY (Plate 158)
[For NEIDPATH CASTLE see under TWEEDDALE (Plate 166)

PLATE 126

New Aberdour, Aberdeen. The ruined Dundarg Castle, looking across Aberdour Bay

Newark Castle, Selkirk. The ruined, mainly 15th century Castle, associated with Sir Walter Scott's '*Lay of the Last Minstrel.*' It stands near the Yarrow Water, a mile south-east of Broadmeadows, off A708

Newbattle, Midlothian. Newbattle Abbey, now a college. The original Cistercian structure was founded in 1140, and the later house became a seat of the Marquess of Lothian

New Bridge, Dumfries; Kirkcudbright. Part of the 'Twelve Apostles' stone circle, consisting actually of 11 stones in two adjacent fields. They are situated off B729, a little to the north-west

Newbigging, Lanark. The Mercat Cross of 1693

New Galloway, Kirkcudbright. The carved 'Adam and Eve' stone in the churchyard of Kells, which is situated a little to the north of the town, on A762

NEW ABERDOUR, Aberdeen. Map 27, **NJ 8** 6.
Stands a little to the south of the red sandstone cliffs of Aberdour Bay, which is overlooked by the ruined tower of *Dundarg Castle*. The little River Dour flows into the bay to the west of the castle. The cliffs in the vicinity are riddled with caverns. See **Pitsligo.** *Iter. 182.*

NEW ALYTH, Perth. Map 20, **NO 2** 4.
See **Alyth.** *Iter. 166.*

NEWARK CASTLE, Fife. Map 17, **NO 5** 0.
See **St. Monance.**

NEWARK CASTLE, Renfrew. Map 8, **NS 3** 7.
See **Port Glasgow.**

NEWARK CASTLE, Selkirk. Map 10, **NT 4** 2.
See **Broadmeadows.**

NEWARTHILL, Lanark. 6,755. Map 9, **NS 7** 5.
Stands partly at an altitude of over 500 ft. *Iter. 87.*

NEWBATTLE, Midlothian. 9,356. Map 10, **NT 3** 6.
On the River South Esk, and well known for *Newbattle Abbey*, now used as a college. Of the former Cistercian Abbey, founded in 1140, the crypt and basement chapel still survive, and are incorporated in the present buildings. The earlier structure was burnt in 1544. There are some notable portraits and interior furnishings, and in the fine park stand two fine sundials. Newbattle Church, rebuilt in 1727, preserves the pulpit and other memorials of Archbishop Leighton, minister from 1641 to 1653. The former "*Sun*" Inn was well known in coaching days. *Iter. 9, 11, 12.*

NEWBIGGING, Lanark. Map 9, **NT 0** 4.
The old Cross carries the date 1693. *Iter. 37, 52.*

NEWBRIDGE, Midlothian. 1,548. Map 9, **NT 1** 7.
Here is a crow-stepped, gabled inn, dated 1683. The grounds of *Ingliston* (1846) are the permanent site of the annual Royal Highland Show. At *Cliftonhall*, to the south-west, lived Euphame McCalzean, burnt as a witch in 1591 after a trial in Edinburgh. *Iter. 15, 16.*

NEW BRIDGE, Dumfries; Kirkcudbright. Map 3, **NX 9** 7.
The bridge spans the Cluden Water. A little to the north-west, off the Moniaive road, are the remains of a large stone circle, known as the "Twelve Apostles," and of which 11 stones are still to be seen, including five in an upright position. See **Irongray.** *Iter. 27, 48, 56, 67, 74.*

NEWBURGH, Aberdeen. Map 27, **NJ 9** 2.
E.C. Wed. A small harbour, standing on the estuary of the River Ythan, in the Formartine division of the county. The river is known for its mussel-pearls and also for fishing. Across the estuary are the Sands of Forvie, now a National Nature Reserve of 1,774 acres. To the south, the coast is flat and sandy. *Iter. 182.*

NEWBURGH, Fife. 2,089. SB. Map 17, **NO 2** 1.
A small Royal Burgh, with a harbour, on the Firth of Tay. It is noted for the manufacture of linoleum. The *Mugdrum* Cross is more than 1,000 years old. The pedestal of *Macduff's* Cross stands on a hill to the south of Newburgh. Opposite the harbour, the Firth is divided by Mugdrum Island into the North and South Deeps. A little to the east are the remains of *Lindores Abbey* (*q.v.*), and to the south-east lies Lindores Loch. **3 m. N.E.** of Newburgh, beyond Lindores Abbey, is the ruined *Ballinbreich Castle*, overlooking the Firth of Tay. The Earls of Rothes once owned this 14th cent. stronghold below *Normans Law*, 936 ft. *Flisk* Church, in the vicinity, dates from 1790. **2 m. S.** is *Pitcairlie House*, mainly 18th cent. *Iter. 131, 132.*

NEW BYTH, Aberdeen. Map 27, **NJ 8** 5.
A small village, founded in 1764, in order to promote home industries, among which hand-loom weaving was formerly practised on a considerable scale. *Iter. 183.*

NEWCASTLETON, Roxburgh. 1,023. Map 5, **NY 4** 8l
Founded in 1793 as a weaving village, *Newcastleton* has hill views to east and west, and is situated in the delightfu. Liddesdale valley, on the Liddel Water, which forms the boundary between England and Scotland for some miles to the south-west. The valley is associated with Scott's "Guy Mannering." The Forestry Commission have planted great new forests on the hill slopes in the vicinity, which together with Wauchope Forest (See **Bonchester Bridge**), form part of the Border Forest Park, extending across the English border. To the north-east of Newcastleton are the *Larriston Fells*, 1,677 ft., beyond which rise the lonely *Cheviot* hills, and to the north-west of the village is *Roan Fell*, 1,862 ft., The English-Scottish border traverses the *Larriston Fells,* which, on their west side, were once crossed by a road linking Liddesdale with the North Tyne valley in Northumberland. The inscribed *Bloody Bush* stone, showing the former toll charges, still stands on the fells some $2\frac{1}{2}$ miles east of the Newcastleton-Jedburgh road. **$1\frac{1}{2}$ m. S.S.W.** is the old Border stronghold of *Mangerton Tower*. See **Hermitage Castle** and **Riccarton.** *Iter. 31, 47.*

NEW CUMNOCK, Ayr. 6,926. Map 8, **NS 6** 1.
E.C. Wed. This mining parish was separated from *Cumnock* (*q.v.*) in 1650, and lies on the River Nith, near its source in the hills, and where it is joined by the Afton Water. The latter flows through the delightful Glen Afton, to the south, overlooked at the head of the valley by *Blackcraig Hill*, 2,298 ft. Glen Afton is associated with Sir William Wallace, and Robert Burns wrote the well-known lines commencing: "Flow gently, sweet Afton." *Iter. 27, 67.*

NEW DAILLY, Ayr. Map 2, **NS 2** 0.
See **Dailly.** *Iter. 74, 85.*

NEW DEER, Aberdeen. 2,968. Map 27, **NJ 8** 4.
See **Old Deer.** *Iter. 183, 186, 189, 197.*

NEW ELGIN, Moray. 2,096. Map 26, **NJ 2** 6.
Iter. 190, 192.

NEW FOWLIS, Perth. Map 16, **NN 9** 2.
See **Fowlis Wester.** *Iter. 145.*

NEW GALLOWAY, Kirkcudbright. 335. SB. Map 3, **NX 6** 7.
E.C. Thurs. GOLF. A tiny Royal Burgh and angling centre, on the River Ken, in the Glenkens district, with Loch Ken immediately to the south. Still farther to the south, the shores of the loch are well-wooded. In *Kells* Churchyard, a little to the north of New Galloway, is the grave of a Covenanter, shot in 1685. There is also a curious carved Adam and Eve stone. Other stones have unusual carvings and inscriptions. Away to the north-west rise the lofty *Rhinns of Kells*, with *Corserine* reaching a height of 2,668 ft. South-westwards, on the *Newton Stewart* (*q.v.*) road, lies *Clatteringshaws Dam* (*q.v.*), with the Cairn Edward Forest, part of the Glen Trool Forest Park, situated in the immediate vicinity. The Glenlee power station in connection with the Galloway Power Scheme lies to the north-west of the town. Some **5 m. S.E.,** and east of the Kirkcudbright road, the Black Water of Dee enters Loch Ken. See **Balmaclellan** and **Dalry** (Kirkcudbright). *Iter. 25, 71, 77.*

NEWHAVEN (Edinburgh), Midlothian. Map 10, **NT 2** 7.
This little fishing port was founded by James IV, c. 1500, the original population being of Dutch, or Danish strain. Some early warships were built here, including the "Great Michael," launched in 1507, on which served Sir Andrew Wood of *Largo* (*q.v.*). *Newhaven* is noted for its fish dinners, and also for the curious dresses worn by the fishwives. The old fishergirl cries of "Caller ou" (fresh oysters) and "Caller herrin'" (fresh herrings) were characteristic of Edinburgh in former days. The "*Peacock*" Inn has long been known for sea food.

NEWHOUSE, Lanark. Map 9, **NS 7 6.**
Iter. 18, 50, 52, 87.

NEW LUCE, Wigtown. 226. Map 2, **NX 1 6.**
Lies in that part of *Galloway* (*q.v.*) known as The Moors, and is situated at the junction of the Main Water of Luce with the Cross Water of Luce, which together form the Water of Luce flowing southwards to *Glenluce* (*q.v.*) and Wigtown Bay. The hilly and narrow road leading northwards to *Barrhill* (*q.v.*) in Ayrshire is gated, and goes through lonely moorlands rising to about 1,000 ft. From 1659 to 1662, Prophet Peden was minister at New Luce. *Iter 78.*

NEWMACHAR, Aberdeen. 1,960. Map 27, **NJ 8 1.**
Iter. 180.

NEWMAINS, Lanark. 6,914. Map 9, **NS 8 5.**

E.C. Wed. This town is situated on the extensive Lanark coalfield, with large iron and steel works. *Murdostoun Castle,* to the north of Newmains, is partly 15th cent., and has an old dovecote. To the east, on the Midlothian border, are the *Gladsmuir* hills. *Iter. 19, 20, 50, 52.*

NEWMILLS, Fife. Map 16, **NT 0 8.**
GOLF. See **Culross** and **Valleyfield.** *Iter. 134.*

NEWMILNS, Ayr. 3,534. SB. Map 8 **NS 5 3.**
GOLF. A small town specializing in muslins. Several Covenanters' tombstones stand in the churchyard. The former Tolbooth dates from 1739. *Iter. 20, 69.*

NEW ORLEANS, Argyll. Map 7, **NR 7 1.**
Situated on the east side of the Kintyre peninsula.

NEW PITSLIGO, Aberdeen, 1,438. Map 27, **NJ 8 5.**
E.C. Wed. A large *Buchan* (*q.v.*) village, to the north-west of which rises the hill of *Turlundie.* See **Pitsligo.** *Iter. 188.*

NEWPORT-ON-TAY, Fife. 3,728. SB. Map 17. **NO 4 2.**
E.C. Wed. A Firth of Tay resort. formerly linked to *Dundee* (*q.v.*) by a car ferry. The fine new bridge of 1966 has 42 spans and is the second longest in Europe. The foreshore is rocky. To the south-west, commencing at *Wormit,* is the famous two-mile long Tay Bridge, built 1883-1888, and replacing its ill-fated predecessor, which was blown down, in 1879, while a train was making the crossing, causing heavy loss of life. **2½ m. S.** of Newport-on-Tay, on the Leuchars road, is the strangely named "*Pickletillem*" Inn. See **Tayport.** *Iter. 92, 126, 127.*

NEW SCONE, Perth. Map 17, **NO 1 2.**
See **Scone.** *Iter. 151, 153.*

NEWSTEAD, Roxburgh. Map 10, **NT 5 3.**
An old-world village, standing on the south bank of the River Tweed, to the west of the point where it is joined by the Leader Water. On Leaderfoot Hill is a monument marking the site of the Roman Camp of *Trimontium,* where excavations, between 1905 and 1910, revealed treasures which are now in the National Museum of Antiquities in Edinburgh. To the south rise the triple-peaked *Eildon* hills. **2 m. E.,** in a bend of the Tweed, is *Old Melrose,* the site of a monastery founded in the 7th cent. *Iter. 13, 41, 43.*

NEWTON BRIDGE, Perth. Map 16, **NN 8 3.**
Situated a little beyond the northern extremity of the delightful *Sma' Glen* (*q.v.*). Here, the by-road leading westwards into Glen Almond threaded by the River Almond, diverges from the main road leading northwards on the line of General Wade's military road towards *Amulree* (*q.v.*). Away to the west, and dominating Glen Almond, rises *Ben Chonzie,* 3,048 ft. *Iter. 89, 140, 141, 147.*

NEWTON MEARNS, Renfrew. 4,009. Map 8, **NS 5 5.**
A mile to the south-east is *Mearns,* on the edge of an extensive and high-lying moorland district. The Church here dates from the late 18th cent. Nearer to Newton Mearns stand the 15th cent. *Blackhouse Castle* and the restored *Pollok Castle,* with its 17th cent. garden architecture. To the south-west, on the Kilmarnock road, is a monument to Robert Pollok, an early 19th cent. poet. See **Eaglesham.** *Iter. 55, 61.*

NEWTONMORE, Inverness. 655. Map 19, **NN 7 9.**
E.C. Wed. GOLF. A Speyside resort, with both a summer and a winter-sports season, situated beneath the foothills of the *Monadhliath* mountains to the west, and with views towards the *Cairngorms* (*q.v.*) to the east. Pony-trekking is a recently-introduced local sport. The Clan Trust Museum contains treasures of the Clan Macpherson. Outside the village, to the south-west, the Spey is joined by the Calder, which has come down through the wild Glen Banchor. To the north-east of the town, the Spey receives the waters of the Tromie, issuing from the long glen of that name, which extends far into the wilds of the great Gaick Forest, a wilderness of lonely hills. **3 m. S.W.,** off the road leading towards *Drumgask* (*q.v.*) and *Loch Laggan* (*q.v.*), near the meeting-point of the Spey and the Truim, is the site of a clan battle, fought in 1386. The site is overlooked to the north by *Craig Dhu,* 2,350 ft., a gathering-place of the Clan Macpherson, and giving its name to their battle cry. In a cave on the steep cliffs of this hill, Cluny Macpherson hid for some years after the '45. The wooded scenery at this point is of much beauty. See **Dalwhinnie, Kingussie** and **Tromie Bridge.** *Iter. 140, 147, 150, 208.*

NEWTON STEWART, Wigtown. 1,881. SB. Map 2, **NX 4 6.**
E.C. Wed. **M.D.** Fri. GOLF. This attractive little *Galloway* (*q.v.*) weaving town and fishing resort is situated on the River Cree, a few miles above Wigtown Bay. Houses in the town are built along the river banks, giving a delightful, almost Venetian appearance. The ornate 19th cent. *Galloway* monument is 57 feet high. The old village of *Minnigaff,* where the churchyard by the ruined Church contains carved tombstones, is linked to Newton Stewart by means of the Cree Bridge, built by John Rennie in 1813 to replace an earlier one washed away by the river. The scenery in the vicinity is of great charm, notably to the north, and there are distant views of the mountains around *Loch Trool* (*q.v.*). Beyond the Cumloden deer-park, and near the line of the Devil's Dyke, are two tall prehistoric stones known as "The Thieves." To the south is the ruined 16th cent. *Garlies Castle.* Immediately to the north-east of the town, and threaded by the Penkill Burn, is Kirroughtree Forest, part of the Forest Park of Glen Trool. **3 m. S.E.,** on the road to *Creetown* (*q.v.*), is the entrance to the pretty Bargaly Glen, threaded by the Palnure Burn. It is overlooked to the east by the great mass of *Cairnsmore of Fleet,* 2,331 ft., a notable lankmark which is associated with John Buchan's "The Thirty-Nine Steps." **4 m. N.W.,** on the Bargrennan road, are the *Cruives of Cree,* a beautiful wooded stretch of the river, which burns has described in verse. See **Kirkcowan.** *Iter. 25, 26, 71, 72, 73, 78, 79, 80, 81, 82.*

Galloway Monument. 1.

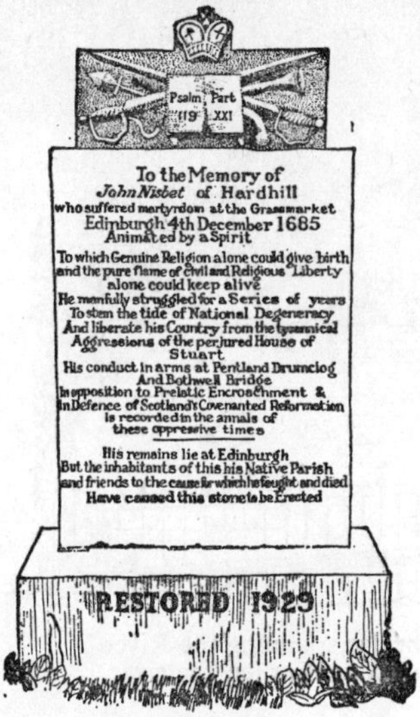

Newmilns, Ayr. One of a number of Covenanters' monuments in the churchyard

New Orleans, Argyll. A house situated on an unclassified road 4 miles south-east of Campbeltown, near the east coast of the Kintyre peninsula

Newport-on-Tay, Fife. The strangely named 'Pickletillem' Inn, which stands some 2½ miles south of the town, on A92

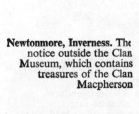

Newton Mearns, Renfrew. The Monument to the poet Robert Pollok, born in 1798. It stands 3 miles south-west, near A77

Newtonmore, Inverness. The notice outside the Clan Museum, which contains treasures of the Clan Macpherson

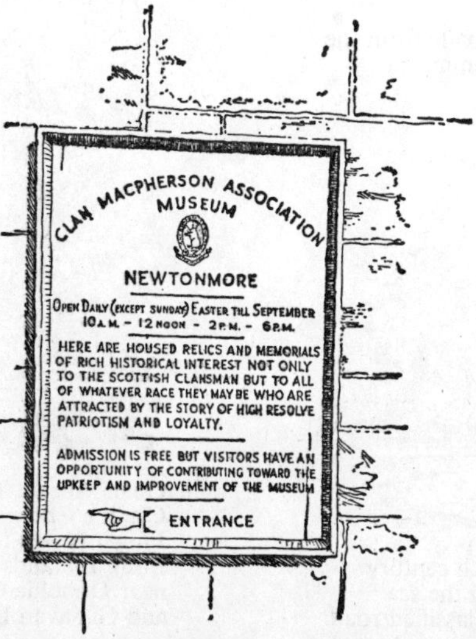

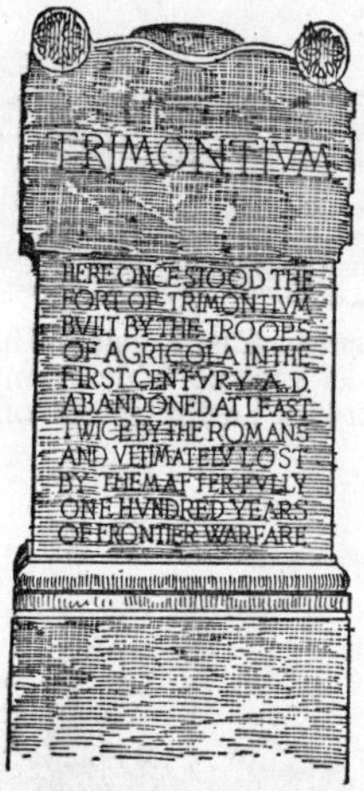

Newstead, Roxburgh. The Monument on Leaderfoot Hill, above the River Tweed, marking the site of the Roman fort of Trimontium

(For NEWTON STEWART see following plate

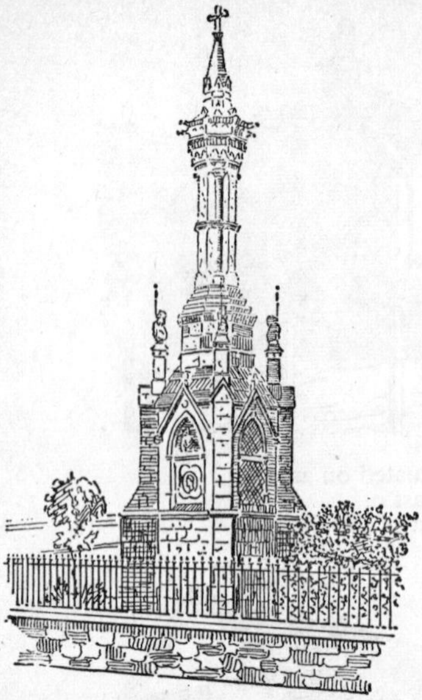

Newton Stewart, Wigtown. The Galloway Monument, erected in 1875 to commemorate the 9th Earl of Galloway, who died in 1873

Newton Stewart, Wigtown. The early 19th century bridge spanning the River Cree, which replaces an older structure wrecked by floods. Earlier, the river was crossed by the Black Ford of Cree

Oban, Argyll. The unfinished building, intended as a museum and art gallery, and known as 'McCaig's Folly.' It is situated on a hill at the back of the town

North Berwick, East Lothian. The archway made from the jawbones of a whale, which stands on the summit of North Berwick Law, 613 feet, off B1347

Oban, Argyll. The Dog Stone, or Clach a'Choin, to which the legendary Fingal is said to have tied his dog Bran. It stands on an unclassified road near Dunollie Castle, between Oban and Ganavan Bay

Oban, Argyll. The remains of the 12th to 13th century McDougall fortress of Dunollie, overlooking the sea between Oban and Ganavan Bay, on an unclassified road

[For NORTH BERWICK see also under BASS ROCK (Plate 15) and TANTALLON CASTLE (Plate 159)

NEWTOWN ST. BOSWELLS, Roxburgh. Map 10, **NT 5** 3.
A railway junction, noted for livestock sales which were previously held at St. Boswells. See **St. Boswells Green.** *Iter. 4, 13, 32, 36, 52.*

NEWTYLE, Angus. 1,580 with Kettins. Map 17, **NO 2** 4.
A *Sidlaw* hills village, with the high points of *Auchterhouse Hill*, 1,399 ft., and *Craigowl Hill*, 1,493 ft., rising to the east. To the south-east of Newtyle, at the commencement of the ascent over the Glack of Newtyle in the Sidlaws, the road to Dundee passes the ruined 16th cent. *Hatton Castle.* See **Eassie.** *Iter. 160.*

NEW YORK, Argyll. Map 14, **NM 9** 1.
Faces *Portinnisherrich* (*q.v.*) from the west bank of Loch Awe.

NIGG, Ross and Cromarty. 454. Map 31, **NH 8** 7.
Overlooks the small Bay of Nigg, an inlet of the larger Cromarty Firth. The Church preserves a curious sculptured stone, perhaps 7th cent. work. To the east rises the *Hill of Nigg*, 666 ft. See **Balintore, Dunskeath, Fearn** and **Logie Easter.**

NORTH BALLACHULISH, Inverness. 120. Map 18, **NN 0** 5.
E.C. Thurs. Faces *Ballachulish* (*q.v.*) across the narrows of Loch Leven, crossed here by a busy car ferry. For motorists travelling south, this ferry can be avoided by making the long, but picturesque detour round the loch by way of *Kinlochleven* (*q.v.*), and rejoining the main road at *Carnach* (*q.v.*), near the entrance to *Glencoe* (*q.v.*). By the door of *St. Bride's* Church stands a copy of the High Cross of *Oronsay* Priory. See **Colonsay.** *Iter. 100, 124, 125, 142.*

NORTH BALLOCH, Ayr. Map 2, **NX 3** 9.
At the head of the pleasant Stinchar valley, where the river is joined by the Balloch Burn. To the south-east is the 1,280-ft. high, lonely Nick o' the Balloch Pass, traversed by the road to *Bargrennan* (*q.v.*). *Iter. 84.*

NORTH BERWICK, East Lothian. 4,414. SB. Map 10, **NT 5** 8.
E.C. Thurs. GOLF. This well-known Royal Burgh, resort and fishing village on the North Sea coast is famous particularly for golf, and there is also a sandy beach for bathing. The harbour is situated between the east and west bays, and in the vicinity of the former is a fragment of the 12th cent. "Auld Kirk." Out to sea, to the north-east, is the famous landmark of the *Bass Rock*, 350 ft. high, with a powerful lighthouse. It was once a Covenanters' prison, and is associated also with R. L. Stevenson's "Catriona." There are traces of old fortifications, and of a chapel, while the former fort on the island was destroyed in 1694. Sea-birds now inhabit the Bass Rock in large numbers. North-west of the resort lies *Fidra* island, with its lighthouse. This island is a bird sanctuary, as are also the nearby *Eyebroughty* and *Lamb* islets. A little to the south of North Berwick is *North Berwick Law*, 613 ft., a fine viewpoint, crowned by a watch-tower dating from Napoleonic times, near which is an archway made from the jawbones of a whale. Farther to the south, off the road to *Haddington* (*q.v.*), is the 16th cent. *Fenton Tower*. **3 m. E.**, on the coast, beyond Canty Bay, are considerable remains of the picturesque, moated *Tantallon Castle* (A.M.), situated on a headland, and dating probably from the 14th cent. and later. The Castle was besieged in 1528, and finally destroyed by General Monk, in 1651. Scott's "Marmion" describes this romantic Douglas stronghold. A 17th cent. "doocot," or dovecote, stands within the two inner ditches. To the south-east of the castle, in the grounds of *Seacliff House*, are slight remains of *Auldhame Priory*. See **Dirleton, Gullane, Tynninghame** and **Whitekirk.** *Iter. 2, 36, 37, 38.*

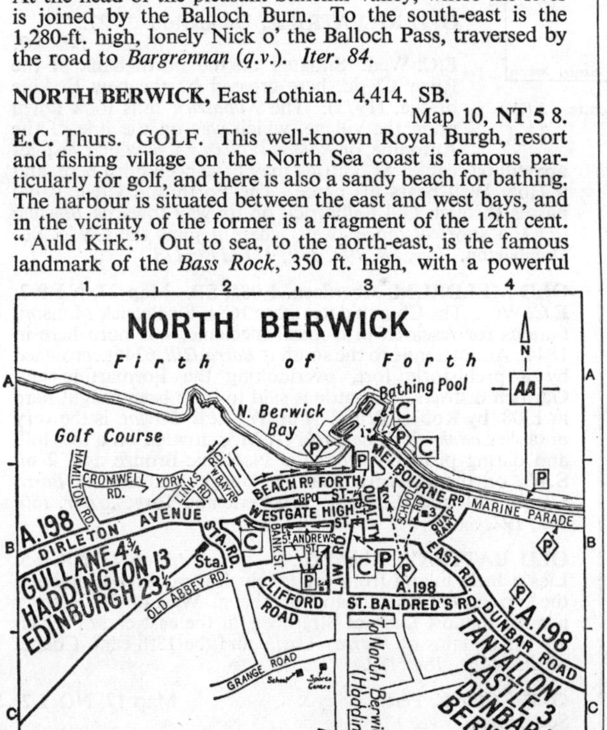

"Auld Kirk" ruins 1 (A3) Tourist Information Centre 2 (B3)
Museum 3 (B3)

NORTH KESSOCK, Ross and Cromarty. Map 25, **NH 6** 4.
A crofting and fishing village, facing the narrows which divide the waters of the Beauly Firth from those of the Inner Moray Firth. It is known as North Kessock to distinguish it from *South Kessock* (*q.v.*) on the Ness estuary, in Inverness-shire, on the opposite shore of the narrows, to which it is connected by car ferry, giving access thereby to *Inverness* (*q.v.*). Above North Kessock, to the north-east, is *Ord Hill*, crowned by a large vitrified fort. At *Coulmore*, to the west, is a Boating Centre. *Iter. 202. 203.*

NORTH QUEENSFERRY, Fife. Map 17, **NT 1** 8.
See **Queensferry, North.**

NORTH UIST, ISLE OF, Inverness. Map 32, **NF 7** 7 etc.
See **Hebrides, Outer** (North Uist). *Iter.* 261.

OA CHURCH, Isle of Islay, Argyll. Map 6, **NR 3** 4.
See **Mull of Oa.** *Iter. 244.*

OAKLEY, Fife. 3,591. Map 16, **NT 0** 8.
In the vicinity, to the west, is situated the *Comrie* coal mine, one of the most modern and up-to-date in Scotland. *Iter. 133.*

OBAN, Argyll. 6,910. SB. Map 14, **NM 8** 3.
E.C. Thurs. **M.D.** Wed. GOLF. A famous West Highland resort, yachting centre, and starting point for picturesque drives in the district of *Lorne* (*q.v.*), notable for its magnificent seascapes and island scenery. Many of the finest excursions can be made by steamer to such well-known places as the islands of Mull, Lismore, Iona and Staffa, which are all described under their own headings. There are also regular steamer sailings to several of the Outer Hebridean islands. Yachting is a great feature of the waters in the vicinity, while during the second week of September is held the annual Argyll Gathering. The island of *Kerrera* faces Oban Bay, being linked by passenger ferry, and is separated from the mainland by the Sound of Kerrera. On the south-western shores stands the ruined *Gylen Castle*. At the opposite end is an obelisk recalling David Hutcheson, who founded the West Highland steamer services. Alexander II died on Kerrera in 1249. Oban itself has a modern R.C. Cathedral of granite, built by Sir Giles Scott, and on a hill behind the town is the curious, unfinished structure known as "McCaig's Folly," and also an uncompleted hydropathic. From Pulpit Hill, to the south, the view (indicator) is remarkable, and sunsets seen from here can be memorable.

On the east side of Oban Bay is the Clach a' Choin, or, "Dog Stone," traditionally associated with Fingal's dog, Bran. Nearby is the ruined McDougall stronghold of *Dunollie Castle*, 12th or 13th cent., overlooking the Firth of Lorne. In the modern mansion of *Dunollie* is preserved the Brooch of Lorne, supposed to have been worn by Robert Bruce. Beyond the old Castle lies Ganavan Bay, with its fine, sandy bathing beach. To the east of the town in Glen

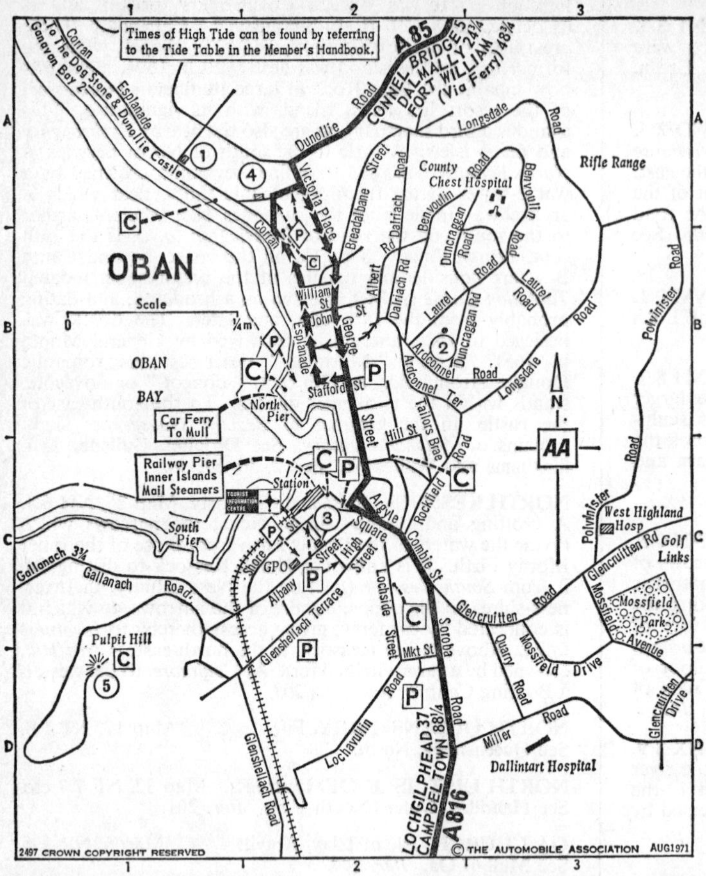

Cathedral (R.C.) 1 (A1)
McCaig's Folly 2 (B2)
Tourist Information Centre 3 (C2)
Town Hall 4 (A2)
Viewpoint at Pulpit Hill 5 (D1)

Cruitten, stands *Glencruitten House*, its park noted for the "Cathedral of Trees." Dr. Johnson and Boswell visited Oban in their tour of 1773, and found a "tolerable" inn. Sir Walter Scott came here in 1814. The road leading southwards from the town towards Loch Feochan and *Kilninver* (*q.v.*) passes near the ruined *Kilbride* Church, and the restored 16th cent. *Lerags Cross.* A little to the east of the Kilninver road is the pretty Loch Nell, on the south-west shore of which is a curious 80-yard-long boulder ridge, known as the "Serpent's Mound." At the far end of the loch, in Glen Lonan, is a tall granite monolith called Diarmid's Pillar, adjacent to which is the burial-place of Diarmid, the ancestor of the Clan Campbell. Another road, with gates and bad bends, leads direct from Oban into Glen Lonan, and provides an alternative route to *Taynuilt* (*q.v.*) and Loch Etive. See **Connel, Dunstaffnage Castle, Lismore** and **Tyndrum.** *Iter. 110, 117, 118, 119, 122, 124, 125, 144, 145.*

OBBE (Isle of Lewis), Harris, Inverness. Map 32, **NG 0** 8. **See Hebrides, Outer** (Harris). *Iter. 257.*

OCCUMSTER, Caithness. Map 30, **ND 2** 3. The chambered *Camster Cairns* (**3 m.** N.) are of note. *Iter. 200.*

OCHIL HILLS, Clackmannan; Kinross; Perth. Map 16, **NN 8** 0 etc. See **Alva, Bridge of Allan, Dollar, Dunblane, Glendevon, Gleneagles Hotel, Glenfarg** and **Tillicoultry.** *Iter. 86, 89, 135, 136, 146.*

OCHILTREE, Ayr. 5,541 with Stair. Map 8, **NS 5** 2. Lies at the junction of the Burnoch Water with the better-known Lugar Water, in a dairy-farming district. A tablet marks the house in which was born George Douglas Brown, whose "House with the Green Shutters" contains much local colour. The former *Ochiltree House* was the scene of the marriage, in 1684, of Claverhouse, while in an earlier house, in 1564, John Knox was married. See **Stair.** *Iter. 21, 27, 68.*

OICH BRIDGE, Inverness. Map 18, **NH 3** 0. See **Loch Oich.** *Iter. 210.*

OLD DAILLY, Ayr. Map 2, **NX 2** 9. See **Dailly.** *Iter. 78.*

OLD DEER, Aberdeen. 2,653. Map 27, **NJ 9** 4. An attractive *Buchan* (*q.v.*) village, visited for the scanty remains of the Cistercian Abbey (A.M.), founded in 1219, and situated a little to the north-west, in the grounds of *Pitfour House.* Excavation has revealed the ground plan of the buildings, but there is little to see, though its setting, near the South Ugie Water, is charming. A monastery was founded here in the 6th cent. by St. Columba, this being recalled by the well-known Book of Deer, incorporating the first known characters in Gaelic script, and now in the University Library at Cambridge. *Iter. 189.*

OLDHAMSTOCKS, East Lothian. 705 with Innerwick. Map 11, **NT 7** 7. A secluded village, once noted for the biennial fairs held on the green by the now-vanished Mercat Cross. The Church has an elaborate 16th cent. sundial.

OLD KILPATRICK, Dunbarton. 3,227. Map 8, **NS 4** 7. **E.C.** Wed. Situated on the north bank of the River Clyde, here crossed by the new Erskine bridge, (1971). The *Kilpatrick* hills look down upon the village, which was on the line of the Antonine, or *Roman Wall* (*q.v.*), of which vestiges are still traceable. St. Patrick may have been born here, and a Holy Well bears his name. The Forth and Clyde canal passes through Old Kilpatrick on its way towards *Bowling* (*q.v.*), a short distance away, where it joins the Clyde. See **Dumbarton.** *Iter. 88, 109, 110, 111, 112, 113.*

OLD MELDRUM, Aberdeen. 1,085. SB. Map 27, **NJ 8** 2. **E.C.** Wed. The Church dates from 1684. Sir Patrick Manson, famous for research in tropical medicine, was born here in 1844. About a mile to the south is *Barra Hill*, 634 ft., crowned by a prehistoric fort, overlooking the Formartine and Garioch districts. A battle is said to have been fought here in 1308, by Robert Bruce. **4 m. W.**, near *Daviot*, is the very notable *Loanhead* stone circle (A.M.), situated on a low hill, and dating probably from the Neolithic-Bronze age, **2 m. S.W.**, on the Inverurie road, is the old mansion of *Barra Castle*, 17th and 18th cent. See **Fyvie** and **Tarves.** *Iter. 180, 187, 197.*

OLD RATTRAY, Aberdeen. Map 27, **NK 0** 5. Lies a little inland from the lonely Rattray Head, dividing the two bays of Rattray and Strathbeg. West of Old Rattray lies the shallow Loch of Strathbeg, at the east end of which are the remains of *Rattray Castle* and the 13th cent. Chapel of *St. Mary. Iter. 182.*

OLD SCONE, Perth. Map 17, **NO 1** 2. See **Scone.**

ONICH, Inverness. Map 18, **NN 0** 6. **E.C.** Thurs. Finely situated on the rock, shingle and sandy shores of *Loch Linnhe* (*q.v.*), looking towards the *Ardgour* (*q.v.*) hills, dominated by *Garbh Bheinn*, 2,903 ft. There is a monument to Dr. Alexander Stewart, a noted Gaelic scholar.

Ochiltree, Ayr. The house in which George Douglas Brown, the author of the '*House with the Green Shutters*,' was born in 1869. In this book, Ochiltree appears as 'Barbie'

Old Kilpatrick, Dunbarton. The Holy Well of St. Patrick. The Saint was by tradition born at Old Kilpatrick

Old Meldrum, Aberdeen. The Loanhead stone circle, which lies some 4 miles west of the town, near Daviot, on an unclassified road

Onich, Inverness. The perforated monolith known as the Clach a'Charra, which stands near the pier on Loch Linnhe

Old Meldrum, Aberdeen. The old mansion of Barra Castle, partly 17th century, which is situated some 2 miles south-west, on A981

PLATE 130

Orchardton Tower, Kirkcudbright. This circular late 15th century tower was built originally by John Cairns and became a Maxwell property. It stands a mile south of Palnackie, on an unclassified road off A711

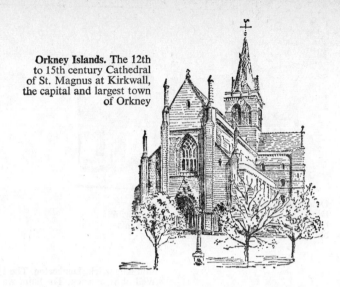

Orkney Islands. The 12th to 15th century Cathedral of St. Magnus at Kirkwall, the capital and largest town of Orkney

Orkney Islands. The tower of the much reconstructed 16th century Bishop's Palace at Kirkwall

Orkney Islands. The great prehistoric chambered tomb of Maeshowe, or Maes Howe, off A965, some 3 miles west-south-west of Finstown

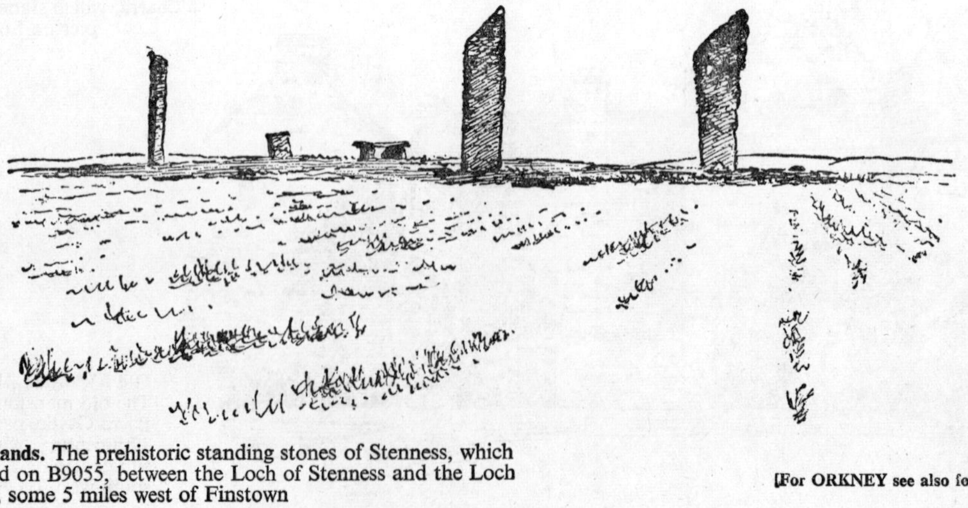

Orkney Islands. The prehistoric standing stones of Stenness, which are situated on B9055, between the Loch of Stenness and the Loch of Harray, some 5 miles west of Finstown

[For **ORKNEY** see also following plate

Near the pier is a perforated monolith, known as the Clach a' Charra. To the north, the Amhainn Righ Burn, on which are waterfalls, debouches from woodedhe ights into Loch Linnhe. *Iter. 100, 124, 125, 142.*

OPINAN, Ross and Cromarty. Map 22, **NG 7 7.** A clachan situated between the Gair Loch and the mouth of Loch Torridon, with views across the Inner Sound towards the distant *Coolin* mountains of Skye.

ORCHARDTON TOWER, Kirkcudbright. Map 3, **NX 8 5.** See **Palnackie.**

ORD, Isle of Skye, Inverness. Map 23, **NG 2 1.** On the south shore of Loch Eishort, with views of most of the great Coolin peaks, spectacular sunsets can sometimes be seen from here.

ORKNEY ISLANDS. Map 33. The *Orkneys* lie about 20 miles to the north of the Scottish mainland, from which they are separated by the turbulent waters of the Pentland Firth, and were known to the Romans as the Orcades. There are, in all, about 70 islands, 28 of which are inhabited, by far the largest being that of the *Mainland*, where the largest mileage of motoring roads will be found, and on which is situated **Kirkwall**, the most important centre. The Mainland is linked by the *Churchill Barriers* to several of the smaller islands to the south. Magnificent cliff scenery, notably in the island of Hoy, sometimes best viewed from a boat; wonderful seascapes; rare bird life; and some famous prehistoric antiquities, are features. The nearest port on the mainland is *Scrabster* (*q.v.*), near Thurso, with a 2½-hour car ferry steamer service to Stromness, and there are air services from the principal Scottish towns to Grimsetter airport at Kirkwall. Other steamer services operate from Aberdeen to Kirkwall. There are also connections to the Shetlands. Owing to their geographical situation, the summer is almost nightless. The climate is mainly mild, and the soil fertile, though virtually treeless. Most of the farming is now carried on by modern mechanical methods. There is an abundance of good trout fishing to be obtained, with free loch fishing. The Picts are said to have been the first colonizers of the Orkneys, being succeeded by the Norsemen. The territory was annexed to Scotland in 1468, being pledged for 50,000 florins by King Christian I of Norway as part of the agreed dowry of 60,000 florins when his daughter Margaret married James III of Scotland. *Iter. 263 to 266.*

THE MAINLAND. 7,713.

This is the largest of the Orkneys, having a deeply-indented coastline, while on it are situated *Kirkwall* and *Stromness*, the two most important ports and towns. There are nearly 200 miles of motoring roads on the island which are well-surfaced throughout. Minor roads giving access to the coast may be poor in places.

Kirkwall (4,688. SB. M.D. Mon.) was created a Royal Burgh in 1486, and is famous for *St. Magnus's* Cathedral, founded in 1137, the buildings being mainly of 12th cent. date. with additions up to 1558. After the battle of *Largs* (*q.v.*), in 1263, the body of King Haco rested here on its return to Norway. The Cathedral was later desecrated by Cromwell's soldiers, and the spire was destroyed by lightning in 1671, but restorations, some 50 years ago, have made good much of the damage. The 133-ft. high tower, built in 1525, is a good viewpoint. In the choir is a notable 15th cent. tomb, and in the north aisle of the nave is suspended a characteristic Orcadian " mort-brod," or memorial, others of which may also be seen. A tablet to the crew of the battleship " Royal Oak," torpedoed in the Second World War, with the loss of more than 800 men, was unveiled in 1948. South of the Cathedral stands the ruined partly 13th cent. Bishop's Palace (A.M.), with its massive mid-16th cent. round tower. Nearby are the remains of the Earl's Palace (A.M.), dating from 1607, and associated with Scott's " The Pirate." A doorway has survived from the 16th cent. Church of *St. Ola*, and near the Cathedral is the old *Tankerness House*, dated 1574. The public library, founded in 1683, is the oldest in Scotland (see **Crieff**). There are picturesque, narrow alleys in the town surfaced mainly with large stone slabs. There is a noticeable absence of footpaths. The pier lies to the north, on Kirkwall Bay.

Kirkwall Airport (Grimsetter) lies to the south-east of the town. Beyond the bay, east of Wide Firth, is *Shapinsay* (400) island, with the 19th cent. *Balfour Castle*. Eastwards of Kirkwall are the smaller bays of Meil and Berstane, each with good sands, and the latter being an inlet of the larger Inganess Bay, to the east of which lies the Tankerness peninsula. South of Kirkwall is the sandy Scapa Bay, near the western shores of which is the road overlooking *Scapa Flow*, the famous naval anchorage, used extensively in both world wars, and which saw the surrender of the German fleet in 1918. Most of the ships were scuttled by their crews in 1919, but a number have since been salvaged. The battleship " Royal Oak " was sunk here by a U-boat in 1939. During the last war, in order to seal up the eastern approach to Scapa Flow, the *Churchill Barriers* were built, linking the Mainland with South Ronaldsay. The new road commences at **St. Mary's Holm, 6½ m. S.E.E.** of Kirkwall, on Holm Sound, and traverses the small island of Lamb Holm, where Italian prisoners, during the war, constructed an ornate little Chapel out of a Nissen hut. Glimps Holm and Burray, with its curious broch, together with the narrow waterways which separate them, are then traversed. **3 m. N.W.** of Kirkwall, off the Finstown road, is *Wideford Hill*, 741 ft. (A.M.), a fine viewpoint. There are curious " weems," or Picts' Houses to the west and north.

Finstown, an attractive village, with one of Orkney's few woods, stands on the Bay of Firth, in which is situated Damsay Island, with its ruined broch. To the south-east of the village, on the bay, is the notable Gallery Grave of *Rennibister* (A.M.). **3 m. W.S.W., at Stenness,** is the very notable **Maeshowe** (A.M.), an enormous burial mound, perhaps Pictish, 36 ft. high and some 300 ft. in circumference, with many Runic inscriptions. A little farther to the west, on a narrow causeway between the Loch of Stenness and the Loch of Harray, and beyond **Stenness** Church, are the famous *Standing Stones of Stenness* (A.M.), comprising two incomplete circles, the *Circle of Stenness* and the *Ring of Brogar*, or *Brodgar* (A.M.), the latter retaining 20 stones. There are also numerous tumuli in the neighbourhood. **7 m. N.E.** of Finstown, near the shores of Wide Firth and facing the island of Gairsay, is the *Hall of Rendall*, where a doocot, having flagstone landing piers for the birds, and dating perhaps from c. 1600, has survived.

Stromness (1,518. S.B.), with its fine harbour, narrow paved street, quaint closes and an interesting museum, faces the hills of **Hoy** across Hoy Sound and looks south-eastwards to historic **Scapa Flow.** The site of *Login's Well* is associated with the explorers Captain Cook and Sir John Franklin. There is a GOLF course. It is the port for *Scrabster* (*q.v.*) and also for Hoy and other islands. Near Waith Bridge, over which the road to Kirkwall passes, is the Neolithic, or Stone Age Chambered Cairn of *Onstan* (A.M.). **9 m. S.E.** of Stromness, near the shores of Scapa Flow, and close to *Orphir* Church (A.M.), is a ruined circular Church, built perhaps by Earl Haakon in the 12th cent. To the east of Orphir lies the sandy Swanbister Bay.

In the extreme north-west of the Mainland lies **Birsay** (839), on the bay of that name, with the Loch of Boardhouse lying to the east. The ruined Palace of Birsay was rebuilt late in the 16th cent. Off-shore, to the north-west, is the tidal island of Brough of Birsay, with a ruined 12th cent. Church. Some **10 m. E.S.E.** of Birsay, past Costa Head, Britain's windiest spot, and by the shores of Eynhallow Sound, is **Evie**, near which stands the large broch of *Gurness* (A.M.). at Aikerness. To the south-west of Birsay Bay lies Marwick Head, reached on foot from **Marwick,** and notable for the Kitchener Memorial. The cruiser " Hampshire," which was taking Kitchener to Russia, was sunk, in June 1916, off the coast in the vicinity.

The very famous prehistoric village of **Skara Brae** (A.M.), dating from the Stone Age, and in a remarkable state of preservation, stands on the south shore of the sandy bay of Skaill, beyond **Aith**, to the west of the **Birsay** to Stromness road. Narrow, covered alleys give access to stone huts, while the smaller remains which have been found point to an occupation of some 250 years. Near the freshwater

Loch of Skaill stands the modernized 17th cent. and later *Skaill House*. Inland, and to the east, lies the Loch of Harray, noted for fishing, to the north of which is **Dounby,** with *Click* mill, an old watermill, in the vicinity.

In the south-east corner of the mainland, known as East Mainland, and situated on Sandside Bay, is **Deerness,** with its ruined broch. A little to the north is a chasm in the cliffs known as the Gloup of Deerness, and beyond it is the Stack of Deerness. The road leading westwards from the Deerness peninsula to Kirkwall passes the head of Deer Sound at St. Peter's Pool. On the narrow isthmus separating it from Taracliff Bay and the North Sea, with Copinsay Island away to the south-east, is the barrow of *Dingy's Howe.* **2 m. N.N.W.** of Deerness, accessible only on foot, and overlooking Deer Sound, is a monument at *Scarva Taing* commemorating 200 Covenanters, wrecked here in 1679.

HOY. 600.

The most spectacular and second in size among the Orkneys, *Hoy* is accessible by steamer from Stromness, and has a number of hills over 1,000 ft. in height, the loftiest being *Ward Hill*, 1,565 ft., noted for its rare plants. From *Linksness*, with its pier, in the north of the island facing Graemsay Island in Hoy Sound, access is gained on foot to the magnificent cliff scenery, riven by steep gashes called " geos." These form the great feature of the north-west coast, from St. John's Head, rising vertically to 1,140 ft., to the celebrated *Old Man of Hoy*, an impressive, isolated rock stack, 450 ft. high. This famous landmark, first climbed in 1966, is visible from Caithness on the mainland coast. Beyond lies Rora Head and another line of cliffs, overlooking the attractive Rackwick Valley, in which is situated the burial-chamber known as the *Dwarfie Stone* (A.M.), associated with Scott's " The Pirate," and inscribed with Hugh Miller's initials. In the south of Hoy are the coloured cliffs of Berry Head, and to the east, beyond the modern *Melsetter House*, with its fine gardens, is the South Walls peninsula, with the inlet of Long Hope. At its mouth lies the island of Flotta, looking westwards to the Scapa Flow naval base of **Lyness.** Hoy is said to be the most southerly breeding-place in Great Britain of the rare great skua.

SOUTH RONALDSAY. 1,150.

This fertile island is now linked to the larger island of Mainland by the *Churchill Barriers*, which traverse the smaller islands of Burray, Glimps Holm and Lamb Holm. On the nothern coast of the island is **St. Margaret's Hope,** associated with Queen Margaret, the " Maid of Norway," who died on board ship on her way to Scotland, in 1290. Hoxa Head, on the north-west side of South Ronaldsay, has a ruined broch. The southern extremity of the island, on which stands **Burwick,** linked by a road to the pretty village of St. Margaret's Hope, is separated from Duncansby Head, in Caithness, on the mainland, by the 6-mile wide turbulent stretch of the Pentland Firth.

ROUSAY AND EYNHALLOW. 300.

The island of *Rousay* is separated from Mainland by the waters of Eynhallow Sound. It has some fine rock scenery on the west coast, on which are also the notable broch and chambered cairn of *Midhope* (A.M.), in addition to other cairns. On the tiny and uninhabited *Eynhallow* Island is a ruined monastic Church (A.M.), and the island is also a haunt of seals and many species of rare birds, among them the skua. Fulmars and eiders also abound.

EGILSAY.

This small island, to the east of Rousay, is noted chiefly for its roofless Norman Church (A.M.), supposed to stand on the site where St. Magnus was murdered, in 1116, and famous for its curious round tower, 48 ft. high, one of the three examples to be found in Scotland. To the south-west is the little island of *Wyre*, or *Veira*, on which are slight remains of *Cobbie Row's Castle* (A.M.), which may be the earliest of all stone-built Scottish castles.

STRONSAY 504.

A strangely-shaped island, in the north-east sector of the group, with three large bays, Milk Bay, St. Catherine's Bay and Bay of Holland. Off the northern shores is the small island of Papa Stronsay and farther north, across the Sanday Sound, is the large and narrow island of *Sanday* (670), with its Neolithic Chambered Cairn of *Quoyness* (A.M.). Beyond Sanday is *North Ronaldsay* (161), the most northerly of the Orkneys, noted for its indigenous breed of sheep, feeding for the most part on seaweed. A stone wall, 12 miles in circumference, has had to be built to keep in order the sheep off the cultivated land.

WESTRAY. 1,011.

On this island, lying in the north-west of the group, is the ruined 16th cent. *Noltland Castle* (A.M.), destroyed in 1746, and noted for its hall, kitchen and fine, winding staircase. The Castle stands a little inland from Pierowall Bay, on the north-east coast, with its ruined Church preserving some inscribed tombstones (A.M.). To the north-east, across Papa Sound, is the island of *Papa Westray*, with a ruined Chapel and a large chambered cairn of Neolithic date, with beehive cells and some rare megalithic engravings (A.M.). In the extreme north-west of Westray is Noup Head, with magnificent, lofty cliffs and a lighthouse. To the south is the Gentlemen's Cave, the hiding-place of several Jacobites after Culloden, in 1746. Off the south-east shores of Westray is *Eday* (197), preserving numerous weems and tumuli, and with Red Head overlooking the Calf Sound, beyond which rises Grey Head on the smaller island of Calf of Eday. See **Shetland Islands.**

ORMISTON, East Lothian. 2,195. Map 10, **NT 4 6.**
A pleasant village, on the Tyne Water, with a 15th cent. Cross, set on modern steps. At *Ormiston House*, to the south, an old house, modernized and enlarged, George Wishart took refuge, in 1545, with Alexander Cockburn. A fragment of the old Church of Ormiston stands near the house, and preserves a notable brass to Alexander Cockburn, who died in 1563. See **Pencaitland.**

ORONSAY, ISLE OF, Argyll. Map 13, **NR 3 8.**
See **Colonsay.**

ORPHIR, Orkney. Map 33, **HY 3 0.**
See **Orkney Islands** (Mainland). *Iter. 264.*

ORTON, Moray. Map 26, **NJ 3 5.**
Pleasantly situated in the Lower Spey valley, with wooded heights rising on each side, and *Ben Aigan*, 1,544 ft., dominating the landscape to the south. *Iter. 171, 189.*

OSE, Isle of Skye, Inverness. Map 22, **NG 3 4.**
Situated on the shores of Loch Bracadale, looking towards the islands of Harlosh, Tarner and Wiay. Glen Ose extends inland to the east and on its southern slopes is the ruined broch of *Dun Arkaig. Iter. 255.*

OTTER FERRY, Argyll. Map 14, **NR 9 8.**
Situated on *Loch Fyne* (*q.v.*), its name derived from " oitir," or sand spit. Across the loch rise the low green hills of *Knapdale* (*q.v.*), and in an inlet of the loch, known as Loch Gilp, are situated *Ardrishaig* and *Lochgilphead* (both *q.v.*). A narrow, winding and hilly road, with gradients up to 1 in 4, and attaining a height of 1,026 ft., leads from Otter Ferry to the shores of Loch Riddon and also to *Glendaruel* (*q.v.*). See **Kilfinan.** *Iter. 102.*

OUTER HEBRIDES, Inverness; Ross and Cromarty.
See **Hebrides, Outer.** Map 32.

OVERSCAIG, Sutherland. 50. Map 29, **NC 4 2.**
On the northern shores of the rather featureless Loch Shin, along which proceeds the road from Lairg to Loch Laxford and *Laxford Bridge* (*q.v.*), on the wild north-western seaboard. Away to the west rises *Ben More Assynt*, 3,273 ft., the highest mountain in the county, while to the north, on the edge of the great Reay deer forest, is *Ben Hee*, 2,864 ft. See **Merkland Lodge.** *Iter. 229.*

OXENFOORD CASTLE, Midlothian. Map 10, **NT 3 6.**
See **Pathhead** (Midlothian).

OXNAM, Roxburgh. 351. Map 10, **NT 6 1.**
Situated in a lonely valley, threaded by the Oxnam Water in a setting of low hills. A little to the north, at *Cappuck*,

The remains of the 16th century Palace of Birsay, on A966, in the extreme north-west of the Mainland. It was a former residence of the Earls of Orkney, and was rebuilt by Earl Robert Stewart, in the style of Falkland Palace (Illustrated on Plate 64)

The broch of Gurness, at Aikerness, with its secondary buildings. It stands near Evie and the shores of Eynhallow Sound, facing Rousay island from an unclassified road off A966

Marwick Head, to the west of B9056, near Birsay, on which stands the Kitchener Memorial. Lord Kitchener lost his life when the cruiser 'Hampshire' was sunk off this coast during the First World War

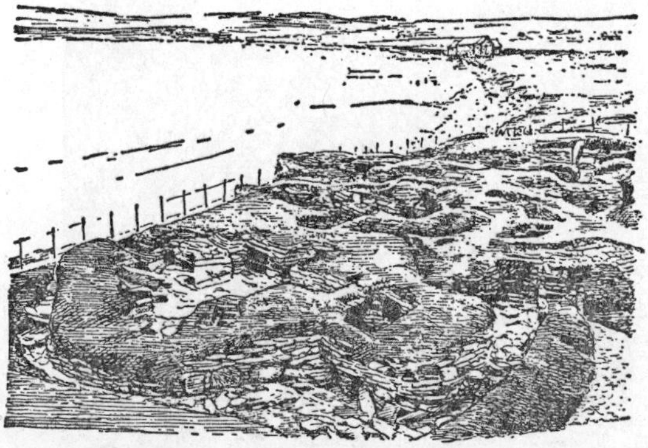

The prehistoric village of Skara Brae, which lies on an unclassified road off B9056, on the Bay of Skaill, near Aith

The island of Hoy, seen from Black Craig, which lies on an unclassified road to the north-west of Stromness

[For ORKNEY see also preceding page

Oxton, Berwick. The Parish Church of Channelkirk, where a church dedicated to St. Cuthbert has existed since before written records. It stands a short distance to the north, on an unclassified road off A68

Oykell Bridge, Ross and Cromarty. The bridge across the turbulent River Oykell, which rises in the massif of Ben More Assynt (3273 feet), Sutherland's highest mountain

Paisley, Renfrew. The restored 17th century Place of Paisley, built originally by the Earl of Dundonald. It was the scene of the wedding, in 1684, of John Graham of Claverhouse and Lady Jean Cochrane

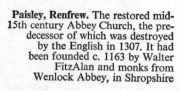

Paisley, Renfrew. The restored mid-15th century Abbey Church, the predecessor of which was destroyed by the English in 1307. It had been founded c. 1163 by Walter FitzAlan and monks from Wenlock Abbey, in Shropshire

Pathhead, Fife. The ruined 15th century Ravenscraig Castle, an old palace of the Sinclairs. It figures as 'Ravensheugh' in Sir Walter Scott's '*Rosabelle*'

[For PALNACKIE see under ORCHARDTON TOWER (Plate 131)

[For PASS OF THE CATTLE see under TORNAPRESS (Plate 163)

a Roman station has been located. The line of the Roman Dere Street, can be traced to the east of Oxnam, on its way towards the *Cheviot* (*q.v.*) ridge, which it crosses, at a height of some 1,500 ft., near the great camp and earthworks of *Chew Green*, to the east of *Carter Bar* (*q.v.*).

OXTON, Berwick. 125. Map 10, **NT 4 5.**
A tiny Lauderdale hamlet, situated a little to the west of the Edinburgh to Lauder road through *Carfraemill* (*q.v.*). A little to the north is the small *Channelkirk* Church, which is associated with St. Cuthbert, who spent his childhood in the district, and in whose honour it was built. A pilgrims' track formerly passed through both hamlets, leading from the *Lammermuirs* to Tweeddale, and it is probable that the Romans also came this way. See **Soutra Hill.**

OYKELL BRIDGE, Ross and Cromarty. Map 29, **NC 3 0.**
Mentioned by Ptolemy, the early geographer, and figuring also in Icelandic Sagas. To the south-east of this bridge over the River Oykell, the river is joined by the Einig, flowing from Glen Einig. A little to the west of Oykell Bridge are some picturesque falls on the Oykell, which has come down from the slopes of *Ben More Assynt*, 3,273 ft., Sutherland's highest mountain. From here it flows south-eastwards through Loch Ailsh, noted for fishing, to form the boundary between Sutherland and Ross and Cromarty for the greater part of its turbulent course. Southwards lies a wilderness of lonely hills in the extensive Freevater Forest. **5 m. N.W.** of Oykell Bridge, on the road to *Inchnadamph* (*q.v.*), near the small Loch Craggie, is a low watershed, from which the views range towards the distant, isolated Sutherland peaks of *Canisp*, 2,779 ft., and *Suilven*, 2,399 ft., with its sharp eastern peak. See **Rosehall.** *Iter. 224, 228.*

OYNE, Aberdeen. 630. Map 27, **NJ 6 2.**
This little village, on the Gady Burn, in the district of Garioch, is overlooked to the south by the afforested mass of *Bennachie*, with *Oxen Craig* rising to 1,733 ft. To the east of the hills is the prominent *Mither Tap*, 1,698 ft., on which is situated a remarkable hill fort. *Harthill Castle*, a ruined tower, standing south-east of Oyne, dates from 1638, and was burnt by the Covenanters. *Westhall* is a 16th cent. tower house. **3 m. E.** stands the 17th cent. house of *Logie-Elphinstone*. See **Chapel of Garioch** and **Insch.** *Iter. 178.*

PAISLEY, Renfrew. 95,344. LB. Map 8, **NS 4 6.**
E.C. Tues. **M.D.** Mon. GOLF. An important Municipal Burgh and industrial town, the world's largest thread-producing centre, and at one time famous for the well-known "Paisley Shawls." In the town is the fine Cluniac Abbey Church, founded in 1163, and destroyed by the English in 1307. The present building dates largely from the mid-15th cent., but the tower, choir and north transept have been rebuilt. The west front, with a notable doorway, and the nave, now the Parish Church, are the finest parts. In place of the south transept is *St. Mirren's* Chapel, built in 1499, in which is an effigy, thought to be of Marjory Bruce, the daughter of Robert Bruce. Part of the former Abbey buildings, on the south side of the Church, on the site of the refectory, are incorporated in the 17th cent. *Place of Paisley*, which has been well restored as a War Memorial. In the town museum are works by Scottish artists, and a collection of Paisley shawls. The Thomas Coats Memorial Church was built in 1894. Professor John Wilson, the "Christopher North" of Blackwood's Magazine, was born at Paisley, in 1785. At 8 Castle Street, was born, in 1774, Robert Tannahill, the weaver poet, who described the *Braes of Gleniffer*, a fine viewpoint, to the south-west of the town. Nearby are the remains of *Staneley Castle*. On the White Cart River, **3 m. E.** of Paisley, is *Crookston Castle* (N.T. Scot. and A.M.), late 14th cent., presented to the Trust in 1931, their first acquisition in Scotland. Open weekdays 10 to 7 (Sun. 2–7), April to Sept.; 10 to 4 (Sun. 2–4), Oct. to March. (See note page 98.) The first American troops to reach Britain in the Second World War came to Paisley in 1942. **2½ m. N.** of the town is *Glasgow* airport. See **Old Kilpatrick.** *Iter. 18, 29, 58, 60, 61, 62, 63, 64, 65, 109, 110, 111.*

PALNACKIE, Kirkcudbright. 177. Map 3, **NX 8 5.**
Situated on a creek of the Rough Firth, an inlet of the Solway Firth. The Urr Water flows just to the north of the village to enter the creek. **1 m. S.** is *Orchardton Tower* (A.M.), late 15th cent., and unique among *Galloway* (*q.v.*) towers in that it is circular. There are grounds for believing that Scott's "Guy Mannering" can be associated with Orchardton. To the south lies a narrow peninsula terminating in Almorness Point. **3 m. N.** are the well-known *Craignair* granite quarries, which have provided stone for the Thames embankment in London. *Iter. 73.*

PALNURE, Kirkcudbright. Map 2, **NX 4 6.**
The Palnure Burn, which has issued from the pretty Bargaly Glen, flows southwards from here to enter the winding Cree estuary. *Cairnsmoor of Fleet*, 2,331 ft., associated with John Buchan's "The Thirty-nine Steps," rises to the north-east. *Iter. 26, 72, 73.*

PANNANICH WELLS, Aberdeen. Map 20, **NO 4 9.**
Lies on Deeside, with views of *Morven*, 2,862 ft., to the north, beyond the river. To the south rises *Pannanich Hill*, 1,896 ft., a good viewpoint. The Wells of Pannanich became known in 1760, and led to the rise of the well-known resort of *Ballater* (*q.v.*), situated a little to the south-west. **2½ m. E.** is *Ballaterach* farm associated with Byron's childhood. See **Cambus o'May.** *Iter. 168, 174.*

PARALLEL ROADS, Inverness. Map 18, **NN 2 8.**
See **Roy Bridge** and also **Loch Lochy** and **Tulloch.** *Iter. 143, 208.*

PASS OF BRANDER, Argyll. Map 14, **NN 0 2**
See **Falls of Cruachan.**

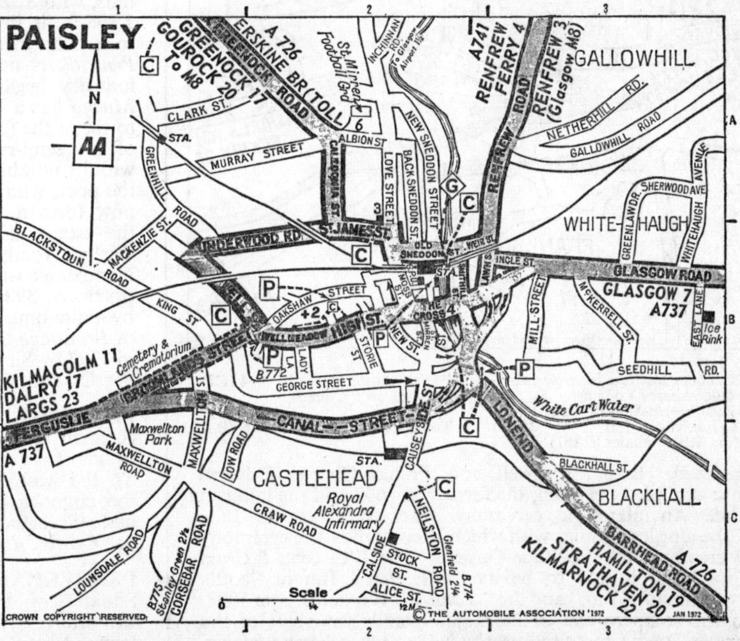

Abbey, part 15th cent., and the 17th cent. Place of Paisley, now a War Memorial	1 (B2)	County Buildings. Information Bureau	3 (A2)
Coats Memorial Church (1894)	2 (B2)	Town Hall	4 (B2)

PATHHEAD, Fife. Map 17, **NT 2 9.**
Situated between Kirkcaldy and Dysart. The ruined 15th cent. *Ravenscraig Castle*, dismantled in 1651, is described in Scott's " Rosabelle " and overlooks the Firth of Forth.

PATHHEAD, Midlothian. Map 10, **NT 3 6.**
To the north, below steep banks, flows the Tyne Water, and beyond the river is *Oxenfoord Castle*, in a fine park. A picturesque ceremonial still observed at the castle is the presentation of a red rose to the reigning monarch when on a visit. *Preston Hall* dates from c. 1794, and *Ford House*, an attractive old house, from 1680. *Southside Castle*, **3 m. W.,** now a farm, is early 17th cent. See **Crichton, Mellerstain** and **Pencaitland.** *Iter. 4, 5, 13.*

PATNA, Ayr. 465. Map 8, **NS 4 1.**
E.C. Wed. Lies on the River Doon, on the edge of a coal-mining and iron-producing area. *Iter. 75, 76, 77, 85.*

PAXTON, Berwick. Map 11, **NT 9 5.**
Between the village and the River Tweed, to the south, stands *Paxton House*, a fine Georgian mansion, attributed to Robert Adam. Farther south, the river is spanned by the fine Union Suspension Bridge, the first of its type, erected originally by Sir Samuel Brown in 1820.

PEEBLES, Peebles. 5,881. SB. Map 9, **NT 2 4.**
E.C. Wed. GOLF. This well-known Royal Burgh and inland resort stands in a delightful setting of green Tweeddale hills, through which the River Tweed, famous for its salmon, flows in one of its most delightful reaches. The town is noted for its tweed mills, and is also a good angling centre. The former Castle has entirely

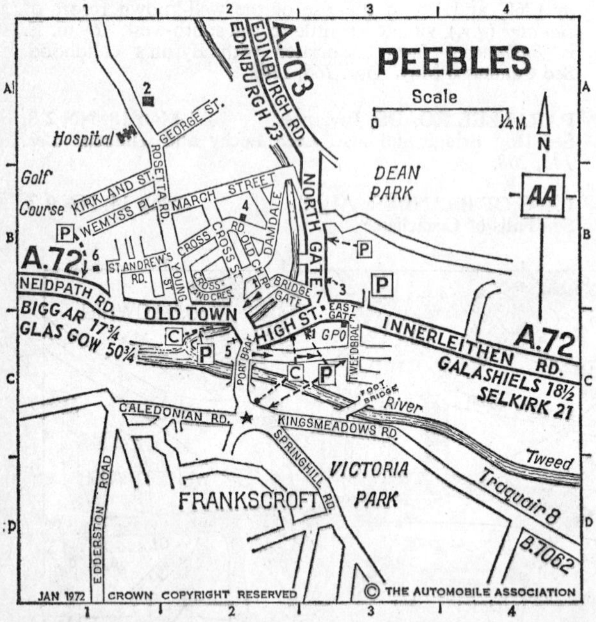

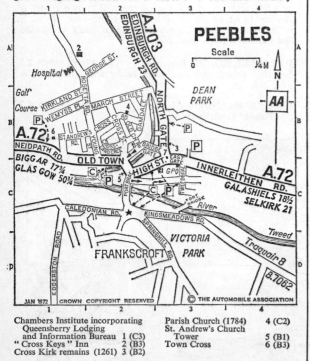

Chambers Institute incorporating Queensberry Lodging and Information Bureau	1 (C3)
" Cross Keys " Inn	2 (B3)
Cross Kirk remains (1261)	3 (B2)
Parish Church (1784)	4 (C2)
St. Andrew's Church Tower	5 (B1)
Town Cross	6 (B3)

vanished. Both Cromwell and Prince Charles Edward have occupied the town, the former in 1649 and the latter in 1745. An interesting ceremony observed yearly in June is the Border Riding, with which is combined the ceremony of crowning the " Beltane Queen." The 17th cent. " *Cross Keys* " Inn is said to be the " *Cleikum* " Inn of Scott's " St. Ronan's Well," and the " *Tontine* " Inn dates from 1808. At the southern end of Northgate stands the shaft of the former Town Cross, and nearby is the *Queensberry Lodging*, dated 1644, and now forming part of the *Chambers Institution*, in which is incorporated an interesting museum. The 4th Duke of Queensberry, famous as " Old Q," was born in the Queensberry Lodging, in 1725. The Parish Church was built in 1784, but there are still some remains of the old Cross Kirk (A.M.), dating from 1261. John Buchan and his sister, Anna Buchan (O. Douglas), the novelist, lived at *Bank House*. R. L. Stevenson and Samuel Crockett also lived in Peebles at different times. The bridge spanning the Tweed, twice widened, was built originally in 1467 and the Peebles arms appear on the present lamp-standards. Mungo Park, the famous African explorer, lived in Peebles at one period. At the western end of the town stood *St. Andrew's* Church, of which only the tower remains. The road following the river westwards reaches, within a mile, the picturesque 15th cent. *Neidpath Castle*, an early Fraser stronghold, having walls 11 feet thick, finely situated on the north bank of the Tweed, and once battered by Cromwell's artillery. The Castle passed later into the hands of the Earls of Tweeddale, and was purchased, in 1686, by the 1st Duke of Queensberry, whose successor, " Old Q.," cut down all the fine timber on the estate. South of the town lies the beautiful and unspoilt valley of *Glensax*, threaded by the Glensax Burn, with *Dunrig* rising to 2,433 ft. at the lonely head of the glen, on the Selkirk border. To the east of Peebles, and bordering the *Innerleithen* (*q.v.*) road, lies Glentress Forest. See **Lyne, Manor, Stobo** and **Traquair.** *Iter. 4, 14, 24, 32, 33, 34, 35, 40, 52, 53.*

PENCAITLAND, East Lothian. 1,206. Map 10, **NT 4 6.**
E.C. Wed. The Tyne Water divides this charming village into two. In Western Pencaitland is an old Mercat Cross, and in Eastern Pencaitland is the Church, dating from the 13th cent., preserving the original north sacristy. There are also three old sundials, a fine 17th cent. west doorway and a laird's loft, while the tower is dated 1631. Beyond the river, to the north, is *Winton House*, dating from 1620, with 19th-cent. additions. This fine structure is somewhat similar in its external details to George Heriot's Hospital, at *Edinburgh* (*q.v.*), and is noted for the tall and finely wrought chimney stacks and the enriched plaster ceilings. **1½ m. S.W.** is *Penkaet*, formerly *Fountainhall*, a beautiful 17th cent. house, with old woodwork and two old dovecotes. See **Ormiston** and **East Salton.** *Iter. 3, 40.*

PENICUIK, Midlothian. 9,913. SB. Map 9, **NT 2 5.**
E.C. Wed. On the North Esk River, south of the *Pentland* hills, with *Scald Law*, the highest peak in the range, rising to 1,898 ft., in the background. To the north of the mountain, in a deep trough, lies the picturesque Loganlee reservoir. *Penicuik* is noted for paper-making. The Scottish cotton industry began here in 1778. The Parish Church of *St. Mungo* has a Doric portico, and its belfry is the 12th cent. tower of the former church of *St. Kentigern*. In the grounds of the semi-ruined *Penicuik House*, dating from c. 1770, with its notable portico, stands an obelisk to Allan Ramsay, the poet, who was born in 1686. Part of the former stables now form a residence, and the Clerk family, owners of the estate, still live there. The " Spear " lodge, on the Carlops road, shows their arms and motto. During the Napoleonic wars, *Valleyfield Mill* was used to confine French prisoners, 300 of whom died there and are commemorated by a monument. **2½ m. S.W.,** near the river, are the remains of *Brunstane Castle*. **1½ m. N.E.** is *Auchendinny House*, built in 1707 by Sir William Bruce, a good example of the period. See **Carlops, Glencorse** and **Roslin.** *Iter. 10, 24.*

PENNAN, Aberdeen. Map 27, **NJ 8 6.**
A small fishing village, on a rocky and precipitous stretch of coast by Pennan Bay, overlooked by Pennan Head. To the west, the Tore Burn, marking the border between the counties of Aberdeen and Banff, flows into the sea, and still farther west is the bold headland of Troup Head. See **Crovie.** *Iter. 182.*

PENNYGHAEL, Isle of Mull, Argyll. Map 13, **NM 5 2.**
Situated on the southern shores of Loch Scridain, with *Ben More*, 3,169 ft., rising away to the north beyond the loch. A narrow road leads southwards from Pennyghael through Glen Leidle to *Carsaig Bay* (*q.v.*). The road which proceeds to the head of Loch Scridain winds through the onely Glen More, in a setting of lofty hills, with *Ben Buie*,

Pathhead, Midlothian. The ' Lion ' entrance gates to Preston Hall a late 18th century mansion

Peebles, Peebles. The Chambers Institute, perhaps incorporating the reconstructed remains of the Queensberry Lodging of 1644. The 4th Duke of Queensberry, known as ' Old Q,' was born here in 1725

Pencaitland, East Lothian. This unusual lodge, on the Pencaitland–Gifford road (B6355), forms an entrance to Saltoun Hall

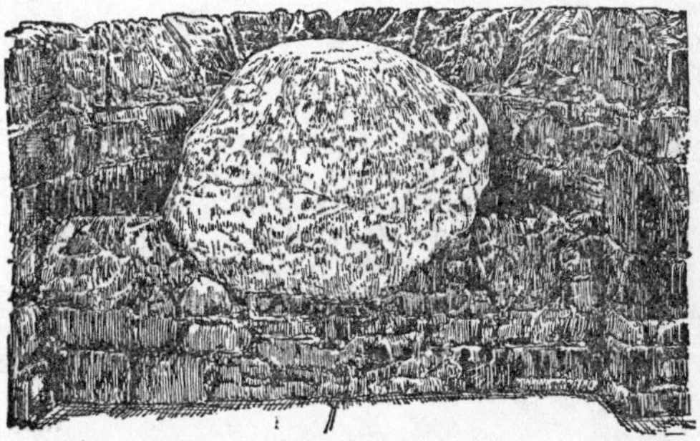

Peebles, Peebles. The White Stone, facing the ' Peebles ' Hydro. At this spot the town used to give an official welcome to distinguished visitors

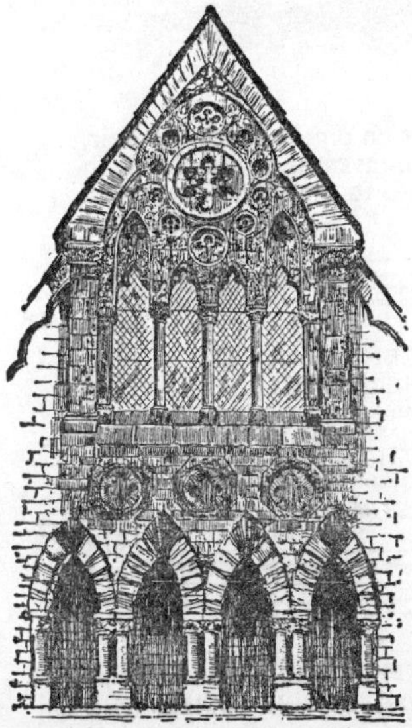

Penicuik, Midlothian. The ornate front of the South Church

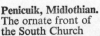

Penicuik, Midlothian. A huntsman and a hunting horn with the motto of the Clerk family, owners of the Penicuik estate. They are placed on the gable of the entrance lodge, which stands on the Carlops road (A766)

Perth, Perth. St. John's Church, 15th to 16th century, where John Knox delivered his famous sermon on idolatry in 1559

Perth, Perth. The 'Salutation' Hotel, which has a brass plate recording its association with Bonnie Prince Charlie and the '45 Rising

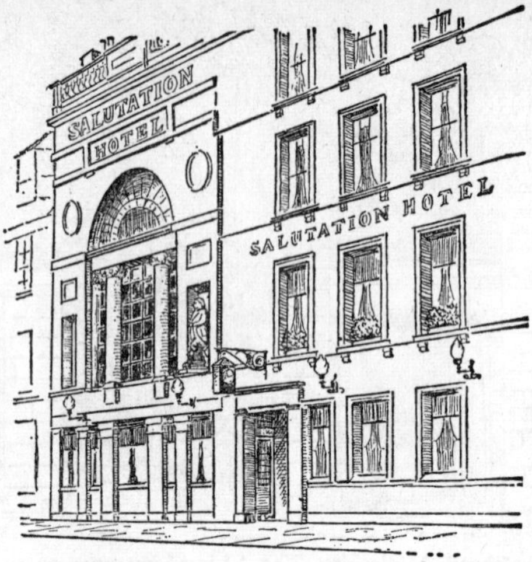
SALUTATION
HOTEL
SALUTATION HOTEL

Perth, Perth. The house of Catherine Glover, the 'Fair Maid of Perth.' Her father was a noted glover, and a niche in the wall of the house once held a statue of St. Bartholomew, the patron saint of the glovers

Penpont, Dumfries. The inscription on the smithy at Keir, where Kirkpatrick Macmillan, inventor of the bicycle in 1839, was born. It stands to the south-east, on an unclassified road

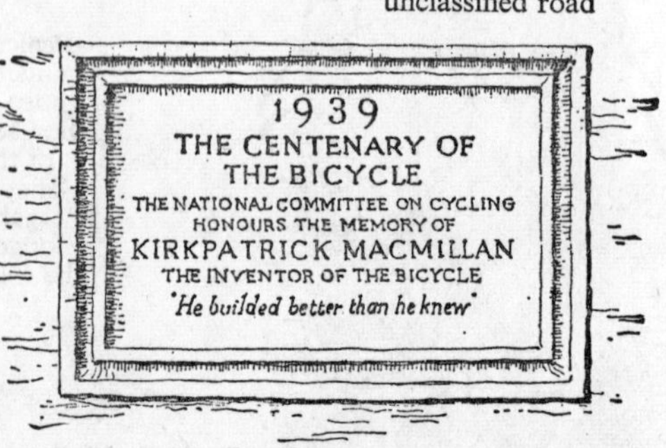
1939
THE CENTENARY OF
THE BICYCLE
THE NATIONAL COMMITTEE ON CYCLING
HONOURS THE MEMORY OF
KIRKPATRICK MACMILLAN
THE INVENTOR OF THE BICYCLE
'He builded better than he knew'

Peterhead, Aberdeen. The statue of Marshal Keith, who was born near the town in 1696

[For PINKIE HOUSE see following plate
[For PETERHEAD see also under BUCHAN (Plate 25)

2,354 ft., rising to the south. Later it reaches the northern shores of the almost land-locked Loch Spelve on the way to *Craignure* (*q.v.*). See **Kilfinichen Church.** *Iter. 249.*

PENPONT, Dumfries. 870 with Tynron. Map 3, **NX 8 9.** Lies on the Scar Water, which, within a short distance, joins the Nith. The village stands on the line of an ancient Pilgrims' track, and James IV travelled this way going from Edinburgh to *Whithorn* (*q.v.*), in 1507. On *Tynron Doon,* 946 ft., to the west, is a prehistoric hill-fort commanding an extensive view, and said to have sheltered Robert Bruce, in 1306. *Auchengibbert Hill,* 1,221 ft., rises away to the north. To the south of Penpont is the long ridge of the *Keir* hills. To the north-east of these hills is the hamlet of *Keir,* in the vicinity of which, at *Courthill* smithy, was born Kirkpatrick Macmillan, the inventor of the bicycle in 1839. The original machine is in the Science Museum, in London, and a plaque here commemorates the inventor. *Iter. 25.*

PENTLAND HILLS, Midlothian. Map 9, **NT 0** 5 etc. See **Carlops, Currie, Glencorse, Penicuik, Swanston** and **West Linton.**

PERTH, Perth. 43,051. LB. Map 17, **NO 1 2.** **E.C.** Wed. **M.D.** Fri. GOLF. The "Fair City" of Perth, known at one time as *St. Johnstoun,* stands between the meadows of the North and South Inch at the head of the estuary of the River Tay, famous for its salmon. The city looks towards the *Sidlaw* hills to the north-east, and the *Ochil* hills to the south-west, while eastwards, on the north shores of the Firth of Tay, stretches the fertile *Carse of Gowrie* (*q.v.*). Near Perth are *Kinnoull Hill,* across the river, to the east, and *Moncreiffe Hill,* to the south-east, both over 700 ft. high, and providing fine views from their summits, the first-named crowned with a view indicator. Perth is an ancient Royal Burgh, once the capital of Scotland, and has a long history, having been on several occasions in the hands of the English. In 1600, the Gowrie conspiracy took place here; in 1651, the city surrendered to Cromwell; and in both Jacobite risings, in 1715 and again in 1745, it was occupied by the insurgents.

The fine, restored Church of *St. John* dates from various periods, the choir having been built in 1450, the nave c. 1490 and the central tower having a 15th cent. steeple. In 1559, John Knox delivered here his famous sermon against idolatry in the Church. Charles I, Charles II and Prince Charles Edward all attended services here, and Scott has introduced it into the scene of his "Fair Maid of Perth." In the rebuilt north transept is Sir Robert Lorimer's War Memorial Chapel. The Church has preserved some notable Pre-Reformation church plate. *St. Ninian's* Episcopal Cathedral is 19th cent. The Old Academy, now a school, has a façade of 1807. In *Balhousie Castle* is the Black Watch Regimenal Museum. The County Buildings occupy the site of the former Gowrie House where, in 1600, the famous conspiracy took place. There is an interesting Museum and Art Gallery. The *Fair Maid of Perth's House* is situated in Curfew Row, near the North Inch, on which took place the judicial Clan combat of 1396, which Scott has so graphically described. Nearby stood the former Blackfriars Monastery, in which James I was murdered, in 1437, after Catherine Douglas, a lady of the Queen, had vainly striven to save him by placing her arm in a door in order to replace a stolen bar. On the North Inch is the fine new *Bell's Sports Centre.* The "*Salutation*" Hotel has associations with Prince Charles Edward and the '45. Perth Bridge (1771) is the work of Smeaton. Perth has today many industries, including dyeworks retaining 19th cent. buildings, and waterworks of 1832 by the river, which it is hoped to preserve. The city is an important touring centre for Central Scotland, and a 70 mile countryside trail for cars starting at Perth and going by way of *Dunkeld, Aberfeldy* and the *Sma' Glen,* has been worked out by the Scottish Wild Life Trust. At *Bridgend,* across the Tay, John Ruskin spent part of his boyhood, and he was married in 1848 at the house of *Bowerswell,* which stands below Kinnoull Hill. The fine *Branklyn Gardens* (N.T. Scot.) are open Mon. to Sat., 10 to 5 (Sun. 2 to 6), Mar. to Sept. **6 m. E.** is *Inchyra House.* c. 1800. **4½ m. S.E.,** on the south bank of the Tay, beyond Moncreiffe Hill, is the ruined 16th cent. *Elcho Castle* (A.M.), retaining its yetts. Open summer, 10 to 7, winter, 10 to 4; Sun., after 2. (See page 98.) See **Abernethy, Bridge of Earn, Huntingtower, Methven, Rumbling Bridge, Scone** and **Stobhall.** *Iter. 86, 90, 91, 130, 131, 132, 135, 145, 146, 147, 148, 149, 150, 151, 152, 153, 154.*

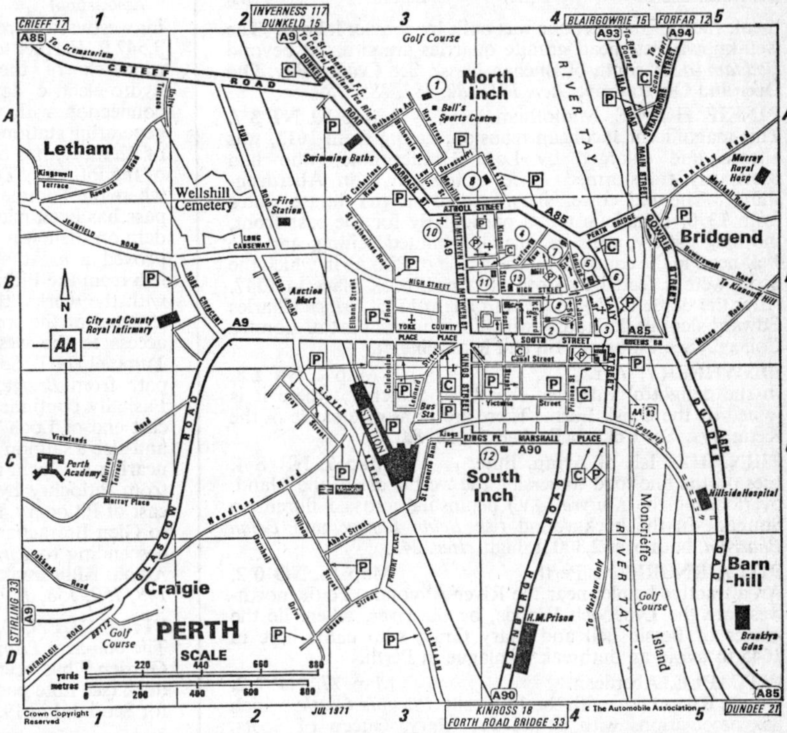

Balhousie Castle	1 (A3)	Municipal Buildings and City Chambers	6 (B4)	St. Ninian's Episcopal Cathedral	10 (B3)
City Hall	2 (B4)	Natural History Museum and Art Gallery	7 (B4)	Sandeman Public Library	11 (B4)
County Buildings	3 (B4)	Old Academy	8 (A4)	Sir Walter Scott's Statue	12 (C4)
Fair Maid's House	4 (B4)	St. John's Church	9 (B4)	Theatre	13 (B4)
Information Bureau (June-Sept.)	5 (B4)				

PETERCULTER, Aberdeen. 1,407. Map 21, **NJ 8 0.** **E.C.** Tues. GOLF. See **Culter** (Aberdeen). *Iter. 152.*

PETERHEAD, Aberdeen. 14,164. SB. Map 27, **NK 1 4.** **E.C.** Wed. **M.D.** Fri. GOLF. An important *Buchan* (*q.v.*) herring fishing port, situated on Peterhead Bay. This is separated by Salthouse Head from Sandford Bay, beyond which is Buchan Ness, the most easterly point in Scotland. The town was founded in 1593 by the Keiths, who, for helping the Old Pretender in 1715, were exiled. On the links to the south are the remains of *St. Peter's* Kirk (1132), The Bell tower of 1592 contains a Dutch bell of 1647. The old Parish Church, or Muckle Kirk, dates from 1806. The Town House dates from 1788, and in front stands a statue of Marshal Keith, born in 1696, at *Inverugie Castle,* **3 m. N.W.,** a ruined 16th cent. structure on the River Ugie. About a mile farther up the river are the remains of the 14th cent. *Ravenscraig Castle.* Peterhead convict prison, adjacent to *Burnhaven* (*q.v.*), lies near Salthouse Head, and the south

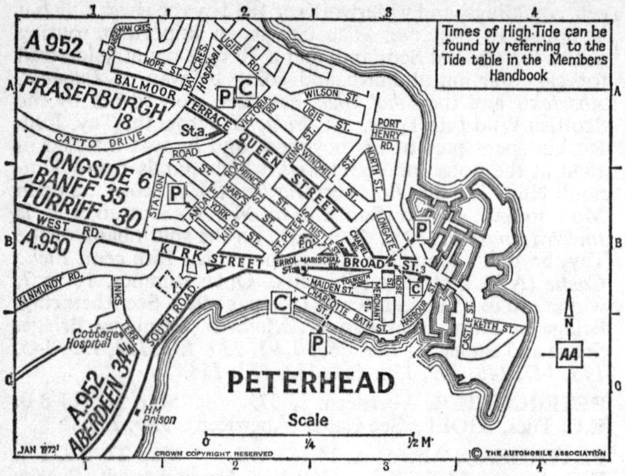

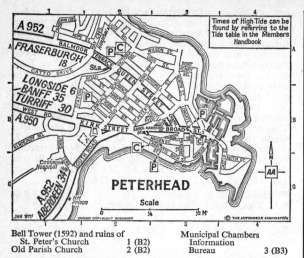

Bell Tower (1592) and ruins of St. Peter's Church 1 (B2)
Old Parish Church 2 (B2)
Municipal Chambers Information Bureau 3 (B3)

breakwater of the harbour was built by convict labour. The well-known Peterhead granite quarries are situated beyond *Boddam* (*q.v.*), south of Buchan Ness. See **Cruden Bay, Old Deer** and **Old Rattray.** *Iter. 181, 182, 187, 188, 189.*

PINKIE HOUSE, Midlothian. Map 10, **NT 3 7.**
This magnificent Jacobean mansion, dating from 1613, was altered and enlarged by Lord Dunfermline, who had previously transformed *Fyvie Castle* (*q.v.*), in Aberdeenshire. The old tower incorporated in the house dates from 1390. Pinkie is noted particularly for the east front, the long gallery, with its splendid painted ceiling, and the well-head in the courtyard. The battle of Pinkie, in which the Scots were defeated by Lord Hertford, took place in 1547. After the battle of *Prestonpans* (*q.v.*) in 1745, Prince Charles Edward slept in the house, which now forms part of Loretto College. See **Carberry Hill** and **Musselburgh.**

PINWHERRY, Ayr. Map 2, **NX 1 8.**
In the delightful valley of the River Stinchar, where it is joined by the Duisk Burn. There are ruins of a castle of the Kennedys. See **Colmonell.** *Iter. 71, 78, 84.*

PIRNMILL, Isle of Arran, Bute. Map 7, **NR 8 4.**
Lies on the fine road traversing the west coast of the island, overlooking the *Kintyre* (*q.v.*) peninsula across Kilbrennan Sound. In the background rise *Beinn Bhreac* and *Beinn Bharrain*, both over 2,300 ft. high. *Iter. 242.*

PITCAIRNGREEN, Perth. Map 16, **NO 0 2.**
An attractive hamlet near the River Almond. To the north-west are the Lynedoch Woods, by the river, where lie the graves of Bessie Bell and Mary Gray, who came here in 1645 to avoid an outbreak of plague in Perth.

PITCAPLE, Aberdeen. Map 27, **NJ 7 2.**
On the River Urie, with the 15th cent. *Pitcaple Castle*, which has associations with James IV, Mary, Queen of Scots, Charles II and the Marquis of Montrose. The last-named slept at the Castle as a prisoner on his last journey to Edinburgh, in 1650. It is open at reasonable times, if convenient, June to Aug. (See note page 98). See **Chapel of Garioch.** *Iter. 175, 178.*

PITCUR, Angus. Map 17, **NO 2 3.**
Situated on the edge of the *Sidlaw* hills, where the Coupar Angus to Dundee road begins to cross the range by way of Tullybaccart Hill. At *Pitcur* is preserved a remarkable "weem," or Pict's House, the key of which is kept at Hallyburton House. See **Lundie.** *Iter. 157, 158, 159.*

PITLESSIE, Fife. 328. Map 17, **NO 3 0.**
In the manse of *Cults*, a little to the north-east, was born, in 1785, Sir David Wilkie, the painter. One of his pictures, "Pitlessie Fair," hangs in the Scottish National Gallery at Edinburgh. The Church font originates from the Crimea. *Crawford Priory*, to the north-east, is 19th cent. *Iter. 93.*

PITLOCHRY, Perth. 2,593. SB. Map 20, **NN 9 5.**
E.C. Thurs. GOLF. A well-known Highland summer resort and touring centre of the *Grampians* (*q.v.*), in a wooded setting on the River Tummel, and sometimes held to be the exact centre of Scotland. The Pitlochry Festival Theatre presents plays during the summer. A little to the south-east, on a tributary of the Tummel, is the picturesque Black Spout waterfall. *Craigour*, 1,300 ft. (N.T. Scot.) reached by path to the north-west, and situated beyond the village of *Moulin* (*q.v.*), is a fine viewpoint, the prospect extending westwards across the Tummel valley to distant *Schiehallion*, 3,547 ft. Farther to the north-east is *Ben Vrackie*, 2,757 ft., the monarch of the nearby district. There are extensive hydro-electric developments in the Pitlochry district in connection with the Tummel-Garry scheme, including the generating stations of Pitlochry and Clunie. A new loch, that of *Faskally*, has been created as a result of the construction of the Pitlochry Dam, and lies on the west side of the resort, where the Tummel flows in a wooded setting. A new salmon-pass has been made for the fish to surmount the 54-ft. high dam on their way to the higher reaches of the river, and has proved a great attraction to visitors, who can watch the fish from the Pitlochry hydro-electric station. In connection with the works, the new Aldour road bridge has been constructed at the south-eastern extremity of the resort, giving access to the west bank of the Tummel and the Linn of Tummel (N.T. Scot.). The Linn is also accessible by footpath from *Bridge of Garry* (*q.v.*). The road passing Loch Faskally continues by the side of the Tummel to reach the east end of Loch Tummel, where there is another new dam and also a salmon ladder. On the farther bank of the Tummel, nearing the loch, is the famous *Queen's View* (*q.v.*), reached from Pitlochry by way of Bridge of Garry. To the north-east of Pitlochry a road climbs on to the moorlands leading to Glen Brerachan, and reaches a height of 1,260 ft., before descending to *Kirkmichael* (*q.v.*) in Strath Ardle. See **Blair Atholl, Killiecrankie** and **Logierait.** *Iter. 120, 139, 140, 143, 148, 150, 158, 159, 162, 167, 168.*

Festival Theatre 1
Information Bureau (Pitlochry Tourist Association) 2
Power Station, Dam, and Salmon Ladder 3

PITMEDDEN, Aberdeen. Map 27, **NJ 8 2.**
The 600-acre *Pitmedden* estate, where the 17th cent. "Great Garden" has been re-created and is now open daily, 9.30 to dusk (see note page 98), was presented to the National Trust for Scotland in 1952. See **Udny.** *Iter. 186, 187.*

PITSCOTTIE, Fife. Map 17, **NO 4 1.**
The wooded ravine of Dura Den, to the north, threaded by the Ceres Burn, is of interest to geologists for its fossils. A collection of these can be seen in the University Museum at *St. Andrews* (*q.v.*). **3 m. N.E.,** at *Magus Muir*, off the St. Andrews road, a cairn within a plantation marks the spot where Archbishop Sharp was murdered by Covenanters, in 1679. His monument is in the Town Church at St. Andrews. There is also a Martyrs' Stone within railings in memory of five Covenanters taken prisoner at the battle of *Bothwell* (*q.v.*) Brig in 1679 and executed here. The stone was set up in 1877. See **Ceres.** *Iter. 129, 132.*

PITSLIGO, Aberdeen. 1,962. Map 27, **NJ 9 6.**
The Church dates from 1633, and is noted for the richly-carved *Forbes* gallery. A little to the north is the ruined Castle, dating from 1577, and farther east are remains of the 17th cent. *Pittullie Castle*. See **Rosehearty.** *Iter. 182.*

PITTENWEEM, Fife. 1,519. SB. Map 17, **NO 5 0.**
E.C. Wed. One of the picturesque Royal Burghs of the

Pinkie House, Midlothian. In this mainly Jacobean mansion Prince Charles Edward slept after his victory at Prestonpans, in 1745. It stands off A1, on the eastern outskirts of Musselburgh

Pitcaple, Aberdeen. The rebuilt Castle, in the predecessor of which the Marquis of Montrose spent the night as a prisoner in 1650

Pitlochry, Perth. The Clunie Memorial Arch, built in the same shape as the water conduits, and marking the completion of the Tummel–Garry hydro-electric scheme in 1952

Pittenweem, Fife. The tower of the Church, which dates from 1592

Pitsligo, Aberdeen. The Church, dating from 1633, which contains the ornate Forbes gallery

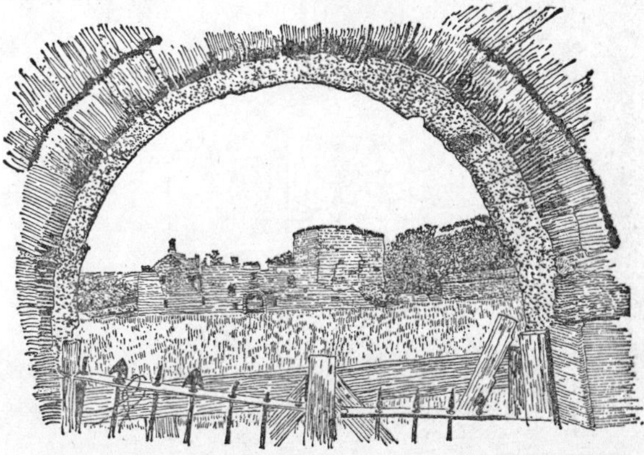

Pitsligo, Aberdeen. The ruined Castle of 1577, once the home of Alexander Forbes, Lord Pitsligo, outlawed after the battle of Culloden, in 1746. It stands to the north, on an unclassified road

[For PITSCOTTIE see under MAGUS MUIR (Plate 119)

Plockton, Ross and Cromarty. The view along Loch Carron from the east side of the village

Pluscarden Priory, Moray. The 13th century Priory, which is being rebuilt by the Benedictines. In 1390, the Wolf of Badenoch burnt down the old church

Pollokshaws (Glasgow), Lanark. Pollok House, the home of the Maxwells, which was built by William Adam in 1752. The estate belongs to the National Trust for Scotland

Polmont, Stirling. The Westquarter dovecote, dating from 1647, which stands to the west, off A9. The arms of William Livingstone of Westquarter appear over the doorway

Poolewe, Ross and Cromarty. The cairn by Loch Ewe in memory of Alexander Cameron, the Tournaig bard, who died in 1933, having spent his whole life by the shores of the loch

county, with old houses grouped around the little harbour. An Augustinian Priory was founded here in 1141, of which slight remains are incorporated in the parsonage. The Church has a picturesque tower, dated 1592, and resembling a castle more than a church tower. A robbery from James Stark, a customs collector, by two men, which took place at Pittenweem in 1736, led to the famous Porteous Riots in Edinburgh. The cave-shrine of *St. Fillan* lies near the harbour. **2 m. N.W.** is *Balcaskie House*, dating from c. 1675, from designs by Sir William Bruce, with terraced gardens. **3 m. N.N.W.** is *Kellie Castle* (N.T. Scot.), 16th cent., with towers and turrets, where Sir Robert Lorimer, the eminent architect, spent his boyhood. The interior is of note and contains Italian paintings. Open Wed. to Sun., 2 to 6, in summer (see note page 98). **3 m. N.E.**, at *West Pitkierie*, is a fluted, octagonal doocot of 1782. See **Leuchars** and **St. Monance.** *Iter. 94, 98.*

PLOCKTON, Ross and Cromarty. 250. Map 23, **NG 8 3.** A fishing and crofting village, part of the *Balmacara (q.v.)* estate (N.T. Scot.), most beautifully situated on a small inlet of Loch Carron, with views of the wild *Applecross (q.v.)* and *Torridon (q.v.)* mountains to the north. The modern *Duncraig Castle*, now a school, stands in a wooded setting to the east of the village, beneath a line of crags facing the shores of the loch. A Douglas fir, some 180 feet in height, grows on the estate. See **Strome.** *Iter. 222.*

PLUSCARDEN PRIORY, Moray. Map 26, **NJ 1 5.** Situated in a fertile valley, overlooked to the north by a well-wooded ridge, to the west of which is *Eildon Hill*, 767 ft. The well-preserved remains of *Pluscarden* have been partially restored by the Marquis of Bute, and are now being rebuilt by the Benedictines, to whom they have been presented. The original Cistercian monastery was founded in 1236, and the choir and transepts remain from the 13th cent. Church, together with the tower and part of the chapter-house. In 1390, the Church was burned by the Wolf of Badenoch, and was later restored. Large circular windows are a feature of the transepts, and alterations to the fenestration of the building took place in 1460, when the Benedictines took over the Abbey. The chapter-house is of interest, and in the calefactory, now used as a Church, is a pulpit, dating from 1680, which was originally in the old High Kirk at Elgin. The " Burgie Necklace " of jet, a Bronze Age ornament, is preserved in the Abbey, which is shown regularly, guides at times. (See note page 98.) *Iter. 198.*

POLLOKSHAWS (Glasgow), Lanark. Map 8, **NS 5 6.** To the north of the White Cart River stands the fine mansion of *Pollok House* (N.T. Scot.) built by William Adam, in 1752, in extensive grounds. It contains rare art treasures and is open weekdays, 10 to 5; Sun., 2 to 5. (See note page 98.) Part of the estate (N.T. Scot.) is now used as a recreation ground. *Iter. 57.*

POLMONT, Stirling. 2,268. Map 16, **NS 9 7.** GOLF. To the north-east of the town, the River Avon, forming the boundary between Stirling and West Lothian, flows into the Forth estuary. The line of the Antonine, or *Roman Wall (q.v.)* is just to the north of Polmont. About **1 m. W.** of Polmont, off the Falkirk road, is the *Westquarter* dovecote, dated 1647 (A.M.). *Iter. 95.*

POLWARTH, Berwick. 350 with Fogo. Map 11, **NT 7 5.** On the green, within a railing, grew once a thorn, associated with verses by Allan Ramsay. The Church, in the grounds of *Marchmount House*, to the south, was rebuilt in 1703, and in the vaults, Sir Patrick Hume, a follower of Argyll in 1685, lay hidden for a month. The mansion was built by William Adam, the father of the even more famous Robert Adam. An oak tree in the park is 128 ft. tall and nearly 15 ft. in girth. See **Carlops.** *Iter. 33, 41.*

POOLEWE, Ross and Cromarty. 1,013. Map 22, **NG 8 8.** Stands at the head of Loch Ewe, where the River Ewe, noted for its salmon, flows into the loch after its short course from *Loch Maree (q.v.)*. On the eastern shore of the loch, about a mile from Poolewe, stands *Inverewe House* (N.T. Scot.), a Mackenzie home, well known for its woodland gardens, semi-tropical plants and palm trees. This is a remarkable fact in view of Poolewe's situation near the 58th parallel, which cuts through Siberia and Canada's Hudson Bay territory. The gardens are shown daily, dawn to dusk; incl. Sun. (see page 98). From the Gairloch road, southwards from Poolewe, there is a magnificent view up Loch Maree, dominated by *Slioch*, 3,260 ft., at its head. A little beyond the River Ewe, to the east, lies Loch Kernsary. Beyond it is the larger Fionn Loch, bordering the lonely Fisherfield Forest, and dominated by *A'Mhaigdean*, 3,060 ft., a notable rock peak, and also *Beinn Dearg Mhor*, 2,974 ft. **4½ m. N.W.** of Poolewe, on the shores of Loch Ewe, is *Inverasdale*, where experimental work in croft rehabilitation has recently been carried out. In both the World Wars Loch Ewe was of considerable naval importance. See **Aulbea, Gairloch and Gruinard Bay.** *Iter. 206, 222.*

PORT APPIN, Argyll. Map 14, **NM 9 4.** This quiet little village lies between Loch Laich, an inlet of *Loch Linnhe (q.v.)*, and Airds Bay, on the Lynn of Lorne, and is a calling place for steamers. It is linked in addition by a passenger ferry to the north-eastern extremity of the island of *Lismore (q.v.)*. The mid-18th cent. *Airds House* stands a little to the south-east of the village. *Appin* **Church,** in the Strath of Appin, is situated **2 m. E.N.E.** of Port Appin, on the Ballachulish to Oban road. Away to the south-east of the Church, this road makes a circuit of the head of Loch Creran, with its mountain background, overlooking the lonely Glen Creran. *Iter. 124.*

PORT ASKAIG, Isle of Islay, Argyll. Map 6, **NR 4 6.** Situated on the Sound of Islay, with a steamer pier, and connected by passenger ferry to *Feolin Ferry*, in the island of *Jura (q.v.)*. **3 m. S.W.**, off the *Bridgend (q.v.)* road, to the right, is Loch Finlaggan, with a ruined island-castle, belonging formerly to the Lords of the Isles. There are alternative routes leading south-westwards from Port Askaig towards *Port Ellen (q.v.)*, the inland one being known as the " glen " road, while the better way is through *Bridgend (q.v.)*, at the head of Loch Indaal. **4 m. N.** of Port Askaig, over a narrow, hilly and winding road passing the Caol Isla distillery, is Bonahaven Bay, with views across the Sound of Islay towards the conical *Papa of Jura*, and also to the more distant coast of Mull. *Iter. 243, 247.*

PORT BANNATYNE, Bute. 1,165. Map 7, **NS 0 6.** A small resort on Kames Bay, facing the Firth of Clyde, looking to Toward Point on the mainland. The waters of the *Kyles of Bute (q.v.)* lie farther to the north-west near the entrance to Loch Striven. The tower of *Kames Castle*, overlooking the bay, is perhaps of 14th cent. date. Inland from Port Bannatyne, to the north-west, is the highest ground in the island, with *Windy Hill* attaining 911 ft. A road leads westwards across the narrow waist of Bute to reach the sandy Etterick Bay, with views over the Kyles of Bute to Ardlamont Point. This road continues northwards as far as *Kilmichael*, where the ancient, ruined Chapel of *St. Michael* is still standing. Another roads goes north-westwards from Kames Bay, and terminates at *Rhubodach*, linked to *Colintraive (q.v.)*, on the mainland, by a car ferry. *Iter. 241.*

PORT CHARLOTTE, Isle of Islay, Argyll. Map 6, **NR 2 5.** On the western shores of Loch Indaal, at its narrowest point. In the vicinity are the graves of some American soldiers drowned in the sinking of the " Tuscania," in 1918. A road leads westwards from the village across the Rhinns of Islay peninsula to *Kilchiaran Bay*, from which a rough and narrow road follows the peninsula towards *Portnahaven (q.v.)* at its south-western extremity. *Iter. 247.*

PORT EDGAR, West Lothian Map 17, **NT 1 7.** A fishery protection vessel base.

PORT ELLEN, Isle of Islay, Argyll. Map 6, **NR 3 4.** GOLF. The main port of the island, with distilleries in the vicinity, *Port Ellen* is situated on a small rocky bay, facing a prominent lighthouse on the Mull of Oa peninsula. A road goes north-eastwards along the coast past *Lagavulin*, where a ruined round tower may once have been a Macdonald stronghold, and reaches, after 7 miles, the churchyard of *Kildalton (q.v.)*. **1½ m. W.** of Port Ellen, facing the sandy

Kilnaughton Bay, is a pillar commemorating the American troops drowned in the sinking of the "Tuscania" in 1918. **4 m. N.W.** of Port Ellen, to the west of the "low" road leading to *Bowmore* (*q.v.*), is *Machrie*, near Laggan Bay, noted for its sands and golf, the splendid course having been constructed on the machair, or sea-turf. A little farther to the north is *Glenegedale* Airport, with regular services to Glasgow (Renfrew airport). Machrie can also be approached from Kilnaughton Bay, to the west of Port Ellen. Another road to Bowmore, known as the "high" road, keeps well inland all the way, and a branch leading north-east from it is known as the "glen" road, and leads to *Port Askaig* (*q.v.*). A better way, however, to the latter, is by way of *Bridgend* (*q.v.*). See **Claggain Bay, Kilchoman** and **Mull of Oa.** *Iter. 243, 244, 245, 246.*

PORT ERROLL, Aberdeen. Map 27, **NK 0 3.**
See **Cruden Bay.**

PORTESSIE, Banff. Map 26, **NJ 4 6.**
This picturesque fishing village, on a sandy coast, stands on a small crescent-shaped bay, with some old cottages. To the east is Portessie Bay, sheltered by Craig Head. *Iter. 199.*

PORT GLASGOW, Renfrew. 22,399. LB. Map 8, **NS 3 7.**
E.C. Wed. GOLF. A shipbuilding town on the Clyde, founded in 1668, and formerly the chief custom-house port of the river before it was deepened and ships were able to proceed up the river to Glasgow. *Newark Castle* (A.M.), on the river bank, dates from the 16th and 17th cents., and is a notable example, preserving a courtyard and a hall. Open weekdays 10 to 4.30 or 7; Sun 2 to 4.30 or 7 (see note page 98). *Iter. 59, 64, 65, 85, 88, 112, 113.*

PORTGORDON, Banff. 910. Map 26, **NJ 3 6.**
The harbour at this little place, which is situated near the Moray border, was built by the Duke of Richmond and Gordon, in 1874. See **Tynet.** *Iter. 199.*

PORTGOWER, Sutherland. Map 31, **ND 0 1.**
A small fishing village, on a rocky stretch of coast, with moorlands rising in the background which culminate in *Beinn na Meilich*, 1,940 ft. *Iter. 200, 231, 233.*

PORTINCAPLE, Dunbarton. Map 14, **NS 2 9.**
On Loch Long, facing Loch Goil and the hills known as *Argyll's Bowling Green.*

PORTINNISHERRICH, Argyll. Map 14, **NM 9 1.**
On the east side of *Loch Awe* (*q.v.*), facing the island of Innis Shearaich. To the north is the smaller island of Innis Connel, on which are situated the remains of *Ardconnel Castle*, an ancient Campbell stronghold. The road leading north along the loch from the village passes, after about two miles, the outflow of the Allt Blarghour Burn, on which are some waterfalls. See **Portsonachan.** *Iter. 119.*

PORTKNOCKIE, Banff. 1,110. SB. Map 26, **NJ 4 6.**
A quaint fishing village, to the west of Cullen Bay, from which it is separated by Scar Nose. See **Findochty.** *Iter. 199.*

PORT LOGAN, Wigtown. 65. Map 2, **NX 0 4.**
A small fishing village in the Rhinns of Galloway, situated on Logan Bay, on the opposite side of which can be seen a remarkable tidal fish-pond. This was commenced in 1788, taking 12 years to complete, and is notable for the extraordinary tameness of the fish, which are fed by hand. It can be seen Mon., Wed., Sat. and Sun., 12.30 to 6.30, 1st Sun. in May to 1st Sun. in Oct. **2 m. N.** is the Georgian *Logan House*, famous for its grounds, shown daily, 10 to 5, April to Sept. (See note page 98), in which many rare plants and trees flourish. See **Drummore.** *Iter. 82.*

PORTMAHOMACK, Ross and Cromarty.
Map 31, **NH 9 8.**
GOLF. A Dornoch Firth fishing village, situated on a narrow peninsula stretching into the Moray Firth, at the extremity of which is Tarbat Ness, with Scotland's lowest average annual rainfall. There is a lighthouse, and a wide outlook over sea and land. Near the Church, to the south-west, are the curiously-named sandhills of *Gaza. Ballone Castle*, probable 16th cent., stands to the south-east.

PORT MARY, Kirkcudbright. Map 3, **NX 7 4.**
See **Dundrennan.**

PORTMOAK, Kinross. 822. Map 17, **NO 1 0.**
Situated on the low ground to the east of Loch Leven, between the *Lomonds* and *Benarty Hill*, and including *Kinnesswood* and *Scotlandwell* (both *q.v.*) within its Parish boundary. *Portmoak* Church, the third to be built here, had, in the early 18th cent., as its minister, Ebenezer Erskine, who founded the Scottish Secession Church. In the churchyard is the grave of his wife and children, with a four-line epitaph. The cottage of Michael Bruce, a local poet of the 18th cent., is now a small museum. *Iter. 98.*

PORTNACROISH, Argyll. Map 14, **NM 9 4.**
Situated on Loch Laich, an inlet of Loch Linnhe in the *Appin* (*q.v.*) district, and looking towards the island of Shuna. *Appin House*, to the north, is 17th cent. On a tiny island off-shore is the prominent and very picturesque sea-girt *Castle Stalker*, dating from c. 1500, an ancient home of the Stewarts of Appin, and associated with James IV, the Royal Arms being carved over the entrance. The Castle is also well seen from the steamers traversing Loch Linnhe. See **Port Appin.** *Iter. 124.*

PORTNAHAVEN, Isle of Islay, Argyll. Map 6, **NR 1 5.**
At the south-western extremity of the Rhinns of Islay, and to the south-east of which is Rhinns Point. The island of Orsay, with its lighthouse, faces Portnahaven. A road leads north-eastwards along the rocky west side of the Rhinns peninsula to *Kilchiaran Bay.* See **Port Charlotte.** *Iter. 247.*

PORT NA LONG, Isle of Skye, Inverness. Map 23, **NG 3 3.**
See **Talisker.** *Iter. 252.*

PORTOBELLO (Edinburgh), Midlothian. Map 10, **NT 3 7.**
A popular resort, with good sands and a bathing pool, much frequented by the citizens of Edinburgh. Linked to Portobello at its eastern extremity, is *Joppa.* The resort was the birthplace, in 1870, of Sir Harry Lauder. The name of Portobello is derived from a Panamanian town of that name, and was given to it by a sailor, who served there in 1739 under Admiral Vernon. A little to the west is *Restalrig* Church, an ancient building, destroyed in 1560, but later restored. The adjacent 15th cent. hexagonal Chapel (A.M.) is considered to be that of *St. Triduana*, who cured ailments of the eyes with water from the spring that bears her name. In the vicinity is *Craigentinny House*, late 16th cent., with large 19th cent. additions. W. H. Miller, an eccentric owner of the house, was buried in a strange-looking mausoleum off the Portobello Road in 1849. See **Duddingston.** *Iter. 2.*

PORT OF MENTEITH, Perth. 2,110 with Aberfoyle.
Map 15, **NN 5 0.**
A small resort on the Lake of Menteith, noted for pike, and the only "lake" in Scotland apart from the little artificial Pressmennan Lake near *Whittinghame* (*q.v.*) in East Lothian. On the largest of the lake's three islands are the remains of *Inchmahome Priory* (A.M.), founded in 1238. Part of the nave, choir and tower arch are still to be seen, and some of the work, notably the fine west porch, is of much interest. R. B. Cunninghame Graham, the writer, who died in 1936 at Buenos Aires, is buried here. Robert Bruce visited the Priory on three occasions. Mary, Queen of Scots, at the age of 5, was sent to the island after the battle of *Pinkie* (*q.v.*), in 1547, and her garden, known as Queen Mary's Bower, is still in existence. From here, the Queen was removed to *Dumbarton* (*q.v.*), prior to sailing for France. On Inch Tulla island is a ruined Castle, once the home of the Earls of Menteith. In the vicinity is *Cardross House*, 16th to 18th cent. Overlooking the lake, to the west, rise the *Menteith* hills, attaining 1,289 ft., and in the vicinity is part of the newly-planted Loch Ard Forest. East of these hills are *Beinn Dearg*, 1,401 ft. and *Ben Gullipen*, 1,344 ft., between which lies the tiny Loch an Balloch. Off the Callander road lies Loch Rusky, which is

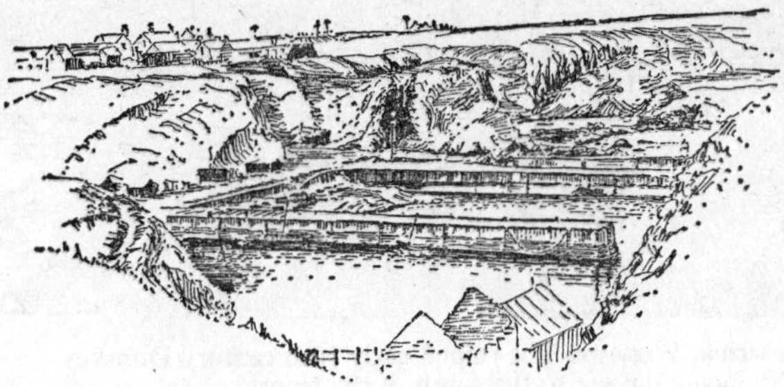

Portknockie, Banff. The fishing harbour, which is sheltered by Scar Nose

Port Glasgow, Renfrew. The 16th to 17th century Newark Castle, on the banks of the River Clyde. The monogram of the builder, Patrick Maxwell (1597), is above the entrance

Port Logan, Wigtown. The tidal fish-pond, in which the fish are tame and fed by hand

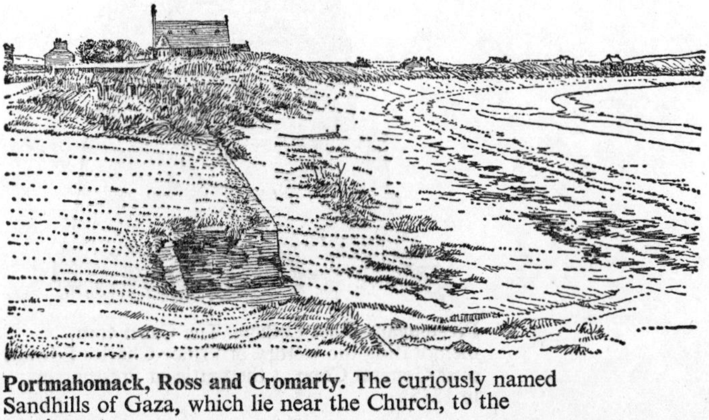

Portmahomack, Ross and Cromarty. The curiously named Sandhills of Gaza, which lie near the Church, to the south-west

Portobello (Edinburgh), Midlothian. The Mausoleum, noted for its decorative panels. It contains the body of W. H. Miller, the eccentric owner of Craigentinny House, who died in 1849. He was known as 'Measure Miller,' owing to his habit of measuring all the books he bought with a ruler which he carried for the purpose

Portpatrick, Wigtown. The ruined early 16th century Dunskey Castle, facing the sea to the south of the resort

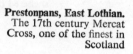

Prestonpans, East Lothian. The 17th century Mercat Cross, one of the finest in Scotland

Prestonpans, East Lothian. Hamilton House (1628), which has been restored by the National Trust for Scotland

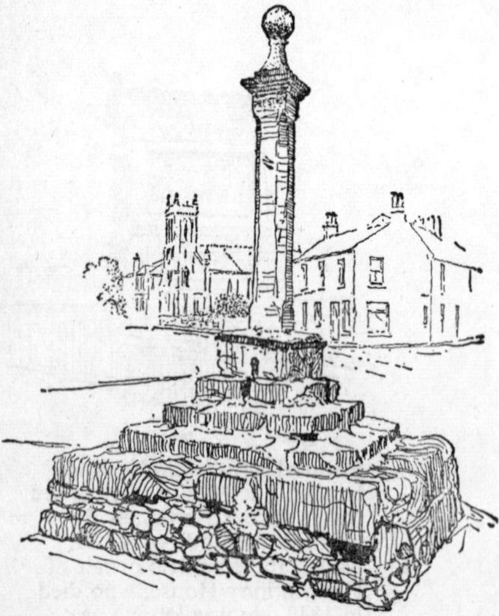

Prestwick, Ayr. The ancient Mercat Cross

Prestonpans, East Lothian. The Cairn commemorating the victory of Prince Charles Edward over General Cope at the battle of Prestonpans, in 1745

PLATE 139

[For PORTREE see under RAASAY (Plate 140)
[For PRESTON see under BUNKLE CHURCH (Plate 25)

sometimes frozen over in the winter. The name *Menteith*, or Monteith, is applied generally to that part of the county lying to the south of Port of Menteith towards the River Forth, on the Stirling border. The flat land south of the Lake of Menteith, merging into Stirlingshire, is known as the Flanders Moss. In the vicinity of the south-western shores of the lake is the tiny Loch Macanrie, where, according to a legend, a king's son was saved from drowning by a girl while hunting. *Iter. 109, 111, 139.*

PORT OF NESS, Isle of Lewis, Ross and Cromarty. Map 32, **NB 5** 6.
See **Hebrides, Outer** (Lewis). *Iter. 260.*

PORTPATRICK, Wigtown. 1,062. Map 2, **NX 0 5.**
E.C. Thurs. GOLF. Now a small Rhinns of Galloway resort. It was formerly a port for steamers to Northern Ireland, but the service was transferred to *Stranraer* (*q.v.*), owing to the danger from severe south-westerly gales. The North Channel, separating Scotland from Ireland, was swum in 1947 by Thomas Blower, who crossed from Donaghadee to Portpatrick in just over 16 hours. The seaward views extend to the Irish coast, some twenty miles distant, and also towards the Isle of Man. The shores are rocky, but there are several sandy bays suitable for bathing. The remains of *Dunskey Castle*, built c. 1510, stand in a strong position on a headland to the south of Portpatrick, where the Craigoch Burn enters the sea. See **Lochnaw.** *Iter. 81, 83.*

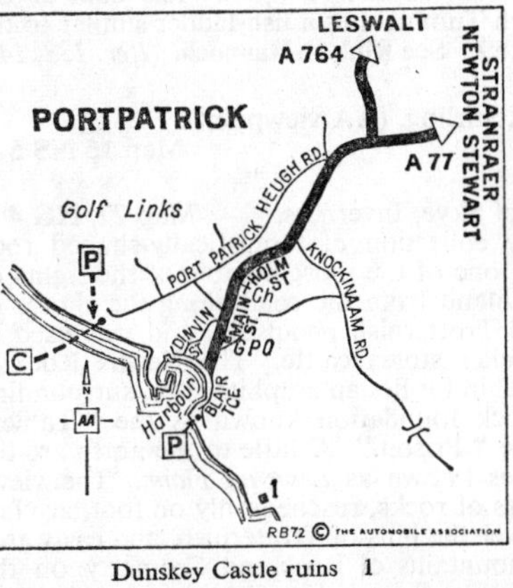

Dunskey Castle ruins 1

PORTREE, Isle of Skye, Inverness. 2,025. Map 23, **NG 4** 4.
E.C. Wed. GOLF. The metropolis of the island, at the mouth of the delightful Portree Loch, with a pleasant harbour and a pier for the steamers. Portree Bay, sheltering the fishing fleet, looks towards *Ben Tianavaig*, 1,352 ft., and also over the Sound of Raasay to Raasay Island (see below). Prince Charles Edward said farewell to Flora Macdonald here in 1746. The name Portree means "King's Haven" and commemorates a visit paid by James V. The old name of the town was *Kiltaragleann*. Off the road leading northwards towards the prominent *Storr* (*q.v.*), a landmark for many miles and the highest point in the long, elevated Trotternish ridge, lie the Storr Lochs, which have been harnessed to a hydro-electric scheme, inaugurated in 1952. A very rough hill road leads north-westwards from Portree to *Bracadale* (*q.v.*), on Loch Beag, an inlet of Loch Harport.

The island of *Raasay*, some 15 miles long, is hilly for the most part, and contains *Raasay House*, now a hotel, where Dr. Johnson and Boswell were entertained in 1773. On the flat-topped *Dun Caan*, 1,456 ft., Boswell performed a solo dance. On the north-east coast of the island is the ruined Macleod Castle of *Brochel*, beyond which lies the small island of Rona, with its lighthouse. See **Coolins, Dunvegan, Sligachan, Staffin** and **Uig.** *Iter. 251, 253, 254, 255.*

PORT SETON, East Lothian. 3.549. SB. Map 10, **NT 4 7.**
A Firth of Forth fishing village. See **Seton.**

PORTSKERRA, Sutherland. Map 30, **NC 8** 6.
A small fishing village on the west shores of Melvich Bay, with some cliff scenery. *Iter. 232, 234.*

PORTSONACHAN, Argyll. Map 14, **NN 0** 2.
Lies on the south shore of *Loch Awe* (*q.v.*), with views of *Ben Cruachan*, 3,689 ft., away to the north beyond the loch. *Iter. 119.*

PORTSOY, Banff. 1,699. SB. Map 27, **NJ 5** 6.
A small fishing port on a rocky stretch of coast, known for Portsoy marble, or serpentine. This marble is coloured light green and pink, and was used for two of the chimney-pieces in the Palace of Versailles. **2 m. E.,** overlooking the Burn of Boyne, in a wooded setting, is the ruined *Boyne Castle*, dating from 1485, an early Ogilvie fortress. **2½ m. W.** is Sandend Bay, sheltered by Redhythe Point and Garron Point. See **Fordyce.** *Iter. 184, 193, 198, 199.*

PORT VASCO, Sutherland. Map 28, **NC 5** 6.
A tiny coastal hamlet at the mouth of the Kyle of Tongue, looking westwards towards Eilean Iosal and Roan Island out to sea. *Beinn Thutaig*, 1,340 ft., rises to the west beyond Strath Melness. *Iter. 225.*

PORT WILLIAM, Wigtown. 539. Map 2, **NX 3** 4.
E.C. Thurs. GOLF. This little port and resort, founded by Sir William Maxwell in 1770, lies on the sandy Luce Bay, in the Machers district, from which a road climbs inland to the well-known house and park of *Monreith* (*q.v.*). There are fine views across Luce Bay. In the vicinity are rocks with cup and ring markings dating from the Bronze Age (A.M.). **2 m. N.E.** of Port William, off the Glenluce road, is *Kirk of Mochrum* (*q.v.*). *Iter. 78, 82.*

POTARCH BRIDGE, Aberdeen. Map 21, **NO 6** 9.
See **Kincardine o' Neil.** *Iter. 165, 168.*

POWFOOT, Dumfries. Map 4, **NY 1** 6.
In former days only a fishing village, but now a pleasant little resort, with sandy shores, situated on the Pow Water, where it flows into the Solway Firth.

PRESSMENNAN LAKE, East Lothian. Map 10, **NT 6** 7.
See **Whittinghame.**

PRESTON, Berwick. 417. Map 11, **NT 7** 5.
The Whiteadder Water, flowing down from the *Lammermuir* hills, passes a little to the south of the village. The shaft of the old Cross is still standing. **2½ m. N.E.,** below the foothills of the Lammermuirs, is the rebuilt Church of *Bunkle*, which preserves a Norman arch said to be the earliest of its period in the country. *Iter. 38, 39.*

PRESTONKIRK CHURCH, East Lothian.
See **East Linton.** Map 10, **NT 5** 7.

PRESTONPANS, East Lothian, 3,207. SB. Map 10, **NT 3** 7.
Once noted for salt-panning and oysters, the former industry having been established here in the 12th cent. by monks from *Newbattle Abbey* (*q.v.*). Sir Walter Scott stayed here as a child, and gained much local knowledge, which he utilized in his novel "Waverley." *Morrisonhaven*, to the west, was once the port of the town. The battlefield of Prestonpans, where Prince Charles Edward defeated General Cope in 1745, is **1 m. E.** *Hamilton House* (N.T. Scot.) dates from 1628, and has been well restored. It can be inspected by arrangement with the occupier. To the north stands the ruined 15th cent. *Preston Tower*, with a 17th cent. dovecote, Nearby is a fine 17th cent. Mercat Cross (A.M.), said to be the oldest extant in Scotland, standing unaltered on its original site. *Northfield House*, a fine 16th or 17th cent. dwelling, lies opposite, with a contemporary dovecote and a sundial dated 1647. In the grounds of the 17th cent. *Bankton House*, now a farm, is a monument to Colonel Gardiner, who died at *Tranent* (*q.v.*), from wounds received at the battle of Prestonpans. Scott's "Waverley" describes the incident. See **Cockenzie, Musselburgh, Pinkie House** and **Seton.** *Iter. 2, 37.*

PRESTWICK, Ayr. 13,441. SB. Map 8, **NS 3** 2.
E.C. Wed. GOLF. Long known as a golfing resort, and now almost contiguous with *Ayr* (*q.v.*), to the south. *Prest-*

wick is now additionally famous for its great international airport, the most important in Scotland. The town has an old Mercat Cross, and the ruined Church of *St. Nicholas*, a landmark for mariners, is said to date from 1163. There is a sandy bathing beach on Ayr Bay, and also a bathing pool, while the views across the Firth of Clyde to the mountains of Arran are very fine. *Iter. 60, 66, 88.*

PRINCE CHARLES EDWARD MONUMENT, Inverness. Map 18, **NM 9 8.**
See **Glenfinnan.** *Iter. 209.*

PUCK'S GLEN, Argyll. Map 14, **NS 1 8.**
See **Benmore Estate** and **Kilmun.**

PUMPHERSTON, West Lothian Map 9, **NT 0 6.**
Noted until recent years for shale-mining.

QUARTER, Lanark. Map 8, **NS 7 5.**
In a field in the vicinity, Gordon of Earlston was slain after the battle of *Bothwell* (*q.v.*) Brig, in 1679.

QUEEN ELIZABETH FOREST PARK, Perth; Stirling. Map 15, **NN 4 0** etc.
See **Aberfoyle, Rowardennan** and **Trossachs.**

QUEENSFERRY, NORTH, Fife. 1,353. Map 17, **NT 1 8.**
E.C. Wed. Situated on the Ferry Hill peninsula, this is the northern terminal point of the two splendid bridges spanning the Firth of Forth, the older carrying the railway, and the new (opened 1964) carrying the road. Both bridges and the former ferry are described below under **Queensferry, South.** There are associations with Queen Margaret, who formerly journeyed this way towards Dunfermline. St. Margaret's Bay, to the north-west, is part of the naval base of *Rosyth* (*q.v.*).

QUEENSFERRY, SOUTH, West Lothian. 5,175. SB. Map 17, **NT 1 7.**
E.C. Wed. Situated on the south shore of the Firth of Forth, facing *Queensferry, North* (*q.v.*). The former ferry boats left from the Hawes Pier, opposite which stands the "*Hawes*" Inn (1683), described in Scott's "The Antiquary" and R. L. Stevenson's "Kidnapped." The little Royal Burgh takes its name, as does also its namesake across the Firth, from Queen Margaret, who formerly journeyed this way between Edinburgh and Dunfermline. A Carmelite Chapel was founded here in 1330, and the existing structure, dating from c. 1500, and restored as a Church in 1890, has a central tower and barrel vaults. In the Burgh museum are preserved the old charters. There is an old Tolbooth, which was remodelled in 1720. *Plewlands House* (N.T. Scot.), dated 1643, has been restored and converted into flats. *Black Castle*, dating from 1626, shows characteristic crow-stepped gables. The picturesque Ferry Fair is held annually in the summer, and the quaint "Burry Man's" procession is another regular annual custom. Overshadowing the town is the spectacular *Forth Bridge*, built 1883-90, to carry the main railway line from Edinburgh to Aberdeen across the Firth of Forth. This great bridge, one of the finest examples of engineering in the world, has a length of 2,765½ yards, including the approach viaducts, and crosses the firth giving a headway of 150 ft., the two main spans each having dimensions of 1,710 ft., and the top of the bridge being 361 ft. above the water. *Inchgarvie Island*, in the centre of the narrows, gives support to the structure, and had formerly a 15th cent. fort, which opposed Cromwell in 1650. The bridge was built by Sir John Fowler together with Sir Benjamin Baker, the contractor being Sir William Arrol. An impressive new road bridge, opened in 1964, has been built to span the Firth west of the railway bridge. This bridge has a length of 2,000 yards, with a centre span of 3,300 feet and side spans of 1,337 feet. It is one of Europe's largest suspension bridges. **1½ m. S.** is *Dundas Castle*, the old building dating from 1416 to 1424, and the modern building from 1818. The house was for many years the seat of the Dundas family, one of the oldest in the country. See **Dalmeny, Port Edgar** and **Hopetoun House.** *Iter. 96.*

QUEEN'S VIEW, Perth. (AA viewpoint.) Map 19, **NN 8 5.**
A famous outlook, visited by Queen Victoria in 1866, and situated on the north bank of the River Tummel, a little to the east of Loch Tummel. Access is by a gate to a rocky spur, from which the river, the loch and a grand array of mountains to the north and west in the *Breadalbane* (*q.v.*) country, dominated by the sharp quartzite cone of *Schiehallion*, 3,547 ft., are seen in all their magnificence. In the nearer vicinity the wooded setting forms a fitting foreground to the general picture. In 1777, Maskelyne, the Astronomer Royal, made use of Schiehallion in connection with his experiments to determine the gravity of the earth. Developments in the extensive new Tummel-Garry hydro-electric scheme have necessitated the building of a dam, and also the lengthening of Loch Tummel, which has inevitably detracted from the beauties of the view in that direction. Loch Tummel itself has roads on both north and south banks, the former being the better, and leading in a westerly direction towards *Tummel Bridge* (*q.v.*). The dam at the eastern end of Loch Tummel has a fish-ladder similar to the one at *Pitlochry* (*q.v.*). See **Kinloch Rannoch.** *Iter. 138, 148.*

QUEEN'S VIEW, Stirling. (AA viewpoint).
See **Auchineden.** Map **15 NS 5 8.**

QUIRAING, Isle of Skye, Inverness. Map 22, **NG 4 6.**
This extraordinary collection of fantastically-shaped rock pinnacles, forming one of the most notable of the sights of Skye, lies a little inland from the road along the shores of Staffin Bay, in the Trotternish peninsula, and was used in olden times to shelter stolen cattle. The Needle Rock is 120 ft. high, and behind it lies an amphitheatre, surrounding a grass-covered rock foundation known as the "Table," while nearby is the "Prison." A little to the north are the rocks and pinnacles known as *Leac na Fionn*. The views from this wilderness of rocks, reached only on foot, are far-flung, and range over the hills of Trotternish, and eastwards to the Torridon mountains of Ross and Cromarty on the mainland. Overlooking the whole collection of rocks, and attaining a height of 1,779 ft., to the north of this road, is *Meal na Suiramach*, a hill from which the view extends over northern Skye and out to sea towards the distant Outer Hebrides in the Atlantic. The inland road linking *Staffin* (*q.v.*) and the Quiraing with *Uig* (*q.v.*) is under complete reconstruction. See **Flodigarry.** *Iter. 254.*

QUOICH BRIDGE, Inverness. Map 18, **NH 0 0.**
Hydro-electric developments on *Loch Quoich* (*q.v.*) have taken place in this neighbourhood. To the north extends the roadless Glen Quoich, which was traversed by General Monk and his soldiers in 1654. Southwards, across the loch, rises *Gairich*, 3,015 ft. See **Kinloch Hourn.** *Iter. 214.*

RAASAY, ISLE OF, Inverness. Map 23, **NG 5 3** etc.
See **Portree.**

RANNOCH STATION, Perth. Map 19, **NN 4 5.**
This remote West Highland railway station is situated almost on the Argyll border, and is the terminal point of the road which leads westwards for 6 miles from the western extremity of *Loch Rannoch* (*q.v.*). Some 10 miles of the wild and lonely Moor of Rannoch lie between Rannoch and the fine new road leading from Tyndrum to Glencoe, but there is no connecting link. To the south-west of the station stretches Loch Laidon, with the *Black Corries* rising to the north. Beyond them stretches the large Blackwater Reservoir in Argyllshire. The lonely Loch Ericht stretches away in a north-easterly direction in the *Grampian* (*q.v.*) mountains to the north of the *Kinloch Rannoch* (*q.v.*(road. Some 3,500 acres of Rannoch Moor are now a Nature Reserve. *Iter. 148.*

RATHO CHURCH, Midlothian. Map 9, **NT 1 7.**
See **Hermiston.**

RATTRAY, Perth. 5,229. SB. with Blairgowrie.
See **Blairgowrie.** *Iter. 141, 152, 159, 166.* Map 20, **NO 1 4.**

Queensferry, South, West Lothian. The partly 17th century, but much altered ' Hawes ' Inn. It is associated with Sir Walter Scott's '*The Antiquary*' and here Robert Louis Stevenson is said to have commenced writing '*Kidnapped,*' in Room No. 13

Queensferry, South, West Lothian. The restored Carmelite Church of St. Mary, founded originally by the Laird of Dundas, in 1330. It is the only mediaeval church of this Order still functioning in Great Britain

Quarter, Lanark. The sign on A723 pointing to the village

Queen's View, Perth. The westerly view along Loch Tummel from the A.A. viewpoint on B8019

Quoich Bridge, Inverness. The bridge across a stream issuing from Glen Quoich, a glen traversed in 1654 by General Monk and his troops. Loch Quoich, now part of a large new hydro-electric scheme, lies west of Tomdoun, on the fringe of the ' Rough Bounds,' in the lonely Knoydart district

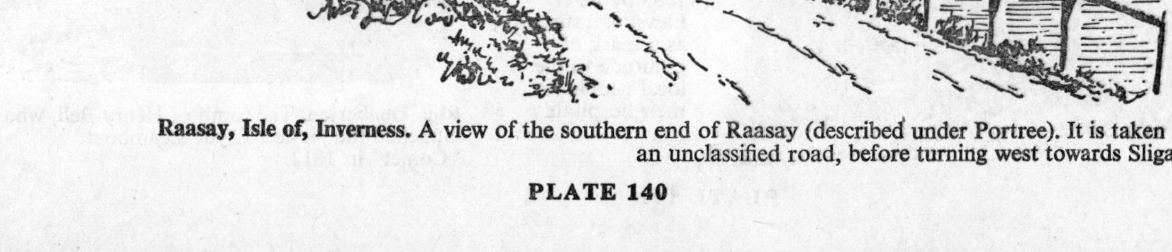

Raasay, Isle of, Inverness. A view of the southern end of Raasay (described under Portree). It is taken from an unclassified road, before turning west towards Sligachan

Reiss, Caithness. The modernised Ackergill Tower, once a seat of the Earls Marischal, which stands on Sinclair's Bay, to the east

Renfrew, Renfrew. Inchinnan Church, once the property of the Knights Templars. The present building was erected by Lord Blythswood early in this century. It stands a mile to the west, off A8

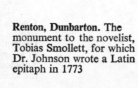

Rest and Be Thankful, Argyll. The inscribed stone at the summit of the pass looking down Glen Croe. The seat which formerly stood there was described in verse by William Wordsworth

Renton, Dunbarton. The monument to the novelist, Tobias Smollett, for which Dr. Johnson wrote a Latin epitaph in 1773

Rhiconich, Sutherland. A well on A838, some 7 miles north-east, placed there in 1883 by Peter Lawson, a surveyor, as a mark of gratitude to the local people for their hospitality

Rhu, Dunbarton. The tomb of Henry Bell, who launched the pioneer Clyde steamboat 'Comet' in 1812

REAY, Caithness. 865. **Map 30, NC 9 6.**
Stands at the head of Sandside Bay, on the lonely Caithness coast, and gave its name to Lord Reay, Chief of Clan Mackay. Their seat was **2 m. N.E.**, near the sea, at *Dounreay Castle*, now a farm, and preserving a 16th cent. tower. *Reay* Church, which dates from 1739, is typical of several in the vicinity, and its belfry has an external staircase. In the churchyard are remains of an older Church, with a carved Celtic cross-slab. The lonely mountains and deer forest of Reay, in the county of Sutherland, lie in the vicinity of *Rhiconich* (*q.v.*), near the wild north-west seaboard. See **Dounreay.** *Iter. 232, 234, 240.*

REDCASTLE, Ross and Cromarty. **Map 25, NH 5 4.**
On the north shore of the Beauly Firth, with the estate of *Redcastle*, an old home of the Mackenzie family. The house retains some 16th cent. work, now incorporated in a modern mansion. See **Muir of Ord.**

REISS, Caithness. **Map 30, ND 3 5.**
Lies a little inland from Sinclair's Bay, at the junction of roads leading to Thurso and John o' Groats. On the shores of the bay stands the ancient *Ackergill Tower*, now modernised. It retains a well 25 ft. deep, and also two 18th cent. dovecotes. *Iter. 200, 238.*

RENFREW, Renfrew. 18,589. SB. **Map 8, NS 5 6.**
E.C. Wed. GOLF. This ancient Royal Burgh, its charter having been granted in 1396, gives the title of Baron to the Prince of Wales, and is generally considered to be the cradle of the Royal House of Stuart. The Parish Church has a sculptured tomb and a 15th cent. effigy on the tower. *Renfrew* is today best known for its important shipbuilding yards on the Clyde, which are well seen from the car ferry over the river, situated to the north of the town, and giving access to *Yoker* (*q.v.*), in Lanarkshire. Westwards from the ferry is the park of *Blythswood House*, where, in 1685, the Earl of Argyll was captured, and later executed at Edinburgh for his share in the Monmouth rebellion. **1½ m. W.** of the town, off A8, near a swing-bridge by the meeting of the Black and White Cart Waters, is the *Argyll Stone*, which was at one time thought to be stained with the Earl's blood. **2 m. S.W.** of the town lies the new *Glasgow* (Abbotsinch) airport, from which there are regular services to some of the outlying Scottish islands. **1 m. W.** of Renfrew, across the Black Cart Water, is *Inchinnan* Church, once the property of the Knights Templar, the present modern building having been erected by Lord Blythswood. In the churchyard are preserved Celtic stones, tombs of the Templars, and also several mortsafes, recalling the days of " body-snatching." *Iter 59.*

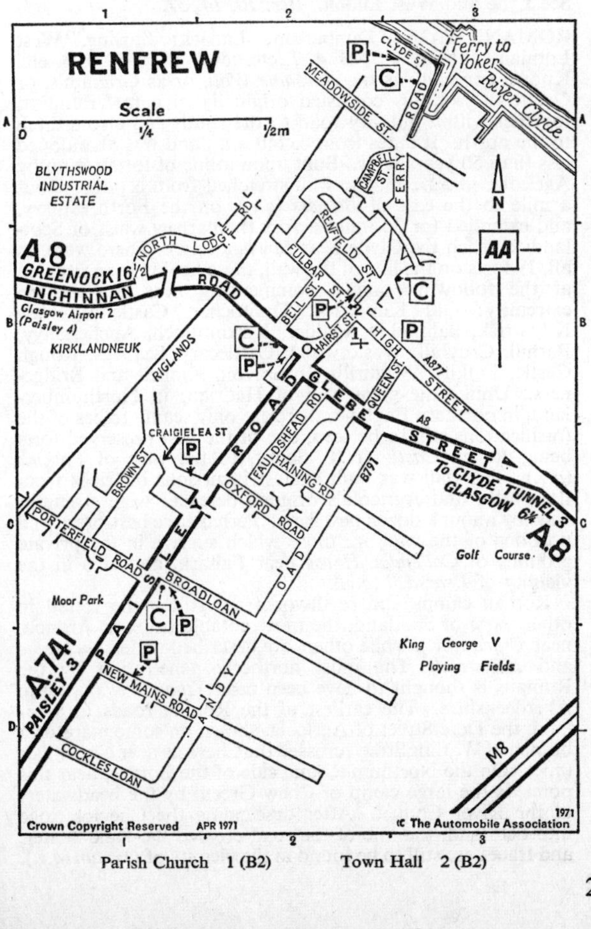

Parish Church 1 (B2) Town Hall 2 (B2)

RENTON, Dunbarton. 4,011. **Map 15, NS 3 7.**
There is a monument to Tobias Smollett, with a Latin inscription written by Dr. Johnson in 1773. See **Alexandria.**

RESTALRIG CHURCH, Midlothian. **Map 10, NT 2 7.**
See **Portobello.**

REST AND BE THANKFUL, Argyll. **Map 14, NN 2 0.**
At the summit of the easily-graded, reconstructed road climbing up Glen Croe from the shores of Loch Long, and at a height of nearly 900 ft., stood formerly a rough stone seat, inscribed " Rest and be Thankful." Wordsworth, after a visit to the pass, described it in verse. The old road, with its steep gradients, is still used for motor trials. Above the summit, to the north-east, rises *Ben Ime*, 3,318 ft., a notable viewpoint, the ascent of which can be undertaken from here. *Ben Arthur*, 2,891 ft., more familiarly known as *The Cobbler*, rises to the north of the glen, while the south side is dominated by the rough, rocky slopes of *The Brack*, 2,580 ft., and farther to the west by the extensive mass of *Ben Donich*, 2,774 ft. This mountain area in *Cowal* (*q.v.*) is included within the Ardgoil Estate of the Argyll Forest Park, while the summits to the north of Glen Croe form part of the Ardgartan Estate. The westerly descent from the head of the pass leads by way of lonely Loch Restil, under the slopes of *Beinn an Lochain*, 3,021 ft., to the west, and then proceeds down Glen Kinglas towards the shores of *Loch Fyne* (*q.v.*). A steep and narrow road gives access from the summit of Rest and be Thankful to the rocky and lonely *Hell's Glen*, and also to *Lochgoilhead* (*q.v.*), at the head of Loch Goil. *Iter. 88, 101, 102, 103, 137.*

RESTENNETH PRIORY, Angus. **Map 21, NO 4 5.**
See **Forfar.** *Iter. 153.*

RHICONICH, Sutherland. **Map 28, NC 2 5.**
A little clachan, where an inn was formerly situated, finely placed at the head of Loch Inchard. It provides magnificent views of the great quartzite peaks of the Reay Forest, away to the south-east, an area given over largely to deer. *Foinaven*, 2,980 ft., dominates the range, with the rocky *Creag Dionard*, overlooking the bleak head of Strath Dionard and its lonely loch farther to the south-east. To the south rises *Arkle*, 2,580 ft., with its rough scree slopes, backed by the peak of *Meall Horn*, 2,548 ft. The whole setting around Rhiconich and the district farther south is one of innumerable lochans, lying among outcrops of Archaean grey gneiss, some of the world's oldest rocks, and has been described as being almost akin to a lunar landscape. On the road northwards to *Durness* (*q.v.*), the Achriesgill Water threads a picturesque little ravine just beyond Rhiconich, and to the north-east extends the lonely Strath Dionard, backed by *Grann Stacach*, 2,630 ft., and *Beinn Spionnaidh*, 2,537 ft. The Amhainn Dionard, draining Loch Dionard, flows northwards into the Kyle of Durness. **4 m. S.W.** of Rhiconich near *Skerricha* is an Adventure School. See **Kinlochbervie** and **Laxford Bridge.** *Iter. 225, 229.*

RHU, Dunbarton. 1,202. **Map 14, NS 2 8.**
E.C. Wed. Faces the Gare Loch and Rosneath Bay, with a pier, and is noted for yachting. Henry Bell, who launched

the steamboat " Comet," in 1812 is buried in the churchyard. A deep glen to the north, known as Whistler's Glen, was mentioned in Scott's " Heart of Midlothian." See **Helensburgh.** *Iter. 102, 111, 116.*

RHUBODACH, Bute. Map 7, **NS 0 7.** On the shores of the *Kyles of Bute (q.v.)*, and also known as *Rudhabodach*, being linked to the mainland by a car ferry to *Colintraive (q.v.)*. At one time cattle bound for Bute were made to swim the strait. See **Port Bannatyne.** *Iter. 214.*

RHUM, ISLE OF, Inverness. Map 23, **NM 3 9.** See **Rum.**

RHYNIE, Aberdeen. 1,157 with Gartly. Map 26, **NJ 4 2.** **E.C.** Thurs. The *Tap o' Noth*, 1,851 ft. (Clashindarroch Forest), visible as far away as the North Sea, and crowned by a vitrified fort, dominates *Rhynie*, the full name of which is *Muir of Rhynie*. Near the Church is in inscribed stone, known as the Crow Stone. **1 m. S.E.** is *Druminnor Castle*, a restored 15th cent. former home of the Forbes family. Open Sun. 2 to 7, Whitsun to Oct. (see note page 98). **2½ m. W.**, off the Dufftown road, is the ruined *Lesmore Castle*, once a Gordon stronghold. This road climbs to a height of nearly 1,400 ft. near the Banff county boundary, with the hill known as the *Buck of Cabrach*, 2,368 ft., rising to the south. See **Leslie** (Aberdeen). *Iter. 165, 167, 177, 190.*

RICCARTON, Ayr. 4,950. Map 8, **NS 4 3.** *Iter. 55.*

RICCARTON, Roxburgh. Map 5, **NY 5 9.** Situated in a remote part of Liddesdale, in a setting of hills, with the *Larriston Fells*, 1,677 ft. high, to the south. **2 m. N.E.**, beyond the Liddel Water, is *Thorlieshope*, well known as the home of Dandie Dinmont in Scott's " Guy Mannering." Away to the east rises *Peel Fell*, 1,975 ft., in the *Cheviots (q.v.)*, on the north-eastern slopes of which, near the boundary between Scotland and England, is situated the remote *Kielder Stone*, a remarkable boulder. The road leading north-eastwards towards *Jedburgh (q.v.)* climbs to 1,250 ft. at Note o' the Gate, in the Lowland hills. To the east of Riccarton, a lonely road penetrates the Cheviots at a comparatively low altitude, crossing the Border after about four miles, and giving access to the North Tyne valley in Northumberland. *Iter. 47.*

RINGFORD, Kirkcudbright. Map 3, **NX 6 5.** A *Galloway (q.v.)* hamlet, on the Tarff Water. **2 m. N.**, to the left of the road leading towards *New Galloway*, is a monument recalling the killing of five Covenanters, in 1685, by Grierson of Lag, whose seat, the tower of *Lag*, is described under *Dunscore*. *Iter. 26, 77.*

RING OF BROGAR, Orkney. Map 33, **HY 2 1.** See **Orkney Islands** (Mainland).

RISPOND, Sutherland. Map 28, **NC 4 6.** This remote little place stands on Rispond Bay, just off the Durness to Eriboll road, with some fine cliff scenery and sandy bays at the northern extremity of picturesque Loch Eriboll. To the north is the island of Eileen Hoan, and across the mouth of the loch, to the north-east, rises Kennageall, or Whiten Head, the most prominent feature in a line of bold, cave-ridden cliffs attaining nearly 850 ft. See **Smoo Cave.** *Iter. 225.*

ROADS TO THE ISLES, Inverness; Ross and Cromarty. See **Fort William, Glenfinnan, Lochailort, Morar, Mallaig,** and also **Fort William, Invergarry, Invermoriston, Cluanie, Kyle of Lochalsh.**

ROBERTON, Roxburgh. 649. Map 10, **NT 4 1.** The Church of this hamlet, on the Borthwick Water, dates from 1650. *Chisholme* and *Borthwickbrae* are 18th cent. houses in the vicinity. A little to the west, on the *Tushielaw (q.v.)* road, beyond the early 19th cent. *Greenbank* toll-house, now incorporated in a farm, is *Firestane Edge*, at an altitude of more than 1,000 ft., a fine viewpoint. Beyond it lies the little Alemoor Loch, drained by the Ale Water. To the south of the ridge stretches the lonely valley of the Borthwick Water, with a range of hills forming the Dumfries border rising at its head. *Iter. 34.*

ROB ROY'S CAVE, Stirling. Map 15, **NN 3 1.** See **Inversnaid.**

ROCKCLIFFE, Kirkcudbright. Map 3, **NX 8 5.** **E.C.** Thurs. A quiet resort, off the main road, on Rough Firth, the estuary of the Urr Water, with small rocky and sandy bays looking towards the Solway Firth. The Mote of Mark (N.T. Scot.) is the site of a prehistoric vitrified fort. In the Firth is *Rough Island* (N.T. Scot.), a bird sanctuary. See **Kippford.** *Iter. 73.*

RODEL (Isle of Lewis), Harris, Inverness. Map 32, **NG 0 8.** See **Hebrides, Outer** (Harris). *Iter. 257.*

RODONO HOTEL, Selkirk. Map 10, **NT 2 2.** See **St. Mary's Loch.** *Iter. 13, 46.*

ROGART, Sutherland. 463. Map 31, **NC 7 0.** *Rovie Lodge*, in Strath Fleet, into which flows the River Fleet, has beautiful gardens. *Iter. 233.*

ROGIE FALLS, Ross and Cromarty. Map 25, **NH 4 5.** See **Falls of Rogie.** *Iter. 204, 205, 206, 221.*

ROMANNO BRIDGE, Peebles. 50. Map 9, **NT 1 4.** **E.C.** Wed. Lies on the Lyne Water. To the south, near *Newlands* Church, are the so-called " Romanno Terraces," on the hillside, which are probably medieval cultivation terraces, known as strip lynchets. **3 m. S.** of Romanno Bridge, in the valley of the Lyne Water, near its meeting with the Tarth Water, is *Drochil Castle*, left unfinished in 1581, its owner, the Regent Morton, having been executed for his complicity in the murder of Darnley. **1 m. N.E.** is the 16th cent. *Halmyre House*, an ancient Gordon residence. See **Lyne** and **West Linton.** *Iter. 10, 14, 37.*

ROMAN WALL, Dunbarton; Lanark; Stirling, West Lothian. Map 8, **NS 4 7** etc. and 16, **NT 0 8** etc. Known generally as the *Antonine Wall*, or as Graham's, or Grime's Dyke, this consisted originally of a turf rampart, together with a military road to the south and also a ditch to the north. It dates from c. 140 A.D., and was abandoned less than 50 years later. Built upon a line of forts set up by Agricola, in A.D. 78, the wall stretched from a point about a mile to the east of *Bo'ness (q.v.)*, on the Forth estuary, and extended for 36 miles across the narrow waist of Scotland to reach the Clyde near *Bowling (q.v.)*. There were, in all, 19 forts on the line of the wall, these having been situated at the following points, commencing near the western extremity: Old Kilpatrick, Duntocher, Castlehill, New Kilpatrick, Balmuildy, Cadder, Kirkintilloch, Auchendavy, Barhill, Croyhill, Westerwood, Castlecary, Seabegs, Rough Castle, Falkirk, Mumrills, Inveravon, Kinneil and Bridgeness. Unlike the great wall of Hadrian, in Northumberland, in northern England, there are only scanty traces of the fortifications still to be seen, one of the best preserved forts being *Rough Castle* (N.T. Scot.), to the west of *Falkirk (q.v.)*. The wall was built against incursions of tribes from the north, and Agricola's original defences were strengthened by about a dozen new forts. Perhaps the best-preserved portions of the wall are those which survive in the private grounds of *Callendar House* near Falkirk, and also in the vicinity of *Bearsden (q.v.)*.

Roman camps and earthworks are still to be found in other parts of Scotland, the most notable being at Ardoch, near *Braco (q.v.)*, while others are described under *Lockerbie* and *Newstead*. The most northerly penetration by the Romans is thought to have been near *Ythan Wel s (q.v.)* in Aberdeenshire. The earliest of the Roman roads in Scotland, the Dere Street of Agricola, shown on some maps as a branch of Watling Street, crossed the Cheviots near *Carter Bar (q.v.)*. On the Northumberland side of the Border, near this point, is the large camp of Chew Green, by the headwaters of the River Coquet. After descending the Cheviot ridge into Scotland, the line of the road crossed the Kale Water, and traces are still to be found in the vicinity of *Oxnam (q.v.)*.

Rhynie, Aberdeen. The Crow Stone, showing Pictish symbols, which stands in a field near the church

Rispond, Sutherland. A view taken from A838, to the west, showing Whiten Head across the mouth of Loch Eriboll

Roman Wall, Dunbarton. A fragment of the Antonine Wall at Duntocher, in Dunbartonshire. The wall was erected around A.D.140, and extended from Bridgeness, east of Bo'ness, on the Forth estuary, to Old Kilpatrick, by Bowling, on the estuary of the Clyde

Roberton, Roxburgh. The former 19th century Greenbank toll house, now a farm, situated on the Tushielaw road (B711), to the west

Romanno Bridge, Peebles. The curious ' Romanno Terraces,' which lie on the hillside to the south, near Newlands Church

PLATE 142

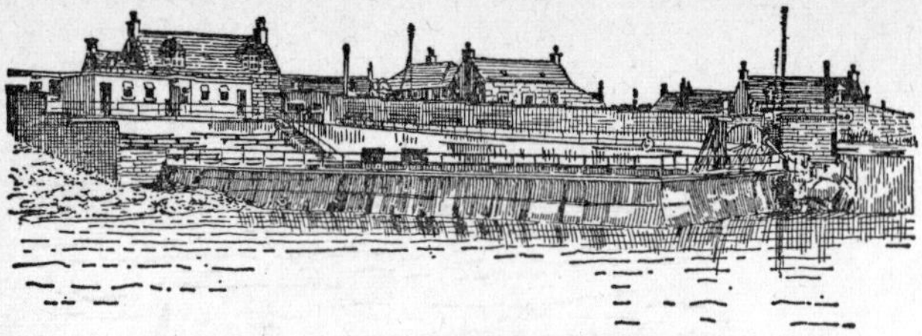

Rosehearty, Aberdeen. A view of the pool in an attractive fishing village in the Buchan district of the county

Roslin, Midlothian. The plaque on the 17th century 'Old Rosslyn' Inn, on College Hill, which was set up in 1950, and records the names of former eminent visitors to the hostelry (see below)

Rothiemay, Banff. The old bridge spanning the River Deveron

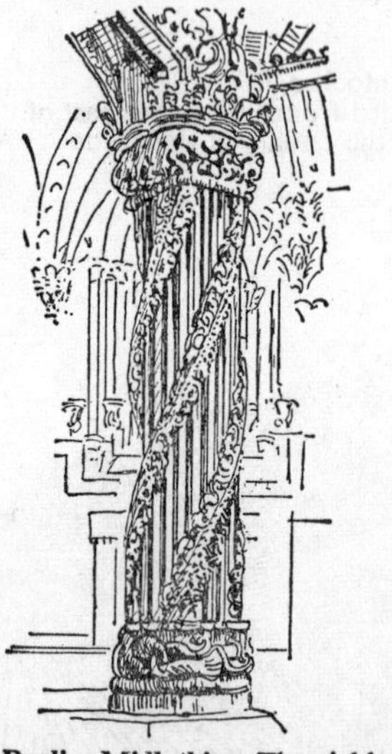

Roslin, Midlothian. The richly carved Prentice pillar in the Church, which was founded by William Sinclair in 1446. This pillar is said to have been carved by an apprentice during his master's absence in Italy to examine the original for the proposed design. On his return, the master killed his assistant in a fit of jealousy

Rosemarkie, Ross and Cromarty. A grave-slab in the churchyard, bearing a Cross on one side and Pictish symbols on the other

[For ROTHIEMURCHUS see following plate
[For ROTHESAY see under BUTE (Plate 26)

ROSEBANK, Lanark. Map 9, **NS 8** 4.
E.C. Thurs. *Iter. 53, 69.*

ROSEHALL, Sutherland. Map 29, **NC 4** 0.
Situated in Strath Oykell, on the Oykell River, near the point where it is joined by the turbulent Cassley, flowing down the long and little-known valley of Glen Cassley, to the north. Near the point where the Lairg road crosses the Cassley are the remains of *Auchness Castle.* There are traces of several brochs in the vicinity, and at *Tutim,* a little to the west, on the Oykell, a fierce clan battle took place in 1408. To the east of the village the road divides, the left fork leading to *Lairg* (*q.v.*) and the right fork to *Bonar Bridge* (*q.v.*). *Iter. 224, 228.*

ROSEHEARTY, Aberdeen. 1,135. SB. Map 27, **NJ 9** 6.
E.C. Thurs. A pretty fishing village, with sands and shelving rocks to the east. To the west, beyond Braco Park, on the coast, is the cave of *Cowshaven,* where the last Lord Pitsligo, outlawed for the part he played in the '45, was hidden by his neighbours. See **Pitsligo.** *Iter. 182.*

ROSEMARKIE, Ross and Cromarty. 500. Map 25, **NH 7** 5.
GOLF. A small, but exceptionally charming *Black Isle* (*q.v.*) resort, on Rosemarkie Bay and the Moray Firth, facing Fort George on the opposite shores of the Firth. The beach is sandy and there is some good rock scenery. In the churchyard is an interesting Celtic sculptured stone. Rosemarkie was once the seat of a bishopric, before this was transferred to *Fortrose* (*q.v.*). To the north-east are cliffs of geological interest, which have been made famous by the writings of Hugh Miller, who was born at *Cromarty* (*q.v.*). *Iter. 203.*

ROSLIN, Midlothian. 1,207. Map 10, **NT 2** 6.
E.C. Wed. This little mining village lies on the North Esk River, in the vicinity of which was fought a battle, in 1303, when the Scots defeated the English invaders. *Roslin* is famous both for its Chapel and its Castle, known also as *Rosslyn.* The former was founded in 1446, by William Sinclair, later Earl of Caithness, and was intended to become a Collegiate Church, but only the choir was built, this becoming the burial-place of the Sinclairs. After being damaged by rioters in 1688, the Chapel was finally restored in 1842. It is noted particularly for its profusion of rich and elaborate carving, showing continental influence, and the outstanding feature of the interior is the beautifully decorated Prentice pillar, rich with foliage. The exterior of the Chapel has flying buttresses and finely-carved pinnacles. There is a vaulted Lady Chapel, only 15 ft. high, and also a crypt, possibly once used as a Chapel. Scott has introduced the Chapel into the " Lay of the Last Minstrel." On a wall of the one-time " *Old Rosslyn* " inn, on College Hill, is an inscribed plaque recording names of former visitors and set up in 1950. Dr. Johnson and Boswell (in 1773), Robert Burns, Queen Victoria (in 1856) and King Edward VII have all visited the inn. The Castle overlooks the North Esk and the picturesque Roslin Glen from the edge of a cliff. The oldest parts date from the early 14th cent., and although nearly destroyed in 1544, the buildings were later restored. The 16th and 17th cent. rooms are now shown daily, 10 to dusk (see note page 98). The Bilston Burn, which flows to the north of Roslin, is of much interest to geologists.

ROSNEATH, Dunbarton. 923. Map 14, **NS 2** 8.
E.C. Wed. A small Gare Loch resort and yachting centre, overlooking Rosneath Bay, in the south-east corner of the narrow Rosneath peninsula. At the south-eastern extremity of the bay is the old Castle. *St. Modan's Well* (N.T. Scot.) commemorates a saint who founded the Church at Rosneath. See **Kilcreggan.** *Iter. 116.*

ROSSLYN CHAPEL, Midlothian. Map 10, **NT 2** 6.
See **Roslin.**

ROSYTH, Fife. Map 17, **NT 1** 8.
A naval base on the Forth estuary, of special importance during both the World Wars. The dockyard Church contains memorials from the more recent of these wars. The former Cunard liner " Mauretania " was broken up here in 1935. Rosyth Garden City stands on ground on which was fought, in 1651, the battle of *Inverkeithing* (*q.v.*). *Rosyth Tower* (A.M.), in the dockyard, carries the date 1561, and is mentioned in Scott's " The Abbot." *Iter. 134.*

ROTHES, Moray. 1,204. SB. Map 26, **NJ 2** 4.
E.C. Wed. On the River Spey, which flows to the south, between *Ben Aigan,* 1,544 ft., on the east side, and *Conerock Hill,* a wooded viewpoint, on the west side. To the north of the town is the pleasant Glen of Rothes, traversed by Edward I of England in 1296, and through which goes the road to *Elgin* (*q.v.*). A ruined Castle stands in a loop of the river to the north-east of Rothes. The town was partially inundated in the great Spey floods of 1829. In the vicinity are *Rosarie Forest,* newly planted, and *Teindland Forest,* known to forest scientists. *Iter. 171, 190, 192.*

ROTHESAY, Bute. 6,524. SB. Map 7, **NS 0** 6.
E.C. Wed. GOLF. A well-known resort and Royal Burgh, which gives the title of Duke of Rothesay to the Prince of Wales. The town stands on the sandy Rothesay Bay, with an open-air bathing station, overlooking the Firth of Clyde, and facing Toward Point on the mainland. There is a good harbour, which is associated with the annual Clyde Yachting Fortnight, held in July. Near the pier, where many of the Clyde steamers call, are remains of the old castle, and also of the chapel of *St. Michael,* the latter probably of 14th cent. date. The Castle (A.M.), largely destroyed in the 17th cent., is a remarkable example of its kind. Open weekdays 10 to 7 or 4; Sun. 2 to 7 or 4 (see note page 98). The present moated structure is 13th cent., and its strong walls enclose a circular courtyard. The original castle, captured in 1263 by King Haco of Norway, is said to have been demolished by Robert Bruce. Scott, in his " Fair Maid of Perth," has introduced the story of the Duke of Rothesay and the castle. The ruined chancel of the old Church of *St. Mary,* with its ancient tombs, stands near the Parish Church, while the *Mansion House* is of 17th cent. date. Behind the town lies the narrow Loch Fad, on the western shore of which stands *Kean's Cottage,* built by Edmund Kean, the famous actor, in 1827. A road traverses the eastern shores of the loch, and provides an alternative route to *Kilchattan Bay* (*q.v.*). The other road to the resort goes along the coast past Bogany Point to reach the model village of *Kerrycroy,* beyond which, in a wooded setting, stands *Mount Stuart,* the palatial modern seat of the Marquis of Bute. Another road leads south-westwards from Rothesay, passing the little Greenan Loch, and giving access to the sandy bays of St. Ninian's and Scalpsie, with views of the island of Inch Marnock. A branch from this road leads northwards to the sandy Etterick Bay, looking across the waters of the *Kyles of Bute* (*q.v.*) to Ardlamont Point. See **Port Bannatyne** and **Rhubodach.** *Iter. 241.*

ROTHIEMAY, Banff. 679. Map 26, **NJ 5** 4.
Here is an old bridge over the River Deveron, which is oined a little farther to the south-west by the Isla, flowing through the strath of that name. A monument at Milltown of Rothiemay commemorates James Ferguson, an early 18th cent. astronomer. *Rothiemay Castle,* in a park beyond the Deveron, preserves some old work and has fine gardens. To the south is the extensive *Bin Forest.* **4 m. W.S.W.** is *Auchanechy Castle,* 16th to 18th cent. *Iter. 189, 193.*

ROTHIEMURCHUS, Inverness. 1,047. Map 25, **NH 8** 0.
Situated on a minor road linking Aviemore with Kingussie along the east bank of the River Spey, and on the fringe of the great Forest of Rothiemurchus, now partly a Nature Reserve. This once formed part of the extensive Caledonian Forest, and contains a wealth of paths and rides, dividing Speyside from the *Cairngorms* (*q.v.*). Through the forest goes the walkers' track leading to the well-known *Lairig Ghru Pass* (*q.v.*). Reindeer have in recent years been successfully introduced into the district. To the south-east of Rothiemurchus Church, and reached by a by-road, on which is the carved *Martineau* monument, is the beautiful *Loch an Eilean,* in richly wooded surroundings, noted for its triple echo. On an island of the loch stands the sinister ruined castle of the Comyns, once a stronghold of the notorious Wolf of

Badenoch. Near the Church, in a bend of the Spey, is the mansion of *The Doune*, 16th cent. and later, with an interesting interior. South of the forest, at the head of Glen Einich, is lonely Loch Einich, one of the wildest lochs in the Highlands, situated at a height of 1,650 ft. in an amphitheatre of Cairngorm peaks, with *Braeriach*, 4,248 ft., to the east, and the great cliffs of *Sgoran Dubh*, 3,658 ft., to the south-west. Beyond *Sgoran Dubh* extends a long line of hills over 3,000 ft. in height overlooking Glen Feshie and its remote forest. Contiguous with Rothiemurchus Forest, to the north-east, is Glenmore Forest, with one of the Forest Parks, described under *Aviemore*, the *Strath Spey* (*q.v.*) resort, some **2 m. N.** of Rothiemurchus, on the opposite bank of the Spey. In the Park is *Loch Morlich* (*q.v.*), and to the south-east rises *Cairn Gorm*, 4,084 ft. There is ski-ing in *Coire Cas* (ski lift), accessible by means of a new road rising to a height of about 2,250 ft. Beyond here, a rough track leads to the *White Lady Shieling* mountain lodge (2,500 ft.) and chair lift, at the foot of *Cairn Gorm*. See **Coylumbridge.** *Iter. 138, 149.*

ROTHIE NORMAN, Aberdeen. Map 27, **NJ 7 3.**
The Fordoun Burn flows here on its way to join the Ythan near *Fyvie* (*q.v.*), with its great castle. *Iter. 184.*

ROUGH BOUNDS, Inverness. Map 23, **NG 7 0** etc.
See **Knoydart.**

ROUSAY, ISLE OF, Orkney. Map 33, **HY 3 3.**
See **Orkney Islands** (Rousay).

ROWANTREE, Ayr. Map 2, **NX 3 8.**
A little to the north two narrow and winding roads fork, the right-hand branch leading over the hills, and attaining a height of 1,421 ft., with *Shalloch on Minnoch*, 2,520 ft., rising away to the east. Later, it reaches *Straiton* (*q.v.*), in the valley of the Water of Girvan. The left-hand branch crosses the lonely Nick o' the Balloch Pass, 1,280 ft. high, and descends towards *Maybole* (*q.v.*). *Iter. 79.*

ROWARDENNAN, Stirling. 40. Map 15, **NS 3 9.**
The road along the eastern shores of *Loch Lomond* (*q.v.*) terminates here, where a steamer pier is situated. From this point there are views across to Glen Douglas, on the opposite side of the loch, with which it is connected by passenger ferry. Rowardennan is a good starting point for the ascent of *Ben Lomond*, 3,192 ft., the monarch of the whole district, and a magnificent viewpoint, notably in the direction of the richly wooded district of the *Trossachs* (*q.v.*), to the east. The lesser summit a little to the west of the Ben is known as *Ptarmigan*, and attains 2,398 ft. To the south-east lies *Rowardennan Forest* in the *Queen Elizabeth* Forest Park. See **Luss.** *Iter. 104, 115.*

ROXBURGH, Roxburgh. 581. Map 10, **NT 6 3.**
The present small village of Roxburgh stands on the west bank of the Teviot and the churchyard contains the grave of Andrew Gemmels, the "Edie Ochiltree" of Scott's "The Antiquary." Of the Castle, situated some **3 m. N.E.** and **1½ m. S.W.** of *Kelso* (*q.v.*), between the Rivers Teviot and Tweed, there are only very scanty remains. The former town of Roxburgh, once adjacent, has entirely vanished, though in the 13th cent. it was one of the four Royal Burghs of Scotland. James II besieged the Castle, once a Royal residence, in 1460, and during the siege is said to have been accidentally killed by the bursting of a cannon in the park of *Floors Castle* (*q.v.*). **3½ m. S.W.** is the late 17th cent. *Fairnington House*. *Iter. 32, 46.*

ROY BRIDGE, Inverness. Map 18, **NN 2 8.**
The bridge spans the River Roy, coming down from Glen Roy, the stream then flowing into the Spean, a short distance to the south in Glen Spean, in the *Lochaber* (*q.v.*) country. A rough and narrow road threads its way northwards through Glen Roy, which is famous for its so-called "Parallel Roads," well seen on the hillside some four miles from Roy Bridge, the uppermost "roads" being about 80 ft. apart, and the lowest situated some 200 ft. below them. These roads portray the most striking evidence of glacial action in Scotland, and have been interpreted as marking the shores of a vanished lake. Montrose made a wonderful forced march through Glen Roy before the battle of Inverlochy in 1645. (See **Fort William.**) The 18th cent. *Keppoch House* is the successor to an older mansion of the MacDonells of Keppoch. One of the young Chiefs of Keppoch and his brother were murdered here in the 17th cent. The assassins, seven brothers, were slain seven years later, by Iain Lom, the family bard, and their gory heads washed in the "Well of the Heads," on the shores of *Loch Oich* (*q.v.*). At Roy Bridge took place the last of the clan battles, fought between the MacDonells of Keppoch and the MacIntoshes on August 4, 1688. This is said to have been the final recorded use of bows and arrows by the Highlanders. The MacDonells were victorious, but their opponents' standard-bearer jumped the River Roy and escaped. To the east, road and railway traverse the Achluachrach Gorge, on the River Spean, in which are situated the *Monessie Falls*, in their rocky setting, seen to great advantage from the railway, though their fall has been reduced since the Lochaber Power Scheme came into operation. Away to the south of Roy Bridge rise the remote peaks of the *Grey Corries*, 3,858 ft., the most easterly in the series of lofty ridges culminating in *Ben Nevis* (*q.v.*), 4,406 ft., the monarch of the British Isles. See **Spean Bridge** and **Tulloch.** *Iter. 143, 208.*

RUM, ISLE OF, Inverness. Map 23, **NM 3 9.**
This mountainous Inner Hedbridean island is a prominent feature in the views from various places on the West Highland mainland, notably from the Ardnamurchan peninsula, Arisaig, Morar and Mallaig. *Rum*, or *Rhum*, is now a property of the Nature Conservancy and difficult to visit. The peaks in its southern half form a splendid group, the highest being *Askival*, *Sgurr nan Gillean* and *Ashval*, all exceeding 2,500 ft. in altitude, and providing fine climbing, as well as being notable viewpoints. At the head of Loch Scresort, on the east side of the island, is the little township and Castle of *Kinloch*, and on the west side, in Glen Harris, is situated a mausoleum. The Cuillin Sound lies between Rum and the island of Skye, to the north. Separated from Rum by the Sound of Canna, to the north-west, is the small island of *Canna*, on which stands the low *Compass Hill*, the iron deposits of which sometimes affect mariners' compasses. The Sound of Rum, to the south-east of Rum, divides that island from *Eigg*, on the south side of which rises the curious *Sgurr of Eigg*, 1,289 ft., a remarkable landmark. This is well seen from *Galmisdale*, with its pier, and is prominent in views from the mainland. Scott's "Lord of the Isles" describes a tragedy in a cave on this island, when several hundred Macdonalds were deliberately suffocated by the MacLeods of Skye in the 16th cent. On the north-west side of the island is the Bay of Laig, with the clachan of Cleadale, and in the vicinity are some "singing sands." Beyond Eigg, to the south-west, across the Sound of Eigg, lies the tiny island of *Muck*, with a laird's residence at *Gallanach* and a small harbour at *Port Mor*. Steamer services link Rum, Eigg and Canna with *Mallaig* (*q.v.*). The four islands of Rum, Eigg, Canna and Muck are known collectively as the *Small Isles*.

RUMBLING BRIDGE, Kinross; Perth. 253. Map 16, **NT 0 9.**
E.C. Wed. This well-known beauty spot, on the River Devon, its name derived from the noise of the river when in spate, gives access to several spectacular and picturesque gorges and falls. The Devon is spanned near the hotel by two bridges, one of which, a narrow arch, dates from 1713, the other being dated 1816. The Devil's Mill and Caldron Linn are the best-known falls, the former to the north-east, and the latter to the south-west of Rumbling Bridge. **3 m. S.E.** stands the restored *Aldie Castle*, overlooking the *Cleish* hills across the Pow Burn. *Iter. 86, 89.*

RUTHERGLEN, Lanark. 24,728. LB. Map 8, **NS 6 6.**
E.C. Tues. Although contiguous with the city of Glasgow, *Rutherglen*, situated south of the River Clyde, has successfully retained its independence, and remains the oldest of the

Rothiemurchus, Inverness. The ancient Comyn stronghold on Loch Eilean, in which the notorious Wolf of Badenoch once lived. The loch lies off an unclassified road to the south-east, in Rothiemurchus Forest, in the foothills of the Cairngorms

Roy Bridge, Inverness. The view up the lonely Glen Roy, to the north of A86, in which lie the famous ' parallel roads,' which have been formed by glacial action

Rutherglen, Lanark. The tower of the Parish Church, which incorporates a fragment of the earlier Norman Church

Rutherglen, Lanark. The Kirk Port of 1663, which retains two sentry boxes dating from the 18th century

Rumbling Bridge, Kinross; Perth. Two bridges spanning the River Devon, dated 1713 and 1816 respectively. A plaque showing the two bridges exists on the wall of the hotel

Ruthwell Church, Dumfries. The famous 18-foot high carved 8th century Cross, which is preserved in an apse built specially for it

Saddell, Argyll. An entrance arch to Saddell Castle, built in 1508. Robert Bruce was concealed in the castle after his defeat at Methven in 1306

St. Andrews, Fife. The remains of the Cathedral, founded originally in 1160. Robert Bruce attended its consecration in 1318

St. Abb's, Berwick. A row of net houses used to store the local fishermen's gear

St. Andrews, Fife. The 14th century Gothic arches known as The Pends, which form part of a once-vaulted gatehouse to the Priory precincts

St. Andrews, Fife. The Club House of the Royal and Ancient Golf Club, founded in 1754, and acknowledged as the ruling authority on the game

[For ST. ANDREWS see also following plate
[For RUTHVEN BARRACKS see under BADENOCH (Plate 13)

Scottish Royal Burghs, having been thus created by David I, early in the 12th cent. The former castle has disappeared, having been burnt by the Regent Murray after the battle of Langside, in 1568, after which Mary, Queen of Scots commenced her flight from the country (See **Clarkston**). In 1679, the Covenanters affixed a delaration to the Town Cross, which led to the battles of Drumclog near *Loudounhill* (*q.v.*), and *Bothwell Brig* (*q.v.*). A gable from the former Norman Church rests against an early 16th cent. steeple containing a Dutch bell of 1635. The Kirk port dates from 1663 and has a pair of 18th cent. sentry-boxes. The present Mercat Cross is modern. Clydesdale horses were at one time tethered in the wide main street during important sales. The town is an important manufacturing centre, noted for chemicals and paper mills, and there are also collieries in the vicinity. **1½ m. S.** is *Castlemilk*, incorporating a 15th or 16th cent. tower, and thought to have housed Mary, Queen of Scots before the battle of Langside. See **Cambuslang**. *Iter. 56.*

RUTHVEN BARRACKS, Inverness. Map 19, **NN 7 9.**
See **Kingussie.** *Iter. 138, 149.*

RUTHWELL, Dumfries. 1,179. Map 4, **NY 1 6.**
The Church lies a little to the north, and the village a little to the south of the Dumfries to Annan road. The very remarkable *Ruthwell Cross* (A.M.) is of the greatest interest to archaeologists, and is preserved inside the Parish Church, in an apse built specially for it. This preaching Cross, 18 ft. high, and probably of 8th cent. date, is one of Europe's most notable examples, and carries an inscription in Runic characters, depicting the earliest phrases extant of written English, in the Northumbrian dialect. The Cross was overthrown in 1642, but was restored again in 1823. At Ruthwell, in 1810, the Rev. Henry Duncan set up Scotland's first savings bank. The local pronunciation of Ruthwell is " Rivvie." See **Brow.** *Iter. 28, 47.*

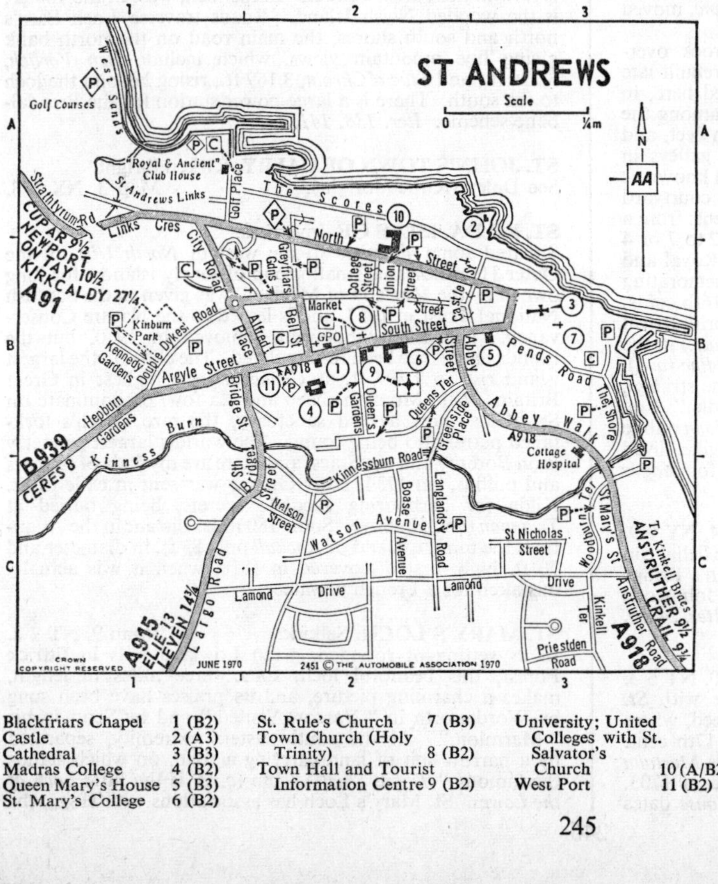

Blackfriars Chapel 1 (B2)	St. Rule's Church 7 (B3)	University; United Colleges with St. Salvator's Church 10 (A/B2)
Castle 2 (A3)	Town Church (Holy Trinity) 8 (B2)	West Port 11 (B2)
Cathedral 3 (B3)	Town Hall and Tourist Information Centre 9 (B2)	
Madras College 4 (B2)		
Queen Mary's House 5 (B3)		
St. Mary's College 6 (B2)		

SADDELL, Argyll. 932 with Skipness. Map 7, **NR 7 3.**
Stands in a picturesque setting on Saddell Bay, at the foot of Saddell Glen, with slight remains of a Cistercian monastery, possibly of 12th cent. date. This is said to have been founded by Somerled, the first Lord of the Isles, from whom sprang the Clan Donald. In the churchyard are some stones carved with Celtic inscriptions, and one of the recumbent effigies may be that of Somerled himself. On the south side of the bay stands *Saddell Castle*, dated 1508, with a machicolated parapet, and once the residence of the Bishops of Argyll. Above the date panel over the door is carved a representation of the " Galley of Lorne." To the west of Saddell rise the highest of the *Kintyre* (*q.v.*) hills, with *Beinn an Tuirc* attaining 1,491 ft. and *Beinn Bhreac* only slightly less high at 1,398 ft. See **Carradale.** *Iter. 122.*

ST. ABB'S, Berwick. Map 11, **NT 9 6.**
A small resort and fishing village, with sands, on a cliff-bound stretch of coast. There is a row of picturesque, tiny buildings used for storing the local fishermen's gear. Towards St. Abb's Head, with its lighthouse, to the north, the red cliffs rise to over 300 ft., forming an impressive headland, and are riddled with the caves of former smugglers. From the small inlet of Pettycarwick Bay the rugged coast scenery is well seen. See **Coldingham.** *Iter. 2.*

ST. ANDREWS, Fife. 11,633. SB. Map 17, **NO 5 1.**
E.C. Thurs. GOLF. This fascinating old University town and well-known summer resort on St. Andrews Bay, looking towards the North Sea, can justly claim to be one of the most interesting in Scotland, and was once the ecclesiastical capital of the country. The town stands on a promontory, and steep cliffs guard the narrow harbour, but north-westwards lie extensive stretches of sand fringing a shallow bay. At this end lie the golf-courses for which St. Andrews is today most celebrated, the Royal and Ancient Golf Club (founded 1754) being the foremost in the world and the ruling authority on the game, which is said to have been played here in the 15th century. There are four courses in all, two of which are kept up by the club and two by the Corporation, and championship meetings take place from time to time. During the annual autumn meeting, the captain for the following year plays himself into office.

St. Andrews was made a Royal Burgh in 1140, and in 1160 the Cathedral (A.M.) was founded, becoming the largest in the country, and having been completed in 1318. James V and Mary of Guise were married within its walls, and in 1559, after sermons delivered by John Knox, a certain amount of destruction of ornaments took place. By 1649 the Cathedral was reduced, mainly by neglect, to a state of ruin. Today, only parts of the west and east ends, together with a portion of the south nave wall are still standing, though the ground plan can still be traced. There are fairly extensive monastic remains, including the chapter house and refectory. Close to the Cathedral stands the small *St. Regulus*' or *St. Rule's* Church (A.M.), with its 108-ft. high tower, dating from the early 12th cent., which is ascended by a spiral staircase. The nave has vanished, but the narrow, roofless choir, with its rounded-headed windows, has survived.

The University is the oldest in Scotland, founded in 1412, and until 1967 included *Dundee* (*q.v.*) University, incorporated in 1897. The United Colleges of *St. Salvator* and *St. Leonard*, founded in 1455 and 1512, and combined in 1747, are famous for the Church of *St. Salvator*, now the College Chapel. This 15th cent. Church has a tall tower, with an octagonal broach spire, and the interior contains the tomb of the founder, Bishop Kennedy; the oldest Sacrament House in a Scottish Church; and John Knox's pulpit, formerly in the Town Church. *St. Mary's* College, founded in 1537 by Cardinal Beaton, preserves a quadrangle between the older buildings, while a thorn tree, planted by Mary, Queen of Scots, still flourishes. The University Museum contains interesting fossils from Dura Den, near *Pitscottie* (*q.v.*). There are still slight remains of the original *St. Leonard's* College, in which John Knox resided, and nearby is the little 16th cent. *St. Leonard's* Chapel, with monuments of interest. The Town Church, *Holy Trinity*, founded in 1412, but so much altered that it is now virtually a new structure, retains its 16th cent. tower, of "Fife" type. The interior contains an elaborately-carved 17th cent. marble monument to Archbishop Sharp, murdered in 1779, at Magus Muir, near Pitscottie. John Knox preached his first public sermon in the Church in 1547. The *Playfair* aisle contains monuments to the family. There are also two choir stalls of c. 1505; some notable modern windows by Douglas Strachan; and a wall tablet to the famous golfer, Tom Morris. The Session House contains interesting relics, including two "cutty" or repentance stools and the branks or scold's bridle. In the grounds of the modern *Madras* College stands the Blackfriars Chapel, dating from 1525, a fragment of the former monastery, founded originally in 1274. In the Town Hall are portraits and among some interesting relics is the headman's axe, as well as a stone dated 1565, which came from the old tolbooth, taken down in 1862. A house in South Street, built by Hugh Scrymgeour in 1523, and now *St. Leonard's* School library, is said to have once housed Mary, Queen of Scots. Nearby are *The Pends* two Gothic arches, perhaps 14th cent., forming the entrance to the Priory precincts, once completely encircled by a wall, the work of Prior Hepburn in the 16th cent., of which considerable portions are still *in situ*. A number of fine old houses may still be seen in South Street, the west end of which is spanned by the *West Port* (A.M.), built in 1589. The *Teinds Yett*, in Abbey Walk, is another old gate. A picturesque custom is the "Kate Kennedy" procession, held annually in the spring. Near the station is the legendary *Blue Stane*, moved from the West Port.

The ruined Castle (A.M.) is situated on a rock overlooking the sea, and was founded in 1200, being rebuilt late in the 14th cent. Cardinal Beaton was murdered here, in 1546, and in the following year John Knox was among the garrison when the Castle was taken by the French fleet, and the prisoners, among them Knox, taken to the galleys in France. In the Sea Tower is a 24-ft. deep dungeon known as the Bottle Dungeon, and to the south-east of the courtyard is an underground passage containing mine fragments from a siege of 1546. Open weekdays, 10 to 7 or 4; Sun. 2 to 7 or 4 (see note page 98). Near the Club House of the Royal and Ancient Club is the Martyrs' Monument, commemorating reformers burnt at St. Andrews in the 15th and 16th cents. The town makes a good centre for the old-world Royal Burghs situated along the Fife coast, from *Crail* (*q.v.*) in the east, to *Culross* (*q.v.*) in the west beyond *Dunfermline* (*q.v.*). **2 m. S.E.** of St. Andrews is Kinkell Ness, with the strange, basalt rock pillars known as the "Rock and Spindle." **2 m. S.W.** is the park of *Mount Melville*, now the *Craigtoun* public park. The 19th-cent novelist, G. J. Whyte-Melville, lived here. See **Ceres, Dairsie, Leuchars** and **Pitscottie** (for *Magus Muir*). *Iter. 93, 94, 128, 129, 131, 136.*

ST. ANN'S, Dumfries. Map 4, NY 0 9.
Lies on the Kinnel Water, which flows through the delightful Raehills Glen, a little to the north-west. St. Ann's Bridge dates from c. 1800. *Lochwood Tower*, a ruined Johnstone stronghold, situated in a wood, was burnt in 1592. *Iter. 24, 46.*

ST. BOSWELLS GREEN, Roxburgh. 1,353. Map 10, NT 5 3.
GOLF. A spacious common links the village with *St. Boswell's*, to the north-east, nearer the River Tweed, where *Lessudden House* is a fine, modernised 16th and 17th cent. house. Across the Tweed, to the north-east, stands *Mertoun House*, designed originally by Sir William Bruce in 1703. There is a dovecote dated 1576. *Old Mertoun House* dates back to 1677. To the north-west is *Newtown St. Boswells* (*q.v.*). In the background rise the triple-peaked *Eildon Hills*. See **Dryburgh Abbey**. *Iter. 4, 13, 32, 36, 41, 43, 46, 52.*

ST. CATHERINE'S, Argyll. Map 14, NN 1 0.
Situated on the eastern shore of *Loch Fyne* (*q.v.*), looking across its waters to *Inveraray* (*q.v.*). To the north-east, the road continues along the lochside to circle round its head, but two branches diverge to the east, leading to Hell's Glen and Glen Kinglas respectively, and meeting again at the summit of *Rest and be Thankful* (*q.v.*), in its mountain setting. *Iter. 102, 103, 137.*

ST. COMBS, Aberdeen. Map 27, NK 0 6.
A fishing village situated under Inzie Head, with Strathbeg Bay lying beyond it to the south-east. *Iter. 182.*

ST. CYRUS, Kincardine. 997. Map 21, NO 7 6.
E.C. Thurs. Lies on the coast, to the north of the estuary of the River North Esk, with some rock scenery north-east of the village, and also bathing from a sandy beach. About a mile in this direction is the ruined *Kaim of Mathers*, a refuge, built in 1421, near which is the promontory of Milton Ness. The former village of Mathers was destroyed by the sea in 1795. There is a 227-acre Nature Reserve at St. Cyrus. **2 m. N.E.**, and west of the Inverbervie road, is the wooded Den Finella, with a waterfall. *Iter. 155.*

ST. FILLAN'S, Perth. 170. Map 15, NN 6 2.
E.C. Wed. GOLF. Charmingly situated at the eastern extremity of Loch Earn, and on the River Earn, where it commences its journey down Strath Earn. To the south rise the wooded slopes of *Dundurn*, 2,011 ft., an ancient Pictish fortified hill, and below is the smaller *Dunfillan Hill*, 600 ft., topped by a rock known as *St. Fillan's* Chair. A ruined Chapel stands in a cemetery near the village, and has long been used as the burial-place of the Stewarts of *Ardvorlich House*, near *Lochearnhead* (*q.v.*). The font from the Chapel is now in the Parish Church. In the loch, west of the village, is the wooded Neish Island. Roads traverse Loch Earn's north and south shores, the main road on the north bank giving fine mountain views, which include *Ben Vorlich*, 3,224 ft., and *Stuc a'Chroin*, 3,169 ft., rising beyond the loch to the south. There is a large power station for the Breadalbane scheme. *Iter. 138, 141, 145.*

ST. JOHN'S TOWN OF DALRY, Kirkcudbright.
See **Dalry** (Kirkcudbright). Map 3, NX 6 8.

ST. KILDA, ISLES OF, Inverness.
Situated some 40 miles to the west of *North Uist*, in the Outer Hebrides, this small group of lonely islands, for long owned by the Macleod of Macleod, was given to the Scottish National Trust in 1957, and is leased to the Nature Conservancy. The inhabitants were removed in 1930, but the islands have since been re-populated. The cliffs on the largest island rise to 1,397 ft. at *Conachair*, the highest in Great Britain. Wild Mouflon sheep and sea-fowl predominate on St. Kilda, now a bird sanctuary, the rare Leach's fork-tailed petrel also being found. The world's largest gannetry is on Boreray and the Stacs, and there are myriads of fulmars and puffins. In 1734, Lady Grange was sent in exile to St. Kilda for harbouring Jacobite secrets, being buried at *Trumpan* (*q.v.*), in Skye. Some 180 miles distant in the Atlantic is the minute island of *Rockall* only 83 ft. in diameter and 70 ft. high, first discovered in 1810, when it was actually mistaken for a French privateer.

ST. MARY'S LOCH, Selkirk. Map 9, NT 2 2.
In its setting of rounded, green Lowland hills in Ettrick Forest, this beautiful loch, some three miles in length, makes a charming picture, and its praises have been sung by Wordsworth in "Yarrow Visited" and by Scott in his "Marmion." At the south-western extremity, separated by a narrow spit of land carrying a road, on which stands the famous "*Tibbie Shiel's*" Inn (*q.v.*), is the little *Loch of the Lowes*. St. Mary's Loch has associations with Hogg, the

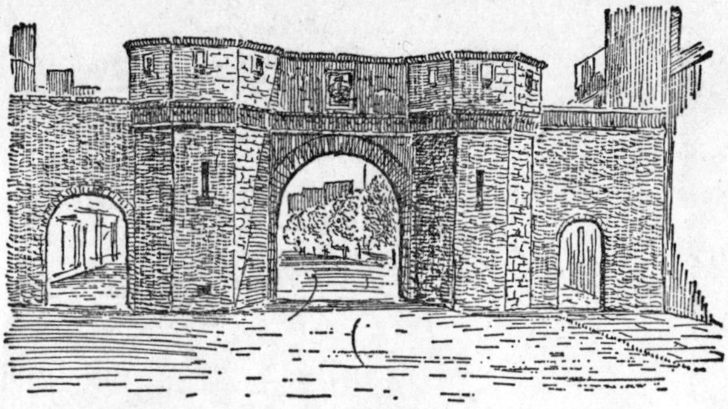

St. Andrews, Fife. The West Port, spanning South Street. Its building contract is dated 18th May, 1589, but it was extensively restored in 1843 and the side arches added

St. Andrews, Fife. The ruined Castle, of 14th to 17th century date, in which Cardinal Beaton was murdered in 1546. A year later John Knox was taken from here to the galleys in France

St. Fillan's, Perth. The ancient ruined Chapel in a cemetery near the village

St. Boswells Green, Roxburgh. The knocker on the entrance door to the 16th to 17th century Lessudden House. It stands at St. Boswells, to the north-east, on B6404, near the River Tweed

St. Cyrus, Kincardine. The 15th century refuge known as the Kaim of Mathers, which was built by a Barclay, in 1421, after he had slain a sheriff of the Mearns. It lies to the north-east, near Milton Ness

St. Andrews, Fife. The ruined early 12th century St. Rule's Church, which has a tower 108 feet high. It was built originally for Bishop Robert. In the nearby cemetery is buried Tom Morris (1821-1908), the famous golfer of early days

[For ST. ANDREWS see also preceding plate
[For ST. MARY'S LOCH see following plate

St. Mary's Loch, Selkirk. A view of the loch, in its setting of hills in the Southern Uplands

St. Monance, Fife. An old dovecote near the ruined Newark Castle, on the cliffs to the south-west

St. Mary's Loch, Selkirk. The statue of James Hogg, the ' Ettrick Shepherd,' which stands near ' Tibbie Shiel's ' Inn, between St. Mary's Loch and the Loch of the Lowes, on A708

St. Vigean's, Angus. The Drosten Stone, in the Church, carrying Pictish symbols and a contemporary inscription

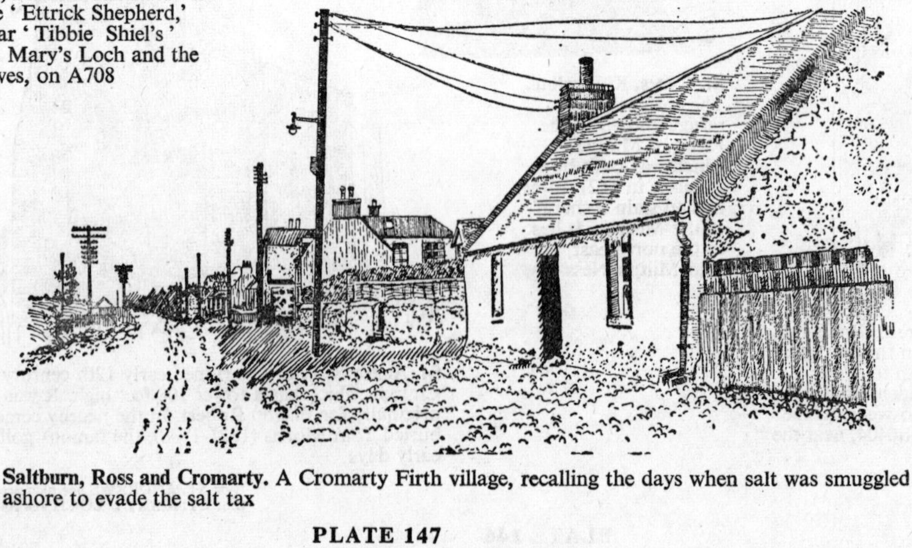

Saltburn, Ross and Cromarty. A Cromarty Firth village, recalling the days when salt was smuggled ashore to evade the salt tax

PLATE 147

'Ettrick Shepherd,' who herded on the hills in the neighbourhood, and his statue stands near Tibbie Shiel's. The Megget Water flows into the loch on the north side, at *Coppercleuch*, while a rough track traverses the valley through which the stream flows, and gives access to the lonely Talla Reservoir, near *Tweedsmuir* (*q.v.*), overlooked by *Broad Law*, 2,754 ft., one of the loftiest of the Lowland hills. To the south of the Megget Water outflow is the picturesquely situated "*Rodono*" Hotel, taking its name from the old barony of Rodonna of which the Megget family formed a part. On the hillside, north of the loch, is the old churchyard of *St. Mary's* Kirk. Farther to the north-east is the ruined *Dryhope Tower*, said to be the birthplace of Mary Scott, the "Flower of Yarrow," who married "Auld Wat of Harden," an ancestor of Sir Walter Scott. (See **Hawick.**) North-eastwards, in the extensive Ettrick Forest, lies the beautiful Vale of *Yarrow* (*q.v.*), one of the loveliest of the Border valleys. See **Ettrick, Ettrick Bridge End, Gordon Arms Hotel** and **Tushielaw Inn.** *Iter. 13, 46.*

ST. MONANCE, Fife. 1,206. SB. Map 17, **NO 5 0.**
E.C. Wed. A charming little fishing port, also known as *St. Monans*, with old houses clustered near the water's edge. A beautiful little 14th cent. Church, restored in 1828, stands almost on the foreshore, having been built by David II, and consisting of an unfinished cruciform structure, topped by a curious stone steeple. A model of a three-masted ship hangs usually from one of the transept roofs. The original "Fifie" fishing boats were built in the town's shipyard, which now specializes in yachts. On the cliffs, to the south-west, are remains of the 17th cent. *Newark Castle*, with an old circular dovecote close by. The Castle was once the home of General Leslie, the Covenanter, who won the battle of *Philiphaugh*, near *Selkirk* (*q.v.*), but was later defeated by Cromwell in the battle of *Dunbar* (*q.v.*). *Iter. 94, 98.*

ST. NINIAN'S, Stirling. 3,932. Map 16, **NS 7 9.**
This old village, known also as *St. Ringan's*, is situated to the south of *Stirling* (*q.v.*). It stands at the junction of roads leading towards Airdrie and Falkirk, with the famous battlefield of *Bannockburn* (*q.v.*) in close proximity to the south-west. **2½ m. S.** of St. Ninian's, and off the road to Denny, is the 16th cent. mansion of *Auchenbowie*. In the vicinity, to the west, is the probable site of the battle of *Sauchieburn*, in 1488, when James III was defeated, wounded and afterwards murdered. *Old Sauchie*, to the west, is a 16th cent. and later house. *Iter. 50, 87, 95, 99.*

ST. VIGEAN'S, Angus. Map 21, **NO 6 4.**
The village lies a little to the north of Arbroath, on the Brothock Water, and is known chiefly for its Church, founded in the 11th cent., but much restored. There is a remarkable collection of inscribed Celtic stones, and outstanding is the so-called *Drosten Stone*, carrying Pictish symbols. **3 m. N.**, near the Brothock Water, is *Colliston House*, dating from 1583.

SALEN, Argyll. 136. Map 12, **NM 6 6.**
A small fishing resort on the beautifully-wooded shores of *Loch Sunart* (*q.v.*), a long and narrow sea loch, which divides Ardnamurchan from Morven, and whose waters mingle with those of the Sound of Mull away to the west. Eastwards rises *Ben Resipol*, 2,774 ft., a splendid viewpoint, and northwards goes the road to *Acharacle* (*q.v.*), at the western end of *Loch Shiel* (*q.v.*), with its memories of Prince Charles Edward and the '45. See **Strontian.** *Iter. 216.*

SALEN, Isle of Mull, Argyll. 119. Map 12, **NM 5 4.**
E.C. Wed. A steamer port on the Sound of Mull, on the narrowest part of the island, and separated by only 3 miles of land from the beautiful sea loch of Loch na Keal. This loch may be the "Loch Gyle" of Campbell's famous poem, "Lord Ullin's Daughter" (See **Ulva Ferry**). Roads traverse both north and south shores of its waters, that on the north side leading later by the shore of Loch Tuath, in which lies the island of *Ulva*, with its caves, and eventually reaching *Calgary* (*q.v.*). The road on the south side of Loch na Keal passes near the north-western extremity of the beautiful inland Loch Ba. Later it gives views of Ulva, beyond which lies the smaller island of *Gometra*, before passing under the magnificent *Gribun* (*q.v.*) cliffs on the way to Loch Scridain, In the background, to the east, rises *Ben More*, 3,169 ft. Mull's highest peak, and a fine viewpoint. To the east of Salen, a road leads along the shores of the Sound of Mull, overlooked by a range of 2,500-ft. high hills. **2 m. N.W.** of Salen, overlooking the Sound of Mull, and near the entrance to Glen Aros, on the inland road to *Dervaig* (*q.v.*), is the ruined *Aros Castle*, once a stronghold of the Lords of the Isles. **2 m. E.** stands the ruined *Pennygowan* Chapel, in which some carved cross-slabs are preserved. See **Craignure** and **Tobermory.** *Iter. 248, 249, 250.*

SALINE, Fife. 1,727. Map 16, **NT 0 9.**
GOLF. At the foot of *Saline Hill*, 1,178 ft., an outlier of the *Cleish* hills, which stretch away north-eastwards, partly in Kinross-shire, their highest point being *Dumglow*, 1,241 ft. Sir Walter Scott stayed here at times.

SALTBURN, Ross and Cromarty. Map 25, **NH 7 6.**
A Cromarty Firth village, adjacent to *Invergordon* (*q.v.*), its name recalling the days of the salt tax, when it was smuggled ashore and hidden in burns. A new pier and large aluminium smelter works have changed the face of the village. *Iter. 201.*

SALTCOATS, Ayr. 14,901. SB. Map 8, **NS 2 4.**
E.C. Wed. A well-known resort, with a harbour, sands and bathing, facing Irvine Bay to the south-east. The resort and steamer pier of *Ardrossan* (*q.v.*) lies to the north-west across a bay. Saltworks were originally established at Saltcoats by James V, in the 16th cent. See **Stevenston.** *Iter. 88.*

SANAIGMORE, Isle of Islay, Argyll. Map 6, **NR 2 7.**
Lies on Sanaigmore Bay, near which, in 1847, the emigrant ship "Exmouth" foundered with heavy loss of life. Away to the north-east, on a rocky stretch of coast, is Ardnave Point, at the mouth of Loch Gruinart. A narrow road leads southwards from Sanaigmore, keeping inland from the rocky coast, in which are some notable caves. It passes near the shores of Loch Gorm, with remains of an ancient castle of the Macdonalds, on the way to the sandy Saligo Bay, in the Rhinns of Islay. See **Kilchoman.** *Iter. 246.*

SANDBANK, Argyll. 1,035. Map 14, **NS 1 8.**
E.C. Wed. Situated on the south shores of the Holy Loch, which is almost encircled by the road from Dunoon to Ardentinny, providing fine marine views for the whole of the distance. A little to the north-west is the entrance to Glen Lean, threaded by the narrow and hilly road leading to the heads of Lochs Striven and Riddon, and thence to *Glendaruel* (*q.v.*) and *Loch Fyne* (*q.v.*). The yacht "Sceptre," the unsuccessful 1958 challenger for the America's Cup, was launched at Sandbank, and the later unsuccessful challenger, "Sovereign," also came from here. See **Ardnadam** and **Holy Loch.** *Iter. 102, 137.*

SANDHAVEN, Aberdeen. Map 27, **NJ 9 6.**
A coastal village, with the ruined 17th cent. *Pittullie Castle* standing a little inland to the south-west. *Iter. 182.*

SANDHEAD, Wigtown. Map 2, **NX 0 4.**
On Luce Bay, with the extensive Sands of Luce, backed by the sand dunes of the Torrs Warren, to the north-east, where a battle between the Picts and the Scots once took place. **2 m. S.W.**, on a by-road away from the coast, is *Kirkmadrine* Church, in the porch of which are preserved several remarkable inscribed stones (A.M.), showing that a very early Christian settlement must have existed in the locality. *Iter. 82.*

SANDWICK, Shetland. Map 33, **HU 4 2.**
See **Shetland Islands** (Mainland). *Iter. 269.*

SANDWOOD BAY, Sutherland. **Map 28, NC 2 6.**
See **Kinlochbervie.** *Iter. 229.*

SANDYKNOWE, Roxburgh. **Map 10, NT 6 3.**
At this farmhouse, situated near the picturesque *Smailholm Tower (q.v.),* Sir Walter Scott spent some of his childhood years, living with his grandfather.

SANNOX, Isle of Arran, Bute. **Map 7, NS 0 4.**
Situated on Sannox Bay, at the seaward end of the picturesque and lonely Glen Sannox. This penetrates into the heart of the granite hills of Arran, the head of the valley being dominated by *Cir Mhor,* 2,618 ft., and *Caisteal Abhail,* 2,817 ft. The hills which overlook the lower half of the valley are *Suidhe Fhearghais,* 1,756 ft., to the north, and *Cioch na'h Oighe,* 2,168 ft., to the south. By traversing a ridge to the south of *Cir Mhor,* access is gained for climbers to Glen Rosa and *Brodick (q.v.).* From the bay, views are obtained towards the islands of Bute and the twin Cumbraes. The road leading north-westwards from Sannox to *Lochranza (q.v.)* traverses the fine North Glen Sannox. See **Corrie.** *Iter. 242.*

SANQUHAR, Dumfries. 2,006. SB. **Map 9, NS 7 0.**
E.C. Thurs. GOLF. A small Nithsdale Royal Burgh, the River Nith being joined, to the east, by the Crawick Water, flowing down from the lonely hills on the Lanarkshire border. These are traversed by a winding and narrow road reaching Clydesdale by way of *Crawfordjohn (q.v.).* The site of the former Town Cross, to which the Covenanters affixed the two famous Declarations of Sanquhar, in 1680 and 1685, is commemorated by a monument. The Tolbooth dates from 1735. The Riding of the Marches festival takes place in the summer. The ruined castle above the Nith belonged once to the Crichtons and later to the Douglases. West of Sanquhar are remains of an earthwork called the "Devil's Dyke," the origin of which is obscure. In the latter half of the 17th cent. the *Lowther* hills, to the east, were a retreat for the persecuted Covenanters, or "Men of the Moss Hags." See **Enterkinfoot** and **Mennock.** *Iter. 27, 48, 49, 67.*

SARCLET, Caithness. **Map 30, ND 3 4.**
On a rocky piece of coast, with the Stack of Ulbster to the south, near Loch Sarclet.

SARK BRIDGE, Dumfries. **Map 4, NY 3 6.**
This bridge over the River Sark, which flows from here into the Solway Firth, forms the border between Scotland and England, and carries the road (built in 1830 to supersede the road via Longtown) leading from Carlisle to Glasgow and Stranraer. The former Sark Toll Bar house was the scene of many runaway marriages. See **Gretna** and **Springfield.** *Iter. 10, 13, 26, 27, 28, 29, 42, 50, 51.*

SATTERNESS, Kirkcudbright. **Map 3, NX 9 5.**
See **Southerness.**

SCALLOWAY, Shetland. **Map 33, HU 3 3.**
See **Shetland Islands** (Mainland). *Iter. 270.*

SCAPA FLOW, Orkney. **Map 33, HY 3 0.**
See **Orkney Islands** (Mainland).

SCARBA, ISLE OF, Argyll. **Map 13, NM 6 0.**
See **Clachan Bridge.**

SCHIEHALLION, Perth. **Map 19, NN 7 5.**
See **Kinloch Rannoch** and **Queen's View.** *Iter. 89, 138, 147, 148, 149.*

SCONE, Perth. 2,977. **Map 17, NO 1 2.**
Famous for the former Abbey and Palace, which stood **2 m. W.** of *New Scone,* a little to the west of the Perth to Blairgowrie road, and between *Old Scone* and the River Tay. It was destroyed in 1559 by a mob from Perth, who had been fired by John Knox's oratory. The mote-hill of Scone was known already in the 8th cent., and the celebrated Stone of Scone, traditionally identified with Jacob's pillow at Bethel, and later the Stone of Destiny at Tara in Ireland, was brought here about a century later, to be carried away to England by Edward I in 1297. It was later placed under the seat of the Coronation Chair in Westminster Abbey, from which it was sensationally taken in December 1950. Early in 1951, the Stone found a temporary resting place in the Abbey at *Arbroath (q.v.),* before being returned to England. All the early Scottish Kings were crowned at Scone until the time of James I. The last King to be crowned here was Charles II, in 1651. The Old Pretender kept court in Scone Palace, in 1716, and 29 years later Prince Charles Edward slept there. The present early 19th cent. Palace on the old site replaces the rebuilt 16th cent. house. Open Mon., Tue., Wed., Thur., Sat., 11 to 5 (Sun., 2 to 5), May to early Oct. (See note page 98). In the park is preserved the old Cross of Scone. South-east of New Scone is *Bonhard House,* with a well-restored dovecote of 1701. See **Dunstaffnage.** For *Iter.* see *New Scone.*

SCONSER, Isle of Skye, Inverness. **Map 23, NG 5 3.**
In their tour of 1773, Dr. Johnson and Boswell dined at an inn here. *Iter. 251, 252, 253.*

SCOONIE, Fife. 3,683. **Map 17, NO 3 0.**
See **Leven.** *Iter. 94, 98, 128.*

SCOTLANDWELL, Kinross. **Map 17, NO 1 0.**
Takes its name from springs which bubble up in a parapeted stone cistern west of the main street. To the north rises *White Craigs,* 1,492 ft., an outlier of the *Lomonds,* and south-westwards is situated *Benarty Hill,* 1,167 ft. *Iter. 98.*

SCOTS DYKE, Dumfries. **Map 4, NY 3 7.**
See **Canonbie.**

SCOTT COUNTRY, THE **Map 10, NT 5 3 etc.**
The Scott country may be taken to comprise that part of the picturesque *Border (q.v.)* country in the *Lowlands (q.v.)* which is threaded by the River Tweed, and has for its centre the town of *Melrose.* Numerous places in the district have achieved fame for their personal links with the great novelist, or are associated, either with his ancestors, or with characters from his works. Of these places *Abbotsford House* is perhaps the best known, having been Sir Walter's last and best-loved home, while to *Dryburgh Abbey* falls the honour of being his place of burial. Although not part of the Scott Country proper, the beautiful *Trossachs (q.v.)* country, in Perthshire, is bound up with the novelist's "Lady of the Lake" and "Rob Roy," and is visited yearly by countless admirers of his genius. Two other places, *Riccarton (q.v.)* and *Gatehouse of Fleet (q.v.),* are particularly associated with "Guy Mannering," and *Caerlaverock (q.v.)* has the tomb of Robert Paterson, Scott's "Old Mortality." See **Abbotsford House, Ashiestiel, Darnick, Dryburgh Abbey, Edinburgh, Ettrick Bridge End, Galashiels, Hawick, Irongray, Kelso, Manor, Melrose, Peebles, St. Mary's Loch, Selkirk, Sandyknowe, Shetland** and **Smailholm.** *Iter. 13, 43.*

SCOTT'S VIEW, Berwick. (A.A. viewpoint.)
Map 10, NT 5 3.
From this point a beautiful view is disclosed, much loved by Sir Walter Scott, looking across the Tweed towards the *Eildon Hills (q.v.).* See **Bemersyde.**

SCOURIE, Sutherland. 51. **Map 28, NC 1 4.**
E.C. Wed. A small crofting village and fishing resort, situated on Scourie Bay, with views to the east of the sharp gneiss cone of *Ben Stack,* 2,364 ft. Palm trees growing in the vicinity of Scourie are thought to be the most northerly in the world. The landscape around this remote Sutherland village is one of innumerable tiny lochans. To the south is the small inlet of Badcall Bay, forming part of the larger island-studded bay of *Eddrachillis (q.v.).* North-west of Scourie Bay, separated from the mainland by the Sound of Handa, is *Handa (q.v.),* now a sea-fowl sanctuary. See **Kinlochbervie, Laxford Bridge** and **Rhiconich.** *Iter.* 225.

SCOUSBURGH, Shetland. **Map 33, HU 3 1.**
See **Shetland Islands** (Mainland).

SCRABSTER, Caithness. **Map 30, ND 0 7.**
On the sandy Thurso Bay, sheltered by Holborn Head, with its curious arched chasms. From the pier, the mail-steamer for Stromness in the *Orkneys (q.v.)* crosses the turbulent Pentland Firth. See **Thurso.** *Iter. 236.*

SEAMILL, Ayr. **Map 8, NS 2 4.**
See **West Kilbride.** *Iter. 66, 88.*

Sandyknowe, Roxburgh. The farmhouse where Sir Walter Scott spent some of his childhood days

Sanquhar, Dumfries. The ruined Castle, above the River Nith, which was once owned by the Crichtons and later by the Douglases

Sark Bridge, Dumfries. The Sark Toll Bar house, on A74, the 'First House in Scotland,' where runaway marriages were performed. Above the entrance door is 'the marriage room' tablet. The former main road to Scotland followed A6071 by way of Longtown and Springfield (see Plate 153), marriages being first performed in the latter village

Schiehallion, Perth. The 3,547-foot high peak, which rises south-east of Kinloch Rannoch. West of the peak lies Glen Sassunn, near which English invaders are said to have fought Robert Bruce

Scotlandwell, Kinross. A stone cistern, dated 1858, in which is contained the spring from which the village takes its name

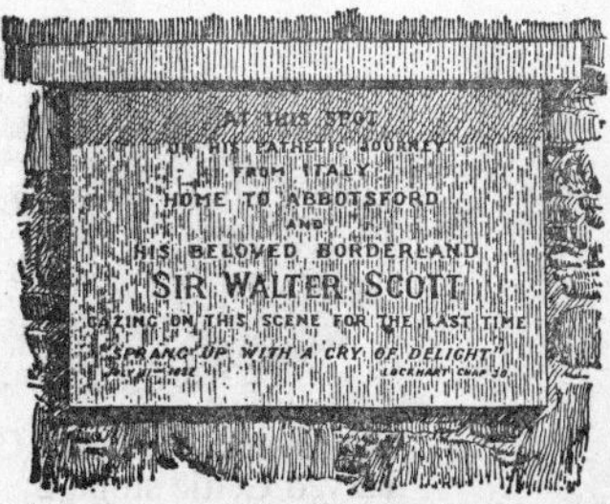

Scott Country. The tablet at Langlee, on the Melrose road (A6091), about 1½ miles south-east of Galashiels, in Selkirkshire. It records Sir Walter Scott's last journey to his home at Abbotsford, on his return from Italy in 1832, shortly before his death.

Selkirk, Selkirk. The Flodden Monument, which was erected in 1913, on the 400th anniversary of the battle, and is inscribed, 'O Flodden Field'

Selkirk, Selkirk. The tablet on the West Port recalling the former 'Forest' Inn, where Robert Burns once lodged

Shandwick, Ross and Cromarty. A carved Celtic stone by the roadside

Seton, East Lothian. The unfinished 15th century Collegiate Church. It stands in the grounds of the Castle, which Robert Adam built in 1790 to replace the old Palace, where Charles I was entertained in 1633

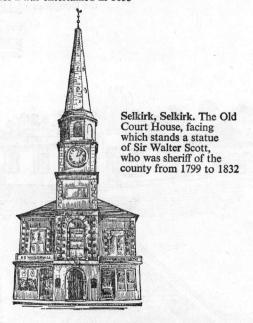

Selkirk, Selkirk. The Old Court House, facing which stands a statue of Sir Walter Scott, who was sheriff of the county from 1799 to 1832

Shawhead, Kirkcudbright. One of a number of examples of modern sculpture by Henry Moore, set up on the slopes of the hills near Glenkiln, to the north-west

[For SHETLAND see following plates

SEIL, ISLE OF, Argyll. Map 14, **NM 7 1.** See **Clachan Bridge.** *Iter. 122.*

SELKIRK, Selkirk. 5,687. SB. Map 10, **NT 4 2.** **E.C.** Thurs. GOLF. A Royal Burgh, on the edge of Ettrick Forest, situated on the Ettrick Water, which has received the waters of the Yarrow a little farther to the south-west. A picturesque Border Riding ceremony is still kept up annually, and the town is today noted especially for its tweed mills. A nightly curfew is sounded from the Town Hall, with its 110-ft. high spire. The Mercat Cross is modern. *Helliwell's Close* is 17th cent. There are statues in the High Street to Sir

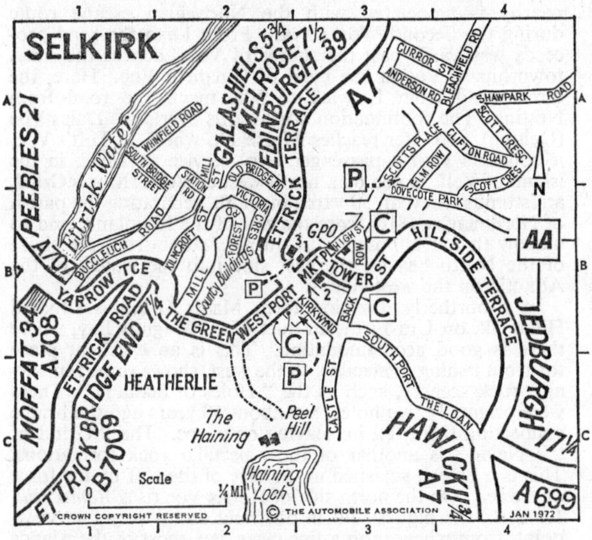

Helliwell's Close, 17th cent., now Information Centre 1 (B3)
Town Hall 2 (B3) Town Museum and Library 3 (B2)

Walter Scott, who was once Sheriff of the county, and to Mungo Park, the eminent explorer. Another monument recalls the tragic news of Flodden Field. In the Town Museum is kept a **flag,** said to have been captured at Flodden, and there are relics of James Hogg, the "Ettrick Shepherd," Mungo Park and Andrew Lang, the writer. Burns lodged at the former *Forest* Inn, now marked by a tablet, in the West Port. Selkirk was once famous for its "Sutors" or shoemakers. South of the town stands *The Haining* (1794-1819), a Palladian house, near which is the shell of an earlier mansion, burnt in 1944. To the south-west of Selkirk, where the Ettrick and Yarrow Waters meet, is *Philiphaugh,* a mansion with fine gardens, recalling the battle, fought in 1645, when Leslie and the Covenanters defeated Montrose. A monument now commemorates the event. (See **Traquair.**) Between the two rivers is *Carterhaugh,* the scene of the ballad of "Tamlane," Nearby, to the north-west, is the park of *Bowhill,* a fine house, enlarged by Sir Charles Barry in the 19th cent., and containing notable portraits. See **Bowden, Broadmeadows** and **Ettrick Bridge End.** *Iter. 11, 13, 14, 41, 42, 43, 46.*

SETON, East Lothian. Map 10, **NT 4 7.** There stood here formerly *Seton Palace,* one of the most magnificent of Scottish buildings, which was replaced by *Seton Castle,* by Robert Adam, dating from 1790. Mary, Queen of Scots is associated with Seton, having been here in 1566, with Darnley, after the murder of Rizzio, and again in 1567, with Bothwell, after Darnley had been murdered. In the grounds of the Castle is the late 14th cent. unfinished Collegiate Church of *Seton* (A.M.), noted for its fine vaulted chancel and apse, with good window tracery. There are also splendid tombs and a good example of a piscina. A little to the north of Seton lie the twin fishing-villages of Port Seton and *Cockenzie* (*q.v.*). *Iter. 2, 37.*

SHADER, Isle of Lewis, Ross and Cromarty. Map 32, **NB 3 5.** See **Hebrides, Outer** (Lewis). *Iter.* 260.

SHAMBELLIE WOOD, Kirkcudbright. Map 3, **NX 9 6.** See **New Abbey.**

SHANDWICK, Ross and Cromarty. Map 31, **NH 8 7.** Here, in a field west of the road, is a carved Celtic Stone.

SHANKEND, Roxburgh. Map 5, **NT 5 0.** On the Slitrig Water, in a setting of Lowland hills. To the south, the line of the ancient "Catrail," or Picts' Ditch crosses the road which leads towards Liddesdale and the English border. The summit of this road is reached at Limekiln Edge, **3 m. S.** of Shankend, at an altitude of about 1,200 ft., overlooked to the west by the strangely-shaped *Maiden Paps,* 1,677 ft. The Catrail keeps to the north of the Paps, and then turns northwards, another stretch being visible in the vicinity of *Galashiels* (*q.v.*). *Iter. 31.*

SHAWHEAD, Kirkcudbright. Map 3, **NX 8 7.** **E.C.** Sat. On the slopes of the hills to the north-west, at *Glenkiln,* are placed a number of modern bronzes by Henry Moore, a head by Rodin, and other carvings.

SHEIGRA, Sutherland. Map 18, **NC 1 6.** See **Kinlochbervie.** *Iter. 229.*

SHERIFFMUIR, Perth. Map 16, **NN 8 0.** See **Dunblane.**

SHETLAND ISLANDS. Map 33. Known locally as *Shetland,* these consist in all of some 100 islands, of which less than 20 are inhabited, and form the most northerly portion of the United Kingdom. By far the largest of these is *Mainland,* on which stands **Lerwick,** the only important town. The islands lie about 60 miles from Orkney and are remarkable for their prehistoric antiquities and for their splendid cliff and sea loch scenery, the local name for the latter being "voes." Knitting, fishing and crofting are the principal industries, Shetland hosiery being known the world over. The land is treeless and the summer is short, but during June and part of July the "Simmer dim" as it is called gives nights with little or no darkness, and the beauty of a "Simmer dim" night has to be seen to be realised. The sea trout fishing in the islands is particularly good and in many places the fishing is free. Shetland wool has a world-wide reputation and Shetland ponies are equally well known. Many of the roads on the Mainland are excellent, but in the lesser islands they range from middling to poor. The Picts are supposed to have been the first colonizers of Shetland and were succeeded by the Norsemen. In 1468, however, when Margaret, daughter of Christian the First, King of Denmark, Sweden and Norway, married James the Third, King of Scotland, Christian by the marriage contract agreed to pay 60,000 florins as her dowry. He pledged the Orkney islands for 50,000 and agreed to pay the balance before Margaret left for Scotland, but could only produce 2,000, and pledged Shetland for the remaining sum due, 8,000 florins. There are air services from the principal Scottish towns to Sumburgh airport on Mainland. Steamer services link Lerwick with Aberdeen, Leith and Orkney (Kirkwall). *Iter. 267 to 270.*

MAINLAND.

This island, which is the most southerly of the Shetland group, has on its eastern shore the capital of the islands, **Lerwick** (5,933. SB. **E.C.** Wed.) standing on Bressay Sound. It is the most northerly town in Britain and is a busy fishing port. King Haco of Norway visited the harbour when on his way to the battle of Largs in 1263. In Lerwick there is celebrated the picturesque festival of 'Up Helly A' every year on the last Tuesday in January. This is a Norse Festival in which a Viking ship is escorted round the town by torch bearers and afterwards burnt. The Festival is supposed to celebrate the return of the sun. In Charles the Second's time, *Fort Charlotte* (A.M.), overlooking the town, was built, but in a subsequent Dutch war it was burnt by a

Dutch frigate together with some of the best houses in the place. Repaired in George the Third's time, it was until recent years used as a headquarters for the Royal Naval Reserve who drilled there in the winter time. After being repaired it took its name from George the Third's Queen. There is a narrow paved street running the length of the old town and narrow "closes" run up to the top of the hill. At the south end of the town a number of the houses are built into the sea. These were in earlier days known as "lodberries," or loading piers, being used extensively before the harbour works were made. Lerwick possesses a fine Town Hall in which there are good stained glass windows.

On the Ward of **Bressay,** which lies across Bressay Sound, there is a fine viewpoint, and near Bard Head, in the extreme south, is the stalactite Cave of the Bard, noted for its echo. The Lerwick GOLF course is at **Bressay** (350). A visit to the island of **Noss,** now a Nature Reserve, should certainly be undertaken to view the myriads of birds which frequent its great cliffs.

A road to Dunrossness, the most southerly parish in Shetland, proceeds southwards from Lerwick, and a short distance from the town *Clickhimin* Loch is passed, at which there is a fine specimen of a "Pictish" broch (A.M.). The road follows the east coast and passes **Sandwick** (761), which is situated on Mousa Sound. Here, at Leebotten, a boat may be hired to convey tourists to the island of *Mousa,* where the best extant specimen of a "Pictish" broch (A.M.) can be examined.

Some eight miles farther to the south is **Dunrossness** (2050), the district so frequently mentioned in Sir Walter Scott's novel "The Pirate" as the abode of Norna of Fitful Head. Here is also **Jarlshof,** the residence of Mr. Basil Mertoun. This place has now acquired considerably more fame than it originally had as a dwelling as being the site of very important archaeological discoveries from the Bronze and Iron age periods and also a Viking age house (A.M.). North of Jarlshof, between the West Voe of Sumburgh and the Pool of Virkie, is **Sumburgh** airport. The main road ends near Jarlshof, but a secondary one leads to Sumburgh lighthouse, where a view of the dangerous "Roost" or current which sometimes upsets seaborne passengers can be obtained. Returning to Dunrossness, a detour can be made by branching off at the Parish Church and continuing in a south-westerly direction to Quendale school, then continuing round the west side of Loch Spiggie to **Scousburgh,** where there are two hotels. Continuing northwards past St. Ninian's Bay and Island, this road later joins the main road at Channerwick. Those who are fond of hill-climbing on foot will have ample opportunity of doing so by tackling *Fitful Head,* 928 feet high, beyond Quendale Bay, away to the north-west, the view from the top being ample reward for the toil involved.

Scalloway, situated some 6½ miles west of Lerwick, is the ancient capital of the islands and seat of the justiciary. It lies at the head of Clift Sound, which is sheltered by the islands of Trondra, Papa and Oxna. Farther down the Sound lie East and West Burra. In this latter isle there was an ancient Christian Church where early Christian sculptured stones have been discovered. *Scalloway Castle* (A.M.), built about 1600 by the notorious Earl Patrick Stewart, is a conspicuous landmark, and to the west of the village lies the Gallows Hill, where witches were formerly burnt. To the north of Scalloway, in the fertile valley of **Tingwall** (1,150), are the lochs of Asta and Tingwall, both good trout fishing lochs. In the loch of Tingwall there is a small hold, or islet, at one time reached by stepping stones, where the Island Parliament met. The loch has been lowered and the stepping-stones are no longer required. Proceeding northwards and westwards, Weisdale Voe is encircled, and the road climbs southwards until the top of the hill is reached, with a fine view at the Scord of Sound.

At **Twatt** a road turns south to *Reawick,* with a fine sandy bay. Farther west from Twatt and just beyond the Bridge of Walls is the village of **Walls** (650), on Vaila Sound. This is the port for the Foula mail boat. *Foula,* with a cliff 1,220 ft. high, is a home of the Great Skua, and here the film "The Edge of the World" was made in 1938. To the north-west of Walls is the district of **Sandness,** a part of the parish of Walls, and across the Sound of Papa is the island of *Papa Stour.* The caves in the island have been described by Dr. Macculloch, a well-known authority, as being the best in Britain. Out at sea from Papa Stour lie the dangerous "Vee Skerries," on which many ships have been wrecked. The islands are the haunt of large flocks of seals.

The main road leading to the North Mainland from Lerwick goes along the loch of Girlsta, to the north-east of which lies the **Nesting** (400) peninsula looking seawards to **Whalsay** (950) island. At South Nesting Bay, a road turns off inland to Dury and **Laxo,** where a gated and switchback branch road goes northwards, passing near Vidlin to reach *Lunna,* with its interesting, ancient church. The old mansion nearby is associated with the Norwegian escape route during the Second World War. From Laxo the road proceeds westwards past the shores of Voe Loch to the small township of **Voe** at the head of Olnafirth Voe. Here, the direct road from Lerwick to Voe meets the road from Nesting. The continuation northwards overlooks Dales Voe (Delting), and later reaches **Mossbank,** where, at Toft's Voe, it connects with a passenger ferry service to *Ulsta,* in the island of Yell. Some **6 m.** north-west of Voe is **Mavis Grind,** an isthmus less than 50 yards in width, separating the parish of **Northmavine** (816) from the rest of the Mainland, and so narrow that it is possible to throw a stone from the shore of the North Sea on the east side into the waters of the Atlantic on the west side.

In a northerly direction from Mavis Grind is situated **Hillswick,** on Ura Firth, an inlet of St. Magnus Bay, where there is good accommodation. This is an excellent place for trout fishing. **Eshaness,** to the west, shows some remarkable rock scenery, such as the "Holes of Scraada." There were originally two holes, but about 50 years ago the bridge connecting them fell in, leaving only one. The "Grind of the Navir" is another of these peculiar rock formations. This is a breach smashed in the face of the cliff by the force of the sea. On the north side of Ronas Voe rises *Ronas Hill,* 1,475 ft., the highest hill in Shetland and a very fine viewpoint, from whence, on a fine clear day, most of the islands can be seen. To the east and north-east lie the townships of Collafirth and Burravoe. The road which passes the heads of the inlets on which they lie terminates at **Isbister,** in North Roe. Still farther north is Fethaland, the northernmost point of the Mainland.

YELL. 1,152.

This island is separated from the Mainland by Yell Sound, and is almost cut in two by Whalefirth on the west side and Raefirth or Mid Yell Voe, as it is sometimes called, on the east side. In the north of Yell is Gloup Voe, almost like a miniature Norwegian fjord. Off the east coast of Yell lies the island of *Fetlar* (127), noted for the breeding of Shetland ponies. Passenger ferries connect *Ulsta* with Toft's Voe (*Mossbank*) in the Mainland and also *Gutcher* with the island of **Unst** at *Belmont.* The mail and passenger steamer "*Earl of Zetland*" from Lerwick calls at *Burravoe, Mid Yell,* to the west of Hascosay, and *Cullivoe,* which are all on the east side of the island.

UNST. 1,151.

The most northerly of the Shetland Islands and scenically and mineralogically perhaps the most interesting. This island is separated from Yell by Blue Mull Sound, access being by passenger ferry from *Gutcher* in Yell. Here, for many years, was the home of the rare Great Skua, which was preserved from extinction by the endeavours of the Edmonstons, the principal proprietors of the island. At the south-east end of the island is *Muness Castle,* built in 1598, but now a ruin. Midway on the isle is the principal port, *Baltasound,* once a very busy herring fishing port, and farther north is situated *Haroldswick,* which has the most northerly post office in Great Britain. Burrafirth, a large sea loch opening to the north, has some very fine caves, and the *Hermaness* district, on its western shores, is now a National Nature Reserve. The Great Skua breeds here, and many other species of birds breed on the sea cliffs. Out at sea is the Mukkle Flugga lighthouse, on its lonely rock, Great Britain's most northerly inhabited place. The mail steamer

The 45-foot high broch of Mousa, the only one that survives to approximately its original height. It stands on the island of Mousa, reached by boat from Leebotten, on the Sound of Mousa, near Sandwick

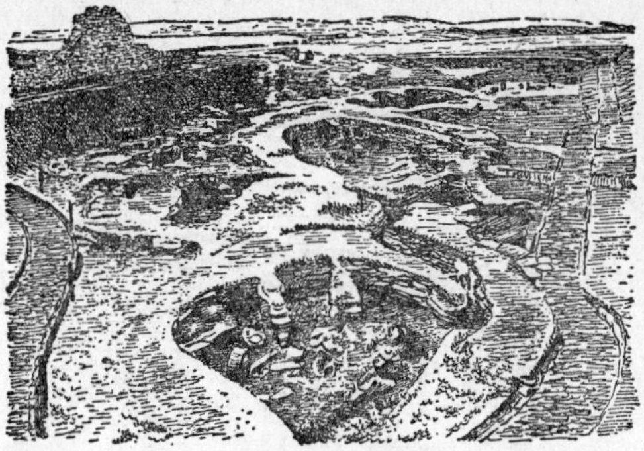

The Bronze Age excavations at Jarlshof, which lie near the airfield at Sumburgh, in the southern extremity of the Mainland. The nearby 16th cent. laird's house has associations with Sir Walter Scott's '*The Pirate*'

The lighthouse at Sumburgh Head, in the extreme south of the Mainland. It was erected by Robert Stephenson in 1820. A dangerous current off-shore at this point is known as the 'Roost'

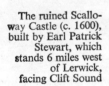

The ruined Scalloway Castle (c. 1600), built by Earl Patrick Stewart, which stands 6 miles west of Lerwick, facing Clift Sound

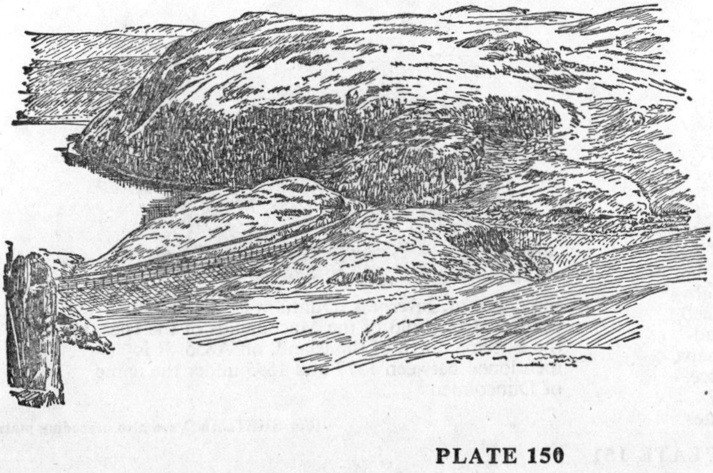

The 50-yard wide isthmus of Mavis Grind, from which a stone can be thrown from the waters of the Atlantic Ocean into those of the North Sea. It lies on A970, some 6 miles north-west of Voe, on Olna Firth

[For SHETLAND see also following plate

Shetland Islands. The broch of Clickhimin, and its secondary buildings, on Clickhimin Loch to the south-west of Lerwick, off A970

Skelmorlie, Ayr. The entrance door of the partly 16th century Skelmorlie Castle, which stands a mile to the south, on A78

Skipness, Argyll. The ruined Castle. Its red sandstone quoins may have been brought from the island of Arran across the narrow Kilbrennan Sound

Skirling, Peebles. Examples of curious wrought-iron work incorporating painted birds and animals, which are a feature of this village

Skye, Isle of, Inverness. The 2,537-foot high Red Cuillin hill of Glamaig, seen from A850, at the head of Loch Ainort, between Broadford and Sligachan. In 1899, Haskabir Thapa, a Gurkha visiting Skye with General Bruce, of Himalayan fame, climbed the hill in 37 minutes and made the descent in 18 minutes

Skye, Isle of, Inverness. Duntulm Castle, a 15th century stronghold of the Macdonalds of the Isles, in the extreme north of the island, off A855. It is mentioned between 1577 and 1595 under the name of Duncolmen

[For **SHETLAND** see also preceding plate

" *Earl of Zetland* " calls at *Uyeasound* on the south side and at *Baltasound* on the east side of the island. Out to sea from Uyeasound is the small island of *Haaf Gruney*, a National Nature Reserve. A new airfield will be the most northerly in Britain. The Artic Circle is only some 300 miles distant.

FAIR ISLE (N.T. Scot.).
This small and lonely island is situated half-way between Orkney and Shetland. There are two lighthouses on it, and a bird-watching station, which was founded in 1948. A Spanish Armada ship was wrecked here in 1588. The female inhabitants of the isle are mostly employed in making the variegated woollen knitwear famous all over the world under the name of Fair Isle hosiery.

SHETTLESTON, Lanark. Map 8, **NS 6 6.**
A town engaged in the coal and iron industry. *Iter. 16.*

SHIEL BRIDGE, Ross and Cromarty. Map 24, **NG 9 1.**
Most beautifully situated at the head of the lovely sea loch of *Loch Duich* (*q.v.*), near the clachan of *Invershiel*, and in the heart of the 15,000-acre *Kintail* (*q.v.*) estate (N.T. Scot.). This includes *Ben Attow*, 3,383 ft., and the famous *Five Sisters of Kintail*, dominated by *Scour Ouran*, 3,505 ft. The road descending from the grand defile of *Glen Shiel* (*q.v.*), between the Five Sisters, to the east, and *The Saddle*, 3,317 ft., to the west, divides here, the eastern fork continuing round Loch Duich towards *Dornie* (*q.v.*), and the western fork climbing the well-known pass of *Mam Rattachan* (*q.v.*) on its way to *Glenelg* (*q.v.*). Another road leaves the Mam Rattachan road, and continues along the western shore of Loch Duich, passing Glen Shiel Church on its way to *Totaig*, facing *Ardelve* (*q.v.*), to which it is linked by a passenger ferry. See **Croe Bridge** and **Inverinate.** *Iter. 207, 220.*

SHIELDAIG, Ross and Cromarty. Map 22, **NG 8 5.**
A little crofting and fishing village, picturesquely situated on Loch Shieldaig, an inlet of Loch Torridon. Beyond, to the north-east, rise the great Torridon sandstone peaks of *Ben Alligin*, 3,232 ft., *Beinn Dearg*, 2,995 ft. and, finest of all, *Liathach*, 3,456 ft. A new road, providing magnificent views, has been built to link with *Torridon* (*q.v.*), at the head of the loch, passing near the Falls of Balgy and the head of Loch Damh. To the south of the road rises the fine peak of *Ben Damh*, 2,958 ft., and also the cone of *Meall a'Chinn Deirg*, 3,060 ft. A walkers' track goes westwards from Shieldaig, and follows the coast to *Applecross* (*q.v.*), giving magnificent views over the Inner Sound towards the islands of Raasay and Skye. The road leading south-eastwards to *Tornapress* (*q.v.*) climbs to over 400 ft. before descending to Loch Coultrie, with views of Coir Each and Coire na Poite, two of the wild corries of *Beinn Bhan*, 2,936 ft., the highest of the Applecross hills, showing characteristic horizontal bands of red Torridon sandstone. *Iter. 223.*

SHOTTS, Lanark. Map 9, **NS 8 6.**
GOLF. See **Kirk o'Shotts** and **Newmains.**

SILVERBURN, Midlothian. Map 9, **NT 2 6.**
A *Pentland* hills hamlet, at the foot of *Scald Law*, 1,898 ft., the highest point in the range, above the picturesque Loganlee reservoir. It can be climbed from here. *Iter. 25.*

SKARA BRAE, Orkney. Map 33, **HY 2 1.**
See **Orkney Islands** (Mainland). *Iter. 264.*

SKEABOST BRIDGE, Isle of Skye, Inverness.
Map 22, **NG 4 4.**
Spans the River Snizort, where it flows into one of the inlets of Loch Snizort Beag. There is a picturesque old churchyard. *Iter. 255.*

SKELMORLIE, Ayr. 1,327. Map 8, **NS 1 6.**
A Firth of Clyde resort, linked to *Wemyss Bay* (*q.v.*), having a fine beach, and giving views across the Firth to Toward Point and westwards to the island of Bute. In the waters of the Firth, opposite Skelmorlie, is a " Measured Mile " where smaller vessels are tested for speed. **1½ m. S.,** on the coast road to *Largs* (*q.v.*), is *Skelmorlie Castle*, parts of which date back to 1502. See **Corrie.** *Iter. 66, 88.*

SKENE, Aberdeen. 2,138 with Echt. Map 27, **NJ 8 0.**
E.C. Wed. North-west of the village, off the Alford road, is the little Loch of Skene. See **Dunecht.** *Iter. 176.*

SKERRAY, Sutherland. Map 28, **NC 6 6.**
A crofting township, with a pier and a sandy bay, looking towards the islands of Roan and Eilean Co'omb.

SKERRYVORE, Argyll. Map 13.
See **Tiree, Isle of.**

SKIBO CASTLE, Sutherland. Map 31, **NH 7 8.**
This impressive modern Castle, built for Andrew Carnegie, is situated just to the south of the Bonar Bridge to Dornoch road, and succeeds a former structure, which was once an episcopal residence. *Iter. 200, 231.*

SKIPNESS, Argyll. Map 7, **NR 8 5.**
Faces the waters of Kilbrennan Sound and the Sound of Bute, from the eastern side of the *Kintyre* (*q.v.*) peninsula, with fine views of the northern half of the island of Arran. There are remains of an ancient Chapel, and also of a large 13th cent. castle, overlooking Skipness Bay. *Iter. 122.*

SKIRLING, Peebles. 263. Map 9, **NT 0 3.**
An attractive village, with a green. It is noted for some curious wrought-iron work and painted animals and birds, which are a local feature, making the village probably unique in Scotland. It was the idea of Lord Carmichael, who also designed his own house here, and died in 1926. The ironwork was carried out by Thomas Hadden of Edinburgh. The former castle was demolished in 1568. *Iter. 35, 53.*

SKYE, ISLE OF, Inverness. 7,772. Maps 22 and 23.
The largest of the Inner Hebrides, known as the " Winged Isle," or " Isle of Mist," and perhaps the most picturesque of all the islands lying off the Scottish mainland. *Skye* is most famous for its range of jagged black mountains, known as the *Coolins*, or *Cuillin*, which provide the most sensational rock scenery in the British Isles. The island is 50 miles long and over 600 square miles in area, and is deeply indented by sea lochs at many points, being thus broken up into a series of individual peninsulas. All these are dominated from far or near by the serrated tops of the Coolins, while no part of the island is more than about 5 miles from the sea. The chief places of interest are linked by fairly good roads, while others are narrow, hilly and less well-surfaced, many being provided with passing-places. Some 165 miles of road fall within the Class ' A ' category. The mild and misty climate gives rise often to weather effects of unique beauty. Crofting and fishing are the main local industries. The name of Prince Charles Edward is inseparably linked with the island, notably in connection with the heroic exploits of his intrepid helper Flora Macdonald, who is buried at *Kilmuir*. In 1773, Dr. Johnson and Boswell paid their memorable visit to Skye, and since that time many thousands of tourists have delighted in the splendour of mountain, lock and coast scenery, which is unsurpassed in Scotland. The seaboard of the island is largely rocky, and bathing is generally from stones or gravel. Some of the finest cliff scenery lies in the Duirinish district, west of Dunvegan, but is only accessible on foot. Among the most notable sights of Skye are the wild and beautiful *Lochs Coruisk* and *Scavaig* in the *Coolins*; the fantastic rock towers of the *Quiraing* near *Staffin*, in the Trotternish peninsula; the famous castle of *Dunvegan*; and the magnificent panoramic view of the *Coolins* rising beyond *Loch Scavaig* as seen from above *Elgol*. The island is most easily accessible for motorists by way of *Kyle of Lochalsh* or *Mallaig* (both *q.v.*), the ferry from the former crossing the narrow strait of Kyle Akin to *Kyleakin*. All places of interest in Skye are described under their own separate headings and the most noteworthy are indexed below. See **Armadale, Broadford, Coolins, Dunvegan, Elgol, Flodigarry, Glenbrittle, Kilmuir, Kyleakin, Kylerhea, Loch Coruisk, Loch Scavaig, Portree, Quiraing, Storr** and **Uig.** *Iter. 251 to 255.*

SLAMANNAN, Stirling. 3,311. Map 9, **NS 8 7.**
A village on the River Avon, with the Black Loch to the south.

SLIDDERY, Isle of Arran, Bute. Map 7, **NR 9 2.** Lies near the southern coastline, at the foot of Glen Scorrodale. *Iter. 242.*

SLIGACHAN, Isle of Skye, Inverness. Map 23, **NG 4 2.** Situated near the head of Loch Sligachan, on the river of that name, and at the northern extremity of the boggy Glen Sligachan, which extends southwards into the fastnesses of the black *Coolins* (*q.v.*). *Sligachan* is a resort of anglers, and is, above all, famous among mountaineers, who from here can climb, among other notable hills, *Sgurr nan Gillean,* 3,167 ft., the great pinnacled Cuillin peak which rises majestically almost directly above the village, to the south. The path down Glen Sligachan gives access to various well-known rock peaks in the range. Farther down the glen, a long and poorly-defined path over the Drumhain ridge leads to the spectacular *Loch Coruisk* (*q.v.*) in its deep basin below the Coolins. *Bruach na Frithe,* 3,143 ft., a magnificent viewpoint, and comparatively easy to climb, is best approached over the Bealach a'Mhaim, south-west of Sligachan. Below the peak lies the gloomy Harta Corrie, in which the Bloody Stone commemorates the final clan battle between the Macdonalds and Macleods, fought in 1601. To the east of Sligachan, in Lord Macdonald's Forest, are the rounded, red granite peaks of the Red Coolins, or Red Hills, among them *Glamaig,* 2,537 ft. and *Marsco,* 2,414 ft., forming a striking contrast to the precipitous Black Coolins. Two roads diverge from Sligachan away from the loch, that to the north leading through Glen Varragill to *Portree* (*q.v.*), and that to the west proceeding through Glen Drynoch towards Loch Harport. This latter road continues thence towards the Duirinish and Vaternish peninsulas of the island, between which lies the famous castle of *Dunvegan* (*q.v.*). Nearing Loch Harport, a rough and narrow road branches southwards, giving access to *Glenbrittle* (*q.v.*), a well-known climbers' rendezvous in the southern Coolins. The road leading alongside Loch Sligachan from Sligachan follows the coast, and later rounds the head of Loch Ainort, on the way to *Dunan* and *Broadford* (both *q.v.*), providing fine views, especially towards the islands of Raasay and Scalpay. See **Bracadale, Elgol** and **Talisker.** *Iter. 251, 252, 253, 255.*

SLOCHD SUMMIT, Inverness. Map 25, **NH 8 2.** The highest point on the main road linking Strath Spey with Inverness and the north, a height of 1,332 ft. being reached, where both road and railway traverse the lonely Slochd Mor gorge. *Iter. 140, 150, 195.*

SLUG ROAD, Kincardine. Map 21, **NO 7 9.** See **Banchory** and **Stonehaven.** *Iter. 190, 191.*

SMA' GLEN, Perth. Map 16, **NN 8 2 and 9 2.** This beautiful, rocky glen, which is situated on the road linking Crieff with Dunkeld, is threaded by the River Almond. It forms one of the loveliest sights in the Perthshire hills, which rise to more than 2 000 ft. on both sides of the heatherclad glen. The road was made originally by General Wade, in 1730. Overlooking the glen, on the eastern side, is *Dun Mor,* 1,520 ft., surmounted by a partly vitrified hill-fort. Below it, between the road and the river, is *Ossian's Stone,* which was moved from its original site by Wade's soldiers, and has been celebrated in verse by Wordsworth. At the northern extremity of the Sma' Glen, at *Newton Bridge* (*q.v.*), the Almond joins the road, from its journey through the upper reaches of Glen Almond, surrounded by lonely hills, dominated by *Ben Chonzie,* 3,048 ft. See **Gilmerton** (Perth) and **Methven.** *Iter. 89, 140, 141, 147.*

SMAILHOLM, Roxburgh. 382. Map 10, **NT 6 3.** Near the church is *Smailholm House,* dating from 1707. To the south-west stands *Smailholm Tower* (A.M.), probably of 16th cent. date, in a romantic and wild situation on a rocky knoll, with fine views all round, especially towards the triple-peaked *Eildon* hills. The land was acquired in the 17th cent. by the Scotts of *Harden* near *Hawick* (*q.v.*), and Sir Walter himself spent some of his childhood years here at the nearby farm of *Sandyknowe* (*q.v.*). Scott later brought Smailholm into the Introduction to the Third Canto of "Marmion," and it also forms the scene of his ballad "Eve of St. John." On *Brotherstone Hill* are the ancient "Brothers' Stones" and the "Cow Stone." *Iter. 7.*

SMOO CAVE, Sutherland. Map 28, **NC 4 6.** A well-known cave, on the wild northern coast of Sutherland, situated in a deep cove in the cliffs, and extending beneath the road. It consists of three chambers, the outermost, which is accessible, being 33 ft. high, 203 ft. long and 130 ft. broad. Sir Walter Scott visited the cave in 1814 and admired it greatly. The name Smoo may be derived from 'smjuga,' a rock. *Iter. 225.*

SNIZORT, Isle of Skye, Inverness. 1,018. Map 22, **NG 4 5.** On Loch Snizort Beag, an inlet of the larger Loch Snizort. A little to the south-west of the Church, on the right bank of the River Haultin, is the notable chambered cairn of Cairn Liath. See **Uig** (for *Kingsburgh House*). *Iter. 253, 254.*

SOAY, ISLE OF, Inverness. Map 23, **NG 4 1.** See **Loch Scavaig.**

SOCIETY, West Lothian. Map 17, **NT 0 7.** A quaintly named hamlet, perhaps a corruption of "Sea City," on the shores of the Firth of Forth, near Abercorn.

SOLWAY FIRTH, Dumfries, Kirkcudbright. Map 4, **NY 0 5** etc. The waters of this inlet divide England from Scotland, and the Firth is noted for its rapid tides. *Criffell,* 1,868 ft., dominates the Firth from its position overlooking the Nith estuary, and forms the finest viewpoint for a panoramic view of the Solway, including within its orbit the distant Lake District mountains of Cumberland, to the south.

SORBIE, Wigtown. 1,109. Map 2, **NX 4 4.** To the east stands the ruined *Old Place of Sorbie.* On Garlieston Bay is the small port of *Garlieston* (*q.v.*). *Iter. 82.*

SORN, Ayr. 3,536. Map 8, **NS 5 2.** This attractive village, on the River Ayr, has a 17th cent. Church, on the walls of which still hang the jougs; its lofts are reached by external stairs. *Sorn Castle,* dating partly from 1409 and partly from 1795 to 1805, lies a little to the north-west. Alexander Peden, the preacher, was born, in the early 17th cent., at a lonely farm on the moors to the north, and ended his days as a fugitive in a cave in this same district. See **Denholm.** *Iter. 35.*

SOUTHDEAN, Roxburgh. 319. Map 5, **NT 6 0.** A little to the south of the Parish Church, in which a window recalls James Thomson, the author of "Rule Britannia," flows the Jed Water. On the river is the ruined *Souden Kirk,* where the Scottish leaders gathered in 1388 before the battle of Otterburn. The Redeswire Raid of 1575 took place in this parish. (See **Carter Bar.**) Among relics excavated from the 13th cent. Church is a super-altar only 9¼ inches long, bearing 5 incised crosses. *Souden Law,* rising above the river, is crowned by a hill-fort, and there are numerous other prehistoric remains in the vicinity. To the south is the long line of the *Cheviots,* dominated by *Peel Fell,* 1,975 ft. and *Carter Fell,* 1,815 ft. *Iter. 44.*

SOUTHEND, Argyll. 488. Map 6, **NR 6 0.** GOLF. A small resort, with fine seaward views over the North Channel to the coast of Northern Ireland. Off-shore, and separated by the Sanda Sound, lies the small island of Sanda. It is traditionally believed that St. Columba first set foot on Scottish soil near Southend. The narrow road leading westwards to the *Mull of Kintyre* (*q.v.*) passes, within a short distance, the slight remains of *Dunaverty Castle,*

Sma' Glen, Perth. 'Ossian's Stone,' which may have marked his grave, lying between the road and the River Almond. Wordsworth has described it in verse. The stone has been moved from its original site

Smoo Cave, Sutherland. The entrance to the famous cave, one of the three chambers of which is accessible. It is situated east of Durness, off A838

Smailholm, Roxburgh. The 16th century Smailholm Tower, near which Sir Walter Scott spent part of his childhood. He last came here in 1831, with the painter Turner, who made a sketch of the building

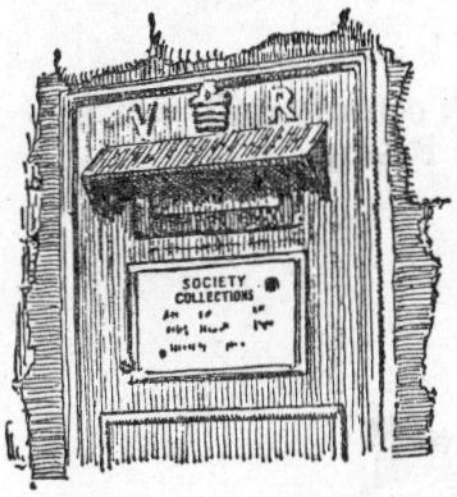

Society, West Lothian. A rare example of a VR letterbox of Queen Victoria's time. The curious name of this tiny village may be a corruption of 'Sea City'

Solway Firth, Dumfries; Kirkcudbright. The historic 7-foot high Lochmaben Stone, which weighs 10 tons. It stands across fields to the south of Gretna, near the Dumfriesshire shores of the Firth, off an unclassified road

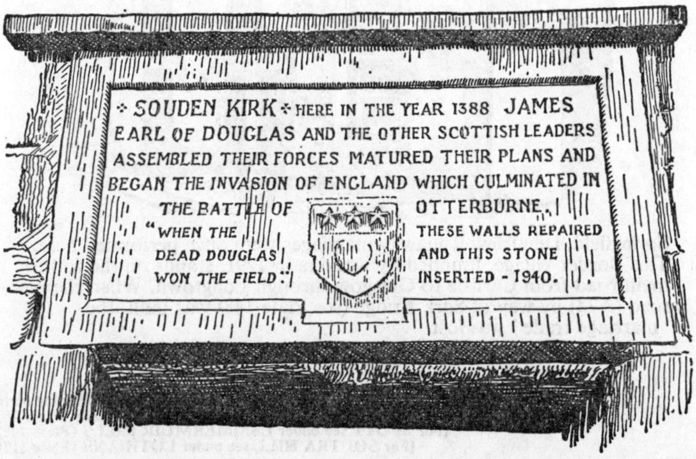

· SOUDEN KIRK · HERE IN THE YEAR 1388 JAMES
EARL OF DOUGLAS AND THE OTHER SCOTTISH LEADERS
ASSEMBLED THEIR FORCES MATURED THEIR PLANS AND
BEGAN THE INVASION OF ENGLAND WHICH CULMINATED IN
THE BATTLE OF OTTERBURNE.
"WHEN THE DEAD DOUGLAS WON THE FIELD".
THESE WALLS REPAIRED AND THIS STONE INSERTED - 1940.

Southdean, Roxburgh. The tablet on the ruined Souden Kirk, near the Jed Water, where the Scottish leaders gathered in 1388 before invading England

[For SOUTHEND see following plate
[For SLOCHD SUMMIT see Plate 174
[For SORN see Plate 172

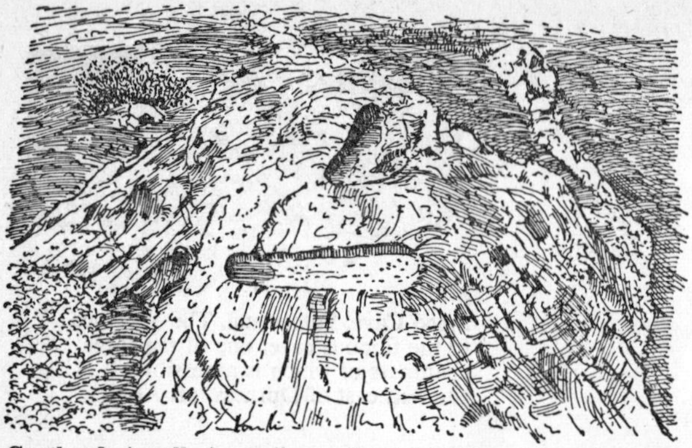

Southend, Argyll. According to local legend these are the footprints of St. Columba, who landed at this point. They are situated near Dunaverty Castle, to the west, off B842

Southerness, Kirkcudbright. The disused lighthouse at Southerness Point. An older name for the village was Satterness

Spean Bridge, Inverness. The Commando Memorial, designed by Scott Sutherland in 1952. They trained in this district during the Second World War. It stands to the north-west, in the angle between A82 and B8004

Spinningdale, Sutherland. The remains of the 18th century mill, which was erected to relieve poverty following the 1745 Rising

Spittal of Glenshee, Perth. A memorial Cross by A93, near Glenshee post office, in memory of an American girl killed here in 1906, when the horse pulling her coach bolted. The original Cross was replaced by her brother 41 years later

Springfield, Dumfries. Runaway marriages were once performed here. This Border village, founded by weavers in 1791, stands on the former main road from Carlisle to Glasgow through Longtown. When the new road (A74) by way of Sark Bridge (see Plate 148) was built, the 'marriage trade' was lost

[For SPYNIE PALACE see following plate
[For SPITTAL OF GLENSHEE see also under GRAMPIANS (Plate 78)
[For SPOTT see under LAMMERMUIR HILLS (Plate 105)
[For SOUTRA HILL see under LOTHIANS (Plate 117)

where, in 1647, the garrison, to the number of some 300, were put to death by the Covenanters under General Leslie. In 1306, Robert Bruce spent several nights here on his way to Ireland. To the north, the road to *Campbeltown* (*q.v.*) traverses the Conie Glen, and a branch road leads first westwards and then north-westwards to terminate at the head of Glen Breakerie, from which a track leads to the coast. Here, under the slopes of *Cnoc Moy*, 1,426 ft., are caves containing stalactites. See **Machrihanish.** *Iter. 123.*

SOUTHERNESS, Kirkcudbright. Map 3, **NX 9 5.** GOLF. A pleasant little resort, also known as *Satterness*, situated off the main road, on a rocky piece of coast, with a disused lighthouse standing on Southerness Point, overlooking Gillfoot Bay, an inlet of the Solway Firth. There are views towards the distant Lake District mountains. *Criffell*, 1,866 ft., rises away to the north, beyond the village of *Kirkbean* (*q.v.*). *Iter. 73.*

SOUTH KESSOCK, Inverness. Map 25, **NH 6 4.** Faces the narrows which divide the waters of the Beauly Firth from those of the Inner Moray Firth. A car ferry connects with *North Kessock* (*q.v.*) on the opposite shore. South Kessock stands on the estuary of the River Ness, and is less than two miles distant from the Highland town of *Inverness* (*q.v.*). *Iter. 202, 203.*

SOUTH NESTING BAY, Shetland. Map 33, **HU 4 5.** *Iter. 270.*

SOUTH QUEENSFERRY, West Lothian. Map 17, **NT 1 7.** See **Queensferry, South.**

SOUTH RONALDSAY, ISLE OF, Orkney. Map 33, **ND 4 8.** See **Orkney Islands** (South Ronaldsay). *Iter. 266.*

SOUTH UIST, ISLE OF, Inverness. Map 32, **NF 7 2** etc. See **Hebrides, Outer** (South Uist). *Iter. 262.*

SOUTHWICK, Kirkcudbright. Map 3, **NX 9 5.** Pleasantly situated off the main road, and on the Southwick Water, which flows into the Solway Firth, with the Mersehead and Barnhourie Sands situated off-shore. In the background, to the north-east, rises *Criffell*, 1,866 ft., a fine viewpoint, with its spur of *Boreland Hill*, 1,632 ft., in the foreground. *Iter. 72, 73.*

SOUTRA HILL, Berwick; East Lothian; Midlothian. Map 10, **NT 4 5.** This well-known viewpoint, at a height of 1,131 ft., on the road leading south-eastwards from Edinburgh towards Lauder, is situated near the meeting point of Berwick, East Lothian and Midlothian. The *Moorfoot* hills rise away to the south-west, while the main ridge of the *Lammermuirs*, their slopes largely given over to sheep, extends north-eastwards towards the distant coast in the neighbourhood of *Cockburnspath* (*q.v.*). There are prehistoric remains in the vicinity of Soutra Hill, and the road itself is on the line of an ancient Pilgrims' Way. This is recalled by the *Soutra Aisle*, the remains of a hospice, or chapel, possibly of 15th cent. date, which stands a little to the south-west, on a lonely moorland road giving access to the valley of the Gala Water. The Romans knew the road across Soutra Hill, and it was used at different times by Edward I, Edward II and James IV of Scotland, among others. The view is very extensive, and stretches from the *Eildon* hills, to the south, away to the *Ochils* beyond the Forth estuary, taking in also *Arthur's Seat*, overlooking the city of Edinburgh. *Iter. 4, 5, 13.*

SPEAN BRIDGE, Inverness. 135. Map 18, **NN 2 8.** E.C. Thurs. GOLF. The bridge, built by Telford, in 1819, spans the turbulent River Spean, which flows through a picturesque reach to enter *Loch Lochy* (*q.v.*) near *Gairlochy* (*q.v.*). About **2 m. W.** on this reach is *High Bridge*, 100 ft. above the gorge, the remains of one of the bridges, built in 1736, on General Wade's road, the line of which deviated from the present road through Spean Bridge. The bridge cost £1,087 6s. 8d. to construct. A preliminary skirmish took place here, in 1745, three days prior to the raising of Prince Charles Edward's standard at *Glenfinnan* (*q.v.*), this being virtually the commencement of the '45. The last repairs to the bridge took place in 1893, but in 1913 part of it collapsed, and nothing has been done to it since. The road leading south-westwards from Spean Bridge towards Fort William crosses an elevated moorland ridge, giving magnificent views of the *Grey Corries*, 3,858 ft., *Aonach Mor*, 3,999 ft., and the great northern corries of distant *Ben Nevis*, 4,406 ft. (*q.v.*), which are usually streaked with snow as late as June, and sometimes right through the summer. A memorial to the Commandos in the Second World War has been erected to the north-west of Spean Bridge. Eastwards extends Glen Spean, which gives access to *Roy Bridge* (*q.v.*), for the famous "Parallel Roads." See **Wade Roads.** *Iter. 143, 208, 210, 220.*

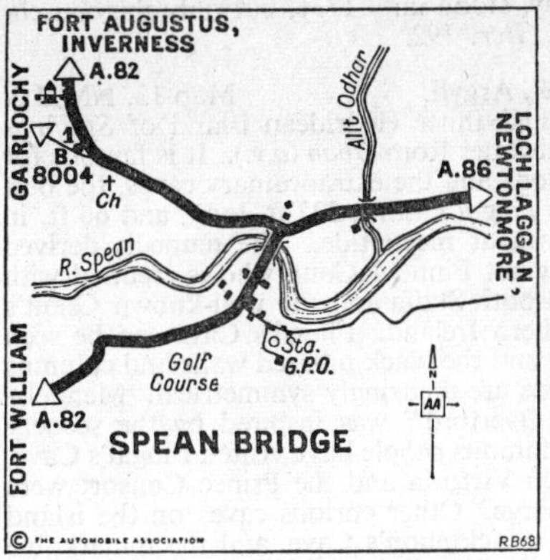

Commando Memorial 1

SPEY BAY, Moray. 200. Map 26, **NJ 3 6.** E.C. Wed. GOLF. A small resort, with a shingle beach, some sand at low ride, and bathing, at the mouth of the Spey, the second-longest river in Scotland, famous for its salmon. The best-known reaches are to the south-west, in the foothills of the Cairngorms, where Speyside, or Strath Spey, is at its best around *Grantown-on-Spey* (*q.v.*) and *Aviemore* (*q.v.*). See **Fochabers.** *Iter. 171, 199.*

SPEYSIDE, Inverness. Map 25, **NH 8 0** and 26, **NJ 1 3** etc. See **Strath Spey.**

SPINNINGDALE, Sutherland. Map 31, **NH 6 8.** On the Dornoch Firth, with the ruins of an 18th cent. mill. See **Creich.** *Iter. 200, 231.*

SPITTAL OF GLENSHEE, Perth. Map 20, **NO 1 6.** See **Glenshee.** *Iter. 141, 152, 160, 167, 168.*

SPOTT, East Lothian. 578 with Stenton. Map 10, **NT 6 7.** In the modern Church is preserved a beautifully-carved early 18th cent. pulpit, with a sounding-board. The jougs still hang near the door, and near the Church gate is an old watch-house. At Spott Loan is a Witch's Stone, recalling the fact that the last witch to be burnt south of the Forth suffered her fate at Spott. In the vicinity there are various prehistoric remains, among them hut circles and cairns.

SPRINGFIELD, Dumfries. Map 4, **NY 3 6.** A village founded by a band of weavers in 1791. Runaway marriages were performed here during the 18th cent. in competition with *Gretna* (*q.v.*). The main Glasgow to Carlisle road formerly went through the village and crossed the River Esk at Longtown before the present A74 road by way of *Sark Bridge* (*q.v.*) was constructed in 1830. *Iter. 51, 67.*

SPRINGHOLM, Kirkcudbright. Map 3, **NX 8 6.** E.C. Wed. See **Kirkpatrick Durham.** *Iter. 26, 70.*

SPYNIE PALACE, Moray. Map 26, **NJ 2 6.** This ruined palace, situated near the shores of the little Loch Spynie, slightly to the east of the Elgin to Lossiemouth road, was formerly the Castle of the Bishops of Moray. The prominent square tower, known as Davie's Tower, dates from c. 1470, and over the main entrance to the courtyard, with its three small towers, are the arms of the early 15th cent. Bishop John Innes. The Church of Spynie, once the

Cathedral of Moray, stood until 1736, but only the churchyard now remains. *Iter. 192.*

STAFFA, ISLE OF, Argyll. Map 13, **NM 3 3.** The tiny, uninhabited Inner Hedridean island of *Staffa* is usually visited by steamer from *Oban* (*q.v.*). It is famous for its basaltic formations and the extraordinary caves, the best known of which is *Fingal's Cave*, 227 ft. long, and 66 ft. in height above the sea at mean tide. The name is derived from the Ossianic giant Finn McCoul, who is credited with the construction of both Staffa and the well-known Giant's Causeway in Northern Ireland. Fingal's Cave can be seen on foot or by boat, and the black pillared walls and columns flanking the aperture are amazingly symmetrical. Mendelssohn's " Hebrides Overture " was inspired by the scenery of the cave. Many famous people have visited Fingal's Cave, and, in 1847, Queen Victoria and the Prince Consort were rowed into it by barge. Other curious caves on the island are the Boat Cave, Mackinnon's Cave, and the remarkable Clam Shell Cave, with its columns suggesting the ribs of an old wooden ship. The last-named is near the usual landing-place, and has in close proximity the Great Causeway, reminiscent of the Giant's Causeway in Northern Ireland. Staffa was introduced to the world, in 1772, by the explorer Sir Joseph Banks, then on his way to Iceland, while Pennant's " Tour in Scotland," written in 1774, provides the earliest description. To the west of Staffa are the tiny *Treshnish* Islands, the most southerly known as the " Dutchman's Cap," from its shape. See **Iona.**

STAFFIN, Isle of Skye, Inverness. Map 22, **NG 4 6.** Faces the sandy Staffin Bay, in the Trotternish peninsula, with Staffin Island off-shore, and has notable cliffs of basalt. A little to the south-east, off the Portree road, is the well-known *Kilt Rock*, best seen from a boat, and farther south still, where the road nears the seashore, the waters of Loch Mealt pour into the sea as a waterfall. The road leading northwards from the village divides into two branches, one continuing along the coast towards *Flodigarry* (*q.v.*), and the other, now under complete reconstruction, narrow and steep, climbing to nearly 900 ft., with a hairpin bend below the fantastic rock masses of the *Quiraing* (*q.v.*). This road provides splendid views of Staffin Bay, on the way to *Uig* (*q.v.*). A hydro-electric scheme, inaugurated in 1952, operates along the road to Portree. *Iter. 254.*

STAIR, Ayr. 5,541 with Ochiltree. Map 8, **NS 4 2.** *Stair House*, a picturesque old building, situated in a bend of the River Ayr, dates from the early 17th cent., and has been modernized. *Iter. 85.*

STANLEY, Perth. 1,930. Map 17, **NO 1 3.** Stands on the River Tay, in the *Strathmore* (*q.v.*) valley. On the river, a little to the north-east, are the Campsie Linn rapids. Off a by-road, **4½ m. N.E.,** near the Tay, are remains of the rectangular enclosure of *Kinclaven Castle*, said to have been destroyed in 1336. *Iter. 148.*

STAXIGOE, Caithness. Map 30, **ND 3 5.** A fishing village having a small harbour, situated on a rocky stretch of coast between the Tails of Elzie and Silkey Head, with the more prominent Noss Head to the north, overlooking Sinclair's Bay. The airport for *Wick* (*q.v.*) lies a little to the south-west of Staxigoe.

STENHOUSEMUIR, Stirling. 7,490. Map 16, **NS 8 8.** See **Falkirk.**

STENNESS, Orkney. Map 33, **HY 3 1.** See **Orkney Islands** (Mainland). *Iter. 263, 264.*

STENTON, East Lothian. 578 with Spott. Map 10, **NT 6 7.** An attractive village, with the 14th cent. Rood well, topped by a cardinal's hat. The medieval Wool Stone, used formerly for the weighing of wool at Stenton Fair, stands on the green. *Biel*, a fine old mansion, now modernized, with 16th cent. terracd gardens, liees to the north-east.

STEPPS, Lanark. 5,244. Map 8, **NS 6 6.** The small Frankfield Loch lies to the south-west. *Iter. 17, 97, 99.*

STEVENSTON, Ayr. 12,050. SB. Map 8, **NS 2 4.** **E.C.** Wed. GOLF. A town of ancient foundation, overlooking Irvine Bay in the Firth of Clyde. There are coal-mines, chemical works, and an explosives factory in the neighbourhood. A yumber of early pumping engines have survived in the district. *Iter. 57, 63, 66, 69, 88.*

STEWARTON, Ayr. 4,490. SB. Map 8, **NS 4 4.** **E.C.** Wed. **M.D.** Thurs. Stands on the Annick Water, and is noted for its woollen mills. See **Kilmaurs.** *Iter. 62.*

STEWARTRY, THE, Kirkcudbright. Map 2, **NX 4 7** and 3, **NX 8 7.** This name is sometimes applied to Kirkcudbright, as an alternative to the title of county. It is derived from the fact that the lordship of the Balliols, when it was taken away from them, was placed under the jurisdiction of a Royal Steward, an office which was held by the family of Maxwell between 1526 and 1747. The Stewartry, together with the adjacent county of Wigtown, comprises the district known as *Galloway* (*q.v.*).

STIRLING, Stirling. 29,769. LB. Map 16, **NS 7 9.** **E.C.** Wed. **M.D.** Thurs. GOLF. A famous old Royal Burgh, known as the " Gateway to the Highlands," and situated on one of the numerous loops of the River Forth. Stirling Bridge spans the river at the north end of the town, and close to it is the Old Bridge (A.M.), dating from c. 1400, and still in use for foot passengers. Remains of the original burgh gate are still to be seen at one end of the structure. This bridge was for centuries of great strategic importance as the sole exit to the north. Until the opening of the new bridge at *Kincardine-on-Forth* (*q.v.*), lower down the Forth, Stirling was the last place where the river could be crossed before the estuary widens. The battle of Stirling Bridge, fought in 1297, in which Wallace defeated the Earl of Surrey, is thought to have taken place near a now-vanished wooden bridge, about a mile upstream.

The history of Stirling is bound up with its great Castle (A.M.), in which several of the early Scottish Kings died. Wallace recaptured the Castle from the English in 1297, but Edward I retook it after a siege in 1304. Later, Stirling became a favourite Royal residence, and within its walls was born James II, in 1430, while both Mary, Queen of Scots and James VI spent some years in the Palace. General Monk took the Castle, in 1651, but Prince Charles Edward failed to capture it in 1746. Stirling Castle stands in a commanding situation, but has long been used as a barracks, though restoration work is in progress. James III built several of the older towers in the 15th cent., and the splendid Renaissance buildings of the Palace date from the following century. The Parliament Hall, 125 ft. long, abuts on the Inner Court, and on the north side of the Court is the Chapel Royal, rebuilt in 1594 by James VI, and preserving early 17th cent. wall-paintings. In the historic, restored Douglas Room are kept various interesting relics. The hereditary keeper of Stirling Castle is the Earl of Mar and Kellie. The Castle is open weekdays, 10 to 4 or 6.45; Sun., 1 to 4. (See note page 98.) The view from the 420-ft. high Queen Victoria's look-out is famous, and extends well into the Highlands. On the Esplanade is a statue of Bruce, and the Ladies' Rock is another good viewpoint, overlooking the King's Knot (A.M.) and King's Garden. Queen Mary's look-out has the inscription: M.R. 1561.

In the town are severai 17th cent. houses; the fine Tolbooth, dating from 1701; the old Mercat Cross, with a modern shaft; and *Darnley's House*, associated with James VI and his son. The uncompleted Renaissance structure known as *Mar's Wark* (A.M.) stands in Broad Street, and dates from 1570, retaining several curious inscriptions. *Argyll's Lodging* (A.M.), one of the most noteworthy of its period in Scotland, was built by the Earl of Stirling in 1630, and for many years was used as a military hospital. The 17th cent. Guildhall, or *Cowane's* Hospital retains old relics and bears a statue of John Cowane, the founder, who

Spynie Palace, Moray. The ruined 15th century Palace, once a castle of the Bishops of Moray. It stands near Loch Spynie, to the east of A941

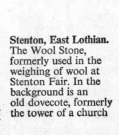

Stenton, East Lothian. The ancient Rood Well, surmounted by a cardinal's hat, and associated with the Abbey at Melrose

Stewartry, Kirkcudbright. Maclellan's Castle, at Kirkcudbright, dating from 1582, and built by Sir Thomas Maclellan of Bombie, a former Provost of the town. The Stewartry is a name applied to the county, recalling its former jurisdiction by a Royal Steward

Stenton, East Lothian. The Wool Stone, formerly used in the weighing of wool at Stenton Fair. In the background is an old dovecote, formerly the tower of a church

Stirling, Stirling. The old Mercat Cross, which has a modern shaft

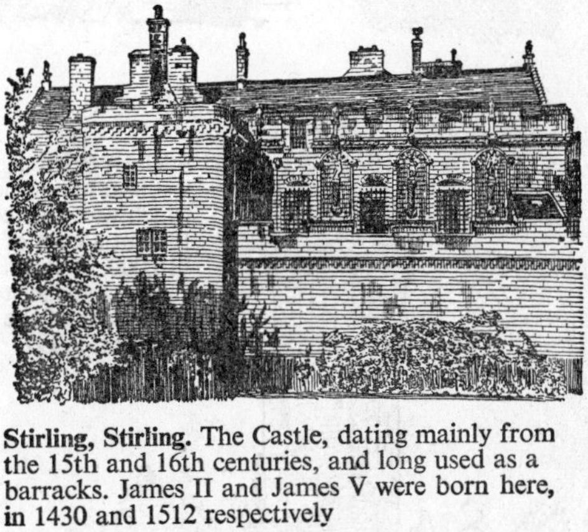

Stirling, Stirling. The Castle, dating mainly from the 15th and 16th centuries, and long used as a barracks. James II and James V were born here, in 1430 and 1512 respectively

[For STIRLING see also following plate

Stirling, Stirling. The 16th or 17th century Darnley's House, perhaps the nursery of James VI and his son Prince Henry, but more probably associated with the Erskines of Gogar. It was reconstructed in 1957

Stirling, Stirling. The Old Bridge of c. 1400, for many years famous as the sole ' Gateway to the Highlands.' One of the arches was blown up in 1745 to prevent the entry of the Highlanders

Stobo, Peebles. The ancient 'jougs,' or iron collar for wrongdoers, which is preserved outside the Church

Stirling, Stirling. The entrance to Argyll's Lodging, built in the 16th and 17th centuries, and used as a military hospital since 1799

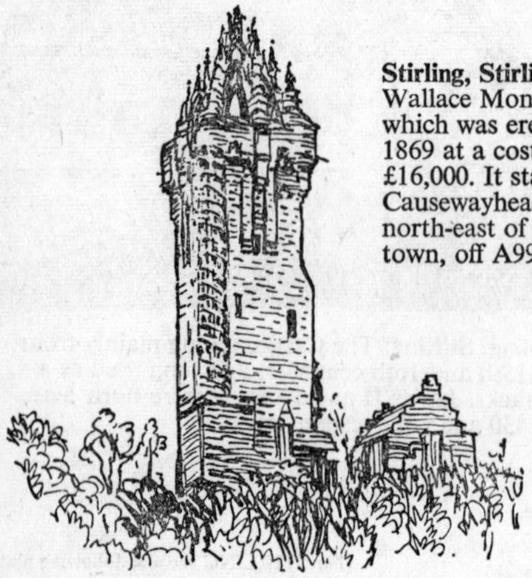

Stirling, Stirling. The Wallace Monument, which was erected in 1869 at a cost of £16,000. It stands near Causewayhead, to the north-east of the town, off A997

Stirling, Stirling. Mar's Wark, dated 1570 and never completed, the Town House of the Regent Mar. It has the Royal Arms above the main entrance

[For STOBO see also under TWEEDDALE (Plate 166)

died in 1634. In the *Smith* Institute are pictures and relics of interest. The fine Church of the *Holy Rude* is mainly of two dates. The nave was commenced c. 1414, and retains a notable oak roof, while the choir dates from between 1507 and 1520, and has, as its outstanding feature, a remarkable five-sided apse. The square 90-ft. high battlemented tower still shows the shot marks made by guns in the 1651 siege. In 1543, Mary, Queen of Scots was crowned in the Church at the age of 9 months, and 24 years later James VI, when a year old, was crowned in the choir, the sermon being preached by John Knox. Between 1656 and 1936 the nave and choir were used as separate Churches. In the former titling ground, now a cemetery, between the Castle and the Church, is a marble representation, in a glass case, of the Covenanting Wigtown Martyrs (See **Wigtown**), who, in 1685, were tied to stakes and drowned by the incoming waters of the Solway Firth.

A little beyond Stirling Bridge is *Causewayhead*, overlooked by the 362-ft. high Abbey Craig, which is crowned by the well-known 220-ft. high *Wallace Monument*, erected in 1869 at a cost of £16,000, containing Wallace's sword, and providing an extensive view. About a mile to the south, near one of the bends of the Forth, in the fertile district known as the "Links of the Forth," are the rather scanty remains of *Cambuskenneth Abbey* (A.M.), founded in 1147, and retaining a fine 14th cent. detached tower, which can be ascended for the view. James III and his Queen were buried before the high altar in 1488, and Queen Victoria erected a monument to them, in 1864. A Scottish Parliament, under Bruce, was held at Cambuskenneth, in 1326. **3 m. E.** of Stirling stands the 17th cent. house of *Stewarthall*. See **Bannockburn, Bridge of Allan** (for *University*), **Dundrennan, Gargunnock** and **St. Ninian's.** *Iter. 50, 87, 95, 96, 99, 108, 111, 112, 133, 134, 135, 136, 137, 138, 139, 140, 141, 142, 144.*

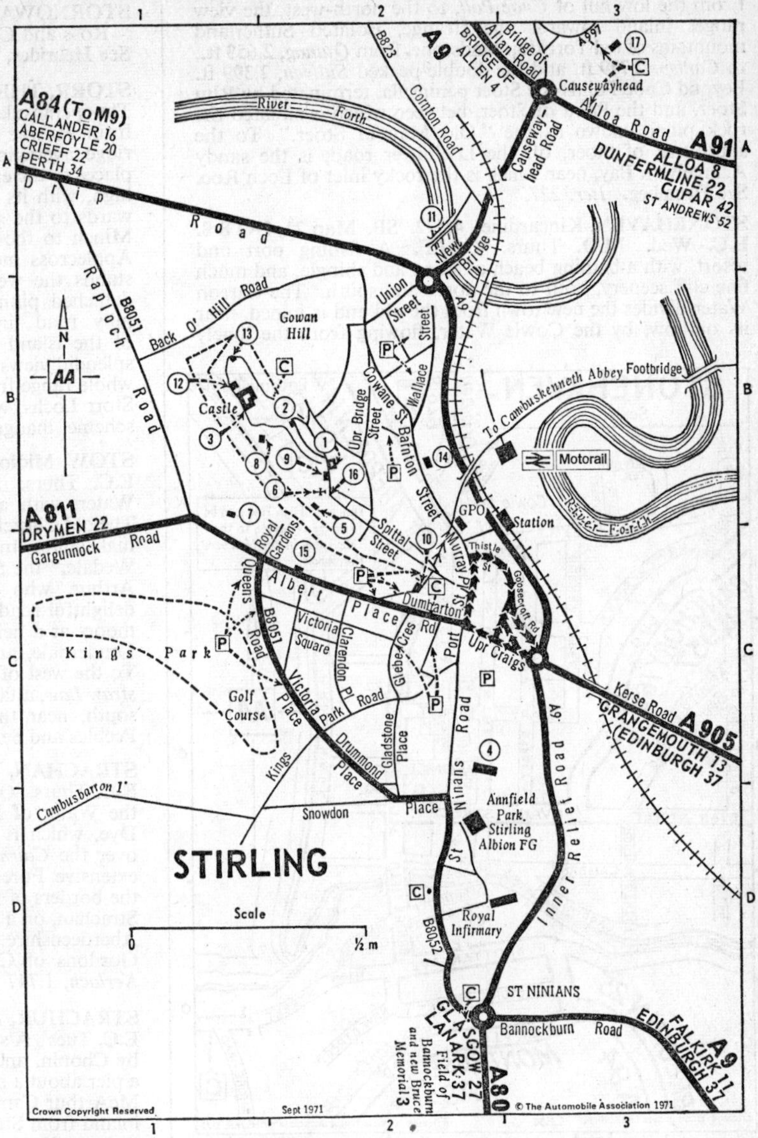

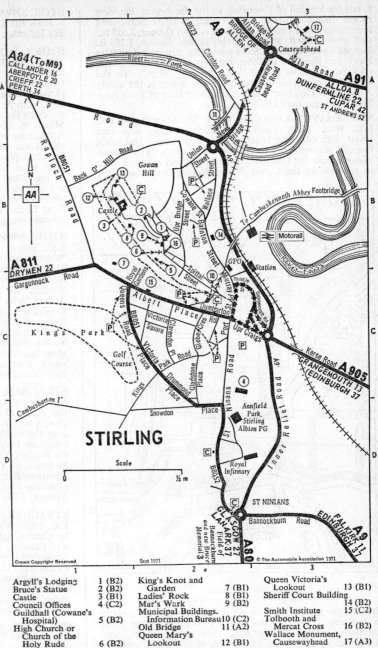

Argyll's Lodging 1 (B2)
Bruce's Statue 2 (B2)
Castle 3 (B1)
Council Offices 4 (C2)
Guildhall (Cowane's Hospital) 5 (B2)
High Church or Church of the Holy Rude 6 (B2)
King's Knot and Garden 7 (B1)
Ladies' Rock 8 (B1)
Mar's Wark 9 (B2)
Municipal Buildings. Information Bureau 10 (C2)
Old Bridge 11 (A2)
Queen Mary's Lookout 12 (B1)
Queen Victoria's Lookout 13 (B1)
Sheriff Court Building 14 (B2)
Smith Institute 15 (C2)
Tolbooth and Mercat Cross 16 (B2)
Wallace Monument, Causewayhead 17 (A3)

The battlefield (1314) of Bannockburn with the new Bruce Memorial lies to the south of the town by exit A80

STOBHALL, Perth. Map 17, **NO 1 3.**
Here, situated on a ridge, on the east bank of the River Tay, is a picturesque and well-preserved group of buildings overlooking a courtyard, the ancient home of the Drummonds (A.M.). The larger house consists of a chapel and tower dating from 1578, the former retaining the old Holy Water stoup, the aumbry, with its original door, and a painted ceiling, above which is a loft. Millais, the painter, lived for a time in the house. Nearby is the dower-house, dated 1761, and attached to it is the gateway, with its heraldic panel, which leads to the whole enclosure. To the south-west of Stobhall are the Campsie Linn rapids.

STOBO, Peebles. 247. Map 9, **NT 1 3.**
The small, restored Church of *Stobo*, overlooking the River Tweed, is of Norman date, with additions in the 16th and 17th cents. The barrel-vaulted porch enshrines a 13th cent. doorway, and the jougs still hang by the porch. *Stobo Castle*, a little to the south-west, is a modern building. On the opposite bank of the river are the remarkable *Dawyck Woods*, some of the best-known in the country, and the place where the horse-chestnut was introduced to Scotland in 1650 and the larch in 1725. There are also Douglas firs, the tallest 133 years old and 131 ft. high, a pinetum and a wealth of Chinese rhododendrons and other shrubs and trees. Gardens open Wed., Sat., Sun., 2-5, May to end of Aug. (See note page 98.) *Iter. 24.*

STOCKIEMUIR, Stirling. Map 15, **NS 4 8.**
From this elevated stretch of moorland a wide panoramic view can be obtained, and glimpses of *Loch Lomond* (*q.v.*), away to the north-west, are sometimes possible. A little to the west, on the slopes of *Auchineden* (*q.v.*) Hill, 1,171 ft., is the curious chasm known as the *Whangie. Iter. 104, 106.*

STOER, Sutherland. 206. Map 28, **NC 0 2.**
A remote little North-West Highland village, on the picturesque, narrow and hilly road linking *Lochinver* (*q.v.*) with *Kylesku* (*q.v.*). There is bathing from the sandy shores of the Bay of Stoer. The neighbourhood is one of innumerable tiny lochans, many of which provide good fishing.

From the low hill of *Cnoc Poll*, to the north-west, the view ranges inland towards the strange, isolated Sutherland mountains of red Torridon sandstone, from *Quinag*, 2,653 ft., to *Canisp*, 2,779 ft. and the double-peaked *Suilven*, 2,399 ft. Beyond Cnoc Poll is the Stoer peninsula, terminated by Rhu Stoer, and the Point of Stoer, between which is situated the rock pillar known as the "Old Man of Stoer." To the south-east of Stoer, off the Lochinver road, is the sandy Achmelvich Bay, near which is the rocky inlet of Loch Roe. See **Drumbeg.** *Iter. 227.*

STONEHAVEN, Kincardine. 4,572. SB. Map 21, **NO 8 8.** **E.C.** Wed. **M.D.** Thurs. GOLF. A fishing port and resort, with a bathing beach of stone and shingle, and much fine cliff scenery, both to the north and south. The Carron Water divides the new town from the old and is joined, near its outflow, by the Cowie Water, flowing from the lonely

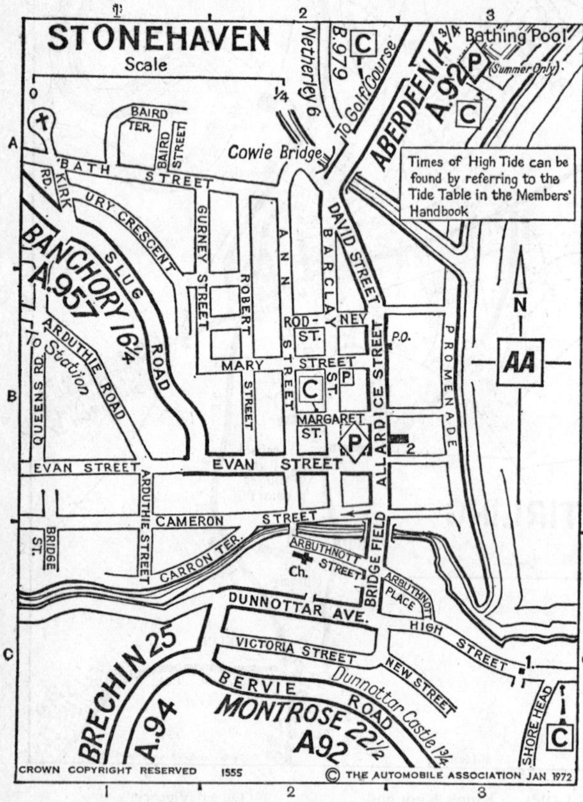

Mercat Cross and 18th cent. steeple 1 (C3)
Town Hall (Information Bureau adjacent) 2 (B3)

hills to the west through an attractive glen. On the quay is a 16th cent. Tolbooth, formerly a storehouse of the Earls Marischal, and used later until 1784 as a prison. Local Episcopal ministers were lodged here in 1745. The building was restored in 1963. Near the harbour stands the Mercat Cross, and also the 18th cent. Steeple, where the Old Pretender was proclaimed king in 1715. At Hogmanay, fireballs made from tallowed rope are carried through the town. The road leading north-westwards from Stonehaven past *Fetteresso Forest* and over the hills to *Banchory (q.v.)* is known as the *Slug Road*. It rises to nearly 800 ft. near *Durris Forest*. To the north of this road, within 4 miles of Stonehaven, is the Roman Camp of *Raedykes*. The road to the east of the camp, leading from Stonehaven to the Dee Valley, is the Elsick Mounth road, used by the Romans. See **Cowie, Dunnottar Castle** and **Muchalls.** *Iter. 151, 155, 156, 190, 191.*

STONEHOUSE, Lanark. 4,051. Map 9, **NS 7 4.** *Iter. 20, 29, 69.*

STONES OF CLAVA, Inverness. Map 25, **NH 7 4.** See **Culloden.**

STORNOWAY, Isle of Lewis, Ross and Cromarty. 5,153. SB. Map 32, **NB 4 3.** See **Hebrides, Outer** (Lewis). *Iter. 256, 258, 259, 260.*

STORR, THE, Isle of Skye, Inverness. Map 22, **NG 4 5.** The peninsula of Trotternish, which extends northwards from *Portree (q.v.)*, has for its backbone a 10-mile-long ridge, averaging some 2,000 ft. in height, precipitous in many places to the east, and dominated by the lofty *Storr*, 2,360 ft. high, with its wild crags. This fine viewpoint looks southwards to the great *Coolins (q.v.)* range; westwards over the Minch to the Outer Hebrides; and eastwards towards the Applecross mountains on the mainland. Below the Storr stands the well-known *Old Man of Storr*, a 160-ft. high detached pinnacle of rock, not climbed until 1955. The hilly road linking Portree with the northern extremity of the island passes below the Storr cliffs, and provides splendid views of the steep contours and varied forms of the whole range from many places. On the Portree road lie the Storr Lochs, which have been harnessed to a hydro-electric scheme, inaugurated in 1952. *Iter. 254.*

STOW, Midlothian. 1,404 with Heriot. Map 10, **NT 4 4.** **E.C.** Thurs. A delightful village, situated on the Gala Water, with a fine pack-horse bridge, dating from 1655. The old Church is in ruins. The modern Church has a 140-ft. high spire. In the vicinity, once known as the "Stow of Wedale," the Saxons are said to have been routed by King Arthur, who founded a Church as a thanksgiving. A delightful road proceeds eastwards from Stow, crossing the moors at a height of over 1,100 ft., before descending into Lauderdale, and reaching the small town of *Lauder (q.v.)*. To the west of Stow rise the lonely *Moorfoot* hills. *Windlestraw Law*, attaining 2,161 ft., is situated a little farther to the south, near the point where the counties of Midlothian, Peebles and Selkirk meet. *Iter. 9, 11.*

STRACHAN, Kincardine. 469. Map 21, **NO 6 9.** **E.C.** Thurs. On the Water of Feugh, near its junction with the Water of Dye, flowing along the long valley of Glen Dye, which is traversed by the well-known road climbing over the *Cairn o' Mounth (q.v.)*. Away to the west is the extensive Forest of Birse, extending to the lonely hills on the borders of Aberdeen and Angus. Some 12 miles west of Strachan, on a by-road, stands the restored, partly 16th cent. Aberdeenshire Castle of *Birse*, a former home of the Gordons of Clunie. To the south-east of Strachan rises *Kerloch*, 1,747 ft. See **Feughside Inn.** *Iter. 163, 174.*

STRACHUR, Argyll. 580. Map 14, **NN 0 0.** **E.C.** Tues. A small resort near *Loch Fyne (q.v.)*, once visited by Chopin, and situated in the *Cowal (q.v.)* peninsula, with a pier about a mile to the north-west. The former seat of the McArthur Campbells dates from c. 1783. The road leading inland from Strachur gives access to *Loch Eck (q.v.)*, a long and narrow sheet of water surrounded by hills. The highest of these are *Beinn Bheula*, 2,557 ft., to the north-east, and *Beinn Mhor*, 2,433 ft., overlooking the western shores of the loch. See **Inveraray** and **St. Catherine's.** *Iter. 102, 137.*

STRAITON, Ayr. 1,864 with Kirkmichael. Map 8, **NS 3 0.** An attractive *Carrick (q.v.)* village, on the Water of Girvan, with a pre-Reformation aisle in its restored Church. To the west, near the river, is the old mansion of *Blairquhan*. A narrow and hilly road leads southwards, climbing over the moors towards *Rowantree (q.v.)*, and attains a height of 1,421 ft., with views of *Shalloch on Minnoch*, 2,520 ft., to the south-east, beyond which lies the remote Loch Macaterick. To the east of Straiton, off the Dalmellington road, is the glen of the Lambdoughty Burn, in which are several waterfalls. One of these is called the Rossetti Linn, having been much admired by Dante Gabriel Rossetti when staying at *Penkill Castle*, near *Dailly (q.v.)*. *Iter. 49, 74, 79.*

STRANRAER, Wigtown. 9,853. SB. Map 2, **NX 0 6.** **E.C.** Wed. **M.D.** Fri. GOLF. An important port for the mail-steamers to Larne in Northern Ireland, having taken the place of *Portpatrick*, which is too much exposed to gales. Stranraer is situated in the Rhinns of Galloway at the head of Loch Ryan, the *Reregonius Sinus* of the Romans, and the

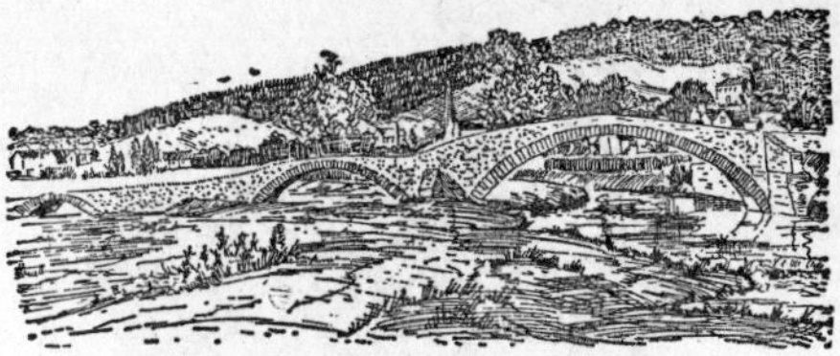

Stow, Midlothian. The pack-horse bridge spanning the Gala Water, which was built in 1655

Stones of Clava, Inverness. Standing stones and burial cairns (N.T. Scot.), dating from the Bronze Age, 1800–1500 B.C. They stand 1 mile south-east of the battlefield of Culloden, across the River Nairn

Strachur, Argyll. The upper reaches of Loch Fyne, which in the vicinity is said to attain its greatest depth of some 82 fathoms

Stranraer, Wigtown. The 16th to 17th century Castle, which at one period was used as the gaol

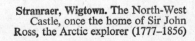

Stranraer, Wigtown. The North-West Castle, once the home of Sir John Ross, the Arctic explorer (1777–1856)

Strathdon, Aberdeen. Poldullie Bridge, which spans the River Don, to the south-west

Strathaven, Lanark. Strathaven, or Avondale Castle, a 15th century ruin, last occupied by the Duchess of Hamilton in the 17th century

Strathmiglo, Fife. The Tolbooth of 1734, built from the stones of a former castle owned by Sir William Scott of Balwearie

Strathmore, Angus; Perth. The cottage at Kirriemuir, Angus, known as ' A Window in Thrums,' associated with Sir James Barrie. Strathmore lies between the Lower Grampian and the Sidlaw Hills

Strathdon, Aberdeen. The Church, with its tall spire, a landmark for many miles around

Strathmore, Angus; Perth. Huntingtower, formerly Ruthven Castle, 15th century, where the historic ' Ruthven Raid ' of 1582 took place, resulting in the putting to death of the Earl of Gowrie. It stands on A85, west of Perth, at the south-west extremity of Strathmore

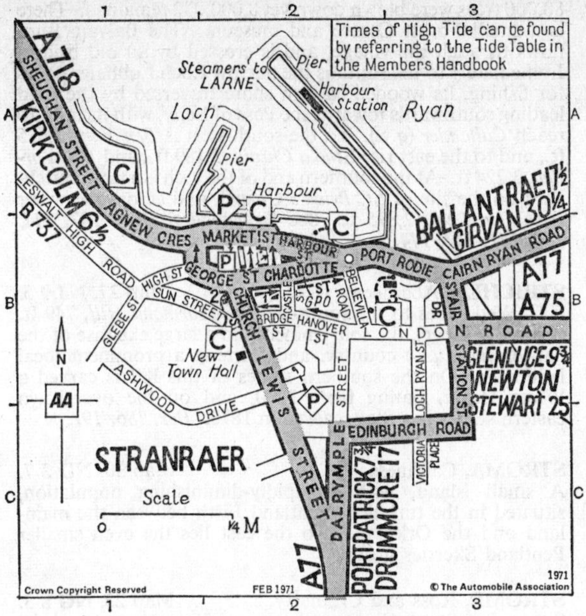

Castle	1 (B2)
Information Bureau	2 (B2)
Municipal Offices, Dunbae House	
North West Castle House	3 (B3)

sea passage from here to Larne is only 35 miles in length. *Stranraer Castle* stands in the centre of the town, and is probably of early 16th cent. date, with some 17th cent. reconstruction, having long been used as a gaol. Claverhouse is said to have lived there, in 1682, when rounding up the Covenanters. Near the pier is a house called the *North West Castle*, formerly the home of Sir John Ross, the Arctic explorer. Stranraer was the home port of the ill-fated cross-channel steamer " Princess Victoria," lost in the great storm of early January, 1953. See **Castle Kennedy** (also for airport), **Innermessan, Kirkcolm** and **Portpatrick.** *Iter. 25, 26, 55, 82 83, 84.*

STRATHAVEN, Lanark. 4,100. Map 8, **NS 7 4.** **E.C.** Wed. **M.D.** Tues. GOLF. A weaving town, situated at a height of over 600 ft. on the edge of an extensive moorland district stretching away to the west. The Powmillon Burn, spanned here by an ancient bridge, threads its way through the town on its way to join the Avon Water, to the south-east. The remains of *Strathaven*, or *Avondale Castle*, dating from the 15th cent., overlook the burn. To the west of Strathaven, on A71, stands the house of *Lauder Ha'*, formerly the home of Sir Harry Lauder, who was born, in 1870, at *Portobello* (*q.v.*). *Iter. 20, 29, 56, 68, 69, 87.*

STRATHBLANE, Stirling. 1,467. Map 15, **NS 5 7.** GOLF. This small resort, on the Blane Water, has calico-printing works. It is situated at the foot of the *Strathblane* hills and the loftier *Campsie Fells*, in which *Earl's Seat*, 1,896 ft., is the highest point of the range. About a mile to the east, on the Ballagan Burn, are the falls known as the Spout of Ballagan. **2 m. N.W.,** off the Killearn road, stands the partly 15th cent. *Duntreath Castle*, in which the medieval stocks and dungeons are preserved. See **Campsie Glen, Milngavie** and **Stockiemuir.** *Iter. 105, 108, 115.*

STRATHCARRON STATION, Ross and Cromarty. Map 24, **NG 9 4.** Lies immediately to the south of the road from Inverness to *Kyle of Lochalsh* (*q.v.*), near the north-eastern extremity of Loch Carron, and is overlooked by the lonely hills of Attadale Forest, in which *Beinn Dronnaig* attains 2,612 ft. See **Lochcarron.** *Iter. 219, 221, 222, 223.*

STRATHDON, Aberdeen. 747. Map 26, **NJ 3 1.** Here, the River Don, noted for fishing, is joined by the Water of Nochty, flowing from the *Ladder Hills*. The spire of the Church is a local landmark, and to the south-west of the village the Don is spanned by *Poldullie Bridge*, dating from 1715. There is attractive river and hill scenery and the new *Tornashean Forest*. The Lonach Highland Gathering is usually held at Strathdon in mid-August. **1½ m. E.S.E.,** near the Don, are slight remains of the 16th cent., but never completed *Colquhonnie Castle*. **7 m. S.E.,** on A97, is a notable viewpoint at *Tillypronie Hill*, 1,213 ft., on the road to Cambus O'May. See **Cock Bridge** and **Glenkindie.** *Iter. 141, 176, 191.*

STRATHFARRAR, Inverness. Map 24, **NH 2 3 and 3 3.** See **Struy Bridge.**

STRATH GLASS, Inverness. Map 24, **NH 3 3.** See **Cannich** and **Struy Bridge.** *Iter. 206, 210.*

STRATHKANAIRD, Ross and Cromarty. Map 29, **NC 1 0.** In the valley of Strath Kanaird, between the remote Rhidorroch Forest and the *Coigach* hills. The valley is traversed by the picturesque Ullapool to Inchnadamph road, which, to the south-west of Strathkanaird, goes by the shores of Loch Kanaird, with Isle Martin lying off-shore. On the north side of the estuary of the Kanaird River, on the coast, stands *Dun Canna*, a ruined broch, with *Ben More Coigach*, 2,438 ft., rising in the background, and dominating the Coigach district. *Iter. 224, 225, 226.*

STRATHLACHLAN, Argyll. Map 14, **NS 0 9.** On Lachlan Bay, a small inlet of *Loch Fyne* (*q.v.*), stands *Castle Lachlan*, in its wooded setting. **2 m. N.E.,** a road climbs over the hills of *Cowal* (*q.v.*) to descend towards *Glendaruel* (*q.v.*), a long and pleasant glen. *Iter. 102.*

STRATHMIGLO, Fife. Map 17, **NO 2 1.** The Tolbooth, dating from 1734, has a spired tower. To the south rise the *Lomond* hills. In the parish are some late 18th cent. weavers' cottages. **3m. N.W.** is the 15th cent. **Balvaird Castle.** See **Falkland.** *Iter. 92, 130, 136.*

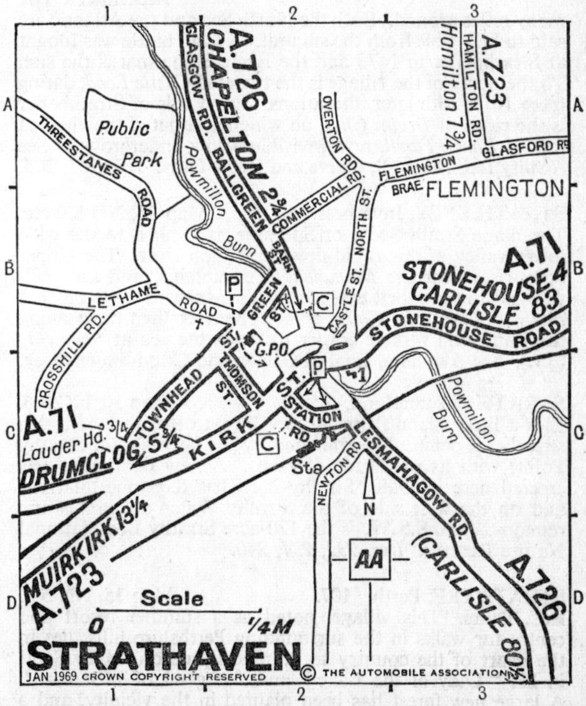

Castle ruins 1 (C2)

STRATHMORE, Angus; Perth. Map 20, **NO 1** 3 etc.
A pleasant, fertile valley, lying to the south of the *Grampian* (*q.v.*) foothills, and north of the *Sidlaw* hills. It extends from south-west to north-east across the area, at first parallel with the River Tay, and later with its tributary, the Isla. The greater part of Strathmore is in Perthshire, but it stretches also into Angus, in the direction of *Kirriemuir* (*q.v.*), where it is known as the Howe of Angus.

STRATH NAVER, Sutherland. Map 30, **NC 6** 4 etc.
Situated in the lonely valley of Strath Naver, largely depopulated in the early 19th cent., and stretching from *Altnaharra* (*q.v.*), on Loch Naver, to the coast at *Bettyhill* (*q.v.*), where the River Naver flows into the sea. The river was known to Ptolemy, the early historian from Alexandria, and is famous for its salmon. There are many prehistoric remains in the valley. See **Syre Church.** *Iter. 232, 235.*

STRATHPEFFER, Ross and Cromarty. 1,110.
Map 25, **NH 4** 5.
E.C. Thurs. GOLF. This well-known Highland spa and resort stands in a sheltered and wooded setting to the north of Strath Conon. There are chalybeate springs here, and as a touring centre Strathpeffer is convenient for the Moray Firth district, and for explorations of the beautiful lochs and mountains of *Wester Ross* (*q.v.*). *Ben Wyvis*, 3,429 ft., the highest mountain in Easter Ross, rises to the north, and is a notable landmark for many miles around. Both the North Sea and the Atlantic are said to be visible from the summit. A Clan battle was fought at Strathpeffer in 1478 and the Eagle Stone marks the site. To the north of the village is the turreted *Castle Leod*, dating from 1616, with later alterations. Eastwards of Strathpeffer is the ridge of *Druim Chat*, on which is situated the vitrified fort of *Knock Farril*, now invisible below undergrowth. See **Achilty Inn, Dingwall, Garve** and **Rogie Falls.** *Iter. 201, 206.*

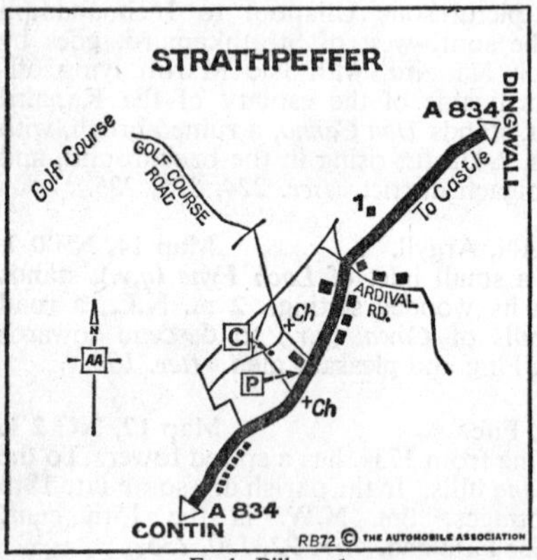

Eagle Pillar 1

STRATH SPEY, Inverness. Map 25, **NH 8** 0 etc.
The name Strath Spey, or Speyside, is applied to the wide lower valley of this rapid-flowing salmon river. The Upper Spey rises near the *Monadhliath* mountains, and the well-wooded lower valley extends north-eastwards between that range and the lofty *Cairngorms.* The river then flows along the Banff and Moray border to reach the sea at *Spey Bay* (*q.v.*). See **Aviemore, Boat of Garten** and **Grantown-on-Spey.**

STRATHY, Sutherland. 758. Map 30, **NC 8** 6.
Lies a little inland from Strathy Bay, to the west of which stretches a peninsula terminated by the headland of Strathy Point, with its multitude of caves. A new lighthouse was erected here in 1958. Strathy itself has flagstone quarries, and on the west side of the Strathy Water are prehistoric remains. **8 m. S.S.W.** is the 120-acre Strathy Bog National Nature Reserve. *Iter. 232, 234, 240.*

STRATHYRE, Perth. 107. Map 15, **NN 5** 1.
E.C. Thurs. This village, noted as a summer resort and centre for walks in the surrounding Perthshire hills, lies in the heart of the country so graphically described by Scott in his "Lady of the Lake" and "Legend of Montrose." A large new forest has been planted in the vicinity, and a Scots pine has attained 116 ft. In the hurricane of 1968 some 80,000 trees were blown down yet 8,000,000 remained. There is a small Forest Centre and museum. The Balvaig Burn flows through the village, and is crossed by an old bridge. Immediately to the south is the narrow Loch Lubnaig, noted for fishing, its wooded eastern shore traversed by the road leading southwards towards the Pass of Leny, with its falls, to reach *Callander* (*q.v.*). To the south-west is *Ben Vane* 2,685 ft., and to the east rise *Stuc'a Chroin*, 3,189 ft., and *Ben Vorlich*, 3,224 ft. At the southern end of the loch is a tiny churchyard on the site of *St. Bride's* Chapel, and across the water rises *Ben Ledi*, 2,875 ft. See **Balquhidder.** *Iter. 107, 111, 139, 141, 142, 144.*

STRICHEN, Aberdeen. 1,711. Map 27, **NJ 9** 5.
E.C. Wed. Lies to the south-west of *Mormond Hill*, 749 ft. (Forest of Deer), the sole eminence in a large expanse of the flat *Buchan* (*q.v.*) country, and forming a prominent local landmark. On the southern slopes of this hill is carved a White Horse, dating from 1700, and on the overgrown eastern slopes is a Stag, carved in 1870. *Iter. 186, 197.*

STROMA, Caithness. Map 30, **ND 3** 7.
A small island, with a rapidly-diminishing population, situated in the turbulent Pentland Firth between the mainland and the Orkneys. To the east lies the even smaller Pentland Skerries group.

STROME, Ross and Cromarty. Map 23, **NG 8** 3.
Situated on Loch Carron, a new road has now replaced the car ferry. Overlooking the loch, on the north side, are slight remains of *Strome Castle* (N.T. Scot.), the building having been destroyed after a long siege, in 1609. There are fine views from here of the distant *Coolins* (*q.v.*) in Skye. The road leading towards the loch on the north side was constructed by Telford, he and the poet Southey being the first to travel over the road in a wheeled carriage, in 1819. On the south side, the road first climbs steeply, before descending to Strath Ascaig, and then crossing the hills towards *Auchtertyre* (*q.v.*). See **Lochcarron** and **Plockton.** *Iter. 219, 220, 221, 222, 223.*

STRONACHLACHAR, Stirling. Map 15, **NN 4** 1.
Here is a steamer pier on *Loch Katrine* (*q.v.*), and a short length of road connects by way of Loch Arklet with *Inversnaid* (*q.v.*) on *Loch Lomond* (*q.v.*). Another road leads southwards towards the shores of Loch Chon, eventually reaching *Aberfoyle* (*q.v.*). A path leading north-westwards from Stronachlachar gives access to the lonely house of *Glengyle*, in Glen Gyle, on the Perthshire border, the birth place, in 1671, of the famous freebooter, Rob Roy, immortalized by Scott. See **Balquhidder** and **Trossachs.** *Iter 105.*

STRONE, Argyll. Map 14, **NS 1** 8.
E.C. Wed. GOLF. A small holiday resort at the mouth of Loch Long, facing the Firth of Clyde, with a pier at Strone Point, at the eastern extremity of the Holy Loch, and looking across to *Hunter's Quay* (*q.v.*). Almost adjoining Strone, to the north, is the little resort of *Blairmore*, also with a pier. See **Ardentinny** and **Kilmun.** *Iter. 102.*

STRONSAY, ISLE OF, Orkney. Map 33, **HY 6** 2.
See **Orkney Islands** (Stronsay).

STRONTIAN, Argyll. Map 12, **NM 8** 6.
Picturesquely situated at the eastern end of *Loch Sunart* (*q.v.*), a long and beautiful sea loch, with richly wooded scenery farther towards the west, on the road to *Salen* (*q.v.*). The loch separates the districts of Sunart and Ardnamurchan, on the north side, from Morven, on the south side. The Strontian River flows through the village into the loch, and in the glen to the north, where the Arriendle Forest Nature Reserve lies, are deserted lead-mines, which once formed an important feature of the locality. Among other rare minerals found at the time was the element strontium, named after this place. The name of Scotstown, by which one of the settlements in the glen is known, recalls the

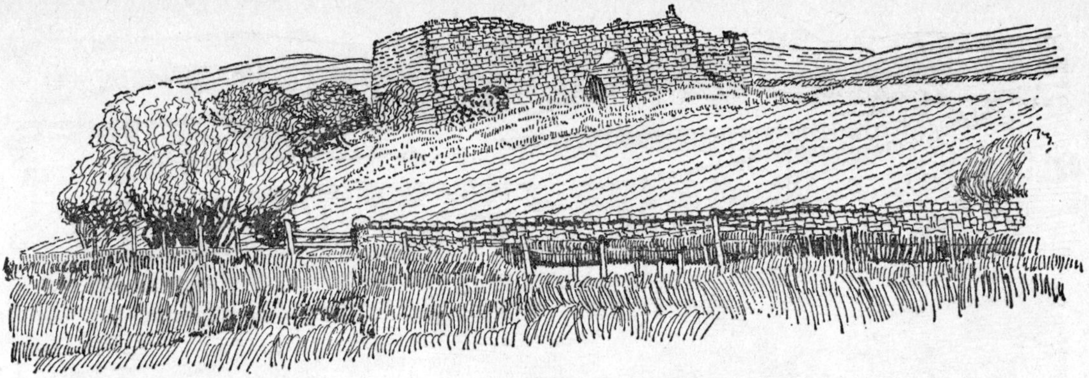

Strath Spey, Inverness. The remains of Castle Roy, an old stronghold of the Comyns, Lords of Badenoch, which stands a little to the north-east of Nethybridge, on B970

Strathpeffer, Ross and Cromarty. An upright stone, bearing incised Pictish symbols. In a clan battle here of 1478, the Munros were defeated by the Mackenzies

Strathyre, Perth. The old bridge over the Balvaig Burn

Strichen, Aberdeen. A White Horse, carved in 1700, and said to be the only one in Scotland, on the southern slopes of Mormond Hill. On the eastern slopes is a carving of a stag (1870), now much overgrown. The hill rises some 2 miles north-east of Strichen

Strome, Ross and Cromarty. The remains of the Castle (N.T. Scot.), destroyed in 1609. It overlooks the narrows of Loch Carron at North Strome

PLATE 158

Struie Hill, Ross and Cromarty. The north-westerly panorama from the A.A. viewpoint, at an altitude of about 700 feet, giving a distant glimpse of Ben More Assynt, the highest mountain in Sutherland

Struan, Perth. The picturesque Falls of Bruar, in Glen Bruar, off A9, to the east

Swanston, Midlothian. A village in which Robert Louis Stevenson spent some of the holidays of his youth between 1870 and 1880

Symington, Ayr. Round-headed Norman windows of 12th century date in the chancel of the old Church, much reconstructed

Tain, Ross and Cromarty. The 17th century Tolbooth, which has a conical spire

Tantallon Castle, East Lothian. The 14th century and later Douglas stronghold, which General Monk dismantled in 1651. It figures in Sir Walter Scott's '*Marmion*,' and stands 3 miles east of North Berwick, off A198

[For TARBERT see following plate

miners who came here in the 18th cent. from the Lowlands. From the glen it is possible to climb the prominent peak of *Ben Resipol*, 2,774 ft., which rises to the north-west of Strontian, and provides a magnificent view from the summit, notably over the waters of *Loch Shiel* (*q.v.*), and southwards to Morven. *Iter. 216, 217.*

STRUAN, Perth. Map 19, **NN 8** 6.
Lies at the junction of Glen Garry with Glen Erochy, and is divided by the River Garry, with its noted falls and salmon leap, from *Calvine*, which stands on the main Perth to Inverness highway. A little to the east of Calvine, and situated actually in Glen Bruar, are the well-known Falls of Bruar, the upper fall being a short distance up the glen, which is dominated to the east by *Beinn Dearg*, 3,304 ft., in the Forest of Atholl hills. A path leads up this glen by means of which long-distance walkers can traverse the lonely hills of the wild Gaick Forest, and after crossing the remote Minigaig Pass eventually reach *Kingussie* (*q.v.*) in the Spey valley. The road which leads westwards from Struan through Glen Erochy, climbing to a height of over 1,000 ft., gives access to the Tummel valley and *Kinloch Rannoch* (*q.v.*). The Clan Donnachie is associated with Struan and there is a small clan museum. See **Blair Atholl.** *Iter. 147, 149.*

STRUIE HILL, Ross and Cromarty. (A.A. viewpoint.) Map 31, **NH 6** 8.
A lofty height overlooking the waters of Dornoch Firth.

STRUY BRIDGE, Inverness. Map 24, **NH 4** 4.
On the River Farrar, near its confluence with the Glass, the combined streams being thence known as the Beauly River. There are roads on both sides of the delightful Strath Glass, which extends to the south-west, these roads meeting later near *Cannich* (*q.v.*). In the 18th and 19th centuries, large numbers of people emigrated from these old Clan Chisholm lands to America and Canada. Westwards from Struy Bridge stretches the long and beautiful Glen Strathfarrar, traversed for some distance by a private road. Hydro-electric developments are taking place in the glen. Cattle-ranching has been introduced into this district. The valley continues into the fastnesses of the Ross-shire mountains, many exceeding 3,000 ft. in height, and in the heart of which lies the lonely Loch Monar, dividing Ross and Cromarty from Inverness. Beyond the loch stretches West Monar Forest, in which *Sgurr a' Chaorachain* attains 3,452 ft., and looks northwards towards the lonely Glencarron Forest. Ptolemy of Alexandria, the early historian, mentions the Farrar River in his writings. Immediately to the north-east of Struy Bridge stands the modernised *Erchless Castle*, once the seat of the head of Clan Chisholm. See **Crask of Aigas** and **Kilmorack.** *Iter. 206, 210.*

SUILVEN, Sutherland. Map 29, **NC 1** 1.
See **Lochinver.**

SUMBURGH, Shetland. Map 33, **HU 4** 0.
See **Shetland Islands** (Mainland). *Iter. 269.*

SUMMER ISLES, Ross and Cromarty. Map 29, **NB 9** 0.
See **Achiltibuie.** *Iter. 226.*

SWANSTON, Midlothian. Map 9, **NT 2** 6.
A tiny hamlet, at the north-eastern extremity of the *Pentland* hills, visited for its associations with the novels of R. L. Stevenson, notably "St. Ives." *Swanston Cottage* was the summer home of the Stevensons between 1867 and 1881, and in it are preserved relics belonging to the author. *Caerketton* and *Allermuir* hills, in the Pentlands, overlook Swanston from the south. See **Colinton.**

SWEETHEART ABBEY, Kirkcudbright. Map 3, **NX 9** 6.
See **New Abbey.** *Iter. 72, 73.*

SWINTON, Berwick. 503. Map 11, **NT 8** 4.
On the Mercat Cross (1769) are several sundials. The Church has a tomb dating from c. 1200. *Iter. 38, 46.*

SYMINGTON, Ayr. 3,134 with Monkton. Map 8, **NS 3** 3.
The small, restored Church shows a trio of round-headed windows, dating from the 12th cent., and also an ancient roof of open-work timber. There is an old toll-house at *Bogend*. *Craigie Castle*, an old Wallace stronghold to the north-east, is in ruins.

SYMINGTON, Lanark. 652. Map 9, **NS 9** 3.
E.C. Wed. To the west rises *Tinto Hill*, 2,335 ft., a prominent landmark for many miles, with a wide view from the summit, extending as far as the English Lake District mountains and the coast of Northern Ireland. Near the eastern slopes of the hill stands the ruined *Fatlips Castle*. Away to the north of Symington, beyond the River Clyde, is *Quothquan Law*, 1,097 ft. *Iter. 35, 53.*

SYRE CHURCH, Sutherland. Map 30, **NC 6** 4.
Situated in the *Strath Naver* (*q.v.*) valley. To the north and south are numerous prehistoric remains, notably ruined brochs and hut circles. At *Skail*, to the north, a stone recalls the inception of the 93rd Sutherland Highlanders, who fought at Balaclava. Westwards from Syre lies the lonely little Loch Syre, and still farther west, beyond Loch Loyal, rises the multi-peaked *Ben Loyal*, 2,504 ft. This fine mountain is seen perhaps at its best from the vicinity of *Tongue* (*q.v.*). See **Bettyhill.** *Iter. 232, 235.*

TAIL OF THE BANK, Renfrew. Map 8, **NS 2** 7.
See **Greenock.**

TAIN, Ross and Cromarty. 1,940. SB. Map 31, **NH 7** 8.
E.C. Thurs. **M.D.** Alt. Fri. GOLF. An ancient Royal Burgh of Easter Ross, on the Dornoch Firth, with a fine 17th cent. Tolbooth having a peal of bells. Nearby is the restored Market Cross. The Collegiate Church of *St. Duthac* was built in 1371, and has some good fenestration. In the churchyard stands a ruined Chapel of *St. Duthac.* The remains of another Chapel to the same saint are on a knoll near the golf links, and to this Chapel fled, in 1306, the wife and daughter of Robert Bruce, who were later given up to Edward I. In the 15th and 16th cents., James IV made regular pilgrimages to Tain, and a road leading southwards from the town, crossing Glen Aldie in the direction of *Logie Easter* (*q.v.*), is still known as the King's Causeway, and recalls the rides of that monarch. His son, James V, also traversed the road on foot, in 1527. Eastwards of the town lies Loch Eye, with the ruined *Lochslin Castle*, and away to the north of the loch, bordering the Dornoch Firth, is a large expanse of sandy links, known as the Morrich More. See **Fearn.** *Iter. 201.*

TALISKER, Isle of Skye, Inverness. Map 23, **NG 3** 3.
The well-known *Talisker* distillery is situated at the village of *Carbost*, on the western shores of Loch Harport, reached along a by-road leaving the Sligachan to Bracadale road in a westerly direction near the head of Loch Harport. A narrow and rough road goes westwards over the hills from Carbost to Talisker Bay, with the imposing mass of *Preshal More* rising to the south of the road near the coast. Away to the south of the bay lies a splendid range of lofty cliffs, accessible only on foot. Another by-road leads north-westwards from Carbost, along the shores of Loch Harport towards Fiskavaig Bay. To the north of this road, near Ardtreck Point, is *Port na Long*, noted for its Harris tweed weavers. *Iter. 252.*

TANNADICE, Angus. 1,045 with Fern. Map 21, **NO 4** 5.
Situated on the South Esk River, in the fertile Vale of *Strathmore* (*q.v.*), looking towards the *Hill of Finhaven* beyond the river. See **Finhaven.** *Iter. 166.*

TANTALLON CASTLE, East Lothian. Map 10, **NT 5** 8.
See **North Berwick.** *Iter. 2, 38.*

TARBERT, Argyll. 1,313. Map 7, **NR 8** 6.
E.C. Wed. On East Loch Tarbert, an inlet of *Loch Fyne* (*q.v.*), and well known as the headquarters of the Loch Fyne herring industry. There are sands providing good bathing, and also a steamer pier. The ruined 14th cent. Castle, which overlooks the harbour, was once the home of Robert Bruce and, at a later period, of James II. To the south-west of the town, about two miles distant, is *Tarbert*

West Pier, used by the steamers which serve Gigha and the Inner Hebridean islands of Jura, Colonsay and Islay. Magnus Barefoot of Norway is said to have been dragged in a galley across the isthmus separating the two lochs, in 1093. North-west of Tarbert rise the hills of South Knapdale, among which *Sliabh Gaoil* attains 1,840 ft. West Loch Tarbert, a narrow sheet of water, some ten miles in length, divides the districts of *Knapdale* and *Kintyre* (both *q.v.*), and exhibits much pleasant, wooded scenery. Roads encircle the loch on both sides, that on the north, somewhat rough and hilly, continuing westwards, and later northwards, to overlook the waters of the Sound of Jura and Loch Killisport. The road along the south side extends along the narrow Kintyre peninsula, with views towards the island of *Gigha* (*q.v.*), and eventually reaches *Campbeltown* (*q.v.*). See **Kennacraig** and **Skipness.** *Iter. 121, 122.*

TARBERT (Isle of Lewis), Harris, Inverness. Map 32, **NB 1 0.**
See **Hebrides, Outer** (Harris). *Iter. 256, 257.*

TARBET, Dunbarton. 162. Map 15, **NN 3 0.**
E.C. Wed. A resort on *Loch Lomond* (*q.v.*), at the eastern extremity of the narrow neck of land separating it from *Arrochar* (*q.v.*) on Loch Long. Across here Haakon of Norway dragged his ships, in 1263, when laying waste the country. From Tarbet, the view across Loch Lomond includes the fine peak of *Ben Lomond,* 3,192 ft., while westwards, beyond Loch Long, rises *Ben Arthur,* or *The Cobbler,* 2,891 ft. The road leading northwards on Loch Lomond's shores reaches, after some 4 miles, the *Inveruglas* (*q.v.*) power-station of the Loch Sloy hydro-electric scheme, which was opened by Her Majesty Queen Elizabeth, the Queen Mother, in October, 1950. *Iter. 88, 100, 101, 103, 110, 111, 137.*

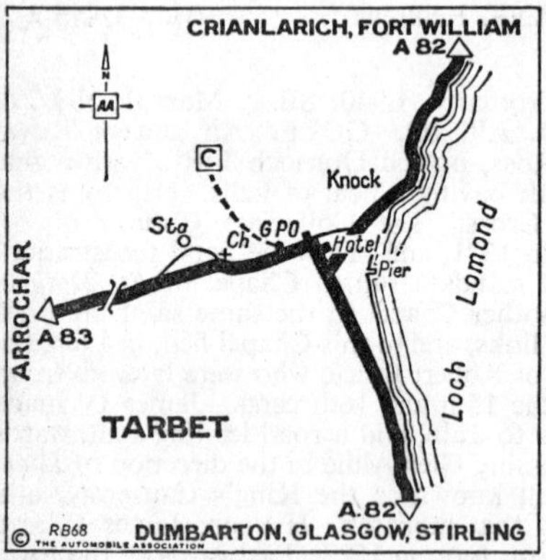

TARBOLTON, Ayr. 7,030. Map 8, **NS 4 2.**
E.C. Wed. Well known for its associations with Robert Burns. The family lived at *Lochlea* farm from 1777 to 1784 and here his father died. At Tarbolton, in 1781, the poet became a Freemason, while one year previously he had founded the Bachelor's Club, which met in the upper part of a thatched house. In 1938, this 17th cent. house became the property of the N.T. Scotland, and now contains Burns relics from the Lochlea period of the poet. The Church has stone stairs leading to the loft and the spire rises to 90 feet. *Willie's Mill,* on the Water of Fail, to the north-east of Tarbolton, has Burns associations, as has also *Failford* (*q.v.*), farther to the south-east. In the vicinity stands *Montgomerie* (1804), where Mary Campbell, Burns's "Highland Mary," was in service. It was known formerly as *Coilsfield,* from the tradition that "Auld King Coil" was killed here by Fergus, King of the Scots. **2 m. N.** of Tarbolton is the prominent 19th cent. *Barnweil* Monument, associated with William Wallace and the burning of the Barns of Ayr. John Knox preached in the ruined *Barnweil* Church. *Iter. 85.*

TARFSIDE, Angus. Map 21, **NO 4 7.**
Lies in the picturesque valley of Glen Esk, in the foothills of the eastern Grampians. The Water of Tarf flows into the Esk at this point. *The Retreat,* Glenesk, is a small museum. Away to the north-west rises *Mount Keen,* 3,077 ft., and to the north-east is *Mount Battock,* 2,555 ft., near which Angus, Kincardine and Aberdeen meet. A walkers' track goes northwards from Tarfside through the hills, crossing a shoulder of the *Hill of Cat,* 2,435 ft., and is known as the Fir Mounth road (2,363 ft.), giving access to Glen Tanner and *Aboyne* (*q.v.*). See **Lochlee.** *Iter. 164.*

TARLAND, Aberdeen. 682. Map 21, **NJ 4 0.**
GOLF. On the outskirts of this village, to the north-east, stands the *House of Cromar,* re-named *Alastrean House,* and donated to the Royal Air Force by the late Lady MacRobert in memory of her three sons, who gave their lives during the Second World War. **4 m. N.E.,** on the Aberdeen road, is the Slack of Tillylodge, a fine viewpoint, the prospect extending westwards towards *Morven,* 2,862 ft., and the distant Cairngorms. About a mile farther stands the ruined *Corse Castle,* dated 1581. **3 m. S.E.,** off the Aboyne road, are the remains of *Coull Castle,* on a rocky knoll near the Church, and in the vicinity is the stone circle of *Tomnaverie* (A.M.), probably dating from the Bronze Age. See **Craigievar Castle.** *Iter* 179.

TARVES, Aberdeen. 1,656. Map 27, **NJ 8 3.**
Here, in the 19th century, the Duthie family perfected the famous Collynie breed of shorthorn cattle. Situated on a by-road, **2 m. S.,** are the interesting remains of *Tolquhon Castle* (A.M.), dated 1584 and 1589, with an entrance between two round towers showing grated windows and a fine carved panel over the door. The courtyard has buildings on all four sides. Open summer 10 to 7, winter, 10 to 4; Sun., 2 to 4 (see note page 98). *Iter. 186.*

TAY BRIDGES, Angus; Fife. Map 17, **NO 3 2.**
See **Dundee, Newport-on-Tay** and **Wormit.** *Iter. 94, 126, 127.*

TAYINLOAN, Argyll. Map 6, **NR 6 4.**
Stands on the west side of the narrow *Kintyre* (*q.v.*) peninsula, looking across the Sound of Gigha towards the island of *Gigha* (*q.v.*), to which it is linked by a passenger ferry. See **Killean.** *Iter. 121.*

TAYMOUTH CASTLE, Perth. Map 16, **NN 7 4.**
See **Kenmore.**

TAYNUILT, Argyll. 415. Map 14, **NN 0 3.**
E.C. Wed. A small resort near the shores of picturesque Loch Etive, where the village of *Bonawe* (*q.v.*) stands opposite the narrows which divide the lower and the upper loch. Near *Muckairn* Church is a monument to Lord Nelson, which was erected in 1805, before his remains had been brought back to England. To the south-east, beyond the River Awe, is the entrance to the gloomy Pass of Brander, threaded by the River Awe, and in which are situated the *Falls of Cruachan* (*q.v.*). The views from Taynuilt are very extensive, taking in *Ben Cruachan,* 3,689 ft., and also the mountains overlooking Upper Loch Etive, the highest of which is *Ben Starav,* 3,541 ft., far to the north-east. Southwards from the village is the wooded Glen Nant, traversed by the road leading to *Kilchrenan* (*q.v.*). Another road, gated and with bad bends, leads westwards by way of Glen Lonan, and passes near Loch Nell on the way to *Oban* (*q.v.*). *Iter. 110, 117, 125, 144, 145.*

TAYPORT, Fife. 2,963. SB. Map 17, **NO 4 2.**
GOLF. Overlooks the Firth of Tay, and was formerly known as *Ferry Port on Craig,* but the ferry service to Broughty Ferry, on the opposite shore, is no longer in operation. The Church has a 17th cent. tower and carries the date 1794. *Scotscraig,* a mansion to the south-west, below Hare Law, preserves an archway dated 1667, the crest recalling Archbishop Sharp, its one-time owner, who was murdered at Magus Muir. (See **Pitscottie.**) To the south-east of Tayport is the Tents Moor, with its forestry plantations, on the western extremity of which are the *Morton Lochs,* an important breeding ground and resting place for migrating birds, around which an area of 47 acres has been declared a National Nature Reserve for the study of wildfowl. Surrounding the reserve is Forestry Commission property, planted mainly with Corsican pine. Part of it forms the 92-acre *Tentsmuir Point* National Nature Reserve. *Iter. 94.*

TAYVALLICH, Argyll. Map 14, **NR 7 8.**
Lies in the *Knapdale* (*q.v.*) district, on a small inlet of Loch

Tarbert, Argyll. The remains of the 14th century Castle, once a stronghold of Robert Bruce. It overlooks the inlet of East Loch Tarbert

Tarbet, Dunbarton. A milestone on A83 between Arrochar and Tarbet

Tarbolton, Ayr. The tall 19th century Barnweil Monument, off B730, some 2 miles north. It commemorates the burning of the Barns of Ayr by William Wallace

Tarbolton, Ayr. The Bachelors' Club, which Robert Burns founded in 1780. It is now the property of the National Trust for Scotland

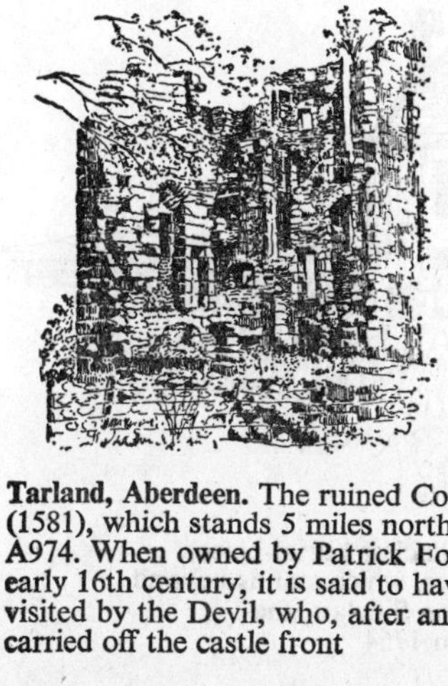

Tarland, Aberdeen. The ruined Corse Castle (1581), which stands 5 miles north-east, off A974. When owned by Patrick Forbes, in the early 16th century, it is said to have been visited by the Devil, who, after an argument, carried off the castle front

Tayport, Fife. The sundial and plaque on the Church, which records its re-building in 1794 by the Rev. Dr. Robert Dalgleish of Scotscraig. The 17th century tower is out of true

[For TARBET see also under HIGHLANDS (Plate 84)
[For TAYMOUTH CASTLE see under KENMORE (Plate 94)
[For TARVES see under TOLQUHON CASTLE (Plate 162)

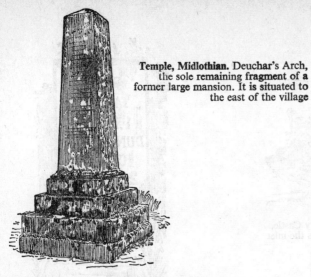

Temple, Midlothian. Deuchar's Arch, the sole remaining fragment of a former large mansion. It is situated to the east of the village

Temple, Midlothian. A churchyard monument, which is perhaps unique, being inscribed with the details of the Will of the Rev. James Goldie, who died in 1847

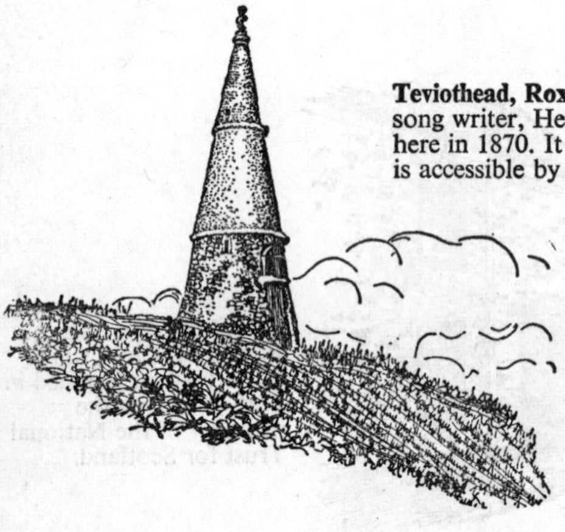

Teviothead, Roxburgh. The Monument to the song writer, Henry Scott Riddell, who died here in 1870. It stands a little to the north and is accessible by a path

Thornhill, Dumfries. The tall column of 1714, surmounted by the 'winged horse' emblem of the Queensberry family

Thurso, Caithness. Pennyland House, in which Sir William Alexander Smith, the founder of the Boys' Brigade, was born in October, 1854

Thurso, Caithness. The Sinclair burial-place, known as Harold's Tower, which stands beyond the Castle, where Sir John Sinclair, the agriculturist, was born in 1754

Sween, with its richly wooded shores. To the west, beyond a small neck of land, is Carsaig Bay, in the Sound of Jura. The road leading south-westwards from Tayvallich terminates at *Keills* (*q.v.*). *Iter. 122.*

TEANGUE, Isle of Skye, Inverness. Map 23, **NG 6 0.** In the fertile Sleat peninsula, facing Knock Bay, an inlet of the Sound of Sleat. On a crag above the bay are the remains of *Knock Castle*, from which the views towards the lofty mainland mountains are very fine. About a mile to the north-west of Teangue, a rough and hilly by-road crosses the peninsula to *Ord*, on Loch Eishort, which is described under *Isle Ornsay*. *Iter. 253.*

TEMPLE, Midlothian. 2,046 with Borthwick. Map 10, **NT 3 5.** This pleasant village is situated on the steep banks of the South Esk River, and is visited for its roofless 13th to 14th cent. Church, which has a 17th cent. east gable belfry. *Temple* was formerly the chief Scottish seat of the Knights Templar, the order having been suppressed in 1312, and the property passing to the Knights of St. John of Jerusalem. In the churchyard of the modern Church is a gravestone to the Rev. James Goldie, on which appears his will. East of the village stands " Deuchar's Arch," the sole remnant of a vanished mansion. **3 m. S.W.,** on the lower slopes of the *Moorfoot* hills, at a height of 900 ft., is the large Gladhouse reservoir, beyond which rises the lonely hill of *Blackhope Scar*, 2,136 ft. See **Gorebridge.** *Iter. 40.*

TENTSMUIR, Fife. Map 17, **NO 4 2.** See **Tayport.**

TERREGLES, Dumfries. Map 4, **NX 9 7.** See **Dumfries.**

TEVIOTHEAD, Roxburgh. 499 Map 5, **NT 4 0.** In the churchyard of the lonely Church, situated among the rounded hills of Teviotdale, is a memorial to Johnny Armstrong, an early 16th cent. Border " reiver," or outlaw. He was associated with the district around *Canonbie* and *Langholm* (both *q.v.*), and was hanged near Teviothead by order of James V. On the high ground a little to the north stands a monument to Henry Scott Riddell, a writer of patriotic songs, the best known of which are perhaps " Scotland Yet " and " Oor ain Folk." Formerly a minister of the parish, he was buried in the churchyard in 1870. *Iter. 11, 30, 45.*

THIRLESTANE, Berwick. Map 10, **NT 5 4.** See **Lauder.**

THIRLESTANE, Selkirk. Map 10, **NT 2 1.** See **Tushielaw.**

THORNHILL, Dumfries. 1,441. Map 3, **NX 8 9.** **E.C.** Thurs. **M.D.** Sat. GOLF. A small town overlooking the pleasant valley of the River Nith, with a backing of Lowland hills, dominated by *Queensberry*, 2,285 ft., to the east. There are tree-lined streets, and a museum with Burns and Covenanters' relics. A tall column, erected in 1714, and restored after gale damage in 1955, is topped by a winged horse, the emblem of the Queensberrys. Near the bridge over the Nith, to the west, is the 15th cent. *Boatford Cross*, marking the old ford and ferry. **2 m. S.,** off the Dumfries road, and near the river, is *Dalgarnock* churchyard, where a Cross commemorates 57 Nithsdale Covenanters, who gave their lives in various parts of the country. See **Carronbridge, Closeburn, Drumlanrig Castle, Enterkinfoot** and **Penpont.** *Iter. 27, 48, 56, 67.*

THORNTON, Fife. 2,500 Map 17, **NT 2 9.** An important mining centre on the East Fife coalfield. *Iter. 93, 126, 130.*

THREAVE CASTLE, Kirkcudbright. Map 3, **NX 7 6.** See **Castle Douglas.**

THRUMSTER, Caithness. Map 30, **ND 3 4.** A tiny Caithness village, with three small lochs in the vicinity. To the north-east is the bare Loch Hempriggs; to the south-west is the Loch of Yarehouse; and to the south, close to the village of *Sarclet*, and almost on the rocky coast between Sarclet Head and the Stack of Ulbster, lies Loch Sarclet. *Iter. 200.*

THURSO, Caithness. 9,074. SB. Map 30, **ND 1 6.** **E.C.** Thurs. **M.D.** Tues. GOLF. Finely situated on the Thurso River, flowing into Thurso Bay. There are good views north-westwards towards the most northerly point on the Scottish mainland, the cliffs of Dunnet Head, and also to the distant cliffs of Hoy, in the Orkneys, across the Pentland Firth. To the north-west of the town are the riven

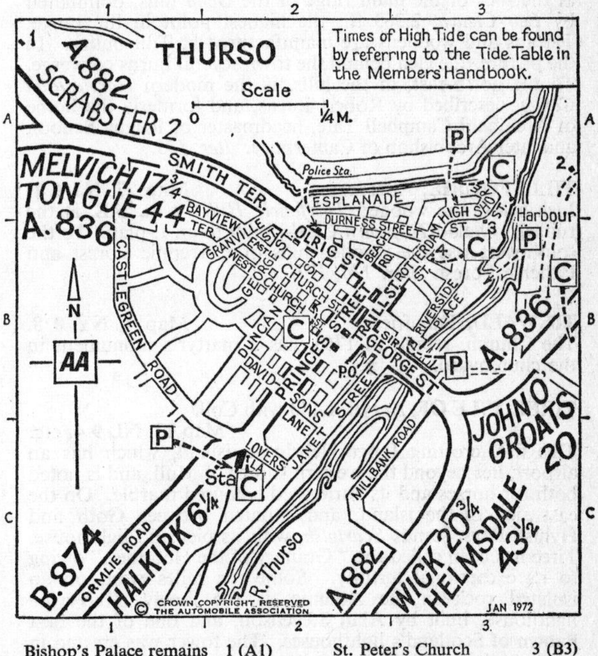

Bishop's Palace remains	1 (A1)	St. Peter's Church	3 (B3)
Castle	2 (A3)	Town Hall, with Library and Museum adjacent	4 (B3)

cliffs of Holborn Head. Once an important port, *Thurso* is today mainly a fishing town and resort, while the quarrying of Caithness flagstones is a local industry, most of the fields and roads in the vicinity being lined by them in place of trees or hedges. The ruined Church of *St. Peter* is a reconstruction of the 17th cent. The town has some 17th cent. houses, and in the Museum is a collection of plants and fossils and a small Runic Cross. At *Thurso Castle*, north-east of the town, and partially demolished, was born Sir John Sinclair, the 18th cent. agriculturist and statistician, to whom a statue stands by the Church. Beyond the Castle stands *Harold's Tower*, the Sinclair burial-place, erected over the grave of Harold, a former Jarl of Caithness, killed in 1196. In Manson's Lane is the ancient Meadow Well. West of the town, on the shores of the bay, are the remains of the medieval *Bishop's Palace*, and in the vicinity is *Pennyland*, where Sir William Smith, the founder of the Boys' Brigade, was born in 1854. Farther to the north-west is *Scrabster* (*q.v.*), the port for the Orkney steamer. **2½ m. W.,** near the foot of Scrabster Hill, is a broch known as " Things Va." See **Bridge of Forss, Dounreay, Dunnet** and **East Mey.** *Iter. 232, 234, 236, 237, 238, 239, 240.*

TIBBIE SHIEL'S INN, Selkirk. Map 9, **NT 2 2.** This well-known anglers' inn stands on the narrow neck of land separating picturesque *St. Mary's Loch* (*q.v.*) from the Loch of the Lowes. Here, many famous names are recalled, among the visitors to the inn having been de Quincey, Brewster and Lockhart, while here also took place one of the " Noctes Ambrosianae " of Christopher North (Professor Wilson) and James Hogg, better known as the " Ettrick Shepherd." See **Ettrick.** *Iter. 13, 46.*

TIGHNABRUAICH, Argyll. 1,500. Map 7, **NR 9** 7.
E.C. Wed. A favourite *Kyles of Bute* (*q.v.*) and *Cowal* (*q.v.*) resort, with a steamer pier, facing the Island of Bute in one of the narrowest reaches of the Kyles. The road from the eastern shores of *Loch Fyne* (*q.v.*) now continues northwards along Loch Riddon towards *Glendaruel* (*q.v.*). Adjacent to Tighnabruaich, to the south-west, is the smaller resort of *Auchenlochan*, also with a pier. See **Kames.** *Iter. 102, 103.*

TILLICOULTRY, Clackmannan. 4,099. SB. Map 16, **NS 9** 9.
E.C. Tues. GOLF. The town stands on the River Devon, at the foot of the main ridge of the *Ochil* hills, dominated by *Ben Cleuch*, 2,363 ft., the highest point in the range. Tartans and woollens are manufactured at Tillicoultry. In the picturesque glen behind the town several burns converge. To the north-east, in the hills, is the modern *Harviestoun Castle*, described by Robert Burns, and formerly the home of Archibald Campbell Tate, headmaster of Rugby School, and later Archbishop of Canterbury. *Iter. 136.*

TILLYFOURIE, Aberdeen. Map 27, **NJ 6 1.**
Lies below the wooded *Tillyfourie Hill.* **2 m. S.E.** is the ruined, ivy-clad *Tillycairn Castle*, built to an L-plan. To the south-west rise the wooded hills of Corrennie Forest and Pitfichie Forest. *Iter. 176, 177.*

TINWALD, Dumfries. Map 4, NY **0** 8.
The Church, rebuilt in 1763, has a martyr's monument in the churchyard.

TIREE, ISLE OF, Argyll. 1,143 with Coll. Map 13, **NL 9** 4, etc.
This flat, crofting Inner Hebridean island, which has an airport, lies beyond the western shores of Mull, and is noted both for horses and its variegated coloured marble. On the east side of the island, and situated between Goth and Hynish Bays, stands *Scarinish*, with its pier and lighthouse. Tiree has been called the " Granary of the Hebrides," owing to its exceptional fertility. Some ten miles west, on an isolated rock in the Atlantic, is the lonely *Skerryvore* lighthouse, built by Alan Stevenson, and one of the best known of Scotland's lighthouses. The tower was erected in 1843, and is 135 ft. high, its construction having been attended by immense difficulties. To the north-east of Tiree, separated by only a few miles of water, is the flat island of *Coll*, devoted mainly to crofting, while there are some remains of early forts, and also the ruined *Breachacha* Castle. Dr. Johnson paid a visit to the island, in 1733, when he inspected the castle. Both Tiree and Coll are connected to *Oban* (*q.v.*), on the mainland, by steamer service, and Tiree has a direct air service from Glasgow.

TIUMPAN HEAD, Isle of Lewis, Ross and Cromarty. Map 32, **NB 5** 3.
The northernmost point of the *Eye* peninsula, with a lighthouse. At the southern extremity is Chicken Head. *Iter. 259.*

TOBERMORY, Isle of Mull, Argyll. 641. SB. Map 12, **NM 5** 5.
E.C. Wed. GOLF. The largest and best-known resort on the island, with a steamer pier overlooking Tobermory Bay, sheltered by Calve Island in the Sound of Mull. There are views of the Ardnamurchan and Morven coast on the mainland to the north and east. The town stands in a pleasant wooded setting, with several waterfalls, and is noted for sea fishing. Its name means St. Mary's Well. Tobermory has long been associated with a Spanish Armada galleon, probably the " Florida," which was blown up and sunk in the bay in 1588. The ship was actually destroyed as the result of the work of a Scottish hostage. Numerous attempts, including some in recent years, have been made to retrieve the treasure which is believed to be hidden in the wreck. Various articles have at different times been salvaged from the galleon, including a cannon, now resting at *Inveraray Castle* (*q.v.*). Dr. Johnson and Boswell visited Tobermory in 1773 and noted 12 to 14 vessels in the harbour. From the pier a service connects with Mingary, near *Kilchoan* (*q.v.*), on the Ardnamurchan coast. To the south-east of the town are the fine grounds of *Aros House*. The road leading westwards towards *Calgary* (*q.v.*) passes near the shores of the Mishnish Lochs, to the north of Loch Frisa, beyond which, after some hairpin bends, it reaches *Dervaig* (*q.v.*), on the narrow Loch Cuan. Away to the north of Tobermory, near the coast, is the modern *Glengorm Castle*, in its fine grounds. See **Salen** (Mull). *Iter. 248, 250.*

TOLQUHON CASTLE, Aberdeen. Map 27, **NJ 8 2.**
See **Tarves.**

TOMATIN, Inverness. 166. Map 25, **NH 8** 2.
E.C. Wed. A Strath Dearn village, in the midst of fir plantations, and situated on the River Findhorn, which has come down from a wilderness of lonely hills away to the south-west, dominated by the *Monadhliath* range. The bridge over the river at Tomatin replaces one built originally by Telford in 1833. From here the river flows north-eastwards through a roadless part of Strath Dearn known as *The Streens*, overlooked by hills rising to more than 2,000 ft., and leading towards *Dulsie Bridge* (*q.v.*), situated in what is the Findhorn's most picturesaue reach. *Iter. 140, 150, 195.*

TOMDOUN HOTEL, Inverness. Map 18, **NH 1 0.**
An anglers' resort, beautifully situated in Glen Garry, where the western end of the enlarged Loch Garry merges with Loch Poulary. The road which climbed northwards over a 1,424-ft. high shoulder of *Creag a'Mhaim* leading to *Cluanie* (*q.v.*) is no longer usable owing to the construction of the Loch Loyne reservoir in connection with the Loch Garry hydro-electric scheme. A new road (**4 m. E.**) now crosses low hills from the north side of Loch Garry to reach the eastern end of Loch Cluanie. Both these lochs are now reservoirs. The continuation of this fine road westwards leads to Cluanie for *Glen Shiel* (*q.v.*) and *Kyle of Lochalsh* (*q.v.*). Westwards from Tomdoun goes a road following the shores of Loch Garry and its continuation Loch Poulary. This road gives access to the very lovely *Loch Quoich* (*q.v.*), its contours also changed due to hydro-electric works, and terminates (very rough and narrow) at *Kinloch Hourn* (*q.v.*). The whole of this *Knoydart* (*q.v.*) or *Rough Bounds* district is one of lonely mountain grandeur, with *Gairich*, 3,015 ft., dominating Loch Quoich from the south, and prominent in the westerly view from Tomdoun itself. Depopulation of this neighbourhood took place in the 18th and 19th centuries, many of the emigrants departing to Canada, to found a new Glengarry. See **Invergarry.** *Iter. 214, 220.*

TOMINTOUL, Banff. 457. Map 26, **NJ 1** 1,
E.C. Wed. The loftiest village in the Highlands, being situated at a height of 1,160 ft. It is well known as an angling resort in summer, and also as a winter sports resort. *Tomintoul* lies on a plateau, with the main range of the *Cairngorms* (*q.v.*) rising away to the south-west beyond the valley of the River Avon, their lonely foothills and distant *Ben Avon*, 3,843 ft., being visible at various points from the road leading north-westwards towards *Grantown-on-Spey* (*q.v.*). To the east flows the Conglass Water, which is crossed by the road climbing north-eastwards, and reaching a height of more than 1,200 ft. nearing the Braes of Glenlivet, before descending to *Tomnavoulin* (*q.v.*) and *Glenlivet* (*q.v.*). South-eastwards from Tomintoul, the famous *Lecht* road, described under *Cock Bridge*, reaches a height of 2,090 ft. near the Aberdeen and Banff border on its way to the valley of the Don, and is liable to be blocked by snow in winter. The Avon flows to the west of Tomintoul, being joined by the Conglass Water, and a road follows Strath Avon and the *Cromdale* hills in a northerly direction towards *Delnashaugh Inn* (*q.v.*), on the threshold of the Spey valley. This point is also accessible by the Glenlivet road, mentioned previously To the south-west of Tomintoul, the Avon flows through the remote foothills of the Cairngorms. Just outside the village, near *Delnabo*, it is joined by the Water of Ailnack. This stream, together with the Water of Caiplach, flows along the Banff and Inverness border in a series of spectacular gorges, most difficult of access, with *Geal Charn*, 2,692 ft., rising in the background. Tomintoul is not the highest village in Scotland, this distinction falling to

Tobermory, Isle of Mull, Argyll. A view of the bay, in which Dr. Johnson, during his visit of 1773, counted 12 to 14 ships. A Spanish Armada galleon was sunk here in 1588, and efforts have been made at various times to salvage treasure from the wreckage

Tolquhon Castle, Aberdeen. The ruined Castle, dated 1584 and 1589, which was built by William Forbes. It stands 2 miles south of Tarves, on an unclassified road off B999

Tomdoun, Inverness. A view looking towards the dam on Loch Garry, off A87, to the east. It is part of a large new hydro-electric scheme extending westwards to Loch Quoich

Tomintoul, Banff. A fountain presented by Robert Grant M.D., in 1915, as a memento of his boyhood

Tomintoul, Banff. A cattle-grid, at a height of 2,090 feet, on the Lecht road (A939), which was built in 1754 as a military road, and leads south-eastwards to Corgarff, in the Upper Don valley

[For TIGHNABRUAICH see under KYLES OF BUTE (Plate 104)

Tongland, Kirkcudbright. A power station in connection with the extensive Galloway hydro-electric scheme

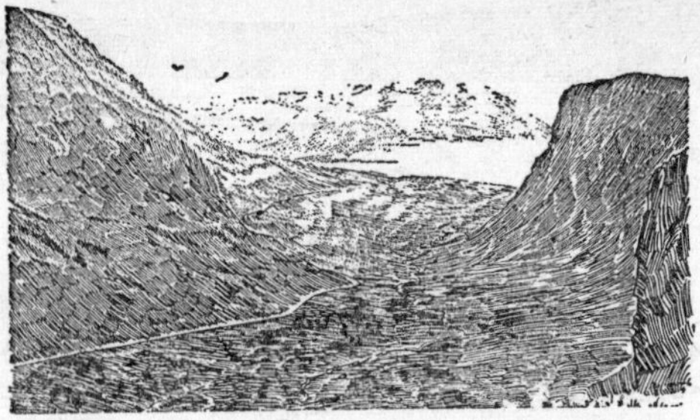

Tornapress, Ross and Cromarty. A view down the famous Pass of the Cattle, or 'Bealach nam Bo' (2,054 feet), which climbs over the hills to descend to Applecross Bay, facing the islands of Raasay and Skye

Tongue, Sutherland. Ben Loyal, 2,504 feet, which rises to the south of Tongue, and is well seen from both A836 and A838

Torphichen, West Lothian. The 12th to 16th century Church, which was once the property of the Knights Hospitallers of St. John of Jerusalem, and outwardly resembles a castle more than a church

Torphichen, West Lothian. A churchyard stone bearing cup marks. It has been associated with an area of sanctuary connected with the church

Torridon, Ross and Cromarty. Part of a moraine deposit, known as the 'Corrie of a Hundred Hills,' which lies in Glen Torridon

[For TORRIDON see also under GLEN TORRIDON (Plate 77)

Wanlockhead (*q.v.*), a Lowland village, situated at an altitude of 1,380 ft. *Iter. 141, 160, 169, 174, 176, 177, 191, 192.*

TOMNAVOULIN, Banff. Map 26, **NJ 2** 2.
Situated in Glen Livet, with the famous *Glenlivet* (*q.v.*) distillery situated on a by-road to the north-west. East of Tomnavoulin is an area of lonely hills and moors, dominated by *Corryhabbie*, 2,563 ft., overlooking Glen Suidhe and Glen Fiddich. The Tomintoul road goes southwards, rising to more than 1,200 ft. beyond the Braes of Glen Livet. *Iter. 169, 177, 192.*

TONGLAND, Kirkcudbright. 1,519 with Twynholm. Map 3, **NX 6** 5.
The dam here was constructed as part of the important *Galloway* (*q.v.*) hydro-electric scheme, which utilizes the fall in the level of the River Ken before joining the Dee at the foot of Loch Ken. The generating station at Tongland was built in 1935. Tongland Bridge, over the River Dee, is a Telford design of 1805. A fish pass for the salmon has been constructed, and is said to be one of the highest in the country. Of the former 12th cent. Abbey, only a mere fragment still remains in the burial-ground near the Parish Church. *Iter. 70.*

TONGUE, Sutherland. 708. Map 28, **NC 5** 5.
E.C. Mon. This pleasant resort, also known as *Kirkiboll*, lies on the Kyle of Tongue, the outer waters of which are known as Tongue Bay. There are exposed sandy shores providing good bathing, while fishing is also to be had. The ruined *Castle Varrich*, situated on the Allt an Rhian, where it flows into the Kyle, is traditionally the former home of an 11th cent. Norse king. *Tongue House*, to the north of the village, is of 17th and 18th cent. date, replacing a one-time home of the Lords of Reay. Beyond it, to the north-east, is the craggy height of *Cnoc an Freiceadain*, 1,009 ft., well seen from the road to *Bettyhill* (*q.v.*). Away to the south, the road to *Altnaharra* (*q.v.*) skirts the shores of Loch Loyal, and westwards rises the multi-peaked, granite *Ben Loyal*, 2,504 ft., one of the finest mountains in Sutherland, though not of great interest to climbers. Ben Loyal is also a prominent feature in the view from the road which rounds the Kyle of Tongue, passing near the little Loch Hacoin, before it turns northwards towards the desolate moorlands of A'Mhoine. See **Melness** and **Reay.** *Iter. 225, 230, 234, 235, 240.*

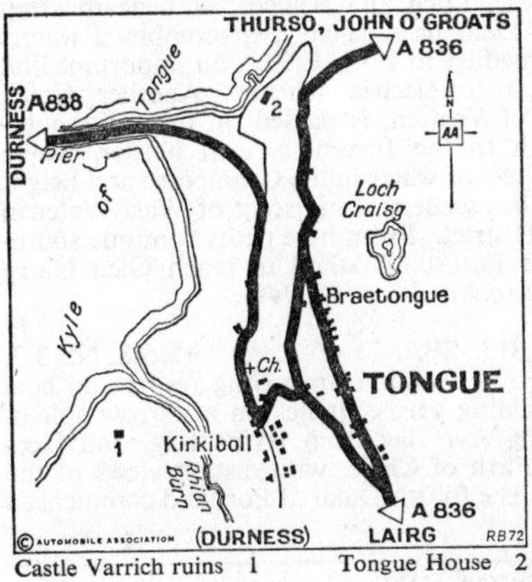

Castle Varrich ruins 1 Tongue House 2

TORGYLE BRIDGE, Inverness. Map 24, **NH 3** 1.
In Glen Moriston, where the road through the glen crosses the Moriston River, with its fine rapids. To the east, the country is well wooded, but westwards the glen becomes bare, with high mountains rising away to the west dominated by *Sgurr nan Conbhairean*, 3,634 ft. *Iter. 207.*

TORNAPRESS, Ross and Cromarty. Map 23, **NG 8** 4.
Lies at the head of Loch Kishorn, an inlet of Loch Carron. This is the starting point of the famous mountain road to *Applecross* (*q.v.*) over the Pass of the Cattle, or " Bealach nam Bo," the nearest approach to an Alpine climb in Great Britain, and liable to be blocked by snow in winter. This rough and narrow, but spectacular road ascends from sea-level to a height of 2,054 ft. within six miles, almost the highest in Scotland, having a maximum gradient of 1 in 4, while near the summit are situated several sharp hair-pin bends. The view from the top is superb, ranging westwards towards the Coolins of Skye and the distant Outer Isles, and eastwards over Lochs Kishorn and Carron to the serried Ross-shire and Inverness-shire peaks. The descent to Applecross is less difficult, but the return journey must be made over the same road. To the south of the pass rises *Meall Gorm*, 2,325 ft., and on the north side is *Sgurr a' Chaorachain*, 2,539 ft., both composed of red Torridon sandstone. Nearer to Tornapress itself is the peak of *Beinn Bhan*, 2,936 ft., with its remarkable, lonely eastern corries, notably Coire na Poite. See **Shieldaig.** *Iter. 219, 223.*

TORNESS, Inverness. Map 25, **NH 5** 2.
On the River Farigaig, with three lochs, those of Ruthven, Duntelchaig and Ashie, lying to the north-east. *Iter. 211.*

TORPHICHEN, West Lothian. 907. Map 9, **NS 9** 7.
This village stands high, in a situation away from main roads, and is visited for its fine Church (A.M.), once belonging to the Order of Hospitallers, or Knights of St. John of Jerusalem. A meeting of the Order, the first for 400 years, was held here in 1947. Outwardly, the structure is more in the nature of a castle than a Church, the upper storeys of the tower, with its saddle-back roof, having doubtless formed part of the original " Hospital," or domestic buildings. A 16th cent. Parish Church has been built over the former nave, and of the original Norman Church, built for the Knights Templar, the chancel arch has survived. Only the foundations of the choir remain. There are 13th cent. transepts, while the crossing, tower and upper storeys are 15th cent. work. A sanctuary stone stands in the churchyard. Torphichen Mill was the birthplace, in 1767, of Henry Bell, designer of the " Comet," one of the earliest steamboats. Near the mill, a bridge, built c. 1800 and repaired in 1930, spans the River Avon. To the south-east rise the *Bathgate* hills, the highest point being *The Knock*, 1,017 ft., a good viewpoint. **2 m. S.W.** is *Bridge Castle*, standing on a rocky eminence, and dating mainly from the 16th and 17th cents., having been formerly in the possession of the Earls of Linlithgow. About **2 m. S.E.** of Torphichen is *Cairnpapple Hill* (A.M.), a Neolithic sanctuary remodelled in the Bronze Age and recently excavated. To the north-east rises *Cocklerue*, once *Cuckold le Roi*, a low hill figuring in a poem by R. L. Stevenson. **See Bowling.** *Iter. 86.*

TORPHINS, Aberdeen. 473. Map 27, **NJ 6** 0.
GOLF. **E.C.** Thurs. **M.D.** Alt. Mon. A pleasant small village to the north of the Dee valley. It may have taken its name from Thorfinn, a Scandinavian ally of Macbeth, the latter having been killed in the neighbourhood of nearby *Lumphanan* (*q.v.*). **2 m. S.** is the ruined *Castle Maud*, which may date back to the time of Robert Bruce. *Iter. 165, 190.*

TORRANCE, Stirling. 3,252. Map 8, **NS 6** 7.
Iter. 107, 113.

TORRIDON, Ross and Cromarty. Map 24, **NG 9** 5.
Lies at the western end of Glen Torridon, perhaps the finest and wildest of the *Wester Ross* (*q.v.*) glens. It is of great interest to geologists for the grand mountains of red Torridon sandstone (N.T. Scot.), some with white quartzite tops, lining both sides of the valley, whicn extends inland in the direction of *Loch Maree* (*q.v.*). West of Torridon is Inner Loch Torridon, its northern shores traversed by a narrow road which continues as far as the hamlet of Diabaig, on the Outer Loch, the latter half of the road being rough and steep with hairpin bends and gradients of 1 in 5. Above the Inner Loch, beyond Coire Mhic Nobuil, rises *Ben Alligin*, 3,232 ft., showing the " Horns of Alligin," and to the north-east is *Ben Dearg*, 2,995 ft., from which all the Torridon peaks can be very well seen. In Glen Torridon, the monarch of the hills is *Liathach*, 3,456 ft., one of Scotland's finest peaks, composed of more than 3 miles of steep terraces or red sandstone, most difficult to climb, and towering over the spectacular corrie of Coire na Caime, to the north. These hills of Torridon stone, capped in places by quartzite, make a striking picture when lit by the rays of the evening sun. Situated in the glen is the curious so-called " Corrie of a Hundred Hills," probably an ancient moraine deposit. North-eastwards are the fine quartzite peaks of *Ben Eighe*,

over 3,000 ft. in height. (See **Kinlochewe.**) A new road has been made on the south side of the Inner Loch leading to *Shieldaig* (*q.v.*). This climbs above the loch, with superb views of the terraced Torridon peaks to the north, notably *Liathach. Iter. 223.*

TORRIN, Isle of Skye, Inverness. Map 23, **NG 5 2.**
Faces Loch Slapin, beyond which, on the Strathaird peninsula, rises the great black *Coolin* (*q.v.*) peak of *Blaven*, 3,042 ft., with its notable rock ridge of *Clach Glas*, well known to climbers. A little to the east of Torrin, on the Broadford road, is the little Loch cill Chriosd, in Strath Suardal, with the ruined Church of *Kilchrist*, probably of 16th or 17th cent. date. See **Elgol.** *Iter. 252.*

TORRYBURN, Fife. 1,744. Map 16, **NT 0 8.**
Lies on Torry Bay, an inlet of the Forth estary, and is a small coal port. In 1822, Alison Cunningham, who was nurse to R. L. Stevenson, and to whom he later dedicated his " Child's Garden of Verses," was born in a house in the village. In a field is the 8ft. high Bronze Age Stannin Stone. Preston Island, in Torrie Bay, once had a coalmine. **2½ m. W.**, on the coast, is the famous little Royal Burgh of *Culross* (*q.v.*). *Iter. 97, 134.*

TORTHORWALD, Dumfries. 1,151. Map 4, **NY 0 7.**
The old, ruined Castle keep of the Carlyles overlooks the fertile Nithsdale valley, to the west, from its 250-ft. high eminence, and is probably of late 14th cent. date. *Iter. 45.*

TOSCAIG, Ross and Cromarty. Map 22, **NG 7 4.**
See **Applecross.**

TOUCH HOUSE, Stirling. Map 16, **NS 7 9.**
See **Gargunnock.**

TOWN YETHOLM, Roxburgh. Map 11, **NT 8 2.**
See **Yetholm.**

TRANENT, East Lothian. 6,288. SB. Map 10, **NT 4 7.**
E.C. Wed. A mining town, situated a few miles inland from the Firth of Forth. Colonel Gardiner, who died here from wounds received at the battle of *Prestonpans* (*q.v.*), in 1745, is associated with Scott's " Waverley." The Parish Church was built in 1800, on the foundations of a much older structure, and in the churchyard are numerous interesting monuments. A nearby doocot dates from 1587. **2 m. S.W.** is the ruined 15th and 16th cent. *Falside Castle*, also situated on high ground. See **Ormiston** and **Pencaitland.** *Iter. 1, 3.*

TRAPRAIN LAW, East Lothian. Map 10, **NT 5 7.**
See **East Linton.**

TRAQUAIR, Peebles. 394. Map 10, **NT 3 3.**
An attractive little village, lying on the Quair Water, one of the tributaries of the Tweed. *Traquair House*, perhaps the Tully-Veolan of Scott's " Waverley," is one of the finest and most picturesque of early Scottish mansions, and is shown, 2 to 5.30, all Suns. from May and all weekdays (except Fri.) from July, until end of Sept. (See note page 98.) It is one of the oldest inhabited houses in the country and was once the home of William the Lion, who held a court here in 1209. The main block dates from 1642, with an older tower and later wings. Mary, Queen of Scots and Darnley stayed in the house in 1566. The main avenue gates have not been opened since 1796, when the 7th Countess of Traquair died, but tradition has it that they were closed already after 1745, not to be re-opened until a Stuart should once more ascend the throne. There are fine gardens at the house known as the *Riggs of Traquair*. South-west of the Church, which has outside gallery stairs, lies *Glen*, with its fine gardens, an early home of the 1st Countess of Oxford and Asquith. To the east of Traquair, on the Selkirk border, rises *Minchmuir*, 1,856 ft., a fine viewpoint, traversed by an old drovers' track linking Peebles with Selkirk, which was used as an escape route by Montrose, in 1645, after the battle of *Philiphaugh* near *Selkirk* (*q.v.*). Montrose is said to have halted at *Traquair House* during his flight. The road leading southwards towards the picturesque Vale of *Yarrow* (*q.v.*) climbs over the hills, and is known as the " Paddy Slacks." It reaches a height of over 1,100 ft. near the meeting-point of the counties of Peebles and Selkirk, on the northern fringe of Ettrick Forest. See **Blairgowrie.** *Iter. 12, 34.*

TRINAFOUR, Perth. Map 19, **NN 7 6.**
Situated in the lonely moorlands of Glen Erochy, on the road linking the Tummel valley with the main Perth to Inverness highway in Glen Garry at Calvine, near *Struan* (*q.v.*). The Errochty River has been harnessed to a hydro-electric scheme, in conjunction with the Tummel-Garry undertaking, and for this purpose the Errochty reservoir and power station have been constructed. To the north of Trinafour, a rough track leading to *Dalnacardoch* (*q.v.*) is part of Wade's original military road, constructed in 1730, and climbing to a height of 1,452 ft. before descending into Glen Garry. The view of the mountains to the north in the extensive Forest of Atholl from the hairpin bend on this track, above Trinafour, is extremely fine. A better route to Glen Garry is to continue through Glen Erochy, as mentioned above. See **Kinloch Rannoch** and **Wade Roads.** *Iter. 147, 149.*

TROMIE BRIDGE, Inverness. Map 19, **NN 7 9.**
To the south extends the long, partly wooded expanse of Glen Tromie, which gives access by paths to the lonely Gaick Forest. Here, Loch an't Seilich, set beneath steep hills, is linked to Loch na Cuaich, their combined waters being taken by aqueduct to Loch Ericht, an important link in the Rannoch hydro-electric scheme. Another Gaick Forest loch, that of Vrotten, is passed on the way southwards by footpath to the Inverness-Perth border, where Loch-an-Duin, a sheet of water in the Grampians at a height of some 1,700 ft., has scenery reminiscent of Wast Water in the English Lake District. From here paths continue southwards through the Forest of Atholl to reach Glen Garry near *Dalnacardoch* (*q.v.*). *Iter. 138, 149.*

TROON, Ayr. 11,315. SB. Map 8, **NS 3 3.**
E.C. Wed. GOLF. A well-known golfing resort and coal port, with ship-building yards. It lies on a narrow spit of rocky land dividing Ayr Bay from Irvine Bay, and faces the waters of the Firth of Clyde, with distant views of the Arran mountains. The fourth Duke of Portland commenced

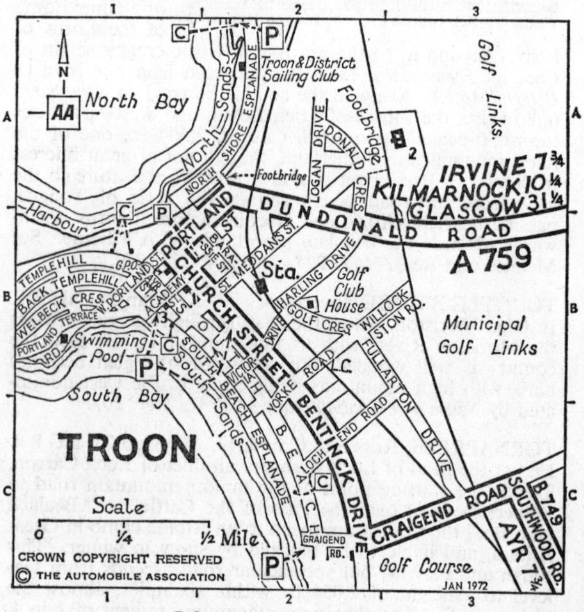

Information Bureau 1 (B1)
Marr College 2 (A3) Municipal Buildings 3 (B1)

Torthorwald, Dumfries. The ruined 14th century Castle of the Carlyles, situated on a hill to the east. One of its earliest owners was given the title of Lord Torthorwald by James VI

Tranent, East Lothian. The dovecote of 1587, which stands near the Church

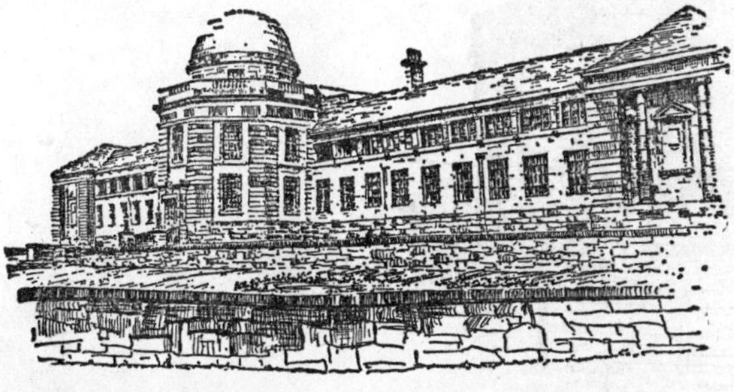

Troon, Ayr. Marr College, erected from the proceeds of a legacy donated to the town in 1919 by Charles Kerr Marr, who was born at Troon

Traquair, Peebles. Perhaps Scotland's oldest inhabited mansion, the present Traquair House, of the 16th century and later. William the Lion hunted in Traquair Forest in 1209, and Mary, Queen of Scots, stayed here with Darnley in 1566

Traquair, Peebles. The main entrance gates to Traquair House, which have been closed since the '45 Rising, and it is said will not be re-opened until a Stuart once again ascends the throne

Trossachs, Perth. The Loch Katrine steamer at the Trossachs pier

Trossachs, Perth. A milestone on A81, between Aberfoyle and Balfron, on the southern edge of the Trossachs. It gives an unusual spelling for Aberfoyle

Tullibardine, Perth. The Collegiate Church of 1446, which contains a remarkable open timber roof

Tullynessle, Aberdeen. The ruined Terpersie Castle, dated 1561. It stands in a farmyard to the north-west, off an unclassified road

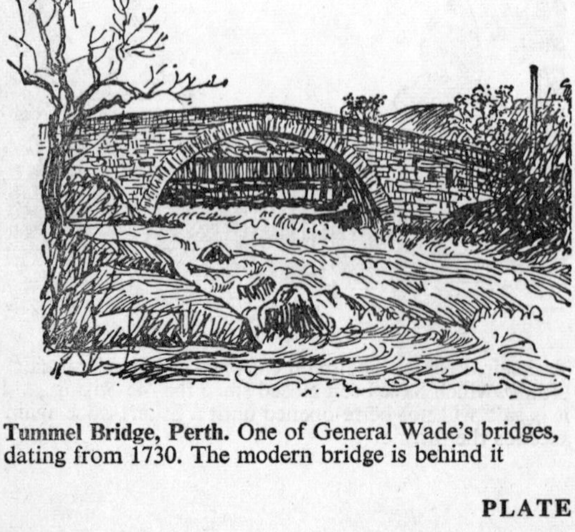

Tummel Bridge, Perth. One of General Wade's bridges, dating from 1730. The modern bridge is behind it

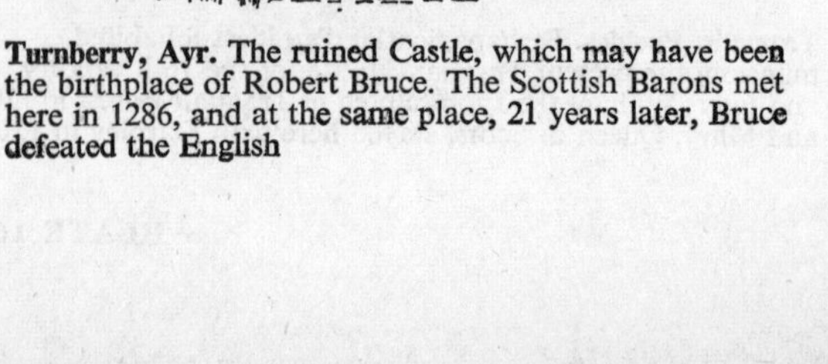

Turnberry, Ayr. The ruined Castle, which may have been the birthplace of Robert Bruce. The Scottish Barons met here in 1286, and at the same place, 21 years later, Bruce defeated the English

the development of the harbour in the 18th cent. *Marr College* dates from 1919. The south sands provide good bathing, and beyond the north sands lie *Barassie* and *Gailes*, both known for their excellent golfing facilities. Off-shore is Lady Isle, a bird sanctuary. Louis Philippe of France stayed, in 1801, at *Fullarton House*, which lies inland to the east. See **Dundonald** and **Symington** (Ayr). *Iter. 19, 88.*

TROSSACHS, THE, Perth. 250. Map 15, **NN 4** 0 and **5** 0.
The fame of the *Trossachs* district is due not only to its extraordinary lovely combination of mountain, loch and woodland, but also to the graphically-written descriptions in Scott's " Lady of the Lake " and " Rob Roy," which have served as an introduction to many thousands of visitors. The word Trossachs means " bristly country," and the richly-wooded gorge of the Trossachs extends actually from Loch Achray to Loch Katrine, though the road through the pass does not follow quite the same course as in Scott's time. Part of the area lies within the newly-created *Queen Elizabeth Forest Park*. The rugged hill of *Ben Venue*, 2,393 ft., to the south, a fine viewpoint, dominates the scene, and overlooks the eastern end of picturesque *Loch Katrine* (*q.v.*) and the Pass of Achray. Here, opposite Ellen's Isle, was the former " Silver Strand," associated with the " Lady of the Lake," but now submerged since the level of the lake was raised in connection with the building of the subterranean aqueduct conveying water supplies for Glasgow. A steamer plies on the loch in summer from Loch Katrine pier, where the public road terminates, to *Stronachachar* (*q.v.*) pier, from which Rob Roy's birthplace at *Glengyle* can be visited on foot. The private road from Loch Katrine pier along Strath Gartney and the northern shores of the loch, which also gives access to Glengyle, can only be used by pedestrians.

A road diverges southwards by the wooded shores of Loch Achray (water-ski-ing), leading over the hills to *Aberfoyle* (*q.v.*), with fine views. To the west of this road, and traversed by paths, is the picturesque Pass of Achray, and also the Bealach nam Bo, or Pass of the Cattle, along which the MacGregors once drove their plunder. The road leading eastwards along the northern shores of Loch Achray passes the " *Trossachs* " Hotel, behind which rise the hills of *Sron Armailte*, 1,149 ft., and *Ben A'an*, 1,750 ft. (to the north-west), both good viewpoints. Later it reaches the well-known *Brig o' Turk*, familiar to lovers of the " Lady of the Lake." This bridge spans the Finglas Water, or River Turk, which has descended from Glen Finglas. Beyond the bridge stretches picturesque Loch Vennachar, with *Ben Ledi*, 2,875 ft., rising to the north, the road following the north bank of the loch towards *Callander* (*q.v.*). To the south of Loch Vennachar lies the smaller Loch Drunkie, which is well seen from the picturesque " Duke's " Road linking the Trossachs with Aberfoyle. See **Inversnaid.** *Iter. 106, 111, 139.*

TRUMPAN, Isle of Skye, Inverness. Map 22, **NG 2** 6.
In an isolated and lonely setting on the narrow Vaternish peninsula, washed by the waters of Loch Snizort and Loch Dunvegan. The ruined Macleod Church was burnt by the Macdonalds, and here is buried Lady Grange, who had been exiled, in 1734, to *St. Kilda* (*q.v.*). To the north of the village is Vaternish Point, and eastwards, in Loch Snizort, lie the Ascrib Islands. *Iter. 255.*

TULLIBARDINE, Perth. Map 16, **NN 9** 1.
The interesting Collegiate Church of *Tullibardine* (A.M.) dates from 1446, and stands in a delightful Strath Earn setting. The most notable feature is the open timber roof, and at the fortified west end of the building is a small tower. The Church, at one time the Atholl mausoleum, is now the burial-place of the Strathallan family. The Castle of *Strathallan* lies a little to the north, near the point where the Machany Water flows into the River Earn.

TULLIBODY, Clackmannan. Map 16, **NS 8** 9.
Situated within a large bend of the River Devon, near the point where it flows into the Forth. The old *Bridgend* Bridge spans the stream. The village was the birthplace in 1811, of the geologist, Robert Dick. *Brucefield* is an early 18th cent. house.

TULLOCH, Inverness. Map 19, **NN 3** 8.
On the River Spean, in Glen Spean, with one of the curious " Parallel Roads " well seen on the hillside to the north. (See **Roy Bridge.**) To the south-east, and traversed only by the railway, are the shores of Loch Treig, surrounded by lofty hills exceeding 3,000 ft. in height. The loch is now included in the great Lochaber power scheme, its waters being carried by means of a 15-mile long tunnel through *Ben Nevis* (*q.v.*). To the south-east of Loch Treig is the lonely Loch Ossian, in Corrour Forest, beyond the shores of which rise the peaks of *Beinn Eibhinn*, 3,611 ft., and *Ben Alder*, 3,757 ft. The road leading north-eastwards from Tulloch passes a reservoir, dominated by the great mass of *Creag Meaghaidh*, 3,700 ft., to the north, and later reaches the shores of *Loch Laggan* (*q.v.*). *Iter. 143, 208.*

TULLOCHGORUM, Inverness. Map 25, **NH 9** 2.
Situated on the north bank of the River Spey, with *Creag an Fhithich*, 1,325 ft., a wooded hill, rising to the west. The name Tullochgorum is that of a well-known 18th cent. Strathspey tune, the words of which were written about 150 years ago by John Skinner, a bishop of Aberdeen.

TULLYNESSLE, Aberdeen. Map 26, **NJ 5** 1.
Lies on the Suie Burn, a tributary of the River Don. A little to the north-west, in the foothills of the *Correen* hills, stands the ruined three-storeyed stronghold of *Terpersie Castle*, dated 1561, and showing the Gordon crest on a window-sill. *Iter. 165.*

TUMMEL BRIDGE, Perth. Map 19, **NN 7** 5.
This bridge was built by General Wade, in 1730, and stands on the line of his military road from Crieff to Dalnacardoch. A power station, in connection with the Tummel-Garry hydro-electric scheme, is now situated nearby on the south bank of the River Tummel. Mendelssohn spent some time at an inn here in 1829. Eastwards lies Loch Tummel, perhaps the loveliest aspect of which is to be obtained from the celebrated *Queen's View* (*q.v.*). Roads traverse both shores of the loch, that on the north side being the finer of the two. Farther east still is the Linn of Tummel (N.T. Scot.), described under *Pitlochry*. To the south of Tummel Bridge, the Wade road climbs over the hills past *White Bridge* (*q.v.*), reaching a height of nearly 1,300 ft., with *Schiehallion*, 3,547 ft., to the west, before descending into Strath Appin. See **Kinloch Rannoch** and **Wade Roads.** *Iter. 138, 148, 149.*

TURNBERRY, Ayr. 500. Map 8, **NS 2** 0.
E.C. Tues. **GOLF.** Situated on the sandy Turnberry Bay, looking across to the mountains of the island of Arran, and well-known for its golf-course. Motor racing is a more recent addition to the attractions of the resort. There are scanty remains of *Turnberry Castle*, to the north, at Turnberry Point, and Robert Bruce is sometimes thought to have been born here, though *Lochmaben* (*q.v.*) disputes this claim. Bruce is said to have landed at Turnberry, in 1307, to commence his fight for Scotland's freedom, which culminated 7 years later at *Bannockburn* (*q.v.*). See **Culzean Castle** and **Dunure** (for *Electric Brae*). *Iter. 80.*

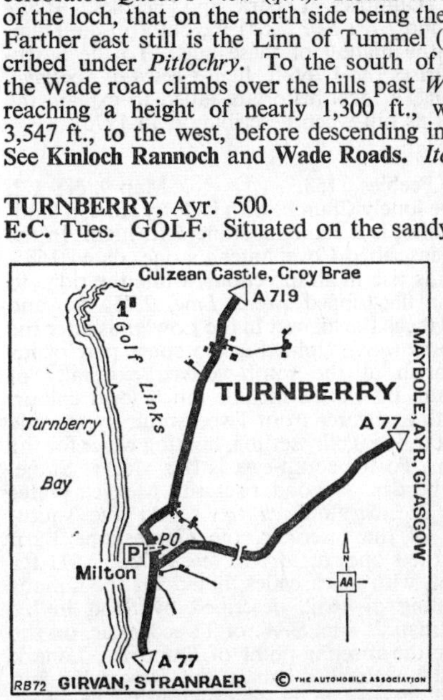

Castle ruins 1

TURNHOUSE, Midlothian. Map 9, **NT1 7.**
In the vicinity lies the airport for Edinburgh. *Iter. 91, 95.*

TURRIFF, Aberdeen. 2,813. SB. Map 27, **NJ 7 4.**
E.C. Wed. **M.D.** Tues. GOLF. Stands on the Idoch Water, which joins the more important River Deveron, forming the Aberdeen-Banff boundary, a little to the north-west. The Knights Templar once had a church here. The present Church has a 16th cent. choir, a double belfry, dated 1635, and also some monuments of interest. The old Market Cross was re-erected in 1865. A skirmish, known as the "Trot of Turriff," was fought here, in 1639, between the Covenanters and the Royalists. To the east, in wooded grounds, stands the 14th to 16th cent. *Delgatie Castle*, the home of the Clan Hay. It is shown Wed. and Sun., 2.30 to 5, July and Aug. (See note page 98.) **4½ m. N.E.** stands *Craigston Castle*, an early 17th cent. structure. **3 m. S.E.,** off the Fyvie road, is *Hatton Castle*, with part of the ancient *Balquholly Tower*. See **Auchterless** and **King Edward.** *Iter. 180, 189, 196.*

TUSHIELAW INN, Selkirk. Map 10, **NT 3 1.**
Lies in a picturesque setting on the Ettrick Water, surrounded by the characteristic green and rounded hills of the Lowlands. **2 m. S.W.** is the ruined *Thirlestane Tower*, associated with Sir John Scott, a follower of the same king. A fine moorland road climbs in an easterly direction from the inn, passing, after five miles, into Roxburghshire, on the way to Hawick. See **Buccleuch, Ettrick, St. Mary's Loch** and **Tibbie Shiel's Inn.** *Iter. 12, 34, 42.*

TWEEDDALE, Peebles. Map 10, **NT 1 3** etc.
An alternative name for Peeblesshire, through the centre of which flows the River Tweed, famous for its salmon-fishing, and which, during its course, is joined by numerous tributaries rising within the county. Perhaps the loveliest reaches of Tweeddale are those which extend from *Melrose* (*q.v.*) through *Peebles* (*q.v.*) itself to the lonely head of the river at *Tweedsmuir* (*q.v.*), associated with the novels of John Buchan. Beyond here, ranges of lofty hills close in near the meeting-point of Dumfries, Lanark and Peebles. *White Coomb*, 2,695 ft. and *Hart Fell*, 2,651 ft., both on the Dumfries border, are the highest of these hills. To the north-west of the latter rises the 1,766-ft. high *Crown of Scotland.* Captain Armstrong, a local historian, failed to explain the curious name of this hill when describing it in 1775.

TWEEDSMUIR, Peebles. 153. Map 9, **NT 1 2.**
E.C. Sat. Near the lonely Church, with its lofty spire, a landmark for many miles, is a standing stone 5 ft. high. In the churchyard is an inscribed Covenanter's stone, dated 1685. Lofty, rounded hills rise in all directions, while the ridge to the east, with the flat-topped *Broad Law*, 2,754 ft., and *Dollar Law*, 2,680 ft., is the highest in the Lowlands after the *Merrick* in *Galloway* (*q.v.*). John Buchan spent part of his youth in this parish at the south-western extremity of *Tweeddale* (*q.v.*) and his novels include much local colour. A track leads south-eastwards from Tweedsmuir by the side of the *Talla* reservoir, in its hilly setting, holding water for the city of Edinburgh. To the south-east is the Megget Stane, near the Selkirk border. Beyond rises the Megget Water flowing towards *St. Mary's Loch* (*q.v.*). At the south-eastern extremity of the reservoir, the Gameshope Burn flows down from the slopes of *Molls Cleuch Dod*, 2,571 ft., by Talla Linn foot, with its cascades, noted for the famous Covenanters' meeting of 1682, described by Scott in his "Heart of Midlothian." **8 m. S.W.** of Tweedsmuir, on the Moffat road, near the meeting-point of Dumfries, Lanark and Peebles, is the watershed where the Rivers Annan, Clyde and Tweed all rise in close proximity. The last-named rises at Tweed's Well, situated at a height of 1,500 ft., a little to the east of the road. At this point on the road, known as *Tweedshaws*, stands a cairn and tablet in memory of the devoted guard and driver of the Edinburgh mail-coach who lost their lives in a great snowstorm in 1831. The highest point of the road lies a little farther south and attains 1,348 ft. See **Crook Inn** and **Moffat.** *Iter. 10, 24.*

TWYNHOLM, Kirkcudbright. 1,519 with Tongland. Map 3, **NX 6 5.**
Barwhinnock, to the north-west, is a notable example of a small Regency mansion, with a walled garden. *Iter. 26.*

TYNDRUM, Perth. 90. Map 15, **NN 3 3.**
E.C. Wed. This well-known angling, climbing and winter sports resort is situated at a height of about 800 ft. in Strath Fillan, near its junction with Glen Lochy. Dominating the latter is the fine peak of *Ben Lui*, 3,708 ft., with its great northern corrie, on the Argyll border, and to the east of which rises *Beinn Oss*, 3,374 ft., above Glen Coninish. On the slopes of *Ben Lui* rises the Fillan Water, which is later known as the Dochart, and after emerging from *Loch Tay* (*q.v.*) becomes the Tay, a river having the largest volume of water in Scotland. Another fine group of mountains lies to the south-east, where Glens Falloch and Dochart meet at *Crianlarich* (*q.v.*). About **2 m. S.E.** of Tyndrum, near the Fillan Water, is *Dalry*, where Robert Bruce was worsted in a skirmish, in 1306, and lost his brooch, which is now treasured in the Macdougall mansion of *Dunollie* near *Oban* (*q.v.*). *Beinn Chaluim*, 3,354 ft. and *Creag Mhor*, 3,305 ft., are the principal heights rising to the north-east of Tyndrum in the Forest of Mamlorn mountains and facing the head of Glen Lochay in the *Breadalbane* (*q.v.*) country. See **Bridge of Orchy.** *Iter. 100, 110, 120, 125, 142, 144, 145.*

TYNET BRIDGE, Banff. Map 26, **NJ 4 6.**
In the vicinity stands *Tynet* Church, one of Scotland's oldest Post-Reformation structures, still in use. *Iter. 178, 198.*

TYNNINGHAME, East Lothian. Map 10, **NT 6 7.**
In the richly wooded grounds of *Tynninghame House*, 18th and 19th cent., to the north-east, near Tynninghame Sands on the coast by the Tyne estuary, are the remains of the 12th cent. Church, now a burial chapel of the Earls of Haddington. This Chapel must have been one of the best examples of parochial Romanesque architecture in Scotland, as shown by the rich carving on the surviving arch of the apse. Beyond the park stretch the links, terminating in a narrow promontory, with a rock known as *St. Baldred's Castle.* Nearby is a cairn dating from the Bronze Age. Farther north are the Peffer Sands. See **East Linton.** *Iter. 2, 38.*

TYNRON, Dumfries. 870 with Penpont. Map 3, **NX 8 9.**
On the Shinnel Water. There is an inscribed martyr's stone in the churchyard. A small National Nature Reserve lies here.

UDDINGSTON, Lanark. 9,167 with Bothwell. Map 8, **NS 6 6.**
E.C. Wed. **M.D.** 3rd Wed. A town situated on the River Clyde, to the south-east of Glasgow. *Iter. 51.*

UDNY, Aberdeen. 1,295. Map 27, **NJ 8 2.**
Situated in the Formartine district, which takes in much of the country between the Rivers Don and Ythan, and also the sandy coast to the east. The Castle retains an ancient four-storeyed tower. See **Pitmedden.**

UIG, Isle of Lewis, Ross and Cromarty. Map 32, **NB 0 3.**
See **Hebrides, Outer** (Lewis). *Iter. 258.*

UIG, Isle of Skye, Inverness. Map 22, **NG 3 6.**
On the picturesque Uig Bay, with a steamer pier, in the Trotternish district, overlooking Loch Snizort, the Ascrib Islands, and the Vaternish peninsula. A little to the north-west, on the coast, is the rugged Stack Skudiburgh, in its rocky setting. Farther north, off the *Duntulm* (*q.v.*) road, near *Port Kilbride*, stands *Monkstadt House*, near which Flora Macdonald and Prince Charles Edward, the latter disguised as "Betty Burke," her maid, landed on June 29,

Turriff, Aberdeen. The double belfry (1635) of the Church. The Knights Templars formerly owned a church here

Tweeddale, Peebles. The Dawyck Woods, at Stobo, to the south of the River Tweed, and south-west of Peebles. They are considered some of the finest in Scotland

Tweeddale, Peebles. The 15th century Neidpath Castle, once battered by Cromwell's guns. It stands to the west of Peebles, on the banks of the Tweed, off A72

Tweeddale, Peebles. Barns Tower, dating from 1488, which stands near Lyne, to the south of the Tweed, on an unclassified road in the vicinity of Manor Church

Tweedsmuir, Peebles. The cairn (1931) at Tweedshaws, 8 miles south-west, on A701, which tells the story of the snowstorm of 1831, when the driver and guard of the mail coach lost their lives

Uig, Isle of Skye, Inverness. A house in the form of a round tower overlooking Uig Bay

Urquhart Castle, Inverness. The ruined Castle, blown up in 1692 to prevent its occupation by the Jacobites. It stands on Loch Ness, off A82, to the south-east of Drumnadrochit

Ullapool, Ross and Cromarty. A memorial clock to Sir Arthur Fowler of Braemore, who died in 1899

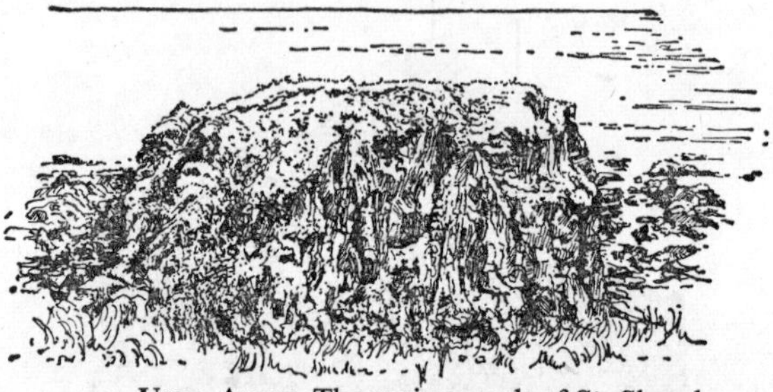

Usan, Angus. The curious rock of St. Skeagh, said from certain angles to resemble an elephant. It is situated near Boddin Point, on an unclassified road to the south-west

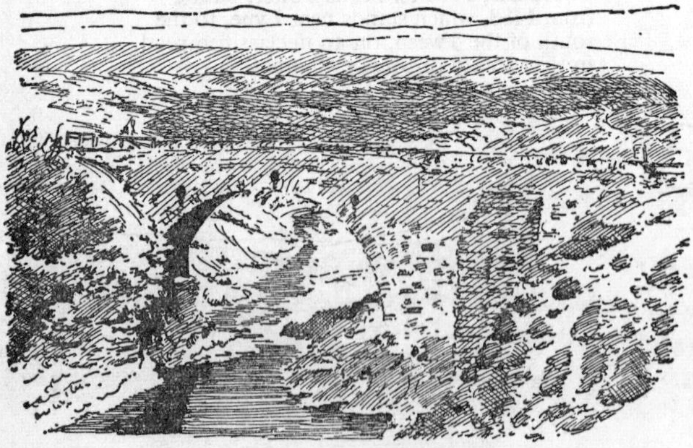

Wade Roads. A by-passed Wade bridge near A9, at Dallnamine, 2 miles south-east of Dalnacardoch, in the Grampian mountains of Perthshire

Wade Roads. General Wade's Sluggan Bridge of 1728 across the River Dulnain. It stands 2 miles west of Carrbridge, Inverness-shire, on the original line of his road from Kingussie to Inverness

1746, from the remote island of *Benbecula* in the Outer Hebrides. Some six miles off the road leading south from Uig towards Loch Snizort Beag stands the successor to the former *Kingsburgh House*, where the Prince sheltered and Flora Macdonald stayed, and where, in later years, Dr. Johnson and Boswell were entertained. A well nearby, to the north, where the Prince quenched his thirst, is still known as Prince Charles's Well. The road leading westwards and then northwards from Uig makes an abrupt double bend before ascending Idrigil Hill, and then leads towards *Kilmaluag* (*q.v.*). The road leading north-eastwards towards the *Quiraing* and *Staffin* (both *q.v.*), is under complete reconstruction. See **Flodigarry, Kilmuir** and **Hebrides, Outer** (Benbecula). *Iter. 253, 254.*

UIST, NORTH AND SOUTH, Inverness. Map 32, **NF 7** 7 etc., and **NF 7** 2, etc.
See **Hebrides, Outer** (North Uist and South Uist).

ULBSTER, Caithness. Map 30, **ND 3** 4.
In the vicinity is the picturesque sea-inlet of the Trollie Pow, with its waterfall, and also a steep descent of 365 steps leading to the little Whaligoe Bay. *Iter. 200.*

ULLAPOOL, Ross and Cromarty. 1,138 with Dundonnell. Map 29, **NH 1** 9.
E.C. Tues. An attractive *Wester Ross* (*q.v.*) fishing town and resort, founded by the Fisheries Association, in 1788, to further the herring industry. It forms a convenient base from which explorations of some of the finest mountain scenery of the North-West Highlands can be made. There is a pier and a safe anchorage, Both bathing and angling are available. *Ullapool* is very beautifully situated on *Loch Broom* (*q.v.*), with grand views towards the head of the loch, and faces *Aultnaharrie* (*q.v.*), dominated by *Ben Goleach*, 2,052 ft., on the opposite shore, to which it is linked by passenger ferry. Beyond Loch Broom, away to the south-east, is the fertile, wooded valley of Strath More, above which rise the lofty peaks of the *Ben Dearg* group. North-west of Ullapool, a rugged and picturesque stretch of road traverses the shores of Loch Kanaird, on the edge of the rugged *Coigach* district, with the low-lying Isle Martin off-shore, before turning inland through Strath Kanaird, with *Ben More Coigach*, 2,438 ft., prominent to the north-west. Farther out to sea are the delightful Summer Islands in Baden Bay, looking towards *Achiltibuie* on the mainland coast. The largest island is Tanera More, and to the south-east lies Horse Island. Motor launches from Ullapool visit the islands. There are several ruined brochs in the neighbourhood of Ullapool, including Dun Canna (See **Strathkanaird**), and also two examples on the farther shore of Loch Broom, south-east of Aultnaharrie. The Ullapool River flows into Loch Broom at Ullapool, having emerged from Loch Achall, to the east, at the extremity of which lies Glen Achall, among lonely hills, with Rhidorroch Forest to the north. See **Achiltibuie, Baddagyle, Braemore Junction, Dundonnell** and **Loch Lurgain.** *Iter. 204, 222, 224, 225, 226, 235.*

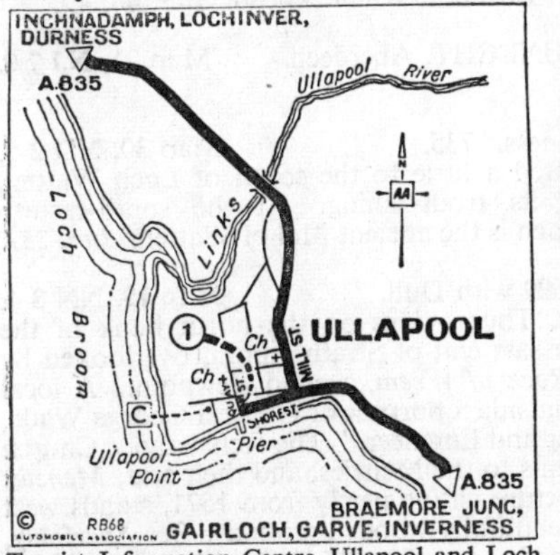

Tourist Information Centre, Ullapool and Loch Broom Tourist Association 1

ULVA FERRY, Isle of Mull, Argyll. Map 12, **NM 4** 3.
Situated a little to the west of the road which skirts the shores of Loch Tuath and Loch na Keal, in the north-west sector of the island. A narrow piece of water, crossed by a passenger ferry, separates Mull from the smaller island of *Ulva* at this point, while beyond the island, to the south-west, are Little Colonsay and the well-known island of *Staffa* (*q.v.*). Ulva has caves, and cliffs of basalt, and was visited in 1773 by Dr. Johnson and Boswell, while later visitors include Sir Walter Scott and David Livingstone. Campbell's famous poem about Lord Ullin's daughter is associated with the island, but it is thought that the " Loch Gyle " in the poem may refer to Loch Goil in the *Cowal* (*q.v.*) district. A little to the west of Ulva is the island of *Gometra*, which shows basaltic columns, and looks out towards the tiny islands of Lunga and Fladda in the Treshnish group. The road leading eastwards from Ulva Ferry winds high above the shores of Loch na Keal, with fine views of *Ben More*, 3,169 ft., to the south, before descending to the lochside. **2 m. N.** of Ulva Ferry, near the shores of Loch Tuath, are the Laggan waterfalls, off the road to *Kilninian* (*q.v.*). *Iter. 248.*

UNAPOOL, Sutherland. Map 28, **NC 2** 3.
On Loch Glencoul, near its junction with Loch Glendhu, and on the road leading northwards to the ferry at *Kylesku* (*q.v.*). This enables cars to cross the narrows which link the two lochs with Loch Cairnbawn, an inlet of the bay of *Eddrachillis* (*q.v.*). The mountain which dominates the remote head of Loch Glencoul is *Ben Leoid*, 2,597 ft. The road leading in a southerly direction towards *Inchnadamph* (*q.v.*) is dominated by the long ridge of *Quinag*, 2,653 ft., with its outlying peak of *Sail Gorm*, 2,551 ft. *Iter. 225, 227*

UNION BRIDGE, Berwick. Map 60, **NT 9** 5.
See **Paxton.**

UNST, ISLE OF, Shetland. Map 33, **HP 5** 0, etc.
See **Shetland Islands** (Unst).

UPHALL, West Lothian. 3,489. Map 9, **NT 0** 7.
The Church, partly of Norman date, has a burial-vault of the 17th cent., and contains some tombs of interest. The manse was once a 17th cent. dower-house of the Dowager Lady Cardross. *Houston*, a 16th cent. mansion, to the south of the village, was the birthplace, in 1819, of Principal Shairp, the writer, who is buried in the Church. *Iter. 16.*

UPLAWMOOR, Renfrew. 1,807. Map 8, **NS 4** 5.
A small village, its name being derived from *Ouplaymuir*. To the south-west, across the Ayrshire border, stands the Adam mansion of *Caldwell*, built in 1772.

UPPER LARGO, Fife. Map 17, **NO 4** 0.
See **Largo.** *Iter. 94, 98, 128.*

URQUHART CASTLE, Inverness. Map 25, **NH 5** 2.
See **Drumnadrochit.** *Iter. 207, 210, 213.*

USAN, Angus. Map 21, **NO 7** 5.
Once a thriving fishing village of some importance, known as *Fishtown of Usan*, its port and mill being mentioned in 1608. It is now a quiet village and coastguard station, with a rocky foreshore, situated between Scurdy Ness and Boddin Point. Near the latter is the curious rock of *St. Skeagh*, and beyond lies the wide expanse of Lunan Bay, sheltered by Lang Craig and Red Head to the south. A track, known as the " King's Codger's Road," once led westwards inland to *Forfar* (*q.v.*) along which fresh fish was conveyed to the former Royal Palace at that town. To the north of Usan is *Ferryden* (*q.v.*), overlooking *Montrose* (*q.v.*) across the estuary of the River South Esk.

VALLEYFIELD, Fife. Map 16, **NT 0** 8.
A garden village on Torry Bay, with the small coal-port of *Torryburn* (*q.v.*) situated a little to the south-east.

VOE, Sutherland. Map 53, **HU 4** 6.
See **Shetland Islands** (Mainland). *Iter. 267, 270.*

WADE ROADS. Map 19, **NN 6** 8 etc., 20, **NO 0** 4 etc., and 25, **NH 6** 4, etc.
A number of great military roads were constructed by General George Wade in the Highlands between 1726 and approximately 1740. Modern research considers, however, that by no means all the roads built for military purposes in this part of Scotland were actually the work of Wade. The road mileage definitely attributed to the General is $234\frac{3}{4}$, and between approximately 1728 and 1737 a total sum of £23,316.0.6 was paid out to him. The most notable road constructed by Wade was that linking Dunkeld with Inverness, involving the crossing of the *Grampians* (*q.v.*), a road

which is very largely followed by the course of the present splendid modern highway. A link road, which commenced at Crieff, followed a northerly course through the Sma' Glen to Aberfeldy, where, what is perhaps Wade's finest bridge, still spans the Tay. The continuation led over the Perthshire hills by way of Tummel Bridge, also Wade's work, to reach the main highway at Dalnacardoch, where, in the vicinity, the Wade Stone is still standing. Part of this link road is incorporated in modern roads, and part is still in existence as a rough track. Beyond Dalnacardoch, the road climbed northwards through Drumochter Pass to descend towards Dalwhinnie, where another famous Wade road diverged to the left into the Upper Spey valley (see below). From here a short spur was constructed to rejoin the more important road nearing Kingussie, at which point Wade reconstructed the well-known Ruthven Barracks, still to be seen, although in a ruinous state. The main highway from Kingussie continued to Fort George, now known as Inverness, a new Fort George having been constructed away to the north-east of the town at a later date.

The road from the Upper Spey led north-westwards to climb the famous Corrieyairack Pass in steep zigzags, reaching a height of more than 2,500 ft., amid a lonely wilderness of hills, before the descent through Glen Tarff commenced. This great road, traversed in 1745 by Prince Charles Edward, gradually fell into disuse, and is today little more than a track, which, in places, is barely discernible, and can only be crossed on foot, involving a long and arduous journey. From Glen Tarff, the road led to Fort Augustus, in the Great Glen, or *Glen More* (*q.v.*), where Wade rebuilt and enlarged the former barracks, and on the remains of which, in 1876, the present Benedictine Monastery was built. Fort Augustus lies on the road which Wade built from Fort William to Inverness through the Great Glen, and along parts of which the line of the present magnificent road now goes. Between Fort Augustus and Inverness, the Wade road kept to the east, and the modern road keeps to the west of Loch Ness. Inverness thus became the meeting-point of what are perhaps Wade's two best-known roads, both of which are to some extent incorporated in the present modern highways.

In 1740, Wade was relieved of his command in Scotland, and four years later he fought in a campaign in Flanders. He played a part in the '45 Rising, but retired when Cumberland took over the supreme command of the English army. After living at Highgate, in London, for some years, Wade died at Bath in 1748, at the age of 75, and was buried in Westminster Abbey, a monument being erected by Roubiliac in his memory.

Perhaps the best known of General Wade's successors was General Caulfeild, who was the reputed author of the well-known lines:

"If you'd seen these roads before they were made,
You'd lift up your hands, and bless General Wade."

Caulfeild was responsible for a large number of the military roads which were constructed in later years, and spent on them some £167,000 in all. Among these were the roads linking Dumbarton with Inveraray (1746-1750); Coupar Angus to Braemar and over the Lecht road to Tomintoul, Grantown-on-Spey and the present Fort George (1748 onwards); Stirling to Tyndrum, Kinlochleven and Fort William by way of the now disused Devil's Staircase near Kingshouse (1748-1751); and Fort Augustus to Bernera Barracks at Glenelg (1750-1784), this road later being abandoned. A map of the military roads was first produced in 1755, and a list of these roads in Scotland towards the end of the 18th cent. gives their total mileage as 1,103. By the year 1800, only some 600 miles of these roads were kept in a state of repair, and in 1814 they were taken over by the Commissioners of the Road and Bridge Act of 1812.

See **Aberfeldy, Corrieyairack Pass, Dalnacardoch, Dalwhinnie, Drumgask, Fort Augustus, Foyers, Inverfarigaig, Inverness, Kingussie, Sma' Glen, Spean Bridge, Tummel Bridge** and **Weem.**

WALKERBURN, Peebles. 932. Map 10, **NT 3 3.**
A textile-manufacturing village, founded in 1854, on the River Tweed. A Border Riding ceremony is held here annually. On *Purvis Hill*, to the north, high above the Tweed, are some remarkable earthen terraces. **2½ m. E.,** on the south bank of the river, is the ruined *Elibank Tower*, dating perhaps from 1595, and built, or enlarged, by one of the Murrays of *Darnhall* near *Eddleston* (*q.v.*). The daughter of this Murray, known as "Muckle Mouthed Meg," married a Scott of *Harden* near *Hawick* (*q.v.*), and has been commemorated in ballads by both Hogg and Browning. *Iter. 14, 32, 33, 52.*

WALLS, Shetland. Map 33, **HU 2 4.**
See **Shetland Islands** (Mainland). *Iter. 268.*

WANLOCKHEAD, Dumfries. Map 9, **NS 8 1.**
The loftiest village in Scotland, standing 1,380 ft. above sea level in a setting of rounded *Lowther* hills, with *Green Lowther*, 2,403 ft., and *Lowther Hill*, 2,377 ft., as the principal summits, both being fine viewpoints. Many of the persecuted Covenanters hid in these hills during the late 17th cent. Lead mines in the neighbourhood of the village were opened originally in 1680, while other metals, including gold and silver, have also been mined, both here and at the nearby almost equally loftily-situated village of *Leadhills* (*q.v.*). The road linking these two villages attains a height of 1,531 ft. on the Dumfries-Lanark border. Leading south-westwards towards the Nith valley, a road traverses the fine *Mennock* (*q.v.*) pass, and attains a height of more than 1,400 ft. just beyond Wanlockhead. *Tomintoul* (*q.v.*), the highest village in the Highlands, stands only 1,160 ft. in altitude, more than 200 ft. lower than Lowland Wanlockhead. *Iter. 48, 49.*

WATERTON-DUNECHT, Aberdeen. Map 21, **NJ 7 0.**
See **Dunecht.**

WATTEN, Caithness. 735. Map 30, **ND 2 5.**
E.C. Tues. Situated a little to the south of Loch Watten, well known for its trout-fishing. At the south-eastern extremity of the loch is the ancient Mill of Watten. *Iter. 237.*

WEEM, Perth. 609 with Dull. Map 19, **NN 8 4.**
E.C. Wed. **M.D.** Thurs. Lies on the north bank of the River Tay, at the east end of Strath Appin, overlooked by the 800-ft. high *Rock of Weem*, a good viewpoint. A local inn has hanging outside a portrait of General George Wade, inscribed "Soldier and Engineer." The Renaissance Church contains monuments to the Menzies, and their seat, *Menzies Castle*, a fine structure dating partly from 1571, stands west of the village in beautifully-wooded grounds. See **Aberfeldy, Dull** and **Wade Roads.** *Iter. 89, 107, 147, 149.*

WEISDALE, Shetland. Map 33, **HU 3 5.**
Iter. 268, 270.

WEMYSS, Fife. Map 17, **NT 3 9.**
See **East Wemyss and West Wemyss.** *Iter. 128.*

WEMYSS BAY, Renfrew. 376. Map 8, **NS 1 6.**
E.C. Wed. GOLF. A popular Clyde coast resort, with a rock and pebble beach and a busy steamer pier. There are good views across the firth to the hills of Bute and Cowal. The Kelly Burn separates Wemyss Bay from the neighbouring Ayrshire resort of *Skelmorlie* (*q.v.*). To the east of Wemyss Bay is the burnt-out *Kelly House*, and to the north near Wemyss

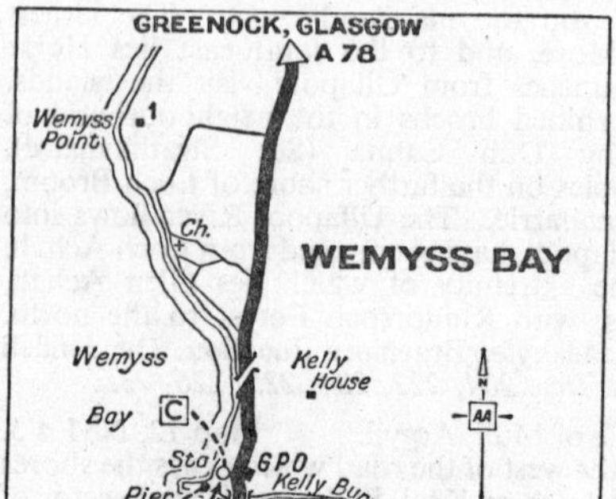

Castle 1

Walkerburn, Peebles. The late 16th century Elibank Tower, 2½ miles east, on an unclassified road south of the River Tweed. Here is said to have taken place the wedding of Scott of Harden and ' Muckle Mou'd Meg '

Wanlockhead, Dumfries. What is said to be the highest petrol pump in Scotland, at an altitude of some 1,500 feet

Watten, Caithness. The old Mill of Watten, which lies at the south-eastern extremity of Loch Watten, on B870

Weem, Perth. The sign of the Inn, where General Wade, ' Soldier and Engineer,' stayed in 1733

Weem, Perth. Menzies Castle, which dates partly from 1571, and stands on the west side of the village, off B846

Wemyss, Fife. The remains of Macduff's Castle, near which stands an ancient dovecote. It is situated at East Wemyss, overlooking the Firth of Forth, off A955

Wester Ross, Ross and Cromarty. The view from the Wester Ross railhead of Kyle of Lochalsh towards the Skye hill of Beinn na Caillich, across the narrows of Loch Alsh

Westerkirk, Dumfries. The Memorial to the engineer and architect, Thomas Telford, born near here in 1757

Westruther, Berwick. One of a pair of gate-houses incorporating milestones and coaching clocks, leading to the former Spottiswoode House. They stand some 3 miles south-west, on the Lauder road (A697). The inscription on the milestone is shown in the small illustration to the right

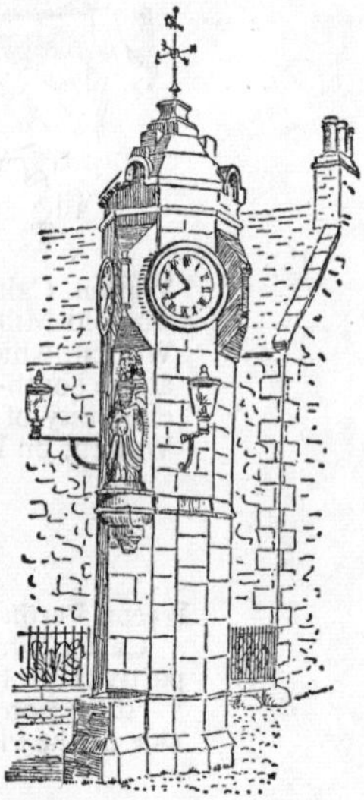

West Linton, Peebles. Lady Gifford's Well, on which is a figure carved locally in 1666

West Wemyss, Fife. The old Tolbooth, with its outside staircase

Whitekirk, East Lothian. The two-storeyed tithe barn, incorporating part of a 16th century castle, which stands beyond the churchyard

Point, stood formerly the 19th cent. *Castle Wemyss.* See **Millport.** *Iter. 59, 64, 65, 66, 88.*

WEST CALDER, Midlothian. 1,058. Map 9, **NT 0** 6. **E.C.** Wed. GOLF. Shale oil mining is carried on in the neighbourhood. See **Mid Calder.** *Iter. 19, 20, 22.*

WESTERGLEN, Stirling. Map 16, **NS 8** 8. Here is a BBC radio transmitter.

WESTERKIRK, Dumfries. 794. Map 4. **NY 3** 9. A lonely Eskdale village, also known as *Bentpath,* surrounded by green Lowland hills. A memorial Cross stands to the memory of Thomas Telford, the famous engineer, who was born in the vicinity, in 1757, and was buried in Westminster Abbey. Among his many achievements in Scotland was the construction of the *Caledonian Canal* (*q.v.*).

WESTERN ISLES. Maps 6, 7, 12, 13, 22, 23 and 32. The name given collectively to the island groups off the West Coast of Scotland, consisting chiefly of the Inner and Outer Hebrides. All these, in addition to Arran, Bute and the Cumbraes, which lie farther south in the Firth of Clyde, are shown, together with their mainland communications, in the special map on pages 34 and 35 of the atlas. See **Arran, Bute, Colonsay, Hebrides (Outer), Iona, Islay, Jura, Millport** (for *Cumbraes*), **Mull, Rum, Skye, Staffa** and **Tiree.**

WESTER ROSS, Ross and Cromarty. Map 22, **NG 7** 2 etc. 24, **NG 9** 6 etc. and 29, **NC 0** 0 etc. This is the name applied to the picturesque and hilly western half of the county of Ross and Cromarty, as distinct from *Easter Ross* (*q.v.*), which comprises the more level country facing the North Sea. The coast of Wester Ross is indented by numerous fine sea lochs, including *Loch Alsh, Loch Carron, Loch Torridon* and *Loch Broom* (all *q.v.*). The rail-head of *Kyle of Lochalsh* (*q.v.*) facing the island of Skye, and also the beautiful little resorts of *Gairloch* (*q.v.*) near the delightful *Loch Maree* (*q.v.*), and *Ullapool* (*q.v.*), between the Teallach range and the Coigach mountains, are two centres for this district. The grand Torridon range and the Ben Eighe National Nature Reserve, both near *Kinlochewe* (*q.v.*), are other outstanding attractions in this North-west Highland landscape. See **Dundonnell, Gruinard Bay** and **Torridon.**

WEST GORDON, Berwick. Map 10, **NT 6** 4. See **Gordon.**

WEST KILBRIDE, Ayr. 4,284. Map 8, **NS 2** 4. **E.C.** Wed. GOLF. The old village lies off the main road, a little inland from the modern resort of *Seamill,* with its good sands, on the Firth of Clyde. To the north-west is Farland Head, with the ruined *Portencross Castle,* over-looking the twin Cumbraes. Off the headland, a Spanish Armada galleon is thought to have foundered. *Kilbride Tower,* or *Law Castle,* stands on high ground off the road to Dalry. See **Fairlie.** *Iter. 66 88.*

WEST LINTON, Peebles. 841. Map 9, **NT 1** 5. **E.C.** Thurs. GOLF. This village, at one time known as *Linton Roderick,* lies at the foot of the *Pentland* hills, at a height of nearly 800 ft. It was formerly well known for its stonemasons, who worked largely on tombstones, and whose craftsmanship, dating from 1666, is displayed on the figure, re-erected in 1861, surmounting "Lady Gifford's Well." The dates 1660 and 1678 occur on a house opposite, the carvings being probably by the same hand. To the north-west, the Lyne Water flows down from the *Windy Gowl,* below the main Pentland ridge. A road, following the stream, climbs into the hills and then becomes a track, which was formerly one of the best known of the old drove roads, and is called the *Cauld Stane Slap.* This track crosses the Pentlands at a height of 1,430 ft., under the slopes of *East Cairn Hill,* 1,839 ft., and cattle were formerly driven over this drove road making for Stenhousemuir near *Falkirk* (*q.v.*). Opposite the track, to the south-west, rises the even higher *West Cairn Hill,* 1,844 ft. **9 m. S. W.** of West Linton, above the hamlet of *Dunsyre* (*q.v.*), rises *Black Law,* 1,460 ft., on which is situated the grave of a nameless Covenanter, slain at Rullion Green in 1666. See **Glencorse** and **Romanno Bridge.** *Iter. 25.*

WESTRAY, ISLE OF, Orkney. Map 33, **HY 4** 4. See **Orkney Islands** (Westray).

WESTRUTHER, Berwick. Map 10, **NT 6** 4. Situated on the southern hill slopes of the *Lammermuirs,* with *Dirrington Great Law,* 1,309 ft., rising away to the north-east. Near the modern Church are remains of the former structure. Two lodges, with clocks over their gables, and milestones, remain from the former *Spottiswoode House,* and stand some **3 m. S.W.,** off the Lauder road (A697). **1½ m. N.E.** is *Wedderlie House,* partly 17th cent. *Iter. 9.*

WEST WEMYSS, Fife. 1,334. Map 17, **NT 3** 9. GOLF. Lies a little to the south-east of the Kirkcaldy to Leven road, and is a small coal-port on the Firth of Forth. The old Tolbooth has a curious inscription. The coast to the north-east is rocky, with caves, or "weems," notable for their Bronze and Iron Age and Early Christian carvings, though some of the caves have collapsed. *Wemyss Castle,* dating from 1421, 1670 and 1880, is of historic interest for the first meeting between Mary, Queen of Scots and Darnley in 1565. See **East Wemyss.** *Iter. 128.*

WHALIGOE, Caithness. Map 30, **ND 3** 3. See **Ulbster.**

WHALSAY, ISLE OF, Shetland. Map 33, **HU 5** 6. See **Shetland Islands** (Mainland).

WHISTLEFIELD, Dunbarton. Map 14, **NS 2** 9. On the watershed between the Gare Loch and *Loch Long* (*q.v.*), looking towards the hills of *Argyll's Bowling Green.* See **Portincaple.** *Iter. 102, 111.*

WHITBURN, West Lothian. 7,791. SB. Map 9, **NS 9** 6. A district of coal mines and iron foundries. *Iter. 18, 86.*

WHITEBRIDGE, Inverness. Map 25, **NH 4** 1. Here, the River Foyers is joined by the Fechlin, which has emerged from Loch Killin, in the hills to the south-east. *Whitebridge* is on the line of General Wade's military road from Fort Augustus to Inverness, constructed in 1732, and the former military rest-house at this point became at one time an inn. The Fort Augustus road first follows the Foyers, and then climbs to a height of 1,275 ft., with good views, on to moorlands, on which is situated Loch Tarf, before des-cending steeply to the wooded Glen Doe. There is a choice of routes leading northwards from Whitebridge, one road being hilly and descending to *Foyers* (*q.v.*) on *Loch Ness* (*q.v.*), and an alternative going by way of *Errogie* (*q.v.*), both routes converging at *Dores* (*q.v.*). A by-road leads south-east to reach the remote hill-encircled Loch Killin. See **Fort Augustus.** *Iter. 211, 212.*

WHITE BRIDGE, Perth. Map 19, **NN 7** 5. At a height of over 1,000 ft. in the Perthshire hills, on the line of one of the Wade roads, and near a road fork of two routes leading northwards to the Tummel valley. Between these roads lies the little Loch Kinardochy, and the westerly of the two roads passes near the loch-side to climb over the moorlands below *Schiehallion,* 3,547 ft., with fine views, before descending later to *Kinloch Rannoch* (*q.v.*). The more easterly of the roads reaches a height of 1,263 ft. shortly after leaving White Bridge. *Iter. 89, 138, 147, 149.*

WHITEHILLS, Banff. Map 27, **NJ 6** 6. This small fishing village lies in a sandy and rocky bay between Stake Ness and Knock Head. The coast to the west is rocky, with a succession of lonely headlands near *Portsoy* (*q.v.*). Inland stands the ruined *St. Branden's* church, preserving Jacobean churchyard tombstones. *Iter. 199.*

WHITEKIRK, East Lothian. 622. Map 10, **NT 5** 8. The interesting 15th cent. cruciform Church has a barrel-vaulted chancel and porch, and a massive tower, surmounted by a wooden spire. The structure was damaged by suffragettes in 1914, and has since been repaired. The carved wooden front of the north gallery is of 17th cent. date. A Holy Well was once situated nearby, and was visited, among others, by Aeneas Silvius, later Pope Pius II. The Church owed its origin to this Well, which was discovered in 1294. Near the Church is a two-storeyed tithe barn, with part of a 16th cent. castle. It was once used for the storage of grain by monks from Holyrood. **2 m. S.W.** stands the mansion of *Newbyth*, with fine walled gardens. **2 m. N.W.** is the late 18th cent. *Leuchie House*. See **Tynninghame.** *Iter. 2, 38.*

WHITE MOUNTH, Aberdeen. Map 20, **NO 2** 8.
The great mountain plateau of the *White Mounth* lies on the Angus border and faces Deeside and Balmoral Forest to the north, which separates it from the more important *Cairngorm* range. *Lochnagar* is the most famous White Mounth peak, its twin summits attaining 3,786 and 3,768 ft. respectively. *Broad Cairn*, 3,268 ft., *Cairn Bannoch*, 3,314 ft., *Fafernie*, 3,274 ft., and *Cairn Taggart*, 3,430 ft., are the other principal heights. Glen Callater, with its loch, to the west, and Glen Muick, also with its loch, to the east, lie on either side of the mountains, and provide means of access from Braemar and Ballater. The only access from the Angus side is by mountain paths from *Braedownie (q.v.)*.

WHITHORN, Wigtown. 983. SB. Map 2, **NX 4 4.**
E.C. Wed. An ancient Royal Burgh, in the bleak Machers peninsula, with the remains of a 12th and 15th cent. Priory Church. It has a good late 12th cent. carved doorway. This Church may have been built on the site of *St. Ninian's* " White House," or " Candida Casa," though *Isle o, Whithorn (q.v.)* claims the distinction that *St. Ninian's* Christian Chapel, built in 397, perhaps the earliest in Scotland, stood near the ruined Chapel at that place. *St. Ninian's Shrine* at Whithorn became an important place of pilgrimage, and was visited regularly by James IV. Whithorn Priory Church (A.M.) is approached by a 17th cent. archway known as " The Pend," which has a panel carved with the Royal Arms of Scotland before the Union; here has been set up a museum in which some carved stones are preserved. These include the 7th cent. *St. Peter's* Stone and the 5th cent. *Latinus* Stone, the latter possibly the oldest in Scotland. There are a number of small 18th cent. houses in George Street. See **Cruggleton** and **Monreith.** *Iter. 82.*

WHITING BAY, Isle of Arran, Bute. 578. Map 7, **NS 0 2.**
GOLF. This attractive small resort, with bathing, lies on Whiting Bay, facing the Firth of Clyde. There is a steamer pier. Inland extends the pretty Glen Ashdale, with its falls. Away to the north-east, beyond Kingscross Point, is Holy Island, described under *Lamlash*. See **Kildonan.** *Iter. 242.*

WHITTINGHAME, East Lothian. 300. Map 10, **NT 6 7.**
E.C. Wed. *Whittinghame House*, built in 1817, was the birthplace, in 1848, of the Earl of Balfour, and in the grounds is his tomb. An old yew tree is said to mark the spot where Darnley's murder was plotted. The old *Whittinghame Tower* stands in the neighbourhood of the house, and dates from the 15th cent. **2 m. S.E.** is the little artificial *Pressmennan Lake*, formed in 1819, the only " lake " in Scotland, apart from the much better known Lake of Menteith, described under *Port of Menteith*. **$1\frac{1}{2}$ m. E.** is the modernized 17th cent. house of *Ruchlaw*, which preserves two old sundials and a dovecote. See **Stenton.**

WICK, Caithness. 7,613. SB. Map 30, **ND 3 5.**
E.C. Wed. **M.D.** Thurs. GOLF. Situated on Wick Bay, where the Wick Water flows into the sea, the important herring fishing port and ancient Royal Burgh of *Wick* has a harbour designed by Telford. It was later improved by Thomas Stevenson, but is accessible to large steamers at high water only. The suburb of *Pulteneytown* was founded by the British Fishery Society early in the 19th cent. In the Parish Church is the old Sinclair Aisle, in which the Earls of Caithness are buried. The quaint Town Hall is surmounted by a cupola. The airport lies about **2 m.** to the north-east. There is much fine cliff and rock scenery, both to the north and to the south of the town. **3 m. N.E.** is Noss Head. with its lighthouse, overlooking the sandy Sinclair's Bay, on the shores of which stand, in close proximity, the ruined Castles of *Sinclair* and *Girnigoe*, both demolished during Clan battles in the 17th cent. The latter had a complicated system of moats, portcullis and guardrooms. **$1\frac{1}{2}$ m. S.E.** is the Castle of *Old Wick* or *Castle Oliphant*, dating from the 14th cent., and known to mariners as the " Old Man of Wick." Nearby are curious rock stacks called the " Brig o' Tram " and the " Brough." See **East Mey, Reiss** and **Staxigoe.** *Iter. 200, 237, 238, 239.*

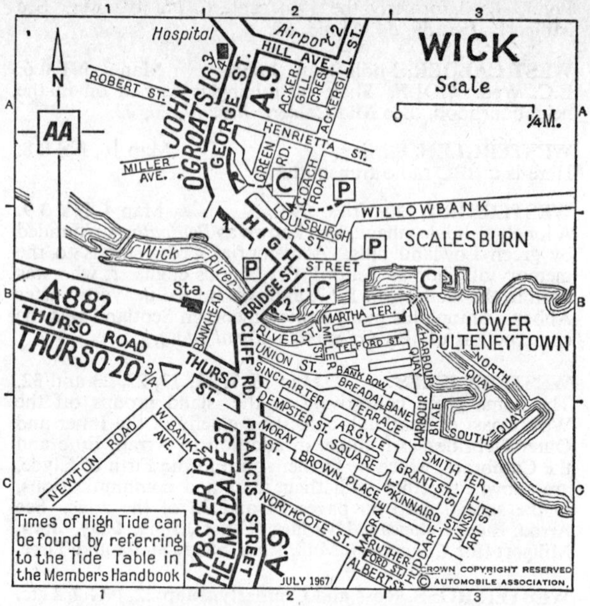

Parish Church 1 (B2) Town Hall 2 (B2)

WIGTOWN, Wigtown. 1,118. SB. Map 2, **NX 4 5.**
E.C. Wed. This old town became a Royal Burgh in 1457, and stands on Wigtown Bay, near the estuary of the River Bladnoch, where there is a derelict quay. The old Cross, dating from 1748, retains its sundial, and is neighboured by a Cross of 1816. In the broad main street is an enclosure, once used to pen cattle. The churchyard contains an inscribed stone in memory of the " Wigtown Martyrs," a woman and a young girl, named Margaret McLauchlan and Margaret Wilson respectively, who are said to have been tied to stakes and drowned at the mouth of the Bladnoch in 1685, because of their Covenanting beliefs. A stone on the shore marks the spot. Another Covenanters' memorial stands on high ground behind the town, from which an extensive view can be obtained. **3 m. N.W.**, off the road to *Kirkcowan (q.v.)*, are the standing stones of *Torhousekie* (A.M.), dating probably from the Bronze Age. They consist of 19 stones and form a complete circle 60 feet in diameter. See **Bladnoch** and **Stirling.** *Iter. 81, 82.*

WILSONTOWN, Lanark. Map 9, **NS 9 5.**
A mining village, standing at an altitude of more than 900 ft., in a district of lonely moors and fells. *Iter. 22, 86.*

WINCHBURGH, West Lothian. 2,625. Map 9, **NT 1 7.**
A centre of the oil-shale industry, which is of considerable importance locally, but has left its mark in places to the detriment of the countryside. **1 m. N.** is the ruined late 16th cent. *Duntarvie Castle*. *Iter. 91, 95.*

WINDYGATES, Fife. 1,446. Map 17, **NO 3 0.**
The village stands a little way inland from the Fife coast, on the River Ore. *Iter. 94, 98, 127, 129.*

WINTON HOUSE, East Lothian. Map 10, **NT 4 6.**
See **Pencaitland.** *Iter. 3.*

Whithorn, Wigtown. Remains of the 12th to 15th century Priory Church, later adapted for parish use. Fragments of St. Ninian's original ' White House,' or Candida Casa, survive on the site

Whithorn, Wigtown. The 17th century Pend archway, carved with the Royal Arms of Scotland before the Union

Wick, Caithness. The old Town Hall, which is surmounted by a cupola

Wick, Caithness. The 14th century Castle of Old Wick, or ' Old Man of Wick.' It stands 1½ miles to the south-east, off A9

Wigtown, Wigtown. The Covenanters' Memorial, which stands on a hill behind the town. It was erected in 1858

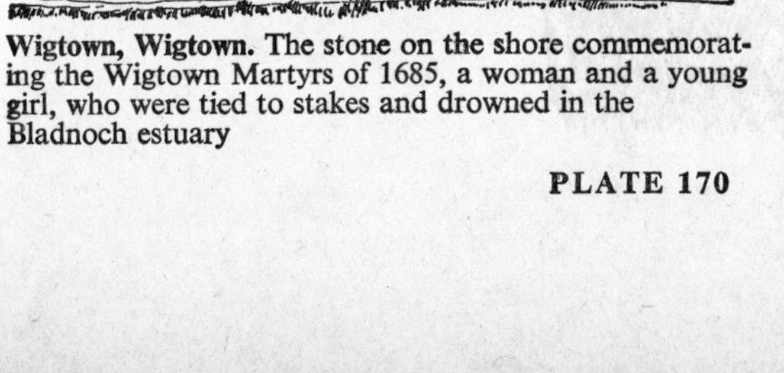

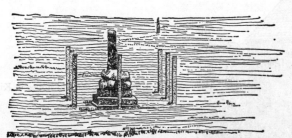

Wigtown, Wigtown. The stone on the shore commemorating the Wigtown Martyrs of 1685, a woman and a young girl, who were tied to stakes and drowned in the Bladnoch estuary

Wormit, Fife. The 2-mile long railway bridge across the Firth of Tay, built 1883–88 to replace its ill-fated predecessor, blown down in 1879. The supports of the old bridge are still visible nearby

Yarrow, Selkirk. The rebuilt Church, which takes the place of two previous structures, both burnt down. Sir Walter Scott's great-grandfather was once minister of the church

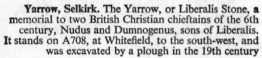

Yarrow, Selkirk. The Yarrow, or Liberalis Stone, a memorial to two British Christian chieftains of the 6th century, Nudus and Dumnogenus, sons of Liberalis. It stands on A708, at Whitefield, to the south-west, and was excavated by a plough in the 19th century

Yetholm, Roxburgh. An old house in Kirk Yetholm, which was formerly the 'Palace' of the Scottish gipsies

WISHAW, Lanark, 74,453. LB. with Motherwell. Map 9, **NS 7** 5.
E.C. Wed. **GOLF.** *Wishaw House*, to the north, and *Cambusnethan Priory*, to the south-west, are Victorian mansions by Gillespie Graham. J. G. Lockhart, Scott's biographer, was born at Cambusnethan manse in 1794. See **Motherwell.** *Iter. 19, 54.*

WISTON, Lanark. Map 9, **NS 9** 3.
The old Church in this village was replaced in the 19th cent. *Tinto Hill*, 2,335 ft., a fine viewpoint, rises to the north.

WORMIT, Fife. Map 17, **NO 3** 2.
E.C. Wed. The first stone of the ill-fated original Tay Bridge carrying the railway into Fife was laid here in 1871. The present bridge was built 1883-88. A fine new road bridge was built some 2 miles farther east. Wormit is said to have been the first Scottish village to have had electricity. See **Newport-on-Tay** (for details of Tay bridges).

YARROW, Selkirk. 384. Map 10, **NT 3** 2.
The beautiful Vale of Yarrow, threaded by the Yarrow Water, and well wooded in places, lies in the heart of the green, rounded hills of Ettrick Forest, in the Lowlands, and has been praised in verse and song by many well-known writers and composers. "The Braes of Yarrow" by Hamilton of Bangour; "The Dowie Dens of Yarrow" by Scott; and Wordsworth's three famous poems, all vividly recall Yarrow Vale. Scott's great-grandfather was once minister of Yarrow Kirk, which has twice been burnt, and which now contains relics associated with Wordsworth and Hogg, the "Ettrick Shepherd." A little to the north-east of the Kirk is the picturesque, derelict *Deuchar Bridge*, dating from 1653. To the south, a by-road leads over the hills to *Ettrick Bridge End (q.v.)*. About ½ **m. W.** of the Kirk, off the Moffat road, is the *Yarrow*, or *Liberalis* Stone, at Whitefield, excavated by chance by a plough during the 19th cent. It commemorates the battle of Yarrow, in 592, when two sons of Liberalis died. Some of the loveliest scenery in the Vale is in the vicinity of *Broadmeadows (q.v.)*, lying to the north-east, in a richly-wooded setting. *Iter. 13, 46.*

YELL, ISLE OF, Shetland. Map 33, **HP 4** 8 etc.
See **Shetland Islands** (Yell).

YESTER HOUSE, East Lothian. Map 10, **NT 5** 6.
See **Gifford.**

YETHOLM, Roxburgh. 651. Map 11, **NT 8** 2.
E.C. Wed. Situated at the foot of the *Cheviot (q.v.)* hills, with the *Cheviot*, 2,676 ft., away to the south-east, across the Northumberland border. Nearer hills, traversed partly by the Border line, are *The Curr*, 1,849 ft. and *The Schel* 1,985 ft., below which lies the lonely valley of the College Burn. The village is divided by the Bowmont Water into *Kirk Yetholm* and *Town Yetholm*, and is overlooked by the Cheviot foothill of *Staerough*, 1,086 ft. Kirk Yetholm was once the headquarters of the Scottish gipsies, and the last "Queen," Esther Faa Blythe, was buried here in 1883. Her so-called "palace" in the village is still pointed out, and her son, who became "King" in 1898, died four years later. The character of "Meg Merrilees," in Scott's "Guy Mannering," is supposed to have been suggested by one of the earlier gipsy "Queens." *Iter. 7, 47.*

YETTS OF MUCKHART, Perth. Map 16, **NO 0** 0.
GOLF. A meeting-place of roads in the hills around *Glendevon (q.v.)*, with the River Devon flowing to the south-east below *Lendrick Hill*, 1,496 ft. **4 m. N.** stands *Glendevon Castle*, mainly 17th cent., now a farm. See **Crook of Devon** and **Rumbling Bridge.** *Iter. 86, 89, 136.*

YOKER (Glasgow), Lanark. Map 8, **NS 5** 6.
Here is a car ferry across the River Clyde, giving access to *Renfrew (q.v.)*. Nearer to Glasgow, a road tunnel under the Clyde links Whiteinch with Linthouse.

YTHAN WELLS, Aberdeen. Map 27, **NJ 6** 3.
Lies in the Strathbogie district of the county. The River Ythan rises in the vicinity and flows eastwards to enter the North Sea near *Newburgh (q.v.)*. 1½ **m. W.**, at *Glenmailen*, are traces of Roman occupation, considered to be the most northerly in Britain. **3 m. N.** stands the ancient house of *Frendraught*, with which a tragedy of 1630 is associated, when the tower was set on fire, causing the deaths of Lord Aboyne and Gordon of Rothiemay.

Explanatory Glossary

Aisle.—In Scotland, sometimes applied to a small building attached to a church, such as an apse or mausoleum. See **Arbuthnott** and **Largs.**

Ambry or Aumbry.—Small cupboard for holding altar vessels, etc.

Archæan.—Of the earliest geological period (See **Hebrides, Outer (Harris)** and **Inchnadamph).**

Bailey.—Enclosure. See Mote.

Bailie or **Baillie.**—Magistrate, cf. alderman.

Barbican.—Outer defence, especially double tower over gate or bridge.

Bartizan.—Battlemented parapet, or turret at top of tower.

Bastel House.—House capable of being defended.

Bastion.—Projecting part of fortification.

Beltane.—May-day Festival when great fires are lit and traditional ceremonies observed. See **Peebles.**

Black House.—Highland cottage of unmortared stones with fire in middle of floor, and interior blackened by smoke. See **Dornie.**

Blindstorey.—Triforium below clearstorey of church, admits no light.

Bothy.—Farm Servants' hut.

Broch or **"Pictish Tower".**—Massive cylindrical drystone tower peculiar to Scotland. Skilfully constructed with intra-mural chambers, stair and galleries. All openings, except entrance tunnel, look on roofless inner court about 40-50 feet in diameter. Period unknown, but relics prove occupation by civilized community engaged in farming, weaving, etc., during early Iron Age. Chiefly found north of Inverness. See **Altnaharra, Glenelg, Orkney** and **Shetland.**

Bronze Age.—From approximately 1800 B.C. to 400 B.C. tools, weapons and ornaments were made of bronze, well designed and serviceable.

Burgh.—cf. borough, a chartered town. (1) Royal Burgh had charter from the Crown. (See **Culross,** etc.) (2) Burgh of Barony was created by the baron. (See **Aberdeen.**) (3) Police Burgh, managed by commissioners.

Cairn.—Pyramidal heap of undressed stones erected as sepulchre, monument or landmark.

Cairn, Chambered.—Enclosing one or more burial chambers or cists. Were round, oval, rectangular, elongated or horned (with horn-like projection, found only in Scotland). See **Kilmartin** and **Orkney** (Maeshowe).

Carse.—Alluvial fertile land alongside a river. See **Carse of Gowrie.**

Chapter House.—Special building in which members of monastic or knightly order met to hear chapters of the rule read and transact business.

Cinerary Urn.—Urn holding ashes after cremation.

Cist.—Prehistoric stone coffin, found in a cairn or underground, sometimes containing a cinerary urn (*q.v.*).

Clearstorey or **Clerestory.**—Section over aisle roofs lighting upper part of church. See **Blindstorey.**

Col.—Depression in mountain chain.

Collegiate Church.—Church served by a staff of clergy (14th and 15th centuries). See **Crichton, Seton,** etc.

Corbel.—Projection of stone or timber which supports part of building.

Corbie-steps.—Crow steps (where the gable has stepped instead of sloping sides).

Covenanter.—Upholder of the Covenants which played an important part in Scottish history. (1) The National Covenant, 1638, repelled Episcopacy and the Scottish Prayer Book (sometimes called "Laud's Liturgy"). (2) The Solemn League and Covenant, 1643, a league with England for the suppression of Episcopacy. The Covenants were declared illegal after the Restoration and the Covenanters took up arms in 1665. In 1685, adherence to the Covenants was declared treasonable and mercilessly repressed. The name "Covenanter" is specifically applied to the persecuted—"the men of the moss hags," hunted down during the "Killing Time," 1685-9. See **Sanquhar,** etc.

Crannog.—Lake-dwelling. See **Cambus o'May.**

Croft.—Small-holding.

Cromlech.—Prehistoric monument consisting of flat stone laid across upright ones.

Crow-steps.—See Corbie-steps.

Culdee (Keledei).—Member of Celtic religious order occupied in maintaining the round of divine service.

Cup-Mark, Cup-and-Ring Mark.—Cup-shaped hollow, sometimes surrounded by concentric rings, found in groups on earth-fast boulders and covers of cists. Purpose unknown. See **Kilmartin.**

Curtain.—Wall connecting towers and surrounding castle enclosure.

Dolmen.—See Cromlech.

Donjon, Dungeon.—Originally the mound or mote: then the tower on the mound; later the strongest tower of a castle; lastly its prison cell.

Doocot.—Dovecote.

Earth House.—Low, curved, subterranean gallery. Also called Pict's House, Fairy House, or Weem (Cave). See **Pitcur.**

Entresol.—Intervening floor between vaulted basement and hall of tower.

Fifteen. The, or The '15.—Jacobite Rising of 1715, attempted to restore the House of Stewart in the person of James Francis Edward Stewart, Chevalier de St. George, sometimes referred to as "the Old Pretender." His standard was raised at **Braemar** (*q.v.*), 6th September, 1715.

First Pointed.—See **Gothic.**

Flamboyant.—"Flame-like" tracery used in late French Gothic, and in Scotland in preference to English Perpendicular. See **Melrose.**

Forty-five, The, or **The '45.**—Attempt renewed by Jacobites in 1745 when Prince Charles Edward Stewart (or Stuart) ("Bonnie Prince Charlie," called the "Young Chevalier" or "Young Pretender"), raised his standard at **Glenfinnan** (*q.v.*). See **Culloden.**

Gabbro.—Black rock, excellent for climbing, found chiefly in the **Coolins** (*q.v.*) of Skye.

Gait, Gate.—Way, road.

Ghillie.—A sportsman's attendant.

Girth.—Sanctuary enclosure.

Girdle, or **Griddle.**—Round iron baking-plate.

Gneiss.—Archaean (*q.v.*) grey rock found near **Inchnadamph** (*q.v.*) and in **Harris.** See **Hebrides, Outer.**

Gothic.—Style of architecture that developed the use of the pointed arch. Prevalent from 12th to 16th centuries. Periods of development styled Early, Middle and Late Pointed, corresponding to Early English, Decorated and Perpendicular in England. "Scottish Baronial" (*q.v.*) Gothic was attempted revival of Gothic forms in mansions of 19th century, characterized by excessive use of pepper-pot **turrets,** battlements, etc.

Haar.—Drizzling rain; mist.

Harl.—Rough-cast.

Haugh, Hauch.—Water-meadow.

Hogmanay.—New Year's Eve.

Howe.—(1) A hollow or sheltered place. (2) A (sepulchral) mound.

Howff.—Resort, or meeting place. See **Dumfries.**

Hut Circle.—Stone foundation of prehistoric round dwelling.

Iron Age.—Period from about 400 B.C. to introduction of Christianity, about A.D. 400 at **Whithorn** (*q.v.*).

Jacobite.—Adherent of House of Stewart after deposition of James VII and II in 1689. See the Fifteen and Forty-five.

Jougs.—An iron collar, with a lock, which was fastened round a wrong-doer's neck and attached by a chain to a tolbooth or churchyard wall for a period of punishment. See **Duddingston** and **Fowlis Easter,** etc.

Kale, Kail.—Greens, or broth made of greens.

Kelpie.—Water-sprite.

L-Plan.—Plan of tower with wing projecting at right angles. See **Craigievar Castle,** etc.

Ballater, Aberdeen. The bridge over the River Dee, which links A93 and A973

Huna, Caithness. A farmhouse with fences made from the local flagstones, in a far northern hamlet

Crail, Fife. An old dovecote standing near the shore of one of the earliest Royal Burghs in the county

Kinnaird, Perth. The restored 12th to 15th century Castle, which overlooks the fertile Carse of Gowrie

Crossraguel Abbey, Ayr. The ruined Kennedy stronghold of Baltersan Tower, which stands to the north-east of the ruined Abbey

Sorn, Ayr. The ancient Church, with its outside staircase, and the 'jougs,' or collar for wrongdoers, hanging on the wall below

Kintore, Aberdeen. The carved Ichthus Stone showing on one side a fish and on the reverse what may represent an elephant

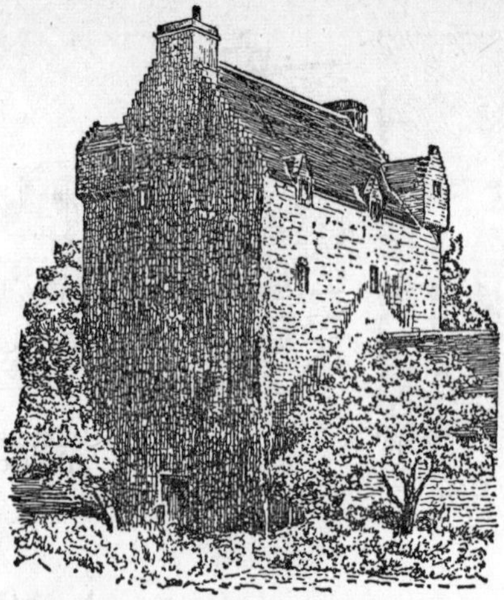

Ettrick Bridge End, Selkirk. Oakwood Tower (1602), showing characteristic crow-stepped gables. It was once the home of Sir Walter Scott's grandfather, and stands 2 miles north-east, on B7009

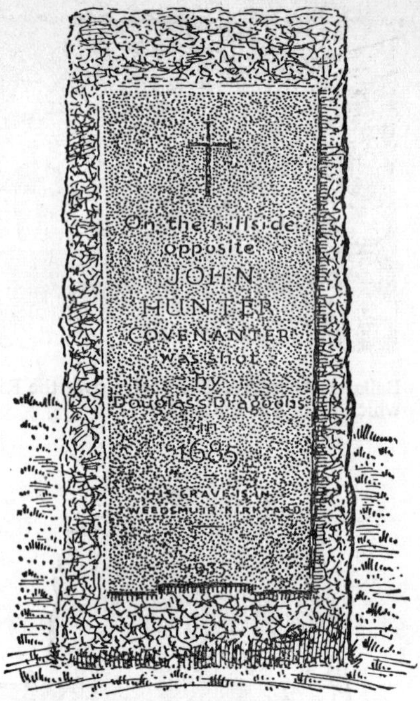

Devil's Beef Tub, Dumfries. The Memorial Stone (1935) to John Hunter, a Covenanter martyr, who was shot near here in 1685

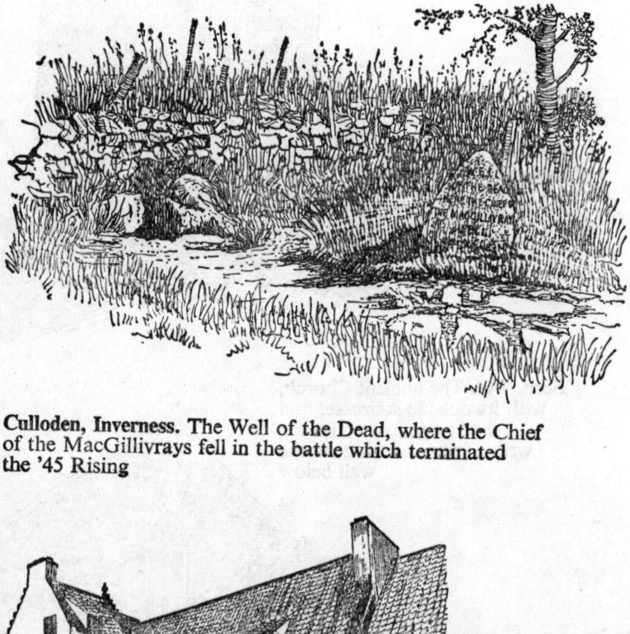

Culloden, Inverness. The Well of the Dead, where the Chief of the MacGillivrays fell in the battle which terminated the '45 Rising

Dunsyre, Lanark. The 'jougs,' or iron collar for wrongdoers, hanging on a wall of the Church

Culross, Fife. The 17th century house known as The Study. This tiny Royal Burgh, now partly in the hands of the National Trust for Scotland, was once famous for its girdles, or baking-plates

Laird.—Landed proprietor.

Links.—Sandy ground, Golf Course.

Machicolation.—Projecting parapet with spaces left between supports to permit of missiles being dropped on assailants. See **Borthwick Castle.**

Manse.—Minister's house. (In Aberdeen, Professor's house.)

Megalith.—Large stone.

Meikle.—Great, much.

Mercat Cross.—At one time a proclamation centre, or where criminals were punished. See **Aberdeen, Inverkeithing, Prestonpans,** etc.

Monolith.—Single block of stone.

Mote, Motte.—Steep-sided earthen mound on which Norman castle stood. A Mote-and-bailey Castle stood on a mote, with bailey or forecourt enclosed by a palisade and ditch, as in the Bayeux Tapestry (early 12th century).

Mounth.—An expanse of mountain. Came to be applied to the passes of the Grampians. See **Cairn o' Mounth** and **White Mounth.**

Neolithic.—See Stone Age.

Norman.—See Romanesque.

Ogee.—A curve produced by the merging of a convex and a concave line.

Ogham, Ogam.—Celtic form of writing on stone. The essential feature is a central line with strokes at right angles to it, and groups of dots representing vowels. See **Golspie.**

Peel or **Pele.**—A tower. Has come to have special reference to Border towers. See **Cranshaws.**

Pend.—Vaulted passage through buildings, usually ending in court, or yard. See **Whithorn.**

Picts.—A mysterious people whose race has never been authoritatively determined. The Romans called them Picti, which may mean "painted." Chiefly in the north-east, they left sculptured stones bearing symbols of unknown significance. (See **Elgin, Ballater,** etc.) Finally dominated by the Scots, losing their language and individuality. Pictish towers—see Brochs. Pict's House—see Earth House.

Pinetum.—Plantation of various kinds of pines grown for botanical or ornamental purposes. See **Stobo.**

Piscina.—Stone basin with drain for rinsing altar vessels.

Policies.—Park or grounds.

Porphyry.—Volcanic rock containing crystals.

Provost.—(1) cf. mayor; (2) cf. dean.

Pulpitum.—The most important screen in a medieval church, with platform on top from which Epistle and Gospel were read. Position varied with position of the quire.

Quire, Choir.—The Eastern part of a monastic, cathedral or collegiate church.

Reek, Reekie.—Smoke, smoky. "Auld Reekie"—name applied to **Edinburgh.**

Reiver.—Outlaw.

Romanesque or **Norman.**—Architectural style, 11th-12th centuries, characterized by the round arch (but see also Transitional).

Runes.—(1) Letters of earliest Teutonic alphabet (*e.g.* **Ruthwell**). (2) Marks of hidden meaning. (3) Secret counsel.

Sacrament House.—Interior niche often elaborately carved, for the reservation of the Elements. See **Cullen, Deskford** and **Fowlis Easter.**

Scaur, Scar.—Precipitous slope.

Scottish Baronial.—Name given to style of building of many late 16th and early 17th century castles, as at **Craigievar** and **Midmar,** etc. (*q.v.*). See also under Gothic.

Sedilia.—Recessed seats south of altar.

Sept.—Branch of clan.

Sett.—Pattern of tartan.

Shieling, Sheiling.—Summer pasture, or herdsman's hut at summer pasture.

Slogan.—Battle-cry.

Souter or **Sutor.**—Shoemaker. See **Cromarty** and **Selkirk.**

Standing Stone.—Monolith of unhewn stone.

Stewartry.—Lands governed through a Steward. Usually refers to the county of **Kirkcudbright.**

Stone Age.—Stage of civilization at which tools and weapons were of stone. Distinction made between the Palæolithic, Older Stone Age, and the Neolithic—New Stone Age, when polished stone and flint implements used, and great sepulchral cairns built; approximately between 2500 and 1800 B.C.

Sutor.—See Souter.

Tacksman.—Tenant (generally a kinsman of the Chief).

Tolbooth.—Once the booth for collecting tolls or taxes. Later, came to refer to the Town Hall. See **Culross, Edinburgh, Tain,** etc.

Transitional.—In architecture, refers to the transition from Romanesque to Gothic, i.e. to the period in which the round and the pointed arch were used simultaneously, late 12th to early 13th centuries. (Note, however, that round-headed doorways were common in Scotland in Gothic times.)

Undercroft.—Basement under church.

Vennel.—Alley. See **Edinburgh** (Castle).

Vitrified Fort.—Hill-fort with walls fused by fire. See **Finhaven,** etc.

Weem.—Cave. See Earth House.

Whaup.—Curlew.

Wynd.—Alley. See **Glamis.**

Yett.—Gate, particularly massive iron-barred grille defending entrance to tower. See **Cawdor,** etc.

Gaelic Place Names

Aber = at the mouth of
Abercorn
Aberdeen
Aberdour
= at the confluence of
Aberfoyle (confluence of the streams)
Aberlour (loud confluence)
Abernethy (confluence of Nethy and Earn)

Ach (from *achadh* = field)
Achaleven (field of the elm)
Achnacarry (field of the weir)
Achray (field of devotion)

Alt, Ald, Auld (from *allt*, stream, burn)
Altnabreac (stream of the trout)
Auldearn (stream of the Earn)
Balaldie (farm at the burn)

Ar (form of Aber)
Arbroath (at the mouth of the river Brothock)

Ard = high
Ardbeg (little height or cape)
Ardchattan (height of abbot Cattan – friend of Columba)
Ardeer (west cape)
Ardentinny (height of the fire)
Ardfern (height of the alders)
Ardincaple (height of the mare)
Ardlamont (height of Lamont)
Ardnamurchan (height of the otter)
Ardrishaig (height of the briars)
Ardrossan (height of the little cape)

Auch (another form of *achadh* = field)
Auchencairn (field with the cairn)
Auchengray (field of the herd)
Auchenleck (field of the floral store)
Auchter (Ochter) (high field)
Auchterarder (upland of the high stream)

Bad = thicket
Badenoch (bushy place)

Bal (from *bail, baile* = hamlet, house, village)
Balerno (barley farm)
Ballachulish (village of the strait)
Ballantrae (village on the shore)
Balmaha (village of the St. Maha – companion of St Patrick)
Balmoral (laird's dwelling)
Balnabruaich (village on the bank)
Bellahouston (village with the crucifix)

Bar = height or hill
Barr
Bardowie (black height)
Barlinnie (height with the pool)

Blair (from *blar* = plain)
Blair
Blairgowrie (plain of the goat)
Blairmore (big field)

Bon, Bun = foot
Bonawe (foot of river Awe)
Bunchrew (at the foot of the trees)

Cal (from *coile* = wood)
Calton (hazel wood)

Cambus = bay, creek
Cambuslang (creek of the boat)
Cambusmore (big bay)

Car (from *carr* = rock)
Carfin (white rock)
Carluke (rock by the hollow)
Carmyle (bare, rounded rock)
Carnoustie (rock of the feast)
Carrick (sea cliff or rock)

Clack, Cloch (from *clach* = stone)
Clackmannan (stone of Mann—legendary figure)
The Cloch (Gourock) (the stone)

Cor (from *coire* = cauldron, circular glen)
Corrie
Corrievreckan (the whirlpool of Brecan – a legendary figure)
Coruisk (glen of the stream)

Craig (from *craeg* = crag, rock)
Craigievar (rock with point)
Craigmillar (rock of the bare height)
Craignure (rock of the yew)

Cul (from *cuil* = corner, rock)
Cullen (little nook)
Culrain (nook with ferns)

Cul (from *cul* = at the back of)
Culloden (at the back of the ridge)
Culnaha (at the back of the kiln)

Dal (from *dail* = field or meadow)
Dalbeattie (field of the birch trees)
Dalgarnock (field with noisy burn)
Dalmeny (field of delay)
Dalnaspidal (field of the spittal or inn)
Dalry (field of the king)

Doug (from *dub* = dark)
Douglas (dark stream)
Dougrie (dark glen)

Dum, Dun = fort, hill
Dumbarton (fort or hill of the Britons)
Dumfries (hill of the shrubs)
Dunbar (fort on the height)
Dunblane (hill of Blann – c. 600 A.D.)
Dundas (south hill)
Dundee (hill of God)
Dunmore (big hill)
Dunoon (castle on the water)

Fin (from *fionn* = clear, white)
Findhorn (Earn with clear banks)
Findlater (white, clear hillside)
Findon (white, clear hillside)
Finhaven (clear river)

Gair, Gir (from *gearr* = short)
Gairloch (short loch)
Girvan (short river)

Gart = enclosure
Gartcosh (enclosure with cave)
Gartness (enclosure by the waterfall)

Inch (from *innis* = island, pasture, links)
Inchcolm (St. Columba's island)
Inchgarvie (rocky isle)
Inchinnan (isle of St. Finnan)
Inchnadamff (pasture of the ox)

Inner (from *inver*)
Innerleithen (confluence of the river Leithen)

Mid Calder, Midlothian. The Parish Church, which has an apsidal choir, re-built in 1541

Kilmarnock, Ayr. The surviving steeple of the former Laigh Kirk, which was burnt in 1668, and replaced by the present building in 1802

Kincardine-on-Forth, Fife. The 17th century Mercat Cross

Edinburgh, Midlothian. The Canongate Church, built in 1688, with a stag's antlers on the gable Cross. The Old Town of Edinburgh has been described as 'Auld Reekie,' referring to the smoke formerly emitted by the closely packed tall houses

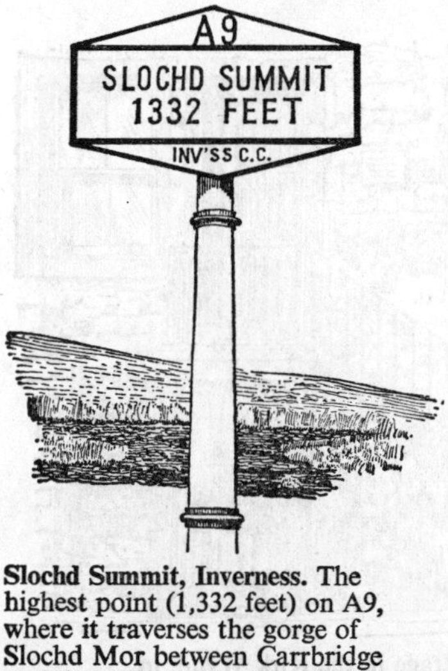

Slochd Summit, Inverness. The highest point (1,332 feet) on A9, where it traverses the gorge of Slochd Mor between Carrbridge and the valley of the River Findhorn on the way to Inverness

Doune, Perth. The old Mercat Cross of a small town formerly well known for the manufacture of pistols

PLATE 174

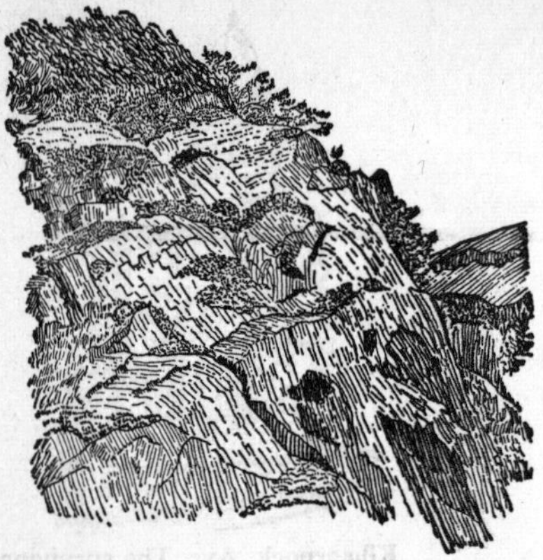

Benderloch, Argyll. Part of the hill known as Beregonium, or Dun Mac Sniochan. On the summit is a prehistoric fort showing traces of vitrifaction, or burning

Closeburn, Dumfries. The 14th century Closeburn Tower, which still preserves the iron 'yett,' or grille, to its first-floor entrance doorway

Latheron, Caithness. A prehistoric standing stone, which is situated near the station

Crail, Fife. The 16th century Tolbooth, into which prisoners were formerly taken through the blocked-up doorway under the window at the side

Auchtermuchty, Fife. The Tolbooth of 1728, which displays characteristic crow-stepped gables

Kirkcaldy, Fife. A cottage in the Kirk Wynd, in which Thomas Carlyle lodged between 1816 and 1818

Inver = mouth of the river, confluence
Inveraray (mouth of the Aray)
Inverness (mouth of the Ness)

Ken, Kin (from *ceann* = head)
Kenmore (big head)
Kennet (chief ford)
Kinbuck (buck's head)
Kinloch (head of the loch)
Kintail (at the head of the salt water)

Kil (from *cill* = cell, church, grave)
Kilbarchan (church of St. Barchan)
Kilbrandon (church of St. Brandon)
Kilbride (church of St. Bridget)
Kilcreggan (church on the little crag)
Kilmacolm (church of my Colm, Columba)
Kilmeny (church of the monk)

Kill (from *coill* = wood)
Killiecrankie (wood of the aspens)

Knock (from *cnoc* = hill)
Knock (a hill)
Knockando (hill of commerce)

Lag = hollow, cave
Lagg
Laggan (little hollow)

Linnhe = pool, sheltered loch
Loch Linnhe
Lynturk (pool of the wild boar)

Lis (from *lios* = garden, enclosure)
Lismore (big garden)

Loch = lake
Lochaber (swamp, standing water)
Lochgelly (clear, white lake)

Mon (from *moine* = moss, moor)
Moncur (moor with the bend)
Monriack (showery moor)
Moniaive (moor with the cry or howl)
Monifieth (moss with the peats)
Montrose (moss on the promontory)

Mor = big
Ben More
Morven (big glen)

Pit = croft
Pitcairn (croft with the cairn or barrow)
Pitcaple (croft of the mare)
Pitsligo (shelly croft)
Pittenweem (land by the cave)

Poll = burn, stream, pool
Polmont (stream or pool on the moorland hill)
Poltalloch (stream of the smithy)

Strath = valley
Strathavon (valley of the Avon)
Strathblane (glen with the little flowers)
Strathyre (valley of the land)

HIGHLAND CLANS AND LOWLAND FAMILIES

THE CLAN MAP on page 36 of the Atlas gives a general idea of the districts occupied by the principal Highland clans, and indicates also the Lowland areas in which certain families were dominant.

HIGHLANDS: It will be understood that the districts outlined were not clan reserves, nor were they clearly delimited by hard-and-fast boundaries like a modern county. Clansmen always moved about freely. Moreover, whereas some clans, notably the Campbells, continually enlarged their holdings, others, as for example the MacGregors, gradually lost every rood of land. Then again, in certain districts there was a mixture of clans from the earliest recorded times; for instance, in Glen Lyon there were Robertsons, MacGregors, members of Clan Menzies and others. Other districts were debatable lands, such as Lochaber, where Camerons, Mackintoshes, Macdonalds and Macleans had conflicting claims. As a general rule, however, a particular clan was in the majority, as the map suggests.

The word clan means " children " or " descendants," and Mac means " son." Thus MacDonald means the son of Donald the " world-ruler " from whom all MacDonalds claim descent. The Chief of a clan is the representative of this common ancestor, and is known to his own people by a patronymic which proclaims this relationship. Hence the Duke of Argyll, head of Clan Campbell is MacCailein Mor, Son of the Great Colin. The tie of blood was always insisted upon, and a remarkable and enduring feature of Highland life was the love the clansmen gave their Chief. Travellers like Dr. Johnson were invariably impressed by it. General Wade reported to the Government that the chiefs " have an Inherent Attractive Virtue, which makes their people follow as Iron Claps to the Loadstone." The Chief was the clan's leader in war, and at home he was responsible for its welfare and conduct, and was the holder of the land it occupied. Legally he had the right of administering justice, which included the power of life and death. This hereditary jurisdiction was taken away after the Jacobite Rising of 1745. At the same time the clans were disarmed and forbidden to wear their national dress. The results of this measure were far-reaching, for it broke up the military organization which was the basis of clan life, and in so doing, it struck a blow at the whole social system of the Highlands. The Chief, who had been the leader and father of his people, became their landlord. The clansman ceased to be a warrior and became a peasant.

HIGHLAND DRESS: The embargo on Highland dress, mentioned above, may seem trivial, but the tartan set the Highlander apart from the Lowlander, and also distinguished clan from clan. There is nothing fortuitous about the sett or pattern of tartan. It was possible to tell where a man lived by looking at his plaid. Writing about 1695, Martin Martin noted that " the women are at great pains first to give an exact pattern of the plaid upon a piece of wood, having the number of every thread of the stripe on it." The belted-plaid was from four to six yards in length and two yards broad. It was plaited from the belt to the knee, thrown round the shoulders and fastened on the breast with a bodkin. It was kilt, plaid and coat in one. The division of this garment into three seems to have come about in the 18th cent., giving rise to the philabeg (or small kilt) as now worn. The arms forbidden by the Disarming Act of 1746 were broadsword, targe, dirk, pistol, or gun. The use of the distinguished and expressive Gaelic language, once universal in the Highlands, was steadily discouraged by religious and educational agencies. The 1961 provisional Census figures show a decline in the number of Gaelic and English speakers from 230,806 in 1901 to 75,508 in 1961, while the number of persons who speak Gaelic alone has dropped from 28,106 to 1,079.

LOWLANDS: On the Border, social conditions in the Middle Ages approximated to conditions in the Highlands. In both cases the people needed land to live on, and a leader who would defend them. Where the Highlander looked to his Chief for protection and leadership in war, the Borderer looked to a Douglas, a Ker, or a Home. An old rhyme tells of the dominance of Lord Cassillis, head of the Kennedy family:

> Frae Wigtown to the town of Ayr,
> Port Patrick to the Cruives of Cree,
> Nae man need think for to bide there
> Unless he court a Kennedy.

Both in the Highlands and on the Border, as surnames became usual, the dependants of a great house—even although they were not kinsmen—adopted the family name, so that it became the commonest name in a district. In the Lowlands, as in the Highlands, the people showed devotion to the head of the family, a " clannishness " that appears to be part of the common Celtic heritage of the race. The sense of mutual obligation, and the way it worked out in practice on the Border, appears in ballads—" Jamie Telfer of the Fair Dodhead," or " Kinmont Willie."

HIGHLAND CLANS: Brief notes follow on some of the clans mentioned in the gazetteer.

CLAN CAMERON: Famous Chiefs were Sir Ewen Cameron (" Evandhu ") who fought at **Killiecrankie** (*q.v.*), and his grandson the " gentle Lochiel " whose influence was decisive in rallying the clans to Prince Charles Edward's banner in 1745. The clan badge is the cranberry or the oak. The slogan is interpreted—" Sons of the hounds come hither and get flesh! " (See **Lochaber** and **Loch Arkaig.**)

CLAN CAMPBELL: The name means " wry-mouthed." The Chief is the Duke of Argyll, known to his people as MacCailein Mor, Son of the

Great Colin, who founded the family of Campbell of **Loch Awe** (*q.v.*), a race of statesmen, with high literary gifts. In 1715 and 1745 they supported the Government. The mythical progenitor of the family was Diarmid (See **Oban** and **Glenshee**). This badge is the wild myrtle or fir club moss, and their slogan "Cruachan!" (See **Loch Awe** and **Inveraray.**)

CLAN CHATTAN: See Clan Mackintosh.

CLAN CHISHOLM: The clan territory is Strath Glass and its lovely tributary glens. (See **Struy Bridge.**)

CLAN DONALD: Donald means "world-ruler." The clan claims descent from Donald, grandson of the great Somerled who broke the power of the Scandinavians and prepared the way for the Celtic Lordship of the Isles. (See **Inveramsay** and **Saddell.**) The clan supported Prince Charles Edward from the outset of his ill-fated adventure (See **Loch nan Uamh, Kinlochmoidart,** etc.). This widespread and once-powerful clan includes the families of Sleat in Skye (the House of the Isles, See **Duntulm**); Glengarry (See **Invergarry**); and Clanranald (See **Acharacle** and **Dalilea**), whose Chiefs decide precedence by lot, if more than one is present at a gathering of Clansmen. Other branches noted in the gazetteer are Clanranald of Lochaber (MacDonells of Keppoch, See **Roy Bridge**), Clan Iain Abrach (MacDonalds of **Glencoe,** *q.v.*) and Clan Iain of Ardnamurchan (See **Kilchoan**). The badge is the common heath. "Fraoch Eilean!"—"Heather Isle" is one of the clan slogans and the various branches have much distinctive pipe music, including the fine Lament, "The Massacre of Glencoe."

CLAN DONNACHIE: The Robertsons of **Struan** (*q.v.*) are believed to be the descendants of the ancient Celtic Earls of Atholl. The badge is the fine-leaved heath, and the slogan means "Fierce when roused!"

THE FARQUHARSONS' lands lie in Aberdeenshire, and the royal estate of **Balmoral** (*q.v.*) was bought from them. Their slogan is "Carn na cuimhne!"—"Cairn of Remembrance!" (See **Monaltrie.**)

THE FRASERS are a family of Norman origin, who first settled in Tweeddale (See **Peebles**) and in the 13th cent. were granted the forfeited estates of the Bissets in Inverness-shire. (See **Kilmorack.**)

GORDON is a "place" name (See **Huntly**). The clan became so powerful in the Highlands that the Chief was known as "Cock o' the North." (See **Fochabers, Aboyne** and **Methlick.**)

GRAHAM is an ancient name, traditionally derived from the hero who overthrew the Roman Wall, locally known as Grim's, or Graeme's Dyke. The family was distinguished by its loyalty to the House of Stewart and produced the two most distinguished soldiers of the Civil Wars, the great Marquis of Montrose, and Graham of Claverhouse, the "Bonnie Dundee" of Scott's ballad (See **Fort William** and **Killiecrankie**). The Chief of Clan Graham is the Duke of Montrose.

CLAN GRANT is a branch of Clan Alpin. The present Chief is Lady Seafield. The clan has many distinguished branches. The badge is the pine or the cranberry, and their slogan "Stand fast, Craigellachie!" (See **Cullen** and **Aviemore.**)

CLAN GREGOR: "'S Rioghail mo Dhream"—"Royal is my Race"—is the motto of this ancient and unfortunate clan which (with Macaulays, Mackinnons and others) claims descent from Griogar, son of King Alpin (c. A.D. 787). The name Macgregor was proscribed from 1603 to 1774. The famous Rob Roy was a MacGregor of Glengyle, but frequently used the name of Campbell. (See **Balquhidder.**)

THE MACDOUGALLS: Like Clan Donald, Clan Dougall is descended from the mighty Somerled, and once had wide domains. These Lords of Lorne were on the losing side in the contest for the throne between Bruce and Balliol, and many of their lands passed to the Campbells, but Dunollie still remains the seat of the Chief. (See **Oban** and **Tyndrum.**) The badge is bell heather and the slogan means "Victory or Death!"

CLAN MACKAY: The Highland designation of the Chief, Lord Reay, is Mac Aoidh—"Son of Hugh." The badge is reed grass or broom, and the slogan means "the White Banner of Mackay!" (See **Reay.**)

THE MACKENZIES: The "z" here represents an obsolete letter formerly rendered by "g" or "y," and an old form is the name of MacKengie. The clan rose to great power after the forfeiture of the MacDonalds, Lord of the Isles. The Chief of the Mackenzies of Kintail was the Earl of Seaforth. Their badge is variegated holly, and the slogan "Tulach Ard!"—(A hill in Kintail.) (See **Poolewe.**)

CLAN MACKINTOSH or Macintosh and **CLAN MACPHERSON:** These are the leading clans of the Clan Chattan Confederacy, and are believed by some authorities to have formed the "Clan Quhele" which took part in the Clan combat at **Perth** (*q.v.*). The badge of both is boxwood or whortleberry, and their slogans are "Loch May!" and "Creag Dhubh!" (See **Drumgask, Moy** and **Newtonmore.**)

THE MACLEANS or **CLAN GILLEAN** belong to the Western Isles and claim descent from Gillean of the Battle-axe, who fought at the battle of Largs. The Chief is Maclean of Duart and the 26th Chief acquired and restored the historic Castle Duart in Mull (See **Craignure**). Ardgour is almost the only clan territory to have been held by Macleans in continuity. Crowberry, holly and blaeberry are the badges of various families, and the clan slogans mean "Death or Life!" and "Another for Hector!" (See **Inverkeithing.**)

THE MACLEODS are an Island family, and the names of the early chiefs suggest that they were of Norse, or mixed Norse and Celtic descent. The historic seat of the Chief is **Dunvegan** (*q.v.*) in Skye. The badge of the Macleods of Harris is juniper, and a famous pipe tune is "The Lament for Rory Mor."

THE MACNABS are a branch of the ancient Clan Alpin, and claim descent from the lay Abbot of Glendohcart (Clann-an-Aba, Sons of the Abbot). Their badge is the heath. (See **Killin.**)

THE MACPHERSONS: See Clan Mackintosh.

THE MACRAES of Kintail mustered strong in the Seaforth Highlanders when the regiment was first raised in 1778. The Chief held from 1520 the post of Hereditary Constable of Eilean Donan Castle. (See **Dornie.**)

CLAN MENZIES fought for Bruce at Bannockburn. The slogan means "Up with the Red and the White!" (See **Weem.**)

CLAN MUNRO'S Chief is Munro of Foulis and the slogan is "Casteal Folais ne theine!"—"Foulis Castle on Fire!" Many noted soldiers came of this clan. (See **Evanton.**)

CLAN STEWART: There are many septs of this royal clan. The Stewarts of Appin played a gallant part in the '45, led by Stewart of Ardshiel (See **Portnacroish**). The badge is the oak and the slogan is "Creag-an-Sgairbh!"—"The Cormorant's Rock."

THE MURRAYS: This powerful family claims descent from Hugh Freskyn (See **Duffus**), a Fleming, whose son assumed the title "de Moravia" because of his wide domain in Moray. The Duke of Atholl is Chief of Clan Murray of Atholl (See **Blair Atholl**). An old saying ran:

Duke of Atholl, King in Man
And the greatest man in a' Scotlan'.

OGILVIE: The Chief is the Earl of Airlie, who claims descent from the Celtic Earls of Angus. His seat is **Cortachy** (*q.v.*) Castle. The family suffered heavily in the Stewart cause.

PLACE INDEX

Many places mentioned in this book do not warrant their own separate Gazetteer entry. Such places are listed alphabetically below with the indication of the particular Gazetteer entry under which they are to be found.

INFORMATION CENTRES AND BUREAUX

Tourist Information Centres able to deal with inquiries from callers in person are listed here. Some of these centres display a special sign TOURIST INFORMATION CENTRE issued by the British Travel Association, Queen's House, 64-65 St. James's Street, London W1 (*T* 01-629 9191).

They are shown on the town plans in the Gazetteer, except for places marked with an asterisk, indicating that no AA town plan is available. Other Information Bureaux, sometimes located at Town Halls, or in Council Offices, are also shown on the town plans.

Aberdeen Aberdeen
Information Bureau,
20 Union Street
T 23456
May 1 to September 30
Information Caravan, in
Stonehaven Road at south
entrance to City.
June to mid-September
Information Kiosk,
The Beach

Aberfeldy Perth
Mid-June to mid-September
Information Kiosk
The Square
T 276

Bonar Bridge Sutherland
April to August
Sutherland Tourist Association,
Bonar Bridge
T Ardgay 333

***Carnoustie** Angus
Carnoustie Publicity &
Development Association,
Council Chambers
T 3335
June to first week September
Information Kiosk on beach
T 2258.

***Castle Douglas** Kirkcudbright
Galloway & Dumfriesshire Tourist
Association,
146 King Street
T 2219

Crieff Perth
Crieff Tourist Association,
James Square
T 578

Dunbar East Lothian
Information Bureau,
Town House
T 3353

Dundee Angus
Information Bureau,
Town Clerk's Department,
21 City Square
T 23141

Dunfermline Fife
Information Bureau,
Carnegie Clinic
Pilmuir Street
T 22911

Dunoon Argyll
Information Centre,
Pier Esplanade
T 7 Ext. 16

Edinburgh Midlothian
Information Bureau,
City of Edinburgh Publicity
Department,
343 High Street
T 031-225 5081
The Scottish Tourist Board,
2 Rutland Place, West End
T 031-229 1561-4

Fort William Inverness
Lochaber Tourist Association,
West End
T 2232

Glasgow Lanark
Information Bureau,
George Square
T 041-221 7371, 041-221 9600

Gourock Renfrew
Information Bureau,
Pierhead Gardens
T 31126

Grantown-on-Spey, Moray,
Improvement and Tourist Association,
31 High Street
T 273

Hawick Roxburghshire,
Tourist Information Centre,
14 High Street
T 2341

Inverness Inverness
The Scottish Tourist Board,
2 Academy Street
T 34353

***Kirkwall** Orkney,
Orkney Tourist Association,
Mouthoolie Lane
T 856

***Leven** Fife
Information Bureau,
South St
T 533

Montrose Angus
Information Bureau,
Town Buildings
T 367

***Newtonmore** Inverness
Spey Valley Tourist Organisation,
Main Street
T 253

North Berwick East Lothian
Information Centre,
Quality Street
T 2197

Oban Argyll
Information Bureau,
Albany Street
T 2466

Pitlochry Perth
Pitlochry Tourist Association,
28 Atholl Road
T 215

***Prestwick** Ayrshire,
Information Centre,
Station Road
T 77084

***Rothesay & Isle of Bute**
Information Bureau,
West Pier
T 751

St Andrews Fife
Information Centre,
Town Hall,
South Street
T 1021

***Shetland Islands**
Shetland Tourist Association,
Alexandra Wharf,
Lerwick
T Lerwick 34

***Skye** Inverness
Isle of Skye Tourist Association,
Portree
T Portree 137

***Stornoway** Isle of Lewis
Western Isles Tourist Association,
21 South Beach Street
T 569

***Tarbert**, Harris, Isle of Lewis
Western Isles Tourist Association,
Post Office.
T Harris 11 and 12

Ullapool Ross-shire,
Mid-May to September
Information Bureau,
Quay Street
T 135

*Wester Ross (Southern) Tourist
Association,
Kyle of Lochalsh.
T 4276

SERVICES TO THE ISLANDS

BY SEA

Regular shipping services for passengers and vehicles are maintained throughout the year to most of the islands. The shipping companies publish timetables giving particulars of all their services, including details of the numerous summer excursions and tours and services to the following smaller islands: Canna, Eigg, Iona, Lismore, Raasay, Rum, and Staffa.

BY AIR

There is no air ferry service for the transport of vehicles between the mainland and the islands, but British European Airways operate passenger services from the mainland towns of Glasgow, Edinburgh, Aberdeen, Inverness, Wick, and Campbeltown to the islands of Islay, Tiree, the Outer Hebrides, Orkney, and Shetland. The airports are shown on the atlas pages 34-35. For full details apply to any British European Airways office or agency.

TAKING A VEHICLE

Three factors govern the decision whether or not to take a vehicle to the islands—the distance from the mainland, the cost of shipping, and the extent of motor roads on the island. Distances range between the half-mile ferry crossings to Bute and Skye and the 270 miles from Edinburgh to Shetland. They can be roughly estimated from the atlas. The chart overleaf shows the return charges for vehicles, and details of road conditions and the extent of roads are given in the itineraries and the gazetteer; the extent of roads can also be ascertained from the atlas.

RESERVATIONS. Booking arrangements vary from service to service. On some services reservations are not accepted, on some they are advisable but not essential, and on others reservations must be made; details are given on the chart overleaf. Acceptance of vehicles depends on traffic conditions and tides. Solo motor cycles are usually accepted without bookings. Applications for reservations should be made direct to the shipping company at the address given; the AA cannot undertake to make reservations.

INSURANCE. Vehicles are carried at owners' risk, and members should make sure that their vehicle insurance policy covers the journey.

MAINLAND GARAGES. If it is not considered worth shipping a vehicle, arrangements can be made for it to be garaged on the mainland. Addresses of convenient garages are given in the *Members Handbook*. It is best to book garage space in advance.

CAR-CARRYING SERVICES

The islands are listed alphabetically. Unless otherwise stated the charges given are for return journeys made within three months. For services where vehicles are driven on board, the charges vary according to the length of the vehicle; where loading is by crane, charges are made according to weight, and a weight certificate (obtainable at any public weighbridge) must be produced at the time of shipment. See the chart overleaf for the method of loading on each service. In addition to carrying charges, pier dues—which vary from 5p to £1—must be paid at some ports on both departure and arrival.

Abbreviations

See Chart overleaf

BR British Railways
M/c/s Motor cycle with sidecar
cr Crane loading
dr Vehicles driven on board
M/c Motor cycle (solo)
T Telephone Number

OPERATING COMPANIES

BF Bute Ferry Co Ltd
Colintraive, Argyll
T Colintraive 235

CG Caledonian Steam Packet Co Ltd
Gourock. *T* for Arran–0475–34568
T for Bute–0475–34567.
See also BR Scottish Region timetable

EM M A Mackenzie, Glenelg,
By Kyle of Lochalsh, Ross-shire
T Glenelg 224

MG David MacBrayne Ltd
Travel Centre, 302 Buchanan St.
Glasgow G1 2NG
T 041-332 9700

NO North of Scotland, Orkney and Shetland Shipping Co., Ltd., New Pier, Stromess.

NS North of Scotland Steamship Co
Matthews Quay, Aberdeen AB9 8DL
T 0224 29111
or
Tower Place, Leith, Edinburgh 6
T 031-554 2661

ST The Scottish Transport Group
Kyleakin *T* Kyleakin 282

WF Western Ferries Ltd, Kennacraig,
By Tarbert (Loch Fyne), Argyll
T Whitehouse (Argyll) 218

The information given is correct at the time of going to press, but the sailing times and charges should be verified with the operating companies concerned, from whom further information can be obtained.

For abbreviations see page 284

Island	Map Page	Island Pier	Mainland Ports	Operating Company	Charge *return*	Loading	Service
ARRAN	7	Brodick	Ardrossan	CG	Car from £5.00 M/c £1.25	dr	Sundays June–mid Sep only. 3 sailings Weekdays June–Sep 5 sailings October–May 3 sailings *Reservation essential*
		Lochranza	Claonaig (Kintyre)	CG	Summer only—details from operating company		
BARRA	32	Castlebay	Oban	MG	Car from £6.98	cr	No Sunday service Oct–May 3 sailings weekly May–Sep 1 sailing weekly *Reservation essential*
		Castlebay	Mallaig	MG	Car from £5.40 single	dr	No Sunday service May–mid Sep only 3 sailings weekly *Reservation essential*
BENBECULA	32	See services to Skye, then via Uig (Skye) and Lochmaddy (North Uist)		MG	See under Skye and North Uist		
BUTE	7	Rothesay	Wemyss Bay	CG	Car from £1.85 M/c 70p	dr	Daily, 3–7 sailings *Reservation essential in Summer*
		Rhubodach	Colintraive	BF	Car from 55p single M/c 20p single	dr	Daily 08.00 (Sundays 09.00)–dusk *No Reservations*
COLL	12	Coll	Oban	MG	Car from £6.53 single	cr	No Sunday service 3–4 sailings weekly *Reservation essential*
COLONSAY	13	Colonsay	Kennacraig (West Loch Tarbert)	WF	Car from £3.30 single	dr	No Sunday service 3 sailings weekly *Reservation advisable*
CUMBRAE, GT	7	Cumbrae Slip (for Millport)	Largs	CG	Car from £1 single	dr	Regular sailings—about every half hour
GIGHA	6		Kennacraig (West Loch Tarbert)	WF	Car from £2.20 single	dr	6 sailings weekly *Reservation advisable*
HARRIS	32	Tarbert	See services to Skye then via Uig (Skye)	MG	Uig-Tarbert Car from £4.10 single	dr	*No Sunday Service* *From Uig usually 1–3 sailings daily* *Reservation advisable*
ISLAY	6	Port Askaig	Kennacraig (West Loch Tarbert)	WF	Car from single £2.90	dr	Sundays 1–2 sailings Weekdays 2–3 sailings *Reservation advisable*
JURA	6	Feolin	Kennacraig (West Loch Tarbert)	WF	Car from £3.80 single	dr	As for Islay then via Feolin Ferry
LEWIS	12 & 13	See service to Skye then via Uig (Skye) and Tarbert (Harris)		MG	Uig-Tarbert Car from £4.10 single	dr	See under Harris
		Stornoway	Kyle of Lochalsh Mallaig	MG	Car from £6.95	cr	*No Sunday Service* Weekdays, 1 sailing daily *Reservation essential*

Island	Map Page	Island Pier	Mainland Ports	Operating Company	Charge *return*	Loading	Service
MULL	12 & 13	Craignure	Oban	MG	Car from £3.20 single	dr	*No Sunday Service* *From Oban* 4 (2 winter) sailings daily
			Lochaline		Car from £2.80 single		*From Lochaline* 2 sailings daily *Reservation advisable*
NORTH UIST	32	Lochmaddy	See service to Skye then via Uig (Skye)	MG	Uig-Lochmaddy Car from £4.10 single	dr	*No Sunday service* *From Uig* May–Sep Mondays–Fridays 1 sailing Oct–April 4 sailings weekly *Reservation advisable*
ORKNEY	33	Stromness	Scrabster (Thurso)	NO	Car from £10.15 M/c £2.30	cr	Sunday service July and August only. Weekdays from Scrabster 1 sailing *No Reservations (Can be arranged May to September)*
SHETLAND	33	Lerwick	Aberdeen	NS	Car from £23.35 M/c £4.50	cr	Monday and Thursday 1 sailing *Reservation essential*
SKYE	22 & 23	Armadale	Mallaig	MG	Car from £1.50 single	dr	*No Sunday Service* May–Sep Weekdays 3–5 sailings daily *Reservation essential*
		Kyleakin	Kyle of Lochalsh	ST	Car from 55p single M/c single 20p	dr	Sundays 10.00–20.45 (Winter 10.15–17.20) Weekdays 08.00†–23.00 *No reservations*
		Kylerhea	Glenelg (summer only)	EM	Car 50p single M/c 15½p single	dr	*No Sunday Service* May–Sep only From 08.30–20.00 or dusk *No reservations*
SOUTH UIST	32	See service to Skye then via Uig (Skye) and Lochmaddy (North Uist)		MG	Uig-Lochmaddy Car from £4.10 single	dr	See under North Uist
		Lochboisdale	Oban	MG	Car from £6.95	cr	*No Sunday service* Oct–April 3 sailings weekly May–Sep 1 sailing weekly *Reservation essential*
		Lochboisdale	Mallaig	MG	Car from £5.40 single	dr	June–mid Sept only *No Sunday service* 3 sailings weekly *Reservation essential*
TIREE	13	Tiree	Oban	MG	Car from £6.53	cr	*No Sunday service* 3–6 sailings weekly *Reservation essential*

† Sailings between 04.30 and 80.00, according to demand

MAINLAND FERRIES

FERRIES are listed alphabetically; the map reference is for the atlas where the name of each ferry is shown in a small panel at the appropriate place. The information given below is correct at the time of going to press; more details are available from the ferry company. At Christmas and Bank Holidays services may be altered.

Space cannot be reserved in advance (except on the Gourock–Dunoon service), and journeys are undertaken at owners' risk. Charges given are for single journeys. On ferries where passengers are allowed to remain in their vehicles, enough room must be left between vehicles for doors to be opened so that they could escape in an emergency.

For abbreviations used on Chart, see page 284

Some ferries do not operate on Sundays. There are often delays due to winds or tides.

Ferries	**Map**	**See notes below**	**Car Space**	**Transit Time** *min*	**Charges** *single*	**Services**
BALLACHULISH *Across Loch Leven* *T* Ballachulish 215	18 **NN** **0** 6	1	6	5	Car 30p–45p M/c 10p M/c/s 20p	Weekdays 08.00 (Sundays 09.00) or dawn if later–dusk (21.30 latest)
CORRAN–ARDGOUR *T* Ardgour 257	18 **NN** **0** 6	–	8	6	Car 30p M/c 10p M/c/s 17½p	Weekdays 08.15 (09.00 December and January, 10.00 Sundays)–dusk (19.45 latest, 20.45 June–August)
DUNOON–GOUROCK *T* 047–558 4497	8 **NS** **1** 7	2	40	20	Car 90p–£1·70 M/c 42p M/c/s 80p	Weekdays 9-10 sailings Sundays 8 sailings (3 October–March)
KESSOCK *Across Beauly Firth* *T* Inverness 33270	25 **NH** **6** 4	–	22	7	Car 30p M/c 10p M/c/s/ 20p	Weekdays 07.15–20.45 Sundays 09.45–17.45
KYLESKU *Across Loch Cairnbawn* *T* Kylestrome 222	28 **NC** **2** 3	3	8	5	Free	09.00–dusk or 21.00
RENFREW–YOKER *T* 041-221 8733	8 **NS** **5** 6	4	14	2	Car 10p M/c 5p M/c/s 10p	Continuous day and night

1. Very congested at times during summer, but may be avoided by using the road round Loch Leven. When approaching from the south telephone Ballachulish 215 from AA Telephone (at junction of A82/A828) and ask about the delay. If towing a caravan or trailer, go round Loch Leven.
2. For full details see BR Scottish Region timetable. Reservation advisable for Saturdays and Sundays—apply to the Caledonian Steam Packet Co Ltd, Gourock, Renfrewshire.
3. A red flag is flown from the pier when bad weather affects sailings.
4. Very congested during rush hours. Rates doubled between midnight and 05.00.

TOLL BRIDGES AND THE CLYDE TUNNEL

Name	Map	Location	Charge
ERSKINE (Renfrew-Dunbarton)	8 **NS** 4 7	8 miles north west of Glasgow	Car 15p
FORTH (West Lothian/Fife)	17 **NT** 1 7	10 miles west of Edinburgh	Car 15p
TAY (Fife/Angus)	17 **NO** 4 2	Linking Newport and Dundee	Car 12½p
CLYDE TUNNEL *River Clyde*	8 **NS** 5 6	On the west side of Glasgow	No charge

BARTHOLOMEW'S
ROAD ATLAS OF SCOTLAND

Showing Ministry of Transport Road Numbers, A A and R A C Telephone Boxes, Mileages and National Grid

SCALE: FIFTH-INCH TO MILE

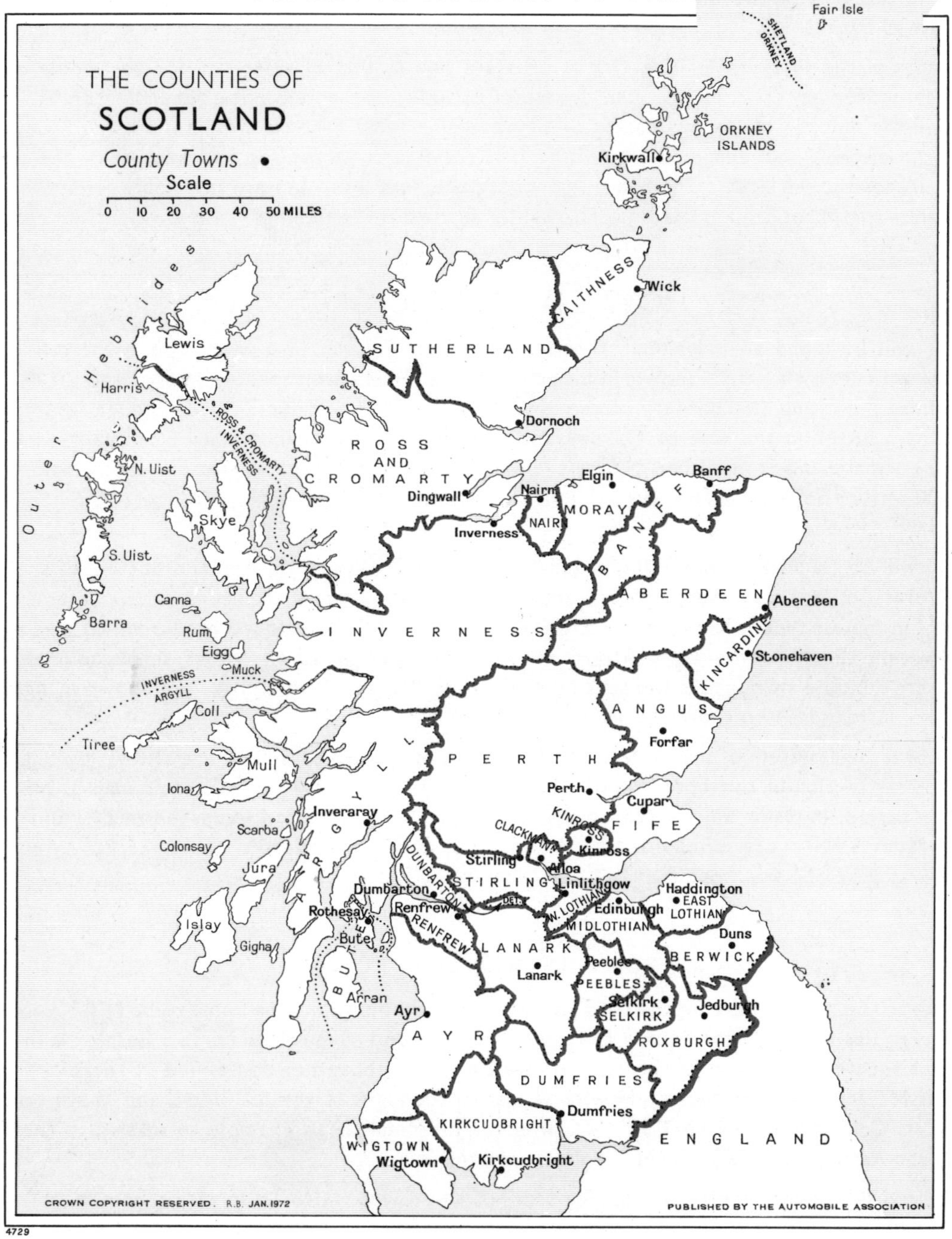

PUBLISHED BY THE AUTOMOBILE ASSOCIATION

4729

CONTENTS

THE NATIONAL GRID AND THE A.A. ROAD BOOK

GENERAL

The Atlas on the following pages has had the network of the National Grid superimposed upon it and the map references in the gazetteer portion of the Road Book give the page number of the Atlas, followed by the National Grid reference. In conformity with the present Ordnance Survey practice, National Grid references in the text of the book are given in the new form of letters and figures instead of in the original form of figures only.

The advantage of the National Grid is that it provides one system of reference for the whole country, which is correct for any scale of map, the degree of accuracy of the reference depending on the scale of the map and the number of ' co-ordinates ' or figures given in it. The co-ordinates are the figures given in the margin of the Atlas, and it will be noted that the figures at the top and bottom of the page are heavier than those at the sides. The heavy figures are the ' eastings ' and are invariably given first in the reference after the Major Square letters. The lighter figures, or ' northings ', are always given second.

HOW TO USE THE GRID

On page iv will be found an index map showing the Major Squares into which the country is divided, each square with its own letters shown in a circle. These letters are repeated in the pages of the Atlas, the thick lines indicating the borders of the Major Squares. The Major Square number formerly used (preceded by a letter in the case of Orkney and Shetland) is shown in brackets below the letters to assist in reference to maps published before the adoption of the letter designation. Each Major Square contains 100 smaller Squares, Square **0** 0 being in the bottom left hand corner and Square **9** 9 being in the top right hand corner.

On page iii will be found a reproduction of Major Square **NT**. Along the top and bottom of the square are the figures **0-9** in heavy type. These are the ' eastings ' and at the sides of the square are the ' northings ' in lighter type. These figures are the ' co-ordinates ' (mentioned above) which give the map reference within the Major Square, and are shown in the margin of the pages throughout the Atlas. ' Eastings ' are denoted throughout the text by heavy type figures. ' Northings ' are shown in light type. Major Square letters are also shown in heavy type in the text.

In the National Grid system of map reference the letters of the Major Square are always given first, and in the gazetteer section of this book, these letters follow the map page, e.g. Glasgow Map 8, **NS 5** 6 will be found on page 8, in Major Square **NS**, smaller square **5** 6. To avoid confusion, the smaller squares into which the Major Squares are sub-divided by the east and north co-ordinates, are spoken of by giving the figures separately, e.g. **1** 4 as ' one four ', **2** 5 as ' two five ', etc.

EXAMPLES

By reference to the map on page iii, the Grid reference for Edinburgh will be found to be **NT 2** 7, indicating that Edinburgh lies within Major Square **NT**, two lines east and seven lines north. Peebles is in the left centre of the square to the right of the vertical line **2** and just above horizontal line 4; therefore its Grid reference is **NT 2** 4 (NT, two, four). Hawick is just to the right of vertical line **5** and above horizontal line 1, and its Grid reference is **NT 5** 1 (NT, five, one). Moffat is an example of a town in the smaller square **0** 0 and its reference **NT 0** 0 (NT, nought, nought).

An alphabetical list of the map references for some of the towns which lie in Major Square **NT** is given above the map.

BIGGAR	**NT 0** 3	EDINBURGH	**NT 2** 7	KIRKCALDY	**NT 2** 9
BONNYRIGG	**NT 3** 6	GALASHIELS	**NT 4** 3	LEADBURN	**NT 2** 5
CARTER BAR	**NT 6** 0	HADDINGTON	**NT 5** 7	MID CALDER	**NT 0** 6
COLDSTREAM	**NT 8** 3	HAWICK	**NT 5** 1	MOFFAT	**NT 0** 0
DUNBAR	**NT 6** 7	JEDBURGH	**NT 6** 2	NORTH BERWICK	**NT 5** 8
DUNFERMLINE	**NT 0** 8	KELSO	**NT 7** 3	PEEBLES	**NT 2** 4
DUNS	**NT 7** 5			SELKIRK	**NT 4** 2

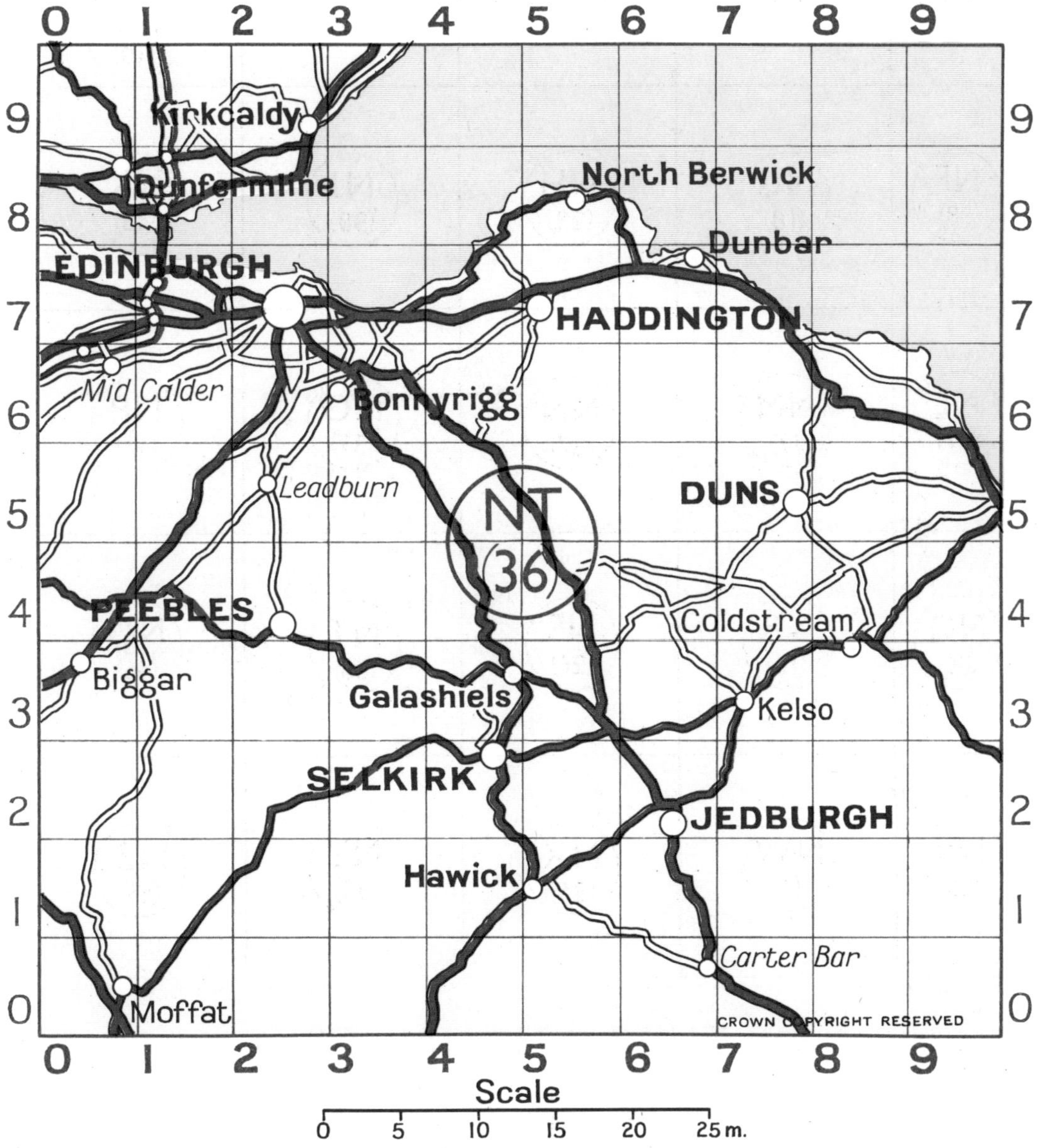

Each Major Square is 62½ miles across and each smaller square 6¼ miles.

INDEX TO MAJOR SQUARE NUMBERS

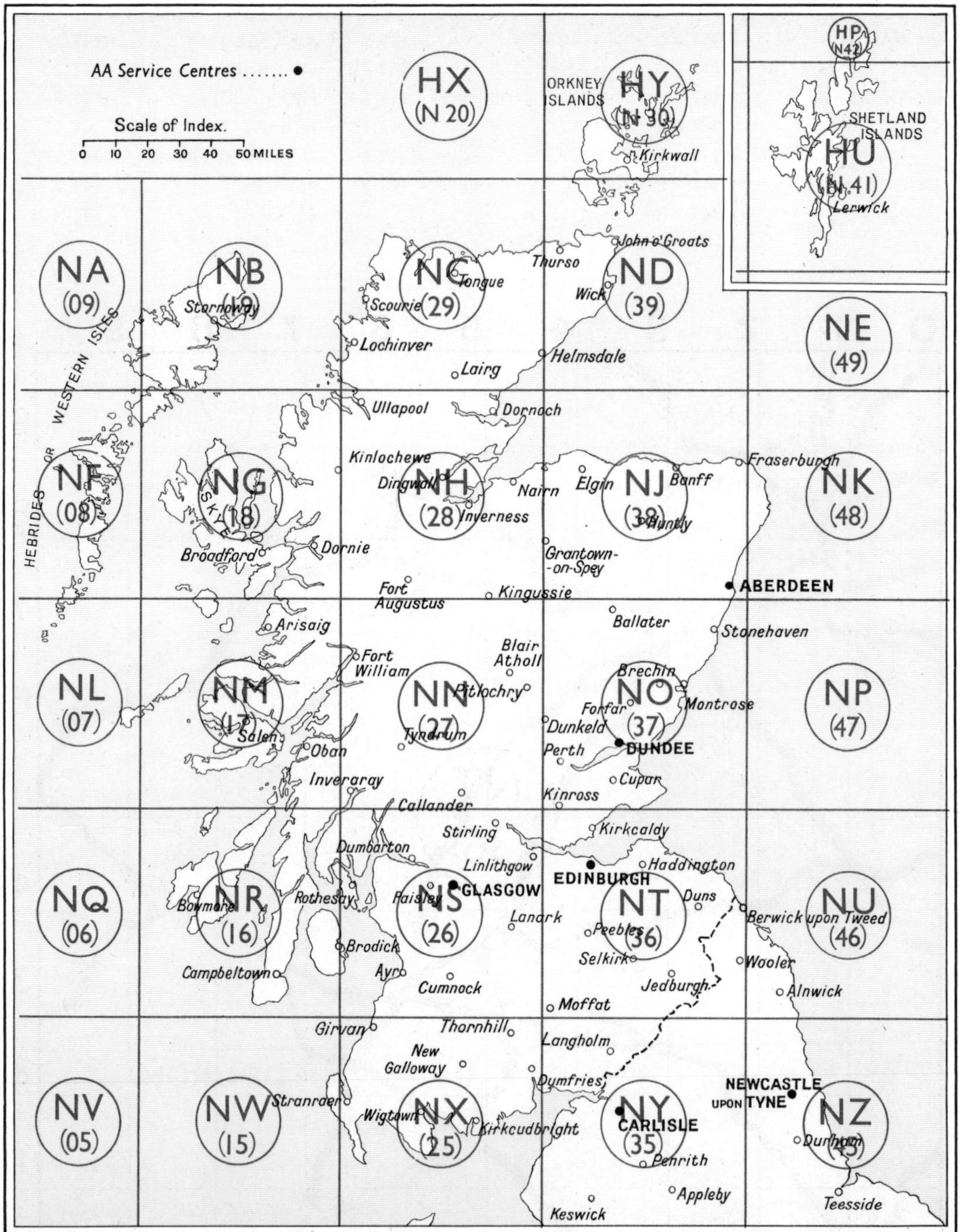

OF THE NATIONAL GRID

The National Grid is superimposed by permission of the Controller of H.M. Stationery Office and the Director General of Ordnance Survey

SCALE OF MAP PAGES 2-31

FIFTH-INCH TO MILE

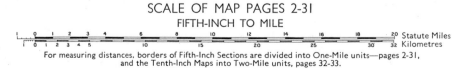

For measuring distances, borders of Fifth-Inch Sections are divided into One-Mile units—pages 2-31, and the Tenth-Inch Maps into Two-Mile units, pages 32-33.

Printed by JOHN BARTHOLOMEW & SON LTD EDINBURGH Published by THE AUTOMOBILE ASSOCIATION

INDEX TO MAP PAGES

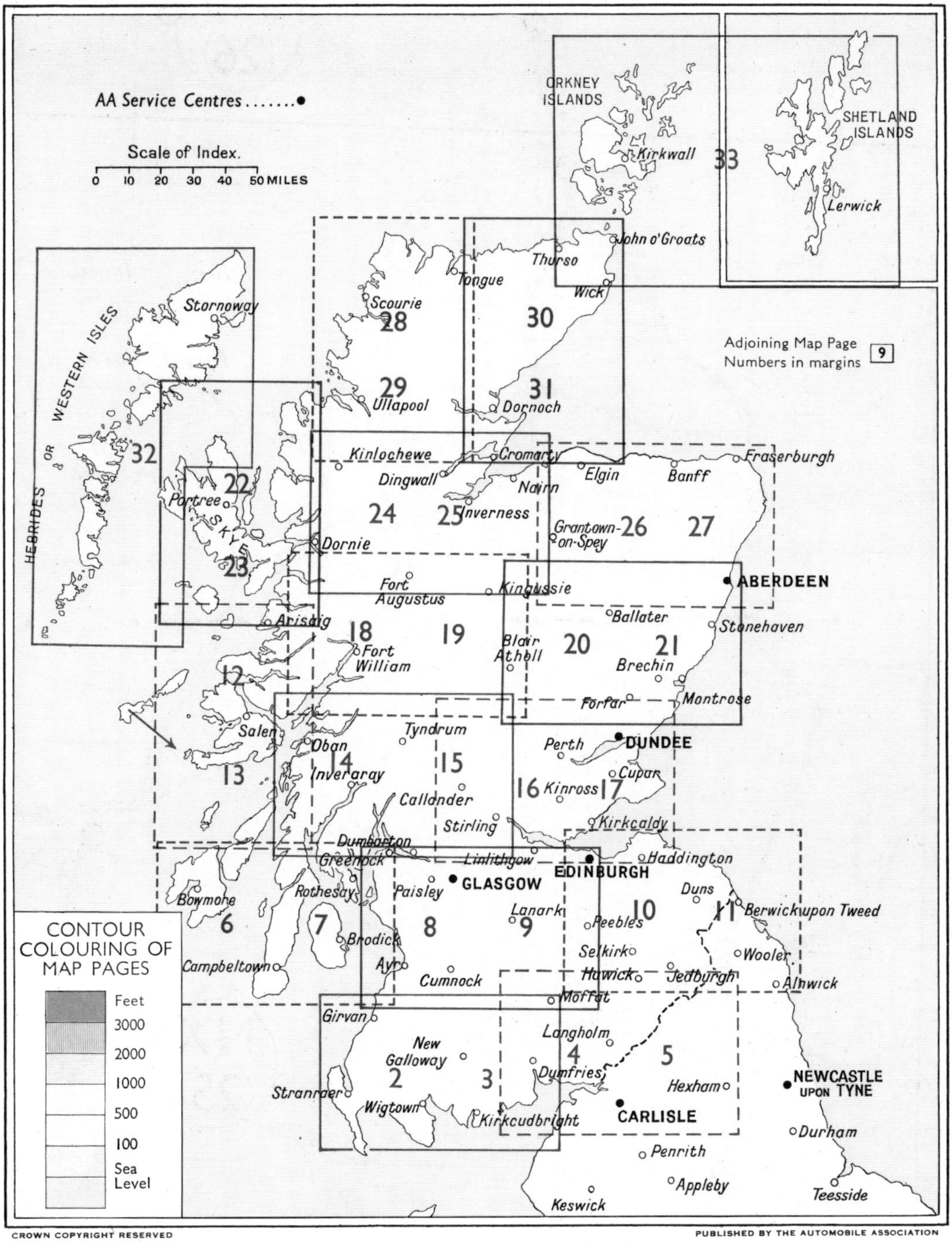

PUBLISHED BY THE AUTOMOBILE ASSOCIATION

REFERENCE TO MAP PAGES, 2-33

- Access Point / Service Area — Motorways
- Dual Carriageways
- Primary and Class "A" Roads
- Class "B" Roads
- Roads requiring special care owing to restricted width and/or rough surface Passing places usually available. (*See note on page 8 of text.*)
- Motorway — Roads under construction
- Other Roads
- Private Roads ....Tracks
- AA and RAC Telephones
- *A 9 A 985 B 8028* — Road Numbers of the Ministry of Transport
- 2 — Distances in miles between Blue Circles
- LC Level Crossing — Railways .... Canals
- County Boundaries
- QUEEN'S VIEW — AA Viewpoints
- ·275 — Heights in Feet
- Airports
- Corran Ferry — Car Ferries
- Car-carrying services (*See also pages 34 & 35 of atlas*)
- Forest Parks

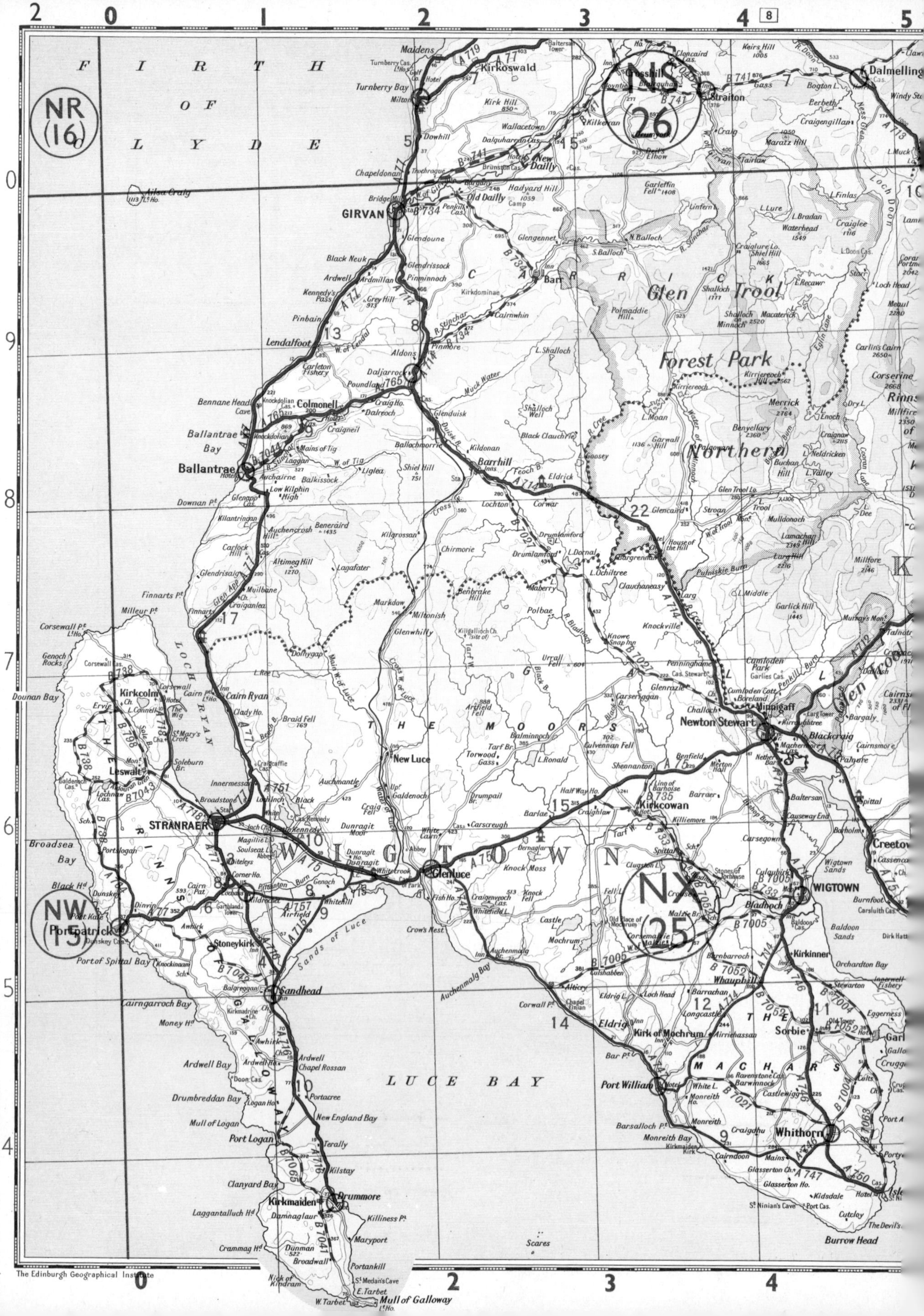
NR (16)
NS (26)
NW (15)
NX (25)
FIRTH OF CLYDE
LOCH RYAN
LUCE BAY
Sands of Luce
Ailsa Craig
Maidens
Turnberry Cas.
Turnberry Bay
Kirkoswald
Kirk Hill
Crosshill
Straiton
Dalmellington
Keirs Hill
Bogton L.
Craigengillan
Maratz Hill
Dowhill
Wallacetown
Kilkerran
Dalquharran Cas.
New Dailly
Old Dailly
Chapeldonan
Hadyard Hill
Bridge Mill
GIRVAN
Penkill Cas.
Glendoune
Black Neuk
Ardwell
Ardmillan
Glendrissock
Pinminnoch
Kennedy's Pass
Grey Hill
Pinbain
Lendalfoot
Barr
Kirkdominae
Cairnwhin
Glengennet
N. Balloch
S. Balloch
Linfern L.
L. Lure
L. Bradan
Craiglee
Waterhead
Shiel Hill
Glen Trool
Forest Park
(Northern)
Shalloch
Shalloch Minnoch
Macaterick
Polmaddie Hill
L. Recawr
Pinmore
Aldons
Daljarrock
Poundland
Carleton Fishery
Colmonell
Knockdolian Cas.
Bennane Head
Craigneil
Dalreoch
Ballantrae Bay
Ballantrae
Mains of Tig
Laggan
Auchairne
Balkissock
Liglea
Low Kilphin High
Ballachmorrie
Glenduisk
Kildonan
Barrhill
Shiel Hill
Muck Water
L. Shalloch
Shalloch Well
Black Clauchrie
L. Goosey
Eldrick
Feoch B.
Garwall Hill
L. Moan
Palgowan
Benyellary
Merrick
Kirriereoch
Enoch
Buchan Hill
L. Valley
L. Neldricken
Glen Trool Lo.
L. Trool
Mulldonoch
Lamachan Hill
Larg Hill
Millfore
Carlin's Cairn
Corserine
Downan Pt.
Glenapp Cas.
Kilantringan
Beneraird
Auchencrosh Hill
Kilgrossan
Lochton
Corwar
Glencaird
Stroan
House of the Hill
Carlock Hill
Altimeg Hill
Lagafater
Chirmorie
Drumlamford
L. Dornal
Bargrennan
L. Ochiltree
Clauchaneasy
Glendrisaig
Finnarts Pt.
Muilbane
Craiganlea
Glen App
Milleur Pt.
Markdow
Miltonish
Benbrake Hill
Maberry
Polbae
Larg
Corsewall Pt.
Genoch Rocks
Corsewall Cas.
Dounan Bay
Kirkcolm
L. Connell
The Wig
Cairn Ryan
Clady Ho.
St. Mary's Croft
Glenwhilly
Dollygap
Main W. of Luce
Cross W. of Luce
Tarf W.
Urrall Fell
Knowe
Knockville
Penninghame
Camloden Park
Garlies Cas.
Glenrazie
Challoch
Cumloden Cott.
Boreland
Minnigaff
Newton Stewart
Blackcraig
Cairnsmore
Braid Fell
Artfield Fell
THE MOORS
Carseriggan
Balminnoch
Culvennan Fell
Tarf Br.
Torwood Gass
L. Ronald
Shennanton
Benfield
Merton Hall
Leswalt
Soleburn Br.
Craigcaffie
New Luce
Auchmantle
Innermessan
Broadstone
Galdenoch Cas.
Lochnaw Cas.
STRANRAER
Craig Fell
Drumpail Br.
Half Way Ho.
Barlae
Craighlaw
Kirkcowan
Killiemore
Barraer
Baltersan
Causeway End
Carsegown
Spittal
Bargaly
Palnure
Creetown
Broadsea Bay
Portslogan
Soulseat L.
Dunragit
Glenluce
Carscreugh
Dernaglar
Knock Moss
Clugston L.
Culquhirk
Stones of Torhouse
Craigenveoch Cas.
Knock Fell
Crouse
Malzie Br.
Bladnoch
WIGTOWN
WIGTOWN (Wigtown county lettering)
Wigtown Sands
Baldoon Sands
Black Hd.
Dunskey Cas.
Port Kale
Portpatrick
Dinvin
Cairn Pat
Corner Ho.
Lochans
Awhirk
Gartland Tower
Stoneykirk
Whitecrook
Fish Ho.
Whitefield L.
Castle L.
Mochrum L.
Old Place of Mochrum
Corsemalzie
Port of Spittal Bay
Knockinaam
Balgreggan
Sandhead
Crow's Nest
Auchenmalg
Auchenmalg Bay
Culshabben
Barnbarroch
Whauphill
Kirkinner
Orchardton Bay
Cairngarroch Bay
Kirkmadrine Ch.
Money Hd.
Corwall Pt.
Chapel Finian
Alticry
Eldrig L.
Loch Head
Barrachan
Longcastle
Airriehassan
Sorbie
Eggerness
Eldrig
Kirk of Mochrum
Ardwell
Chapel Rossan
Ardwell Bay
Doon Cas.
Drumbreddan Bay
Logan Ho.
Portacree
Mull of Logan
Port Logan
New England Bay
Terally
Kilstay
Bar Pt.
Port William
White L.
Monreith Ho.
Ravenstone Cas.
Barwinnock
Castlewigg
MACHARS
Craigdhu
Whithorn
Barsalloch Pt.
Monreith Bay
Monreith
Kirkmaiden
Cairndoon
Mains
Glasserton Ch.
Glasserton Ho.
Kidsdale
Port Cas.
St. Ninian's Cave
Cutcloy
Burrow Head
Isle
Clanyard Bay
Laggantalluch Hd.
Drummore
Kirkmaiden
Damnaglaur
Killiness Pt.
Maryport
Crammag Hd.
Dunman
Broadwall
Portankill
Nick of Kindram
St. Medan's Cave
E. Tarbet
W. Tarbet
Mull of Galloway
Scares
RINNS
A77
A714
A751
A747
A746
A750
A718
A716
A75
A712
B741
B734
B7044
B7043
B7045
B7042
B7041
B7065
B7027
B7005
B7052
B7004
B7021
B7063
B733
B735
The Edinburgh Geographical Institute

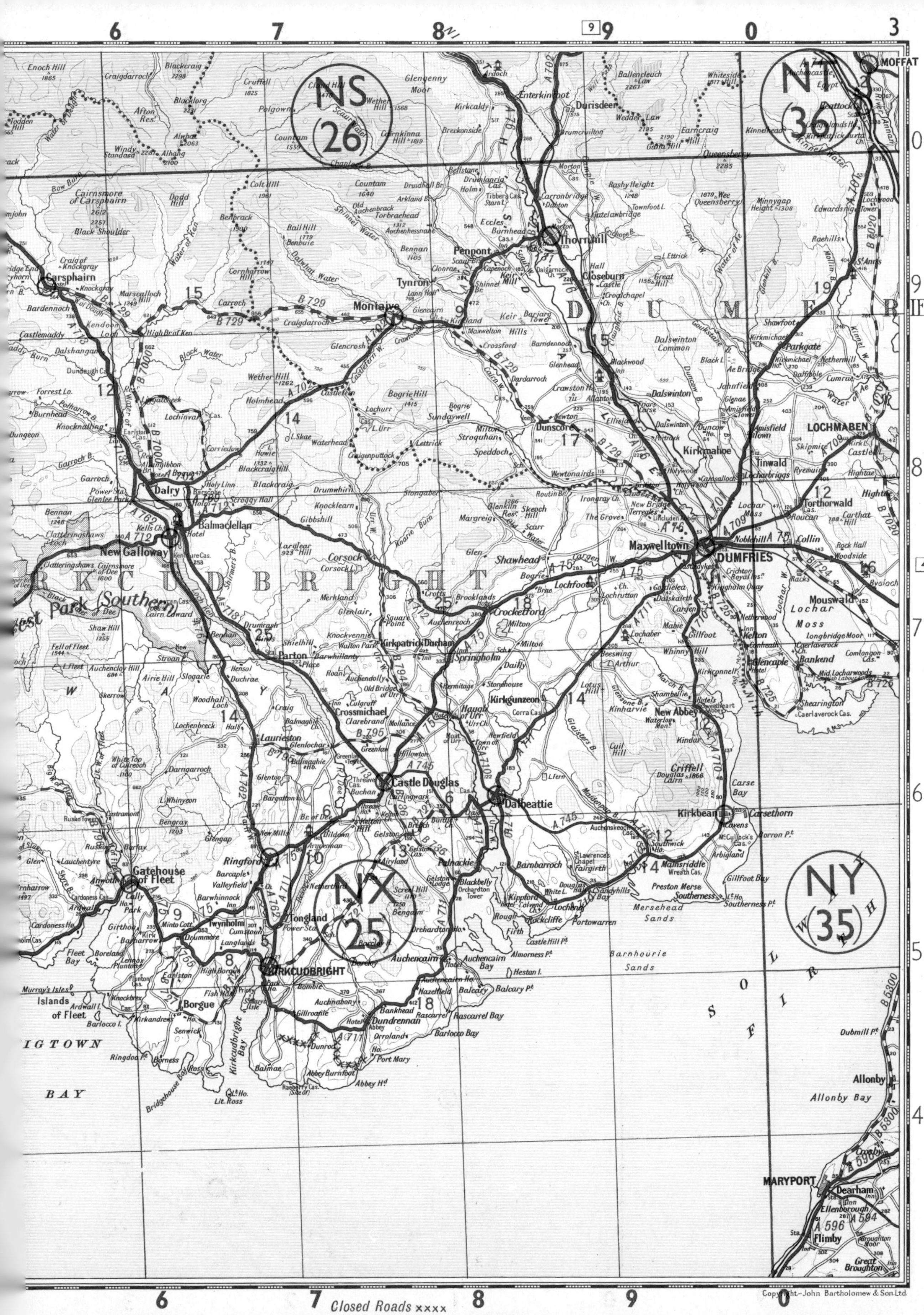

Closed Roads xxxx

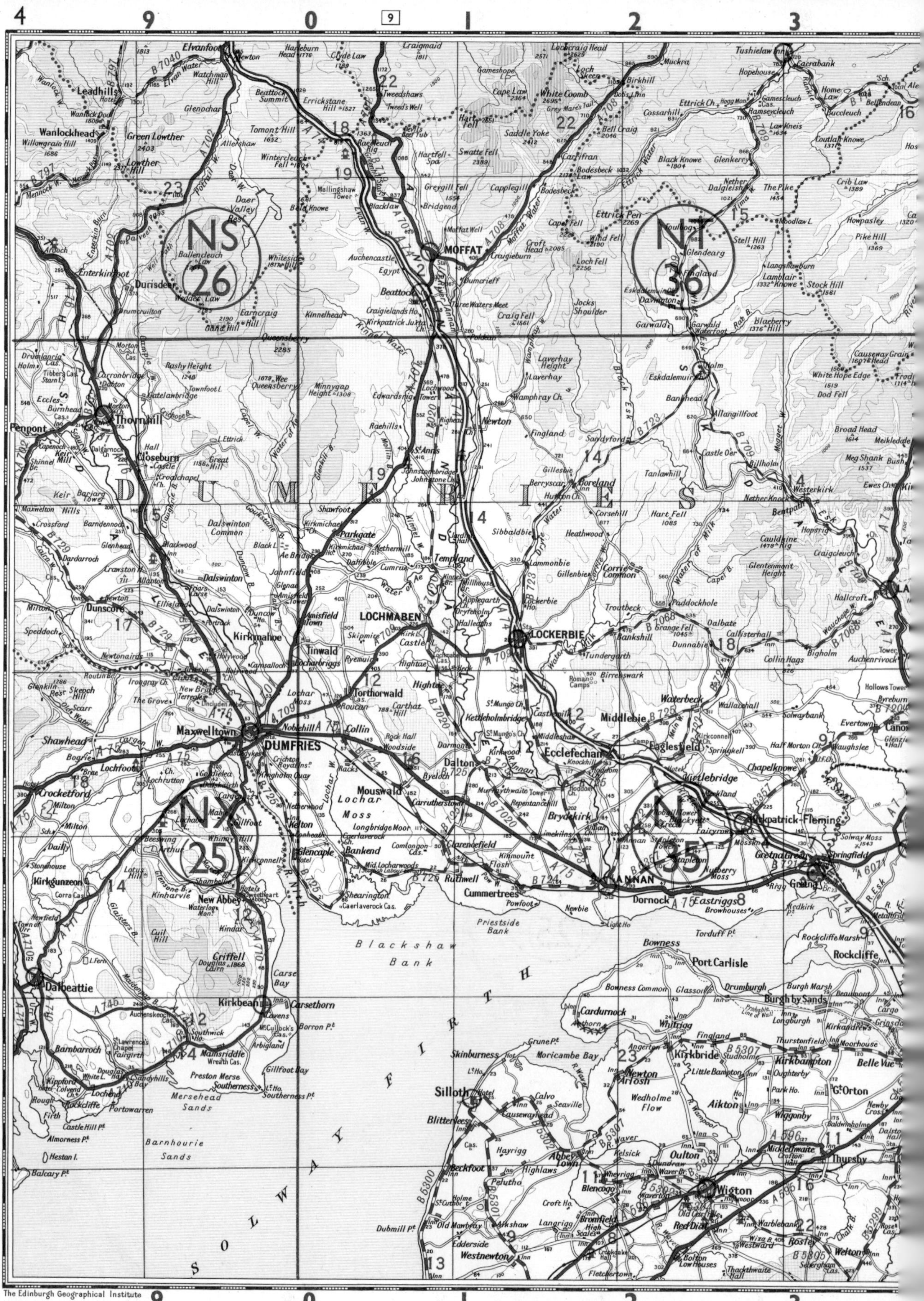

The Edinburgh Geographical Institute

Closed Roads xxxx

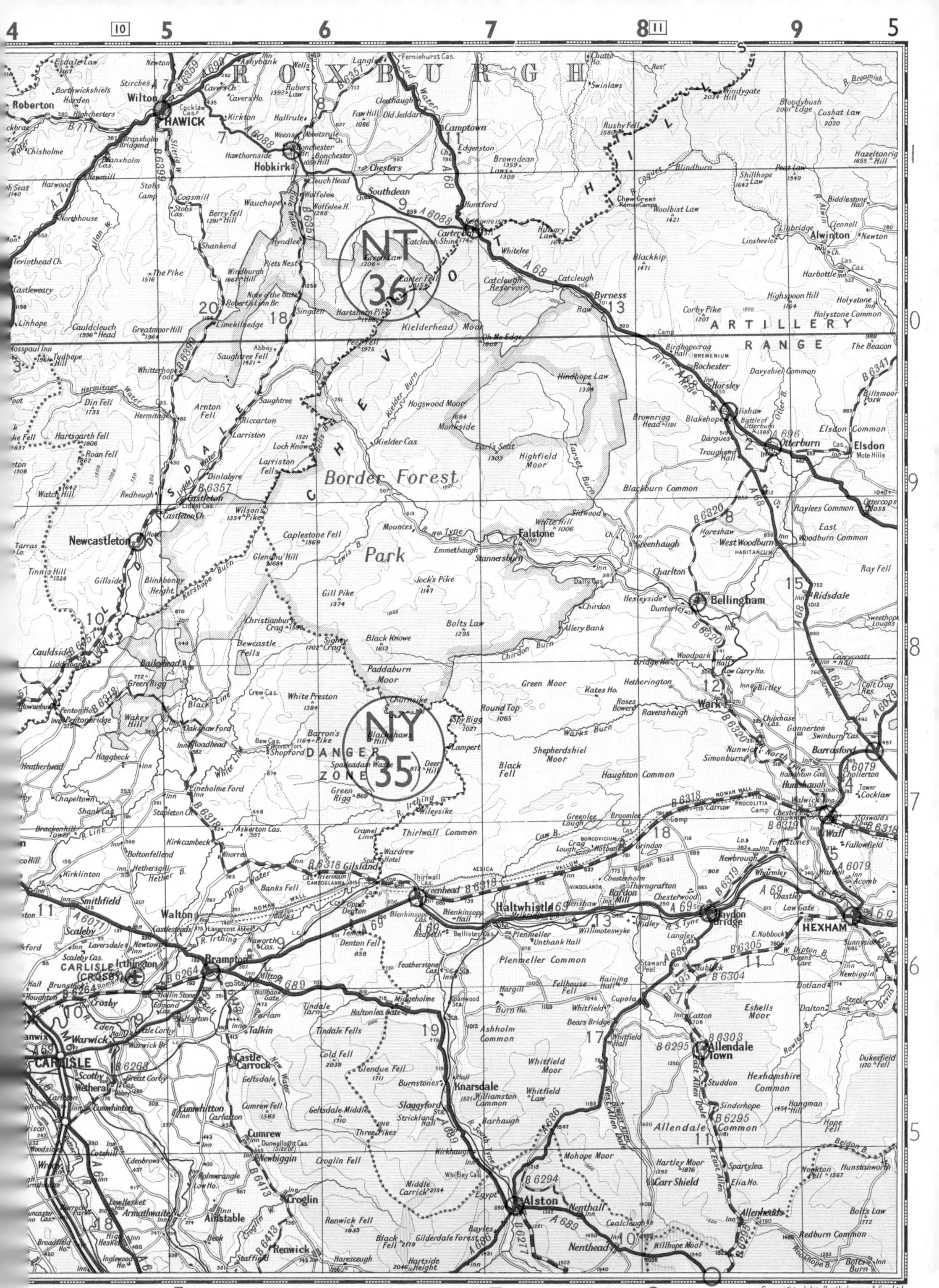

Closed Roads xxxx

13

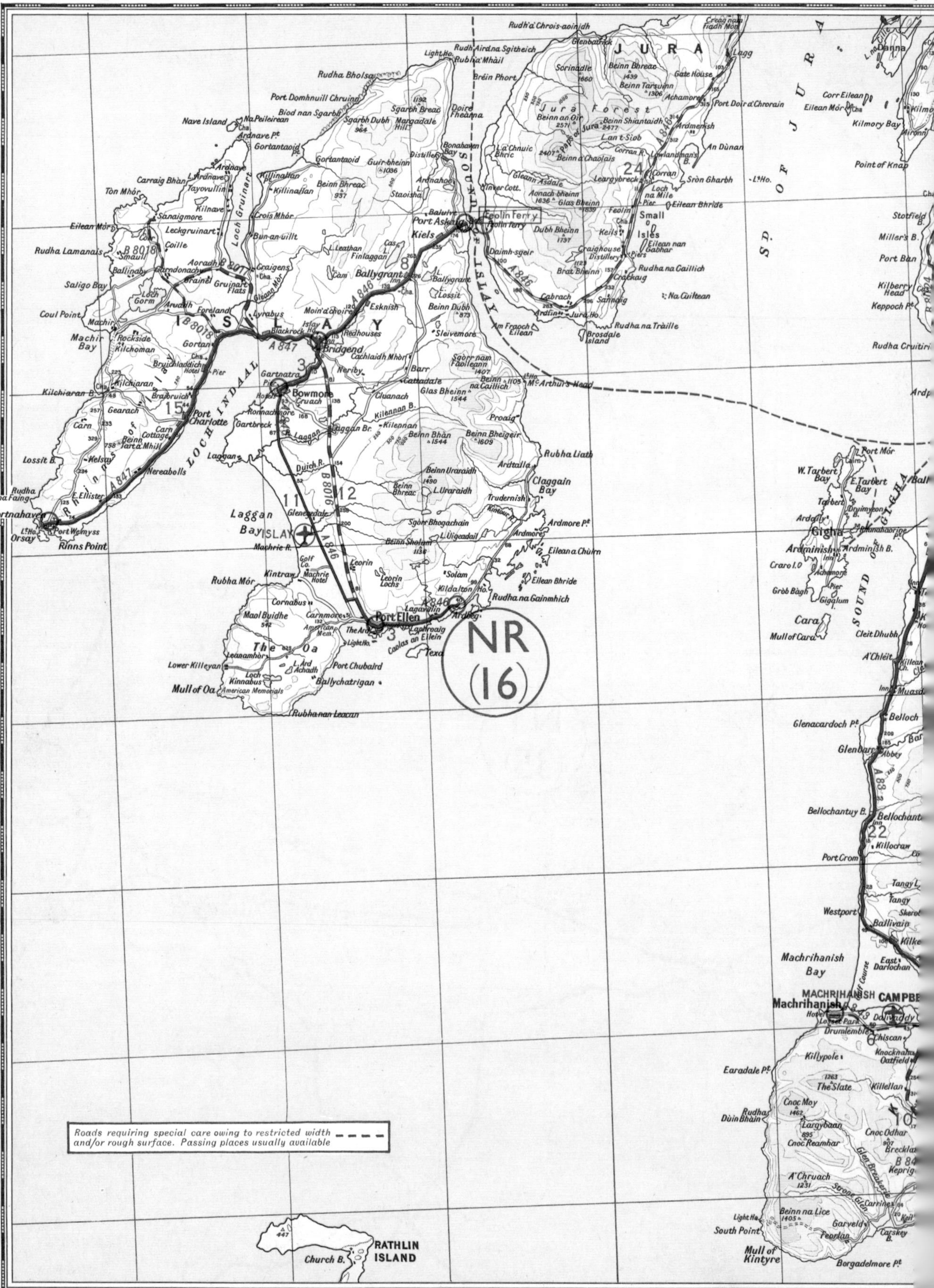

The Edinburgh Geographical Institute

2 3 4 5 6

8
9
0
14
1
2
7
GOUROCK
DUNOON
Dunoon Ferry
GREENOCK
Kirn
Ashton
Prince's Pier
Gourock Bay
Castle Levan
Cloch Pt.
The Gantocks
Bishop's Seat
Dunloskin
Invervegain
L. STRIVEN
Kilfinan
Rudha Beag
Kilfinan B.
Ormidale
Springfield
Fearnach
Beinn Bhreac
Colintraive
Tighnabruaich
Kames
Millhouse
Blairs Ferry
Kilbride
Carry
Ardlamont
Ardlamont Pt.
Kilmichael
Glenmore
Gleckmabae
Kames B.
Port Bannatyne
Ardbeg
ROTHESAY
Craigmore
Ardencraig
Ascog
Kerrycroy
Mountstuart
Bogany Pt.
Toward Pt.
Innellan
Dunan
Wemyss Bay
Skelmorlie
Meigle Bay
Inverkip
Largs
Largs Bay
Fairlie
Kelburne
Tarbert
W. Tarbert
Skipness
Skipness Pt.
Claonaig
Clachan
Whitehouse
Inchmarnock
SOUND OF BUTE
GREAT CUMBRAE
Millport
Little Cumbrae Island
Kilchattan
Kilchattan B.
Garroch Hd.
Cock of Arran
Lochranza
Catacol Bay
Pirnmill
Corrie
Sannox Bay
Goat Fell
Cir Mhor
Brodick
Brodick Bay
Merkland Pt.
Corrygills
Lamlash
Lamlash Bay
Holy Island
Kingscross
Whiting Bay
Kiscadale
Dippin Head
Kildonan Cas.
Pladda
Bennan Hd.
Lagg Inn
Sannochie
Kilmory
Corriecravie
Brown Head
Kilpatrick
Blackwater Foot
Drumadoon Bay
King's Caves
Tormore
Machrie Bay
Dougrie Pt.
Imachar
Shiskine
Ballymichael
ARRAN
KILBRENNAN SOUND
NR (16)
NS (26)
FIRTH OF CLYDE
ARDROSSAN
Saltcoats
Stevenston
West Kilbride
Seamill
Portencross
Farland Hd.
Hunterston
Dalry
Drakemire
Burnside
Carradale
Carradale Bay
Dippen
Saddell
Saddell Bay
Ugadale Pt.
Ardnacross Bay
Grogport
Crossaig
Cour Bay
Davaar I.
Campbeltown Loch
New Orleans
Feochaig
Ru Stafnish
Polliwilline B.
Sanda
Sheep I.
To Cushendall
Sound
Lady Isle
Dunure
Culzean Bay
Culzean Cas.
Maidenhead Bay
Maidens
Turnberry Bay
Kirkoswald
Kirk Hill
Dowhill
Dalquharran Cas.
8
9
0
1
2
2

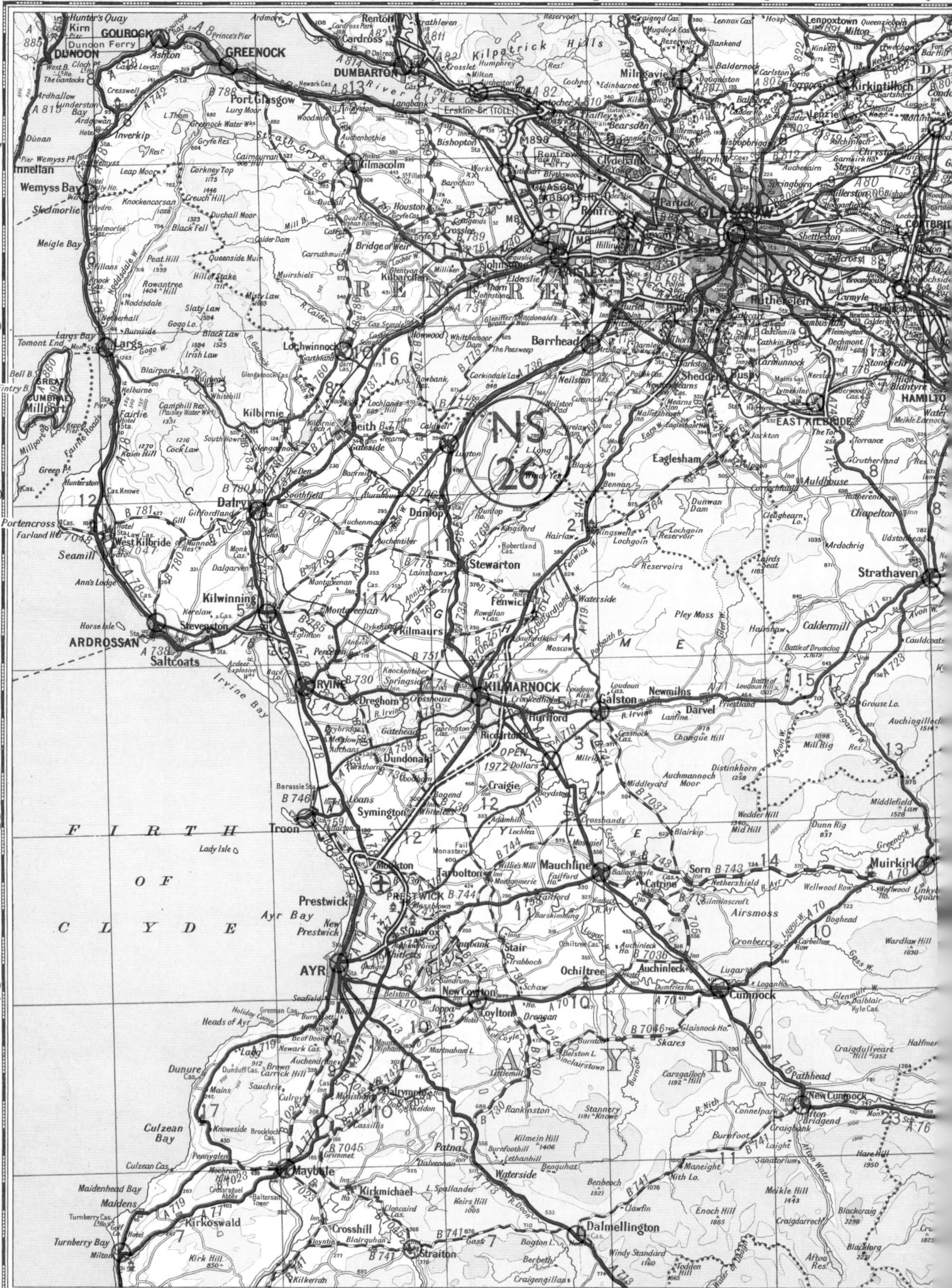

The Edinburgh Geographical Institute

2 3 4 [2] 5 6

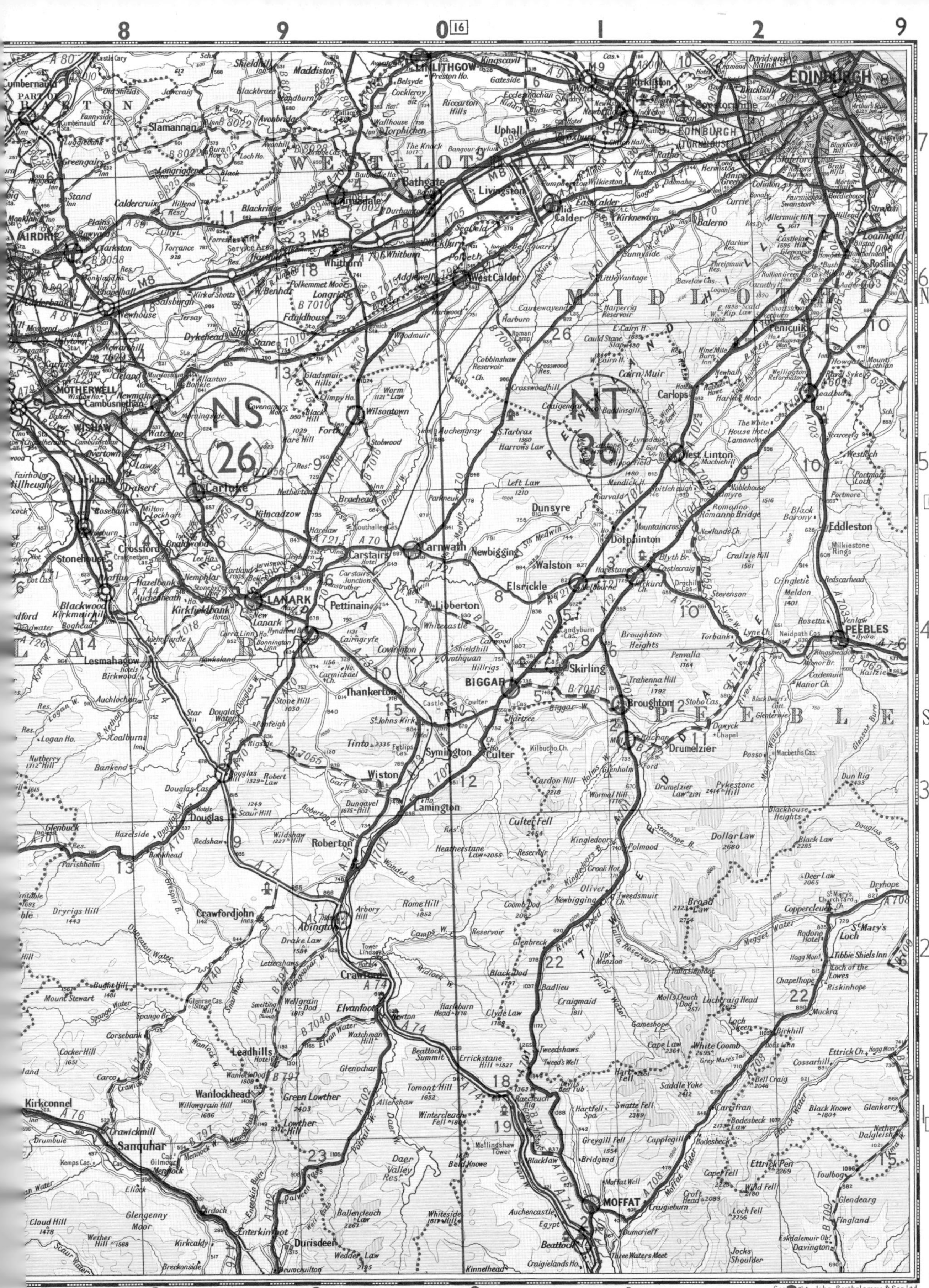

Copyright-John Bartholomew & Son,Ltd.

Closed Roads xxxx

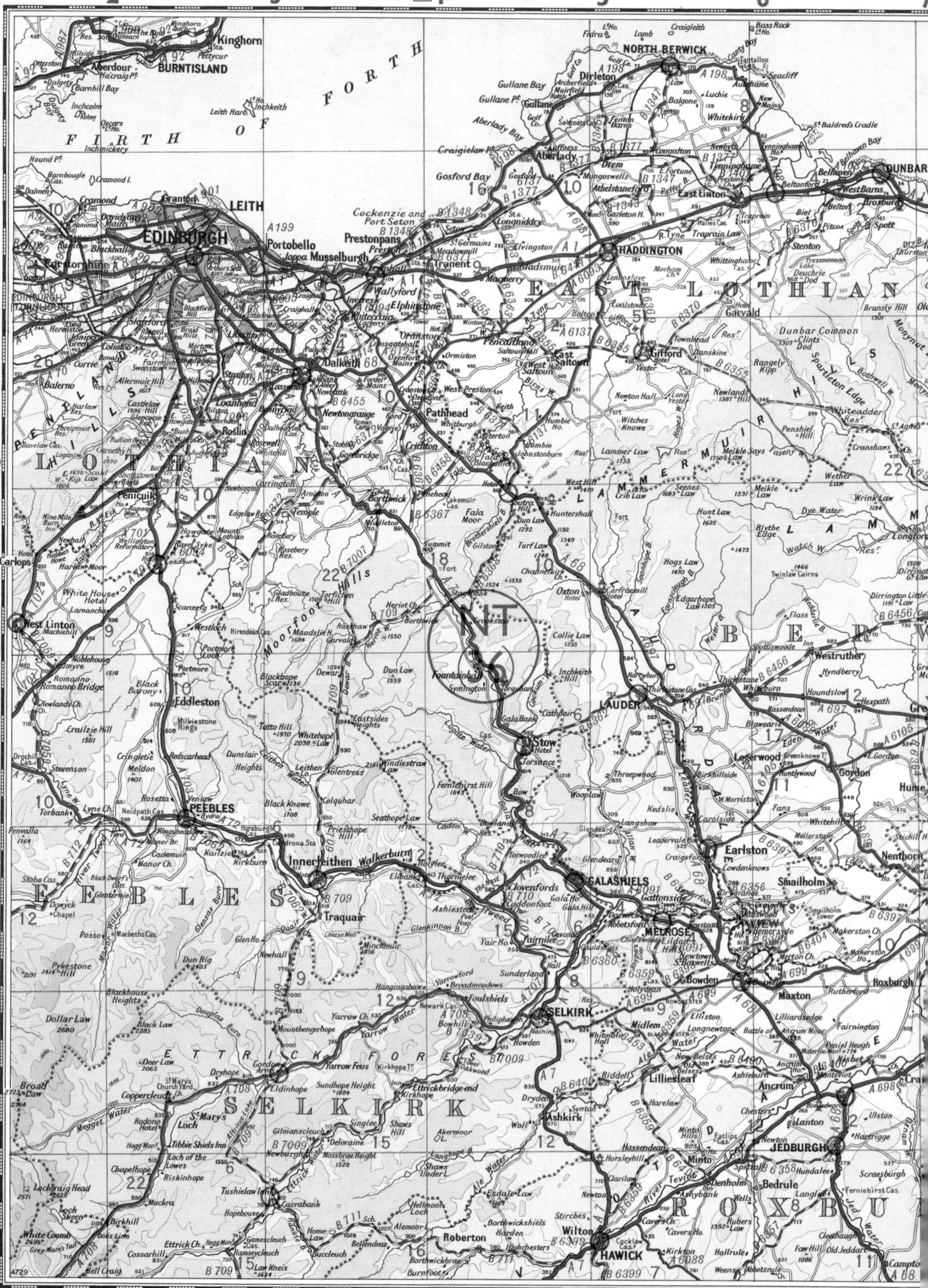

The Edinburgh Geographical Institute

Closed Roads xxxx

8
9
0
1
2
NU
(46)
NT
(36)
Skateraw Harbour
Bilsdean
Reed Pt.
Cove
Pease Sands
Dunglass
Cockburnspath
Craig Taw
Fast Cas.
St. Helen's Ch.
St. Abb's Head
Lt. Ho.
Brown Rig
Meikle Black Law
Moorhouse
Coldingham Moor
Coldingham Loch
Northfield
St. Abbs
Coldingham B.
Ecclaw Hill
Grantshouse
Kilspindie Cas.
Coldingham
Eyemouth
Press Cas.
Houndwood
Moor Ho.
Horseley Hill
Reston
Redhall
Burnmouth
Drake Mire
Auchencrow
Ayton
Cockburn Law
Billie Cas.
Millerton Hill
Ayton Hill
Hilton Bay
Primrosehill
Whiterig
Preston
Lintlaw
Lamberton
Chirnside
Mordington
Marshall Meadows B.
Edington
Foulden
Halidon Hill
Needles Eye
Knock Hill
Edrom
Edrom Newton
Manderston
Ninewells
Hutton Cas.
Whiteadder
Mordington Water
Dunslaw
Duns
Allanbank
Blackadder Ho.
Allanton
Hutton
Paxton
Sharper Head
BERWICK-UPON-TWEED
Tweedmouth
Spittal
Langton
Gavinton
Cheeklaw
Kelloe
Blackadder
R. Tweed
Union Br.
Nisbet
Whitlaw
Hilton
Fishwick
East Ord
Longridge Towers
Caldra
Mount Pleasant
Whitsome
Horndean
Horncliffe
Richardson's Stead
Fogo
Crawfoot Bank
Ladykirk
Scremerston Colliery
Fogorig
Charterhall
Swinton
Upsettlington
Norham
Allerdean
Cheswick Ho.
Swintonmill
Swinton Bridgend
Ladykirk Ho.
Shoreswood
Oxford
Rowieston Chapel
Bughtrig
Simprim
Grindon
Goswick
Leitholm
Ruthven
Twizel
Felkington
Ancroft
Emanuel Hd.
Lindisfarne or Holy Island
Antonshill
George's Field
Tillmouth Park
Duddo
Holy Island Sands
Holy Island
Beal
Orange Lane
Hatchednize
Old Heaton
Donaldson
River Till
Bowsden
Cathedral
Guile Pt.
Eccles
Hirsel
Lennel
Barmoor
Kyloe
Fenwick
Fenham Flats
Longstone
Wormerlaw
COLDSTREAM
Homebank
Pallinsburn Ho.
Etal
Crookham
Fordcommon
Lowick
Kyloe Hills
Buckton
Ross
Birgham
Eden Hall
Cornhill on Tweed
Wark
Carham
Branxton
Ford
Brownridge
Coalshank
Detchant
Elwick
Farne Islands
Ednam
Flodden Field
Holburn
Middleton Hall
Budle Bay
Budle Pt.
Bamburgh
Farne I.
Frierlaw
Pressen
Kimmerston
Cockenheugh
Belford
Easington
Glororum
Sprouston
KELSO
Maxwellheugh
Potsclose
Mindrummill
Paston
Howtel
Flodden
Fenton Town
Fenton Ho.
Doddington
Spindlestone
Bradford
North Sunderland
Seahouses
Milfield
River Till
Hetton B.
Spylaw
Belfordmoor
Ellford
Lempitlaw
Mindrum
Kilham
Kilham Hill
Coupland Cas.
Ewart Park
Doddington Br.
Warenton
Bellshill
Adderstone
Lucker
Beadnell
Blakelaw
Shotton
Westnewton
Glen
Chatton
Chattonpark
Warenford
Newham
Beadnell Bay
Vencheo Hill
Kirknewton
Yeavering Bell
Akeld
Wooler
Swinhoe
Mainhouse
Kirk Yetholm
Town Yetholm
Humbleton
Haughhead
Rosebrough
Chathill
Frogden
Primside Mill
College B.
Earle
Chillingham Castle
Ellingham
Tughall
Newton by the Sea
Linton Ch.
Dikeside
Middleton Hall
North Middleton
Middleton South
Newtown
Lilburn
Botany
Preston
Brunton
Newton Seahouses
Morebattle
Corbet Tr.
Preston Hill
Carey B.
Hepburn
Cateran Hill
Brownyside
North Charlton
Christon Bank
Embleton
Embleton Bay
The Curr
Lambden B.
Lilburn
Bewick Br.
Old Bewick
Bewick Moor
South Charlton
Castle Pt.
Dunstanburgh Cas.
Gateshaws Tower
Whitton
Attonburn
Hounam Law
Langleeford
Langlee Crags
Ilderton
West Ditchburn
Rock
Dunstan
Craster
Mowhaugh
Bowmont W.
The Cheviot
Hedgehope Hill
Wooperton
New Bewick
Percy's Cross
Eglingham
Rennington
Stamford
Cullernose Pt.
Howick
Hounam
Craik Moor
Comb Fell
Dunmoor Hill
Hedgeley Moor
Beanley
Bannamoor
Hefferlaw Tower
Hall
Chatto Ho.
Dere Street
CHEVIOT
Brandon
Branton
Powburn
East Bolton
Shipley
Heckley Ho.
Longhoughton Steel
Loughoughton
Swinlaws
Windygate Hill
R. Breamish
Ingram
Glanton
R. Aln
Hulne Abbey
Hulne Park Tower
Alnwick Abbey
Denwick
Boulmer
Bloodybush Edge
Cushat Law
Cochrane Pike
Great Ryle
Bolton
Broome Park
ALNWICK
Hawkhill
Rushy Fell
HILLS
Prendwick
Eslington Hall
Whittingham
Broomwood
Lesbury
A 1
A 1107
A 697
A 698
A 699
A 6105
A 6112
A 1167
B 6437
B 6438
B 6355
B 6356
B 6460
B 6470
B 6396
B 6350
B 6352
B 6401
B 6351
B 6353
B 6354
B 6349
B 6348
B 6346
B 6347
B 6341
B 1342
B 1340
B 1339
7
6
5
4
3
2
8
9
0
1
2

RUM
SOUND OF RUM
EIGG
SOUND OF EIGG
Muck
SOUND OF ARISAIG
LOCH NAN UAMH
NORTH MORAR
LOCH MORAR
SOUTH MORAR
ARISAIG
Arisaig
MOIDART
Kinlochmoidart
LOCH SHIEL
SUNART
Salen
Strontian
LOCH SUNART
ARDNAMURCHAN
Ardnamurchan Pt.
Sanna Point
Ockle Point
Kilchoan
NM
17
MORVERN
Lochaline
SOUND OF MULL
TOBERMORY
Dervaig
Calgary
Salen
COLL
Arinagour
LOCH TUATH
ULVA
Gometra
Treshnish Isles
LINNHE
A 830
A 861
A 884
B 8007
B 8043

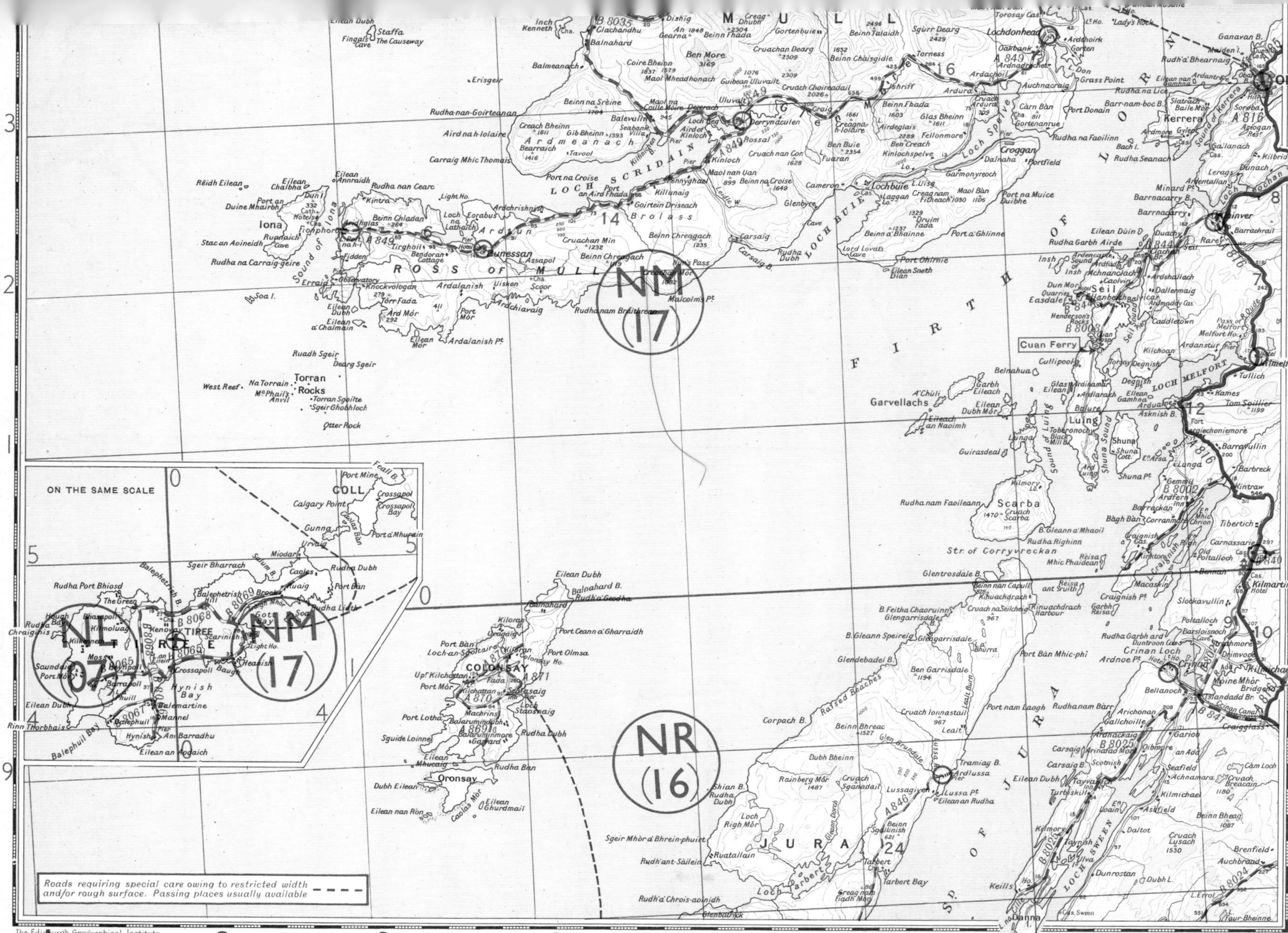

The Edinburgh Geographical Institute

Copyright-John Bartholomew & Son, Ltd.

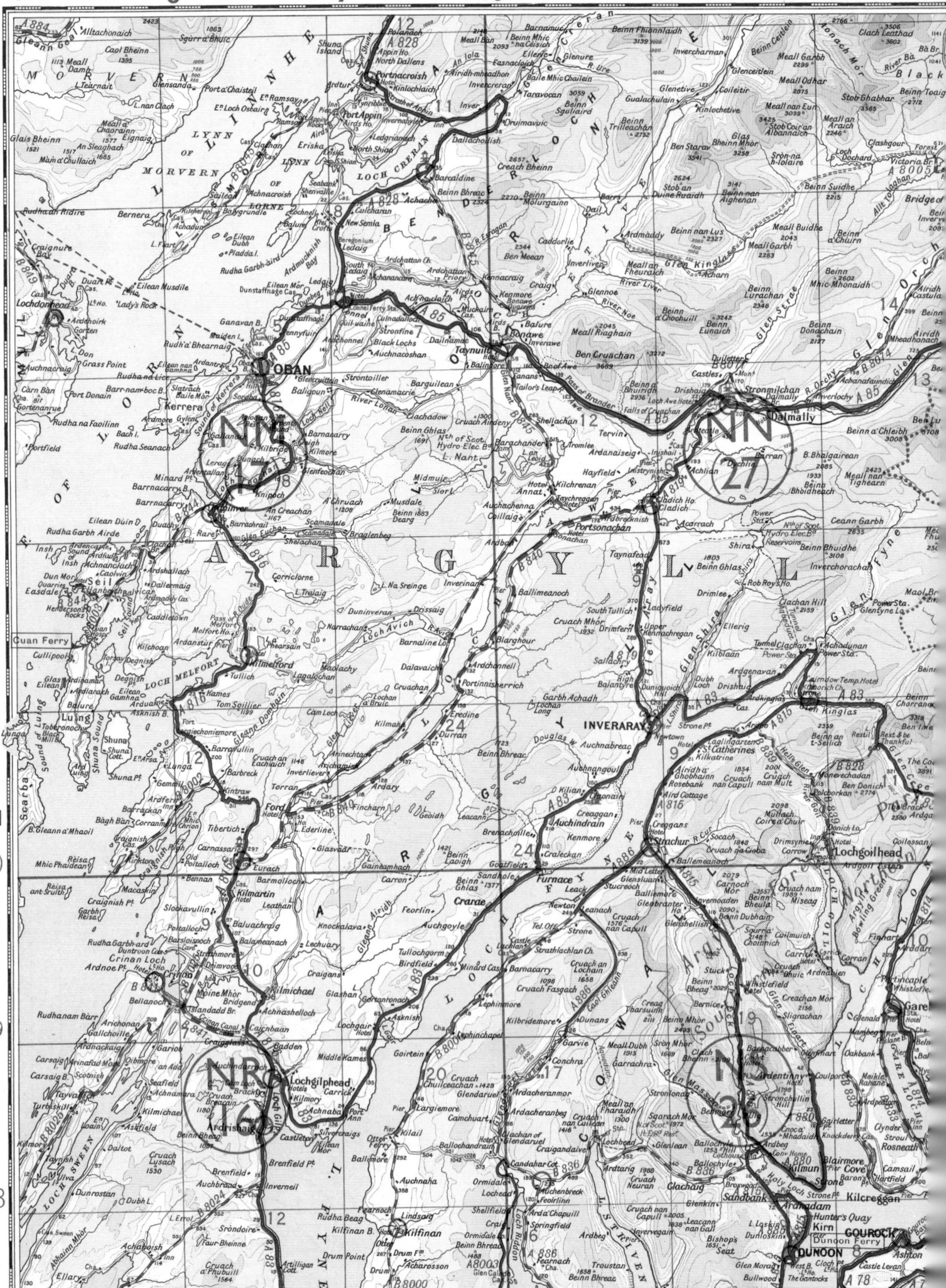

The Edinburgh Geographical Institute

Roads requiring special care owing to restricted width and/or rough surface. Passing places usually available - - - -

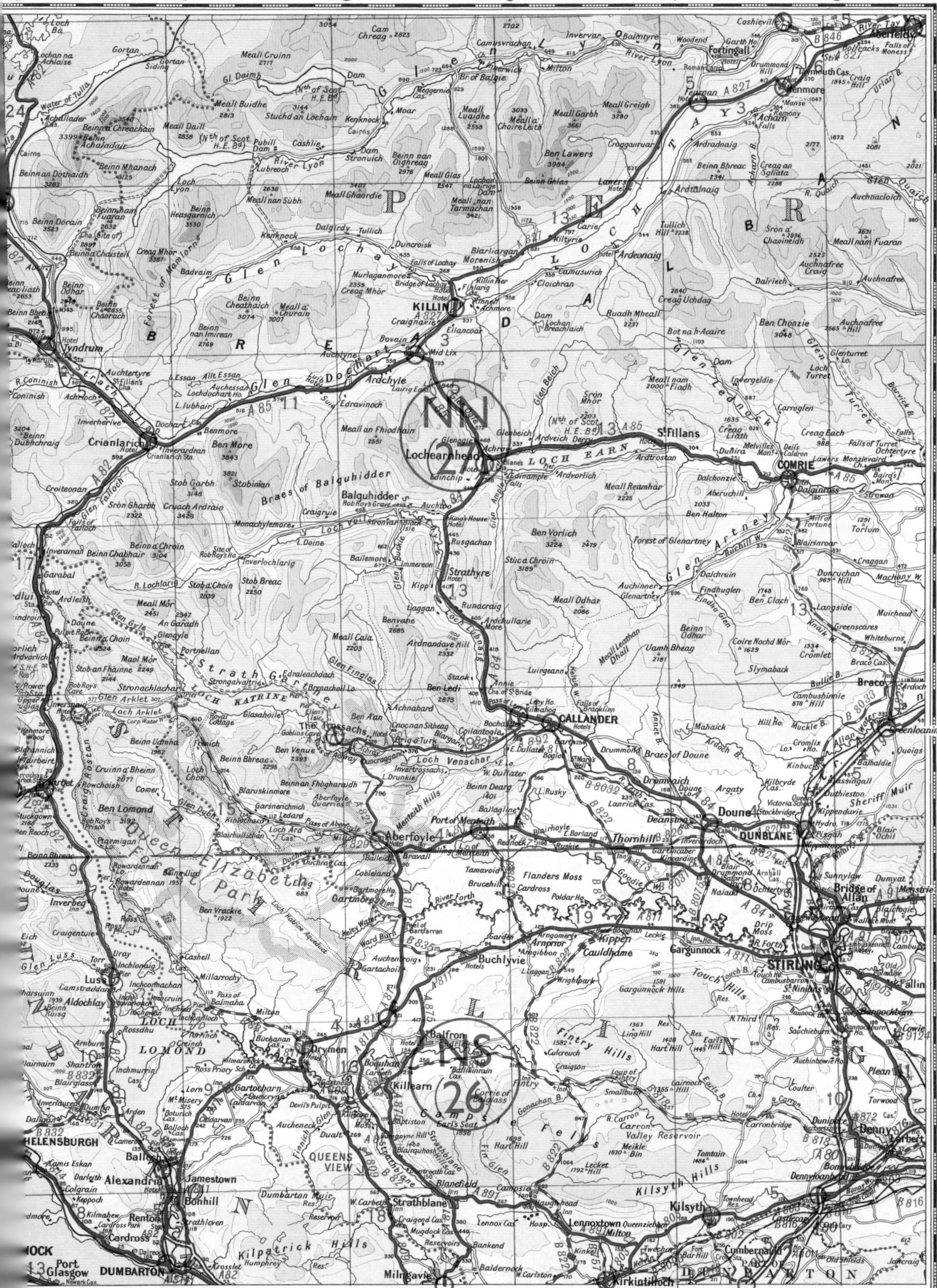

PERTH
BREADALBANE
STIRLING
DUNBARTON
LOMOND
NN 27
NS 26
Tyndrum
Crianlarich
Killin
Lochearnhead
St Fillans
Comrie
Balquhidder
Strathyre
Callander
The Trossachs
Aberfoyle
Port of Menteith
Doune
Dunblane
Bridge of Allan
Stirling
Thornhill
Kippen
Gargunnock
Buchlyvie
Balfron
Drymen
Killearn
Strathblane
Milngavie
Kirkintilloch
Lennoxtown
Kilsyth
Cumbernauld
Denny
Larbert
Falkirk
Bannockburn
Braco
Greenloaning
Aberfeldy
Kenmore
Fortingall
Fearnan
Lawers
Ardeonaig
Luss
Tarbet
Arrochar
Inversnaid
Inverbeg
Balloch
Alexandria
Jamestown
Bonhill
Renton
Cardross
Dumbarton
Helensburgh
Port Glasgow
Loch Tay
Loch Earn
Loch Katrine
Loch Venachar
Loch Lomond
Loch Lubnaig
Loch Voil
Loch Ard
Lake of Menteith
River Forth
River Lyon
River Tay
Glen Lyon
Glen Lochay
Glen Dochart
Glen Falloch
Glen Artney
Glen Lednock
Strath Fillan
Strath Gartney
Braes of Balquhidder
Braes of Doune
Forest of Glenartney
Queen Elizabeth Forest Park
Flanders Moss
Campsie Fells
Fintry Hills
Gargunnock Hills
Touch Hills
Kilsyth Hills
Kilpatrick Hills
Ben Lawers 3984
Ben More 3843
Stobinian 3821
Ben Lomond 3192
Ben Vorlich 3224
Ben Ledi 2873
Ben Venue 2393
Ben Chonzie 3048
Stuc a Chroin 3189
Beinn Dorain 3523
Sheriff Muir
Carron Valley Reservoir
Queens View
Copyright - John Bartholomew & Son Ltd.

16 6 7 [19] 8 9 0

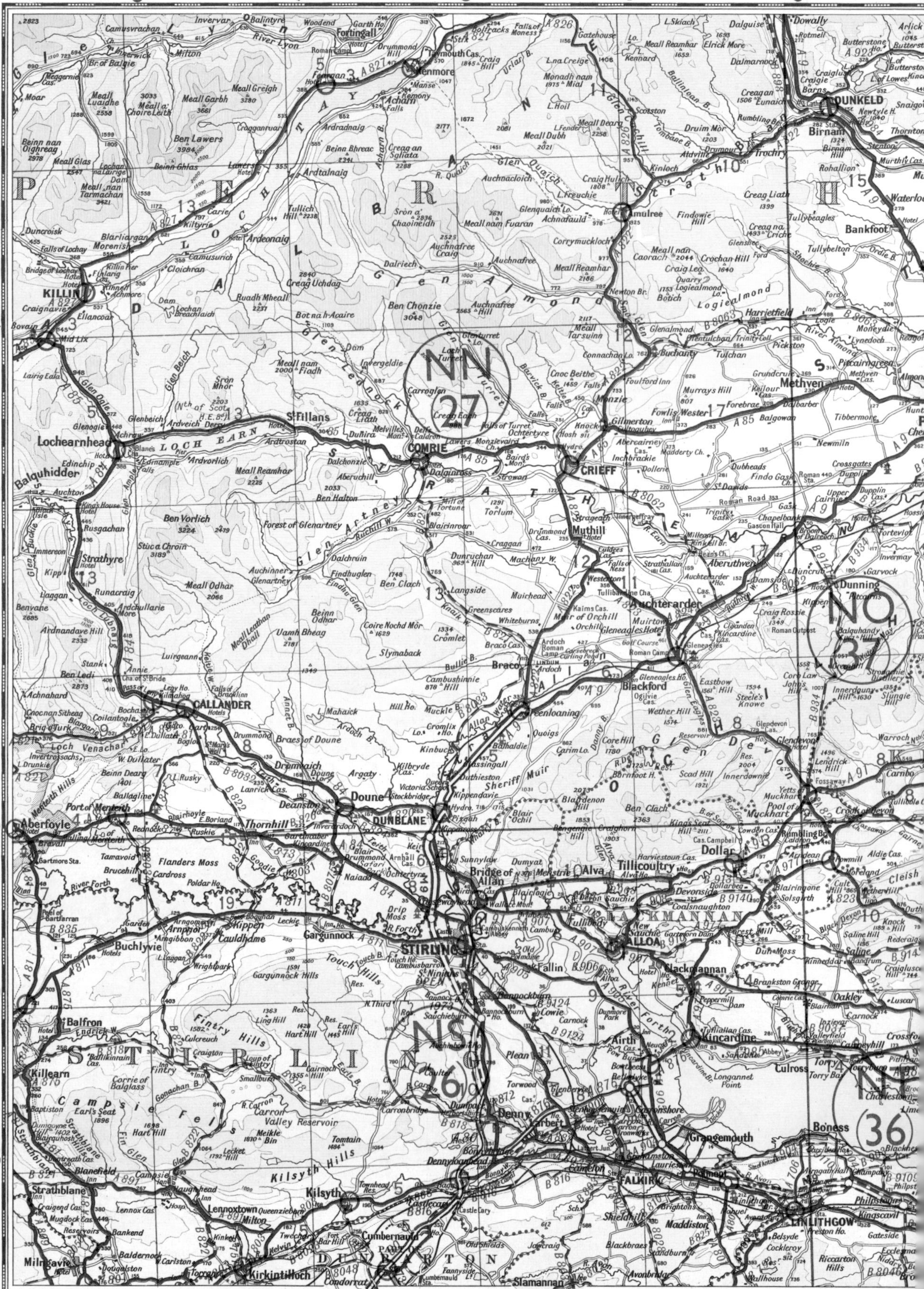

The Edinburgh Geographical Institute

6 [8] 7 8 9 [9] 0

Closed Roads xxxx

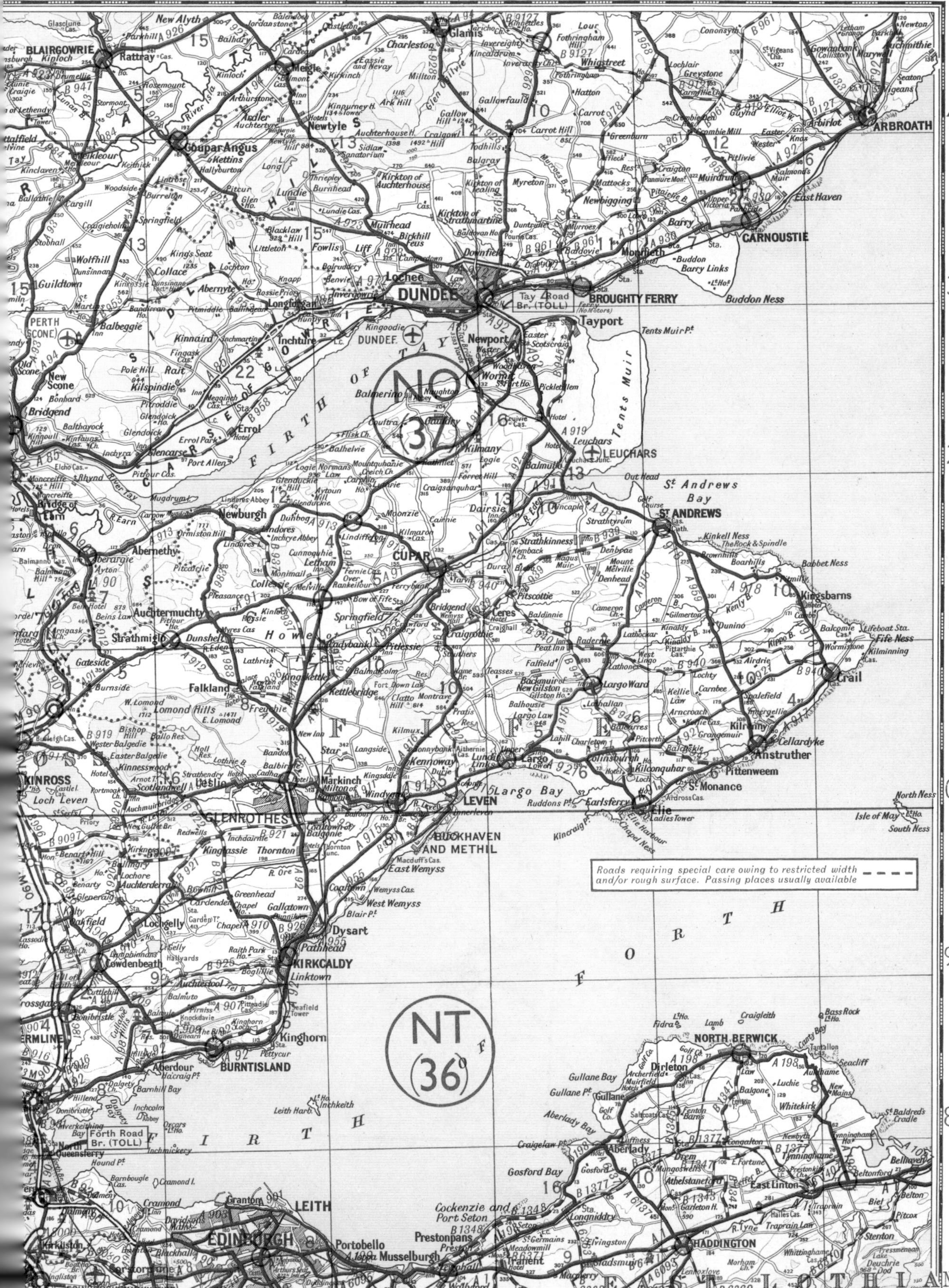

Closed Roads xxxx

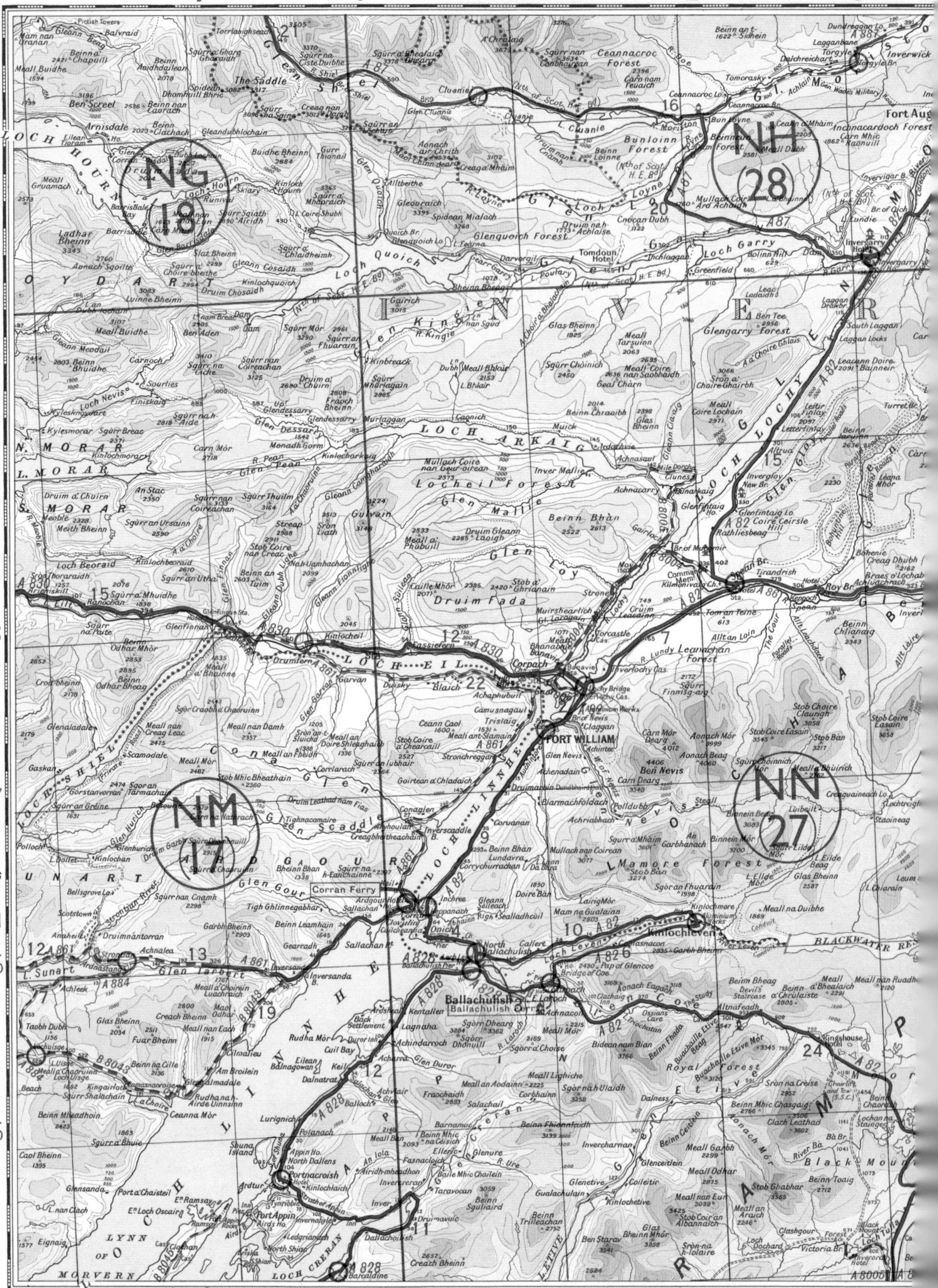

The Edinburgh Geographical Institute

Roads requiring special care owing to restricted width and/or rough surface. Passing places usually available

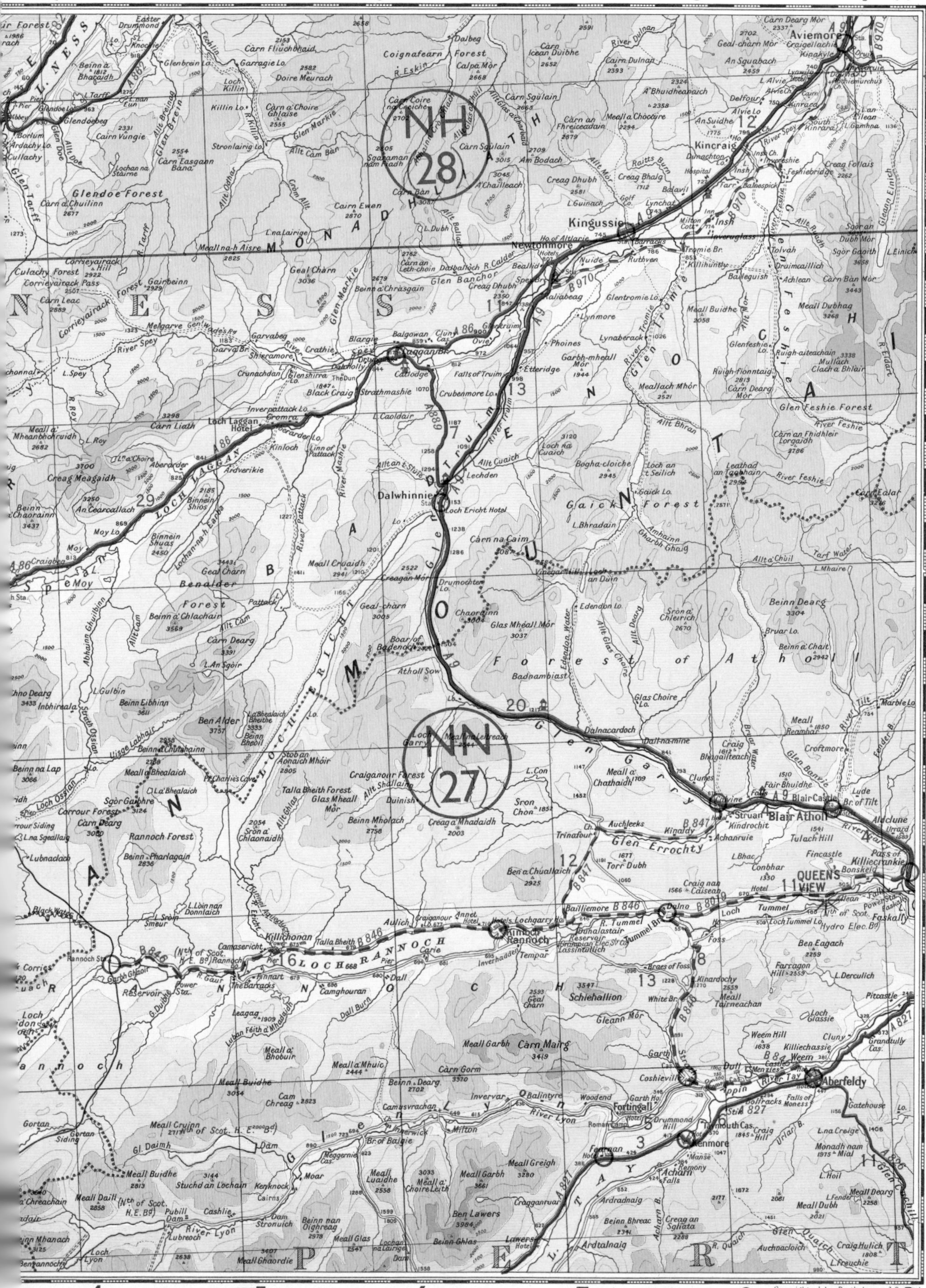
NH
28
NN
27
Aviemore
Kincraig
Kingussie
Newtonmore
Laggan Br.
Dalwhinnie
Blair Atholl
Killiecrankie
Pass of Killiecrankie
Queen's View
Kinloch Rannoch
Aberfeldy
Fortingall
Kenmore
Fearnan
Rannoch Sta.
Loch Laggan Hotel
Loch Ericht Hotel
Glendoe Forest
Corrieyairack Pass
Corrieyairack Forest
Coignafearn Forest
M O N A D H L I A T H
I N V E R N E S S
G A I C K
Gaick Forest
Forest of Atholl
Glen Feshie Forest
Benalder Forest
Ben Alder
3757
Creag Meagaidh
3700
Rannoch Forest
Craiganour Forest
Talla Bheith Forest
Schiehallion
3547
Càrn Mairg
3419
Ben Lawers
3984
LOCH LAGGAN
LOCH ERICHT
LOCH RANNOCH
Loch Tummel
Glen Garry
Glen Errochty
Glen Lyon
River Lyon
River Spey
River Tay
T A Y
R A N N O C H
P E R T H
A 9
A 86
A 889
A 827
A 826
B 846
B 847
B 8019
B 970
Hydro Elec. Bd
Copyright - John Bartholomew & Son Ltd.

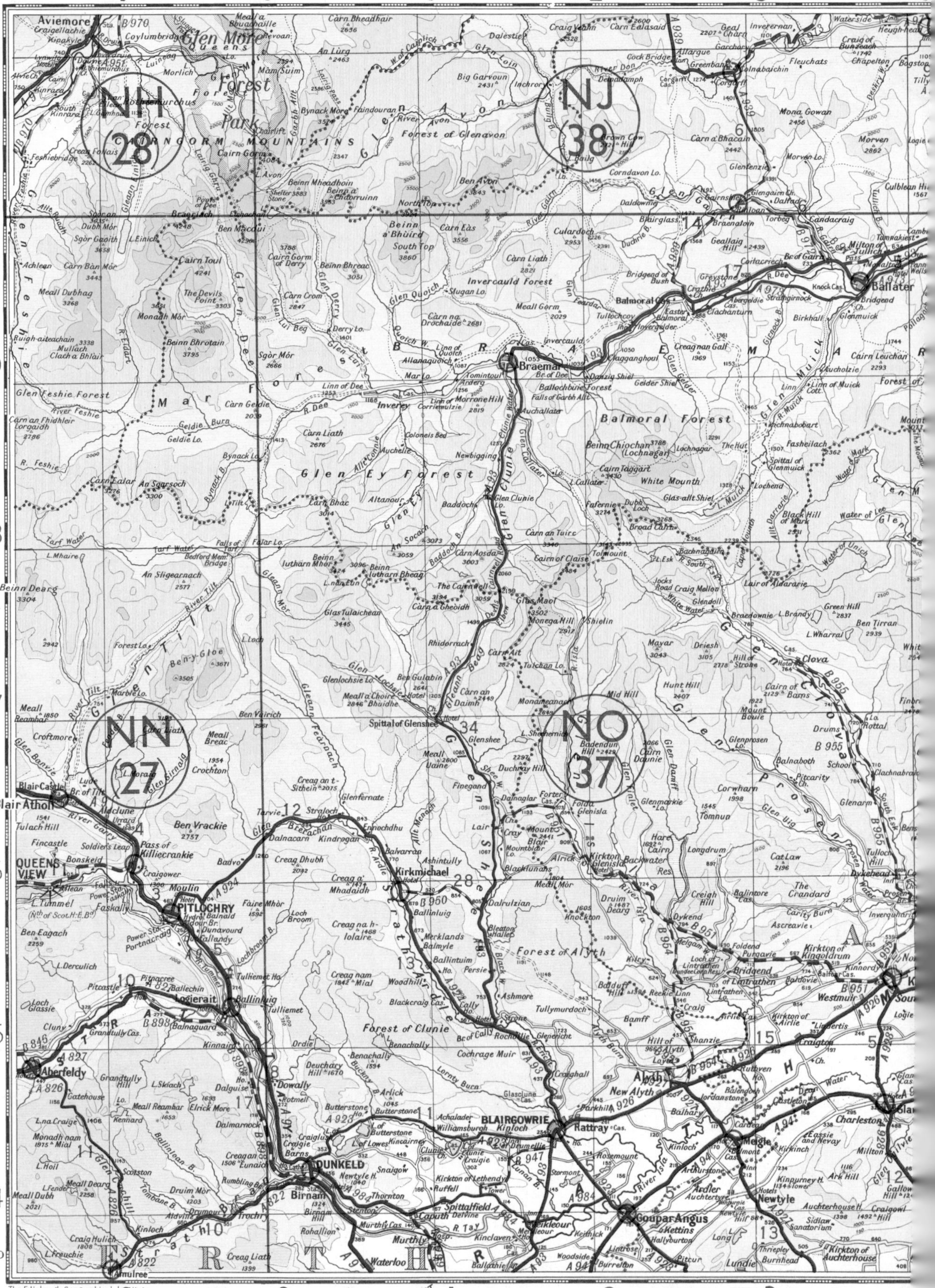
20
25
9
0
1
2
26
3
4
Aviemore
Glen More
Forest Park
CAIRNGORM MOUNTAINS
Cairn Gorm 4084
Ben Macdui 4296
Braeriach 4248
Cairn Toul 4241
Glen Avon
Forest of Glenavon
Ben Avon 3843
Beinn a' Bhùird
NH (28)
NJ (38)
Cock Bridge
Corgarff
Ballater
Balmoral Cas.
Braemar
Invercauld Forest
Mar Forest
Glen Feshie
Glen Feshie Forest
Linn of Dee
Inverey
Balmoral Forest
Lochnagar
White Mounth
Glen Muick
Glen Clova
Clova
Glen Ey Forest
Glen Clunie
Glen Shee
Spittal of Glenshee
Glas Maol
Beinn a' Ghlo
Glen Tilt
NN (27)
NO (37)
Blair Castle
Blair Atholl
Pass of Killiecrankie
Queens View
Moulin
PITLOCHRY
Ben Vrackie
Kirkmichael
Strath Ardle
Forest of Alyth
Glen Prosen
Glen Isla
Kirkton of Glenisla
Logierait
Ballinluig
Aberfeldy
Forest of Clunie
Dowally
DUNKELD
Birnam
BLAIRGOWRIE
Rattray
Alyth
Meigle
Coupar Angus
Newtyle
Kinloch
Strath Braan
Amulree
Murthly
Caputh
Spittalfield
Kirriemuir
18
16
17
0
1
2
3
9
8
7
6
5
4
P
The Edinburgh Geographical Institute

27

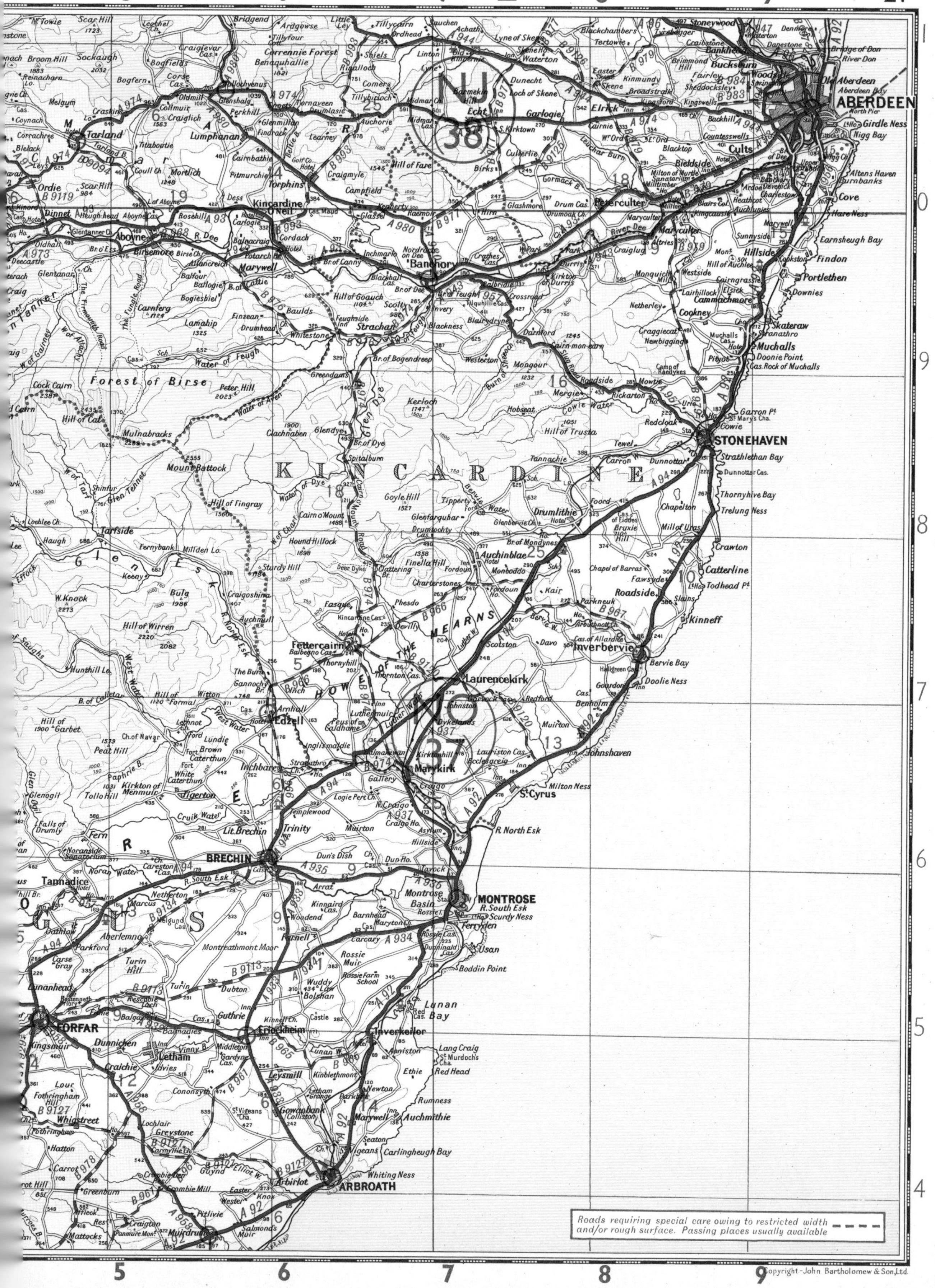

ABERDEEN
Girdle Ness
Nigg Bay
Old Aberdeen
Bridge of Don
River Don
Bucksburn
Dyce
Cults
Bieldside
Peterculter
Maryculter
Cove
Altens Haven
Findon
Portlethen
Downies
Skateraw
Muchalls
Doonie Point
STONEHAVEN
Garron Pt.
Cowie
Strathlethan Bay
Dunnottar Cas.
Thornyhive Bay
Trelung Ness
Crawton
Catterline
Todhead Pt.
Kinneff
Inverbervie
Bervie Bay
Doolie Ness
Gourdon
Johnshaven
Milton Ness
St. Cyrus
R. North Esk
MONTROSE
Montrose Basin
R. South Esk
Scurdy Ness
Ferryden
Usan
Boddin Point
Lunan Bay
Inverkeilor
Lang Craig
Red Head
Ethie
Rumness
Auchmithie
Carlingheugh Bay
Whiting Ness
ARBROATH
Arbirlot
Muirdrum
Carnoustie
Friockheim
Letham
Guthrie
Dunnichen
FORFAR
Aberlemno
Tannadice
BRECHIN
Lit. Brechin
Trinity
Edzell
Fettercairn
Marykirk
Laurencekirk
Auchinblae
Fordoun
Drumlithie
KINCARDINE
HOWE OF THE MEARNS
Banchory
Strachan
Kincardine O'Neil
Aboyne
Dinnet
Tarland
Lumphanan
Torphins
Echt
Garlogie
Westhill
Forest of Birse
Mount Battock
Cairn o' Mount
Clachnaben
Kerloch
Glen Esk
Tarfside
Hill of Fare
Stoneywood
Tillyfourie
NJ
38
NO
37
A 92
A 94
A 90
A 93
A 933
A 934
A 935
A 937
A 957
A 958
A 974
A 980
Roads requiring special care owing to restricted width and/or rough surface. Passing places usually available

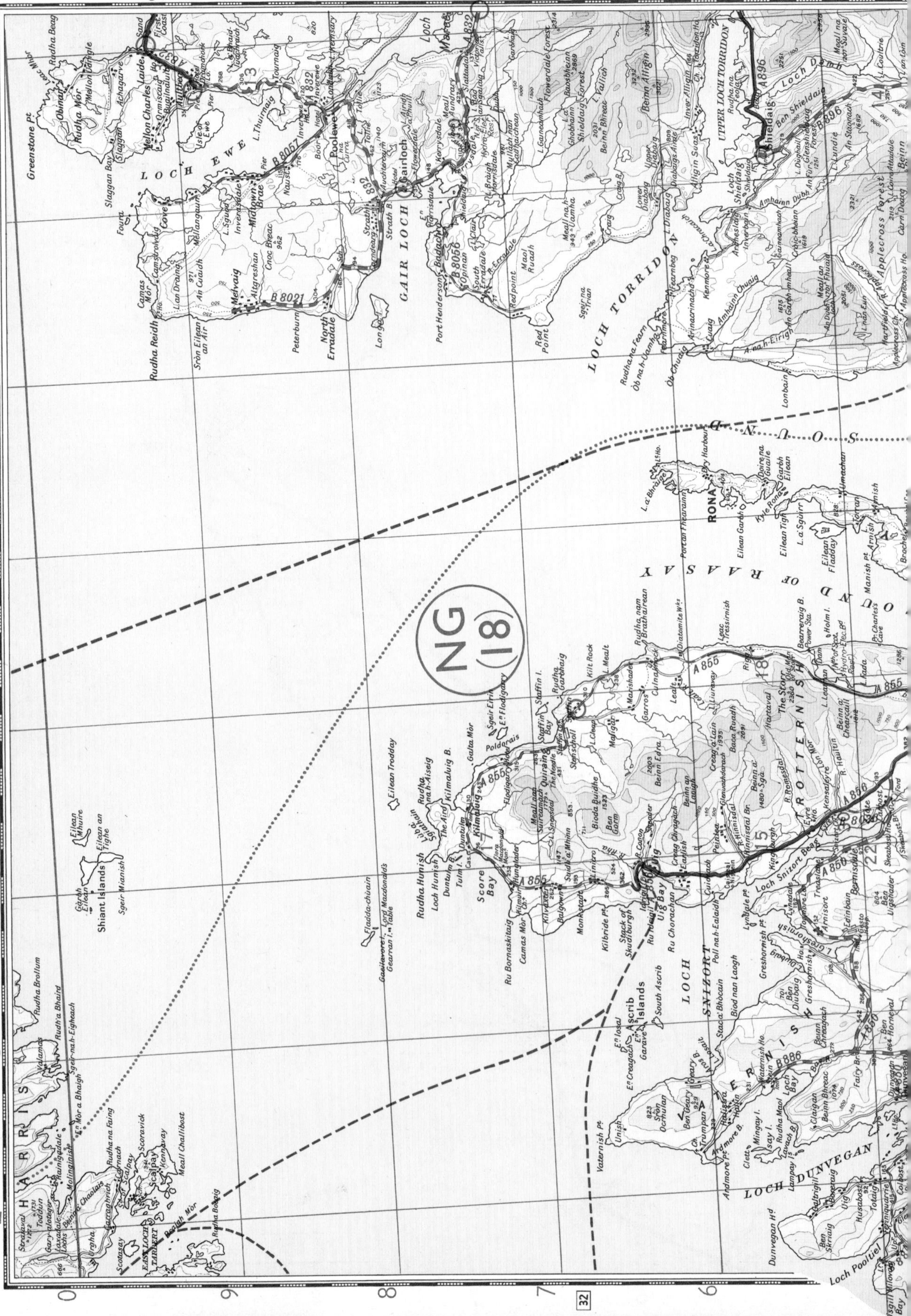
NG
18
LOCH EWE
Poolewe
Gairloch
GAIR LOCH
Loch Maree
Greenstone Pt.
Rudha Mòr
Mellon Charles
Laide
Aultbea
Isle of Ewe
Cove
Melvaig
Rudha Reidh
North Erradale
Badachro
Port Henderson
Opinan
South Erradale
Red Point
Redpoint
LOCH TORRIDON
UPPER LOCH TORRIDON
Shieldaig
Beinn Alligin
Diabaig
Alligin Shuas
Inveralligin
Applecross Forest
Kenmore
Cuaig
Fearnmore
Rudha na Fearn
RONA
SOUND OF RASAY
Staffin Bay
Staffin I.
Kilt Rock
Culnaknock
The Storr
TROTTERNISH
Quiraing
Kilmaluig
Duntulm
Rudha Hunish
Score Bay
Uig Bay
Uig
LOCH SNIZORT
Ascrib Islands
South Ascrib
VATERNISH
Vaternish Pt.
LOCH DUNVEGAN
Dunvegan Hd.
Loch Pooltiel
Lampay
Isay I.
Shiant Islands
Eilean Trodday
Gearran I.
Lord Macdonald's Table
Eilean Fladday
Scalpay
HARRIS
Rudha Brollum
Rudha Bocaig
EAST LOCH TARBERT
Scotasay
Rudha Beag
A 832
A 896
B 8021
B 8056
B 8057
A 855
A 856
A 850
B 886
Loch Snizort Beag
Bernisdale
Kensaleyre
Portree
Loch Bay
Fairy Br.

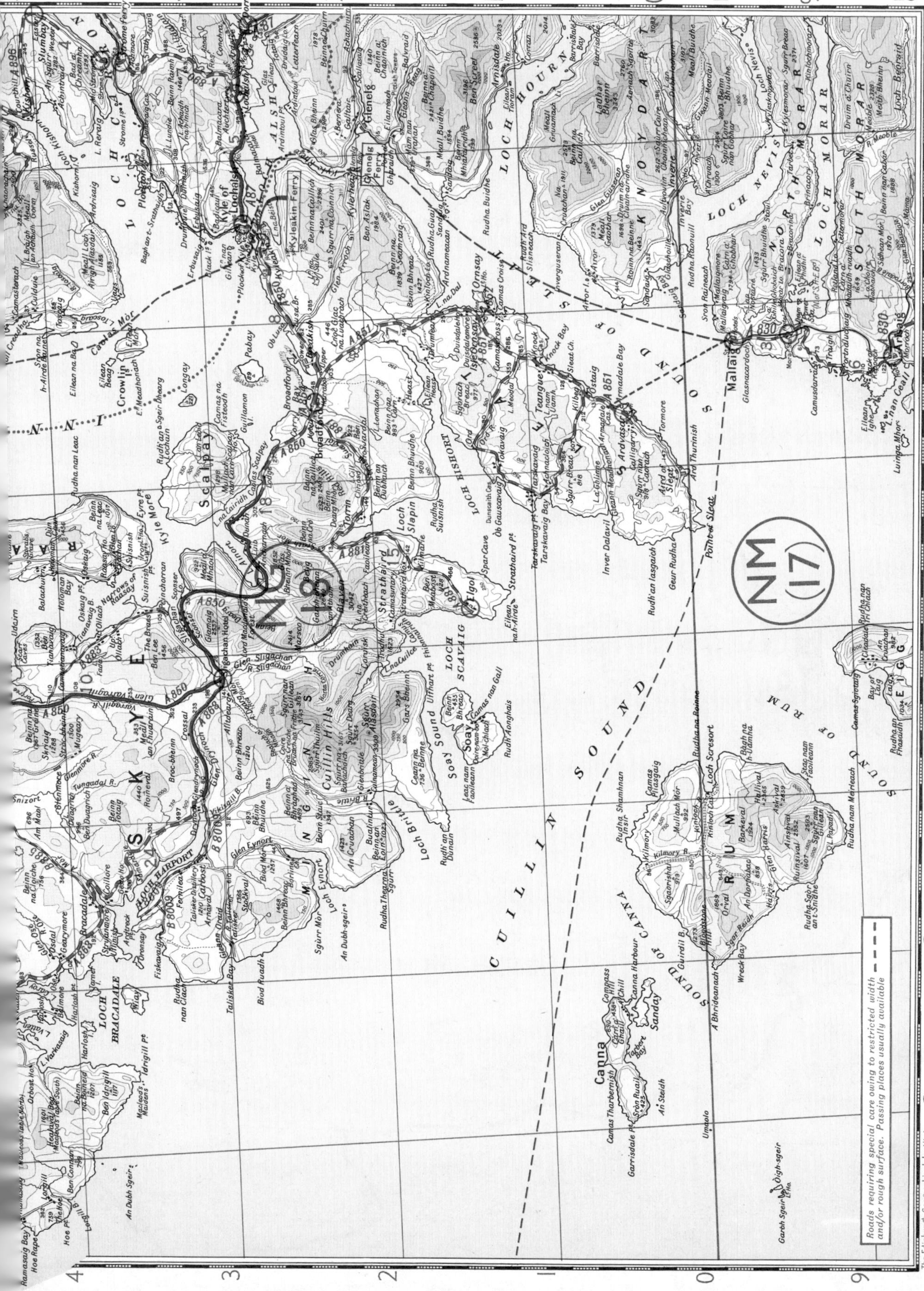
NG (18)
NM (17)
SKYE
RAASAY
Scalpay
Pabay
Soay
Canna
Sanday
RUM
EIGG
CUILLIN SOUND
SOUND OF SLEAT
SOUND OF RUM
SOUND OF CANNA
LOCH HOURN
LOCH NEVIS
LOCH MORAR
KNOYDART
NORTH MORAR
SOUTH MORAR
Kyle of Lochalsh
Kyleakin
Broadford
Mallaig
Arisaig
Glenelg
Dornie
Plockton
Armadale
Elgol
Sligachan Hotel
Cuillin Hills
LOCH BRACADALE
LOCH HARPORT
LOCH SCAVAIG
LOCH EISHORT
Loch Slapin
Loch Eynort
Loch Brittle
Roads requiring special care owing to restricted width and/or rough surface. Passing places usually available

9 0 1 2 29 3 4

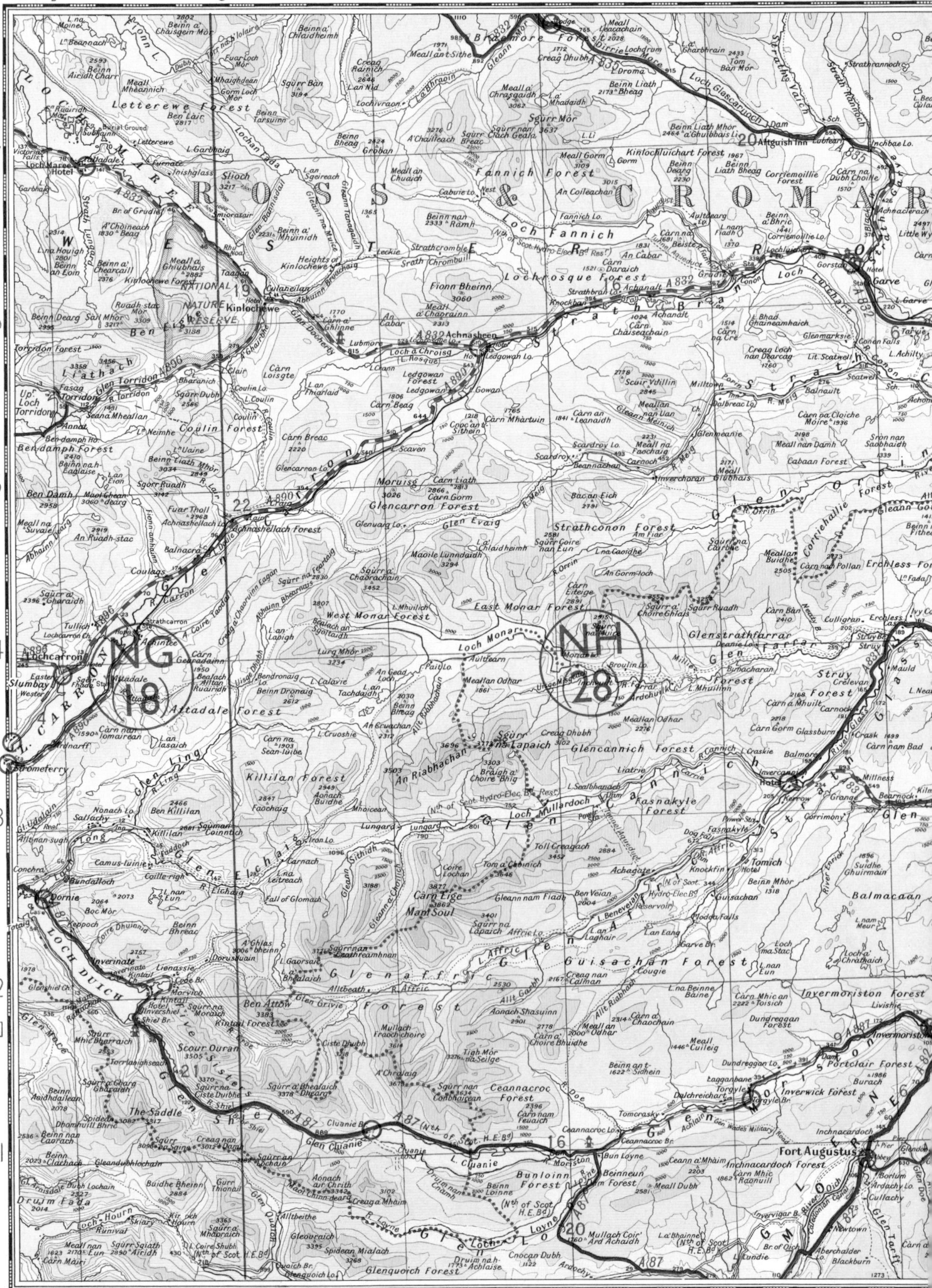

The Edinburgh Geographical Institute

9 0 1 18 2 3 4

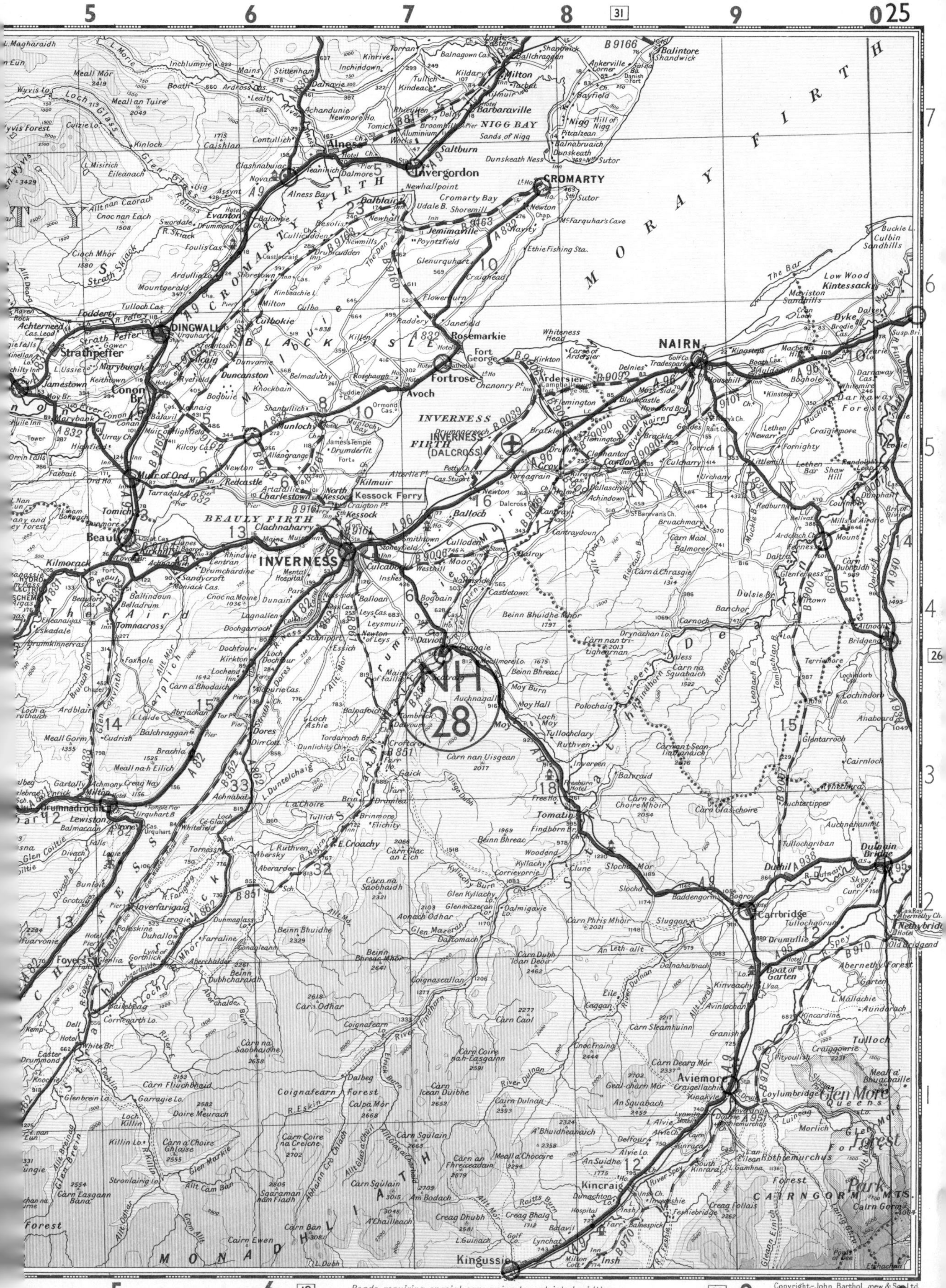

Roads requiring special care owing to restricted width and/or rough surface. Passing places usually available ----

19

20

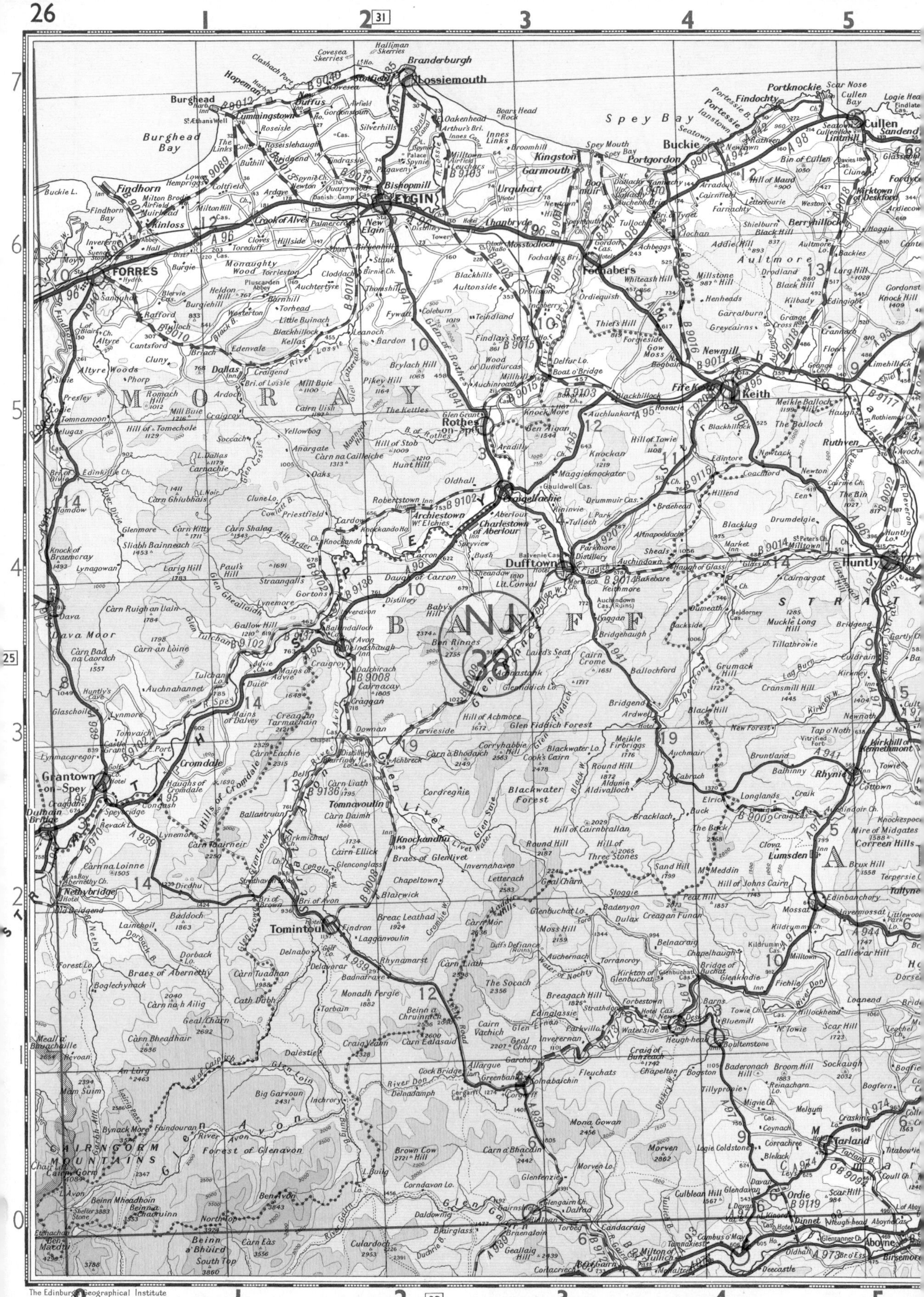

Closed Roads xxxx

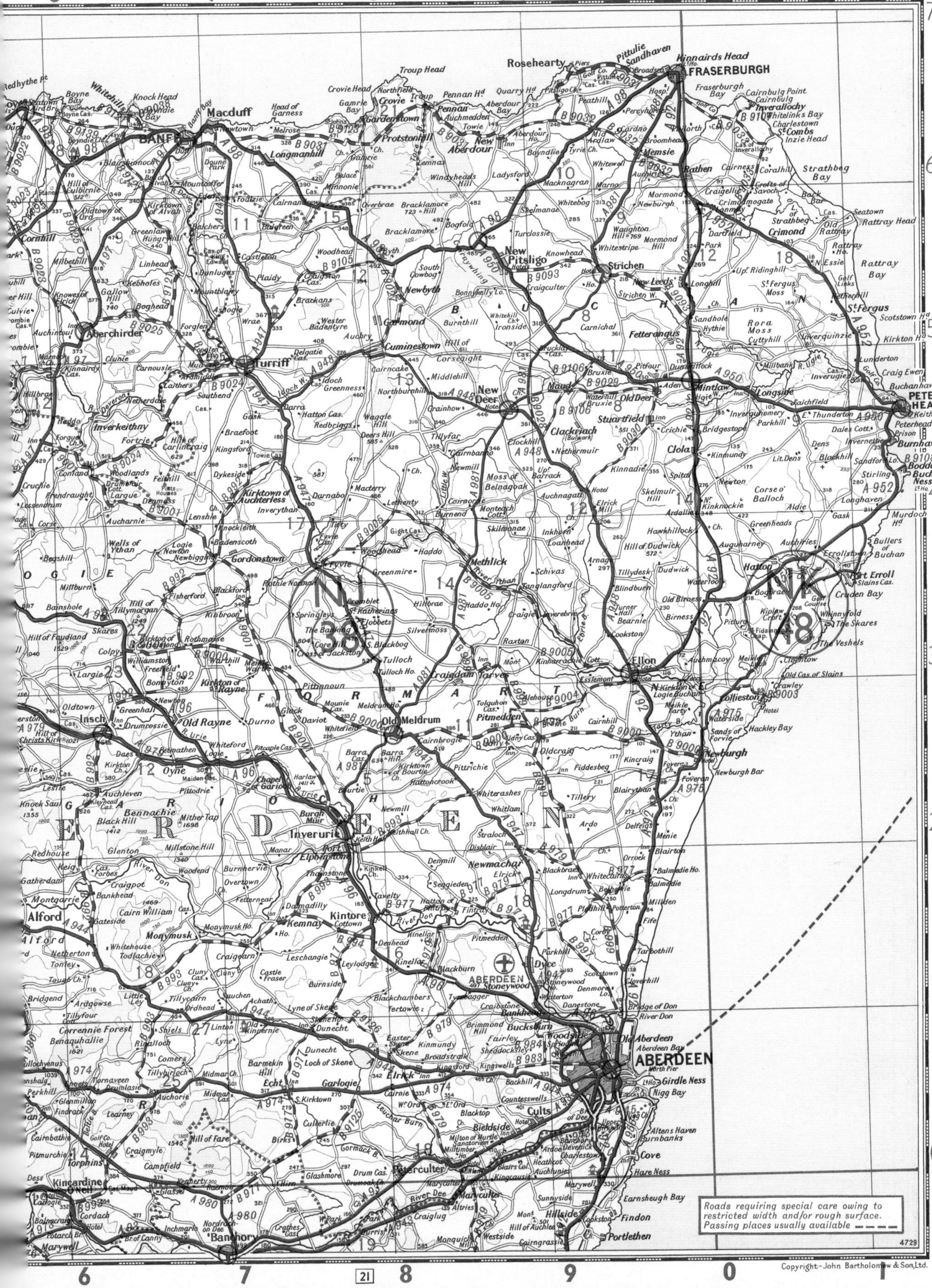
FRASERBURGH
Kinnairds Head
Rosehearty
Pittulie
Sandhaven
Fraserburgh Bay
Cairnbulg Point
Inverallochy
Whitelinks Bay
Charlestown
St. Combs
Inzie Head
Strathbeg Bay
Rattray Head
Rattray Bay
Crimond
St. Fergus
Scotstown Hd
Kirkton Hd
PETER-HEAD
Keith Inch
Peterhead Bay
Burnhaven
Boddam
Buchan Ness
Longhaven
Cruden Bay
Port Erroll
Slains Cas.
The Skares
The Veshels
Collieston
Hackley Bay
Newburgh
Newburgh Bar
Troup Head
Crovie Head
Gamrie Bay
Gardenstown
Pennan
Pennan Hd
Aberdour Bay
New Aberdour
Macduff
BANFF
Boyne Bay
Whitehills
Knock Head
Redhythe Pt
Longmanhill
Turriff
Aberchirder
Cornhill
Cuminestown
New Pitsligo
Strichen
New Leeds
Mintlaw
Old Deer
Stuartfield
Maud
New Deer
Fetterangus
Longside
Methlick
Fyvie
Ellon
Tarves
Pitmedden
Old Meldrum
Insch
Old Rayne
Oyne
Chapel of Garioch
Inverurie
Port Elphinstone
Kintore
Kemnay
Monymusk
Alford
Newmachar
Dyce
ABERDEEN Airport
Stoneywood
Bucksburn
Bankhead
ABERDEEN
Aberdeen Bay
Old Aberdeen
Girdle Ness
Nigg Bay
Cults
Bieldside
Peterculter
Maryculter
Echt
Garlogie
Banchory
Kincardine O'Neil
Torphins
Cove
Findon
Portlethen
Bennachie
Mither Tap 1698
Hill of Fare
Mormond Hill
NJ 36
NK 48
B U C H A N
F O R M A R T I N E
G A R I O C H
A B E R D E E N
Roads requiring special care owing to restricted width and/or rough surface. Passing places usually available
4729

21

Roads requiring special care owing to restricted width and/or rough surface. Passing places usually available
NC
(29)
Cape Wrath
Durness
Kyle of Durness
Loch Eriboll
Loch Hope
Ben Hope
Kyle of Tongue
Tongue
Loch Loyal
Ben Loyal
Strath More
Foinaven
Arkle
Ben Stack
Loch More
Loch Merkland
Scourie
Badcall
Laxford Br.
Rhiconich
Kinlochbervie
Kylesku Ferry
Loch Glencoul
Eddrachillis Bay
Drumbeg
Clashnessie
Pt. of Stoer
Altnaharra
Loch Naver
Strath Vagastie
The Crask
Strath Beag
Strath Dionard
Ben Klibreck
Ben Hee
A 838
A 836
A 894
B 873
Sutherland

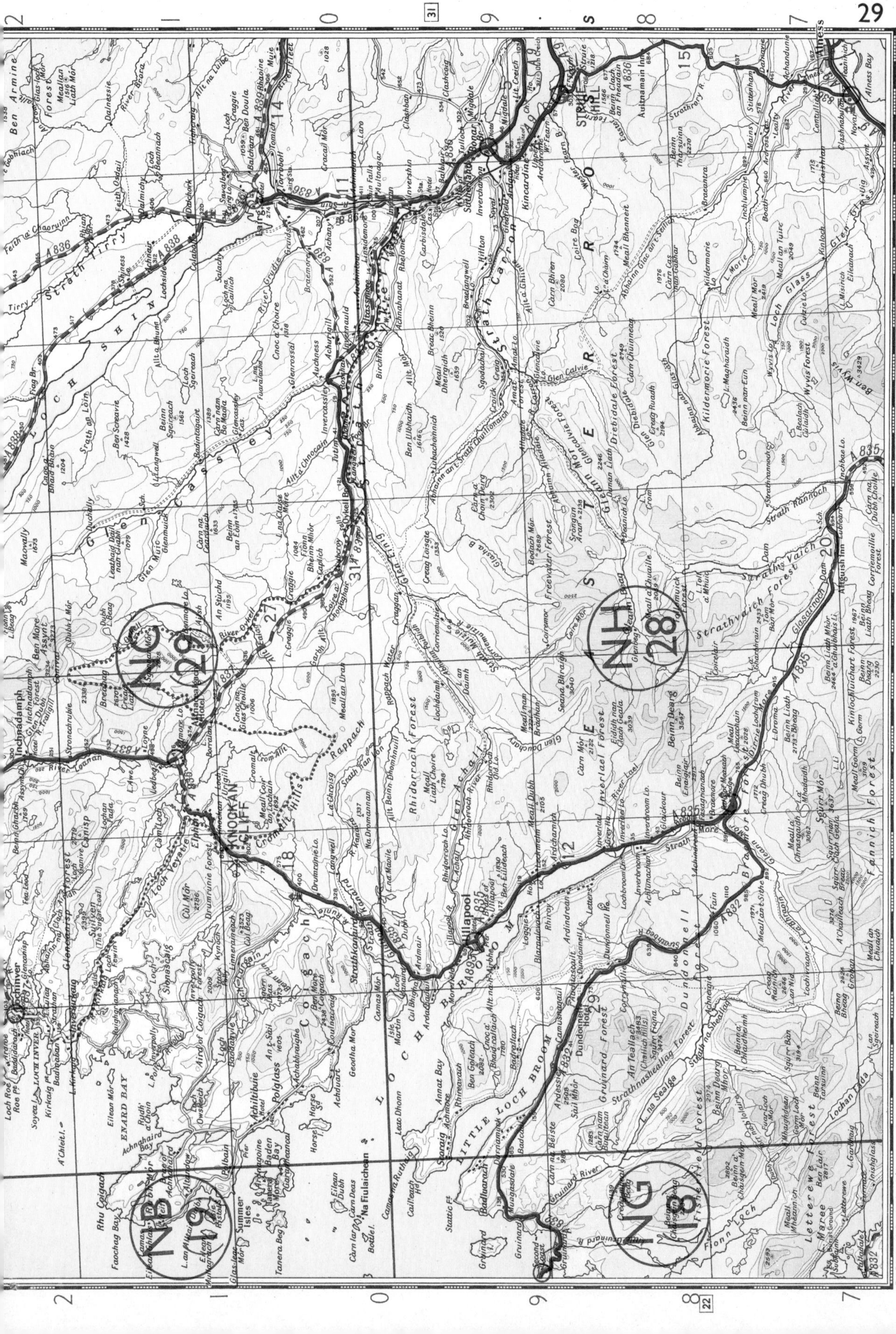
Ullapool
Inchnadamph
Lochinver
Knockan Cliff
Summer Isles
Little Loch Broom
Loch Broom
Strath Carron
Alness
Dundonnell
Strathkanaird
Glen Achall
Rhidorroch Forest
Freevater Forest
Inverlael Forest
Fannich Forest
Letterewe Forest
Loch Glass
Loch Shin
NC 29
NH 28
NG 18
NB 19

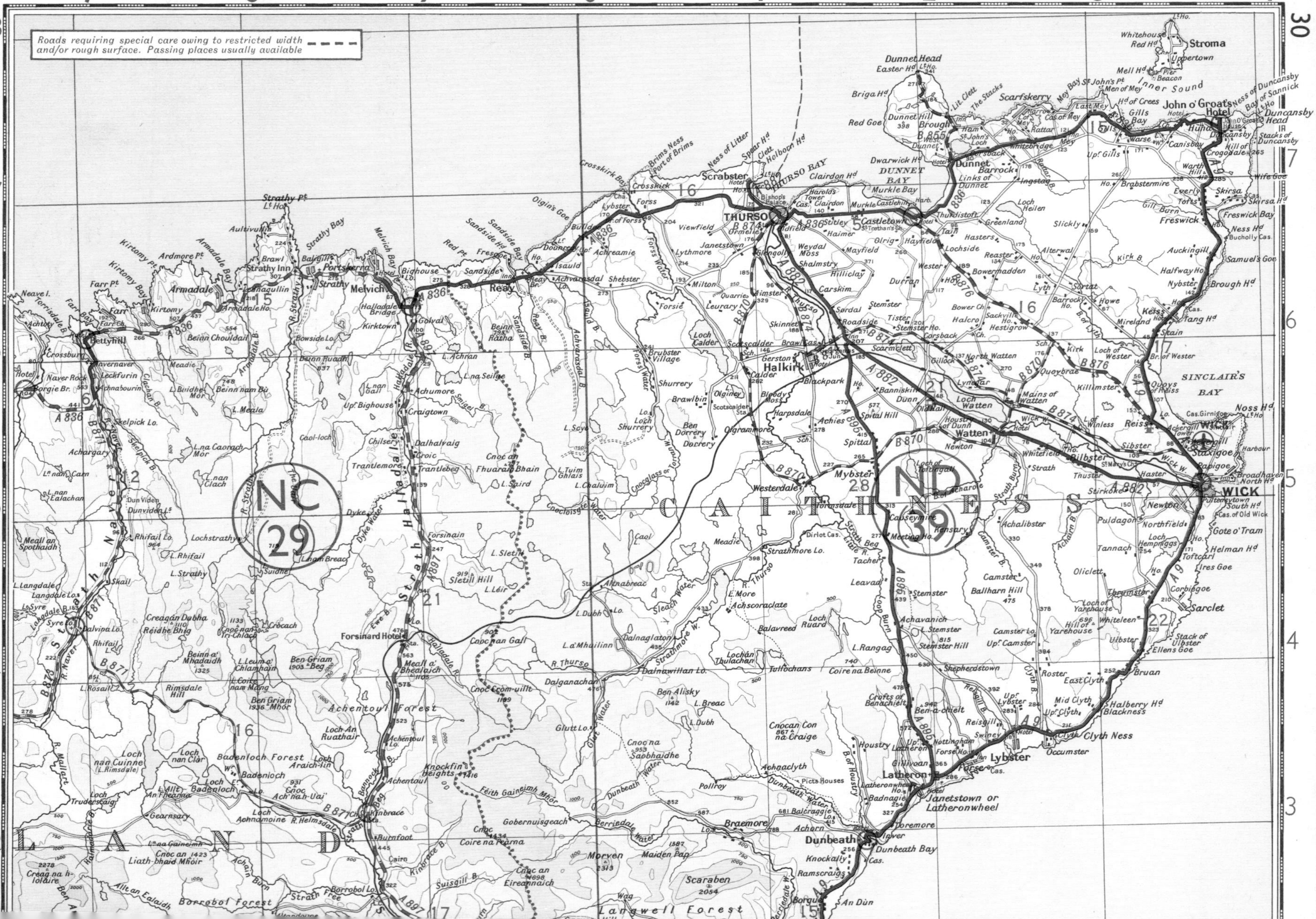
Roads requiring special care owing to restricted width and/or rough surface. Passing places usually available
C A I T H N E S S
S U T H E R L A N D
NC (29)
ND (39)
THURSO
WICK
John o' Groat's Hotel
Duncansby Head
Stroma
Dunnet Head
Dunnet Bay
Thurso Bay
Sinclair's Bay
Scrabster
Castletown
Halkirk
Watten
Keiss
Lybster
Latheron
Janetstown or Latheronwheel
Dunbeath
Reay
Melvich
Portskerra
Strathy Inn
Armadale
Bettyhill
Forsinard Hotel
Kinbrace
Strath Halladale
Achentoul Forest
Badenloch Forest
Borrobol Forest
Langwell Forest
Morven 2313
Scaraben 2054
Maiden Pap 1587
Clyth Ness
Noss Hd
Sarclet
Pentland Firth
Inner Sound
Strathy Pt
Brims Ness
Crosskirk Bay
Sandside Bay
Melvich Bay
Armadale Bay
Kirtomy Bay
Farr Bay

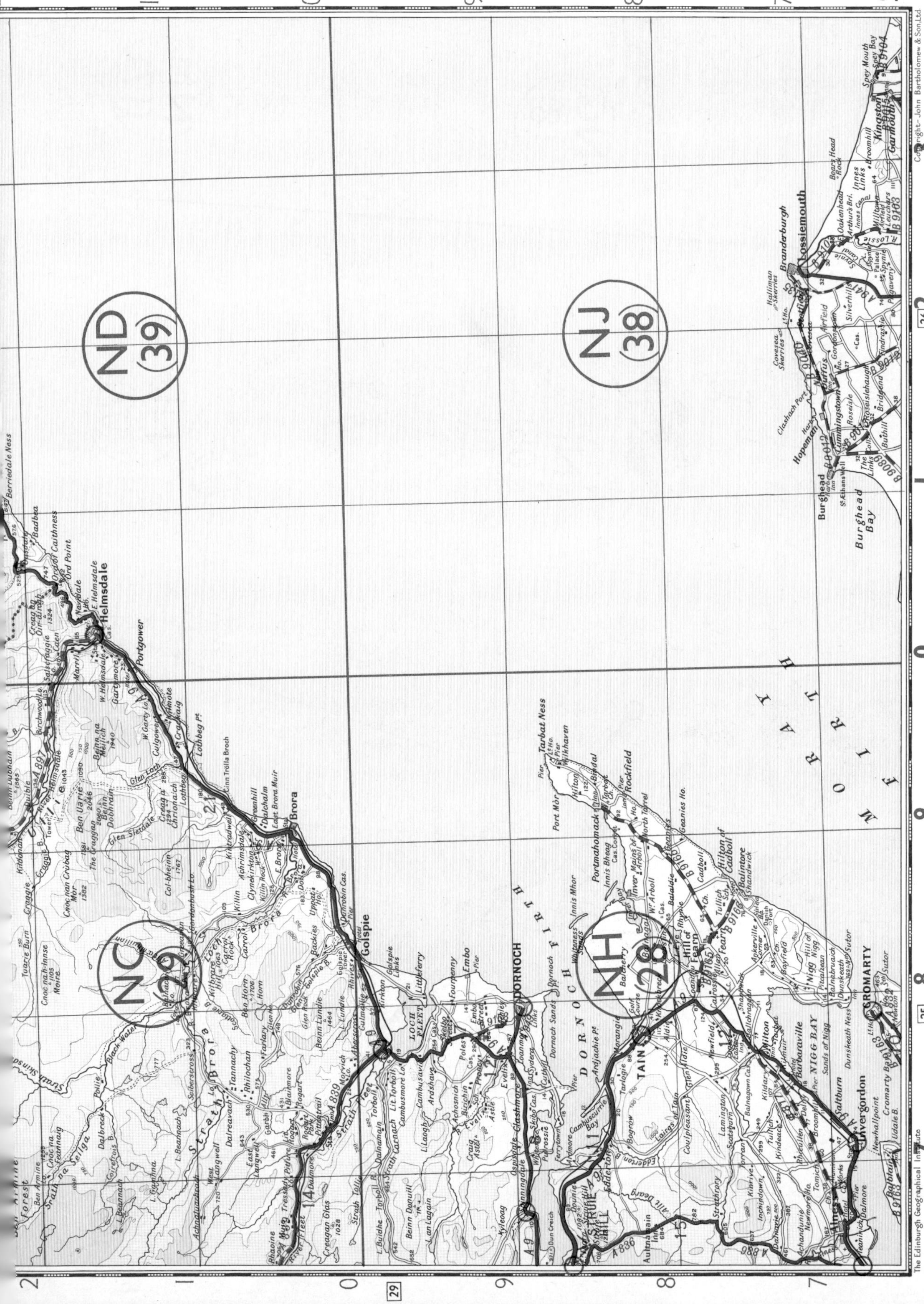
ND
39
NJ
38
NC
29
NH
28
Helmsdale
Portgower
Brora
Golspie
DORNOCH
Embo
TAIN
Portmahomack
Tarbat Ness
Hilton of Cadboll
Balintore
Invergordon
CROMARTY
Alness
Burghead
Hopeman
Lossiemouth
Branderburgh
Kingston
Garmouth
Spey Bay
Burghead Bay
DORNOCH FIRTH
MORAY FIRTH
NIGG BAY
Closed Roads
25
26
29
Copyright - John Bartholomew & Son, Ltd.
The Edinburgh Geographical Institute

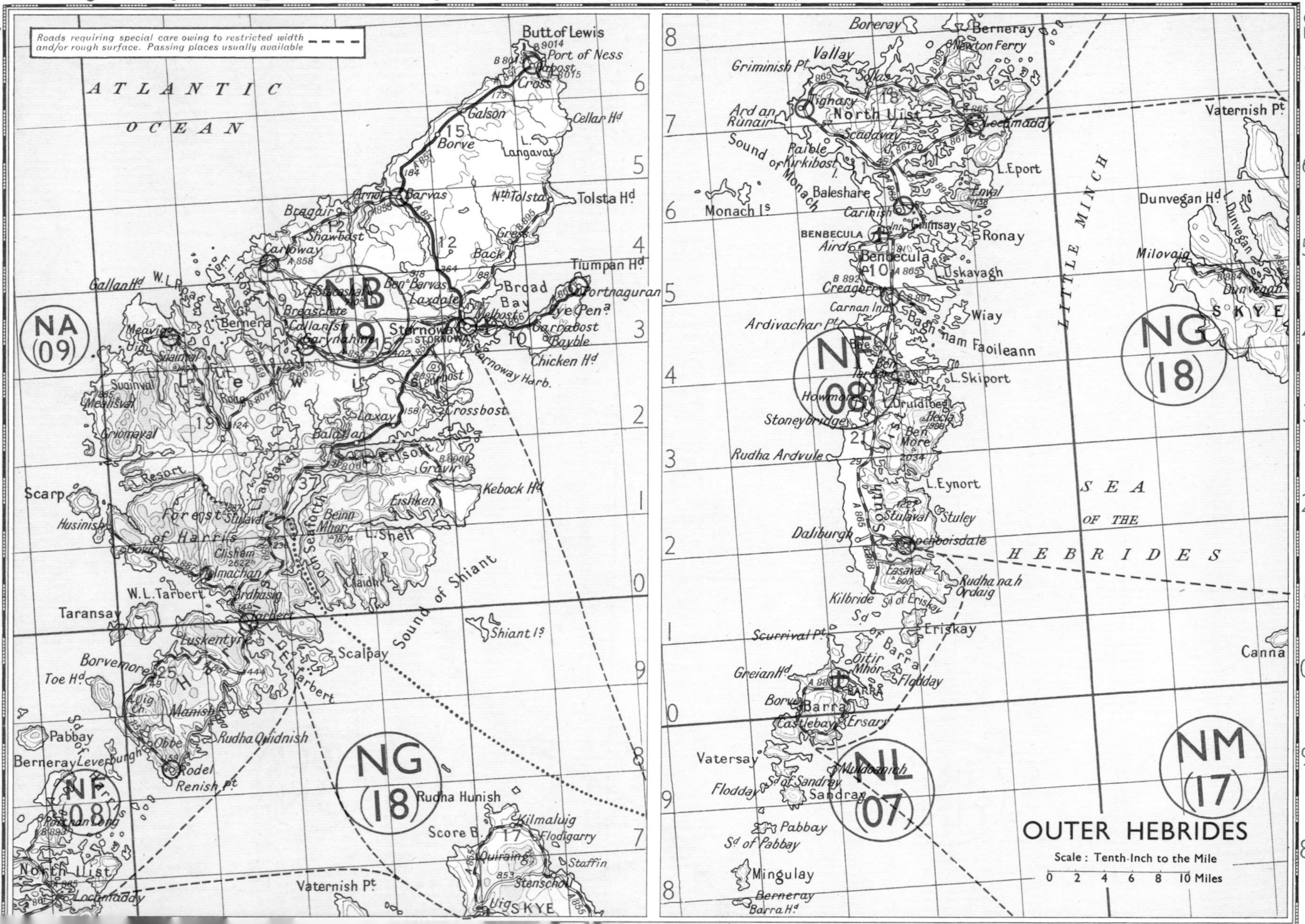
OUTER HEBRIDES
Scale: Tenth-Inch to the Mile
0 2 4 6 8 10 Miles
Roads requiring special care owing to restricted width and/or rough surface. Passing places usually available
ATLANTIC OCEAN
LITTLE MINCH
SEA OF THE HEBRIDES
Sound of Shiant
NA (09)
NB (19)
NG (18)
NF (08)
NL (07)
NM (17)
Butt of Lewis
Port of Ness
Cross
Cellar Hd
Galson
Borve
L. Langavat
Barvas
Nth Tolsta
Tolsta Hd
Tiumpan Hd
Broad Bay
Portnaguran
Garrabost
Bayble
Chicken Hd
Stornoway
Stornoway Harb.
Laxdale
Crossbost
Laxay
Balallan
Gravir
Kebock Hd
Eishken
L. Shell
Shiant Is
Bragair
Shawbost
Carloway
Gallan Hd
Bernera
Breasclete
Callanish
Garynahine
Meavaig
Uig
Mealisval
Griomaval
L. Resort
Scarp
Husinish
Forest of Harris
Clisham 2622
Loch Seaforth
W. L. Tarbert
Tarbert
Taransay
Luskentyre
Scalpay
Borvemore
Toe Hd
Pabbay
Berneray
Leverburgh
Obbe
Rodel
Renish Pt
Rudha Quidnish
Rudha Hunish
Score B.
Kilmaluig
Flodigarry
Quiraing
Staffin
Stenscholl
Uig
SKYE
Vaternish Pt
North Uist
Lochmaddy
Boreray
Berneray
Newton Ferry
Vallay
Griminish Pt
Sollas
Tigharry
Ard an Runair
Scadavay
Sound of Monach
Paible
Kirkibost I.
Baleshare
Carinish
Grimsay
Ronay
L. Eport
Eaval
Monach Is
BENBECULA
Aird
Benbecula
Uskavagh
Creagorry
Carnan Inn
Wiay
Bagh nam Faoileann
Ardivachar Pt
L. Skiport
Howmore
Stoneybridge
Druidibeg
Hecla
Ben More 2034
Rudha Ardvule
L. Eynort
Stulaval
Stuley
South Uist
Daliburgh
Lochboisdale
Easaval
Rudha na h Ordaig
Kilbride
Sd of Eriskay
Eriskay
Sd of Barra
Scurrival Pt
Greian Hd
Oitir Mhor
Fladday
Borve
Barra
Castlebay
Ersary
Vatersay
Muldoanich
Flodday
Sd of Sandray
Sandray
Pabbay
Sd of Pabbay
Mingulay
Berneray
Barra Hd
Dunvegan Hd
L. Dunvegan
Milovaig
Dunvegan
Vaternish Pt
Canna

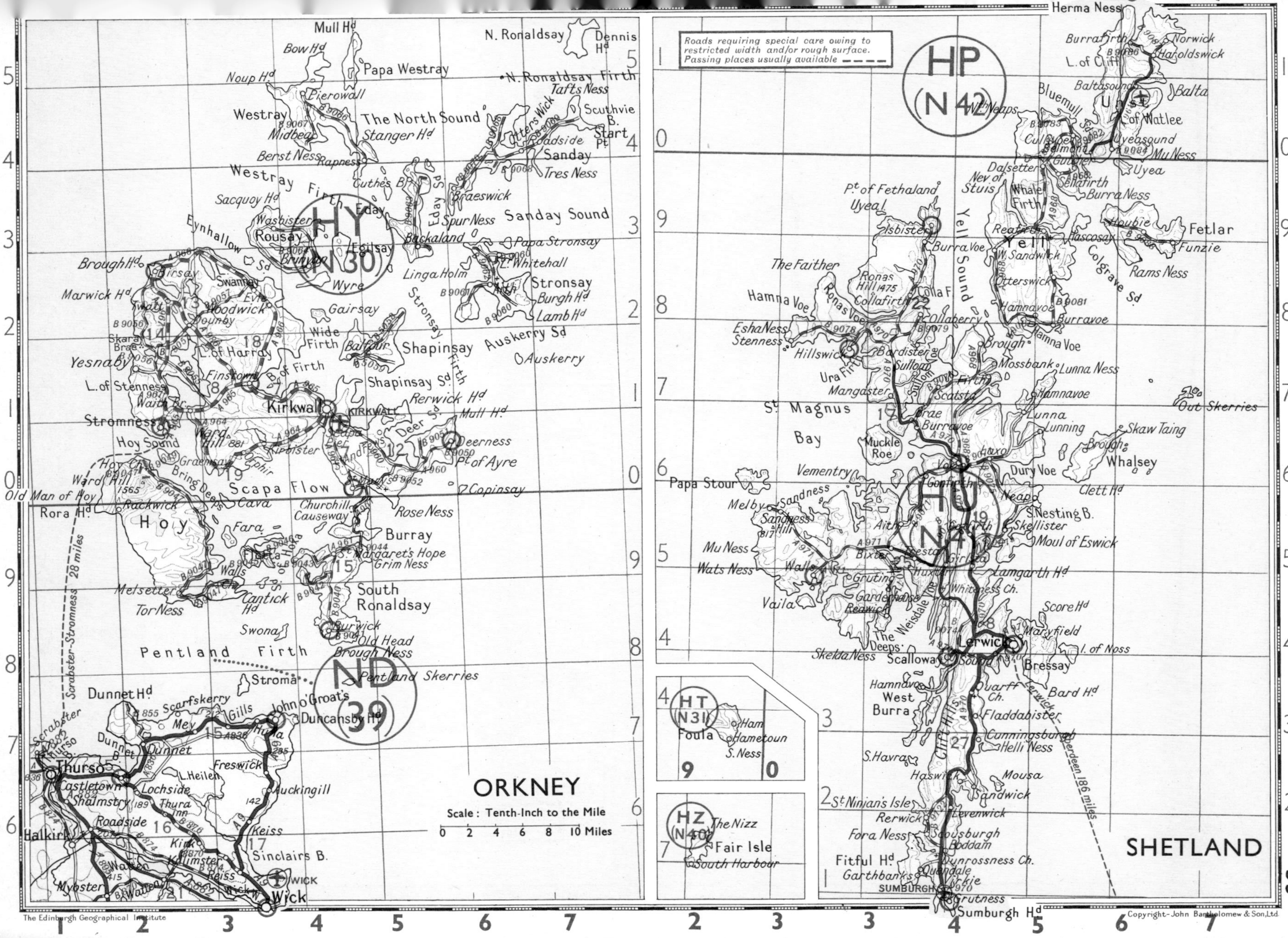
ORKNEY
Scale: Tenth-Inch to the Mile
0 2 4 6 8 10 Miles
SHETLAND
HY (N 30)
ND (39)
HP (N 42)
HU (N 4)
HT (N 31)
HZ (N 40)
Roads requiring special care owing to restricted width and/or rough surface. Passing places usually available
Scrabster-Stromness 28 miles
Aberdeen 186 miles
N. Ronaldsay
Dennis Hd
Mull Hd
Bow Hd
Papa Westray
Noup Hd
Westray
The North Sound
Sanday
Sanday Sound
Westray Firth
Rousay
Eday
Egilsay
Wyre
Stronsay
Shapinsay
Kirkwall
Stromness
Hoy
Scapa Flow
Burray
South Ronaldsay
Pentland Firth
Pentland Skerries
Stroma
John o'Groat's
Duncansby Hd
Dunnet Hd
Thurso
Wick
Copinsay
Auskerry
Herma Ness
Unst
Yell
Fetlar
Yell Sound
Whalsey
Out Skerries
St Magnus Bay
Papa Stour
Lerwick
Bressay
Scalloway
West Burra
Mousa
Sumburgh Hd
Foula
Fair Isle
The Edinburgh Geographical Institute
Copyright-John Bartholomew & Son, Ltd.

MAINLAND FERRIES AND SERVICES TO THE ISLANDS

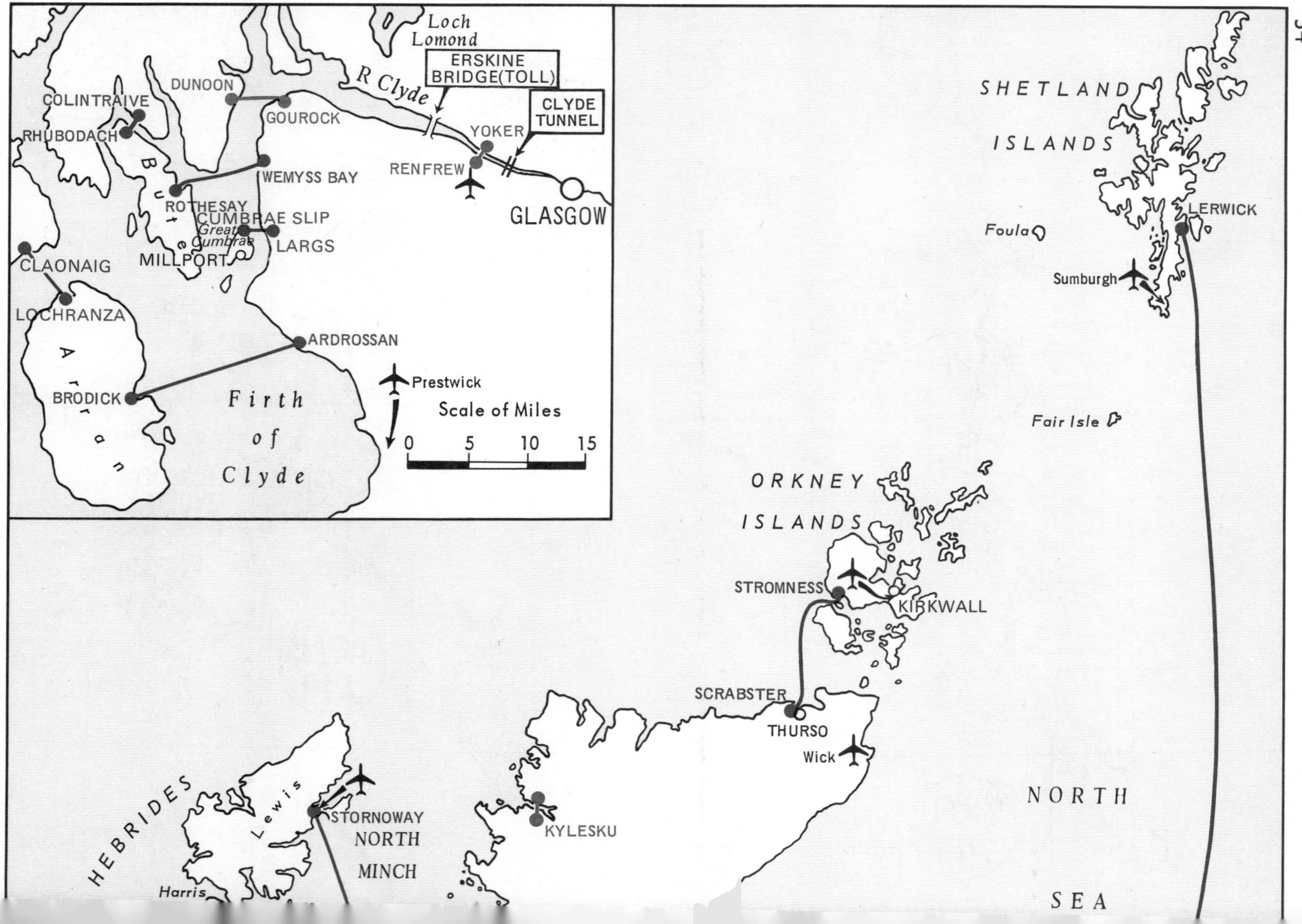

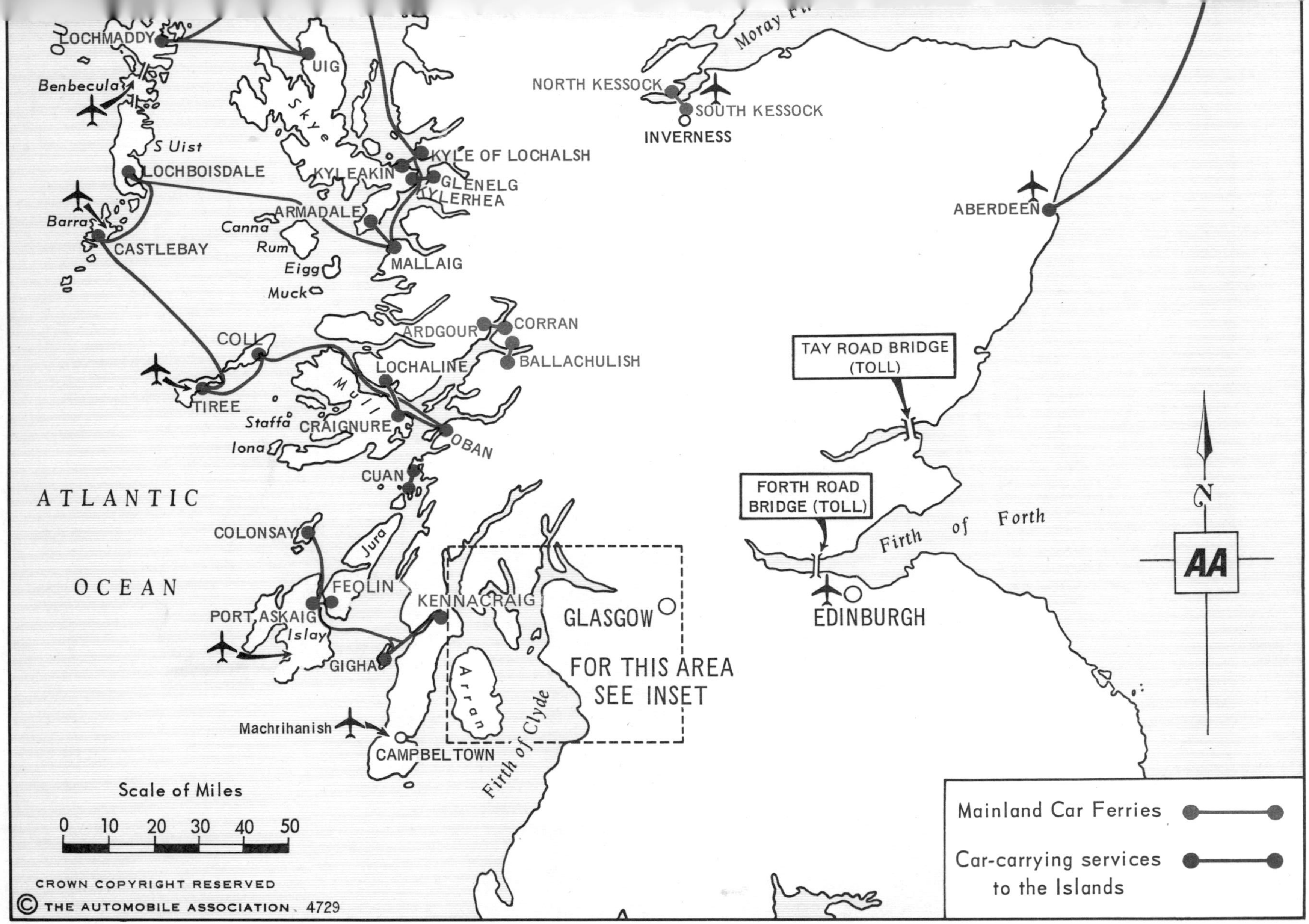
LOCHMADDY
UIG
Benbecula
Skye
S Uist
LOCHBOISDALE
KYLE OF LOCHALSH
KYLEAKIN
GLENELG
KYLERHEA
ARMADALE
Barra
Canna
CASTLEBAY
Rum
MALLAIG
Eigg
Muck
NORTH KESSOCK
SOUTH KESSOCK
INVERNESS
Moray
ABERDEEN
ARDGOUR
CORRAN
BALLACHULISH
COLL
LOCHALINE
Mull
TIREE
Staffa
CRAIGNURE
OBAN
Iona
CUAN
ATLANTIC
OCEAN
COLONSAY
Jura
FEOLIN
PORT ASKAIG
Islay
KENNACRAIG
GIGHA
Arran
Firth of Clyde
Machrihanish
CAMPBELTOWN
GLASGOW
FOR THIS AREA SEE INSET
TAY ROAD BRIDGE (TOLL)
FORTH ROAD BRIDGE (TOLL)
Firth of Forth
EDINBURGH
N
AA
Scale of Miles
0 10 20 30 40 50
Mainland Car Ferries
Car-carrying services to the Islands

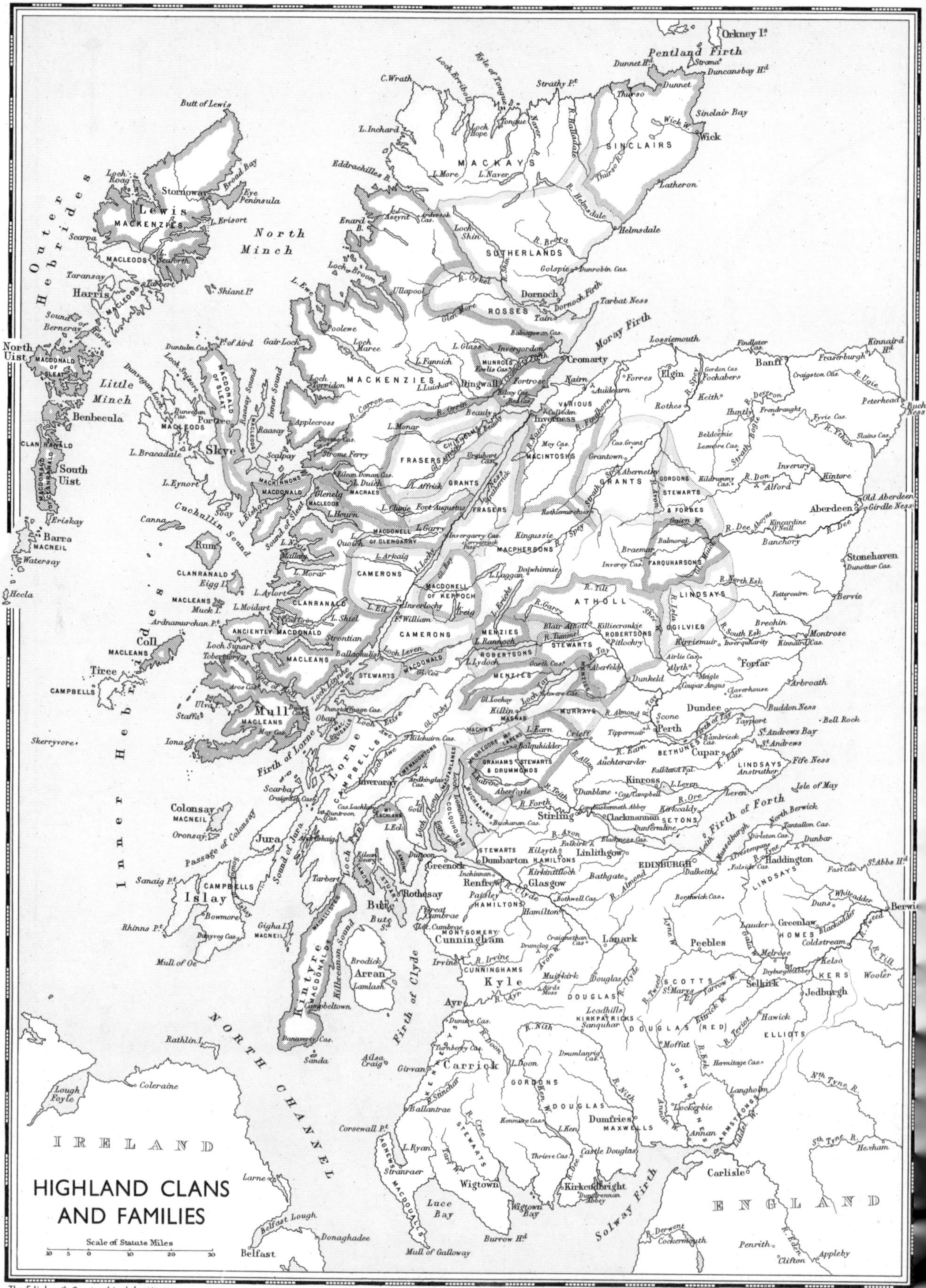

HIGHLAND CLANS AND FAMILIES

The Edinburgh Geographical Institute